The Selected Papers of Jane Addams

VOLUME 1

PREPARING TO LEAD,

1860–81

The Selected Papers of Jane Addams

VOLUME 1

Preparing to Lead,

1860–81

EDITED BY

MARY LYNN McCREE BRYAN,

BARBARA BAIR, AND

MAREE DE ANGURY

UNIVERSITY OF ILLINOIS PRESS

URBANA AND CHICAGO

FRONTISPIECE: Jane Addams, born 6 September 1860,
in a portrait taken when she was about twelve.
(Samuel V. Allen, Freeport, Ill.; SCPC)

Library of Congress Cataloging-in-Publication Data
The selected papers of Jane Addams / [edited by Mary Lynn
McCree Bryan . . . et al.].
v.   cm.
Includes bibliographical references and index.
Contents: v. 1. Preparing to lead, 1860–81 / edited by M.L.M. Bryan,
B. Bair and M. De Angury
ISBN 0-252-02729-9
1. Addams, Jane, 1860–1935—Correspondence.
2. Women social workers—United States—Correspondence.
3. Women social reformers—United States—Correspondence.
4. Women pacifists—United States—Correspondence.
I. Addams, Jane, 1860–1935. II. Bryan, Mary Lynn McCree.
HV40.32.A33S45   2003
361.92—dc21   2001005638

Every word we utter sets in motion a breath of air that extends around the earth, and for these wandering utterances earth has a scheme, a scale of moral music, which controls the casts of thought, and the contagion is literally and figuratively "in the air." An echo seems to hand our speech, not word for word, but line by line, up to the recording angel, and just as our breath, in that case, strikes the rock, so our words strike a negative mind, and go forth into the universe of electric thought.

—L.J.A. [Laura Jane Addams], "Plated Ware," *Rockford Seminary Magazine,* April 1878, 62

Contents

Illustrations

Acknowledgments

The work of the Jane Addams Papers project could not have been undertaken without the agreement, support, and assistance of many agencies and individuals. The editors of this project are exceedingly grateful to all who have been supportive in our enterprise.

From the very beginning of the Jane Addams Papers project in the mid-1970s we have had the support of the National Historical Publications and Records Commission and the National Endowment for the Humanities. Both agencies encouraged the development of this project. Throughout the entire project—including the gathering, organizing, and annotating of documents for the microfilm edition of *The Jane Addams Papers* and the preparation of *The Jane Addams Papers: A Comprehensive Guide*, we have benefited also from the financial and moral support of many other foundations and individuals. Their help was essential to the progress of the project.

Not surprisingly, the work associated with this particular volume has been supported by grants from the National Historical Publications and Records Commission and the National Endowment for the Humanities. The latter provided a mix of direct and matching funding. We are extremely grateful to the Lilly Endowment, Inc., Indianapolis, Indiana, and in particular to program officer Susan Wisely and her staff, who have had faith in our project. The Lilly Endowment has provided the lion's share of a one-for-one National Endowment for the Humanities match. In addition, we have had important timely support from the Spencer Foundation and the Franke Family Charitable Foundation, both of Chicago, Illinois. The following individuals provided funding for the project in honor and memory of Mary Addams Hulbert, great-niece of Jane Addams: Anne C. Baeck, Katharine L. Eisler, Virginia Lee Laurence, Elizabeth W. Martin, William C. and Maria Stevenson, and Steven E. Zemmelman. Betsy G. Miller and Barbara Sicherman also gave financial and moral support. The Barbara Penny Kanner Award of $500 for excellence in bibliomethodology that the Jane Addams Papers project's *The Jane Addams Papers: A Comprehensive Guide* received from the Western Association of Women Historians was not only wonderful recognition for our guide to our microfilm edition of the Addams Papers, but it also helped us meet our NEH match.

In addition to these outright gifts, the project has received generous in-kind support. The Bryan Pontiac Cadillac Company, Fayetteville, North Carolina, provided access to long-distance telephone, photocopying, and mailing and shipping options. All of the editors also provided in-kind project support. We work at our homes using space and equipment we provide for ourselves. Duke University, Durham, North Carolina, and in particular the history department, has generously served as the project's academic home since 1983. It has lent its extraordinary academic reputation to the project, acted as a haven for the funds we have secured, and furnished accounting and reporting expertise so important to those who fund projects such as ours. In addition, we have made special use of the libraries of the following institutions: Duke University, the University of California at Santa Cruz and Berkeley, and especially the interlibrary loan services of the Cumberland County Library, Fayetteville, North Carolina. We are deeply grateful to all who have been so supportive in helping us secure a solid footing for our project.

Without the assistance, encouragement, and permission of the relatives of Jane Addams this endeavor would have been impossible. Great-nieces, the mates of great-nephews, great-great-nieces and great-great-nephews, and distant step-cousins have been most helpful in providing access to Addams, Weber, Hostetter, and Haldeman materials in private hands. They have given their permission for the project to move forward, and they have remained interested in our progress and products. Mary Addams Hulbert opened her home and her family collections and shared her wonderful memories on many occasions. John Brittain, Mary Hulbert's nephew and son of her sister Louise Hulbert Brittain Torchia, and his wife Geraldine have become just as encouraging as Mary Hulbert was during her life. No less supportive and every bit as attentive to the project was Alice Haldeman-Julius DeLoach, a major figure in preserving Addams and Haldeman family records and artifacts. Mary Lynn McCree Bryan visited with her many times at her homes, first in Roswell, Georgia, and later in Florida. Her daughter Marcet Bliss has assumed her mother's role and been most helpful to the project. Elizabeth Linn Murray also lent support and encouragement. Having assisted her father James Weber Linn with his biography of Jane Addams, she understood from experience the daunting task we had assumed. Jane Linn Morse and her husband Chuck Morse have also been very encouraging and have made family materials available to the editors. They facilitated a marvelous visit with Myra Reynolds Linn, the widow of Jane Addams's nephew Stanley Linn. Kay and Ben Schneider made their Hostetter family materials available to the project and were especially helpful in sharing the papers of Sarah Hostetter. Another Hostetter relative, David Sandburg, who has been work-

ing on the Hostetter genealogy, has assisted us in sorting out various generations and individuals associated with his family. Paul Fry, nephew, and Jean Fry
Joyce, niece, of near-family member Mary Fry, companion to Jane Addams's
stepmother Anna Hostetter Haldeman Addams, have provided access to Addams, Fry, and Cedarville, Illinois, materials. Their moral support and reassur-
ance, as well as memories of their Aunt Mary, the Addams homestead, and Cedarville events have been extremely valuable.

This project would also not have been possible without all of the work that
went into locating, gathering, organizing, and annotating the Jane Addams
papers that were published in the microfilm edition. We remain indebted to
those editors who worked on that project, among them Nancy Slote, Jane
Colokathis, Beth Durham, Peter Clark, Frank A. Ninkovich, David N. Ruchman,
Barbara Starr, Sue Weiler, Lynn Weiner, Julie Johnson Bradbury, Kathy Brown,
Tina Certo, Nan Cohen, Lynn Getz, Barbara S. Kraft, Mary Lou Laprade, Susan
Starbuck, and Ann D. Gordon. The documents that appear in this first volume
of the selected printed edition come primarily from five major collections of
Addams-related materials, most of which appear in the microfilm edition. These
are the Jane Addams Collection, Swarthmore College Peace Collection, Swarthmore College, Pennsylvania; the Jane Addams Memorial Collection, Manuscript
Collection, University of Illinois at Chicago; the Mrs. S. A. Haldeman Manuscripts, Lilly Library, Indiana University, Bloomington; Rockford Archives, Rockford College, Rockford, Illinois; and the Ellen Gates Starr Collection, Sophia
Smith Collection, Smith College, Northampton, Massachusetts. The editors are
very grateful to the archivists and manuscript librarians of these collections for
their help and support, especially to Wendy E. Chmielewski, director of the
Swarthmore College Peace Collection; Mary Ann Bamberger, assistant special
collections librarian, University of Illinois at Chicago; Sandra Taylor, curator of
manuscripts, Lilly Library; Joan Surrey Clark and Mary P. Pryor, archivists of
the Rockford College Archives; and (all at the Sophia Smith Collection), Susan
Boone, reference archivist, Amy Hogue, curator of manuscripts, Karen Eberhart,
archivist specialist, and Mary Elizabeth Murdock, former director.

We owe special thanks to Ronald Beam and to the Cedarville Area Historical Society for permitting the project to publish portions of the Jane Addams
1875 diary; for spending time with the editors, looking through the society's
collections of Cedarville artifacts and manuscripts; and for being a patient and
helpful guide to the Cedarville community as it was in Jane Addams time and
as it is now. Ronald Beam directed us to local resources, developed a map of the
community as it was in Jane Addams's day, and generally kept us apprised of
doings in the community that might affect our project.

Numerous individuals helped us conduct research in far-flung repositories.
Without their careful and timely efforts on our behalf, we could not have pro-
vided a great deal of the annotation for the Addams documents. Richard R.
Seidel, historiographer and archivist for the Episcopal Diocese of Chicago, con-

ducted research throughout Chicago and northern Illinois for us and was un-
flagging in his efforts to secure data. His reports were thorough and detailed.
We appreciate his expert assistance and friendship. Jean Marken from Thom-
son, Illinois, conducted research on the Hostetter and Haldeman families in the
Mount Carroll, Illinois, area, and members of the Stephenson County Genealogical Society, particularly Lois DeGarmo, have been extraordinarily helpful in
efforts to identify distant Addams relatives who lived in the Stephenson County area and citizens from Freeport and Cedarville known to the Addams family
during the last half of the nineteenth century. Carole Lemley Montgomery, assistant editor with the project during 1994, handled special research on the early days of Cedarville. Elizabeth Stevens, assistant editor for Volume 2 of this
selected edition, conducted research on Jane Addams's tours of Europe while
work on this volume was in progress.

We are extremely grateful to Samuel J. Rogal, chair, Division of Humanities and Fine Arts, Illinois Valley Community College, Oglesby, Illinois, for sharing data he has gathered on Mary E. Holmes. Beverly Scott provided valuable
information about Ellen Gates Starr's participation in the Society of the Companions of the Holy Cross. Doris J. Malkmus at the University of Iowa gave us
access to her research on Shimer College and its founders. Jim Bade and Mary
Mau made available the diaries they were editing of various members of the
Clingman Family of Cedarville. It was through Mary Mau that we received access to a previously unpublished Jane Addams letter. Gerald J. Brauer and his
staff at Ellwood House Museum in De Kalb, Illinois, were very generous in sharing data about the Ellwood family. We counted on the Illinois State Historical
Library and Illinois State Archives for access to county histories and census data.
John Daly, director of the Illinois State Archives, and various staff members,
particularly Charles L. Cali, Kim Efird, Jr., Becky Tipps, and M. Cody Wright,
were helpful with questions concerning land, corporation, public health, vital
statistics, the general assembly, and insurance records of the state of Illinois.

In Illinois, we are also grateful for the help of many other institutions and
individuals. Among libraries, manuscript collections, and archives we consulted in the Chicago area were the Chicago Historical Society, Chicago Theological Seminary Hammond Library, McCormick Theological Seminary McGaw
Library, Meadville Theological School of Lombard College, Moody Bible Institute Library, Archives Branch of the Federal Archives and Records Center of the
National Archives and Records Administration, Newberry Library, Chicago
Public Library, and University of Illinois at Chicago. We thank Patrick M. Quinn,
university archivist, Northwestern University, and David K. Himrod, assistant
librarian for reader service at the United Library of the Garrett Evangelical
Theological Seminary and Seabury-Western Theological Seminary, both in
Evanston, Illinois. Still others provided important information: Arthur Miller,
archivist and librarian for special collections, Donnelley Library, Lake Forest
College; Robert T. Chapel, archives technical assistant, University Archives,

University of Illinois at Urbana-Champaign; Karen Deller, special collections assistant, Bradley University, Peoria, Illinois; Jo Rayfield, university archivist, Illinois State University, Normal; and Carley R. Robinson, curator of manuscripts and archives, Knox College, Galesburg. In addition to the librarians and archivists at Rockford College who have been most attentive, we have received help and encouragement from John L. Molyneux and others at the Rockford Public Library and from Karl Moehling and John Peterson, proprietors of the Book Stall of Rockford. In Freeport, Stephenson County, Illinois, employees in several county government offices were helpful, especially those associated with the clerk of the circuit court, the recorder, county clerk, and probate court. Various employees and volunteers at the Stephenson County Historical Society in Freeport shared manuscripts, books, and artifacts with us.

Conducting research in Iowa was not an easy task; several people at different institutions, however, smoothed our way and provided important missing pieces of our research puzzle. They were Emma Lee Hill of the Keokuk Public Library; Mary Bennett, special collections librarian and Jeffrey A. Coon, reference librarian, at the State Historical Society of Iowa, Iowa City; Tyler O. Walters, university archivist, and Becky S. Jordan, special collections, both at Iowa State University, Ames; Florence Morgan at the Newton Public Library; and Betty Haas, corresponding secretary, Old Fort Genealogical Society, Inc., Fort Madison. Buena Vista College, Buena Vista, provided data on John Manning Linn's tenure as an early president of the institution.

We had numerous helpers in Philadelphia, Pennsylvania: Ward J. Childs, city archivist, Philadelphia, Department of Records; Development Officer Cynthia Little and Reference Librarian Daniel N. Rolph, the Historical Society of Pennsylvania; and Kenneth J. Ross, reference librarian, Presbyterian Church (U.S.A.). They were extremely helpful in developing biographical data on various cousins, aunts, and uncles of Jane Addams who lived in the Philadelphia area and identifying an assortment of Presbyterian ministers who maintained a relationship with the Addams family during their Cedarville years. Of most assistance outside Philadelphia were the Historical Society of Berks County; Diane Windham Shaw, special collections librarian and college archivist, Lafayette College, Easton; Sharon Gothard, history room of the Easton Area Public Library and District Center; and Kay Schellhase, archivist, the Evangelical and Reformed Historical Society, Lancaster. Esther Leiby, assistant librarian, Sinking Spring Library, and various volunteers at the Adamstown Public Library helped us gain access to information about both communities during the eighteenth and nineteenth centuries.

We appreciate the reference assistance of Paul Machlis, collection specialist at the McHenry Library, University of California, Santa Cruz, as well as the services of the staff members of the Doe (Main) Library, the Bancroft Library, and the Flora Lamson Hewlett Library of the Graduate Theological Union, all at the University of California, Berkeley. Kim Ball of the Georgia Historical Society

Library in Savannah helped us unravel the story of Mary and Fred Greenleaf. Information on the Valparaiso Male and Female College came from the archives of Valparaiso University in Indiana. In Kansas, we had the assistance of Terri Harley of the Girard Public Library and Randy Roberts at the Pittsburg State University. Willard B. Arnold III of the Waterville Historical Society in Maine; Susan Ravdin, assistant in special collections, Bowdoin College Library, Brunswick, Maine; Alice C. Dalligan, Burton Historical Collection, Detroit Public Library; and various staff members of the Bentley Historical Library and the University of Michigan Archives, Ann Arbor, also ably assisted. Cynthia Steinke of Edina, Minnesota, conducted research for us in St. Paul among the Minnesota Historical Society's records of the Breck School. In Missouri, we had the assistance of Jason D. Stratman, library assistant–reference at the Missouri Historical Society, St. Louis, and researchers at the Carondelet Historical Society, also in St. Louis. Elaine S. Pike, special collections assistant, Vassar College Libraries, Poughkeepsie, New York; Karen Reagan, head, public services, Rare and Manuscript Collections, Cornell University, Ithaca, New York; and Alicia Mauldin, archives technician, U.S. Military Academy, West Point, New York, were also helpful. We are grateful to the many volunteers who manage the Family History Center, Church of Jesus Christ of Latter Day Saints, Fayetteville, North Carolina, for access to indexed U.S. Census returns and other public records. In Ohio we had adept help at handling a variety of requests, from queries about a long-defunct women's seminary to help with verifying a locally manufactured piano. We are grateful to Constance J. M. Conley, assistant librarian, and Carl Thomas Engel, librarian of genealogy and local history, Morley Library, Lake Erie College, Painesville; librarians in Antiochiana, Antioch University, Yellow Springs; Roland M. Baumann, archivist, and Gertrude Jacobs, a volunteer, both at Oberlin College, Oberlin; Helen Clark Sudyk, clerk of the Huntsberg Congregational Church; and Patricia M. Van Skaik, head, history department, and Alfred Kleine-Kreutzmann, curator of rare books and special collections, both of the Public Library of Cincinnati and Hamilton County. In South Dakota, librarians at the Aberdeen (Alexander Mitchell) Public Library sent us information on the history of their area, including the development of the Groton Collegiate Institute. Ann Allen Shockley, associate librarian for special collections and university archivist, Fisk University, Nashville, Tennessee, was very responsive to our research request. Nancy Slote, former associate editor on the Jane Addams Papers project and now associated with the King County Library System in Seattle, conducted research for us in the state of Washington on an assortment of families associated with Jane Addams's. Also helpful in Washington was the Grays Harbor Genealogical Society in Cosmopolis and Sandy Lauritzen at the Aberdeen Timberland Regional Library in Aberdeen. In Wisconsin, Beth Merkel at the University of Wisconsin–Stout; Laurel Towns of the De Pere Historical Society, White Pillars Museum, De Pere; and Lois R. Stein and Cait Dallas of the Kenosha County Historical Society and Museum at

Kenosha provided valuable information. Fred Burwell, college archivist, and his staff in the Beloit College Archives, Wisconsin, ably supported our efforts to locate information on John Weber Addams, George Bowman Haldeman, Roland Salisbury, their classmates, their careers, and their era at Beloit. Chris Nelson, reference librarian, and various other staff members of the Beloit College Library, were extremely helpful as well. Peter T. Maiken, director, news and publications, at Beloit College, now retired, provided guidance on the Blaisdell family associated with both Rockford Female Seminary and Beloit Academy and College. William H. Barton, research historian at the Wyoming State Archives and Historical Department, Cheyenne, was also helpful.

We are grateful to Charles Brock for the technical assistance he provided with project computer systems. Special students from the Department of History, Methodist College, Fayetteville, North Carolina, ably assisted us with the preparation of initial drafts of the manuscript. Rush Beeler, professor of French emeritus, University of North Carolina, Wilmington, helped with the translation of languages other than English in the documents we present. The talented N. Eason Bryan served as our photographer. We are grateful as well to repositories that gave us permission to include photographs from their collections.

We benefited from advice offered by our experienced advisory board, consisting of Anne Firor Scott, William K. Boyd Professor Emeritus, Department of History, Duke University; Allen F. Davis, professor of history, Department of History, Temple University; and David Chesnutt, editor, Papers of Henry Laurens, University of South Carolina. We are very grateful to the scholars, unknown to us, who have reviewed our work as presented through applications to the National Endowment for the Humanities, the National Historical Publications and Records Commission, and private foundations, and who have supported our efforts. We are also grateful to scholars, including Kathryn Kish Sklar and Beverly Wilson Palmer, who have discussed our project with us at various stages. In addition, we had the pleasure of other discussions with documentary editors, including Candace Falk, Emma Goldman Papers; Ann D. Gordon, Papers of Elizabeth Cady Stanton and Susan B. Anthony; and Esther Katz, Margaret Sanger Papers; and with a group of scholars developing biographies of Jane Addams, among them Gioia Diliberto, Katherine Joslin, Lucy Knight, Barbara Kraft, and Barbara Garland Polikoff.

We are particularly indebted to those who served as readers for the manuscript of this volume. Their fresh perspective as well as their comments, suggestions, and corrections were most helpful. In particular we wish to recognize Ferris Olin, the former associate director, Institute for Research on Women, and now curator, Women's Archives, Mabel Smith Douglass Library, Rutgers University, New Brunswick, New Jersey, for her comments on our treatment of Ellen Gates Starr; and Christie Farnham, associate professor of history, Iowa State University, particularly for her consideration of Jane Addams's Rockford Female Seminary years and for women's education in general. Additional support came from Dana Frank, professor of American studies, University of California, Santa Cruz. The following people have read and commented on the entire manuscript: Nancy Slote, for fifteen years associate editor on the Jane Addams Papers project; independent biographer Frances von Rosenberg; and Allen F. Davis, professor of history at Temple University and a biographer of Jane Addams and historian of the social settlement movement.

We are grateful to Joan Catapano, editor-in-chief and associate director at the University of Illinois Press, for her enthusiastic support of our project. Willis G. Regier, director of the Press, and the Press's editorial board deserve our thanks, too. They have committed the University of Illinois Press to becoming a publisher of works by and about Jane Addams. We also wish to recognize the Press's staff, especially Mary Giles, Theresa L. Sears, Copenhaver Cumpston, and Mary Lou Menches, who guided this work so ably through its production phase.

Many, many other people have helped us along the way. Even though we do not have their names, we are nevertheless extremely grateful to them. This work, truly a team effort, would not have been possible without those individuals and the organizations, institutions, and agencies we have identified. Thank you, one and all.

We dedicate this work to Jane Addams and to all who have, wittingly or unwittingly, followed and will follow in her footsteps, who demand social justice and peace, and who labor to make this shrinking world a better place for all.

Introduction

Jane Addams remains one of the most famous among American women. Her life spanned significant times. She was born in a rural Illinois hamlet as the nation moved toward the Civil War, and she died in Chicago in 1935 as Adolph Hitler was coming to power in Germany. She founded the world-renowned social settlement Hull-House in Chicago in 1889 and was a leader of many of the reform efforts that swept America in the late nineteenth and early twentieth centuries. After taking a difficult stand for pacifism in World War I, she became the first American woman to receive the Nobel Peace Prize. For historians, she has become the woman who best represents the reform agenda and actions that helped define the Progressive Era. During her lifetime in the public eye, everyone knew who she was. In America her name became almost a household word. The plain, direct, solid image that her name often conjures up was accurate for Addams in part, but it conveys far from the whole truth about the intelligent, talented, energetic, caring, complex, and enigmatic woman who gained international recognition as a reformer, champion for social justice and peace, philanthropist, and humanitarian. A feminist role model, writer, and spokeswoman for urban reform, Jane Addams was among the most influential women in the United States. For thousands of people worldwide she came to represent the finest of American womanhood and the best of pluralistic democracy. Jane Addams was an icon in her time, a touchstone for her era.

One of the primary objectives of the Jane Addams Papers project is to bring the story of this remarkably influential figure in American history to a wide audience—from postgraduate scholars and researchers to students and the general reading public. With the publication of this and the volumes to follow we hope to reveal more of the person Jane Addams was. We expect to present sufficient and appropriate evidence of her life so that the full measure of her achievements and contributions to American history can be understood.

Laura Jane Addams began life on 6 September 1860 in Cedarville, Illinois.

She graduated from nearby Rockford Female Seminary, receiving one of the first college degrees it offered. After a period of debilitating illness followed by two European tours split by time in Baltimore and Cedarville, she found her way to Chicago, which became her home for the remainder of her life. There in 1889 Jane Addams and Ellen Gates Starr, her friend and Rockford Female Seminary classmate, co-founded Hull-House. It became America's best known and most influential social settlement. Addams assumed leadership of the American social settlement movement when it stood at the forefront of a variety of social and economic reform efforts that were developed in the 1890s, and she continued to shape American urban life into the twentieth century.

The late 1800s was a period of rapid industrialization and urbanization in the United States. A large influx of impoverished immigrants, predominately from eastern and southern Europe, provided cheap labor to fuel economic growth. These newcomers clustered primarily in eastern and midwestern American cities that had developed where industry and transportation converged. Dilapidated neighborhoods crammed with poor working people of a variety of nationalities and ethnic backgrounds generated major human problems, including conflict between laborers and capitalists, among different cultures, and within families. There was political corruption, a lack of appropriate city services, poor housing, and little chance to learn English. Working conditions were deplorable, and wages exceedingly low. Health-care opportunities were limited, and children and young people had few possibilities to grow up healthy, educated, and secure.

To meet the reform challenge, Jane Addams attracted to her causes an impressive assembly of like-minded men and women. Together they forged a network of leaders who influenced needed reforms. They investigated urban problems around them and helped lead movements that resulted in restricting child labor and sweatshops; improving working conditions, with shorter hours and higher wages in industry for men and women; and developing greater protections for consumers. They supported the growth of unions and served as intermediaries in the great disparity between the power of industrialists and the working poor. They led the struggle for improved educational opportunities for all, including better public schools and the development of vocational education and public kindergartens. They initiated educational programs to help immigrants learn English, improve their literacy, and prepare themselves for U.S. citizenship. They promoted child welfare, offering well-baby clinics, nursery care, public parks, playgrounds, and camps for secure, healthy play environments, educational play opportunities for children, and safe social settings for youths and young adults. They created and helped sustain organizations that provided immigrant and juvenile protection. They worked for woman suffrage, secure living conditions, and expanded rights for women. They supported the creation of civil service, worked for civic reform, and fought corrupt politicians. They brought access to the arts, including a variety of arts education as well as arts appreciation opportunities, for thousands of workers and their families and promoted the preservation of arts and crafts, especially those associated with various immigrant groups. They worked to improve the urban environment including access to adequate water and sanitation facilities, better and more affordable housing stock, and clean streets and alleys. They supported efforts to improve health care and encouraged the development of clinics and education about diet, and they promoted cleanliness within tenements. In the process, these social reformers created a new profession: social work. Addams also helped establish private, nonsectarian philanthropy in America and, by her example, made it more acceptable for single, middle-class women to lead active, productive lives outside the traditional family structure.

Jane Addams was a founding member or active supporter of hundreds of reform organizations. Among the international and national organizations were the International Juvenile Court Committee and International Save the Children Fund, the American Association for the Advancement of Science, American Association for Labor Legislation, American Association for Old Age Security, American Association for Study and Prevention of Infant Mortality, American Civil Liberties Union, General Federation of Women's Clubs, Mobilization for Human Needs—1933 and 1934, National American Woman Suffrage Association, National Association for the Advancement of Colored People, National Child Labor Committee, National Conference of Social Work, National Education Association, National Federation of Settlements, Progressive Party, and the Progressive National Service Committee. Among the local organizations with which she involved herself were the Adult Education Council of Chicago, Chicago Board of Education (of which she was a member from 1905 to 1909), Chicago Commons Settlement, Chicago Urban League, Chicago Woman's Club, City Homes Association of Chicago, Civic Federation of Chicago, Frederick Douglass Center, Immigrants Protective League, Juvenile Court of Cook County, Juvenile Protective Association, Wendell Phillips Settlement, and the Woman's City Club.

Jane Addams was a major force in helping to create a public conscience for the reform agenda that she and her colleagues espoused. Often sought as a speaker, she made numerous lecture tours for her causes. She spoke to thousands, young and old, men and women, rich and poor, and powerful and powerless, people of diverse ethnic, religious, and political backgrounds and philosophies. Her remarks and activities were carried so regularly and by so many newspapers (the primary means of public communication in America of her day) that her access to the public was almost like that of a journalist with a regular syndicated column. By her actions on behalf of humanity, she made news. People wanted to know what she did, where she went, what she thought, and what she said. Because she captured America's interest, she had access to newspapers—and then radio—to promote her views and keep herself and her causes in the news.

Jane Addams also became a prolific writer. Through her eleven books—including the autobiographical *Twenty Years at Hull-House* (1910) and *The Sec-*

ond Twenty Years at Hull-House (1930)—and hundreds of newspaper and journal articles, she helped educate the public and establish a climate in which social reform came to be considered possible as well as necessary. Before women had the vote, she worked tirelessly with lawmakers, journalists, educators, philanthropists, industrialists, union leaders, reformers, and leaders at all levels of government to see that reforms were carried out. Pragmatic, persistent, organized, intelligent, energetic even in her declining years, an excellent communicator, skilled at managing people, a leader of unquestioned ability among both men and women, and noted for her commitment to mediation and compromise as problem-solving mechanisms, Jane Addams was also acknowledged for her sincerity, integrity, seeming gentleness enhanced by an aura of spirituality, and great sense of social justice anchored in her dedication to the democratic ideal. She must have been startled yet pleased when, only in her thirties, she was respectfully and affectionately labeled the "grandmother" of the settlement house movement in America. Jane Addams seemed to combine the most acceptable attributes of the independent woman and the Victorian lady. She won the hearts and minds of both men and women and became identified among the public by a number of flattering sobriquets. Among them were "gentle Jane," "feminine conscience of the nation," "genius of Hull-House," "Chicago's first citizen," "the only saint America has produced," and "first lady of the land." Later, when she fell from public grace because of her stand for peace during World War I and because many came to believe she supported the Russian Revolution in 1917, the phrases became critical and derisive: "the most dangerous woman in America" and "the reddest of the red." Yet it was her image as the "essential American" and the "angel of Hull-House" that prevailed.

Jane Addams seemed to bring out the best in people. She had the ability to give undivided attention to one person at a time, to let each sense her empathy. Yet she never seemed to lose her perspective; she almost never failed to keep her emotional distance, to separate an issue from a personal problem. Perhaps that was the trait her nephew and biographer James Weber Linn had identified (and chided her about) when he wrote to Ellen Gates Starr, "How shall I get at and properly set forth, without exaggeration, her impersonality? It makes her so mad when I speak of it to her—she denies it almost with oaths!" Linn's letter of 4 May 1935 is now in the Starr Papers in the Sophia Smith Collection at Smith College.

While many revered Jane Addams and admired and loved her for the concern they perceived she exhibited for them, she apparently shared genuine personal, emotional relationships only with those closest to her. In her adult life these were most notably Ellen Gates Starr and, later, Hull-House patron Mary Rozet Smith. As a child and young adult she had adored her father and as an adult kept his memory dear. She respected her stepmother and loved her siblings. Some years after the death of her father, Jane Addams found herself to be the matriarch of the Addams family, drawing upon her earlier, youthful role as family peacemaker. By the time she co-founded Hull-House, her siblings, their mates, and their children—her nieces and nephews and eventually her great-nieces and nephews—looked to her for guidance. She seemed constantly to balance their needs in light of her vocation, her public identity, and her own private requirements. She took her role as family leader seriously, yet as she performed it she seemed to lack the kind of emotional warmth that nieces and nephews and their progeny craved from her. It may be important to remember that in addition to the "impersonality" identified by James Weber Linn, by the time they were old enough to want her individual attention she was reaching the end of her life, her health was poor, and she was much in demand from the public. She may have had little time or energy to develop close emotional ties with her young people, who remained as much in awe of their great-aunt as her public was.

Even while devoting herself to the various causes she supported, traveling hundreds of miles each year, and maintaining a public persona, she preserved a ladylike, well-mannered sense of decorum and propriety. Although she seemed to have little vanity about her person or attire, she enjoyed having access to the trappings of wealth—automobile rides, comfortable living accommodations, and good food. Throughout the years her circle of friends and associates, ever respectful of her talents and fame, became almost personal guardians. This was especially so after poor health began to plague her during her late fifties. Addams seldom traveled or took a vacation alone. She spent increasing amounts of time away from Hull-House as her fame grew, but usually at the home of close Chicago friends and Hull-House supporters Mary Rozet Smith or Louise de Koven Bowen. Someone seemed always to be with her.

Her dedication to the cause of world peace was a natural progression from her commitment to social justice and to improving the lot of humanity. She knew that war was destructive for humankind and for the improved quality of life for all that she was fostering. Worried that America's participation in the European conflict that became World War I would hurt her country's move toward social reform, Jane Addams became a leader in the national and international peace movements. She was the primary force behind the founding of the Woman's Peace Party in 1915, the International Committee of Women for Permanent Peace in 1915, and the Women's International League for Peace and Freedom in 1919. Jane Addams was also an active leader in a number of other national and international peace organizations, including the American Peace Society, Anti-Imperialist League, Fellowship of Reconciliation, League of Nations Association, League to Enforce the Peace, World Conference for International Peace through Religion, and World's Court League. Toward the end of her life, as Germany began to arm and dictate under the leadership of Adolph Hitler, Jane Addams and her friends worked through a number of organizations, including the American Committee against Fascist Oppression in Germany, Hospites (a special committee of social workers to help their German colleagues), and the National Committee to Aid Victims of German Fascism, to save those in danger of losing their lives in the Nazi onslaught.

Castigated in public by many Americans for what they saw as her refusal to support the American war effort after the United States entered the war in 1917 and for maintaining her vocal and steadfast commitment to peace and antifascism, Jane Addams was surprised and disheartened by her loss of honor among the American people. Yet she held to her pacifist principles and carried on. It was only as America recovered from World War I and the Red Scare period that she began to regain her former standing with the people of America. Yet the relationship would never be quite the same. Times had changed. The experience of the world war and then the Great Depression beginning in 1929 carried the nation on to new concerns and leaders. Removed from the cutting edge of history, Jane Addams spent the last years of her life continuing to direct and support Hull-House and its programs and promoting world peace.

She received public recognition for her work in 1931 with the award of the Nobel Peace Prize, which she shared with Nicholas Murray Butler. During her lifetime, numerous other accolades came her way, including honorary degrees and memberships, clubs and schools named in her honor, and recognition by national organizations whose mission she had helped craft and carry out. In annual contests sponsored by a variety of magazines and newspapers she was usually named one of the ten outstanding living American women and often chosen as the most admired woman in America. Her death on 21 May 1935 after surgery to remove cancerous lesions of the bowel caused public dismay throughout the world. Newspapers everywhere carried word of her passing. In Chicago, the events associated with her funeral at Hull-House and burial in the Cedarville cemetery made front-page news. Cartoonists who had made her the butt of their jokes in earlier times now mourned her loss, and journalists sang her praises. Walter Lippmann hailed her as witness and example of the best in the tradition of American democracy. "She had compassion without condescension. She had pity without retreat to vulgarity. She had infinite sympathy for common things without forgetfulness of those that are uncommon," he noted in his "Today and Tomorrow" column on 22 May 1935 in the *New York Herald Tribune.*

How could someone so significant in her era be lost to all but scholars— primarily historians—by the end of the century in which she made her mark? One answer is that Jane Addams, a woman, a social reformer, and a peace advocate, became buried by the weight of more recent history, which has been largely maintained and written by men. Until the last forty years of the twentieth century, American history was primarily the story of politics, economics and trade, and war, recounted in the context of great male leaders. Addams and her accomplishments did not fit that matrix. In addition, by 1935 the world was beginning to be consumed by the actions of dictators who would foment one of the century's watershed events, World War II, and its aftermath, the cold war, which was punctuated by political repression and periodic, localized military actions or mini-wars. The American people—indeed, the world—may have craved peace but lived with a different reality, one for which the philosophy and achievements of Jane Addams had little perceived relevance.

Then, during the 1960s, as women began to reassert their rights and claim equal status in society and the work place, they initiated a search for their history and the leaders and social movements of their past. As they began to develop their history and insist that it become part of the mainstream of the American story, they discovered that they needed to secure evidence—manuscripts, documents, photographs, artifacts, and the like—from which that history could be constructed. Especially since the 1970s, numerous collections of appropriate materials related to women have been identified, gathered, and organized to support scholarly research. The Jane Addams Papers project has been part of that effort.

The Project

The Jane Addams Papers project began in 1976. Its goal was to locate, identify, gather (in original or facsimile form) from many disparate sources, and organize as comprehensive as possible a body of documents that Addams had created or acquired and make those documents readily available to scholars and the general reading public. To do so, we devised a set of integrated publications consisting of three parts. The first two, designed primarily for use by specialized scholars, are a comprehensive microfilm edition composed of material gathered after an extensive organized search from more than a thousand collections, both private and public sources, predominately in the United States, Canada, and Europe, along with a detailed guide to its contents. The eighty-two-reel microfilm edition, with approximately two thousand images on each reel, is divided into five series: correspondence, writings, personal documents, Hull-House Association Records, and periodical clippings. It was issued by Microfilming Corporation of America and University Microfilms International between 1985 and 1986. The 684-page *Jane Addams Papers: A Comprehensive Guide* was published in 1996 by Indiana University Press. It includes, among other things, a correspondent-subject index to the Addams correspondence and writings in the microfilm edition, a bibliography of Addams's writing, genealogical information on the Addams family, and a calendar of the correspondence of Jane Addams. The third and final product is the printed edition of the selected, annotated, and indexed papers of Jane Addams, of which this is the first volume.

Although some of Jane Addams's writings have been reprinted and the first of her two-volume memoir *Twenty Years at Hull-House* has become a classic, her correspondence and private papers have never been published in volume form. This series will fill that void. We have chosen a biographical framework for the multivolume edition, presenting documents in chronological order. The edition is not purely biography nor autobiography, yet it has elements of both.

Neither is it meant to be only a group of transcriptions of selected Addams papers; at its core the work will provide accurate transcriptions of key Addams documents. It is meant to present Jane Addams in the context of the time in which she lived and worked. Further, it is meant to provide appropriate, compelling evidence, primarily from first-person sources created at or near the time that the events took place, of Addams's ideas, activities, relationships, and achievements. Our goal is not to interpret the life of Jane Addams as much as it is to provide the data and the context from which readers may make their own interpretations or judgments.

Selection

The documents that appear in this edition have been selected primarily from among those that compose the microfilm edition of *The Jane Addams Papers*. From time to time, we also include documents that have come to light since the microfilm edition was published as well as material that by definition of the scope of papers presented in the microfilm edition were omitted from it but provide evidence of a significant influence in Addams's life.

We have selected from an assortment of documents: correspondence to and from Jane Addams, diaries, memoranda, address books and calling cards, personal history documents, deeds, tax and financial records, wills and probate records, classroom notes, essays, publications, writings and works edited, speeches, interviews, and testimony, reviews of publications, poetry, research files maintained by Jane Addams, periodical clippings files, minutes, announcements, and records relating to organizations with which Jane Addams was associated, family documents and correspondence, photographs, and the records of organizations Jane Addams founded or directed.

In making our selection, we relied heavily, although not entirely, on the correspondence, diaries, writings, and speeches of Jane Addams. We considered each document in light of the following criteria: its centrality to Addams's life story, her philosophy, her work, achievements and the times in which she lived, how revealing it is of her as a person, how telling it is of the role Addams played in the variety of movements with which she was associated that are central to the development of American interests at home and abroad, and how available the document is to researchers and readers through other published sources.

The papers of Jane Addams are voluminous, yet not all that she created or were sent to her have survived. Fire, flood, the wastebasket, space constraints, theft, carelessness, and Jane Addams acting as her own archivist and censor have affected the body of material that remains. There are obvious holes. No Jane Addams correspondence, for example, seems to be extant for the years 1874 and 1875, yet there are letters to and from the young Addams for the years before and after. Letters Jane Addams wrote during the last half of 1880 seem to be lost, and although there are some written to her from the fall of 1881 through the summer of 1882, almost none she wrote have survived for that period. A lifetime of letters between Jane Addams and her sister Alice Addams Haldeman is present only in part. Many of Jane Addams's letters to her sister are extant, although few of Alice Haldeman's letters to her apparently exist. Jane Addams may have destroyed them herself, or perhaps they were destroyed in 1963 when wrecking ball and water made mush of settlement papers stored in the Hull-House basement. Early correspondence between Jane Addams and Ellen Gates Starr, her classmate and the settlement's co-founder, has endured, although Starr destroyed some letters. It is difficult to determine just how much of the later-life correspondence between the two friends has survived.

Jane Addams placed her papers and the books she considered peace related in the Swarthmore College Library in 1932 as the inaugural collection of the Swarthmore College Peace Collection. Numerous additions from a variety of sources, including Hull-House, Addams family members, and close associates, have been made to the collection since Addams's death, broadening its scope to include documentation relating to her entire life. After her boon companion Mary Rozet Smith died in 1934, Jane Addams's letters to Smith, beginning in 1890, were returned to Addams. She apparently reread them, keeping some and destroying others. She reread Mary Smith's letters to her and destroyed almost all of them. At about the same time, Jane Addams was sorting correspondence and documents from her family and personal files to give to her nephew James Weber Linn for the biography he began writing in 1934. She admitted to him that she was destroying family material that she considered to be of a highly personal nature. In some cases, she sent Linn old letters for background information with the admonition that he was to destroy them after he read them. A large group of such documents eventually found their way to the Library of Congress and the University of Illinois at Chicago. The Library of Congress gave the Addams papers to Swarthmore to be added to those already there. Linn's descendants placed some documents in the Jane Addams Memorial Collection at the University of Illinois at Chicago. Family papers that had been lodged in various nooks and crannies at the Addams home in Cedarville eventually found their way to Swarthmore and into various family and private collections. Family members have placed an assortment of Addams, Haldeman, and Hostetter family material, including Jane Addams correspondence, in a number of repositories including Swarthmore, University of Illinois at Chicago, and Indiana University. The essay in *The Jane Addams Papers: A Comprehensive Guide* (65–76) on the provenance of the documents provides a record of what happened to various segments of those that belonged to Addams.

Correspondence

The Addams correspondence is uneven. Generally, the letters Jane Addams wrote during her youth and early adulthood were the longest, most complete, and the most personal to survive. Many were to family members or close friends. The events, ideas, and relationships they describe were from a time when the pace at which she lived her life was slower, easier, and less complicated than the tempo and issues of her adult life after the founding of Hull-House. During the period before 1900, Addams had more reason to share thoughts and ideas completely in letters, for that was the primary means of communication among family and friends who lived in different towns—to say nothing of different states or countries.

In the extant Addams correspondence before 1912, letters written by Jane Addams predominate in number over those sent to her. Jane Addams did not ordinarily keep copies of the letters she wrote before 1912. Those that compose this segment of the Addams correspondence have been gathered primarily from the family, friends, and organizations that received them.

After 1912, extant letters received by Jane Addams overshadow the number of surviving letters—copies or originals—that she wrote. If fame brought little time for her to write personal letters it also brought an increase in the number of letters Addams received, not only from an ever-widening assortment of family, acquaintances, colleagues, and close friends but also from strangers. Considering the complicated issues and relationships among those active in the reform movements with which Addams was associated and the fact that her life was moving at an ever-increasing pace, she may have been unwilling to take the time to put her feelings, ideas in progress, and specific opinions in a form she could not readily retract. In addition, she lived through a period when the telephone, telegraph, typewriter, and increasingly efficient means of travel in and between cities, throughout the country, and between countries became effective influences on the written record. There was no longer an incentive to write a long, informative letter to a good friend, family member, or associate whom she might telephone or see within the day. Many of the surviving letters that Jane Addams wrote during the 1915–35 period of her life, although by no means all of them, concern her peace activities. They focus on her public role in a variety of events and indicate her stand on an assortment of timely issues. With the exception of correspondence to family members, they are not often as revealing of her actions or thoughts nor as personal in content as are her early letters. That is one of the reasons we have chosen to present a larger percentage of letters from the approximately eight thousand pieces of correspondence associated with the 1860–1915 period than from the approximately eighteen thousand items of correspondence associated with the 1915–35 period.

From her first extant letter in 1868 up until 1900, holograph documents comprise most of the surviving Addams papers. A few letters to and from Addams were written by Addams and her correspondents in pencil, but most were scribed in ink—and often in difficult-to-read handwriting. From 1900 until 1935, and in increasing numbers, typewritten letters characterize the Addams correspondence. Fame and the fast-paced reform efforts with which she and her coterie of co-workers were involved dictated the necessity of having ready secretarial help. That resulted in the opportunity to dictate a note or response and get it on its way quickly.

Jane Addams wrote letters by hand, especially personal ones, to family and intimate friends all of her life. They progress from the smudged pages of an eight-year-old attempting her first letters with misspelled words formed from misshapen, printed letters through the development of legible penmanship and communications that improve in length and complexity of thought. By the mid-1890s, however, her handwriting once again had become difficult to follow. As the pace of her life began to speed up, her holographic letters, often written in haste and to close friends familiar with her phraseology, syntax, and grammar, began to devolve into groups of words that raced across each page. An initial letter of the alphabet followed by a long dash or pen stroke parallel to the bottom of the page and sometimes, although not always, ending with a letter could be difficult to decipher.

During the late 1890s, perhaps in recognition of her need to generate a greater amount of correspondence and writing, and because it was a newfangled way to communicate, Jane Addams tried to learn to use a typewriter. Her attempt was short-lived. Although she wrote and typed several letters and a series of lectures, she never achieved speed or accuracy and soon gave up this means of communicating.

All mail that came to her personally, or on behalf of Hull-House or any other organization she led, was answered—if not by Jane Addams then by someone she delegated to respond for her. Grace and Edith Abbott, renowned social reformers themselves, recalled that Addams had no secretary when they first became residents at Hull-House. According to them, after she gathered and reviewed the mail each morning, she would present letters to an assortment of appropriate settlement residents for response. Close friends also served as secretaries from time to time, especially when she was ill or away from the settlement. Even Ellen Gates Starr found herself performing secretarial duties. Many letters handled in this manner begin "Miss Addams has asked me to write to you." Soon, however, a secretary for Jane Addams became the norm. Some were Hull-House residents who took on that responsibility as their settlement job; others were professionally trained and lived away from the settlement, coming in to work daily. Addams dictated responses and then sometimes corrected them by hand as she signed each letter and sent it on its way.

Jane Addams seems to have been raising funds almost constantly to support a variety of causes. At Hull-House, she maintained contribution records for each donor arranged so that on the annual anniversary of each gift she could automatically write and request additional support. By 1915 those letters were form letters; she would identify which version she wanted sent. Her secretary had a pad of stationery, a Jane Addams signature signed in an appropriate place, and could type and mail the letters without Addams ever seeing them. Hull-House

Examples of the handwriting of Jane Addams. The 23 January 1869 letter
reveals the incorrectly formed letters and misspelled words of a child
learning to write. Her letter of 6 March 1881 to her father is extremely
legible for Jane, and her letter of 30 May 1931 to her niece Esther Linn
Hulbert is an example of the hurried scrawl that characterized her holograph letters in later life. (JAPP)

had a similar arrangement with regard to requests for autographs or photographs of Jane Addams. The Women's International League for Peace and Freedom and the International Committee of Women for Permanent Peace had her permission to use a stamp with a replica of her signature on specific kinds of correspondence, for example circular letters that went out to each of the organizations' branches and their officers.

As she found the time to do so, Jane Addams wrote from many different venues, whether a desk, table, or book in her lap. She dashed off letters as she waited in someone's office for an appointment or for the start of a meeting, or when she was on a train or boat, on in a hotel room. In most cases, letterhead stationery from a hotel or travel conveyance or a friend's home where she was lodging reflects where she actually was when she wrote each letter. But that was not always so. She had a habit of taking hotel stationery with her and using it to write while traveling. She also sometimes used the stationery of an organization—most often Hull-House, her home—while traveling. She usually remembered, however, to mark through the letterhead and record the date and place from which the letter was written.

Her standard close for the letters of her adult years was "Faithfully yours." It was almost always followed by her full signature, "Jane Addams," even to family members and intimate friends like Mary Rozet Smith. Her choice of signature seemed to follow her preference for being addressed formally as a person, yet that was not always so. Although named Laura Jane Addams, she had never been called Laura. As a child, to family and friends she was Jennie Addams, and she signed her childhood letters as Jennie or Jennie Addams. During her first year at Rockford Female Seminary she was listed in the school catalog as Laura Jane Addams, but in newspaper articles about school functions she was identified as Jane or Jennie Addams.

Her position on the matter of address obviously affected Ellen Gates Starr. In a letter to Jane Addams on 27 July 1879 (found in the Starr Papers in the Sophia Smith Collection at Smith College and reprinted in transcribed form in its entirety with the documents in this volume) she wrote:

> Now, my lady, I have a pretty serious bone to pick with you. I almost forgot it. I staid with Katie [Hitchcock] & Mary [Downs] one night & something was said about my saying "Miss Hitchcock" & her calling me "Miss Starr" & I observed that I should have been most happy to have appeared a little less formal with some of the girls, but never was allowed that privilege, as they all <u>insisted</u> on calling me "Miss Starr". Katie replied that she had always done so because she thought I preferred it. I asked her whence came that remarkable idea, & she said Jane said so. I was pretty wrathy Miss Addams, I do assure you. After I had <u>besought</u> of you as much as I considered consistent with my dignity, to call me something else, & you had cruelly refused to do so for so long, I didn't expect of you the additional cruelty of misrepresenting me.

From her days at Rockford Female Seminary to the end of her life, Jane Addams seems always to have been "Miss Addams" to everyone except family and her most intimate friends such as Ellen Gates Starr, Mary Rozet Smith, and Louise de Koven Bowen. To them she was "Aunt Jane" or "Jane." She was most often "JA" or sometimes "gentle Jane" to other friends, among them Florence Kelley, Julia Lathrop, and Alice Hamilton.

Diaries

Jane Addams seems to have begun keeping a diary at the urging of her parents. Her father John Huy Addams apparently kept a diary for at least part of his life, although only a six-month portion, July–December 1844, is extant. Stepmother Anna Haldeman Addams also kept a diary sporadically before she wed John Huy Addams, and it, too, is extant. The young Jane Addams was not a regular diarist. Although she may have tried to keep one earlier, the oldest existing ex-

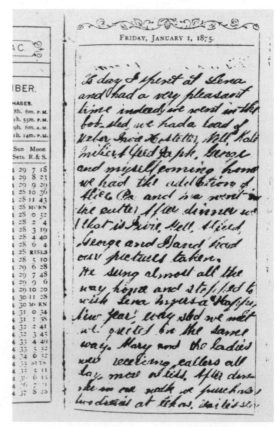

The first page of the earliest extant diary that Jane Addams kept. It was written during the first eight months of 1875, when she was fourteen. (CAHS)

ample belonging to her was one she wrote as a fifteen-year-old in 1875. Portions of it are presented in this volume.

No diary has survived for her years at Rockford Female Seminary or the time immediately following those years, and there is no evidence from correspondence or other writings that Jane Addams attempted to continue the discipline during this period of her life. She apparently had her 1875 diary with her at the seminary, because portions of its pages are filled with drafts of a classroom essay or two and with jottings that later appeared in the seminary magazine. While she was at Rockford Female Seminary she did keep notebooks, two of which are extant. In them she recorded class notes, ideas for various sections of the seminary magazine, and favorite quotations from readings and lectures. She also used the notebooks to record thoughts during a summer visit to Nantucket in 1882 and from the fall of 1882 and winter of 1883 as she recuperated from an operation performed by her brother-in-law Harry Haldeman to correct her spinal curvature.

Jane Addams created a record of her first European trip begun in the fall of 1883 and lasting until the early summer of 1885. That extant diary reveals brief, almost illegible handwritten entries describing quick, timely impressions composed as she traveled. No log has survived in which she recorded her activities for the 1885–87 period of her life, when she spent winters in Baltimore and summers in Cedarville. During her second European trip, she apparently kept a notebook and recorded her thoughts and reactions to what she was experiencing. That record is apparently no longer extant. During both her first and second European trips, sister Alice Addams Haldeman collected Jane Addams's long, descriptive letters, shared among her siblings as circular letters, and copied them into a series of three notebooks. This record, although not in Jane Addams's hand and preserved with some omissions—primarily personal asides—from the original letters, serves as a diarylike account of her travels. It was not until she and Ellen Gates Starr founded Hull-House in 1889 that Addams once again began to record the events in her life with any regularity. And then it appears that she relied on a diary chiefly as a means of keeping her appointments straight. A diary with extremely brief entries reflects activities at Hull-House during the first year of its existence, 1889–90. Diaries that Jane Addams may have kept for the period from 1891 through 1893 are missing; those for the years from 1894 to 1923 and one for a 1925 trip to Mexico are extant. Calendars for the following years survive: 1914–15, 1918–1925, 1927–32, and 1934. The entries in both kinds of documents are brief, written in a cramped, almost illegible hand, and primarily reflect her daily appointments.

Speeches and Writings

If Jane Addams had no time for indulging in lengthy, thoughtful diary entries, nor for writing numbers of long, informative letters during her busy adult life, she seems to have made time for preparing thousands of speeches and articles. These became the primary vehicles through which she shared her thoughts, promoted actions, and indicated her hopes for the American people. She wrote hundreds of articles and speeches as well as eleven books, edited several publications, and produced poems, endorsements, book reviews, letters to editors, statements, and speeches. The Macmillan Company was her book publisher. Her other written work appeared in an assortment of periodicals, ranging from scholarly journals like the *Proceedings* of the American Academy of Political Science to popular periodicals such as *Ladies Home Journal, Good Housekeeping,* and newspapers. Sought after as a speaker, during her lifetime she presented thousands of speeches on a variety of topics to an assortment of diverse organizations. She wrote and spoke anecdotally, using personal experiences, many from Hull-House, to make her points. She was committed to the ideal of world peace, the creation of a new social contract, and the idea that new relationships among classes, genders, and national or ethnic groups in America could lead to greater democracy and better quality of life for all. As Nancy Slote points out in "Introduction to the Writings" in *The Jane Addams Papers: A Comprehensive Guide,* "Her stories always included a basic message: inaction would lead to the perpetuation of unnecessary suffering and ultimately to the breakdown of the social contract" (95).

Classroom essays, the texts of debates and of exhibition and graduation addresses, and articles written for the *Rockford Female Seminary Magazine* offer the earliest evidence of Jane Addams's ability as a writer and speaker. The subjects she treated are varied and in part reflect assignments provided by her teachers, but as a body of work this documentation reveals the formative stages of life-long personal interests. Two issues stand out: her interest in the position of women in society and her recognition that she and her sister graduates, as part of the first generation of college women, had an obligation to make special contributions to society. There is more than one version of several of her seminary writings. In some instances there are drafts as well as a final manuscript version of a work; in others there may be only a manuscript and/or a published version. Many manuscripts from her seminary years bear marks correcting spelling, sentence structure, grammar, or organization. In some instances it is difficult to know whether the corrections were made by Jane Addams or by one of her teachers. Although she continued to write for the seminary magazine and published two articles during the eight years after her graduation in 1881, it was not until she had founded Hull-House and assumed a leadership position as a social reformer that she began her career as a noted writer and public speaker.

Jane Addams understood the power of the spoken and written word, and she used her skills as writer and speaker not only to support her reform agenda but also to provide an income for herself. She apparently liked to write and was proud of her talent with words. Throughout her life, she gathered a huge collection of reference material and used it as she prepared speeches and articles (see the microfilm edition of *The Jane Addams Papers,* documents series, reels 31–37). An avid reader, she sought to educate herself in order to educate the people who listened to her. In the process of preparing to write, she had an opportunity to consider and organize her thoughts on a subject. Putting them onto paper must have given her a sense of the logic and suitability of her position.

She used the material she had prepared in many different ways. Some articles began as speeches, particularly at the beginning of her public life. She wrote a series of lectures, gave them in public, and then edited and published some in periodicals before issuing them all in *Democracy and Social Ethics* (1902), her first book. Jane Addams was an excellent extemporaneous speaker. Sometimes she had a written text, and many times she used the same text for more than one speech. On many occasions she probably spoke without any supporting notes or perhaps from an outline scratched roughly and perhaps quickly on a piece of paper. Although she made more than a hundred speeches each year for a great many of her adult years, only a few speech manuscripts or outlines for speeches are extant. Some articles were written originally as articles, and like her speeches they were often revised and reconstructed for different publications. At times she created a new manuscript using an old one. She would cut up a copy of the manuscript of an old article and, pinning portions together in a different arrangement with straight pins, begin to draft a new one by hand. It is likely that she employed this technique in writing the manuscripts for her books. None of those manuscripts survive, however, except for a portion of her last book *My Friend, Julia Lathrop* that reflects this style of preparation.

Addams's extant speeches and writings appear in the microfilm edition of *The Jane Addams Papers* on reels 30 and 45–49. An index to subjects, coauthors, titles, and publishers, two bibliographies (one presented chronologically and the other by title), and a discussion about the search for Jane Addams's writings and speeches and their organization in the microfilm edition may be found in *The Jane Addams Papers: A Comprehensive Guide* (95–232).

Volume 1

We have designed this series to appeal to many different audiences. Local historians and scholars of Illinois history will find this first volume useful, as will academics and public historians working in the fields of women's, family, social, or cultural history; the history of religion, education, and social movements; and Victorian America. It is also intended for a more general audience, including readers interested in biography and the life of Jane Addams, among them high school and college students, teachers, and patrons of public and university libraries.

We focus on particular themes in each volume. For this first volume, on the childhood and formal education of Jane Addams, we have identified major influences in Addams's life that might have set her on her path to greatness as a social reformer, humanitarian, and pacifist. We consider not only the evidence from papers that belonged to Jane Addams and her family but also data developed through research in other primary resources. Much of this historical evidence falls into five thematic categories: family, community, education, women's role in private life and society, and religion and ethical development.

The earliest influence on Jane Addams was the family into which she was born. Primarily through John Huy Addams's activities, it was one of the leading families of northwestern Illinois. This prominence had an early and profound influence on Jane Addams. Through the Addams family story, readers will have an opportunity to see the development of a midwestern pioneer family that came to Illinois with little but a dream and stayed to achieve financial prosperity and a reputation for integrity, leadership, and concern for the welfare of others. The development of their livelihood, the ideas and institutions they valued, their relationships with one another and with others in their community, and their wide-ranging friendships, activities, and contributions to their community were all influences on the young Jane. Her parents, John Huy Addams and Sarah Weber Addams, took responsible roles in the events and activities coincident with the development of the frontier prairie region in which they chose to settle. Both were deeply involved in their traditional spheres of influence. John Huy Addams assumed a particularly strong, visible, and respected position as a farmer, stock-raiser, miller, banker, insurance provider, Republican politician, lay religious leader, and humanitarian. He was a driving force in bringing the railroad to the region. He also helped to create schools and to develop a private lending library. He supported churches and other frontier religious organizations, developed community and business organizations, and helped those who wanted work or could not work. Sarah Addams, and her daughters after her, took responsibility for nursing the sick, providing advice and assistance to emigrants as they passed through on their way west, teaching in Sunday School, and supporting community and religious organizations. A philanthropic impulse seems to have been a natural part of Addams family life. In addition to Jane Addams, her two sisters who lived to maturity also engaged in work of a humanitarian-related philanthropic nature as adults.

Through biographies of each member of Jane Addams's immediate family, father, mother, siblings and their mates, stepmother, and stepbrothers, readers will have an opportunity to explore the complicated Addams family dynamic. Within its structure, Jane Addams experienced and reacted to a variety of childhood female friendships and traditional female tasks; to the deaths of her mother, a sibling, her near-mother childhood nurse, and her adored father; to a stepmother whose style and attitude were very different from the mothering she had been used to; to interaction with a stepbrother approximately her own age who became a recluse closely attached to his mother; to the marriage of each of her siblings and to their departure from the family home; to the mental illness of her brother; and to the alcoholism of a stepbrother who became her brother-in-law. It is clear that John Huy Addams, noted by all who knew him for honesty, integrity, dedication to humanity, kindness, and good judgment, was his daughter's hero and a vital connection in her sense of family.

Under the tutelage of her mercurial stepmother Anna Haldeman Addams, Jane Addams gained poise. She also acquired valuable experience by practicing mechanisms for coping with a prickly personality. With Anna Addams as a guide, Jane Addams also may have learned that play could be educational as well as fun; that being useful to others had high value; that the arts—theater, poetry, literature, fine art, and music, especially—were basic enrichment factors to well-rounded lives; and that social elegance and grace had a useful place in relationships with others. All of these influences became important factors in the development of Hull-House.

Readers will also have an opportunity to investigate the development of communities in northwestern Illinois during the last half of the nineteenth century. The village of Cedarville, where Jane Addams was born and where her first friendships blossomed, was another major influence on her growth. It remained a small community where everyone knew everyone and there were divisions along ethnic and religious lines, yet most worked together and apparently respected one another. We have conducted extensive primary research on Cedarville, nearby Freeport, and the surrounding region of Stephenson County, Illinois. Readers will find information on the growth and then stagnation of Cedarville; on a number of families and individuals in the community with whom the Addams family interacted, schoolmates and adults, including village physicians, ministers, teachers, shopkeepers, millers, farmers, and the like; on village organizations and institutions; and on Cedarville's relationship to the larger community of Freeport for which it served as an early suburb. In Cedarville, villagers held events to raise funds for worthy community endeavors. There was a debating society, a village band, agricultural fairs, old settlers' parties, and entertainment provided by lecturers and traveling shows. Many of these kinds of activities would become part of the program structure at Hull-House. The development of Freeport and Rockford, Illinois, and their surrounding areas, their economy, the growth of business enterprise and commercial connections, their institutions, and Addams family associations are also part of the Addams story. The influence of railroads and the development of Chicago as a center of trade, commerce, business, and culture on the communities in which Jane Addams grew up are considered as well.

Because this period of Jane Addams's life is the one most closely associated with formal education, we have tried to provide evidence of the variety and types of educational experiences and influences to which she was exposed. Through these documents readers may explore the history of small-town midwestern private and public schools, especially in Illinois, including the issues of curriculum, pedagogy, and teacher training. Other major educational influences on the young Jane Addams were the positive attitude of her family toward the importance of education for all children and the availability of learning opportunities less formal than organized school. Self-education through reading both the classics and current literature, access to a library and encouragement to use it, education through playing games and interacting socially with others, listening to lecturers and story-tellers, siblings sharing their interests and expertise with younger family members, learning with a competitive and close peer group, being read to by adults, and studying music and attending concerts and plays were all influential in the Cedarville years of Addams's life. Again, remnants of these educational influences appeared later in the strong focus on education at Hull-House. They helped establish her lifelong dedication to improving educational opportunities for all.

Through the vital Rockford Female Seminary years, readers have an opportunity to explore evidence about the development of women's education from secondary school through college, especially during the middle part of the last fifty years of the nineteenth century in America. There is information about women's seminaries, efforts to create college-level institutions and postgraduate education for women, equality for women's schools with men's schools and debates over coeducation, and curriculum development for women's education and efforts to move it to parity with the college curriculum for men. Readers will be able to explore the religious and missionary influence in female education; inter-campus relations, especially between men's and women's schools; and daily life in a seminary environment, including school routine, rules, and activity requirements as well as social relationships among students and teachers. Other elements in the education theme concern the difference between a midwestern seminary and an East Coast woman's college education and the preparation of male and female students for public lives. The development of college journalism and the importance of debate and literary societies, scientific organizations, oratorical contests, and organized social occasions are strong elements in the educational theme. The contribution and importance of women pioneers in women's education and the significance of Jane Addams's teachers as role models and friends are also major aspects of this first volume. These college years were critical for the young Jane Addams. She found comfort in a female community that she would later replicate in part at Hull-House. She discovered her leadership talents and honed her writing and speaking skills. She became an individual in her own right. Finally, she began in earnest to struggle with her relationship with God, an effort that would continue throughout her life.

Just as education was a part of everyday life in the Addams family, some aspect of religious teaching was present, too. Jane Addams was exposed to an assortment of religious influences, from the faith of her father, a self-professed Quaker but engaged in activities associated primarily with the Presbyterian church, to visiting speakers and ministers who often came to the Addams home to share a meal or spend the night. A constant regimen of Sunday School, church, social outings, and community sings—all associated with traditional religion—was also part of the environment. It is during this part of her life that Jane Addams's personal spiritual quest is most evident, especially in contrast to that of Ellen Gates Starr. Their letters reveal their differences in perspective about religious matters and the importance to them of their relationship with God. In addition, the moral lessons that formed the basis of Jane Addams's behavior toward others were fostered and imparted in a setting that relied entirely on beliefs associated with Protestant teachings. Among elements in the religious theme are the central role that traditional organized religion played in the development of the frontier; the primary position of Christianity in the life of many frontier families and the variety and amount of family and community activity connected with religion; the importance of moral values associated with religion as the rules by which family and community function; the place of American Protestantism in the last half of nineteenth-century America and its influence on social movements, including the Social Gospel; the influence of traditional religion in education; and the influence of theology.

All the Jane Addams papers are a rich resource for women's history. Readers and researchers using material in this volume can consider, among other things, the private and public roles of women; the position of women in traditional family relationships; activities of women in a frontier or rural village setting; what constitutes a proper career for women, including teaching and missionary work and, in the domestic realm, being educated mothers; what constitutes an appropriate education for women; the growing cadre of women in science and their influence on the first generation of college women; issues of health and illness as it concerned women; debates over women's natures, capabilities, and the social stereotypes of the proper place for women in family and society; the development and significance of women's organizations and movements, including temperance organizations, missionary societies, and alumnae associations; and the growth in legal rights of women.

This volume is the work of a team of three editors working together for our fourth historic partner, Jane Addams. Although we three are physically separated by the United States—one is located in California and two in North Carolina—all participated in all aspects of preparing this work for publication. Making use of computer technology, the old-fashioned telephone, the still more old-fashioned postal service, and meeting at least once a year for editorial conferences, we maintained a working relationship and friendship. We selected documents, transcribed them, verified them through at least two readings, and conducted research to provide the context for them and identify people, places, organizations, events, or ideas mentioned in them. We worked together to design the editorial apparatus by which they are presented and wrote annotation, exchanged and read one another's work, and rewrote annotation. We prepared the manuscript for publication. We visited and maintained relationships with a variety of repositories, individuals, and organizations; kept appropriate records; helped other scholars with reference questions; and promoted our project every chance we got. In addition, we raised the funds that made the publication of this first volume in the series possible. We are proud to record the life, accomplishments, and contributions of Jane Addams.

Editorial Method

In addition to a contents page and list of illustrations, each volume of the selected edition of the Jane Addams papers will contain a list of documents presented in the volume and a list of abbreviations used by the authors of the documents and by us. An introduction for each volume will be preceded by acknowledgments and followed by the main body of the text, which is composed of documents with annotation. Back matter may include an appendix containing longer biographical profiles on individuals who were especially important in the life of Addams and also a bibliography.

Throughout this work, all documents are presented in chronological order. Correspondence appears in sequence, according to the date on which it was written or the date on which we believe it may have been written. Speeches usually appear in the arrangement by the date on which each was given rather than published. Published periodical articles appear at their date of publication, and unpublished essays, announcements, and assorted documents are presented by the date that appears on them or one we are able to determine for them. When we have more than one version of a document from which to select, we will usually opt for the extant final rendition of the item and place it at the appropriate date sequence. Documents written on more than one day are placed in order according to the first date. When we include two documents of the same date, we will place them in sequence according to their content and in consideration of the relationship of each to other documents near them in the sequence.

Documents are arranged in sections. An introduction for each section provides a context for the documents and annotation associated with them. Each document is identified by a title or header—the name of the person to whom a piece of correspondence is addressed or from whom it was received or the title of a writing or a type of document. In some cases, a headnote providing information we believe will benefit readers before they read the document appears immediately under the header and before the document. Letters are presented in standardized letter form, with the salutation flush left and the place and date-line flush right. The complimentary close is run into the last line of the text of the letter, and signatures, appearing on a separate line, are followed by any post-script, enclosures, or attachments to the letter. Diary entries are presented with the date of the entry flush left at the beginning of the text for that date. Essays, writings, speeches, announcements, and other documents are presented in straight text format.

Transcriptions of all documents are literal, with some exceptions. We do not employ the editorial device [*sic*] to indicate errors made by the authors of the documents we present. The childhood letters of Jane Addams are replete with misshaped letters and misspelled words. When a misshaped letter is the symbol for another letter, we have preserved it without alteration and without footnote explanation. For example, Jane Addams often mixed the letters *m* and *n,* writing "Nis" when she apparently meant "Mis." We believe that readers will know what Jane Addams meant and so let "Nis" stand. Sometimes letters of the alphabet were formed incorrectly, but they represent no other letters or numbers. In those instances, we do not present the mis-drawn letters but silently correct the letters. Jane Addams often reversed the letters *s, j,* and *p* and the number *9*. We present them accurately formed within the words and sentences in which they appear. When the misspelling of a word creates a new word that, considering its use in the context of the document text, we believe the author did not mean, we present the word as the author wrote it and suggest in an annotation the word we believe was likely intended. For example, if Jane Addams wrote "who" when we believe that, given the structure of the sentence, she meant to write "how," we have presented the word *who* as she wrote it and offer our alteration in brackets or explained in a footnote. When we judge that a word is so misspelled that a reader might not be able to determine what the author meant (and if we believe we know), we correct it. If the word can be corrected by adding letters, we do so, inserting appropriate letters in brackets. If the word can only be corrected by deleting portions of it, we make that correction in a footnote. We have been sparing in correcting authors' spellings, and readers will find misspellings rife, especially in the letters and writings of Jane Addams in her childhood and youth.

Jane Addams and many of her correspondents were not careful about punctuation, capitalization, and grammar in their handwritten documents. Sometimes she ended sentences with a period; at other times her periods resembled commas. Occasionally, she used a dash, and sometimes her sentences had no end mark. When there is no mark or a mark other than a period, and the next word begins with a capital letter and definitely denotes a new sentence, we have assumed a sentence end. We treat commalike periods and dashes as periods and silently replace them with periods in the text. When there is no punctuation at the end of a sentence, we have usually inserted a period in brackets. A reader interested in the sentence-ending grammar of Jane Addams may consult the microfilm edition of *The Jane Addams Papers,* which offers facsimile copies of the text for most of the documents presented in this edition.

Other punctuation throughout the document texts is presented as the authors wrote it—with two exceptions. When an author used quotation marks and omitted the second set of the pair—as Jane Addams often did—we have added the second set in brackets if we could determine where they should be placed. If we could not decide where they were meant to be placed, we used annotation to indicate that the second of the pair is missing from the original text. In a very few instances we have added a comma in brackets to help readers differentiate appropriate elements in the text. That usually occurs in a string of names, where the author and correspondent knew the individuals but today's reader may not. For example, the author could have written "Sarah Alice Mary Catherine" with no punctuation. These could either be the names of two sisters of Jane Addams, or four individuals with these first names, or any combination. If we know how the names should be presented, we will add commas in brackets in appropriate places.

When writing informally and to close friends and family, Jane Addams used two methods of paragraphing. In most instances she followed standard procedures by indenting the beginning of each new paragraph. In some instances, however, perhaps to save paper, she changed subjects in the middle of a line, leaving a great deal of space between the end of one sentence and the start of another. We have taken these as paragraph breaks and silently standardize them as such. Any doubts about accuracy may be put to rest by consulting the photocopy of the document in the microfilm edition of *The Jane Addams Papers.*

Superscripts and subscripts appear on lines rather than above or below them. Interlineations are also presented on the line and where the author meant to insert them. They are enclosed in angle brackets. Text written by the author on the side of the main body of the text, and sometimes perpendicular to it, has been treated as an interlineation and inserted in the text if it is clear from the author's marks where it goes. If, however, it is not possible to determine where the author meant to put it, we place it in a footnote. In both cases, we indicate in footnote annotation where the marginal text appeared on the original document. Text written across or perpendicular to previously written text in a document appears as ordinary text in our transcription.

The abbreviations and symbols that Jane Addams and other authors used are maintained unless we judge them to be unknown to modern readers or impossible to duplicate using modern print technology. Words underlined with a single or a double line are reproduced as underlined; however, words and phrases underlined three or more times are underlined once and accompanied by a descriptive footnote. Words written in the Cyrillic alphabet are reproduced using letters from that alphabet and translated in a footnote. Canceled words, phrases, or paragraphs that are relevant and readable are indicated by a line drawn through the type. If necessary, they are annotated with a footnote. Single crossed-out letters or numbers, and partial words as well as mistakenly duplicated words, are silently omitted unless particularly relevant. Letters, words, or phrases that we cannot decipher because of poor handwriting, cross-outs, mutilated pages, or the like will be indicated by the word *illegible,* italicized and surrounded by italicized brackets.

We identify enclosures or attachments and summarize their contents in annotation. In the few cases when we present the text of enclosures or attachments, the documents will be preceded by the words *enclosure* for something sent with the letter or document or *attachment* for something added after the document or letter was received. With regard to annotation, we handled enclosures and attachments as if they were part of the document to which they are appended.

Infrequently (and primarily to avoid repeating information already provided in previous documents or annotations) we may present only a portion of a document. When that is the case, we employ ellipsis and indicate by a summary statement in footnote annotation the nature of the omitted information.

We use brackets—sparingly and only to clarify information—to indicate that we have added information to document texts. When document text is mutilated or missing and we can determine with certitude what the missing elements would have been, we insert them, in brackets, where they belong. Most often we add information in the date and place lines. When a document has a partial date or no date and we have been able to determine what the date should be, we add that information in brackets where the dateline should be. When we are aware that an author has provided an incorrect date or place, we retain the author's information and place the correct information in brackets beside it. In some instances, authors write documents on more than one day, yet the dateline they place on the document carries only one date. Similarly, documents may be written in more than one place. If we are aware of omissions from either the date or place line, we add that additional information in brackets. If there is uncertainty about an element we supply, we put that element, along with a question mark, in brackets.

Some documents contain drawings. When we do not reproduce them we provide statements describing each drawing. The statements appear in bold italic print and within a pair of virgules or slant lines at the location of each drawing in the original document.

As a general rule, we do not reproduce letterheads on stationery; however, when Jane Addams wrote a letter from Hull-House and the letterhead "Hull-House" is the only place information, we use "Hull-House, [Chicago, Ill.]" as the place line. If we consider the information contained in a letterhead pertinent to the document, we place that information in a footnote. Because the majority of the documents in the selected edition appear in the microfilm edition of *The Jane Addams Papers,* those who wish to see letterhead information may do so by reviewing each document in its original form.

We have prepared annotation for each document to help readers understand its significance to the narrative story of the life, times, and achievements of Jane Addams. Annotation takes several forms. There are section introductions that provide a context for the documents. In addition, some documents have been treated with editorial comment in headnotes as well as in footnotes. Each document also is identified by a source note that appears at the end of the document and before the beginning of the footnotes. It is composed of the physical description of the document given in abbreviated form (see Abbreviations) and names the collection and repository in which the original document will be found as well as the document's reel and frame number in the microfilm edition of *The Jane Addams Papers*. Other special aspects of the document itself will be presented in this location.

In creating annotations we relied predominantly on research in primary sources. Our research has taken us to other correspondence and documents in the papers and the published writings of Jane Addams. In addition, we have focused on family and friends' manuscript collections in a variety of repositories and in private hands; published letters and diaries; county histories, travel guides, local newspaper sources, and popular literature for the period; county records (including marriage and death records, deeds, and court records); plats and maps; state archival records (including records for the Illinois General Assembly and for the insurance department and the corporation division of the Office of the Secretary of State); city directories, advertisements, dictionaries, college catalogs, and assorted publications issued during the period; miscellaneous materials from college and university archives, manuscript repositories, historical society, public library, and private collections and church archives; cemetery records; and census returns. We have consulted standard biographical sources and compendia for a variety of subjects, including art, literature, and music, and consulted secondary sources on special subjects. With the exceptions of James Weber Linn's *Jane Addams: A Biography* and Winifred Wise's *Jane Addams of Hull-House,* biographies written with the approval and participation of Jane Addams during her lifetime, we have not relied on the work of other biographers of Jane Addams.

Because we expect that a wide audience will consult the volumes of the selected edition, we have prepared annotation to take into account the likely knowledge and context level of readers from high school through postgraduate scholars, including the general reading public. We use annotation primarily to assist readers at all levels in understanding the content of the document.

As a general rule, annotation will be used to identify persons, organizations, historical events, and relationships mentioned in the texts of the documents to the degree that they clarify the importance of the document. When we supply information in the text of a document in brackets we will sometimes employ annotation to explain our rationale for doing so. Annotation is also used to explain the archaic use of words and special jargon, correct spelling errors, and translate phrases of text in languages other than English. It is used to explain documentary relationships that are not immediately obvious and provide leads to other documents and materials that might offer more information about the annotated item. Annotation also directs readers to other documents, usually additional correspondence, personal documents, writing, and material located in the microfilm edition of *The Jane Addams Papers* or to other manuscript collections and repositories. We use annotation as a cross-reference to direct readers to other documents or appropriate annotation in the selected edition. In addition, annotation indicates the existence of documents that are mentioned in the texts of documents in the selected edition. Through annotation, we provide bibliographic references for quotations, for article or book titles, and for speeches, meetings, or gatherings. Annotation also reveals significant variations in different texts of the same document, explains aspects of the text not reproduced in the publication, and describes special physical characteristics of documents, including form, spelling, grammar, punctuation, and symbols. Footnotes for each document and headnote, if there is one, are presented at the end of the document text after the document source citation line.

Generally, identification for people, places, organizations, events, or ideas appears at their first mention in either editorial annotations or the document texts. Biographical notes for individuals we judge to be of sufficient importance to the life of Jane Addams to be treated with special emphasis appear in the Biographical Profiles at the end of all document text and annotation in the volume.

Within the annotations—section introductions, headnotes, footnotes, and special biographical notes—we only provide bibliographic citations for the source of direct quotations or, infrequently, to direct readers to further information on a topic. When we quote from original correspondence we provide the collection and repository in which the original letter is located and (if the material is in the microfilm edition of *The Jane Addams Papers*) a citation to the location of the document in the microfilm. We employ a short form of all titles cited. Full bibliographic information for these titles and other sources that we have consulted during the process of creating the manuscript appears in the Bibliography.

Abbreviations and Symbols

Document Descriptions

A	Autograph
AD	Autograph Document
ADS	Autograph Document Signed
AL	Autograph Letter
ALI	Autograph Letter Initialed
ALS	Autograph Letter Signed
AMs	Autograph Manuscript
AMsI	Autograph Manuscript Initialed
AMsS	Autograph Manuscript Signed
D	Document
HD	Holograph Document
HDS	Holograph Document Signed
HL	Holograph Letter
HLS	Holograph Letter Signed
HMs	Holograph Manuscript
HMsS	Holograph Manuscript Signed
Ms	Manuscript
Mss	Manuscripts
MsS	Manuscript Signed
PD	Printed Document
PDS	Printed Document Signed
TD	Typed Document
TMs	Typed Manuscript
TMsS	Typed Manuscript Signed

Manuscript Collections and Repositories

BC	Beloit College Archives, Beloit College, Beloit, Wis.
BC, EB	Emerson-Bannister Collection, Beloit College Archives, Beloit College, Beloit, Wis.
CAHS	Cedarville Area Historical Society, Cedarville, Ill.
CAHS, Addams	Addams Family Collection, Cedarville Area Historical Society, Cedarville, Ill.
CHS	Chicago Historical Society, Chicago, Ill.
ISA	Illinois State Archives, Springfield
ISU	Illinois State University, Normal
IU, Lilly, SAAH	Mrs. Sarah Alice Haldeman Mss, Lilly Library, Indiana University, Bloomington
JAPP	Jane Addams Papers Project, Fayetteville, N.C.
JAPP, AHHA	Anna Hostetter Haldeman Addams Files, Jane Addams Papers Project, Fayetteville, N.C.
JAPP, DeLoach	Alice DeLoach Collection, Jane Addams Papers Project, Fayetteville, N.C.
JAPP, Hulbert	Mary Addams Hulbert Collection, Jane Addams Papers Project, Fayetteville, N.C.
JAPP, JA	Jane Addams Collection, Jane Addams Papers Project, Fayetteville, N.C.
JAPP, JHA	John Huy Addams Collection, Jane Addams Papers Project, Fayetteville, N.C.
JAPP, Schneider	Kaye Schneider Collection, Jane Addams Papers Project, Fayetteville, N.C.
PSU, EHJ	Emanual Haldeman Julius Collection, Pittsburg State University, Pittsburg, Kans.
RC	Rockford College Archives, Rockford College, Rockford, Ill.
RC, PP	Presidents Papers, Rockford College Archives, Rockford College, Rockford, Ill.
SC, Starr	Starr Collection (Ellen Gates Starr and Family), Sophia Smith Collection, Smith College, Northampton, Mass.
SCHS	Stephenson County Historical Society, Freeport, Ill.
SCPC	Swarthmore College Peace Collection, Swarthmore College, Swarthmore, Pa.
SCPC, JAC	The Jane Addams Collection, Swarthmore College Peace Collection, Swarthmore College, Swarthmore, Pa.
SHSW	State Historical Society of Wisconsin, University of Wisconsin, Madison
SHSW, Smith	Smith Family Collection, De Pere, Wis. (Correspondence of Addie B. and Sara Elizabeth Smith), State Historical Society of Wisconsin, University of Wisconsin, Madison

UIC, JAMC	Jane Addams Memorial Collection, University of Illinois at Chicago
UIC, JAMC, Detzer	Mrs. Karl Detzer (Dorothy Detzer) Collection, Jane Addams Memorial Collection, University of Illinois at Chicago
UIC, JAMC, HH Assn.	Hull-House Association Records, Jane Addams Memorial Collection, University of Illinois at Chicago
UIC, JAMC, HJ	Haldeman-Julius Family Papers, Jane Addams Memorial Collection, University of Illinois at Chicago
UIC, JAMC, HJ Supp.	Haldeman-Julius Family Papers, supplement, Jane Addams Memorial Collection, University of Illinois at Chicago
UIC, JAMC, Smith	Louise Smith Papers, Jane Addams Memorial Collection, University of Illinois at Chicago
UIUC	University of Illinois at Urbana-Champaign
UM, BHL	Bently Historical Library, University of Michigan, Ann Arbor

Individuals

AH	Anna Hostetter
AHH	Anna Hostetter Haldeman
AHHA	Anna Hostetter Haldeman Addams or Anna Haldeman Addams
EGS	Ellen Gates Starr
GBH	George Bowman Haldeman or George Haldeman
HWH	Henry Winfield Haldeman or Harry Haldeman
JA	Jane Addams or Laura Jane Addams
JHA	John Huy Addams or John H. Addams
JML	John Manning Linn or John M. Linn
JWA	John Weber Addams or Weber Addams
LJA	Laura Jane Addams or Jane Addams
MCA	Mary Catherine Addams or Mary Addams
MCAL	Mary Catherine Addams Linn or Mary Linn
SAA	Sarah Alice Addams or Alice Addams
SAAH	Sarah Alice Addams Haldeman or Alice Haldeman
SW	Sarah Weber
SWA	Sarah Weber Addams or Sarah Addams

Frequently Cited Published Sources

PJA	*Selected Papers of Jane Addams*
JAPM	*The Jane Addams Papers.* Edited by Mary Lynn Bryan et al. Microfilm, 82 reels. Ann Arbor: University Microfilms International, 1985–86.
NAW	*Notable American Women, 1607–1950.* Vols. 1–3 edited by Edward T. James, Janet Wilson James, and Paul S. Boyer. Cambridge: Harvard Uni-

versity Press, 1971. Vol. 4 edited by Barbara Sicherman and Carol Hurd
Green. Cambridge: Harvard University Press, 1980.

NCAB   *The National Cyclopaedia of American Biography.* New York: James T.
          White, 1897.

OED   *The Compact Edition of the Oxford English Dictionary.* [New York]: Ox-
          ford University Press, 1971.

RSM   *Rockford Seminary Magazine*

Organizations, Institutions, or Events

ACWA   Amalgamated Clothing Workers of America
AWSA   American Woman Suffrage Association
CPSAS   Chicago Public School Art Society
DAR   Daughters of the American Revolution
NWSA   National Woman Suffrage Association
RFS   Rockford Female Seminary, Rockford, Ill.
SCHC   Society of the Companions of the Holy Cross
WCTU   Woman's Christian Temperance Union
WTUL   Women's Trade Union League
YMCA   Young Men's Christian Association

Symbol

@   kiss

Part 1

EARLY INFLUENCES:

CHILDHOOD AND FAMILY

IN CEDARVILLE,

1860–77

Introduction

L aura Jane Addams was born at the beginning of autumn in 1860 in Cedarville, Illinois. The eighth child born of Sarah Weber Addams[1] and John Huy Addams,[2] she shared her name with Laura Jane Gorham,[3] called Jennie, a teacher and family friend who lodged in the Addams home. From the beginning the new infant was called Jennie like her namesake. She would eventually be known simply as Jane Addams.

It is significant that Addams, who became a great pacifist, was born at the beginning of America's descent into civil war. At her birth on 6 September 1860, the country was divided over the future of its union. Rhetoric over the issues that split the nation had become increasingly strident. Discussion of the controversies dominated newspapers, letters, speeches, and debates and could be heard in the halls of government and in churches, schools, and general stores. Wherever people gathered, the concerns fueling the growing regional division were the all-consuming topic. Armed conflict seemed inevitable. Abraham Lincoln[4] was elected the sixteenth president of the United States in November 1860. South Carolina seceded before the end of 1860, to be followed by ten other states. The first shots of the Civil War were fired at Fort Sumter in the Charleston, South Carolina, harbor on 12 April 1861, before Addams had reached her first birthday.

John Huy Addams was a staunch Unionist[5] and a friend of Lincoln. They had been Whigs together and helped found and develop the Republican Party in Illinois. Lincoln was presented as a hero in the Addams home. His picture hung on the wall in John Huy Addams's room, and a photograph of him with his young son Thomas ("Tad") was featured in the Addams parlor. In the chapter on Lincoln in her memoirs *Twenty Years at Hull-House* (1910), Jane Addams recalled that she "never heard the great name without a thrill." She came to see

Lincoln as the savior of democracy in his time. Lincoln's birthday was later celebrated each year at Hull-House with great reverence and patriotism. Addams remembered her father's small packet of letters from Lincoln (apparently no longer extant) that began "My dear Double-D'ed Addams" and the pleasure she took in listening to her father reminisce about his friendship with Lincoln.[6] In addition to raising a company of Illinois volunteers from his area for the Union army,[7] Addams, it has been claimed, may have provided support for runaway slaves seeking freedom in the North through the Underground Railroad.[8]

Addams family relatives, like many of their neighbors in Cedarville and the surrounding area of Stephenson County (one of the northern tier of Illinois counties at the southern border of Wisconsin), had emigrated west beginning in the late 1830s. These settlers came from New England or, like the Addamses, from Pennsylvania or other mid-Atlantic states. Most of them were farmers who worked their own land. By the late 1840s and 1850s, however, there was a growing cadre of businessmen and entrepreneurs who were pushing industrial development west with the railroads. The results of the Panic of 1837 and the poor harvests in 1835 and 1837 had induced them to leave the rapidly developing urban East. They believed that industrious individuals would find opportunity on the secured frontier of the Midwest; basic agrarian skills were still valued, the air was clean and land was cheap, and families could obtain wealth through hard work.

When Illinois had sufficient population to become a state in 1818 its northern precincts were barely settled. Chicago was a muddy village of a few cabins, and although a growing community at the nexus of water, road, and soon rail transport, it was not incorporated until 1833 with a population of 350. The last Native American uprising in Illinois, in which a band of the Sac and Fox led by Black Hawk[9] attempted to reclaim lands they had ceded in northern Illinois, was quelled in 1832. Shortly thereafter the remaining bands of Winnebago were induced to sell their claim to northern Illinois lands and move to Wisconsin. The fertile rolling prairies of northern Illinois, dotted with choice stands of hardwood and bubbling springs and crossed liberally by swiftly flowing streams and rivers, were opened to white settlement.

Among the emigrants who began to arrive in the Stephenson County area in 1839 and 1840 were several families from John Huy Addams's birthplace, Sinking Spring, Pennsylvania.[10] The Millers, Mulls, and Ruths were relatives and close friends of the Addams family.[11] The young John Huy Addams had grown up with some of them, sharing chores, playing childhood games in their fields and barns, and attending school and religious and social occasions with them. Members of these families, some related by marriage, probably came seeking the freedom that frontier life offered, to escape the growing confinement of the developing urban area in Berks County, Pennsylvania, around Philadelphia and Reading, and to secure economic opportunity.

Philip H. Reitzell who had wed Mary Ruth, a cousin once removed of John Huy Addams, purchased a mill on Richland Creek in Stephenson County at what would eventually become Buena Vista, Illinois. Their children and other pioneers connected with Sinking Spring established themselves on farms in the surrounding countryside.[12] Their letters back to Pennsylvania must have been full of information about the opportunities that the Stephenson County area offered. The young John Huy Addams, who returned to Sinking Spring to teach and help his father after he had completed his apprenticeship to miller Enos L. Reiff[13] in 1842, was determined to make his life there. "Mill's are doing very little," he wrote to Reiff. "The Business is indeed discouraging so much so that by the advice of some of my friends I concluded to stay out of it so far as <to> carrying it on for my self. . . . I am at present at the Business intended when I left my school is large indeed, quite beyond my expectatations and larger than ought to be. I have 49 on my list. . . . My Business for next summer is not for certain yet—The West most likely will take up my time if a good comrade can be procured."[14]

Accordingly, two weeks after they said their marriage vows Sarah Weber Addams and John Huy Addams began their journey to permanent residence in northern Illinois. They had been married on 18 July 1844 before Reformed min-

Sarah Weber must have looked something like this when she agreed to wed the young John Huy Addams. This photograph was taken when she and her sister Elizabeth Weber Reiff went to Harrisburg, Pennsylvania, where each had her photograph made. (A. G. Keet, Harrisburg, Pa.; JAPP)

ister Jacob Christian Becker at Sarah Weber's home in Kreidersville, Pennsylvania. Sarah Weber's father, Col. George Weber,[15] who was investigating property to buy in the West, went with them. They traveled by horse and cart, railroad, and boat through New Jersey to New York City, then up the Hudson River to Niagara Falls, and via steamer through the Great Lakes to Chicago.

The Addams-Weber party probably headed west on the Old State Road[16] across the northern Illinois prairies in a buggy drawn by a bay mare named Dolly that John Huy Addams had purchased in Chicago, the ten-year-old city they left behind. With its population of about eight thousand, Chicago was just starting to sprawl out of its swampy beginning and onto the flat, wide-open expanse of plain that surrounded it. They went in search of their Sinking Spring friends in the Freeport area of Stephenson County, approximately 120 miles away.

The young Addams couple settled among the Miller and Reitzell families and began their new life. Sarah helped Mary ("Polly") Ruth Reitzell with the household chores, including cooking, sewing, gardening, preserving foods, cleaning, and washing. She visited in the homes of other settlers and, with her husband and other members of the household, attended Sunday church meetings wherever they were held, in a grove, cabin, or an open field. Soon pregnant, she became as anxious as her husband about securing a proper home, farm, and livelihood.

Over the first five months, John Huy Addams visited mill and farm sites in northwestern Illinois, alternately riding out through the prairie to investigate mills available for purchase and helping his hosts with farming and milling activities. He assisted Philip Reitzell with the repair of his millpond dam, dug potatoes, repaired fences, harvested corn, wheat, and flax, butchered his first hogs, and built a bench "settee." He also explored the countryside, meeting other farmers and millers, and began to make friends with residents in Freeport, a small village on the Pecatonica River, where mail for the area arrived by stagecoach and merchants, preachers, farmers, millers, and lawyers gathered to share information.[17]

From the beginning, he had determined that the mill property he favored was located on the south side of Cedar Creek about three miles south and east of Buena Vista, six miles directly north of the village of Freeport and among the properties of other Pennsylvania-German emigrants. Built in 1837 by Dr. Thomas Van Valzah from Lewistown, Pennsylvania, the saw- and gristmill was the first in Stephenson County. The owners wanted at least four thousand dollars for the mill and approximately four hundred acres of land. John Huy Addams did not have sufficient resources of his own to purchase the property.[18] After he discovered that his father-in-law would not assist him, he hoped that his father, Samuel Addams,[19] would make up the difference and sent a request for support to him via his father-in-law, who returned to Pennsylvania in August. He received favorable news three months later and negotiated the deal for the mill property in December 1844.[20]

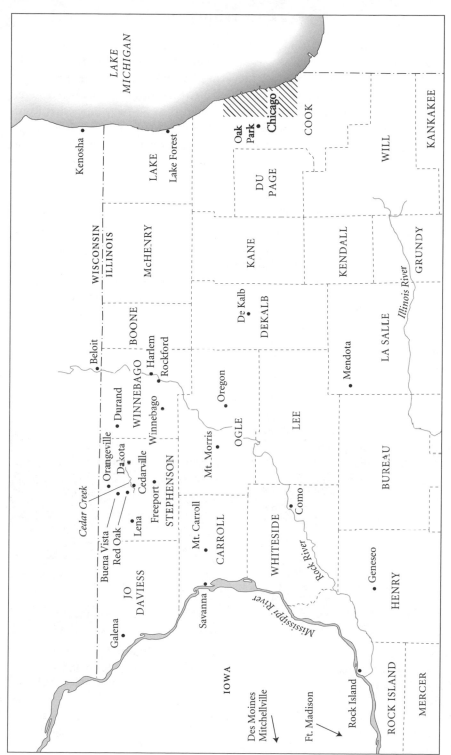

The Northern Illinois Region.

On 7 January 1845, Sarah and John Addams established their new life together at the mill site. Their home was in an eight-by-ten-foot, one-room log cabin, one of the three out-buildings they had purchased with the mill property.[21]
It was located on the opposite side of Cedar Creek from the mill and sheltered
by a tall cliff on which John planted the seeds of the Norway pines that Sarah
had brought with her from home.[22]

Among Sarah Weber Addams's early home furnishings were a churn and
two tubs that her husband had purchased in Chicago; a desk, table, and three
bedsteads he had ordered made from cherry wood and maple in Freeport during the fall of 1844 by a Mr. Small; and chairs purchased from E. Hyde, a Freeport merchant. The couple also had household effects in four large trunks and
miscellaneous boxes brought on their wedding trip and stored in Chicago until they had their own home.

It was expected that new settlers would spend their first two years or so in
simple log homes. Here they lodged while they put the bulk of their labor and
resources into the enterprise that they had chosen to support them and assured

When John Huy and Sarah Weber Addams finally secured the mill property they favored on Cedar Creek, they moved into a small cabin near the mill. On the bluff behind the cabin they planted the seeds of pine trees that they had brought with them
from Pennsylvania. That bluff became renowned in the area as Pine Hill for the striking stand of pine that grew from the seeds. Jane Addams and her friends were frequent visitors to the site, which could be seen, as it is here, from the front of the Addams home and Jane's birthplace across Cedar Creek. (JAPP)

themselves that they wished to remain in the place in which they had settled. The Addams family was more than typical. Before Sarah gave birth on 25 June 1845 to their first child, a girl they named Mary Catherine, called Mary,[23] John had constructed a new, larger log home on the south side of Cedar Creek. They moved there on 14 April 1845. It consisted of two rooms, a living–dining room and a bedroom for the couple in addition to a sleeping loft for their children and a lean-to kitchen. Until 1854 that cabin was their home.

Health hazards were a notable part of pioneer life. Typhoid fever, pneumonia, and a host of childhood diseases, including whooping cough and scarlet fever, were prevalent in Stephenson County, sometimes in epidemic proportions. Houseflies and other vermin such as lice and bedbugs flourished where housing without bathing and other sanitation facilities was the norm. Women were particularly vulnerable to many diseases and conditions associated with childbearing. Each pregnancy must have come with the attendant fear of incapacity or death. Sarah Weber Addams was certainly aware of the dangers. Fevers and ague as well as malaria were universal and the bane of pioneer existence. Like other pioneers, the young Addams family suffered an assortment of illnesses. In his 1844 diary, John Huy Addams frequently mentioned that he or Sarah was not feeling well from such ailments and causes as the ague, bilious fever, bowel complaint, the need for a physic, bed bugs, "musquitoes," and homesickness.

From the end of July until early November 1846, their physician, Charles G. Strohecker, who was married to a distant Addams relation, Elizabeth Reitzell, called on the Addams family thirty-seven times.[24] Many of the visits were to treat Sarah, and most of the medications prescribed were quinine.[25]

Although Sarah Weber Addams may not have been physically robust, she was determined and committed to a pioneer life in Illinois. It was difficult for her to leave family behind in Pennsylvania not knowing when or if she would see them again and to relinquish the comforts of an established home, community, and friends for she knew not what.[26] The few brief letters that survive from the first two years after the couple established themselves on Cedar Creek reveal their pride in their new home as well as Sarah's longing and homesickness for family.

The couple managed and developed their resources carefully. That first year, John was pleased with the output of his mill and the prices his goods received,[27] and Sarah planted a large garden and began her orchard. Over the next nine years the Addamses had four more children: Georgiana, born on 20 June 1849, died on 12 April 1850; Martha[28] was born on 17 September 1850; John Weber,[29] called Weber or Web (pronounced Weeb or Weeber), was born on 19 February 1852; and Sarah Alice,[30] called Alice or Allie, was born on 5 June 1853.

In 1845, with his small family in basic but suitable housing, John Huy Addams turned to the paramount task of securing a livelihood. He used profits from his milling operation to purchase more farmland and improve his milling capacity. By 1846 he was able to rebuild the gristmill, adding at least one run of stones[31] and other improvements valued at approximately four thousand dollars. He constructed a larger barn in 1848 and continued to acquire more farmland.[32] In 1858, at a cost of ten thousand dollars, he built a three-and-one-half-story frame gristmill with three run of stones, grain storage, and a flour bolter. He operated this mill for the remainder of his life. The mill runs were powered by the force of water from the pond that Van Valzah had created by damming Cedar Creek when he constructed his mill. Addams maintained the dam and pond, the latter stretching about a mile to the north and east of the mill site.[33]

Providing an appropriate education for their children was important to the Addamses. Like their parents, they saw it as one of their responsibilities. Each had received a formal education above the primary level, and John Huy Addams had taught school. From their own experiences they knew how valuable a suitable education would be for all of their children, both male and female.

Addams became active in helping to develop Cedarville schools and in creating a community library. He served on the committee that raised the funds and organized the construction of the first schoolhouse in Cedarville in 1846. He selected and recruited teachers, helped initiate the private high school, and was a

The mill that Jane Addams knew as playground and family livelihood. Although she was attracted by the "excitement" that the sawmill offered, she revealed in her autobiography *Twenty Years at Hull-House* that "the flouring mill was much more beloved. It was full of dusky, floury places which we adored, of empty bins in which we might play house; it had a basement with piles of bran and shorts which were almost as good as sand to play in" (11–12). She also associated it with her father, whom she adored. John Huy Addams constructed the mill in 1858 to replace the one that he had purchased in 1844 from Dr. Thomas Van Valzah. The 1858 mill was improved by his son John Weber Addams during the 1880s but ceased operations by 1905. (JAPP)

Another favorite childhood haunt for all of the Addams children was the family barn constructed in 1848 and still in use in the last years of the twentieth century. (JAPP)

member of the board of directors when the Cedarville public school became Stephenson County District School No. 5 in 1880. In addition, the couple was especially supportive of those who came to teach in Cedarville from other communities. At least one teacher lodged with them, and several were frequent guests in their home for meals and social occasions. Some became close family friends.

To add to the educational opportunities available to all the citizens of the community, John Huy Addams, Abner B. Clingman,[34] Josiah Clingman,[35] and Adrian W. Lucas[36] formed one of the early lending libraries in Illinois. Organized as the Union Library Company of Cedar Creek Mills on 7 March 1846, it consisted primarily of basic nonfiction works on philosophy, history, and economics.[37] It was located in the Addams home and available for circulation to the citizens of Cedarville, who joined the company by buying one share of stock for two dollars. Addams served as librarian. After 1854, when his family moved into their new brick home in Cedarville, the library was located on shelves in the second-floor parlor. The Addams family had a private library, too. It seems to have consisted of a broad range of reading matter, from novels, poetry, and children's books to works of science, philosophy, history, biography, and religion.[38]

Dr. Van Valzah, who had owned the Cedar Creek Mill site, had hoped that the small collection of families beginning to cluster around his mill would become the county seat for Stephenson County. Unfortunately, Freeport won that political prize. By the time Jane Addams was born, Freeport was rapidly outpacing Cedarville in population and development. Freeport was begun in 1835 by the William ("Tutty") Baker and Benjamin Goddard families on the site of a large Native American village of the Winnebago tribe on the Pecatonica River. By 1840 its population of 491 was served by several stores, a ferry, a saloon, ho-

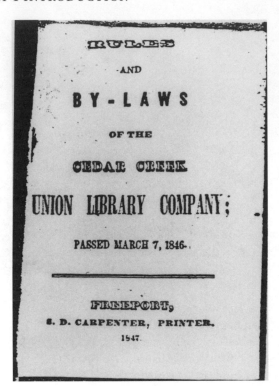

RULES

·AND·

BY-LAWS

OF THE

CEDAR CREEK

UNION LIBRARY COMPANY;

PASSED MARCH 7, 1846.

FREEPORT,
S. D. CARPENTER, PRINTER.
1847.

Jane Addams had access not only to the family library but also to the collection of the Cedar Creek Union Library Company, one of the earliest community lending libraries in Illinois. (JAPP; *JAPM,* 28:853–56).

tel, school, post office, and stagecoach stop. According to the U.S. census of 1860, all of Buckeye Township, in which Cedarville was the principal town, had a population of 2,367; Freeport alone had within its three political wards a population of 5,399. By 1870 the population of Freeport was more than ten thousand. In addition to being the political center for the county, it was a transportation hub where railroads going east and west, north and south crossed, and where railroad roundhouses and repair shops provided ready employment. By the 1880s the town had a considerable number of brick and stone structures; two newspapers; an assortment of churches, schools, social clubs, hotels, manufacturers of farm equipment, foundry and machine shops, iron works, pump factories, carriage makers, lightning rod and churn manufacturers, coopers, brick and lumber yards, breweries, and mills; a concert hall; a tannery; a sugar manufacturer; and at least four banks, one of which, the Second National, was owned by John Huy Addams. Although the large, elegant homes of the landowners, developers, merchants, and manufacturers had begun to grace the lengthening city streets, even more prevalent were the growing number of small houses built cheek-by-jowl in which the new immigrants who provided some of the work force lived.

But there was something special about Center Precinct, the first name given to the area in which Cedarville developed. "Its situation is singularly beautiful, presenting every variety of landscape to the artistic eye, without the quality of sameness which palls by its very monotony," wrote M. H. Tilden.[39] Sarah Hostetter,[40] Jane Addams's step-cousin, childhood playmate, and a frequent visitor to Cedarville, remembered, "From each hilltop there opens to view a wonderful panorama of fertile fields stretching away into the distant hills and finally lost in the line of the horizon."[41] The area developed was on a rise and surrounded by gently rolling prairie. Cedar Creek, providing the water power for the Addams mills, largely defined the northern border of the community. It ran through limestone formations that included caves and watered glens, its hilly banks full of cedars and hardwood trees and wildflowers.

In 1849 resident George Ilgen[42] determined that the area around Cedar Creek Mills should be incorporated as a town. Marcus Montelius,[43] who had been Stephenson County surveyor since 1847, laid out lots and streets. By 1860 the early cluster of frontier cabins was already well established as a permanent village with churches, schools, merchants, and businesses. Increasing population and improvements in village structures appeared coincident with the brick kiln established by James Canfield in 1850.[44] At first called Harrison, the village was named Cedarville in 1853, probably for the numerous cedars that grew in profusion near the limestone formations that helped define the area.

Cedar Creek ran to the north of the Addams home and was the site of the Addamses' millpond and mill. In all seasons, it was an exciting and ever-changing playground for Jane, her stepbrother George Haldeman, and their friends. (CAHS)

The town of Cedarville (first named Harrison), Illinois, is perched on a rise about five miles directly north of Freeport, Illinois. The photographer who took this picture was positioned south of Cedarville, looking north toward the southern entrance to the village from Freeport. Members of the Addams family frequently journeyed back and forth on this road between the two communities. (JAPP)

For this winter view of Cedarville, the photographer stood on Pine Hill on the north-west side of the community and looked south. The Addams mill is to the left in the foreground. Steeples of the village churches punctuate the skyline. (JAPP)

Cedarville developed slowly until the 1870s, when the nineteenth-century population high of approximately eight hundred began to decrease.[45] The most substantial business was John Huy Addams's milling operation, which provided employment for the surrounding farmers, for millwrights and millers, and for teamsters and coopers. In addition, a flaxseed mill started by Addams, Joseph F. Jackson,[46] and Richard Glennan[47] in 1856 was converted to a woolen mill during the Civil War and was operated by Jackson until the mid-1880s. John W. Henney[48] continued the Henney Wagon and Carriage Works started by his father, Jacob. It grew so rapidly that by 1879 he had moved it to larger quarters in Freeport. Two other carriage factories, one operated by John W. Shaffer[49] and the other by Joseph B. McCammon,[50] and a factory owned by Joseph P. Reel[51] and Andrew J. Seyler[52] to produce an improved and patented middlings purifier[53] were also located in the village.

In addition, Cedarville had cabinetmakers, carpenters, plasterers, stone and brick masons, stone cutters, blacksmiths, harness makers, shoemakers, a tinsmith, an inn keeper and hotel keeper, a watchmaker, seamstresses, tailors, and milliners. In 1860 there were two permanent preachers, one Methodist and the other Lutheran, at least one attorney, a dentist, two physicians, teachers, and a smattering of servants and extra farm laborers. Along the dusty streets among brick, log, and frame homes were two stores, one of which served as the post office, two church buildings, a town hall, a school, and a cemetery. The community erected a small stone jail in 1870, but it was so little used that the bars were removed from its windows and it became a meeting hall, with space beside it for one firefighting wagon operated by volunteers. If there was a service Cedarville did not have, citizens could draw upon those located in Freeport. A Freeport purveyor supplied the Addams family with oysters for special occasions, and by 1870 the family could secure flowers in winter from a greenhouse there as well.

The sense of community in Cedarville seems to have been strong. Everyone knew everyone, many were from similar Pennsylvania backgrounds, and mutual support and concern for the welfare of all prevailed. Jane Addams grew to maturity influenced by this close-knit environment where neighbors, no matter what their religious preference or livelihood, were respected and accepted so long as they abided by generally accepted community mores based on Christian ethics. Organizations and community institutions evolved to meet need. Area teachers gathered in institutes. There was a debating society and a local band. A fair, farmers' union, grange, and agricultural institute were organized to support the agricultural community. The town hall was the frequent site of local and traveling entertainment. An old settlers' organization was formed to preserve connections with pioneers and the history of the area. Many community organizations developed from church groups. There were Sunday School teachers' meetings, temperance revivals and a temperance lodge, community sings, and Bible study classes. There were socials to support various community

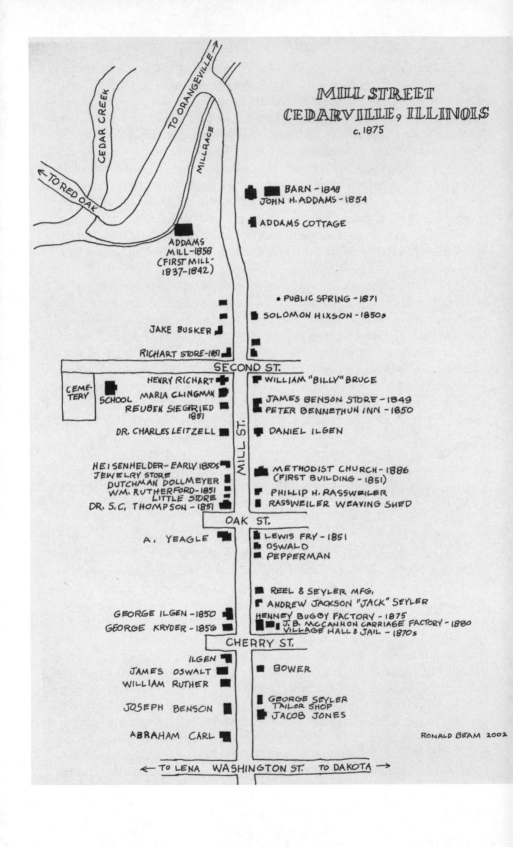

MILL STREET
CEDARVILLE, ILLINOIS
c. 1875

CEDAR CREEK

TO ORANGEVILLE →

MILLRACE

← TO RED OAK

ADDAMS MILL - 1858
(FIRST MILL - 1837-1842)

BARN - 1848
JOHN H. ADDAMS - 1854
ADDAMS COTTAGE

• PUBLIC SPRING - 1871
SOLOMON HIXSON - 1850s

JAKE BUSKER
RICHART STORE - 1851

SECOND ST.

CEMETERY
SCHOOL
HENRY RICHART
MARIA CLINGMAN
REUBEN SIEGFRIED 1851
DR. CHARLES LEITZELL

MILL ST.

WILLIAM "BILLY" BRUCE
JAMES BENSON STORE - 1849
PETER BENNETHUN INN - 1850
DANIEL ILGEN

HEISENHELDER - EARLY 1850s
JEWELRY STORE
DUTCHMAN DOLLMEYER
WM. RUTHERFORD - 1851
LITTLE STORE
DR. S.C. THOMPSON - 1851

METHODIST CHURCH - 1886
(FIRST BUILDING - 1851)
PHILLIP H. RASSWEILER
RASSWEILER WEAVING SHED

OAK ST.

A. YEAGLE

LEWIS FRY - 1851
OSWALD
PEPPERMAN

REEL & SEYLER MFG.
ANDREW JACKSON "JACK" SEYLER
HENNEY BUGGY FACTORY - 1875
J.B. McCANNON CARRIAGE FACTORY - 1880
VILLAGE HALL & JAIL - 1870s

GEORGE ILGEN - 1850
GEORGE KRYDER - 1856

CHERRY ST.

ILGEN
JAMES OSWALT
WILLIAM RUTHER

BOWER

JOSEPH BENSON

GEORGE SEYLER
TAILOR SHOP
JACOB JONES

ABRAHAM CARL

RONALD BEAM 2002

← TO LENA   WASHINGTON ST.   TO DAKOTA →

and church projects. Cedarville residents could easily spend part of Saturday, all of Sunday, and several evenings during the week engaged in activities associated with various religious organizations. By 1870 there were at least five formally organized religious groups in Cedarville: the Methodist Church, the Lutheran and Reformed Church, the Evangelical Association, the Presbyterian Church, and the Union Sunday School.[54]

Despite the facts that Sarah Weber Addams had joined the Reformed Church in Kreidersville, Pennsylvania, on 7 November 1839, and her brother George Weber, Jr., was a missionary for the Reformed Church, she and John attended and supported all four Cedarville churches. Although John Huy Addams was a regular churchgoer, there is no evidence that he ever became a formal member of any church.[55] His mother Catherine Huy Addams had been a Quaker. Jane Addams reported that when she asked her father, "'What are you?'" he replied, "'I am a Hicksite Quaker.'"[56] Addams believed strongly in the power of God and relied on his faith for daily guidance. He usually devoted Sundays to his religion, attending services, reading his Bible, and praying. Dedicated to bringing

PRESBYTERIAN CHURCH

OPPOSITE: One of the main streets in the village, Mill Street was home to many of the village's businesses. It bridged the millrace and connected with the road to Red Oak and Orangeville just past the Addams compound on the north side. (Created by and printed with the permission of Ronald Beam)

The Cedarville Presbyterian Church was attended by all members of the Addams family. It was in this structure, built in 1876, that Jane joined the church in the fall of 1888. All of the Addams children eventually became members of the Presbyterian church. (JAPP)

the uplifting influence of religion to his community, he was instrumental in developing the Union Sunday School and served as one of its teachers. For thirty-one years until his death, he was a leader in the Cedarville Bible Society and the Stephenson County Bible Society. He was also an organizer of the German Presbyterian Society of Richland in Buckeye Township, Stephenson County, Illinois.[57] The family preference for religious service was the Presbyterian Church. All of the Addams children who lived to maturity eventually joined the Presbyterian Church, including Jane.

As the years progressed, John Huy Addams was regarded throughout northern Illinois as a hard-working, prudent, wise, and successful businessman. He was a civic leader who also became well known and respected among his neighbors as a spokesman and politician for the Republican Party.

While her husband expanded his influence, Sarah Weber Addams worked as a helpmate and partner. She seemed to have an ability to command with ease and dignity. John made certain that she was familiar with the operation of all of the family businesses, including the mills and farms. While he was away on business or while he served in the state legislature, he relied upon her to be vigilant in the care of their enterprises and to serve as his means of communication with those in his employ. In January 1857, for example, he wrote to tell Sarah to have his millers raise the price of flour. In a note written to him while he was away in the legislature in January 1861, she reminded him that she had paid the taxes due on the Iowa land they owned.[58] John Huy Addams often called upon his wife to use her cooking skills for the benefit of his milling business. Using flour produced in the family mill, she baked a perfect loaf of bread. Her husband liked to present such loaves to women in the region as an example of what they could do if they would only use his flour instead of some other miller's.

Like other pioneer women, Sarah's major responsibility was maintaining her home and raising her family. At first she probably did all her own work, but as her family increased she had one or two hired girls or helpers, especially when she was pregnant. The Addams family grew its own fruits and vegetables and preserved them. Sarah Weber Addams cooked, washed dishes, sewed, knitted, washed and cleaned clothes, cleaned house, cared for the children, created and participated in community social and religious events, and performed volunteer service. In addition, she served as midwife helper, ministered to the ill, gave newcomers useful practical advice about life on the prairie, and helped develop community social organizations.

Because her husband was so often away, Sarah had most of the responsibility for raising the Addams children, supervising their health, household duties, education, participation in community life, interactions with others, friendships, and discipline. Two family stories concern disciplining John Weber Addams and Sarah Alice Addams, both noted for their irrepressible sense of adventure. When any of the children misbehaved in an extraordinary way, their mother would place them in detention in the under-stair hall closet. All knew that its door was closed but never latched. Weber Addams recalled he was often there, and no matter how he yelled or kicked the door she would not release him—nor would he release himself—until she believed he had served adequate detention time for his misbehavior.

Particularly worried about the perils of the millrace near which Weber and Alice loved to play, their mother warned them over and over to play elsewhere. Time after time they forgot or ignored her admonition. To teach them a lesson, she surprised them one day when they were playing near the race by pushing Weber, whom she considered to be the leader, into the pond. As he was pulled toward the millrace, she hurried to the bridge over it and fished him out, bedraggled and frightened, before he came near the dangerous mill wheel. A horrified Alice looked on.

In 1854 the Addams family moved into a commodious home built especially for them. Here the couple's last four children were born. Horace, born on 15 February 1855, lived only two months; George Weber, born on 3 April 1857, lived only two years; Laura Jane, born on 6 September 1860, grew to maturity; and the last child, a daughter, was stillborn on 10 January 1863.

Constructed of the soft red brick made in Cedarville, the new Greek revival, two-story house was soon painted grey. It was nestled against a hillside, and

The birthplace of Jane Addams. Although the interior of the house has been altered over the years, the exterior has remained much the same as it was when it was built. The two-story, bay-window addition on the right was added by Anna Haldeman Addams, the second wife of John Huy Addams. At the end of the twentieth century the house was in use as a private residence. (JAPP)

the view from its frame front porch looked west toward the Addams mill and the bluff of pines across the millstream. It was five bays wide, with two windows on either side of a centered door surrounded by dark, garnet-red glass in the transom above and to about two-thirds of the way down either side. Although difficult to see through from the outside, the glass provided the central hall with a warm glow, especially when the sun began to settle toward evening.

A large kitchen with a fireplace and dutch oven and a dining room, formal parlor, and Jane Addams's parents' bedroom were all on the first floor. On the second was the less formal family parlor, where the Union Library of Cedar Creek Mills was shelved; a small spare room; the girls' bedroom, with two bedsteads and simple pegs for clothing; two additional bedrooms (one of which was for John Weber Addams); and the helpers' quarters. The well was up the hill, just behind the kitchen and connected to the house by a wooden porch that could be entered from the kitchen or the dining room. The privy was approximately seventy-five feet to the northeast. Although the house was apparently

CEDARVILLE MILLS. *JOHN H. ADDAMS* PROP.*
CEDARVILLE. STEPHENSON CO. ILL.   RES. OF HON. JOHN H. ADDAMS, CEDARVILLE, STEPHENSON CO. ILL.

The Addams home, farm, and mill in Cedarville as it appeared from the north looking south. On the far left is the Addamses' barn and to the right of that is their home; below both structures is the millpond. To the right is the mill and, to the far right, Pine Hill. The village of Cedarville is in the background of the drawing and to the south of the Addams property. Line drawing from the *Combination Atlas Map of Stephenson County Illinois, Compiled, Drawn, and Published from Personal Examinations and Surveys* (Geneva, Ill.: Thompson and Everts, 1871): 28.

heated by stoves in various rooms until a central heating system was installed, the basement room and kitchen had fireplaces. There were two staircases into the basement, where food was preserved and stored, one from the kitchen and one from the dining room; a front staircase from the entrance hall to the second floor; and a back staircase from the helpers' room to the kitchen.

We know little about the first two years of Jane Addams's life. She was the family baby and surrounded by a lively and loving assortment of siblings, parents, mill- and farmhands, relations and near-relations, a servant or two, and members of the close-knit Cedarville community. When she was born, her sister Mary was fifteen, Martha was eleven, Alice was seven, and her brother Weber was eight. All were attending school in Cedarville and had chores and responsibilities in the Addams home and businesses. Weber was learning to care for stock, and the girls were acquiring the skills of successful home management from their mother.

By 1862 the forty-three-year-old Sarah Weber Addams was expecting the couple's ninth child. Shortly after New Year's Day 1863, John Huy Addams left for Springfield and the opening of the Illinois General Assembly. As usual, Sarah remained behind to manage family, household, and business. Her husband was probably very anxious about her health. When Sarah had been pregnant in 1857 he had written repeatedly from Springfield, urging her to hire extra help and be careful.[59] In 1863 his concern proved to be tragically accurate. As on many previous occasions, Sarah went to help with the birth of a neighbor's child. Before her return home, her own labor began unexpectedly—two months early. The result was a stillborn daughter who was followed, a few days later, on 14 January 1863, by Sarah's own death. A stunned community and bereaved family buried their friend, wife, and mother and sought to carry on.

Although no extant records reveal Jane Addams's reaction to her mother's death, it must have been a watershed event in her young life. She recalled that time as one of mystery and confusion. According to her nephew and biographer James Weber Linn, she believed she had a dim recollection of the occasion. She recalled herself pounding on the closed first-floor bedroom door, demanding to see her mother and hearing her mother tell the family, "'Let her in, she is only a baby herself.'"[60]

The shock of her mother's death and fear that others might also abandon her became worries in Jane Addams's young, developing mind. She was, however, immediately enfolded in the loving ministrations of her oldest sister Mary (seventeen at their mother's death), who was ably assisted by "Polly" Beer,[61] Sarah Weber Addams's childhood nurse. Polly Beer's connection with Sarah must have been comforting for her young charge, but if Polly shared stories about Jane's mother with the child the maturing Addams did not reveal them in the extant written record.

Beer, and especially Mary Catherine Addams, served as Jane Addams's surrogate mothers during the next six years of her life. Mary was also grieving over

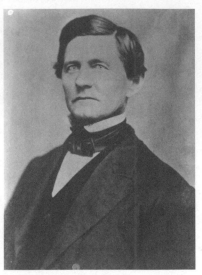

The Addams family about the time Jane was born. Sarah Weber Addams was forty-four and John Huy Addams about forty. The four Addams children who lived to greet their new sibling in 1860 were, clockwise from the top left, Martha, Mary Catherine, John Weber, and Sarah Alice. (JAPP and C. S. German, Springfield, Ill., JAPP)

her mother's passing and revealed that deep sense of loss and loneliness in a letter to her mother's sister, Elizabeth Weber Reiff: "Oh! how lonesome and sad it is without her. Sometimes it seems as if I could not live another day without her."[62]

The young Mary Addams became the head of the household operations and provided guidance and nurturing for all the Addams children. She had learned to manage a home by helping and observing her mother and various domestic helpers. Apparently similar to her mother in personality, she was a careful, loving, and selfless person, willing to assume responsibility and manage for the good of the family. Her dreams of attending Rockford Female Seminary in Rockford, Illinois, were delayed. Instead, like her mother, she assumed community responsibilities, teaching Sunday School, maintaining community friendships on behalf of the family, and helping those who were ill or in need.

It was Mary Addams as much as John Huy Addams who imparted family teachings concerning manners and appropriate and moral behavior to her sisters. Evidence of her influence appears in letters to her younger sister Alice, who attended Rockford Female Seminary, and it is likely that the young Jane Addams was treated to similar behavior-shaping love. On 30 September 1869, Mary advised Alice, "Am glad that you are settled with your room-mate. . . . I think if you try to do your part towards making it pleasant, you & Miss [Emma] Faris will get along very well: We should always try to remember that we have our happiness very much in our own hands."[63] "You must learn to be contented without always looking forward to something ahead in the future," Mary had admonished earlier. She also addressed her sister's problem with her weight and with eating as a form of self-gratification: "We should eat to live, and not live to eat: I wish you would set yourself re[s]olutely to work to break yourself thinking so much about your food. This fault as, in every thing else in our daily life, you can ask the help of God to overcome: but I will not weary you, remember it is because I love you that I speak as I do."[64]

As their siblings Martha, Alice, and Weber continued in the local school and their father returned to the legislature and to the management of his farms and business interests, Mary and Jane remained at home. Their relationship became especially close and significant for Jane, who recalled, "My horrible dream every night would be Mary's death and no one to love me."[65] For the remainder of her life, Jane Addams felt a special responsibility to Mary, not only as her sister but because she had served as a substitute mother. Shortly after Mary left the Addams home to be wed in November 1871, Jane wrote to tell her beloved sister that she was so lonesome for her that she cried although she was careful no one saw her. In 1889 she told her friend Ellen Gates Starr, "I owe so much to Mary in so many tender ways."[66]

Jane Addams often visited Mary Addams Linn and her growing family. Mary's husband, Presbyterian minister John Manning Linn,[67] was frequently away from home, leaving his often-pregnant wife to cope by herself. Jane stayed with Mary and helped when she could. She encouraged her other siblings to assist, too, and often secured nursing services and domestic help for Mary. With Mary's death in 1894, Jane Addams not only served as the executor of her estate but also, and more important, became surrogate mother for her four children and legal guardian for the three who were minors.[68] For the remainder of her life she maintained a special relationship with them and their families.

Jane Addams was small in stature and slender as a child. She had large, gray eyes; a sallow complexion; a straight nose and thin lips with a dimpled chin; and long, light-brown hair. Alice Addams recalled her sister as "a sweet dainty <u>little</u> girl with an earnest serious little face peering from long <light> brown curls."[69] She would not weigh more than a hundred pounds until she was out of her teens and never be taller than five foot three and a half. She had a slight curvature to her spine, which was likely the result of tuberculosis of the spine or Potts disease, probably a consequence of typhoid fever she had suffered when she was about four and a half.[70] Writing years later, Jane Addams's niece Marcet Halde-man-Julius reported that the Addams family, Mary in particular, was "lenient" with young Jane. "The others gave up to her and were quickly responsive to her moods and childish tempers. Playing much alone, she grew introspective; un-crossed, she came to feel that her own way was without question the right one. She was lovable but, not surprisingly, in this atmosphere of indulgence she was also willful. She was delicate too, and the fear that they might lose her often fell

Laura Jane Addams, called "Jennie," was four when this photograph, the oldest known extant of her, was taken. Sarah Weber Addams had been dead two years, and her eldest sister Mary Catherine, assisted by her mother's childhood nurse Mary ("Polly") Beer, acted as a surrogate mother. (JAPP)

like a shadow upon the hearts of her father and older sisters."[71] Jane was a serious, reserved little girl, intelligent and inquisitive. She probably had already affected the "dreamy" or "spiritual" quality that would be evident for the rest of her life. Step-cousin Sarah Hostetter, who met her for the first time when she was about thirteen and Jane about nine, recalled, "She was always neat and fresh-looking and did not get mussed and dirty like most children. She wore tiny gold earrings, our wonder and admiration. Ah, but she was so sweet and gentle and good, everybody loved her."[72]

With Mary Addams and Polly Beer in charge of the household, John Huy Addams remained free to pursue his business, political, and civic interests. He continued to represent several northern counties, including Stephenson, in the Illinois General Assembly, and he served on a number of senate committees that required him to travel about the state. He visited Chicago and ports along the Mississippi, including St. Louis, to find the best markets for his farm produce and mill products. By 1864 he had formed the Second National Bank of Freeport, of which he was president, and started two new insurance companies. He was away a great deal, and his absences may have been troubling for his youngest daughter, who worried about being left alone in the world.

In the years after her mother's death, Jane Addams's attachment to her father grew, as did her respect and love for him. Her most important goal was to comport herself so her father would continue to love her. Although she published nothing about her memories of her mother—nor indeed about her siblings—she devoted the first two chapters of her autobiography *Twenty Years at Hull-House* to her father. She used stories about her childhood relationship with him to illustrate her dedication to the values—including honesty, responsibility, civic duty, thoughtfulness for others, perseverance, organization, and diligence—that he prized. When asked years later to identify the aspect of her father's character she most valued, Addams wrote, "He was respected for his stern honesty and the tricksters either in politics or in the legislative halls were afraid of him. He was the uncompromising enemy of wrong & of wrong doing. He was a leader as well as a safe and fearless advocate in right things in public life— at best." She surmised that her "most vivid recollection" of her father was "the fact that he was a man of purest and sternest integrity and that bad men feared him. This fact was proverbial at Springfield, where as a senator & in other public positions, he distinguished himself both as an able man and an honest man."[73]

John Huy Addams was reserved but sensitive. He was also logical, pragmatic, intelligent, conscientious, and thoughtful, a gentle man who had a quiet sense of humor. He was a kind and apparently affectionate parent who engendered love and respect among his children. Mary Addams's extant letters to her father report on doings in the Addams household and transmit Jane's kisses, indicating as early as January 1865 the demonstratively affectionate bond between father and daughter.[74] Addams, with a sure authority, expected his children's adherence to the principles he held dear. He reasoned with and instructed the children, talking with them rather than down to them. He also required their obedience and appropriate behavior. Yet there are indications he was a reluctant disciplinarian.

Jane Addams admired her father's imposing looks, his public persona, his character, and the way others responded to him with careful and honest respect. Years later she recalled that at one point in her young life she was so in awe of him that she did not want strangers to know that such a "homely little girl" with a crooked back belonged to her "handsome father." In public, when both were present, she sought to appear as the child of her uncle, James Huy Addams,[75] to spare her father embarrassment. She also recalled her flush of pleasure when her tall, slender father, with his full head of dark-brown hair, grey eyes like hers, and neck beard, would playfully bow and doff his black-silk stove-pipe hat in her direction on a public sidewalk in Freeport. He became a role model, mentor, and the idol she did not want to disappoint. His probable expectations for her future in a traditional female role as wife and mother, as well as her initial unwillingness to go against him, may have caused her some pain and uncertainty when she identified and eventually acted on goals that were different from those he seemed to envision for her.

By 1866 Martha and Alice Addams had started boarding school at Rockford Female Seminary, Weber was a student in the Freeport school system, and Jane became a student in the Cedarville public school. Her first teacher, Julia Eastman,[76] remembered her as a "kind-hearted child, not precocious but gentle and with a pathetic countenance that one could not forget."[77] According to Eastman's assistant Agnes Bennethum, the class Jane first attended "was kind of a kindergarten." "Jane Addams," she recalled, had only come "to school [that first year] a few days when she fell off a bench and hurt herself and could not come back to school."[78]

"Jennie likes her school very much indeed; she can scarcely wait from one day to another so that she can go," Mary Addams wrote to Alice in 1867.[79] Her classmates and playmates were the children of millers who worked for her father. Some were neighbors from the village, others were the children of area farmers. One or two were the offspring of area relatives, most notably cousins, the children of her Aunt Lavina Hinnersheetz Addams and Uncle James Huy Addams, who lived on a farm about a mile west of the family home.

Jane Addams usually walked to the schoolhouse located south of her house. Surrounded by a playground, it was at the west end of Second Street on a hill near the first town cemetery.[80] She was a student in a two-room school environment where the younger children were divided from the older and two teachers taught a variety of subjects at a mixture of grade levels to children of different ages and intellectual development. Among teachers who served the Cedarville schools while Jane was a student were Julia Eastman; John H. Parr,[81] perhaps her favorite teacher (1870–73 and 1875–77); C. W. Moore[82] (1873–75); and Eva Pennell[83] (1875–77).

By 1868, when Jane began to correspond with family and friends, she had learned to form letters, spell words and write sentences, do simple arithmetic, and read. On 28 January 1870, she wrote to her sister Alice, "[I] study geography and arithmetic and spell and read in the fourth reader."[84] Between 1870 and 1875, the years for which records exist, she studied reading, spelling, writing, and arithmetic. In general, her highest grades came in arithmetic, followed by reading, writing, and, last, spelling, at which, despite great efforts, she could not seem to excel. A whole year of grammar was substituted in 1872 for what in 1870 and 1871 had only been two months of study. For the 1874–75 school year, history and chemistry appeared on her grade record; by 1875, natural history, algebra, and Latin took their place. Jane Addams was a conscientious, persistent, and bright student. She always received high marks in deportment, and on a grading scale of one to ten, where ten was perfect, her grades generally ranged from 8.1 to 9.8 (As and Bs).[85]

In the Cedarville school, Jane and her classmates were subjected to several different teaching techniques. There were textbooks to study, papers to write, examples and problems to work, sentences to parse, and rules and facts to memorize. A literary society, with constitution, bylaws, officers who were elected

Jennie Addams began school when she was five. Her report card for the month of June 1873 was signed by one of her favorite teachers, John H. Parr. She always received high grades in deportment. (CAHS)

every two weeks, and a publication, helped students learn about organization, working together, and politics. Students gave an assortment of classroom presentations and had opportunity to stand and reply to questions put to them by teachers and other students. They organized oral exhibitions that were presented on Fridays to parents, friends, and school officials. The Friday events helped them prepare for the public oral examinations held at the end of each term so everyone could appraise each student's readiness to advance to a new level of study. By the time Jane Addams graduated from the Cedarville school in the early summer of 1877, she was able to stand and speak in front of others with ease.

One of the most famous, and to some of Addams's biographers and interpreters surprisingly prophetic, stories is connected with her earliest school days. The event probably took place before the fall of 1867, when the Haldeman Stone Steam Flour Mill in Freeport was closed. On a visit with her father to the mill, she recognized and described for the first time the "horrid little houses so close together" that were so prevalent in the "poorest quarter" near the mill.[86] Although she omitted her father's explanation for the conditions in her version of the story, she remembered telling him with assurance that she would one day have a large house amid such small, rude houses, the implication being that from her dwelling she would provide assistance for her less fortunate neighbors.

Jane Addams apparently understood at a very early age that there were varying degrees of wealth and associated responsibility. She had been taught that her family's success placed her in a position of relative wealth and that she had the concomitant duty to use it wisely and help others less fortunate. Sarah and Mary must have served as powerful community-service role models for young Jane in this respect. Earle A. Berry,[87] a teacher in Cedarville after she matriculated at Rockford Female Seminary, was often a guest in the Addams home. He recalled John Huy Addams recounting the story of his young daughter's comments in Freeport.[88] Perhaps Jane identified the story as significant not only because of the eventual creation of Hull-House and because of the ideas she wished to impart by presenting it in her memoirs but also because her father thought the story special.

Before she was eight Jane Addams once again experienced death in the circle of her immediate family. She was aware of the deaths of others, including playmates and their parents, and she had lost pets, but none of those losses came as close as that of her mother. Jane's sixteen-year-old sister Martha was a senior at Rockford Female Seminary when she became ill with typhoid fever in early 1867. She died at the school on the twenty-third of March. The family, once again, was devastated. Mary Addams shared her grief and attempted to console Alice, who returned to Rockford Female Seminary after Martha's burial in order to continue her studies. "Sometimes it seems to me that it cannot be possible that I shall never see Martha again," Mary confided on 17 April 1867, "very often I think of her as at Rockford." Most of Mary's letters to Alice at Rockford Female Seminary in the spring of 1867 carry her lamentations over their dead sibling.[89]

Alice, meanwhile, reacted to Martha's death by making a commitment to join the Presbyterian Church. Martha had done so shortly before her death, and she had wanted Alice to join, too.[90] That suited Mary, who encouraged among her siblings the certitude that they could all be reunited with Martha in heaven. "[T]hough she cannot come to us, we may go to her," she reassuringly wrote to Alice three weeks after their sister's death.[91]

If Jane Addams's mother's death was blurred in memory, Martha's death and the ceremonies associated with it must have been more traumatic for the six-year-old Jane because she was more aware. It may have been at this juncture that the feelings and fears expressed in the recurring dream she remembered having "night after night" as a child were most poignantly felt.[92] She recalled dreaming that she was totally alone in the world, everyone having disappeared to the cemetery, and that she was responsible for constructing a wheel without knowing how. She remembered vividly being overwhelmed and terrified, later in life recounting her reaction at the age of six to the death of a relative—probably her sister. All the family save she attended the funeral and burial. She was left at home in the care of Polly Beer and a visitor. Jane recollected her reaction to the mystery of death and its awful finality and the fear that it would come for her or others she loved, leaving her alone. She sat in the middle of the stairway of the Addams home, and in that "moment of loneliness and horror" she experienced, "only the blank wall of the stairway seemed to afford protection . . . against the formless peril."[93] She also recalled the oppressive and unsettling feelings she experienced at seeing her first burial. The mother of one of her classmates had died, and their teacher took the class to the interment. Jane was "totally unprepared to see what appeared to be the person herself put deep into the ground."[94]

The year 1868 brought great change for the Addams family. On the seventeenth of November, John Huy Addams remarried. His new wife was Anna Hostetter Haldeman Addams,[95] a forty-year-old widow six years his junior. She had moved to Freeport in the late 1850s with her first husband, William J. Haldeman.[96] There Haldeman owned and operated the Stone Steam Flour Mill until his death from tuberculosis in 1866.[97]

Like the Addams family, Anna Haldeman had Pennsylvania roots. Like Jane, her mother had died when she was young; also like Jane, she was nurtured by her oldest sister, Susanna ("Susan") Hostetter Bowman.[98] At sixteen she emigrated with her physician brothers John Lichty Hostetter[99] and Abraham Hostetter[100] to Mount Carroll[101] in Carroll County, Illinois, about thirty-five miles southwest of Freeport. She lodged there with her brother, John L. Hostetter. By the time she was nineteen she had wed William J. Haldeman, whose family owned a mill in Mount Carroll. The couple had four sons. Two—John Hostetter Haldeman and William Nathaniel Haldeman, both born in the 1850s—died in early childhood. The other two—Henry Winfield Haldeman,[102] called Harry and sometimes Hal, and George Bowman Haldeman,[103] called George—were

Anna Hostetter Haldeman, ca. 1866, in mourning clothes shortly after the death of her Freeport, Illinois, miller husband William J. Haldeman. John Huy Addams envisioned her as a potential wife and mother for his children. (Miller Brothers, Mt. Carroll, Ill.; JAPP)

twenty years old and seven years old respectively when John Huy Addams courted their widowed mother in 1868.

It is likely that neither Addams nor Anna Hostetter Haldeman entered what was a second marriage for each with the same ardor or comfort they had felt for their first partners. Yet they both saw the new match as beneficial. Although initially reluctant to enter the relationship, Anna had good reasons to consent to Addams's offer of marriage.[104] She needed security and a father for her sons. She was also attracted to the public life and position she assumed she would have as John Huy Addams's wife. She recognized that he had a houseful of children who would benefit from the lessons an experienced and able wife and mother could provide. For his part, Addams wanted a mother for his children. He was no doubt lonely, and he saw in Anna Haldeman a suitable intellectual companion who was socially accomplished, witty, and entertaining. In addition, she was an attractive woman, tall and slender, with chestnut hair and bright hazel eyes.

Anna came into the Addams home expecting to have an active social life enlivened by and enlivening the halls of the Illinois General Assembly and the homes of Springfield on the arm of her state senator husband. Described by her granddaughter Marcet Haldeman-Julius as "beautiful, high-spirited and cultured," she was also temperamental and self-centered.[105] Anna brought with her a love of culture and social refinement that the Addams family with its simpler pioneer ways seemed to lack. She considered herself attuned to the intellectual vanguard of her day. She read the classics as well as popular literature and loved music, theater, and poetry. In addition, she enjoyed games of all kinds, humorous stories, lively conversation about substantive issues, good manners, beautiful surroundings, fine food, and an elegantly appointed table. Her favorite saying translated from German was "Whatever is beautiful—that belongs to me."[106] Anna detested household chores, including sewing, cooking, baking, preserving foods, cleaning, and gardening. She also rejected the role of community samaritan that had been filled so ably by Sarah Weber Addams and her daughter Mary. She brought her two sons into the Addams home with her.

Married in mid-November 1868 by John Huy Addams's friend the Rev. Isaac Carey[107] of the First Presbyterian Church of Freeport, the newlyweds headed soon after to Pennsylvania and Maryland to meet both sets of relatives. Their children remained in the Addams home in Cedarville, getting acquainted with one another under the care of Mary Addams and Polly Beer. The new couple returned home to Cedarville in time for Christmas and to comfort young Jane, who had whooping cough. Children, parents, and Polly—all still in the honeymoon phase of the new family relationship—worked to establish good permanent bonds.

Early in January, Addams left for the General Assembly, soon to be visited in Springfield by his new wife. The rest of the new family also dispersed. Alice returned to Rockford Female Seminary, and Weber returned to Beloit Academy in Wisconsin. Harry Haldeman, who had expressed enthusiasm over his mother's marriage and the new family structure,[108] began to study medicine in Freeport with Dr. Levi A. Mease.[109]

Mary Addams, freed from caretaking duties, took music and china painting at Rockford Female Seminary and traveled to see family and friends in the East. Anna called on life-long Addams family friends in Cedarville early in the year and then spent time with her husband in Springfield. She returned to the Addams home in Cedarville and settled into a round robin of visits from close friends and Mount Carroll Hostetter relatives, including sisters, nieces, and nephews. She also turned her attentions to the two youngest members of the family.

Life in the Addams home changed dramatically under Anna Haldeman Addams's influence. Authority for the welfare of the home and children shifted away from Mary Addams and the cherished family housekeeper Polly to John Huy Addams's new wife. "The new head of the household was just and equal in her treatment of Jane and George, though she was too honest to pretend that

John Huy Addams and Anna Hostetter Haldeman soon after their marriage in 1868. (J. Haldt, Philadelphia; SCPC)

she loved them equally," wrote Marcet Haldeman-Julius years later.[110] As the children of her beloved first husband, Harry and George Haldeman were especially dear to their mother, and they remained so all of her life. She wanted them to have all of the opportunities for success possible. Although Harry soon left Cedarville, George, the apple of her eye, remained with her to grow to maturity in the new Addams family under her dominating influence.

Without doubt the young Jane Addams bore the brunt of the change at home, for she was with her stepmother daily. She had been used to the gentle, steady directions of an older sister for whose affection and attention she had no rival. Now she was suddenly competing with her stepbrother George. She also had to learn to adapt to her stepmother's uneven personality as well as to Anna Haldeman Addams's sense of order, propriety, and responsibility—all of which were so very different from Mary's habits and attitudes. Although Mary remained in the Addams household for a time, it was clear that Anna was in charge. That may have been a relief to Mary; on 11 January 1869 Anna wrote to her husband that Mary was blossoming with her lack of family responsibility and her newfound freedom.[111] Anna was concerned about Mary's marital status (as was Mary). Although Mary joked with her sister Alice about approaching another birthday as a single woman, Anna Addams attempted to help secure at least one appropriate suitor for her eldest stepdaughter, setting her sights briefly on her nephew John H. Bowman as a possible match.[112]

Jane, separated from her siblings, also found that her father was no longer as accessible to her as he had been. Now he had a wife, and his business and political life also continued to keep him away from home. Except for Polly (whose household work was also directed by Anna and who spent blocks of time away from the Addams home visiting friends and relatives), Jane was primarily in the care of her stepmother. She was surrounded by two new stepbrothers, by the Hostetter relatives who frequently came to visit, and by Anna's friends.

The new Mrs. Addams seemed intent on bringing discipline and training as well as intellectual and social improvement to the home. She led the Hostetter relatives to believe that the "Addamses were somewhat primative in their manners and mode of life, having been with out a mother for some time" but that she had stepped in to remedy this situation. John Huy Addams's new wife "remodeled the house [and] corrected the children's manners until it was a fitting place to entertain the many noted people who would naturally be the senator's guests."[113]

Although the domestic environment in the Addams home was probably not quite as basic and colorless as Anna would recall, she did bring a certain sense of fun, adventure, sophistication, and polish to her new surroundings. Anna had grown up among brothers and sisters who were intellectually able, creative, and successful. Her relatives in Mount Carroll were community leaders—physicians, farmers and stock breeders, and newspaper publishers—who constructed homes that became islands of intellectual activity and fun. They often attended public lectures presented by scholars at Mount Carroll Seminary. They read widely in the popular literature of their day; loved music, poetry, games, and the theater; and took up avant-garde, nontraditional theories and associations, among them theosophy and phrenology. They held annual reunions and hosted an assortment of parties attended by family and friends.

Once in charge in Cedarville, Anna Haldeman Addams saw to it that the clothing pegs disappeared from upstairs bedrooms, to be replaced by wardrobes. China, silver, and napery were more abundant at the table, and an upright piano was positioned in the parlor. Eventually, bays of three windows were added to the south side of the first-floor parlor and to the family parlor above. A small private office was built off the main first-floor hall near the kitchen so John Huy Addams did not have to conduct his business in the first-floor parlor, and a bathroom was installed on the second floor.

With the arrival in the Addams household of Anna Haldeman Addams and her children came an emphasis on music. "[M]usic has been my abiding star—it sings to me," she explained in a letter to her son Harry. "[M]y brain—records it—and repeats it—[it] lulls my weary soul," she continued. "Music is the only 'truth' that makes me feel free, to fly away from Earth and care—to a sphere beyond this temporal life."[114] Anna composed poetry and sang while she played a small guitar. She was noted for her ability to keep children spellbound with her readings, stories, and songs. Harry was a talented violinist and pianist. He studied music at the Mount Carroll Seminary and then for the two years between 1866 and 1868 at the Conservatory of Music in Leipzig, Germany. During the late 1860s it was Anna's expectation that Harry would eventually support his brother George and her by becoming a concert musician and a music teacher. Although he taught music the remainder of his life (even while a physician and later as a banker), he never succeeded as a professional. He wrote music, poetry, and plays, yet apparently none of the attempts by him or his mother during the early 1870s to have pieces published were successful.[115]

Anna Haldeman Addams hoped that she could also encourage musical talent in her son George and in the Addams children. With little consideration for her talent in art or for her wishes, Alice Addams was instructed to take music lessons at Rockford Female Seminary, primarily because her stepmother preferred she do so. Mary Addams, who was used to giving Alice direction, had the task of breaking the unwelcome news to her. "Pa & Ma think you better go on with your music because you can at least learn to play enough to be some gratification to your friends," she wrote, encouraging her that "some other time you can take painting."[116] The results were not promising. Shortly after the Addams family purchased a new Hazelton piano in April 1875, Jane recorded in her diary on 4 May, "Allie tried to play but hammered that everlasting Russian March and bird waltz. And scrat[c]hed the piano all up with her foot."[117]

Although Jane Addams and George Haldeman were given piano and singing lessons and attended community sings, neither possessed any special musical talent. In fact, Sarah Hostetter recalled that "when a girl" Jane "could not sing a tune. She had a good conception of rythm but [was] never quite sure of pitch." She did, however, have a sense for the emotional and dramatic. "It was a rare treat when we could persuade her to sing 'The Mistletoe Bough'," Hostetter remembered. "She liked the tragedy and its music and always rendered it most dramatically the sentiment the rythm but mostly [in] a monotone."[118]

The Haldemans brought a healthy disregard for traditional religious practice with them, too. Like her brothers and their families in Mount Carroll, Anna Haldeman Addams was attracted to the theosophic system of Swedish scientist, philosopher, and mystic Emanuel Swedenborg (1688–1772), whose ideas led to the founding of the New Jerusalem Church. Swedenborg claimed that he had been given the correct interpretation for humanity of the true inner doctrine of the divine word. He had achieved this by direct insight into the spiritual world with the permission of God. Visions and interactions with spirits and angels had prepared him for this task, setting forth the teachings of the "New Church," which had begun with the Second Coming, an event that Swedenborg and his followers believed had taken place in 1757. Swedenborgianism held that religion should be perceived in close relation to life and that the life of religion was to do good. His doctrines were meant to bind members of all established Christian Churches into one religious alliance.

At different times, Swedenborgianism was associated with mesmerism, spiritualism, and homeopathy. It attracted a mixture of advocates, among them intellectuals, those with disdain for religious traditions, eccentrics, and liberals. There was something for everyone in an organization of beliefs that revered love, wisdom, and usefulness. Robert and Elizabeth Browning, Henry Ward Beecher, and Thomas Carlyle were among those influenced by Swedenborgianism. The Hostetters attended New Jerusalem Church gatherings and bought and read its publications.[119] The Abraham Hostetters joined the New Jerusalem Church as a family in 1862 and daughters Susan Mattie and Sarah were educated for two years at the Waltham New-Church School in Massachusetts. Charles Linnaeus Hostetter (a nephew of Anna Haldeman Addams who worked in Chicago during the 1860s)[120] wrote several letters informing her of his activities and those of her friends at New Jerusalem Church gatherings there. His brother Abram Bowman Hostetter[121] gave up studying for the New Jerusalem Church ministry after one year. Shortly after her first husband's death, Anna Haldeman Addams despaired over the tangle of financial and family problems she found facing her. Her brother John L. Hostetter turned to Swedenborgian teaching in lending her advice. "Our natural instincts prompt us to dislike and even hate those whom we think have injured us," he reminded her in a letter written on 26 May 1866 from Mount Carroll, "but viewed in the light of the New Jerusalem Church insofar as they

The new Mrs. John Huy Addams, about forty, came to the Addams home with her two sons, Henry Winfield Haldeman and George Bowman Haldeman, to become wife to Addams and mother to his children. (Allen and Williams, Freeport, Ill.; JAPP)

are governed by envy and hate, malice[,] revenge or any of the direful passions, they become objects of commisseration, for our energies to be expended upon for their release from the power of evil spir[i]ts."[122]

After her marriage to John Huy Addams, Anna made an effort to engage in some traditional religious activities. She went to the Presbyterian Church although she was an irregular attendee, and her son George attended Sunday School and church with Jane. In a letter dated 27 February 1873 from Mendota, Illinois, Harry Haldeman, reflecting on institutionalized religion, advised his mother: "I hear your new Minister has arrived—I hope you—Will like him—dont get to argueing too much but—I sincerely hope you Will hold your own against the orthodoxical—pack—of Subterfuges—he may have with him." Harry Haldeman became an atheist.[123]

Anna Haldeman Addams shared a part of her religious philosophy with her stepdaughter Alice. She wrote to her on 19 August 1871 to observe that human beings "are constantly progressing—or retrograding—there is no climax of perfection attainable in this life: Developement, developement, is the Soul's demand." She went on to describe her concept of what should ideally be strived for in life. "The highest development is to see and know the 'Lord in all His works.' To love Him above all things—and fellow beings as ourselves: For this high end, we must lose sight of our selfishness, by trying to make others—as happy as we would wish to be: (that is to do all in our power, to make others so)." She did not see these ideals well manifested in the rising generation. "Not wishing to moralize," she told Alice, "I could not help saying what—I have, because I see so many heartless young people growing up selfish and, perfectly regardless of any one: But themselves and their own enjoyments."[124] No doubt she also shared her perspective with Jane.

Another influence the new Mrs. Addams brought to the Addams home was her interest in phrenology, an analytical method of describing mental ability and human character and actions based on the shape and contours of the skull. It had originated in Vienna and was developed and made popular in the early part of the nineteenth century in England and America by German physician Franz Joseph Gall (1758–1828) and his followers.

Phrenology, as Madeleine B. Stern has put it, "was to the American nineteenth century what psychiatry and psychoanalysis" became to the twentieth century."[125] Phrenologists asserted that the brain was composed of many small component parts that worked together as an aggregate. Each faculty or character trait associated with mental function was believed to have a corresponding organ in the brain. The size of these various regions of the brain indicated the strength of particular attributes within a given individual and determined their distinctive personality. Because the organs that made up the brain were believed to have specific locations in the skull, phrenologists claimed to be able to analyze ability and identify strengths and weaknesses of character by measuring the unique size and shape of each person's head. They also taught that mental functions and personality traits could be developed by increasing the size of their respective organs within the brain through exercise.

These theories made individuals potentially the masters of their own minds. Each was free to decide how they felt about different strengths of character and to increase attributes they considered desirable and diminish those they deemed undesirable. Its advocates embraced phrenology as a means of self-reform and a route to larger, societal reform. Many seized upon it as the "lever that would prevent crime and improve the condition of the insane, obviate incompatibility in marriage and vocational maladjustment, and restore the nation's health—physical and spiritual." The result was a current of optimism. To believers in phrenology, "all things were possible."[126]

The ideas that individuals could improve if they chose and that organic change was possible were powerful personal motivators. By extension, phrenology also offered new hope to existing reform movements. Because phrenologists did not argue that mental attributes associated with the brain organs were different for men and women, their theories gave support to those who promoted equality as an argument for women's rights. That phrenology could also be used (its practitioners argued) to identify proper mates made possible more open discussion of sex, choice, and love with liberating aspects for women.

The Addams, Hostetter, and Haldeman families were familiar with the theories associated with phrenology. John Huy Addams and Abraham and John L. Hostetter were all educated during the 1830s in Pennsylvania, when and where phrenological ideas had found ready acceptance.[127] It is likely that Addams was exposed to phrenology through his formal education. So was William J. Haldeman. One of the few extant volumes from his library is George Combe's *Moral Philosophy* (1844) marked "William Haldeman / R[ock] R[iver] Seminary."[128] The influences were not limited to the formal halls of learning. The Union Library Company of Cedar Creek Mills, located in the Addams home in Cedarville, contained several volumes promoting phrenological theories. Among them were two works by George Combe, one by J. Stanley Grimes,[129] and one by J. G. Spurzheim.[130] Phrenological ideas were already known to Jane Addams before Anna Hostetter Haldeman became her stepmother. Her father had subscribed to *The Student*—a periodical issued by the phrenological publishing house in Boston owned by the Fowler family—for his children's enjoyment.

Although there was much general interest in phrenology, Anna Haldeman Addams seems to have made a particularly strong commitment to its teachings. It probably appealed to her intellectual elitism. It may also have provided hope that her sons could improve themselves, helping one to combat his alcoholic excesses and the other to circumvent his reclusive tendencies. She saved William's volume by Combe, and in 1881 she cared enough about phrenology to secure the volume by J. G. Spurzheim from the John Huy Addams estate.[131] Among her possessions was a three-dimensional replica of a human head with the various attributes measured by phrenology marked on it in their proper location. She was attracted to phrenological lectures, and in 1876 sought a phrenological consultation for herself, George, and stepdaughter Jane. The reading for Jane Addams is printed in this volume.[132]

It is difficult to know how much the ideas of self-knowledge, self-improvement, and social reform promoted by the phrenological theorists affected Jane's thinking. Although it is certain that she was exposed to the doctrines of phrenology during her formative years, she left scant evidence in her adult public or private writings about her knowledge of these beliefs or their significance to her. As she grew older, popular acceptance of the theories waned. She, like others, remained skeptical of phrenological practices, which had become the subject of amusement in many quarters, including later at Rockford Female Seminary.

Swedenborgianism and phrenology were not the only forms of social reform to which Jane Addams was exposed in her family. Both Anna Addams and John Huy Addams were strong supporters of temperance. Together with their older children, they often attended temperance revival meetings in Cedarville and Freeport. Although alcohol may have been used for medicinal purposes in the Addams home, no wine or other alcohol was ever served at the Addams table.[133] Mary, Alice, and Weber became active members of Constance Lodge No. 937 of the Independent Order of Good Templars. The lodge was established in Cedarville in 1866 but lost its charter on 20 April 1872 due primarily to a dwindling membership.[134] After its demise, public temperance meetings were held monthly in Cedarville.

The Addams children remained quite conscientious regarding their temperance ideals. Even after her marriage to the Rev. John M. Linn, Mary participated actively in temperance organizations in the towns of northern Illinois where they lived. While Alice was touring Europe in the summer of 1875, she was apparently tempted by German wine on a special occasion. Her father wrote that he was "pleased that you did not waive your Temperance principals at the pleasant banquet you describe do not think you lost any prestage from any sensible person."[135] Although for the rest of her life Jane Addams supported temperance, becoming a member of the Woman's Christian Temperance Union and a staunch supporter of prohibition in her later years, she may not have been as careful as Alice during her own adventures in Europe.[136]

The one family backslider on the temperance issue was Harry Haldeman, who was probably an alcoholic. A Hostetter family history described him as a man who "drank too much."[137] Cautious because of Harry's behavior, Anna Haldeman Addams was deeply concerned about her younger son George when he first left her watchful eye to attend Beloit Academy. Trying to assuage the fears he knew she had, George wrote to his mother in detail about attending Sunday School and church and, by implication, staying away from saloons and similar influences. On 23 September 1877 he reported, "I have not experienced any temptations as yet, although I expect them. . . . I never go out nights at all, making it a point to go down town in the day time if we need anythng."[138]

In keeping with some aspects of their interest in moral reform, Jane Addams's parents also shared similar conservative views about the role of women in society. Despite accepting the idea that women were intelligent, they believed they had neither a place in politics or public office nor the need for the vote. John Huy Addams had been quite firm on this issue for some time. During a trip to Niagara Falls in 1844 he recorded in his diary that "upon treading on Canada shore a feeling of derision crosses one's mind thinking that all this country is subject to the government of a Women—for republicans this will not do[.]"[139] Anna Addams maintained that there were ample ways for women to achieve in the private realm. "I am writing this on the volume—called 'Eminent Women of the age,'" she wrote to Alice in July 1871, "and, tho' we can not all become Eminent, in, a world wide form we can be eminent—among— friends and, associates, for a cultivated mind, and, heart—actuated with reason, and good common sense."[140]

Debate about woman suffrage appeared frequently in Freeport and other Illinois newspapers, especially during the 1869–70 period when Illinois was preparing for and holding a constitutional convention. Leaders of the woman suffrage movement hoped that the new Illinois constitution would include the right for women to vote. Shortly after the Illinois Woman Suffrage Association was formed on 11 and 12 February 1869 in Chicago, its new president Mary Livermore,[141] accompanied by Elizabeth Cady Stanton,[142] went to Springfield to the legislature to argue their case. John Huy Addams described the event in a letter to Anna Haldeman Addams, sparing little sarcasm in the process. "The Strong minded Women are in the City—Women's Suffrage on the Advance," he reported. "Two of its most noted champions addressed a very large Audiance in Rudolph Opera House last night [19 February 1869] including Many Gran[d] Senators and dignified Representatives and in addition to all that our Gallant and honered (Speaker) Leut Governor [John] Dougherty Presided and in [a] little speech introducing the fair ones (although are abomnable ugly) gave his adhesion to the principles they advocate—Oh y[e]s Fogy Ladies take heed." Addams's derision extended from his political colleague to the visiting activists. Although he reserved some respect for the Illinois representative, his views of the less self-effacing Elizabeth Cady Stanton were not kind. "Mrs Stanton from New York & Mrs Livermore from Chicago were the speakers," he wrote to Anna. "And am proud to say that our Western lady made by all comparison the best address— although she stated that she by no means claimed to be an Orator and only appeared upon the urgent solicitation of their Woman General in the Movement Mrs Stanton to acompanee her to this place—Her remarks were well arranged and Arguments strong & convincing—Mrs Stanton's were rambling and rather bordering on the Egotistical which you know is no fancy of mine—but you are weary of this."[143]

It is likely that the young Weber Addams shared some of his father's objections to woman suffrage. He certainly echoed his views when he prepared a negative argument to the question "Res. That Woman should be allowed the right of suffrage" for the debating club of Cedarville on 21 May 1870. Woman, Weber argued, was created as "an helpmate & assistant to man & not as a Co-partner with equal rights & priveleges." Singling out Elizabeth Cady Stanton and Mary Livermore especially, he held that it is not the "senate God Loving Woman, who asks the right to vote and hold office; But a few Ambitious creatures, who prefer the Dirty, Bar Room & the praise of a few Logey Loafers to the hundred duties of a Wife & the praise of God." Pronouncing that the statutes of the United States and Illinois adequately protected the "civil, social & marital relations of man & woman," he rhetorically asked, "What then would be the condition of the Morals of our Country, if the Mother, who is especially qualified by Providence to teach her children the principles of right & justice, should, like Mrs. Stanton, leave her little ones to contend, unguarded, against the temptations of life & become a politician & office seeker[?]"[144]

Although they frowned on women in politics, Jane Addams's parents wished to be certain that women had necessary legal rights, especially to hold and manage their own property. Long before any of his daughters were married, John Huy Addams supported legislation in Illinois that permitted a married woman, rather than a trustee (often a woman's husband), to hold, manage, and convey her assets.[145] Addams expected all of his children to inherit real estate and money from him. He and both of his wives had made considerable effort to teach their children how to manage financial resources. Each was encouraged to keep a record of income and expenditures. Jane even kept a record of the pennies she placed in the collection box at Sunday School.[146]

Both John Huy Addams and Anna Haldeman Addams assumed that their children would live their adult lives within a traditional marriage structure like the ones they themselves had chosen. In that traditional model, the males were to be responsible for the family's protection and livelihood and for business matters and politics. The females were to undertake the creation and management of home, rearing children, and maintaining community ties. The Addams children were prepared accordingly.

Mary Addams, Polly Beer, and finally Anna Haldeman Addams initiated Jane into the traditional skills of female culture. As with most girls of the period, she was also surrounded during her girlhood and teen years by a growing assortment of female friends. Drawn from her own family, including her sisters and female cousins and step-cousins, as well as from the families that the elder Addams couple befriended, these friends included the daughters of millers (most of whom helped operate the Addams mill and lived in close proximity to the Addams home), farmers (especially those in the Cedarville area who were Republicans and either Presbyterians or Methodists), ministers, merchants, and businessmen. After Anna Haldeman Addams arrived, Jane also became involved with the young children of her stepmother's friends. Most of these friendships (those among family excepted) did not survive to adulthood. Being introduced to the importance of a female community, the girls corresponded and visited in one anothers' homes. Throughout her teenage years, Jane Addams's list of correspondents increased. By 1877, when she kept a brief record of the letters she sent and received, she counted among her correspondents an assortment of aunts, uncles, cousins, and sisters, a minister and two teachers, and also a list of female friends.[147]

Some friendships grew from proximity. Some of the long-distance friendships began in the Cedarville area before the families of Jane's friends moved away. Others were long-distance from the start. That was the case with female cousins in particular. The girls shared their experiences cooking and sewing and discussed their progress in school and favorite pastimes. Games gave way to parties and social occasions that were often organized around church activities and included boys. Although Jane Addams mentioned the exploits of female and male classmates who became emotionally attached to one another, she never referred in extant documents to feelings she may have harbored for any young man, including her stepbrother George. Considered as a potential mate for him by some of the family, she treated George in her 1875 diary and in correspondence in an unemotional manner simply as a brother and a friend.

When Jane Addams was very young she began to be given household responsibilities. As a youngster, she was assigned the task of keeping the glass chimneys on oil lamps clean. As she grew older, it became her duty to fill the water pitchers in each bedroom and be sure the wash basins were clean and that fresh toweling was available.[148] She learned about food preservation and preparation, partly from Mary Addams and Polly Beer although mostly from cooks hired by Anna Haldeman Addams (who acted as the judge of quality). The second Mrs. Addams disliked cooking and gave her youngest stepdaughter a chance to practice her kitchen arts whenever the cook took a day off or left employment. In her teenage years, Jane experimented in the kitchen, creating a variety of sweet dishes, waffles, cookies, and taffy.[149] By the time she was old enough to learn from participating fully in many of the tasks required of a woman to maintain a smoothly functioning home in the late nineteenth century, those tasks had been turned over to full-time household help.

As a child, Jane shared a bedroom with her sisters. By the time she was in her teens it had become her room except when her sisters visited, and she was responsible for its decorating and cleaning. Although she assisted with spring cleaning, neither she nor her stepmother bore the duty alone. Anna Addams usually hired local women to share in the task. Jane may have assisted with the washing and ironing, but it is doubtful that she ever undertook those chores on her own for the entire family. Like other girls from well-to-do Victorian families, she was raised to have enough experience and knowledge to judge whether servants had performed their jobs adequately.

Sewing was another basic skill required of pioneer women. Sarah Weber Addams was apparently a proficient seamstress. In 1845, shortly after she and

John Huy Addams arrived in Stephenson County, she helped organize a sewing and reading circle to raise money to furnish a meeting house.[150] She sewed to meet her family's needs from bed linens to dresses and taught her older daughters the skill as well. When she died, her eldest daughter, Mary, aided by Polly Beer, an able knitter, took her mother's place as the family seamstress. Assisted by friends and near family, she made and altered dresses, cloaks, and undergarments for her sisters at Rockford and for Jane. Mary probably taught Jane how to sew. After Anna Haldeman Addams came into the Addams household, Mary continued to serve as the primary seamstress until she married in 1871. From that time on, Anna relied primarily on professional seamstresses for major alterations on clothing and for new dresses for herself and Alice and Jane, both of whom were responsible for their own mending.

By 1870 Jane Addams was engaged in learning and practicing decorative needlework. She may have done so at the urging of her sister Mary, who by 1871 was serving as one of two superintendents for the Department of Fabrics and Fancy Articles at the first Cedarville Agricultural Fair. The next year Jane Addams won a prize for making the best housewife in the Department of Ladies' Fancy Work at the fair.[151] Many of her friends were also taking up decorative needlecraft. An art form that could add special beauty to a home and was seen as an appropriate feminine skill, decorative sewing in the late nineteenth century became popular with women of wealth who had enough leisure to undertake "fancy work." Jane's practice of needlecraft, including knitting, became a life-long personal hobby.[152]

In many ways it was not female friends or family members that provided Jane with her closest companionship as a child. Encouraged by both parents, she and George, with only nine months' difference in their ages, became inseparable playmates, quickly forming their own special peer group. Mary Addams commented to her sister Alice that "Jennie and Georgie . . . never seem to be quite as contented as when they are here alone, without any company."[153] Temperamentally and intellectually the two seemed well matched. Both were bright and inquisitive and eager for knowledge, neither was physically robust, and both had new family relationships to adjust to. They went to school together, took the same subjects in the same classroom from the same teacher, and studied together. They attended church and church-related activities together. They played at games together, including croquet, chess, authors, and natural history. They took piano lessons together, practiced together, and played duets. They read similar books and listened to the same stories from their parents. They shared friends and childhood experiences. They roamed the fields and woods, exploring the caves of Cedar Creek and the rivulets that emptied into the Addams mill pond. They went boating on the pond in summer and skated on it or glided on sleds down slopes toward it in winter. They created make-believe worlds and events and recreated heros from eras gone by, sometimes in the mill but more often in the Addams orchard or the pastures and woods of the surrounding area. Sometimes they were crusaders brandishing play swords or knights from King Arthur's Round Table. Sometimes they were fighting Black Hawk or searching for pieces of pottery or projectiles left by Native Americans who had lived in the area such a short time before them.[154] For a time they collected specimens of various plants and animals and celebrated their discoveries by bringing them to an altar of stone they had erected upon which to sacrifice their treasures. Jane recalled placing numerous dead snakes on the altar along with English walnuts splashed with cider and even a favorite book or two burned as an offering to a specially created deity. After Anna Haldeman Addams and George arrived, Jane's dolls disappeared, to be replaced by more challenging intellectual pastimes and adventures. Sometimes she was in the lead, but more often it was George. Among their intellectual pursuits in addition to schoolwork, music lessons, and reading were writing poetry, communicating in specially created alphabets, and investigating natural and scientific phenomena.

Their interest in science was fostered by Harry Haldeman, who focused on science himself as he studied medicine, and by Anna Haldeman Addams's physician brothers. John L. Hostetter, who believed that women should be educated as physicians in their own medical schools, was probably especially encouraging. By the end of 1873, George and Jane were investigating almanacs. They created the Science of Almanacs Association, whose members were themselves, with George identified as "chief," and a secret password: "Quinaxzimoto." Not

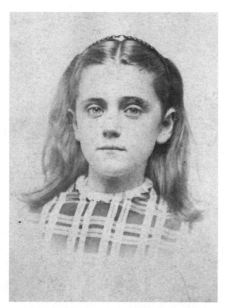

Jane Addams and her new stepbrother George Haldeman were both about eight when their parents married. The children became fast friends and shared a close sibling relationship.(W. B. White, Freeport, Ill.; JAPP)

surprisingly, they resolved to use Hostetter's U.S. almanac in their studies and to collect almanacs.[155]

On one outing in the spring of 1874 when they were about fourteen, George persuaded his stepsister to help him investigate the contents of an owl's nest. Jane was to hold the free end of a rope wrapped twice around a maple tree and knotted around her stepbrother's waist as he climbed down the face of a near fifty-foot cliff to the nest resting in the crotch of a tree that hung from the cliff over Cedar Creek. A portion of the cliff gave way as he felt his way down its face. The rope whipped from Jane's hands, and George plunged downward, to be caught in the branches of the owl's tree. Jane, who feared the worst, discovered that her stepbrother had survived the fall. With her rope-burned hands she held the rope taut and pulled as George climbed back up the cliff again. They trudged home together, her hands handkerchief-wrapped, to share their frightening story with parents. When Anna Haldeman Addams wrote to her son Harry about the episode, he replied, "I was quite astonished at the adventure of George and Jen—and the Owl's nest quite daring but quite too reckless—for the comfort of others concerned."[156] During the summer of 1874, while George Haldeman was visiting his brother, Harry, in Mendota, they made up a chemistry set for Jane, and Harry explained each compound to her in his letter transmitting it.[157]

It was also in 1874 that Jane and George took up the study of anatomy. Sarah Hostetter, who visited them in the summer of 1875, recalled:

> Jane had a passion for collecting bones of all sorts. Her dresser was a work of art with yards and yards of the vertebrae of snakes strung & festooned about! They were pretty too bleached white and clean as they lay in sun & shower along a creek and hillside. A little more uncanny were the bones of a human arm in the bottom dresser drawer, that Jane at the instigation of a doctor brother had prepared herself. The writer today has a card of black pasteboard with figure of skull and crossbones cut carefully out of white paper and pasted on the black back-ground signed on the opposite side in purple ink Jane Addams 1875. It was felt a great compliment to receive this card at the time and after the long years a treasure indeed. A curiosity of the time when our heroine was so interested in Anatomy she thought a card with skull and crossbones a very suitable "coat of arms" so to speak.[158]

Sarah Hostetter also remembered Jane Addams's love for wildflowers, trees, and the study of botany, which had been added to her Cedarville school curriculum for the spring of 1875. The interest that Jane and George shared in all manner of scientific investigation continued to grow until both went away to school.

Travel had long been a part of Jane Addams's world. With her sister Mary, she had visited Martha and Alice Addams at Rockford Female Seminary. When only seven, she had gone with Mary by railroad to stay with the family of Henry C. and Jennie Forbes in Union County, about four hundred miles away from Cedarville in southern Illinois. After the Haldeman and Addams families were joined, journeys became frequent. George and Jane sometimes went to Mount

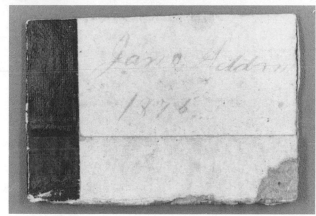

This skull and crossbones card was the one that step-cousin Sarah Hostetter recalled receiving from Jane Addams during the summer of 1875 when the young Miss Addams was intrigued with bones. Jane wrote her signature and the date "1875" in purple ink on the reverse of the card. (JAPP)

Carroll to visit Anna's family, where they played games and went swimming and boating on the Waukarusa River, also known as Carroll Creek, near the homes of cousins and step-cousins. While she visited Mary Addams Linn and her family, George often went to stay with his brother Harry. Their parents took both children on summertime vacations as well. Most often these were to the cool north, where John Huy Addams could explore property to purchase and a variety of business opportunities. In drawings, George recorded a family trip by stagecoach to Madison, Wisconsin, in 1873 to see, among other things, the famous eagle "Old Abe" who perched in the capitol building there and had been the mascot of a Wisconsin regiment during the Civil War.[159]

By the time she reached her late teenage years, reading to learn and for pleasure had become a hobby as well as a habit that Jane Addams would appreciate for the remainder of her life. Books, magazines, and newspapers were available in the Addams home. Her father had barely reached Illinois when he subscribed to the *U.S. Gazette* and several local newspapers. The family had ease of access to holdings of the Union Library Company of Cedar Creek Mills in their home, as well as to their own growing collection of books. At least some of these were children's books.[160] She recognized how significant a library had been to her father and that images of him reading influenced memories of her childhood.

> I imagined him in the early dawn in my uncle's old mill reading through the entire village library, book after book, beginning with the lives of the signers of the Declaration of Independence. Copies of the same books, mostly bound in calfskin, were to be found in the library . . . and I courageously resolved that I too would read them all and try to understand life as he did. I did in fact later begin a course of reading in the early morning hours. . . . Pope's translation of the "Iliad," even followed by Dryden's "Virgil," did not leave behind the residuum of wisdom for which I longed, and I finally gave them up for a thick book entitled "The History of the World" as affording a shorter and an easier path.[161]

In Jane Addams's teenage years, "serious" reading was interspersed with popular literature. John Huy Addams encouraged his daughter to undertake "historic reading" by paying her a nickel for each Plutarch *Life* she read and could adequately report to him and a quarter for each volume of Washington Irving's *Life of Washington*.[162]

Jane was exposed to poetry at school and through her stepmother, who loved it. Anna Haldeman Addams encouraged her two youngest charges to read and write poetry, and Jane engaged in the practice for the remainder of her life, drafting poems primarily for special occasions.[163] As a teenager, she became especially familiar with the work of Henry Wadsworth Longfellow[164] and Walt Whitman[165] and with the poems of Irish poet Thomas Moore,[166] a favorite of her stepmother.

As many young girls of her day did, Jane Addams read widely in the books of American female authors, novelists, and essayists. Her favorite may have been Louisa May Alcott,[167] although she also read the works of Mary Abigail Dodge (who wrote under the pseudonym Gail Hamilton),[168] Elizabeth Stuart Phelps Ward,[169] Dinah Maria Mulock Craik,[170] and Harriet Beecher Stowe.[171] Among English authors, she was not particularly fond of the work of Sir Walter Scott[172] but thoroughly enjoyed the novels of Charles Dickens[173] and discussed them with her friends.

While John Huy Addams had an intellectual impact upon his daughter, Anna Haldeman Addams was also important in Jane's development. She helped her move gracefully from girlhood to young womanhood, encouraged her healthful growth with outdoor play and horseback riding, and instilled in her a need to be useful and proper. Through her stepmother, Jane's intellectual interests became more catholic and she discovered the valuable connection between play, fun, and learning. She acquired polish in manners, speech, and dress and an appreciation of culture that permitted her easy admission to the society to which her father's position and wealth gave access. Marcet Haldeman-Julius believed that her aunt had been "schooled in the enjoyment of moderate luxuries, with compensating admonitions of thrift—to distinguish between what was best and what was only costliest." The result was that she developed a "grand air, the air of one to the manner born, yet without the shallow vice of ostentation." Haldeman-Julius held that "this habit, essentially patrician was instilled into Jane Addams by her second mother[.]"[174]

Although Harry Haldeman wrote to his mother in 1870 to assure her that her stepdaughters, including Jane Addams, loved her,[175] Jane's relationship with Anna became one of respect and obedience rather than devotion. Over time, little genuine sense of warmth grew between them. They were, according to Marcet Haldeman-Julius, who knew both of them well, "tempermental opposites."[176] Both were determined to have their own way but sought it differently. The uneven, quixotic, mercurial, high-spirited Anna was demanding, demonstrative, and vocal, whereas the quiet, serious-minded, pragmatic Jane used calm reason to persistently and logically get her way. Used to the relatively placid household of her sister Mary Addams, Jane probably did everything she could to recreate and maintain that even-handedness with her stepmother. In the process, she must have discovered and cultivated a variety of coping mechanisms, paramount among them the tactics of compromise, mediation, and reconciliation. She would hone and use these practices to great advantage as an adult. As the Addams child who probably knew Anna Haldeman Addams best— including her moods, wishes, and wiles—she was often called upon to smooth relations between her stepmother and other Addams family members, with hired help, and with the Cedarville community.

From the start, in November of 1868, everyone in the combined Addams-Haldeman family tried hard to make their new relationship successful, but by the end of the first year the discord that would result in permanent division and strain had appeared. The last six months of 1869 and the first few in 1870 were a critical time in the newly constructed family. Jane Addams and George Haldeman were beginning to interact as brother and sister. Alice, away at Rockford Female Seminary for most of the year, seemed pleased with her stepmother's interest and attention. Polly Beer and Mary Addams worked at fitting in with Anna's vision of how the Addams house should operate. Anna Haldeman Addams was becoming more comfortable and more assertive in her new role. Although John Huy Addams did not take her to Springfield with him as much as she might have liked, she still had a pleasant life. She had no financial worries, and there were servants to do her bidding. Her two sons were near and there was almost always a friend or Hostetter family member visiting.

Anna's relationship with John Weber Addams was another matter. From the fall of 1867 through 1868, Weber was a student at Beloit Academy, a young men's preparatory school connected with Beloit College and begun by the Congregational and Presbyterian Churches in 1846.[177] Early in January 1869 Weber Addams returned to Beloit to continue his studies. When he came home ill at the spring mid-semester, Anna helped care for him. He did not return to school.

Improving over the summer, he matriculated the next fall at the University of Michigan, Ann Arbor. Within two weeks, however, he discovered that the pressures of university study were too great for him, and once again he returned home ill. His sister Mary was called home from her extended visit with relatives in the Philadelphia area to accompany him to stay with the Henry C. Forbes family in southern Illinois with the hope that he would recover quickly in their care. Hints of a highly unpleasant confrontation between Anna and Weber survive in family correspondence.[178]

Weber's outburst in late 1869 was directed primarily toward Anna Haldeman Addams and her relatives. The Addams home was full of Hostetter and Haldeman folk. Not only was George Haldeman there and, of course, Anna, but also the brilliant, cynical, and outspoken Harry, so much like his mother, and Mary Peart[179] from the East. She would wed Charles Linnaeus Hostetter. Anna Haldeman Addams had experienced Weber's illness in the spring and apparently had little sympathy for him at this repeat. In fact, she may have seen his inability to compete at school as mental ineptitude or laziness on his part—especially when she compared his abilities and achievements with those she attributed to her own elder son. She may also have believed Weber's antagonism toward her was a result of her relatively new position in the family as stepmother.

Weber rambled through the southern Illinois countryside and worked at an assortment of tasks requiring physical labor on Colonel Forbes's fruit farm. He wrote to his father on 1 December 1869 regarding his progress under the Forbes's guidance. "My tongue is entirely cleared off and I feel very well indeed. . . . I shall continue on with the perscription . . . if I continue to grow better as fast as I have for the last two days I shall not need any more medicine. Took a pill last night before going to bed. Slept <u>very</u> soundly until I had a passage whci[which] occured sometime after midnight when I slept 'like a brick' until morning." In the same letter he directed, "Shall expect you <u>not</u> to show this to Ma as for her to know what I have written concerning the effects of Doctor Zucker's medicine and what the change of <u>food</u> climate and c[are?] has done for me would be very disagreable to me."[180]

Later in December, Mary Addams wrote to her father about Weber:

> Last evening I read Mrs. Forbes part of Ma's letter while he [Weber] was sitting by; some time after when we were in the room alone he made some remarks about <u>Mary Peart</u> and <u>Harry</u>, when I got up and went out of the room, after I came in he talked about something else; he has not said one word to me about Ma; altogether I think he is <u>much</u> better, but not altogether settled on <u>that</u> one subject . . .
>
> Mr. Forbes said he believed if home matters was what troubled Weber it would be better for him to go right from here East, as he was so much better it would not be best for him to go home until he was well or at least until we saw if <going East> would make him entirely well.
>
> . . . Sunday evening while he was writing so steadily, Mr Forbes seated himself with a book almost opposite Weber so that he could observe him, but thought

Weber would think he was . . . reading; he said Weber seemed to notice it immediately and looked at him sort of strangely.[181]

Weber was showing indications of the paranoid schizophrenia that was to
plague him for the remainder of his life. Little was then known about the condition or how to treat it successfully. When Mary Addams wrote to Miranda
Addams[182] about Weber's symptoms, her cousin responded that she knew of one
other case like Weber's and wondered if Mary was safe with him. Mary agreed,
writing that "sometimes I almost dread going East with him, but . . . I will go
and do the best I can."[183]

One of the consequences of the unfortunate events of the fall of 1869 was
that neither Harry Haldeman nor Weber Addams ever again lived in the Addams
home. When Weber returned to the Cedarville area about Christmas 1869 he
lived on one of his father's farms. He began to learn the mill trade and to manage a stock farm. His father watched over him, and Weber did not have to interact with Anna or her family.

By 1870 Harry Haldeman was twenty-one, four years older than Weber
Addams and still not totally independent or gainfully employed. In addition,
he may have continued to drink. None of this would have pleased John Huy
Addams, and it is likely that he challenged Harry to become independent and
successful. On 18 January 1870 Harry wrote to his mother:

> Considering—the many dismal Scenes I have gone through—the vices I have in-
> dulged in—and the willingness of friends to lend a helping hand—to assist . . . me
> out of the Slough of despondence into which I have fallen—I have made wonder-
> full progress in reform—and Shall continue to rise. I have but little love for per-
> sons who could have aided me materially . . . but—who would Sooner have Seen
> me descend to ruin—than encourage me to attempt, that which they knew I could
> accomplish, With credit to my Self—(I refeer to my medical Studies). But the day
> will come—the day Shall come—when I will throw my resentment in their teeth
> and their esteem to the dogs—which I have done allready[.]
>   Destiny—is my Star—Renown my hope—and Reputation my object—therr
> aime in life is littleness—with minds about as expansive as a five cent peice—
> Onword! . . . You know Mother under what Sort of circumstances I have had to
> contend—you know how often I have started out to seek employment. . . . Few
> have had to learn so much in so little time as I—few have gone as low and re-
> formed—I have but few feelings with the world in common—and fewer with
> unfeeling relations and Friends—all of whom I hate with an intensity not to be
> Soothed.[184]

Harry was embittered and disaffected by the turn of events, especially with
John Huy Addams and stepbrother Weber. While Weber was having trouble dealing with his stepmother, Harry developed an equivalent estrangement from his
stepfather.[185] He moved to Mendota, Illinois, approximately sixty miles south and
east of Freeport, where he lived until 1873. Relying on the skills he had been learn-

ing while he was attending classes in music and science in Leipzig, Germany, from 1866 to 1868, he continued to study medicine under the tutelage of new mentors, the physicians Cook of Mendota.[186] At the same time, to earn his living he gave music lessons, tuned pianos, and presented recitals. He resisted visiting the Addams home, and he also began to court his stepsister Sarah Alice Addams.

While all this family discord began brewing, John Huy Addams decided not to run again for his Illinois senate seat. He was tiring of the long hours and days in Springfield. "The pleasure of enjoying the Society of my dear family is far preferable and very, very much more to my taste and inclination," he wrote to Anna.[187] There were probably several other reasons for his decision. There was a new Illinois constitution in 1870 that increased the size of the senate. It also made private legislation illegal and as a result altered the way the senate would operate. With his business interests continuing to grow, John Huy Addams may have seen this as a good time to bow out of political life gracefully. There was his new wife to understand and family differences to moderate. Addams family lore holds that he did not return because of the "social wars" in which Anna engaged in Springfield and that Anna nagged him, sometimes loudly, to seek further political office. It was also becoming clear that the matter of the health of his son Weber was a serious one. He would have to commit Weber to a mental institution in June 1872, the first of what would prove to be a series of hospitalizations.

Things were changing for Mary Addams as well. After nursing Weber, she spent more and more time away from the Addams home on her own affairs. She visited friends and relatives, attended church functions and conventions, and began to be courted. On 11 November 1871 she wed John Manning Linn, Cedarville's Presbyterian minister. Thereafter, Mary and her family moved frequently from one small northern Illinois town to another, following her husband's calls to serve various congregations. Often the financial means to acquire a house large enough for her growing family came from her inheritance after the death of her father. That Mary Addams Linn's life was not easy was clear. Her first child, John Addams Linn,[188] was born in 1872. A miscarriage[189] in 1874 may have been followed by another the next year, for James Weber Linn (her second child)[190] was not born until 1876. Financial problems and uprooting continued to be major factors throughout her married life as more children were born into the family.[191]

In the mid-1870s Anna Haldeman Addams and John Huy Addams faced a new family dilemma. Alice Addams and her stepbrother Harry Haldeman declared that they intended to marry. The two had corresponded and courted while Alice was at Rockford Female Seminary, first as a student and later as a graduate resident serving as a tutor while she studied art. Harry had been a struggling musician studying medicine in Mendota and had attended medical school for a time at the University of Michigan, Ann Arbor, beginning in 1873. Neither parent thought the other's child appropriate as a mate. Alice, an attractive young woman already tending to the fleshiness that would characterize her later life, was headstrong, demanding, selfish, charming, spirited, artistic, creative, intelligent,

Mary Catherine Addams and Presbyterian minister John Manning Linn were photographed in the same studio in Freeport about the same time that they were married in November 1871 and went to live in Lena, Illinois. Jane Addams admitted that she cried sad tears when Mary left the Addams home on her wedding day. (D. T. Weld; JAPP)

and outspoken. She was a risk-taker who loved challenge and adventure. Harry, slender like his father, was also outspoken as well as brilliant, irreverent, eccentric, creative, egotistical, and unsettled. He drank, tended to live a bohemian lifestyle, and seemed unable to secure adequate livelihood to provide security for a family. Anna and John must have been relieved when Harry took up a medical practice in the fall of 1874 in Fontanelle, Iowa, more than two hundred miles away from Alice; the young people, however, remained committed.

On 3 January 1875 Harry wrote to his mother to defend his relationship with Alice and make an effort to respond to a letter (no longer extant) that Anna had addressed to him on 1 January, apparently questioning his judgment. He made a strong case for his ability to support a wife, his need of a wife, and his commitment to Alice. He presented arguments that he knew would be dear to Anna Haldeman Addams's heart: how much money he had saved in the three months he had been practicing in Fontanelle; how his practice had grown; how, if married, he would have twice the business because a married physician received considerably more obstetrical business, which paid well; how he was well organized, dedicated to being a doctor, and God-fearing; and how, most of all, "I love Alice Sincerely—She is a true woman, and I hope you will appreciate her—

and be—kind to her. I would not do, nor be guilty of a mean action on her account for the world, I hope someday—to make her as happy—as heart can wish. My every exertion is for her—and—her good will—and affection—stimulate me to untireing perseverence."[192]

As she often did in personal matters, Anna sought the advice of John L. Hostetter, the brother to whom she felt closest. Although her letter to him has not survived, his response indicates that despite Harry's arguments Anna remained opposed to the relationship. "I beg of you dear sister not to look at it in the light you do," he wrote. "Divine Providence has a guiding influence in the sacrament of marriage, and our own plans are sometimes not, in accordance with the final good." In the same letter he encouraged Anna to support Alice, his favorite step-niece, in her request for a European trip. "Alice is ambitious to be a true helpmate to Harry," he argued. "To be this she feels she has yet much to learn, such an opportunity would not likely occur again. It can in no wise interfere with their engagement to each other. . . . From my knowledge of Alice's sentiments, I know that nothing but the grim messenger can ever estrange the love she bears him."[193]

In a letter dated 8 March 1875 and written to his mother shortly before Alice came home from Rockford to make preparations for her trip, Harry reconfirmed that he expected to marry Alice in the fall. He also concluded that the Addams family was still embattled over the couple: "From what I could make out in your letter, I was led to conclude there was a war of Some sort going on at your House about me and Alice."[194] Unfortunately, Anna's response is not extant. Alice Addams went to Europe, and on her return she and Harry Haldeman were wed on 25 October 1875 in Cedarville. They settled together in Fontanelle.

Anna Haldeman Addams's life had become less satisfactory than that she had anticipated, and she became discontent. Although her younger son, George, was by her side and friends and relatives were frequent visitors, she was relegated to the social milieux of Cedarville and Freeport, neither of which she found fulfilling. Because John Huy Addams had chosen to take himself out of the Illinois General Assembly, there were no longer as many opportunities for social intercourse with the political and cultural elite of the state. Harry had wed, to her mind, the least acceptable Addams daughter. In addition, he was available to her only through correspondence and, by 1873, infrequent and short visits. John Huy Addams, who had the task of dealing with his schizophrenic son, also spent considerable time away on business, leaving Anna to the unpleasant (to her) mercies of housekeeping or local visiting.

John L. Hostetter's prophecy at Anna and John Huy Addams's marriage that "there will sometimes occur differences of opinion" had, not surprisingly, come to pass. Unfortunately, the "calm deliberate concessions" he suggested were apparently not the techniques used to assuage the discord.[195] No doubt there were many happy, memorable, and pleasant occasions and relationships associated with the reconstructed Addams family. The gatherings of neighbors, fam-

Jane Addams's sister Sarah Alice, seen here while on a tour of Europe in 1875, and Jane's stepbrother Henry ("Harry") Winfield Haldeman, seen here as he looked in 1874, caused great consternation in the family when they decided to marry. To the dismay of both parents, they wed in October 1875 and went to live in Fontanelle, Iowa, where Harry had a medical practice. (Loescher and Persch, Berlin, and G. W. Barnes, Rockford, Ill., both SCPC)

ily dinners, visits with relatives from near and far, shopping in Freeport, traveling, and roaming the countryside and mill were only a few. But the stresses of the personalities and the problems associated with the Addamses swirled about the impressionable Jane and must have been among the defining influences in her young life.

By the time she was ready for Rockford Female Seminary, Jane Addams may have looked forward to a respite from the difficult relationships and the tense interactions she experienced within the Addams family structure almost as much as she longed for the intellectual challenge of seminary life. She had experienced strong women—her mother, sisters, and stepmother. With the exception of her father, in her immediate family she had also found weak men—mental illness in her brother, alcoholism in her stepbrother Harry, and an unsuccessful provider in her brother-in-law John Manning Linn. It is likely that she also found George Haldeman wanting and too willing to submit to the demands of his mother, with whom she was sometimes at odds. Through Mary Addams Linn, she saw the heartache and difficulties of child bearing, miscarriages, and the physical hardship frequently resulting from managing a household alone. She knew the trauma that mental illness and alcoholism could cause in a family and the anxieties and uncertainties associated with living in a blended family with a complicated stepmother. At seventeen, Jane, growing into a mature young woman, probably did not aspire wholeheartedly to a traditional female lifestyle, yet was uncertain what her future would hold. Rockford Female Seminary would take her one step closer to sorting out what that future would be.

Notes

1. See Biographical Profiles: Addams, Sarah Weber.
2. See Biographical Profiles: Addams, John Huy.
3. "In the parlor on the second floor" of the Addams home, Cedarville school teacher and family friend Julia Eastman Brace recalled, "stood a marble top stand. On the stand was a large perfumery jar—ten or twelve inches tall. Around the neck of the jar was a blue ribbon attached to which was a white card with these words: 'To Laura Jane Addams from Laura Jane Gorham,' whom Jane Addams was named after" (*Freeport Journal-Standard,* 13 Jan. 1932).

Laura Jane ("Jennie") Gorham (1835–1914) was born in Vermont, the daughter of Mercy Humphrey Gorham and Alonzo Gorham, who came to Illinois from Vermont. She was a graduate of RFS in the class of 1858. JHA hired her in 1859 to initiate the Cedarville Academy, a select school for area children who wished to teach school or to seek higher education. She taught in Cedarville for five years and boarded with the Addams family part of that time. After SWA's death, Jennie Gorham helped care for JA, who was a toddler. She married Henry Clinton Forbes (1833–1903) on 3 Sept. 1861. Until Nov. 1865 Forbes served in the 7th Cavalry, Illinois Volunteers, during the Civil War and was a breveted colonel. The Forbes family remained long-time Addams family friends. They had at least five children, including Robert Humphrey (b. 1867), Bertha Mary (b. 1869), Stuart Falconer (b. 1872), and Marjorie (b. 1882). From Cedarville they moved in May 1866 to South Pass (Cobden) in Union Co., Ill., where they lived on a forty-acre fruit farm. Col. Forbes managed the local school, with four other teachers, for the next thirteen years. Thereafter they also lived in Delavan (1879), Polo (1880), and Princeton, Ill. (1886) while Col. Forbes taught school. In 1891 the Forbeses moved to Urbana, Ill., where Col. Forbes became librarian for the State Laboratory of Natural History, a position he held at the time of his death. Jennie Gorham Forbes belonged to the Congregational church and was active in missionary work. During the last part of her life she made her home in Urbana and then in Seattle, Wash., where she died of "softening of the brain" in the home of her daughter, Mrs. J. W. Wilson, on 1 Dec. 1914, and was cremated (Washington State, Forbes, Laura Jane, [death certificate]).

JHA's younger sister, Susan Jane Addams Mull, may have thought that JA was her namesake. While MCA and SAA were visiting in the Philadelphia and Reading, Pa., area during the summer of 1865, MCA wrote to their younger sister Martha, who was at home with JA, of her Addams and Weber relations: "[T]hey are all very very anxious to see Jennie, especially aunt Jane" (19 July 1865, IU, Lilly, SAAH). Susan Jane Addams (1827–1914) was the ninth child of Catherine Huy Addams and Samuel Addams. She grew up in Sinking Spring, Pa., attended school there, and married Edwin E. Mull, also from Sinking Spring. They had three children, all cousins to JA: John Addams Mull (1850–94), William Henry P. Mull (1852–1920), and Catherine Elizabeth Mull (1860–65). Toward the end of her life Susan lived in the Philadelphia home of her niece, Harriet C. Addams Young's daughter Clara L. Young.

4. Abraham Lincoln (1809–65) was elected president on 6 Nov. 1860. The major campaign issue was the future of slavery in the United States The Democratic Party was divided. The southern pro-slavery wing of the party selected John C. Breckinridge of Kentucky as its candidate, while the northern antislavery wing selected Stephen A. Douglas, like Lincoln from

Illinois, as its candidate. The Constitutional Union Party, composed of former Whigs and moderates, nominated John Bell of Tennessee. The split in the Democratic Party helped make Lincoln's candidacy successful. He won 1,866,000 votes, with 1,375,000 for Douglas, 845,000 for Breckinridge, and 589,000 for Bell. Lincoln carried Illinois and received a total of 180 electoral votes to only 12 for Douglas.

Lincoln, who with determination and eloquence guided the country during the Civil War, was elected to another four-year term in 1864. He won over Democratic candidate Gen. George B. McClellan, who ran on a platform supporting the cessation of hostilities between North and South. When Lincoln was assassinated by actor John Wilkes Booth on 14 Apr. 1865 (he died the next day), a few months into his second term and just days after the Civil War ended, the country mourned. The Addams family was no exception. JA recalled that on the day Lincoln died the two American flags flying from the front gateposts of the Addams home were draped with black. Her father, "in tears," told her that "the greatest man in the world had died" (Addams, *Twenty Years*, 23).

5. Not all of the Addams family relations approved of the Civil War or of JHA's support for the Union cause. His brother-in-law George Weber, Jr., a Reformed church missionary, made his position clear. "These are terrible times," he wrote to his Weber siblings. "I am afraid we will not have peace untill we subject ourselves to one another under our fundamental principles framed by our Constitutional Fathers. . . . May the right prevail I am opposed to <the> War out & out it is inconsistent with a professed Christian nature but we become exhalted in need" (George Weber, Jr. to Bro. & Sister, 17 Jan. 1863, SCPC, JAC). This letter could have been addressed to one of two couples who lived in Pennsylvania, or quite literally to one brother and one sister of George Weber and Sarah Addams Weber. Sister Elizabeth Weber Reiff was married to Enos L. Reiff. Brother Devault Weber was married to Mary Ann Hiester Weber.

6. Addams, *Twenty Years*, 31. Few of JHA's letters written from the Illinois General Assembly before Lincoln's election as president have apparently survived. There are seventeen that he sent to his wife SWA between 4 Jan. and 13 Feb. 1857. On 5 Feb. he informed SWA that he had declined an invitation to a party given by Benjamin S. Edwards, a Springfield attorney (and brother of Abraham Lincoln's brother-in-law Ninian Edwards, who was married to Mary Todd Lincoln's sister Elizabeth P. Todd) but accepted one issued by Lincoln. In a letter the next day from the senate chamber in Springfield, JHA reported that he had "attended Mr Lincolns party last night" and that "there was a great crowd. All past off well—The ladies were out in hoops and quite a number of them" (JHA to SWA, 6 Jan. [Feb.] 1857, JAPP, JHA).

7. The Addams parlor also featured a framed roster of the "Addams Guards," the unit recruited from the Stephenson Co. area by JHA. It served as Company G of the 93d Regiment, Illinois Volunteers and was mustered into U.S. service on 13 Oct. 1862 in Chicago. The regiment joined the fighting at Memphis and after battles at Vicksberg and Chattanooga was part of Gen. William Tecumseh Sherman's march through Atlanta and up the East Coast. The regiment participated in the Grand Review on 24 May 1865 in Washington, D.C., and was mustered out on 23 June 1865.

8. According to Addams family lore, runaway slaves were brought to the Addams barn hidden in wagons of mill or farm produce and led into the Addams home under cover of darkness. They were secreted in an attic room until it was time for them to move on, and the process was reversed. Winifred E. Wise (b. 1906), who wrote the children's biography *Jane Addams of Hull-House* (1935) with JA's blessing and assistance, and James Weber Linn, in *Jane Addams: A Biography* (1935), referred to the Addams home as a stop on the Underground Railroad. We have found no other extant documentation to substantiate that claim, however.

9. Black Hawk ("Chief Ma-Ka-Tai-me-she-Kia-Kiak") (1767–1838), opposed the Treaty of St. Louis that in 1804 granted Native American lands to Indiana Territory and, with Tecumseh, fought with the British in the War of 1812. He and his followers invaded Illinois from

Iowa in 1832 to regain their tribal lands. Defeated at the Bad Axe River, Wis., he and his followers returned to Iowa, where he was deposed by Chief Keokuk. He was taken to Washington, D.C., to meet President Andrew Jackson in 1833 and returned to live in his Sac village on the Des Moines River, where he died.

10. Sinking Spring, a small village near Reading in Berks Co., Pa., was first settled in the 1730s by Welsh and German immigrants. It was during the early settlement that Daniel Miller's (1789–1844) forebears became large landowners on the east end of the community, and Peter Ruth (d. 1771) purchased property on the west end. As early as 1767, John Huy (1751–1837), one of JA's great-grandfathers, began to build an inn that had some walls that were two feet thick. The inn was next to the sinking spring (from which the community gained its name), which usually flowed freely in the spring but by fall had retreated into the limestone fissures from which it arose. Isaac Addams (1747–1809) came from Adamstown, approximately eight miles south and a little west, to wed Peter Ruth's daughter Barbara (1744–1832). One of their children, Samuel Addams (1782–1854), married Huy's daughter Catherine (1787–1866). They became the parents of JA's father and later operated the inn, where JHA was probably born.

In 1831 the town of Sinking Spring was formed, and as the community grew, streets in the village were named for prominent early citizens. The children of many of these families intermarried, and while some of their progeny stayed in the area, many left for the developing west. When JHA and SWA arrived in Stephenson Co. in 1844, among the settlers from Sinking Spring already there were John Ruth, John and Hiram Miller, and Mary Ruth Reitzell. Thomas and John Mull visited in Stephenson Co. during the first five months the Addams couple lived there. Jacob Latshaw, a tinsmith, and James Huy Addams, brother of JHA and an auctioneer, would follow later.

11. Elijah and Hiram Miller were farmers, carpenters, and innkeepers. John Miller was a merchant who began a tanning business that became the property of the Thomas Mull family by 1840 (when he moved west to Stephenson Co., Ill.). Thomas, Aaron, and Rueben Mull were landowners, farmers, and merchants, and Henry Mull was an innkeeper. The Mull family home was constructed in the village in 1802. Elijah and William K. Ruth were merchants and also owned a hotel. Christian Ruth donated the property on which the St. John's Reformed Church was constructed in 1794.

12. Philip H. Reitzell (1793?–1850) brought his family to Stephenson Co. from Pennsylvania in 1840. They helped found the First Presbyterian Church in Freeport. His wife, Mary ("Polly") Ruth Reitzell (1801?–79), was widowed at age forty-eight and continued to live in Buena Vista, Ill., until her death. Her cousin Hannah Hain (1809–87) was married to JHA's brother Charles Huy Addams (1809–52), who served as justice of the peace in Sinking Spring. The Reitzell children—George, John, Jonathan, Franklin, Henry, Charles, Cyrus, Elizabeth, and Mary—spilled into the surrounding countryside on farms and in homes of their own. Many married, had families, and continued to live in the Cedarville area.

John Reitzell (b. 1797?) and Jonathan Reitzell (1798?–1879) and their families owned and operated farms in Lancaster Twp. to the southeast of Cedarville in Stephenson Co. Franklin and Henry, followed by Charles (1833–1905) and Cyrus, continued the family milling operation at Buena Vista until 1874, when it was purchased by Jacob Schatszell. All four brothers had farms. George Reitzell became postmaster of Freeport in 1849 and served the county as sheriff in 1852–53. Elizabeth Reitzell wed physician Charles G. Strohecker in 1850, and they continued to live in the area, too.

13. Enos L. Reiff (1808?–70) was JA's uncle by marriage. On 10 Sept. 1840 he wed SWA's sister, Elizabeth Weber (1815–97?), JA's maternal aunt. The Reiffs, who were second cousins, apparently lived their entire lives in a stone house in Ambler, Pa., a village that in the U.S. census of 1880 had a population of only 251. The gristmill operated by the Reiff family since the late 1700s was run during the middle part of the nineteenth century by Enos Reiff and then by his children. It was located on the west side of Wissahickon Creek opposite the cen-

ter of the village, which developed in the western corner of Upper Dublin Twp. in Montgomery Co. The Reiffs had three children. Joseph L. (1841–93) was a favorite of his aunt SWA; Sarah ("Sallie") Weber (1847?–85) never married; and Enos W., the youngest, married Elizabeth Trotter. That couple had three children.

14. JHA to Enos L. Reiff, 26 Jan. 1843, SCPC, JAC.

15. George Weber (1790–1851) was JA's maternal grandfather. He was born in Towamencing Twp., Montgomery Co., Pa., the eldest child of Elizabeth Reiff Weber (1769–1825) and John Weber (1768–1815). On 17 Nov. 1812 he married Sarah Beaver (1786–1846), and they had eight children: Devault (1813–80), Elizabeth (1815–97?), Margaret (1816–52), Sarah (1817–63), George, Jr. (1819–88), John Harrison (1826–91), Mary Ann (1822–24), and Catherine (1824). When his father died in 1815, George Weber took over the mill at Perkiomen, Pa., and operated it until 1819. Then, after a brief stay in Philadelphia, the Webers relocated to Kreidersville in Allen Twp., Northampton Co., Pa., where Weber purchased property in 1823 and established himself as a miller and storekeeper.

While living in Kreidersville, George Weber became a captain of a company in the 26th Regiment, Pennsylvania Militia and succeeded Jacob Kern as colonel in 1828. For the remainder of his life he was known as Col. Weber. Through his efforts, the first Sunday School at the Stone Church near Kreidersville was organized in 1825. He was also instrumental in founding Lafayette College in Easton, Pa., where he served as trustee between 1826 and 1849.

After he moved his family to Mercersburg, Pa., about 1840, he was selected to serve as associate judge of Northampton Co. in 1850. During the 1840s he began to explore the possibility of relocating his milling and mercantile business, as well as his family, to Illinois. It seems entirely possible that the trip he made to Illinois with newlywed daughter SWA and her husband JHA to explore mill property in the late summer of 1844 was not his first. Shortly after he returned to Pennsylvania from Illinois in 1844 he decided to purchase an interest in mill sites and property in Como, Ill. The mill, one of the largest and most modern in the area, began production by 1845. Col. Weber continued to improve its operation and added a sawmill by 1847.

Just before he was to move his wife Sarah Beaver Weber to Illinois permanently, she died in Sept. 1846 while he was in Illinois. He remained there and continued to develop his enterprise. Two of his sons, John Harrison and George, Jr., and their families joined his Illinois undertaking in Como. The whole family lived together in one house and operated the mill and its store into the mid-1850s. Col. George Weber died suddenly in 1851 and was buried in Como, Ill.

16. The Old State Road was an established roadway generally traveled by 1835. It was made a state road by State Road Act of 15 Jan. 1836. Officially laid out by 5 June 1837, the Old State Road that JHA described in his diary stretched from Meachum's Grove just to the west of Chicago near the DuPage Co. line to Elgin, Belvidere, Rockford, and on to Twelve Mile Grove. The road ended at Galena, Ill., in Jo Daviess Co. on the Mississippi River. The road is now Illinois Route 20 from the Stephenson Co. boundary, with Winnebago Co. on the east to Lena, Ill., and a county blacktop road from Lena to the west Stephenson Co. boundary with Jo Daviess Co.

17. JHA, "Journal, 1844," contains a day-by-day account of JHA's activities from 29 July until 19 Dec.

18. Of his first sight of the mill property he finally purchased, JHA wrote: "[G]ot to the Cedar Creek Mills looked round and the more We looked at Them the better pleased asked the price $4 Thousand dollars with some Hundred acres Land" ("Journal, 1844," 12 July [Aug.], 1844).

19. Samuel Addams (1782–1854) was JA's fraternal grandfather. He was one of six sons of Barbara Ruth Addams (1744–1832) and Isaac Addams (1747–1809). When Isaac Addams married Barbara Addams, she was the widow of his brother William Addams (d. 1774). Isaac and Barbara Addams inherited town lots and the Addams farm and home in Adamstown from

Isaac's father William and from his brother William. Samuel Addams's grandfather William Addams (1703?–73), who owned 246 acres of land around his iron ore smelting mill, was the founder in 1761 of "Addamsburry" or "Addamsville," eventually incorporated in 1850 as Adamstown in Lancaster Co., Pa.

Samuel Addams was a farmer, miller, and merchant. In 1813 he began one of the first mercantile establishments in Adamstown and located it in a log structure. By 1820 he had sold it and gone to manage his father-in-law's inn and farm in Sinking Spring. On 14 Jan. 1808 Samuel Addams wed Catherine Huy (1787–1866), then twenty-one, the daughter of Margaret Gernant Huy (1764–1843) and John Huy, of Dutch descent and early residents of the Sinking Spring area. They had ten children who lived to maturity: Charles Huy (1809–52), Rebecca Margaret (1810–89), Mary B. (1813–92), Elizabeth (1815–51), Harriet C. (1817–97), James Huy (1820–86), John Huy (1822–81), Lydia W. (1825–92), Susan Jane (1827–1914), and Isaac H. (1830–48). JHA was the seventh child and third son born to the couple.

20. For a while, it seemed likely that the mill was not for sale. It had been sold to settler David Neidigh (1806–80) when physician Van Valzah returned to Pennsylvania in 1842. Neidigh was also an emigrant from Pennsylvania. He, in turn, was selling the property to partners Conrad Epley (b. 1810?) and John W. Shuey. Neidigh, meanwhile, remained to become a farmer. Epley wanted to sell, but Shuey would have to be convinced, and so a discouraged JHA, fearful that his father might let him down, continued to explore other options as he anxiously awaited his father's response. When a letter finally came indicating that his father would provide the additional funds he required for the purchase, JHA convinced Shuey to sell. Epley became a miller in Rock Run Twp. in Stephenson Co., where he was in business with his brother James. The young JHA completed the agreement to buy the Cedar Creek property on 19 Dec. 1844. In his diary on 18 Dec. 1844 he recorded that he had convinced Conrad and Shuey to sell for "$4200 without entering, $165 Dollars for his Mill seat. Said his 80 woodland would not come more than $2.25 per acre" ("Journal, 1844").

21. The structure may have been the cabin originally constructed by John Goddard, who along with Barton Jones was the first claimant of the property. John and Joanna Goddard were the first settlers of the Cedarville area. They came with John's brother Benjamin Goddard and his family from New England in Dec. 1835 and apparently moved to Freeport about 1837. Goddard built a cabin, and he and Barton Jones established a mill site claim that they sold to Van Valzah in 1837.

22. The trees on Pine Hill were a distinctive feature associated with the Addams property. Family members, including JA, appreciated their history and beauty. In 1899 AHHA wrote to son HWH, "The Pine Hill stands out like a grand bower—for Santa Claus" (29 Dec. 1899, UIC, JAMC, HJ). JA's uncle George Weber, Jr., may have been referring to Pine Hill when he wrote to JA of her mother SWA that "Those trees & many other marks of handy work of hers speak some of the interest she had not only for the family" (9 June 1882, SCPC JAC; *JAPM*, 1:954). In 1997 only one of the pine trees that JHA planted on the bluff remained.

23. See Biographical Profiles: Linn, Mary Catherine Addams.

24. Charles G. Strohecker (b. 1820?), a physician who practiced in Buena Vista, Ill., was born in Pennsylvania. In 1850 he married Elizabeth Reitzell (1828?–96), daughter of Philip and Mary Ruth Reitzell. They had three children: Eugene R. (b. 1852?), Mary E. (b. 1854?), and Jennie G. (b. 1856?). By 1860 Elizabeth Strohecker was a widow, living with her widowed mother in Buckeye Twp. The U.S. census of 1880 indicates that she had become housekeeper for her brother Charles Reitzell, that Eugene R. was working as a druggist, and that Jennie G. was a teacher. Both were living with their mother in Buena Vista. By the early 1900s Jennie G. Strohecker had moved to Sioux Falls, S.D.

25. [Physicians Invoice], C. G. Strohecker to JHA, [25 July–6 Nov. 1846], SCPC, JAC. The amount the Addams family owed for Strohecker's services—including his visits from Buena Vista, Ill., and medication he supplied—was $23.75.

26. There is, however, no evidence that SWA ever returned to Pennsylvania, although Pennsylvania relatives visited Illinois. Among the first to come were Samuel Addams and Col. George Weber, who visited the couple together in the spring of 1845. The one came to be certain of his daughter's welfare and, one suspects, to measure the deal JHA had struck against that which he had made for a mill on the Rock River south of Freeport at Como. The other came to appraise the couple's welfare and prospects and to see his investment (see John H. Weber and George Weber, Jr. to Enos L. and Elizabeth Weber Reiff, 3 May 1845, IU, Lilly, SAAH). It is likely that SWA did visit with family members, including her father and two brothers and their families, after they settled at Como, Ill.

27. "In this state," wrote JHA on 12 Jan. 1845 to his brother-in-law Enos L. Reiff, "the millers get ⅛ for wheat & ⅐ for Buckwheat & corn—I pay the man about $4600 for this property—and as far as I have come am highly pleased with it—Wheat is worth $.50 cts here & 66 to 68 at Chicago on the Lake flour at Galena—the Lead mines to which we send is worth from $3.75 to $4.00 per Bbl" (IU, Lilly, SAAH). By Apr., wheat had become scarce, and the price in Chicago was up to eighty cents. Addams could buy small lots of wheat to process for forty-five cents cash (see John H. Weber and George Weber, Jr. to Enos L. and Elizabeth Reiff, 14 Apr. 1845, IU, Lilly, SAAH).

28. See Biographical Profiles: Addams, Martha.

29. See Biographical Profiles: Addams, John Weber.

30. See Biographical Profiles: Haldeman, Sarah Alice Addams.

31. A "run of stones" is a pair of large, grooved, horizontal millstones—one fixed and one rotating on the other and powered by animal, water, air, or motor—used to grind grain. The process of grinding grain using millstones was widespread in the U.S. until late in the nineteenth century, when the use of steel roller mills became prevalent.

32. In 1997 the barn JHA had constructed was still standing on its original foundation.

33. Spring floods destroyed the dam that created the millpond at least four times. The first stone dam was reconstructed by the family after a flood in 1866. It was repaired in 1876. Once again destroyed by a flood in 1896, it was replaced with a log and brush structure that fell to another flood in 1905 and was not replaced.

34. Abner Briggs Clingman (1797–1895), a farmer born in Pennsylvania, grew up in the Miami River Valley of Ohio. He and his wife Sarah Woolever Clingman (1805–72), also born in Pennsylvania, had eleven children between 1823 and 1845. They were married in 1822 and farmed in Ohio until 1839, when they settled in Stephenson Co. near Clingman relatives. Clingman, a Buckeye Twp. pioneer, served as a Stephenson Co. commissioner in 1846 and may also have served in Company A of the 46th Regiment, Illinois Volunteers during the Civil War. He died in Halsey, Linn Co., Oreg., at the home of his son George Washington Clingman (1829–1909).

35. Josiah Clingman (1808–65), a relative of Abner B. Clingman, was a farmer married to Maria Simpson (1809–1916). Both were born in Scioto Co., Ohio, and came to Illinois in 1835. First settling in Peoria in Putnam Co. in 1836, they moved to LaSalle Co. Finally, in 1837 they purchased farmland in Buckeye Twp. and settled in a log cabin that in 1838 became the first polling place for state elections in their area. After Josiah Clingman's death on 28 Mar. 1865, his widow remained on the family farm until 1874, when she moved to a house on Mill St. in Cedarville. She lived there with her daughter Ann Eliza Clingman (1838–1907) and other family members until her 107th year. On 12 Dec. 1906, when she was one hundred years old, Cedarville gave her a celebration. According to Clingman lore, JA sent one hundred carnations, one hundred long-stemmed red roses, and an engraved gold teaspoon. Other sources indicate that JA sent the roses, and other members of the Addams family provided the carnations and teaspoon.

The Clingmans were closely associated with the Addams family in community endeavors. Josiah Clingman helped found the Cedarville Cemetery, served as one of the early township supervisors, and helped organize and build the Cedarville Methodist Church. Throughout the Civil War he actively recruited troops for the Union cause.

The Addams and Clingman families were also close friends. JHA served as conservator for the two youngest Clingman children, still minors at the time of their father's death, and both attended college with the Addams children. The youngest son, Ethol B. Clingman (1851–1920), went to the Univ. of Michigan with JWA, and Sophia Clingman (1849–1935) attended RFS and was a good friend of Martha Addams.

The Clingmans had ten children: George W. (1831–61), Mary (1834–1906), Ann Eliza (1838–1907), Thomas S. (1840–62), Jason (1843–1933), William M. (1845–1936), Edwin (b. 1847?), Sophia, Ethol B., and Chester. Chester was deceased by 1850. Two were lost during the Civil War, and several married into other Stephenson Co. families.

36. Adrian W. Lucas (1802?–75?) was born in Ohio and came to Stephenson Co. in 1837. He was a farmer. He and his wife Elizabeth W. Lucas (1800?–78), known in Cedarville as "Aunt Betty" and also born in Ohio, had at least two children, neither of whom survived their parents. The Lucases helped found the First Presbyterian Church of Freeport in 1842. Lucas was also active in the 1847 effort led by JHA to bring the first railroad to Stephenson Co. At the founding of the Old Settlers' Assn. of Stephenson Co. on 1 Jan. 1870, he was elected as a vice president.

37. The initial list of the holdings of the Union Library Co. of Cedar Creek Mills numbered sixty-nine titles. A brochure describing its rules was issued in 1847 and is extant (see *JAPM*, 28:852). Titles were evidently added to the library as late as the 1860s, because it ultimately had at least 107 titles. AHHA eventually boxed and stored the library in the Addams barn, where it was discovered by Ellen Starr Brinton, first curator of the SCPC, on a visit to the Addams home in 1951. Sixty-three titles survive in the Rare Book Room of the Coleman Library at Rockford College in Illinois (see *JAPM*, 28:851–69). Two other titles are located in the CAHS.

38. Remnants of the Addams family library exist in a small collection of fifty-eight volumes also located in the Rare Book Room of the Coleman Library at Rockford College. Three childhood books, including JA's New Testament Bible, which she acquired in 1867, are in the CAHS. The Emanuel Haldeman-Julius library (part of the PSU, EHJ) of more than two thousand titles is composed not only of volumes that were part of the Addams family library but also, according to bookplates and inscriptions, of volumes that belonged at one time to William J. Haldeman, HWH, SAAH, and Marcet Haldeman-Julius. A bibliography of the library is available from the EHJ Collection. Some of the Addams family books may also have found their way into the library of the JWA family in Cedarville. There is no known catalog of that library and no indication of what became of the books the family owned.

SAAH made a listing of approximately thirteen hundred volumes that comprised a large part of her personal library, which served as a lending library for Girard, Kans., until a public library was created in 1901. The catalog exists in JAPP, DeLoach.

Marcet Haldeman (1887–1941) inherited her mother's library in 1915 and added to it over the years following. Toward the end of her life, when she was spending increasing amounts of time at the Addams home in Cedarville, she had portions of her library (including the Addams family and Sarah Alice Addams Haldeman libraries) moved to Cedarville. (The volumes that remained in the Haldeman-Julius home and offices in Girard became the core of the Emanuel Haldeman-Julius Library).

After Marcet Haldeman-Julius died in 1941, her children Henry Haldeman-Julius (1919–90) and Alice Haldeman-Julius DeLoach (1917–91) inherited the Addams home and its contents through her estate. DeLoach recalled that in the late 1950s, when Henry Haldeman-Julius sold the Addams home, she had to remove the contents that belonged to her. She arranged for long-time family friends Louise J. and Lloyd E. Smith (publications editor for the publishing empire of Marcet and Emanuel Haldeman-Julius in Girard, Kans., that included the

Little Blue Books, Big Blue Books, and the socialist newspaper *Appeal to the Reason*) to take all the books from the house. The Smiths rented a van and removed more than three thousand pounds of books to a warehouse in Racine, Wis. They offered to give books to DeLoach and to an assortment of Haldeman friends. DeLoach selected books that could be identified as being from the Union Library Co. of Cedar Creek Mills and a few Addams family school books (most are in the collection at Rockford College). Schuyler M. Watts (1879?–1973), who was an editor and proofreader for Haldeman-Julius publications as well as a friend to Marcet Haldeman-Julius, identified approximately two hundred titles he wanted (primarily biographical and historical studies about Lincoln and the Civil War). He later gave them to the EHJ Collection, Porter Library, PSU, as the library of JHA. Some are identifiable because of his signature on endpaper or title page. As a hobby, Lloyd E. Smith spent years repairing volumes and presenting them as gifts to PSU and to an assortment of other colleges and universities across America. According to DeLoach, the Smiths missed gathering approximately fifteen books from the Union Library Co. of Cedar Creek Mills as well as some prints JA brought back from Europe. DeLoach was told that these were burned by the family that purchased the Addams home in the late 1950s.

39. Tilden, *History of Stephenson County,* 537.

40. See Biographical Profiles: Hostetter, Sarah.

41. S. Hostetter, "Home and Girlhood," 3. In a speech to the Scientific Assn. that she helped found at RFS when she was a student there, JA presented her view of the area in which she grew up. "In the northern part of Illinois about ten miles from the Wisconsin line, the regular and, undulating prairie is abruptly broken by a range of hills lying along a small stream. These hills are from 50 to 80 ft in height, most of them rising perpendicularly from the bed of the stream with the exception of a broken range containing some of the highest points which surrounds the adjacent low ~~long~~ land giving it the appearance of an ancient lake with two openings one to the east and one to the west through which Cedar Creek flows. And this same territory now a broad green meadow dotted with houses and mills ~~and~~ with a village lying on its southern bank, was no doubt once covered with mud & water inhabited by ante deluvian creatures who roamed at will in its slimely depths" ("[Address on Illinois Geography]," 26 May [1878]); *JAPM,* 45:1780–81).

42. George D. Ilgen (1800–64), known to some as the founder of Cedarville, arrived in the Cedarville area about 1841 and purchased land there. He was born in New Jersey. His wife, Maria ("Polly") Ilgen (1798?–1870), was born in Pennsylvania. By 1880 one of their twelve children, Daniel G. Ilgen (1840–1900), had become a merchant in Cedarville.

43. Marcus Montelius (1810–76) was a native of Pennsylvania and thirty-eight years old when he laid out the town of Cedarville for George D. Ilgen. In 1847 he had been designated Stephenson Co. surveyor. He also platted the towns of Buena Vista and Orangeville in the county. The U.S. census of 1870 for Buckeye Twp. identified him as a retired surveyor with real estate valued at $31,200. His wife, Catharine Montelius (1814–94), was born in Pennsylvania. A daughter, Elizabeth (b. 1856?), born in Illinois, was living with them. Along with JHA, Montelius was among those who incorporated the Cedarville Cemetery Assn. in 1855. At his death, he was a member and president of the board of the Buckeye Mutual Insurance Co.

44. James Canfield was born in New Jersey before 1809. Although the U.S. censuses of 1860, 1870, and 1880 for Buckeye Twp. list him as a farmer, brick from his kilns was used to build structures in several Illinois towns, including Mt. Carroll. His wife Sarah (b. 1821?) was born in eastern Canada. After their first child Toba (b. 1840) was born in Illinois, they had at least five other children: Bertrice, Victor, Luther, Emile, and Minnie.

45. U.S. censuses of 1860, 1870, and 1880, Stephenson Co. By 1890 Cedarville had become a sleepy farm village with a population of 376. It had a newly constructed school, village hall, and jail (seldom used); telephone service to Freeport had been installed in 1881. In 1910 the population had dropped to 250. AHHA took credit for keeping the interurban railroad operat-

ing out of Freeport from coming to Cedarville between 1905 and 1910. Electric service for lighting was instituted in 1915, but it was not until after World War II that Cedarville had a municipal water system. By the late 1900s the town was becoming a bedroom community for Freeport. Once again the population soared to more than eight hundred.

By the 1990s, most of the original village streets had been paved, and the layout of the community was the same as it was in JA's youth. Many of the original houses survive, including the two-story Addams home and barn. The Addams mill was dismantled in 1911 to be used as a barn on a farm situated on the west side of Cedar Creek and inherited by the family of SAAH and HWH. In 1967 its remains were given to Rockford College. The Cedarville Cemetery started by JHA in 1855 contains the graves of JA, her parents, her siblings and their spouses, and succeeding generations. Among those buried nearby on the gently sloping hill are the playmates and their parents with whom JA interacted as she grew up in the village.

46. Joseph F. Jackson (1821–1901) was born in Clinton Co., Pa., where he learned the tanner's trade. When he came west, he taught school and farmed. In 1847 he married Sarah F. Barber (1828–1907), born in Union Co., Pa., who came with her parents, the John Barbers, to Cedarville in 1843. The Jacksons had seven children: Sarah E., Emily, John, Clara, Effie, William, and Mary. Jackson, a Republican, was elected as a county supervisor and held a number of school offices.

47. Richard Glennan does not appear in Stephenson Co. in the U.S. census of 1860, nor is there any information available on Glennan in Stephenson Co. histories or in the cemetery records that we consulted.

48. John W. Henney (1842–1926) was born in Center Co., Pa. He migrated to Illinois with his parents, Jacob (1814–1902) and Lydia (1809?–91) Henney in 1854. In 1868 he began producing carriages, and JHA bought the first one. By 1876 he had organized the Henney Buggy Co. In 1868 Henney married Agnes A. Bennethum (1845–1942), also a native of Pennsylvania. The couple had five children: Lilly May (1872–80), Mary Estelle (1876–1967), Iva Evelyn (1882–1968), Arthur (1869–77), and John W. Henney, Jr. (1883–1946). John W. Henney, Jr., went into business with his father in 1916, manufacturing motor hearses, ambulances, and livery coaches.

49. John W. Shaffer (1831–1905), born in Pennsylvania, was a wagonmaker and blacksmith who opened his shop in Cedarville in 1859. By 1880 he employed six men and built sixty vehicles a year.

50. Joseph B. McCammon, born in Pennsylvania about 1851, was a member of the Cedarville band. In 1880 he had five employees in his shop and produced ten thousand dollars' worth of vehicles. By 1900 factory mass-produced conveyances had put his small shop, and that of John W. Shaffer, out of business.

51. Joseph P. Reel (b. 1825?) lived with his wife Susan (b. 1827?) in Cedarville between 1864 and 1883. The Reels had at least one child, Virginia (b. 1850?). All were born in Maryland. Reel was well known as a millwright and master builder.

52. Andrew Jackson Seyler (1840–1914) was born in Pennsylvania and emigrated with his parents to Illinois in 1846. In 1865 he established a business as a millwright. With Joseph P. Reel, Seyler invented, manufactured, and sold a middlings purifier so that millers could make graham flour from wheat middlings. JHA used the purifier in his mill. For a brief period of time in the early 1880s, the firm, located on Mill St. south of the Addams mill in Cedarville, sold one hundred purifiers annually.

53. A middlings purifier is machinery and a process associated with milling flour. Middlings are medium-sized particles of wheat kernel produced when the endosperm portion of the kernel is milled into fine flour. When purified, by passing the middlings through a process that further extracts larger and unwanted portions of the kernel, they may be used to produce some types of flour or livestock feed.

54. With the help of circuit riders, Methodists began to organize a church in Buckeye Twp.,

Stephenson Co., as early as 1839. Between 1849 and 1850 they built the first church building in Cedarville. It was located on Mill St. just south of the Addams home. JHA was one of the three backers of this first church. During the 1860s and 1870s, services were held there on alternate Sundays. In 1886 that church building was razed to make way for one larger. The second church structure erected in the village was the Lutheran and Reformed church. Its cornerstone was placed in 1851, and its brick building, forty feet by forty-five feet, completed by 1854. Services were held on alternate Sundays with the Methodists. The basement rooms in the structure were used as public school rooms between 1852 and 1854. The Evangelical Assn. erected the third house of worship in Cedarville in 1856, a forty-foot by fifty-foot brick structure on Harrison St. in the southeastern section of the village. The village's first organ was installed there. A new building erected in 1887 burned in 1947, and the congregation replaced it with a new church in 1949 at the corner of Oak and Cedar streets. The Presbyterian church was not officially organized until 1872 and shared accommodations with the Methodist church during its first two years. By 1874 it had moved to space in the Lutheran and Reformed church, which it used before completing its own gothic structure in 1876 that had a spire ninety-eight feet high. JA's brother, JWA, served on the committee charged with building the church, and JHA was a member of the committee that built the parsonage.

55. JHA's diary for the last half of 1844 indicates that he attended religious services every Sunday if possible. He seemed to prefer those held by Calvin Waterbury, who served from 1842 to 1847 as the founder of the First Presbyterian Church and as the first Presbyterian minister in Freeport. He befriended Waterbury and other Presbyterian ministers. In his diary on 3 Nov. 1844, JHA wrote that he had "spent a pleasant evening with Mr. Waterbury—went to meeting heard a very good Sermon after which the Lord's Supper was distributed in a very Solemn manner" ("Journal, 1844"). That JHA may have participated in communion is not sufficient evidence to claim that he was a member of the Presbyterian church. On the frontier, members of different Protestant denominations often shared ministers and services.

Calvin Waterbury (1811?–74), a New School Presbyterian minister, returned to act as pastor of the First Presbyterian Church in Freeport between 1860 and 1861. He also served churches in Stone Church, N.Y., and Kingsport, Tenn. He and his wife Priscilla (b. 1812?) had at least four children: Mary, William, Edward, and James. He died in Rotherwood, Tenn.

56. Addams, *Twenty Years*, 16. Hicksite Quakers were more liberal, pragmatic, and less doctrinaire members of the Society of Friends. Elias Hicks (1748–1830) was an American Quaker. After completing his apprenticeship as a carpenter and becoming a farmer, he began his first itinerant preaching tour between Vermont and Maryland in 1779. He attacked slavery and was influential in securing passage of an act declaring free after 1827 all African Americans born in New York and made free by the Act of 1799. He took a practical, rather than a doctrinal, view of his religion and was opposed to any specific pronounced creed, a position he stated in *Doctrinal Epistle* (1824). During 1827–28 his followers, who identified themselves as liberals and were called "Hicksites" by other Friends, broke with their doctrinaire orthodox Friends. Among the Addams family library was the second edition of *Journal of the Life and Religious Labours of Elias Hicks* (1832).

57. With two Stephenson Co. friends, JHA organized the German Presbyterian Society of Richland on 29 Dec. 1845. The young and relatively new settler-miller was elected one of the three trustees to serve as a leader of the society for three years. The organization, which made the first attempt to form a Presbyterian congregation in the Cedarville area, met in the Richland schoolhouse, located midway between the Reitzell brothers' mill on Richland Creek and the Addams mill approximately three miles to the southeast on Cedar Creek. The society survived until about 1853, the year a second, formal, attempt was made to organize a Presbyterian congregation. It was in that year on 16 June that an infant daughter of JHA and SWA, likely SAA, born on 5 June 1853, was baptized in the Presbyterian church. JML led the final and successful attempt on 3 May 1867 to organize a Presbyterian church in Cedarville.

58. See JHA to SWA, 8 Jan. 1856 [1857], JAPP, JHA; MCA and SWA to JHA, 9 Jan. 1861, SCPC, JAC.

59. See JHA to SWA, 5 Jan., 7 Jan., and 12 Jan. 1857, JAPP.

60. This story appears in the second paragraph of chap. 2, "A Different Child," in Linn, *Jane Addams,* 22. In his preface to this work, Linn indicated that besides providing him with her own files of correspondence, diaries, clippings, and records from which to write the biography, his Aunt Jane "read over and annotated" a draft of the first eight chapters, discussed with him the next three chapters, and agreed with his general design for the remainder (vii–viii).

61. Mary ("Polly") Beer (sometimes spelled Bier or Behr) had been with the Weber side of the family since before SWA's birth. She migrated to Illinois in 1848 with another branch of the family and joined the Addams household in Cedarville around the time of SWA's death. She became a nurse and mother figure for JA. See Biographical Profiles: Beer, Mary ("Polly").

62. 1 Aug. 1863, IU, Lilly, SAAH.

63. UIC, JAMC, HJ.

64. MCA to SAA, 15 Mar. 1869, UIC, JAMC, HJ.

65. JA to SAAH, 20 Aug. 1890, IU, Lilly, SAAH; *JAPM,* 2:1203.

66. 24 Jan. 1889, SC, Starr; *JAPM,* 2:1005.

67. See Biographical Profiles: Linn, John Manning.

68. John Addams Linn, born in 1872, had already reached his majority, while James Weber Linn, born in 1876, Esther Margaret Linn, born in 1880, and Stanley Ross Linn, born in 1883, were all legally minor children when their mother, MCAL, died on 6 July 1894.

69. SAAH to Mrs. [Jean] Holden, 31 Jan. 1904, IU, Lilly, SAAH.

70. Winifred E. Wise has indicated that the bout with typhoid fever, which probably occurred before JA was five, left her with "tuberculosis of the spine" and "her curly brown hair straight" (*Jane Addams of Hull-House,* 17).

71. M. Haldeman-Julius, "Two Mothers," 9–10.

72. S. Hostetter, "Home and Girlhood," 6.

73. Addams, "[Statement on John H. Addams]."

74. See MCA to JHA, 24 Jan. 1865, SCPC, JAC.

75. Addams, *Twenty Years,* 8. James Huy Addams (1820–86), sixth child of Catherine Huy Addams and Samuel Addams and the uncle of JA, was born on 16 Mar. 1820 in Berks Co., Pa. Like his brother, James grew up in Sinking Spring, Pa. Before he followed JHA to Cedarville in 1850 in the company of the Jacob Latshaw family, and from the age of eighteen, he was an auctioneer in Sinking Spring. In 1843 he married Lavina (or Lavinia) Hinnersheetz (1825–93) of Berks Co. By 1844, in addition to auctioneering, he was farming, eventually entering the grain and coal business that he sold when he came west. Four of the couple's eleven children were born in Pennsylvania: Alvin (1844–63), Agnes (1845–1905), Austin H. (b. 1847), and Elizabeth (1849). The youngest seven were born in Illinois: Augustus (1851–93), Samuel (1853–95), Nathan (1855–70), William (1857–59), Charles H. (1859–83), Elizabeth Belle ("Lizzie") (1861–1900), and John H. (1862–93). Although the Addams cousins sometimes played together, the two Addams brothers and their families seem not to have been especially close. JHA was apparently wealthier, more respected, better known, and more successful than his brother James.

James Huy Addams was a Republican and held township and school offices. He was a farmer and auctioneer in Cedarville and was reputed to have lived in the first brick home in the county. With JHA he helped establish the Buckeye Mutual Fire Insurance Co. in 1867, serving on its board and as its first agent. After an extended illness, James Huy Addams died in Cedarville on 20 Sept. 1886. He is buried in the Cedarville Cemetery with his family, including Lavina Addams, who died on 9 Feb. 1893 at their farm home located on the road to Red Oak, Ill.

76. Julia Eastman (Brace) came with her parents, Edward N. and Susan Eastman, from New Hampshire to Cedarville in 1860, when she was fourteen. She became a schoolmate of JA's sister MCA in the select school started by Laura Jane Gorham and eventually became JA's first teacher in Cedarville before she moved to Iowa, married, and raised a family there.

77. *Freeport Journal-Standard,* 13 Jan. 1932.

78. Gustason, "Looking Back: Damsel's Decisions." Agnes A. Bennethum (1845–1942), born in Pennsylvania, grew up in Cedarville and married John W. Henney, Sr., in May 1868. She was also JA's Sunday School teacher and presented her with a Bible in 1867. See also n. 48.

79. 9 Apr. 1867, UIC, JAMC, HJ.

80. The two-story, fifty-five-foot by thirty-foot building constructed of red brick was opened in 1855 to provide a better facility for the public school that had been operating in the basement of the Lutheran and Reformed church. Until 1857, when it became the premises for the select school called the Cedarville Academy, the second floor of the 1855 building was used as a public hall. The Cedarville Academy, a private high school to prepare students to be teachers or attend college, was operated by Laura Jane Gorham and Henry C. Forbes. By the mid-1860s, when JA was a student there, the second floor had become the public high school, the private school having been abandoned about 1866. By 1889 the structure was razed to make way for a new school.

81. John Harvey Parr (1851–1935?) was JA and GBH's favorite Cedarville teacher. He was born at Granville, Ill., in Putnam Co., the oldest of eleven children of James (b. 1830) and Elizabeth Fidelia Moore Parr (b. 1836). One brother, Lewis B. Parr (1854–1947), in 1879 married Emily L. Wright (1853?–1931), a Cedarville friend of the Addams family, and settled on a farm in Harlem Twp., Stephenson Co. Another brother, Samuel Wilson Parr (1857–1931), became a distinguished chemist and member of the faculty of the Univ. of Illinois, Urbana-Champaign.

Probably educated in the Granville Academy, John Parr entered the three-year program at Illinois State Normal Univ. at Normal in the fall of 1866 when he was fifteen. Upon graduation, in 1870, young Parr, only nineteen, began his career as teacher at Cedarville. MCA commented to SAA that JA and GBH "seem to be very much interested in their school. I think Mr. Parr tries to make it pleasant, and I think they cannot help but learn; he is quite young looking" (17 Oct. 1870, UIC, JAMC, HJ). Parr remained in Cedarville until 1873, when he accepted a teaching position at Saybrook, Ill., where his father lived as a farmer. After two years there, he returned to serve as principal and teach at Cedarville for a year. He was often a visitor in the Addams home and was an instructor at numerous teachers' institutes held in the Stephenson Co. area.

Parr taught at the Rock River Seminary, Mt. Morris, Ill., between 1876 and 1878 as instructor of the natural sciences and mathematics. He may have received his position partly through his friendship with the Edwards family. Richard Edwards (1822–1908), Illinois State Normal's president and the author of the series of reading texts used in the Cedarville school, had served as a trustee of Rock River Seminary in the 1870s. His son Richard Arthur Edwards (1851–1947), Parr's friend and classmate at Normal, served as instructor in Latin, Greek, and reading during the 1873–74 school year. Upon completing the A.B. degree at Princeton he returned to Mt. Morris as instructor in Latin and Greek for the two school years (1876–78) that Parr was at Mt. Morris.

When Rock River Seminary closed at the end of the 1877–78 academic year, Parr chose to enter the ministry. He enrolled at the Chicago Theological Seminary (Congregational) in the special course, a program for those who had not had a complete literary or classical education. He returned the following year as a member of the junior class and graduated from the regular program in 1882, when he was ordained to the Congregational ministry. His first appointment was the First Congregational Church, Wilmette, Ill., where he successfully helped erect a new church building and create a number of church societies from 1882 until 1884. In that year he became principal of the Tillotsen Institute, Austin, Tex., under the sponsorship of the American Missionary Assn. That appointment was short-lived, however, for by 1885 he was living at Quitman, Ga., and was without a ministerial charge.

In 1887 Parr returned north to resume his ministerial career, serving for a year in Bandaw, Ill. (now part of Chicago). In 1888 he left the ministry permanently and became principal at the Collegiate and Normal Institute, Paxton, Ill., until 1892. While in Paxton, he married Flora Pennell (1852?–1920), an Illinois State Normal Univ. classmate who had been born in Illinois and was the sister of JA's 1875–76 school-year teacher Eva Pennell. Before she wed Parr in Dec. 1890, Flora Pennell was a student at Vassar (1873–74), and she taught reading and was a preceptress at Illinois State Normal Univ. from 1877 until 1890. The Parrs' one child, Dorothy, was born in Mar. 1893. In 1892 the Parrs returned to Chicago to found the Chicago Preparatory School, where he served as principal and she as teacher. They closed it in 1900 and moved to Macatawa, Mich. By 1905 the couple was in Castle Park, Mich., where he taught school and was proprietor of the Summer Hotel. His last teaching post seems to have been in Washington, D.C., from 1912 through 1915. From 1917 until about 1930 he farmed in Baton Rouge and then in Baker, La. We have been unable to discover where and when Parr died.

82. C. W. Moore taught high department students and managed the Cedarville school. He and his wife, whose name may have been Emma and who was also a teacher, were frequent participants in numerous teachers' institutes held regularly throughout Stephenson Co. The Moores were probably in Cedarville for two school years, from 1873 to 1875. For the 1872–73 school year, Moore taught in Ridott Twp. in Stephenson Co. During the 1875–76 school year, the couple moved to Lena, Ill., where Moore was principal.

83. Eva Pennell (b. 1857?), from Normal in McLean Co. in central Illinois, may have been among the early students at Illinois State Normal Univ. While she taught in Cedarville, she roomed and took board with the Clingman family on Mill St. During the summer of 1878 she visited JA in Cedarville, and on 21 Aug. 1878 she wrote to thank JA for a delightful time (see SCPC, JAC; *JAPM*, 1:331–33). She was the daughter of Evelyn A. Pennell (b. 1822?) and W. A. Pennell (b. 1815?), born in Vermont, who by 1848 had migrated to Illinois, where they had at least six children, all daughters. She was the sister of Flora Pennell, who wed JA's teacher John H. Parr. In 1880 Eva took a year away from teaching to study. She spent it in Chicago with a married sister, Mary Pennell Barber, her husband, A. H. Barber, and ten-month-old nephew, Charles Bryant Barber. She explained to JA in a letter of 8 Jan. 1880 that John H. Parr called on the Barber household frequently (see SCPC, JAC; *JAPM*, 1:455–62, and JHA to JA, 17 June 1878, n. 7, below).

84. UIC, JAMC; *JAPM*, 1:136. Among school texts used by JA and her stepbrother GBH are the following, extant in the Rare Book Room of the Coleman Library, Rockford College: Richard Edwards, *Analytical Fourth Reader* (1867); Daniel W. Fish, *Progressive Intellectual Arithmetic; on the Inductive Plan* (1863); Daniel W. Fish, *Robinson's Progressive Practical Arithmetic* (1872); and *Sanders' New Speller, Definer, & Analyzer* (1854) (all owned by JA). In addition, the following are in UIC, JAMC: Richard Edwards and Mortimer A. Warren, *Analytical Speller* (1870); *Mitchell's School Atlas* (n.d.); D. M. Warren, *System of Physical Geography . . . a Treatise on the Physical Geography of the United States* (1863) (all owned by GBH); and D. M. Warren, *Common-School Geography: An Elementary Treatise on Mathematical, Physical, and Political Geography* (1867) (owned by JA).

85. See JA grade cards, 1870–75, CAHS; *JAPM*, 27:13–19.

86. Addams, *Twenty Years*, 15.

87. Earle A. Berry (b. 1856), born in Wisconsin, and his wife Laura (b. 1856), born in Illinois, taught in Cedarville at the time the U.S. census of 1880 was conducted. In 1881 when JHA died, the Berrys were teaching in the Mt. Morris, Ill., public school, where Earle A. Berry was principal. By 1935 the Berrys were living in the Kansas City, Mo., area.

88. *See Kansas City* (Mo.) *Star*, 28 May 1935, SCPC, JAC.

89. UIC, JAMC, HJ; see also 24 Apr., 27 Apr., and 29 May 1867, UIC, JAMC, HJ; and 5 June 1867, IU, Lilly, SAAH.

90. See MCA to Martha Addams and SAA, 7 Mar. 1867, IU, Lilly, SAAH. JWA joined the Presbyterian church the next year (1868).

91. 17 Apr. 1867, UIC, JAMC, HJ.

92. Addams, *Twenty Years,* 5.

93. Addams, *Long Road,* 146–47.

94. Addams, *Long Road,* 154–55.

95. See Biographical Profiles: Addams, Anna Hostetter Haldeman.

96. William J. Haldeman (1823–66) was born on 31 Oct. 1823 to Tamar Johnson Haldeman and Henry Haldeman in Kimberton, Chester Co., Pa. The Haldemans had at least five other children: Tamar, Isaac, Nathaniel, Henry, and Abraham. William was educated in local schools and apparently attended Rock River Seminary in Mt. Morris, Ill., during the early 1840s. He had followed his brother Nathaniel (1811–80) to Mt. Carroll, Ill. Nathaniel, who arrived in Mt. Carroll in 1840, had helped establish the town. Trained as a miller, Nathaniel and his associates organized Emmert, Haldeman & Co. and built the first substantial gristmill in Mt. Carroll. It began operation in 1843. In that same year Nathaniel Haldeman led the effort to move the county seat of Carroll Co. from Savanna to Mt. Carroll. William J. Haldeman became associated with his brother in the milling business as a miller and as a merchant. He ran the mill store located at Stag Point near the mill on Carroll Creek. The store did a substantial business and served customers from throughout the county. William J. Haldeman devised an especially successful way of shipping butter as far as New Orleans without refrigeration by packing it in twenty-five-pound kegs that were then placed in a hogshead and covered with brine. He purchased goods for his business from St. Louis and New York City.

By 1846 William, tall, slender, and blue-eyed with sandy hair, began to court the eighteen-year-old Anna Hostetter, who had come to Mt. Carroll with her physician brothers in April 1845. They were wed on 15 Sept. 1847 in Anna's sister Susanna ("Susan") Hostetter Bowman's home in Cumberland Co., Pa. They began their married life in Mt. Carroll, where William continued to operate the mill store. By 1857 he had sold his interest in the store to develop and operate the Stone Steam Flour Mill in Freeport, which burned within a year of his death. William and Anna Haldeman had four sons, only two of whom (Henry Winfield Haldeman, born 21 June 1848, and George Bowman Haldeman, born 9 June 1861) lived to maturity.

William J. Haldeman was a gentle, intelligent man who readily shared his feelings of love and devotion in letters to his wife when they were separated. He was dedicated to the cause of temperance and spoke publicly at least once on the subject. He was thoughtful of his wife and highly concerned for her health and welfare. A caring father, he kept their older child, Harry, with him in Freeport while Anna stayed with her sister Susan Hostetter Bowman in Mt. Carroll before and after the birth of their fourth child. Until Anna Haldeman finally brought their new son George to live with them in Freeport in 1862, William and Harry Haldeman lived for a time in a hotel and then a boardinghouse. William saw to Henry's every need—his clothes, his health, his schooling, and his music lessons. By 1856, William was being treated for lung disease. He died in Mt. Carroll on 11 Mar. 1866 (see also Biographical Profiles: Addams, Anna Hostetter Haldeman, and nn. 97 and 108).

97. William J. Haldeman was buried in a vault overlooking the Haldeman mill store in Mt. Carroll. In 1919 his granddaughter Marcet Haldeman-Julius moved his remains and those of the two Haldeman children who had died in infancy to the Cedarville Cemetery to be buried with other members of the William J. Haldeman family.

98. Susanna ("Susan") Hostetter Bowman (1812–83), noted in the Hostetter family for her mild, gentle manner, became JA's step-aunt. The oldest child of Magdalena B. Lichty Hostetter (1793–1835) and Abraham Hostetter (1777–1843), she was the sister who cared for AH during her childhood. She was born in Lancaster Co., Pa. On 25 Aug. 1836, on a farm in Cumber-

land Co., Pa., near Harrisburg, she married George Bowman (1813–92), a wealthy farmer. Before coming west in 1845, AH had lodged with the Bowman family. The Bowman couple moved to Illinois in 1858 to join other Hostetter family members in the Mt. Carroll area. The Bowmans settled to the north of the other Hostetters in a large home called Oakland, and they farmed. Their two sons, John H. (1838?–1901) and Abram (b. 1840?), were born in Pennsylvania, as were their two daughters, one of whom died as an infant and Anna Martha (1849–1920).

99. AHHA's brother John Lichty Hostetter (1821–77) became JA's step-uncle. He was born in Lancaster Co., Pa., and came to Mt. Carroll in 1845, where he established a medical practice. He and his brother Abraham Hostetter were both graduates of the Univ. of Pennsylvania Medical College. He married Mary Anne Irvine (1828–67), daughter of John Irvine (1790–1873), a miller, and Amanda M. Fitch Irvine (1809–1900), who had emigrated from Pittsburgh, Pa., to Mt. Carroll. Mary Anne Irvine, a small, delicate woman, had been a student in Miss Penny's seminary for girls in Pittsburgh. She loved music and brought her piano, made about 1830 by Stoddard-Durham, with her from Pittsburgh. The Hostetters had five children: Mary Irvine, Virginia, John I., Annie, and Helen O. Four of these JA step-cousins lived past childhood, although Annie died shortly after she was born in 1856.

Hostetter published the first newspaper in the county (*Mount Carroll Tribune*). He volunteered as a surgeon and served in the 34th Infantry, Illinois Volunteers during the Civil War. On his return, he once again took up the practice of medicine in the Mt. Carroll area.

John L. Hostetter was described in Hostetter family lore as "brilliant . . . literary and poetical" (JAPP, Hostetter Genealogy File). He believed that women should enter the medical profession and spoke openly in favor of women's medical schools. He may have had a strong influence on SAAH (who was his favorite step-niece and the wife of his physician nephew, HWH) and JA's decision to enter medical school in 1881.

AHHA was particularly close to John L. Hostetter and his children. She lodged with him after she came to Mt. Carroll from Pennsylvania until she married her first husband William J. Haldeman two years later in 1847. Brother and sister shared a love of music, poetry, and writing. He served as AHHA's confidant and advisor. After the death of his wife Mary Ann Irvine Hostetter in 1867, AHHA encouraged John to give up his medical practice in Mt. Carroll and establish himself in Freeport where she lived. Although he stayed in Mt. Carroll, the two remained life-long intellectual soulmates.

Evidence of Anna Addams and John Hostetter's special bond survives in a collection of letters John Hostetter wrote to her over his lifetime. Although some are filled with advice or family news, others indicate his poetic nature and reflect his emotional attachment to Anna. "It is night," he wrote in one. "That mysterious stillness pervades the world. The crowd is quiet, and every creature is at rest. In all this silence I fancy I can hear something like far off melody, indescribable but audible, and I have wondered some times whether this is not what poets and philosophers have called the 'music of the spheres,'

"Years ago when sitting at my windows in the city the distant chimes of the church bells sounded something like this. I often wonder too whether others hear it as I do—It is the more striking also, because of the contrast to the rattling and noise of the day-street, and the jar & crash of busy locomotion of the day, or the breakers dash, or the din of arms, or the thunder's roar or the trump of discord, or the shock of men. The sound is, as it were from other worlds, not jaring with even the sound of our own breathing in the stillness, nor the whispering of the winds in the leaves. . . . It is inexpressibly soothing and is, perhaps great Nature's lullaby song, to sing her weary creature's to rest.

"I would not write this to any one, because most practical well meaning but rather obtuse people would laugh at it as stuff but to you, who, although you may consider it a vagary, can appreciate things above mere natural sound, I merely mention it as curious" (2 June 1870, UIC, JAMC, HJ Supp.).

100. Abraham Hostetter (1818–72) became JA's step-uncle. He traveled west from Pennsylvania with his wife, Catherine Bowman Hostetter (1822–72), JA's step-aunt (whom he wed on 25 Nov. 1841 in Lancaster Co., Pa.); three children, Charles Linnaeus, (1842–1919), Samuel Bowman (1843–46), and Emma (d. 26 Oct. 1845); his brother, John L. Hostetter; sister, AH; and close friend, Alexander Officer (1820–97?). After surviving the great Pittsburgh fire of 1845 the group continued by boat to St. Louis, where Abraham Hostetter (who was, like his brother John, a physician) bought a stock of drugs. The party then traveled north on the Mississippi River, landing at Savanna, Ill., and went overland approximately thirty miles. They arrived in Mt. Carroll, where they settled, in Apr. 1845.

Dr. Abraham Hostetter purchased a small house, built a two-story addition, and opened the ground floor as the first drugstore in Mt. Carroll, to which was soon added a stock of building supplies. He and his brother John began an extensive medical practice serving the region around Mt. Carroll. By 1852 he had given up his medical practice, sold the drugstore, and moved to farmland in Salem Twp., where he constructed a small home. In 1857 he formed a partnership with friends from the East Coast and created the banking firm of Hostetter, Reist & Co., which existed until the Civil War.

Abraham and Catherine Hostetter had nine children, four of whom died in infancy. Including Emma and Samuel Bowman, there was Alice Mary (1849–50) and Frank George (1853–59). Those who lived to know JA were Charles Linnaeus (called Linnaeus, or "Linn"), Abram Bowman (sometimes called Abe) (1847–1921), W. Ross (called Ross) (1851–1918), Sarah (1856–1938), and Susan Mattie (1860–1936). All were well educated. The Hostetters built a large, two-story stone and timber home called Wilderberg on their farm two miles north of Mt. Carroll. They lived there and farmed the property until 1872, when both Abraham and Catherine Hostetter became ill. Abraham died of angina, and four months later Catherine died of cancer. Both were buried in the Oak Hill Cemetery in Mt. Carroll.

101. Mt. Carroll was originally settled about 1836. In 1841 Nathaniel Haldeman, brother of AHHA's first husband, William J. Haldeman, and J. P. Emmert constructed their flour mill there on Carroll Creek. The town was not platted until Carroll Co. residents voted in 1843 to move the county seat from Savanna on the Mississippi River ten miles inland to Mt. Carroll. By 1844 a courthouse had been erected to join the mill, the three-story log mill store (probably built in 1842), and a few scattered and simple homes. The first stone building in Mt. Carroll was a hotel constructed in 1844, the year the first lawyer came to town and the post office was established. The first regular stagecoach transportation to Galena, Ill., was greeted with much cheering in 1846.

When the Hostetter party arrived in Apr. 1845, a saloon and a Methodist church had been established, although the latter, organized in 1839, would not build its first building until 1851. By 1869, when JA began to visit Mt. Carroll periodically, the community had at least five other churches: Presbyterian, Baptist, Lutheran, Church of God, and Dunkard or German Baptist.

After a succession of private select schools, the public school system emerged in the late 1850s, probably encouraged to a great degree by the creation of the Mt. Carroll Seminary in the early 1850s. The seminary became a focus for educational and cultural activities in the small community that did not reach a population of twenty-five hundred until 1878.

In addition to the Emmert, Haldeman & Co. Mill, there was a foundry (1853–66) that made plows and stoves, a tanning mill factory (1855–60), and, as time passed, several blacksmiths, carriage makers, and carpenters put up shop. By the late 1870s the largest manufacturer in the community was a brick-making concern. The primary focus of Mt. Carroll and the surrounding area was agriculture. The town was incorporated in 1855 and boasted a succession of newspapers, several banks, and several stores.

By the late 1900s Mt. Carroll was still primarily a trading center for the surrounding farmland, which produced an abundance of wheat, oats, corn, dairy products, and cattle. Its population in 1990 was fewer than two thousand, and it preserved a village atmosphere much like that which might have characterized it when JA was a child. Various generations of the Hostetter and Haldeman families owned farmland and businesses and maintained substantial homes in or near Mt. Carroll. They were cultural, social, educational, political, business, and agricultural leaders in the community.

102. See Biographical Profiles: Haldeman, Henry Winfield.

103. See Biographical Profiles: Haldeman, George Bowman.

104. Some of the letters JHA wrote to AHH during their courtship have survived, although only one of her letters to him for this period is apparently extant (see AHH to JHA, 4 Nov. 1868, SCPC, JAC). John L. Hostetter wrote a congratulatory letter to his sister the day before her wedding took place. He offered encouragement and admonition, admitting that "the announcement created some surprise" but that the "news was not unpleasent partly on acct. of your isolated and lonely condition, and partly because Mr Adams is a gentleman who will endeavor to make life pleasant to you." JHA, he advised, "deserves your highest and best efforts, to make him happy. On my own part," he continued, "I would counsel forbearnce always, as in every family, there will sometimes occur differences of opinion which require calm deliberate concession on both sides. If you will," he concluded, "you can do much toward making others, as well as yourself—happy" (16 Nov. 1868, SCPC, JAC). Later in her life, AHHA told Marcet Haldeman-Julius that she "'had qualms'" but "'thought that he would make a good father for my sons and I <u>knew</u> I would make a good mother for his children'" (M. Haldeman-Julius, "Two Mothers," 12).

105. M. Haldeman-Julius, *Jane Addams as I Knew Her*, 4.

106. M. Haldeman-Julius, "Two Mothers," 13.

107. Isaac Eddy Carey (1823–1902) was born at Locke, N.Y., on 29 July 1823, the son of James and Elizabeth Eddy Carey. He graduated from Yale Univ. in 1849 and then studied theology at Auburn Theological Seminary, a Presbyterian institution in New York from which he graduated in 1853. He married Eliza A. Wright (1825–71) on 1 Jan. 1851. Ordained to the Presbyterian ministry at Springville, N.Y., in 1854, Carey served pastorates at Springville (1853–54); the First Presbyterian Church, Freeport, Ill. (1854–57); Fulton Street Presbyterian Church, Freeport (1857–60); and the First Presbyterian Church, Keokuk, Iowa (1860–62). He then returned to the First Presbyterian Church, Freeport (1862–73). During that time he married JA's father and stepmother on 17 Nov. 1868. After serving at the First Presbyterian Church, Waterloo, Iowa (1873–75), he became a Congregational minister and was pastor for Congregational churches at Huntsburg, Ohio (1875–83) and Claridon, Ohio (1883–90). His retirement years were spent first at Claridon and later at Oberlin. Carey died in Huntsburg on 6 Mar. 1902. He was survived by his second wife, Lucy A. Irwin Carey, whom he had married 5 Aug. 1873, and seven children.

Carey served as an instructor at Beloit College for one year and as a trustee there in 1872–73. He was the author of several publications, mostly patriotic sermons, including *Abraham Lincoln: The Value to the Nation of His Exalted Character* (1865), *Brief History of Presbyterianism in Peoria* (1860), *Conflict and the Victory* (1864), *Discourse of Rev. Mr. Carey on the Death of Abraham Lincoln* (1865), *Ecce Deus—Ecce Homo* (1893), *God Doing Wonderful Things in Behalf of the Nation* (1863), *War an Occasion for Thanksgiving* (1861), and *Sectarian Divisions and Kindred Subjects* (1873). His obvious admiration for Abraham Lincoln may have been a common bond with JHA.

108. In a letter written soon after his mother's remarriage, HWH reported that he had been to Cedarville and had a "splendid time." He had also been to Mt. Carroll, where all save his uncle Nathaniel Haldeman seemed to be pleased with his mother's marriage to JHA. In the flush of hopefulness and excitement he felt about his mother's prospects shortly after she was married he signed the letter as "Henry W. H. Addams" (HWH to AHHA, 30 Nov. 1868, UIC, JAMC, HJ). Nathaniel Haldeman may have been less than happy about the responsibility that descended upon him because of AHHA's marriage. By the terms of his late brother's will, if

Anna remarried he became sole executor of William J. Haldeman's estate, which was apparently in disarray primarily because Anna had been unable to sell or operate the steam mill property in Freeport. He also became the legal guardian of GBH (William J. Haldeman, Will, 20 Jan. 1864, UIC, JAMC, HJ).

109. Dr. Levi A. Mease (1820–81) was born in Union Co., Pa., and migrated to Ohio with his parents when he was nine. He attended school in Ohio and studied medicine there before coming to Stephenson Co. in 1845, where he established a medical practice. He graduated from Rush Medical School, Chicago, in 1851 and from Jefferson Medical College, Philadelphia, in 1856. He practiced medicine in Freeport for thirty-five years and was chosen first president of the Stephenson Co. Society of Physicians and Surgeons. Dr. Mease was married twice. His first wife, Sarah Jane Patton (1827–50), died at twenty-three. They had four children, two of whom lived to maturity. Angeline A. Fisher became the doctor's second wife in 1851, and they had two children. Mease died in 1881 and was buried in the City Cemetery in Freeport.

110. M. Haldeman-Julius, *Jane Addams as I Knew Her*, 4.

111. See AHHA to JHA, 11 Jan. 1869, SCPC, JAC.

112. On 21 June 1869 MCA wrote to SAA, "Yes mam, next Friday will be my birthday; am sorry you are worred because my name is still Mary C. Addams, but what 'cant be cured must be endured,' so you might just as well be easy about it" (UIC, JAMC, HJ; see also John H. Bowman to AHHA, 7 Nov. 1869, UIC, JAMC, HJ). John H. Bowman (1838?–1901) was the oldest child of Susan Hostetter Bowman and George Bowman. He was born in Cumberland Co., Pa., and attended Mt. Carroll Seminary. He served in Company B of the 7th Cavalry, Illinois Volunteers, during the Civil War from Oct. 1864 to Oct. 1865 and returned to Mt. Carroll to farm and become a stock breeder. He died in Chicago, where he was active as a livestock trader.

113. S. Hostetter, ["Reminiscences"], 4.

114. 24 Sept. 1893, UIC, JAMC, HJ.

115. AHHA's nieces Sarah Hostetter and Mary Irvine Hostetter Greenleaf studied and taught music, and her great-niece Rose Reichard, daughter of Virginia Hostetter Reichard and D. Harvey Reichard, became a violinist who studied with violin virtuoso Eugène Ysaÿe (1858–1931) in Europe.

116. MCA to SAA, 18 Feb. 1869, JAPP, DeLoach.

117. Addams, "Pocket Diary, 1875[–81]"; *JAPM*, 28:1562.

118. "Few Reminiscences," 9.

119. Among surviving volumes in the Addams family library at Rockford College are *General Convention of the New Jerusalem in the United States of America. Book of Public Worship, for the Use of the New Church Signified by the New Jerusalem in the Revolution*, prepared by order of the General Convention (1848), and Emanuel Swedenborg, *Four Leading Doctrines of the New Church, Signified in the Revelation, Chapter XXI, by the New Jerusalem . . . Translated from the Latin of Emanuel Swedenborg* (1859). *Great Harmonica: Being a Philosophical Revelation of the Natural, Spiritual, and Celestial Universe* (1853) by Andrew Jackson Davis is one of the volumes in the EHJ Collection, PSU, owned originally by William J. Haldeman.

120. Charles Linnaeus ("Linn") Hostetter (1842–1919) was one of JA's step-cousins. He was the eldest of nine children (five of whom lived to maturity) of Catharine Bowman Hostetter and Abraham Hostetter. He was born on 18 Nov. 1842 in Cumberland Co., Pa., and emigrated with his parents to Mt. Carroll, Ill., in Apr. 1845. He was educated in a district school in Carroll Co. and at Mt. Carroll Seminary. Entering above the level of freshman, he graduated from the first Univ. of Chicago with a B.S. in 1865 after serving during the Civil War in the 134th Infantry, Illinois Volunteers. He attended Union College of Law in Chicago and read law in Chicago with Abraham Lincoln's son Robert Todd Lincoln. At the same time, he worked as a teller in the John Young Scammon Bank and was active in New Jerusalem Church affairs in Chicago. He wed Mary Peart in 1885, and the couple had one child (see n. 179).

Hostetter family lore holds that for "a short time [he] had in his posession the original copy of the Emancipation Proclamation. He considered this a great honor. The document was rolled on a piece of stick which looked like part of a broom handle. Later this original copy was lost" (S. Hostetter, ["Reminiscences"], 8).

After his parents died, he returned to Mt. Carroll to serve as head of the Abraham Hostetter family. He lived at Wilderberg and farmed its two hundred acres, raising, among other things, shorthorn cattle, which he introduced to the region; ginseng root; and orchids. He also practiced law and had an insurance business, the Mt. Carroll Mutual County Fire Insurance Co., which he began in 1888. Because of the latter he became active in the Illinois Assn. of Farmers Mutual Insurance Cos.

Linn was one of AHHA's favorite nephews. They shared an interest in the New Jerusalem Church and in literary matters. He was an active Republican, serving for several years as chair of the Republican Carroll Co. Central Com. Later in life he became interested in writing history. Among his efforts was a monograph for the American Historical Association on the British occupation of the Illinois country from 1763 to the time of the surrender of Kaskaskia to George Rogers Clark, a memoir of the first Univ. of Chicago during the American Civil War, and a Carroll Co. history.

After the death of Mary Peart Hostetter, Linn's sister Sarah went to live with him at Wilderberg as his hostess. She continued the annual Christmas reunions for all the family as well as the special July Fourth celebrations and picnics to which friends and neighbors were invited. The latter occasions consisted of Linn Hostetter reading the Declaration of Independence and then all assembled would sing the National Anthem and "America." Fireworks crackled and fizzed all day. Charles Linnaeus Hostetter died on 9 June 1919 in Mt. Carroll and is buried in Oak Hill Cemetery, Mt. Carroll.

121. Abram Bowman Hostetter (1847–1921), was the nephew of AHHA, step-cousin of JA, and the second son of Dr. Abraham Hostetter and his wife Catherine Bowman Hostetter. He was married to Harriet Stackhouse Irvine on 19 May 1875 in Mt. Carroll. According to Hostetter family lore, Abram Hostetter "was a gay, inventive soul, always bursting with ideas and such a twinkle in his eye" ([C. L. Hostetter and R. Hostetter], "Abram—Abe," in "[Hostetter Family]"). Like his siblings, he enjoyed playing chess and was good at it. After attending Mt. Carroll Seminary he graduated from a course of general studies at the first Univ. of Chicago. Determined to be a New Jerusalem Church minister, he began to study with Frank Sewall (1837–1915) in Glendale, Ohio, only to realize within the year that he would never be able to support a family on his minister's salary.

He came home to Mt. Carroll and became involved in agricultural pursuits for the remainder of his life. When his father died in 1873 he inherited two hundred acres of farmland. Here he and his bride, Harriet Stackhouse Irvine Hostetter (1848–1903), who had been born in Mt. Carroll and was the child of Amanda M. Fitch Irvine (1809–1900) and John Irvine, Sr. (1790–1873), built their home, East Wilderberg. Here also he established a thoroughbred shorthorn stock farm with great success. The Hostetters had one child, Adaline (1878–1938), who graduated from Mt. Carroll Seminary with a major in music in 1902 and studied music with her aunt Sarah Hostetter at the Breck School in Minnesota from 1897 to 1898.

Abram Hostetter served as state secretary for the Illinois Farmers Institute, organized in 1895 to help educate farmers for improved agricultural processes, and he started lending libraries for small county schools. After his wife died in the Illinois Hospital for the Insane in Jacksonville and his daughter married A. Rudolph Burquist (1879–1936) and moved to Duluth, he also moved to Duluth to be near family. There he served as a county agent, working to help improve potato crops in northern Minnesota. Abram Bowman Hostetter died in Duluth after a stroke and was buried next to his wife in Oak Hill Cemetery, Mt. Carroll.

122. IU, Lilly, SAAH.

123. UIC, JAMC, HJ. HWH may have been referring to Lewis H. Mitchell, the Presbyteri-

an minister in Cedarville from 1874 until 1878. Marcet Haldeman-Julius labeled her father an atheist (*Jane Addams as I Knew Her*, 6).

124. IU, Lilly, SAAH. SAA was visiting Addams cousins in the East and had taken her cousin Clara L. Young (1849–1926), daughter of Nathan and Harriet C. Addams Young (her father's sister) to visit Mary Peart, a cousin of AHHA's, who lived in Columbia, Pa.

125. Stern, *Phrenological Dictionary*, ix; see also Stern, *Heads and Headlines*.

126. Stern, *Phrenological Dictionary*, ix.

127. George Combe (1788–1858), a Scotsman who followed Gall, lectured to huge audiences in the Philadelphia area and throughout Pennsylvania during the late 1830s. At that time, phrenology was generally accepted by both laymen and doctors as a new science. It had been created by educated and scientific men using the scientific method of their day. Initially, it attracted and convinced the intellectuals of the early nineteenth century, including scientists, physicians, writers, educators, the social elite, and the reform-minded. Among the thousands who experienced a phrenological reading were Louisa May Alcott, Nathaniel Hawthorne, Henry Wadsworth Longfellow, Mark Twain, Walt Whitman, Horace Mann, Booker T. Washington, Clara Barton, Henry Ward Beecher, Susan B. Anthony, Elizabeth Cady Stanton, Helen Keller, Thomas A. Edison, Samuel F. B. Morse, Andrew Jackson, Abraham Lincoln, and Theodore Roosevelt. By mid-century, however, scientific method was out-distancing the tenets of phrenology, and physicians were ignoring its theories. It was becoming a business and the darling of charlatans and hucksters, who saw phrenology as a way to make a living by traversing the country, lecturing and giving skull "readings."

128. Addams library collection, Rare Book Room, Coleman Library, Rockford College; see also the list of books belonging to the Addams family (*JAPM*, 28:857–68).

129. J. Stanley Grimes was one of the "most notable of the elaborators of phrenology, . . . a brilliant but erratic man, who evolved what he called 'Etherology,'" (Riegel, "Introduction to Phrenology to the U.S.," 78). An author, lecturer, and the first president of the Buffalo Phrenological Society in 1839, Grimes combined phrenology and hypnotism into the system of ideas he promoted.

130. Johann Kaspar Spurzheim (1776–1832), a German physician and author, was one of the founders of phrenology.

131. A note in AHHA's hand on the front endpaper of the first American edition of Spurzheim's *View of the Elementary Principles of Education, Founded on the Nature of Man* (1832) indicates that she acquired it "at the appaizment" of JHA's estate in 1881.

132. For the phrenological reading of JA's head, see Phrenological Reading, 30 July 1876, below. Readings for GBH and AHHA are also extant (see *JAPM*, 28:729–35).

133. JHA recorded on 19 Aug. 1844 that he "took a dose of Brandy for bowel complaints" ("Journal, 1844").

134. The *Freeport Weekly Journal* of 1 May 1872, in reporting the lodge's end, wrote that a careful "observer will tell you that Constance L[odge] has done considerable towards elevating [the?] morals of the community, and kept . . . young men out of the snares of the tem[pted?]." A new lodge associated with the Independent Order of Good Templars was organized in Cedarville in May 1879.

135. 19 July 1875, SCPC, JAC.

136. See JA to MCAL, 6 Dec. 1883; see also Sarah Hostetter to Susan Hostetter Mackay and Henry Mackay, 2 Dec. 1883, JAPP, Schneider.

137. [C. L. Hostetter and R. Hostetter], "Harry Haldeman and Family," in "[Hostetter Family]."

138. UIC, JAMC, HJ.

139. "Journal, 1844," 3 Aug. 1844. JHA was referring to Queen Victoria (1819–1901). In 1844 Canada was a colony of Great Britain and ruled by Queen Victoria.

140. 6 July 1871, IU, Lilly, SAAH.

141. Mary A. Livermore (1820–1905), teacher, lecturer, suffrage leader, and reformer, worked in support of the Union effort during the Civil War, temperance, and woman's rights. She lived in Chicago between 1857 and 1869. During that time, she assisted her husband, the Rev. Daniel Parker Livermore, in editing and publishing the Universalist publication *New Covenant*. In 1869 she founded a woman's rights newspaper, *The Agitator*, which merged with the *Woman's Journal* of the American Woman Suffrage Assn. (AWSA) in 1870. She was its editor until 1872. Serving initially as vice president of the AWSA (formed in 1869 as an alternative to the Natl. Woman Suffrage Assn. [NWSA] organized by Susan B. Anthony and Elizabeth Cady Stanton), Livermore became its president between 1875 and 1878.

142. Elizabeth Cady Stanton (1815–1902) was a leader for woman's rights. With her primary cohort Susan B. Anthony she worked tirelessly for woman suffrage. In May 1869 the two women formed the NWSA, and she served as its president for the next twenty-one years.

143. 20 Feb. 1869, SCPC, JAC.

144. JWA, "Res. That Woman should be allowed the right of suffrage. Negative," JAPP, Hulbert. JWA may have presented his arguments in 1871 shortly before the Nestor Debating Club was formally organized in Cedarville on 13 Dec. 1871. Its members, men and women, met in the Buckeye School House. According to a news item in the *Freeport Journal* (11 Jan. 1871), debate on the woman suffrage issue was won by the women, who argued the affirmative persuasively.

145. See "An Act in Relation to the Rights of Married Women in Certain Cases," Illinois General Assembly, Approved 14 Feb. 1857, Illinois State Archives, General Assembly, RG 600.001 Bills, Resolutions, and Related General Assembly Records.

146. See cash account in Addams, "Pocket Diary, 1875[–81]"; *JAPM*, 28:1667–70.

147. See Addams, [Correspondents, 1877]; *JAPM*, 27:139.

148. See Wise, *Jane Addams of Hull-House*, 22; Addams, "Pocket Diary, 1875[–81]," 24 Jan. 1875; *JAPM*, 28:1511.

149. As a child, JA seems to have been partial to sweets, a preference she never outgrew. The following recipe for chocolate cream candy was said by her great-niece Alice DeLoach to be one of her favorites: "Two cups of white sugar—One half cup of cream—Boil eight minutes—After boiling put in vanilla to taste. Stir till cool. Melt chocolate then roll candy in balls and dip into it" (*JAPM*, 27:146).

150. See John H. Weber and George Weber, Jr., to Devault Weber and Margaret Weber, 3 May 1845, IU, Lilly, SAAH.

151. A "housewife" is a small case that holds sewing notions, including needles and thread. See *Freeport Journal*, 23 Aug. 1871; *Freeport Journal*, 2 Oct. 1872.

152. An assortment of articles JA embroidered or knitted survive in private hands as well as in the CAHS and the UIC, JAMC. Among them are a hand towel, decorated with an *A* embroidered in white floss, and knitted baby clothes and blankets. JA's awareness of the importance of this decorative art in her own life may have contributed to her creation of handcraft opportunities for immigrant women through a variety of programs at Hull-House, the social settlement she co-founded in Chicago in 1889. Other factors were at work there as well, including the maintenance of traditional skills within industrial society, fostering understanding between generations of immigrant women, and the desire to encourage the presence of beauty in tenement dwellers' lives. The skill also provided women with a means of adding to their family's income.

153. 21 Aug. 1871, UIC, JAMC, HJ.

154. All of her life, JA remained intrigued by Native American artifacts. On at least one of her trips to the West (that in 1894 with SAAH) she gathered examples of Native American pottery, weaving, basketry, and artifacts to exhibit at Hull-House. She encouraged friends who lived in the western states to supply examples of Native American arts and crafts to add to the collection. SAAH and HWH also collected Native American artifacts.

155. G. Haldeman, "The Science of Almanacs Association"; *JAPM*, 27:7. *Hostetter's Illustrated United States Almanac* was issued by cousins of AHHA and her Mt. Carroll siblings. It was published by the Hostetter Co. of Pittsburgh, Pa., between 1861 and 1909. These same cousins, led by Dr. and Col. Jacob Hostetter, also manufactured Hostetter's Stomach Bitters in Pittsburgh.

156. This vignette of one of their adventures appears in Wise, *Jane Addams of Hull-House*, 35–36. AHHA's letter to HWH in which she apparently recounts the story is no longer extant (see HWH to AHHA, 14 May 1874, IU, Lilly, SAAH).

157. See HWH to JA, 3 Apr. 1874, SCPC, JAC; *JAPM*, 1:162–65.

158. "Few Reminiscences," 6–7. The card of black pasteboard is extant in the JAPP (see illustration, p. 45). JA's collection of bones probably began in earnest in 1872 when a massive segment of a cliff above Cedar Creek broke off, revealing a fissure. JA described it to her RFS Scientific Assn. classmates. "This fissure was a cavern literally filled with bones, bones of various forms & sizes. The first research brought forth only vertabrae, hundreds in number & apparently those of snakes, some of them evidently belonging to immense rattle snakes, others very small & delicately formed, but the mass consisting of vertabrae belonging to the ordinary sized serpant. Some of them imbedded in the sand browned & blackened <through> ~~with~~ age and moisture, others were bleached & whitened lying on the surface & around the mouth [of the?] den. . . . [We] found vertabrae that evidently did not belong to reptiles, ribs which had a decided character as those of mammalia, skulls of rodents, minute leg bones & scapulas & to crown all wee delicate shells of some remote period & round seed pods entire and unchrushed" ("[Address on Illinois Geography]," 26 May [1878]; *JAPM*, 45:1784–86). The find spurred her on to more exploration, and she reported that she found more bones in other bluffs along Cedar Creek.

159. G. Haldeman, "G.B.H. Things of Interest in Madison Wis."; *JAPM*, 27:5–6. The travelers were JHA and AHHA, GBH, JA, and SAA. Events GBH depicted include visiting the Wisconsin state capitol building and the Univ. of Wisconsin, a boat ride at twilight, visiting Devil's Lake, mountain climbing, riding in a train and stagecoach, and attending Presbyterian church on Sunday. Old Abe, the "Wisconsin war eagle," was carried on a special perch by the 8th Infantry, Wisconsin Volunteers (the Eagle Regiment) into thirty-nine engagements as well as in parades and on marches during the Civil War. Noted for his fierce screams during battle, this symbol of Wisconsin dedication to the Union cause died on 26 Mar. 1881.

160. Among extant Addams family children's books, not school texts, that are in the Addams family library, Rare Book Room, Coleman Library, Rockford College, are Samuel G. Goodrich, *Balloon Travels; or, Robert Merry and His Young Friends, over Various Countries in Europe*, edited by Peter Parley (1855); Margaret Hosmer, *Little Rosie's Christmas Times* (1869, inscribed "To Jennie / from Aunt Harriet [C. Addams Young]. This book belonged to Jane Addams, of Cedarville, Ill."); and Adelaide Ann Procter, *Poems of Adelaide A. Procter* (1871, signed "Jane Addams / Sept 6 1875 / Cedarville, Ill."). There are two childhood books at the CAHS: John Bunyan, *Pilgrim's Progress from This World to That which Is to Come* (inscribed "Merry Christmas / to Jennie Addams / From her / Teacher / 1875") and *Pepper and Salt* [Conundrums] (1874, signed "Jane Addams").

161. Addams, *Twenty Years*, 12–13. Neither Pope's *Iliad* nor Dryden's *Virgil* are extant in the Addams family or the Union Library Co. of Cedar Creek Mills collections in the Rare Book Room, Coleman Library, Rockford College. Neither appear in the original listing of titles of the Union Library Co. of Cedar Creek Mills. What JA refers to as "History of the World" may have been Royal Robbins's *Outlines of Ancient and Modern History and a New Plan . . .*, 2 vols. in 1 (Hartford: Belknap and Hammersley, 1845), Union Library Co. title no. 24 (see *JAPM*, 28:856). This volume is among those extant in the Coleman Library at Rockford College.

162. None of these works appear in the list of the Union Library Co. of Cedar Creek Mills or in its surviving volumes at Rockford College. Among the holdings of the library of SAAH

were three volumes of Plutarch's *Lives* and Washington Irving's *Life of Washington*, 5 vols. (1855–59) (S. Haldeman, "[Catalog of the Library]").

163. For a sampling of JA poems, see *JAPM*, Writings, especially reel 45.

164. Henry Wadsworth Longfellow (1807–82), American poet, was noted during his lifetime for his often simple, sentimental, and moralizing works. Among his more famous shorter poems are "Village Blacksmith," "Wreck of the Hesperus," and "Children's Hour." Longer works include *Evangeline* (1847), *Song of Hiawatha* (1855), and *Paul Revere's Ride* (1861).

165. Walter ("Walt") Whitman (1819–92), an American poet who spent most of his adult life as a newspaper writer and editor, also worked as a carpenter. His first edition of *Leaves of Grass*, which contained twelve of his poems, was published in 1855. For the remainder of his life he continued to revise and issue enlarged editions of this work until the final one in 1892. Although he published other works during his lifetime, *Leaves of Grass* was his touchstone. His innovative use of free verse and his subject matter, including the celebration of individualism, may have inspired later poets to be experimental.

166. Thomas Moore (1779–1852) was the Irish Catholic son of a Dublin grocer. He became a fashionable figure among the liberal-minded aristocracy in Regency England. He wrote songs, poems, and prose. Among his best remembered pieces are *Lalla Rookh* (1817); *Life of Byron* (1830); a biography of the English poet George Gordon, Lord Byron, his good friend; and *Irish Melodies* (1807–34), songs that lent themselves to a social evening around the piano. Moore was a favorite of JA's stepmother AHHA, who sang and quoted his work.

167. Louisa May Alcott (1832–88), born in Germantown, Pa., grew up in New England and became the author of numerous children's stories and novels. To help support her family she worked as a servant and seamstress, governess, and companion before becoming a professional writer. Letters she wrote home as a nurse during the Civil War were published as *Hospital Sketches* in 1863, which was followed in 1864 by her first novel, *Moods. Little Women*, her most famous book, appeared in 1868–69. Her moralistic novels usually provide a view of family life in Victorian America from the female perspective and experience (see Vallie E. Beck to JA, 30 Mar. [and 2 Apr.] 1876, nn. 2 and 3, and JA to Vallie E. Beck, 3 May 1877, n. 5, below).

168. Mary Abigail Dodge (Gail Hamilton) (1833–96), a teacher in the 1850s, became a successful essayist and editor, writing first for the antislavery *National Era*. She also wrote for the *Independent, Congregationalist, Atlantic Monthly*, and *Our Young Folks*. Among her books of essays were *Women's Worth and Worthlessness* (1872) and *Woman's Wrongs: A Counter-Irritant* (1868). She produced humorous pieces with a moral, centered about ordinary experience and current events. She espoused self-development and self-reliance from a feminist point of view. Although she initially supported woman suffrage, she felt it would not prevent economic discrimination and eventually renounced her position. Women, she believed, could be more influential in providing spiritual leadership in the family.

169. On the life and work of Elizabeth Stuart Phelps Ward, see The 1875 Diary of Jane Addams, 17 Jan. 1875, n. 44, below.

170. On the life and work of Dinah Maria Mulock Craik, see JA to Vallie E. Beck, 3 May 1877, n. 4, below.

171. Harriet Beecher Stowe (1811–96), author of *Uncle Tom's Cabin* (1852) and other works, was born in Litchfield, Conn. The daughter of Congregational minister Lyman Beecher and his wife, Roxanna Foote Beecher, she was educated in an atmosphere of New England propriety and religious teaching. Harriet Beecher developed a lifelong interest in theology and in ideas for helping others. In 1836 she married Calvin Ellis Stowe, a professor in Cincinnati. They had six children. *Uncle Tom's Cabin*, a novel about the ills of slavery, captured the attention of readers north, where it was lauded, and south, where it was seen as an unfair rendering. The work was translated into many foreign languages and issued abroad. In addition to abolition and to helping emancipated slaves find new lives, Stowe was also supportive

of the temperance and woman suffrage movements. She wrote other novels, poems, and articles, most of which had a religious tone, as well as housekeeping manuals.

172. Sir Walter Scott (1771–1832) was made a baronet in 1820. He grew up in the Tweed River Valley, where he absorbed Scottish legend and lore, and studied law in Edinburgh. He published popular ballads of the Scottish border, a series of metrical romances modeled on medieval narrative form (e.g., *Lady of the Lake*), and a series of historical novels. See also JA to Vallie E. Beck, 3 May 1877 (n. 3, below).

173. Charles Dickens (1812–70), born in Portsmouth, England, is noted for his entertaining novels with a social conscience. He achieved enormous popularity from his work during his life. Revealing the less beneficial results of the Industrial Revolution in working-class British society, he produced unforgettable, often eccentric, heroes, heroines, and villains whose actions spotlighted such social abuse as child labor and debtor's prison. After schooling interrupted by work in a shoe-blacking factory in London, he found initial employment as a law clerk. He soon found his way to a news reporter's job on London's *Morning Chronicle*. In 1836 he published his first volume of stories *Sketches of Boz*. These were followed by fourteen novels, assorted stories, travel books, sketches, and essays. In addition, he was the editor of two popular magazines, *Household Words* and *All the Year Round*. Dickens made two tours of America, to great acclaim, and continued throughout the latter part of his life to give public readings of his works in England. His novels were *Oliver Twist* (1838), *Nicholas Nickleby* (1839), *The Old Curiosity Shop* (1840), *Barnaby Rudge* (1841), *A Christmas Carol* (1843), *Martin Chuzzlewit* (1844), *Dombey and Son* (1848), *David Copperfield* (1850), *Bleak House* (1853), *Hard Times* (1854), *Little Dorrit* (1857), *A Tale of Two Cities* (1859), *Great Expectations* (1861), and *Our Mutual Friend* (1865). He was at work on his fifteenth novel, *The Mystery of Edwin Drood*, when he died. See also The 1875 Diary of Jane Addams, 17 Jan. 1875 n.5; JA to Vallie E. Beck, 30 Mar [and 2 Apr.] 1876, nn. 6 and 14; and Vallie E. Beck to JA, 10 Aug. 1877, n. 9, all below.

174. M. Haldeman-Julius, "Two Mothers," 17.

175. See HWH to AHHA, 18 Jan. 1870, IU, Lilly, SAAH.

176. M. Haldeman-Julius, *Jane Addams as I Knew Her*, 5.

177. Beloit, Wis., at the confluence of Turtle Creek and the Rock River, fifteen miles north of Rockford, Ill., forty miles southeast of Madison, Wis., and approximately one hundred miles northwest of Chicago, is situated among rolling hills on the Illinois-Wisconsin border. Originally a Winnebago settlement, the first white settlers arrived as trappers and traders, followed by pioneer farmers and merchants in the 1820s and 1830s. Beginning in 1837, a large part of the town of Colebrook, N.H., moved to the tract that had been acquired by Dr. Horace White on behalf on the New England Emigrating Company. The village grew under the successive names of Turtle, Blodgett's Settlement (for Caleb Blodgett from Vermont, one of the early claimants of the property on which the village developed), and New Albany. Finally, in Mar. 1856, it was incorporated as the city of Beloit. Soon after settlers arrived, they built a church and created the coeducational Beloit Academy.

Beloit College was conceived out of a series of four conventions held by the former New Englanders active in the movement to create a quality frontier college to foster higher education in their community. This group of clergy and laity became known as the Friends of Education. The college charter was enacted into law by the Territory of Wisconsin in Feb. 1846, and Beloit College granted its first degrees in 1851. The school had a strong Yale connection through its faculty and administration and also its board of trustees, including Aaron Lucius Chapin, the first president of the school, who served from 1849 to 1886 and was also a force in the administration of Rockford Female Seminary. The board of trustees emphasized quality and classical education and also prided itself on its openness to educational innovation.

The quiet college town developed slowly. In 1886 local businessmen began an effort to interest industry in coming to Beloit. One of the first industries to do so was the Berlin Machine Works in 1887, and development continued. By 1935 there were approximately sixty industrial plants near the community, producing everything from pumps to fireworks and hosiery.

178. A series of letters from MCA and JWA to their father JHA between Oct. and Dec. 1869, as well as letters from HWH to his mother in early 1870, indicate the family discord (UIC, JAMC, HJ; JAPP, Hulbert).

179. Mary Peart Hostetter (1847?–1902), a cousin of AHHA, was the daughter of Quakers Elizabeth Hernley Peart and Daniel Peart, who lived in Columbia, Pa. When she and Charles Linnaeus Hostetter were married in Mt. Carroll on 3 Mar. 1885 she had been living in Philadelphia, where she was educated. She and her husband had one child, Heber Peart Hostetter (1886–1953). Mary Peart Hostetter was an avid reader and life-long student. She was an active member of the Mt. Carroll Woman's Club and served as treasurer for the organized district federation of Woman's Clubs. She is buried beside her husband in Oak Hill Cemetery, Mt. Carroll, Ill. (see n. 120).

180. JAPP, Hulbert.

181. Friday evening [10 Dec. 1869], JAPP, Hulbert.

182. Miranda Eve Addams (1836?–1911), one of JA's cousins, was one of three children born to Rebecca Margaret Addams (1810–88, the daughter of Samuel and Catherine Huy Addams) and Richard Addams (son of William and Eva Van Reed Addams), first cousins who shared Isaac and Barbara Ruth Addams as grandparents. She never married and is said to have initiated the first day nursery in Philadelphia. In 1888 she wrote to AHHA, reporting that "We are at present time adding repairs to our Nursery. Were you ever on a building Committee? if you have been, you can sympathize with me, that is part of my occupation now." Her commitment to the enterprise must have been strong, for she continued, "Oh I wish I could take all these tender babes for my own, they are like rays of sunshine to me" (31 Dec. 1888, UIC, JAMC, HJ Supp.).

From 1860 until her death she lived with members of the Young family in Philadelphia, helping care for the children of the family. After the death of Harriet C. Addams Young and Nathan Young, she remained at 6320 Overbrook Ave., living with their daughter Clara L. Young, who also never married. Before 1890 JA usually visited Miranda Addams and the Young family on her trips east. Miranda Addams is buried with other members of the Young family in Laurel Hill Cemetery in Philadelphia, Pa.

183. MCA repeated Miranda E. Addams's comment in her letter to JHA, Friday evening [10 Dec. 1869] (JAPP, Hulbert). MCA and JWA did not go east.

184. IU, Lilly, SAAH.

185. HWH's break with the Addams men seems to have been permanent. When his mother was ill for several months with erysipelas in 1873, the fact that "Mr Addams" (as he referred to his stepfather) wrote to him was so surprising that HWH said it "set me in a Regular stew" because it made him think that his mother was worse off than she probably was (HWH to AHHA, 22 July 1873, IU, Lilly, SAAH).

186. Among leading physicians in Mendota, Ill., during the last half of the nineteenth century were the doctors Cook. William John Cook arrived in Mendota in 1854, to be joined in 1855 by his son Edgar Humphrey Cook, a graduate of Western Reserve Univ. His sons Edgar P. and Charles Edgar also joined the practice. It is with this family that HWH continued his study of medicine. Edgar P. Cook, who became head of the Illinois State Medical Society and remained active in its development, recommended HWH when he entered the Univ. of Pennsylvania Medical School. He and HWH maintained a life-long friendship. Dr. Charles E. Cook (1859–1931) established hospital facilities for patients at his home in Mendota, and HWH may have worked with him there.

187. JHA to AHHA, 27 Feb. 1869, SCPC, JAC.

188. John Addams Linn (1872–1919) was JA's eldest nephew. He was born in Lena, Ill., the year after MCA and JML were married. He spent his childhood moving with his family throughout small communities in northern Illinois. During his mother's pregnancies and various episodes of illness he was often in the care of aunts and uncles or family friends. He attended public schools and joined JML in South Dakota while his father helped start the Groton Collegiate Institute between 1885 and 1886. In 1893 he graduated from Lake Forest Univ. After considerable thought, he decided to join the Episcopal church and become a priest. Four years later, in 1897, John Addams Linn graduated from the Western Theological Seminary in Chicago. During this period of his life he was often a Hull-House resident.

John Addams Linn, who worked tirelessly to help others, seems to have been an extremely sensitive and somewhat frail young man given to nervousness. While living at Hull-House, and certainly after the death of his mother, he became particularly close to JA. As he was making his momentous decision to join the Episcopal church and enter the seminary, he consulted his Aunt Jane, first telling her that he had "come to consider you [JA] as a second mother." He continued, "I have always thought of you as a sort of monitor, as the one who would back me up in any good thing or be the first to turn me from a wrong path" (John Addams Linn to JA, 17 Dec. 1893, SCPC, JAC; *JAPM*, 2:1471–74). On her part, JA was there on his special occasions, his graduations, ordination, and wedding, and to participate in at least one Palm Sunday service that he conducted.

Linn began his service to the Episcopal church at the First Trinity Church in Petersburg, Ill. (1897–98). Between 1898 and 1902 he was assistant at the Church of St. Mary the-Virgin, in New York City. In 1901 he was ordained as a priest. For six years, from 1902 until 1908, he served as rector of St. Paul's Church in Mishawaka, Ind. While there, he helped the parish build a new church. In 1908 he became master and chaplain of the Episcopal-sponsored Howe School for boys in Indiana. By 1913 he was once again living in New York City, where he taught at the Trinity School.

On 10 Sept. 1903 John Addams Linn married Ethel Winthrop Storer (1881–1952) of New York City. Their only child, John Winthrop Linn (1905–82), was called Winthrop. The Linns were divorced in 1915. After the former Ethel Linn married Frederick Warner Allen, Winthrop Linn legally added his stepfather's family name to his own and became John Winthrop Linn Allen.

When America entered World War I, John Addams Linn worked with the Young Men's Christian Assn. (YMCA). Between Dec. 1917 and his death in Oct. 1918 he served as one of the YMCA chaplains in the 1st Division of the American Expeditionary Force in Europe, primarily at the front with the 5th Field Artillery. Unusual for a YMCA chaplain, "Dad" (he was forty-six), as he was affectionately known among the men, was in the active fighting associated with the Cantigny, Soissons, and Argonne battles and several other operations and engagements. On 8 Oct. 1918, while the battery he was with was under fire, he was killed by a shell that landed among a group of men to whom he was serving biscuits, cigarettes, and chocolate. John E. Steen, Linn's supervisor, reported that "Linn was one of our very best secretaries and in his regiment he was counted a good soldier. . . . [H]e shared the fortune of his regiment and stuck to his job. This made him much beloved by the soldiers" (John E. Steen to Mr. Carter, [ca. Oct. 1918], JAPP, Hulbert). In recognition for his unusual commitment and bravery, the U.S. awarded him a silver star posthumously. In his honor, the men of Battery D with whom he had been serving financially supported a French war orphan, Lucien Eugene Delauney, for a year. JA continued the support for a number of years, sending money regularly through the Paris office of the Red Cross. Linn was buried near more than fifty other soldiers at the Chaudron Farm, the Commune of Exermont at Exermont (Ardennes) France. JA visited his grave in Apr. 1919. His final resting place was the Argonne cemetery at Romagne, Montfaucon, France.

189. Regarding MCAL's probable miscarriage, see HWH to AHHA, 14 May 1874, IU, Lilly, SAAH.

190. James Weber Linn (1876–1939), best known as the first biographer of his aunt JA, also achieved fame as one of the most influential and memorable professors of English at the Univ. of Chicago. Weber Linn (or "Teddy" as he was sometimes called later in life because of his resemblance to the crusty, outspoken Theodore Roosevelt) was born on 11 May 1876 in Winnebago, Ill., the second child of MCAL and JML. As his family moved about northern Illinois he attended several different public schools. By the time he was sixteen, the Linn family was living in Storm Lake, Iowa. There, Weber Linn became a student at Buena Vista College and worked in its commercial department. He is credited with creating the school's first football program.

In 1893 Linn became a student at the Univ. of Chicago and graduated in 1897 with an A.B. degree. After working a few months at the *Chicago Record* and returning to the Univ. of Chicago for graduate study, he joined the Univ. of Chicago English department as an assistant. Linn served forty-three years as a faculty member at the university, achieving the rank of professor in addition to great respect as a teacher, writer, and friend of students. From 1908 until 1920, when he resigned, he was dean of men in the university's college. The university estimated that fifteen thousand students passed through his classes and that he could call at least five thousand of them by their first names. An unnamed former student, writing about Linn in the *Freeport Journal-Standard* shortly after his death in 1939, recalled him as one of the "rare teachers" who "succeeded brilliantly. His composition classes (yes, composition classes!) were exciting, absorbing, endlessly amusing. As a critic he was precise yet stimulating, sometimes merciless but never unjust" (undated clipping, JAPP). "He really put the fear of God into us," another recalled. "[I]t took time and many meetings before you got through his rough exterior to the sensitive interior." That same former student remembered how generous he was with his time and thoughtful advice for his students. "Mr. Linn set young men's feet in the proper paths with a clearer understanding of their futures than they had themselves. . . . He was continually giving young men such advice which had great significance in their lives" (Breckinridge, "James Weber Linn," 8–9). Novelist James T. Farrell, also a former Linn student, recalled that Linn warned students how difficult it was to earn a living as a writer. Linn explained that his own ambition was to be a writer, but to support his family he also became a teacher and journalist. Farrell "saw in Linn a man of knowledge and education." He continued in his memorial to Linn, "I never came to understand how much he helped me until he was no more" ("James Weber Linn").

Linn was the author of an assortment of novels and biographies as well as six textbooks on English composition and literature and periodical articles. For more than sixteen years he wrote a column, "Round about Chicago," for the old *Chicago Herald,* the *Herald Examiner,* and finally for the *Chicago Daily Times.* He began to work on the biography of JA after she was awarded a share of the Nobel Peace Prize of 1931. *Jane Addams: A Biography,* first issued by D. Appleton-Century Co. in 1935, the year JA died, and reissued in 1938, was undertaken by Linn with the help and blessings of JA. Widely reviewed, Linn's rendition of her life was haled as "adequate, trustworthy, and authoritative." It was seen by some critics as an appreciation of JA's life work and influence in American life.

On 26 Mar. 1904 James Weber Linn wed Mary Howland (1877–1951) of Cambridge, Mass. The couple had three daughters. Jane Addams Linn (1906–71) married James Waller Rogers; Elizabeth ("Bips") Howland Linn (1908–97) married John B. Allen, was widowed, and then married Robert H. Murray; and Constance Linn (1912) lived but a day. As a young man, Linn was often a resident at Hull-House. After their marriage, the Linn couple maintained a communication with JA and the settlement.

In addition to his work as a scholar and journalist, Linn led an active social and political life. He was a member of the Tavern, Quadrangle, and University clubs in Chicago. He served as secretary for the Illinois Century of Progress Comm. in 1933 and 1934. In 1938 he ran for and was elected to the Illinois House of Representatives from the Fifth District, which surrounded the Univ. of Chicago. He paid particular attention to matters relating to education during his brief tenure in the state legislature. James Weber Linn died from complications arising from leukemia on 16 July 1939 while vacationing in Lakeside, Mich. Graveside services were conducted for him on 18 July 1939 when he was buried (his wife was later buried near him) with other members of the Addams family in the Cedarville Cemetery.

191. Other children born to the Linns were Esther Margaret Linn (1880–1955), Stanley Ross Linn (1883–1945), Mary ("Little Mary") Addams Linn (1885–88), and Charles Hodge (1887).

192. UIC, JAMC, HJ Supp.

193. 22 Jan. 1875, JAPP, DeLoach.

194. IU, Lilly, SAAH.

195. John L. Hostetter to AHHA, 16 Nov. 1868, SCPC, JAC (see also n. 104).

To Sarah Alice Addams

This earliest extant Jane Addams letter is replete with the misformed letters and the misspelled words of a child learning to write. It is inscribed by pencil in capital letters. "Dots," or periods above the line, with spaces between them, appear between nearly every word, a teaching technique used to help young students learn to form words. In this letter Addams ran the words teachers' meeting *together as "TACH-ERMITTING." Perhaps she thought it was one word or perhaps she forgot to include the dot between these words. The young Jennie Addams was apparently somewhat dyslexic. She had difficulty for many years writing the letters of the alphabet correctly and, for an even longer time, spelling words correctly.*

In the document printed below, and in other early childhood letters, we have corrected only misformed letters that do not correctly represent others in the alphabet. Sometimes Addams reversed letters like B, D, J, P, and S and some numbers. These have been corrected in the texts; however we have not altered the letter D, mistakenly used here by Addams for B, the letter N for M and vice versa, the letter P for R, and the letter T for D. Thus, in the following letter, the word DED *appears when Addams obviously meant* BED *and* NIS *when she probably meant* MIS. *Misspellings are rife throughout her childhood letters, and we have chosen to keep the words as she wrote them. In some instances she spelled the same word differently and incorrectly more than once in the same letter. In most of her extant letters written before 1870–71, Jane Addams did not mark the ends of sentences with periods. When the text is read aloud, we believe the meaning will be clear.*

[Cedarville, Ill.]   [1868?][1]

DEAR · SISTER · ALICE[2] ·
   AS · I · TAKE · MY · PEN · IN · HAND · TO · LET · YOU · KNOW · THAT · I · AM · WEL · AT · PRESSENT · HOPIN · THAT · YOU · ARE · THE · SAME · DID · YOU · GET · DOWN · SAE · POOR · CITY[3] · FLEELS · VERY · LOMC-SONE · SINCE · YOU · ARE · GONE · POOR · PONTO[4] · FLEES · VERY · LOM-SOME · TO · I · WAS · UP · TO · MR · TEMPLETONS[5] · DAY · BEFOR · YES-TERDAY · WITH · IDA · COBBLE[6] · AND · COMMING · HOME · WE · WAS · COUGHT · IN · A · STOPM · AND · HATTO · STOP · IN · AT · NIS · COB-BLES · TILL · THE · STORM · WAS · OVER · POLLY[7] · CAME · HOME · TO · NIGHT · MARY[8] · AND · ELLEN[9] · HAS · GONE · TO · TACHERMITTING[10] ·

AND · POLLY · HAS · GONE · TO · DED · POLLY · PAPA[11] · ELLEN · MARY
SENDS · THIRE · LOVE · AND · I · SEND · LOVE · AND A BIG · 🐌

AL, printed in pencil (JAPP, DeLoach; JAPM, 1:115–16).

1. This undated letter was probably written in 1868, before the marriage of JHA and AHH on 17 Nov. 1868. In extant childhood letters, beginning with those in 1869, JA conscientiously remembered to send greetings from "Ma" (her name for stepmother AHHA) to the recipient of her letter. This letter lacks a mention of "Ma." Another clue to the date is the mention of Ponto, the family dog, and "kitty." JA's brother JWA also referred to these pets in his letter of 17 Jan. 1868 (see below). Neither pet is mentioned in letters after 1868.

2. JA's sister SAA was a student at RFS (located in Rockford, Ill., approximately thirty miles east of Cedarville) from the fall of 1866, when she enrolled in the preparatory course, until 1872, when she graduated from the collegiate program. She had been at home for a visit.

3. A family cat. Cats seemed to have been favorite pets for JA. When she and her sister MCA were visiting the Henry C. Forbes family in South Pass, Ill., in the fall of 1867, MCA wrote to SAA at RFS: "[T]hey have three cats here and that suits Jennie" (10 Oct. 1867, UIC, JAMC, HJ).

4. A portrait of Ponto, the family dog, appears in *JAPM*, 27:2. Attributed to JA by Addams and Haldeman family lore, the unsigned pen and ink drawing is more likely the work of SAA, who at her own urging was permitted to take drawing lessons while a student at RFS. During her adult years she continued to draw and paint and developed an avid interest in photography.

5. Alexander Templeton (b. 1835?) born in Union Co., Pa., farmed six hundred acres in Buckeye Twp. in Stephenson Co., Ill., and lived in the village of Cedarville, several blocks south of the Addams home, near the Jacob Latshaws and the Daniel Cobles. The son of pioneer Stephenson Co. settlers, in 1870 his family consisted of his wife Elizabeth Wright Templeton (b. 1833?); children Mary (b. 1864?) and John (b. 1867?), both born in Illinois; and Elizabeth Miller (b. 1798?), retired, born in Pennsylvania. The Templetons, including Alexander's siblings James A. and Walker of Dakota Twp. in Stephenson Co., were Republican in politics and Presbyterian in religion.

6. Ida Coble (b. 1860?), born in Illinois, was the daughter of Julia A. Coble (1833?–1914) and cabinetmaker Daniel P. Coble (1836?–66), both born in Pennsylvania. Ida Coble's brother Charles (1865?–1920) was also born in Illinois.

7. Mary ("Polly") Beer.

8. JA's eldest sister MCA, who in many ways acted in the role of a mother to JA in JA's youth. MCA wrote to JHA and SAA to report the toddler's cute observations long before JA could write herself. "[Jennie] just now asked me when her little finger would be as long as the others," MCA wrote to JHA on 1 Feb. 1865 (SCPC, DG 1). On 24 Sept. 1866 she wrote to SAA to report that "Jennie said I should 'wrap her in the carpet, and send her to Rockford, and then when the girls unwrapped the carpet they would say, Oh! my where did this little girl come from'" (UIC, JAMC, HJ).

9. Ellen, whose last name is unknown, was working in the Addams home as a domestic helper. Family correspondence indicates that Ellen had relatives in the Cedarville area with whom she may have lived; by the summer of 1869, however, she planned to go east. She is not listed in the Addams family household in the U.S. census of 1870.

According to JA's niece Marcet Haldeman-Julius, the Addams family often had two "'hired girls.' But those girls were not regarded as servants. . . . Usually they were the young daughters of neighboring mothers who saw an opportunity for them to receive training for their own future households under the guidance of such an excellent cook and manager as Sarah Addams" (M. Haldeman-Julius, "Two Mothers," 5). It is likely that this practice continued after SWA died, although there may only have been one helper during some periods to assist

MCA and Polly Beer. For the U.S. censuses of 1860, 1870, and 1880, only one servant is listed as living with the Addams family.

10. Meetings for teachers associated with the Union Sunday School were held regularly, judging from the extant correspondence of MCA. The Stephenson Co. Sunday School Union was part of the American Sunday School Union movement started in 1824 to promote secular and religious education in rural areas and emerging communities throughout the United States. In Cedarville, the Union Sunday School, begun in 1868, usually met on Saturday and Sunday in the Lutheran and Reformed church located on Cedar St. parallel to and one street east of Mill St., which ran past the Addams home at the north end of town. JHA, one of its founders, and his daughter MCA were among its teachers in Cedarville. As Cedarville churches became strong enough to support their own Sunday Schools, Union Sunday School became exclusively the Lutheran and Reformed church.

11. JHA.

From John Weber Addams

Beloit. College [Wis.]   Jan. 17. 1868

Dear. Jeeny.

I. received your. letter. to. day. and. was. glad. to. get. it. especially. because. you: wrote. it.[1]

I. was. glad. to. receive. your. love. and. kiss. and. to. hear. that. you had. got. so. far. along. in. your. Second Reader. But. I. guess. you. for.got. to. tell. me. where. your spelling. lesson. was. and. <how> many. times. you: were. up. head.[2]

About. this. time. I. guess. you. are. up. at. the. festival.[3] and. are. eating. your. supper. I. wish. you. a. good. time. How. is. ponto. "*/drawing of dog/*". does he. ever. follow. you. to—school? and kitty ("./*drawing of cat/*" waht. a. kitty) does. she. ever. get. sick.?

I. suppose. you go. to bed. ev.ery. night. at. eight. oclock, well. I. go. to. bed. at. ten. oclock. and. get. up at. six oclock. almost. every. day.

Please. to. Give. this note. to. Pa. an.d. give. him my. love.

Give. my. love. to. Poll.y, and. tell. her. that, I. like. the. cuffs. firstrate, and. Give. my. love. to. Kate, Ally, Mary, Pont. and. Kitty. and. Big. Tom.[4] and tell Ally. that. it. would not. hert. her. or. me. one. bit. if. she. would. write. to. me. and. write. as. good. a. letter. as. you. did. .

Here is. a. Big. Kiss 𝒶 for. you. and I. send. my. love. with. it. .

Hoping. that. this. will. find. you. all. well. I. remain. Your. Dear. Brother.

W.eb.

ALS, printed in ink (JAPP).

1. JA's letter to her brother JWA is apparently not extant. By 1868 JWA could write script; he printed this letter to his youngest sister, however, using the method by which she was learning to write, spell, and identify words. He placed "dots" or periods at the end of most words, on the line rather than raised above it.

2. JA attended public school each year in Cedarville from at least the age of six until she

was ready to go to RFS at age seventeen. In a 5 Nov. 1866 letter to SAA at RFS, MCA announced that "Jennie goes to school" (UIC, JAMC, HJ Supp.). Julia Eastman (Brace), JA's first teacher, recalled more than sixty years later that the "winter of '65, Jane Addams came to school and it was my pleasure to enroll her as one of my pupils" (*Freeport Journal-Standard*, 13 Jan. 1932). In a letter to JA, written on 8 May 1868, JWA asked about her progress at school in the second reader, inquired about the chickens she was helping to raise with the guidance of Polly Beer, and mentioned the playhouses she and her classmates were constructing at school (see UIC, JAMC, HJ; *JAPM*, 1:112–13).

3. Held on 17 Jan. 1868, the festival sponsored by the Union Sunday School was a fundraising effort. MCA helped plan the event, which was reported in the 22 Jan. 1868 *Freeport Journal*. All who attended shared supper; sampled cakes, cookies, and breads made by festival organizers; listened to entertainment, including vocal and instrumental music; and participated in a post office where everyone got a letter. The proceeds amounted to $112.20. This was not the first fund-raising festival sponsored by the Union Sunday School, nor would it be the last. On 31 Jan. 1867, MCA wrote to her father that the festival "took in eighty-nine dollars or thereabouts" in spite of the cold (UIC, JAMC, HJ). Festivals to support the Union Sunday School were also held in January 1869, 1870, 1871, and 1872 (see JA to SAA, 15 Jan. 1869, n. 3, below).

4. In order, Kate Miller, SAA, MCA, a dog, and two cats. Kate Miller was a distant Addams relation, although she is not referred to as a relative by JA. In 1870 Katherine ("Kate") E. Miller (1843?–post 1917), twenty-seven and born in Pennsylvania, lived in Freeport with the family of her brother, livery owner and carriage maker Isaac Hayne (or Hain) Miller (1826?–96), born in Pennsylvania, and his second wife Helen B. (1841–1922), born in England. The siblings were the children of farmer Daniel Miller (1789–1844) and his wife Mary ("Polly") Hain Miller (1801–84) of Sinking Spring, Pa. Kate Miller was a frequent visitor in the Addams home. Near the time of her mother's death, she returned to her home in Sinking Spring, where she lived until her own death.

When JA's parents arrived in the Cedar Creek area of Stephenson Co. in 1844, they lodged for a time with Elizabeth Ruth Miller (b. 1805), JHA's first cousin once removed, and her husband John (b. 1801?) and their family. JHA's grandfather Isaac Addams (1747–1809) had married Barbara Ruth (1744–1832). Isaac H. and John Miller may have been cousins. It is more likely, however, that the family connection was through Kate Miller's mother, Mary Hain. A brother of JHA, Charles Huy Addams was married to Hannah Hain. The Miller and Hain families intermarried over several generations, and Mary Hain Miller and Hannah Hain, although not sisters, may have been cousins.

To Sarah Alice Addams

This is the first extant letter in which Jane Addams mentions her new stepmother, Anna Hostetter Haldeman Addams. On 2 and 3 January 1869, Anna wrote to John Huy Addams, who had left Cedarville on 1 January to attend the opening of the Illinois General Assembly (4 January), where he was a member of the senate, representing Stephenson County: "Well last night Allie [Sarah Alice Addams] slept with me, and in a degree could make amends—for her Father's absence, by being so warm; and lovingly twining her arms about me[.] To be termed 'mother'—or 'Ma' by such warm-hearted kind—children (does not after all make the position a hard one,) As I had supposed for me to fill."[1]

[Cedarville, Ill.]   1869 7 JAN

MY DEAR · SISTER · ALLIE ·

I · HOPE · YOU · ARE · WELL · I · HAVE NOT · NO · INK · WE · WENT · UP · TO · THE · STORE · TO · MALE · SOME · LETTER[2] DID · YOU · GET · DOWN · SAFF[3] · MA SAID · SHE WANTS · YOU · TO · WRIGHT · TO · HER · ONCE · A · WEEK · AND · SHE · WILL · ANSWER · YOU · WILL · YOU · PLEAS · ANSWER · THIS · SOON · MARY · AND · ELLEN · WENT · TO · TEACHERS · MEETIN · LAST · EAVING · WE · ARE · ALL · WELL · EXSE[PT .] I · HAV · THE · HOO[PING · C]O[UGH · T]HAIRE · ARE · [NOT ·][4] MUTCH · NEWS · IN · SEDERVILLE, NOW

I GUSS I WIEL · CLOSE, FOR THIS TIME[5] · MARY · SENDS · HER · LOV · MA · SENDS · HER · LOV · AND POLLIE · SENDS · HER · LOV · AND · I · SENDS · MY · LOVE AND A · BIG 🐚

JENNIE

ALS, printed in pencil (JAPP, DeLoach; *JAPM*, 1:118).

1. SCPC, DG 1.

2. In 1865, when Andrew Johnson became president, the Cedarville post office was moved from Republican Jackson Richart's store a block south of the Addams home to Democrat James Benson's store farther south on Mill St. It returned to Richart's store after Ulysses S. Grant, a Republican, took office in Mar. 1869.

3. SAA returned to school at RFS after Christmas holidays to begin classes on 2 Jan. 1869. She was enrolled as a junior.

4. Page torn at crease in paper; portions of words missing.

5. JA was inconsistent in applying the practice of placing "dots" between all of the words she wrote. In this line, she forgot to insert separating dots between all the words in the sentence except "WIEL · CLOSE."

To Sarah Alice Addams

CEADERVILL ILLINOIS   ·1869 JAN 15

NY · DEAR · SISTER · ALLICE ·

I · HOPE · YOU · ARE · WELL · I WAS · UP · AT · MAGIES[1] · YESTERDAY · AND · HAD · A · NICE · TIME · WE · HAD · A · NICE · TIME · AT · MAGIS · WE · HAD · COMPY · YESTEDDAY · IT · WAS · MRS · DREWSTE · AND · MISS · MOLTON[2] ARE · YOU · LOESOME · SINCE · YOU · LEFT · HOME · WILL · YOU · PLEAS · ANSWER · THIS · SOON · MA · SENDS · HER · LOVE · AND · SEYS · SHE · HOPS · THAT · YOU · ARE · WELL · I · WAS GLAD · TO · RECEIVED · YORE · LETTER · I · GAVE PA · 45 · KISS · INSTEAD · OF · 25 · THAT · YOU · SENT · IN · YOURE · LETTE · PA · SENDS · HIS · LOVE TO · YOU · THAY · IS · NOT · MUTCH · GONE · ON · IN · SEADVERVILL · NOW · THIRE · ARE · GONTE · TO · BE · A · FESTIVAL · HERE · AWEEK · FROM · TO · DAY

One of the earliest stores in the Cedarville village was owned and operated by Jackson Richart and his family. John Huy Addams, in a stovepipe hat, is on the wooden sidewalk. Others in the photograph are Jackson and Charlotte C. Richart and their son Henry with his wife Susan and their children. The store was located at the northwest corner of Mill and Second streets. Jane Addams walked by it daily on her way to school, which was up a hill and to the west on Second Street beyond the store. (JAPP)

· OF · OUR SUNDAY · [SCHOOL ·][3] I · COULDUF · HAD · SONE · INK · THIS · TIME · BUT · I · KANT · WRITE · GOOB · WTTH · INK · MY · COUGH · IS · A · LITTE · BETTER MAGIE · IS · WELL · I · HAVENT · PANTED · ENY · IN · MY · BOOK[4] · SINCE · YOU · LEFT · I · GIVE · MY · LOVE · TO · MISS · SMITH[5] · I · WISH · I · COULD · SEE · YOU · BUT · I · GUESS · IT · IS · OF · NO · YOCE · BECAUSE · YOU · ARE · NOT · HEAR · BUT · WILL · COME · HOME · SOOME · AS · I · HOPE · YOU · WILL · PA · CAME · HOME · THIS · MORING · I · AM · GOIN · TO · WRIGH · TO · WEBBE · TO · DAY[6] · WE · ARE · ALL · WELL I · HAVENT · BINE · TO · SCHOOL · SINCE · YOU · LEFT · I · GIVE · YOU MY · LOVE · AND · A 🐱 I · GUESS · I · WILL · CLOSE · FOR · THIS TIME ·

                                                          JENNIE

ALS, printed in pencil (JAPP, DeLoach; *JAPM*, 1:119–21).

1. Josephine Maggie Stahl (1860–1911) was a JA childhood friend. JA corresponded with her and visited her in Lena, Ill., after the Stahl family moved there from Cedarville. Maggie was one of five children of Hannah Irwin Stahl (1829–69) and widower John Stahl (1823–1910) of Union Co., Pa. Widower Stahl and his family may not have come to Stephenson Co. permanently until 1871. They lived in various small communities in Stephenson Co., including Cedarville (where John Stahl and his brother Aaron, beginning in 1871, operated the Addams mill), Lena, and Ridott Twp. (where by 1878 he owned the Ridott Mills). Maggie Stahl attended Cedarville and Lena schools and never married. She was a teacher. At the time of her death in a Freeport hospital from kidney failure after surgery to remove her cancerous uterus she was serving as the matron at the Settlement Home in Freeport.

The Stahl and Addams families were linked through the marriage of JA's cousin Augustus Addams (1851–93), son of JHA's brother James Huy Addams and Lavina Hinnersheetz Addams, to Amelia Bell Stahl (1854?–91), sister of Maggie Stahl.

The Settlement Home where Maggie worked had originally been established in the late nineteenth century by the local Methodist Conference through three deaconesses, Olive G. Webster, Margaret Niblo, and Eva M. Bailey. In 1894 the Sunday School, English instruction for the foreign-born, and cooking, sewing, and manual-training classes proved too much for Freeport Methodist churches to support. The enterprise was turned over to the King's Daughters, a benevolent organization formed in Freeport in 1888. The institution was reorganized as the Settlement Home in 1904, at which time it became nonsectarian, and incorporated in 1909. The Home, which had different locations at various times in Freeport, provided a broad spectrum of social settlement–type activities: a lounge, reading room, employment bureau, mother's club, Sunday School, and industrial school. In 1926 it changed its focus to specifically work with children and became the King's Daughters Children's Home. It was still operating in Freeport in the 1970s.

2. Given her childhood penchant for confusing the letters B and D, we suspect that JA is actually referring to Emily L. Brewster, wife of Freeport grain dealer J. K. Brewster, and to Bridget Molton or Moulton, born in Ireland, who lived in the Brewster household and was a seamstress.

3. Similar to the festival in Jan. 1868, this one was held on 22 Jan. 1869, to raise money for the support of the Union Sunday School. As MCA described the event, "The festival on Friday evening passed off very well [and] there were a great many there: it was almost impossible to go in to supper, there was such a crowd," she wrote. "I did not have time to visit very much: though there were a great many there that I knew. The amount cleared was most ninety-nine dollars ($99.00) not quite as good as last year, but still a good sum, for my part I am about tired of festivals" (MCA to SAA, 25 Jan. 1869, UIC, JAMC, HJ). By 1872 Cedarville seemed to be tiring of the festival experience, too. "The festival passed off pleasantly," JHA reported, "the crowd was not great but quite pleasant and netted $45.00" (JHA to SAA, 6 Jan. 1872, SCPC, JAC).

4. SAA encouraged JA to develop any latent artistic talent by drawing and painting in a book for that purpose. The drawing book has not survived. JA's extant letters during the 1869–70 period, especially those addressed to SAA, contain numerous small drawings of houses, trees, flowers, and people.

5. Lucy M. Smith (1844–1909), a teacher at RFS and in 1850 one of the seven living children of Ezra C. and Sarah Smith, was born at Coburg, Ontario, Canada. Two years later she emigrated with her parents, making the three-week trek with horse and buckboard to a small farm near Beloit, Wis. She was probably educated in local schools nearby. Although apparently of modest means, her parents must have believed in educating their children. Her brother Lathrop E. Smith (1837–1928) attended Beloit Academy from 1854 to 1858 and became a member of the freshman college class at Beloit in 1858. He left without graduating in his junior year to become a newspaper editor. Lucy Smith entered RFS in the junior class of the Collegiate Dept., 1863–64, graduating with the class of 1867.

Immediately following graduation, Lucy was engaged by RFS as a teacher of rhetoric and the English language in the Normal and Preparatory Dept. During the 1870–71 school year she also taught German. Lucy Smith remained at RFS from 1867 until the end of the spring term of 1884. That autumn she began teaching at Ferry Hall, the Young Ladies Dept. of Lake Forest Univ. in Lake Forest, Ill. (later Ferry College of Young Ladies and then Ferry Hall Seminary). Initially she was engaged to teach English composition, but from 1887 she was listed as instructor in history and English literature. After teaching at Ferry Hall for fourteen years, Lucy Smith resigned in the spring of 1898 and moved to Madison, Wis., where she lived with Lathrop and his family. She died at Madison and was buried in the Smith family plot at Beloit.

6. JWA had returned to Beloit Academy in Beloit, Wis., shortly after 1 Jan. 1869.

To Sarah Alice Addams

CEADERVILL [Ill.]   MARCH 2 [and 3] 18[69]

MY · DEAR · SISTER · ALLIE ·
    I · HOPE · YOU · ARE · WELL. DID · YOU · REACH · SAFE · MARY · CAME · HOME · ON · MONDY · GEORGIE[1] · IS · WRIEING · TO · YOU · TO · I · DO · NOT · KNOW · WAT · TO · SAY · AS · YOU · HAVE · BINE · HOME · BUT · I · GUESS · I · CAN · THINK · OF · SOMTHING · IF · I · TRY · SAM · ADDAMS · IS · HERE KNOW[2] · WE · STARTED · TO · SCHOOL · YESTERY · AND · HAD · A · NICE · TIME · THE · SCHOOL · WILL · CLOSE · AT · THE · END · OF · THIS · WEEK · MAMY · IS · IN · FREEPORT · YET · I · SEND · MY · LOVE · TO · ELLA[3] · IS · MIS · SMITH · WELL · IF · SO · I · SEND · MY · LOVE · TO · HER · AND · A BIG · LOT · OF · KISSES · TO · HER · HERE · THAY · ARE · 1 @ 2 @ 3 @ 4 @ 5 @ 6 @ 7 @ 8 @ IS · THAT · ENOUGH · ILE · SEND · SOME · TO · ELLA · TO · HEAR THAY · ARE. 1 @ 2 @ 3 @ 4 @ 5 @ 6 @ 7 @ 8 @ 9 @ · IS · THAT · ENOUGH · I · HOPE · SO · I. SEND · A · DOUT · AS · MUTCH · LOVE · AS · I · DO · KISSES · WE · ARE · ALL · WELL · I · HAVE · NOT · RED · THAT COMPISION[4] · YET · BUT · I · WILL · WREAD · IT · OF · ON · FRIDY · AND · SEND · IT · TO · YOU · MAGIE · IS · WELL · I · WAS · AT · HER · HOUS · YESTRY · EAVING ·
    WENDSY · EAVING · WE · HAVE · JUST · BINE · DOWN · TO · THE. ICE · AND · HAD · A · NIE · TIME · WE · PLAYED · THAT · THE · ICE · BELONED · TO · THE · KING · AND · WERE · THE · WATER · WAS · THAT · WAS · HIS · BATHING · PLCES · I · GUESS · ILL · CLOSE · FOR · THIS · TIME ·

                                                              JENNY

ALS, printed in pencil (UIC, JAMC; *JAPM*, 1:126–27).

1. GBH.
2. The visitor was likely Samuel Huy Addams (1842–69), a favorite of the JHA family. Probably named for his and JA's grandfather Samuel Addams, he was the son of JA's paternal uncle Charles Huy Addams and aunt Hannah Hain Addams. Samuel Huy Addams served in Com-

pany A, 11th Infantry Regiment, Illinois Volunteers during the Civil War. At the time of his death, he was living in Freeport in the home of Capt. William Young, former commander of Company G, 46th Infantry Regiment, Illinois Volunteers. AHHA informed SAA that Samuel had taken his own life. "He was taken ill Tuesday and on Wednesday morning, ended his life by a wound at his <u>throat</u>—the Dr. said it was temporary insanity—certainly in a clear sound mind he could not have done so rash and horrible an act" (MCA and AHHA to SAA, 8 June 1869, UIC, JAMC, HJ). He was buried in the Cedarville Cemetery. JA also had another cousin named Samuel Addams (1853–95). He was a son of Lavina Hinnersheetz Addams and James Huy Addams and lived in Cedarville.

3. Ella D. Cook, from Ottawa, Ill., was a student with SAA in the junior class in the Collegiate Dept. and in the fourth class of the Conservatory of Music of RFS. She did not graduate with SAA's class in 1872.

4. JA's composition is not extant.

To Sarah Alice Addams

[Cedarville, Ill.]   Jan 15th [and 16th] 1870

my dear sister

I hope you are well[.] i would have wruten to you before but i expected you to write first as you are the oldest[.] you must excuse mistaks because this is my first attemp ir writeing[.][1] I received a letter fron nellie[.] she said she was comeing over as soon as she was well[.][2] i cant think of eny thing to say so i will try to do the best I can[.] i wrote to nellie this Morning in writeing[.] pleas answer my letter soon[.] so pleas dont foget to do it for my sake[.] i wood rather talk with you than to write but as I cant I must do the best I can with writeing[.] georgeie is writeing to you too[.] it is not the 15th eny more but it is the 16th[.] mary and papa and weder and polly are all gone to curch[.] we just cane hone fron cunday school[.][3] ma did not go because she did not fell well enough[.] we had a pretty full chool this sunday[.] it was hailing wen we whent to sunday school but when we cane home it stoped[.] yesterday we had lots of fun <fun>[4] slideing down hill with ida and charlie coble[.][5] we had three sleds idas codles and georgeies and weders[6] sleds and when we got tird we whent in the mill to warn ourselves and played in thare till we got warm[.] maggie was down yesterday and we played King dan queen and had lots of fun[.] polly dident go to curch as i thought she did[.] she cane hone a little while a go so you see i was mistakeing in telling you so dut i guess you will excuse me because you now <now>[7] this is ny first attemp[.] i send lots of love[.] so good by from

Jennie to Allie

ALS (JAPP, DeLoach; *JAPM*, 1:133–35).

1. JA was progressing in her efforts at penmanship. Her letter of 19 Mar. 1869, which she addressed to SAA, was a mixture of script and printing. She formed letters by using script but created words using the printing technique of separating each letter in a word (see JAPP, DeLoach; JAPM, 1:128–29). Perhaps JA did not recall that she wrote at least one earlier script letter, dated 20 [21 and 22] May 1869 and addressed to SAA (see JAPP, DeLoach; JAPM, 1:130–31). In both of these letters she still used dots to separate each word.

2. Helen ("Nell" or "Nellie") O. Hostetter (1860–75), step-cousin of JA, niece of AHHA, and daughter of Mary Anne Irvine Hostetter and John Lichty Hostetter of Mt. Carroll, Ill., was ill with scarlet fever. She grew up in Mt. Carroll, was a JA playmate, and attended Mt. Carroll Seminary.

3. As a child, JA was frequently exposed to formal religion. She attended community sings held at the Methodist church and went to Sunday School and services in various churches. Although there is correspondence that indicates that members of the Addams family attended revivals and temperance meetings in the Cedarville and Freeport areas, there is no explicit evidence that JA did.

4. Printed above the written word *fun*.

5. Charles and Ida Coble lived a few blocks south of the Addams home.

6. JWA.

7. Printed above the written word *now*.

To Sarah Alice Addams

Cedarville Ill   No[v.] 6 1870

My dear sister

I hope you are well[.] I wrote to Clara[1] last sunday but She hase Not ANCerd Me yet[.] george and I whent to freeport and got our piCtures taken[.] we got some taken to gether and some taken a part but those taken together wereent good[.][2] Ma and pa whent to Mr Shaffer[3] furnael[.] Mary whent to the teaChers instute tea[4] and webar whent to and george and polly and I are all alone[.] we go oure teaChers Name is Mr parr[.][5] we had 30 Calers the last I Counted[.] then Mary read us a Cupple stoures before She whent[.] I whent to Sunday SChoal to day in the Marning and afternoon[.] you know you told me a vearCe quenCh Not the Spiret[.] the Sunday we had verCes Commencing with [V.?] we all had the Class I Mean the tearCher to the fokes I heare[.] george Sends his love and So do I

Jennie L. Addams

ALS (IU, Lilly, SAAH; *JAPM*, 1:138–39).

1. Clara L. Young (1849–1926), JA's cousin and the daughter of JHA's sister Harriet C. Addams Young (1817–97) and her husband Nathan (1810?–90), a partner in Fox, Cope and Young, grocers, lived in Philadelphia. Clara never married, and after the death of her mother she and her cousin Miranda E. Addams lived together in the Young home. Toward the end of her life she made her home with her brother Charles and his family in Kansas City, Mo., where she died. She is buried in Laurel Hill Cemetery, Philadelphia, Pa.

2. In his letter of 30 Oct. 1870, to SAA, GBH indicated the photography session took place on 29 Oct.(see UIC, JAMC, HJ). No photograph identified as JA or GBH in 1870 or at ten years of age is apparently extant in any of the collections that we searched. Photographs of JA and GBH, with labels that indicate that they were eight and twelve years of age, are extant; each set, however, could have been taken in 1870 (see illustration, p. 43).

3. J. Wilson Shaffer (1827–70) served in the U.S. Volunteers between 1861 and 26 Aug. 1864, when he retired as a breveted brigadier general. One of the directors of the Second National Bank of Freeport, Ill., organized by JHA, he was a Republican. He had died on 31 Oct. 1870 in Utah after serving only eight months of his appointment by President Ulysses S. Grant as territorial governor.

4. During the 1870s, increasing numbers of young women were becoming teachers, continuing a trend that had begun during the war years. Many had little education and no experience in giving instruction. "Teachers, as a rule, were on a par with their surroundings. If they could read, write, and cipher to the 'single rule of three,' their educational qualifications were deemed sufficient," reported nineteenth-century Illinois historian John Moses (*Illinois Historical and Statistical* 2:993).

In recognition of the need to improve the skills of Illinois teachers, in 1857 the General Assembly created the Illinois State Normal School, which became Illinois State Normal Univ. in Normal. It began classes to prepare teachers in that year near Bloomington, Ill., with an initial class of eighty-eight students in the normal school and forty in the model school program. Its first class of much-sought-after teachers graduated in 1860.

Despite its increasing class sizes, however, the Normal School was insufficient to meet the demand for skilled educators, and teachers' institutes became the primary means for promoting better instructional skills until more teachers' colleges were created. County and township institutes, which lasted from one day to one week, were held at different locations in Stephenson Co. to promote better methodology and share teaching tools. Although not compulsory, the sessions were well attended by teachers as well as by those interested in teaching. It was not unusual to find more than a hundred people, most of them women, in attendance. The institutes provided an opportunity for socializing and finding new jobs.

5. John H. Parr.

To Sarah Alice Addams

Cedarville [Ill.]   Mar 5 1871

My dear Sister Allie

I hope you are well[.] I Sent you a valintine But Mary Said that She thought you dident get it But that you got georgies[.] Weber went up to his farm yasterday.[1] and yesterday George and I went down By the Creek an in comeing home We Came to a little Stream and ~~We~~ I Couldent get aCrost[.] George he got acrost But got one foot in the water But dident get it wet unaCont of his Boots[.] he fixed Come Stones for Me and Coxed Me to come over[.] I wanted to go Back from ware we started from But he dident want to[.] at liat I tried it and got My feet wet.[2] George went up to Mrs Carls[.][3] I would of gone to But I had Company[.][4] We are all pretty well[.] I when up to Mr Carterights in dacakto[.][5] Ma and pa and I all whent up with the tow Bells Fanely[6] last week and Comeing home

the water was wery high[.] a Sleigh hadto get out and Cane in our Big Sled an-
cot of the high water and We Couldent hardely get through But I Must quit[.]
pleas excuse Mastakes[.] I Send lots of Love and kisses[.] Right Soon[.] from

L. Jennie Addams to her Sister Allie

ALS (JAPP, DeLoach; *JAPM*, 1:141–42).

1. By 1870, JWA had begun to learn the milling trade and to farm several hundred acres of
land owned by his father northeast of the Addams home.

2. GBH described the incident of the wet feet on Cedar Creek in the following manner:
"[T]he water was high yester day a we was going around the creek and Jennie got a wet foot.
and we made a Little River thowgh an a Little Island. and then we tred to dam it up and then
after Jennie got a wet foot we went home" (GBH to SAA, 5 Mar. 1871, UIC, JAMC, HJ).

3. Two Carl families lived in Buckeye Twp. according to the U.S. census of 1870. Abraham
Carl (1831–1903) a farmer listed in the U.S. census of 1860 as a miller, and his wife, Sarah H.
Carl (1831–76), had five living children, two of whom, Edgar, ten, and Alice, twelve, attended
school. Mrs. Susan Kryder Carl (1840?–1923), a dressmaker and a widow, lived in Cedarville
with her four children, Raphael, eleven, Mary, ten, Francis M., nine, and Alice (1863–1946),
all of whom were schoolmates of GBH and JA. Her husband Henry C. Carl had died in 1864
of wounds he received in the Civil War. GBH described his visit in a letter of 5 Mar. 1871 to
SAA. "And yesterday I went up to Mellie Carts [Mary Carl] and we we[nt] up in the barn in
the Straw and put a straw under our hair on each Side of our heads and then played we were
Bulls and crept on our hands and knees and run at each other and then we went to the wood
pile and got the saw Back," he reported. "Played se saw and walked on stilts and I am beginning to know how and we went up in the Corn Crib and tryed to make pig pens out of corn
cobs" (UIC, JAMC, HJ).

4. Classmates Ada S. Jackson and Emma Swartz were visiting (see JA to SAA, 12 Mar. 1871,
below).

5. Barton H. Cartwright (1810–95), said to have organized the first Protestant church in Iowa
in 1834, was the Methodist Episcopal minister in Dakota in Stephenson Co., Ill., five miles
northeast of Cedarville. Dakota was platted in the late 1850s after the Western Union Railroad identified its proposed route. The first enterprise in the village was a warehouse in anticipation of trade and transport. By 1860 there were seven houses and a school, blacksmith,
cabinet shop, and general store. The village was incorporated in 1869. There were also three
congregations in Dakota: Presbyterian, Methodist, and Evangelical Lutheran. During the
summer of 1860 the Methodists had constructed a frame building large enough to seat three
hundred. By the late 1870s the congregation numbered one hundred.

6. Thomas (1819–96) and Robert (1813–94) Bell, born in Pennsylvania, came to the Cedar
Creek area, Stephenson Co., in June 1843. Thomas married Jane W. Young, and Robert married Eliza Ann McCool, both from Union Co., Pa. Each couple had five children. The brothers successfully farmed land in Lancaster, Buckeye, and Harlem twps. They were Republicans,
Methodists, and close friends of the Addamses. Thomas Bell was a carpenter by trade, and
Robert Bell became chair of the Lancaster Mutual Fire Insurance Co. when it was organized
in 1869 (the company was still in operation in Freeport in 1970). He also served as superintendent of the County Poor Farm for three years during the mid-1870s and by 1879 had opened
the Tremont House Hotel in Freeport, selling it after two and a half years and purchasing
the Pennsylvania House Hotel in 1882.

To Sarah Alice Addams

Cedarville [Ill.]   March 12 1871

My dear sister Allie

you asked Me in yore Last Letter how[1] my comapy was[.] they was Eda Jackson and Emmie Swartz.[2] the Reason George dident go Mr Cratwrights was because he hato go to school[.] the Reason I dident go to school was because I wasent well and Ma thought the ride would do me good. we go to school and I will tell you about it on fridy[.] instead of doing as Most all schools do We have a Littery Society and we have a President and a Vice President to it and a Secretary and Assistent Secretary[.] George Magars[3] is President and Carrie Richard is Secretary[.][4] the Vice President is only to take the Presidents Place if he is adsent and the Assistent Secretary is to take the Place of the Secretary. the President Calles of the Names of thoes who have Pecies on eny thing, but the Best part of all is the Littery Gassete[.] all the scolars Put in what evryething they Like and wanto. the Secerty puts down evry thing we do and Reads it in the Next Meeting and she Calles the Roll. they was Something in the Last papper real funny[.] it was called Henry Coble and this was what it Read as well as I can Rembar it. Henry Coble is a boy that goes to our School[.] I cannot exactly describe him But I will do the Best I can. just amegine to Bean Poles about 20 feet high and on then a pair of Pants so short that they dont Reach half way down. and on that a Log 6 feet high and a feet in diemeter and on that a coat so big that it Reaches down to the end of the pants. and on the top of the Log is a squash wich henry Made hinself and wich he cales his head and for a hat he has a old basket and as for arms he has his Coat sleaves stuffed full of feathers and sawdust[.] if you immagine that you have henry Coble. it is know sundy school time so good by[.] write soon and pleas excuse Mistakes[.] from yore Loving sister

L Jennie Addams

ALS (JAPP, DeLoach; *JAPM*, 1:143–45).

1. JA seems to mean *who* rather than *how*.

2. Ada S. Jackson (b. 1858?) was the daughter of Mary J. Jackson (b. 1831?). Emma Swartz (b. 1857?) was the daughter of Evangelical clergyman Simon Swartz and his wife Sarah of Cedarville.

3. The only George Magars, Mager(s), Mayer(s), Major(s), or Majer(s) living in or near Cedarville, according to the U.S. census of 1870, was the three-year-old-son of Jonathan Mager or Mayer, a laborer, and his wife, Sarah—obviously, not the president of the literary society.

4. Caroline ("Carrie") Richart (1853–1932) was the daughter of Cedarville merchant Jackson Richart and his wife Charlotte C. Richart. In 1878 she wed William Angle (1851?–1923) of White Rock, Kans., where the couple lived until 1898, when they returned to the Angle farm in Cedarville. They had six children. In 1904 the Angles moved to Freeport.

To Sarah Alice Addams

Cedarville [Ill.]   Dec 3th—71

Dear Sister

The reason I did not write to before was because I did not know you had written to George and I guess you was disappointed not to hear twice week from home: Mary came home last eaveing and expects to stay till Tuesday and expects Mr Linn on Monday:[1] It has been snowing hear to day it seems as if all the Sundays were stormy: It is good skateing and has been for a couple of weeks: George and Frank Stahl[2] went up to the head of the dam on skates yesterday and George broke in twice but did not get wet only his feet: We will have three days vacation this week: Wenday Thursday Friday and then Saturday that will make four day whrite strait along. Polly knit George and I each a pair of new mittens mine are red and Georgeies are grey: The bell ringers are comeing to Freeport and mebey we will go to hear them: We are all well and I hope this will find you the same: Mr March[3] preached hear to day but I did not go he preaches so long: Mrs Carey is very sick with the dropsy they do not think she will live:[4] I have got a new water proof it is a great deal nicer than any other ever was: Budd goes visiting a good deal all alone:[5] Mary Templeton[6] had the chicken pox but is over it now: They was a crasy man came hear last eaveing and this Morning he wanted to tune and play on our Piano: The lS.S. has a new Organ:[7] We are agoin to have a Chrimas tree and George is in a dilogue they are agoin to have: They all send love: Please give my love to all inquiring frinds not forgeting your self good By it getting late from your ever loving

Sister Jennie

ALS (IU, Lilly, SΛΛH; *JAPM*, 1:146–47).

1. On 6 Sept. 1871, MCA wrote to SAA that "today Mr. Linn took his things to Durand. He was here on Monday evening: and yesterday afternoon we took a ride: we were gone about three hours. We expect now to be married about the middle of November" (UIC, JAMC, HJ). MCA and Presbyterian minister JML were married on 9 Nov. 1871 in Cedarville. They went to live in Durand, Ill., about eighteen miles to the northeast, until 1872, when Linn became pastor in Lena, Ill.

2. Frank Floyd Stahl, son of Hannah Irwin Stahl and John Stahl and brother of JA's friend Maggie Stahl, eventually lived in Lena, where he was in the marble business.

3. The Rev. A. March preached for the newly organized Presbyterian congregation in Cedarville.

4. Eliza Ann Wright Carey, wife of the Rev. Isaac Carey, did not live long. She died on 22 Dec. 1871 at the age of forty-six (dropsy, which she may have had, is characterized by an excessive accumulation of fluid in a serous cavity or in the subcutaneous cellular tissue). The Careys had wed in 1851 in Auburn, N.Y., while Isaac Carey was attending Auburn Theological Seminary. When Eliza Carey died, three children remained at home: Jane W. was seventeen, M.E. was thirteen, and Iowa ("Ida") May was ten. Known to her friend and playmate JA as Ida May, she was born in Iowa (see also the introduction to part 1, n. 107, above, and the introduction to part 2, n. 54, below).

5. This family dog died in 1874.

6. Likely the seven-year-old daughter of Alexander and Elizabeth Templeton.

7. "IS.S." may mean the Lutheran Sunday School. A Burdette organ was purchased by the Union Sunday School and installed in the Lutheran and Reformed church in Cedarville. F. J. Burdette, president, moved the Burdette Organ Co. from Erie, Pa., to Freeport in 1894. Mary ("Mamie") Irvine Hostetter (see JA to AHHA, 11 Oct. 1872, n. 6., below), niece of AHHA, gave a piano concert in Cedarville in Apr. 1872 to help pay the balance due on the new instrument. The 1 May 1872 *Freeport Journal* reported that the "programme, which was some[what] varied and comical, was well executed [and] seemingly highly appreciated by the . . . audience in attendance."

From Sarah Alice Addams

Forest Hill Seminary[1] [Rockford, Ill.]   Dec 7. 1871

My Dear Jennie

Finally after a long wait I received a letter from you & was very much pleased to get it.

We have just returned from "a parlor Concert & sociable" given for one of the churches here. There was a great many there & though we had a real nice time we no doubt would have enjoyed it more if there had been fewer.

It is almost twelve o'clock and I can write you but a few lines, as I must blow out my light & go to bed. Miss Howen, (whom I wrote in my last letter home was sick) is a great deal worse[.] Her father mother & sister are all here. Her father just came this evening, & the doctors say than cannot give much encouragement though they have not quite given up all hope.[2] One of the young ladies too is quite sick & a number have taken cold, but otherwise we are all well. Yesterday after school went with Mamie to call upon her Auntie who has been in Chicago since before the fire[3] & returned just about an half hour before we went there. we had a real pleasant time. Mamie expects to go over tomorrow evening and spend the Sabbath. It will do her good as she has not been away from the Seminary except to church for the past ten weeks & is sadly in need of a change.[4]

Miss Smith,[5] Miss Sill,[6] Mamie, Anna Dean, Adile Brown[7] send a great deal of love to you[.]

My love to all, with a great share for yourself.

Did you write that letter to Uncle Harry[8] that you spoke of writing, he would be glad to hear from you. I had a letter from Uncle John[9] & also one from Uncle Dewalt[10] they both sent love to you all at home. Maybe Uncle John will be over at Cedarville a few days in the Holidays[.] But I must bid you good night. Write soon to your loving sister

                                                                    Alice Addams.

ALS (IU, Lilly, SAAH; *JAPM*, 1:148–50).

1. RFS was sometimes referred to as Forest Hill Seminary because its grounds, like Rockford, which was known as "Forest City," had so many trees (for more on RFS, see part 2 below).

2. Elizabeth Haven taught history and English at RFS from the fall of 1870 until she died in Dec. 1871. "The death of Miss Haven was very sad," JHA wrote. "I held her in much esteem, in the acquaintance I had with her [will?] cast a Gloom for a Merry Chistmas at the Seminary—what a warning to be always ready" (JHA to SAA, 19 Dec. 1871, SCPC, JAC 1).

3. The Great Chicago Fire, which burned three and a half square miles of the city, occurred on 8 and 9 Oct. 1871. This pivotal event in the development of Chicago killed 250, left nearly 100,000 people homeless, destroyed more than 17,000 buildings, consumed $200 million worth of property, and was the talk of the country. JHA, who sent his mill products to Chicago for sale and whose former brother-in-law John Harrison Weber (see n. 8, below) and his family lived there, visited the city on 12 Oct., three days after the fire had been extinguished. Two days later he wrote to his daughter, "I just returned from Chicago this morning—I will not pretend to give you description as you have seen accounts which it almost seems impossible to exaggerate. The destruction is simply fearful" (JHA to SAA, 14 Oct. [1871], SCPC, JAC).

4. Mamie may have been Mary White Marston, class of 1871, who served during the 1871–72 school year as a resident graduate at RFS. It would have been difficult for her to go home to San Diego, Calif., except during the summer. No other classmate named Mary or Mamie lived so far away.

5. Lucy M. Smith.

6. Anna P. Sill (1816–89), founder and principal of RFS. For information on Sill's life and career, see the introduction to part 2, nn. 6, 10, and 13, below.

7. Adile C. Brown of Chicago, Ill., and Sara Anna Dean of Monona, Iowa, were enrolled in the junior middle class in 1871. Brown, also a student in 1871–72, did not graduate from RFS; Dean, however, did so in 1873. She married Frank D. Hinckley, chief grain inspector in Milwaukee, and they had five children.

8. John Harrison ("Harry") Weber (1826–91), brother of JA's mother SWA, was born in Kreidersville, Pa., and educated in local schools. He married Caroline Catherine Houck (1828–92) of Mercersburg, Pa., and they had three children, cousins to JA: George Adam (1848–1923), John C. (1851–81), and Edward Yale (1863–1930). Uncle Harry Weber had come west with his father, Col. George Weber, to work the mill and mill store in which his father was a partner at Como, Ill. After his father died in 1851, Harry Weber moved his family to Chicago, where by 1856 he was in the mercantile business. He began as a wholesale milliner in the firm John H. Weber and Co., selling hats, caps, straw goods, and parasols. In 1860 the firm was reorganized as Weber, Williams and Yale and reorganized once again in 1863 as Weber, Williams and Fitch. By 1868 Harry Weber had become associated with Thomas Cogswell in Cogswell and Co. as agents for the Waterbury Clock Co. in Chicago. This enterprise was short-lived, because by 1869 Harry Weber had become a furrier doing business at 296 Clark St. After the Great Chicago Fire, he moved his family to New York City, where he was a member of the firm of Ferry, Conrow and Co., manufacturers of fur hats. He was also a partner in the firm of Solley and Weber in New York City. His sons George Adam and Edward Yale were his partners in the Brooklyn Knitting Co., formed in 1887.

9. John L. Hostetter.

10. Devault Weber (1813–80), brother of JA's mother SWA and eldest son of Sarah Beaver Weber and Col. George Weber, was born in Kreidersville, Pa. He married Mary Ann Hiester (1818–93) of Chester Co., Pa., in 1840. After primary school in Easton, Pa., Weber attended Lafayette College, also in Easton, in 1841, where his father was a trustee. He studied hydraulics and civil engineering but because of ill-health did not graduate. He became so expert in hydraulics that he was often called upon to help settle disputes involving water rights. Between 1851 and 1854 he operated the flour mill of his Uncle John C. Weber (1799?–1860) near Jeffersonville, Pa., and then converted it into a weaving mill that he continued to operate for several more years. The Devault Webers' only child, John H. (1842–43), died before JA was born.

To Sarah Alice Addams

Cedarville Ills   Jan 14 1872

My dear sister
    Georgie recived your letter and as it is my turn to awncer I will do so now; Tell Mamie I will not write to her but will send the pictures in with this letter of yours;[1] Ma came home on Friday we did not expect her till Sturday; I went in yesterday day to have my teeth filled but he found that all that needed filling were filled:[2] Mr Guiteau's[3] expect to move but had not decided yet they thought they would though; A man fell off of the Court house last week and was killed.[4] I had my heir up in tins last night and I coulded get fixed to get to sleep for ever so long, but they curled nicely this morning. But such a time as I had about those tins I went and told Mrs Lacshaw[5] and she said she would tell him and when I went up to get them she had forgotten them and the next time she forgot it again and she felt so ashaned she cut them her self: But I must stop all send love from

Jennie

ALS (UIC, JAMC; *JAPM*, 1:152–53).

1. The enclosure is missing.
2. The Addams family dentist in Freeport was Dr. George P. Kingsley, a graduate of the Baltimore College of Dental Surgery, founded in 1840. Apparently, JA had bad teeth. Throughout her life she consulted dentists in Cedarville, Rockford, Europe, and Chicago for repair work. Most often she seemed to require fillings to replace decayed areas or make extractions. Her visits to the dentist increased during the early 1920s according to her calendars and diaries, and by 1924 she had acquired dentures.
    That the condition of her teeth was a personal trial is certain. While at RFS, she wrote a scientific paper entitled "Teeth" in which she imagined primitive man's view of his world and opined, "But what was his chagrin when he began to examine the means by which he hoped to accomplish to his end. When he compared his puny body to the immense bulk of the elephant, or his muscular power to that of the mastodon. Still his vexation and chagrin were not complete until he examined his teeth until he found what a failure they were. He could neither eat grass like an ox, flesh like a lion or nuts as a squirrel, they were good for every thing and therefore of no use to him, he could cope with none of his powerful enemies with simply his teeth as a defense. They were hardly sufficient even to supply his temporal wants let alone to conquer the world with" ("Teeth"; *JAPM*, 45:1666–67). "Speak to me of this paper," her teacher commented. Poses without smiles seem to have been standard for subjects photographed during the late nineteenth century, and JA was no exception. There are no extant photographs of her smiling until after she had acquired dentures. One wonders, however, whether the condition of her teeth played a role in the sober, sometimes bland, visages of her that are the norm for photographs during the first sixty years of her life.
3. Luther W. Guiteau (1810–80), born in Utica in Oneida Co., N.Y., was a devotee of the Oneida Community and a follower of John Humphrey Noyes (1811–86). He and his first wife, Jane Howe Guiteau (1814–48), married in 1833, settled in Freeport in 1838, and had six children. After losing his mercantile business in 1841 he worked at various jobs in Freeport, successfully repaying all of his debts. He served in the Freeport post office, was elected clerk of the circuit court, and was the first commissioner of schools in Stephenson Co. When JHA organized the Second National Bank of Freeport in 1864, he hired Guiteau as bookkeeper. Within a year Guiteau had become cashier of the bank, a position he held until his death.

Cedarville public school students, 1872. Jane Addams is the second from the left in the first row (standing). She is holding a dark hat with ribbons. Her stepbrother George Haldeman is seated in front on the ground, the third from the left in the front row. John H. Parr, one of the Addams family's favorite teachers, is holding a hat and a book, the fifth from the right near the center of the first row (standing). (RCA)

He married a Freeport widow named Maria Blood (b. 1824?) of Cazenovia, N.Y., in 1854, and they had two children, Luther and Flora Z. (1854–1936). The Guiteau and Addams families were friends, visiting in each other's homes.

4. A new, four-story stone courthouse and jail was constructed between 1870 and 1873 in the Freeport town square to replace the original hand-hewn timber structure built in 1838. No extant Freeport newspaper or Stephenson Co. history carries an account of this incident.

5. Jacob (1817?–90) and Harriet Latshaw (1818?–95) built a tavern and inn adjacent to the Benson store on Mill St. in Cedarville in 1851. The couple had migrated from Sinking Spring, Pa., with the James Huy Addams family in 1850. JML lodged in their Cedarville inn until his marriage to MCA. Jacob Latshaw was the Cedarville tinsmith and also operated a sorghum mill. The Latshaws had one daughter, Della (b. 1852?). The family belonged to the Presbyterian church in Cedarville, and Harriet Latshaw taught a class for the Union Sunday School.

To Anna Hostetter Haldeman Addams

Cedarville [Ill.]   October 11th 1872

Dear Ma

We received your kind note this eveing and was very glad to get it only wish it was longer.[1] The Bantum are getting very tame[.][2] we can catch them and pat them, this eveing they run to meet me when I came from school and, this eveing the hen laid a little egg[.] Christain found it. I got nine for my essay and George the same. This eveing we went up for a music lesson but found Miss Tobias gone.[3]

Mary has the Boy named John Addams Linn.[4] Mr Linn was <here> last night and went home in the morning, he came to a funeral about four miles from here and so came all the way. Thank you very much for remembering the lace[.] I thought as you had so many thing to think of you would forget it. The boys up at school have formed a company and march up at school along the sidewalk and keep step, George is captain and takes his sword and he has had all his flags up; they have a drum horn and flute and two of the boys bring flags, tomorrow they are agoin to have a grand parade and are agoin to start from here, George is ago-in to take his fife and mouth organ, and expect to have a grand time marching through town. Give my love to Nell[5] and as she is not goining east till after the wedding couldent she come home and spend a week with us when you come[.] I should like it very much. But Good bye I most close, give my love to Mamie[,] Jennie[,] Uncle John[6] all inquiring friends but be sure and keep plenty for your-self. George Pa Allie all send love. from your loving daughter

L Jennie Addams

P.S Dont forget about Nellie. L.J.A.

ALS (JAPP, DeLoach; *JAPM*, 1:156–57).

1. AHHA was visiting the John L. Hostetter family in Mt. Carroll.

2. By 1868 JA was learning to raise chickens with the help of Polly Beer (see JWA to JA, 8 May 1868, UIC, JAMC, HJ; *JAPM*, 1:112–13). Tending to the Addamses' flock may have con-tinued to be one of her responsibilities.

3. Mary M. Tobias (b. 1849?) was a music teacher. She lived in Cedarville with her parents, Simon Tobias (b. 1822?), a life insurance agent, and his wife Leah (b. 1827?), both of whom were born in Pennsylvania. JA and GBH took piano lessons, beginning in 1869. When HWH left the Addams household in Jan. 1870 his piano went with him, and AHHA talked her hus-band into acquiring another, and lessons continued through at least 1875. Mary Tobias seems to have taught her pupils on Sunday evenings, using the piano in the Reformed church.

4. John Addams Linn was JA's first nephew. He was born on 9 Sept. 1872 to MCAL and JML at their home in Lena, Ill.

5. Helen ("Nell" or "Nellie") O. Hostetter.

6. Dr. John L. Hostetter and his two daughters, Mary Irvine and Virginia ("Jennie"). Mary Irvine Hostetter Greenleaf (1848–1913), known in the family as Mamie, the daughter of John and Mary Anne Irvine Hostetter, was a favorite niece of AHHA and a step-cousin to JA. Educated in Mt. Carroll, she was a talented musician. According to Hostetter family lore, "She was short, stocky, and enjoyed being waited on" ([C. L. Hostetter and R. Hostetter], "John Hostetter," in "[Hostetter Family]"). As a young woman she gave music lessons to children in Mt. Carroll and Freeport. In 1873 Mamie married Frederick W. Greenleaf (1847–1903), el-dest son of Frances J. Foss Greenleaf and Simon Greenleaf, who would become publisher of the *Savanna* (Ill.) *Times* in 1875. After graduating from the U.S. Naval Academy, Frederick Greenleaf served in the navy until kidney disease forced him to retire from active service in 1884. Mamie lived in Mt. Carroll while her husband was away on duty and often taught music there. The Greenleafs settled in Augusta, Ga., where he became an instructor of science and mathematics in the Academy of Richmond. The couple had two children, Dorn (1877–78) and Ray (1883), both of whom died in infancy.

In the late 1890s, when Frederick Greenleaf returned to active duty during the Spanish-American War, the couple separated and divorced. After the war, he served in Savannah, Ga., as head of the hydrographic office in the Customs House. The Greenleafs were reunited in marriage on 17 Jan., just three days before Frederick died on 20 Jan. 1903. Their life's journey apparently delighted the romantic hearts of Savannah. A lengthy article on Frederick recounting the couple's reunion appeared in the Savannah Morning News on 18 Jan., three days before his obituary on 21 Jan. Mamie Greenleaf buried her husband in Oak Hill Cemetery in Mt. Carroll. After his death, she continued to teach music in Augusta and later in Ardmore, Okla. Throughout her life she was often a guest in the Addams home, where she and her music provided companionship for her aunt AHHA and cousin GBH.

Jennie Hostetter (1850–1934) also was born and grew up in Mt. Carroll. She was married there in Oct. 1874 to D. Harvey Reichard, and the young couple opened a store and pharmacy in Mitchellville in Polk Co., Iowa. According to Hostetter family lore, she was a handsome woman of regal bearing. The Reichards had two daughters, Rose and Mary Barbara ("Babs"). HWH and SAAH lived in Mitchellville, too, between 1878 and 1884 and then moved to Girard, Kans. AHHA maintained a lifelong relationship with the Reichards. In 1903 she sent Rose Reichard, accompanied by her mother, Virginia, to Europe for the summer to study violin. Sometime after 1904, Rose married Herbert Marshall, and the couple moved to Seattle, Wash. Babs Reichard wed Herbert Bartlett Wyman, Jr., in 1904, and the couple settled in Des Moines, Iowa.

From John Greenleaf Whittier

By 1873 Jane Addams had been introduced to the popular poetry of her day. Anna Haldeman Addams encouraged her charges Jane Addams and George Haldeman to read and to write verse. Anna shared a love of poetry with her brother John L. Hostetter and with her elder son Harry Haldeman. His correspondence with his mother between 1870 and 1873 is full of the poetry he wrote as well as the poetry of others he found meaningful enough to quote.

It is not surprising that the young Jane was reading the poetry of John Greenleaf Whittier (1807–92), nor that she found "Barbara Frietchie" intriguing enough to write him a fan letter. Steeped in the lore of the Civil War, she had grown to maturity in its aftermath, which colored every aspect of the period. The heroism and exploits of the male figures who participated in the struggle were memorialized in organization, stone, story, and song and were well known to her. In Whittier's famous and popular poem, female heroism and courage were celebrated. Jane Addams evidently wondered at how closely Whittier's fiction approximated real events.

John Greenleaf Whittier was a Massachusetts editor and poet of Quaker upbringing. He wrote romantically of rural life and New England history and championed themes of social justice. He was an ardent Abolitionist and lecturer at antislavery meetings. Founder of the Liberal Party, he was also the editor of Pennsylvania Freeman *(1838–40) and other periodicals, including the* National Era *(1847–60), to which he contributed many poems and articles. His poetry written in opposition to slavery was collected in* Voices of Freedom *(1846). In his later life (1859 to his death) he wrote increasingly of the religious inspirations of nature.*

"Barbara Frietchie" first appeared in the October 1863 Atlantic Monthly *and then was reprinted in* In War Time and Other Poems *(1864). Written in couplets, it is a literary account of a historical incident of female heroism that occurred in*

reaction to Stonewall Jackson's entry into Frederick, Md., on his way to the battle of Antietam in September 1862. Barbara Hauer Frietschie[1] (1766–1862) was an elderly woman who raised the Union flag in defiance. "'Shoot, if you must, this old gray head, But spare your country's flag,' she said," wrote Whittier. Jackson, in admiration for her bravery, ordered his troops to march on.

Amesbury [Mass.]   2nd Mo. [Feb.] 15—1873.

My dear fr'd.

Barbara Frietchie is <u>real</u>. I have her photograph taken after she was 90 yrs. old; a scrap of her silk dress, and a walking stick from the oaken frame of her house. I had the facts from Mrs. E. D. N. Southworth[2] of Washington in the first place, & they have been confirmed by ample evidence since. Miss Dorothea S. Dix,[3] the philanthropist, visited Frederic City & wrote me a long letter about the brave old lady, who had then just died.

I thank thee for thy generous appreciation of my writings. I am glad to know that they have given pleasure to thee.

I am very truly Thy friend

John G. Whittier.

ALS (SCPC, DG 1; *JAPM*, 1:159–60).

1. See *NAW* 1:673. Whittier spelled his heroine's name "Frietchie."
2. E. D. E. N. (Emma Dorothy Eliza Neville) Southworth (1819–99) of Georgetown, Va., was a popular nineteenth-century domestic novelist who wrote more than sixty sentimental romances, including *Curse of Clifton* (1852), *Missing Bride* (1855), *Hidden Hand* (1859), and *Maiden Widow* (1870). During the Civil War she served as a nurse in a Union hospital near her home.
3. Dorothea I. Dix (1802–87), a humanitarian and reformer, served as superintendent of nurses for the Union army during the Civil War.

The 1875 Diary of Jane Addams

Cedarville, Ill.

Two diaries provide the most detailed information about Jane Addams's life during the period from March 1873 to February 1876.[1] One was kept by Jane herself during 1875. Selections from it are presented below. The other was written by one of Jane's close girlhood friends, Kitty Lutts,[2] between June 1873 and June 1874 while she lived with her widowed grandmother Maria Simpson Clingman on the Clingman family farm north of Cedarville. Like her friend Jane, she took music lessons from Mary Tobias in Cedarville, attended Cedarville public school, and participated in an assortment of social events and parties for young people her age. Her diary is one of the several family diaries edited by Clingman descendants James Bade and Mary Ellen Mau and shared with us in draft form in 1997 as Cedarville Clingmans. Jane Addams's name appears frequently in the brief one- or two-sentence entries.

During the summer of 1873, Kitty recorded a boat ride with Jane on the Addams millpond and described a school picnic that both girls attended. After going to a party at Jane Addams's home on 25 September 1873, Kitty wrote: "We played croquet and took a boat ride and went to the head of the dam and then came back and ate supper. And then we all got weighed."[3] On 6 November 1873 she reported that she went to hear bell-ringers in the evening with Jane Addams and spent the night with her. Kitty proudly noted in her diary that on her fifteenth birthday, 18 January 1874, Jane Addams and their mutual friend Maggie Stahl pulled her ears, a teasing birthday recognition. On 2 and 3 March, Kitty spent the night with Jane because the water in Cedar Creek was so high she could not safely cross it to get to the Clingman farm. Then, on 23 March 1874, Kitty went with Jane Addams, George Haldeman, and four others to a concert. On 10 June 1874 Kitty had dinner at the Addams home, with ice cream and strawberries for dessert. She stayed the night again with Jane on 16 June 1874. As she prepared to leave Cedarville to join her parents and siblings in Missouri, the two friends seemed to spend even more time together. They saw one another in Freeport on 18 June and attended the school picnic in Buena Vista, after which Kitty spent the night with Jane on 20 June. On 21 June they went to Sunday School and church together and met for one last time on 23 June before Kitty left for Missouri on 24 June. The two friends corresponded for a time, but their friendship did not survive to adulthood.[4]

Jane Addams, about fourteen, and childhood friend Clara Belle Lutts, 1874. (Samuel V. Allen, Freeport, Ill.; JAPP)

Jane Addams was fourteen when she purchased a pocket diary. It measured approximately six inches by three inches, and she bought it for seventy-two cents on New Year's Day 1875. From 1 January until 28 June 1875, she faithfully recorded her activities and feelings in it—often with misspelled words and incomplete sentences. Except for sporadic entries in August 1875, the remaining pages of the diary contain drafts of articles and notes she wrote a few years later while a student at Rockford Female Seminary. Her stepbrother George Haldeman also purchased a diary at the beginning of 1875. In an account book dated 1875–76 that George kept are one or two diarylike entries for a few dates in 1875.⁵

In a letter of 28 January 1873, Dr. John L. Hostetter wrote to his sister Anna Haldeman Addams that she should "tell George and Jenny that Irvie⁶ has written in his diary regularly each day."⁷ Perhaps George and Jane gave their cousin John Irvine Hostetter a diary, or perhaps all of the cousins had diaries and their parents were encouraging them to record in them regularly.

Jane Addams's 1875 diary reveals some of her activities and reactions to events around her. It records a period full of change in the Addams family. Her sister Mary, Mary's Presbyterian minister husband John M. Linn, and their firstborn son John Addams Linn moved from Lena, Ill., further east to Winnebago, Ill. Sister Alice, at Rockford Female Seminary as a resident graduate tutor and taking art lessons, became engaged to their stepbrother Harry Haldeman, Anna Haldeman Addams's son, much to the dismay of both Anna and John Huy Addams. Alice's parents decided to send her on a chaperoned tour through Europe with other Rockford Seminary students, and she left in May. Also in May, step-cousin Abram Bowman Hostetter was married to Harriet Stackhouse Irvine in a ceremony in Mount Carroll. Shortly after that, Jane's step-cousin and sometime playmate Nellie Hostetter died unexpectedly while on the way to visit her recently married sister Virginia Hostetter Reichard in Iowa.

Jane Addams's diary mentions all of those events and provides a six-month window on life in the Addams home in Cedarville. The routines of her life fill each page: school, church and Sunday School, friendships, family times and company, pastimes and hobbies, and responsibilities in the Addams home. The number of entries devoted to school is one indication that it was a primary focus in her life. Her sense of humor, competitiveness, need to learn, and will to achieve are all there. There is undisguised pleasure in besting her teacher and her stepmother.

In the volume's front matter, its publisher provided a title page that gave the signs of the zodiac. That was followed by a one-page calendar for 1875, a table of the differences in time between an assortment of U.S. and European cities and Boston or New York City, an interest table, and a Chicago almanac with a prediction of the moon and sun rising and setting for each day of 1875. A blank page was labeled with each day of the year for recording comments. Because page size was small, Addams's entries were of necessity brief. In most cases she filled the entire page with comments. As back matter, the publisher provided several pages marked "memoranda," a format for recording cash transactions labeled "cash accounts," and pages for cash ac-

counts memoranda. Addams used the cash account format for the months of Janu-
ary through March to record the money she had received and spent. We have select-
ed diary entries that reveal what she did and thought and shed light on her role in
the community and family. The entries, arranged chronologically, are presented by
month and include the period from January through the end of June.

1. There is apparently no extant JA correspondence for the period from Mar. 1873 to Feb. 1876.

2. Clara Belle ("Kitty") Lutts (1859–1947) was the daughter of Mary Clingman Lutts, born in Ohio, and M. Grove Lutts, born in Pennsylvania. She was the granddaughter of Maria Simpson Clingman and Josiah Clingman. When Kitty Lutts was born, her parents lived on a farm in Harlem Twp. in Stephenson Co. By 1870 they had moved to an eighty-acre farm in Kent Twp. in the same county, south and west of Cedarville. In June 1873, when the Lutts family, including Kitty's brothers Edward (1862–1935) and Rufus (1870–1965), moved to a farm in Missouri, she remained in Cedarville. A year later she joined them in Missouri.

When the Lutts family left Missouri for a farm in Earlham, Iowa, in 1880, Kitty Lutts went with them. In 1889 she wed William Knox (d. 1928), and they settled on a farm near Earlham. The couple had at least two children, Lorena (1889–1978) and Harold (b. 1903). In 1902 Kitty and her husband moved to an eighty-acre farm they had purchased in Missouri. After 1903 they moved farther west to Neosha Falls, Kans., where Kitty's widowed mother joined them until her death in 1906. After Knox died, Kitty went to live with her daughter Lorena Knox Rudolph in Pennsylvania.

3. Bade and Mau, *Cedarville Clingmans*, 185. It is likely that the Addams mill had one of the few scales in the village. Getting to weigh oneself was a treat.

4. On 30 May 1880, Kitty wrote to JA: "O! when will we meet? how I long to see you" (SCPC, JAC). See also JA to Clara B. Lutts, 14 [and 17] Jan. 1880, below.

5. G. Haldeman, "Account Book, 1875–76."

6. Step-cousin John Irvine ("Irvie") Hostetter (1857–1923), like his father John L. Hostetter, became a physician. He was born in Mt. Carroll, Ill., and attended Mt. Carroll Seminary. After receiving his medical degree from Chicago Medical College, Ill., he settled in Colo, Iowa, in 1880, where he practiced until his retirement about 1912. In 1885 he married Lillian C. Hull, and they had two children, John Hull and Mary Greenleaf.

7. John L. Hostetter to AHHA, 28 Jan. 1873, UIC, JAMC, HJ Supp.

Friday, January 1, 1875.

To day I spent at Lena[1] and had a very pleasant time indeed, we went in the bob-sled, we had a load of Weber, Irvie Hostetter, Nell, Kate Miller, Alfred Zaph,[2] George and myself coming home we had the addition of Alice Pa and Ma went in the cutter. After dinner we (that is Irvie, Nell, Alfred, George and I) and had our pictures taken.[3]

We sung almost all the way home and stopped to wish Lena Myers[4] a "Happy New Year," evry sled we met we greeted in the same way. Mary and the ladies were receiving callers all day, more or less.[5] After dinner on our walk we purchased two diaries at Chas. Waite's store.[6]

1. Lena, located in the rolling hills of northwestern Illinois, originally settled about 1835 and named Alida, is approximately ten miles directly west of Cedarville. It was surveyed in 1853 after the Illinois Central Railroad, which began service in 1854, was laid out. By 1860, with a

population of about six hundred, Lena became a shipping point for agriculture supplies and produce. During the 1880s the community boasted 1,500 residents, seven churches, two grain elevators, two hotels, forty assorted stores, and a weekly newspaper, public school, opera house, bank, wagon factory, mill, lumberyard, and cooper shop. Between 1872 and 1875, MCAL and JML lived in Lena, where JML was a Presbyterian minister. Laura Shoemaker, whom JWA would marry on 16 Mar. 1876, also lived in Lena (see Biographical Profiles: Addams, Laura Shoemaker).

2. Alfred Zapf, fifteen in 1880, lived in Freeport and was the son of Edward Zapf (1831–74), a baker and merchant there who had died in the state mental hospital in Elgin, Ill., and his wife, Elisabeth (1836–89).

3. For the photograph see SCPC, JAC.

4. Probably Lena Meyer, six in 1875, and daughter of carpenter Henry Meyer, forty-seven, and his wife Caroline, forty-one, who lived with at least two other children, Anna, twelve, and Louisa, ten, in Erin Twp. in Stephenson Co., southeast of Lena.

5. In an article entitled "Did You Call?" the *Freeport Journal* of 6 Jan. 1875, observed, "The weather (about calling hours) was of an undefinable character, and what your coffee-fed Londoners would call 'nasty'." It was the custom to spend New Year's Day calling on neighbors and friends to wish them well in the coming year.

6. Gen. Charles Waite, born in 1837 in Orange Co., Vt., was a veteran of the Civil War. A druggist who later became a banker in Lena, he opened his store in 1869. He married Emily Clement of La Porte, Ind., in 1866, and they had three sons, Charles C., Daniel, and Frederick P.

Saturday, January 2, 1875.

. . . In the evening, George, Alice and I went to singing,[1] but Oliver and Emma[2] came and she did not stay until it was out. We bought a singing book[3] this evening.

1. A community sing was held most Saturday evenings in the Methodist church in Cedarville, with George W. Barber presiding. The Addams family, including JA and GBH, attended regularly, although it clearly was not an activity favored by JA. In her 1875 diary on Saturday, 10 Apr., she recorded: "We went to singing and joys of joys it is the last night" ("Pocket Diary, 1875[–81]"; *JAPM*, 28:1549). JA and GBH had participated in group singing in Cedarville since at least the fall of 1869.

2. JA was referring to Oliver Zipsie (b. 1865) and Emma Zipsie (b. 1862), her and GBH's classmates. They were the children of farmer and shoemaker Jacob (1814?–75) and Catherine (1818?–87) Zipsie. The family lived in Buckeye Twp.

3. It was likely that the Addams family purchased a collection of hymns gathered and issued by George W. Barber; the only singing book identified from the records of books once owned by the family, however, was a Presbyterian hymnal with the date 1876 inscribed and the signature of JHA. We were unable to locate a copy of any Barber collection of hymns.

. . . Monday, January 4, 1875.

This morning school began and we had the addition in our room of seven new scholars.[1] It was very cold and we all set around the stove. Mr Moore[2] called George and I up to his desk to ask us what we would study this term in place of history finly concluded on Philosophy.[3] This evening Pet Stahl[4] came over and we played jack-straws and old maid and had lots of fun. Mrs Stahl is not very well. After Pet was gone Ma, George and I played snap.

1. No complete list of children attending the Cedarville public school with JA exists. In 1875 she and GBH were students in the High Dept. There were 109 students enrolled during the May–June 1875 period, with an average daily attendance of 82 (*Illinois Monitor*, 16 June 1875).

2. C. W. Moore was not a teacher favored by JA and GBH. Shortly after the new school year began in 1873, AHHA must have reported this to her son HWH. He replied on 23 Nov. 1873, "I am sorry the children dont—take avery enthusiastic interest—in school—however children seldom do—I've no doubt—from what you and Alice say—the new—teacher is n't—the most—promising in the world—but—then—he <u>may</u>—improve" (UIC, JAMC, HJ).

3. Later referred to by JA as "natural philosophy," on 2 Feb. she reported in her 1875 diary, "We had a big time in our philosophy class about the pendulem" ("Pocket Diary, 1875[–81]"; *JAPM*, 28:1515). On 8 Feb. her class studied sound and on 11 Feb. the velocity of light. She wrote on 19 Feb.: "[I]n our philosophy class about umber and pemumbra Mr Moore put a diagrahm on the boa[r]d of the sun and earth to illustrate and got me so I did'ent understand it at all, and got real provoked" ("Pocket Diary, 1875[–81]"; *JAPM*, 28:1519).

4. One of JA's classmates at school in 1875 was Fairy Mabel Stahl (1864–1932), also called "Pet." She was the daughter of Sarah E. Winklebeck Stahl (1838–1918) and Aaron Stahl (1834–1904), both born in Union Co., Pa. They came west in 1858 and settled initially in Lena. In 1871 Aaron joined his brother John in operating JHA's flour mill in Cedarville, Ill. The Stahls eventually returned to Lena. Pet Stahl attended Cedarville and Lena schools. She and JA's friend Maggie Stahl were cousins. She married Irvin J. Kiplinger on 19 June 1883. In 1910 the Kiplinger family moved to Freeport, where they operated Kiplinger and Son, a lumber and coal business, and lived for the remainder of their lives.

. . . *Wednesday, January 6, 1875.*

This morning Pa went to town, Ma intended going but finly concluded she wouldent.[1] This afternoon Miss Echart[2] came up to visit the school and of course I failed in Latin.[3] This afternoon about three o'clock, Emma went home and I had the extreme pleasure of getting supper.[4]

This evening Pa came home and brought us each a new book. After supper Ma[,] George and I pladed a game of four handed chess. And Ma & I were beaten.

1. JA's step-cousin Sarah Hostetter recalled that "Promptly at nine o'clock on Wednesday & Saturday mornings the carriage was at the door, and year after year . . . [JHA] would be met driving the well kept gray team, so well trained they knew where to avoid the bumps in the road and how to straddle the ditches" ("Few Reminiscences," 2). In another written reminiscence, she indicated that he would have dinner at the Pennsylvania House Hotel. "We could always meet him there and go to Cedarville for a gay visit" ("[Reminiscences]," 4).

2. No one by the family name of Echart appears in the U.S. census returns for 1870 or 1880 in the three townships in which Cedarville was located. JA's Miss Echart may have been a distant relative who was visiting. Two uncles of brothers JHA and James Huy Addams were married to women from an Eckert family in Pennsylvania. Peter Addams (1784–1852) married Susan Eckert (d. 1842), and Isaac Addams (1779–1884) married Catherine Eckert.

3. JA and GBH had studied Latin for most of the 1874–75 school year. JA recorded on 19 Jan. 1875: "This morning Mr Moore gave me eight latin papers to correct and it kept me very busy indeed all day" ("Pocket Diary, 1875[–81]"; *JAPM*, 28:1508). On 3 May 1875 she commented, "We have translations in latin every day now and it is quite interesting" ("Pocket Diary, 1875[–81]"; *JAPM*, 28:1561). JA's manuscript translations of "Caesar's Commentaries on the Gallic War," books 1–4, chap. 36, are extant. She wrote them carefully into copybooks that are in the RCA and may be seen on *JAPM*, 27:20–116.

4. Emma, whose last name is unknown, was the cook in the Addams household in 1875. Unlike the other domestic servant who was a laundress and cleaning maid, she did not live with the family. Perhaps she was the daughter of a nearby family and earned extra money cooking while continuing to live with relatives.

JA noted in her diary whenever Emma was not available to get meals, for that chore evidently fell on her. In an entry of 25 Mar. 1875, she reported that "Emma went home to day and I had to get supper" ("Pocket Diary, 1875[-81]"; *JAPM*, 28:1541). Just four days later, on 29 Mar., she complained, "This morning got up very early and had breakfast ready by six o'clock. . . . Emma came home just about noon, if we would of been sure of her coming I would of gone to Lena to day and cam back Wednesday but I could'ent" ("Pocket Diary, 1875[-81]"; *JAPM*, 28:1543). Now and then JA assisted Emma. "I helped Emma get supper and things past off very plesantly and socibaly all around," she wrote on 25 May 1875 ("Pocket Diary, 1875[-81]"; *JAPM*, 28:1572).

JA, remembered by her step-cousin Sarah Hostetter as a good cook, frequently practiced cooking sweets. She attempted taffy, gingersnaps, and sugar cookies with some success. As she indicated in several 1875 diary entries, however, she had difficulty with crullers that were too sweet (see JA, "Pocket Diary, 1875[-81]," 19 Jan. 1875; *JAPM*, 28:1508); "dreadful waffles" that stuck or burned (see 18 May 1875, below); and a crumb pie that had "too much butter and it all run together" ("Pocket Diary, 1875[-81]," 20 Feb. 1875; *JAPM*, 28:1524). She did not impress her stepmother AHHA with her prowess. On 3 Apr. 1875 the diary entry states: "I tried to make pies and they were all right I thought but Ma thought otherwise" ("Pocket Diary, 1875[-81]"; *JAPM*, 28:1545).

Keeping good domestic help was a chronic Addams family problem. With the exception of Polly Beer, treated as near-family because of her long association as nurse with the Webers and Addamses, servants in AHHA's home came and went with some frequency. U.S. census returns of 1860, 1870, and 1880 for Cedarville list the names of three different servants for the household. On 8 Feb. 1875, JA wrote: "Our new girl came this afternoon and our old one left. I think I will like this one better. If appearances have any thing to do with it. I will certainly" ("Pocket Diary, 1875[-81]"; *JAPM*, 28:1518). "Our new girl irons beautifuly and is real nice and modest," she praised the next day ("Pocket Diary, 1875[-81]," 9 Feb. 1875; *JAPM*, 28:1519).

Thursday, January 7, 1875.

This morning I got the breakfast as Emma has not yet arrived.

After I went up to school we (that is the philosophy class) sent up a petion to Mr Moore to have our class recite in the afternoon, he did not exactly scold but he did not like it very well. This evening Lizzie[1] came home with me to spend the night[.] Pet Stahl came over and we had a very nice time playing snap and old maid. Lizz won two games of snap and George one.

1. JA's cousin Elizabeth Belle ("Lizzie") Addams (1861–1900), daughter of Lavina Hinnersheetz Addams and James Huy Addams, aunt and uncle of JA, was born in Cedarville, graduated from the Cedarville public school, and lived with her parents and siblings on the road to what became the village of Red Oak, Ill., in 1887, two miles west and a little north of Cedarville. She attended Northern Indiana Normal School and Business Institute in Valparaiso, where she was enrolled in the Commercial Dept., a member of the class of 1886. On her grave marker in the Cedarville Cemetery her name appears as Mrs. Lizzie Addams Tilten (or Tilton).

... *Saturday, January 9, 1875.*
This morning it is so cold Pa did not go to town. In the forenoon George
and I drew and painted pictures. In the afternoon Pet and Mrs Stahl came over.
We drew a while and then played charades. I mended my purple dress which
was out at the elbows. We did not go to singing as it was too cold. But Ma, George
and I played four handed chess and afterwards Natural History.
It is still cold though not as cold as it was this morning.

Sunday, January 10, 1875.
This morning it is still cold, but not as severe as it was last night.
Mr Barber[1] was not at Sunday School[2] and Mr Montelius[3] tought our class.
We were very sorry Mr Barber was not there.
Mr Wrights[4] were not in too church and Mr Mitchell[5] had a big time too
get any one too sing, he asked me if I could lead.
Alice Tobias[6] sit with me in our pew.
Mr Michell wes here too dinner. His text was, Golry too God in the highest,
and on earth good peace to men.[7]

1. George W. Barber (1835–1913) was active in planning musical concerts and holding community sings on Saturday evenings in the Cedarville Methodist church. According to the *History of Stephenson County, 1970*, he enjoyed something of a national reputation for his popular collection of gospel hymns, which appears to have had a considerable circulation in the
neighborhood to promote community sings. Unfortunately, no copies of this work seem to
have survived. He was the leader of the fifteen-member Cedar Cliff Band, sometimes called
the Cedarville Band or the Independent Band of Cedarville after he and his brother Samuel
organized it in 1873. With JHA he helped initiate the Buckeye Mutual Fire Insurance Co., created on 13 Apr. 1867, and the Cedarville Farmers Union Club in 1871. The Barber family, including George and his brothers Samuel and Thomas, came to Cedarville in 1843 with a group
of fifty-four emigrants in three wagons from Union Co., Pa. They bought land, established
stock farms for thoroughbred Jersey cattle, and became active Republicans and Methodists.
    2. Union Sunday School.
    3. Marcus Montelius.
    4. JA received an undated award of merit from Sunday School teacher J. Lawson Wright
sometime during her youth. She could have been referring to him and to his wife Rose Clarridge Wright. The Wrights were married in 1871. J. Lawson Wright, born in Union Co., Pa.,
in 1837, was one of five children of Pascal and Jane Lawson Wright, emigrants to Stephenson
Co. in 1838, both of whom died in 1872. He attended local schools and graduated from Illinois State Normal Univ., Normal, in 1873. After teaching school for ten years in Ogle, Carroll, and Stephenson counties, he established a book and stationary store in Freeport with a
succession of partners. An alderman in Freeport, he was also a Mason and a Presbyterian.
    JA might also have been referring to either of two brothers of Pascal Wright. John and
William Wright followed their sibling to Stephenson Co. in 1843 from Union Co., Pa. John
A. Wright (1825?–89), who was a farmer and served as treasurer of the building committee
for the Presbyterian church in Cedarville, was married in 1862 to a second wife, Mary B. Heise
Wright (1830–1901). William Wright, born in Pennsylvania in 1820, was a farmer, Presbyterian, and Republican and was married to J. Runner Wright.
    5. Lewis Henry Mitchell (1846–1904) followed JML as minister of the Cedarville Presbyterian church. He was a graduate of the Univ. of Wisconsin in 1872 and had attended the Union

Seminary of New York and the Presbyterian Theological Seminary (McCormick Theological Seminary) in Chicago. After being ordained in 1874, he served churches in Cedarville and Dakota, Ill., from 1874 until 1878, when he went to Portage, Wis. After serving during the 1880s and until 1893 in various communities in Minnesota, he held churches in the Chicago area during the 1890s, going to Pasadena, Calif., between 1901 and 1904, where he died.

6. Alice Tobias (b. 1861?) was the daughter of Simon and Leah Tobias and sister of JA and GBH's piano teacher Mary Tobias. She attended public school with JA and GBH.

7. The phrase "good peace to men" is written perpendicular to the text and in the right margin of the page.

Monday, January 11, 1875.

This morning there was a light snow. It is not so very cold. On my [way] to school I met little Susie Midigh[1] and walked up the hill with her, and had quite a conversation. This evening I had to stay after School to spell neighing.[2]

Pa went to Freeport to day as it was so <stormy> Saturday he could not go, he brought home a pair of forceps and this evening ma pulled one of his back teeth.

Nothing of very much importance happened to day. I tried an experimet with sealing wax.[3]

1. JA seems still to have been confusing capital *M* and *N*. This is likely Susan Neidigh (b. 1870), the daughter of David Neidigh (b. 1815?), a farmer born in Pennsylvania and prominent in the Evangelical Assn. of Cedarville, and his wife Mary (b. 1845?), who was also born in Pennsylvania. By 1880 the Neidighs had at least nine children.

2. Judging from her grades and extant documents written by JA during her youth, she found spelling her most difficult subject. Her spelling scores during the five years between 1870 and 1875 fluctuated each month, from a low of 3 to a high of 8.6 of a possible perfect 10. On 25 Mar. 1875 she explained that she and GBH received perfect scores in arithmetic, reading, and Latin and bemoaned, "But alas in spelling!" ("Pocket Diary, 1875[81]"; *JAPM*, 28:1541). JA, GBH, and their classmates participated in round after round of spelling bees. Eighteen 1875 diary entries contain descriptions of various contests. In none of the entries does JA identify herself as an individual winner.

3. The phrase "sealing wax" is written on the right side of the text near the bottom of the diary page and perpendicular to the text.

Tuesday, January 12, 1875.

This forenoon Pa came up and visited our school.

This evening at five o'clock we had quite a dinner-party.

They were here, Ida and Mrs Bucher,[1] Mr and Mrs Templeton, and small daughter,[2] and Mr and Mrs Moore,[3] and last but not least Rob Bucher. We had a turkey roast and other good things.

In the evening we played snap and old maid. George and I played a duet, and George played the German Rhine.[4] Pet and Mrs Stahl are sick.

1. Catherine Bucher (1831?–1918) was the widow of Samuel R. Bucher (1827?–74), the first physician in Cedarville. She and her two living children, Ida M. (1856–1922) and Samuel Robert (1868–97), lived in a brick house on the corner of Cedar and Mill streets, a few short blocks south of the Addams home. Dr. Bucher's practice was assumed by Dr. Smith C. Thompson (1850–1933) in 1874. Thompson graduated from Rush Medical College in Chica-

go, in 1872 and practiced for a year there at St. Luke's Hospital before coming to Cedarville. Ida M. Bucher married Thompson in 1879, and the couple continued to reside in Cedarville. After the death of Dr. Charles G. Strohecker, Bucher followed by Thompson became the Addams family physicians. It was probably Bucher who attended SWA at the birth and death of the ninth Addams child and at her consequent death.

2. Likely Alexander and Elizabeth Templeton and a new baby. By the early 1880s the family had moved to Cleveland, Tenn.

3. School teacher C. W. Moore and wife, Emma.

4. JA and GBH had been taking piano lessons for at least five years.

... *Thursday, January 14, 1875.*

This morning it is eighteen degrees below zero.

We went to school as usual working examples goes very slowly. In the evening after supper George and I shelled corn for a while and then George, Ma, and I played history natural. Ma beat one game and so did George and I came very near it. This morning Pa showed me how to work a couple of examples, it seems as if we never could get the whole ninte seven of them.[1] ...

1. JA is referring to a set of ninety-seven arithmetic problems labeled "Promiscuous Examples," appearing on pages 334 through 341 of *Robinson's Progressive Practical Arithmetic* by Daniel W. Fish (Chicago: Ivison, Blakeman, Taylor & Co., 1872). Her copy of this text with her name on the front endpaper is part of a small collection of Addams family books in the Rare Book Room of the Coleman Library of Rockford College, Rockford, Ill. During the 1874–75 school year, JA studied arithmetic and algebra. Throughout the six months of 1875 diary entries, there are several that indicate that she was not the only one who struggled to complete this set of mathematics problems successfully. Various family members and her teacher, C. W. Moore, had some difficulty as well, a fact that obviously gave her secret pleasure. Her diary entry for 26 Jan. reads in part, "This morning I had an example that I would get $2.30 too much, and Mr Moore said 'O that is very simple' and tried it and came $8.52 out of the way it made me feel quite grand" ("Pocket Diary, 1875[–81]"; *JAPM*, 28:1512). She finished the examples, as well as two weeks of study about the metric system, on 26 Feb., according to her 1875 diary.

... *Sunday, January 17, 1875.*

This morning we got up pretty late, and had to be in a great hurry with my work, and then got to Sunday S. long before any body else. We had rather an interesting lesson, and I learned that we should try and remember the goodness of God. Went to the M. Church[1] but there were very few people there, as old Mr Plowman[2] was buried to day. And so Mr Conley[3] dismissed the rest of us. This afternoon finished the "gates Ajar.["][4] And begun "Pickwick Papers"[5] which I think will be interesting.

1. Sunday School and Methodist church.

2. Listed in the U.S. census of 1870, Thomas Plowman, seventy-five and born in Maryland, lived and worked as a day laborer and carpenter in Buckeye Twp. His tombstone in the Freeport City Cemetery indicates that he died on 16 Jan. at age eighty-two. His wife Mary, born in Pennsylvania, was sixty-five when she died in 1862. They had at least four children.

3. The Rev. James M. Conlee (1833–95), appointed in the fall of 1874 to serve the Methodist Episcopal churches in Dakota and Davis, Ill., by 1875 was an ordained elder and also preaching in Cedarville. He preached in various communities in northern Illinois until he retired in 1888.

4. According to her 1875 diary, JA began reading *Gates Ajar* on 13 Jan. "[T]hink I will like it there is not much in the story itself but there is a good deal in the book" ("Pocket Diary, 1875[–81]"; *JAPM*, 28:1505). Elizabeth Stuart Phelps (1844–1911), born Mary Gray Phelps, began writing *Gates Ajar* when she was twenty. Published in 1868, it was the first of what would become fifty-seven books, some of which were feminist novels of women in careers, and hundreds of stories, essays, and poems to be issued during her life. Of particular note was *Doctor Zay* (1882), a novel about a female physician. Exceedingly popular before the end of the nineteenth century, *Gates Ajar,* an anticlerical novel relating the process in Christian redemption, sold eighty thousand copies in America and one hundred thousand in England.

Phelps was educated at Abbott Academy in Andover, Mass., and then in Mrs. Edwards School for Young Ladies. She was certainly influenced by the scholars and the orthodox religious climate at Andover Seminary, where her father and grandfather taught. Both her mother, Elizabeth Stuart Phelps, and her father, Austin Phelps, were published writers. After her mother's death in 1852 she took her name. Her father remarried twice, providing her with two stepmothers, neither of whom she apparently felt close to. When she was forty-four, she married twenty-seven-year-old Herbert Dickenson Ward, a graduate of Andover Seminary.

5. Charles Dickens's (1812–70) *Pickwick Papers: The Posthumous Papers of the Pickwick Club* was serialized in monthly sections between Apr. 1836 and Nov. 1837 and published in novel form at the end of 1837. Written when Dickens was twenty-four, it is a humorous collection of separate tales revolving around Samuel Pickwick, founder of the Pickwick Club, and the travels, observations, and misadventures that members of his club experience. Cedarville teacher Eva Pennell would recall with pleasure the Dickens parties given by Sarah Hostetter and her siblings in which guests dressed as their favorite characters, including those from the *Pickwick Papers.* In a winter 1876–77 party, Charles Linnaeus Hostetter played the role of Mr. Wardell of Dingley Dell from *Pickwick,* and Abe Hostetter was Pickwick himself. Other guests came attired as characters from various Dickens works and were treated to a supper of oyster stew, sandwiches, and pickles. Dickens parties were popular. Illinois Gov. and Mrs. Richard J. Oglesby hosted a "Dickens' Disciples" party in the Governor's Mansion in Springfield on 15 Feb. 1885 as a benefit for a local choir.

Monday, January 18, 1875.

To day went to school and every thing went off as uasal.

This evening there was a spiritual or magic preformance up in the hall.[1] George, Pet and I went first and there was not any one there but a few of the band.[2] After awhile Mr and Mrs Stahl, Ma and Emma and that was about all who came, but a few boys[.] The most wonderful feat was the transfrormation of a man from a basket to a locked and sealed box, tied up with a hudred feet of rope by <two of> the audience. Came home sleepy . . .

1. In 1875, the Cedarville Town Hall was located near the northeast corner of Cherry and Mill streets.

2. JA was referring to the Independent Band of Cedarville, also called the Cedar Cliff Band, composed of approximately fifteen members and organized on 8 July 1873 to play at a variety of public functions in and around Cedarville. This Cedarville institution was finally disbanded after seven of its members entered the U.S. Navy during World War II.

... Saturday, January 23, 1875.

This morning Pa and Ma went to town and left George and I to keep house. I got through my work about ten o'clock and we took our sleds and went sliding on the creek we would start on the ice under the bridge and slide clear down to Mr Hixson's.[1] This afternoon I gave my drawers a thorough reading[2] up. Just as we were eating supper Mr Mitchell came to spend the night. This evening George and I played or rather went to singing but it did not last long.

1. Solomon Hixon (1824–84), a member of the Evangelical church of Cedarville, was born in Union Co., Pa. He made barrels for JHA's Cedar Creek Mills between 1855 and 1867, after which he became a farmer. In 1853 he married Margaret Snyder (1834?–64), and after she died he married her sister Mary in 1866. Among the Hixon children, six of whom lived to maturity, were Luther and Mary, ages eleven and seven in 1870, and William and Ada A.
2. JA may have meant *read[y]ing*.

... Friday, January 29, 1875.

To day we had our monthy examnation and every thing went off nicely. Ma came up in the afternoon to visit us and hear our latin recite.[1] I am begining to be interested in "Pickwick Papers" I did not like them very much at first. I have worked sixty six examples,[2] it begins to go a little faster now. To day we had a written examnation in philosophy and it seems to me he picked out the hardest things he could find. George has a sore throat now.

1. Public oral recitations and examinations were the norm in public schools throughout Stephenson Co. In addition to those held once a month attended by parents, school officials, school board members, and the public, there were term-end examinations and also Friday recitations in the Cedarville public school.
2. JA was still working "Promiscuous Examples" in *Robinson's Progressive Practical Arithmetic*.

Jan. 1875 entries: AD (Addams, "Pocket Diary, 1875[–81]," CAHS; *JAPM*, 28:1499–514).

... Friday, February 5, 1875.

To day we had a meeting of our society and an election of officers.[1] We began the meeting with a declaimation by Alma Richart[2] and topped off with "The Day is Done."[3]

Pa and Ma were the only spectators we had. The best preformance was a dilogue entitled "Old and New["] which brought down the house as the saying is. Albert Tobias[4] was elected President and Mary Templeton secetary. Mr Moore does not like our choice of secetary at all, but the boys did it for fun and it cannot be helped[.]

1. The school literary society was described by JA in her letter of 12 Mar. 1871 to SAA (see above).
2. Alma Richart (1863?–1954) was the daughter of Cedarville merchant Jackson Richart and his wife Charlotte C. Richart. After her mother's death in 1914, she married Charles Johnson. The couple moved to Fostoria, Iowa, where she died.

3. On 25 Jan. JA wrote, "I finished learning, 'The Day Is Done' which I intend to speak next meeting, I think it is perfectly beautiful" ("Pocket Diary, 1875[–81]"; *JAPM*, 28:1511). Henry Wadsworth Longfellow published "The Day Is Done" in *Poems* (1845).

4. Albert Tobias (b. 1858?) was a brother of JA's classmate Alice and her music teacher, Mary.

... Friday, February 12, 1875.

This afternoon Mrs Moore was up too visit the school. We had quite a little excitement about a broken window pane, and who was the auther of the mischief. This evening Eda Jackson[1] brought down my dress.

I cracked some nuts and Kate[2] and I made some taffy. After which I put away the wash (which the new girl ironed beatifuly) and Pa, Kate, George, Ma and I played proverbs and enjoyed ourselves in so doing until bed time.

1. Classmate Ada S. Jackson. According to a diary entry for 8 Feb. 1875, JA had Ada's mother, Mary J. Jackson, fit an old dress to be remade.

2. Kate Miller came from Freeport for a visit on 10 Feb.

Saturday, February 13, 1875.

This morning Kate went home with Pa. I gave my room a thorough cleaning and sweeping. I bought a couple of valentines and sent one to Kitty Lutts[1] and one to John.[2] In the afternoon I made some tarts and pies. George read aloud in "Pickwick."

We did not go tonight[3] as Mr Barber is sick. But stayed at home and played natural history and so forth until bed time when we retired to that useful article of furniture.

1. By 1875 the Lutts family was living in Allendale in Worth Co., Mo.
2. John Addams Linn.
3. JA was referring to a community sing.

... Wednesday, February 17, 1875.

This morning Pa went to town Ma intended going but the ride yesterday was to much for her and she was threatened with the erysipelas.[1] Mr Moore at last got that example for which I am deeply grateful. This finishes up the primeous example[2] and we are both done.

Mr Rocky came down this evening to pow wow[3] Ma's face and George and I were sent out in the dining room to spend an awful dull evening and he had to stay three hours.

1. Erysipelas, caused by streptococcus, is identified by fever and an abnormal inflammation and swelling of the skin, producing pain and deep-red color. Also referred to as "St. Anthony's fire" or "the rose," it usually affects the head. AHHA suffered from the condition periodically. Lydia Addams Albright (1825–92), sister of JHA who had been visiting the Addams family in 1873, wrote on 28 Apr. on her return to Pennsylvania: "I am glad you are rid of your Erysiplas, it is not very pleasant is it?" (IU, Lilly, SAAH). Correspondence with her son HWH indicates that AHHA was still ill into the summer of 1873. At that time she was

being treated by her physician brother John L. Hostetter and by Addams family physician Dr. Samuel R. Bucher. The summer vacation the family took to Madison, Wis., in 1873 was planned in part to aid AHHA's recovery.

Erysipelas seems to have been one of those diseases, like typhoid fever, malaria, and scarlet fever, to which pioneers were frequently subjected as epidemic events. When AHHA suffered episodes of the condition, no medications were apparently effective at halting its course, which usually lasted ten days to two weeks. Sometimes the disease persisted longer or recurred. In extreme cases, when brain membrane or other internal organs became infected or when the infection resulted from some other illness, such as typhoid fever, erysipelas could be fatal. It was apparently so in the case of Henrietta Bupp Shoemaker, mother of JWA's wife Laura Shoemaker Addams.

2. JA meant *Promiscuous Example*. She had reported in her 15 Feb. 1875 diary entry that "Mr Moore at last discovered how to work the ninety-first and so I only have one more to work but I don't know how long that will take. I expected to get done last week, But how vein my expectations" ("Pocket Diary, 1875[–81]"; *JAPM*, 28:1522).

3. Among Pennsylvania German farm people, powwow doctors were sometimes called upon to conjure away illnesses. AHHA, whose Hostetter ancestors came from Germany to settle in Pennsylvania, had spent her youth in the heart of Pennsylvania German country and spoke its unique patois. Several families named Rocky lived to the north of the Cedarville area. In the townships immediately surrounding Cedarville (Buckeye, Harlem, and Lancaster), there was a John Rocky, fifty-three in 1870, who was a farmer from Pennsylvania and lived in Lancaster Twp. with his wife Catherine, fifty-two, and three children: John, twenty-six, and William, twenty-three, who were also farmers, and Charles, sixteen. We have been unable to tell from the sources available whether John Rocky was the powwow doctor consulted.

... *Friday, February 19, 1875.*

. . . Weber is twenty three years old to day and was here to dinner. This evening after supper George and I played boxing match.

... *Wednesday, February 24, 1875.*

This morning went to school, just before noon Miss Hockman[1] had a falling fit and was very sick, it produced quite an excitement up at school and the little room was dismissed.

Things went a little better in our latin class. Ever since this big meeting has commenced Eda Jackson has been sitting and crying all the time, it looks disgusting. She wants to get Albert Tobias to ~~but~~ mourn for his sins but cannot.[2]

This evening Ma[,] George and I played shanty with cards

1. Anna Hockman (1846–96), daughter of Ephraim Hockman, a farmer, and his wife, Mary, instructed younger students in the Cedarville public school in 1875 and also taught Sunday School. Never married, in 1875–76 she took a teaching position in Yellow Creek Twp. in Stephenson Co. yet continued to live with her parents in Buckeye Twp. in Stephenson Co.

2. Illinois was involved in the resurgence of the temperance movement that spread across the United States after the Civil War. Although largely an issue identified with evangelical Protestants, by the 1860s and 1870s temperance began to appear as an issue in national and state politics and political parties. Illinois had passed temperance legislation that went into effect on 1 July 1872 despite strong and determined opposition, much of it from German brewers. Local temperance clubs and branches of national temperance organizations arose in many communities as a variety of temperance lecturers carried their crusades across the state.

The *Illinois Monitor,* published in Freeport, on 13 Feb. 1875 announced that Francis Murphy (1836–1907), a "reformed saloon man," would hold a meeting in the Freeport opera house on 23 and 24 Feb. The same newspaper on 27 Feb. judged the event quite successful. Murphy, who was born in Ireland and immigrated to the United States, served in the Union army during the Civil War and as a chaplain in the Spanish-American War. By 1870 he was on his way to becoming recognized as a gospel temperance evangelist. Beginning in Maine, where he helped organize temperance clubs, Murphy criss-crossed the country from his headquarters church in Pittsburgh and spoke several times in northern Illinois. He estimated that his campaign gathered ten million pledges for abstinence nationwide.

Thursday, February 25, 1875.

To day I finished my essey[1] and as I had nothing else to do I was doing nothing. Mr More siad Jennie are you idle, I said yes sir I have nothing to do so he sent me to the board to work examples for a long while.

After recess we spelled down and had a spelling match. Mat. Graham[2] and George chose for the match and our side beat, but Jennie Sills[3] spelled down the school and she was on the oppposite side. This evening read.

1. JA's diary entry for 26 Feb. 1875 reads in part "To day I finished my essay and practised *my* it after school, he [C. W. Moore] sit there and did not say a thing when I begin or ended, which I think was not very nice" ("Pocket Diary, 1875[–81]"; *JAPM,* 28:1527). This essay is not extant.

2. According to the U.S. census of 1870 only one Graham family lived in the three townships that composed Cedarville. Samuel Graham (1814–82) was a cabinetmaker born in Pennsylvania. His wife Rebecca Lutts Graham (1814–83) and son George, twenty-nine and a day-laborer, were also born in Pennsylvania. Mary, probably a daughter, nineteen and living at home, was born in Michigan; James, fourteen in 1870 and born in Illinois, attended school. With the family was one child named Martha Vantilbert (or Vantilburg), thirteen in 1875, who may have been JA's Mat (or Mattie) Graham. Ellen Catherine Vantilburg, who died in Jan. 1862 at the age of twenty-three, was the wife of W. H. Vantilburg. She may have been the daughter of Samuel and Rebecca Graham, because the U.S. census of 1860 lists a Catherine Graham as living in the Graham household. In addition, her grave in the Cedarville Cemetery is near those of the Graham family.

3. Cedarville cooper Jacob Sills (1819–91) and his wife Catharine (1817–1912) had three daughters, one of whom, Mary J., was seventeen in 1875 and attended school with JA and GBH.

. . . Sunday, February 28, 1875.

To day Mr Barber came to sunday School again and it seems awful nice and interesting. Mr Conly preached a pretty good sermon to day full of imaganation.

Ma was sick this morning but was up when we came home. Emma lost her way comeing home from church and was late and so I got dinner. This <evening> a tried writing a romantic tale[1] and had lots of fun for George illustrated as we went along. This evening read the lesson, after which preformance I went to bed.

1. This story is not know to be extant.

Feb. 1875 entries: AD (Addams, "Pocket Diary, 1875[–81]," CAHS; *JAPM,* 28:1515–28).

Monday, March 1, 1875.

This morning George has one of his old spells and of course connot go to school.[1] So Jennie Sills had to start alone in the higher arithmetic. He gave us an awful long lesson for too morrow.

This evening I stayed to practice my essey. The girls that have got up that dialoge feel quite discouraged[2] . . .

1. From time to time during the 1870s family correspondence carried cryptic references to GBH's "spells" or illnesses. In her 1875 diary entries for 26 and 28 June, JA mentioned an extended nosebleed that he had suffered.

2. Two days later, on 3 Mar., JA recorded, "The girls have a spendid dilouge only they do not know it very well yet and Mary Smith does not seem to care, and she has the princapal part. Next Friday after we elect officers, we girls intend to have the society named and a constitution that is if we can" ("Pocket Diary, 1875[-81]"; *JAPM*, 28:1530). Mary Smith, fourteen, was the daughter of Martin Smith, a cooper, and his wife Mary, who lived near the Addams family in Cedarville (see The 1875 Diary of Jane Addams, 27 Apr. 1875, n. 1, below).

. . . *Friday, March 5, 1875.*

To day is the eventful one.[1] We had quite a number of visitors and Mary Templeton did very nicely as sectary. Chartie Addams[2] and Mell. Carl had a real funny dialogue and made every body laugh. Albert Tobias our president did not give any one any chance to elect officers or do any thing else for he omited that part all together, so of course our fine plans amount to nothing. Every body said it was a very good meeting.

Mr and Mrs Moore were here to tea.

1. Apparently JA wrote the first sentence of this entry in anticipation of her female classmates giving their dialogue and naming their literary society. Unfortunately, she did not report on the reception given the dialogue.

2. JA meant to write *Charlie.* Charles H. Addams (1859–83), seventh child of James Huy Addams and Lavina Hinnersheetz Addams, was JA's cousin. Educated in the Cedarville school, he attended the Northern Indiana Normal School and Business Institute in Valparaiso, graduating from the Teachers' Dept. in the class of 1880. He died in Cedarville in 1883, probably of tuberculosis, after an illness of several weeks.

. . . *Sunday, March 7, 1875.*

This morning All of our class[1] were there the first time since last fall, we did not have a very interesting lesson to day. Went to church Mr Mitchell preached and after dinner came down and spent part of the afternoon. This evening George and I helped and had Alice make out her will for fear she might be swallowed by a whale or find a grave in the briny deep.[2]

Pa went to hear Mr Conely preach and the rest of us spent a very quit evening at home.

1. Union Sunday School.

2. On 6 Mar. JA wrote, "This evening Alice came home . . . [and] a whole bevey of Freeport and Rockford girls, and young men came out. We had an oyster supper and a very nice

time. . . . It was pretty near eleven o'clock when I went to bed and asleep" ("Pocket Diary, 1875[–81]"; *JAPM*, 28:1531). SAA was planning a trip to Europe.

. . . Thursday, March 11, 1875.

This forenoon Mame Greenleaf came out to see us.[1]

This afternoon pretty near all the scholars went down to the white school house[2] as it is the last day. There was only fourteen of us and after recess we did not have any regular school but spelled and hunted words out of words until four o'clock. This forenoon Mr Moore invited the whole school to a kind an entertainment at his house next saturday evening. This evening listen to music etc. . . .

1. JA's step-cousin Mamie Hostetter Greenleaf left the next day.

2. Built in 1846, the first small school building constructed south of Cedarville by subscription was soon outgrown. The next school building, frame, was twenty by thirty feet. It was built near the site of the first cemetery in Cedarville, on a hill at the west end of Second St. JA likely refers to this second school house. The third school building, the first made from brick and that at which JA and GBH were students, was built on the same site as the second structure.

. . . Saturday, March 13, 1875

To day it is quite warm and the snow is melting like every thing[.] George and I went to see the creek it is getting pretty high.

This evening went to the entertainment and had a very pleasant time, first we played Simon's says thumbs up and other such plays. We were then entertained by five or six tableax. After that we had refreshments of nuts and candies, we then talked and were sociable for a little while, it was ten minutes to ten when we came <home.>

Sunday, March 14, 1875.

Went to Sunday School as uasal. As Mr Barber was not there we went into Mrs Latchaw's class and as she devoted most of her time to her own scholars we could not hear much she said, so Molly Brown[1] and I sat in the coner of the seat and whispered and looked around like two naughty little girls as we were. . . . After dinner George and I practiced the "Star Spangled banner" we are getting it nicely.

1. Mary ("Molly") Brown, who also attended school with JA, was fourteen in 1875. She was the only child listed in the U.S. census of 1870 for parents John F. Brown, forty-two, and his wife Sarah, thirty-five. The Browns were all born in Pennsylvania. An itinerant farmer, John F. Brown and his family no longer lived in Buckeye Twp. in Stephenson Co. in 1880.

Tuesday, March 16, 1875.

This morning there is a dreadful storm and there were only fifteen in our room and seven boys in the other. This evening Lizzie and Charlie[1] staid here all night, we first played hide and go seek and lots of fun, we then played old maid and of course I was it, we end off with shanty and asked all sorts of silly foolish questions and had lots of fun, it is getting awful stormy and snowy but looked as if was looking as if it would clear off a while ago.

1. Cousins Elizabeth Belle ("Lizzie") Addams and Charles H. Addams.

Wednesday, March 17, 1875.

This morning went to school and we had a few more scholars, the roads are blown shut so from the storm Pa did not go to town until noon, this evening I went up town and took my blue skirt up to Ellen Syler[1] to see if she could fix it and then went up to Mr Kostenborder's[2] for Polly's dress and there was the funniest little old woman there sewing carpet rags I ever saw. This evening we played old maid and so on and had a passable time.

1. Ellen Seyler, born in Pennsylvania, was twenty-nine in 1875. She was the daughter of George Seyler (1815–91), a tailor who lived and worked in Cedarville from 1846, when he left his home in Centre Co., Pa., and his wife, Mary Potts Seyler, also of Pennsylvania.

2. Daniel Kostenbader (1823–1903), single, was a farmer and carpenter in Cedarville. A native of Pennsylvania, he and his brother Aaron came to Cedarville in 1847 to join their brother Andrew, who was working on David Neidigh's farm. His older sister Margaret or Marguth Kostenbader (1821–88) kept house for him and may have been a seamstress, although the U.S. census of 1870 does not indicate an occupation for her. The Kostenbaders lived near the family of Simon Tobias in Cedarville.

. . . Monday, March 22, 1875.

. . . I have had an awful headache to day and this evening can hardly see for it.

Tuesday, March 23, 1875.

This morning feel a great deal better but kind of top heavy yet. This noon we discovred quite a love sick piece of poetry on Eda Jackson's slate to her absent Albert.[1] We that is Mat. Graham and I copied it, she would be raving and tearing mad if she knew it. She has been crying all day in our class she tried to read but broke down all on a heap and said she could not read and so we did not. This afternoon we elected officers for next Friday, John Coble[2] as president and Lizzie Addams Sec',[3] I got two letters to day.

1. Ada S. Jackson and Albert Tobias.

2. John Coble (b. 1860?) and his sister Mary (1863?–1946), children of Elizabeth and John E. Coble (1818–82), a farmer, from Pennsylvania, were JA's classmates.

3. It seems that JA actually served as secretary of the class literary society until the next election. In his "Account Book, 1875–76," GBH recorded that on 23 Mar. he was elected president but declined to serve and John Coble was elected in his stead with Elizabeth Belle Addams elected secretary. The entry for 24 Mar. reads: "Lizzie Addams refuses to act as secretary after a long hesitation Mattie Graham rises and says Jennie Addams[.] Geo P. Barber

seconds, carried by a unanimous vote." Barber was the son of Thomas Barber (1831?–94), a Republican farmer from Pennsylvania, and Jane E. Patton Barber (1837?–94), a couple who in 1880 had other children: Samuel, Nellie, and Sallie.

... *Friday, March 26, 1875.*

This forenoon I went ~~of~~ over in the little room for a while and it is very amusing to hear them read and spell. Just before dinner Mr Richart[1] and Pa were up while we examined in philosophy and I got ten every time but once and then nine and a half.

This afternoon I acted as secetary and every thing would off gone nicely if John Coble would not of been such a booby.

Our dialogue took splendidly we had forty two visitors more than we ever had before for a long time.

Awful high water today.[2]

1. Jackson Richart (1817–1900) came to Buckeye Twp. in Stephenson Co. in 1837 from Ohio. He owned a general merchandise store in Cedarville in what had been the first brick home in town, constructed by Samuel Sutherland in the Pennsylvania-Georgian style. He lived there with his family, including wife Charlotte C. Ault Richart (1824–1914), and seven children, four of whom survived to maturity. These were sons Henry (1845–1921), who worked in the store, and Cyrus (d. post 1900), who lived in Kirwin, Kans., and daughters Caroline (1853–1932), seventeen in 1870, and Alma (1863–1954), seven and a classmate of JA. A Republican, for a time Richart served Cedarville as postmaster and the township as justice of the peace, assessor, supervisor, and town clerk. He was also an active member of the Old Settlers' Assn. and participated in early efforts to bring railroads to Stephenson Co.

2. Line written in the right margin of the diary page and perpendicular to the page of text.

... *Sunday, March 28, 1875.*

... George and I were trying to learn to play on the jew's harp and finely learned how to make it go and that was all. This evening had our lesson and singing.

... *Tuesday, March 30, 1875.*

This fore noon George and I nearly killed our selves playing hop scotch but had a good deal of fun. This noon for dinner we had a roast turkey and quite a party of old ladies to help eat it.

After dinner of course George and I had to play our duet and did so with some grumbling.[1]

This evening Pet was over and we played a little of every thing out doors, it is very warm the thermometer has stood at eighty all afternoon.

1. They probably attempted the National Anthem, on which they had been practicing.

Mar. 1875 entries: AD (Addams, "Pocket Diary, 1875[–81]," CAHS; *JAPM*, 28:1529–44).

Thursday, April 1, 1875.

Last night a took Georg's wash basin and pitcher away and he had to wash elsware and that was the first fool. Then I soaped the looking glass and made it look as if it was broken. At breakfast Pa tried to take something out of an empty dish and sugared his potatoes and eggs. George and I had it hot and heavy up stairs, he emptied my drawer put the key inside and locked it. I found his private keys and made an exebition of his things. He came up stairs and told me Ma wanted to see me and I came down. So it was all day.

. . . Friday, April 9, 1875.

This afternoon the little room was let out at three of the clock and we were kept in until four. Miss Hockman came over in our room. We had a selection of officers and after a great deal of nominating George Messner[1] was elected President and Mat Graham Secretary. I had my angry passions stirred up considerly against Mr Moore this evening. . . .

1. According to the U.S. census of 1870, there was no Mesner or Messner family living in the Cedarville area in 1870; in the 1880 census, however, one George Mesner, age eighteen, boarded with the John W. Shaffer family and helped in his carriage works as a carriage painter. Mesner was born in Illinois, although his parents were born in Pennsylvania. It is likely that he was the son of the Henry Messners, who lived in Cedarville for a time while the Rev. Messner was a pastor for the Evangelical Assn.

. . . Sunday, April 11, 1875.

. . . This evening tried to sing but did not make much of a secess out of it. Had our lesson and retired from the stage.

. . . Wednesday, April 14, 1875.

This morning Pa and Mr Mitchell went to Freeport.

This evening after school Pet and I went after spring beauties and found a good many.

After supper Pet came over and we played croquet[1] and I white-washed both her and George.

Mr and Mrs Moore came down to spend the evening just as we were enjoying a game bamboozle. After that we played authers until Pet went home.

And I read until bed time.

1. In early Apr., Mr. and Mrs. C. W. Moore brought their croquet set to the Addams family lawn. JA seemed especially fond of the game; she had played it since at least 1871. On 21 Apr. 1875, she wrote, "This evening after supper George and I stood the two Mr Mitchells in croquet and they beat us but not very badly" ("Pocket Diary, 1875[–81]"; *JAPM*, 28:1555). JA was referring to the Presbyterian minister and his brother Edward Mitchell, who was visiting. According to JA biographer Winifred E. Wise, JA and GBH often played so late into the dusk that they had to place white handkerchiefs over the wickets to see where the ball should go.

. . . *Saturday, April 17, 1875.*

This morning Pa went to town.

I did most of my work up before dinner. Ma is not very well to day. This afternoon George and I pracised the "Star Spangled Banner" until we know it just about perfectly, that is as near as we can get it.

This evening we formed a sort of a spelling school and had lots of fun. Pa is about the best speller among us all.

I have finely got my habit.[1]

1. With the encouragement of her parents, JA took up horseback riding. AHHA was an accomplished horsewoman, according to her granddaughter Marcet Haldeman-Julius ("Two Mothers"), and it is likely that she believed JA needed to be, too, and convinced JHA. JA first mentioned riding in a diary entry on 6 Apr. 1875. On 7 Apr. she reported that she went to George Seyler's, the Cedarville tailor. Her record of succeeding visits on 8 and 16 Apr. indicates that she was being fitted for riding clothes. Diary entries and correspondence reveal that JA rode horseback from 1875 until she graduated from RFS. Her extant letters for the period disclose a certain pride in being able to ride distances. Although she never indicated dismay at having to ride, she remembered that doing so hurt her back (see JA to Vallie E. Beck, 3 May 1877, below). Winifred E. Wise, who interviewed JA for a biography for young people, *Jane Addams of Hull-House* (1935), reported, "The jogging pained her back so much that she hated riding" (50). Mary Fry, housekeeper and companion to AHHA and other family members, believed that JA was allergic to horses (Fry, *Generous Spirit*, 109).

. . . *Tuesday, April 20, 1875.*

To day went to school played ~~school~~ <ball> at intermissions and played a little of every thing in school time.

Pa was up to visit the school and he saw those verses on the outside of my Botany[1] and looked so funny I almost had to laugh out loud.

Mr and Mrs Moore were here to tea. I went riding in my new habit after supper and the saddle turned and I had to jump to save my self from a fall.

This seems like Friday just as much as can be.

1. JA's botany book is not extant.

. . . *Friday, April 23, 1875.*

This morning just as we were finishing up breakfast we saw a wagon coming with very jingling bells on the mules and a young fellow came in and said he had brought the piano and sure enough a perfectly splendid handsome upright Haselton at the cost of $700. It is ment to represent ebany and is as beautiful as can be.[1]

Went to school and had the question box and got out at three o'clock.[2]

This evening we learned the coaxing polka.

1. "The Hazelton seems to be *the* piano of the period," observed the editor of the *Freeport Journal* in his "Local Matters" column on 13 May 1874. Hazelton instruments, made by three

brothers and their assistants in Cincinnati, Ohio, were sold by Pelton and Pomeroy, Freeport merchants identified as selling musical instruments and jewelry. This piano replaced the one purchased by the Addams family between 1870 and 1871.

2. The question box was a regular Friday afternoon event. On 12 Mar., JA recorded in her 1875 diary that four questions had been addressed by various classmates to her. Because she was unable to answer them, she had until the next Friday to secure the answers and share them with classmates. Any student could put a question addressed to someone else into the box. Sometimes JA did not receive any questions.

Saturday, April 24, 1875.

To day went to town with Pa and had five dollars to spend for the fixing up of my room.

All forenoon I was shoping bought a table and cover and a pair of book-shelves for my room. They is a Phrenologist at the Penn. House[1] and I heard her old forth quite a string of gab. This afternoon I went up to visit Mary Van'reed[2] and enjoyed my self very much.

This evening came home and played on the new piano most of the evening.

1. In 1848 the Pennsylvania House, a frame hotel of forty rooms, was constructed by Jacob Meyer on the corner of Stephenson St. and Van Buren Ave. in Freeport. In 1862 the structure was acquired by Isaac S. Zartman and moved two blocks west, where it remained until it was demolished in 1911. JHA was fond of having his meals there on the days he went to Freeport.

2. Mary L. Housman Van Reed (1850?–1917) and husband Mabry A. Van Reed (1841–1915) were married by 1866. Mabry, born on 3 Oct. 1841, was the son of JHA's sister Mary B. Addams Van Reed (1813–1892) and her husband John. While the former Mary Housman was born and grew up in the Philadelphia area, Mabry was born and educated in Reading, Pa. At the start of the Civil War, he enlisted and served more than three years, part of the time as secretary to breveted Gen. Alfred Pleasonton, who led cavalry actions at Antietam and Gettysburg and in Missouri.

Mabry Van Reed brought his family to Springfield, Ill., in Jan. 1869 and begged the help of his uncle JHA in finding employment. It was in JHA's nature to help those in distress, especially if they were war veterans and family. Accordingly, the Van Reeds lodged in Cedarville for a year, where Mabry worked for JHA before moving his family permanently to Freeport, Ill. In Freeport, he held various jobs. He was a stationary engineer (one who runs a stationary engine) employed at the Freeport Waterworks, at Elias Bamberger and Son's sawmill, and in other businesses.

Mary and Mabry Van Reed provided a hint of Addams family scandal. Their first child, Edith, was born when Mary was only thirteen and when she and Mabry had been wed only six months. In an attempt to hide the fact of her pregnancy, young Mabry agreed to have the doctor who attended the birth give away the child. When the couple discovered that the doctor had placed Edith in an almshouse, however, they retrieved her and moved west. Shown Mabry's letter of 28 Jan. 1868[1869?] to JHA explaining this history, the newly wed AHHA commented, "Truth stranger than fiction[.] Retribution follows wrong doing" (SCPC, JAC).

The Van Reeds had two children. Edith (birthdate uncertain, d. 1930) was a teacher in Freeport and played the organ in Grace Episcopal Church there (where her family were members); she became Mrs. J. M. Hutchinson of Lowell, Mich. The Van Reeds' son Frederick became a resident of Stanislaus, Calif.

When Mabry Van Reed died as a result of a fall from a cherry tree, his obituary appeared on the front page of both Freeport newspapers. He was praised as "a kindly man, whom it was a pleasure to meet and an honor to know" (*Freeport Journal Standard,* 3 July 1915) and a "highly respected citizen . . . well known" and "admired . . . for his fine character, and pleasant disposition" (*Freeport Daily Bulletin,* 3 July 1915). In addition to his participation in the activities of the Grand Army of the Republic, he was also a Mason. He and his wife were buried in Oakland Cemetery in Florence Twp. south of Freeport.

Sunday, April 25, 1875.

To day we were all at Sunday School and had a very interesting lesson.

Pa and I went to hear Mr Conely preach he had rather a lengthy but good sermon.

He gave me a new view about thearters card playing and so forth he said that they might not be worng in them selves but it was going very near the precipice where the least influence would thow you over. In other words it was going as near hell as possible and go to heaven.

Monday, April 26, 1875.

To day went to school and things went on in the same hum drum way. Mr Moore trying to be witty and totally fails, tries to be cross and does not fail. Yesterday afternoon wrote a piece of poetry on the old piano, but to day did not feel very poetical.[1]

This evening pricticed my piece called the "Petrified fern." We Elected a president and as there was such an award[2] pause I nominated Eda J——— and she was elected, she has been hinting for that position all winter.

1. JA's poem is not extant.
2. JA probably meant to write the word *awkward.*

Tuesday, April 27, 1875.

This morning I was awaken from my slumberous repose as by the tramping of many feet up and down stairs and through hall and this is mere interduction for house cleaning has fairly begun. To day they cleaned the little front room Georges room the spare room. A pretty good day work considering all the time Mrs Smith and Eliza spent in fighting.[1]

Pa is not very well this evening he ate some of the detestable pudding for dinner.

1. Magdalena Mary Smith (1826–97) was married to cooper Martin Smith (b. 1823?), according to the U.S. census of 1870. Both were born in Europe and had several children, one of whom, Mary, was a classmate of JA and GBH, and another of whom, Eliza, was born in Ohio in 1852(?). They lived near the Addams family and may have been hired by AHHA, especially to help with spring cleaning.

Wednesday, April 28, 1875.

Pa got real sick last night and is unable to go to town this morning as uasal he is obliged to lie in bed most of time.

This evening I got excused at recess as Ma is not very well either. My room was cleaned to day and I was very busy fixing it and the parlor and helping to put down the hall carpets. Mrs Stahl and Pet were here this evening and saw how clean we were. I am just slitely tired this evening felt as if I was pressed.

Thursday, April 29, 1875.

To day we spelled at school, we first had a match and George, Alma Richart[,] Meda Seyler[1] and I stood Mat Graham[,] Eda Jackson[,] Mary Smith and Charles Coble and beat them too. We then had a spelling ~~match an~~ down, and I went of the stage one the word paralysis. Mat Graham cane off victor. This evening sewed on my curtains and put them up. Fixed my room generally, and am generally tired.

1. According to the U.S. census return for Cedarville in 1880, Almeda Seyler, sixteen and born in Illinois, was the granddaughter of George Seyler and Mary Seyler and the daughter of Andrew J. Seyler (1840–1914), a widower born in Pennsylvania.

Apr. 1875 entries: AD (Addams, "Pocket Diary, 1875[–81]," CAHS; *JAPM*, 28:1544–60).

. . . Sunday, May 2, 1875.

This morning went to Sunday School, and had the subject of Samson for our lesson and came to the conclusion that he was decidly <u>not</u> a good man.[1] Pa's class came to somewhat different conclusion. I did not go to church but took John[2] home and put him to bed and asleeep.

Weber came down.

This afternoon John and I went to call on Mrs Mitchell[3] and Mrs Bucher. This evening Mr Guteau and Mr and Miss Crone[4] came to tea.

1. The story of Samson appears in Judges 13–16. On 16 May 1875, JA had an opportunity to reverse her opinion of Samson. She reported, "This morning Mr. Mitchell preached on the charater of Samon namely weather he was I good or a bad man, he took the stand that he was a good man, it was a powerful sermon and had augements but still I do not know weather I am convinced or not. Mr Barber after church asked me what I thought of Samson now?" ("Pocket Diary, 1875[–81]"; *JAPM*, 28:1568).
2. MCAL and her son John Addams Linn visited from 1 May to 3 May.
3. Mrs. Mitchell was Rev. Lewis H. Mitchell's mother. She and his brother Edward came to Cedarville on 9 Apr., and they lodged at the Latshaws.
4. Likely Luther W. Guiteau and Second National Bank of Freeport director Jacob Krohn (1832–1901) and his wife, Dora Fleischman Krohn (1834?–93). Jacob Krohn was prominent in Freeport. He arrived in 1855 after immigrating from Prussia, where he learned the tobacco trade in which he was involved in Freeport. Elected alderman and twice as mayor, Krohn also served on the board of education and on the building committee for the courthouse constructed in the early 1870s. He became president of the Second National Bank after the death of JHA. Krohn was exceedingly active in the Masons and Oddfellows Lodge in Illinois. He and his first wife had eight children: Bertha, Moses, Lena, Maimie, Emma, Rosa, Carrie, and Edna. His second wife was Mrs. Carrie Feilter from Cincinnati, Ohio.

. . . Tuesday, May 4, 1875.

This morning went to bed or rather school which is almost as bad.

This evening Allie Tobias and Susan Mark[1] came down to see us before Allie leaves as she intends to go to morrow.[2]

Allie tried to play but hanmerd that everlasting Russian March and bird waltz. And scrathed the piano all up with her foot.

George and [I] played The Star Spangld banner also, the coaxing polka and I thind we exucuted them nicely.

1. Susan Mark (b. 1848?), the daughter of Rebecca (1817–1904) and Henry Mark (1807–76), a boot and shoemaker in Cedarville, lived in Buckeye Twp. and was prominent in the Evangelical Assn. in Cedarville. Like her sister Sarah, a year older, she lived at home and became a dressmaker. Their brother Thomas (b. 1859?) was a classmate of JA and GBH.

2. SAA was about to leave for a summer tour of Europe in the company of a group of women from RFS and chaperoned by AHHA's good friend Vicenta M. Fensley (see JA to Vallie E. Beck, 26 Feb. 1876, below). SAA toured Germany, where she took art lessons, Austria, Italy, Switzerland, France, Belgium, and Great Britain, returning home in late Sept. 1875. An account of her travels is extant in a series of letters to her father, JHA (SCPC, JAC).

Wednesday, May 5, 1875.

This morning Pa went to town it is raining some what.

This morning recess Alma Richart, Mary Smith and I went down to the rocks to get some flowers to anylze, we climbed down that place and got very heavy feet with the wet sand, and then did not get any flowers but had to go behind the School house, and then found some blood root and some ladies tobacco which we could not anylize.[1]

This evening Pet was here and we played nock up.

1. JA and her friend Pet Stahl also gathered spring beauties, fern, walking fern, moss, and columbine for their study of botany.

. . . Friday, May 7, 1875.

To day is the grand day for our exercises and we had a good many visitors. Mrs Moore, Miss Rutter,[1] Mr Mitchell[,] Pa and Ma and a couple girls. Aunt Betsey bean went off very nicely I dressed Alma up in Ma's chigon and curls, she had on an a long dress and all.[2] The only balk in it was that I could not get the door open and had to go in and get Mr Moore. Gorden Heitz[3] spoke and he would first scratch one leg and then the other in quite a killing way.

1. This was probably one of the five daughters of Jacob Rutter (1818–91), a Cedarville blacksmith and carpenter, and his wife Mary Hartman Rutter (1813–80). The sisters' names were Sarah A., Anna C., Mary E., M.J., and Susan R. H. The elder Rutters had come to Stephenson Co. in 1854 from Pennsylvania.

2. Apparently JA had written a play or dialogue, no longer extant, for Alma Richart to perform with her. JA had a great-aunt named Mary Weber Bean (1793–1889), wife of William Bean (d. 1855), the son of Jesse Bean of Lower Providence. The Beans lived in Pennsyl-

vania and had six children: Jesse, William, Hannah, Edwin H., Theodore W., and Anna L. Mary Weber Bean was the sister of JA's mother's father, George Weber. JA also had two distant cousins named Elizabeth Bean but no Aunt Betsy Bean.

3. Gordon Heitz, ten in 1875, was the son of Anna Heitz, forty-two, and John Heitz, fifty-three, a farmer from Pennsylvania who lived in Buckeye Twp. in Stephenson Co.

... Monday, May 10, 1875.

This morning I went to school. And this afternoon as it was quite warm and we all kind of had the spring fevers, we were sitting under I[1] tree, and I got up three dialogues, to which Mr Moore objected saying that three were almost too [many] unless we got a good many single piecs.

So Eda Jackson let her angry passions get the better of her, and we had a little passage of arms on the spot. Mr Moore was victorous.

1. JA intended to write *a tree.*

Tuesday, May 11, 1875.

This morning as there are a good many single pieces coming in Mr Moore concluded that three or four dialogues would not be too many and so every body is quite peaceful[1] and contented except ~~Alma~~ Eda Jackson who still has some bitter thoughts ~~in~~ rankling in bosom. As Matt. Graham has played "quits" Alice Carl is sitting with Pet, and as I am alone Eda J. seems very anxious I should sit with her. I decline.

1. JA began immediately to secure her dialogues. On 12 May 1875 she indicated that she had "finely found one to suit me pretty well called the origin of gold" ("Pocket Diary, 1875[−81]"; *JAPM,* 28:1566).

... Thursday, May 13, 1875.

This afternoon was the time for spelling down and so accordingly we were all in order after recess. Mary Smith, George and I stood Eda Jackson, Meda Seyler[,] Alma Richart and Willliam Ilgin.[1]

I do not know what ailed me, but I do know that I spelled miserably and felt ashamed of my self. Every thing has been going wrong lately maybe it is because I complain so much. I[f] so I must quit it, I find it in every page of my diary.

1. William Ilgen, thirteen in 1875 and born in Illinois, was the son of Cedarville carpenter Louis Ilgen (1830?–1915) and his wife Susan, forty-four, both of whom were from Pennsylvania. The Ilgens had two other children, George O., eighteen, and Luther, sixteen, who died in 1881.

... Saturday, May 15, 1875.

... Yesterday we discovered that we must of made a misculculation for we had it that school would be out on the second of June and lo and behold it is the ninth just a week longer, and just a week to much. This afternoon we put the kitchen in order which was quite a job.

. . . Tuesday, May 18, 1875.

This evening after school I took it into my head to make waffles, so out to the kitchen I went, but those dreadful waffles would'nt bake any way that I could fix it, they would either stick to the pan or else burn up altogether.

This evening Mr Linn[1] and I took a horse back ride, he rode Fan and I rode his little horse and taought he to lope and we had a splendid time. This evening James Carey[2] came to call.

1. JML and MCAL, with their son John Addams Linn, arrived on 17 May. MCAL and her son planned to spend two weeks in Cedarville while her husband attended a Presbyterian convention in Cleveland, Ohio.
2. James Carey (b. 1854?) was the son of Presbyterian minister Isaac E. Carey and Eliza A. Carey. In 1875 the Rev. Carey lived in Waterloo, Iowa, with his new wife, the former Lucy A. Irwin, whom he wed on 5 Aug. 1873. James Carey and JWA had been childhood friends.

. . . Thursday, May 20, 1875.

This morning crept like a snail unwillingly to school.

And just as unwillingly crept through all of the exercises.

This afternoon Mrs Moore came up to visit the school. We had a spelling match and William Ilgin who is a very poor speller went shifting from side to side no one wanting to claim him. It presented quite an amusing spectacle.

We then spelled down.

Friday, May 21, 1875.

This morning did up my work and played around with John[1] until school time.

This evening when I came home, Pa and Ma had already arrived and had a great deal to tell about, it sounded so nice that I almost wished that I had gone, but on the whole am glad I did not.[2]

This afternoon we had the question box and Mrs Moore was up again but went over in the little room and did not <hear it.>

1. JA doted on her first nephew, John Addams Linn. On 8 Mar. 1875 she recorded, "This evening I and George amused John by spinning my top. This evening Mary gave me a picture of him[.] I enjoyed myself very much. This evening I told stories until John went to sleep and I could'ent tell any more" ("Pocket Diary, 1875[–81]"; *JAPM*, 28:1532).
2. On 19 May 1875, JA commented, "This morning Pa and Ma left for Mount Carroll to attend Abe's wedding, it took them a good while to get started and kept me pretty busy trotting around but at last they got off" ("Pocket Diary, 1875[–81]"; *JAPM*, 28:1569). The Addamses were going to the wedding of AHHA's nephew Abram Bowman Hostetter to Harriet Stackhouse Irvine.

. . . Monday, May 24, 1875.

This morning went to school. Clara Jones[1] and I changed our seats over to the unoccupied one on the boys side in the coner it is ever so much pleasanter than it was over at the grave yard side.[2]

I expect Eda Jackson will be provoked she wanted to sit over there with me and now of course she cannot, but I don't care for I will be sure to get into trouble if I sit with her.

1. Clara Jones was thirteen in 1875. She was the daughter of miller Jacob Jones, fifty-three, and Ann, fifty, both born in Maryland. Their other children were Laura, nineteen, Ida, eighteen, Franklin, sixteen, Samuel, twelve, and Martha, nine.
2. The first Cedarville Cemetery was at the west end of what became 2d St. on the same hill as the school and to the west of the school. When the two-story brick school building was constructed near it in the mid-1850s, a group of community leaders, including JHA, determined that the cemetery should be moved. The school needed a playground, and the cemetery required more space. Accordingly, in 1855 JHA provided the land on which the new burial ground was laid out to the north and west of the community and off the road to Red Oak. The Cedarville Cemetery Assn. was also formed by JHA, Marcus Montelius, Adrian W. Lucas, Josiah Clingman, Peter Woodring, and John Wilson in 1855. JHA served as its first secretary and treasurer.

May 1875 entries: AD (Addams, "Pocket Diary, 1875[–81]," CAHS; *JAPM*, 28:1560–75).

Wednesday, June 2, 1875.
This morning Pa went to town and the rest of us stayed at home. Things went off passably well at school to day. John[1] is just as cute as he can be and talks and carries on all the time and we will miss him dreadfully when he goes away.[2] This evening I read in "Old Curiosity Shop"[3] I have finished the first volume and like the story every so much, I think that Nell is just perfect.

1. JA spent considerable time entertaining John Addams Linn and being entertained by him during the Linns' visit in Cedarville. She recorded John's sleeping habits in her diary and frequently took the little boy on walks. On 30 May 1875 she noted, "This afternoon wrote a letter to Alice and John sent one, two, ten, eight, nine kisses. He has been just as good and cunning all day as can be" ("Pocket Diary, 1875[–81]"; *JAPM*, 28:1575).
2. The Linns were leaving Lena on 7 June to live in Winnebago, Ill., approximately thirty miles southeast of Cedarville and to the east of the village of Pecatonica. JML was to be the pastor of the Presbyterian Church of Winnebago, which had a membership of 140. The congregation, organized in 1869, built its church for $4,300 in that same year. The village of Winnebago was platted in 1853 after the Galena and Chicago Union Railroad, eventually known as the Chicago and Northwestern, was completed through Winnebago Co., which is immediately east of Stephenson Co. The town of six hundred people served as a transportation center for agricultural products, primarily wheat, corn, and meat, produced in the surrounding area. By 1875 Winnebago had several stores, carriage, pump, and furniture manufacturers, a school, and seven churches.
3. Dickens's *Old Curiosity Shop* (1841) tells the story of "Little Nell" Trent and her grandfather, keeper of the shop of the novel's title. The novel, first published in serial form, was enormously popular in America, where Little Nell's perils riveted readers. Mobs of people who had been following the story and were eager to know her fate gathered at the docks to greet the ship that arrived with bulk copies of the issue that contained Dickens's description of her demise.

... *Monday, June 14, 1875.*

This morning it is quite wet and drizzly but in spite of that George and Sarah took quite a lengthy boat ride up the dam, they went soon after breakfast and did not return until we had eaten dinner.

I am glad I did not go, for they got awful tired and tuckered out.

Polly and Weber left for Uncle George Weber's[1] this morning or noon rather.

This afternoon had a pretty nice time generally.

1. George Weber, Jr., (1819–88), born in Kreidersville, Pa., was the brother of JA's mother, SWA. His only formal higher schooling seems to have been as a preparatory student during the 1841 academic year at Lafayette College, where his father, Col. George Weber, was a trustee. He committed himself to serve the Reformed Church and began appropriate studies in Pennsylvania. JHA recorded in his diary on 4 Oct. 1844 that he hoped George Weber would do well "and also that he would not become too much excited but to keep with in bounds that he may not get prejudice against him in his enthusiasm and prevent him from doing good amongst his fellow beings" ("Journal, 1844").

On 30 Nov. 1848 Weber married Maria (sometimes Mariah) W. Hoffeditz, daughter of Juliana Roth Hoffeditz (1795–1860) and Theodore Ludwig Hoffeditz (1783–1858), who served the Reformed Church as a minister primarily in Pennsylvania. At the time, Weber was a merchant in Siegfried's Ferry, Pa. In 1849 the young couple went west to join Col. George Weber and work in his ill-fated milling and mercantile venture in Como, Ill. After his father died in 1851, George Weber, Jr., and his family began a journey throughout the Midwest dictated by Weber's life as a Reformed minister and missionary.

Before Weber became an ordained minister in the Ohio synod of the Reformed Church in 1853, the couple lived in Orangeville, Ill., where Weber served the Reformed Church community of twenty-four. While there, in 1852 he officiated with two other Reformed Church leaders at the laying of the cornerstone for the Lutheran and Reformed Church built by 1855. Perhaps the Webers went there because it was near George Weber's sister in Cedarville, only six miles directly south of Orangeville, and perhaps because Polly Beer, the family nurse, had cousins who lived nearby. They stayed in Orangeville until 1857.

Weber served in Dayton, Ind., in 1858, and after that he practiced primarily as a Reformed Church missionary in Forreston, Ill., in 1861, Cedarville in 1862, and Freeport in 1863 and 1864. He and his family were in Central City, Iowa, in 1865. Back in Illinois, he worked in Summum in 1866 and 1867, Elroy in 1868, and Sterling between 1863 and 1873. Then the family returned to Iowa. Between 1874 and 1880 they were in Blairstown, home of one of Weber's former classmates from Lafayette College, L. Christian Becker. The Webers finally moved to Vinton, where George worked also in Millersburg from 1881 until his death while on a visit in Pennsylvania in 1888. An obituary in the 28 Nov. 1888 *Reformed Church Messenger* recounted that most of George Weber's life had been spent in missionary work in the Midwest and that he was "not eloquent in the pulpit, . . . [but] in the sick chamber" due primarily to a lack of formal training.

The Webers had ten children, and three of the five who died in infancy were buried in Como. To keep his family fed, Weber tried his hand at being a merchant and a farmer. JHA lent him money to purchase a farm in Iowa. When, after JHA's death, Weber could not repay the note, JA and her sisters forgave it. In addition, from time to time they also sent small gifts of money to the family. By the time George Weber, Jr., died, Maria Weber was paralyzed and an invalid, cared for by some of her children. She died in Vinton, Iowa, in 1889. The five children who lived to maturity were Mary, Grace, Charles, George Cyrus, and Samuel Devault Weber.

... *Sunday, June 20, 1875.*

This morning just as we were preparing for Sunday School Weber came in and said very bad news. Nellie Hostetter and Susie[1] started to see Ginnie got as far as Rock Island when Nellie was taken sick and could not go on this was Teusday[.] Wednesday Uncle John[2] went down. Friday night she was very low that is the last news. Pa Ma and Aunt Susan[3] and myself went to the Sunday School institute this forenoon. We had fourteen people here to dinner.

Did not go this afternoon.

1. Susan Mattie Hostetter (1860–1936) was the youngest child of Catherine Bowman Hostetter and Abraham Hostetter. She was AHHA's niece and JA's step-cousin. She and her cousin Helen were going to visit Helen's sister Virginia, who lived with her pharmacist husband D. Harvey Reichard in Mitchellville, Iowa.

Susan Hostetter was acknowledged in the family as a beauty. She had sparkling brown eyes and a pink and white complexion topped by a head of black, curly hair. A lively girl, she grew to love games, parties, and all manner of social occasions. After her parents died in 1872, her father of angina and her mother of cancer, she and her sister Sarah were sent by their brothers Charles Linnaeus, Abram, and Ross, to the Waltham Mass., New Church School for two years. They then attended Mt. Carroll Seminary in their hometown, Mt. Carroll. Although Susan completed all of the requirements, she did not graduate because she refused to pay the five dollar fee for her diploma.

In 1883, when JA hoped to have her as a traveling companion on her first European trip, Susan stayed home to marry Henry Mackay (1854–1916), a young lawyer she met through his sisters, who were classmates of hers at Mt. Carroll. Her sister Sarah went instead, and JA, Susan Hostetter Mackay, and Sarah Hostetter remained lifelong friends. Susan spent the remainder of her years at Northwood, the two-story white frame home she and her husband constructed on land left to them by her father. At Northwood, she and Henry had three children. Robert Partello Mackay (1888–1944) never married, Catherine Hostetter Mackay (1891–1975) married physician Cary Pratt McCord (1886–1979), and Sarah Davina Mackay (1884–1966) married Clem C. Austin (b. 1882).

Although Susan was unwell most of her life, suffering from tuberculosis in her right shoulder and from the cancers that may have been the results of experimental x-ray treatments to halt the spread of tuberculosis, she was a vivacious and active participant in life at Northwood. She was particularly good at chess, which she taught all of her children. She wrote poetry and songs as well and took up photography in the 1890s. She was also a serious botanist.

Under her guidance, Northwood became known for its hospitality. Of particular renown were the New Year's Eve parties, beginning in the first year of the Mackay marriage, which became an annual custom. After Henry died in 1916, Susan continued to live at Northwood, making it a haven for her children and grandchildren. She looked forward to the visits of JA, infrequent though they were. She died in her sleep in the summer at Northwood and was buried in Mt. Carroll.

2. Helen's father, Dr. John L. Hostetter.

3. Susanna ("Susan") Hostetter Bowman.

Monday, June 21, 1875.

This morning are still suspence having not head[1] a word from Carroll or about Nellie.

This afternoon received a telegram as follows, "Nellie is dead. Funeral Teus-day at [4?] P.M. diliver at once.["]

I don't know how I feel, I don't believe I can fell,[2] I don't relize it.

Ma and Aunt Susan intend to go on the twelve o'clock train.

This evening Mr Mitchell came down and we played croquet. I wonder how I acted, I wanted not to give in to it.

1. JA probably meant to write the word *heard* or *had*.
2. JA probably meant *feel*.

Tuesday, June 22, 1875.

George is not at all well or else we would of gone to Carroll.

So this morning while he was lying down I brought my motto "God is Love" and worked at it while [he] watched me and helped with his suggestions. By dinner I had the first word worked, and by evening the first two.[1]

This evening I called on old Mrs Mitchell and Mrs Stahl. Expect Ma to morrow.

1. On 18 June 1875 JA recorded in her diary that she bought a piece of canvas and the silk to work it. She also bought a work basket in which to keep her sewing.

Wednesday, June 23, 1875.

This evening Ma came home from Mount Carroll and told us all about it, it seems just like a dream to me, I can't pound it down into reality.

This forenoon we spent in the library I working on my motto and George playing bank we enjoyed it very much.

By this afternoon have my motto all finished and every one tinks it is very pretty.

. . . Sunday, June 27, 1875.

This morning Mary, John, Weber, George, Bertha[1] and I went to hear Mr Linn preach, he had a passable discourse.[2]

After church Mary interduced me to some lady and she took me around and must of interduced me to about fifty or sixty girls, right in a string. I went in a class and Mr Linn and I stayed to Sunday School and the rest of them went home. Enjoyed it pretty well.

1. Unknown but likely domestic help.
2. On 25 June 1875 JA, JWA, and GBH went to Winnebago to visit the Linn family in their new home.

Monday, June 28, 1875.

To day stayed at home most of the time or rather at Mr Linn's and spent a very quiet day, playing with John and amusing our selves in various ways.

George's nose keeps bleeding continualy and sort of worries me but he says he feels some better than he did[.][1] I wrote home to day and we have decided to stay until after the Rockford commencement[2] and go home Saturday with Mary.[3]

1. JA and GBH, whose almost constant nosebleeds seemed better by 30 June, planned to remain with the Linns until 3 July, when they would return to Cedarville.

2. Commencement exercises took place at RFS on Thursday morning, 1 July 1875.

3. Throughout the remaining summer months of 1875, JA, her stepmother, and stepbrother George entertained guests and traveled. After JA and GBH returned from Winnebago, Ill., GBH went to stay several weeks with brother HWH in Fontanelle, Iowa, while AHHA journeyed to Mitchellville, Iowa, to visit the Reichards. When Polly Beer visited the George Weber, Jr., family in Blairsville, Iowa, JA was looked after in Cedarville by Permilia "Pem" Tate, to whom she referred as "Miss Pemmie." Tate, from Mattoon, Ill., was a student and classmate of SAA in the Preparatory Dept. of RFS from 1869 to 1871, when she became acquainted with AHHA. She was unable to complete her senior year at RFS and graduate. According to the 30 June 1875 *Freeport Journal*, Pem Tate was the sister of Elizabeth A. Wurts Harding (wife of Capt. John R. Harding) of Freeport. Before the end of the summer, JA, GBH, AHHA, and Miss Pemmie had journeyed to JA's Hostetter step-relatives in Mt. Carroll and step-cousin Sarah Hostetter had paid a return visit.

Pemmie Tate was not a hit with everyone. HWH was concerned that his mother would take her too much into her confidence about the Addams family problems. "I would be very guarded in my conversations with Miss Tate," he advised, "and say nothing about any of the family at all. Don't try to get sympathizers—there's nothing more dispicable—we all have our troubles and unless We speak of it casually to each other—it should never be hinted at—that we are otherwise than happy;—all people carry—news—they can't help it—its second nature, and the fewer confidants We have and make the better are we off" (HWH to AHHA, 8 July 1875, IU, Lilly, SAAH).

June 1875 entries: AD (Addams, "Pocket Diary, 1875[-81]," CAHS; *JAPM*, 28:1576-89).

To Vallie E. Beck

In 1876 the sixteen-year-old Jane Addams added another name to her list of family and friends with whom she corresponded regularly. Vallie Emily Beck was born in Fort Madison, Iowa, in 1860, where she lived until her death in 1933. She was the only living daughter of Joseph Marcus Beck (1823–93), an attorney who became chief justice of the Iowa Supreme Court, and Clara C. Rinehart Beck (1833–85), daughter of Fort Madison physician William Rinehart (1803–68) and Mary Van Reed Rinehart (1813–71), who was born in Union County, Pennsylvania.

Jane Addams and Vallie Beck addressed one another as "cousin" because both shared distant Van Reed relatives. After meeting Judge and Mrs. Beck at her cousin Mary Reitzell Brawley's[1] home in Chicago, Mary Catherine Addams wrote to her sister Alice on 24 February 1870, "Mrs. Beck's Mother is a cousin of Pa's I think."[2] The Addams and Van Reed families of Pennsylvania, with mills on the Cacoosing Creek near Reading, intermarried in several different early generations. Jane Addams's aunt Mary B. Addams married John Van Reed; her great-uncle William Addams's first wife was Eva Van Reed, and one of their children, Amelia Addams, wed John H. Van Reed. William Addams's second wife was Catherine Huy Van Reed, widow of John Van Reed. And one of the children of this second marriage was Valeria Addams, who wed John H. Knapp in 1855. By 1856 the young Knapps were living next door to the Beck family in Fort Madison. It is also possible that the connection may have been strengthened by a Huy family relationship. John Huy Addams's mother's maiden name was also Catherine Huy.

It is impossible to know how Vallie Beck and Jane Addams met. It could have been through Valeria Addams Knapp, but more likely the introduction was the result of the friendship between Anna Haldeman Addams and the Soule and Fensley families, who settled near the Knapp and Beck families in Fort Madison about 1870. Vicenta M. Fensley[3] had befriended Anna in 1866 while visiting in Freeport, Ill., shortly after the death of Anna's first husband William J. Haldeman. Fensley lived in the Soule household and helped with the care of the Soule children. By 1873 Jane Addams and one of those children, Sarah Soule, called "Tadie" and also born in 1860, were conducting a correspondence, none of which is apparently extant. Tadie and her siblings visited with the Addams and Haldeman children in Cedarville with Vicenta Fensley, who traveled there periodically. In addition, Vicenta and Anna corresponded[4] and in 1875 she chaperoned Alice Addams on her tour through Europe.

The Vallie Beck–Jane Addams correspondence extended for a five-year period between 1876 and 1881. Because of their diverging intellectual and social interests, evident in their letters, their teenage friendship did not survive to adulthood.

Cedarville Ill   Feb. 26 1876

My dear Cousin

Was very much surprised but none the less pleased at the receipt of yours of the 26th ult. It was very kind in you to write and I hope we shall enjoy the correspondence if it so proves.

Received my last letter from Tadie[5] last week she is very punctual in writing. I too think her home must be delightful, but from her verbal description of her former one should imagine that a very pleasant locality also. I will begin by answering your inquiries. I go to school from home attending the Cedarville Public, and like it very much. Study the three R's, Latin, Algebra and Book keeping. Now have I your permission to ask you one? If so I will put the patent one of the day. "Are you going to the Centennial?"[6]

Ma received a paper from Oakland[7] containing the news of Mrs Fensleys[8] death it seems very sad indeed.

Please do not think I did not appreciate your letter by not answering sooner, but we have been giving several school entertainments in order to raise our portion of the funds necessary to represent the Ill educational interests at the Centennial Exhibition[9] and I have had my time very fully occupied.

Pa and Ma unite with me in sending thier kindest regards. Yours Truely

Jennie Addams

ALS (SCPC, JAC; *JAPM*, 1:167).

1. Mary Reitzell Brawley (1831?–post 1911), a distant JA cousin, was a daughter of Philip H. and Mary Ruth Reitzell. She was eighteen in 1850 when she married Francis W. S. Brawley (1825–98). He was a young attorney, born at North East in Erie Co., Pa., who was admitted to the Illinois bar and began practicing law with Martin P. Sweet in Freeport in 1847. He edited the *Freeport Bulletin* for a year and served twice as superintendent of schools for Stephenson Co. He was postmaster in Freeport from 1852 until 1858 and city attorney from 1860 to 1869. He was a Stephen Douglas Democrat. For a number of years both Brawleys were active with the board of education of Freeport and leaders in the Freeport Episcopal Church. In 1869 the couple moved to Chicago, where Francis Brawley practiced law, establishing the firm of Brawley and Dunne. The Brawleys lived on Chicago's South Side at 3010 Lake Park Ave. until 1906. By 1911 Mary Reitzell Brawley had been widowed and was living with her niece Jennie Strohecker, a teacher in Sioux Falls, S.D.

2. MCA to SAA, 24 Feb. 1870, IU, Lilly, SAAH.

3. Vicenta M. Fensley (1838?–1910) was the sister of Frances Fensley Soule (1835–1909), who was married to Joseph T. Soule (1822?–1890 or 1900). Joseph T. Soule was a sea captain who moved his family from the East Coast to West Coast, stopping for a while in several different towns in Illinois and Iowa. He was the founder of Soule, Davis and Co., later Soule, Kretsinger and Co., a predecessor to the Iowa Farming Tool Co. in Ft. Madison.

4. For the Fensley-Addams correspondence, see UIC, JAMC, HJ Supp. and IU, Lilly, SAAH.

5. Sarah ("Tadie") Soule was the eldest daughter of Capt. Joseph T. and Mrs. Frances Fensley Soule. By the early 1880s the Soule family was living in Hoquiam, Wash., where they owned and operated a fleet of sailing vessels. One account indicates that Capt. Joseph Soule died at sea in 1890, while another indicates that someone with a similar name died in 1900 at the Sailors' Snug Harbor, New York, N.Y. The Soule children remained in Hoquiam. Thomas C. Soule, born in Ft. Madison, Iowa, in 1874, operated a tug and barge company, a logging operation, and shingle mill. John F. Soule became a merchant and lumberman, secretary of the North-Western Lumber Co. in Hoquiam, and, like his brother, a city leader. JA's friend Tadie became Mrs. Sarah Soule McMillan. Two other sisters wed Josiah O. Sterns and Albert H. Kuhn.

6. In 1876, in the midst of an economic depression, the United States was preparing to celebrate its centennial. The idea for the "United States International Exposition" was born at the end of the Civil War when some were looking for ways to acclaim a united country; little financial support or planning was provided from government or private sources, however, until 1875. "The Centennial," as the event came to be known, opened on 10 May 1876 and closed 159 days later on 10 Nov. Nearly ten million people visited Fairmont Park near Philadelphia, Pa., where exhibits, food, and a variety of events filled two permanent buildings and hundreds of temporary structures set among specially constructed landscaped lawns, gardens, fountains, and paths. It was the first international exposition to be served by public transportation constructed especially for it. Another innovation was the creation of a Women's Pavilion. The Centennial's organization set the standard for several international expositions that followed. Although poorly attended at first, excitement about the exposition grew by word of mouth, bringing increasing numbers to witness exhibits from states, twenty-four of which erected buildings; foreign countries, with nine nations building fifteen buildings; and special exhibits focusing on agricultural and industrial innovations. Here for all to see for the first time in one place was America's might as the world's newest economic and industrial giant.

7. Oakland was the family home of Susan Hostetter Bowman and George Bowman near Mt. Carroll. It was situated in section 5 of Salem Twp. in Carroll Co. on 172 acres of farmland that the Bowmans bought about 1850. Oakland was constructed of brick produced in Cedarville after 1858, when the Bowman family moved permanently to Mt. Carroll from Penn-

sylvania. AHHA spent more than a year, from 1861 to 1862, living with the Bowmans at Oakland, coincident with and after the birth of her fourth child, GBH, and while her husband, William J. Haldeman, was living in Freeport with their older son HWH and running the Stone Steam Flour Mill.

8. Eliza Bunting Fensley, wife of Capt. John Martin Fensley of Albany, N.Y., was born in Portland, Maine. During the last year of her life she lived with her two daughters and grandchildren in the Soule family.

9. Planners for the Centennial wanted to have a large exhibit on the condition of education in America. In 1875, U.S. Commissioner of Education John Eaton asked each state to prepare material for the exhibit. Illinois Superintendent of Public Instruction Samuel M. Etter called leading educators together to plan their state's contribution. The Illinois State Teachers Assn. took a major role in promoting participation statewide. Materials indicating the development of education, teaching techniques, and the results as seen in students' work were gathered from private and public schools, including primary, graded and ungraded schools, high schools and seminaries, normal schools, colleges and universities, other educational and charitable institutions, and the Museum of Natural History. The exhibit was organized and prepared.

Although Centennial judges seemed generally unimpressed with the educational exhibits as a whole, the Illinois effort, primarily because of the award-winning presentation of the Illinois Industrial Univ., one of the Morrill Act of 1862 institutions that would be renamed the Univ. of Illinois, was thought one of the better displays. JA's father had served on a committee of the Illinois General Assembly that had selected the location for the university and promoted its creation.

The entire exhibit on behalf of Illinois education was expensive. When state government could provide none of the money to support the exhibit, planners decided to rely on county superintendents, their teachers, and parents and children to raise the needed funds. JA, her classmates, and the citizens of Cedarville participated in the effort. Statewide, $4,652 was secured to support the Illinois educational exhibit.

To Vallie E. Beck

When Jane Addams and George Haldeman missed the wedding of John Weber Addams to Laura Shoemaker on 16 March 1876 because they were home with mumps, Jane read to pass the time. She described her reaction to Charles Dickens's Pickwick Papers: *"Pickwick[1] made us laugh which operation was very painful, and almost every thing else seemed dry." Going on, she pronounced: "Speaking of Miss Alcotts 'Eight Cousins'[2] I like it, but not nearly so well as some of her former works, I have read and re-read 'Little Women'[3] and it never seems to grow old. The first series of 'Young America Abroad' is all I have to judge Oliver Optic[4] from, and I think that they are most decidedly not 'illusions,' optical or any other kind; although it contains some events which are rather improbable; but as Miss A. writes in a good deal the same strain, I think it was rather poor taste in her to criticize him." She added, "I am also on probation from that light kind of reading at present, and I suppose am singing my feeble praises for about the last time."[5]*

John Weber Addams and Laura Shoemaker were married in the Shoemaker home in Lena, Illinois. (S. H. Verbeck, Lena, Ill., and Lena Art Gallery, both SCPC)

Cedarville Ill   Mar. 30 [and Apr. 2] '76

My dear Cousin

I am enjoying a quiet afternoon sandwiching "Martin Chuzzlewit"[6] and letters up in my room; Pa and Ma are visiting Sister Mary at Winnebago, George has a young friend spending his vacation with him, and so I am "left alone in my glory."[7] I am ever so much obliged to you for your kind invitation, but am sorry to add it is impossible for me to accept. I hav'ent the least doubt but that I should have the nicest kind of a time and would not miss the "gay,"[8] for I cannot number dancing among my accomplishments, and my knowledge of "cards" is very limited indeed. But as I have a number of friends in Iowa including my sister and an uncle,[9] it may be in "the far distant future, etc.["]

We all expect to go east about the first of May,[10] and between now and then I suppose will find time really is fleeting, especially when fully occupied. But as Cedarville is east of you and consequently nearer the great magnet, I should be delighted if you could find it convenient to pay us a visit, I could safely promise you picnicing, boating, horse back rides and so forth, but nothing very far out of that line, for you know "we are six miles from a lemon."[11]

I have often heard Alice speak of Miss Jessie Hubbard,[12] and have met her when visiting at Rockford; she and her sister used to seem to me, to be the spice of the institution.

Apr 2.

At that point I concluded to read awhile and continued to do so until the tea bell rang.

You asked if I understood working on Turkish toweling,[13] I think I do in theory, although I have never worked on it. Alice had a beautiful toilet set made of it; given to her for a wedding present by one of the Rockford girls, I studied it quite a while and think I can do it. I cannot tell wether Tadie had reference to Geo. or Harry as being good chess players as both of them play very nicely.

I think I can sympathize with you in regard to "standard authors" especially "history" for if they were all as interesting as Dickens I think I could really enjoy them but possibly I have not been "worked up" to that fine and appreciative point.

I have read <five> of above mentioned authors works, and as I am a little inclined to "over do" things when I get started, I now have an arrangement with Pa, that I am to read a certain amount of history first, and the rest of the day can read "standard" that is a little more interesting.[14]

Please do not think I wish to appear learned, or any thing of that sort, but I think you will understand me.

Pa and Ma unite with me in sending kindest regards to the family. Yours very Truely

Jane Addams.

ALS (SCPC, JAC; *JAPM*, 1·179–87).

1. JA began reading *Pickwick Papers* in Jan. 1875 (see The 1875 Diary of Jane Addams, 17 Jan. 1875, n. 5, above).

2. *Eight Cousins* by Louisa May Alcott was about the fictional Campbell family. It was published in 1875, with a sequel, *Rose in Bloom*, issued in 1876 (see also JA to Vallie E. Beck, 3 May 1877, n. 5, below).

3. *Little Women*, initially published in two volumes between 1868 and 1869, has become Louisa May Alcott's most widely read work. It is said to be based on Alcott's own experiences growing up in Concord, Mass. (see also JA to Vallie E. Beck, 3 May 1877, n. 5, below).

4. Oliver Optic was the pseudonym of William Taylor Adams (1822–97), a Boston writer and teacher who produced many juvenile books and stories for magazines. His rags-to-riches moralizing made much of his work (such as the Onward and Upward series of novels published in 1870) similar to that of Horatio Alger, but he also wrote many adventure stories, including the Young America Abroad series and his Great Western series of novels published in 1875–82. He edited *Oliver Optic's Magazine for Boys and Girls* from 1867 to 1875. JA may very well have seen Alcott's work about girls as similar to William Taylor Adam's writings about boys, and thus her criticism of "Optic" as unfair.

5. JA to Vallie E. Beck, 16 Mar. 1876, SCPC, JAC; *JAPM*, 1:175.

6. Charles Dickens's *The Life and Adventures of Martin Chuzzlewit* was published in serial form from Jan. 1843 to July 1844 and as a book in 1844.

7. Apparently a paraphrase of the line "But we left him alone with his glory" from stanza eight of *Burial of Sir John Moore at Corunna*, the best-known work of Charles Wolfe (1791–1823), an Irish poet and priest. The poem, written in 1816, was first published anonymously in the *Newry* (Ireland) *Telegraph* ([1817]).

8. A "gay" was likely a party for young men and women. The definition does not appear

in the *OED* or in any of the dictionaries of the period that we consulted. Neither dancing nor card playing were activities favored in the Addams family. JA may have danced on occasion; her correspondence, however, indicates that she usually left a party before the dancing began. She did play whist and on more than one occasion won the booby prize.

9. SAAH and her husband HWH lived in Fontanelle, Iowa. Uncle George Weber, Jr., brother of JA's mother SWA, lived, along with his wife Maria Hoffeditz Weber and their children, in Blairstown, Iowa. Among other possible friends were step-cousin Virginia Hostetter Reichard and her husband D. Harvey Reichard in Mitchellville and relatives of at least two Cedarville families who were Addams friends, the Clingmans and the Eastmans.

10. The Addams family planned to visit the Centennial Exposition and relatives in Philadelphia, Pa.

11. Once again, JA is paraphrasing from a piece of current literature. Mary Abigail Dodge (writing as Gail Hamilton) issued *Twelve Miles from a Lemon* in 1874. The first sentence in the opening essay, which has the same title as the book, reads, "When Sydney Smith declared merrily that his living in Yorkshire was so far out of the way, that it was actually twelve miles from a lemon, all the world laughed." The author continues, "But the world little knows—the great, self-indulgent world, that dearly loves comfort, and ease and pleasure, . . . what it is to live twelve miles from a lemon. A lemon means ice and a market, all good things in their season, and all men eager to wait upon you" ([7]). Cedarville was six miles north of Freeport.

12. Jessie F. Hubbard of Cedar Rapids, Iowa, graduated from RFS with a diploma in music in 1876. She was a junior preparatory student during the 1870–71 academic year, when both SAA and MCA were attending the school, and in 1871–72 she enrolled in the RFS Conservatory of Music. She married George K. Barton, a merchant, and lived in Los Angeles, Calif.

13. Embroidery on turkish toweling.

14. JA was becoming an avid reader, consuming the popular literature of her day, works she referred to as "standard," with relish while avoiding more "serious" works. Among the other books by Dickens that she had read were *Pickwick Papers* (1837), *The Old Curiosity Shop* (1840), *Barnaby Rudge* (1841), and *Bleak House* (1853).

To Vallie E. Beck

Cedarville [Ill.]   May 1 '76

Dear Cousin Vallie

Please continue to call me Jennie or any thing that pleases you, do not think I mean "to stand aloof on my dignity" or any thing of that sort, I am simply Jennie at home, although I usually sign myself Jane—if it is one of the homelist in the catalogue.

I don't believe the old addage is always true, and am not at all afraid to become familiar,[1] and so most willingly accept your kind permission to address you as Vallie, for I like you ever so much and dislike to be so formal.

I was almost astounded to hear any thing about Vassar[2] that was not highly complimentry, for I had a floating idea in my mind that it was one of the schools that was just about perfect.

I have read about it and have met several people who have personal knowledge of the institution and they all praised it highly, but "There are many men of many minds."

We hardly expect to start on our trip untill the middle of the month. We will not remain in Philadelphia but a part of the time.[3]

We had quite an adventure ~~quite adventure~~ the other afternoon, Susie Hostetter a niece of Ma's about my age was visiting us, and she, Geo and myself took a boat-ride,[4] there was a real high wind when we started, and were soon struck with the brilliant idea of sailing at our ease, instead of having the labor of rowing, two saplings were made stand duty as masts, whilst a water proof was hoisted in lieu of a sail, it certainly did not look "white and gustling" but never the less we were on our way rejoicing even being so daring as to breathe the hope that we might ship-wreck on the rocks or some thing of the sort, just to relieve the monotany of <u>plain</u> sailing you know. George did the steering and not knowing exactly how to manage it, run us against the cliff with a good deal of force as preface from which pleasant situation it took us about half an hour to relieve ourselves. I was pilot and called out to Geo. that there was a stump ahead, he, in his frantic efforts to avoid it, run straight into it, giving the boat such a jar that it threw me (who was standing up to ajust the sail) off of my feet and half way out the boat, they with thier united exertions managed to save me, and after examining my hair and finding it had not turned gray, concluded I would recover from my fright in due course of time, and we proceeded to run into a snag and from thence into the opposite shore with a bang!! After this we went for about half a mile without difficulty, the wind grew higher and it sailed just splendidly.

But in making some changes one of our oars fell over board, and in trying to rescue it and not looking where we were going to, found ourselves floated high and dry on a mud bank.

This was a desperate situation, for we had not thought of the going home ward, we could not possibly get off with one oar and the wind was blowing a perfect gale. After our first laugh had subsided we looked blankly at one another, George waded into the mire half knee deep and tried to shove us off, which was a failure. We finely abonded the boat and gain[ed] the shore, walked around to where we lost the oar, and with the aid of trees and hard work, bore it off in triumph. We went back to the boat and rowed it home. Sue and I walked, feeling decidedly cheap, may be wet feet had some damping effect upon our spirits. Arrived at home found we had been gone just four hours and a half.

Please excuse me for not answering before, but we have had a great deal of company lately and have been quite busy "I will try to be good and not do so anymore."

All send kind regards. Yours etc

                                                      Jane Addams.

ALS (SCPC, JAC; *JAPM*, 1:189–94).

1. JA may be referring to Maxim 640 of Publlillius Syrus, repeated by Shakespeare and Aesop: "Familiarity breeds contempt."

2. Vallie Beck's letter to JA, apparently with a criticism of Vassar, is not extant. Vassar College, Poughkeepsie, N.Y., was chartered in 1861 and opened in 1865. Named for Matthew Vassar (1792–1868), who provided financial support for its creation, it has been heralded as the first major women's college in the United States. Although other colleges that admitted women were established before it, among them Oberlin and Antioch in Ohio and Georgia Female College in Macon, Vassar set a new standard in entrance requirements. It also boasted an excellent and trained faculty, modern and sufficient buildings and equipment, and stringent performance requirements for graduation that were similar to those of male schools. The purpose of the school, as stated in its first prospectus as written by the president, John H. Raymond, was to provide physical education, as well as a four-year course of intellectual training that featured English, Latin, French, or German, algebra, geometry, natural philosophy, botany, zoology, mineralogy, geology, physical geography, anatomy and physiology and hygiene, outlines of history, theoretical and practical ethics, in addition to a group of electives, moral and religious education, domestic education, social education, and opportunities for professional education in teaching, telegraphy, phonography (shorthand), and bookkeeping.

3. JA and her family did go east during the summer of 1876. The Addams family held a reunion at Harriet C. Addams Young and Nathan Young's house, 536 North Fourth St., in Philadelphia. Rebecca H. Addams, Mary B. Addams Van Reed, Lydia M. Addams Albright, Harriet C. Addams Young, Susan Jane Addams Mull, JHA, and James Huy Addams attended. It is also likely that their spouses and some of their children were there, too. In addition to JA, from the JHA family, GBH and AHHA were present. Although they may have visited other family members in the Philadelphia area, and perhaps some of the Weber family in and around Reading, Pa., the big event of the summer was attending the Centennial.

There is no definite record of what they saw at the Centennial, but it is likely that at the very least they visited the Machinery Hall, the Horticultural Hall, Memorial Hall, and the building constructed by Illinois. The Women's Pavilion could have made a significant impression on the sixteen-year-old JA. Here Emma Allison stood every day at the controls of her six-horsepower Baxter steam engine, which ran six looms and a printing press. Also on display were the inventions of more than seventy-five women patent-holders covering all manner of creation, from dressmaking systems and the manufacture of clothing, kitchen tools, and furniture to flares produced for the U.S. Navy. There were scientific and medical exhibits.

Among educational exhibits was a model kindergarten, evidence that the movement begun by Frederick Froebel in the 1830s was getting a strong foothold in the United States. There were examples of work turned out by women who taught at all levels of education throughout the United States. There were special exhibits from Smith, Wellesley, and Mt. Holyoke in Massachusetts, as well as from RFS and from the Women's Medical College of Pennsylvania. What an opportunity for a young woman beginning to think seriously about education after high school to be able to compare and contrast educational institutions. Exhibits of painting, sculpture, and the decorative arts graced the pavilion. A library contained books by women as well as a comfortable place to sit and read. Philanthropic women received special notice. The Women's Centennial Committee, which raised almost $175,000 to create the Women's Pavilion, issued a listing of philanthropies under the direction of women. It identified 822 charitable organizations from throughout the United States and hung pictures of representative institutions associated with that list on the walls of the pavilion for all to see.

4. GBH, Susan Hostetter, and JA were sailing on the Addams's millpond on Cedar Creek.

While the siblings of John Huy Addams were gathered for a family reunion in Philadelphia during the summer of 1876, all apparently had their photographs taken by the award-winning photographer F. Gutekunst at 712 Arch Street. This photograph of (left to right) Jane Addams, Anna Haldeman Addams, and George Haldeman was taken about the time that they ventured forth to the cabinet of John L. Capen, phrenologist, for a reading. (JAPP)

Phrenological Reading

By 1876 America's fascination with phrenology was on the wane; Anna Hostetter Haldeman Addams's was not. When the Addams family visited Philadelphia for the reunion and the Centennial Exposition during the summer of 1876, she took Jane and George with her to see John L. Capen, M.D.,[1] for a phrenological consultation. Capen read Jane's skull on at least two different occasions, 28 and 30 July 1876. It seems likely that she was pleased with what he revealed about her. She carefully presented it in her own hand so that it was clear and easy to read. While copying Capen's statement about her supposed lack of talent as "a good copyist," she made two glaring errors in the spelling of the words from *and* to, *one of which Capen would not have made. She must have meant the word* form *but wrote instead* from. *It is also likely that the difference between the written letters* M *and* N *was still an issue for the fifteen-year-old, given her spelling of the word* menorize *in the last paragraph in the body of the text.*

George and Jane's interest in phrenology continued after their return to Cedarville. They formed the Capenic Phrenological Society of the Northwest, with George as president and Jane as secretary. Jane Addams received a playful letter written by her former teacher John H. Parr and his friend Richard Arthur Edwards on 8 January 1877, a response to a letter she had written inviting them to join. In accepting honorary membership in the Capenic Phrenological Society of the Northwest, Parr and Edwards, using appropriate phrenological vocabulary, promised to "constantly endeavor to develop the good organs and restrain the growth of the bad. So that long after these organs have lost their material existence, their ghosts, like good angels, may hover round the places we now inhabit, filling the very atmosphere with the spirit of Reverence, keener Perception, a deeper love of the Beautiful, a loftier Patriotism, and, &c"²

Philadelphia, Pa.
The Contents of Jane Addams' head, as examined by John L. Capen Phrenologist, July 28. 1876
Age—15 years, 8 months, 22 days
    Size of head ¼ to ½ inch larger than average adults. Mental powers greater than physical. With care will enjoy a good degree of health through out her life. Vital power not great; but still an element of toughness in her that will endure a good deal. Rather an evenness of temperament but shows marked traits of character. Has strength of feeling and energy. Large positiveness if she thinks a thing is true, she thinks it with all her might. Great sensativeness and timidity, lack of self esteem consequently <lack of> confidence in herself. Social, but not fond of general society, fond of her own select society and circle of friends and

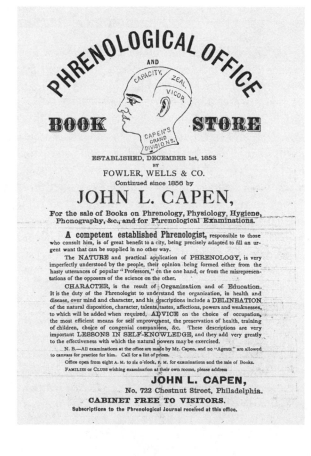

Broadside distributed by John L. Capen advertising his phrenological cabinet. (*JAPM*, 28:729)

home folks. Intellect beyond average, inclined to be sober, serious and earnest. Strong will and inclined to be very obsanate. As a business women would be a good bookkeeper, financeir and arithmetician but a lack of sharpness as in making bargains or trading. Strong in her likes and dislikes, very affectionate, thinks a great deal of her friends and will always stand by them.

Womanly and matronly. True, steady and uniform, self sacrificing until she finds she is imposed upon then would become very indignant. Strong reasoning powers. Gratitude large; consciencousness great. Form medium, very large firmness. Memory average, large originality dislikes to imitate others, or memorize, prefer to be original. Inclined to be inventive especially of things of a mechanical nature. Dislikes to be over persuaded. She would make her mark in drawing designs, although her ideas of size and from[3] are to poor to become a good copyist. Not enthusiastic, in any project will become slowly interested and by reason, but when interested will be zealous and presevearing and loath to abond it. Her mind will always become interested before she takes hold with her hands. ~~Large~~ <Small> veneration and great preseverance. Prudent and careful. Moral faculties very much larger than religious. Inclined to be skeptical, as for intance, if some one was trying to make her believe a thing against her principle of right and wrong and even say that the Lord said so, she would begin to doubt if the Lord ever did say such a thing wether it was'ent man that said it. She would never be a proselyte, not sectarian, thinks ever one has the right to believe what they please. Will do any thing from principle, believe nothing without a good reason. Melody poor, but good harmony, would hardly come up to the average through the first courses of music but do better afterward. Large imagination but under good control, if she builds castles in the air always has some good foundation for them. She will be a good chess player, in philosophy and mathematics very good; as a linguist in foreigh languagues would hardly come up to the average. If subject to mortifications, great disapointment or anxiety in the next five years would be apt to stunt the growth of her mind and injure its strength; inclining then to become meloncoly.

Hope large, if it has any foundation. Natural disposition cheerful.

At school <among a large number> will not be showy or brilliant on account of her lack of confidence in herself, being sensitive and easily mortified, also not being able to menorize so easily as others; but will be steady and presevering, sticking to a thing when the majority give it up, and will come out near the head at last.

Philadephia Penna.
922[4] Chestnut Street.

P.S. July 30.
Prespective faculties fair but no so large as reflective. Should cultivate her talent for drawing and music.

HD authored by John L. Capen and copied by JA. UIC, JAMC, Detzer; *JAPM*, 28:736–741.

1. Dr. John L. Capen had been trained in the New York office of the Fowler family, primary purveyors of phrenology in America. By the mid-1850s, Lorenzo and Orson Fowler, together with their sister Charlotte, half-brother Edward, half-sister Almira—the latter two homeopathic physicians—and their mates, children, and converts, had created a phrenology empire consisting of publications, stores, educational opportunities for those who wanted to learn the would-be science, lectures and public appearances to amaze and to promote, and a practice of reading heads and creating a museum of famous heads. Their books and journals, including the *American Phrenological Journal, Student* (to which the Addams children subscribed) and *Illustrated Life*, carried the phrenological message far and wide across the expanding United States, as did their lectures and readings and those of the practitioners they trained. In the process, the Fowlers became writers, educators, editors, publishers, speakers, and public figures whose work was supported at different times by eminent public figures and intellectuals. Their doctrine of reform through self-knowledge was appealing and set the stage for promoting hundreds of societal reforms, among them penal reform, better understanding of the insane, more attention to the early care and education of children, marriage counseling, women's rights, sex education, vegetarianism, temperance, and giving up tobacco. The Fowlers also promoted water as a cure-all. By the mid-1850s, with phrenology at the height of its popularity nationwide, they opened branches of their enterprise in Boston and Philadelphia.

Two years after the Philadelphia branch at 231 Arch St. had opened in 1853, its management was taken over by John L. Capen. He was still in charge of the Phrenological Museum, Book Store and Office located at 722 Chestnut St. when the Addams family visited during the Centennial. Capen's readings of AHHA and JA's heads are both extant. The reading for GBH exists only as notation in *New Illustrated Self-Instructor and Physiology; with Over One Hundred Engravings; Together with the Chart and Character of Miss Jane Addams, Mr. George B. Haldeman as Marked by John L. Capen July 31, 1876 (JAPM, 28:731–35)*. The phrenological study done by Capen of AHHA's head survives in its original form handwritten by Capen (*JAPM, 28:730*).

2. SCPC, JAC; *JAPM, 1:198*.

3. JA probably meant to write *form*.

4. JA mistook Capen's *7* for a *9* when she copied the address.

To Vallie E. Beck

Cedarville Ill   May 3 1877

My dear Vallie

Housecleaning now rules and reigns with all its untold horrors, please accept that simple explanation for the apparent unappreciation of your last kind letter.

I spent my spring vacation in visiting Sister Alice, and had a very pleasant two weeks trip, it was my first views west of the Mississippi and I was delighted with Iowa and more so with the people, they were all so very kind and hospitable; But Harry and self took a twenty two mile horseback-ride over the boundless prairie, out of sight of fences or humans, it was perfectly glorious and reminded one of "forever and forever."[1]

Your description of "talented" cousins was real funny, I think they are nice, but I always have to feel my insignificance so deeply when I see them, that it makes me feel bad. I have one however that has entirely the reverse affect, for she inspires one to a sort of hero worship, her name is Anna Young prehaps you "have heerd on her" she has just been married to Mr Mohr and they made us a flying visit on their wedding tour, returning yesterday, we enjoyed their society very much.[2] I think bridal parties are so <u>interesting</u>, don't you? You spoke of reading Scott, I have "never partaken very freely of his great genius." I suppose of <u>course</u> I shall enjoy him, but as a rule, (dreadful to relate) "instructive novels" are a to me a bore. I have a cousin who raves over Scott and is one of his most devoted admirers, of about every thing he said or did.[3] I most decidedly think Mrs Craik's books pure, and all I have read struck me as being quite moral and "good." I think her works are so interesting and facinating without being thrilling.[4]

I have never thought much about the "ism" you spoke of, I think there is a good deal of force in the theory, but when love does <u>not</u> beget love it is apt to produce dislike or what is worse hatred, rarely indifference. I am a great admirer of Platonic love or rather pure sacred friendship, I think it is so much higher than what is generally implied in the word love.

I have not yet read the "Rose in Bloom" and after reading what you said about Charlie I don't exactly care to, would rather finish the story to suit myself, for he was my favorite of the eight cousins. I think as you said, that those are the characters one most admires, and I think Rose might of influenced him and brought him out all right, if she had sufficiently exerted herself. I diden't think any of the Campbell family were particularly brilliant or remarkable excepting Mae and Charlie may be Miss Alcott wanted to show what is in the <u>average</u> boy and girl for they are so very seldom "brought out." I think Miss A. must have an ideal hero in her mind that runs through all her works more or less, for Charlie is somethings like "Laurie" in <u>Little Women</u> and Tom in ["]Old Fashioned Girl" don't you think so.[5] I received you note from Chicago, thank you very much for it. And <u>now</u> I intend to assert my rights and insist on your coming to see me very soon indeed, it is'ent any thing of a ride from here to Chicago, and you could arrange it to miss very little time from your studies, say come some Saturday and spend the following Sunday, and just as much more time as you could possibly spare, we would meet you at the depot and take you <there> just when you thought you would have to go; we have a fine piano and you would not need to lose one bit of practice. I do want to see you so bad and it is not probable I shall be in Chicago in the next two months. Now <u>do</u> try and come, we would all extend you a hearty welcome in our home, and Pa and Ma unite with me in sending a very urgent invitation.[6]

It will do you good to have a few days country quit for I know you intend to work hard.

Please write soon and I will be daily expecting a "yes" or a <u>very</u> good reason for a negative reply. Eveyours

Jane Addams.

ALS (SCPC, JAC; *JAPM*, 1:218–23).

1. JA's first trip west of the Mississippi River took her to Fontanelle, established in 1855 as the first county seat of Adair Co., Iowa, to visit her sister SAAH and her husband, stepbrother and physician HWH. HWH had established his practice in the village in the fall of 1874 and brought his bride there on their wedding trip in Oct. 1875. The town had a bank, newspaper, hotel, school, and assorted businesses located on a town square by the time JA visited.

2. Anna E. Young (1847–1915) was one of the children of JA's aunt Harriet C. Addams Young and uncle Nathan Young, who lived in Philadelphia. In April 1877 she married James Nicholas Mohr (1844–1921). After their wedding trip to the west, the Mohrs also settled in Philadelphia. The Mohrs had no children who lived to maturity. James N. Mohr was the son of Angeline Maderia Mohr and John H. Mohr (1804–57), whose ancestors were founders of Mohrsville, Pa., where he was born. He spent his career in the paper business. Throughout the 1890s and until 1913, when he may have retired, he was vice president of Reading Paper Mills.

3. We do not know which of JA's many step-cousins liked the work of Sir Walter Scott. The Scottish lyric poet's historical novels included *Kenilworth* (1821) and *Ivanhoe* (1819).

4. Dinah Maria Mulock Craik (1826–87), married to George Lillie Craik, a partner in the Macmillan and Co. publishers, wrote novels as well as children's stories, poems, and essays. Among her works was *John Halifax, Gentleman* (1857), which stresses the moral that personal integrity is more important than good breeding or material riches. Her other novels include *Life for a Life* (1859), *Ogilvie* (1849), *Olive* (1850), *Head of the Family* (1851), and *Agatha's Husband* (1853). It is likely that JA had become familiar with Craik through her children's stories and was in the process of graduating to her adult fiction.

5. Alcott's *Rose in Bloom* was not issued until 1876 and was a sequel to *Eight Cousins*. It features Rose, a "modern" woman raised in a household of boys, who conquers her feelings of vanity and materialism and finds fulfillment through adopting a baby girl and founding a home for working women. Lonely, sensitive Laurie, the neighborhood boy in *Little Women*, longs to be part of the inner circle of the young women next door and eventually achieves his goal through marriage to one of the sisters. In *An Old Fashioned Girl* (1870), Tom Shaw, irresponsible and self-centered but basically good, is like the household of women with whom he is surrounded, spoiled by shallow, newfangled expectations associated with wealth and urban life.

6. Vallie Beck was studying music in Chicago. Although Beck's direct response is not extant, on 30 May 1877 JA wrote to her, "Received your very welcome letter, and was made twice happy by the news it contained. We shall now most certainly expect you very soon indeed; do come before it grows so warm for I am sure you will enjoy it more than you will later. . . . I will be most happy to visit you at your home some future time, but cannot make any definite promises, and I hope you won't consider your visit as contracting a debt, for I shall enjoy it more than you shall" (SCPC, JAC; *JAPM*, 1:224).

From Vallie E. Beck

Keokuk, Iowa.   Friday, Aug, 10th 1877

My dear Jennie;

Since I received your last kind letter, my time has been consumed in entertaining company and visiting; as you have frequently "been there yourself" you can appreciate my seeming neglect in not answering your last letter, which I assure you was no exception for all of your affusions unless indeed it was more interesting and characteristic (if that were possible.)

I spent nearly a week in Burlington, where I enjoyed myself very much, being among lively people mostly, but this is the place that I enjoy visiting, the family being old friends of ours and consisting of some of the nicest people I have ever had the good fortune to meet.[1] But aside from this, I feel more at home and easy, whether I forget restraint and "company manners" or because my friends are so kind and clever.

If you have ever visited Keokuk,[2] you are aware the people are very hospitable and although so are at the same time rather, removed than otherwise from freeness, which to me is a great compliment. There are some quite pretty drives around the place and nearly every day I have spent the mornings out riding. Keokuk sports a boulevard which if spoken of with less flourish would be quite fine, but, the [most?] <of> Keokukions are too proud of spouting to not give vent occasionally to a fit of boasting about, "our drives". But we can easyly forgive their weakness if we only have an opportunity to drive to Wild Cat Springs[3] which is several miles north on the Ills. shore. Yesterday morning we went up there and found it a charming place not <only> the Springs but the surrounding country, also. Wild Cat creek is peculiar, considering the fact that few of the small streams in this immediate vicinity are rocky bound. The water is unusually clear and is fed by springs all the way; is colder than usual for creeks, and has numerous small cascades. Quite near the Springs are picknick—ks grounds which are popular with the young people here, there being many nooks in the rock in which almost any congenial couple declare innumerable ferns are to be found. When we recollect the meaning of Fern[4] in the language of Flowers it is not hard to understand why they are declared so numerous.

Unfortunately(?) I found no ferns there as my companion was an old gentleman long ago past the age in which "ferns" are sought. May be it is just as well for I assure no young gentleman I have so far met, could persuade me that "ferns" are as plentiful as some young ladies choose to believe.

One of my friends is a West Point Cadet and is at home on his first furlough. His discriptions and anecdotes of the W.P. life are very interesting to me for I have always been entertained in reading about the place and have wished often that I might sometime spend a season on the Hudson and part of the time at "The Point." Judging from what I have heard and read the gentleman is a typical West-Pointer, being gay, free, light hearted and almost too easy on the Subject of religion; a fine horseman. I should like you to meet him for like many Pointers his manners are captivating. He has two brothers who are quite as agreeable as he. His sister is one of my friends and I am her most devoted admirer and have been always her truest and most loving friend. She is beautiful, a type of Grecian beauty, a blond, is quite accomplished, and is just my style.[5] There is but one other lady whom I admire more than her. Well I have "gushed" enough for once. Please excuse it I shall do so no more in future and on the same subject.

Since visiting here I have read Howells' Forgone Conclusion[6] which for me is merely a readable book, containing peculiar characters but, unsatisfactory ones;

as to the plot, there was none and the only one that interested me was Don Ippolito: also read "Kismet", one of the "No Name["] series, a book which failed to interest me and one which I easily forgot and think wasted my time in reading.[7] Am now reading Wm Black's "Princess of Thule."[8] Before I left Home I finished Bleak House[9] and found it very interesting but alittle tediou[s]ly (if the two may be combined). Esther was a character to forever be admired and extolled, but are there any such? Have you ever been so fortunate as to meet such an one?

If I should meet an Esther, probably my perverse disposition would show its self by not allow me to like her and by really give me a sort of dislike for her old maidish ways. But as for Ada I never did like peaches and cream which were overly sweetened.

Esther's husband is the sort of man to admire and cannot be too much sought after and Guardian is the kind of people one always respects but has a certain pity regarding them.

Really you must excuse my pitying you but I do if you have waded through this lengthy letter in one installment, but the temptation was to me irresistable for I have deprived myself the pleasure of writing to you for so long.

Please do write soon and let me know when we may expect to have your delightful company and the longed for visit. My kindest regards to your parents. Your very sincere friend

Vallie E. Beck.

ALS (SCPC, JAC; *JAPM*, 1:228–40).

1. Vallie Beck was visiting the home of Mary Ann Bowen Howell (d. 1903) and Judge James B. Howell (1816–80). Judge Howell had emigrated to Iowa in 1841, settling in Keosauqua, where his first wife Isabella Richards Howell died and where he purchased his first newspaper, the *Des Moines Valley Whig*. In 1849 he and his newspaper, renamed the *Gate City*, moved to Keokuk, where in 1850 he wed Mary Ann Bowen. He became active in Republican politics, and in 1870 the Iowa legislature elected him a member of the U.S. Senate to fill an unexpired term. In 1871 he was appointed one of the three judges of the U.S. Court of Southern Claims, serving until shortly before his death. There were seven children born to the Howells, three of whom died in infancy.

2. Keokuk, Iowa, is located at the confluence of the Des Moines and the Mississippi rivers just north of Ft. Madison and also in Lee Co. The settlement, begun in 1820 at the foot of a segment of rapids on the Mississippi River, was named in 1829 for the chief of the Sac tribe who had been friendly to the settlers. Ft. Des Moines barracks, constructed in 1834, were occupied until 1837, when the troops were moved further west to Ft. Leavenworth, Kans. Platted in 1837, Keokuk had a population of two thousand by 1848. The post office opened in 1841, and soon there were churches, stores, and a school and hotel. The Civil War brought more population and more development. The growth of Keokuk was aided by the construction of the Des Moines Canal 1867 to 1877, intended to bypass the Mississippi River rapids and promote transport on the river, and by the Keokuk to Hamilton, Ill., bridge across the Mississippi, which was completed in 1871. By 1870 the community boasted a medical school, library, opera house, and fire department in addition to several banks, railroads, newspapers, and numerous commercial and manufacturing establishments. The community of fifteen thousand was proud of its wide streets and handsome homes.

3. Wild Cat Springs, a site of wooded ravines and bluffs bordering Cheney Creek on the east side of the Mississippi River near the town of Hamilton, Ill., possessed an old cave where a terrible cat was supposed to live. It was a favorite location for picnics, chautauquas, and reunions for people from Keokuk, Iowa, Clark Co., Mo., and nearby parts of Illinois. The site had been the property of the Brown family for a number of years, and when Vallie Beck visited it, she and her friends probably paid a small fee to Alice and Homer D. Brown, its owners. The site was acquired by Hamilton as a public park in 1954.

4. Since ancient times ferns have been recognized for their magical powers. They were used as medicine, for charms and curses, for protection to ward off evil, as a cure, and to attract (Vallie Beck may have been making an oblique reference to that use). It is difficult, however, to know exactly what she meant. The language of flowers, associated in America primarily with the Victorian era, had no universal vocabulary for symbolically matching flowers with specific human traits of character or feelings. Writers of the books in which floral vocabularies appear, called "language of flower books," have selected their own different and special meanings. In some cases, authors agree on the meaning associated with a flower, in others they do not. According to Beverly Seaton, "There is almost no evidence that people actually used these symbolic lists to communicate, even if the parties agreed upon what book to use for their meaning" (*The Language of Flowers: A History,* 2). This letter seems an exception. Vallie Beck must have thought JA would understand what she meant. According to several different flower vocabularies, the fern could be used to symbolize sincerity, secrecy, confidence, fascination, or solitary humility.

5. The four Howell children who were Vallie Beck's friends were: Jesse B., who became the manager of the *Gate City;* Lida Gordon, who despite her "Grecian beauty" remained in Keokuk and never married; Daniel Lane, a graduate of the U.S. Military Academy at West Point in 1879, became a career soldier who served in the Spanish-American War and retired to California as a colonel; and James Frederick, who served as a captain in the Spanish-American War and continued in the army until his retirement to Long Island, N.Y., as a colonel.

6. William Dean Howells (1837–1920), an American magazine editor, short-story writer, and novelist who was U.S. consul to Venice during the Civil War, published *Foregone Conclusion* in 1875. Later in her life, quite unexpectedly, JA encounterd Howells in person. She was speaking before what she believed to be a difficult audience in New York City. To calm herself, and, she hoped, successfully make her points, she chose to address her remarks to one older man in the audience. After the speech he came forward to congratulate her on her presentation and to thank her for the particular attention she had paid him. He introduced himself as William Dean Howells.

7. *Kismet,* a novel by Julia Constance Fletcher (1858–1938), whose pseudonym was George Fleming and who lived most of her life in Venice despite her American parentage, was published anonymously in 1877 as part of a series entitled "No Name." Among her other novels are *Nile Novel* (1877), *Vistigia* (1882), and *Truth about Clement Ker* (1889).

8. William Black (1841–98) was a Scottish novelist and a war correspondent during the Franco-Prussian War. *Princess of Thule* was published in 1873. His other novels include *Daughter of Heth* (1871) and *Macleod of Dare* (1879), all stories of Scotland.

9. Dicken's *Bleak House* (serialized in 1852–53) was a satire of the old Court of Chancery and the great social costs of its corrupt and inefficient bureaucracy.

From Devault Weber

Norristown [Pa.]   September 3d 1877

Dear Niece

The hot weather is now about over with us, I feal more like writing, and I find an unswered letter[1] from <you> dated March 9. 1877, among my pack,

Your Cousin Joseph Reiff[2] got Started at last he was to see us a few days before he Started, which seamed the hardest part, which I urged him to over-come and all would go well, which he has proved by a letter from him from Vinton Iowa Aug 25. 1877[.][3] I must her give you a part of his letter, After Spend-ing a very pleasant time with you all at Cedarvill, he left for Como,[4] as follows, (Como Seams to be deserted place indeed no business going on whatever, the mill is Standing idle and all Shut up. I was greatly disappointed that I could not gain admittance the man in charge was just coming out of the Mill as I got there, I told him who I was and the reason that I wished to go inside but he positively would not permit it on any account he said he was very sorry but his orders forbade the admittance one & all. I have Since found out the cause & it Seams their is Still trouble about the property[.] the parties who have the mill are <u>lawing</u> with other parties who have a clame gainst the Same and as possession is nine thenths of the game, they might have suposed I had been sent their for that purpose as my telling who I was did not make it so, to them as they did not know <me>. I saw at a glase that the property had cost an amence amount of money. The Mill race is 35 ft wide 5 ft deep their has been no water in it for about Six years, the grass is growing in the middle from the Mill to the dam there are also Many fences built accross it Roads &c.

After looking all around out side the Mill I started for the grave yard[.] I had no guide & was compeled to see & find the best I could, the grave yard is about 1 ¼ miles up the race near the dam after looking a long time I found Grand Fathes grave it is enclosed in a lot by a fence 18 ft long by 15 ft wide the head lying East 30 Steps west to the race & 42 Steps to the dam north east their are Six other graves in the lot four of Uncle Georges children & Dr Hoffendizs Daughtr and R. Russell, their is one side of the fence lying down[.][5]

I wished very much as I stood their all alone by the side of his grave that you and mother could have been their also. Indeed Uncle I assure you it was a <very> great Satisfaction for me to be their as it brought many thoughts to my mind of the days of my chilhood[.)]

My dear Ni[e]ce it is no hardship to pen this Sketch of Joseph discripton down[.] I have read it over agan & again and have weeped over it as it appears like my only funeral procession to my Fathers grave[.]

I cannot help with my present sollem thoughts to give you a discription of your Grand Mothers[6] grave and resting place, in October 1869 I was written to from Mercersburg Pa that all the dead was to be removed from the old grave yard in Mercersburg town <to> outside the limits of the town to a Cemetery & thus I should attend to remove my Mother.

I made arangement and Started October 18th 1869 with the intenton to remove her to My Cemetery Lot at Norristown. I arived in Mercersburg 7 ½ Oclockp.m., and found that Brother Harrison[7] had araived their a few days before from the West, and <had> Mother taken up & removed to the Cemetery about a mile out of the town to a family lot he bought of his own then and had that day removed Mother body and placd a marble slab as faullows, The Marble Slab was firmly surported by Square oblong blue limestone Slabs cut and dresed & fermly cemented together, Surported by a stone foundation wall, on high ground overlooking the sorounding County, and Brother <Harrison> had left for New York the Same day, I arived their, It was a beautiful Moon light night, and I felt overcome after hearing the result of Mother Removal by Brother Harrisons Brothernlaw who I hapened to Meet on my arival at mercersburg who told me all. I asked him if he would not walk out to the Cemety[.] I could see it as well to night by moonlight as by day, and which I would rather do, he consented when their he explane all, he left me alone awhile seeing my anguish. Oh such sacred moments at the dead of night the silent dead all around bending over the domb of a departed parent are never to be forgotten, with soft and lingering Steps I withdrew from the holy grounds, and <join> my friend <at the gate>. Mr Shively with whom I remand all night and as I would had to reman over a day I prefered returning by Stage next morning by dayligh when I agan Saw the grave from the road as we passed[.]

The inscription on her hansom Marble Slab is as follers =

> Scacred to the memory of
> Sarah Weber, Wife of George Weber born
> July 30 A.D. 1786 died July 9 A.D. 1846
> aged 59 Years 11 Mo. & 9 days
> "The Lords will be done"

Now will you be so kind & send me a discription of where and how your Mother[8] is buried and all a bout it, I had bought a large lot before I left to remove Mother in 1869. and hoped Some day to remove Father and Mother to it, I have a Famely Monument, and a rocky <to an only child> with Image of Hope and Faith, which I will <som day> send you a discription[9] of.

I did not think when I commenced this letter of making it of so Sollem a compositon but looking over your Cousin Josephs letter I could not help it. And as you never had heard of your Grand Mothrs I thougt it best and well for you to know[.]

Your Aunt[10] and I have enjoyed good health this Summer and Send our love to you all give me Mary Linns P. Off. address[.] I must write to them some day[.] Your Affectionate Uncle

Devault Weber

NB, Your Aunt & I last evening attende Francis Murphys temperance Reformed lecture. Over a thousand people attended he is a powerfull lecturer[.] A great Many old drinker here have reformed under his instrumentaly, a blessd Revival here it is needed[.]

ALS (SCPC, JAC; *JAPM*, 1:242–48).

1. JA's letter of 9 Mar. 1877 to De Vault Weber is not extant. It probably provided him with an account of Polly Beer's death, which took place on 7 Jan. 1877 on a farm to the north of Cedarville and with JA in attendance (see Biographical Profiles: Beer, Mary ["Polly"]).

2. Joseph L. Reiff (1841–93) was the eldest of three children of one of JA's mother's siblings, Elizabeth Weber Reiff, and her husband Enos L. Reiff. He never married and lived in Ambler, Pa., where he built a home near the flour mill his father operated and which he owned after the death of his sister Sarah ("Sallie") Weber Reiff in 1885.

3. Joseph Reiff was visiting his uncle, George Weber, Jr., and his family.

4. Como, Ill., located on the north bank of the Rock River in Whiteside Co., was platted in 1838. It was supposedly named for Lake Como in Europe, which the Rock River at that location was said to resemble. By the 1840s there was a ferry across the river and bridges across Elkhorn Creek, a tributary of the Rock River, and stores in the village as well as a hotel and stagecoach stop, post office, blacksmith and plow manufacturer, school, and gristmill, one of the most modern in the area. When in the mid-1850s the Chicago and Northwestern Railroad passed Como by a mile and a half on one side, the village began to disappear. Addams family lore suggests bad feelings between Col. George Weber and his son-in-law JHA were created over the major role Addams played in securing a more northerly route for the Galena and Chicago Union Railroad (which later merged with the Chicago and Northwestern Railroad) to benefit Freeport and Cedarville.

JA's grandfather, Col. George Weber, had chosen to establish his milling and mercantile business in Como. By 1845 a large gristmill costing approximately forty-two thousand dollars was built, with a millrace stretching from Elkhorn Creek through the village. Possibly constructed in part by Hezekiah Brink, the mill and a mill store became the property of Weber and the Smith brothers, Leman and Howard. Weber wrote to his son-in-law, miller Enos L. Reiff, "We are getting along with our building here verry well, but not quite as fast as expected. I have the Dam Race & forebay, complected & the water in, & will have the Sawmill running Shortly. I am pleased to see that Milling has been good for some time back with you (its better here)" (1 Jan. 1847, SCPC, JAC). During the late 1840s the mill and store served the entire Rock River valley and more than half of the county's inhabitants.

Weber convinced two of his sons and their families to emigrate west and join his business venture as merchants. John Harrison Weber, called "Harry," wrote to the Reiffs shortly after their arrival in Como in June 1848:

> Our house is a two story one, with two large rooms below and four above. Father occupies one, Polly [Mary Beer] & Lucy [Louise Hensy] one, & we the other, the remaining one we have in readiness, should any of our friends favor us with a vist, and sojourn with <us> for more than a day, the parlor below is large & roomy as well as the dining room, from the latter a door leads into the kitchen which makes it very convenient, we are about as far from the Mill & store, as three fourths of the distance from your house to Ambler, the Mill is the finest I have ever seen, and can do an immense amount of work, the store is a very fine building and arranged inside so as to be very convenient, last week we unpacked our [new?] goods and have been kept very busy since, yesterday we sold one hundred & fifty dollars worth of goods we can realize good profits on goods here, grain is very scarce at present as farmers have nearly all sold out to make room for the coming

crop which looks fine and promises an abundant yield the Mill is still running day & night. (J[ohn] H[arrison] W[eber] to Brother & Sister [Elizabeth and Enos L. Reiff], 10 June 1848, SCPC, JAC)

In addition to Harry, the U.S. census of 1850 indicates that the household included his wife, Caroline C. Weber, twenty-one; their first child, George A. Weber, two; and Harriet M. Hake, eighteen and born in Pennsylvania. The latter was probably a relation of Harry's wife, whose maiden name was Houck. Also in the household were Mary ("Polly") Beer, forty, born in Pennsylvania; George Weber, Jr., thirty-one, born in Pennsylvania and like his father and brother identified as a merchant; his wife, Maria, twenty-five and born in Pennsylvania; and the young couple's son, John L. Weber, ten months old and born in Pennsylvania. William Hoffidity or Hoffeditz, identified as a laborer, age twenty and born in Pennsylvania, was probably Maria Weber's brother. John Cross and Jacob Seiple, ages eighteen and twenty-one, were laborers, and Louise Hensy, sixteen and also born in Pennsylvania, was a servant.

Then Col. George Weber, who was intestate, died suddenly in 1851. His children continued to operate the mill and store for a time, but by the mid-1850s both had left Como and the milling business. The Harry Weber family moved to Chicago, and the George Weber, Jr., family to northern Illinois. By the 1880s the mill property had fallen into ruin. In 1879 and again in 1881, the mill was advertised for unpaid taxes, and in July 1881 a flood washed away part of the mill's foundation. The mill may have been sold in 1882 as a site for malt manufacturing, although there is no evidence that it was ever used for that purpose. By 1885 Como was a ghost town except for its post office, which was disestablished in 1905. In 1886 the mill, not used in twenty years, burned, and the reported loss was fifteen hundred dollars.

5. In the early 1980s, genealogists recorded the grave markers remaining in the Como Cemetery. Broken grave stones with partial information for the following Weber relatives remained: Col. George Weber; John T. [or L.] Weber (1819 [1849]–50), son of George and Mara [Maria] H.; Benjamen Weber (d. Aug. 26, 187?), son of G. and M. W. Weber; and Gertrude (d. 1863, age 2 months, 18 days), daughter of G. and M. W. Weber. Missing are the stones for one of the Weber children, the Hoffeditz daughter, sister to Maria W. Hoffeditz Weber, and R. Russell.

6. Sarah Beaver Weber, JA's grandmother and the mother of JA's mother, was the fourth child of Devault Beaver (1756–1837) and his wife Margaret Schaeffer Beaver (1748–1843) of Chester, Pa. Born on 30 July 1786, she married Col. George Weber on 17 Nov. 1812 and died in Mercersburg, Pa., after a short illness on 9 July 1846. The Webers' eight children were Devault (1813–80); Elizabeth (1815–97?); Margaret (1816 52?); Sarah (1817–63), the mother of JA; George, Jr. (1819–88); John Harrison (1826–91); and Mary Ann and Catherine, both of whom died in infancy. Until 1840 the Webers lived in Kreidersville, Pa., and then they moved to Mercersburg. Sarah Weber was an active member of the Reformed Church.

7. John Harrison Weber.

8. SWA was buried in the Addams family plot of the Cedarville Cemetery. Property for the cemetery, located on a hill to the northwest of Cedarville and on the road that passes the Addams home and continues on to Red Oak, had been given to the community by JHA in the mid-1850s. SWA, JHA, all of their children and their spouses, and some of their grandchildren and great grandchildren are buried there, as are AHHA, her first husband William J. Haldeman, and their children. Polly Beer is also buried in the Addams plot.

9. "In the year A.D. 1869 we removed our son's remains from Brown's graveyard, Coventry twp., Chester Co., to the Montgomery Cem., Norristown, in lots No. 76 and 77, Section L, and in December, 1873, we erected over his remains a Rockery Monument with a child of Hope together seven feet high imported from Italy, and also a monument with figure of Faith fourteen feet high" (Beaver, *History and Genealogy of the Bieber, Beaver, Biever, Beeber Family*, 335).

10. Mary Ann Hiester Weber.

Part 2

"AN EDUCATED WOMAN":

ROCKFORD FEMALE SEMINARY,

1877–81

Introduction

In the fall of 1877, seventeen-year-old Jane Addams left Cedarville to begin school, as her older sisters had before her, as a boarding student at Rockford Female Seminary in Rockford,[1] Illinois. In doing so she was conscious of participating in something larger than herself. She and her class-mates were aware that they were taking part in important transitions in women's education. As they moved into their rooms at Rockford, they joined with other middle-class women of their generation who were seeking higher education in ever-growing numbers. The options available to women in education were also improving. Jane Addams's career at Rockford Female Seminary serves as a microcosm of the social shift from seminary to college. It also reflects late-nineteenth-century debates about the merits of single-sex institutions versus co-education and about the differences in standards between men's and women's schools. At Rockford, Addams studied and participated in campus life as female administrators and alumni worked behind the scenes to upgrade curriculum and improve academic recognition for their school. "Throughout our school years we were always keenly conscious of the growing development of Rockford Seminary into a college," she recalled. "The opportunity for our Alma Mater to take her place in the new movement of full college education for women filled us with enthusiasm, and it became a driving ambition with the undergraduates to share in this new and glorious undertaking."[2]

Female seminaries were traditionally viewed as training grounds where women were prepared to support themselves and serve society as teachers or missionaries. Alternately, a good seminary education could prepare young women to become good wives, often of churchmen, and instructive mothers able to raise moral, cultivated families. This was probably a good part of the attraction that

Rockford Female Seminary held for John Huy Addams as a destination for his daughters, including his youngest. Jane's childhood had been shaped by the widening democratization of learning, including her formal education in the Cedarville district school, access to her family's books and periodical publications, and the fact that the Cedar Creek Union Library was housed in her home. Her range of knowledge was also molded by the dictates of local church services and socials, by her domestic duties and familial relations in her home. The larger influences of Victorian popular culture were also a factor, from the day-to-day politics of domesticity, to prevailing ideas about self-training and the fulfillment of talents, to the novels she enjoyed that featured self-sacrificing but often feisty heroines. While her stepmother had introduced important new elements of reformist thought and arts appreciation into the Addams home, Jane's strongest personal intellectual influence since her earliest years had been her father.

Within the family, the question was not whether Jane Addams should seek higher education but how and where. With choices between the brand new women's colleges of the eastern seaboard and the family tradition of attendance at Rockford Female Seminary, it was John Huy Addams's long-standing support for the Rockford school that won out. He and Anna Haldeman Addams had many practical and emotional reasons to send their youngest daughter to Rockford. In addition to the proximity of the Cedarville-Freeport area to Rockford by train, the family was connected to the school through ties of friendship and loyalty as well as tragedy. Both Alice and Mary Addams studied there and Martha Addams had died there, the victim of typhoid fever. Rockford teachers were well known to the Addamses, especially to the women, and John Huy Addams had lent financial support to the school. He selected a Rockford graduate to head the select school he started in Cedarville in 1859. More important, he was a member of the Rockford Female Seminary Board of Trustees from 1876 to 1878, when decisions about Jane's scholastic future were being made. It was the family's close connection to the seminary that she emphasized in recalling these events, characteristically downplaying her preparedness in the process. "As my three older sisters had already attended the seminary at Rockford, of which my father was trustee," she wrote, "I entered there at seventeen, with such meager preparation in Latin and algebra as the village school had afforded."[3]

Despite her demure explanation of why she followed in her sisters' educational footsteps, Jane Addams harbored other desires and goals. She later confessed that as a teenager she had been "very ambitious to go to Smith College" for her post-Cedarville education (Vassar had also held its attractions) but had acquiesced to her "father's theory in regard to the education of his daughters," which included a long-range plan of "a school as near at home as possible, to be followed by travel abroad in lieu of the wider advantages which an eastern college is supposed to afford."[4]

Addams knew other girls who began studies at Rockford Female Seminary and then entered Vassar College or Smith College for more advanced study, and for most of first year at the seminary she privately longed for the same chance for herself. She discussed with friends her desire to transfer from what she referred to as a "fresh-water" women's school to a degree-granting college on the eastern seaboard.[5] The dreams of attending a first-class women's college were deferred, however. As she began to see the ways in which she could develop and grow in knowledge and leadership skills within the seminary environment, the hope for the East Coast college experience was set aside for a time and not rekindled until graduation approached.

When Addams came to Rockford, the school, under the leadership of veteran educator Anna P. Sill,[6] had one foot in the educational mandates of the past and another in those of the future. Working at odds with most of the members of the seminary's all-male Board of Trustees, Sill quietly pushed the boundaries of conventional notions about women's intellectual abilities. She lobbied to expand the curriculum beyond traditional ideas of the kinds of training women should receive. She and her teachers sought to make the sciences and ancient languages as open to women students as they were to the men at men's schools, and they challenged long-held assumptions about the proper exclusion of women from study that would prepare them for professions and public roles. At the same time, however, that Sill and her supporters made behind-the-scenes statements about equity and women's capabilities, they continued to embrace ideas about cultivating women's virtues and instilling a sense of special mission for uplift and moral influence that had dominated the way middle-class women were prepared for adulthood throughout the century. For Sill, producing well-educated and moral mothers, teachers, church members, and foreign or domestic missionaries remained the motivation behind the push for better female education.

At Rockford as at other female seminaries, strides to open and improve women's minds—and change men's minds about what women could do—occurred largely within the ideological parameters set by the school's Protestant origins at mid-century. Women's advancement in the late 1870s and early 1880s was still defined at Rockford as much in religious terms as in intellectual ones. Sill and her teachers embraced conventional Victorian images of women at the same time they were busy reconstructing them. Girls were taught that their futures were a matter of the soul, perhaps even more than of the mind, and it was first and foremost tenets of piety and conversion, self-transformation, and dedication to a greater good or a sense of mission that shaped their training. Their fervor for making an advanced place for themselves in the wider world was in part an evangelical kind of feminism. As they attended mandatory daily chapel exercises and marched off in a long line, two by two, to Sunday services, their visions of social reform and salvation were closely intertwined. Under Sill's stern and watchful eye—and under the testing of the seminary's Board of Examiners, which was made up largely of ministers—theological notions of sin, conversion, and salvation took their places beside more secular and sociological concepts of self-help, self-education, and social improvement in the lives of Rockford students.

The burden of choice regarding an education at a traditional midwestern seminary versus a more avant-garde eastern women's college may well have been, on John Huy Addams's part, as much a judgment about the merits of the new female education as a matter of loyalty to Rockford. In addition to the pragmatic reasons he had for maintaining a family connection to Rockford, he saw a seminary education as sufficient training for the kind of futures he envisioned for his daughters. His support of women's rights fell far short of embracing the career- and public-oriented assumptions about the role of educated women in society that the eastern women's schools represented. In this, he was supported by his second wife. A few months after their marriage in November 1868, Anna Haldeman Addams wrote to Jane's father about a group of mothers and their babies whom she had met during a visit to a neighbor's home in Cedarville. "'Woman's rights' would hardly look upon them as filling their highest prerogative" she confided to her husband, who was away fulfilling public roles as businessman and legislator, "but would do away with baby and cradle and ape instead a statesmanship or professorship."[7] Jane's parents were thus in close agreement in having baby and cradle foremost in mind for their daughters, including the youngest. At the same time, they supported the rights of women within certain middle-class domestic parameters—especially when it came to rights of inheritance, personal finances, or property. Although he scoffed at suffragettes, if not entirely at woman suffrage, John Huy Addams had worked in the Illinois senate on behalf of legislation that would guarantee property rights to married women.[8]

All these ruminations over women's proper roles in society and an educational destination aside, fate had it that Jane Addams attended Rockford Female Seminary at a critical turning point in its history. In the end, she participated in high-profile ways in the landmark changes through which the school progressed from a seminary to a degree-granting college. From the time she entered Rockford fresh from Cedarville in September 1877—a small, slim, somewhat bent and serious young girl with large, soulful eyes—to the time she spoke confidently from the podium on the topic of the status of women as valedictorian of her graduating class in June 1881, the seminary completed a decades-long process of development from preparatory to collegiate status. Addams saw firsthand the fruition of that process, which had begun many years earlier with Sill's founding of the school as a girls' academy in 1849. When the all-male Rockford Female Seminary Board of Trustees finally relented on the issue of women earning degrees in 1881, she was among the first to be granted a bachelor of arts. That degree, officially awarded in June 1882, symbolized the claim of women to equal status, and equal opportunity, with men.[9]

Anna P. Sill was the driving force behind the elevation of women's academic training at Rockford Female Seminary. An experienced teacher and administrator, Sill had come to Rockford from New York state at the end of the 1840s.[10] She arrived in northern Illinois at the behest of those who had chosen Rock-

ford as the preferred site for a new female academy, which area Congregationalists and Presbyterians planned as a sister school to Beloit College. Sill saw
herself from the beginning as serving divine purposes while establishing the
groundwork for a quality seminary for young women. She wrote in a diary entry
of 11 June 1849 that she had "commenced school, and laid the foundation of
Rockford Female Seminary. Opened with fifty-three scholars. O Lord, fit me for
my work and glorify thyself thereby."[11] She believed that part of her mission was
to offer educational chances to young women from both poor and middle-class
families, a policy that in the 1870s would benefit some of the young women who
became friends of Jane Addams's.

Along with key women teachers at the seminary, Sill, a woman of imposing
demeanor and strong will, was a role model and exemplar of female leadership
for the young Jane Addams, who regarded her with a mixture of respect and
recalcitrance. When Addams started school at Rockford Female Seminary, the
elderly Sill's religious conviction and devotion to excellence in education for
women had defined the basic character of that institution for almost three decades. Sill was as impressive in appearance as she was in wielding authority. A
teacher on her staff for several years recalled that in 1852 Sill "was about thirty-
six years old, a woman of such splendid physique and majestic beauty that any
artist might have rejoiced to find such a model for a Greek work of art."[12] Years
later, a classmate of Addams's similarly remembered "Miss Sill" as "a tall and
slender lady, very capable, very orthodox, and with a commanding presence."[13]

Their principal understood very well the desires that Addams and other
talented students had to be part of the new educational chances emerging for
women. Sill's dedication to winning better educational opportunities for her
girls—within the conservative parameters in which she viewed such advances—
was tireless. In the midst of battling with conservative Rockford Female Seminary Board of Trustees members over the benefits of separate women's education versus coeducation, she wrote to the Rev. Joseph Emerson,[14] the seminary
board president and a professor at Beloit College, during Addams's sophomore
year: "You see how sensitive I am at any limitation of their [young women's]
privileges in securing a liberal education equal in culture to young men. . . . I
believe in colleges for women and if young I should seek the best college education I could find, whether at Wellesley, Vassar, or Smith College, Mt. Holyoke
Seminary, or Rockford Seminary." At issue was not only raising standards while
maintaining women's separate education but also the availability of quality
opportunities for girls who lived in the South and the West. The understand-
able lure of the East was still on Sill's mind two years later. "Am I wrong in asking that the young women of the West who want a collegiate education in a
woman's college should be allowed this without going east?" she queried Emerson in frustration. "I know there is wealth enough in Rockford to put this
institution on a college basis."[15]

While engaging in these behind-the-scenes battles, Sill had become, by the

1870s, quite anachronistic when it came to social aspects of the school and ideals of female deportment—at least from the viewpoint of her girls. Old-fashioned on issues of social behavior and always concerned for the maintenance of the pristine reputation of the school in public opinion, Sill carried on the tradition of antebellum women's schools by imposing tight rules and schedules of religious instruction that strictly regulated the lives of students and faculty. The rules and expectations were spelled out in annual catalogs. At the beginning of each school year, students were asked to pledge themselves to observe the rules and in accordance to write out the regulations by hand, signifying their understanding of the guidelines of behavior. Rules were set regarding visitors, respectful conduct, prompt attendance, maintenance of quiet during study hours, observance of the Sabbath, and other aspects of campus life. Students were encouraged to dress plainly and leave jewelry and extra spending money at home. All student expenditures, large and small, were to be reported and recorded in account books maintained by the administration. Jane Addams's handwritten pledge of "faithful and cheerful observance of all the regulations" was completed along with all the others.[16] Students and parents alike were reminded in no uncertain terms that "the Seminary is the result of benevolent efforts on the part of friends of Christian Education both East and West, and it is expected to be decidedly religious in its character and influence."[17]

Many girls appreciated Sill's unwavering emphasis on self-improvement and right living, especially in hindsight. Former student Emma Goodale (Garvin) reflected that the "hard study and discipline was good for us all and must have helped me in my life work—made me perhaps ready to do my best with whatever I had to do and find pleasure in simple, homey things."[18] But Sill's austerity often elicited rebellion more than admiration. Lizzie Smith, a spunky friend and classmate of Jane's, dared privately voice the fact that Sill's autocratic control was not always greeted in a positive manner by those subjected to her authority. Lizzie had gone astray in regard to her observance of the rule requiring Sill's prior approval for girls receiving "calls from young gentlemen in town." Reprimanded and remanded to her parent's care, she spent a short respite at home over a holiday and returned, reformed, to school. "Miss Sill's ways are mysterious and sometimes unpleasantly so, as you know," Lizzie wrote home to her sister Addie, a former Rockford student, during the autumn of 1880, the beginning of Lizzie and Jane's senior year.[19]

While many Rockford students were free in sharing their feelings about Sill's regimented administration, Jane Addams, as in all things, was—in most cases—circumspect about her differences with the principal. Although not as outspoken as her friends and classmates about her criticisms, she privately did not agree with Sill's dogmatic emphasis on conversion and Christianity nor with her limited ideas of the proper fields of female usefulness, particularly her desire that seminary girls prepare themselves for lives of missionary work. In this, Addams had the good fortune to be among a class of rebels who were united in their interest in analyzing, and in some cases attempting to overthrow, time-worn school traditions. Her friends passed around a paper that each was asked to sign, pledging that they would be strong in withstanding Sill's expectations that they become missionaries. When it came to directly negotiating difficulties with Sill, however, Addams's classmates were adamant regarding the best approach: "let Jane do it."[20]

Although she served as an able diplomat between the students and Sill, Jane remained inwardly conflicted and tactfully defiant. Upon one occasion she questioned Sill's incorrect pronunciation of the name *Don Quixote,* which led to the entire class being suspended for two days. After they had been reinstated, Addams borrowed her friend Nora Frothingham's hymnal during chapel exercises and devilishly wrote on the flyleaf: "Life's a burden, bear it. / Life's a duty, dare it. / Life's a thorn-crown? Wear it / And spurn to be a coward!."[21] As James Weber Linn reported, "She was . . . unable to accept conventions of thought, at Rockford or later," and in her solid way during her student years she went about overturning some of Sill's prided traditions.[22] The issues involved remained with her, along with the tensions they created. As Linn put it, choosing the present tense at the end of his aunt's life in 1935, "Her instinctive conflict, both in theory and spirit, with Miss Sill, is a matter of importance in her life. For the consciousness of this conflict tangled and confused her not only while she was at Rockford, but for years afterward." Her mixed feelings about Sill and Sill's dictums, and her desires to both conform and reform, caused the young Addams a good deal of uneasiness. She struggled, for "Miss Sill was not a person to be opposed in conviction lightly; she was too fine, too passionate, and too grimly sure that *she* was right for any young girl, however precocious and determined to preserve her 'mental integrity,' to differ with comfortably."[23]

The religiosity that framed the educational experience at Rockford was countered, however, by more secular influences. The seminary curriculum contained both conventional and innovative elements. Older standards combining the "useful" (applied subjects such as geometry, geography, and English grammar) with the "ornamental" (fine arts and art history, and instrumental and vocal music) were increasingly supplemented with liberal, intellectual, and scientific learning. The school was divided into normal, preparatory, and collegiate divisions. The Conservatory of Music and the Department of Drawing and Painting attracted "special" students as well as those regularly enrolled in the collegiate and preparatory divisions. Within the collegiate department, students could pursue classical, scientific, or literary "courses" of training (or majors), with additional Greek, French, and German courses as electives (or minors). The various courses or tracts were outlined carefully in seminary catalogs.

Addams studied the standard collegiate curriculum at Rockford. When she began school at the seminary, forty-four students were enrolled in the collegiate department, and 180 were studying at the school overall. Only seven girls were in her entering class. In her first year, her courses included, in the first "series" or semester, Latin (with the study of Virgil and Latin prose composition); natural science (physiology and hygiene, civil government); ancient history; critical readings in English literature and rhetorical composition (including learning weekly selections from Goldsmith, Wordsworth, and Tennyson); and Bible history (beginning with Genesis, Exodus, and the gospels). She enrolled in these courses as well as German and music. In her second series of 1877–78, she shifted from physiology to botany and added university algebra (at which she excelled, as she did in German). The musical interest, although it lasted through her first year at the seminary, was short-lived; she did, however, complete the entire four-year course in German. An excellent student overall, the lowest scores Jane Addams received during her career at Rockford were in her first year's courses in Bible history. In mathematics and science she progressed from algebra to classes in geometry, trigonometry, astronomy, and chemistry. She began the Greek course of study in her second year and shifted year to year from ancient to modern and medieval history.

At Rockford as at other seminaries, lines were blurred between the humanities and the sciences. Literature, philosophy, and natural science—what was then called moral, mental, and natural philosophy—were the cornerstones of coursework. Philosophic attention to nature and the perfectibility of the soul melded, somewhat tenuously, with modern theories of science, including discussion of evolutionary theory in biology and cosmogony and a new emphasis on natural history. That field, in its various forms (botany, mineralogy, meteorology, zoology, and taxidermy), was sweeping not only the Rockford campus— mainly in extracurricular ways—but also popular study circles, lyceums, and other informal educational settings of the day. Seminary girls were schooled,

Anna P. Sill, principal of Rockford Female Seminary from 1852 to 1884, in a portrait taken in her early days at Rockford Female Seminary. Anna Sill was near the end of her reign as the head of the seminary when Jane Addams was a student. (RC)

as educated young men long had been, in "arts" education focused on languages, classics, and the study of rhetoric, logic, and effective elocution. There was also emphasis on the study of the Bible and on developing a good knowledge of canonical literary and historical texts. The essays, drafts of debates, and creative writing that Jane Addams produced at the seminary—samples of which are printed as documents in this volume—reveal a strong background in the "Great Men" approach to history and culture. Steeped in the perspectives of Thomas Carlyle, she often employed his model of heros and heroism to her topics, making questions of idealism, courage, character, and personal endeavor central to her arguments and examining the types of behavior and choices that cause an individual to make a difference to society.

Like other educators of the time, Sill was concerned with deportment in all its forms. Girls were evaluated on ladylike behavior as well as scholarship, and the two ratings were factored into one another to determine a final grade point average. Jane Addams, after four years at the school, graduated with a 9.862 average for scholarship. Factored with a perfect 10 for deportment, that resulted in an overall average of 9.931.

Sill was keenly interested in the development of her young charges' bodies as well as their characters and souls. Like other pioneers in female education, she associated physical strength and good hygiene with the ability to take on larger roles in society. Accordingly, physical education at Rockford Female Seminary was designed to counteract Victorian stereotypes of female weakness and try to reverse the very real effects of illness upon young people's lives. For an hour each day, students were expected to walk a continuous circuit laid out on planks on the grounds; twice a week they participated in gymnasium. Jane was excused from the latter because of her back. Championing the physicality of women in outdoor life was a challenge to those who doubted middle-class women's inherent abilities and vigor to act and do.

Ideas stemming from the era of the founding of the seminary lauded the role of education in the optimum development and improvement of individual faculties. The idea of self-culture, primarily an intellectual dictum, was also considered to have physical, moral, and spiritual dimensions.[24] Conventionally understood as an imperative for males whose duty it was to develop fruitful public lives of work and citizenship, the idea of self-culture was adapted by those active in reforming women's education and applied to the experiences of females. Female educators contradicted beliefs propagated by physicians, authors of advice manuals, and others that women's assumed inferior intellectual abilities were due to a supposedly necessary focus on reproductive functions. Reformers attacked the fashionable associations made between femininity, ill-health, and pallor—sometimes carried to the point of chronic invalidism. They observed that students were emerging from their educational experiences "pale, thin, [and] bent."[25] Anna P. Sill wanted to be sure that her school did not perpetuate such trends. She wrote to a trustee that "women need the best kind of mental discipline and physical strength and true <u>heart</u> culture for <u>home</u> and <u>social duties</u> and benevolent work in this progressive era."[26]

Physical education was thus seen as a remedial measure to counteract popular visions of women's prevailing ill-health. Within the religious framework of seminaries for females, a physical regimen was considered to be one more form of self-discipline—of self-fulfillment through what commentators called "habits of *self-control,* punctuality, and order."[27] These brought "temper and feeling into . . . proper subjection" and led students to adapt "themselves to the daily and hourly duty of acting out the beauty and symmetry of the precepts of our Saviour."[28] Walks and weights joined daily prayer, chapel services, silent times, and assigned seating at meals in applying outer and inner order to seminary student life. In this environment Jane Addams thrived—perhaps in spite of the regulation. Some five feet three inches tall and still weighing less than a hundred pounds, she gained in beauty and vitality at Rockford. Despite her relative frailty and a spinal deformity that would lead to extreme pain as she continued to mature, she was energetic and winsome—"slight and pale, spirited and charming"—and inspired deep affections through her eager enthusiasms.[29] Friends remembered her good-humored fearlessness in confronting wintery snowdrifts by sleigh and the vigor with which she arrived for visits at her sister Mary's house or dashed through the Rockford hallways.

While Anna P. Sill and other educators were concerned with building stronger bodies and counteracting the connections drawn between femininity, illness, and disease, the true emphasis of self-culture at Rockford was in developing the intellect. Self-culture meant exposure to the finest in thought and artistic expression in order to bolster moral character and prepare girls to undertake useful, God-directed service in the world. Jane Addams and her close friends very much embraced the Arnoldian concept of culture prevalent in their day and took as personal directives the quotable self-culture dictums that Matthew Arnold, one of her favorite poets, wrote.

Arnold equated culture with a certain kind of learning and emphasized the responsibility of an enlightened person to broadly disseminate knowledge to others of all walks of life. In *Culture and Anarchy* (1869) he urged the learning of works by great thinkers and an effort to make "the best that has been thought and known current everywhere" in order that "all men live in an atmosphere of sweetness and light."[30] These words, intended for males, were absorbed by the young women of Rockford, who similarly pondered what Arnold's advice to "attain the mighty life you see" meant for them.[31]

Addams's reading list during her Rockford years included Bacon, Carlyle, De Quincey, Emerson, Hugo, Longfellow, Scott, Shakespeare, and Tennyson as well as Goethe, Homer, Plato, Virgil, and Xenophon. She cherished poems that urged self-reliance, self-development, and higher awareness and writing that cultivated refinement and moral introspection while instilling the idea of social uplift. She also read and debated works by Sand, de Staël, and Eliot. She was particularly attracted to these women writers and the modes of womanhood they, and the female characters they created, represented. She, at least publicly, disdained the kind of serialized romance fiction that many other Rockford girls enjoyed, and she was not as entertained by Dickens as some of her fellow classmates.

Rockford students in general were well instructed in the proper selflessness of self-culture—especially for women, who were expected not so much to succeed, like men, as individuals but as individuals in the service of others and the greater good. Edification through self-culture was encouraged at Rockford, both in the classroom and out. Addams and her friends engaged in various kinds of informal education. They also met for discussion, went to hear visiting lecturers, participated in church and missionary meetings, and prepared after-school literary society and natural science association programs.

Jane Addams participated fully in school life. Whatever initial doubts she had about her situation, her seminary experience was deeply fruitful and rewarding. She was greatly enriched by the close friendships she developed and by her edifying relationships with the dedicated teachers who became mentors. The high standards that she met in her formal schooling and the extracurricular activities in which she engaged would shape her life as a feminist and reformer.

Addams excelled in her studies and emerged early on as a student leader. She became an officer, as her sister Alice had been before her, in the campus literary society, the Castalians. The Castalian Society (which in combination with

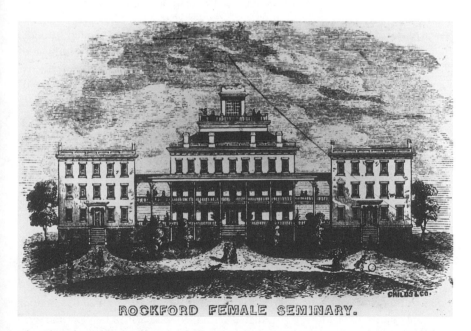

ROCKFORD FEMALE SEMINARY.

The Chapel, Middle, and Linden halls, Rockford Female Seminary campus. (Childs and Co. RC)

its competing sister society the Vesperians made up the Pierian Union at Rock-ford) was—like student literary and debating societies at other men's and wom-en's colleges—at the center of the seminary's extracurricular intellectual and social life. It was under Pierian Union auspices that the *Rockford Seminary Magazine* was published to voice the thoughts and opinions and report the ac-tivities of the student body. Addams was part of the magazine's staff during her first years at the seminary and became editor-in-chief during her senior year. Under her leadership, the magazine's format was revamped and modernized. As often as not, the periodical provided a vehicle for gentle intellectual and political rebellion in relation to the Rockford administration as well as outreach and exchange with other schools, including men's and coeducational colleges.

Her experience as editor and policy-setter at the magazine was directly re-lated to Addams's increasing involvement, during her junior and senior years, in public speaking and debate. In an era when oratory and elocutionary train-ing were seen as pivotal stepping stones in preparation for full participation in public life and leadership roles for male students, she took an active interest in building programs at Rockford that developed and displayed the public-speak-ing skills of young women. Doing so proved to be an important factor in her future. Formulating arguments for on-campus Castalian Society debates and attending and participating in off-campus oratorical contests with other schools gave her practice at articulating her viewpoints in ways that would sway vari-ous audiences. Oral presentations were at the center of key rites of passage for Rockford students. At the end of each academic year, a board of outside exam-iners, many of whom were ministers and had college educations, tested students in oral examinations, and seniors prepared talks to present as the main part of their commencement ceremonies. Highlights of Addams's public-speaking ca-reer at Rockford Female Seminary came in organizing the Junior Exhibition of 1880, which was similar to the event held at brother-school Beloit and open to the public, and in her valedictory address of 1881, which underscored her lead-ership at the school and capped the four years of training she had received there. During her last two years at the seminary she emerged as one of its most force-ful debaters and orators and figured strongly in Sill's efforts to win inclusion for Rockford girls in regional coeducational oratorical competitions.[32]

Journalism and public speaking were not the only collegiate areas in which Addams made new strides for girls. Her academic interests were well balanced. She loved ancient languages, classical literature, European history, and writing. She was also attracted to the natural and biological sciences. Just as her love for the outdoors at Rockford was a continuation of the many hours spent playing with her stepbrother George Haldeman around the millpond and meadows of Cedarville, so her collegiate interest in the sciences had been piqued by amateur science projects she had once conducted with George. Early in her seminary ca-reer she became one of the founding members of the Rockford Female Seminary Scientific Association, an after-school club that sought to supplement the regular, albeit archaic and underfunded, science curriculum.[33] Her interest in natural history led her, among other things, to tackle learning the art of taxidermy.

Taxidermy in Addams's time was advancing beyond mere hobby. Like public speaking, it had larger ramifications for women's opportunities to interpret the world. Mastering oratory was, for female students, a matter of entering traditionally male territory, competing against male students, and developing skills designed for use in public, professional, or political contexts previously assumed to be reserved for men. Taxidermy also had pioneering aspects in terms of gender. Botany and the development of herbariums had for some time been an acceptable path of scientific pursuit for women. Identifying and preserving fauna as a means of scientific interpretation was considered largely a masculine enterprise, whereas women's skills in those areas were regarded mainly as a decorative art. In the late nineteenth century, male taxidermists gained popular fame for reproducing the animal world for the masses through displays in the nation's burgeoning natural history museums. Prowess in the scientific technique of taxidermy was related to the messages conveyed through the depiction of the animal world in such exhibits, in which the males of the species were typically presented in positions of grandeur and dominance. Addams bridged science and art when she tried her hand at the practice.[34] Under the tutelage of Rockford's young new natural science teacher Mary E. Holmes,[35] Jane demonstrated a special interest in studying and preserving birds of prey.

Debating and scientific inquiry were combined when Addams prepared lectures and participated in debates on scientific subjects with friends in the scientific association that Holmes sponsored. Addams's self-identified penchant for the linguistic and scientific—and her preference for "masculine" fields and logic over "feminine" genres and emotional interpretations—was reflected in an argument she developed for a February 1878 debate regarding the place of music and the arts in the educational curriculum. In "Resolved that the Ornamental branches are necessary to a Complete Education. negative," she used an evolutionary framework to argue that the strong-minded had "outgrown the arts," which were "relics of barbarism," and that the "highest cultivation is gained through science and languages."[36]

Jane Addams's attraction to the sciences was as much a matter of personality as of intellect. She advocated the objectivity that she felt the study of the sciences brought to learners. That emphasis on the value of objective reasoning applied also to her notion of self-development. She valued precision as well as openness of mind. Accuracy, she reasoned, was a necessary first step toward morality and justice as well as self-knowledge. At Rockford she strove to discipline herself. As she later put it in her memoirs, paraphrasing her graduation essay on "Cassandra," she wanted to "detect all self-deceit and fancy in herself and learn to express herself without dogmatism."[37] She spurned sentimentality and the overt silliness and emotional displays of affection she saw rampant in much of schoolgirl culture, describing herself as "of serious not to say priggish tendency."[38]

Despite a self-proclaimed proclivity toward prudishness, Addams could often be found at the center of Rockford's social life. The particular brother-sister school connection between Rockford Female Seminary and Beloit College, where George Haldeman was a student at the same time Jane was in Rockford, was an important source of socializing for Rockford girls. Addams traveled with other seminary students to Beloit for special programs and lectures. Beloit boys also came to Rockford to attend chaperoned mixers, which included parties in the homes of the city's elite. Fanny Jones Talcott,[39] who had graduated from the seminary, and Charlotte Emerson (Brown),[40] a former seminary instructor, held literary society meetings, musical soirees, and rowing parties to entertain the girls and introduce them to young people from the town.

These occasional forays out into a mixed-gender world beyond the campus were, however, more the exception than the rule. The most important aspect of social life at Rockford Female Seminary was the women's culture cultivated and insulated by the separate-sex nature of the school. As one of Addams's classmates laughingly put it, James Alcock,[41] the jack of all trades at the school, was the only male aside from Daniel Hood,[42] the much respected head of the music department, to regularly frequent the seminary grounds. Jane found many role models among the excellent female teaching staff and formed lifelong friendships with several faculty members as well as with other students, many of whom went on to high achievements.

Among the faculty members who had particular impact upon Addams's intellectual development and sense of self was Sarah Anderson (Ainsworth).[43] Anderson, the school's accountant, was one of the first points of contact for new girls at the seminary. In Jane Addams's first year, Anderson taught gymnastics. By Addams's second year she had become an English teacher and remained so until her promotion within the school's administration. Anderson became a mentor to Addams and, in time, one of her best friends and confidantes. They went on summer trips together when Addams was a student and traveled to Europe together in 1887–88. In the years immediately following Addams's graduation in 1881, she and Anderson corresponded, confiding in one another their feelings about their postgraduate educational opportunities and professional hopes. Anderson was also part of the ongoing connection that Addams maintained with Rockford Female Seminary after graduation. Both women would become involved, along with Fanny Jones Talcott, in the pathbreaking admittance of women to the previously all-male bastion of the Rockford Female Seminary Board of Trustees. In 1890, when Hull-House was newly founded and Addams was active with the seminary board, she supported Anderson's appointment as the new principal of the seminary. Anderson oversaw the official change of the seminary's name to Rockford College in 1892, finally fulfilling Anna P. Sill's dream of full collegiate status for her school. She served as principal of Rockford College until 1896, when she resigned and married, moving away from Rockford.

Other teachers were influential as well. Mary E. Holmes guided Addams's scientific pursuits, serving as a role model of the possibilities of science as a pathway for the professional woman and encouraging Addams's interest in medical education. Caroline Potter (Brazee),[44] who taught European literature and history and believed strongly in intellectual discipline, was another significant instructor. She taught Addams in critical reading, outlines of history, American literature, modern history, geometry, ancient history, rhetoric, English literature, word analysis, medieval history (Addams's favorite), ancient literature, and criticism, courses spread throughout her four years at the seminary. Feared by many, Potter was fond of Addams and fostered the young woman's interest in the humanities. It was she whom Addams singled out in her memoirs as a pivotal influence. Sarah Blaisdell[45] was another.

The instructor of ancient languages at Rockford, Blaisdell taught Addams and a small circle of seminary students in Latin and Greek. Addams in turn used public-speaking opportunities to draw modern messages of courage and inspiration for women from Greek and Roman myths. Recognizing Addams's willingness to pursue independent study, Blaisdell tutored her through the classics and the two shared private Sunday sessions, translating biblical passages from the Greek. It was another way of stepping into what was considered masculine intellectual terrain, for the Greek testament was not typically part of a young woman's study but was a regular offering for boys at Beloit, where Blaisdell's brother James[46] was a professor.

Addams held the private sessions with Blaisdell very dear. While Anna P. Sill's emphasis on evangelicalism was manifested in regular church-going, obligatory daily chapel attendance, weekly prayer meetings, missionary society activities, and semiannual revival events, Addams found her soul more greatly nurtured by the quiet spirituality of her meetings alone with Blaisdell. "The only moments in which I seem to have approximated in my own experience to a faint realization of the 'beauty of holiness,' as I conceived it," she recalled, "was each Sunday morning between the hours of nine and ten, when I went into the exquisitely neat room of the teacher of Greek and read with her from a Greek testament."[47] Addams and Blaisdell engaged in this weekly ritual for two years. At the time of this closeness, Addams was still a teenager and Blaisdell was approaching the end of her long teaching career. When she retired at the end of 1881 it was Addams who gave tribute to her during seminary graduation ceremonies. Blaisdell remained an honored friend to Addams in the years after each had left Rockford.

Rockford Female Seminary afforded students a chance to become a part of a community of women led by women and also to develop individual direction and identity within close-knit circles of classmates and fellow students. Addams was already comfortable with the intimacy of small-town community from her life in Cedarville, but at Rockford she found a community of like-minded peers. At the boarding school she was part of what she called a "group of ardent girls who discussed everything under the sun with such unabated interest" who stud-

Sarah Blaisdell, an instructor of ancient languages, taught at Rockford Female Seminary as a full-time faculty member from 1866 to her retirement in 1881. Jane Addams cherished her private sessions with Blaisdell, and they remained friends until Blaisdell's death in 1906. (RC)

ied, exercised, went to church, and socialized together, shared special foods from home in their rooms, and discussed the contents of their hearts and minds.[48] Addams remembered with a kind of joy the routine of seminary life, including the clean simplicity of the daily regimen in which each girl rose to make her own fire in the woodstove and tidy her room before joining the others around the breakfast tables downstairs. On at least one occasion, school-girl inquisitiveness and sharing extended past intellectualism into some more directly experiential experimentation, as Addams joined other students enamored of Thomas De Quincey's *Confessions of an English Opium-Eater* in trying some of the substance themselves over a school holiday. Their experiment was brought to an abrupt end by the intervention of a faculty member.[49]

Eva Campbell (Goodrich),[50] Katie Hitchcock,[51] Mattie Thomas (Greene),[52] and Ellen Gates Starr[53] were among Addams's close friends in her first years at school. At the beginning of her time at Rockford, Addams also corresponded with her distant cousin Vallie Beck and a childhood friend, Ida May Carey.[54] She compared her own experience at the seminary with what those friends were finding at their respective girls' schools. While Carey wrote to Addams that the "sentimental 'spooning' malady" that Addams had said "infests Rockford" also existed at Lake Erie Seminary in Painesville, Ohio, where she was a student, both girls dissented—at least on paper—from active participation in the overtly emotional schoolgirl culture of crushes, pairing, dating, and romantic relationships among young women.[55]

As a schoolgirl, Addams repeatedly stressed belief in the value of detachment at the same time she formed very close female friendships. Some of these relationships lasted throughout her life. They occurred in conjunction with her seemingly unswerving adherence to Victorian rules of propriety in private life as well as in public behavior, including her buttoned-up, lifelong conservatism about the body. There is no doubt however, that the range of female friendship that Carroll Smith-Rosenberg's pathbreaking work describes—"from the supportive love of sisters, through the enthusiasms of adolescent girls, to sensual avowals of love by mature women" in a world where men were often marginal —occurred at Rockford Female Seminary as at other nineteenth-century female schools and as a pattern in Addams's own life.[56]

Relationships between girls within the "female world" or women's culture of women's schools were fed by intense conversations and confidences. The schools created environments that made possible an intimacy of communication that Victorian boundaries between women and men largely barred. This element of communication certainly characterized Addams's relationship with her best friend, Ellen Gates Starr. Starr and Addams met during Addams's first year at Rockford Female Seminary. When Starr left school after the 1877–78 year to make a living teaching, a rich correspondence grew between her and Addams, accelerating in the 1880s. However intellectualized the young women sought to make their topics of discussion, the letters are heartfelt testimony to the close friendship the two had established and the "soulmate" function they found fulfilled in one another. In many ways the two friends were opposites. Starr, for example, was deeply aesthetic and pious, whereas Addams was logical and filled with religious doubts. While bridging these differences, the teenagers built one another's self-confidence. Addams's relationship with Starr helped her form an important identity in the eyes of another, which aided her in differentiating herself from her family and her background in Cedarville. With the security and support of Starr's friendship and close ties to others, especially teachers, and the increasing respect that sister-students accorded her accomplishments, Addams emerged at Rockford as a particularly independent thinker and leader.

For many school girls of Addams's generation, the powerful attraction to other girls and the centrality of women to their lives was age-specific, part of their teenage experience. Most of Addams's cohorts at Rockford went on to marry. Several defied the standard either-or choice between career and marriage and balanced teaching, professional, and social reform or missionary work with raising families. A strong minority, including Addams and Starr, did not marry. They remained single, returned to families of origin, or partnered with other women. Economics and ambitions entered into these choices, as well as sexual preferences and orientations. For many who trained at Rockford, marriage was the expected answer to a lack of personal financial independence, just as using skills obtained in the classroom was a means of support for those who found themselves by fate or choice on their own.

Addams had personal financial means and rejected traditional marriage, choosing instead a life-long commitment to another woman. For her, the comfort of community, the women's culture, and standards of high female professional and intellectual achievement of Rockford were recreated in new form in the residential community—made up largely of women—at Hull-House. There she enjoyed as an adult the combined benefits of a mutually supportive community of friends, where everyone had similar goals yet undertook their own tasks and responsibilities. In the settlement she recreated the professionalism, action, and intellect she had seen modeled in Rockford faculty along with the kind of close camaraderie and polite affection among women that she had enjoyed among seminary students. Even the dormitory life-style she had savored at Rockford was like that shared by the residents at Hull-House, with their separate rooms and communal meals. As she put it in *Twenty Years:* "Perhaps this early companionship showed me how essentially similar are the various forms of social effort, and curiously enough, the actual activities of a missionary school are not unlike many that are carried on in a Settlement situated in a foreign quarter."[57] The emotional connection between the female "worlds" of Rockford and Hull-House was reinforced by the presence in both contexts of Hull-House co-founder Ellen Gates Starr and the continuing interest and concern in the settlement project of Sarah Anderson, whose ongoing friendship with Addams and Starr linked the college and Hull-House years.

In addition to being a time for the development of leadership skills and a foundation of female mentorship and friendship, Addams's college years were a period of spiritual questioning and growing philosophical maturity. She absorbed the messages taught at Rockford: Each person must strive to discover a personal calling and fulfill it well, and individuals had a duty to try to bring the real into as close a conjunction as possible with the ideal. Combined with the missionary and service philosophies that dominated Rockford Female Seminary, these beliefs reemerged later in life in her dedication to rights, labor, social justice and peace issues, urban reform, collective living, and the creation of large-scale structures for social change.

In the meantime, she struggled a great deal with self-doubts and feelings of failure in regard to her goals of self-improvement. Her lovely Sunday morning sessions translating the Gospels from the Greek in Sarah Blaisdell's room aside, she was subjected at Rockford to heavy peer pressure to convert to an active commitment to Christianity. As she remembered, "during the four years it was inevitable that every sort of evangelical appeal should have been made to reach the comparatively few 'unconverted' girls in the school. . . . I was singularly unresponsive to all these forms of emotional appeal."[58] In addition to chapel and prayers, Bible study, including the memorization by each girl of the entire Book of Hebrews, was also mandatory; Sundays were scheduled with a series of church-related activities; and students were expected to be active in the campus Society of Mission Inquiry.[59] The pressure only became greater in the senior year, when faculty urged students relentlessly toward careers in missionary work. The formidable Miss Sill was known to call individual students into her rooms to discuss their spiritual state. Addams fulfilled all the expectations for social participation in religious rituals and events while remaining immune to both the evangelical fervor and the missionary calling. She also stuck to her beliefs in a kind of female-centered force of Nature, or pantheism, and to a historical view of Jesus during an extended correspondence with Ellen Gates Starr about the incarnation of God in Christ. While Starr followed in her aunt Eliza Allen Starr's attraction to devout spirituality, Addams followed in the footsteps of her father, who had embraced rationalism and private mental integrity above all else. She finally had to tell her friend that she thought they should stop discussing religion. Soon after that she wrote to a family friend, the Rev. T. H. Haseltine, for help sorting out her beliefs, especially her lack of feeling of closeness to Jesus as a personal deity. Haseltine responded with reassurances and encouragement for her to try to remain receptive to the kind of personal knowledge of Christ that more evangelical understandings of doctrine demanded.[60] She managed to find her own way amid all these expectations. "This passive resistance of mine, this clinging to an individual conviction," she later stated, "was the best moral training I received at Rockford College."[61]

Notes

1. Rockford, Ill., was settled by New Englanders. A city of industry and commerce in the time that JA attended school there, it began as a prairie village and mill site on the Rock River in 1834. Located east of Cedarville in Winnebago Co. in northern Illinois, some eighty miles northwest of Chicago, Rockford burgeoned as a city in the mid-nineteenth century. Its economic health was based on the damming of the Rock River. The Water Power Co., created by business leaders in 1851, provided the hydraulic power that made foundries and other manufacturing enterprises possible. In 1852, the year Rockford was incorporated as a city, railroad service was established, linking regional farms to the Chicago grain market and creating supply lines for eastern-milled lumber to be used in Illinois construction. By 1860 the population had doubled to 6,979.

Rockford "was a Whig stronghold and hotbed of abolitionist feeling in the 1850s," with support for temperance and anti-slavery causes high in its churches and social organizations (Lundin, *Rockford*, 48). Voters approved a local liquor prohibition law in 1856. The city contributed six companies of volunteers to the Union army effort during the Civil War. In the 1870s when JA attended RFS, the city's skyline included the steeples of Baptist, Catholic, Congregational, Lutheran, Methodist, and Presbyterian churches. During that period Rockford was called "Reaper City" because of the high concentration along the riverfront of factories producing reapers, plows, and other farm machinery. The city had many residents who were from Sweden. During the 1870s, Swedish immigrants made up approximately one-quarter of the population. The U.S. census figure for the city's population during JA's senior year at RFS was 13,129. In the twentieth century, Rockford became the second-largest city in Illinois.

2. Addams, *Twenty Years*, 53–54. By 1870, approximately one-fifth of American higher education students were women. In 1890 women made up about one-third of the total. Addams's education at RFS came right in the midst of this period of growth and reform. She and her cohorts benefited from the pioneering efforts of antebellum female educators who had endeavored earlier in the century to open liberal education to women and improve the stan-

dards of education within separate female schools. They also came to seminary at a time when elite colleges for women were gaining ground in the East (Vassar opened in 1865, Smith and Wellesley in 1875, and Bryn Mawr in 1880). Although JA identified with the wave of graduates of her generation who were trained at the women's colleges of the East, the RFS curriculum had much in common with that offered to earlier students who attended antebellum female colleges, including study in ancient languages, mathematics, and the sciences.

3. Addams, *Twenty Years*, 43.

4. Addams, *Twenty Years*, 43. If this was indeed JHA's plan for his daughters it was rather unevenly applied: MCAL never traveled to Europe, before or after her marriage; Martha Addams died before her chance to go; and SAA was sent in part to separate her from her attachment to HWH. JA went first in the company of her stepmother and later with friends and still later as a political activist. On the male side of the family, JWA did not travel abroad, but both GBH and HWH traveled or studied in Europe. HWH spent almost two years at Leipzig before his mother and JHA were wed, and GBH joined JA and AHHA in Europe for a brief period in 1886.

5. Addams, *Twenty Years*, 47.

6. Anna Peck Sill (1816–89) was born in Burlington in Otsego Co., N.Y. She was the youngest of the ten children of farmers Abel Sill (1773?–1823?) and Hepsibah Peck Sill. Raised from the age of seven by her mother, Sill was educated in local district schools. She trained from her youth to become a teacher. Deeply religious, she was moved to seek higher education out of spiritual conviction and because of a missionary concept of social change rather than because of individualistic ideas of personal achievement. She recorded in her diary that the "primary motive which led me to acquire an education was that I might lay it at the Savior's feet, and thus be some service to his cause" (quoted in Townsend, *Best Helpers*, 17).

Anna P. Sill was well grounded as a teacher before she founded RFS. When she was twenty she left home to teach in a district school in Barre near Alton, N.Y. During breaks in the sessions, she attended classes at a school in Albion, N.Y., and the following Sept. she enrolled full time at Albion Female Seminary (later Phipps Union Seminary), which had been founded in 1833. In 1839 she began teaching at the seminary in addition to taking classes, and she remained in Albion for the next five years as a teacher/pupil. Beginning in Oct. 1843, she opened a school of her own, a seminary for young ladies that was located on Main St. in Warsaw, N.Y. By the end of the first year she was teaching 140 scholars in music and painting, languages, reading, orthography, arithmetic, and grammar. She closed the school in Mar. 1846 and considered offers from various schools to serve as principal. She chose to go to the three-year-old Cary Collegiate Institute, a boarding school for girls and boys near Batavia (also called Careyville), N.Y., as head of the Girls' Dept. She left Careyville in 1849 to found RFS in Rockford (see also n. 10). Beginning as an academy for young girls, by the early 1860s the higher education department of the seminary was well established, and in the decades that followed Sill oversaw the school's expansion and continued good reputation.

Sill faced down internal opposition from the male trustees of RFS in arguing for the merit of women earning collegiate degrees, and she ultimately saw her goals achieved. She guided RFS for thirty-five years and succeeded during that period in elevating it from a girls' school to one offering a four-year collegiate course for women. By the time of JA's graduation in 1881, Sill "was a woman of nobility, but her elasticity was gone" (Linn, *Jane Addams*, 63). Internal squabbling and dissent over gender equity and moral censorship issues, in addition to society's increasing trends toward secularization and the gender integration of educational institutions, weighed heavily on the seasoned administrator during the 1880s. After taking a leave of absence at the end of the 1882–83 academic year, Sill formally tendered her resignation to the RFS Board of Trustees on 30 Jan. 1884. She officially ended her tenure as principal at the end of the 1883–84 term. She was succeeded as principal during her lifetime by Martha Hillard (MacLeish), an 1878 Vassar graduate who served as head of the school from 1884 to 1888, and by Univ. of Michigan graduate and Wellesley College teacher Anna Bordwell Gelston, who was principal from 1888 to 1890. In the spring of 1889, Anna P. Sill's last surviving brother and his wife and two children died of pneumonia. Sill contracted the illness herself while helping to care for them. She recovered but returned to Rockford in May 1889 in a weakened state. She died on 18 June 1889 in her rooms at RFS.

7. AHHA to JHA, 11 Jan. 1869, SCPC, JAC.

8. For more discussion of these attitudes in the Addams family and JHA's political career, see the introduction to part 1 and Biographical Profiles: Addams, John Huy.

9. For more on these events, see June 1881 documents below and *PJA*, 2.

10. Anna P. Sill came to Rockford through personal connections. While teaching at Careyville, she became friends with another teacher, Eliza Richards, and her brother Benjamin Richards. The Richardses had a sister and brother-in-law, Mr. and Mrs. Lorenzo Dwight Waldo, who lived in Rockford, and when they traveled to Illinois to visit in 1848, Eliza Richards decided to stay and open a private school for girls. At the same time, regional Protestant church conference members in Wisconsin and Illinois were beginning to search for a principal to head a female seminary to complement the all-male Beloit College in Wisconsin (for information on Beloit, Wis., see introduction to part 1, n. 177, above). An offer to head the new school was made to Anna P. Sill, perhaps through Eliza Richards's recommendation or perhaps through the influence of the Rev. Hiram Foote of Racine, Wis., an old friend of Sill's from her childhood in New York. Foote was involved in the search, and he later became a trustee of RFS, serving from 1852 until his death in 1889.

Sill accepted the position. She left Careyville and arrived in Rockford in May 1849. She started the new school that summer. Eliza Richards's cousin, Hannah Richards, came west with her and worked with her in the new enterprise. Sill's long-range vision was the creation of an institution that would parallel the quality of education offered by Mary Lyon's Mt. Holyoke Seminary in South Hadley, Mass. Despite these hopes for the future, RFS initially operated primarily for younger students. The majority of the first students who enrolled were under ten years of age. In the beginning years, Hannah Richards was in charge of the youngest girls and head of the Culinary Dept.; Eliza Richards divided housekeeping work with Hannah and taught music; and Anna P. Sill worked with the most advanced and older students. Sill was officially head of the school's Dept. of Mental and Moral Philosophy as well as its principal. Eliza Richards married within the year and was succeeded at RFS by her younger sister, Malinda Richards, who came from Bennington, N.Y., to join Sill's staff. Hannah Richards remained with Sill at the school as a teacher of history and belles lettres into the 1850s.

11. Quoted in Cedarborg, "Early History," 12.

12. The teacher quoted here is Mary E. B. Norton, who taught natural history and botany at RFS from 1859 to 1875, quoted in Cedarborg, "Early History," 71.

13. Alderson, "Memoirs," 35. RFS student Addie B. Smith told her mother, upon first observing Anna P. Sill, "I like her very much & think she is very pretty for her age. She is a little prim & excentric but very nice. I suppose she is very religious for she does all the praying & reading & has us all kneel when she prays" (Addie B. Smith to Annie M. Jordan Smith, 23 Sept. [1876?], SHSW, Smith). JA's friend Mary Ellwood referred less graciously to Sill as an "old cow" (Mary Ellwood to JA, 25 Sept. 1881, SCPC, JAC; *JAPM*, 1:798).

14. Prof. Joseph Emerson, D.D. (1821–1900) was a longtime member of the RFS Board of Trustees and a confidante of Anna P. Sill. The second son of the Rev. Ralph Emerson (1787–1863) and Eliza Rockwell Emerson (1797–1875), he was born in Norfolk, Conn., and raised in New England. In 1830 his family moved to Andover, Mass., where he was educated at Phillips Andover. He attended Yale Univ. as an undergraduate, then trained in the ministry and earned his divinity degree from Yale Theological Seminary, graduating in 1847. He taught mathematics and Latin at Yale while studying toward his degree. He joined the Beloit Col-

lege faculty in 1848, arriving in the Beloit-Rockford area just before Anna P. Sill's founding of RFS. He was ordained as a minister in Beloit in February 1860 and taught at the college for forty years. He retired from the classroom in 1888 due to poor health but remained a member of the RFS Board of Trustees until his death.

15. Anna P. Sill to Joseph Emerson, 10 July 1879 and 26 Apr. 1881, BC, EB; see also Vallie E. Beck to JA, 2 Feb. 1878, n. 3, below. RFS began granting degrees in 1882; its name was not changed to Rockford College until a decade later.

16. See two extant pages from JA's hand-copied version of the rules and expectations: "Manual of Rockford Seminary—1878–&79," RC; *JAPM*, 27:196. The quotation regarding "faithful and cheerful observance" is from the first page of her pledge (*JAPM*, 27:196). Four rules are represented in what remains of JA's pledge. The first included respectful deportment and courtesy toward teachers and staff members with basic "lady-like behavior." The second demanded "Prompt attendance . . . at every duty," including "recitations, practice hours, study hours, meals, domestic work, room work, family devotions, chapel exercises, church and all special appointments by teachers." The third mandated "Perfect quiet" at "study and recitations hours in all places; and after retiring at night." Rule four limited access to "other young lady's" rooms (*JAPM*, 27:196).

17. RFS *Catalogue*, 1879–80, 31; *JAPM*, 27:312.

18. Emma Goodale Garvin shared these reflections with Rockford College historian Hazel Cedarborg (Emma Goodale Garvin to Hazel Cedarborg, 22 Mar. 1925, RC). Garvin in many ways fulfilled Anna P. Sill's dream in regard to her girls making their way in the world. The daughter of missionaries, she married a minister and served as a missionary with him overseas. For information on the life of Emma Frances Goodale Garvin, see Announcements in the *RSM*, [19 or 26 Sept.?, 3 Oct., 10 Oct.] 1879, n. 13, below.

19. Sara Elizabeth Smith to Addie B. Smith, 13 Oct. 1880, SHSW, Smith. Both Addie B. Smith (Wells) and her sister Sara Elizabeth ("Lizzie") Smith of De Pere, Wis., were students at RFS during JA's time at the school. Addie B. Smith was a special student in music from 1876 to 1879. A "special student" designation was given to girls who had graduated from another institution but wished to pursue specialty studies at RFS. Lizzie Smith began school at RFS with JA in 1877–78. Along with Kate Tanner (Fisk) and Annie Sidwell, she was one of the nine "partial collegiates" listed between the students in the preparatory and collegiate divisions in that year's *Catalogue* (8; *JAPM*, 27:122). By the following year, all three had regular collegiate status, and they all graduated with JA in the class of 1881. For further information on the lives of Sara Elizabeth Smith and Addie B. Smith, see Announcements in the *RSM*, Mar. 1879, n. 13, below.

Rules regarding gentlemen callers appeared as part of the regulations all students pledged to uphold (see, for example, the 1870–71 RFS *Catalogue*, 25). Lizzie Smith ran into trouble during the first semester of the 1878–79 school year when she and her more wayward friend Ella Waterman violated Anna P. Sill's strict regulations regarding contact with outsiders. The two repeatedly snuck away from their dormitory rooms in the evenings to meet and talk with boys at a cottage on the school grounds. Lizzie's sister wrote to their mother on 18 Dec. 1878, relaying the news that Lizzie had "broke the Seminary rules very shockingly . . . flirting . . . with some fellows who come up to the Seminary grounds for that purpose" (Addie B. Smith to Annie M. Jordan Smith, SHSW, Smith). The girls confessed to Miss Sill, who expelled Waterman from the school and temporarily suspended Lizzie Smith, whom she believed had been led astray by her bolder acquaintance. Lizzie Smith's troubles at the seminary and Sill's disciplinary action are documented in Anna P. Sill to Annie M. Jordan Smith, 12 Dec. 1878 and Sara Elizabeth Smith to Annie M. Jordan Smith, 13 Dec. and 15 Dec. 1878, SHSW, Smith.

20. JA's friend Nora Frothingham (Haworth), quoted in Linn, *Jane Addams*, 48. For more information on Eleanor ("Nora") Frothingham Haworth, see Announcement in the *RSM*, Apr. 1878, n. 9, below.

21. Frothingham, quoted in Linn, *Jane Addams*, 48.

22. Linn, *Jane Addams*, 48.

23. Linn, *Jane Addams*, 44.

24. The multilayered concept of self-culture propagated by William Ellery Channing, Joseph Story, and Unitarian thinkers in the late 1830s and 1840s was closely related to nineteenth-century moves toward greater democratization of education or the idea of uplift, through learning, for people of all classes. It was well captured, in Victorian terms, in the content and title of Transcendentalist James Freeman Clarke's (1810–88), *Self-Culture: Physical, Intellectual, Moral, Spiritual* (Boston, 1880), published in JA's junior year at RFS, or in John S. Blackie's *On Self-Culture, Intellectual, Physical, and Moral . . . for Young Men and Students* (1874). Instruction and training were considered essential for the development of individual talents, intelligence, and conscience; like muscles that went without exercise, talents and moral and intellectual abilities that were not fostered disappeared. See also Howe, *Making the American Self*, 256–69; Kett, *Pursuit of Knowledge*, 81–87; and JA to Eva Campbell, 25 [and 29] July 1879, n. 9, below.

25. Women's physical education advocate Diocletian ("Dio") Lewis (1823–86), quoted from *Our Girls*, 357–58, in Woody, *Women's Education*, 2:101.

26. Anna P. Sill to Joseph Emerson, 10 July 1879, BC, EB. Sill's dedication to bringing good physical education to RFS girls was matched by Emma Willard (1787–1870) of Troy Female Seminary, Troy, N.Y.; Mary Lyon (1797–1849) of Mt. Holyoke Seminary, South Hadley, Mass.; Mary Ann Evans (1841–1921) of Lake Erie Seminary, Painesville, Ohio; and other early leaders in women's education. Despite the progressive aspect of Sill's dedication to compulsory physical activity, the specific forms in which exercise was dictated at RFS during JA's time there—the daily walk, the occasional gymnastic quadrilles, and regular household duties—were relatively conservative. The required one-mile walk a day and the quadrille form of calisthenics done at RFS were actually older formats of female exercise, introduced most prominently in a circular published by Mary Lyon in 1835 and instituted in the early years of Mt. Holyoke. By the 1860s, many women's schools, including Mt. Holyoke and Vassar and RFS in 1865, shifted to the "New Gymnastics" systems of graceful aerobic drills as outlined by Dio Lewis, and, in the 1880s, weight-bearing exercises as advocated by Dudley Allen Sargent (1849–1924), a Yale-educated physician and professor of physical culture at Bowdoin College, Yale, and Harvard who developed a new system of personal training based on the individual body.

27. Henry Barnard, from *American Teachers* (n.d.), 338, quoted in Woody, *Women's Education*, 1:399.

28. From an article in *American Journal of Education* (n.d.), quoted in Woody, *Women's Education*, 1:399.

29. The observation on JA's spirit and charm is that of a Beloit College undergraduate who confessed "that I fell in love with Jane Addams that day" (commencement day, 22 June 1881) "and never got over it" (quoted in Linn, *Jane Addams*, 63). For more information about JA's physical condition and treatments for her spine, see *PJA*, 2.

30. Matthew Arnold, quoted in Kett, *Pursuit of Knowledge*, 142.

31. Matthew Arnold, "Self-Dependence," stanza 7, line 4, from *Empedocles on Etna, and Other Poems* (1852).

32. Various samples of Addams's RFS essays, debates, speeches, and orations—as well as *RSM* editorials—are reprinted below. For more information on JA's involvement in oratory and Anna P. Sill's ambitions for RFS's participation in coeducational regional oratory associations (including discussion of the often-repeated claim that JA debated with William Jennings Bryan in her senior year), see JA to JHA, 8 May 1881, below.

33. The make-do nature of the study of the sciences at the seminary was one of the ways that the education available there contrasted sharply with the conditions at eastern wom-

en's schools. Vassar College at the same time had many rooms filled with scientific apparatus, a medical lecture hall, and an entire floor of a building dedicated to the cabinets of geology and mineralogy and scientific teaching collections.

34. For more detailed discussion on JA's interest in the art of taxidermy, and the gendered aspects of taxidermy as an art and science in the late nineteenth and early twentieth centuries, see JA to SAAH, 23 [and 24] Jan. 1880, below.

35. Mary Emilie Holmes (1850–1906) was a pioneer for women in science. As a Ph.D. graduate of the Univ. of Michigan in 1888, she was among the first women in the country to earn a doctorate in earth sciences, and in 1889 she became the first woman inducted into the American Geological Society. A graduate of RFS in the class of 1868, she began teaching natural sciences there in 1877. Later in her life, Holmes turned to missionary and educational work. For more detailed information on the life of Mary E. Holmes, see Announcement in the *RSM*, Apr. 1878, n. 4, below.

36. *JAPM*, 45:1719, 1721.

37. Quoted from JA's discussion of "Cassandra" in *Twenty Years*, 61; for the text of "Cassandra," see Graduation Essay, 22 June 1881, below.

38. Addams, *Twenty Years*, 49.

39. Fanny Jones (Talcott) (d. 1925) graduated from RFS in the class of 1860. She married Rockford businessman and RFS trustee W. A. Talcott (d. 1900), and she and her husband were important boosters of the seminary. She was awarded an honorary M.A. degree in June 1882 during the first commencement in which the school granted earned baccalaureate and honorary master's degrees. JA received her A.B. in the same ceremony. In 1883 Talcott became, along with JA, one of the first female members of the RFS Board of Trustees, a position she held until her death. In addition to her involvement in women's education at RFS, as a fundraiser, trustee, and officer of the RFS Alumnae Assn., Talcott was state regent of the DAR and president from 1904 to 1906 of the Rockford Woman's Club. For more on the Talcott family and Fanny Jones Talcott's involvement in RFS, see JA to AHHA, 2 June 1881, n. 2, below.

40. Charlotte Emerson (Brown) (1838–95) was part of an influential academic family involved in both Beloit College and RFS. She was the daughter of the Rev. Ralph Emerson and Eliza Rockwell Emerson of New England and Rockford and the sister of RFS trustee Joseph Emerson. Charlotte Emerson was born on 21 Apr. 1838, in Andover, Mass., and educated at Abbott Academy in her hometown. She taught in Montreal before coming to Rockford in the Civil War era. She received "permanent" appointment to the RFS faculty as "'Teacher of History and English Literature" and was listed as "Teacher of French and German" in the 1878–79 and 1879–80 RFS *Catalogue*. She was JA's German teacher in 1879–80. In addition to her expertise in modern languages, she was reputed among RFS girls to be an excellent elocution teacher. "When Charlotte went into the Seminary two years ago," her mother wrote in 1867, "she made elocution a special object." She had, her mother added, studied elocution under Dr. Barber in Montreal (Eliza Emerson to Mrs. Banister, 1 July 1867, BC, EB). An Emerson family history reported that Charlotte Emerson "possessed remarkable magnetic and organizing powers" and was "an accomplished writer and speaker" (Emerson, *Ipswich Emersons*, 323).

Before her marriage, Charlotte Emerson's home in Rockford functioned as a center for literary, musical, and artistic gatherings. She was the host of the La Matinée Club, a group "for improvement and intercourse in the French language" (*RSM* [Apr. 1879]: 103) and of the Euterpe Club, a musical society headed by Daniel Hood, whose members gathered at her home to play piano solos and songs. She also sponsored an annual spring party for seniors from Beloit College and RFS. Charlotte Emerson became the corresponding secretary of the Congregational Board of Ladies of the Society of Mission Inquiry in 1878 and was reappointed in that capacity in 1879–80. On 18 Feb. 1880 she wrote to JA to suggest that they put together a colloquy on "Heroines of German Drama," including suggestions for the casting of various RFS girls and with JA as the "character of Kriemhild" (SCPC, JAC; *JAPM*, 1:482–83). She remained in touch with JA after JA's graduation.

Charlotte Emerson married the Rev. William Bryant Brown (b. 1816) of East Orange, N.J., on 20 July 1880. Brown was a Congregational pastor who served parishes in Henrietta, N.Y., Andover, Mass., and Newark, N.J., and was secretary of the American Congregational Union. He had been educated at Oberlin College, Ohio, and received his D.D. degree from Princeton Univ. in 1877. Charlotte Emerson Brown was an organizer and the first president (1890–94) of the General Federation of Women's Clubs of the United States, which grew to become the largest national organization of women in the country by the end of the century (Linn, *Jane Addams*, 60–61).

41. James Alcock, (sometimes spelled Alcott and almost always referred to by students and faculty as "James") (1834–81), worked for twenty-one years at RFS "as general attendant of the seminary and grounds, and his countenance and pleasant ways are remembered throughout the city, and by all the students who have attended that institution during all those years" (obituary for James Alcott, Sill, "Scrapbook"). For more detailed information on his life, see Katie L. Hitchcock to JA, 31 [30] Sept. 1879, n. 2, below.

42. Daniel Hood (1833–1928), the "first male member of the faculty," came to RFS in 1858 and received a permanent appointment in 1869. His salary was based on a percentage of the fees that students paid the college for music lessons, and he taught in a cottage provided for him on campus. He established the RFS Conservatory of Music, built it into the largest academic division on the campus, and headed it for decades. Hood's music program attracted special students, many of them planning to become private music teachers, community concert performers, church musicians, or simply wishing to enjoy accomplished music performance within their families. Regular RFS students also studied music or music history as part of their larger curriculum. JA, who had no particular talent for music, enrolled in the Conservatory of Music only briefly in 1877.

By all accounts, Daniel Hood was well liked. Special music student Addie B. Smith wrote home to her mother that "I have just begun taking music lessons and like the Prof. very much. He is fine looking, has grey hair and whiskers, is of very erect [stature] and seems about forty" (Addie B. Smith to Annie M. Jordan Smith, 28 Sept. [1876?], SHSW, Smith). Charming and gregarious, he was described generally as a man "of a genial disposition and a pleasing personality" who was said to radiate happiness to those around him (Cedarborg, "Early History," 252; see also obituary, ca. 17 Mar. 1929, Daniel Hood file, RC). While a teenager, he had been the organist for St. Peter's Church in Salem, Mass., and for a major congregation in New York City. In 1853 he married Maria Greenough (1835–80) of Brooklyn, N.Y., who was said to have come from a "bright and happy" background and to "at eighteen" have "married the lover of her choice, Prof. D. N. Hood, who, five years later removed with her and their infant daughter to Rockford, then a struggling town in the remote west" (*RSM* [Mar. 1880]: 75). Maria Greenough Hood's health failed soon after arriving in Illinois, and she suffered from "physical weakness and almost constant pain," mainly "reign[ing] perfectly in the true Woman's Kingdom of her home" (*RSM* [Mar. 1880]: 76). Daniel Hood, meanwhile, became very active in the Rockford and Chicago communities as well as at RFS. He earned a statewide reputation as a fine musician. He served as an organist and musical director for various Rockford and Chicago churches, including, in his twenties, the State St. Baptist Church of Rockford, where the Rev. Edward Cushing Mitchell, also a young man at the time, hired him in 1859, and, in the 1870s and 1880s, the Second Presbyterian Church in Chicago. Hood also taught private piano lessons, performed as a concert pianist, and was involved in organizing community concerts as the director of the Rockford Musical Assn. Two of the Hoods' three daughters grew up to become music instructors with their father at RFS. Nettie G. Hood was teaching at RFS when she married Frank D. Emerson in Rockford on Christmas Day 1877. The Hoods' second daughter, Carrie (1859–80), was an instructor of vocal music at RFS during

JA's time there. Both Carrie and her mother died tragically of illness during JA's junior year (see also EGS to JA, 29 Feb. 1880, n. 5, below). Daniel Hood retired from RFS in 1895 and moved to Woburn, Mass. He died on 16 Mar. 1928 in Ipswich, Mass., at the age of ninety-four.

43. See JA–Sarah Anderson correspondence and Biographical Profiles: Ainsworth, Sarah Anderson.

44. Caroline A. Potter (Brazee) (1837–1932) of Rockford was one of the first students to enroll when Anna P. Sill founded the new female seminary in her hometown. She was twelve when she met Sill, and her family had been among the initial supporters of the school. She graduated in the second graduating class of the school in 1855 and spent much of her life teaching ancient and modern history and, occasionally, lecturing in English literature at RFS. The 1878–79 RFS *Catalogue* (of JA's sophomore year) listed her as "Teacher of English Language, Literature and History." JA remembered that although she was very attracted to the sciences in her RFS years, "My genuine interest was history, partly because of a superior teacher" (*Twenty Years*, 47). She also worked closely with Potter in journalism, for Potter was the supervisor of the *RSM* when JA joined the staff and eventually became the editor of the magazine. RFS alum Mabel Clapp Wadsworth recalled that "Mrs. Brazee was one of the strongest spirits Miss Sill ever had to aid her—a born teacher and molder of minds—always bringing out the best in every girl and making even ancient history so vivid and real that we never knew what time meant in her classes" (Mabel Clapp Wadsworth to Friend, 12 Mar. 1895, RC). On 15 May 1880, JA wrote to EGS that she was busy watching Caroline Potter: "By the way I have been studying Miss Potter of late and I wish you were here to assist me in the delightful task, for as I may have remarked to you before, this year preimmently I have taken people for my observation and conversation for my recreation!! How lordly and conceited that does sound, 'the proper study of mankind is man' is a much more graceful way of putting it" (SC, Starr; *JAPM*, 1:505).

Caroline Potter was a leader in the RFS Alumnae Assn. Along with JA, she applied for degree status and was granted an honorary M.A. in 1882. She left RFS at the end of the 1882–83 school year and married Col. C. M. Brazee of Rockford later in 1883. After being widowed in 1886, she lived the rest of her life within view of the RFS campus, literally keeping her eye on RFS affairs. She participated in the seventieth commencement exercises of RFS in 1925 and died in Rockford at the age of ninety-five. Caroline Potter Brazee was a cousin of Adeline Potter Lathrop (b. 1836?), a RFS graduate in the class of 1854, who was the first president of the RFS Alumnae Assn. (and president again in 1884) and mother of Hull-House reformer Julia Clifford Lathrop (1858–1935), the subject of JA's *My Friend Julia Lathrop* (1935). In that tribute to her friend, JA also fondly remembered times with Caroline Potter at RFS, writing "The hours spent with her in 'critical readings,' as she called them, were not quite class work nor quite recreation, but those readings after the lapse of more than fifty years, are still surrounded with a sort of enchantment, first evoked I think by Milton's 'Comus'" (15–16).

45. Sarah Blaisdell (1823–1906) was the mainstay of the RFS Dept. of Ancient Languages. She began teaching at RFS during the Civil War and was given a permanent appointment as a teacher of Latin and Greek in July 1866. During the following 1866–67 school year, when JA's sister Martha was a student at RFS, Blaisdell came to visit the Addams family in Cedarville. The young JA was fascinated with her and followed her incessantly around the house.

Blaisdell was born in Lebanon, N.H., into a family accustomed to public service and reform politics. Her father, Elijah Blaisdell (1782–1856), was a lawyer and judge, and her parents were both temperance supporters. Her mother, Mary Fogg Blaisdell (married 1804, d. after 1827), was her father's first wife. She gave birth to eleven children, four boys and seven girls. Sarah Blaisdell was the youngest daughter and the tenth child. After Mary Fogg Blaisdell's death, Elijah Blaisdell wed Mary Kingsbury Taylor in 1838.

Sarah Blaisdell was known among RFS students for her strictness and her desire for perfection and also for a keen sense of justice. Carrie Longley may well have spoken for JA when she recounted to Rockford College historian Hazel Cedarborg in a 16 Feb. 1925 letter that "Miss Blaisdell, teacher of Latin, sister of Prof. Blaisdell of Beloit was most feared, but by those who knew her intimately greatly beloved. Strict in administering the rules, although she did not believe in having them, but very just and impartial in her ruling" (RC). Upon first coming to the seminary, Addie B. Smith wrote to her mother that "we all have directions & rules dosed out to us daily by Miss Blaisdell, a very nice old maid who has lost her lover. She looks a little like Mrs. Crane [apparently an acquaintance of the Smiths'], grey curls hanging down on both sides of her face, and very nice & prim" (Addie B. Smith to Annie M. Jordan Smith, 23 Sept. [1876?], SHSW, Smith). It is unknown whether Addie's news regarding Blaisdell's lost lover was a fact or a schoolgirl legend. Blaisdell retired from teaching at the end of JA's senior year, in 1881, and moved to Beloit, where she lived near her brother at 731 Mechanic (now Harrison) Ave. She was joined at the turn of the century by a sister who had raised her family in Boston—probably Mary Ann Blaisdell Tyler (1819–1905). Another sister, Rhoda Morse Blaisdell (1821–98), also lived with her.

Blaisdell remained in touch with the Addams family, and she and JA corresponded after both left RFS. JA's thoughts turned appreciatively to Blaisdell when JA first visited Greece in the mid-1880s. In 1902 Blaisdell wrote to AHHA to say that she was no longer able to get out as she once did but that she maintained ties to "some of my dear Rockford girls and have great comfort in their abiding love. The Rockford College is said to be prospering. . . . I am not able to visit as I did for many years after I left it as a teacher." She referred to the situation of sharing a house with her sister in her old age as "well for her as well as for myself. Beloit is my home and I am happy in it. She [Mary Ann Blaisdell Tyler] also likes Beloit and the people . . . we both have much to make life comfortable and to be thankful for. She can walk, make calls & go to church. I can read aloud to her, sew, and we can both think. . . . The children & nephews and nieces are kind & loving, real joys to us" (Blaisdell to AHHA, 17 Jan. 1902, UIC, JAMC, HJ).

Sarah Blaisdell suffered a stroke and died in Beloit on 12 Oct. 1906 at the age of eighty-three. The *Beloit Daily Free Press* praised her as a "woman of high attainment" and proudly headlined "Jane Addams Her Friend." "She was always foremost in the local missionary movements, and her council was sought and heeded on all affairs affecting the moral welfare of the community," the newspaper reported, also noting that Blaisdell had been a mentor to many, including "Jane Addams of Hull House fame, with whom Miss Blaisdell had a warm friendship." The *Beloit Daily News* (12 Oct. 1906), similarly stressed Blaisdell's friendships with JA and Sarah Anderson Ainsworth, as did the Beloit College *Round Table* (19 Oct. 1906). See JA–Sarah Blaisdell correspondence below.

46. Sarah Blaisdell's younger brother, the Rev. James Joshua Blaisdell (1827–96), was a graduate of Dartmouth College, Hanover, N.H. (1846), and of Andover Theological Seminary, Mass. He came from a ministry at a Presbyterian church in Cincinnati to Beloit College in July 1859. He became chair of rhetoric and English literature and later professor of mental and moral philosophy or, as JA put it, "Christian Ethics" (*Twenty Years*, 52). The superintendent of Beloit city schools, a supporter of temperance, and a conservationist, he gave regular public addresses, including lecture series in ethics and logic. He also taught Greek to the "few students who desired it" (Blaisdell, *Story of a Life*, 10). He was kind to JA and helped in her Greek education, giving and loaning her books that included the copy of the Greek testament she used in study and proofing her Greek oration on Bellerophon for the 1880 RFS Junior Exhibition. The oration, JA reported, "was written with infinite pains and taken to the Greek professor in Beloit College that there might be no mistakes, even after the Rockford College teacher [Sarah Blaisdell] and the most scholarly clergyman in town [probably Rev. William S. Curtis] had both passed upon it" (*Twenty Years*, 46; see also Introductory Speech at the Junior Exhibition, 20 Apr. 1880, below). Upon the death of JHA in the summer of 1881, James Blaisdell came to see JA to "inquire how far I had found solace in the little book

[the Greek testament] he had given me so long before" (Addams, *Twenty Years*, 52; see also 53). James Blaisdell's wife, Susan Ann Allen Blaisdell (b. 1828), was a graduate of Mt. Holyoke, and their son, the Rev. James Arnold Blaisdell (1867–1957), who was born in Beloit and a graduate of Beloit College (1889), became a professor of biblical literature and college librarian at Beloit in 1903 and president of Pomona College, Claremont, Calif., in 1910. Like his father and grandfather before him, he supported the temperance cause.

47. Addams, *Twenty Years*, 51.

48. Addams, *Twenty Years*, 48, see also 46–47.

49. On the fascination with De Quincey, the opium craze, and this incident, see Draft of Essay, [ca. 1878], below, and Addams, *Twenty Years*, 46.

50. Eva Maria Campbell (Goodrich) (1854–1938) was the daughter of farmers and civic activists in Pecatonica, Ill., a town located between Cedarville and Rockford. She was JA's roommate at RFS in 1878–79. Like EGS, she left RFS without graduating but continued to regularly correspond with JA about their respective lives in and out of school. Campbell was in the modern languages program with JA during the 1878–79 school year, and she wrote for the *RSM* in the spring of 1879. Unlike JA, she was musical, and her primary study at RFS was in the Conservatory of Music. She taught music after leaving RFS, and in the summer of 1879 married educator and widower Lewis Goodrich and settled in her hometown. Eva Campbell Goodrich had three children and a stepson. After twelve years of marriage, she and her family moved to Fairmount, Nebr., where they operated a farm. She died in Fairmount in 1938. For more information on the Goodrich family, see EGS to JA, 20 Aug. 1879, n. 1, and Eva Campbell Goodrich to JA, 31 Aug. 1880, n. 2, below; see also JA–Eva Campbell Goodrich correspondence below.

51. Kate ("Katie") Hitchcock came to RFS from Des Moines, Iowa. She was one year ahead of JA in coursework, and the two girls had many interests in common. They worked together during JA's first years on the staff of the *RSM* and were both active in the RFS Scientific Assn. They also were among the few RFS girls studying Greek—Hitchcock and JA were two of the three Greek-language students listed in the 1878–79 RFS *Catalogue*. She and JA were elected to chair the two committees of the Castalian Society to plan programs in JA's second year at the school. Unlike JA, Hitchcock was artistic. She was enrolled in RFS's drawing and painting program as well as in the regular curriculum. Hitchcock was unable to complete her senior year at the school. The Nov. 1879 edition of the *RSM* reported that "Katie Hitchcock, '80, is prevented by ill health from joining her class this year, but writes that she shall consider our alma mater as hers also" (245). See JA–Katie Hitchcock correspondence below.

52. Martha ("Mattie") Thomas (Greene), (d. 1936), a member of the class of 1881, was from Lansing, Iowa. She gave the Latin oration at the Junior Exhibition in Apr. 1880 (when JA gave the Greek oration) and was literary editor of the *RSM* in 1881, when JA was editor-in-chief. She was a member of the Castalian Society and secretary of the Presbyterian Branch of Home Missions Society in Rockford. She taught at RFS (1881–82) and other schools before marrying Dr. Joel Henry Greene in Lansing, Iowa, on 21 Jan. 1885 and settling in Dubuque. Mattie Thomas Greene was very active in the Presbyterian Church Missionary Society in Dubuque and an officer in the Dubuque Woman's Club. The Greenes had three children, two sons and a daughter, born between 1886 and 1895. Mattie Thomas Greene remained in touch with both JA and Sarah Anderson, corresponding with them after leaving RFS. She and her husband lived in Champaign-Urbana, Ill., from 1914 to 1922, in St. Paul, Minn., from 1922 to 1929, and in Chicago from 1929 to 1931. They lived with their daughter Lois Greene Zeitlin (b. 1887) in her home in Urbana from 1931 until their deaths five years later. Mattie Thomas Greene died on Christmas Day, 1936. See JA–Mattie Thomas correspondence below.

53. See JA-EGS correspondence and Biographical Profiles: Starr, Ellen Gates.

54. Iowa ("Ida") May Carey (Abbott) (b. 1861) was an old childhood friend of JA's from

the Cedarville area. Her father the Rev. Isaac E. Carey (1823–1902) was former Freeport Presbyterian minister and Beloit College instructor and trustee (introduction to part 1, n. 107). Ida married George E. Abbott, a banker, of Cheyene, Wyo., and the couple had two children. George Abbott died in 1942, having outlived his wife, whose death date is not known. See also Ida May Carey to JA, 5 Dec. 1877, n. 1, below.

55. See Ida May Carey to JA, 5 Dec. 1877, below. There is no question that the primary loving and emotionally supportive relationships of JA's mature life were with other women, especially EGS and Mary Rozet Smith.

56. Smith-Rosenberg, *Disorderly Conduct*, 53.

57. Addams, *Twenty Years*, 49.

58. Addams, *Twenty Years*, 49.

59. The Society of Mission Inquiry met monthly on the RFS campus. Meetings were held in the RFS chapel, and both RFS faculty and members of the student body participated. Meeting agendas included opening exercises; reports on missionary activities in various parts of the globe; book reports, readings, or lectures on various mission topics; and singing, Bible study, and prayer. Each June at the First Congregational Church of Rockford the society presented a formal annual address. The society collected contributions and distributed them through its Benevolent Fund to worthy causes, including famine relief, foreign and domestic missions, Fisk Univ., Bible societies, educational groups, and miscellaneous charitable needs. The society had various committees or boards of activities. The two main ones—the Congregational Board of Ladies and the Presbyterian Board of Ladies—reflected the two primary Protestant denominations represented by RFS. Instructors Sarah Anderson, Sarah Blaisdell, Charlotte Emerson, Mary E. Holmes, and Caroline Potter were all active participants in the organization, as were many of JA's friends. JA seems to have participated sparingly in the society during her first years at the school. In her junior year she read a paper on "Conservatism of the Japanese" at the 9 Jan. 1880 meeting as part of a discussion on Japanese missions. Although participation was officially not mandatory, Sill strongly encouraged RFS girls to be active in the group.

In JA's senior year (1880–81), Sill orchestrated a minor shake-up in the organization in order to encourage better student participation. In that year, JA was already responsible, by virtue of her capacity as class president, for gathering and delivering the class of 1881's financial contributions to the society. With Sill's reorganization at the beginning of the academic year, her responsibilities grew. At the Oct. 1880 meeting, "the Principal and her assistants[,] feeling greatly the lack of vital interest among the pupils in this great cause," instituted a new plan, namely that "three sister organizations [be] formed" as auxiliaries and "each pupil to be at perfect liberty to join which ever she prefers; each society to hold its regular m[ee]t[in]gs on the first sabbath evening of the month" ("Society of Mission Inquiry, RFS Minutes"). These auxiliary meetings were held in addition to the regular Friday afternoon monthly meetings of the main Society of Mission Inquiry. The three newly created auxiliaries were the Congregational Society (also called the Congregational Branch of Foreign Missions, with Annie Sidwell chosen as president), the Presbyterian Society (or Presbyterian Branch of Foreign Missions, with Nora Frothingham as president), and the Home Missions Society (or Branch of Home Missions, which, the recording secretary's notes explained, included both Presbyterian and Congregational work). Sarah Anderson was the Home Missions Society president, and JA was the vice president. The remaining offices in the Home Missions Society slate— corresponding secretary, recording secretary, and treasurer—all went to JA's friend Mary Ellwood. JA was not named among the officers listed when the *RSM* reported the formation of the three new missionary societies in the fall of 1880 (*RSM* [Dec. 1880]: 265).

60. Rev. T. H. Haseltine to JA, 13 June 1880, below.

61. Addams, *Twenty Years*, 56.

From Vallie E. Beck

In late 1876 and early 1877, Jane Addams's friend and distant cousin Vallie Beck studied voice and piano at the Hershey School of Musical Art in Chicago. In the fall of 1877 she became a student at Glendale College[1] near Cincinnati, Ohio, from which she graduated in 1879. In their first year away from home, she and Jane compared notes about life at their respective schools.[2] Addams began classes at Rockford Female Seminary on 20 September 1877.

Glendale F[emale] College. Glendale, O.   Oct. 4th 1877

My dear Jennie;

Perhaps the cause of your silence is the same as mine; in order to prevent a discontinuance of our correspondence (which, to me, at least, has been the source of much pleasure) I shall try to give you something more than a school girlish letter. The heading of this would indicate my inability to write in a different manner, but, I dred being called a boarding school girl, for they are so headless and foolish, as a class. I came here via Chicago and whilst in the city saw Mrs. Brawley[3] for the first time and was very much pleased with her. My anticipations were quite exhalted, but were by no means crushed, after seeing her. Mama considers her a very fine lady and I could not do otherwise than consider her the same, for who could meet her and think differently. She said you expected to be at the Rockford school this year and I suppose you are now there, as a five day boarder, and you may be thankful that you have not to spend Sabbath at school.[4]

Until this last summer I have been always anxious to attend boarding school and have always regretted Papa and Mama did not consider me well enough to go. But this fall when I found I must go I did not have the same longing for the experience I heretofore have had. If it were possible I should much prefer returning to Chicago and continuing under my former instructors there, but as vocal music is the first consideration after my health and I had sore throat and a severe cold (not the result of carelessness) the whole time I was there, you may know it took no more to convince me that I could not endure the climate; of course I made little or no progress in vocal music. Mme Rivé[5] was the attraction here and I assure you she is worthy her reputation as a teacher of Vocal Music; but I consider my first teacher Mrs. Hershey[6] of Chicago her equal. The former is very peculiar and affectionate: she calls her pupils "love, honey, darling, deary" &c. If you have ever seen her daughter you may judge something of her form—she is fleshy, clumsy & homely. Those who have expected to see an energetic little French woman for Mme. Rivé are disappointed in meeting so ungainly a German woman. This is a good strict, Presbiterian school which doubtless is a recommendation to you; the teachers are kind and as linient as possible. The principal, Miss Sheldon, is a lady of superior ability. This is a beautiful village; is built up mostly by business men from Cincinnatti whose homes are here, this place being only fifteen miles from Cincinnati. There are some pretty places here. The famous Stanley Mathews[7] resides here and is highly respected, as is Pres. Hayes.[8] Indeed Ohio is well satisfied with the Government at present it being mostly controlled her citizens.

The first tea bell has rung and this must be closed to go out on the evening train, although I have not said nearly all I wish to. Please write to me soon for your letter will give me much pleasure; I fear you have been waiting to hear from me, please do not so again. Well the gloss has worn off of boarding school for me and I have been very homesick, but I am thankful that I have learned to appreciate my home.

The 2nd bell! Write soon. Your sincere friend Vallie E. Beck

Direct to G. F. College.
Glendale, O.
Do not fear that I got the whole contents of this letter it would need a double pair of gold glasses to make out the <u>exquisite</u> little scrawl[.] Ever lovingly

Ma[9]

ALS (SCPC, JAC; *JAPM*, 1:254–61).

1. Glendale Female College was located in Glendale, Ohio, some fifteen miles north of Cincinnati, in the Ohio Valley. It was founded in Sept. 1854 under the auspices of the Presbytery of Cincinnati by the Rev. John Covert and his wife, who served as lady principal. It was originally called the American Female College. In Apr. 1856 management was transferred to the Rev. Joseph G. Monfort, the Rev. S. S. Potter, and the Rev. Ludlow D. Potter (and their wives, all of whom had teaching experience), and in the following year the name of the seminary was changed to Glendale Female College.

The institution began as a kind of finishing school and academy rather than a college preparatory school or college. It operated a public school for day pupils as well as the private boarding school for more advanced students. Like RFS, it improved its college-oriented curriculum over time. At school ceremonies in 1879 Ludlow D. Potter pointed out that Glendale Female College was among the first institutions for women "to adopt the regular classification and four-fold division of studies, in the form and under the designation historically known as applied to college for males—Freshman, Sophomore, Junior and Senior" (*History of Cincinnati and Hamilton County*, 446). Potter also stated that enrollment at the school had stayed fairly steady through the years, except during the Civil War and a period of economic crisis in the mid-1870s. In 1892–93 the college had 105 students, 35 of whom were residents. Boarding arrangements at Glendale Female College were very similar to those at RFS, with two girls per room and each student expected to furnish her own tableware and supplies. The main building at Glendale was an impressive one, with three stories and fifty rooms and an extension with dining room, art room, and fourteen music practice rooms. Like RFS, Glendale emphasized a "FAMILY AND HOMELIKE" atmosphere, and the activities of the girls were strictly supervised (Faran, ed., *Glendale Ohio*, 71). Just as at RFS, students marched together from campus to church on Sunday, walking in rows of two, and religion was an important part of the daily curriculum.

After the turn of the century, the college found it difficult to compete with coeducational universities and better-equipped private schools. It became increasingly burdened financially and closed at the end of the 1920s. The campus buildings were demolished to make way for residential housing in 1940.

2. Vallie Beck returned to Ft. Madison after she finished her coursework at Glendale. She eventually taught music there as Vallisca Beck. She never married, and family responsibility claimed her. After the death of her mother, she served as housekeeper for her widower father and then, after his death, for her brother William (1857–1936), a lawyer who also never married.

3. Mary Reitzell Brawley was living on the South Side of Chicago (see JA to Vallie E. Beck, 26 Feb. 1876, n. 1, above).

4. JA, as a full-time regular boarder, returned home only for the winter holiday and summer vacations. In the 1877–78 school year, the winter holiday extended from 22 Dec. 1877 to 2 Jan. 1878, and summer vacation began after commencement on 27 June. Students from outside Rockford were required to board at the school and were limited in their visits home unless special arrangements were made with the institution.

The 1878–79 RFS *Catalogue* promised that boarding arrangements would resemble the "simplicity of a family circle, rather than the usual boarding school life" (29; *JAPM*, 27:188). In addition to decorating and caring for their own rooms, most boarders also performed general domestic duties through the school's Industrial (or Domestic) Dept. in exchange for a reduction in tuition. As JA recalled, the "regime of Rockford Seminary was still very simple in the 70's. Each student made her own fire and kept her own room in order. Sunday morning was a great clearing up day, and the sense of having made immaculate my own immediate surroundings" (*Twenty Years*, 51–52). The RFS 1877–78 *Catalogue* stipulated that "Each young lady" should furnish "her own table napkins, teaspoon, table fork, also a pair of sheets and pillow cases; a blanket, a comfortable, a bedspread or quilt, and towels. Carpets are rented by special arrangement in the correspondence, or are furnished by the occupants of the room" (27; *JAPM*, 27:131). JA took up residence in a "high-ceilinged corner room on the second floor of Linden Hall." She brought her own carpet, and "the room was already furnished with a walnut bed, two study tables, a rocker, and shelves for schoolbooks and for the required 'Bible, *Sabbath Hymn and Tune Book*, a dictionary, and standard poetic works'" (Wise, *Jane Addams of Hull-House*, 62–63). Her window looked out upon the seminary grounds and the Rock River. Carpet rentals for those who did not bring their own averaged $5 a year. Students were also financially responsible for their own gaslight (at approximately $6 a year); fuel for the woodburning box stoves fitted into the glazed-brick fireplaces in their rooms (about $10 a year); and laundry (costing between $14 and $24 a year, depending on whether girls paid for just washing, or both washing and ironing, for a dozen pieces per week). The estimated charges were listed in the school's catalog and were in addition to fees for board and tuition, which cost $175 per academic year for regular students and $115 per year for the daughters of clergy.

Domestic training through the performance of household duties had been part of "both the theory and practice of the seminary" movement since its inception in the early 1800s; by the turn of the twentieth century, most women's schools had evolved the practice into course curriculum and formal domestic science departments (Woody, *Women's Education*, 1:399). In the late 1800s, RFS students wrote home about sweeping the hallways, disposing of their own slops, and participating in culinary work in the kitchen. For students from middle-class families used to household help, this could come as something of a shock. One student re-membered, "Many girls came who had had very little training in any way. I did not like the domestic work. But for some of the girls who did not know how to peel potatoes because they had never done it, I thought it was time they learned" (Florence May Smith to Hazel Cedarborg, n.d. [ca. 1925], RC). There is no indication that JA participated in this kind of formal work through the Industrial Dept. as a supplement to her tuition.

Despite the emphasis on family atmosphere, the boarding process was strictly regulated according to a set routine. "You see we have a bell for almost every movement we make" wrote student Addie B. Smith to her mother. "There is one right near our door. It rings when it is time for meals, for classes, to get up in the morning, to go to bed at night and besides lots & lots of other times that I don't understand yet." In the same letter, Addie gave a good descrip-tion of a typical room at RFS and of the seminary setting. "We have our room all swept and the bed made & pail emptied," she reported one Sept. Saturday morning:

> We have tin pails in each room & have to carry down our slops. It is not heavy though and we don't have far to carry it. Our room is real nice. It has a neat carpet on it, has very high ceiling and is real airy. We have a nice little stove, a stand, a table with a leaf to let up & down, a bureau with four drawers in it, a large wood-box, a good set of book shelves, two chairs, two looking glasses, a broom, and a poker & fire shovel. Then we have a little room off of the bed room which is large enough for closet & wash-room both. It has hooks around on all sides for our dresses, has a carpet on it & a window in half of the door for which I have made a little white draw-curtain. There is also a wash stand in it with two drawers and a place to put our sponges bottles brushes & mugs etc., also two wash bowls & all the necessary crockery. So you may see how nicely we are fixed. The things we want to get now are some pictures, a triple spread and a few ornaments. We

The Chapel and Middle and Linden halls, at the heart of the Rockford Female Semi-nary campus, in 1881. (RC)

are going to make some boquets of grasses and pretty leaves. They are beginning to turn here on the grounds. It is lovely around the Seminary. On the right is the river, which is just as picturesque as can be. There are some falls in sight, then some little rapids, and then another little stream empties into it on the opposite side. Down a short distance the river becomes wider then branches off on either side of an island which is as perfect as a picture. The trees are so near the water that the branches almost dip into it. (Addie B. Smith to Annie M. Jordan Smith, 23 Sept. [1876?], SHSW, Smith)

5. Caroline Staub Rivé was a member of the Glendale Female College faculty and "one of the best-known music teachers in this part of the country" (Faran, ed., *Glendale, Ohio*, 72). She had previously taught at the Ohio Female College at College Hill and came to Glendale Female College in 1856 along with Rev. and Mrs. John Covert, founders of the college. She was born in France of German heritage. She was a superb soprano soloist and teacher who had been at the Paris Conservatory as a contemporary of Swedish coloratura Jenny Lind (1820–87), the best-known concert singer in Europe, who debuted in America in 1850. Caroline Staub Rivé was married to the French painter Leon Rivé. The couple emigrated from Paris to New Orleans, where the three children they had brought with them from France died in a cholera epidemic. They moved to Baton Rouge, La., and Louisville, Ky., before coming to Cincinnati about 1854. Their daughter, born in Cincinnati, was the famed pianist Julie Rivé-King (1854–1937), who was praised for her brilliance in a concert career that extended from the mid-1870s into the early 1900s. She received early training from her mother before studying in New York and Europe, where she made her debut in 1874. Caroline Staub Rivé's husband was killed in a railroad accident in the same year.

6. Sara Hershey-Eddy was a highly respected musician, pianist, and vocal instructor who founded the Hershey School of Musical Art in Chicago. Of Pennsylvania Dutch (German) heritage, she was born in Lancaster Co., Pa., and educated in Philadelphia and Europe. She was the daughter of Benjamin and Elizabeth Hershey. After studying music in Philadelphia, she came west with her parents and taught in Muscatine, Iowa. In 1867 she went to Berlin for conservatory training in vocal techniques, elocution, and acting and went on to study operatic voice and oratorio in Milan and London. She returned to the United States with plans to establish a music school in Chicago. These plans were averted by the Chicago fire of 1871, and Hershey began teaching in Brooklyn, N.Y., instead. She worked as a concert singer and church soloist and taught at the Packer Institute in New York before becoming the head of the Dept. of Music at the Pennsylvania Female College in Pittsburgh. She moved to Chicago and founded the Hershey School of Musical Art in 1875 and became very well known as a mentor of successful professional singers on the European model. The Hershey Music Hall was built under her direction in 1876. Sara Hershey married Clarence Eddy on 1 July 1879.

7. Stanley Matthews (1824–89) was an influential and controversial lawyer and politician who became an associate justice of the U.S. Supreme Court during the Garfield administration. Matthews, born in Cincinnati and educated at Kenyon College, Gambier, Ohio, was a veteran of the Civil War. He served as a state senator in the 1850s and was active in the Presbyterian Church General Assembly on antislavery issues. In 1876 he lost a hotly contested race for the 2d District of Ohio congressional seat when it was revealed that, when he was district attorney for the Southern District of Ohio in 1858–61, he had chosen to use private information to prosecute an Ohio citizen who had given succor to a runaway slave in violation of the Fugitive Slave Law. In 1877 he was elected as a U.S. senator from Ohio, an office he held until 1879. President Rutherford B. Hayes, his friend, nominated Matthews as associate justice of the Supreme Court in 1881, but he was accused of having excessive bias in favor of railroad conglomerates during his senatorial career and the nomination failed. He was nominated again by President James A. Garfield. That nomination was confirmed in 1881, and he served on the Supreme Court until his death.

8. Rutherford B. Hayes (1822–93) was elected president of the United States in 1876 and served from Mar. 1877 to Mar. 1881. Hayes was born in Delaware, Ohio. Like Matthews, he was a graduate of Kenyon College and a veteran of the Civil War. He worked as an attorney and served as a Republican member of Congress and as governor of Ohio for several terms before succeeding Ulysses S. Grant in the presidency. His wife, Lucy Webb Hayes (1831–89), a graduate of Wesleyan Women's College, Macon, Ga., was a devout Methodist and an activist in the antislavery and temperance movements. She was the first First Lady to have graduated from college.

9. JA must have shared this letter with AHHA, who returned it to JA with this note, written perpendicular to the text of the Beck letter and in the top margin on the first page of the document.

From Vallie E. Beck

G[lendale]. F[emale]. College. Glendale, Ohio   Nov. 3rd 1877

My dearest Jennie;

Your very welcome letter of 21st inst., was received in due time: need I say that it relieved me of considerable anxiety? for, groundless fear! I almost gave up the hope of ever again hearing from you: and indeed you must not think me fickle, because I considered it doubtful if I ever received (not read, for if you never wrote me another letter I should re-read with pleasure, those you have written), another of your charming letters. Why I almost wonder how one who writes so well as you can spend their time on a correspondent so dull as I, that was one reason I feared a discontinuance on your part (I should have been like the Brook I fear, "on and on forever,") because I am aware how fully occupied your time must be and appreciate your letters the more for that. As to homesickness, that is something I was used to conside[r] an indication of instability, but to my surprise, I found after a few days here, that it was something not controlled by the will and therefor succumbed to it. Now my dear, confess, you were homesick because you could not help it and not because you wished to be "fashionable" as you would have me believe, were you not?[1] To me it was an ache that I could place, to be shunned as a snake, although it was indiscribable yet as real as ever I wish any thing to be. At first discouragement seemed to be my trouble, next thing despair (of course a mild form, but oh! so real) seized me and then I took, what a woman too often resorts to, a cry; about it's being "good", I cannot assure you, but I certainly felt better after I finished "the tide from the briny deep" as one of the girls called it in her essay yesterday. Essays! Our Saturday mornings work and how I dislike it: why it irritates me to think of it, and then such subjects as they do give, why they would be the very one for young students in theology and are certainly unsuited to wild schoolgirls. It is the exceptional pupil who can write well on "Out of the darkness into the Light" "Pictures from Memorie's Gallery" &c. Our section teacher is very entertaining and intelligent but I must say she can not choose nice topics. School friendships! What do they amount to? (I forgot my grammar then): dozens of girls have been inseperable, then a grand fuss, no speaking and sworn enemies, all within the short time of seven weeks. I have made two or three pleasant acquaintances, but [no] friends, or enemies yet: the latter I do not intend to have and perhaps shall have none of the former, shall certainly never race around the halls hugging and kissing every girl good night and that seems to be the way to secure a host of "most intimate friends" and admirers and have the reputation of being so sweet! I dislike a sweet girl! she is usually a sickly little blonde, with thin yellow hair, washed out blue eyes, pug nose, a sickly smiling mouth[,] lisps, loves every one alike (as also she deceives them), feeds on candy and the kisses of her friends, breaks all the rule[s] and reports "perfect" every day. (Draw from imagination, no reference to present acquaintances, oh no!) The girls I admire are those who possess dignity, grace and minds of their own: those who do their own living, who rely upon themselves, are honest, true but with all, are not eccentric. I like an honest, dignified and intelligent gentleman, one whose aim is not glory, not selfishness but to do his best and benefit others. Those are my types, I hear you ask, have you met them? and I say yes, (and one describes you, I think!). How many pupils have you in your school?[2] Have you much ground around the school?[3] How do you like the teachers?[4] In short please tell me all about the school when you write for I am interested in all that concerns you. I envy your room by yourself, I could not have a room alone unless I should go to the third story, but with a room-mate secured the best room in the house, second to the lady principals.

My room mate and I agree well enough but she is not congenial, although if she is neat, honest and not too peculiar I do not know if that should make much difference. I wish you attended this school with me, for I know we would do more than agree. Please write soon, for your letters will be doubly enjoyable now that I have so few pleasures. Your sincere friend & 42nd cousin

Vallie E. Beck.

ALS (SCPC, JAC; *JAPM*, 1:262–71).

1. JA also confessed to missing home at the beginning of her life at RFS: "After the first weeks of homesickness were over, however, I became very much absorbed in the little world which the boarding school in any form always offers to its students" (*Twenty Years,* 43).

2. Regular collegiate students made up a minority of all students studying at RFS. The size of collegiate first-year, second-year, junior, and senior classes varied, but during JA's time at RFS approximately ten girls were enrolled in each class. There were often three times that many in each class of the preparatory school, and many older girls attended school part time as special students.

3. The RFS campus was erected within the boundaries of Rockford on spacious grounds purchased from Buell G. Wheeler in 1852. The hilly, tree-lined site was often referred to as Forest Hill. The Congregationalists and Presbyterians on the Com. of Location for the Female Seminary negotiated over the proposed sites for the school for girls and young women for five years after Beloit College opened. The school in Beloit included both a collegiate section and an academy for boys. They formally chose Rockford in 1851 and recognized Anna P. Sill's school on 1st St. as the Preparatory Dept. of what would become the full female semi-

nary. Classes were transferred to the new RFS campus in 1853, a year after the land was purchased. The physical plant of RFS was concentrated in three main buildings: Middle Hall,
built in 1852; Linden Hall, built in 1854; and Chapel Hall, built in 1866.

4. JA was forming close relationships with some of her teachers. The RFS faculty was made
up of seventeen teachers, including a librarian, in addition to principal Anna P. Sill.

From Ida May Carey

Lake Erie Seminary—[Painesville, Ohio]   Dec. 5—1877—

My Dear Fellow:—

Am I just a trifle outside of limit?

I sue for pardon: have been home to eat my Thanksgiving dinner, & opportunity for writing has not presented itself, until now. My recess extended from
Tues. night to Fri. noon.

By the way, are you aware that my stern sire is the fond & doting parent of
two months-old twin boys? Truly, "Truth is stranger than fiction."

I have arrived at an era in my existence when nothing can surprise me. I saw
the babies for the first time when I was at home. They are splendid little fellows:
fine heads, fortunately constituted, happy dispositioned, in short are well worthy the <u>respectable</u> name of Carey.[1]

Two wks. from this morning, I shall start for home, (W.V.) the term closing
at that time, for a vacation of two wks. Hope to return next term, & bring a
friend, one Belle Barnes, with me.

Ida May Carey. (David, Painesville,
Ohio; SCPC)

Reviews commence tomorrow. Some of the girls have five & six examinations. I shall have but one, I blush to confess. Someway I don't feel as if I had accomplished as much as I ought.

This term has been truly delightful, though, & I don't think my time has been utterly wasted. I have made great plans about reading, next term. Am ashamed that I have read so little this term. I read so very slowly. How is it with you? Have been reading "Knickerbocker's New York,"[2] & find it stupendously entertaining. We have written our last compositions for this term, thank the good stars! I had to read one entitled, "The Funny Column," before the Sem. Picture my intense embarrassment & awkwardness.

The girls here are afflicted with the same sentimental "spooning" malady which, you say, infests Rockford. I heartily agree with you, old fellow, that it is both disgusting & horrible, & demoralizing to us as women. I have invariably found that "Familiarity breeds contempt."[3]

Indeed, the girls carried the thing so far as to actually <u>flirt</u> with <u>one another</u>, in a way similar to the different sexes. For a time, there was quite an excitement over the affair. Miss Bentley[4] brought it up in Sem. ex. in such a sarcastic yet sad & reproving way, that we were all filled with shame. I believe in kissing one's friends at the proper time, but as to bestowing them <her kisses> promiscuously on one & all, the sacredness of a kiss loses its charm. I believe that the true, deep friendships & loves are those which make no obstreperous demonstrations—as it were. Dear Pythias,[5] I think that in you, I have found my affinity, & <I> picture to myself the delightful, quiet times we might have "of an evening," reading aloud to each other, & holding earnest conversations. "Hui me infelicem!"[6] Pythias, you are quite <u>too</u> aggravating. Are you afraid to trust to me the secret of your heart? Then you do not love me, for there can be no <u>true</u> love, without <u>perfect</u> trust. But since you continue so obstinate—dare I say?—I will pave the way, commanding you to follow and I will make then, the astounding revelation that I have four male correspondents,—had five, but found it painfully necessary to discard the youth who rendered himself obnoxious. I have two boys in Beloit College: one is Roger Leavitt[7] of Waterloo, Ia; the other is Herbert Sylvester[8] whom I have never seen. Will tell all next time, <u>provided</u> you reciprocate in your <u>next</u>. What is his name in Beloit? Write soon.[9] Yours devotedly

Damon

ALS (SCPC, JAC; *JAPM*, 1:272–75).

1. Ida May Carey's father, the Rev. Isaac E. Carey, married his second wife, Lucy A. Irwin Carey, on 5 Aug. 1873 and had seven children with her, including twin boys born in 1877 (see also introduction to part 1, n. 107, JA to SAA, 3 Dec. 1871, n. 4, and introduction to part 2, n. 54, all above).

2. Diedrich Knickerbocker was the fictitious chronicler of Washington Irving's (1783–1859) burlesque *A History of New York, from the Beginning of the World to the End of the Dutch Dynasty, by Diedrich Knickerbocker* (in seven books, first published in 1809 and revised in 1812,

1819, and 1848). Often described as American literature's first great comedy, the Knickerbocker stories satirized epic poetry and other literary classics as well as Jeffersonian democracy and heroic visions of the Dutch occupation of the state. Irving's work was the source of the name of the Knickerbocker Group of New York City writers and of the *Knickerbocker Magazine* (1833–65), a New York literary monthly founded in tribute to Irving's comic wit.

3. Several letters in extant correspondence from JA's first year at RFS indicate a fascination about female relationships and love. At RFS as at other women's schools, what historian Christie Farnham has called patterns of "intense emotional identification and love," including sometimes an "erotic component in these crushes," took place within the schoolgirls' ongoing creation of a context of romantic beauty. As Farnham has put it, "Part of the appeal of romantic friendships may have stemmed from the attractiveness to the Victorian mind of the rituals involved" (*Education of the Southern Belle*, 157). Among the girls whom JA knew at Rockford, memorization and recitation of romantic poetry, writing affectionate notes, taking daily walks, and picking flowers and arranging floral bouquets for one another were all part of the school milieu. As Farnham has observed about schools in the South, "If such tokens of attachment were acceptable, they often served to initiate exclusive relationships," best friendships that "became highly visible among the community of students and teachers by displays of ritualized attentiveness" (158). So it was at Rockford, where student Lizzie Smith wrote home to her mother, naming the couples that had emerged among her own circle of friends. Carroll Smith-Rosenberg has emphasized the positive aspects of such relationships in terms of building young women's sense of "inner security and self esteem" (*Disorderly Conduct*, 64), and it is true that JA and her friends gained self-confidence during the process of valuing and validating one another. Farnham, however, has cautioned that spooning among girls could also be destructive and lead to ostracism and animosity as the girls jockeyed for preference among one another and moved through attachments that were of a "short-term, serial nature" (*Education of the Southern Belle*, 159). These two aspects to same-sex friendships existed simultaneously at RFS. On the one hand, JA benefited from what Smith-Rosenberg has described as a kind of apprenticeship or mentoring system like that which existed between female teachers and administrators and students. On the other hand, just as rivalries emerged among members of the two literary societies at Rockford (which also functioned as social sororities), so jealousies and hierarchies existed among the girls, as did tensions over strict rules of behavior between the students and Anna P. Sill. In memoirs or letters home, schoolgirls reported memories of being selected as a partner by a popular girl in the Sunday ritual of walking two by two to church, or—as in Lizzie Smith's case—of the disdain and repulsion she felt for sleeping in the same bed with a new roommate who was of a different socioeconomic class and whom she found to be unattractive.

In Apr. 1878 Carey inquired what JA was reading. She herself was starting Hawthorne's *The Marble Faun* and asked for JA's advice on "Lucile," especially on its passage regarding the nature of honest love. Carey repeated her rejection of what she and JA regarded as sentimentality, lest JA should read something into a request for a quotation about love: "I assure you," she wrote, "I meant nothing sentimental in that quotation, for a sentimental person, is one whom I detest with my whole being. Heaven knows this school is reeking in sentimentality & I have had my turn at it, & one dose was sufficient to send all my love-sick propensities to the four-winds. How is it at R—? Do the girls lower themselves to this contemptible flirting with one another? Let me have your opinion" ("Damon" [Ida May Carey] to JA, 14 Apr. 1878; IU, Lilly, SAAH). Perhaps Carey protested too much and may actually have been more interested in schoolgirl relations than she professed (see also Vallie E. Beck to JA, 6 Dec. 1877 and 2 [and 4] May 1878, below).

4. Luette A. Bentley (d. 20 July 1922) of Streetsboro, Ohio, graduated from Lake Erie Female Seminary in 1865 and became a faculty member there the following fall. She was assistant principal from 1878 until 1898 when she became dean. Her aunt was a New England

physician, and Bentley did postgraduate study in medicine in New York during summer breaks from teaching physiology and hygiene at Painesville. Her scientific teaching was considered very progressive in the 1880s, and at her death she was described as a scholar whose research interests had been far in advance of her times. She lived and worked in close partnership for more than forty years with principal and president Mary Ann Evans, who came to the school from Mt. Holyoke in 1868. The two women retired together in 1909. They traveled extensively, and beginning in 1917 they shared a small house on campus provided for them by the school. Bentley was buried in Hudson, Ohio.

   Like RFS, Lake Erie Female Seminary, which offered higher education to women in a noncoeducational setting, was popularly referred to as a Mt. Holyoke of the West. It was based on the ideal of a quality curriculum for middle-class girls, incorporating high educational standards and a boarding-school plan in which students performed domestic work, and supported with a public endowment. All the original faculty members were from Mt. Holyoke.

   Lake Erie Female Seminary was located in Painesville, fifteen miles to the east of Willoughby, Ohio. It was the successor to the Willoughby Female Seminary, which had burned to the ground in 1854, just seven years after its founding. The cornerstone for the new female seminary in Painesville was laid in July 1857, and classes opened in Sept. 1859. All students were required to board at the school, and the course of study placed an emphasis upon ancient languages, mathematics, and science. The school was affiliated with the Presbyterian Church, and daughters of clergy, including Ida May Carey, received a discount in their annual tuition and board. The seminary's main building was enlarged in stages over several years, with parts under construction during Carey's time at the school. As at RFS, physical exercise was emphasized for Lake Erie students, and the basement of College Hall was used as a gymnasium. Just as Anna P. Sill and Sarah Anderson presided over the transition of RFS from seminary to college, so Bentley and Evans guided Lake Erie Seminary into collegiate status. The school's name was changed to Lake Erie Seminary and College in 1898 and to Lake Erie College in 1908. Ida May Carey graduated from the school in June 1881.

   5. Damon (as Carey signs this letter) was a shepherd singer in Virgil's eighth "Eclogue," and his name is associated with love and friendship. Damon and Pythias were also Pythagorean Greeks who became immortalized in classical legend for their intimate friendship. The story of fraternal love was popularized in the Irish poet and novelist John Banim's (1798–1842) *Damon and Pythias; a Tragedy in Five Acts*, which was produced in London in 1821 and was an inspiration in the founding of the Knights of Pythias fraternal organization in 1864. Carey continued to sign her correspondence to JA as "Damon" and to "trust to your imperturable good-nature & our long-established friendship . . . the kind of good, solid, sensible friendship, which will endure through any amount of wear & tear" (28 July 1878, SCPC, JAC; JAPM, 1:308–10).

   6. This Latin phrase translates as "Oh, unhappy me!"

   7. Roger Leavitt was a student at Beloit College in 1877–78, as was his friend Herbert Sylvester. Leavitt (b. ca. 1861) graduated in the class of 1882. He entered the academy section of Beloit College as a Middle Preparatory Dept. student in 1876 and completed the collegiate course, spending a total of six years studying at the school. He was one of twelve students at Beloit who were from Iowa hometowns in the 1877–78 term. He worked with Prof. James J. Blaisdell and roomed at a series of boardinghouses near the Beloit College campus, including, in 1878, the home of Luther L. Greenleaf, where GBH also boarded during part of his time as a Beloit College student (see also JA to JHA, 8 May 1881, n. 25, below). Like GBH, Leavitt was active in debating at Beloit. He presided over Beloit oratorical contests and in 1880 won 1st prize at the Beloit College 33d Anniversary Declamation Contest. He spoke on the subject of Savonarola at his school's Junior Exhibition on 29 Mar. 1882, and at the 35th commencement of Beloit College in June 1882 he spoke on the subject of Longfellow and Emerson. He became president of the Interstate Oratorical Assn. in 1882, having won the endorsement of

William Jennings Bryan, whom he first met during a train trip to an association meeting in 1881 (see also JA to JHA, 8 May 1881, n. 24, below). Leavitt was the treasurer of Beloit's Delian Society in 1881 and literary editor of the Beloit College *Round Table* in 1882. He became a banker in Cedar Falls, Iowa, and remained a strong supporter of Beloit College. In 1923 he became a member of the college's board of trustees, filling the unexpired term of his friend and JA acquaintance Rollin D. Salisbury, who died that winter. Leavitt left his scrapbook of memorabilia about Beloit College to the college's archives.

8. Charles Herbert Sylvester, known at Beloit College as "Syl," was from Boscobel, Wis. By 1880 he had left the college to study law at home. He passed the Wisconsin bar in 1882 and began to practice law.

9. Carey later chided JA for her failure to correspond regularly. The following summer she wrote to report that she had failed her algebra and ancient history examinations and described herself "as impenetrably stupid in Mathematics." She also told JA that she indulged herself in a fantasy of spending the "vacation with you in your most charming of homes. Ah, my friend, that were a bliss which far surpasses my wildest dreams. I have not forgotten those cool retreats among those immense boulders, nor how we used to row up & down in the shadows of the cliffs. What enjoyable <times> we would have picnicing, & reading poetry, & talking, all through these tranquil summer days. And here I <u>sigh</u>, if you please" (28 July 1878, SCPC, JAC; *JAPM*, 1:309–10).

Draft of Essay

The following essay is a reminder of the centrality of the Civil War and its imme-diate political aftermath to those of Jane Addams's generation. Many social activists in northern Illinois, including leading citizens of Rockford, had been involved in the antislavery movement and in the war. Jane Addams and her acquaintances had experienced the war, Emancipation, and the death of Abraham Lincoln as backdrops to their early childhoods, and they came of age during Reconstruction. Addams herself had been raised within a strong Republican household. Her first year at Rockford Female Seminary coincided with the first year of the administration of Rutherford B. Hayes. Herein Addams protests the mandates of the Compromise of 1877, which brought an end to further civil rights reforms and the adoption of what would prove to be a long-standing federal policy of appeasement toward state-level institutionalization of white supremacy. While concentrating on party politics, the young Addams illustrates the limits of the northern liberal imagination in regard to race and the envisioning of full systems of racial equality.

[Rockford, Ill.]   5 Dec. 1877

The Present Policy of Congress.

Grant, who for eight years has represented our highest political power and has been our main prop and stay, has <u>now</u> sublimely departed to foreign shores,[1] for the purpose of enjoying his hard earned honors, and[2] as he stands on the deck of the stately steamer, smoking his cigar with the air of a man who has done his duty, and is swiftly borne from sight, the whole nation turns its attention to Hayes and his "policy";[3] for <u>he</u> as well as congress proudly claims ownership to

a "policy" and intends[4] to settle at once the civil rights question.[5] "War has always been the mint in which the worlds history has been coined,["] it is an old
story, but it is a new one to this generation of Americans.[6] We are learning many
strange matters from our fresh experiances and we hardly know how to deal with
the present state of affairs[.] Our late war was inevitable, it might have come a
little sooner or a little later, but come it must. The disease of the nation was
organic not functional, it needed the knife, not soothing herbs,[7] war was its only
remedy and we are better and stronger for it. Thousands died on both side[s],
to have stopped before the end was attained, or if Congress now yields one inch
of the principle then advanced, will make all that terrible loss of life mere butch-
ery. If they carry out the intention with which they first resented the outrage,
the earth drinks the blood of martyrs fallen in a noble sacrifice.

But the negroes are free, that is a settled fact, and something must be done
with them, the plight of the nation reminds us of the Vicar of Wakefield,[8] who
paid an enormous price for his family portraits and then did'ent know what in
the world to do with them, as it was impossible to get them into the house, much
less keep them there.

We understand Hayes to be an honest, principled gentleman, but just a trifle
ethereal and visionary, who is rather attempting to conciliate the south, forgetting that "~~weakness~~ meekness is weakness", and that they should be treated with
justice and not mercy <alone>. He believes in putting the right man in the right
place, regardless of his party principles, but "to prevent opinion from organizing itself under political forms, is very desirable, but it is not in accordance ~~to~~
<with> the theory or practice of self government." Hayes should remember "to
the victor belongs the spoils" and not put a democrat, his political enemy, into
office when there is an honest republican to be found in the neighborhood.[9]

It will be remembered that of the three vacant seats in Congress two belong
to Louisiana and one to South Carolina, they should be filled at once.[10]

Patterson[11] says that Hayes forgets it is to the republicans of South Carolina, who stood true to thier principles during the entire campaign, that he owes
his election. Little did these men think, as they tried their best, and did every
thing for his election, that the first thing he would do would be the removal of
the troops whose presence alone enabled them to exercise the functions of thier
office. His policy means the abandonment of political friends for the concilia-
tion of political foes.

<One> half <of> the people of the U.S. believe he was elected by fraud, <the
other half> recognize him as fairly elected, but if he deserts the big republican
north, for the sake of soothing the big democratic south, he will find "midst a
whole country full friends he has none."[12]

AMsS (UIC, JAMC, Detzer; *JAPM*, 45:1684–90).

1. Ulysses S. Grant (1822–85) was elected president of the United States in 1868 and 1872 and
served in that office from Mar. 1869 to Mar. 1877. He was well known to the Addams family—
indeed, to all of northern Illinois—for he lived in Galena, less than fifty miles west of Free-

port near the Iowa border. Like Rutherford B. Hayes, Grant was originally from the Cincinnati area. He was born in Point Pleasant, Ohio, and raised in Georgetown. He married Julia Boggs Dent, the daughter of a St. Louis slaveholding planter and merchant, in 1848, and they settled in Galena, where Grant joined his father and brothers in a leather goods business. West Point–trained and with experience in the 1846–48 Mexican War, Grant joined the Union army in 1861 and rose to command the Union forces during the last part of the Civil War (from Mar. 1864 through war's end in Apr. 1865). He was endorsed for the presidency by the Republican Party on a Radical Reconstruction platform and as president continued the federal occupation of the South. During his presidency, the Fourteenth Amendment, granting citizenship to freed people, and the Fifteenth Amendment, granting freedmen (but not women) the right to vote, were adopted and the Civil Rights Act of 1875 was ushered through the U.S. Congress. Grant attended the inauguration of Hayes and then departed with his family on a global tour to Europe, Asia, and Africa. They traveled abroad from the spring of 1877 to the fall of 1879. In 1881 Grant moved to New York City and invested his life savings in a brokerage firm that went bankrupt in 1884. He died of cancer in July 1885, shortly after completing his memoir, which became a classic of American literature and saved his family from financial ruin.

2. The original manuscript has been edited lightly in a few instances by another hand, presumably that of JA's history and English teacher Caroline Potter, who, at the end of this essay, gave JA a grade of "93–." Most of the spelling and grammatical errors have been left without correction. Here the comma following "honors" has been changed to a period and the "a" of "and" marked for capitalization.

3. According to the Compromise of 1877 forged by Republicans and Democrats in Jan. as a negotiation over the disputed presidential election of 1876, Hayes agreed to remove federal troops from the South and appoint at least one southern Democrat to his cabinet. The arrangement signaled the end of the Reconstruction era.

4. In the original, the word *they* has been inserted between "and" and "intends" and "intends" has been edited to the singular, making the phrase "and they intend to settle."

5. Grant had stated in his second inaugural address on 4 Mar. 1873 that slaves had been freed but not made citizens, nor did they possess civil rights, wrongs that should be corrected. Hayes, in his 5 Mar. 1877 inaugural address, spoke of the pacification of the country, signaling a turn away from federal commitment to enforcement of Reconstruction-era congressional acts regarding racial equity or future federal interference with state laws undercutting those reforms.

6. JA quotes poet, social commentator, essayist, and Harvard Medical School dean Oliver Wendell Holmes, Sr. (1809–94), from his essay "Bread and the Newspaper," on the public reaction to events at the beginning of the Civil War. The essay was first published in Sept. 1861 and was reprinted as the lead piece in Holmes's collection entitled *Papers from an Old Volume of Life* (1883), 1–15. The full sentence from which JA quotes reads: "War has always been the mint in which the world's history has been coined, and now every day or week or month has a new medal for us" (13).

7. Here JA uses the metaphor of illness to describe the war. In "Slavery: An Allogory," a 24 Mar. essay of an unknown year but written during her time at RFS (possibly for her civil government class in the first semester of 1878–79, or the modern history course of the second semester in the same academic year), she used the equally lethal image of a hemlock tree, with roots representing the spread of the institution of slavery. In her allegory, the tree is planted by Dutch colonists and left uncultivated to take root on its own. In a "free soil" versus slave South analogy (and a mixed metaphor of plant and human body), JA has the southward-probing roots of her mythical tree drawing "from the fresh soil the clear pure waters of liberty and changing it into the poisonous sap that coursed through every vein" (*JAPM*, 46:3). In the allegory, abolitionism is represented by the storms that buffet the tree, and the Underground Railroad and escaped slaves by sap that leaks out of fissures in northward-

moving roots. At the end of the essay she offered a key that explained that the roots were to represent the avariciousness of slave dealing; the sap, the slaves (who are "freed" at the end of the allegory when lightning strikes the tree, splitting it in half and uprooting it); and the leaves, "gain—cotton" (*JAPM*, 46:6).

8. A reference to *The Vicar of Wakefield* (1766), a novel by Oliver Goldsmith (1730?–74) that traces the fall from prosperity and good fortune of the Rev. Dr. Primrose and his family.

9. JA is quoting William Learned Marcy (1768–1857), who was a senator from New York from 1831 to 1832. In a Jan. 1832 speech before the U.S. Senate, Marcy defended an appointment of his friend Martin Van Buren, saying, "To the victor belong the spoils of the enemy," thus giving rise to the term *spoils system* in American politics. Hayes appointed David M. Key (1824–1900) of Tennessee as postmaster general, thus fulfilling his pledge to put a southern Democrat on the cabinet.

10. The election of 1876 led to great confusion in Florida, Louisiana, and South Carolina when Republicans disallowed Democratic victories because of massive intimidation that had taken place in certain parishes. Under Hayes's administration, federal troops were withdrawn from the South Carolina statehouse on 3 Apr. 1877, bringing about the fall of Republican Gov. Daniel H. Chamberlain and putting the Redeemers (conservative Democrats) in power. In Louisiana, where both Republican and Democratic governors and legislatures had taken office in Jan., troops were removed on 20 Apr., leading to the governorship of Conservative-Democrat Francis Nicholls.

11. John James Patterson (known derisively as "Honest John") (b. 1830) was a Republican politician, editor, and businessman from Pennsylvania. He edited the Juniata, Pa., *Sentinel* and the *Harrisburg* [Pa.] *Telegraph*. He was also engaged, in a corrupt way, with banking and the management of railroads. He served in the Union army during the Civil War and was a carpetbagger after war's end, moving to South Carolina, where he was elected to the U.S. Senate in 1872 and served one term.

12. Hayes came into office on an extremely close and highly disputed vote. He actually lost the popular vote to his opponent, Samuel J. Tilden (1814–86) of New York, with Tilden polling 51 percent to Hayes's 48 percent, with a margin of difference of fewer than 250,000 votes. Tilden, however, was only one electoral vote away from victory when Republican officials ruled many Democratic ballots in Florida, Louisiana, and South Carolina invalid, and returns in South Carolina were tainted in confusion. The situation was resolved by a Congressional Electoral Comm., which convened on 20 Jan. and voted in Feb. 1877, strictly along party lines, to give the votes from all three disputed states to Hayes. Hayes was declared elected on 2 Mar. and inaugurated on 5 Mar. 1877.

Voters in Rockford, a traditional Republican stronghold, voted overwhelmingly for Hayes (who received 4,505 votes in Winnebago Co. to Tilden's 1,568 in the 1876 election). The northern Illinois county had similarly backed John C. Frémont, Abraham Lincoln, and Ulysses S. Grant—the Republican candidates in 1856, 1860 and 1864, and 1868 and 1872, respectively, and would give similar support to James A. Garfield, the Republican candidate (and victor) in 1880.

From Vallie E. Beck

Old Maids Retreat. Glendale, Ohio   Dec. 6" 1877.

My dear Jennie.

In order to express my appreciation of your charming letter, I must make an immediate reply to it and even then I fear I shall not have made you understand how I value your letters. Indeed judging from your deeds, I should think you credited me with no regard for your ever welcome letters, for you write so seldom and only tantalize with your (to me) such short letters. I try to pay my debt of gratitude to you—for your kindness in writing at all—by answering and writing as lengthy letters as I have time but yet this perhaps does not satisfy you. My dear possibly you are hard to please (I shall not say fastidious, for that is a quality I much admire and I am now scolding you and one never should censuor people for traits we admire in them.) Now in your last you said you admire cold people, they are few and far between, can that be the reason you like them? But seriously you and I agree exactly in regard to that. My own particular style, is a dignified (rather haughty) proud—not vain—and cold person; yet I like them capable of graceful acts and with these characteristics must be combined intelligence and considerable experience. I have three such friends and hope I shall have frequent opportunities of meeting such people and improving their acquaintances. And since I know that is your style also, I shall cultivate such touches in my own character. Apropos—Taidee Soulé has considerable of this in her composition, or at least had when I knew her and do hope it has been fostered. By no means do I wish you to think me conscious of only these traits when in the presence of my friends of whom, I have just spoken, for there are certain others, such as honesty that I price as highly a[s] dignity. I hate deceit and flattery and after I discover either one <in> a person I forwith drop them and even since here have found myself trusting a certain person allmost unduly because my dislikes for her have become so intense, simply because I have discovered her deceitful.

We are now having charming weather for our daily exercise.[1] Alternately muddy and cold, with each day a rain, snow or (as today) a sleet to give a variety: you know it is so monotonous to have pleasant days right along. But 12 days without a ray of sunshine was not conducive to the lightest and most joyous of spirits and then I have not the most congenial room mate in world. Yet I am quite sure I prefer her to any one else in the school. I have an odd idea that best friends should keep their distance for familiarity usually follows if too much intimacy is indulged, and you know well the old addage concerning that.

Well to return to our discourse, we are out every morning before it is quite light, before the sun is up (do not criticize that if you are studying astronomy) and must walk about 6 squares in about fifteen minutes and although this might not be so very objectionable if taken after a hearty breakfast yet I assure you I do seriously regret going out after cold coffee and bread.

That reminds me, thanksgiving I received a large box of eatables from home. Every thing came through in fine condition and I all but made my self sick; if I had it would have been disagreeable enough, I assure you, for few favors are granted for some time after Thanksgiving, because if you have received a box, every thing from a sore finger on up, is called a slight fit of indigestion; you will soon be over it. I do enjoy winter picnics and I had an enjoyable time, notwithstanding lack of dishes, cold room (unusual however) and such slight inconveniences as those.

I leave for home two weeks from tomorrow to spend the holy days; do write to me before I leave, please <u>answer immediately</u>. You observe a constant fear of rising, dinners, study, tea and other bells and about destroyed even the poor penmanship I have heretofore had. Your loving friend-cousin

Vallie E. Beck

ALS (SCPC, JAC; *JAPM*, 1:276–79); UIC, JAMC, HJ; *JAPM*, 1:280.

1. While Vallie Beck took part in pre-dawn physical exercises at Glendale Female Seminary, RFS girls were required to walk on the grounds for an hour each day and to participate in evening calisthenics in the school gymnasium. According to authorized biographer Winifred Wise, "Jenny promenaded dutifully, but, because of her back, she did not take gymnasium" but did ride horseback, according to a regimen set by JHA and AHHA (*Jane Addams of Hull-House*, 63). James Weber Linn reported that "the prescribed physical exercise was very dreary—every day each girl must walk for one hour on the wooden walk about the grounds, making the same narrow circuit twenty or thirty times in damp weather. Jane preferred even that to her stepmother's prescribed Saturday morning horse-back riding, which hurt her spine" (Linn, *Jane Addams*, 49; see also The 1875 Diary of Jane Addams, 17 Apr. 1875, n. 1, above, and JA to Eva Campbell, 25 [and 29] July 1879, n. 7, below).

The "Editorial Notes" in the Jan. 1878 *RSM* began with an observation on mid-winter walking at RFS: "As the cold, bleak days of winter come o'er us, we girls are apt to neglect our daily exercise, on the plea that it is so monotonous walking over the same paths again and again without anything to divert our minds." The editor announced the rumor that "the skating rink is again to be numbered among the out-door amusements for the winter, and if this report proves true, let one and all come to the rink with skates in hand; and I hope that now, after Christmas, no one will be obliged to come empty handed" (36).

That JA had a sense of humor about the RFS walking regimen was clear. In diary notes written at RFS (and printed here in poetic form, as JA broke the lines in the narrow pages of the diary), she wrote the following ditty: "Must I then / exercise, said I to / myself / With nothing to / see or to view, / Go round & round / the horrid old walk / and encounter / nothing new? / I put on my hat / & went out the door / I did it with a snarl / & a phew / The only reason I did / it at all / was just because I / had to" ("Pocket Diary, 1875[–81]," printed date 30 Sept. 1875 [written 1879?]; *JAPM*, 28:1626).

A few pages later in the same diary, she drafted a scenario by hand for the "Home Items" section in the *RSM:* "Two students exercise as hard as possible—1st student ([walking] 'Walking brings forth wisdom'[)] 2nd student[, '] De Quincey says walking makes beautiful Eyes.' 1st student 'Ah well we all know what we need most' 2nd St[udent]. 'let's walk'" ("Pocket Diary, 1875[–81]," printed date 5 Oct. 1875 [written 1879?]; *JAPM*, 28:1629). The piece appeared printed in the following modified form in the July 1879 *RSM:* "Two students exercising as hard as possible. / FIRST STUDENT:—'Walking brings forth wisdom.' / SECOND STUDENT:—'Yes, and De Quincy says walking makes beautiful eyes.' / FIRST STUDENT:—'Ah, well! we all know what we need most.' / SECOND STUDENT:—'Let's walk!'" (201).

After four years at RFS, JA had gained some perspective on the walking issue. One of her editorials as editor-in-chief of the *RSM* written in her last semester at the school was about attitude being the key in the walking routine—and in the larger issue of rules and confinement at RFS, as well. "Exercise is as essential for the preservation of good health as either food or pure air," she reminded readers:

While we may think it tiresome to walk within the gates for an hour daily, we can in this, as in many other things make it an agreeable or disagreeable duty, according to the way we go about it. . . . . It is very easy, by thinking over a matter for some time, to convince ourselves in regard to it, thus we may make ourselves believe that we are the most abused persons in the world,—shut up within four walls, we might as well be in a prison. Then we may start out with a different view of things, with the intention of getting all the enjoyment possible in one hour; the sky, the air, the trees never seemed so perfect, and we wonder, while searching for zoological or botanical specimens, if people walking along the dusty street do not envy us our green grass and cool shade. ([May 1881]: 152)

From Vallie E. Beck

Glendale, Ohio.   Feb. 2" 1878

My dear Jennie;

My seeming neglect is quite excusable, allow me to assure you, and so you will think if you have ever passed an examination. Before those which ended yesterday commenced, I had no anxiety whatever concerning them, for I knew not what to expect, never having been through any. For several weeks passed every one has been on the qui vive concerning them and I have remained as placid as Neptune—a la Virgil[1]—because I feared nothing; but hereafter I shall know what to expect and—I presume—shall act as insanely as many of the girls did, their only greeting being "examinations begin next week! are you scared?" (the latter word I particularly dislike)[.] "Oh, dear day after tomorrow, I shall die, I just know I shall, I can't live through it" &c &c[.] If anyone wishes to make himself particularly disagreeable to me just let him call me a school girl: they are usually so gushing, and young: that is they seem to have no idea of the propriety or decorum. I do hope I shall never be afflicted with the giggles, laugh when the blessing is asked, laugh when some one fails in their lessons, laugh when the President makes remarks or lectures us, on the whole laugh at this and laugh whenever it is improper to laugh.

And talk! how unhappy the quiet girl is deemed; she that can talk the most and gossip in an easily hateful (do you understand?) is the popular girl: at least such an one is our "general favorite." Who does not understand the desultory habit of many women? i.e. gossip.

They seem to have nothing excepting the affairs of the affairs of their neighbors to interest them. If they would only review what they read: women do read, but they seem to have no faculty of reviewing what they read and enlarging upon it: digesting it and discussing. Now I know one lady (this is gossip, but it is necessary to illustrate what I have written, and I shall tell you who she is, our lady principal) who is a student of Shakespeare—this proper name may be spelled in any way and yet be correct—and has read nearly everything, but who has no original ideas on the subject, can not give a criticism on any work she has read. It seems impossible to draw her out she does not know what to say, therefor say nothing unless to gossip in a flippant manner about this that and the other character. The only criticism she has ever made upon any author in my hearing, was that Victor Hugo[2] had not the facination over her that he had over many and that she did not consider his stories entertaining, but thought his power in the portrayal of character wonderful and his discriptive power vigorous and she was held in awe by some of his situations. Now that was the most extensive observation I have ever heard the lady make. But really in this and other matters I must practice what I preach. That is the most difficult matter to appreciate; others estimate me as I rate them and consequently I have few friend[s]. I never think when I say others gossip and for that reason find fault with them, that I am doing the same thing and they are saying the same of me.

But you have probably met at sometime, one whom you considered a lady "to the core," so why should I continue this harangue about those who are not ladies.

Just now one of the girls was here who was so kind(?) as to tell me the remark of another about me; it seemed strange that just after I had written that; I should be told of an unkind remark. However I felt a little complimented about it because it had an undertone of something like envy, just a trifle.

Now please write to me soon: do not wait for examinations as an excuse. Altho' I have not so many studies yet my time is well occupied with 4 hours of practice and three studies.

When do you expect to enter Vasser? Please write me your plans. Of course you look forward with the greatest pleasure to your days at V. and I wish you all success and a realization of your ambitions and anticipation.[3] Your prospects are bright, I know, and you I am very sure, will do nothing to marr but much to bring them into greater brilliancy.

The bells have rung for tea. Again I must close an unfinished letter. Your sincere friend

Vallie E Beck.

ALS (SCPC, JAC; *JAPM*, 1:288–92).

1. A reference to Neptune, the Roman god of the sea, and Virgil (70–19 B.C.), the Roman poet and author of the *Aeneid*, the epic poem of the adventures of Aeneas and his Trojans in the settlement of Italy.

2. Victor-Marie Hugo (1802–85), French Romantic poet, playwright, and novelist, spent the years from 1851 to 1870 in exile after the 1848 revolution and is best known for *Les misérables* (1862). The novel was popular among JA's cohorts and the subject of discussion. "Have you read 'Les Mis<er>abiles'?" Ida May Carey asked JA. "I have heard so much about it" (28 July 1878, SCPC, JAC; *JAPM*, 1:310). EGS inquired during the following summer, "Do you cultivate Hugo's style of writing?" (11 Aug. 1878, below). JA discussed Hugo's hero Jean Valjean in "The Passion of revenge and mercy as a producing element in Literature" ([1880–81?], *JAPM*, 46:113–19).

3. JA maintained a hope that she would transfer from RFS to earn a degree at either Smith or Vassar College. Although Vallie Beck mentions Vassar in this letter, it was Smith College, the new women's school popularly known among RFS girls as "Smith's" from its early name

Miss Smith's College, endowed by Sophia Smith and opened in Northampton, Mass., in Sept. 1875, that most attracted JA. Vassar College in Poughkeepsie, N.Y., bridged the secondary training of female seminaries and the classical course of study of colleges. At Vassar, requirements in such areas as mathematics and ancient and modern languages were equal to those at men's colleges. While RFS sought to be the Mt. Holyoke of the West, Vassar sought to be for women "what Yale and Harvard are to young men" (Jewett, "Origin of Vassar College," quoted in Horowitz, *Alma Mater*, 29).

There were several personal connections between RFS and both Smith and Vassar. For example, the fall issue of the *RSM* printed in JA's first year announced that Julia Lathrop, who was born in Rockford and graduated from RFS in 1878, "has gone to Vassar" (194). Lathrop received her bachelor's degree from Vassar in 1880 and a decade later became a resident of Hull-House. While the Mt. Holyoke plan served as the model for RFS's founding, it was Vassar, with its modernized approaches and full liberal arts curriculum for women, that was looked to as the standard for improvements in the RFS courses of study made during JA's tenure at the school. Smith College trustees had done a good job in advertising their school in western states during JA's adolescence, convincing the public that they "meant to open, not a High School for Girls, not a Seminary, but a College in very truth" and creating a demand among westerners for admission. The object of the college, stated clearly in the first promotional circular issued by the trustees in 1872, was to furnish the "means and facilities for education" for women "equal to those which are afforded in our colleges to young men" (Hanscom and Greene, *Sophia Smith*, 98, 115).

By the end of her second year at RFS, JA had decided that the small seminary had its advantages. She urged her friend Eva Campbell to not "give up the idea of coming back, Eva, I beg of you, for it seems to me that we can both do better work at Rockford next year than any place I know of" (25 [and 29] July 1879, below). The dream of attending Smith did not die, however, but was merely deferred, to reappear again as an ambition in JA's junior and senior years and yet again as each new school year approached in the years immediately following her graduation. As her senior year drew to a close, JA, like her classmate Mary Ellwood, was looking forward to a year at Smith to follow completion of the course of study at RFS. Degree status became a possibility at RFS just as JA was finishing her four years there. Before that, Smith offered what (until to 1881–82) RFS did not—a bachelor's degree and an elevated course of study for women. JA traveled to the Smith College campus in the summer of 1882, but she never attended the school (see *PJA*, 2). She did, however, receive an honorary LL.D. degree from Smith in 1910.

Announcement in the
Rockford Seminary Magazine

Several other Rockford Female Seminary students shared Jane Addams's keen interest in science. Just before she entered the seminary, the Rockford Female Seminary Board of Trustees were encouraged to foster the student body's desire to study the sciences by providing better materials and greater outlets for expression. In reporting on the public examinations at the end of the 1876–77 academic year, the school's Board of Examiners commended the "enthusiasm shown, and advances made in the study of the natural sciences. In the departments of zoology and botany the young ladies, considering the material at their hand, and the time spent upon these branches, did remarkably well." The board "call[ed] upon the friends

of the Seminary to furnish it, as speedily as possible, with the specimens, appara-
tus and books for the study of these sciences, which it so much needs."[1]
   The girls could be exuberant in their pursuit of science. The April 1878 Rock-
ford Seminary Magazine carried a rather surprising editorial about the sad fate
of a campus cat who had been stalked and killed by science students so they could
dissect it, including details about the process. Jane quickly joined in making the new
scientific association's programs a success. She prepared a talk on Illinois geogra-
phy and reptiles, and delivered it to her "scientific sisters" in May 1878.[2]
   In the notice below the magazine editors announce the organization of the sci-
entific association, with Addams as a member of its executive committee.

[Rockford, Ill.]   APRIL 1878

   We have the pleasure of announcing that since our last issue a "Scientific
Association" has been organized, under very favorable circumstances, and we
infer from its meetings thus far that it will be a live, working society. They have
already announced lectures upon Botany, by Mr. M. S. Bebb,[3] of Fountaindale,
one of the first botanists of our State, and upon the Structure and Diseases of
the Eye, by Dr. Henry P. Fitch, of Rockford, whose star as physician and oculist
is quite in the ascendant. Its officers are: President, Miss Mary E. Holmes;[4] Vice
President, Miss Mary Downs;[5] Secretary, Miss Addie F. Merrill;[6] Treasurer, Miss
Kate L. Hitchcock; Curator, Miss Addie Stephens;[7] Executive Committee, Misses
Ellen G. Starr, Jennie Addams, Hattie Smith,[8] and Nora Frothingham.[9]

PD (*RSM* [April 1878]: 81).[10]

   1. RFS Examining Com. to the RFS Board of Trustees, 26 June 1877, Sill, "Scrapbook."
   2. See "[Address on Illinois Geography]," 26 May [1878], *JAPM*, 45:1779–87, and introduction to part 1, nn. 14 and 158, above. The poor status of scientific study, particularly the lack
of opportunity in laboratory sciences, remained an issue at RFS for years. The RFS Scientific
Assn. supplemented regular science curriculum. JA enrolled in a physiology course in her first
semester and in a botany class in her second. She took no formal science courses in her second year at the seminary but enrolled in astronomy in the first semester of her junior year
in 1879–80 and in her senior year took a geology-mineralogy class.
   3. Michael Schuck Bebb (1833–95), a self-trained naturalist, was a prominent Illinois botanist whose specialization was the genus Salix (willows). His herbarium, which he began
collecting in 1856, was deposited after his death at the Field Museum of Natural History,
Chicago. The *RSM* reported in July 1878 that "Mr. M. S. Bebb lectured on Botany before the
Scientific Association, in May." He spoke on the three main botanical areas of the United
States and then drew a comparison between the flora of Europe and America. Bebb was said
to have "a very affable manner of speaking, and certainly his kindness in lecturing before the
Scientific Association deserves the most cordial thanks of its members" (139).
   4. Mary E. Holmes (1850–1906), JA's science teacher at RFS, was the daughter of a Rockford Presbyterian minister, Mead Holmes (d. 1906), and Mary D. Holmes (d. 1890), a church
activist. After a childhood spent in Ohio and Wisconsin, where her father worked as a pastor, she came to Rockford with her parents in 1864. She was one of two children. Her brother, Mead Holmes, Jr., enlisted in a Wisconsin regiment of the Union army and was killed in
action in battle at Murfreesboro, Tenn., in 1863. Holmes benefited through her brother's early

education. As a result of listening in on his lessons, she was able to parse and translate in Greek, Latin, and French at the age of eight. She began her first herbarium at the age of five. In her childhood she created at her family's home a virtual zoo of tamed squirrels, woodchucks, raccoons, foxes, gophers, thrushes, and other small birds and animals. The habit continued into adulthood, when the Holmes residence was home to a menagerie of cats and dogs as well as many tamed woodland animals, including several chipmunks, "squirrels—black, gray, red, and flying—robins, mocking birds," a bald eagle, several types of owls, and a bear ("Miss Mary Holmes and Her Cat," clipping, Sill, "Scrapbook"). Holmes excelled in her public school education, passing county-certified examinations in all subjects with perfect scores by the age of thirteen. She entered RFS at the age of fourteen and graduated in 1868, after which she studied with Daniel Hood and completed the RFS program in his Conservatory of Music, specializing in organ performance and graduating in 1870. She taught Spencerian penmanship at RFS in 1868–70, helping to train students for secretarial and clerical work. From 1877 to 1885 she taught natural sciences (botany and chemistry) at the seminary. Under her tutelage the RFS Scientific Assn. was formed, and RFS girls gave public laboratory demonstrations for members of the Rockford community.

According to a historian of Rockford College, Holmes had "an excellent reputation as a scientist. Her classes in chemistry seem to have been unusually well conducted, and her methods advanced. She lectured in and around Rockford." In 1876 the *RSM* "spoke of hers and Miss Mary E. B. Norton's attainments. Her researches, they said, 'find appreciation beyond the limits of Rockford. In a catalogue of Illinois plants, published this year by Harry N. Patterson, her name stands third upon the list of botanical authorities, no other lady's name appearing except that of Miss E. B. Norton'" (Cedarborg, "Early History," 258). In 1877–78 Holmes published articles in the *RSM,* including "Chemistry—Its Rise, Diffusion, and Progress" ([Oct. 1877]: 209–12). She gave a toast on "Earnestness and Enthusiasm the Keys to Success" at an RFS Alumnae Reunion. On that occasion, she observed, "The very air we breathe is redolent with earnestness and enthusiasm. Our Alma Mater, this home with her 870 loyal daughters, is turning these keys in as many households and family circles, and unlocking the mysteries of literature, mathematics, science and religion to thousands" (*RSM* [July 1878]: 170).

When RFS began conferring degrees in 1881–82, Holmes petitioned to be included, and the situation became a battle between Anna P. Sill and the more conservative members of the board. Sill wrote to Joseph Emerson, a RFS Board of Trustees member and her confidante, on 8 Dec. 1881 to inform him that "Miss Holmes applies for a degree and asks what studies farther she shall pursue or what examinations she must pass" (BC, EB). The Rev. Wilder Smith looked over Holmes's application and approved it, citing familiarity with her scholarship, but other board members wanted her to take examinations. In a 6 May 1882 letter, Sill said that the "faculty recommended that Miss Holmes should receive A.B. and the Executive Committee, including two of the Special Committee, voted that she receive this degree; and so will recommend to the Board of Trustees without any examination." A letter of 1 June 1882 records that examinations were nevertheless required and that the Rev. William S. Curtis and Smith administered them (RC, Anna P. Sill Papers).

In 1885 Holmes left RFS to do postgraduate work at the Univ. of Michigan. According to university records, she earned a M.A. degree in the Literary Dept. in July 1886 and a Ph.D., with a dissertation on the morphology of corals, in Feb. 1888 (other sources cite her degrees as a M.A. and Ph.D. in geology and paleontology in 1887). She was elected the first female fellow of the Geological Society of America in 1889 (see Holmes's responses to Univ. of Michigan Alumnae Questionnaire, Aug. 1889, UM, BHL). Holmes continued to conduct scientific research after earning her degree, traveling on a series of geological research trips in 1887–92. In her Rockford home, she compiled an amazing array of scientific specimens, including more than a thousand birds and animals preserved through taxidermy; more than two thousand species of shells; a gigantic herbarium; and extensive collections of algae, minerals, and fossils, "all meticulously numbered, labeled, and catalogued."

Holmes was also a gifted artist, and her house was decorated with paintings she had done of natural subjects. In addition, she had prepared several hundred "botanical, histological, and geological slides" and field drawings (Rogal, *Educational and Evangelical Missions*, 24, 25). Moreover, she combined her fascination with earth sciences and natural history with a dedication to educational reform and pedagogy. She delivered a paper before the Women's Dept. during the World's Congress Auxiliary of the World's Columbian Exposition in Chicago in 1893. The talk was published as "Methods of Presenting Geology in Our Schools and Colleges" in 1893. In it she argued that if geology was to be truly appreciated as a "life force, a life inspiration to the masses generally and to those in our high schools and colleges, we must begin with the little children" (quoted in Rogal, *Educational and Evangelical Missions*, 20).

Coming from a religious family, the backdrop for Holmes's scientific pursuits and teaching had always been activism within her church. She served as the organist for the Westminster Presbyterian Church of Rockford for decades and was very active in Rockford-area women's organizations, including the Society of Mission Inquiry, for which she was corresponding secretary of the Presbyterian Board in 1879–80. In 1890 she became president of the Westminster Church Woman's Home Missionary Society. Her mother had helped found the group in mid-Feb. 1876 and had been its former president. After her mother died, Holmes became the head of the group and remained so until her own death. Missionary society meetings were held in her home. Members worked to raise funds to build and promote Christian-sponsored schools. They also collected clothing and school books to send in care packages to other women working in the field as missionary teachers in remote areas of the United States. And, under Mary E. Holmes's direction, they banded together to write a collaborative novel. Called *His Father's Mantle: By the Ten* (1895), the story was of a pastor and his wife who go to the rural Pacific Northwest as missionaries. Various women members of the Freeport Presbytery missionary societies also joined with Holmes to write *Aida Rocksbege* (1897), the story of a woman who discovers after her mother's death that her mother was of African American heritage and then dedicates her life to establishing a "seminary in the rural South to mold leaders out of impoverished Black children of various ages" (quoted by Rogal, *Educational and Evangelical Missions*, 43, 48–49).

If not strictly autobiographical, *Aida Rocksbege* proved somewhat prophetic of Holmes's activities in the latter part of her life. After her mother's death in 1890, she became increasingly involved in the Presbyterian Board of Missions for Freedmen. She had worked for the board on an unsalaried basis since 1886, traveling to many cities to give speeches and presentations to win support for the church's program of education for African Americans. She also helped oversee the beginnings of the Monticello Academy in Monticello, Ark., but was subjected to antagonism from the white community of that town, who objected with great hostility to her close collaboration with the Rev. C. S. Mebane, the school's pastor-principal, an African American. Mebane received death threats and was forced not only to close the school but also to leave town. Holmes subsequently founded the Mary Holmes Seminary in West Point, Miss., in memory of her mother, who had been an ardent abolitionist.

The Mary Holmes Seminary, funded by the "ladies of Illinois" (Holmes's friends in the Rockford and Freeport areas) was built with the cooperation of the citizens of Jackson, Miss., the Woman's Board of Home Missions of the northern states, and the Board of Missions for Freedmen. Its first site was in Jackson on "land donated by Negro citizens of the vicinity" (Board of Missions for Freedmen, *Annual Report* [1891]: 7–8; Parker, *Rise and Decline*, 281). The school opened in Sept. 1892 with a capacity student body enrolled in primary, elementary, and high school divisions. Curriculum focused on domestic training and the industrial arts.

In 1941 the school became Mary Holmes Junior College. Holmes was also editor and publisher of the *Freedman's Bulletin,* a monthly publication devoted to African American issues.

As the Rockford newspaper put it, she "died in the harness" at her family's home on South 1st St. on 13 Feb. 1906. She was fifty-five. At her death, she left "one of the finest private scientific collections in the west. . . . visitors [had] come hundreds of miles to examine the treasures which silently . . . tell the story of Miss Holmes's many years of patient research" ("Death Calls Mary E. Holmes," unidentified Rockford newspaper clipping, n.d., [ca. 13 Feb. 1906]).

5. Mary B. Downs (1858–1940) was a friend of JA, EGS, Sarah Anderson, and Katie Hitchcock, and a colleague of JA's on the *RSM* staff. She was born in Ridgefield, Ill., the daughter of Elizabeth Perkins Downs, whose New England family had pioneered in Dundee, Ill., and the Rev. John V. Downs, a Presbyterian minister and missionary who served in several Illinois locations, including Elgin and Chicago. Mary Downs came to RFS from Hyde Park, Ill. She graduated as valedictorian of the class of 1879 and became a teacher in Chicago (see also Mary Downs to JA, 14 Nov. 1880, nn. 5 and 8, below).

6. Addie F. Merrill was the business editor of the *RSM* in 1879. Her sister Emma was also a student at RFS. They were from De Witt, Iowa. Addie Merrill was in the class of 1879, and her sister in the class of 1880. Fellow student Addie B. Smith reported to her mother, Annie M. Jordan Smith, on 3 Mar. 1878, that "Addie Merrill asked me to walk to church with her so I did. She is the leader of the stylish girls in school and it seems kind of funny that she should want me to walk with her for I guess she thinks I'm an awfully innocent little creature and wouldent flash or do the things she does for the world. And then she is real tall and cute and about two years older than I." Smith concluded, "The other Addie is just a little wild but from a real good family" (SHSW, Smith). Addie Merrill and Mary Downs apparently had their differences during their graduating year. Downs reported to JA that she had written to Merrill in the summer of 1879 and "apologized for the rudeness with which I had some times treated her and 'agreed to disagree': she answered very pleasantly and there the subject was dropped as far as the harmony of the class is concerned" (23 May 1880, SCPC, JAC; *JAPM*, 1:508).

7. Ada ("Addie") Maria Stevens (sometimes spelled "Stephens") was from Toledo, Iowa. In addition to being the curator of the Scientific Assn., Stevens was also the librarian for the Vesperian Society. She was a member of the class of 1880 but did not continue school through graduation, probably for financial reasons. She left RFS for the last ten weeks of the 1877–78 school year with the intention to "change from the position of scholar to that of teacher" (*RSM* [Apr. 1878]: 84). She became very ill in the following year, and the Feb. 1879 edition of the *RSM* reported that the "girls who spent the vacation away from Rockford were rejoiced to find Miss Addie Stevens, who has been ill for some time, able to resume her duties at the Seminary. Lest her sickness should prove contagious, she had been removed to the house of Mr. Alcott, in the Seminary grounds. She was cared for very kindly, and was visited by both teachers and pupils, when it was thought safe for them to do so" (28).

8. Harriet ("Hattie") A. M. Smith (Etnyre) from Oregon, Ill., was a member of JA's close circle during her first years at RFS. In addition to being in the Scientific Assn., she (along with JA and Katie Hitchcock) was one of the three Greek-language students in the 1878–79 course of study. She was also in the Conservatory of Music program. Although not expected to return in 1879–80 because of illness in her family, she did come back for her senior year and graduated from RFS in 1880. She taught music and married Edward D. Etnyre, a manufacturer, with whom she had six children. The Etnyres lived in San Diego and Sacramento, Calif., and in Oregon, Ill.

9. Eleanor ("Nora") Frothingham (Haworth) (1860–1949) from Manchester, Iowa, was a classmate of JA's in the class of 1881. She earned excellent grades and graduated second in their class. She and JA met at their first day at school when Nora provided paper so JA could write entrance examinations. Frothingham also silently helped JA with a confusing zoology question. Asked "the difference between a dog and a cat paw" a "puzzled Jenny . . . looked across the aisle at Nora and held up five fingers. Nora spread out her hand and then hooked

the fingers back like cat claws, thus cleverly answering Jenny" (Wise, *Jane Addams of Hull-House*, 62). Nora Frothingham roomed with Mattie Thomas in 1878. At RFS, she was particularly interested in Latin studies and was active in the Vesperian Society. She wrote frequently for the *RSM* in 1879 and 1880. In her senior year she became the historian of JA's class and president of the Presbyterian Branch of Foreign Missions. She was appointed recording secretary of the Society of Mission Inquiry at RFS for the 1879–80 school year. Despite her religious dedication, she was known for her rebellious antics. In late Nov. 1880 she parodied the role of Topsy from Harriet Beecher Stowe's *Uncle Tom's Cabin* at a Pierian Union spoof of literary characters. At the end of her senior year, the class sibyl predicted that Frothingham would join the circus. On Class Day 1881 she presented a satiric oration: "Chaucer was certainly a woman" (*RSM* [July 1881]: 208). Although Wise describes Nora as small and vivacious, classmate Helen Harrington remembered her as "a brilliant student, and a steadfast friend, much beloved by her classmates" (Alderson, "Memoirs," 31).

After graduation, Frothingham taught music and German in Manchester, Iowa (in 1881–82), Morrison, Wis. (in 1884), and Corning, Iowa (in 1885). She married the Rev. Barnabas C. Haworth, a missionary with the Presbyterian Church, and the couple had five children. They lived in Tokyo, Japan, where Frothingham became principal of a school for foreign children. Upon her return to the United States, she served as secretary of the San Francisco League of Women Voters. She received her M.A. from the Univ. of Washington, Seattle, in 1911. She died on 5 Oct. 1949.

10. See also Announcements in the *RSM*, Mar. 1879, below.

Excerpt from Essay in the
Rockford Seminary Magazine

This essay, "Plated Ware," was the first article published under Jane Addams's initials while she was a student at Rockford Female Seminary.[1]

[Rockford, Ill.]   APRIL 1878

PLATED WARE

. . . Minds drift along with the current of the times, listen to the discussions in print and conversation, and shift the phases of thought just as we imperceptibly do our mode of dress. "There are no bad men, no bad herbs; there are only bad cultivators." Out of every twelve men you'll find one red headed one, and very likely one skeptic and one villain. Likewise the changes of thought are subject to law, and come with regularity; *we* are the rebound of the hard, austere religious ages.

It has been supposed that the planets of the universe are knit together by a principle of musical harmony; "by one pervading spirit of tones and numbers all things are controlled." Innumerable voices fill the heavens with everlasting harmony, control the movements of the universe, and produce the seasons. For terror, joy, or sadness, how vast is the compass of notes, and how varied the effect. The vain distress gun sounds from a sinking ship, the sprinkling of cold earth that falls echoing from a coffinlid, must surely go forth into the vast universe of sound, and plate *some* mind with a tinge of pensiveness and melancholy.

Every word we utter sets in motion a breath of air that extends around the earth, and for these wandering utterances earth has a scheme, a scale of moral music, which controls the casts of thought, and the contagion is literally and figuratively "in the air." And echo seems to hand our speech, not word for word, but line by line, up to the recording angel, and just as our breath, in that case, strikes the rock, so our words strike a *negative* mind, and go forth into the universe of electric thought.[2]

L.J.A.

PD (*RSM* [Apr. 1878]: 60–62; *JAPM*, 45:1754–56).[3]

1. In the same issue of the magazine, the RFS Chess Club—of which JA was a member—printed what was probably a collaborative poem that had been drafted in JA's hand: "The Origin of Chess" (*RSM* version, *JAPM*, 45:1750–53; AMs version, *JAPM*, 45:1745–49). The poem was prefaced with a short explanation: "A Chinese queen whose two sons were warring upon each other, driven frantic by grief, in her lonely palace, pictures the battles fought between the brothers, and upon a miniature field opposes to each other mimic hosts. This was the origin of the world-renowned game of Chess" (69). The first stanza of the poem was: "Once in the flight of ages past, / Before Confucious lived and died, / Before the Chinese wall was cast, / Or ever porcelain was descried, / Within her garden lived a queen, / Almond-eyed queen of Celestial glory, / Slender and lissome as the almond-tree, / Fair as the bloom of the fragrant tea, / Wise and good, renowned in story" (69).

The formation of the RFS Chess Club was announced in the "Home Items" section of the Jan. 1878 *RSM* (32). "A chess club!" the notice began. "Sure enough, why can't we have one? We can have one. Accordingly six of our number met to organize on the 7th of December, 1877. The constitution was drawn up, to which each member signed her name, promising to join head and hands in pursuit of the science of chess. The choosing of a name was deferred. The time appointed for meeting was every other Friday night, alternating with the literary societies. Much pleasure and benefit is anticipated by the members" (32). JA apparently remembered the Chess Club fondly, for she included wry mention of it in *Twenty Years*. She reported that the club drew girls who were acutely self-conscious about the grand mission of female education being mounted by the seminary leaders. They conscientiously dedicated themselves to making good use of their time, fostering "an atmosphere of intensity, a fever of preparation" (44). That attitude was epitomized by a motto they posted on the wall of the Chess Club room—at least for a time: "We worked in those early years as if we really believed the portentous statement from Aristotle which we found quoted in Boswell's Johnson and with which we illuminated the wall of the room occupied by our Chess Club. . . . 'There is the same difference between the learned and the unlearned as there is between the living and the dead.' We were also too fond of quoting Carlyle to the effect, ''Tis not to taste sweet things, but to do noble and true things that the poorest son of Adam dimly longs'" (45).

2. JA began this essay by describing Vulcan on Mt. Aetna with his forge, tossing thunderbolts toward earth and creating "invulnerable armors to be worn by mortal heroes . . . but sometimes yielding to the softening influence of his heavenly birth, he would form gentle golden maidens, [to] teach to mortals the subtlety of electricity, and the arts which embellish life, and promote civilization." She then detailed how, in the creation of plated ware (such as a metal shield), a thin plate of gold is applied to the outside of an object forged of inferior metal and fixed by an electrical current: "each little spark does its duty, and the article, forming the *negative* pole, is beautifully and evenly covered. . . . Just as easily, and in a similar manner, are minds and characters of every age plated with a certain cast of thought" (60).

3. See also the AMsS version of "Plated Ware," signed L.J.A., June 1878; *JAPM*, 45:1697–704, and fragment, *JAPM*, 45:1705–7.

Clipping from Anna P. Sill Scrapbook

The Castalian Society and the Vesperian Society were the two literary societies active at Rockford Female Seminary. Joined together, they made the Pierian Union.¹ The two societies functioned as reading groups and social sororities, sponsoring receptions, debates, programs, and parties. The Rockford Seminary Magazine *also operated under the official mantle of the Pierian Union. Jane Addams was an officer or member in the Castalian Society and a member of the staff of the magazine throughout her college years. Here, she and her good friend Ellen Gates Starr participate in a Pierian Union program.*

[Rockford, Ill.]   [ca. April 1878]²

Pierian Union Entertainment

The members of the Pierian Union could not have made a finer evening for their entertainment on Thursday evening.

First there was music by Misses Spafford³ and Tanner,⁴ who rendered Dorn's "Rayon du Soliel" with pleasing effect. The essay entitled "The Pictures of Our Lives," by Ellen G. Starr, was a carefully written and well read production.⁵ After music, by Lizzie L. Allen,⁶ there was an

original colloquy,

which discussed the "Influence of literary style." It was participated in by Misses Ellen G. Starr, Kitty M. Dick,⁷ Corinne Williams,⁸ Lizzie W. Pomeroy,⁹ Jennie L. Addams, Kate L. Hitchcock, Lizzie A. Wright,¹⁰ Hattie S. Leach,¹¹ Laura Keeney¹² and Laura J. Rezner.¹³ The colloquy was written by one or more of the students of the Seminary, and was a thoughtful, critical production, and evinced a careful study of the authors discussed, including Carlyle, Emerson, Victor Hugo, and others. The disquisition upon Hugo was particularly appreciative. The young ladies who engaged in the colloquy represented a tea-party, and while the conversation was in progress, refreshments were passed, and the representation moved off with becoming ease and naturalness.

After a piano interlude by Miss Lilly G. Beckman,¹⁴

thirteen young ladies

filed into the chapel and on to the rostrum, to the time given by the piano, and proceeded to give a gymnastic exercise. They were all dressed in loose frocks gathered at the waist, and hanging to the ankles. They were well-formed, vigorous, bright-eyed young ladies, and evidently enjoyed the exercise in gymnastics. The muscular movements are intended to strengthen the arms, the body and the lower limbs, and is most fortunately designed for this most excellent purpose. The young ladies who attend the Rockford Female Seminary are certainly in no danger of growing weak and puny for lack of exercise, so long as this admirable system of physical culture is a part of the school's discipline.¹⁵ And the *personnel* of the institution evinces the benefits of the system, for the beauty and bloom and vigor of the "seminary girls" are the envy and admiration of the town. "The Benefits of Imitation" was another carefully prepared essay, written by Miss Stella E. Foote.[16] Then came a song, "Beautiful Venice," by Misses Allen and Longley,[17] which elicited

ROUND AFTER ROUND OF APPLAUSE

and the two young ladies were persuaded thereby to repeat the musical gem.

A drama came next, the parts in it being taken by Misses Kitty L. Tanner, Helen M. Betcher,[18] Hattie M. Ellwood,[19] Addie M. Smith,[20] Mary K. Wykoff,[21] Mary A. Baker[22] and Nettie Leonard.[23] It represented a longing, sighing seeker after happiness, who was ministered unto by the other members of the company, under various guises, offering her everything that earth can afford, including love itself, but she rejects them all until Religion, beauteous in pure white and resplendent with stars and buoyant with wings, comes to her and crowns her with immortal happiness.

A beautiful feature of the drama was a Cupid with darts and wings, represented by little Mamie Potter.

This drama closed the entertainment, which was very select, well executed, and highly pleasing to the audience.[24]

PD (Newsclipping, ca. Apr. 1878, Sill, "Scrapbook").

1. The Vesperian Society later became Kappa Theta (in 1901), and the Castalian Society was renamed Chi Theta Psi in 1902. Although the RSM stated that the "great object of our Literary and Scientific Societies is to strengthen the self-confidence of the members in preparing and presenting intellectual entertainment," they also had a strong social function, with members of the one group in friendly rivalry with members of the other ([July 1879]: 205). As JA's friend Corrine Williams Douglas remembered, the Castalian Society "held itself proudly aloft as the repository of intellect, with an Emersonian motto and real programs, and which rather looked down with a condescending tolerance upon the more frivolous and worldly-minded Vesperians. The first few weeks of each school year were given over to a maddeningly exciting game of politics to see which society should capture the most and the most desirable new girls. The very storm centers of these campaigns were the public entertainments, to which neophytes and enemies were alike invited" (quoted in Linn, Jane Addams, 51).

2. This Pierian Union meeting was reported in the "Home Items" section of the RSM (Apr. 1878): 81, perhaps by JA, whose article "Plated Ware" appeared in the same issue (see Excerpt from Essay in the RSM, Apr. 1878, above). Castalian and Vesperian programs were regularly reported in the seminary magazine throughout her time at the school.

3. RFS special student Bertha Eugenia Spafford of Rockford was enrolled in the Dept. of Modern Languages and the RFS Conservatory of Music in 1877–78.

4. Katherine ("Kate," also "Kit" or "Kitty") Louise Tanner (Fisk, sometimes spelled "Fiske") of Rockford was enrolled as a student with "partial collegiate" status in 1877–78. She later graduated with JA's class of 1881. A contralto with a fine voice, she studied music at RFS and became a professional musician. She performed as a concert soloist in Chicago, New York, and London. She was engaged to marry Franklin P. Fisk, a principal of a Chicago high school, during her senior year at RFS. In her personal address book from the 1880s JA recorded "Kit Tanner Fiske, 532 W. Adams, Chicago," next to the addresses of fellow RFS friends Addie M. Smith Strong, Laura Ely Curtis, and Phila Pope (JAPM, 27:1196, see also 1197). Later in the same book there is an entry for a "Mrs. F. P. Fisk, 578 West Monroe St Chicago" (JAPM, 27:1200). In the early 1900s the Fisks made their home in New York, where she was a member of the Universalist Church. She was an active alumna of RFS and returned there to give a number of song

recitals, including a Feb. 1892 fundraiser to help with the purchase of a pipe organ (with Julia Officer, an 1878 graduate of RFS, who was a professional music teacher in Chicago at the piano). Fisk also performed solo in Sept. 1910.

5. The differences between "Emotional Ellen" and "calm Jane," as Winifred Wise described the friends, was evident in their styles of writing and speaking. Although both gained reputations at RFS for being fine writers and persuasive speakers, EGS was given to "flowery Latin translations" and "learned articles," often on questions of art history or religious philosophy. While she swayed audiences to her views by evoking emotion and sensibility—of God, of the ideal, or of the beautiful—JA did so by employing logic and appealing to a sense of what was right or pragmatic. "'Ellen writes just like Ruskin,'" swooned RFS classmates (*Jane Addams of Hull-House*, 69).

6. Lizzie Lee Allen of Rockford was a junior in the Preparatory Dept. at RFS in 1877–78. She was also enrolled in the Conservatory of Music.

7. Probably a reference to Marion Ophelia Dick of Sycamore, Ill., who was in her senior year in the Preparatory Dept. in 1877–78. She was also enrolled in the Dept. of Drawing and Painting and the Conservatory of Music.

8. Corrine Stanton Williams (Douglas) (1860–1934), JA's friend and a pioneer for women in the field of law, was one of the seven members of JA's first-year class in 1877–78. A relative of Grover Cleveland and of Abraham Lincoln's secretary of war Edwin Stanton, she was born on 15 Nov. 1860 into a prominent Wyoming, Iowa, family. Her family had a strong connection to RFS. Her grandmother taught at the seminary in 1847, and her mother was one of the first students of the institution. In addition, two of her daughters attended RFS, as did her niece.

During her seminary career, Williams was a close colleague of JA's on the *RSM* staff and paired with her for Pierian Union debates, sharing her interest in the humanities and the sciences (see Draft of Debate Argument, 13 Nov. 1878, below). Williams graduated from RFS in 1880, one year before JA. Her fellow *RSM* staff members noted at her graduation that her "name calls up a confused mingling of French novels, strong-minded women, and of early persecutions of America" (*RSM* [July 1880]: 209). Williams served as president of the Scientific Assn. from 1879 to 1880 and also as the head of the Castalian Society. Her articles for the *RSM* included essays on Confucius and Alexander the Great.

Williams taught in Winton, Iowa, after graduation and in 1884 went to Europe to pursue her interest in astronomy, which she had studied at RFS. She met and married Hamilton Douglas (d. 1922) in 1886 while they both were earning law degrees at the Univ. of Michigan. Douglas received her law degree in 1887 and shortly after was admitted into the Michigan bar. At the time, it was rare for a woman to enter the profession; according to the U.S. census of 1880 there were only seventy-five women lawyers in the United States when Douglas graduated from RFS.

In Oct. 1886 Douglas joined with five other women lawyers and law students in Ann Arbor to form the Equity Club, which worked to overcome the sexual discrimination and professional isolation they faced during the late 1880s. The club remained in existence for four years. During that time it expanded into a larger network of thirty-two women and became a "correspondence club for women lawyers and law students throughout America and in other countries as well," constituting, in effect, the "first national organization of women lawyers in American history" (Drachman, *Women Lawyers*, 1). "Woman's right to a professional training is no longer a mooted question," Douglas declared to fellow club members on 7 May 1887. "It is a settled fact. . . . Women as well as men have the duty laid upon them of making the world better." She then mentioned the growing acceptance of women doctors and equated the call for "lady-lawyers" to that for "lady-physicians." She also strongly defended rearing children as a worthy calling and described the pursuit of a profession as a goal that could exist simultaneously for women with the care and nurturing of a family. At the same time, she defended women who had chosen not to marry but to devote their energies to improving the happiness of others in the profession. She pointed out that not everything in such matters is a question of choice. For women who remained single by choice or fate, the legal profession could be a needed "means of support." For married women, it could be "a means of becoming to their husbands more nearly what the word 'help-meet' means" (quoted in full in Drachman, *Women Lawyers*, 48–50). One Equity Club member, Belva Lockwood (1830–1917), became in 1879 the first woman admitted to practice before the U.S. Supreme Court.

Soon after she earned her degree, Douglas and her husband moved to Atlanta, Ga. There they raised five children—the first born in Nov. 1887. The state of Georgia at the time did not admit women to legal practice, so although Douglas assisted her husband behind the scenes she was unable to work in her own right as an attorney. Indeed, her husband claimed to others in their early years in Atlanta that she had studied law not to pursue it on her own but in order to be of help to him. She had become the "help-meet" she analyzed in the 1887 Equity Club letter. In addition to raising their children and aiding her husband in his practice, she turned to bettering conditions for working women and widening opportunities in female education. In 1890 she founded a technical school for girls in Atlanta: the Commercial High School for Girls. Although its curriculum centered on training girls for domestic employment and business careers, it also, through Douglas's influence, offered courses in science, history, and advanced mathematics, a departure for trade-oriented institutions. Douglas became the first principal of the school in 1888. In 1922 it became coeducational, and its name was changed to the Atlanta Commercial High School.

As a northerner living in the South, Douglas had to act carefully within a very traditional white, middle-class, southern social environment that frowned on women's participation in public life outside home and family. In order "to address social problems in her neighborhood Douglas adopted a socially and intellectually progressive approach to the problems she identified, while addressing them with traditional and conservative methods" (Drachman, *Women Lawyers*, 220). She won support for her endeavors by arguing that better educations for girls and better protections for working women would enable them to be better wives and mothers. She was a member and president of the Atlanta Woman's Club and an officer in the Atlanta Business Woman's Club, which was eventually absorbed by the Atlanta Woman's Club. In addition, she worked on behalf of bringing anti-tuberculosis campaigns into poorer neighborhoods and chaired the local Red Cross committee on the blind.

Douglas's daughter, Helen Douglas Mankin, a Rockford College graduate who completed law school in 1920, designed the Red Cross button. Georgia had opened the bar to women in 1916, and Mankin encouraged her mother to apply for admission when she did. Together, the two were admitted to the bar in Atlanta. After her husband died in 1922, Corrine Douglas took his place in the family firm of Douglas, Douglas, and Andrews. Their son, Hamilton Douglas, Jr., was dean of the Atlanta Law School. Corrine Williams Douglas, who was given an honorary M.A. degree at Rockford College in 1930, died of pneumonia on 20 Jan. 1934 (*Atlanta Constitution*, 21 Jan. 1934). An Atlanta newspaper paid tribute to Douglas at her death, saying, "Georgia may well honor the memory of this fine and constructive woman whose determined and virile contributions to progressive movements have aided so materially in the development of the state" (clipping, [ca. May 1934], RC). Some of Corrine Williams Douglas's memories of JA and their time together at RFS are quoted in Linn, *Jane Addams* (see particularly 47 and 51–52).

9. Lizzie Wright Pomeroy of Lee Center, Ill., was a member of the junior class in the Collegiate Dept. of RFS in 1877–78. She was also enrolled in the Conservatory of Music.

10. Elizabeth ("Lizzie") Amelia Wright of Lone Rock, Wis., was a special student at RFS in 1877–78. She was enrolled in the Dept. of Modern Languages and the Conservatory of Music.

11. Harriet Shepherd Leach of Rockford was one of two graduates from other schools pursuing special studies at RFS in 1877–78. She was enrolled in the Dept. of Modern Languages and the Conservatory of Music.

12. Laura L. Keeney of Rockton, Ill., was a member of the RFS junior class in 1877–78 and enrolled in the Dept. of Modern Languages. She graduated in 1879.

13. Laura Jane Rezner (1855–86) of Freeport was a senior in the Collegiate Dept. in 1877–78 and graduated from RFS in 1878. The "Personals" section of the Feb. 1879 *RSM* announced, "Laura Rezner is teaching in Ashton, Lee [C]ounty, Ill., this winter" (27), and in Jan. 1880 that "Laura Rezner is teaching near Freeport" (23). During the 1880s Rezner lived with her parents, Robert F. and Elizabeth Rezner, on their eighty-acre farm in Lancaster Twp., four miles north of Freeport and not far from Cedarville. She taught school nearby and was a member of the Presbyterian Church. Laura Jane Rezner died on 5 Apr. 1886.

14. Lillian ("Lillie") Beckman (sometimes spelled "Beekman") of Byron, Ill., was a senior in the Collegiate Dept. at RFS in 1877–78. She was also listed in the 1877–78 RFS *Catalogue* as a "resident graduate" of the Conservatory of Music (13; *JAPM*, 27:124). She graduated from RFS in 1878 and became a teacher at the Academy of the New Church in Bryn Athyn, Pa. An able musician as a student, she regularly played the piano for class events and Pierian Union meetings in 1878. She was also the "mystic class prophetess" for Class Day 1878 (Cedarborg, "Early History," 407). The Oct. 1878 issue of the *RSM* reported, "Lillie Beekman, class of '78, is studying medicine" (205). The Jan. 1880 issue announced, however, that "Lillie Beekman is soon to begin teaching music in Oregon," Ill. (23). In the 1880–81 RFS *Catalogue* the "Class of 1878 Alumnae" section listed her as a teacher in Byron, Ill. She taught school for many years and in 1903 was a member of the faculty of the Normal Dept. of the Academy of the New Church.

15. Outside lecturers visited RFS to promote female physiological vigor and hygiene, and RFS provided brochures that gave instructions for making gym suits. Schoolgirls in 1877–78 wanted new garments designed to emphasize freedom of movement, an outgrowth of progressive thinking regarding dress reform, especially rebellion against tight lacing and heavy skirts. Soon after JA started school at RFS, the *RSM* reported, "Good news for the gymnasts! The gymnasium is to be renovated with fresh paint, paper, curtains, etc., so as to make it a much pleasanter place for our exercises. Under our enthusiastic teacher, the practice is entered into with much interest and no little amusement. And when the bright, new suits make their appearance we shall doubtless enjoy the hour even more" ([Oct. 1877]: 189). The editorial in the same issue reminded girls that "This branch of our education surely equals any other in importance. . . . We hear, read and see much of the feebleness and nervousness of American women, the causes of which are laid to their ambition to educate themselves as highly as the other sex, and often, to our mode of dress." The editor urged the introduction of weight training with dumbbells so girls could build strength in the same way as men did. She then called for better gym outfits that would allow for freer movement in the name of "dress-reform . . . eagerly discussed by several of our number." She went one step further in the cause of female liberation and equality, comparing the confinement of RFS girls to campus with male students' ability to move about in the wider world: "The rules of many of our seminaries and colleges for women render it impossible for us to exercise as freely and therefore as profitably as our more fortunate brothers can, for while we are restricted by imaginary boundaries or picket fence, they roam at will over the country, ever finding something new to divert their thoughts for a time from their hard studies" (200).

The dress-reform gym suits did arrive, and student Addie B. Smith loved them—and the gymnastics classes led by Sarah Anderson. Gleefully, she wrote home about doing the Laucen Quadrille and wearing her navy-blue flannel suit ("You know we mustn't wear our corsets in gymnastics" she reminded her mother). The garments were "made with short kilt pleated skirts and very loose sailor waists with oval collars"—dark blue for the blondes and "cardinal flannel for the brunettes." "I wish you could see us all in our suits when going through our exercises in the gymnasium," Addie wrote in another letter. "We are arranged so that the navy blue and the cardinal red come alternately in the lines and it looks real pretty. I have my suit on now [while writing to her mother from her room] with the stockings and slippers. I always feel like having a good waltz when I don this thing" (Addie B. Smith to Annie M. Jordan Smith, 7 Mar. 1878, 11 Apr. [1878], SHSW, Smith). While Addie B. Smith emphasized the beauty and freedom of gymnastics, JA and her cohorts at the RSM were more rueful. They noted that gymnastics were increasingly popular among the RFS girls. The awkward tossing of Indian clubs by novices was a subject of some lampooning ("Indian clubs have been added [to] the gymnasium, and the consequence is that girls are afraid of each other. No extremely tragic scene has as yet been enacted" [RSM (Apr. 1881): 103]).

Indoor physical education for girls was updated at RFS in the decade after JA's graduation. A brand new gymnasium facility was opened in 1887, and the theories of Dudley Allen Sargent, director of the gymnasium at Harvard Univ. (beginning in 1879) were put into practice. Illustrations of hearty young women clad in loose outfits and using weight machines graced a newspaper article on the new gymnasium, including a description of the school's latest sports facilities.

Closely related to gymnastics was the issue of dancing, officially frowned upon by Anna Sill. In 1878 regimented calisthenic demonstrations by gym-suited girls were part of RFS public examinations and Pierian Union meetings, but dancing was another matter. Sill maintained a question box, and students could submit written queries that she would answer during morning devotions or evening prayer. Addie B. Smith reported to her mother that at one chapel exercise in Apr. 1878 Sill attempted to answer the "question 'Why do you consider it unladylike to dance round dances?' She discoursed at quite a length on the subject but her arguments were not at all convincing to me. I could see that most of the girls were just laughing in their sleaves" (Addie B. Smith to Anna M. Jordan Smith, 11 Apr. [1878], SHSW, Smith).

16. Stella E. Foote (Warren) of Belvidere, Ill., was a member of the RFS class of 1878 and a student in the Dept. of Modern Languages. She married Edwin A. Warren, a farmer, and raised four sons on their farm a mile north of her hometown. She was active in the Mission Society and Sunday School of the Presbyterian Church of Belvidere.

17. Carrie Alfreda Longley (Jones) of Danvers, Ill., was a senior in the Collegiate Dept. at RFS in 1877–78 and graduated in the class of 1878. She became a teacher and was principal of Belvidere High School for twelve years before marrying Frederick Jones, a farmer. She and her husband lived in Bloomington and Belvidere, Ill. She was a member of the Ladies' Amateur Musical Society and the Belvidere Congregational Church.

18. Helen M. Betcher of Red Wing, Minn., was a special student at RFS in 1877–78. She was enrolled with JA in the Dept. of Modern Languages and in the Conservatory of Music.

19. Harriet ("Hattie," also called "Puss" by close family and friends) May Ellwood (Mayo) (1861–1934) of De Kalb, Ill., was a junior in the RFS Preparatory Dept. in 1877–78. She finished her work in 1879 and graduated from the RFS Conservatory of Music in 1880. Ellwood was from a wealthy family. Her sister, Mary Patience Ellwood (Lewis), was a senior in the Preparatory Dept. in 1877–78 and a first-year student in the Collegiate Dept. in 1878–79. JA became close to the Ellwood family. She visited their home in De Kalb and in the summer of 1883 traveled to Europe with the Ellwood sisters (see EGS to JA, 27 July 1879, n. 10, below, and PJA, 2).

20. Two Addie Smiths attended RFS during JA's time there. One was Adele ("Addie") M. Smith (Strong) of Newton, Iowa, and the other was special student Addie B. Smith (Wells) of De Pere, Wis. Adele (also called "Add," "Adda," "Ada," or "Addie") M. Smith (Strong) (d. 1914) was originally from Newton, but during at least part of her RFS years her parents lived in Chicago. She attended school at RFS for the spring semester of 1877–78, and in Nov. 1879 she became JA's roommate. While at RFS, Smith was the secretary of

the Congregational Branch of Foreign Missions (1880) and leader of the Vesperian Society (1881). She was also a very good friend of Mary Ellwood and spent Thanksgiving 1880 and other holiday breaks with the Ellwood family in De Kalb. She graduated from RFS in the class of 1881. Like JA, her ties with RFS remained strong. She became president of the RFS Alumnae Assn. and a trustee of RFS.

She married Joseph H. Strong (d. 1941), a stockbroker, in 1884. JA received the unexpected news about the marriage while traveling in Europe, and she was concerned by what she heard about the match. As she wrote to her sister, "There has been a report among our girls—it came to me through two people so is probably not reliable and I would like to be able to contridict it—that Addie Smith did not marry so happily as she might. What do you know of Mr Strong?" (JA to SAAH, [10] June 1884, UIC, JAMC; *JAPM*, 1:1530; see also JA to SAAH, 16 Feb. 1884, UIC, JAMC; and *JAPM*, 1:1376–85). The Strongs had two sons and made their home in Chicago. She was a member of the Christian Science Church and the Chicago Woman's Club. At graduation, classmates described her as the "only aristocrat of our class" (*RSM* [July 1881]: 199). Adele M. Smith Strong was eulogized by the Rockford College Board of Trustees as "an inspiration to those who were permitted to work with her." Henry Wadsworth Longfellow's "A Psalm of Life" (a JA favorite) was quoted in tribute to her spirit of action and her well-spent life (Rockford College Board of Trustees, "Minutes of the Annual Meeting," 15 June 1914, RC).

21. Mary ("May") McKnight Wicoff (sometimes spelled "Wycoff") of Galesburg, Ill., was a special student at RFS in 1877–78. She was enrolled in the Conservatory of Music and also in the Conservatory's Vocal Dept. Wicoff left school in 1878 (see Vallie E. Beck to JA, 2 [and 4] May 1878, n. 1, below).

22. Mary Agnes Baker of Harvard, Ill., was a senior in the Preparatory Dept. in 1877–78 and a first-year RFS student in 1878–79. She graduated in 1882.

23. Nettie Leonard (who married a man of her same last name) finished her education at RFS in 1888. She lived in Wichita, Kans., and Lewiston, Maine. She married Arthur N. Leonard, Ph.D., a professor of German. She was the president of the Wichita Ladies' Library Club and active in the Baptist churches of Wichita and Lewiston.

24. Lizzie Smith described a Castalian program that had taken place on 22 Feb. 1878:

> We (the 'Castalians') were to give a public in the eve it being Washingtons birthday. A public meeting is only public in that the other society is allowed to attend it. We had a rehersal about 4 o'clock and Addie & I found that we were to be in the comb band, which consisted of seven girls with combs and a leader with a great wooden tuning fork. Then we thought of clappers and Addie got James [Alcock] to get her some bones, which she used in some of the pieces. At night every one said the band was splendid. The whole meeting was thoroughly a patriotic one, each of the members as her name was called responding with a patriotic sentiment, all the tunes being national ones. The band struck up America on the combs first then the audience joined in singing it; the rest of music was wholly instrumental, comb and partly bone.

She then named the tunes they performed. Next in the program came "a poem The Progress of the 1st Century of the U.S. illustrated by Tableaux among which was the invention of the sewing machine with some one sewing on a machine" (Sara Elizabeth Smith to Annie M. Jordan Smith, 24 Feb. 1878, SHSW, Smith).

From Vallie E. Beck

G[lendale]. F[emale]. College. Glendale, Ohio.   May 2nd [and
                                                                    4th] /78

Had anyone else implied that I was or am fickle, my dearest Jennie, and in a less conciliatory manner, I should have at once resented the implication with spirit. But your short sentence at once gave me pain and pleasure: upon the first it grieved me to think that you could mistrust my friendship for you, that you could think me so wavering as to give up my warm affection to old friends for new faces and people. I trust however you now think better of my stability of character. On the other ha<n>d, I could not restrain a feeling of great gratification, for your language certainly did flatter in the use "love" but you must cut off the "lost" because above all things be truthful. As I think this was only a little ruse of yours, to bring an answer to you[r] letter which was received with such pleasure some weeks since, I shall not lay too much stress upon the language—which, I might construe is a profession of most ardent affection. But shall only appropriate sufficient to give a satisfied and agreeable feeling of superiority, because one of my ideas in regard to you, is that you are quite as choice as am I, in the selection of friends.

This is sufficient to prepare the way for excuses—which seem to be an inevitable part of my letters just as P.S.'s are so many people's—and they are quite sufficient to satisfy even your ideas of right. In the first place, I went to Cin'ti just after the receipt of your letter, and of course had no opportunity to answer it then, although I wished to do so: The next week or so I was quite as busy as ever I have been, so again possessed "the will, but not the way." Afterwards one of my acquaintances in the school was taken seriously ill—a complete prostration of the nervous system resulting from over-study[1]—and my room and bed being much more comfortable than was her own, my roommate kindly consented to allow her to come in this room. As she was in need of constant attention, I had nearly sole care of her during the days for two weeks and more, during which time she was in bed with the exception of one day. Her father came for her and they returned home day-before-yesterday and only since that time have I been free to answer your "reproach". Am I pardoned? do forgive me freely and reinstall me in your kindest feelings immediately: I know you are no longer provoked, tried, nor hurt by my only seeming neglect of your dear love, as you have now given me the privelege to make such implications.

We are now counting the weeks and from this time until June does not seem such a spanless time as it did in February. I look forward to my summer vacation as one of most enjoyable times and as bringing with it a visit from you: remember you must come to Ft. Madison this summer: I will not take "no" for the answer.[2]

May 4".
And here I broke off to spend the rest of the time in bed: my second sick-
headache. Pray that it may be my last. I was like the sea-sick traveller, who, you
know, was at first so sick that he feared he might die, then really thought he
should and lastly was afraid he should not! My head is so sore today that I feel
as though Niagara Falls had been whirling over it. (Apt illustration.)

The honors for this year's senior class have been decided: much dissatisfac-
tion is expressed and none are pleased with the result. The class is so small this
year, that we thought the faculty would find little, if any difficulty in settling the
awards, as everything indicated that first honor would be bestowed upon a
young lady from Pa., but for some unaccountable reason (of course they will
not explain) they gave her only the lowest or third honor. She has been here for
three years and has had fine grades in scholarship and unobjectionable deportment. Probably that is if no more attention is paid to scholarship and deportment next year we shall draw for the honors and the lucky girl will take her
valedictory with christian fortitude. Such is life—Boarding school life. I sincerely
hope this is not an example of real life after we leave school.

My head is beginning to assert its power and I am determined not again to
yield to it so shall stop this occupation before it entirely subdues(?) me.

Show your forgiveness by a speedy answer. Ever sincerely your friend

Vallie.

ALS (SCPC, IAC; JAPM, 1:293–300).

1. Here Vallie Beck refers in a matter-of-fact way to the nervous maladies that were assumed
to especially affect middle-class Victorian women who pursued intellectual interests. Indeed,
the presumed nervous or sensitively high-strung nature of women was widely accepted, if
not culturally mandated, and those expectations were born out in behavior. A study of the
health of students at women's colleges listed "Psychic nervous conditions, sensitiveness, neu-
ralgic headaches, fainting, insomnia, and continuous worry" at the top of the list of problems, followed by "defects of posture," "defects of the respiratory organs," and "derangements
of the digestive organs" (Woody, Women's Education, 2:125). Although Beck's acquaintance
suffered from prostration, Beck reports experiencing migraine headaches. Breakdowns due
to depression or exhaustion were common, and both JA and her good friend EGS experienced them as young women.

The conditions to which Vallie Beck refers at Glendale Female College also existed at RFS.
RFS benefactor Ralph Emerson (1831–1914), the brother of Charlotte Emerson and son of the
Rev. Ralph Emerson and Eliza Emerson, wrote to his wife Adaline Elizabeth Talcott Emerson (b. 1837) on 2 Feb. 1876 to express dismay and surprise at one of their young daughters,
who "fire[d] off the following at the breakfast table. 'I think it is just wicked the way they go
on at the seminary. They are having a revival over there and all the girls are very much excited and some of them are sick of nervous diseases and lots of the others so nervous they don't
know what to do'" (BC, EB). The Emersons had several daughters, including Adaline Eliza
(b. 1859), Harriet Elizabeth (b. 1861), Mary (b. 1863), Charlotte Bell (b. 1865), and Dora Bay
(b. 1869). RFS student Addie B. Smith wrote to her mother Annie M. Jordan Smith on 12 May
1878 that a girl she liked was leaving school because of a nervous disorder: "She is one of the
prettiest girls in the school," Addie reported, and "so full of life," but "real nervous natural-

ly and sometimes when she is not very well she can not control herself and goes into hysterics. Lately she has had quite a time and had been very intimate with another girl who is nervous too and May Wickoff, the girl who was here just now got so bad that she just screamed sometimes and a few days ago her older sister came to see her and is going to take her home with her" (SHSW, Smith).

Although psychological symptoms often were given precedence, the prevalence of physical illness at RFS, as at other boarding schools, was very real. Rooms in Linden Hall, especially during the 1850s and 1860s, were crowded and poorly heated and ventilated. Infectious disease was a danger to all, and the food by all accounts was poor. Efforts to supplement diets with food or sweets from home were frowned upon for fear of spreading disease. "Parents and friends should not send boxes of provisions to the students, as hitherto they have been a fruitful cause of sickness. Good health is not only essential to success in study, but in after life, and no present gratification nor any school attainment can compensate for its loss," warned the RFS *Catalogue* of 1877–78 (28; *JAPM*, 27:132; see also JA to JHA, 6 Mar. 1881, n. 9, below). A high incidence of illness among schoolgirls and their family members is mentioned in the RFS literature, including girls being taken ill or needing to leave school and return home because of family illness. The Addams family knew the reality of illness at RFS firsthand; JA's sister Martha had died at Rockford in Mar. 1867.

JA made frequent references to efforts at RFS to prevent illness, including exercise and tonics. In entries she made at RFS in her old 1875 diary, she wrote, "Brace up / Clark's tonic / huge doses!" and, on a set of later pages, she wrote of a series of four lectures on health given by Dr. Anne Hall, who questioned the girls about the content of her talks. JA observed that "her gran[d] object was to give practical knowledge & advice, taking for granted that we were already sufficiently grounded in the scientief side of her subject. When she <the Dr.> recommended <such things as [*illegible*] meal [*illegible*]> an hour of outdoor exercise, retiring early, never eating between meals & so forth[,] her hearer strongly suspected her of being in league with the faculty" (Addams, "Pocket Diary, 1875[–81]," printed dates 28 Sept. 1875, 17 and 18 Nov. 1875 [written 1880?]; *JAPM*, 28:1625, 1650, 1651). In the back of the same diary, JA jotted notes on the healing uses of plants: "Pennyroyal. aromatic. Used in pain and nausea in the stomach. Is rather stimulating, is used chiefly for children. Sweet flag. (Calamus) aromatic. Is used for the bowels and dyspepsia. May apple. Catharic. Used as a physic. Dandelion Mild Diuretic. Used in Dyspepsia attended with derangement of the liver also in certain forms of Dropsy" ("Pocket Diary, 1875[–81]," printed memoranda pages [written 1881?]; *JAPM*, 28:1666).

Despite incidences of, and perhaps because of precautions, instructions, and policies to prevent, ill-health at RFS, many emerged from their training at the seminary in better physical condition than they had been when they entered. Members of the RFS Board of Examiners, who questioned the girls at the end of the school year, observed that they were "gratified to note the appearance of vigorous health, indicating that the cultivation of the mind is not allowed to be carried on at the expense of the body" ("Report of the Examining Com.," [ca. June 1881], clipping, Sill, "Scrapbook"). The latter observation also may have pertained to popular nineteenth-century fears and medical theories that females, in developing the use of their minds, could deplete their physical powers, particularly the vitality of their reproductive organs and the health of their nervous systems.

2. No evidence has been discovered that JA visited Ft. Madison, Iowa, in the summer of 1878. She did travel to Mitchellville, Iowa, in 1879 with Sarah Anderson and came home with her father. It is possible that they stopped at Ft. Madison on the return trip. In early Aug. 1878 she wrote to decline an invitation to visit the Becks (see JA to Vallie Beck, 3 Aug. 1878, below). SAAH's move to Iowa was officially announced to the RFS community in the "Personals" section of the Oct. 1878 *RSM*: "The address of Mrs. S. Alice (Addams) Haldeman, of '72, is changed to Mitchellville, Iowa, where her husband, Dr. Henry Haldeman, is pursuing his chosen profession" (225).

From John Huy Addams

Although Jane Addams's memoirs of her youth in Twenty Years *revolve around the importance of her father in her life, little of the warm intimacy or deep nature of conversation she recalled, or the strong guidance and moral mentorship she identified as so important to her own development, are evidenced in his writings. Few examples of his letters to his daughter are extant, and the ones that have survived focus primarily on mundane matters. The rich debates that Jane Addams remembered may have been entirely oral ones, reserved for talks between father and daughter. Conversely, the one extant letter from Rockford Female Seminary years from Anna Haldeman Addams to her stepdaughter is familiar in tone, full of advice, and contains information about shared acquaintances. Jane wrote both parents letters that were descriptive of her activities and responsive to the concerns and interests she believed they might have. Her youthful correspondence with her stepmother, whom she effectively omitted from mention in her memoirs, was friendly. Here, John Huy Addams repeated much of the local Cedarville news already imparted by his wife in an earlier letter.*[1]

Cedarville [Ill.]   June 17 /78

Dear Jenny

Your kind and interesting letter received on my return from Freeport Saturday[.]

Pleased to hear of your continued good health. I enclose you ten Dollars—which please acknowledge sent you ten Dollars sometime ago presume it came duly to hand[.][2]

Presume the folks wrote you that Lena was taken sick rather singularly last week.—but is better and around again her hand is healing.[3] Mr Thomas Hutchins[4] was buried last Thursday[.]

Am glad to your vacation[5] is so near at hand am sorry that I cannot see that I can be down at the commencement as the inducements you hold out are of a character worthy of consideration and perhaps such prominent positions to be envied[.]

We have no news of any importance that will interest you. Mr Parr[,][6] Miss Martin[,][7] Mr Mitchell[8] are away Miss Martin will take the school again for next year—but Mr Parr does not intend to return.

This is a beautifull morning[.] Ma and I just returned from a ride which was quite enjoyable.

Weber took supper with us last evening[.] Laura & Sarah[9] were visiting with Edward Bell's near New Pennsylvania[10] for few days—but were well[.]

Let us hear from you have no time to say more all send love[.] Affectionately your Father

John H Addams

ALS (IU, Lilly, SAAH; *JAPM*, 1:304–5).

1. AHHA wrote to JA on 11 June 1878, commenting on JA's letter to her written the previous Sabbath and noting that she was "glad my child is so cheerful." JA was evidently very
happy with her "retrospect of the past" year and a self-evaluation that "her school work has
been well-done" (IU, Lilly, SAAH; *JAPM*, 1:301).

2. Tuition and board were paid directly to the RFS administration, but the girls were expected to keep strict accounts of their use of discretionary funds and report personal bud-
gets to RFS financial secretary Sarah Anderson each month. JA's reported expenses, as recorded in her financial "Report [Account] Book" for 1879–80, averaged fifteen dollars a
month. Routine purchases included matches, books, stamps, and stationery. Church and
missionary fees needed to be paid, as did "buss fare" (a 29 Oct. entry at twenty-five cents) or
other costs of occasional travel. Extracurricular lessons in elocution and other subjects also
cost money, as did seasonal needs such as buying Christmas presents and valentines. JA also
sometimes added apples to the regular RFS diet or ran out of gloves or socks. A small portion of the money her father sent went to recreation. RFS girls enjoyed archery, and in May
1880 JA purchased a bow and some arrows for a dollar ("Report [Account] Book, [1879–80]";
JAPM, 27:331).

3. In her 11 June 1878 letter, AHHA had written that "Lena was doing nicely; until—yesterday—when she took a nervous spell—and, has been rambling and talking—rather out of
her mind." JA's brother-in-law HWH was away studying at Northwestern Univ. Medical
School in Chicago, so the family called a local family physician, Smith C. Thompson, to help
Lena with "some quiet remedies," and SAAH spent the night at her bedside (AHHA to JA,
11 June 1878, IU, Lilly, SAAH; *JAPM*, 1:301–2). Lena may have been either a domestic servant
or a family friend being cared for within the Addams household. There was no one named
Lena in the Addams family.

4. Addams is referring to Isabela Wallace Hutchinson (or Hutchison), the wife of Thomas
Hutchinson (1798–1888), a farmer. She died on 11 June 1878 at age seventy-three and was buried
in the Cedarville Cemetery. The Hutchinsons were married for fifty-four years and had at
least eight children, most of whom remained in the Stephenson Co. area.

5. JHA apparently meant to write: "Am glad to hear your vacation is so near at hand."

6. AHHA had written that Mr. Parr was to give a picnic on 12 June 1878, and "then he will
hie himself to Mt. Morris, to pass commencement—with his brother John" (11 June 1878, IU,
Lilly, SAAH; *JAPM*, 1:302). Members of the Parr family were familiar to residents of Cedarville, and John Harvey ("J.H." or John H.) Parr, who had taught JA at the Cedarville school,
was finishing a two-year stint as instructor at Mt. Morris Seminary (previously Rock River
Seminary, introduction to part 1, n. 81, above). This may be a reference to Lewis B. Parr (1854–
1947), the second of eleven children (eight of whom were boys) born to James and Elizabeth
Moore Parr. Educated in the local schools, Lewis B. Parr lived with his parents until he was
almost twenty-five, when, on 9 Oct. 1879, he married Emily L. Wright (1853?–1931), daughter
of John and Margaret Ewing Wright of Harlem Twp. in Stephenson Co. The Parrs settled on
a farm of 180 acres in Harlem Twp., and Lewis B. Parr became noted for raising Norman and
English draft horses. He was also a director of the school district for six years before 1887 and
a Republican. The Parrs and their three children—Emily A. (1880?–97), William E., and
Maggie—were members of the Presbyterian Church. In 1900 the Parrs moved to Rockford.

7. AHHA wrote that "Miss Martin has her lambs gathered, on the same site Miss Pennell—
had her fold last year—to regale them with flowers—and, pleasant memories—" (11 June 1878,
IU, Lilly, SAAH; *JAPM*, 1:302). Maggie Martin and Eva Pennell were teachers in the Cedarville school. Maggie Martin (b. in 1855 in Ohio and a Freeport resident with her family in 1870)
participated in a Dec. 1872 Teachers' Institute held in Cedarville and "exhibited her method
of oral instruction in language (grammar). Her pupils, some of them quite young for such a
study, were fully prepared to analyze any sentence and give distinctions in the use of words
without hesitation" (*Freeport Weekly Journal*, 11 Dec. 1872). Eva Pennell was seventeen, very

close in age to fifteen-year-old JA (with whome she became friends) when she began teaching in Cedarville. Pennell's sister Flora wed JA's teacher John H. Parr (see also introduction to part 1, nn. 81 and 83, above). Pennell corresponded with JA from Illinois State Normal Univ., Normal, where she was probably studying while living with her family. Clara B. Lutts wrote to JA on 25 Aug. 1878 to say that she learned that "Miss Pennall was up visiting in your town" that summer (SCPC, JAC; *JAPM*, 1:335). When JA was a junior at RFS, Eva Pennell wrote from Chicago to report that she "took this year to rest from teaching" and was "engaged in scholastic persuits, but to a very limited degree." She spoke warmly of Dickens parties given by Sarah Hostetter ("We can transform our friends into some of Dickens characters and imagine ourselves in London"); told JA of a friend of hers who was interested in dissection; and asked, "Is medicine still your aim?" She also asked after AHHA and commented, "You know I always was in love with her." She closed by asking JA to write to her "of school your studies &c." (8 Jan. 1880, SCPC, JAC; *JAPM*, 1:456, 457, 459, 459–60).

8. Possibly Edward Mitchell, brother of the Rev. Lewis Henry Mitchell, pastor of the Cedarville Presbyterian Church, or Rev. Mitchell himself, who left the Cedarville church for a post in Portage, Wis., in 1878.

9. References to JWA; his twenty-two-year-old wife Laura Shoemaker Addams, whom he married in Mar. 1876; and their toddler daughter Sarah ("Sadie") Weber Addams, born on 26 Feb. 1877 (d. 19 Dec. 1951, see Biographical Profiles: Addams, John Weber, and Addams, Laura Shoemaker).

10. New Pennsylvania was in the neighboring township of Waddams, six miles northwest of Cedarville. It later became McConnell, Ill. The Edward Bells do not appear in Waddams Twp. in the U.S. census of 1880.

To Vallie E. Beck

Cedarville Ill   Aug 3—'78

My dear Vallie

I know it is horrid to begin every letter with a stale apology, but this time I feel thoroughly ashamed of myself, and, as I would rather be thought a bore than to be considered indifferent to your very pressing invitation, I shall therefore explain that my long delay was not owing to indifference, but to that indescribable human trait which leads us to put off any thing we dislike to do as far as possible, and to dodge disagreeable facts until the very last moment, and the fact is, that I am very sorry and very reluctant to refuse your kindness and forego the pleasure of seeing you, but I guess that it is inevitable.

We have had company during <all> the summer, I have a friend visiting me now who will probably be here through August, the state-fair is held in Freeport this fall,[1] and will of course draw numerous spectators, so that my vacation is about planned and the time used up.

Please give my love to your mother and my sincere thanks for her kind invitation.

I wish I could have a visit from you, and rest assured that we will all be delighted to see you, whenever you can come.

I am very much disappointed, for I know I should enjoy a visit to Ft Madison above all things, and have thought long and much upon "the ways and means" but I can't possibly leave home just now, I have occasionally repeated during the course of this letter the following pat quotation and have derived comfort therefrom—"There is never a 'might have been' that touches with a sting, but reveals also to us an inner glimpse of the bright and beautiful 'may be'," and in the far away future I 'may be' will behold you although my summer of '78 must pass without that felicity.

"Such is life" we are constantly deluding ourselves by vain and fickle hopes[.] I have passed a very quiet summer and fear I have accomplished little in the way of reading or study although I had planned to do somewhat of both. During the <u>warm</u> weather, I, like Egar Poe's raven "sat & perched and nothing more" and found the occupation so delightful that I have continued to sit and do nothing ever since.[2]

The orb of day is fast declining & if I light a torch the mosquitoes will be simply fearful. I therefore close as my last alternative. Truly your friend

Jane Addams.

ALS (SCPC, JAC; *JAPM*, 1:311–15).

1. Until 1893, when permanent grounds were secured for the Illinois State Fair in Springfield, the fair was held each year in different venues throughout the state, beginning in Oct. 1853. In 1859, 1877, and 1878 it was held in Freeport, the latter two years in Taylor Park in the east part of the city.

2. In making this reference to stanza seven of Edgar Allan Poe's (1809–49) tragic poem "The Raven," written in New York in 1844 and published in *The Raven and Other Poems* (1845), JA misspells Poe's given name as "Egar." Stanza seven of "The Raven" reads: "Open here I flung the shutter, when, with many a flirt and flutter, / In there stepped a stately Raven of the saintly days of yore. / Not the least obeisance made he; not a minute stopped or stayed he, / But, with mien of lord or lady, perched above my chamber door— / Perched upon a bust of Pallas just above my chamber door— / Perched, and sat, and nothing more" (see also JA to JHA, 6 Mar. 1881, n. 9, below).

From Katie L. Hitchcock

In this letter, Jane Addams's friend Katie Hitchcock refers to several mutual acquaintances and to her work with Addams on the staff of the Rockford Seminary Magazine. The magazine was produced by students four or five times a year until 1879, when it was revamped and began to come out on a monthly basis during the academic year. It included articles, essays, speeches, lectures, and poetry by students, faculty, visiting luminaries, and alumnae as well as news about social and academic life, selected coverage of seminary events, and news or opinions from other college campuses. Jane became part of the staff during her first year at Rockford Female Seminary and contributed entries for the "Home Items" section and sold advertising. In the spring of 1878, she began publishing pieces in the magazine.[1] She worked during her sophomore and junior years as a writer, and in 1879–80 she was pro-

moted to edit and help prepare the "Home Items," "Clippings and Exchanges," and
"Literary Department" sections, which featured witty news and anecdotes about
goings-on at Rockford and other campuses and literary articles or short entries about
what Rockford girls were reading.[2]

Des Moines. [Iowa]   Aug. 11. 1878.

My dear Jane.

What must you think of me!

I am almost afraid you will send this letter back unopened.

Your unexpected epistle was received with agreeable surprise by myself, after a somewhat protracted delay, caused by your directing it to the care of "S.
Request"—a personage unknown to your correspondent.

No relation of mine, my dear. I suppose you must have meant, to write "<u>Hon.
S. P. Wisner</u>."[3] But oh Jennie, I was so glad to hear from you.

It is perfectly shameful of me to wait so long before writing.

You may rest assured that "<u>constancy</u>" is a jewel undimmed as yet by any
thought of mine although you cannot help sorrowing over the dimness of the
jewel "consistency". I hope you will understand what I have been trying to say
above. I can't.

There would be no point in my expressing my fear lest it should be Greek
to you, would there?—for I expect by this time you have commenced the "Anabasis".[4]

Alas—I have not opened my Greek grammar[5]—all these weeks—and I
greatly fear that will be the state of the case at the end of vacation.

There is so much going on all the time—I have been out enough this summer already to last the rest of the year.

You received Lillie Beckman's picture, didn't you?

Carries[6] and mine came before I left Cedar Rapids. They were both very
good, one being a little darker than the other however.

Did you ever notice how much stronger Miss Beckman's face appears in the
photograph than in the original. So many people after they find out that picture isn't the photograph of some actress remark upon the strength of character and intellect that face has in addition to its beauty.
I must confess it's somewhat agravating.

I heard the other day that Miss Wright,[7] who taught at Rockford, year before last, is coming back again next year.

If this is a fact we can hardly hope to see our "whilom" teacher, Miss Lucy
Smith,[8] that is, if Miss Lucy is well enough to come back.

I hope she will be. What have you heard from Hattie?[9]

Jennie, did you see how the Senior editor changed your home item[.][10] I
rather wondered that no audible objection was made to the position of those
boots when I read the article aloud in the editor's scantum.[11]

It was done unbeknosost to me.

I wonder how Miss Anderson[12] is this summer.

How we would feel if she should n't come back next year. I can't bear to think of the possibility. I bought "The Queen's Neck-lace" by Alexander Dumas[13] to read in the cars. Miss Potter[14] recommended it. I did not find it as entertaining as I anticipated.

Henry Ward Beecher[15] is coming here to lecture this month. (What did I write the whole of his name for) I shall try and hear him, of course.

Bessie heard Joseph Cook[16] in the spring. She was disappointed in his appearance.

Carrie is well. I can hardly tell yet whether she will go back next year or not.

Jennie I intended to write a longer letter when I commenced but Minnie[17] has just returned from mission-school and wants me to go to the young people prayer meeting.

Good-bye dear. Your friend

K. L. Hitchcock.

P.S. Aren't you tired of hearing your relations say, "What a beautiful herbarium"?[18]

ALS (SCPC, JAC; *JAPM*, 1:316–21).

1. JA wrote essays, articles, poems, short, amusing vignettes, and editorials during her four years on the *RSM* staff. On her first works, "Plated Ware" and "The Origins of Chess," see Excerpt from Essay in the *RSM*, Apr. 1878, above.

2. In June 1879 the *RSM* reported in the "Personals" section that "Jane Addams, '81, has been appointed as successor of Maria Nutting, editor of 'Home Items,' who has recently left us [she had been in poor health, and went home to recover, see n. 10]. 'Nuttie' will heartily congratulate the editors and rejoice with them when she observes their success in securing so able a conductor for the deserted department" (163–64). JA drafted notes for "Home Items," and also some editorial remarks, in the empty pages of the old diary she had begun in 1875 (see Addams, "Pocket Diary, 1875[–81]" [with pages printed with dates in 1875 and entries written in 1875 and others written ca. 1879–81]; *JAPM*, 28:1591–1666). Besides her "Home Items" and "Clippings and Exchanges" work in 1878–80, in the second semester of her sophomore year (1878–79) JA published an essay, "The Element of Hopefulness in Human Nature," and a synopsis of "Marks," a collaborative play performed by the members of the Castalian Society. "One Office of Nature" (see Essay in the *RSM*, June 1879, below) and "Follow Thou Thy Star" (see Essay in the *RSM*, July 1879, below) came out in the summer issues. In the second semester of her junior year (1879–80), she wrote "The Macbeth of Shakespeare" (see Essay in the *RSM*, Jan. 1880, below) and an editorial entitled "The Chivalry of Study" (*RSM* version, *JAPM*, 46:170–72; AMsS version, *JAPM*, 46:164–69). JA began writing editorials regularly, beginning with the Nov. 1880 edition of the magazine (see also Mary B. Downs to JA, 14 Nov. 1880, n. 1, below). Her "Self Tradition" appeared as the lead article in the Apr. 1881 edition of the magazine (97–100).

3. There was an entry for "R. S. Wisner, 507 Sycamore St., Des Moines, Iowa" in JA's personal address book (SCPC, JAC; *JAPM*, 27:1200).

4. A reference to Xenophon's (ca. 430–ca. 355 B.C.) *Anabasis*, a history of the expedition of Cyrus and the retreat of the Greeks.

5. JA began studying Greek in her second year at Rockford. RFS girls were given a list of books to study over the summer to prepare for their next year's classes, and both Katie Hitch-

cock and JA studied Greek in 1878–79 and 1879–80. The full Greek course at RFS consisted of Greek lessons and grammar (using Alpheus Crosby), Xenophon's *Anabasis,* and exercises in composition in the student's first year of study; Herodotus, Xenophon's *Memorabilia,* Homer's *Iliad,* and exercises in composition in the second year; Greek grammar, Demosthenes, Greek drama, and exercises in composition in the third year; and Plato, Greek drama, and exercises in composition in the fourth year.

In addition to Greek in 1878–79, JA took mathematics (plane geometry and trigonometry), ancient history, modern history, civil government, German, American literature, and Shakespeare. Her study of classical languages continued with Greek and Cicero classes in the first semester of 1878–80 and Greek and Horace courses in the second semester. In her senior year she studied German and Latin (JA student transcript, 1881, RC; *JAPM,* 27:462).

Bolstering the standards for the study of ancient languages at RFS was one of the ways by which Anna P. Sill worked toward collegiate status for the school. Indeed, the existence of classical studies was an area that traditionally differentiated colleges from seminaries and men's from women's schools. When the RFS Board of Trustees was seriously discussing beginning to offer degrees in the late 1870s, Sill proposed a Division of Classical Study as one of the programs for degree-earning work. She wrote frequently to her friend Joseph Emerson about school policies. "How will it do to take Wellesley as our standard," she asked Emerson in an Apr. 1881 letter, "or Smith College and make equivalent with our course and add enough to take a degree in the Classical Course[?]" Perhaps, in addition to increasing the hours of Greek in the curriculum, classes and recitation time should be planned to match those of Wellesley ("15 recitations per week of 40 minutes each"), she suggested in June (25 Apr. and 2 June 1881, BC, EB). The RFS Examining Com. in 1881 recommended that more encouragement be given RFS girls to undertake the full course of Greek study. "In view of the small number of pupils in Greek," the report noted, "the committee would suggest that the Greek course be made prominent before the minds of the young ladies, and rendered attractive to them, especially in connection with the extension of the course of study which is contemplated" ("Report of the Examining Com.," [ca. June 1881], clipping, Sill, "Scrapbook").

By the time JA was finishing at RFS, the "collegiate" course included three years of Latin and two years of Greek (with two more years possible as electives), and the content of the Greek classes strongly paralleled the courses offered at Beloit College. Beloit students also studied the Greek testament, as did JA in her private Sunday sessions with Sarah Blaisdell.

6. Caroline ("Carrie") Hitchcock, probably Kate Hitchcock's sister, was also from Cedar Rapids, Iowa. She was a special student enrolled in the modern languages program and studying water color painting. She did not return to RFS for the 1878–79 school year.

7. Mary Page Wright (b. 1848) was born at West Jersey in Stark Co., Ill. Her parents were the Rev. Samuel G. Wright, a home missionary, and Minerva Hart Wright. Mary P. Wright was educated at Adrian College, Adrian, Mich., and graduated from RFS in 1871. In 1874 she was elected superintendent of public schools for Coffey Co., Kans., and by so doing "furnished the Supreme Court the test case in the decision that sex is no disqualification for that office" (Eagle, ed., *Congress of Women,* 305). She taught at RFS in 1876–77. The Oct. 1877 *RSM* reported that "Miss Mary P. Wright, who was teacher with us last year, is now assistant teacher in the High School at Newton, Iowa" (195); the "Personals" section of the Oct. 1878 *RSM* announced, "The address of Miss Mary P. Wright, of '71, is Brookville, Kansas" (225). She became a missionary after teaching at RFS. The "Personals" section of the May 1881 *RSM* announced that she had been appointed to a mission in "Eastern Turkey" (145). She served there for eight years with the American Board of Commissioners for Foreign Missions of the Congregational Church. By 1892 she was living in Rogers Park, Ill., and she spoke at the Women's Congress at the 1893 Chicago World's Fair. In her talk, "Woman's Life in Asiatic Turkey," she described the life of the average Turkish woman as "monotonous and sad . . . because: (a) They are held to be essentially inferior to man. (b) They are ignorant, most of

them being unable to even read. . . . (c) Because of the miseries of polygamy, the seclusion of Moslem women in their harems, and (e) [d] The subjection of Armenian wives to their mothers-in-law" (Wright, "Woman's Life," 305). She also recounted questions she received from Turkish women and girls about the United States and their professed amazement at American women's relative freedom of movement and expression, and greater social equality with men.

8. Lucy M. Smith graduated from RFS in 1867 and was granted an honorary M.A. in 1882. She taught rhetoric and English language in the RFS Preparatory Dept. Smith was "both teacher and nurse. 'Tall and slim, clad in black,'" she cared for students when they were ill (Cedarborg, "Early History," 256). Carrie Longley (RFS class of 1878) recalled to a historian of the school that "Miss Lucy Smith teacher of Rhetoric was greatly beloved, and her mild, loving reproof had often more effect than Miss B[laisdell]'s sternness" (Carrie Longley [Jones] to Hazel Cedarborg, 16 Feb. 1925, RC). Anna P. Sill was Smith's advocate when Smith applied to receive a master's degree in 1881–82 and wrote to Joseph Emerson on 6 May 1882 to name Smith among the six faculty members and alumnae whom she felt worthy of a degree (BC, EB; for more detailed information on the life of Smith, see JA to SAAH, 15 Jan. 1869, n. 5, above).

9. Probably a reference to Hattie Smith. For more information on Hattie Smith, see EGS to JA, 11 Aug. 1878, n. 4, below.

10. Hitchcock referred to the editing of one of JA's pieces for the "Home Items" section of the *RSM*. The masthead of the magazine does not list the senior editor of the *RSM* in 1877–78, but Caroline Potter was the faculty sponsor and oversaw the journal's production. Hitchcock's mention of the editor who changed JA's "Home Items" piece is almost certainly a reference to Maria Nutting, who was in charge of that feature until she left school in May 1879.

Maria Gilman Nutting (known to classmates as "Nuttie") (d. 1936) was born in Boston. She left school temporarily in the spring of 1879—the May 1879 issue of the *RSM* reported that "'Nuttie' has gone, leaving sorrow in many hearts, and especially in the hearts of the sister editors and her classmates" (131)—but returned the following year and graduated in 1880. Her cohorts on the *RSM* staff wrote that Nutting "was sent to Rockford Seminary for the purpose of receiving discipline, which she very sadly needed. During the last few years she became resigned to her fate, and now, as she is about to leave forever, she looks back upon misapplied hours and the anxiety she has caused her teachers, with feelings of remorse" (*RSM* [July 1880]: 209). Nutting became assistant principal and taught mathematics and several other subjects at an institute in Hopkinton, Iowa, in the 1880–81 school year and was the librarian at RFS from 1882 to 1884. She taught Latin at Lake Geneva Seminary, Wis., in 1885. In the mid-1880s she went to Turkey and Asia as a missionary and began writing a series of Christian books. In 1887 she was running a mission kindergarten in Turkey. Her books, which have Christian messages, include *Baby Helen, Joy,* and *Cordelia,* all written before 1904. Nutting worked as a missionary in Turkey for twenty years. In 1904 she returned to Randolph, Wis., and later moved to Berkeley, Calif., where she was an ardent supporter of woman suffrage and active in the League of Women Voters and Women's Civic League. JA visited her in 1935 in Berkeley. When Nutting died she directed that she be dressed in the simple clothing she was wearing when she passed away, wrapped in a missionary shroud, and cremated, with the ashes sprinkled in her garden.

11. The July 1878 edition of the *RSM* featured a lead essay on "Florence and Edinburgh" by JA's good friend EGS. The "Home Items" section was atypically lengthy because of reporting on the recent commencement. In addition to news about lectures and Class Day exercises, "Home Items" contained a reference to boots, perhaps an inside joke in the editorial department. In an imaginary dialogue about the work of playwright Benjamin Jonson (1572–1637), one student pitied Jonson's difficult life (he killed a fellow actor in a duel, was imprisoned, and fell in and out of court favor), whereas another pondered "Footprints on the sands of

time," a reference to lines 25–28 of Henry Wadsworth Longfellow's "A Psalm of Life": "Lives of great men all reminders / We can make our lives sublime / And, departing, leave behind us, / Footprints on the sands of time." A third student, "still gazing at her stout walking boots," commented, "'Oh, how I wish I could make a footprint as big as my foot'" (138).

12. A reference to Sarah Anderson.

13. Alexandre Dumas (1803–70) was a popular French novelist best known for *The Count of Monte-Cristo* and *The Three Musketeers* (1844–45). He also wrote a series of romantic novels about European history. His *The Queen's Necklace* (1849–50), a sequel to *Memoirs of a Physician* (1846–48), was one of the romances about Marie Antoinette that he wrote in collaboration with Auguste Maquet. His son, also named Alexandre Dumas (1824–95), was a dramatist.

14. Caroline Potter also taught English and history.

15. Henry Ward Beecher (1813–87), clergyman, reformer, and lecturer, was the brother of educator and reformer Catharine Beecher and of abolitionist writer Harriet Beecher Stowe. He was educated at Amherst College, Mass., (1834) and Lane Seminary, Cincinnati, (1837), and licensed to preach by the Cincinnati Presbytery in 1838. He was a pastor in Indianapolis for ten years before being called to shepherd the Congregational Plymouth Church in Brooklyn in 1847, where he remained for the rest of his career. He had a vibrant presence, exuding charm and vitality, and earned the reputation as one of the outstanding orators of his generation. In 1844 a short series of his lectures on such topics as gambling, idleness, and women was published as *Seven Lectures to Young Men,* and in 1872–74 the lectures he had given at Yale Univ. were printed in three volumes as *Yale Lectures on Preaching.* His public reputation was compromised by scandal in 1874, however, when he was named as the transgressor in an adultery suit brought by Theodore Tilton, a former protegé and parishioner in Beecher's church. The trial ended with a hung jury. After it was over, Beecher lectured throughout the country, in part to recoup financially from the enormous legal fees he had incurred. He withdrew from the Assn. of Congregational Ministers in 1882 because he refused to believe in a literal hell and he also embraced the concept of evolution. His *Evolution and Religion* was published in 1885.

16. Joseph Cook (1838–1901), author and lecturer, was a graduate of Harvard College (1865) and Andover Theological Seminary (1868). After studying in Europe, he settled in Massachusetts, where he became the unordained minister of the Congregational church in Lynn. There, during the early 1870s, he delivered a series of lectures on the factory system, child labor, working women, wages, self-help, industrialization, urbanization, and vice. By the end of the series he was speaking to standing-room-only audiences. In 1873 he began a series of "Monday lectures" at Tremont Temple in Boston, speaking on the relationship between science and religion, politics, and other reform issues. The popularity of these lectures led to national fame and, in 1880–83, a lecture tour abroad. He was a popular speaker at Beloit College, and his lectures won admiration from GBH, a student at Beloit. AHHA wrote to JA on 11 June 1878 that "George was sorry you could not hear Cook he enjoyed him ever so much" (IU, Lilly, SAAH; *JAPM,* 1:301). "I heard Joseph Cook last Thursday evening," Sarah Anderson reported to JA. "He lifted me up and out—what an advantage to a lecturer is such a body, such a head—our admiration and interest are at once enlisted" (22 Apr. 1883, SCPC, JAC; *JAPM,* 1:1062). Cook lectured on the "New Birth of Scientific Necessity" in 1880. In that same year his volumes *Labor, with Preludes on Current Events* and *Socialism, with Preludes on Current Events* were published in Boston and received positive reviews in the influential *Harper's Monthly* magazine in Oct. His compiled *Boston Monday Lectures* were published in eleven volumes between 1877 and 1888.

17. Although this Minnie may have been someone in Katie Hitchcock's family, two Minnies were enrolled in RFS during JA's time there, Minnie Black and Minnie Marks. Sarah Anderson also had a cousin, Minnie Redburn.

18. Part of the botany class that JA took in the second semester of her first year entailed

the making of a herbarium (a book in which plants and flowers are collected, pressed, and identified). Compiling a herbarium was a kind of ritual at RFS. The girls, singly and in groups, often went out along the railroad tracks in search of specimens and took field trips to look for spring flowers. RFS maintained an encyclopedic school herbarium, with specimens donated through exchanges from alumnae and others in different parts of the country. Mary E. Holmes taught the botany classes and led the herbarium rage on campus. She had begun her own herbarium as a small child, and it had grown to include many hundreds of species. Holmes contributed an essay on botanical papers to the *RSM* ([June 1877]: 103, 111) and also wrote a poem and essay, "An Hour with My Herbarium," as an *RSM* "Alumnae Dept." item ([Apr. 1878]: 89). At her death, Holmes's herbarium cabinets in Rockford included approximately ten thousand specimens from all over the world, obtained through exchange with members of scientific societies in other countries. On 10 June 1878, Lizzie Smith, JA's classmate, had written to her mother, Annie M. Jordan Smith, about making a herbarium: "I have to work real hard today putting the names of my flowers into my herbarium as we have to hand them in tomorrow and then she will let us have them again to put in any new flowers we may have before examination in two weeks" (SHSW, Smith). JA's own herbarium can be seen on *JAPM*, 1A:17–19.

From Ellen Gates Starr

Durand, [Ill.]   Aug. 11, 1878.

Dear Jane;

Whatever happens! It <u>happens</u> to be Sunday, and the most convenient day in the week to write. <u>I</u> have kept my part of the bargain to the letter, which cannot be said for <u>you</u>, madamoiselle. I was shocked at you, "my love" that you should break the charm for that miserable charity. I do not like "newsy" letters, but I have one bit of information to communicate which may surprise you. My unsanctified feet will not pollute the sacred walks of the R.F.S. for the year 1878–9. I am going to Mt. Morris.[1] You see I have cut you out entirely. I do not say I am not sorry, but I do this voluntarily and willingly, for when duty calls and bread & butter, (figuratively speaking) it behooves me to respond. Seriously, Mr. H.[2] has offered me two classes to teach which will be a great assistance to me, both in a pecuniary sense and as regards my own improvement; and I shall go on with my Latin, and I think begin French, and pursue whatever other branches I can most advantageously to myself. Mr. H. has given me the general history.[3] I am delighted, but feel that it was desperately audacious in me to ask for it. It will be such an advantage to me to teach it, for I shall study all the time I can "<u>procure</u>" and you know "Whoso bloweth not his own horn, the same shall not be blown."

I do not know whether Hattie Smith is in Oregon,[4] but I think I shall write to her and ask her to come to Mt. Morris, for school opens Aug. 26. Isn't it uncomfortable? I should like so much to see her before she goes back to Rockford. My brother[5] is still here, and I assure you I have made the most of that privelige. I sit in his room a great deal while he is at work, and he likes to have me. He never <u>asks</u> me to, that isn't like him; but sometimes when I am passing the door he says "There is a cool breeze here," and then I always go in. He has been doing a crayon copy of Beatrice Cenci[6] for mother's[7] birthday. She always admired it so much. I think it very beautiful; a great deal better than the photograph he copied, for he put in some shadows which are in the original which were indistinct in the photograph. My sister[8] sent her two lovely panels painted in oils, and Auntie[9] gave her two panels in water colors exquisitely framed.

It seems to me that a frame should be to the picture what the dress should be to the wearer, and the setting to the jewel. So many people apparently disregard this. I often think the picture is used as a mere excuse for hanging up the frame. Like the "clothes-screens" idea. Astonishing, isn't it, how things are reversed. Katie[10] has made me a short visit. I asked her to spend Sunday, and hear Mr. Haseltine, but she did not. She plays in church at home, I think. I wrote to Eva[11] inviting her to visit me, but as I have received no reply I conclude that she is not at home. I was rather disappointed in Lillian's[12] picture when I looked at it carefully. It isn't so pretty as she is. Lillian has rather regular features, and with all the rest of her graces she is exceedingly pretty; but her features are not sufficiently classical for a profile. She has too much chin, and her nose has a slight ascension, so to speak; a fact which I never observed in the original. My brother fell in love with Katie's forehead, and my mother quite fell in love with Katie. As to myself, I venerate Kate Carnefix.[13] She has crotchets which are despicable in Miss Sill. I have a contempt for them in her. In Katie I regard them with something of the feeling one might have towards a constitutional weakness in a strong man. I think <u>Dr. Manette</u> <u>partly</u> illustrates what I mean.[14] It is something which I wish to avoid in her. I wish she were without it, but, even if I could, I would not take the responsibility of removing it.

Really, Jane, (I say it as in the privacy of your room in east connection) I am a little disappointed in Mr. Haseltine. If he wasn't a minister, or if I hadn't heard him preach, I should be inclined to think his eccentricity and reticence a sign of depth; but one doesn't expect a man to reserve his best thoughts in the pulpit. As a minister I consider him rather a failure, as I believe you said you did. I haven't seen enough of him to have opinion of him confirmed otherwise. As a model of self-control he is certainly a success. As a Latin teacher, though he undeniably understands his business, <(I mean Latin, not teaching)> he leaves his pupil altogether too much to her own devices, as far as my observation has extended. He <u>never</u> asks me to parse.[15] One cannot guess at Caesar. If I cannot read it, he explains the construction. That may be, but I imagine there would be trouble with Miss Blaisdell on that point. I have read one book and part of the second. I think I should have gotten through with three as I intended if I had returned the middle of Sept. As it is I shall not, but shall enter the class and read more. That man will sit for the longest time without saying a word than any adult person I ever saw. One of my friends said she thought one day she would try how long he would remain silent, but she became ashamed of herself and spoke. Auntie came Friday, and Saturday Mother asked the Haseltines to tea. She didn't know they were

going so soon and had neglected it. If ever you have the "opportunity" ask Mr.
H. if he ever met my Aunt Miss Starr, and then try to find out what he thought
of her. I would give a good deal to know. It was too funny; those two people together. Auntie is as charming a person as I know, and a beautiful conversationalist when she is interested, but she is very deaf, and you know how low Mr. H.
speaks. I meant to tell him, but did not have an opportunity, and I don't think
she heard a dozen words that he said. Her remarks had no connection whatever
with his, which were very few, and I don't think the stupid man got it through
his head till nearly the last of the time & then he didn't raise his voice any. I should
like very much to have you meet Auntie, for though you don't like deaf people
in general, I think you would like her. Now of course all this that I have said about
good Mr. H. is perfectly dreadful and an evidence of my total depravity. I shall
not blame you in the least if you are quite indignant. We all like and respect him
very much, and the rest of the family are exceedingly sorry to have him go; but
that he is very eccentric cannot be denied. I would give a generous slice of my
future happiness to see Miss Anderson's little round face. She was so good as to
ask me to write to her and I think I shall do so today. I liked and enjoyed a great
many people at the seminary, but Miss Anderson possesses my affections. I suppose as I am not coming back I may expect to hear from you again; at least when
school opens you will tell me who is there and how it seems. I presume I shall
like people at Mt. Morris, too. I shall try to reserve some time this year for reading, outside of class work.

My brother told me the other day that I ought to be ashamed that I had never
read Childe Harold;[16] and I "confessed and denied not, but confessed" that I was.
I am also ashamed that I have written so much and said so little, but as you have
discovered the same peculiarity in my conversation, you will not be surprised.
I hope I shall receive the "momentums" you promised. Pardon my extreme te-
diousness, and believe me very much your friend,

Ellen Starr.

Have you read "93"?[17] I am in the midst of it and enjoy it thoroughly. It isn't
so thrilling as "The Tale of two Cities"[18] but I think more useful because more
general.

Do you cultivate Hugo's style of writing? I am going to read Carlyle's[19]
French Revolution[20] next. Tell me what you are intending to read, and I wish,
Jane, that you would inform me from time to time what Miss Potter's classes
are doing. I should like to read the same things for the sake of companionship
if for nothing else.

E.S.

ALI (SC, Starr; *JAPM*, 1:322–29).

1. Mt. Morris Seminary, originally known as Rock River Seminary, was a coeducational
school in Mt. Morris, Ill., which was at the time of the school's beginnings in the 1840s a
sparsely settled prairie village. Founded by the Methodist Episcopal Church in 1839, the school

opened in 1840 and attracted students from northern Illinois and southern Wisconsin. AHHA's first husband, William J. Haldeman, may have been an early student. The school was the first institution of higher education in northern Illinois. An elementary school for the town's children was added to the seminary in 1841 under the direction of Fanny Russell. The Rev. Daniel J. Pinckney became the school's first principal in 1842. Within ten years the school had successfully outgrown its original building, and in 1852 the Illinois legislature incorporated the school as a university. Hard times came in 1869, when the entire faculty resigned and those individuals who were approached to serve as principal declined the offer. The school was reopened in 1873 with a four-person staff, including a new principal, N. C. Dougherty; a Latin and Greek professor, Richard Arthur Edwards; Maria Hitt, who taught music; and preceptress Lottie M. Smith. By 1878, still under Dougherty's leadership, the school was again in "prosperous condition," and the faculty had expanded to include instruction in reading and grammar, science and mathematics, music, languages, and the arts (*History of Ogle County,* 478). In 1879 the school was sold to the Church of the Brethren and renamed Mt. Morris Seminary and Collegiate Institute. In 1884 the name was changed yet again to Mt. Morris College. The school merged with another Church of the Brethren school, Manchester College, North Manchester, Ind., in 1932. In the 1990s the buildings were still in use, housing a business enterprise.

2. "Mr. H" is a reference to the Rev. Theodore H. Haseltine (1837–84), the Protestant minister in EGS's hometown of Durand, Ill., in 1878, and her Latin tutor. Durand is near the Wisconsin border, almost due north of Pecatonica, Ill., and approximately equidistant northeast and northwest between Freeport/Cedarville and Rockford. The Durand Methodist Episcopal Church was organized there in 1840, and in 1877 it had 125 members, with some one hundred children in its Sunday School. The Haseltine family had strong connections to RFS, and EGS was well acquainted with Haseltine; his wife, Mary; and their three children, Sadie E. (b. 1868?), Warren E. (b. 1873?), and Theodore (b. 1875?). Haseltine was also on friendly terms with AHHA.

Haseltine was born in Middletown, Vt., the son of the Rev. William B. Haseltine, who became a pastor in Wisconsin in 1856, and Sarah W. Haseltine, who died soon after the family's migration west. Theodore Haseltine was educated at Ft. Edward Seminary, N.Y., and Union College, Schenectady, N.Y., where he graduated in 1861. He taught classical languages for more than ten years, marrying Mary Edmond, a fellow teacher at Jennings Seminary in Aurora, Ill., in 1865. He became a minister in the Rock River Conference in 1870 and served in several Illinois parishes, including those of Yorkville (1874–75), Durand (1877–78), LaSalle (1880–82), and Grant Park (1883–84).

Haseltine's period in LaSalle was particularly trying and left him in poor emotional health; he experienced a breakdown during his next assignment. As he described his daily life as a LaSalle preacher to AHHA, "My regular work Preaching twice on Sunday, leading a Bible class, & usually attending a Temperance meeting. This is usual Sunday's work, all of which needs some preparation during the week. Then on Monday eve I have a young people's meeting to lead. In this we converse about some previously announced topic. Then I lead a prayer meeting every Wednesday evening. Every two weeks we have a church social. Almost every afternoon I spend in calling. Then I have a great many funerals." Haseltine also traveled to give lectures, and planned to teach at an institute in Aug. 1881, the month that JHA died. He told AHHA about his children and described LaSalle as "a very wicked city. . . . What shallow basis for social grade here!" He also had opinions about the quality of preaching going on at the Methodist church in Cedarville, where the minister was trying "to produce a 'resurrection.' . . . I am heartily—heretofore unexpressed—ashamed of a church that allows such teachers" (31 May 1881, UIC, JAMC, HJ Supp).

Haseltine attended RFS senior examinations and reviewed Latin classes while JA was a student there in 1880. She later turned to him for spiritual counsel (see T. H. Haseltine to JA,

13 June 1880, below), and he wrote to comfort and guide her after her father's death. Although he seemed to have wielded influence to secure EGS a position as a teacher-student at Mt. Morris, Haseltine was not a member of the board of trustees or of the faculty of Mt. Morris Seminary in 1878.

3. EGS was not officially listed among the faculty members or preceptresses of Mt. Morris Seminary in 1878–79. Her Latin classes were directed to the elementary-level students at the school, while upper-level classical courses were offered by the regular Latin and Greek instructor Richard Arthur Edwards, a friend of JA's grade-school teacher John H. Parr. Mt. Morris had no regular teachers of history or French on its faculty in 1878–79. The *RSM* reported in the fall of 1878 that "Ellen Starr is engaged as teacher at Mt. Morris" and the following spring that "Ellen Starr spent a few days with her friends at the Seminary" ([Apr. 1879]: 100; [Oct. 1878]: 205).

4. Hattie Smith, who was from Oregon, Ill., on the Rock River and just a few miles southeast of Mt. Morris, may have been away visiting. She wrote to JA from Independence, Iowa, on 28 Aug. 1878, replying to a 23 July 1878 letter from JA. She inquired about how JA's study of Greek was progressing. The girls had discussed their mutual desire to go to school in the East, and in her 28 Aug. letter Smith asked how things were proceeding on that front within the Addams household: "What does your father say of Smith College by this time? Do you know, I can't get my father to say anything pro nor con; and I shall go right on and do just as I think best" (SCPC, JAC; *JAPM*, 1:339). She seemed to share EGS's general assessment of the regimented life at RFS, referring to her "dread" of returning to the school and another year there as "persecution" (SCPC, JAC; *JAPM*, 1:342). Unlike EGS, however, she decided to return after the 1877–78 school year. She took a leave from RFS in the first semester of the 1879–80 year but returned and graduated in 1880. She later became a music teacher.

5. EGS had two brothers, William Wesley Starr (1851–1913), who was eight years older than she, and Albert Childs Starr (1861–1935), who was two years younger and the baby of the family. Albert Starr studied pharmacy in Chicago and became a cotton-broker with his sister Mary's husband, Charles M. Blaisdell, in Chicopee, Mass. He married Jeanne Josephine Stutz in 1893, and they had two daughters, Josephine Stutz Starr and Elizabeth Angela Starr.

William Wesley Starr, the eldest child in the family, was born in Deerfield, Mass., in Jan. 1851 and came west with his parents at the age of four. He attended schools in Laona Twp. in Winnebago Co., Ill., and in 1870 went to Chicago to study drawing under the instruction of his aunt, Eliza Allen Starr. He then went to Boston and studied at the Lowell Institute of Art from 1872 to 1878. In 1878 he began a tour of Europe with his aunt. He studied the old masters and stayed for a year in Rome. He returned to the United States and was employed as a crayon artist in Grand Rapids, Mich., for two years before moving back to Chicago, where he shifted his artistic pursuits to sculpture. In 1889 he moved back to Durand, Ill., where he created busts and public art sculptures of several leading Chicago citizens, among them a bust of Henry Wilmarth of the Wilmarth family who were patrons of EGS's efforts on behalf of the arts and urban reform.

6. Beatrice Cenci (1577–99) was a Roman noblewoman who was condemned to death by Pope Clement VIII. She conspired with others in the assassination of her brutally sadistic father, Francesco Cenci, in 1598. The pope refused to show her mercy, however, and after her execution he confiscated the Cenci properties. The tragedy, mystery, and martyrdom of Beatrice Cenci has inspired painters, poets, and writers.

7. EGS's mother, the former Susan Gates Childs (1821–1900), married Caleb Allen Starr (1822–1915) in Massachusetts in 1848. She was the daughter of Samuel and Electa Gates Childs of Deerfield, Mass. Caleb Starr, also born in Deerfield, was the son of Lavina (sometimes spelled "Lorina" or "Lovina") Allen Starr and Oliver Starr, who like the Childs were farmers of modest means. Caleb Starr was educated in district schools and at a local academy. He sold books door to door, and between nineteen and twenty-four he worked as a sailor out of

Calcutta and other international ports. Leaving the sea in his mid-twenties, he returned to Deerfield to help his parents with their farm and to marry. The family farm was entrenched in debt in the 1840s, however, and in the early 1850s Caleb and Oliver Starr decided to move to acreage in Illinois in the hope of improving their financial situation. They named the new property Spring Park.

Susan Gates Childs Starr came west with her husband in 1855 and helped him farm in Laona Twp. in Winnebago Co. for twenty-two years. The exchange of close family and friends in Deerfield for the relative isolation of a prairie farm was a difficult transition for her to make, however, and while her husband engaged in regional business life she was more confined and suffered from bouts of melancholia. Her artistic talent was manifested in traditional sewing crafts, particularly embroidery. She did not share her husband's penchant for public activism. In 1877, the year EGS started school at RFS, the Starrs moved from their farm and into the town of Durand, where Caleb Starr opened a drugstore (see also Biographical Profiles: Starr, Ellen Gates).

8. EGS's older sister, Mary Houghton Starr (1849–1934), was another member of the family who became an artist. She was educated in Cambridge, Mass., where she lived with her aunt Eunice Wellington and returned home to Illinois for the summers. She studied painting for two years in Paris and specialized in portraiture. In 1884 she married Charles M. Blaisdell, a merchant, in Chicopee, Mass., and then made her home in New England. The couple had no children.

9. EGS's aunt, Eliza Allen (born Ann) Starr (1824–1901), was an important role model for EGS (see also Biographical Profiles: Starr, Ellen Gates). Eliza Allen Starr was an author, lecturer, and art teacher of renown in the Chicago area. Along with her brother Caleb, she was influential in shaping the ideas and moral values of EGS. In particular she provided a role model of female independence and achievement, and many of her ideas about public art and the political aspects of aesthetics were put into practice by her niece at Hull-House and in public programs. She was also important to EGS for her devout religious commitment, especially her conversion to Catholicism.

Eliza Allen Starr was born in Deerfield, Mass. She was educated at the local district school, where she was taught by Caroline Negus, a well-known painter of miniatures, and at Deerfield Academy. In 1845 she went to Boston for art instruction and opened her own painting studio. She taught drawing in Brooklyn and Philadelphia and worked for two years as a private art tutor to a wealthy Natchez, Miss., family before returning to Boston in 1854. Raised in the Unitarian faith, she went through a decade-long quest toward a more religious experience. Her cousin George Allen (1808–76), a professor of Latin and Greek at the University of Pennsylvania, a former Episcopal vicar, and in 1847 a Roman Catholic convert, helped influence Eliza toward a conversion to Catholicism. At Christmas in 1854 she was baptized into the Roman Catholic Church in Boston. For the next few years, she seriously considered entering a convent but was dissuaded from doing so because of chronic ill health.

In 1856 she moved to Chicago, where she established a studio in rented rooms. She lived and worked there for the next forty-five years, teaching drawing and painting from life models, nature, and casts to children from Chicago's leading families. She moved into her own studio in 1863 and in 1878 to St. Joseph's Cottage, yet another, and newly constructed, studio. Her home on Huron St. on the North Side of Chicago was a block away from St. James Church and near the Kirkland School, where EGS taught. Both William Starr and EGS were frequent visitors to, and sometimes residents of, her salonlike household.

In the 1870s and 1880s, Eliza Allen Starr became well known nationally for her extensive public lecture series on art history, talks she initially presented in the homes of Chicago friends. With help from wealthy patrons, she toured Europe in 1875–77, collecting reproductions and photographic materials for use with her lectures and for her book *Pilgrims and Shrines* (2 vols., 1883–85). Among her many writings, including those illustrated by her own etchings, were books of poetry (*Poems,* 1867, and *Songs of a Lifetime,* 1887); lives of saints; guides to collections of Catholic art; and treatises on religious aspects of art. Dedication to arts education took a more institutionalized turn when Eliza Allen Starr founded the art department at Saint Mary's Academy near South Bend, Indiana. Her public lecture series on "The Literature of Art," conducted with slides and photographs, in addition to her published poetry and writing on art, focused on spiritual themes, collections of Roman Catholic art, the religious depiction of women, and shrines. She became popularly known through publication of essays, poems, and devotions in such periodicals as the *Catholic Mirror* and *Catholic World.* Radical in her methods—she insisted on students drawing from nature or from casts rather than copying master works—she was know in her interpretation of art for qualities of tenderness, whimsy, and originality. She was also conservative in her valuation of the proper parameters of painting. Her interest in the confluence of spirituality and artistic expression was nearly all-consuming. She received recognition from Pope Leo XIII for her contribution to public understanding of religious art (especially her *Three Archangels and the Guardian Angel in Art* [1899]) and was affiliated with a Dominican order of nuns (the Third Order of Saint Dominic) as a lay member.

Frances Willard described Starr's St. Joseph's Cottage as a "center of art and education, of charitable enterprises and social influence" (Willard and Livermore, *Woman of the Century,* 679). Starr was also a prominent member of the Fortnightly Club, a group of influential and wealthy Chicago women who were deeply involved in cultural affairs and projects for civic reform. EGS's family connection to this network proved important to her and JA when they founded Hull-House at the end of the 1880s. In 1905 James J. McGovern published *Life and Letters of Eliza Allen Starr,* an edited collection printed by Lakeside Press in Chicago and containing geographical sketches, correspondence, a diary of Starr's visit to the Vatican, and some unpublished poems and lectures. Some of Eliza Allen Starr's books, general lectures, and lectures for art courses, along with her will and obituaries, have been preserved as parts of SC, Starr.

10. Katie Hitchcock.

11. Eva Campbell.

12. Lillian Beckman.

13. Catharine (sometimes spelled "Cathrina" or "Kate") A. Carnefix (Graham) (b. 1857?) was from a pioneer family whose members were among the first white settlers of Stephenson Co. Her parents, S. M. and Sarah Carnefix, were both born in Virginia. They were residents on a farm in Stephenson Co. in 1860, along with six children from three (Kate) to nineteen. By the time of the U.S. census of 1880, Sarah had been widowed; her sister, Rosanna, had become a teacher; and Kate herself taught music. Kate Carnefix was a good friend of EGS's at RFS, where she belonged to the Castalian Society. She was a member of the class of 1878 and in June 1878 served as marshall for class exercises. She returned in the 1878–79 school year to continue her musical studies with Daniel Hood. She came back to Rockford to see friends graduate from RFS in 1881. The following year she married David F. Graham, a banker whose parents, Margaret Young Graham and J. H. Graham, were also Stephenson Co. pioneers. The Grahams had two children and lived in Rock City and Freeport, Ill. Kate Carnefix Graham was active in Christian Endeavor, the Presbyterian Church, and the Freeport Culture Club. Despite her residence in the area, she was not buried in either the Freeport Cemetery or the Cedarville Cemetery.

14. A possible reference to Dr. Manette, a fictional character in Charles Dickens's *Tale of Two Cities* (1859) who is a French physician unfairly imprisoned in the Bastille. Manette recovers from dementia in England after his release from captivity.

15. The following words are written along the right and left margins of page ten, perpendicular to the text of the letter: "Under no considerations repeat what I have said about Mr. H's teaching. He may do differently in a class, & his reputation as a teacher is very high. He

says if I read it right he knows I understand the construction, & of course I can parse it"
(*JAPM*, 1:326).

16. A reference to *Childe Harold's Pilgrimage*, a poetic narrative of adventure by romantic poet George Gordon, Lord Byron (1788–1824), written in four cantos between 1809 and 1818.

17. Victor Hugo's historical novel *Quatre-vingt-treize* (Ninety-three) (1873), about Royalist insurrections in Brittany and the Vendeé during the French Revolution.

18. *A Tale of Two Cities* was set in Paris and London during the French Revolution. One of Dickens's historical novels, the book was modeled on Carlyle's *The French Revolution: A History* (1837).

19. Thomas Carlyle (1795–1881) was a Scottish historian and commentator whose major works included lives of Oliver Cromwell, John Sterling, and Frederick the Great. He was also an extremely important intellectual influence upon both JA and EGS. His essays and lectures included analyses of industrialism and modernism, character, self-discipline, and heroic ideals. In *Democracy* (from *Past and Present*, 1843), he analyzed the poverty, hunger, and disorder caused by the massive unemployment of industrial workers and proposed a concept of "heroic" leadership, to arise not from the grass roots but from within an active aristocracy who would deal with the problems of those below them in the social hierarchy. The concept was similar to what JA and EGS later attempted through Hull-House (see also Excerpt from Editorial in the *RSM*, Mar. 1881, below).

20. *The French Revolution: A History* was written in London. Told from the viewpoint of a narrator sympathetic to the revolutionaries, it spans French history from the death of Louis XV (1774) through the taking of the Bastille, the Reign of Terror, the fall of Robespierre, and other events leading up to the insurrection of Vendémiairie in 1795, offering along the way vivid portraits of Lafayette and many others.

Draft of Debate Argument

In her first semester at Rockford Female Seminary, Jane Addams enrolled in a rhetorical composition class with Caroline Potter, where she practiced, among other things, writing critical essays that argued in the affirmative or negative on given topics.[1] By her sophomore year she was using these skills in debates as a member of the Castalian Society. On at least two occasions, she and fellow Castalian member Corrine Williams[2] presented a debate about the relative impact of Mme. de Staël[3] and George Sand.[4] They did so once at a program in November 1878 and again, with similar but largely rewritten arguments, at another program on 13 April 1880. The earlier version is presented here.[5]

[Rockford, Ill.]   [ca. 13 Nov. 1878]

Affirmative.

Resolved; that the French women have had more influence through literature than polotics.

Rep. women[:] George Sand and Mdé Dé Staël.

If a man makes up his mind to do something worthy of rememberance, or utter one thought so illuminated that his name shall not be forgotten as soon as his body is turned into dust, he must[6] either enter the region of literature or polotics, the one the outgrowth of a nation's mind, the other of her will or powers of self control.

Literature & polotics then are the two spheres of action wherein men hope to gain immortal honor and the applause of the world. To suppose the woman could have any influence whatever in either, is but a modern discovery. The imperious will of man is at last forced to admit, that woman like himself posesses an intellect, that she exerts a potent influence in the age in which she lives and that this influence is felt throughout the epoch making or marring its proportions.

The question then, is not what it might, with propriety have been twenty years ago, does woman exert an influence? for that is proven without a doubt, but in which of the two great spheres of action is her influence felt the most?[7]

Naturally one would say that her influence is the greater in polotics, for that requires the persuasive powers, the tongue, her natural weapon, whilst literature demands solid brain in which she is supposed to be rather deficient.

But if we can prove that the woman of France has had more influence through literature than polotics, the statement will hold concerning all womankind of the civilized world)[8] and we can assert that woman's intellect is as vigorous in power as her charms are persuasive in society.[9]

Aurora Dupin, better known throughout two hemispheres as Geo Sand, was a genius, but more than that she was a woman, "no man could have written her books for no man could have had her experiance even with a genius equal to her own;" and this long and bitter experiance is expressed with a passionate earnestness in all her works.

Her life in childhood was irregular, moody and eccrentric, at ten she had the thoughts & feelings of a woman, at fourteen she was a philosopher and a sage, at sixteen she had embraced the Roman Catholic faith with her whole soul & seriously thought of entering a convent, and at eighteen she was married, and married to what? an ordinary commonplace despotic baron, the last creature in the universe that the quivering soul of genius should have wedded, but her heart was on fire and her poetic brain transfigured him. Alas! delusions can not last and in three months they were so spiritually divorced that all the laws of civilziation could not hold them together.[10]

Her history from this time is that of a strong & fervid soul misguided prehaps but struggling upward to the light.

For this passionate and daring young woman by one great decisive step sundered herself forever from the bonds of what we call society, nothing was sacred and nothing was settled. She evolved from her own heart and brain her own law of life, the world was all before her where to choose, and what use did she make of her splendid gifts? With all her force of character Geo Sand's soul and brain were exurberantly[11] and splendidly feminine, she was a French-woman keenly attractive in the bloom of youth and earnestness of passion, she might have held a salon rivaling in brilliancy that of M'de dé Staël or Md'e Roland,[12] but she scorned always to act & plan through others, and exert but a petty personal influence over a few worldly wits of fashion or polotics, she wished not to tell men what laws to make, but to touch thier hearts & deepest morals and save her fellow-women from an experiance as bitter as her own. She retired to her plain, bare garret & launched with brilliant success into the world of letters. She wrote with eagarness throwing the full force of her vigorous mind and genuine experiance into her work. She wrote in defense of her ideal, boldly attacking the peculiar marriage system of the French and declaring the social independance and equality of woman her relations to man, society and destiny.

Her first novels, "Indiana," "Valantine" and "Lelia" followed in quick succession, the latter having a celebrity that arose to senation and frightening those whom it did not fascinate; its influence was felt throughout all classes and the heart of every woman <in France> throbbed in sympathy with Geo. Sand; for thcy too[13] as Lelia had left the passionate enthusiasm, the vague and feverish longing "for things outside the narrow orbit of thier sex which the dark organic forces bid them tread.["] They saw the secret longings of thier own hearts printed in black and white before them and called a new philosophy[.] For these novels are philosophies not mere stories; the woman who wrote them had already laid her bold hand upon the tree of knowledge of good and of evil. "She was not to be saved like a woman through ignorance, but like a man through knowledge <wisdom> which has its heavenly & earthly side." She was ardent in her philanthropy, striving to exalt individuality above sociality, and to point out to her fellow women the delicate limits between the opposing vital forces, between what we owe to ourselves and what we owe to others. She gave the social questions of the 19th cent. an electric shock, "For the first time in the history of the world woman spoke out for herself with a voice as powerful as that of man. For the first time in the history of the world woman spoke out as a woman, not as the plaything, the pupil, the satellite or the goddess of man." "And there is hardly a woman's heart anywhere in the civilized world which has not felt the vibrations of Geo Sand's thrilling voice. Women who never saw one of her books, nay who never even heard her "[']nom de plume' have been stirred by emotions of doubt, fear and ambitions which they never would have known but for Geo Sand."

Compare[14] then this world wide powerful influence, as lasting as literature itself, to the vain & glittering ambition of M'de Dé Staël, gifted, wealthy and popular she drew brave warriors & proud statesmen to her feet, she may have greatly influenced, and who doubts it, the polotics of her day, but of _her_ day only, she was ever acting through others and never for herself, & _now_ when we read of those men, her tools, we instinctively feel a contempt for them, she did not bring out thier true manhood & individuality, but used [t]hem for her own interests, and what were those interests. The main object of her life was to make a constitutional monarchy of France and she could n't do it. France to day is probably just what it would have been if M'de dé Staël had never lived, her influence died with her, with all her scheming her life was a failure and failure is the word we can write on the life of every woman who influenced France through her personal charms and magnatism rather than through her intellect.

But[15] if we follow Geo Sand through her long & brilliant career we find success in every department. The choicest spirits of the day gathered round her in her plain bare garret. Da Lammanias[16] unfolded to her his theories of saintly and visionary philosophy[.] Liszt and Chopin[17] bound her in the enchantment of thier wonderful melodies, Pierre Leroux[18] instructed her in religion, De Balzac,[19] Quintet[20] & de Musset[21] were among her friends & teachers and we can trace thier individual influence in all her writings in her philosophies, poems & dramas; she accepted fearlessly these influences, transforming to the watchword of an enthusiastic crusade the idea which was in the minority & opposition, she now burst upon the world as spokesmen for thier moral, political & religious views, & such was her power that even the weak appeared strong and the cowardly brave, seen through her genius; she brought out what was best in these men and makes us honor instead of despise them.

But when the revolution of '48 came, which swept away all trace of M'de dé Staël's power, for all hopes of a constitutional monarchy was now at an end and all former laws were overturned, then Geo Sand, this splendid, fiery woman, appears as the world's peace maker, the apologist of mankind; she shows the French men & woman how to start again and start again <aright>. In[22] all her books she paints men not only as they are and ought to be, but as they can be. She declares the emancipation of woman & her social equality has faith in her possibilities and hope in her steady progress.

George Sand has secured in literature a classic place and in the heart of every woman in France undying loyalty.

And I quote a high authority when I say that "hers is probably the most powerful individuality displayed by any modern French woman.["] That the influence of M'de Roland was but a glittering unreality, that of M'de dé Staël only a boudoir & coterie success when compared with the power exercised over literature, human feeling & social law, by the energy, the courage, the genius, even the very errors & extravgences of Geo. Sand.

AMs (UIC, JAMC, Detzer; *JAPM*, 45:1795–807).

1. For other debate essays by JA, see "Blindness is preferable to deafness," 5 Jan. 1878; "Resolved: that the Ornamental branches are necessary to a Complete Education. negative," Feb. 1878; and "Resolved: 'That the British form of government tends to develope better statesmen than the American form,' Aff.," 19 Nov. 1880 (all *JAPM*, 45:1708–14, 1715–21, and 46:253–62). The third debate was delivered at a Pierian Union program at which JA and Lizzie Smith argued the affirmative and Helen Harrington and Alice Atkinson the negative. Sarah Blaisdell, Ella Williams, and Emma Briggs judged, ruling in favor of the affirmative. The program was reported in the "Home Items" section of the Jan. 1888 *RSM* (13). Lizzie Smith wrote to her mother about the experience (see Mary B. Downs to JA, 14 Nov. 1880, n. 6; see also Draft of Debate Essay, [ca. Apr. 1879?], below).

2. In notes jotted in her old 1875 pocket diary, probably during her senior year at RFS, JA wrote a tribute to her friend and fellow debater Corrine Williams: "Dedicated[:] Ever con-

nected in my mind & surrounded by an the same halo of glory & the names Md de'Stáel & 'Corinne' Williams the one the champion of the liberties of Fran[ce] the other cham[p]ion of woman<hood>'s best & noblest quali[ti]es. To the latter I dedicate this humble effort, with the old proverb she so richly deserv[e]s[:] Bis vincit, qui se vincet in victoriam" ("She conquers twice, who masters herself in victory"—a proverb of humility in the midst of success) (Addams, "Pocket Diary, 1875[–81]," printed date 1 Nov. 1875 [written 1880?]; *JAPM*, 28:1642).

3. Germaine de Staël (Anne-Louise-Germaine Necker, 1766–1817), novelist, political activist, and comparative cultural critic, was born in Paris, the daughter of Jacques Necker, the French finance minister under Louis XVI. She grew up within the intellectual influence of her mother Suzanne Curchod's literary salon, developing superb conversational skills and sophisticated philosophical knowledge and political understanding at an early age and emerging as an unconventional woman of genius. She entered into an arranged marriage with the Swedish ambassador to Paris, Baron Eric-Magnus de Staël (d. 1802) in 1786. Rebelling against social constrictions regarding female sexuality, she took many lovers and had two children, Auguste and Albert, with Count Louis de Narbonne. She maintained a salon in her home and during the Jacobin Terror worked diligently to save friends from execution. After falling in love with Benjamin Constant, a fellow supporter of the moderate republican cause, she worked with him from 1795 onward in French opposition politics and produced literary works that are often compared with his. In 1797 she gave birth to their daughter, Albertine, who would become the Duchess of Broglie. In that same year, she and Constant founded the Club Constitutionnel and presented ongoing vocal opposition to military dictatorship and tyranny. De Staël wrote prolifically throughout the late 1790s and into the 1800s. Her *De l'influence des passions sur le bonheur des individus et des nations* (On the influence of the passions on the happiness of individuals and nations) (1796) addressed the issue of revolution and recommended that for the individual, the "only real system for avoiding pain is to direct one's life solely in accordance with what one is able to do for others" (quoted in Szmurlo, "Germaine Necker," 466). She wrote in favor of mercy for Marie Antoinette and urged multinational cultural awareness and tolerance. The publication of her revolutionary novel *Delphine* (1802) led to banishment from Paris. She became the center of a literary salon of comparative cultural historians in Germany in 1803 and in 1805 toured Italy, after which she wrote her best-known novel, *Corrine ou l'Italie* (1807), which contrasted patriarchal militarism and dictatorship with national independence and the liberation of women. Its publication made Napoleon target de Staël as a dangerous threat to his authority, and she traveled from country to country in political exile. She continued her opposition to Napoleon while living in London, where she married another lover, John Rocca, in Oct. 1816. She returned to Paris after Napoleon's downfall and died there after suffering severe illness in July 1817. Her *Considérations sur la révolution française* was published after her death (1818). De Staël argued for recognition of the interdependence between a nation's literature and culture and its sociopolitical institutions, and she believed in the political responsibility of a writer to influence popular thought, especially in the interest of liberty and democracy. Her two novels focused on female characters, *Delphine* and *Corrine*, address patriarchal repression and present the theme that, for women, happiness comes in fulfilling destinies for which they were given ability and talent.

4. George Sand (Amantine-Aurore-Lucile Dupin, baronne Dudevant) (1804–76), outspoken leftist activist and prolific French romantic novelist, playwright, and autobiographical writer, had, like Mme. de Staël, a strong father figure, an unhappy marriage, and a series of lovers as well as a life of political dedication and intense literary output. The daughter of an aristocratic military officer who died when she was four, she was raised primarily by her proletarian mother and by her father's mother. Her grandmother arranged for private tutoring and sent her to convent school, where she was known for both her rebelliousness and her mysticism.

At age eighteen she married Baron Casimir Dudevant. Although somewhat dashing, her husband was not her intellectual equal. His primary interests were hunting, liquor, and the sexual pursuit of other women. The union, which brought young Aurore much pain, soon resulted in separation. She had two children, Maurice and Solange, and embarked upon a series of liaisons, including pivotal affairs with writer Jules Sandeau (who under the name J. Sand wrote *Rose et blanche* [1831] with her) and poet and dramatist Alfred de Musset, as well as long companionships with musician Frédéric Chopin and artist Alexandre Manceau. She was legally separated from her husband in 1836 and supported herself and her children by writing. She was well known for adopting an androgynous persona, complete with masculine hair-styles and clothing, the habit of smoking, and a male pseudonym. The female characters she created defied the stereotypes of feminine weakness.

Sand was an activist in the Revolution of 1848, although disillusion over subsequent political events caused her to withdraw from active political participation—including a refusal to run for political office when encouraged to do so—but she continued to address political issues in her writing. She wrote expansively on issues pertaining to women, including the inferior status of their education and the inequities and often abusiveness of marriage and the professional privileges unjustifiably reserved for men. Her first novels, *Indiana* and *Valentine* (both 1832) and *Lélia* (1833), explored marriage as a repressive institution for women, the problems of friendship across class boundaries, female sexuality, and the Pygmalion motif. In the 1840s she turned to such themes as religion, mystical Christian socialism, political evolution, art, idealism, and utopianism. She also examined the role of women and workers' organizations in creating social change. She is most popularly known for *Jeanne* (1843), a novel based on the life of Joan of Arc, and for other novels of rustic pastoral life. Her *Lettres d'un voyageur* (1837) is an example of travel writing, and *Histoire de ma vie* (1854), her major autobiographical work, includes accounts of her childhood and convent schooling.

Sand wrote more than sixty novels, dozens of plays, short stories, novellas and essays, and some sixteen thousand letters. She was supported by patrons and spiritual advisors and in turn devoted much of her life to aiding others, including the poor of her neighboring countryside and working-class poets to whom she gave financial help and artistic counsel.

5. The first extant manuscript (composed ca. 1877–78) in which JA argues the affirmative in this debate is printed here. It was probably the text delivered on 13 Nov. 1878 as a companion piece to Corrine Williams's negative argument, which remains extant (*JAPM*, 27:197–212). Williams noted that the debate on Sand and de Staël, with "Positive—Jane Addams" and "Negative—Corinne Williams" was "Read at Castalian Public, Nov. 13—1878." She added, wittily, that her rebuttal to JA's affirmative was "Written for Harper's Magazine, but not yet published."

A second version of the affirmative argument in the debate, containing lines that JA re-used in her Junior Exhibition speech of 20 Apr. 1880, was probably the text she presented at a Pierian Union program on 13 Apr. 1880 (see *JAPM*, 45:1808–18, and a fragment of a version 45:1819–23). The *RSM* of Apr. 1880 reported that Prof. J. R. J. Anthony was busy on campus training students in oratory in his elocution classes and that JA's junior class had "wearily wended their way to chapel to receive their fifth elocution lesson," only to be happily greeted by presents left to bolster their spirits by the sympathetic members of the sophomore class (116). In the midst of all this intense elocutionary training the Vesperians gave a program in which JA's friend Mattie Thomas argued the affirmative and RFS language and music student Lizzie White (whose piece was read by Ella Nichol) argued the negative in "Resolved; that the civilization of the nineteenth century tends to fetter intellectual life and expression" (*RSM* [Apr. 1880]: 116). The Pierian Union program of 13 Apr. 1880 focused on "Representative French Women." It featured French songs, speeches on outstanding French women, and the debate between JA and Williams, "Resolved; That the French women have had more influence through literature than politics. Representative Women, George Sand and Mme. De

Staël" (*RSM* [Apr. 1880]: 117–18). The literary society programs were clearly in part practice events leading up to the formal Junior Exhibition, which was open to the public and at which JA gave the Greek oration on Bellerophon (see Introductory Speech at the Junior Exhibition, 20 Apr. 1880, below). She and Williams may possibly have recycled the debate they had given earlier in 1878, either under assignment from Prof. Anthony in the interest of revising and improving their performance or perhaps in the interest of lessening their preparation load in the midst of the busy events of the spring of 1880.

6. There are several places where text has been interlineated in a smaller script. These comments may have been inserted by Caroline Potter, but the author has not been definitively established. The additions in a different hand have not been transcribed, except where noted. (For an autograph version of the text see *JAPM*, 45:1795–807.)

7. Question marks were inserted here and in other instances throughout the manuscript. These were added by another hand, possibly by Caroline Potter, who may have marked the draft in the process of commenting on it for inflection. It is also possible that the quotation marks were placed to indicate pauses or emphasis in the oral delivery of the speech.

8. JA here inserts a close parentheses, but no open parentheses appears in the draft.

9. Thus ends JA's introductory remarks; she left extra space before continuing with her comments on Aurora Dupin (George Sand). By the time she did the second extant version of the debate, her introductory arguments were more sophisticated and focused on the status of women, but she still used the theme of direct versus indirect influence:

> Some one has said that the region of fame is restricted to literature and polotics. If so woman certainly in all ages has had a potent influence. . . . Yet during the last cent. & especially the last fifty years of it, there has been a change in the conditions & ambition of woman not that her influence has been noticeably more powerful but her aspirations have taken a new direction. She has discovered that she posesses an intellect as acute if not as powerful as that of man, by the use of which her influence may be as vigorous in power as her charms are persuasive in society—We see it in her education, it has passed from accomplishments and the arts of pleasing to the developement of her intellectual force & her capabilities for <u>direct labor</u>. She wishes not to be a man or like a man but she claims the same right to independant thought & action.

JA then commenced to argue that the literature of George Sand had been instrumental in beginning "such a revolution in the ideal of womanhood," recycling some of the phrasing she used in the above version of the debate (*JAPM*, 45:1809–11).

10. Divorce had been legal in France up to 1816, when it was abolished and not reinstated until a period of social reform in 1884. Under Napoleonic code during much of the nineteenth century, French wives were basically defined as the property of their husbands, and although legal sanctions against adultery were slight for men (restricted to fines in special circumstances), they were stringent for women and included possible penalties of imprisonment. The inequities in marriage law were among the recurrent themes in Sand's writings.

11. Some of the misspellings in the draft are marked with a slash striking out the incorrect letter. This word appears to be the only one in the draft that JA herself corrected in that manner.

12. Jeanne Roland (1754–93) was an advisor and companion to the Girondists, the moderate republican party of the French Legislative Assembly in the early 1790s. The wife of French economist and politician Jean Marie Roland de la Platiere, she was executed in 1793, decrying upon the scaffold the crimes done in the name of liberty.

13. A line or slash mark is drawn diagonally through the center of the text, beginning at "for they too" and ending at "printed in," which in the manuscript version includes the bottom ten lines on the page (*JAPM*, 45:1801). On the next page, three faint diagonal lines strike through the text. Although they begin most strongly at "woman who wrote them" and

end at "its heavenly," which in the manuscript version is mid-page, they seem to be deleting the entire passage (thirteen lines) from the top of the page, beginning with "black and white." In effect, it is a continuation of the same deletion begun the page before (*JAPM*, 45:1802).

14. A faint diagonal line is drawn through this entire manuscript page, which extends from "Compare then this world wide powerful influence" to "a constitutional monarchy" (*JAPM*, 45:1803).

15. This passage of the text has definitely been marked for deletion. Four parallel diagonal lines are drawn through the text, beginning at "But if we follow Geo Sand" and ending at "and visionary philosophy," which in the manuscript version is the last paragraph on a page. On the next page, "Liszt and Chopin" through "the cowardly brave, seen" has also been marked for deletion (*JAPM*, 45:1804–5).

16. Religious reformer Abbé Félicité de Lamennais, Sand's spiritual advisor.

17. Franz Liszt (1811–86), a Hungarian-born child prodigy, gained great fame as a virtuoso pianist upon coming to Paris in 1823 and was at the center of the postrevolutionary circle of artists, intellectuals, and musicians that framed romanticism in the French capital in the 1820s and 1830s. After the Revolution of 1848, Liszt divided his time between Weimar, Rome, and Budapest, composing and conducting as well as teaching a new generation of accomplished musicians. He befriended Frédéric Chopin (1810–49) upon Chopin's arrival in Paris in 1831 (via Vienna from his native Warsaw) and in 1836 introduced Chopin to George Sand. The musician and the writer began an affair that lasted more than a decade, during which Sand supported and nursed Chopin, who was in poor health when they met. Although Chopin grew increasingly ill, his time with Sand was also the most productive period of his composing career. The couple separated because of tensions between Chopin and Sand's son Maurice, and after the split Chopin ceased composing. He died of tuberculosis in Paris in 1849, leaving behind some 206 published compositions, mostly for solo pianoforte.

18. Philosopher, economist, and social reformer Pierre Leroux (1797–1871) had a strong intellectual impact upon Sand. Her novels were influenced by his religious theories of humanitarian pantheism and socialism, expounded in such works as *De l'égalité* (1838) and *De l'humanité, de son principe et de son avenir* (1840).

19. French novelist Honoré de Balzac (1799–1850), although best known for his composite work *La Comédie humaine* (17 vols., 1842–48), produced almost a hundred novels and stories between 1829 and 1848, a period during which he struggled financially and turned for support to a series of close women friends.

20. Edgar Quinet (1803–95) was a French politician, revolutionary, writer, and poet.

21. Alfred de Musset (1810–57), a French romantic lyrical poet, playwright, and novelist, was passionately attracted to Sand and traveled with her to Italy in 1833–34.

22. This passage, beginning at "In all her books" and going through the end of the paragraph ending with "steady progress," is deleted with four diagonal slashes through the center of the text (*JAPM*, 45:1806).

Draft of Essay

When she described her student years, Jane Addams recalled the desire of Rockford Female Seminary girls to supplement the intellectualizing of reading with more tantalizing experience. Thomas De Quincey's Confessions of an English Opium Eater,[1] *an account of the writer's opium addiction and the hallucinatory dreams that he experienced under the influence of the drug, was among the books that she and her cohorts devoured in their spare time. In her memoirs she claimed,*

At one time five of us tried to understand De Quincey's marvelous "Dreams" more sympathetically, by drugging ourselves with opium. We solemnly consumed small white powders at intervals during an entire long holiday, but no mental reorientation took place, and the suspense and excitement did not even permit us to grow sleepy. About four o'clock on the weird afternoon, the young teacher whom we had been obliged to take into our confidence, grew alarmed over the whole performance, took away our De Quincey and all the remaining powders, administered an emetic to each of the five aspirants for sympathetic understanding of all human experience, and sent us to our separate rooms with a stern command to appear at family worship after supper "whether we were able to or not."[2]

What follows is an essay Jane Addams wrote for a science class that focuses more on opium as a social vice than on the botanical aspects of the poppy plant.

[Rockford, Ill.]   [ca. 1878]

Poppy

"We will almost always find poppies springing up amidst the corn; as if it had been foreseen by nature that wherever there should be hunger that asked for food, there would be pain that needed relief."[3] The golden corn gives life & nourishment & has a positiv[e] influence upon the thought & acts of men; the gaudy flower springing up amongst it ~~has a~~ exerts a negative influence fully as powerful. Nature has been ransacked for narcotics. Something to dull, stupify & soothe the nervous symtem[4] is a predominant human weakness.

Tabacco one of the mildest narcotics is used among 800[,]000[,]0000 of the human race. The consumption of opium is <likewise> enormous, <but> the number of opium eaters cannot be computed because of the facility with which they conceal their vice, but the supposition is almost an established fact, that the drug is more largely used as a narcotic than is generally ~~supposed~~ <believed>.[5] Opium is a favorite stimulant with many underfed & over-worked artisans & laborers, it takes the place of food & is used from the same principle that much alcoholic drink is consumed. In some parts of the East it is administered as a restorative even to hor<s>es, and the messengers & palanquin bearers of India, under the support of opium, journey almost incredible distances, for by checking the natural waste of the nervous energy, it enables the system to support fatigue, beneath which it otherwise must inevitably sink. Measures of a severe nature have been ~~made~~ <taken> in China to check the use of opium & have been utterly unsuccessful. However meek the Chinese is in most things he will not submit to the withdrawal of his favorite drug.[6]

The use is universal & it may reasonably be called a national vice, out of forty five inmates of an insane asylum thirty five are addicted to opium.[7]

The confirmed eater of the East seldom lives beyond the age of forty, his muscles become contracted & deformed, his enjoyment gradually deminishes as his system becomes habituated to the drug. From time to time he must increase the quantity which he takes but at length no amount will produce any effect. When the victim must bear his miserable condition & gradually die.

It is difficult to comprehend the probable result of the habit of opium eating upon the Oriental races. Or what would have been their physical & mental characteristics if they had not consumed such quan[ti]ties of this drug.[8] It is certain that it would have been widely different from what it is now, whether for the better or worse it is hard to tell.

Thus we see what a powerful influence the poppy order Papaveraceae, <genus> species Papaver, species somniferium,[9] has had upon the civilization of the world.[10]

AMsS (UIC, JAMC, Detzer; *JAPM*, 45:1691–96).

1. English author, essayist, and magazine writer Thomas De Quincey (1785–1859), who was a neighbor of William Wordsworth and Samuel Taylor Coleridge and part of the social circle of the Lake District school of British writers, began taking opium in 1804 to relieve neuralgia and the pain of a chronic gastric disorder. By 1813 his opium addiction had led him to a daily intake of more than eight thousand drops, a severe dosage. It was more than six years before he gained some control over his dependence on the drug. He published parts of *Confessions of an English Opium Eater* anonymously in the *London Magazine* in Sept. and Oct. 1821 and brought the work out in its entirety in 1822, with a revised and greatly expanded edition in 1856. The book was written in the first person and has three parts: the first focuses on De Quincey as an unhappy schoolboy and as a runaway in London; the second part, "The Pleasures of Opium," describes his first encounters with the drug; and the last, "The Pains of Opium," includes vivid accounts of his extraordinary nightmares and their moral, spiritual, and physical horrors. In her memoirs, JA described remembering a scene from De Quincey's "The Vision of Sudden Death" and the pivotal influence that memory had on her one day in 1883 when she traveled into the slums of East London on an omnibus. The moral lesson of the story—of intellectualizing versus dealing with the immediacies of life and death—was brought home to her in a very real way (*Twenty Years*, 70).

2. *Twenty Years*, 46. Some Addams biographers feel the account of experimental opium use by JA and her friends is apocryphal. It is not known which teacher intervened in the experiment, although it likely was Sarah Anderson, who was of the younger generation of teachers on the faculty and was a friend to JA, EGS, and many of the students.

3. JA reused this wording in *Twenty Years*, when she explained the motto that her class adopted in their junior year: "We took for a class motto the early Saxon word for lady, translated into breadgiver, and we took for our class color the poppy, because poppies grew among the wheat, as if Nature knew that wherever there was hunger that needed food there would be pain that needed relief" (48).

4. JA apparently meant to write the word *system*.

5. JA is correct: Statistics on opium use are difficult to reconstruct because addicts tended not to publicize their condition. According to surveys of physicians and pharmacists, military medical examinations, and opiate import statistics, the rate of opium addiction in the United States increased steadily from the 1870s through the 1890s, with an estimated 4.59 users per thousand users in the 1890s. Chicago pharmacists reported an average number of almost five addicts per drugstore in 1880 (about two per thousand in the population), whereas the rate in Iowa towns in 1885 was just under two (or fewer than one per thousand in the population). Government estimates of the problem of addiction were much higher than those reported by drugstores.

During the nineteenth century, the typical American opiate addict was a "middle-aged white woman of the middle or upper class" who was "addicted to morphine" or opium use

(Courtwright, *Dark Paradise*, 1). By the turn of the century, opiate use shifted dramatically to lower-class urban males. Part of the change was because of the legal status of the drug; opiate addiction was frowned upon socially but not legally prohibited in the 1800s. That changed with the enactment of the Smoking Opium Exclusion Act of 1909 and the Harrison Narcotic Act of 1914, which limited legal access to opiates and required physicians and pharmacists to register the fact that they dispensed narcotics, which in effect criminalized opium use and shifted procurement to the black market. Historian David Courtwright argues that opium use actually peaked in the 1890s before these legal strictures were put in place; he attributes the changes not to the laws but to the nature of medical practice. He also posits that some, if not a great deal, of the supposedly nervous disorders attributed to women in the period were actually the result of iatrogenic use of opium and morphine for a wide range of ailments, including such common chronic conditions as headache, stress, dysmenorrhea, asthma, and bronchitis. The widespread introduction of hypodermic injection during the Civil War increased the general administration of opium and morphine by doctors to patients (and the possibilities for more efficient self-administration). During the period that JA and her cohorts were fascinated with the drug, physicians were dispensing it liberally. Most addictions stemmed from use that had begun under medical care and among those members of society who had access to such care, which meant fewer African American and European immigrant addicts. Indeed, some upper-class use of physician services may have centered on client demand for opiates. At the same time that middle-class white women were imbibing the drug under their physicians' recommendations, nonmedical drug use was occurring among Chinese immigrants (most of them young and male) who smoked opium and among white prostitutes in urban areas. The drug was also associated with the white underworld. Underworld opium use was supplanted by heroin after the turn of the century. Medical use of opiates declined at the end of the 1890s, in part due to the introduction of aspirin as an alternative pain reliever in 1899.

6. JA is again correct in observing that, especially in temperance times, opiate use was a substitute for alcohol, particularly among women, because of the strong stigma against middle- and upper-class women drinking. To the extent that "women stranded in rural areas" or "of high social station" sought "some euphoric agent," opiates were the source of choice (Courtwright, *Dark Paradise*, 60).

7. Opium use was introduced into China by traders from Arabia in approximately 700 A.D. It was originally smoked in combination with tobacco, but by the eighteenth century it was typically smoked alone, mainly by the upper class. By the nineteenth century, its use had spread to the poor, including laborers and soldiers, in part because of the increase in opium traffic. The British had developed a lucrative trade in exporting opium from India to China. Domestic cultivation of poppies in China was common by the 1870s, and estimates of opiate use among the Chinese population varied from about "1 out of 166 to 9 out of 10" (Courtwright, *Dark Paradise*, 67).

8. This association of opiate use and psychopathology became more prominent in medical literature and popular perception as the nineteenth century progressed, perhaps in a confusion of cause and effect in cases of delirium.

9. The word *somniferum* means "sleep-inducing."

10. When she graded this paper, Mary E. Holmes praised the social analysis that JA offered in regard to the poppy but let her student know that she had expected something both more botanical and scientifically pragmatic. She marked a few of the misspellings in the text and at the end of the essay wrote: "I intended your essay to be all of this which is very good, and more, pertaining to the distinguishing characteristics of the poppy as regards petals, sepals, stamens & etc. Also the manner of obtaining the opium. M.E.H." (UIC, JAMC, Detzer; *JAPM*, 45:1695). JA later referred to the juxtaposition of cornfield and poppy in her chapter on Tolstoyism in *Twenty Years* (274–75).

Announcements in the
Rockford Seminary Magazine

These short notices in the Rockford Seminary Magazine *describe some of the extracurricular activities of Rockford Female Seminary girls, including the Scientific Association and literary society in which Jane Addams had ongoing leadership roles.*

[Rockford, Ill.]   MARCH 1879

The Scientific Association organized last year has accomplished a considerable amount of work for its age.[1] It has secured quite a valuable collection, consisting of birds, minerals, charts and books of geological survey, &c. At its last meeting it elected the following officers: President, Miss Holmes;[2] Vice-President, Jane Addams; Secretary, Hattie Smith; Treasurer, Mattie Thomas; Curator, Addie Stevens.

At a later meeting of the Castalians elected for the half-year: for President, Corinne Williams; Vice-President, Eva Campbell; Secretary and Treasurer, Lizzie Smith.[3] In order to utilize all the working talent in the society Jane Addams and Kate Hitchcock were chosen as chairmen of two committees, each to consist of half the members of the society. One committee is to furnish the program of one society meeting and the other for the next.

PD (*RSM* [March 1879]: 66).

1. The new Scientific Assn. thrived at RFS. It was reported in the Apr. 1879 *RSM* that the "Scientific Association has lately purchased a collection of native birds, forty-five in num-

Sara Elizabeth ("Lizzie") Smith of De Pere, Wis., graduated with Jane Addams in the class of 1881. (De Pere Historical Society/White Pillars Museum)

ber, among which are a goodly number of waders; we would particularly mention a fine white heron, the special pet of enthusiastic scientists. . . . At the last meeting of the Scientific Association, the origin and growth of prairies was discussed with lively interest, especially by the Iowa members. The resolution passed at a previous meeting, to speak entirely without notes, was carried out with good effect" (97, 98). In May, the Scientific Assn. acknowledged receipt of a "gift of six volumes, finely illustrated, 'The Geological Survey of the State of Indiana,' from His Excellency Governor [James D.] Williams" (*RSM* [May 1879]: 127). The Scientific Assn. continued to grow in membership in 1879–80, and its cabinet displays were augmented when more than one hundred flora specimens were donated to the group by 1876 RFS graduate Florence Hyde Popenoe in the fall of 1879 (*RSM* [July 1879]: 201; [Dec. 1879]: 276).

2. In the fall of 1879, teacher Mary E. Holmes stepped down as president of the group and was replaced by student Corrine Williams. By the fall of 1880, the Scientific Assn., "whose ambition it formerly was to increase the cabinet & sustain scientific interests in the community," had evolved into a more insular campus club, the "sole object of its members being self improvement." Members met every morning at 8 to exchange notes, using the *Popular Science Monthly* as their text to become, as JA wrote anonymously in the student magazine, "well-informed on the latest scientific investigations" [Dec. 1880]: 266; see also JA's handwritten draft in "Pocket Diary, 1875[–81]," printed date 12 Nov. 1875 [written 1880?]; *JAPM*, 28:1648). *Popular Science Monthly,* initiated by E. L. Youmans (1821–87) in 1872, was part of the wider self-education movement begun specifically, as historian Joseph Kett has put it, "to spread the materialistic doctrines of Spencer and Darwin" and, as Youmans put it, to enable members of the general population who had received some higher education "to carry on the work of self-instruction in science" (Kett, *Pursuit of Knowledge,* 178, Youmans quoted on 149). JA and her RFS friends were tapping into this popularization of study while still part of an educational institution in order to supplement what was missing from the seminary curriculum and to mirror the kind of community-based study society that was becoming common among older middle class women of their era.

3. When Sara Elizabeth ("Lizzie") Smith (1861–1939) graduated from RFS in 1881, it was reported that "her trials have been many, but the trials of her teachers have been more" (*RSM* [July 1881]: 199–200). Lizzie Smith was the younger sister of Addie B. Smith (Wells) (1859–1935). The Smith girls were from a well-to-do family of De Pere, Wis. They were the daughters of Benjamin F. Smith (1836–1914) and Annie M. Jordan Smith (1833–1912). Although later migrants to the Midwest, in many ways the Smiths were the equivalents in the De Pere–Green Bay communities to the Addamses in Cedarville and Freeport. Annie M. Jordan was born and raised in Maine, where she was educated at Gorham Seminary in Gorham. She moved to De Pere with her parents in 1851. Benjamin F. Smith immigrated to Wisconsin from Ontario, Canada, with his father in the same year and became involved in the lumber mill business. The two were married in 1857, and after the marriage Benjamin F. Smith entered into a partnership in the mercantile business with his father-in-law, Dominicus Jordan. He became one of the civic leaders of De Pere, operating the town's general store and other enterprises. In 1895 he helped organize the National Bank of De Pere and served as one of its directors until his death. He also was a founder and major shareholder in the Union Building Loan and Savings Assn. of Green Bay and De Pere, the Pochequette Oil Co., the National Iron Co., and the Green Bay Water Co. A lifelong Republican, he was involved in regional politics, serving as a member of the De Pere City Council and the Brown Co. Board of Supervisors. The Smiths were both active members of the De Pere First Presbyterian Church, and Annie M. Jordan Smith was a charter member of the DAR. In addition to their two daughters, the Smiths had one son, Horace J. Smith. The Smith children all received their primary education in the De Pere public schools, which their parents supported. Annie M. Jordan Smith took a keen interest in her daughters' careers at RFS, and she was one of the parents who donated items for use by the RFS Scientific Assn.

Both of the Smith girls were artistic, and both studied at RFS to better pursue ladylike lives of well-to-do domesticity and civic contribution. Addie began her studies at RFS in Sept. 1876. She was a special student in modern languages, drawing, painting, and music. She also excelled at the piano and was among the small group of RFS girls that Daniel Hood involved in the community musical society. In 1878–79, Addie was courted by letter by a good friend from De Pere, Allison G. Wells (1855–1921), a young man who was close to all her family members. She married him in De Pere on 8 Sept. 1880, and he entered into business partnerships with her father, over time developing interests in grain, elevator, and milling operations. He also operated A. G. Wells Co., a mercantile company that had a dock that supplied commerce on the Fox River. The birth of their first child, Hugo S. Wells (1883–1957), on 10 Jan. 1883 in De Pere was reported in the March 1883 edition of the *RSM*. Hugo and his brother Leland A. Wells (1892–1963) carried on the family businesses after their father's retirement. Addie B. Smith Wells presided over a large, architect-designed, Tudor manor–style house built in 1909 on Broadway St. in De Pere. The home was known for its beautiful gardens.

After attending high school in De Pere, Lizzie Smith joined the class of 1881 at RFS. Possessed of a great joy of life, Lizzie wrote home of crowding friends into dormitory rooms (raising Miss Sill's ire because of the noise), organizing illicit candy making or shopping excursions, and being entertained by the girls across the hall who made fangs out of orange rinds at Halloween. She was also of a self-confessed aesthetic sensibility, drawing floor plans of her room and of Castalian socials for her mother; serving on committees in charge of decorating the chapel or the class parlor for important social events; and describing in detail the latest turn of fashions in hats, dresses, and hair styles. She also wrote home about her interest in boys.

Although Lizzie Smith and JA were involved in the same Castalian Society functions, and Smith served as vice president of their sophomore class, the two were not close personal friends. Indeed, they ran with opposite crowds at RFS. "Lizzie seems to enjoy going with the more lively girls a good deal and I want her to do so just as much as she likes to for she has to be good and sober enough of the time without going with sober girls out of school hours besides," her sister wrote to their mother. JA was clearly one of the "sober" crowd, one of a circle with Mattie Thomas, whom Addie named as being among those "too prosy to interest Lizzie" and too busy studying "a great deal out of school hours" (Addie B. Smith to Annie M. Jordan Smith, 3 Mar. [1878], SHSW, Smith). JA's and Lizzie's separate social cliques had been set by their sophomore year. Indeed, during their senior year Lizzie wrote to her sister that her friends were exchanging bangle bracelets with "Clique of '78" "inscribed on the band" (Sara Elizabeth Smith to Addie B. Smith, 13 Oct. 1880, SHSW, Smith). In describing the patterns of friendship at RFS to her mother, Lizzie wrote, "Our old set is now narrowed down to six, three couples and we are looking forward to the reunion [of the full clique of 1878] at commencement." She then named the way the girls had long ago "paired off," JA not included in the reckoning (7 Nov. 1880, SHSW, Smith). Lizzie was a good friend of JA's roommate, Addie M. Smith, however, and studied vocal music with her (she named Smith as part of the circle of six, in a couple with Hattie Wells).

JA's friend Helen Harrington later remembered that "Lizzie Smith, who touched life lightly on the social side, was among the first, if not the first, woman librarian in the free Public Library of her home town in Wisconsin" (Alderson, "Memoirs," 34). Lizzie had written to her mother that she was not sure how she would occupy her time when she came home, except perhaps to pursue china painting more seriously. "I am convinced that I won't know what to do with myself after I get through here," she wrote on 20 Nov. 1880 (SHSW, Smith).

When the RFS class of 1881 neared graduation, they engaged in a spoof wherein classmate-soothsayers predicted the future for each (see Excerpt from Article in the *RSM*, [18 June] 1881, below). The soothsayers predicted that "Lizzie Smith will early change her life of gaiety and youthful folly for one of self-sacrifice and solemn purpose" (*RSM* [July 1881]: 200). They turned out to be more accurate than they could have guessed. Lizzie returned to De Pere after graduation, where she cared for her mother. As she explained years later, "On returning to my pleasant, New England–like home surroundings, where woman's place was thought to be in the home, or the schoolroom, I became the companion of an invalid mother, for whom I did the marketing and other errands" (Sara Elizabeth Smith to Maxine Ferguson, 22 Feb. 1931, RC).

Despite her keen interest in meeting boys in Rockford, Smith never married. Her destiny turned much more bookish than her career at RFS seemed to have promised. She became a genealogist and amateur historian, helped run a volunteer subscription library service, and attended library school courses at the Univ. of Wisconsin. She helped organize the De Pere Public Library and served as a member of its board of directors and in the Brown Co. library system for more than thirty years. She was also active in the Wisconsin State Woman's Club and served as a president of the local De Pere Woman's Club branch. Like her mother and sister, she was involved in the local chapter of the DAR. During World War I, she worked as a filing clerk for the Brown Co. War Office in Green Bay.

When she died following a stroke in Aug. 1939, the hometown newspaper referred directly to the best-known members of the "sober" crowd at RFS, JA and Kittie Waugh McCulloch (sometimes spelled "McCullough"). Her obituary's headline read, "Miss Sarah Smith . . . Outstanding in Community Life; Was Former Classmate of Famous Women."

Draft of Debate Argument

Rockford, Ill.   [ca. April 1879?][1]

Resolved; that the invention & use of machinery is a hinderance to the increase of wealth in a country.

It is said that one half of the world do not know how the other half live, but Horace Greeley[2] solved the mystery for he discove[r]ed that they lived off of the other half. Horace Greeley was a philosopher, he knew that men must live, and if one half of the people posess the wealth of a country the other half by all sorts of ways & means, foul and fair will manage to live off of them.[3]

Every human being is worth on an average $6000[,] that is every child that is born into the world brings with him that sum of money.[4] If he is not in a position to use his faculties or if he trains his hands & brain in a wrong direction throwing himself into a market which is already overcrowded, then he is a loss to the world of $6000, he saps just that much capital and vitality from the half "other half" by making them support him.

But if a man can earn one dollar <beyond his living> then he becomes <to that extent> a capitalist, he has created wealth & is entitled to it, for he has added to the surplus of the nation. And if he earns enough capital so that he can depend upon it for his living, so that he can use his hands[,] strength and brain for himself without waiting for his neighbor to pay him wages for them, <then> he is indepenant and has a new incentive to labor, he has bought his own time and can afford to spend a day reading a book or building a schoolhouse[.] "Although at evening he can neither clothe nor feed himself with either";[5] he has grown beyond the point where he must scramble[6] every minute in order to ma[i]ntain his physical existence and has reached a higher plane.

Fred Douglas[7] in a 4th of July oration to the negroes a few years <ago> told them that the next ten years would decide thier fate, if in that time they did n't earn some surplus money and posess capital they could never rise from thier degraded position, that what they wanted to do now was not to direct thier energies to getting an education, getting religion &c but to getting rich, that wealth alone would make them respected & give them an equal footing with thier equals. That ever working for wages was for them almost as degrading as slavery & that in order to be independant and valuable citizens they must have money, & that was thier first step to progress.

It is evident then that the wealth of a nation depends on the individual wealth of its average citizen, & its prosperity is the condition of its common people; in order to be a self-dependant power it must preserve a bold peasantry, its native strength, and keep its money in the hands of as many people as possible, the mass of people must hold the wealth or it is not secure, held in the hands of a few capitalists it may be swept away by every wind of trade, "combrous wealth" & accumulated capital produce but a sickly greatness & hasten to decay for they distroy men & tend to make the laboring classes servile. A nation may posess broad lands & rich resources & yet be poor, until its citizens have converted them into wealth, until every rood[8] of ground is utilized & every material substance has a fixed value & personifies a certain amount of labor, of muscle or brain.

There is no principle of political economy more firmly established than that vice in the social state is the sym[p]tom & incident of idleness, & ~~the~~ <we> find that the sphere of vice is at the top & bottom of society, these being the regions in which idleness reigns. It is then the first duty of a nation to give its people something to do, to keep them busy & virtuous. To secure them the enjoyment of what they produce & save, & to encourage every man to become free & independant, to encourage his ingenuity & desire for property & thus increase the wealth of the country. And this is just what the invention & use of machinery does not do. Every new invention draws away capital from the smaller industeries & concentrates it in a few great buildings filled ~~in~~ with costly machinery. The laboring classes must leave thier petty trades, thier multitude of smaller industries in which they were enterprising, intelligent & independent and rush to the large manufacturing towns, run the noisy machinery day by day which requires but little skill or thought & thier condition gradually makes them dependant & ignorant, meanwhile the wealth of the community is concentrated in a few hands & is not secure, it is subject to panics & losses & the nation m[a]y lose it at any time. In New England after the invention of the imporved loom & the great increase in the production of woolen goods, the great mass of the population would not submit to the drugery of the factory operative & came west. Thier places ~~was~~[9] filled by foreigners, of a low grade of intelligence to whom the work was fitted & the character of the county gradually deteriorated vice & ignorance increased. But after [a]while wool production was superseded by a new demand & consequently invention. The old machinery is out of date, it stands idle the loss of that much capital[.][10] The poor operatives, foreigners though they be, are only skilled in that one thing; they are turned adrift and tramp.[11] Alas! drudges must be men & women more's the pity. We do not doubt that machinery increases the civilization & advancement of a county, but we assert that it is a hindrance to the increase of wealth & prosperity.[12]

AMsS (UIC, JAMC, Detzer; *JAPM*, 45:1644–52).

    1. See also M.G.N. (Maria G. Nutting), "Machinery and Wealth," *RSM* (Apr. 1879): 88–90, a printed essay on "Resolved, that the invention and use of machinery have aided in the increase of wealth," representing the counter-argument to that which JA argues here.

    2. Horace Greeley (1811–72), journalist and reformer, founded the low-priced *New York Tribune* as a quality newspaper for working people in 1841 and published it for more than thirty years. He used his position as a leading journalist and a radical Republican Party activist to champion antislavery, pacifism, social reform, and labor causes. Throughout his career he was a consistent voice for the impoverished and landless. Greeley is perhaps best known for his advice to workers who had few prospects in the urban East: "Go West, young man." The phrase "How the Other Half Lives" was later used by a another prominent journalist and reformer, Jacob Riis (1849–1914), as the title of his 1890 muckraking book on the slums of American cities.

    3. Another hand, undoubtably that of Caroline Potter, set off the two instances of "off of" in this paragraph with parentheses and marked them with a question mark.

    4. At the end of the essay, Potter wrote, "Name your authority for estimating the worth of every person at $6000" (*JAPM*, 45:1652).

    5. Here and elsewhere quotation marks were added by another hand.

    6. Potter marked the word *scramble* with parentheses and commented "no," apparently discouraging that word choice.

    7. Frederick Douglass (1817–95), abolitionist and orator, is best known for his autobiography about his emergence from slavery, *Narrative of the Life of Frederick Douglass* (1845), which has been reprinted in many editions and languages. His was a pivotal voice in abolitionism, and he was an informal advisor to the Lincoln White House. In the years after the Civil War Douglass was one the nation's most prominent public spokespersons for racial and social justice causes. Between the end of the war and JA's second year at RFS, he gave some 550 public speeches, appearing on lyceum circuits and before audiences along the eastern seaboard. Although he spoke on a wide variety of topics, many of his speeches focused on the issues of securing economic independence and political rights for African Americans. In 1870 Douglass moved from Rochester, N.Y., where he had established the antislavery newspaper *North Star* in 1847, to Washington, D.C., in order to edit the weekly *New National Era,* which he ran until 1874. He held a series of political positions in Washington during the Grant and Hayes administrations and served on the U.S. commission to Santo Domingo (now the Dominican Republic) in the early 1870s.

    JA is possibly referring here to Douglass's 5 July 1875 oration delivered at Independence Day festivities in Washington, D.C. The speech, "The Color Question," was reported in the *Washington National Republican* on 8 July 1875 and in the *New York Times* on 7 July 1875. It is reprinted in *The Frederick Douglass Papers,* ed. Blassingame, McKivigan et al., ser. 1, 4:414–22. "As a people we have gained much during the last ten years," Douglass observed to black Washingtonians. "But the fact is . . . our progress and present position are due to causes almost wholly outside of our own will and our own exertions" (416). He encouraged black people to seize greater control over their own destinies and to abandon habits of subservience born of slavery. He noted that white political support and black gains in political office were waning and urged African Americans to develop with "their own independent and earnest efforts" their own leaders, newspapers, and sources of income (420). Douglass had recently made a brief foray into banking, serving as president of the beleaguered Freedman's Savings and Trust Co. for five months until its demise in July 1874. He testified before the U.S. Senate about his role in the Freedman's Bank in Feb. 1880. Douglass's more famous Independence Day address, "What to the Slave is the Fourth of July?" was delivered at a meeting of the Rochester Ladies' Anti-Slavery Society at the Corinthian Hall in Rochester, N.Y., more than two decades earlier, on 5 July 1852, and later published by Douglass in pamphlet form as well as reprinted in the *New York Herald* on 12 Aug. 1852 and *The Liberator* on 20 Aug. 1852 (see Douglass, *Frederick Douglass Papers,* ser. 1, 2:359–88).

8. A rood is a unit of land that, in the British system, equals a quarter of an acre.

9. Potter corrected this by writing in "were" above.

10. JA is referring here to the shift from native-born labor, mainly of young, single, workers drawn from the rural countryside, to immigrant labor and family systems in New England textile mills, specifically the woolen mills of Lowell. When William Crompton (1806–91) successfully introduced the use of a loom for the manufacture of figured woolens in 1840, workers whose skills stemmed from the era of hand weaving were effectively displaced, and production speeded. The shift from water to steam power in the late 1840s also spurred the industry, more than doubling the number of productive cotton mills and increasing the demand for low-paid labor.

11. For an earlier essay on related themes of poverty, social class, and labor in which JA addresses the issue of unemployed transients, see "Tramps," *JAPM,* 45:1757–62.

12. JA received a grade of "very good" for this essay (*JAPM,* 45:1652). On its last page, and under her signature, she jotted a note: "1810 & 1811 the destruction of the property in England Luddites." It was a reference to the early-nineteenth-century English workers who deliberately destroyed new labor-saving machinery to protest against the diminishment of skilled work and labor rights that the introduction of the machinery represented. Below the comment on the Luddites, Potter added a note about the life of Cicero (*JAPM,* 45:1652).

From Eva Campbell

Battle Creek, Ida Co., Iowa,   June 18, 1879.

Dear Jane;

How strange that you should have neglected me in <u>this wise</u>. I was growing desperate. I imagined all sorts of things; for I could not think everything was going along smoothly or I should hear either from <u>Jane</u> or Adda Smith.[1] In that <u>line</u> you sent me you said there was trouble at the Seminary;[2] and that you would write full particulars in your next, which would soon be forthcoming. I have waited and waited until my patience is nearly exhausted. Your letter came yesterday. I read it; but it did not satisfy me. It only made me homesick to see you. A letter is a poor excuse after the privilege we have had. I believe <u>now</u> that we did talk considerably; for it seems as though I am just a query box because I want you should tell me so much. I received a letter from Miss Starr since I came to

Iowa. She said she supposed I had heard that Emma Merrill[3] and Ada Stevens[4] were suspended, sent home. Where do you girls expect I am going to get my news if you are all supposition? You, Jane, should keep me posted. Your first duty after the welfare of the home friends is <to> your old chum.

Miss Potter to Europe![5] Miss Clapp to China![6] Adda returned home on account of sickness! Emma and Ada Stevens sent home! and what next? Give me particulars in regard to Em & Ada. Beloved, who cared for you when you were sick? I wish I might have been present to have ministered to your temporal wants. Do you like toast, eggs, and jelly when you are sick?

"The first part of the epistle sounds" all right. It is just like Jane only not half enough of her. How is Shakespeare, Scott, and all the rest?

Did you read Merchant of Venice,[7] and Last Days of Pompeii?[8] If so, did you have questions upon them? Are you as well satisfied with your Modern as Ancient history?[9] I have read Kenilworthy,—intensely interesting, The Bride of Lamiermoor, and I am now reading Legend of Montrose.[10] I finished Merchant of Venice this week; but I am going to review it. If you have the questions on it please send them to me. I think Portia is the most wonderful female character I have found in my reading of Shakespeare. Portia's brilliant character sets off the shadowy power of Shylock. Can you imagine the humility of the Jew? "Tarry, Jew; The law hath yet another hold on you." Shylock must have thought himself in the presence of a supernatural being. Could not the learned doctor see the end from the beginning? I don't consider Jessica a very common character. I think Nerissa mimics her mistress so admirably well that we can but call her a character worthy our notice. She and Gratiano are as well matched as Portia and Bassamio. Shylock stands immovable, fixed. "Vengence is mine, I will repay" saith the Jew. Portia comes like a messenger sent from heaven to rescue the poor Merchant of Venice. You need never apologize for the disconnected sentences after you read the preceeding.

Please send me the programmes for Conservatory concert, and Commencement exercises.[11] Do you have public examinations?[12] Has Miss Black gone home, and if so <or not so,> how are her hands.[13]

Did I tell you that I have access to a public library? O, Jane, I have all the liberties here that anyone could ask for. I am resting. I have not practiced much as the piano is badly out of tune. I hope to have it repaired before many more weeks. I read, study, write letters, do work on that sofa pillow, and ride. I go out riding real often. I went to a picnic a couple of weeks ago. I had a real nice time for me. I usually enjoy such gathering about as well as my room-mate. I have met qu<i>te a number of people. I find some of them very nice; but I don't care to waste much of my sweetness on these western prairies.[14] My time is too precious to spend it talking with people just to keep up a conversation. I brought my French books. I made a great mistake when I left my Latin books at home. Have you returned those books to Miss Sill? I hear from my Mother[15] twice a week. She is real well. My cousin[16] has a class in painting at Evansville, Wisconsin.

You ask if I am going to return to the Seminary next fall. I cannot now answer you, but think it doubtful.[17] I am just as unsettled as ever, but I calculate to remain here until matters <u>are</u> settled. Mother wrote in her last letter that she and father were going east in October. She wants me to accompany them. I don't think I shall go. I must graduate in my music, study Modern history with Miss Potter, if she returns to the Seminary, and be able to read French more fluently before I leave school entirely. Don't take another room mate until you hear that I cannot return.[18] So you are surely going back there next fall. Has Kate decided to stay and graduate?[19] What was the trouble with the Senior class that they failed on class day?[20] Is Miss Benedict back to graduate with her class?[21]

If it is going to make it very inconvenient or unpleasant for you to not know definitely in regard to my returning next fall, you may act regardless of me, for I don't much think I shall return to Ill. until after school opens. You shall hear from me, however, during the summer. How I should enjoy reading with you this vacation; but I must be content where I am.

Do write again before you leave the sem. "Fair thoughts and happy hours attend on you!" Your <u>friend</u>,

Eva Campbell.

I shall not weary you with long stories this evening; but come and see "<u>us</u>" and we will talk, read Shakespeare, ride, and have a good time in general. I think it will be "awful nice" to receive Jane and Miss Starr at my own home.

Hoping to hear from you soon, and that you are soon to visit me, I subscribe myself once more, Your sincere friend,

Eva Campbell.

ALS (SCPC, JAC; *JAPM*, 1:351–57).

1. A reference to Addie M. Smith, who sometimes went by "Ada" or "Adda."

2. This reference to "trouble at the Seminary" is cryptic, but apparently it had to do with a rebellion of sorts among the students over the sequestered nature of campus life. The July 1879 *RSM* contained an unsigned editorial stating that RFS girls should be allowed to branch out more and have the means to establish better social connections within the town. "Our chief complaint here has ever been that our life in Rockford has been rather isolated and unsocial," the editorial stated, "that the Rockford people have been strangers to us and that we have not had the privilege of receiving that culture derived from mingling in their society" (204). The editorial recommended that rules be obeyed but that occasional public receptions should be held at the school, that Pierian Union meetings should be made public, and that some rooms should be reserved for "open society." Although the editorial appealed to the need to acquire greater and more ladylike daintiness in order to justify greater social intercourse between the town and campus, the statement was in fact quite a rebellion against Anna P. Sill's strict rules that kept girls protected by constant chaperoning and relative isolation.

3. Emma Francesca Merrill, sister of Addie F. Merrill, was a member of the junior class in 1878–79. Despite her apparent suspension, which was not reported in any formal way in RFS publications, she was present at RFS to see her sister graduate in June 1879, and she graduated with the class of 1880. Emma Merrill, from De Witt, Iowa, seems an unlikely candidate for suspension. She entered a convent at the age of eleven but changed her mind and came

to study at RFS. Described as studious and humble during her time at Rockford, she lived with her parents in De Witt after graduation.

4. Ada ("Addie") Maria Stevens of Toledo, Iowa, was a student in the modern languages program at RFS in 1877–78. She left for the last ten weeks of the school year in the spring of 1878 but returned in 1878–79 and was active in extracurricular activities in spring of 1879. She was a member of the class of 1880 but did not return to RFS for the 1879–80 school year.

5. Caroline Potter, who traveled to Europe in the summer of 1879, held a reception at her home in Rockford for RFS girls before she left on her travels. When she returned, she applied knowledge she had gained on the trip in the classroom, giving a series of popular lectures on the lives and homes of English writers and analyses of aspects of English literature.

6. Sarah (or Sara) B. Clapp (Goodrich) (d. 1923), was from Wauwatosa, Wis., on the outskirts of Milwaukee. She was the daughter of the Rev. L. Clapp and a member of the RFS class of 1877 and, as a senior, president of the Society of Mission Inquiry. After graduation, she taught at RFS for two years (in 1877–78 and 1878–79) and in the fall of 1878 attended the American Board of Foreign Missions meeting in Milwaukee with Anna P. Sill. The details of her planned departure from RFS to become a missionary were reported in the *RSM* in May 1879:

> Miss Sara B. Clapp, who has taught in this Seminary since her graduation in 1876 [1877], has resigned her position and accepted an appointment as missionary to China, where she will be associated with Miss Diamond, in her work in Kalgan, a city which is five days' journey though only one hundred and forty miles from Pekin. She expects to leave her home in August, and to sail from San Francisco September 1st. She will be accompanied by Dr. Henry Porter and wife. The beautiful sunshine of her life has been the health and brightness of many lives, and sad hearts will mourn her departure. The eloquence of this act of devotion will touch many souls which do not respond to eloquent words. May the cross she has taken be no burden, but a support to her. May the comfort she carries to others enter her own soul, and may the peace which passeth all understanding abide with her. (131)

Clapp sent Anna P. Sill a postcard from China, telling her that she had successfully arrived and was soon to go to her station. She sent an account of her travels, "A Short Trip into Mongolia," for publication in the *RSM* ([Nov. 1880]: 229–34) and signed it "Sara B. Clapp-Goodrich, Kalgan, China." On page 247 of the same issue students were greeted with an announcement of the marriage of Sara B. Clapp to the Rev. Goodrich in Peking, China. Chauncey Goodrich, D.D., a translator of the Bible and composer of hymns, was dean of the Theological College in Fungchou, four miles outside Peking. The couple had four children and remained in China through the siege of Peking in 1900, becoming associated with the Medical, Theological, and Woman's College founded after the destruction. Sara B. Clapp Goodrich was a leader in the movement against the tradition of footbinding for Chinese women. She traveled frequently, including trips home to visit Wisconsin and Illinois as well as to Europe and the Mideast.

7. Shakespeare's *The Merchant of Venice* was written ca. 1596. Portia's plea for mercy from Shylock and shrewd legal response to his refusal during the trial scene is considered one of the most forceful passages that Shakespeare wrote for women.

8. *The Last Days of Pompeii* (1834), a novel by the prolific English writer Edward Bulwer Lytton (1803–73), the first Baron Lytton, is a love story set just before and during the destruction of the city.

9. JA took Bible history for her history and literature requirement in her first year (1877–78), ancient history in the first semester of her second year (1878–79), and modern history in the spring semester. Her enrollment in history courses was completed with another semester of modern history in the second semester of the 1879–80 school year.

10. *Kenilworth* (1821), *The Bride of Lammermoor* (1819), and *Legend of Montrose* (1819) are all novels by Sir Walter Scott. The last two titles made up the third part of the "Tales of My Landlord" series.

11. The annual Conservatory of Music concert was held by RFS at the Second Congregational Church on Monday evening of commencement week. Addie F. Merrill, Addie B. Smith, Mattie Thomas, and Carrie Hood were among the musicians who participated in an evening of selections from Schuman, Chopin, Liszt, and other composers. JA later told Eva Campbell that she was unable to find her copy of the program. It was reprinted in the *RSM* (July 1879): 207. As a musician herself, Eva Campell would have been particularly interested in the concert. Commencement exercises for 1879 began at nine in the morning in RFS's Chapel Hall, with the seven seniors dressed in white silk. Ella C. Smith gave the greeting for the class, and the seniors each gave a talk. Their individual presentations were interspersed with musical selections. The commencement program is reprinted in the *RSM* (July 1879): 208.

12. Public examinations of the RFS Collegiate Dept. were held on Monday and Tuesday of commencement week in 1879. Public examinations at RFS were held twice a year, in Feb. and June. Examinations were oral and held over a two- or three-day span. They were conducted by subject, with teachers and a board of outside evaluators made up of leading ministers and professionals from the community acting as examiners. In 1879 seven out of the eight examiners were ministers: four from Rockford and those remaining from Madison, Wis., Davenport, Iowa, and Seward, Nebr. At least one day of the examinations was open to the public (usually the day including musical performances and the showing of art portfolios), and townspeople would attend for edification and enjoyment.

A typical day's examinations might include translations and parsing of Virgil, along with accounts of the poet's life and the history of the Trojan War; an exercise in Shakespeare, including recitations from various plays; questioning on natural philosophy, including explanation of the construction and mechanics of a steam engine and a telegraph system; a session on Milton similar to the ones on Virgil and Shakespeare; and a botany session in which each student was expected to be prepared to analyze any of one hundred designated flowers and classify seventy-five specimens in a herbarium. Mathematics, including mental arithmetic and chalkboard demonstration, rhetoric, grammar, geography, and fields of history were subjects of examination for other days. As much as five days of written examinations preceded the oral examinations in some subjects. Outside examiners were impressed with the RFS students' performance in June 1877 but recommended that the school modernize its approach to biblical study in order to include more critical evaluation of biblical history and literature and to encourage the girls to think more about "political, ethical, and religious movements" (Anna P. Sill to Joseph Emerson, n.d., re 20 June 1877 Report of Board of Examiners, BC, EB). "We have examinations in Botany tomorrow," Lizzie Smith wrote home to her mother in 1878, "and oral examinations two days and public one day. . . . All my classes will be examined in chapel before the examining committee sometime before school is out. I dread it but hope I will do myself justice at least" (Sara Elizabeth Smith to Annie M. Jordan Smith, 16 June 1878, SHSW, Smith). In a 20 June 1882 meeting, the RFS Board of Trustees voted that "public examinations be dispensed with at the discretion of the faculty" (RFS Board of Trustees, "Minutes of the Annual Meetings," 1882; *JAPM*, 1A:148). JA described her own feelings about public examinations in a reply to Eva Campbell (see 25 [and 29] July 1879, below).

13. Minnie Black was a RFS student whose hands were injured while she was at school in the spring of 1879. She was cared for by Sarah Anderson and sent home to recover. The *RSM* of Nov. 1880 reported that "Minnie Black is one of us again" (249), and Lizzie Smith wrote, "Have I told you that Minnie Black has returned this year and her hands look much better than expected to see them. . . . She is still having something done to them daily so that they will probably be even better than they are now" (Sara Elizabeth Smith to Annie M. Jordan

Smith, 3 Oct. 1880, SHSW, Smith). Sarah Anderson spent Christmas vacation of 1880 at the home of Minnie Black. In June 1881 the *RSM* reported that "Minnie Black went to Beloit Friday morning the 13th instant, to attend an entertainment given by the Sophomores of the College, and to visit her brother who is a member of said class" (172). Black was not listed in *RFS* catalogs among regular students. "Minnie" may possibly have been the nickname of Mary Celia Black of Dallas City, Hancock Co., Ill., a senior in the RFS Preparatory Dept. in 1878–79. She was also enrolled in the RFS Dept. of Drawing and Painting in 1880–81. Sarah Anderson wrote to JA about Minnie Black in 1882.

14. JA repeated this phrase in her answer to Eva Campbell of 25 [and 29] July 1879 (see below). Campbell was probably paraphrasing Thomas Gray's (1716–71) "Elegy Written in a Country Churchyard" (1750): "Full many a flower is born to blush unseen, / And waste its sweetness on the desert air." For Campbell, the "desert air" became the western prairies.

15. Eva Campbell was the daughter of Cynthia E. Hoit Campbell (b. 1828) and Jeremiah Campbell (b. 1818), Pecatonica, Ill., farmers who were both originally from Vermont. Jeremiah Campbell's first wife was Cynthia Hoit's sister, Susan Hoit Campbell (1824–42), who died leaving one child. Jeremiah and Cynthia Campbell were married in Oct. 1843 and had four children of their own, Eva (b. 1854) being the youngest. Eva had one sister, Emma (1852–64), who died young, and two brothers and a step-brother who lived to maturity and became farmers. The Campbells were well-to-do. In 1877 they sold their farmland to their sons, retaining their house and eighty acres, where they enjoyed the "comforts of a happy and splendid home" (*History of Winnebago County*, 605). They were Republicans and Universalists, and Jeremiah Campbell had served as a school trustee and road commissioner.

16. Eva Campbell had a cousin, Lois Campbell (b. 1858), whose father, David, was Eva's paternal uncle. He, like Eva's father, was a farmer and involved in Pecatonica school administration. She had several other cousins, and it is not known if Lois Campbell was the one studying in Evansville.

17. Eva Campbell did not return to school; she married instead and began raising a family.

18. Addie M. Smith became JA's roommate in 1879 after Eva Campbell decided not to return to RFS.

19. Katie Hitchcock became ill when she was a junior in 1879 and did not return for the 1879–80 school year.

20. The senior class of 1879 held no Class Day. The "tradition" of having a Class Day for pending graduates began with fanfare in 1878. Aside from the class of 1879's lapse, the practice became a ritual at RFS.

21. Susan Wheat Benedict (Gordon) did graduate with her class in 1879. She taught for two years and then married Prof. Henry Evarts Gordon of the Univ. of Iowa, Iowa City, and had four children. After living in Trinidad, Colorado, and Massachusetts, the Gordons returned to Iowa City, and lived there in 1903. Susan Gordon was active in the Congregational Church.

Essay in the *Rockford Seminary Magazine*

In this sample of Jane Addams's work as an essayist for the Rockford Seminary Magazine *we see evidence of her combined interests in science and philosophy. These thoughts on nature also illustrate the confluence of her study of romanticism and classical literature, including the attraction to ideas of transcendence, the association of the natural world with the instinctual, the conception of Nature as a woman, and the Demeter-like connection of fertility and Mother Earth.*[1]

[Rockford, Ill.]

ONE OFFICE OF NATURE.

It is said that Pagan religion is but an allegory, a symbol of what man felt and knew about the universe. To the wild, primitive man all was yet new, and the universe flashed in upon him, beautiful, awful and unspeakable. He stood face to face with nature, free and unencumbered, his wild heart filled with wonder and worship, and all things were the emblem of some god. "The world, which is now divine only to the gifted, was then divine to whosoever would turn his eye upon it." In our time it requires a man of genius or a poet to strip off the nomenclatures and scientific heresays and show us the beauty in every star and every blade of grass. We count it a proof of a poetic nature that organizes the divine beauty in every object and can discern the loveliness of things. We have lost the open sense and child-like greatness of the primitive nations, and yet there comes to every man holy hours when he can look into the broad gates and rural solitudes of nature.

One of the sublimest passages in the life of the great Luther[2] is where he is once returning home from Leipsic and is struck by the beauty of the harvest fields, "How it stands, that golden yellow corn on its fair taper stem. The meek earth at God's kind bidding has produced it once again," and with a sudden rush of tenderness the great reformer bows his head as simply as a child and thanks God just for bread.[3] There are passages like this in every life, high or low, and man may still have true communion with nature. Why then does not every human being reclaim his lost birthright? Why is not every stone mason a poet or every farmer a prophetic priest before nature's altar?

There are only a few men who still retain the primitive insight and gain the full reward of the study of nature. A Hugh Miller[4] or an Audubon,[5] who become scientists from the love they bear to the work and who never lose the joy and zeal of their first investigation; a Titian[6] or a Correggio,[7] who reproduce on canvas, with truth and delicacy, the wonderful impressions they receive from the scenes around them; a Scott[8] or a Coleridge,[9] who bind you in the charm of their wonderful descriptions and give you a glimpse into the hidden beauty of forest and meadow: yet these few men, still holding this communion, are the great men, and they each draw their peculiar inspiration from the same living source. We might say that there is no other source to draw from, and that all genuine thought and impressions may ultimately be traced to the study of nature.

Man again and again wanders away and loses himself in a maze of rationalism and ideal philosophy, yet nature remains calm and unchangeable, and in due time receives him again and starts him aright.

We have two striking examples of this in these latter times. The first is among the human philosophers. Probably no man ever came into the pure presence of nature who was more unworthy to know her secrets than Wolfgang Von Goethe,[10] yet he came in a moment of repentance and kindly nature received him.

In his ear all Germany was overcivilized, entangled in a morbid feeling of oppression; she was weighed down under a load of books and modern philosophies,
surrounded by a rolling miscellany of facts and sciences, and german life had a
narrowness and hardness. Goethe bore the curse of his time; he was filled full of
its skepticism, hollowness and a thousand fold contradictions, till his heart was
like to break; yet it was given to him to change the chaos into creation, and to
dispose with ease of the distracting variety of claims. He turned away from all
the confusion and studied with human eyes the unity and simplicity of nature.
It was he who suggested the leading idea of modern botany, that the leaf is the
unit of growth, and that every plant is only a transformed leaf. In optics again
he rejected the artificial theory of seven colors and considered that every color
was the miniature of light and darkness in new proportions. He did away with a
great deal of the sham learning and cant of the age by teaching to modern scientists the high simplicity of nature. Many of the theories he formed from his discoveries were false, yet even these theories unlocked the narrow ties of the old
order, and human nature breathed freer. Goethe was the deliverer of his time;
he studied nature throughout his long life, and his last words, while waiting for
his eighty-second birthday, were a welcome to the returning spring.

We have another prominent example of the same thing—of man growing
confused and bewildered and being brought back again to truth through nature—in the natural school of poetry of which Wordsworth[11] is the representative man. His predecessors, a Pope[12] or Dryden,[13] had written and studied artificial forms, laboriously imitating the classic poets, their thought and expression
trammeled and unnatural. Wordsworth broke away from all this, freed himself
from all affected forms of expression. He clothed everyday incidents with poetry, shed a charm over the common aspects of earth. He made the world appear a more beautiful and happier place; ordinary human life a nobler and diviner thing. He studied nature with a long and genial intimacy and founded a
new period in English literature.

As all wealth and material objects can be traced back to the kindly bosom
of mother earth, so we may trace all philosophies to the study of nature.

Worthy old nature! She goes on producing whatever is needful in each season of her course; produces with perfect composure, knowing that even as she
feeds and nourishes her children with corn and wine, so likewise she contains
that which would make them wise and learned, till even the meanest with delicate fancies and tender thoughts, if they would but read the "open secret" and
study her.[14]

J.A.

PD (*RSM* [June 1879]: 154–56; *JAPM*, 46:20–23).

1. For earlier essays on related naturalistic and spiritual themes, see "The Office of Rivers,"
24 Nov. 1877, and "The night hath Stars (To develope the imagination)," 20 Feb. 1878, both
JAPM, 45:1677–83, 45:1722–28; see also Draft of Essay, 28 Jan. 1880, below. EGS was a particu-

lar admirer of JA's "One Office of Nature," and she later taught the piece to her students at Miss Kirkland's School for Girls in Chicago. "My dear, it is exquisite," she wrote to JA. When she read the essay aloud to her class, one student commented, "'If your friend could write that at nineteen I should think she would write books now'" (EGS to JA, 28 Apr. 1885, SC, Starr; *JAPM*, 2:50, 51).

2. Martin Luther (1483–1546), rebellious Protestant theologian and reformer, was the primary instigator of the Reformation in Germany. He was a member of the Augustinian order and became disturbed by the corruption he saw manifested in the upper echelons of the Catholic Church. After he nailed his famous *Theses* to the door of the Wittenberg, Germany, church, attacking papal indulgences, he was subjected to a papal ban (1521), left the monastic order, and married. He created the Lutheran Bible, the translation of the Old and New Testaments into German (1522, 1534), and wrote or adapted many hymns of joy and triumph. The canonical hymns "Away in a Manger" and "A Mighty Fortress Is Our God" are both attributed to him. He rejected the doctrine of works and believed in justification by the faith of the individual. When JA traveled in Germany in Jan. 1884 she visited the Castle of the Wartberg where Luther had been confined and wrote home of his influence. She mused at one point to JWA, "One learns to have a new respect for Luther and wonder how one man could do so much" (27 Jan. 1884, UIC, JAMC; *JAPM*, 1:1359).

3. JA referred here to Thomas Carlyle's profile of Martin Luther, originally delivered as a lecture in 1840 and printed as "Lecture IV: The Hero as Priest," part of *On Heroes, Hero-Worship, and the Heroic in History* (1841): "Returning home from Leipzig once, he is struck by the beauty of the harvest-fields: How it stands, that golden yellow corn, on its fair taper stem, its golden head bent, all rich and waving there,—the meek Earth, at God's kind bidding, has produced it once again; the bread of man!" Carlyle concluded that "there is a great free human heart in this man" and that it was Luther's humility and capability for emotion, as much as his political victories and triumphs, that made him "a true Great Man; great in intellect, in courage, affection and integrity. . . . A right Spiritual Hero and Prophet; once more, a true Son of Nature and Fact, for whom these centuries, and many that are to come yet, will be thankful to Heaven" (Carlyle, *On Great Men*, 68, 69, 70).

4. Hugh Miller (1802–56), a stonemason by trade, was also a writer on geological subjects and editor of *Witness,* the publication of the non-Intrusionists, a group within the Church of Scotland who felt that congregations should have a say in calling their pastors rather than having to accept ministers who had been appointed by patrons and whom individual congregations may not have wanted. Miller was the author of several works, including *The Old Red Sandstone* (1841), *Footprints of the Creator* (1847), the *Testimony of the Rocks* (1857), and an autobiography, *My Schools and Schoolmasters* (1854).

5. Ornithologist John James Audubon (1785–1851) was famous for his beautiful paintings of birds, notably the color prints that appeared in *Birds of America* (serialized from 1827 to 1838) and *Ornithological Biography* (1831–39). Audubon was born in Haiti and educated in France. He lived near Philadelphia beginning in 1804 and began his wildlife paintings by going into the Kentucky wilderness. He gave drawing lessons and was also engaged in portrait painting and taxidermy. Many of his writings were published in the twentieth century, including *Audubon's America* (1940), *Journal* (1929), and *Letters* (1930).

6. The great sixteenth-century Venetian School painter Titian (Tiziano Vecelli, 1488?–1576), was trained in the studios of Gentile Bellini and Giovanni Bellini and worked as an assistant to Giorgione. Noted at the height of his career for his strong and spectacular use of color and the energetic physicality of his subjects, Titian is often credited by art historians as the founder of modern painting. After painting a successful portrait of Emperor Charles V, Titian was appointed court painter at Bologna in 1533 and befriended by the emperor, who was but one of his wealthy and influential patrons. Famous for his portraits, mythologies, historical paintings, altars, and frescos, Titian's work includes the *Assumption of the Virgin* (1516–18), *Feast*

of Venus and *The Andrians* (both 1517–18), the *Bacchus and Ariadne* (1523–24), *La Bella* (ca. 1536), the *Venus of Urbino* (1538), and various other Venuses, reflecting his visit to Rome and interest in classical antiquity, painted in the 1540s. Later erotic-mythological works include the Diana paintings, the *Rape of Europa* (ca. 1559–62), and the *Punishment of Actaeon* of the late 1550s or early 1560s. Influenced in mid-career by Michelangelo and Mannerist style, the freer style and use of color and light of his later work anticipated Impressionism. One of his landmark final paintings, *Crowning with Thorns* (ca. 1570), a study of the persecution of Christ, used somber tones and lighting, prefiguring the style of Rembrandt in the seventeenth century.

7. Sixteenth-century northern Italian painter Correggio (Antonio Allegri, 1489/94?–1534) was master of the proto-Baroque. Working most of his career in Parma, he became known for his voluptuous and passionate interpretation of mythological/religious subjects and his dramatic use of chiaroscuro (the balance of light and dark in a picture and technique in creating shadow). He was influenced by the Roman High Renaissance, especially by the work of Leonardo da Vinci, Michelangelo, and Raphael. He developed a painterly style that anticipated the Baroque in its softness and emotional qualities. He is well known for his frescoes, notably the *Assumption of the Virgin* (painted ca. 1522–30) in the dome of Parma Cathedral, a masterpiece of illusion and perspective featuring angelic flying figures, and for his series the Loves of the Classical Gods, notably *Jupiter and Io* (ca. 1532).

8. The Scottish novelist and romantic lyric poet Sir Walter Scott was also a translator of Goethe. His work was influenced by early study of French and Italian romantic poetry and modern German poets as well as by Scottish ballads and historical and traditional materials. His early verse romances gave way to a steady stream of historical novels, all widely read by JA's peers. The novels were originally published anonymously but acknowledged by Scott in 1827. The *RSM* "Home Items" section lampooned the influence of Scott among RFS schoolgirls. The following appeared in the May 1880 issue: "It is not safe to venture near the northeast corner, west of the garden now, for the 'Rob Roy Archers' practice there, and notwithstanding they have a target, hit whatever happens to be nearest to them. The 'Highland Plaids' practice on the east side of chapel; so beware of turning corners suddenly" (151). When JA made her first trip to Europe (in 1883–85), her traveling party reread Scott's novels for their autumn 1883 tour of Scotland and drove about the Highlands with a copy of *Rob Roy* (1817) at hand (see JA to SAAH, 30 Sept. 1883, UIC, JAMC; *JAPM*, 1:1175–90).

9. Samuel Taylor Coleridge (1772–1834) was an English romantic poet whose works include "The Rime of the Ancient Mariner" (*Lyrical Ballads* [1798]) and "Kubla Khan, a Vision in a Dream" (composed 1797, published 1816), the lines of which came to him in his sleep. Coleridge also wrote, with his friend Robert Southey—with whom he shared Pantisocractic political convictions—the play *The Fall of Robespierre* (1794). Like Thomas De Quincey, Coleridge suffered from poor health that led, in 1806, to opium addiction. During her Oct. 1883 tour of the Lake District, JA visited the churchyard at Grasmere, where Wordsworth and Coleridge are buried (see JA to MCAL, 3 Oct. 1883, UIC, JAMC; *JAPM*, 1:1192–97).

10. Johann Wolfgang von Goethe (1749–1832), German lyric poet, dramatist, and theater director, divided much of his professional efforts between scientific discovery and literature. His experiments led to a new theory on the nature of color and light (published in *Zur Farbenlehre* in 1810) and to innovative ideas about the connections between animal and plant life. He is best known for his poetic and dramatic version of *Faust* (begun in 1770, written in two parts, and finished in 1832). His *Goetz von Berlichingen* was translated into English by Sir Walter Scott in 1799. JA greatly admired Goethe as a pivotal man of his time, and when she traveled in Weimar in January 1884 she visited his tomb and the sites associated with his life. She sent her brother "a little piece of moss from Weimar—a souvinoir of Göethe & Schiller who are associated with everything in the town" (JA to JWA, 27 Jan. 1884, UIC, JAMC; *JAPM*, 1:1360; see also JA to MCAL, 13 Jan. 1884, UIC, JAMC; *JAPM*, 1:1333–37). JA wrote about

Goethe in her RFS work on more than one ocassion (see, for example, JA, "An Allogory," n.d. [ca. 1877–81], and "[Essay on Johann Wolfgang von Göethe]," n.d., [ca. 1879?], *JAPM*, 45:1603–8, 1610–13). In the latter essay she observed, "It is said there has been but two great men in these later times, one was Napoleon, the other Wofgang von Goethe" (*JAPM*, 45:1611).

11. William Wordsworth (1770–1850) was English romantic poet and a good friend of Samuel Taylor Coleridge, with whom he wrote *Lyrical Ballads* (1798, 1800, 1802), a collection of poems that included Wordsworth's "Lines Composed above Tintern Abbey," which captured the romantic vision of the natural world: "Knowing that Nature never did betray / The heart that loved her" (lines 123–24). The *Lyrical Ballads* were a revolt from the artifice that characterized the literature of the day. The poems in the collection emphasized the romantic, the supernatural, and (especially in the case of Wordsworth), the wonder that could be found in the commonplace and everyday. Because of their clear break from the literary formulas of the day, the poems of Wordsworth and Coleridge incurred an initially poor reception from critics but later reached a huge and abiding popular audience.

12. Alexander Pope (1688–1744), English essayist, satirist, poet, and translator of Homer's *Iliad* (1720) and the *Odyssey* (1725–26), is best known for such poetical works as "Rape of the Lock" (1712) and his poems of lost or abandoned love, the elegy "Verses to the Memory of an Unfortunate Lady" and "Eloisa to Abelard" (both published in collected form in 1717). A major edition of Pope's works was edited by Whitwell Elwin and W. J. Courthope and published in the 1870s and 1880s.

13. John Dryden (1631–1700) was a prolific poet, playwright, translator, and author of prose. He wrote fourteen plays between 1668 and 1681, including *All for Love* (1678), a story of Anthony and Cleopatra. He was named poet laureate of England in 1668 and in the 1680s he wrote a series of didactic, satirical poems. He converted to Roman Catholicism in 1686. He also published several translations, including the complete works of Virgil (1697) and portions of work by Ovid, Homer, and others. He was buried in Westminster Abbey in the grave of Chaucer. Sir Walter Scott published an edition of Dryden's collected works in 1808.

14. Soon after publishing this essay, JA wrote to EGS that her own spiritual searching had led her to a kind of feminine deism or panentheism (in which the creator spirit is manifested in the natural world): "Back to a great <u>Primal Cause</u>, not Nature exactly, but a fostering mother, a necessity, brooding and watching over all things, above every human passion & yet not passive, the mystery of creation" (11 Aug. 1879, below). She also referred to Nature personified as a woman in "Follow Thou Thy Star" (Essay in the *RSM*, July 1879, below). See also "The Study of Nature" (*JAPM*, 46:24–29).

To Eva Campbell

In this letter, Jane Addams wrote of the impact that a missionary address given by the Rev. James G. Merrill[1] at the 1879 Rockford Female Seminary commencement ceremonies had upon her at the end of her second year at the school. Through Merrill's speech and other influences at the seminary she heartily absorbed the idea of the responsibility of the individual to work toward fulfilling a greater purpose or cause. As she reported in her description of Merrill's speech in the letter below, she was giving serious thought to the concept that "God devotes each era to some special work" and that "there is a grand general aim to be discovered in each Century." It would take Addams several years, and some false starts, to adequately discern the aim intended in terms of her life's intention or special work. The results,

when they came, were manifested in the settlement house movement that she did
much to establish in the last decade of the century.

Mitchellville Iowa   July 25 [and 29] 1879

Dearly Beloved;

If you would cut my acquaintance & never speak to me again I would not
blame you, for I would think you were justified by appearances, neither would
I blame myself for I would consider myself justified by circumstance. Therefore
before you judge at all read the following, then sit down and write to me & you
will make me the happiest girl alive.

You don't know how glad I was to get a letter from my old chum—it was
just like her—impatient yet under full control—well, it came just at a time when
it did me good—right in the midst of examinations. I was hot, fussy & tired yet
made a desperate effort to keep calm, and succeeded pretty well until it came
time to read my essay & then I was excited, for indeed Eva the idea of a schoolgirl propounding her ideas to a set of men as smart as they were, struck me as
being silly, the committee had asked a good many questions, I knew that they
were learned; and some of them brilliant, I that I[2] was very far from being either—hence my trepidation & the good your letter did me.

I did n't mean to talk so much about the state of my feelings—which were
really of very little consequence—but you know my dear, our conversations were
~~very~~ often like that, we started off on something trivial & very soon found ourselves saying things we thought a good deal about,—that is the way it is with
you[r] letter—I thought a good deal about that.

I meant to answer it first thing when I came home, I will explain why I did
n't & then go on to say lots of things I want to; write them all with the tacit
understanding that we are as good friends as we were that Sunday we read
"Romeo & Juliet"[3] or that Friday night when we stopped in the midst of our
room-work to talk on some pretty big subjects—, by the way I expressed some
opinions then I don't believe at all now—but never mind maybe you don't remember the talk as well as I do. Well as I was about to remark first thing when
I came home we had a lot of company from the east, they had hardly gone when
George[4] took a run of a sort of a bilious fever, we were very much worried & of
course busy all the time taking care of him, by the time he was up and dressed,
the third week of July had come around, the time Miss Anderson & I had arranged for our trip,[5] so off we started & here we are. We have just had a jolly
time, have been to picnics! parties, teas rides & visits, in fact have been rushed
every minute since we came here, spent a day in Des Moines, saw all the wonders of the capital and city and called on Katie Hitchcock which was better than
either; of course I could enter into elaborate descriptions of all this, greatly to
my own gratification, but no doubt you would find it decidedly like the things
you have been doing the last weeks, the only difference being, we only have one

week of it and enjoy the novelty, whilst you are beginning to be tired of it,—as we all would be pretty soon. I admire your pluck, my friend, "do not waste sweetness on the western prairies."[6]

Who should come here Monday night but Pa in order to escort us home to day—Thursday, so yesterday morning Miss Anderson started on to Newton to visit an uncle of hers, I was going to meet her this morning, we would call on the Sem'y girls there and then all go on together this afternoon, but alas! my kind father is worn out, is quiet sick in fact and so I won't leave him, I am kind of sorry, for in one way I wanted to see those Newton girls, I wish you could have been in my place.

This morning I arose at the pensive hour of five & took a long horse-back ride over the prairies, we had a splendid time, it is the second early ride I have had since I came here a week ago.[7] I just came home a few minutes ago from my ride, Harry & Alice were up late with Pa & hav n't gotten up yet, so I am sitting alone in the office in the fresh, morning air, writing to you—the air someway seems to act as a stimulant, for I find the epistle grows painfully long & as yet I have said nothing.

Now I want to say something about our rooming to-gether, it seems to me Miss Campbell that it was one of the understood things, if we were both ever in that institution at the same time that we were to room in sweet companionship, of course as long as there is the least chance of your coming back I will make no other arrangement, and I hope to goodness that you will come back; I applied in your name and mine, for our old room in Linden hall and if we could n't have that one for Ella Smith's[8] old room, I could n't <think> of any room that we would really like better, unless it would be the one opposite Miss Blaisdell, & I thought I would write to you about that first & try to see if I could get it next fall, that is if you wanted it, consider well the circumstances and all the surroundings thereof, Miss Blaisdell is a staunch friend of ours and of course we don't want to be rash & lose her, still if we mean to keep the rules why do we need to be afraid?

Don't give up the idea of coming back, Eva, I beg of you, for it seems to me that we can both do better work at Rockford next year than any place I know of, let's go to work & do it, helping each other all we can & not make all our resolutions at the end of the year, I have been thinking my friend that what we need is a more systematic plan of recreation, that we want to recreate as hard as we study, we can do a good deal more & better study if we try it that way; we will make the <experiment.>

Commencement passed off very much as usual, beginning with the Bacculearate sermon & going straight through, but the Missionary address on Monday evening was something unusual for it was perfectly splendid, it was given by a Mr Merrill of Davenport his subject was "The relation between true culture & the missionary work".[9] I wished with might & main that you could hear it, from the very time he started in until the last word. I wish I could give you a synopsis of it, but I am afraid I can't at this late day. He started in by defining culture in a way that made us all despair of ever reaching it, or at least but partially, & then he discour[s]ed on the missionary work until he made you perfectly enthusiastic—God devotes each era to some special work, there is a grand general aim to be discovered in each Century; in our time it is Missionary work, never before in history has there been such an opening of countries, such an outgoing & sending forth of religions & civilization—our aim is culture, we try hard for it in all ways we hear of, we find that "self-culture[10] but impals a man on his personal pronouns", think of your soul spinning around on a great I, the trouble is we ignore the means at hand, we should throw ourselves into the tide of affairs, feel ourselves swayed by the great ~~tide~~ <flood> of human action as "a sponge is lifted & filled by the oversweeping wave;" the great object of this age seems to be missionary work, throw yourself into that & you will be cultured in your own time & age, will give you a breadth & sweep as nothing else will. Then he spoke of the mere knowledge you must gain, the finest linguists in the world are missionaries, the finest scholars in almost every department have been missionaries. But the idea that impressed me most was the breadth it gave you, just think, Eva, of having expansiveness of soul enough to pray, actually pray for a South African, a man barbarous & brutal, you never expect to see him, he speaks a different language from you own, coarse & uncouth, he seems like an animal and yet you can honestly pray for him, you will be great, cultured in a free sense, it sort of opens to me a possibility that I never thought of before; may be I have given you enough of it, to see why I wanted you to hear it so much; <now> to me, praying for that man seems a utter impossibility, but it seems to me you were reaching toward it when you used to talk to Miss Munson,[11] I think I am doomed to reach on toward self-culture.

The anniversary address was given by Dr Nickole[12] of Milwaukee, he was just as polished & scholarly as he could be, I think I liked his address even better than Mr Merrill's but he did not give me any distinct ideas it was more impressions, vague but powerful, I will remember it longer & it will do me more good, but I can never repeat it, nor quote it to any-one else, for that reason, <I suppose> I retain it—it is easier to pray for a million South Africans than one—may I end up kind of flat? "We miss the abstract when we comprehend" I did n't comprehend. Selah!

I hav n't your letter with me and I guess it is fortunate for it would take until evening to answer all of your questions.

Now, my dear, I don't want to tell you all about that fuss for it is over so long ago and sounds stale, wait until I see you—only two months—and I will sit down and talk with you for hours, tell you all the particulars, enter into all explanations, but really I can't do it now, I'm disgusted with the whole thing; I have no doubt you know the main facts by this time any way. You asked about Minnie Black, she went home about two weeks before school was out, her hands were a good deal better, but it will be about a year before she gets full use of them.

I suppose you heard of the watch she gave Miss Anderson, poor Miss Anderson she remained faithful to the last, put on the final bandages whilst poor Mrs Black stood looking helplessly on!

You asked about our modern history, I worked real hard on it and feel better satisfied than I did with my ancient, it may be only because we spent more time & that it is fresher, but I really think I have a better general idea of things, I of have more of the philosophy of history and so on, I suppose all that is natural from the very nature of things.

I returned those French books all right to Miss Sill, and have the Latin Prose safely among my books, I hope I will have the extreme pleasure of putting them on a shelf mixed up with yours next Sept. By the way, I want to congratulate you on the reading you have done since I saw you, you are getting along splendidly, and if you study every-thing as carefully as you evidently did the "Merchant of Venice" you are all right, someway I didn't enjoy that as much as I expected to. I think it was because we had wasted our best energies on McBeth[13] and hated to start in on anything new, although some parts of it are awfully exciting, do you remember that place where the Jew exclaims "A Daniel! A Daniel! come to judgement" in my first brilliant production next fall I intend to draw a parallel between Portia & Daniel;[14] I have no doubt it will be a fizzle but I mean to try it. I hav n't <had> hardly any time to read during the summer, have finished the "Last Days of Pompeii" and enjoyed it very much. I know that some of the scenes in there are as vividly impressed upon my memory as if I had seen them, we won't have our questions on the book until next year, & she didn't give us any questions on the "Merchant of Venice."

I have read about two hundred pages in Motley's "Rise of Dutch Republic"[15] and mean to finish it this summer, I think it is going to be as interesting as can be when I get into it a little more. I found some-thing in Carlyle the other day on the subject of reading that just suits me, it is in a letter of advice to a young friend, I wish I could copy the whole thing for I know you would like, but I will write down the part that struck me so particularly, and if it will do you as much good as it did me I will be glad of it.[16]

"As to the books which you—whom I know so little of—should read, there is hardly anything definite that can be said. For one thing, you may be strenuously advised to keep reading. Any good book, any book that is wiser than yourself, will teach you something—a great many things, indirectly & directly, if your mind be open to learn. This old counsel of Johnson's[17] is also good, & universally applicable;—'Read the book you do honestly feel a wish & curiosity to read.' The very wish & curiosity indicates that you, then & there, are the person likely to get good of it. 'Our wishes are presentiments of our capabilities;' that is a noble saying of deep encouragement to all true men; applicable to our wishes and efforts in <regard to> reading as to other things. Among all the objects that look wonderful or beautiful to you follow with fresh hope the one which looks wonderfullest, beautifullest. You will gradually find, by various trials (which trials, see that you make honest manful ones, not silly, short, fitful ones)[.] What is for you the wonderfullest, beautifullest—what is your true element & province, & be able to profit by that.[18] True desire, the monition of nature, is much to be attended to. But here also" &c &c &c[.] Some-way or other that entire quotation just suits me, Carlyle has a way of saying things once in a while that strike, as it were my key-note, just exactly what I have been hunting for.

Eva, I wish I had your letter here to tell you the things you asked about, I won't seal this epistle until I get home and can put in the two programmes. Mary Downs' essay was just perfectly splendid,[19] I was as proud of her as I could be, do you know sometimes I have had my doubts whether Mary Downs really was so very smart, or whether her general manner just made her appear; Well on commencement day I was thoroughly ashamed of myself, & never again will I doubt her ability. I think maybe Miss Weigrin's[20] would impress people as being the most finished & scholarly of any of them.

I declare, Eva, I hav n't any idea how this letter sounds. I have just written along as fast as I could write regardless of time & space, but if you dare make any remarks of the character you did that time we got that awful long one from Miss Starr, I will never forgive you. Write to me soon and I will promise not to bore you with such a long letter again. Yours sincerely,

Jane Addams.

Cedarville [Ill.]July 29

> My dear I have <u>lost</u> the musical programme, cannot find it high or low. Yours in deep sorrow

JA

ALS (Private Collection, photocopy, JAPP; *JAPM*, 1:362–73).

1. The Rev. James Griswold Merrill (1840–1921) was the pastor of the Congregational Church of Davenport, Iowa, from Dec. 1872 to Aug. 1882. The son of a minister, Merrill was born in Montague, Mass. He was educated at Phillips-Andover Academy, Andover, Mass., and was an 1863 graduate of Amherst College in Amherst, Mass., and of Andover Theological Seminary in 1866. He was licensed by the Andover Assn. of Congregational Ministers at Lowell, Mass., in 1866, and ordained in Mound City, Kans., where he was pastor of the Congregational Church and in the service of the Congregational Home Mission Society from 1867 to 1869. In Oct. 1866 he married Louisa Wilder Boutwell (d. 1919) in Andover. After leaving Iowa, he was pastor of Congregational churches in St. Louis, Mo., (1882–89), and Portland, Maine, (1889–94). Merrill was the editor of the *Christian Mirror*, which was later absorbed into the *Congregationalist*.

In 1899 Merrill became dean of faculty and professor of logic and moral science at Fisk Univ. and in 1889 was named interim president. He became president in 1901 and served until 1908, when he resigned because of his wife's ill-health. Under his administration, he defied those who believed that education for African Americans should be restricted to the industrial arts. Fisk, Merrill argued, should "not expect to make farmers, carpenters, masons, laundrywomen, dressmakers of its students, but to teach them the underlying principles of Chemistry and Physics as applied to modern industry and agriculture" ("Narrative of Administration," n.p.).

Among Merrill's innovations at Fisk was the founding of a summer seminar for African American teachers, giving instructors already working in the classroom exposure to the latest pedagogical theories and teaching methodologies. He also introduced new electives into the Fisk curriculum, including courses in classical studies, botany, floriculture, meteorology, architectural drawing, climatology, agricultural chemistry, and economic entomology, with an emphasis on combining pure science with practical applications so students would be able to assume leadership roles in industry and business. Merrill's mission at Fisk, as stated in his inaugural address, was to promote a "Christian view of humanity" that "embraced the brotherhood of all mankind" and to encourage students in developing a strong sense of "Christian manhood" and recognition of their duty in honoring others through philanthropy ("James Griswold Merrill: Pastor-Friend," n.p.).

The evangelical style introduced with his inauguration permeated Merrill's administration of the school. He put Fisk on a more secure financial basis, developed a building and endowment fund, promoted the policy of developing a biracial faculty, and encouraged the fundraising and public-relations work of the famed Fisk Jubilee Singers. He remained a member of the Fisk Univ. Board of Trustees until his death on 22 Dec. 1920. After leaving academics, Merrill returned to the ministry and was pastor of Congregational churches in Somerset, Mass. (1909–12) and Lake Helen, Fla. (1912–17). Two sons and one daughter were living at the time of his death. Merrill was the author of *Children's Sermons* (2 vols., 1876–78).

2. JA evidentally meant to write *and that I was.*

3. *Romeo and Juliet* (ca. 1595) was Shakespeare's first romantic tragedy and based on an Italian romance by Matteo Bandello that had been translated into English.

4. A reference to GBH.

5. Sarah Anderson traveled from her hometown of Geneseo, Ill., to meet JA in Moline, Ill., in mid-July 1879. The two stayed in Moline with Anderson's aunt, Sarah Andrews Ainsworth (d. 1891), sister of Sarah Anderson's mother, Mary Andrews Anderson, and wife of Henry A. Ainsworth, a former Geneseo resident and Moline businessman. In 1896 Sarah Anderson became Ainsworth's second wife (see Biographical Profiles: Ainsworth, Sarah Anderson). Anderson and JA went from Moline to Mitchellville, Iowa, where they stayed with JA's sister SAAH, whose husband, HWH, had recently established a medical practice there after graduating from Northwestern Medical School in Chicago. They made short trips from Mitchellville to visit other Iowa friends, including Katie Hitchcock in Des Moines.

6. JA is quoting from Eva Campbell's letter to her of 18 June 1879, above.

7. Although it has been said that JA disliked riding because it hurt her back and she had a severe allergy to horses, here she seems to have enjoyed the early-morning romp over Iowa terrain.

8. Ella C. Smith enrolled at RFS as a senior in 1878–79 and is listed in the RFS *Catalogue* for that school year. She was from DuQuoin, Ill. A fellow student reported in a letter home that "Ella Smith, May B[lakesley]'s roommate from last year" would graduate in 1879 (Addie B. Smith to Annie M. Jordan Smith, 24 Sept. 1878, SHSW, Smith). She did so and delivered the introductory greeting to teachers, trustees, families, and alumnae at the beginning of the June 1879 graduation ceremonies.

9. The ceremonies of commencement week were opened on Sunday with the baccalaureate sermon by the Rev. John Kennedy ("J.K.") Fowler (1848–1908) of the Rockford First Presbyterian Church and Merrill's missionary address. Educated at Union Theological Seminary, New York, Fowler was ordained in 1874 in Rochester, N.Y. He served as pastor of the First Presbyterian Church in Rockford from 1878 to 1884 and later was a minister to churches in El Paso, Tex., Los Angeles, Calif., La Crosse, Wis., and Cedar Rapids and Clinton, Iowa. The July 1879 issue of the *RSM* reported that Merrill's talk was "not one of those dull, tiresome addresses, such as we have listened to times before, when our tired heads were filled with dates and statistics of various missions, but a scholarly discourse, showing in a delightful way the

effect of missionary efforts upon literature and a knowledge of the languages" (206). Both Fowler and Merrill served on the June 1879 RFS Examining Com.

10. In her 1878–79 RFS copybook, JA mentioned "Dr Nicols June 1879—"talk and recorded its theme ("every life an ideal—"). She also took notes on Merrill's "Mission day address June 1879." She wrote, "self culture impals a man upon his personal pronouns"; mentioned "Platonic theory"; and went on to write that "every man has an idea fixed in him, embodied in his inner self. . . . Christian religion confirms this. . . . God alone knows, go completely under his will, & you are all right, the more surrender the better." The point JA clearly was pondering from Merrill's talk was the assertion that the best route to true self-culture was not a focus on self, self-reliance, or self-improvement but on duty and reverence to God. She went on to observe, also from Merrill, that God alone knows the seeds planted in each individual, and through faith, and the careful study of nature, individuals come to know their duty and reverence to man, "all great men" being "but the expression of thier time." By contrast, "life made under self-culture fixed in yourself cannot yield to the grand sea about you" ("[Copybook, 1878–May 1879]"; *JAPM*, 27:168). The issues of acquiring solid self-knowledge—and the ability to act according to that knowledge against a sea of expectations—would occupy JA for the decade after she made notes on Merrill and Rev. G. P. Nicholls's lectures in June 1879.

The notion of self-culture was a very popular element of mid-nineteenth-century American intellectual life. Based on the cultivation of all facets of the individual to the greater good (usually through a conscious program of self-study and self-improvement, including exposure to canonical writings in literature and philosophy), the idea of self-culture encompassed physical, mental, emotional, and spiritual aspects of living. Proper self-culture was thought to take place in a well-rounded way, including development and training of the muscles, the mind, the attitude, and the soul, in order to best live according to the talents God had granted.

Focused on a romantic ideal of the self, prominent proponents of self-culture used a male or "Great Men" paradigm in examining the cultures of the past and applying them to the present as models to emulate, especially for young men preparing to be citizens. The urge toward male self-improvement was manifested by mid-century in young men's societies and gentlemen's clubs, college and professional literary societies, and mutual-improvement associations, as well as in such broader contexts as the public library movement, public lyceums and chautauquas, and the popularity of literary magazines. Self-culturalists called upon ideals of bravery and leadership represented in warriors, the ideal of philosophic contemplation modeled by the Greek philosophers and Christian monastics, and the democratic and Enlightenment ideals that held that ordinary persons are obligated to develop whatever particular abilities they possess.

As ideas of self-culture became more democratic as the 1800s advanced, women faced a dilemma in how best to position themselves in regard to their intellects and expectations of their futures. In extending ideas of self-culture to women, educators, members of the clergy, and reformers often framed the female pursuit of learning within a Christian context and focused on the idea of a young woman's duty to train herself to act according to her full potential, serving God's will for her life in the process. In this way, the liberal concept of self-culture (or self-improvement and the full realization of potential) was expanded past its narrower male-leadership application and became part of the ideas behind the preparation of college girls for public roles as well as private life.

In his talk, Merrill addressed the overly self-centered perspective that could too easily lie at the heart of conducting oneself according to self-culture precepts. The moral challenge that college-educated women faced was how best to take the self out of self-culture, or, as historian Joseph Kett has framed the problem, "To elevate the soul, self-culture had to be devoid of any selfish goal" (*Pursuit of Knowledge*, 83). Educators such as Anna P. Sill solved this conundrum by emphasizing the duty of girls to devote their talents to the good of others—especially, as Merrill emphasized in his talk, as missionaries abroad. JA here struggles with these concepts of balancing individualism and collectivism and her own potential relation to peoples of other cultures.

11. Poet, composer, and music teacher Eva Munson (Smith) (1843–1915) was born in Monkton, Vt., the daughter of William Chandler Munson (d. 1867) and Hannah (or Hanna) Bailey Munson. Munson attended Mary Sharp College in Winchester, Tenn., until her family moved to Rockford, and she graduated from RFS in the class of 1864. She taught vocal and instrumental music, and after her father's death became head of the Music Dept. at Otoe Univ. in Nebraska City, Nebr. She married druggist George Clinton Smith in Nebraska City in 1869 and continued to teach music and elocution. Eva Munson Smith had a beautiful singing voice and was active in directing and singing in church choirs. She was also a composer, having begun writing music as a child, and published many compositions, including the popular "Woodland Warblings," "Home Sonata," and "I Will Not Leave You Comfortless." In tribute to women's largely unrecognized contributions to religious music, she compiled a collection entitled *Woman in Sacred Song: A Library of Hymns, Religious Poems, and Sacred Music by Woman* (1885; 2d expanded ed., 1887). The book was published with an introduction by Frances Willard and featured biographical sketches of women hymn writers, poetry written by 830 women, and some three thousand hymns. Willard included a profile of Eva Munson Smith in her *Woman of the Century* (1886). In 1874 Smith moved with her husband to Springfield, Ill., where for many years her home was the center of a network of Illinois temperance and religious workers. She was a superintendent for oratorical contests for the WCTU and an officer in the organization. She was also the vice president of the Illinois Equal Suffrage Club for nineteen years and historian for the DAR. The Smiths had no children.

12. Rev. G. P. Nicholls of Milwaukee, Wis., delivered the annual address on Tuesday evening. He spoke on the theme "Ideals—the Advantage and Necessity of Ideals." The July 1879 *RSM* summed up the address as imparting the idea that "As artists have had an ideal, for which they have aimed, so we in our lives should have an ideal to strive for, which is far above the real" (207).

13. See Essay in the *RSM*, Jan. 1880, below; see also Linn, *Jane Addams*, 57–59.

14. JA apparently had the idea of comparing the legal scene featuring Portia, heroine of Shakespeare's *The Merchant of Venice*, with one of the stories about the Hebrew prophet Daniel, who was held captive in Babylon, interpreted the dreams of Nebuchadnezzar and handwriting on the wall for Belshazzar, and was thrown, by order of King Darius, into a lions' den, from whence he was delivered, through divine protection, unharmed. In Shakespeare's play, Shylock says to Portia, "A Daniel come to judgement! Yea, a Daniel! O wise young judge, how I do honour you!" (*The Merchant of Venice*, act iv, sc. i). This is a direct allusion to the story of Daniel's role in the case of Susanna, as told in the apocryphal books of the Old Testament. The story of Susanna is conventionally detached from the book of Daniel but appears prefixed to the beginning of Daniel in the Greek text of the Bible.

In addition to writing to Eva Campbell about the parallels between the two stories, JA recorded in her notebook, "Daniel—compare with Portia in Merchant of Venice" ("[Copybook, 1878–May 1879]"; *JAPM*, 27:169). There is no such comparative piece by JA extant or evidence of it as a production. It is possible that she was thinking of preparing it as a Pierian Union tableau or evening performance.

15. John Lothrop Motley (1814–77), an American-born writer and diplomat who lived much of his life in England, published *The Rise of the Dutch Republic* in three volumes in 1856. Born into a prominent Boston family, he was educated at Harvard University and in Europe. He began what would be a lifelong study of the history of the Netherlands in 1847. He served as American minister to Austria in 1861–67 and to Great Britain in 1869–70. His political and religious history of the Dutch Republic stressed parallels between the United Provinces and the United States and depicted the Protestant movement as a source of liberation. Motley

heralded the rise of Protestantism in northern Europe and contrasted a heroic image of William of Orange with an unfavorable depiction of the Catholic Philip II, whom he presents as a dictatorial scoundrel. His other major work was the *History of the United Netherlands* (4 vols., 1860–67).

JA described the summer reading regimens of her friends at RFS: "When we started for the long vacations, a little group of five would vow that during the summer we would read all of Motley's 'Dutch Republic' or, more ambitious still, all of Gibbon's 'Decline and Fall of the Roman Empire.' When we returned at the opening of school and three of us announced we had finished the latter, each became skeptical of the other two. We fell upon each other with a sort of rough-and-tumble examination, in which no quarter was given or received; but the suspicion was finally removed that any one had skipped" (*Twenty Years*, 47–48).

16. JA copied directly from a letter written by Thomas Carlyle to an unidentified male correspondent ("Dear Sir—") from Chelsea on 13 Mar. 1843. Carlyle wrote in reply to the other's request for advice "to forward you in your honourable course of self-improvement." JA quoted directly from the third paragraph of Carlyle's letter, which is reprinted in full in *Collected Letters*, ed. Ryals, Fielding, et al., 16:81–83 (the passage JA quotes and the direct quotation regarding self-improvement, are both from 16:82).

17. A reference to English writer Samuel Johnson (1709–84), who was the son of a bookseller and author of *Johnson's Dictionary* (1755), a guide to the English language, *The Lives of the Poets* (1778–81), an edition of Shakespeare, travel diaries, volumes of sermons, and many other works. Thomas Carlyle, an extremely prolific letter writer, enjoyed quoting or paraphrasing "old Johnson" from *Johnson's Dictionary* when giving advice—especially when it came to issues of perseverance and discipline in writing. As he wrote to his brother Alexander, "have a faith that as, old Samuel Johnson said 'useful industry will be rewarded'" (18 Nov. 1840, in *Letters of Thomas Carlyle*, ed. Marrs, 510, see also 369). He recommended Johnson's *Lives* as reading matter to his brother John, adding that Johnson "has great power of head, and his insensibility to the higher beauties of poetry does not extend to the most complicated questions of reasoning" (Mar. 1821, in *Early Letters*, ed. Norton, 1:341). On another occasion, he told John that "nothing that Samuel wrote is unworthy of perusal: I recommend his works especially to your notice; they are full of wisdom, which is quite a different thing and a far better one than mere knowledge. You will like him better the older you grow" (11 Nov. 1823, in *Early Letters*, ed. Norton, 2:239). In the latter letter, Carlyle also recommended that John should read Gibbon's history—all twelve volumes—and all of Shakespeare's plays in addition to *Don Quixote* and the works of Swift, Fielding, Pope, Southey, Coleridge, Wordsworth, Irving, and numerous others, all as a basis of good general reading (see also Carlyle's discussion of Johnson, Rousseau, and Burns in "The Hero as Man of Letters").

18. The following item matching this portion of JA's letter appeared as an unsigned "filler" piece in the June 1880 *RSM*. It was printed on a half-page between the end of the "Alumnae Dept." section and the beginning of accounts of Class Day exercises in the "School Dept." section:

> The following is an extract from Carlyle's letter of advice to a young man. It is valuable to every one:
>
> As to the books which you whom I know so little of, should read, there is hardly anything definite that can be said. For one thing, you may be strenuously advised to keep reading any good book. Any book that is wiser than yourself will teach you something,— a great many things, directly and indirectly, if your mind be open to learn.
>
> This old counsel of Johnson's is also good, and universally applicable: "Read the books you do honestly feel a wish and curiosity to read. The very wish and curiosity indicate that you then and there are the person likely to get good of it. Our wishes are presentiments of our capabilities." That is a noble saying of deep encouragement to all true men,

applicable to our wishes and efforts in regard to reading as to other things. Among all the objects that look wonderful or beautiful to you, follow ever with fresh hope the one which looks wonderfullest, beautifullest. You will gradually find by various trails [trials] what is for you,—the wonderfullest, beautifullest,—what is your true element and province, and be able to profit by that. (172)

19. Mary Downs's valedictory message and her valedictorian speech were reprinted in *RSM* (July 1879): 190–92, 195–99. Her talk on "Helen and Iphigenia" used the story of the "results of a moment's weakness and a consequent deed of heroism—the weakness of Helen [in killing Agamemnon] and the suffering of Iphigenia," who "offered her life for her country's honor," as a parable illustrating the extent to which the "history of all mankind" could be measured "by deeds of strength and weakness," nobility and injustice (195, 196, 197).

20. Victoria H. Wigren (sometimes spelled "Wiegren") spoke on "Two Epochs in Swedish History" at the 1879 RFS graduation ceremony. In the previous year she had written essays on Julius Caesar and on Greece for the *RSM* (Jan. and Apr. 1879 issues). She was the daughter of the Rev. John Wigren, pastor of the Swedish M.E. Church of Rockford, and his second wife, Mary C. Johnson Wigren. Wigren had preached at Mercer in Iroquois Co., Ill., before coming to Winnebago and Rockford in the mid-1870s. After graduation Victoria Wigren taught in Dayton, Iowa.

From Ellen Gates Starr

Harlem, [Ill.]   July 27, 1879

My dear Jane,

I have been reading this morning, a little book by Horace Bushnell,[1] on the "Character of Jesus." I should like to read it with you, and talk about it. There are some very pleasing things in it, & very sensible things, too. Do you know, Jane, there is something in myself incomprehensible to me, in my views & feelings concerning religious subjects, & especially this subject of the divinity of Christ. I should be glad to believe it. I don't see any thing logically inconsistent or impossible in it. To believe him other than divine, leaves him, to my mind, as great a miracle as to believe him divine. There is, too, a kind of reality to me in thinking of him as divine. And yet when I ask myself if I believe it, I know that I don't. The reality is about like that of certain characters in fiction, Dicken's especially. I think of the Peggottys & David & Agnes, Paul & Florence Dombey as real persons who have lived.[2] I think of the divine Christ like that. There is to me in ceremonies commemorative of him a solemnity which belongs to that reality of seeming. God is more a reality to me every day of my life. I think more of a reality for my thinking about Christ as divine. It is as if I had realized God in Christ without having realized Christ, I wonder if you get my idea. I often find myself holding little conversations with persons, in my mind. I talk with you that way quite frequently, & a great deal better than we ever really talk together. I suppose every one feels, more or less, a sense of injustice to self in all actual conversation. My "charge" has been absent for three weeks, working in the fields,[3] so the "work of regeneration" has necessarily been suspended, & I have returned to Cicero.[4] I do not feel as if I was absolutely getting the youth

Ellen Gates Starr, later co-founder,
with Addams, of Hull-House. (Photograph by H. Rocker & Co., 77–78–80
State Street, Chicago. Sophia Smith
Collection, Smith College)

into the Kingdom, though the old <u>Cain has</u> not displayed itself so conspicuously
as before. But even should it return I do not think I agree with you in the opinion that it would be worse than if I had never attempted to effect a change. I
think heaven and hell are in the condition of the soul, and certainly the condition of a soul who has experienced a <u>single</u> good impulse, is better than that of
one who has experienced none.

I have read four orations. The last five pages of the fourth oration against
Catiline I read yesterday P.M. That is the most I have ever read in a day. I havn't
done much studying lately. The weather has been severe & the flesh weak. I shall
read one more, and then review. That will be as much as I can do well in the
month I have left. I have read Kenilworth, <u>The Vicar of Wakefield</u>, The Monastery, and am at present perusing The Abbot.[5] If I have any more time while I
am here, I think I shall take one of Dicken's. I havn't read any of his for a long
time, Scott educates the mind; Dickens the heart. I don't think a person who
can read some of his scenes without tears, or at least the feeling which produces
them is entitled to the respect due to me in sympathy with humanity. My school
closes the 29th of Aug. I go to Chicago to begin school there the 8th of Sept.[6] I
had once decided to return to the sem. next year, but I had the opportunity of
going into a private school there, which a lady opened last year, & which, though
of course small now, has good prospects, and I thought I might not have another chance, so I accepted that one. I am expected to teach drawing there, &
of course I shall have to go to taking lessons again, & it will take up a good deal

of time. She also wishes me to take History & Composition & Literature, & perhaps some classes in elementary mathematics. I told her just about how much I was competent to do, & I don't think from what she said there will be any thing I shall have difficulty with. The pupils will be young this year, as the school is young. Miss Holmes,[7] the principal, says I shall have plenty of time to study. I mean to have a French teacher as soon as I can, & go on with that, & my Latin & Literature & History. I don't ever want to go into the public schools. I shall be quite near my Aunt, & shall take drawing lessons of her. She is anxious to have me go there, & will do all in her power for my enjoyment. I hope my brother will go there next fall, too. He thinks of it, & it will be pleasant for me. I have enjoyed my riding as much as I anticipated. The pony is just as nice as she can be, & has a very easy gait. She & I do not afford a frame for quite so much "scenery" as we did at first. I have made several calls in the neighborhood. Of course these people don't call on me. I don't suppose it occurs to them to do it, but they seem to enjoy my calling. I went to see an old Scotch lady one day. She was real nice. She talked about Scotland, & showed me pictures. I heard afterwards that she was greatly gratified by my attention. I enjoyed it. The minister's wife is really a very pleasing woman. I quite enjoy her. I have also been to see Dr. Butler,[8] the catholic priest. You know I wanted to go while I was at the sem. but I wouldn't subject myself to a refusal. I had a right jolly call. He is stuffed with egotism like all the catholic clergy, but he is "nice" decidedly. I never saw him before since I was a child, & I awaited his appearance; not with fear & trembling exactly, but with the anticipation of an awfully stiff time of it. But he startled me entirely off my dignity by exclaiming, "Well! So this is little Nellie, is it? You little rascal, why didn't you come to see me before? Well, child—&c[.]" In relating a rather touching incident of his experience he observed "my old paddy soul was stirred within me." He called me "child" treated me like one, in a way that was not in the least offensive. I _felt_ like one & had a real good time. He asked me to come any time without ceremony, & I am going again sometime. He would assist me with my Latin, but I am almost ashamed to let him see how little I know about it. He writes, reads & speaks it, also French, German & Italian as easily as English. Dr. Clarke[9] says he is the smartest clergyman in Rockford, & I havn't a doubt of it. Now, my lady, I have a pretty serious bone to pick with you. I almost forgot it. I staid with Katie & Mary[10] one night & something was said about my saying "Miss Hitchcock" & her calling me "Miss Starr", & I observed that I should have been most happy to have appeared a little less formal with some of the girls, but never was allowed the privilege, as they all _insisted_ on calling me "Miss Starr". Katie replied that she had always done so because she thought I preferred it. I asked her whence came that remarkable idea & she said Jane said so. I was pretty wrathy, Miss Addams, I do assure you. After I had _besought_ of you as much as I considered consistent with my dignity, to call me something else, & you had cruelly refused to do so for so long, I didn't expect of you the additional cruelty of misrepresenting me; & I fully expect of you another elaborate mark for my testament.

Johney Haseltine asked his mother "What ma[k]es some of the men grunt when they are kneeled down in c[hu]rch?" I hope you will not forget to copy those questions on Macbeth. I intend to join a Shakespeare club this winter, if I can. You cheated me out of Beloit commencement nicely.[11] I rec'd a letter from Katie complaining bitterly of you. I forgive, however, even that. Please write to Your friend

Ellen Starr.

ALS (SCPC, JAC; *JAPM*, 1:374–85).

1. Horace Bushnell (1802–76) was a Congregational pastor of the North Church of Hartford, Conn., who in his anti-Calvinistic theological writings emphasized the goodness of human beings, the mercy of God, and the teachings of the New Testament. His writing on the character of Jesus stressed the unity of the Deity. In *Nature and the Supernatural* (1858) he criticized transcendentalism. His major works include *Christian Nurture* (1847), *God in Christ* (1849), and *The Vicarious Sacrifice* (1866). His writings were collected during JA's college years in 1876–81.

2. EGS refers to characters in Dickens's *David Copperfield* (1850) and *Dombey and Son* (1848).

3. After teaching in Mt. Morris, EGS tutored and taught for the summer of 1879 in Harlem, Ill., a small farming community and railroad stop located on the Rock River near Rockford. A historian of the small village wrote in 1877 that "a little section of Scotland has been literally transplanted in Harlem Township," and, as EGS recounts here, many of the townspeople were Scottish immigrants (*History of Winnebago County*, 941). The community had a small public school, begun in the 1840s in a log building that initially served many functions, including as a school, community center, and church. By 1877 the public school was operating as the Harlem Consolidated School. In the 1870s the village also had a Methodist and a Presbyterian church. Close proximity to Rockford made it possible for EGS to visit the city during her stint teaching in Harlem. The seminary magazine noted that "Miss Starr, who is teaching school near Rockford, occasionally visits her friends at the Seminary" (*RSM* [July 1879]: 203).

4. Marcus Tullius Cicero's (106–43 B.C.) writings include many orations and epistles as well as works on moral and political philosophy. He is best known for his opposition to Catiline, who organized a conspiracy to overthrow the Roman government in 63 B.C. Cicero was warned of the planned insurrection—which was to be set in motion by his own assassination—and publicly accused Catiline before the senate. Catiline fled and later fell in battle.

5. Sir Walter Scott's *The Abbott* (1820) was the sequel to *The Monastery* (1820).

6. EGS began teaching in Chicago in Sept. 1879, first briefly at Miss Holmes's new school, then at Miss Rice's, and finally for an extended time at Miss Kirkland's School for Girls. All these schools were run by women who knew each other well and were connected to the network of influential Chicago matrons with whom EGS's aunt Eliza Allen Starr was friends (see *PJA*, 2).

Mary J. Holmes's school was at 571 Division St. Her home address was listed in city directories as 487 N. LaSalle Ave., from 1884, the same address as that of Rebecca S. Rice's school. By 1891 the address of Miss Rice's school was listed as 479 Dearborn Ave. and Mary J. Holmes's residence as 44 Scott St., a few doors down from the new location of the Kirkland School.

Miss Rice's School for Young Ladies and Children (later called Girls' Higher School) opened in Chicago in 1876. It was headed by Rebecca S. Rice (1836–1911), a graduate (A.B. 1860, A.M. 1863) and former professor of mathematics and astronomy at Antioch College, Yellow Springs,

Ohio. Rice had previously taught in Green Plain, Xenia, and Dayton, Ohio, in the 1860s and was an instructor in French and mathematics at the Antioch Academy preparatory school from 1866 to 1870. She left her professorship at Antioch College, where she taught from 1873 to the end of the 1875–76 school year, to found the private school in Chicago.

Designed to prepare students for college, Miss Rice's School emphasized the study of English literature, languages, science, art, music, and history. A school catalog announced that the "object of the school is to teach all branches of a sound education in as natural a manner as possible" (*Young Ladies' School*, 1). The curriculum focused on the reading of classics and of criticism of those canonical works, followed by the writing of student compositions based on the readings. Students also received instruction in modern languages, specifically French, German, and Italian (they were urged to have a speaking and reading ability in two languages by the time they were sixteen). They studied physiology, gymnastic exercise, and elocution, and electives were available in Latin and mathematics. The school was divided into kindergarten, primary (seven to nine years of age), intermediate, and advanced grades. The lower grades included both male and female students, with boys admitted up to the age of ten. The higher school was open to girls only. Private classes were available to pursue special studies, and the school operated art (drawing and painting) and music departments, with lessons taught by Chicago-area artists and musicians.

In 1879 the school was located at 481 North LaSalle St. The 1879 faculty included Rebecca S. Rice, principal; Evelyn Darling, first assistant; Eva Fowler, second assistant; Alice A. Farrar, kindergarten teacher; Eugene von Klenze, modern languages instructor; Sarah H. Stevenson, Ph.D., lecturer on physiology and hygiene; and "Miss Ellen Starr, Drawing Teacher." A catalog describing the school's programs announced that "Primary instruction in Drawing will be given, this year, by a Competent Instructor, to all the members of the School. Advanced classes in Drawing and Painting will be formed as desired . . . a course of Lectures on Art is expected . . . open to ladies and members of the School" (*Young Ladies' School*, 2). The 1888–89 catalog promised that the course of instruction would provide "preparation for our best colleges" and that "Real Higher Schools for women are greatly needed in the West, and it is the hope of the Principals to meet the need, in quality and extent of work, in this school" (*Girls' Higher School*, 1). During the 1880s the school was located at 487 and 489 LaSalle St. and then later moved to 479 and 481 Dearborn Ave. By 1888 Gertrude Estabrook had taken over EGS's old job as instructor in drawing and painting at the school.

Rebecca S. Rice became the first woman member of the Antioch College Board of Trustees in 1888 and served in that position until 1898. In that year she closed her Girls' Higher School and became associated with the Univ. School for Girls, which had been founded by Anna R. Haire, A.B., Smith College, and S. Louise Mitchell, Ph.B., Lake Forest Univ., in 1897. Like Rice's school, the Univ. School for Girls admitted pupils at kindergarten, primary, intermediate, and academic levels. It was affiliated with the Univ. of Chicago and received backing from such luminaries as education reformer John Dewey, Smith College president L. Clark Seelye, and the Rt. Rev. Charles E. Cheney, rector of Christ Church, Chicago, and presiding bishop of the Reformed Episcopal Church.

Rice's good reputation and her strong connections in prominent religious and educational circles in Chicago, helped win a following for the new school. She served along with Haire and Mitchell as a principal of the school at least through 1900, and probably through the duration of her involvement in the school, which ended in 1904 when she retired to Yellow Springs. She taught again for one school year at Antioch Academy in 1909–10 and died at Yellow Springs on 4 May 1911.

7. EGS became a very close friend of Mary J. Holmes, who is mentioned often in her correspondence to JA. The two were frequent companions and spent Sundays together, surveying different church pastors and congregations in the Chicago area.

8. The Rev. Thaddeus Joseph Butler, D.D., was the pastor of St. Mary's Catholic Church in Rockford. Born in Limerick, Ireland, and educated in Dublin and Rome, he came to the United States in the late 1850s and at the outbreak of the Civil War became chaplain of the Irish Brigade of the Union army. He had a fine singing voice and was well known as an orator. In 1877 Butler was described as "a scholar and a thinker" who "ranks among the most eminent of Europe and America" (*History of Winnebago County,* 470).

9. At least three Dr. Clarks practiced medicine in Rockford and had connections to RFS: Lucius Clark (1813–78), Dexter Clark (d. previous to 1878), and D. (Dexter) Selwyn Clark (b. 1839). EGS may be referring to D. Selwyn or possibly to an entirely different "Dr. Clarke." Lucius Clark was born in Amherst, Mass., graduated from Geneva Medical College, N.Y., in 1835, and moved to Rockford in 1845. He reportedly mortgaged his home to help supply the financial support for the founding of RFS, and he was one of the original members of the Board of Trustees. He resigned in 1877 after serving for twenty-seven years and died at his home in Rockford on 5 Nov. 1878. He was memorialized for his "fatherly kindness and tenderness, and delicate benevolence" in the Feb. 1879 issue of the *RSM* (33) and for his "beneficent ministry" in the *Rockford Daily Register Gazette* on 15 Nov. 1878. Lucius Clark's younger brother was Dexter Clark, a leader of the Second Congregational Church of Rockford and superintendent of the church's Sunday School, where many RFS students were involved. Lucius's son, D. Selwyn Clark, came to Rockford with his family at the age of six. He received his medical degree from the College of Physicians and Surgeons in New York City in 1865 and served as a surgeon during the Civil War. He married Eva F. Townsend of Springfield, Pa., in 1872, and operated a private practice in Rockford. He succeeded his father as a member of the RFS Board of Trustees and served in that capacity for many years, including during JA's time at the school. Eva Townsend Clark was a member of the RFS Endowment Com. in 1877 and 1878, and the Clarks were active boosters of the seminary. Eva Townsend Clark was secretary of the RFS Alumnae Assn. when it petitioned for women to become members of the RFS Board of Trustees (see *PJA,* 2).

10. References to Katie Hitchcock and Mary Ellwood. Mary Patience Ellwood (Lewis) (1863–1903) was a member of a very wealthy and prominent De Kalb, Ill., family. She was the daughter of Harriet Miller Ellwood (1837–1910) and Isaac Leonard Ellwood (1833–1910). They were married on 27 Jan. 1859 and had seven children, five of whom—two sons, William (1859–1933) and Erwin Perry (1873–1943), and three daughters, Harriet (1861–1934), Mary, and Jessie (1869–1956)—lived to maturity. Isaac L. Ellwood was a very successful barbed-wire manufacturer and financier whose wealth made him influential in political circles. He owned the I. L. Ellwood Manufacturing Co. of De Kalb and managed the American Steel and Wire Co., a corporation formed in 1898. He was lauded at his death as the "richest man in Illinois" (*Aurora Beacon,* 12 Sept. 1910). The Ellwood mansion, designed by George O. Garnsey of Chicago and built on spacious grounds on North 1st St. in De Kalb in 1879, was a local showcase (it is now open to tours as the Ellwood House Museum). Mary Ellwood began school at RFS in 1878 and graduated with JA as vice president of the class of 1881. The girls remained good friends and corresponded after leaving school. Following an agenda that she and JA had discussed regarding their time after graduation, Ellwood attended Smith College in 1881–82 and in 1883–84 went on a tour of Europe with her sister Harriet "Hattie" (or "Puss") Ellwood (Mayo), aunt Alida Ellwood Young, and JA (see *PJA,* 2). Mary Ellwood married John H. Lewis, a De Kalb banker, on 1 Oct. 1884, and they had two children, James E. Lewis (1887–1932), and Harriet Louise Lewis (Buckingham) (1895–1973?). Mary Ellwood Lewis was active in club and church work and became the president of the De Kalb Ladies' Club. She died in Dec. 1903.

11. JA and EGS had apparently planned either to go to the Beloit College commencement together or to meet there, but JA decided to stay at home in Cedarville (see JA to EGS, 11 Aug. 1879, below).

Essay in the *Rockford Seminary Magazine*

This essay illustrates the potent intellectual influence at Rockford Female Seminary of Thomas Carlyle's classic treatise on great men and destiny, On Heroes, Hero Worship, and the Heroic in History (1841). Engaging in the kinds of questions Carlyle raised, Jane Addams wrestled with the themes of idealism, life's purpose, ambition, self-hood, and fate, all of which would engage her mind for years and eventually lead her to found Hull-House. This essay on heroism was published anonymously as the lead item in the "School Department" section of the seminary magazine.[1] It was followed by a piece on "Hero-Worship" written by Addams's friend Nora Frothingham.[2]

[Rockford, Ill.]   JULY 1879

"FOLLOW THOU THY STAR."[3]

The belief in Astrology is no more. The divine art, first devised on the plains of Chaldea,[4] has been proved to be but an illusion. The primitive wisdom of the earlier sages has been swept away by the irresistless flood of modern science.

Yet no one wonders that the wild primeval man, seeking to peer into the blank future, and unincumbered by any religious superstitions, should strive to read from the illumined book of heaven, the destiny of man; and that after a time was beholding the immutable laws of nature, the stars in their orbits,[5] eternally unchanged and unchangeable, he, is[6] his primitive wisdom, should attribute the same immutability to the affairs of man; and we easily see how fatality was one of the first elements of the early philosophers.

A trace of these philosophies still remains, fatalism yet wields a powerful influence in the world, and every man vaguely believes in a destiny. He feels the spark of the heroic slumbering in his heart, he knows that there is one thing he can say or do that will kindle his true inner nature, present him to the world as he really is in his truest moments, and command admiration from all mankind. Could he but determine his life-purpose, clearly see and understand this vague object for which he must strive, he should *then* strike the key-note of his existence, come into sympathy with nature, and harmony with mankind. Every man realizes this, for this inner con[s]ciousness is great Nature's gift, which she bestows upon all, and there is not one in a thousand who does not sorrowfully throw it away. The moment comes to him to comprehend his life-purpose, but his faculties are locked up, and offer no resistence, he dimly sees it and yet his powers are paralyzed. He may make an effort, and almost grasp it, the thought that most thrills his existence, trembles for utterance, but is gone before he can frame it in language. He sees for one instant his ideal self, grasps for it, but fails, falls back and ever after follows a false destiny, realizing that the happiest, noblest and best part of his life is never to be acted out, that he is everafter to be haunted by a harassing doubt, a vague regret, that he will ever be in discord with the world, his life a daily fret and jar, that the pure ideal of a noble existence was once possible, that he felt it near, but lost it.

It is this same feeling, an idea of not being appreciated, of being something better than his neighbor realizes, that causes the occasional uprising of the lowest dregs of society; in a vague, ignorant way they are trying to gain a footing, they want a chance to work out their ideals, *bread* is but the nominal object, if this was given them they would be still unsatisfied, for "it is not to taste sweet things, but to do noble and true things, and vindicate himself under God's heaven, as a God-made man, that the poorest son of Adam dimly longs."

The religion that requires the most fasting and self-sacrifice, is the religion that in the end gains the most followers. It appeals to the heroic in man, and lifts him above the common place.

But in this age of advancement we are losing the old belief in the starry vision, a certain ethic rationalism denies all mysteries of the truer and diviner hidden in the heart and brain. Religion is growing very easy, and requires no self-sacrifice. Science demands from its devotees only an exertion of the brain, and not a complete surrender of life and all its pleasures. None devotes himself to one purpose with the terrible earnestness of old. It is only the poet who succeeds in speaking his life word, or an occasional fanatical reformer who truly strives to follow his star. These too in time must cease. If hero worship dies there can be no heroes. "If the eye had not been sunny, how could it look upon the sun." Unless each man follow independently his own star no one man can be a hero.

PD (*RSM* [July 1879]: 183–85; *JAPM*, 46:30–32).

1. See also AMsS version, 26 Feb. 1879, *JAPM*, 45:1831–37. JA wrote "The School Dept of Magazine" across the last page, with her signature and the date (*JAPM*, 45:1837).

2. E.[leanor] ("Nora") Frothingham, "Hero-Worship," *RSM* [July 1879]: 185–88. Frothingham wrote of how, across history and time, there is evidence of the human need to worship a power beyond the self and also the urge to act upon the "divine spark in human nature asserting itself above the trivial and earthly parts of man's existence" that spurs them to develop heroic powers (186). Pondering "these long dead men"—William Wallace, Abraham Lincoln, Napoleon, Julius Caesar, and Martin Luther—Frothingham concluded, "We are influenced by the heroes dead and gone, perhaps more than if they were men living to day" (188).

3. For her title, JA was probably quoting from Dante's *Inferno*, canto xv, lines 55–56: "'If thou,' he answer'd, 'follow but thy star, / Thou canst not miss at last a glorious haven.'"

4. Chaldea, an ancient region on the Euphrates River and the Persian Gulf, was originally part of Babylonia, home to the Chaldean, or neo-Babylonian, Empire.

5. See also Draft of Essay, 28 Jan. 1880, below.

6. JA meant to write *in*.

To Ellen Gates Starr

Cedarville Ill   Aug 11—1879

Beloved Friend;

You confuse me by writing about so many things at once, I don't exactly follow your transition of moods—yet I truly thank you for all you said to me concerning your "incomprehensible views." I catch you[r] idea, of course I do. Don't you see that you are all right. What do you understand by being saved? I don't know, of course, whether I have the correct idea or not, but what I call it is this—that a people or a nation are saved just as soon as they comprehend their god; almost every nation has a beautiful divinity to start with, if they would only keep right to that they would be all right, but they don't, they keep getting farther away & lowering their ideal until at last they are lost. Comprehending your deity & being in harmony with ~~your~~ his plans is to be saved. If you realize God through Christ, it don't make any difference whether you realize Christ or not, that is not the point. If God has become nearer to you, more of a reality through him, then you are a Christian, Christ's mission to you has been fulfilled. Don't you see what I mean. If you have a God you are a Dieist, if you more clearly comprehend that God through Christ then you are a Christian. I am afraid I havn't expressed my idea very clearly, if you read Tennyson's "In Memoriam"[1] & look out for it, maybe you can see something that will be exactly what you need; I did once but I am far enough away now, & I beg of you not to think that I am trying to "preach," it don't sound like what I meant it should if you think that. I wish I was where you are. Christ don't help me in the least, I know it is because I don't appreciate him, some times I can work myself into great admiration for his life & occasionally I can catch something of his philosophy, but he don't bring me any nearer the Deity. I think of him simply as a Jew living hundreds of years ago, surrounding whom there is a mystery & a beauty incomprehensible to me, I feel a little as I do when I hear very fine music—that I am incapable of understanding. This is the nearest that I get to it & it is very rare— as a general thing I regard it with indifference, think of the Jewish faith just as I do of Mohammadism or any other system of religion. Lately it seems to me that I am getting back of all of it—superior to it, I almost feel. Back to a great <u>Primal Cause</u>, not Nature exactly, but a fostering mother, a necessity, brooding and watching over all things, above every human passion & yet not passive, the mystery of creation. I make a botch trying to describe it & yet the idea has been lots of comfort to me lately. The idea embodied in the sphinx—peace.

Every time I talk about religion, I vow a great vow never to do it again, I find myself growing indignant & sensitive when people speak of it lightly, as if they had no right to, you see I am not so <u>unsettled</u>, as I <u>resettle</u> so often, but my creed is ever <u>be sincere</u> & don't fuss. I begun with an honest desire to say something that might help you & end by trying to describe something in myself which is intangible—"impals a man on the personal pronoun."[2]

I give you my blessing, my dear, & I'm quite sure you are all right. I think your plans for the next winter are beautiful for situation & prospect, & I congratulate you. No doubt in after years it will be a source of just pride to you, that you were at the smash up of one school & bravely went to work to help found another, and yet I am disappointed to think that you are not coming back to Rockford, that our "social intercourse" is probably over for all time—it is queer though, but a fact that I am glad when I know some people just so much and then stop—Mary Downs for instance—not that I am afraid to go any farther, but there is a sort of a fascination to me, you remember them & retain the impression they leave, go steadily on your own way and meet some-one else, who will sort of finish out what they begun, ~~where as~~ had you kept on with the same person it would probably have been all right, but it is better & more variety so.

I don't feel exactly that way in regard to your going away; but then I don't feel so very bad on the same principle, that two people honestly going ahead are better if they don't "<u>meet</u>" too much—don't need to "descend" you know— "The condition which high friendship demands" &c[.]

I have no doubt at the end of your year at Chicago you will gain a good deal more than if you had been that time in our noble institution, there is something in being in a big city, in giving some-what as well as taking all the time, in gaining the ability ~~to~~ not to move in ruts—that will give you a self-reliance & an education a good deal better than a boarding-school will, & I think that you have a pretty prosperous look-out.

And now, my friend, in regard to a few slurs you made. I can't for the life of me see why you girls did n't go to Beloit, in fact I think you were simple not to— my coming did n't make any difference, because duty seemed plainly appoint me to stay at home and amuse three old ladies & one young man—it did n't extend to all of you, and I shall ever feel personally aggrieved because of your accusations. Miss Anderson & I called on Katie in Des Moines and the first thing she began on was that but—I silenced her. By the way Miss Anderson & I had a lovely trip to gether, spent about a week at my Sister Alice's, in that time surveyed Des Moines & the surrounding country & had a good time generally but I think I enjoyed Miss Anderson more than anything else, she is one of the few people you would enjoy a trip with even to the Great Dessert.

I have had a very quiet summer since then, we have had a good deal of company, but someway I hav n't paid very much attention to them, they have mostly been ministers and sometimes school teachers. All the study I have done has been on comparative anatomy, George & I took up the subject together this summer[3] & have become very much interested, I have been meandering through Motley's Rise of the Dutch Republic and find it a good deal more fun than I expected, it isn't dry in the least. I hav n't quite finished the "Monestay", you did n't say how you liked it, the White Lady[4] has a peculiar attraction for me, there is some-thing glorious ~~to me~~ in the idea of being without a soul, doing what you please without being responsible to your-self, when I was little, I liked the story of "Undine"[5] better than any other, it may be an impression of the same thing— something as foolish [as] people, when the[y] feel an inherited impression think it is a p[r]oof of a pre-existence. I am like-wise reading Carlyle's "Sartor Resartus",[6] there is some-thing in Carlyle that just suits me as no one else does. I am sort of disgusted with general reading, it seems to me it weakens, you read a great many things you would find out yourself if you would take it cool & wait, my admiration for a well-read person is mingled with just a little bit of contempt that they had to <u>read</u> to find out all about it.

Last Sunday I took a long walk & read Thomas á Kempis,[7] it may have been sentimental, but I liked him; now I want to beg your pardon, when you used to keep a copy of him around so much, I was wont to think you did it for show. I don't think so anymore, but may be you did. That reminds me, you demand another book-mark. I won't do it. I don't remember making the speech Miss H. referred to,[8] but I suppose I did, I very likely thought so too, and it is against my principles to apologies[9] for expressing a candid opinion—excepting in cases of lettuce.

You[r] distinction between Scott & Dickens my dear, is quite fine & sounds like a quotation—I mean that I can use it for one—you are perfectly correct in regard to Mr Dicken's, when I first came home from school I felt too tuckered out to attack any thing new, but reread "Little Dorrit"[10] & "Dombey & Son" and enjoyed them too, I could no more do that with one of Scott's than anything.

I know that there is very little time between the 29th of Aug & the 8th of Sept, but I wish that you could take some of it, to come & visit me, I would be simply delighted, will meet you in Freeport any day you may mention & will take you back just when you think you must go. Comply with my simple request. My mother is not at home, otherwise I am sure she would add her invitation with my own.

Those questions on McBeth just struck me this minute. I intend to stop & copy them, you see what you have done,—deprived yourself of six more pages of this valuable epistle, by requesting paltry questions on Shakspeare. Yours &c.

Jane Addams.

Postscriptum & N.B.

Don't think I took this kind of paper just because you did, far be it from me to be so strikingly original, it way[11] it is that I hav n't space to write with a pen, it seems to me the 11th of Aug always comes on the most bewildering days, I am having my room repaired, the man whitewashing the ceiling is prone to streak, so I sit & watch him; if it wasn't for [hon]or I would n't attempt writing at all. I have you essay on "Soul Culture",[12] I don't like it & yet I am posessed to read it every once in awhile, whenever you want it, write for it & your commands shall be obeyed by Your friend

Jane Addams

ALS (SC, Starr; *JAPM*, 1:386–96).

1. Victorian poet Alfred, Lord Tennyson (1809–92) published his long elegy *In Memoriam* in 1850, the same year he became poet laureate. Tennyson was extremely popular in his lifetime. *In Memoriam* contained his reflections on human existence, the nature of faith, and the relationship between mankind, Nature, and God. Inspired by the death of Tennyson's closest friend, the young astronomer Arthur Henry Hallam (1811–33), it is also a celebration of friendship between men. The first stanza of the poem, based in part on John 20:24–29, in which Jesus responds to Thomas's doubts about his authenticity, may very well have been what JA was recommending that EGS read for guidance in her own period of doubting:

"Strong Son of God, immortal Love, / Whom we, that have not seen thy face, / By faith, and faith alone, embrace, / Believing where we cannot prove." EGS replied to JA about *In Memoriam* in a letter written on 29 Feb. 1880 (see below).

2. JA is quoting from the Rev. James Merrill's commencement-week lecture on soul culture (see JA to Eva Campbell, 25 [and 29] July 1879, above).

3. GBH was following in HWH's footsteps in pursuing an interest in medicine and natural science. When she was home, JA joined him in scientific reading and experimentation. They read Charles Darwin and engaged in work with a microscope and a dissection pad. Although JA enjoyed the fieldwork aspects of scientific inquiry, she lapsed in laboratory applications. In her memoirs, she remembered Cedarville summers and berated her abilities in comparison to those of her stepbrother: "In the long vacations I pressed plants, stuffed birds and pounded rocks in some vague belief that I was approximating the new method, and yet when my stepbrother who was becoming a real scientist, tried to carry me along with him into the merest outskirts of the methods of research, it at once became evident that I had no aptitude and was unable to follow intelligently Darwin's careful observations on the earthworm" (*Twenty Years*, 62).

4. A reference to the White Lady of Avenel, a spirit or sylph whose supernatural presence in Sir Walter Scott's *The Monastery* (1820) restores Sir Piercie Shafton to life after he has been mortally wounded and performs other miracles. The White Lady was an archetype of several German folk legends, probably derived from goddesses in Teutonic mythology.

5. *Undine* was a fairy romance written by Baron Friedrich de la Motte Fouqué (1777–1843), German poet, dramatist, and prose writer. Undine, like the White Lady of Avenel, is a sylph. She comes mysteriously to a fisherman couple whose daughter has been drowned, and they raise her in their lost child's stead. Undine later marries and moves back and forth from the watery to the earthly realms in reaction to her husband's disloyalty. JA made notes about Undine in 1878–79: "'He restorest my soul' keeps <you> near reality. You lose your own soul, in fuss [e]tc, he restores it—'Undine' [e]tc" ("[Copybook, 1878–May 1879]"; *JAPM*, 27:169).

6. JA had been reading Thomas Carlyle since she was a child. His *Sartor Resartus: The Life and Opinions of Herr Teufelsdröckh*, part fiction, part autobiography and essay, was originally published in *Fraser's Magazine* in 1833–34 and in book form in the United States in 1836. *Sartor Resartus* ("the tailor, re tailored, or patched together") is divided into two sections. The first is a discourse on the philosophy of clothes—the symbolic "clothes" or emblems and rituals of governmental and religious institutions versus their inner religious or political workings (or the outer appearances or costumes of an individual versus the reality of the inner self). The second is a biography of a fictional professor, Diogenes Teufelsdröckh ("God-Begotten Devil's Dung"), which is based in part on Carlyle's own life story and personal spiritual crisis. As in EGS's essay on "Soul Culture," Carlyle emphasizes the progressive development or growth of the individual's spiritual nature.

7. Thomas à Kempis (1380–1471), a German Augustinian monk, was the author of Christian mystical works, the best-known of which is *De Imitatione Christi*, which was translated from Latin into English in the mid-fifteenth century. It is an outline of the gradual progression of the human soul to Christian perfection and ultimate unity with God.

8. A reference to Katie Hitchcock and the issue of using first names (see introduction to *PJA*, 1, above).

9. JA probably meant to write *apologize*.

10. Dickens's *Little Dorrit* was published in serial form in 1855–57. In the Feb. 1880 issue, the editor of the *RSM* "Literary Notes" section observed, "We think there are very few girls who are not well read in Dickens, but we never knew before the difference of opinion they held concerning him. For two days last week, for some unknown reason, Dickens was discussed on all sides. We were surprised to find that 'Little Dorrit' was the general favorite, even taking precedence over 'David Copperfield' and 'Nicholas Nickleby'" (49–50).

11. JA may have meant to strike through "it way" but neglected to do so.

12. Choosing a title that may have been a pointed critique of the concept of "self-culture," EGS wrote an essay entitled "Soul Culture," which was printed in the *RSM* (Dec. 1880): 284–86, during JA's stint as editor-in-chief of the magazine. Based strongly on the ideas of Carlyle, it was an essay on developing intellect and character, progressing past the sentiment of childhood, and becoming able to perceive the world in symbolic (or archetypical) as well as literal terms. EGS used the contrast between the Venus de Medici and the Venus de Milo to illustrate the difference between mere beauty in form and true beauty that emanates from artists' souls and is given expression in their art. She quoted Victor Hugo on the mysterious nature of the conscience within and ended on a note of angst characteristic of Victorian writers by pointing out the impossibility of obtaining true perfection, of crossing the "gulf between our real and our ideal selves" and thus achieving lasting satisfaction (286).

From Ellen Gates Starr

Harlem, [Ill.]   Aug. 20. 1879.

Dear Janie;

Tonight our beloved Eva becomes Mrs. Lewis Goodrich.[1] Think of it! I presume you have heard it from her before this time. She told me she should write to you. I met her at Brown's last Sat. unexpectedly, & we went to the Holland house[2] & had a most charming visit. I met Mr. Goodrich. He is splendid. I also went to her dressmaker's to see her in her wedding dress. She seems very happy. The dear good girl. I hope she always will be. If this isn't safe, no marriage is. She has known him so long. I have learned tonight to my great joy, that I need not go to Chicago until the 13th. I shall certainly accept your pleasant invitation if nothing unusual occurs to prevent, I think the last of the week.[3] Will let you know when to meet me. Now, Jane, Eva wants you & I to visit her together in her new home. Wouldn't it be nice? While she is a bride you know. And Mr. G. said he should be very glad to see us. Can you go back with me? I hope you can. I did not write Aug. 11. because I did not know as it was to be an institution after that fatal disregard of its observance, I move, however, that it be reinstituted, & see who will keep it longest? The minute either of us gets (pardon, becomes) tired of it, drop it at once. You & I do not use any of "<un>enforced ceremony,"[4] that the immortal William speaks of. I have been out to tea tonight, & had a lovely time. They are really charming people, "They" being the Johnson's.[5] The youngest son, aged 14, & myself, are quite enamored of each other. They have quantities of chickens; beautiful dove-colored ones, almost. The Woodards[6] have them too, & ducks, & ever so many sheep & cows. I help Mrs. W. feed the chickens almost every night. The country is beautiful now. Mr. W. has a very handsome pasture between the house & the river, & his 200 sheep on it make a fine picture. Across the river are corn fields & grain fields, I take my walk there often. I enjoy the threshing as much as any thing in the country. The hum of the machines in the distance is peculiarly in harmony with the sort of subdued hazy atmosphere of late summer & fall. Give me the country or city. Forever excuse me from nasty little towns. It occured to me after I had written, (things always occur <u>afterward</u> to me) that Miss Hitchcock was the one to address on the magazine question. I saw one at the Carpenters,[7] but your article didn't seem to be there.[8] I believe I never yet have made any remark which you have honored me by regarding with favor, of which you did not remark that it "sounded like a quotation." Very much your friend,

Ellen Starr.

ALS (SCPC, JAC; *JAPM*, 1:400–405).

1. Eva Campbell married teacher Lewis Goodrich in Pecatonica, Ill., on 20 Aug. 1879. The wedding was announced in the *RSM* (Nov. 1879): 244, and the staff editorialized that "Eva (Campbell) Goodrich, a student at the Seminary for the past two or three years, has gone out from its walls to return no more as a pupil, but has stepped into the bonds of matrimony" (245). Goodrich (1840–1914), a widower, taught in Pecatonica. He first came to the town in 1854, the year Eva Campbell was born. He worked in the classroom until he became the principal of the Pecatonica school in 1871. Campbell's cousin Laura was his first wife. She married Goodrich in Dec. 1872 but died in July 1876, leaving a young son named after his father. Eva Campbell was thus well acquainted with Lewis Goodrich before her marriage to him.

2. References to businesses in Rockford. Charles W. Brown & Co. was a dry-goods store located in the Holland House block. Merchant Charles W. Brown married Elizabeth Starr of Florida in 1867. John Holland, a banker and railroad promoter, was one of the leading boosters of Rockford civic affairs in the 1840s and 1850s. His Hotel Holland, built in 1848, was four stories tall, the largest and finest hostelry in the city, with 150 rooms. It was one of the most prominent buildings in the city in the nineteenth century. EGS and Eva Campbell apparently ran into each other at the dry-goods store and then went down to the hotel to talk.

3. EGS became very ill with a severe sore throat at the end of Aug. 1879. She wrote to JA on 3 Sept. 1879 that she had made "vigorous use of potassic chlorate & quinine & alcohol" and did not think she had diptheria. "I shall be obliged to give up my visit for this week. If you do not go back to school next week, & have no engagements which will render if inconvenient to you, I think I can come Tuesday" (SCPC, JAC; *JAPM*, 1:412–15). School started at RFS for the 1879–80 school year on 18 Sept. 1879.

4. EGS refers to dialogue in Shakespeare's *Julius Caesar* (act 4, sc. 2), in which Brutus says, "'Thou hast describ'd \ A hot friend cooling. Ever note, Lucilius, \ When love begins to sicken and decay, \ It useth an enforced ceremoney" (lines 22–25).

5. Possibly a reference to the Johnson family, who owned a 125-acre farm in Harlem Twp. Jeremiah Johnson (b. 1804?) came to Illinois in 1837; he married Julia Doolittle (Johnson, b. 1804?) in New York in 1830.

6. Possibly a reference to Mary Perry Woodward (b. 1832?) and her husband Allen (b. 1833?), who were both originally from Oneida Co., N.Y. The Woodwards were farmers and owned 153 acres of land in Harlem Twp. in 1877.

7. Possibly a reference to Carrie and Cora Carpenter of Rockford, RFS graduates in the class of 1878. Both became teachers after graduation, first in Rockford and then, in the early 1880s, in Golden, Colo. Carrie Carpenter married Robert E. Jones of Golden in June 1885 and died of an illness the following Aug. Cora Carpenter continued to teach and visited RFS frequently in the 1880s and 1890s.

8. The July 1879 issue of the *RSM* was devoted largely to the commencement activities of June and to news and work of the graduating senior class. JA's article "Follow Thou Thy Star"

(see Essay in the *RSM*, July 1879, above) was published anonymously, which is probably why, to EGS, it "didn't seem to be there."

Announcements in the
Rockford Seminary Magazine

Jane Addams was elected president of the Castalian Society at the beginning of her sophomore year at Rockford Female Seminary.[1] She presided over the welcoming ceremonies by which the Castalians greeted the Vesperians and new girls at the school were recruited to join one of the societies. The accounts of festivities below appeared in the "Home Items" section of the first issue of the seminary magazine printed in the 1879–80 school year. The report on Addams's presentation to the Vesperians was clearly prepared by a member of the Vesperian Society, perhaps by rival Vesperian president Hattie Wells,[2] who was active with her on the Rockford Seminary Magazine *staff.*

[Rockford, Ill.]   [19 or 26 Sept.?, 3 Oct., 10 Oct.] 1879

A very pleasant surprise in the way of a Phantom party was carried out by the Castalian Society the first Friday evening after our return.[3] Neat invitations, enclosing masques, were sent to all the members of the school, and by half past seven the parlors and reception rooms were thronged with ghostly figures. The Castalian Society wish to express their thanks for the beautiful offering of flowers clustered in the design of a lyre, which was presented by the Vesperian Society. Their fragrance filled the parlors during the entire evening, and the act of courtesy added not a little to the good feeling which was prevalent during the evening.

. . . Friday evening, October 3d, witnessed a strange transformation in the usual stately decorousness of the parlors and unassuming elegance of the reception rooms; for their sacred precincts had been invaded and ruthless hands had changed the furniture and decorations from their usual places, much to the surprise of good old Father Brown,[4] who looked upon us from his picture with startled glances. The exercises of the evening were presented in the back reception room to a large and appreciative audience of Castalians and "new girls." The first on the programme was a grand "Pinafore" duet by Addie M. Smith and Nora Frothingham. After this a poem, composed for the occasion by Belle Rose,[5] on our motto, "They build too low who build beneath the stars," was read. Nettie Pitman[6] then sang in her usual pleasing manner, a "dainty wee Scotch ballad." "Rockford Female Seminary for Women," a poem composed by Berty Hodge,[7] was listened to with great attention and occasional "peals of girlish laughter." After a Barcrolle by Mattie Thomas the Society and friends were invited by the President in a few well chosen words to adjourn to the parlors. As soon as the parlors were filled Jane Addams stepped forward and with the following speech, presented in behalf of the Castalian Society a beautiful blue silk pennant banner with our Vesper star painted upon it.

PRESIDENT OF THE VESPERIAN SOCIETY:—During these later times we have often wished to express our good will to you, our sisters, in some more enduring and visible form than mere words.

We beg now to present this testimony of our loyalty, and although it brings not with it the sweet fragrance of delicate flowers, nor yet suggests the heavenly music lyre, still we cherish the hope that it may prove a rallying point for your forces, an incentive to renewed effort, a memorial of the holy stars.

As its design is that of many stars clustered into one, so may you be. Your many members, each shining with a strong and individual light, may be so united through harmony and good fellowship that their light may blend, until it be like the pure and undiminished radiance of a fixed star in heaven.

Miss President, may we offer this toast:—"Vesperia, may her radiance never be dimmed by a denser mist than the sparkling spray of Castalia's fountain."[8]

To say that we were surprised is unnecessary, and delighted and pleased still more unnecessary. The evening closed with refreshments of ice cream and cake, an ending not at all disagreeable to Seminary girls.[9]

. . . At the last Castalian public, programmes were distributed among the audience, of which the following is a copy:

CASTALIAN SOCIETY.
Chapel, October 10th, 1879.
PROGRAMME[10]
Roll Call.

MUSIC—. . . . . EMMA CARLSON.[11]
ESSAY—"Gypsies,". . . . . LAURA ELY.[12]

Gypsey Camp.
RECITATION— . . . . EMMA GOODALE.[13]
SONG—"Gypsey's Warning," . . . . . NETTIE BURTON.[14]
ESSAY—"The Gypsies of Fiction:
Meg Merrilies their Queen,". . . . . JANE ADDAMS.[15]
RECITATION——
"Meg Merrilies' Curse," . . . . MARY EARLE.[16]
SONG— . . . . ALICE FELCH.[17]

PD (RSM [Nov. 1879]: 239, 241–42, 243).

1. JA was voted president of the Castalians in late Sept. or early Oct. 1879; Emma Dunbar was elected vice president; Edith Evans, secretary; and Edith Price, treasurer and librarian.

2. The Vesperians elected Hattie Wells as president at the beginning of the 1879–80 school year (it was she who was the recipient of JA's presentation at this party). The rest of the Vesperian officers were all friends of JA's. Mattie Thomas was chosen as vice president, Ella Browning as secretary, Nora Frothingham as librarian, and Kittie Waugh as treasurer.

Harriet ("Hattie") Wells (Hobler), called "Kinke" by classmates, was a member of the RFS class of 1882. From Geneva, Ill., she was the business editor of the *RSM* when JA headed the staff; she was also one of the first RFS students to earn a bachelor's degree, along with JA, in 1882. In addition to sharing an interest in journalism, she and JA promoted RFS participation in intercollegiate debating. Wells was listed as a "partial collegiate" in the 1878–79 RFS *Catalogue* (8). In 1879–80 she was a sophomore in the Collegiate Dept., and she was a junior during JA's last year at the school. Wells became an instructor of Latin at RFS in the mid-1880s and served as the secretary and vice president of the RFS Alumnae Assn.

Wells married Edward C. Hobler, a manufacturer, and had two boys, one of whom died at a young age. They lived in Batavia, Ill., where she taught art classes from her home and was active in the Episcopal Church. She chaired the scholarship committee of the Chicago Rockford Assn., the booster-alumnae club made up of graduates who lived in the greater Chicago vicinity. Hattie Wells, along with JA's friends Caroline Potter Brazee and Kittie Waugh McCulloch, was among the five graduates who compiled the school's *Jubilee Book,* a biographical register prepared by the RFS Alumnae Assn. for the fiftieth anniversary of the school in 1904.

3. The 1879–80 school year officially began on Thursday, 18 Sept. 1879. Sept. 26 was the Friday of the first full week of classes.

4. A reference to a portrait of the Rev. Hope Brown (b. 1798?), affectionately known as "Father Brown," who was the financial agent of RFS from 1856 to 1870. Brown was a minister in his late fifties when he was appointed as the school's first administrator by early trustees who were concerned about the seminary's lack of a president or chief financial officer. Sill, as principal, in effect functioned as both academic head and financial president of the seminary for many years. Male trustees hired Brown at an annual salary of $700 at a time when Anna P. Sill was paid $300 and most RFS teachers received much less. He was supposed to spearhead fund-raising and oversee the school's grounds, buildings, and residents, but he functioned much as a social host and handyman when he was on campus. The trustees intended that Brown exercise a curbing influence over Sill, but he served amiably and humbly in his position, declined to challenge her authority, and was always ready to lend a kindly hand to students who needed rides or help in town. The Browns' golden wedding anniversary on 12 Apr. 1881 was announced in the "Home Items" section of the May 1881 *RSM* (138–39), and older students were encouraged to write in and share their fond memories of him.

5. L. Isabella ("Belle") Rose (d. 1885) of Rockford attended the Normal Dept. at RFS and graduated from it in the class of 1871. Rose taught kindergarten in New York and music and German in Rockford. She was enrolled in the RFS Dept. of Modern Languages in 1878–79 and 1879–80. Although some sources list her as graduating from the RFS Collegiate Dept. with SAAH in the class of 1872, another describes her "as taking her degree in 1882" (Hobler, Brazee, et al., *Jubilee Book,* 90). In 1883 she married Z. M. Cypert, a lawyer, and moved to Powhatan, Ark., where she became active in church and social life and served as the organist for her congregation. She had no surviving children at the time of her death.

6. Janette ("Nettie") Pitman of Corvallis, Oreg., was a senior Preparatory Dept. student in 1879–80. She had been a student in Rockford since 1878. She was enrolled as a student in the Dept. of Drawing and Painting and the Conservatory of Music and specialized in the conservatory's Vocal Dept.

7. Sarah Ellen ("Berty") Doak Hodge (d. 1883) of Hopkinton, Iowa, was a member of the RFS class of 1880 and a graduate of the RFS Conservatory of Music. She was the daughter of the Rev. Dr. Samuel Hodge, a Hopkinton minister actively involved in RFS school life. Berty Hodge was born at Washington College, Tenn., on 20 Feb. 1859. She moved in early childhood to Hopkinton, where her father became the president of Lenox College. She graduated from Lenox College and entered RFS in Sept. 1878 as a "graduate from other schools in special studies" (RFS 1878–79 *Catalogue,* 10; *JAPM,* 27:179). While specializing in music, she wrote

for the *RSM*, participated in Pierian Union activities, and, in 1878–80, was vice president of the RFS Society of Mission Inquiry. She was a classmate of JA's in German.

After Hodge graduated from RFS, she returned to her hometown, where she taught German and vocal music at Lake Forest Academy/Hopkinton Institute. She wrote to JA on 14 Aug. 1880 to say that she was "keeping house and taking care of Mamma" (who was disabled with rheumatism) and getting ready to start teaching in Sept. (SCPC, JAC; *JAPM*, 1:551). Because of her mother's illness, she felt she did not have the option to move away from home. She was visited by Nora Frothingham and by Mary E. Holmes in the summer of 1880 and enjoyed exchanging German manuscripts with friends and sharing literary criticism. She hoped JA would write to her and signed her letter "With much love" (*JAPM*, 1:550–53). In 1881–82 Hodge taught at Washington College, Tenn., and in 1882–83 she took private music pupils in Jonesborough, Tenn. Berty Hodge became mortally ill with pneumonia and died after a week's illness on 28 Mar. 1883. The *RSM* printed her obituary in its Apr. 1883 edition (128–29).

8. "Castalia's fountain" is a reference to the spring on Mt. Parnassus near Delphi. In Greek myth, Castalia was a nymph who threw herself into the fountain at Delphi to escape the advances of Apollo. The spring was considered sacred by Apollo, god of poetry, and by the Muses, and renowned for its purifying qualities by Greeks consulting the Dephic Oracle. Its waters are metaphorically associated with poetic inspiration.

9. Earlier in the day of the 3 Oct. 1879 party, Castalian Lizzie Smith confided in a letter to her mother that she, JA, and the other Castalians planned to play a practical joke on the Vesperians. As reported, the Vesperians had given the Castalians a lyre made of flowers. The Castalians, in turn, planned to give the Vesperians a faded, five-cent "basket of pansies as a joke," to be soon followed, after polite thanks from the seemingly snubbed Vesperians, by the real gift: "a beautiful banner with the shape of a star on it & tassels." "Wont the Vesperians feel cheap," Lizzie Smith gloated, "when it is presented with a nice little speach and toast by Jane Addams who is going to wear a new silk gown. They will of course have made all manner of fun of our flowers and they will feal dredful little when the banner comes" (Sara Elizabeth Smith to Annie M. Jordan Smith, 3 Oct. 1879, SHSW, Smith).

10. For a copy of the printed program distributed at the 10 Oct. 1879 Castalian Society meeting, see also UIC, JAMC; *JAPM*, 27:336.

11. Emma Christiana ("Emmy") Carlson of Andover in Henry Co., Ill., was a first-year student at RFS in 1879–80. She was enrolled in the Dept. of Modern Languages, the Dept. of Drawing and Painting, and the RFS Conservatory of Music. In 1880–81 she was a sophomore in the Collegiate Dept. of the seminary.

12. Laura Elizabeth Ely (Curtis) of Argyle in Winnebago Co., Ill., was a student in the Dept. of Modern Languages in 1878–79, when, like Hattie Wells, she was enrolled as a "partial collegiate" student at RFS. In the 1879–80 school year, Laura Ely was reclassified as a junior and graduated in the class of 1881 with JA. She married Edwin L. Curtis in Apr. 1882. The couple lived in Chicago before relocating to New Haven, Conn., where Curtis became a professor of theology at Yale Univ. Laura Ely Curtis traveled for a year and a half in Europe and became vice president of the Study Club of New Haven. The Curtises had four children, the first of whom, a daughter, was born in 1883. Laura Ely Curtis was one of the RFS friends with whom JA kept in touch after graduation.

13. Emma Frances Goodale (Garvin), from Wyoming, Iowa, was a member of the class of 1880. In her senior year, she was a student in the RFS Dept. of Modern Languages and Dept. of Drawing and Painting and president of the student wing of the Society for Mission Inquiry. She gave the president's address on Founders' Day on 11 June 1880. Goodale was born in Marash, Asia Minor, where her parents served as missionaries. She was brought to the United States at the age of five. After graduation, she became the assistant principal of a high school in Mechanicsville, Iowa. In 1884 she married the Rev. James F. Garvin (d. 1923), and they became missionaries in in Valparaíso, Chile.

In 1925 Emma Goodale Garvin responded to a query from historian Hazel Cedarborg regarding her years at RFS. She wrote about the awe she felt for Anna P. Sill and of the "queer kind of honor system used—the girls called it 'The Confessional'" in which girls had to hold forth to Sill in her rooms. During her RFS years, Goodale was best friends with Corrine Williams. She was also close to JA, Nora Frothingham, and Mattie Thomas, all of the class of 1881. She recalled that she and JA "used to get out our German together," and that she always visited JA when home on furlough from missionary duties. Of JA, Garvin wrote, "She, of course, was the outstanding girl of the school. She was very much beloved and we all felt that she would do great things someday." Garvin also remembered RFS teachers fondly and felt that the seminary had given its students a good preparation for life (Emma Goodale Garvin to Hazel Cedarborg, 22 Mar. 1925, RC).

14. Annette ("Nettie") Burton of Golconda in southeastern Illinois was a student in the Dept. of Modern Languages in 1878–79. In 1879–80 she was enrolled as a special student at RFS. She continued her modern languages study and graduated from the RFS Conservatory of Music in the class of 1880, along with Hattie Ellwood, Berty Hodge, and Corrine Williams.

15. This essay by JA was on the most colorful female character in Sir Walter Scott's novel *Guy Mannering* (1815). The title JA placed on the two extant AMs versions of the essay was "The Gipsies of Romance—Meg Merrilies thier Queen." One of these versions was dated 15 Oct. 1879 (*JAPM*, 46:40–48, 49–56). JA also wrote a dramatic scenario of *Guy Mannering* and broke the action into five acts. Act 2 has two scenes: "Scene I—Meg Merriles stops Bertram Sr on the highway & pronounces her curse upon his house—Scene II—child Stolen—." Act 5 begins with the "prison burning, Bertram saved through gipsey—" and ends with scene "III Bertram proclaimed by Meg & recognized by populace—" (*JAPM*, 27:339, 340).

16. Mary O. Earle (Payne) was a graduate of the RFS class of 1877. She taught in Rockford in 1879 and in Lake View, Mich., in 1880–81. She married Frank H. Payne, a physician and surgeon whom she assisted in his work. The Paynes lived in Fremont, Mich., and Chicago. After her husband's death (before 1904), Mary Earle Payne lived in Berkeley, Calif. She should not be confused with Mary E. Earle (Hardy), who was a graduate in the RFS class of 1867 and a teacher at the seminary in 1869 and 1870. Mary E. Earle married Prof. Asa Hardy, a teacher and merchant, and made her home in Unionville, Ill., and Cleveland, Ohio. She was the author of poems and literary pieces published in the *RSM* during JA's time at the school.

17. Alice M. Felch (Sheaf) of Rockford graduated from the RFS Conservatory of Music in the class of 1871. She married John P. Sheaf of Holcomb, Ill., ca. 1880.

From Katie L. Hitchcock

Des Moines, Iowa.   Sept. 31 [30], 1879.

Dear little "Junior" Jane:

Oh, if I could only be with you and see you! You were not wrong in thinking that I felt more than I wrote.

Indeed, I have dreaded writing to either you or Miss Anderson—I am so school-sick and sitting down to write only makes me realize the more positively that I am not going to see you face to face.

You needn't tell our worthy principal nor the "Seniors", but if I feel better I believe I will come for the last "twenty". I don't care very much for graduating—I never did as you are well aware, still I am sorry, oh so sorry that I cannot be with you this year and sorry too not to finish the course after all.

Thank you ever so much for the offer of yourself as room-mate. I appreciate the honor—and would have been glad to accept. Jane, I bequeath to you,
my rocking chair—also a small red footstool which Mary Downs gave to me,
which Lizzie Ide[1] gave to her. You may have the green vases too if you <u>want</u> them.
I would be ever so much obliged to you if you <would> see to packing my things,
although I am sorry to trouble you. Ask James[2] to get a box and then just throw
the articles in and send them to me here at Des Moines.

Please send by freight—C.O.D. My dear girl, there is an old trunk belonging to me some where in Miss Blaisdell's hall. I don't want that trunk. I will not
be haunted by it any longer. I do not think there is any thing in it worth sending to me but my blankets. I think I left an old sack[3] and a skirt or two in it.
Perhaps Mrs Rogers[4] will know of some poor but worthy individual to whom
they will be of service. If there are any papers in the trunk please send them to
me, but I don't think there are.

Burn up the pieces of my clothes if there are any.

You can write me the amount James requires to pay for the packing-box.

My dear, I am so sorry to trouble you. Don't hurry about it—but attend to
it when ever it is most convenient for you.

Oh Jane, I can see you sitting all alone in the Greek class. How I wish I was
by your side. Tell Miss Blaisdell I am going to keep up my Greek of course. Give
her my love and sorrow. I will write to Miss Anderson to-morrow. I was so glad
to hear from her.

Jane, I hope you will write to me this winter. I shall miss school so much. I
would write a longer letter, but I am going to ride and want to send this to-day.
Remember me to James and Mrs Rogers.

You know my friends, dont you? Emma Goodale was so kind to write to me.
She will hear from me soon. Give my love to "Nutty".[5] Don't think because I
have not written before to Miss Anderson or yourself that my friendship is on
the wane. It isn't by any means. Good by, dear friend.

K. L. Hitchcock.

ALS (SCPC, JAC; *JAPM*, 1:418–21).

1. Lizzie V. Ide (Knox) of Leavenworth, Kans., was a RFS graduate and senior class president in 1878. Her mother died in 1879, and Lizzie, as the Jan. 1880 *RSM* reported, began "keeping house for her father" (23). In May 1880 she married Lorenzo A. Knox (d. 1898), a boot
and shoe merchant in Leavenworth. They had three children, and Lizzie was active in hospital work and philanthropic causes as well as in the Sunday School of the Congregational
Church. She was also an officer in Leavenworth's Saturday Club.

2. James Alcock (sometimes spelled "Alcott") (1834–81) was the jack-of-all-trades on the
RFS campus. He did repairs and renovations, maintained the buildings, and helped students
with a myriad of errands and small tasks. "The editors are enjoying a freshly painted, newly
carpeted and furnished sanctum. Thanks unto James," JA reported in the July 1879 edition
of the *RSM* (201). Born in Warwickshire, England, Alcock came to Rockford in 1856 (or, according to one obituary, 1858). He was hired as an occasional laborer at RFS on a monthly
rate in 1860 and worked on that basis for the next three years. In the summer of 1864, the

RFS Exec. Com. voted to confer with Alcock about expanding his tasks as "Man of all work" and put him on salary for the next year.

The committee endorsed building a house for Alcock on campus in early July 1869 and later that month again approved "building a house for James Alcock; and recommended the pattern for house, 16 x 26 feet, with an Ell 14 x 18, and wood shed, to be finished within the cost of $600.00" (RFS Exec. Com., "Minutes of the Exec. Com. Meetings of the RFS Board of Trustees," 14 July 1864, 8 July and 19 July 1869). In the fall of 1869, the "committee app[ointed] to confer with James Alcock in relation to his services for the current year, reported that he be allowed house rent & firewood, and five hundred & fifty dollars ($550.) for the year" (RFS Exec. Com., "Minutes of the RFS Exec. Com. Meetings of the Board of Trustees," 2 Nov. 1869). The salary was a good one in a time when most of the teachers at RFS were making between $150 and $300 a year.

One RFS alumnae remembered that the "heavy work" at RFS "was done by James Alcock ('the most promising man of the West' Miss Sill called him because he was always ready to promise any thing the girls wanted but took his own time to perform), and in the kitchen two strong service girls under the direction of the matron" (Carrie Longley to Hazel Cedarborg, 16 Feb. 1925, RC). The students sent James to shop in town for such items as chocolate or sugar so that they could make candy.

Although his home life was rarely mentioned, James Alcock's family was plagued by tragedy. He married Julia Darling (b. 1837) in 1860. The couple lost a series of children in infancy during the 1860s: Forest Hill, named for the site of RFS (Dec. 1865–Mar. 1866); Nellie (Apr.–July 1867); and a third, unnamed, infant. In 1869 Anna D. Alcock was born. On 7 Mar. 1878, RFS student Addie B. Smith wrote to her mother:

> James was in here just now and says his little girl is very sick with congestion of the lungs and dyptheria. Poor man, I feel real sorry for him. His wife is a sort of invalid and very peevish and Annie is all the comfort he has. He works so hard and it is so monotonous for him too I should think. You know he has been here seventeen years and I never saw such a faithful and goodnatured fellow though he is tormented all the time with the girls' errands. Don't seem like the Seminary could run without him for he is the only man on the premises. (SHSW, Smith)

JA's father JHA was among the parents who appreciated what James Alcock did for RFS students. Putting class differences aside, he invited Alcock to visit the Addams home in Cedarville.

Alcock died at the age of forty-seven, suffering from an abscess of the liver. He was survived by his widow and twelve-year-old daughter. His funeral took place in the Seminary Chapel and was attended by representatives of the many civic and fraternal groups with which Alcock had been engaged, including the Masons, Odd Fellows, Knights of Pythias, and Foresters. The RFS Trustees made provisions for the care of his widow and child. The local newspaper memorialized him as a "man of highest principles, genial disposition, and we have yet to hear of any who knew him who did not have the highest regard for him. The young ladies looked upon him as one of their best friends. He was always ready and anxious to lend his help, or whatever character might be required, and by his kindly attention and faithfulness rendered himself dearly beloved" (Sill, "Scrapbook"). The pastor overseeing Alcock's funeral service, the Rev. F. P. Woodbury, chose for his text Luke 16:10: "He that is faithful in that which is least is faithful also in much."

3. A light-colored, loose-fitting, blouselike garment, often worn with a dark skirt.

4. Betsy Rogers, the cook for many years at RFS, befriended many of the schoolgirls. She was listed officially as the superintendent of the Domestic Dept. in RFS catalogs.

5. "Nutty" (or "Nuttie") was the nickname of Maria Nutting.

From Ellen Gates Starr

482 Hurlbut St., Chicago [Ill.]   Oct. 12 [and 19]. 1879.

My dear Janie;

I suppose you are today laboring over some dreadful chapter of Hebrews, while I am attending McVicker's,[1] & taking every possible means of losing the orthodox heaven. Mr. Haseltine is in town, attending conference, and he went with me this morning to hear Swing.[2] This evening he & Miss Holmes & I are going to hear Mr. Herford[3] if it doesn't rain. I confess I am disappointed in Swing. One might as well hear his sermons as <u>read</u> them. They don't gain anything. This morning he preached a regular presbyterian sermon. Perfectly orthodox on the subject of original depravity, & quite so, I judged, on the atonement. I am sorry dear old Dr. Collyer[4] has gone, or I should attend Unity regularly. His farewell sermon was really touching, & his congregation about heart-broken. <u>His</u> sermons gain everything in the hearing. I have attended two Episcopal churches, but do not fancy them;[5] Miss Holmes is an Episcopalian, & a southerner, but she is just as nice as she can be. I am just on the verge of falling in love with her. You don't know what a tony Latin teacher I have. He is teaching me the continental pronunciation. Don't tell Miss Blaisdell, or she will renounce me. My Italian teacher is a native, & very fine. I havn't yet got in a minute for French, & am afraid I shall have to give it up. I have classes in Eng. Hist. & Literature, & of course I have to do a great deal of work for them. I also have beginning Latin classes, & some Mathematics, (which I shall get rid of as soon as Miss H. can afford to have a special teacher.) and my drawing, too, takes a great deal of my time. I <u>like</u> my work <u>very</u> much. I teach from nine till three, with an hour & a half at noon. Am reading Chaucer with my girls. I have read four of the tales, & two in class.[6] I have set my heart on your coming to see me; & I do so much want to take you to Aunties. I wish you would make a little exertion to come. I wrote to Miss Anderson way in vacation, & I am <u>sure</u> I directed it right, but she has never answered it. Tell her I am sorely grieved, but I send my best love. I have been to hear McCullough as Brutus in Julius Caesar.[7] He is simply grand. Also Robson & Crane as the two Dromio's.[8] They are really wonderful. One has an <u>exceeding</u> peculiar voice, which the other imitates <u>exactly</u>, & the effect in the scene where they carry on conversation, one in the house & the other outside, is very striking[.]

Oct. 19.

Miss Holmes & I have spent the enduring day in pursuance of our religious duties, & a small fortune on car fare besides. We are so far up on the N. side, that it is a journey to the fine churches on the S. side; & when we arrived at the Episcopal cathedral, whither we were bound, we found there were no services. We met with the same disappointment last Sunday night. Arrived at Mr. Herford's church, & found some other man lectured; so went to Dr. Gibson's,[9] the one you & I liked so much. I was astonished to see Prof. Hood[10] at the organ. I thought he no longer played there. I am going to hear Herford, & then stop this sight seeing, & adventure hunting, & go to church to worship. Have you seen any thing of Eva? If any one at the Sem. has Mary Down's address, I wish you would get it & send it to me. I would go out to H.P.[11] & see her, if I knew where she was; & I want her to come & see me, too. Auntie is anxious to see her, too, for the sake of the poem. I have just read "Maiden and Married Life of Mary Powell."[12] How charming it is! Miss Holmes & I are reading Romola[13] together. I have a card, & can get all the books I want from the Public library, & have also some friends who have very nice libraries. One of my girls took me to drive in Lincoln park last Wednesday. I enjoy the lake so much. The drive is beautiful.

I hope you & Miss Anderson will come to Chicago together, & come to see me. I am thoroughly enjoying myself. I think I enjoy both myself & others, more & more. I even enjoyed last summer in that horrid place. My lovely visit at your home is one of the things to be enjoyed more & more. Give my love to your Mother when you write to her. I am sure I shall see her again, & know her better even if I do not see her.

Also, give my love to Miss Potter. I suppose she has returned, & begun her work by this time. I wish I could enjoy it with you. I wrote Miss Blaisdell but she has never answered. I wonder if she rec'd it. With the best of my wishes & sympathy. Your friend[14]

Ellen Starr

ALS (SCHS; JAPM, 1:423–29).

1. McVicker's Theater, on Madison between State and Dearborn streets, seated more than seventeen hundred people. It was used as the meeting place for the Rev. David Swing's Central Church of Chicago from Dec. 1875 until 1880. Swing drew such enormous audiences—with capacity crowds in the theater seats and thousands attending Sunday School—that the new Central Music Hall was built primarily for his use, and his congregation moved there in 1880. McVicker's Theater had previously been used by Swing's former church, the Fourth Presbyterian, while a new church building was being built after the Chicago fire of 1871. Swing preached there under the Presbyterian mantle from 1871 to 1874.

2. David Swing (1830–94) was the controversial head of the Central Church of Chicago. Born in Cincinnati, he earned his bachelor's degree at Miami Univ., Oxford, Ohio (1852). He taught Latin and Greek and worked as an occasional preacher in Ohio until 1866, when he was called to become the minister of the Westminster Presbyterian Church of Chicago (which in 1868 united with the North Church and became known as the Fourth Church). He oversaw the rebuilding of the church, then the largest church edifice in the city, after the 1871 fire. He was also editor of The Alliance (1873–82), in which he printed a weekly sermon, and he became widely known for his original and liberal views. In May 1874 he was charged with heresy on several counts brought by the Rev. Francis L. Patton, who was a supply minister to Jefferson-Park Presbyterian Church until 1879 and then became a professor at the Princeton Theological Seminary.

Swing was particularly charged with failing to pay enough notice to the theory of original sin and the eternity of damnation. Tried before the Chicago Presbytery, he defended himself and was acquitted. The trial was big news. Proceedings were published by Jansen, McClurg of Chicago in 1874, and a *World's Edition of the Great Presbyterian Conflict, Patton vs. Swing* was printed by George Macdonald of Chicago in the same year. Swing chose to leave the denomination because of the experience but continued to preach until "his own congregation . . . urged that Professor Swing, with his peculiar views, ought not to occupy a Presbyterian pulpit" (Andreas, *History of Chicago*, 3:827). He accordingly resigned in Nov. 1875. In the following month a new church was organized for him by those more open to his interpretations, and he began preaching independently as pastor of Central Church, using theater and music hall space in downtown Chicago. Swing was described as awkward and homely in physical appearance but poetical and charming in the delivery of his sermons. He died in Chicago in Oct. 1894. His works include *Truths for Today* (1876) and *Motives of Life* (1879).

On 28 Dec. 1879, EGS wrote to JA that she had "met Prof. Swing at one of my friend's. He is worse than plain. He doesn't look wholesome. I was informed that he paid me the compliment of thinking me interesting. Nevertheless I am rather going back on him. I havn't been there [to one of Swing's services] for a long time" (SCPC, JAC; *JAPM*, 1:451). Swing and the group of people with whom EGS became acquainted in these years would later be very helpful to JA and her in the early years of Hull-House.

3. The Rev. Brooke Herford was pastor of the Church of the Messiah in Chicago (formerly known as the First Unitarian Church), located at Michigan Ave. and 23d St. south of the central city. Herford was from Manchester, England. He became the permanent pastor of the church beginning in Jan. 1876, succeeding the Rev. Robert Laird Collier, pastor from 1866 until the death of his wife, Mary Price Collier, in 1875. The church was destroyed in the fire of 1871, and the early 1870s were rebuilding years. "With the accession of Mr. Herford, the church entered upon a new era of prosperity," becoming free of its indebtedness in 1879 (Andreas, *History of Chicago*, 3:824). Collier returned to the pulpit while Herford made a trip home to see his family in England. The church continued to grow in wealth during Herford's leadership. He resigned on 21 Apr. 1882 in order to accept a call from the Arlington St. Unitarian Church of Boston.

4. The Rev. Robert Collyer (1823–1912) was the founding pastor of Unity Church of Chicago. During the Civil War, he ministered to soldiers on battlefields from the Potomac to the Mississippi. EGS's future employer, Elizabeth Stansbury Kirkland, was a good friend of Collyer and a parishioner of Unity Church. Collyer decided to leave Chicago in mid-1879, and EGS was disappointed that he would not be her pastor. She wrote to JA on 28 Dec. 1879 to say she still had not found a substitute for him and that "Mr. Collyer is my idol" (SCPC, JAC; *JAPM*, 1:451).

Robert Collyer was born in Yorkshire, England, and worked as a child in linen mills. He apprenticed to a blacksmith at the age of fourteen. He began preaching in 1849, and immigrated to the United States in 1850, working as a blacksmith and as an itinerant Methodist preacher. He moved to Chicago in 1859 and became first the visiting minister at the First Unitarian Church, and then in 1860, the pastor of Unity Church. Collyer's determination and faith were manifested to his congregation when the church burned down in the Chicago fire of 1871, and he preached the Sunday sermon from amidst its ashes. A new church was erected on the old site and dedicated in 1873. Collyer became the pastor of Messiah Church in New York in June 1879 and died in New York City.

5. Among the churches EGS attended on a trial basis were the Cathedral of Saints Peter and Paul at Washington and Peoria streets, first opened in 1861, and Trinity Church at Michigan Ave. and 26th St., which was rebuilt and opened with seats for one thousand in Nov. 1874. She may also have attended the Anglo-Catholic Church of the Ascension at the corner of LaSalle and Elm streets. Church records document that EGS was baptized at Grace Church on Wabash Ave. between 14th and 15th streets on Chicago's South Side but confirmed in 1884 at the church around the corner from where she lived—St. James on Chicago's North Side.

6. A reference to Geoffrey Chaucer's (ca. 1345–1400) *Canterbury Tales*, which was written around 1387 and printed for the first time around 1478.

7. John McCullough (1832–1903), an American actor known for heroic parts, was a powerfully built tragedian who specialized in Shakespeare. He played Hamlet in St. Louis in 1874, Macbeth in Washington, D.C., in 1875, Richard III and King Lear in New York in 1877, and Othello in 1881. He also appeared in lead roles in Banim's drama *Damon and Pythias* and in John Howard Payne's (1791–1852) tragedy *Brutus*. EGS also saw the Othello performance in 1881 and evaluated it in a letter to JA on 6 Mar. 1881 (SC, Starr; *JAPM*, 1:596–608).

8. William Henry Crane (1845–1928) was an American comic actor. Born in Massachusetts, he began acting on stage in 1863. He paired with Stuart Robson (1836–1903) in many productions in the 1870s and 1880s, including their specialties, Shakespeare's *Comedy of Errors* and *Merry Wives of Windsor*. EGS saw them in *Comedy of Errors*, where Crane and Robson played the two Dromios—identical twin servants who had been separated at birth, are involved in a confusion of identity, and are reunited in the final act. Although Crane, who was hefty, and Robson, who was slight, were far from identical, Crane used the device of perfectly mimicking Robson's distinctive voice (characterized by rapid shifts from tenor to soprano and strange cadences) in order to indicate the brotherly relationship. An 1891 theater history noted that during the 1879–80 season, "Mr. Crane created a genuine sensation by his wonderful imitation of the peculiarities of voice and manner of his partner, Mr. Robson, though physically totally dissimilar in their grand production of the *Comedy of Errors*" (Willard, *History of the Providence Stage*, 248).

9. Possibly Rev. John ("J.M.") Gibson, pastor of the Second Presbyterian Church of Chicago, Wabash Ave. and 20th St., from 1874 to 1880. EGS mentioned him again in her 29 Feb. 1880 letter to JA (below). Gibson was born in Scotland. He immigrated to Canada with his minister father in 1855 and was educated at Toronto Univ. and Knox Theological College in Toronto. He served as pastor of the Erskine Church in Montreal from 1864 to 1874 and as a lecturer in Greek and Hebrew exegesis at Montreal Theological College from 1868 to 1874. After he left Chicago in 1880 he became pastor of St. John's Wood Presbyterian Church in London. He was the author of several books, including *The Ages before Moses* (1879) and *The Foundations* (1880), a series of lectures on evidences of Christianity published in Chicago, and editor of a book of Robert Browning's poems, *Pomegranates from an English Garden* (1885).

10. Prof. Daniel Hood of the RFS Conservatory of Music (see introduction to part 2, n. 42, above).

11. Probably a reference to Hyde Park Twp., Ill., which became part of Chicago in 1889. It has kept its name recognition as a neighborhood on the city's South Side and the location of the University of Chicago.

12. Anne Manning (1807–79), an English novelist, wrote a series of novels focused on historical women and written in diary form, even imitating old styles of spelling and expression and printed in antique fonts. Her *Maiden and Married Life of Mary Powell* (1849), a mock diary of Mary Powell, chronicles her from her seventeenth birthday in 1643, through her courtship and early marriage to poet John Milton, and ends in Oct. 1846. The book is the story of Powell's disillusionment with marriage and her refuted effort to flee back to her family. *Deborah's Diary* (1858), the sequel to *Mary Powell*, was written from the perspective of the Miltons' daughter. Both books were initially published anonymously and later brought out under one cover and attributed to Manning.

13. George Eliot (1819–80) wrote *Romola* (1863) on a visit to Florence in 1860–61. The novel is set against the historical background of Florence in the fifteenth century and features profiles of several historical figures, including the political theorist Niccolò Machiavelli (1469–1527) and religious reformer and prophet Girolamo Savonarola (1452–98), who is tried and executed by the end of the book. The main story follows the fate of the heroine of the title, who is

the loyal daughter of a blind scholar. She is married by a rogue, Tito Melema, learns to despise him, and is redeemed by her discovery of the virtues of self-sacrifice. A lengthy tribute to George Eliot appeared in *RSM* (Mar. 1880): 66–75. JA re-read *Romola* in Europe during her travels in 1884, and it became the subject of study groups at Hull-House in the 1890s. She wrote admiringly about the character of Savonarola while at RFS ("George Eliot's view of Savonarola," n.d., "Savonarola," n.d., and "Darkness versus Nebulae," 14 June 1880, all *JAPM*, 45:1622–23, 1653–61, 46:207–15; see also Draft of Essay in the *RSM*, Jan. 1880, n. 7, below).

14. EGS wrote in the margin of p. 5 of her original letter: "I had a very pleasant visit with Mr. Haseltine. How did you enjoy his visit in Cedarville? Were you disappointed in him?" (*JAPM*, 1:426). The Rev. T. H. Haseltine, who served as a minister in Warren, Ill., and other towns, visited Cedarville and Freeport in the fall of 1879. He was a friendly correspondent of AHHA's and was involved tangentially in RFS social circles. JA continued to have sporadic contact with him as a spiritual advisor over the next few years (see T. H. Haseltine to JA, 13 June 1880, below).

To Anna Hostetter Haldeman Addams

Rockford Sem'y [Ill.]   Oct 21" 1879.

My dear Ma—

I started to write a letter Sunday but was interrupted and here it is Tuesday night before I know it. I have just come from a recitation in English Literature, we had Bacon[1] for our subject to day and got every much interested in him, discussed & compared his philosophy, so that just now I feel very firm in the resolve never to reason but stay in the induction method. If you observe anything peculiar in this epistle you maybe sure it is because I am trying my unfledged powers. Miss Potter makes her recitations as interesting as can be, she is feeling sort of fresh and learned from her trip, and describes the birthplace and surroundings of each man we come to, until we almost feel that we have been there and seen him; we quite congratulate ourselves in being the first class, for of course afterwhile it will lose its novelty & she will get tired of talking.[2] There is one of the new girls I will always associate with that recitation, she is one of the queerest persons I ever saw, she always talks in exactly the same key & her voice never varies the least bit up or down only when she gets excited she talks louder, she has been to my room three or four times to see me, and I am growing quite interested in her. She has pretty good ideas of things but scarcely any expression.

Corinne Williams & I spent Saturday afternoon at Winnebago, went out on the one o'clock train and came back on the evening freight, I just had a lovely time, the visit was short but I enjoyed it, it seemed so good to see the children again.[3]

I had a long letter from Miss Starr yesterday, she likes her position in Chicago very much and goes out quite a good deal, has heard all the noted ministers and seen several celebrated actors and musicians. Mr Hazeltine was in

Attorney Corrine Williams Douglas with one of her five children, ca. 1890s. She and Jane Addams were friends, traveling companions, and sometimes debating partners when they were students at Rockford Female Seminary. (Rockford College *Jubilee Book*, 1904, RC)

Chicago to spend last Sunday and she went with him to hear Swing. Miss Starr was very much disappointed in him and I judge Mr. H. was rather.

Miss Starr sent her best love to you Ma, it just did me good to get her letter. So many of the old girls whom I enjoyed have left, she is one of them. Miss Anderson and I find we have to make up for them in each others society and it seems to me we have better times together than almost ever before, although they are necessarily short.

Mrs Gardiner[4] came down from Lena Friday afternoon and of course as she had just seen you could tell me all the home news. I am afraid from what she said that you have had a busy worried fall and changing girls again of course will be perfectly wretched. Now Ma, I wish if you think you need me you would write and I would come home for a couple of weeks, or if you would feel better to go I see Harry[5] why I most certainly come home and initiate the new girl, it seems to me I ought to have discipline enough by this time to study by myself, and anyway I wish if you need me you would write. Excuse this short letter I will write very soon again to make up for it.

With much love to Pa & yourself[.] Ever your loving daughter

Jane Addams.

ALS (UIC, JAMC; *JAPM*, 1:430–32).

1. A shrewd and often ruthless English politician and an eloquent writer, legal theorist, and philosopher, Francis Bacon (1561–1626) was born in London, educated at Trinity College, Oxford, and trained in the law. He entered Parliament in 1584 and, after serving as an advi-

sor to Queen Elizabeth, rose in rank from attorney general to lord keeper and became lord chancellor in 1618. He was removed from office and briefly held in the Tower of London in royal disfavor after bribery charges were brought against him in 1621. His major philosophical works included *Advancement of Learning* (1605), *Novum Organum* (1620), and *De Augmentis* (1623), the latter two published originally in Latin. During the eighteenth century a theory circulated that Bacon was the true author of works attributed to William Shakespeare.

JA began studying Bacon's *Essays* in class in Oct. His *Essays; or, Counsels, Civill and Morall* (published in three expanding editions in 1597, 1612, and 1625) was a collection of reflections and quotations from other authors on various themes such as greatness, nature, conduct, truth, wisdom, friendship, and death. JA's account book indicated the purchase of a copy of Bacon's *Essays* in Nov. 1879 (see "Report [Account] Book, [1879–80]"; *JAPM*, 27:325).

The Jan. 1880 issue of the *RSM*, which contained many references to materials JA had dealt with in her literary studies, included an editorial that made an example of Bacon's essay on friendship. The allusion was in the context of the close friendships formed between sets of RFS girls and pledges to meet for reunions in the future. One group of four promised to get together when the youngest of them was fifty, and another group of five vowed to reunite for vacations together during the summers so they could talk of the books they had read and the opinions they had formed during the past year ("Then they separate and each takes up her individual life work again, the happier and younger for the meeting"). "Bacon in his famous essay on the subject sets forth two distinct fruits of friendship," the editorial continued, "the first is the ease and discharge of the fullness of the heart," opening with "'griefs, joyes, fears, hopes, suspicions, counsels and whatsoever lyeth upon the heart to oppress it, in a kind of civil shrift of confession.' The second fruit is that making of daylight in the understanding out of the darkness of confusion of thoughts . . . 'his wits and understanding do clarify and break up in the communicating and discoursing with another.'" In a very JA way, the editorial concluded that the girls at RFS should not waste their friendships in gossip or trivia and talk "about fancy work and nothing in particular" but "really gain these two benefits set forth by the wise Bacon" (*RSM* [Jan. 1880]: 30–32).

2. The Jan. 1880 *RSM* reported that the "lectures given by Miss Potter on Thursday afternoon of each week, to the English literature class, have been both interesting and instructive, and quite largely attended by ladies from town" (20).

3. A reference to MCAL's children, John Addams Linn and James Weber Linn.

4. Caroline F. Williams Gardiner (b. 1827) of Lena, Ill., was originally from New York City. She was the mother of RFS student Julia E. Gardiner. She and her husband, the Rev. Abraham Sylvester ("A.S.") Gardiner, were strong supporters of RFS and often visited Rockford to hear lectures, participate in programs, or dine with the students. A.S. Gardiner (b. 1824) was minister of the Presbyterian Church of Lena. He graduated from the Univ. of the City of New York and practiced law in New York City before becoming a minister in 1850–51. He and Caroline F. Williams married in 1852, and they had three children. Both of their daughters attended RFS. The Gardiners moved from Illinois to New Hampshire after Julia's graduation in 1882 and to Pennsylvania later in the 1880s (see also Announcement in the *RSM*, May 1881, n. 3, below).

5. HWH. JA apparently meant to write "if you would feel better to go to see Harry, why I most certainly could come home and initiate the new girl."

To Myra Reynolds

[Rockford, Ill.]   [Oct. 1879]

Miss R.[1] Head Ed of Vassar Miscellany.[2]

We wrote to Yale at the same time we wrote to you, and expected the same courtesy from them you have shown us—a reply, and as we considered <our request> a dignified & reasonable one ~~request~~, the fulfillment of which would require but little effort, we expected an article as well.[3] ~~and~~ It was with this thought that we wrote you as we did. We have not yet heard from Yale College & but hope that an article from you will not depend upon that as we are very desirous to ~~have one article <contribution>~~ from you learn [*one word illegible*] the societies <of Vassar>[.] We thank you for your well wishes and <we> are ~~happy~~ <glad> to say our plan seems to promise success. The last paper we heard from was the "Bowdoin Orient".[4] Yours re[5]

Jane Addams Lit

ALS draft (SCPC, JAC; *JAPM*, 1:422).

1. Myra Reynolds (1853–1936), English scholar and professor, was born in Troupsburg, N.Y., the daughter of a minister and a school principal. She was educated at the State Normal School, Mansfield, Pa. (1867–70) and taught school before she entered Vassar College, Poughkeepsie, N.Y., in 1876 at the age of twenty-three. Her younger sister, Kate, was already a Vassar student in the class of 1877. Reynolds edited the *Vassar Miscellany* from 1878 to 1880. She graduated as valedictorian of her class in 1880 and became head of the Dept. of English at Wells College in Aurora, N.Y., from 1880 to 1882. After two more years of teaching, she returned to Vassar as a professor of English in 1884. Aside from a stint as "lady principal" of Woodstock College, Woodstock, Canada, in 1887–88, she retained her position at Vassar until she left to attend graduate school at the Univ. of Chicago in 1892. She was granted a M.A. degree by Vassar in 1891 and was a Vassar trustee from 1908 to 1920.

Reynolds taught at the Univ. of Chicago for the rest of her career, receiving her Ph.D. there in 1895, becoming an assistant professor in 1897, and rising to full professor in 1911. She was a member of the committee that planned the Univ. of Chicago Settlement in 1894, and she headed the Nancy Foster Hall residence for women at the university for more than thirty years. Reynolds published a revised version of her doctoral thesis as *The Treatment of Nature in English Poetry between Pope and Wordsworth* (1909) and among her other works was *The Learned Lady in England, 1650–1760* (1920). She retired from the faculty in 1923 and died in Los Angeles. Myra Reynolds's niece, also named Myra Reynolds (1890–1974), married JA's nephew Stanley Linn (1883–1945), son of her sister MCAL and JML, in 1915. They had four children.

2. The *Vassar Miscellany* was published from 1872 to June 1915. It was a continuation of the student newspaper, the *Vassar Transcript,* and contained articles about the Poughkeepsie campus and college life in general, student stories and poetry, personal notices, and, like the *RSM,* quotations from various exchanges. JA praised the *Colby College Echo* in the Nov. 1879 issue of the *RSM,* and in Dec. 1879 it was the *Vassar Miscellany* that came in for special praise— perhaps editorial decisions made in part to persuade the editors of those newspapers to participate in JA's planned "College Societies" series.

3. JA wrote this draft while she was in the process of soliciting feedback from her counterparts on the staffs of college magazines at East Coast schools who regularly contributed copies

of their publications to RFS for use in the "Clippings and Exchanges" section of the *RSM*. "Clippings and Exchanges" in the Nov. 1879 issue ended with the following notice: "We found our sanctum somewhat in disorder on our return, and some of the exchanges arriving during vacation may have been lost, but we acknowledge the receipt of the following: *Oberlin Review, The Tripod, Bowdoin Orient, Vassar Miscellany, University Press, The Dickinson Liberal, The College Courier, The Round Table, The Colby Echo, The Volante, The News Letter, College Journal, Collegian and Neotorian, K.M.I. News, College Record*" (248).

In managing the "Clippings and Exchanges" department, JA wanted to try to solicit actual articles from other student editors about their schools. She wrote: "Write to different Colleges to the Literary editors, asking their opinions on Popular subjects, as the marking system or honors—Societies—General reading outside of class work &c[.] Find out what Books are taken most from the societies libraries, deduce—criticize society work." A few entries earlier, she jotted down ideas for editorials, using her distinctive spelling style: "Editorials—1[.] Societies—rediculous for literarires to act so—waste time &c[.] The only good to have up—literary tonic—2[.] The fear of being Pedantic, what ails girls—3[.] Phaganism—Discovery Northwest paggase [passage]—The humans mind can do most any thing if they just keep at it." On the next page she wrote, "Clippings & Exchanges three or four pages—Beloit peculiar editorial—'iron customs['] —Vassar[,] Colby Echo—Give a list of the exchanges received at the opening of the year—also those which came during vacation" ("Pocket Diary, 1875[-81]," 24 Oct., 20 Oct., 21 Oct. [1879? 1880?]; *JAPM*, 28:1638, 28:1636, 28:1637).

The Dec. 1879 issue of *RSM* contained "College Societies" (270–72), a feature headed with an editorial note that informed readers, "following from Beloit College is our first communication in the series concerning college societies—ED." (270). The Beloit article was about its two debating societies and about the pros and cons of debating as a practice, including its social benefits in fostering the "spirit of fraternity" (272). The piece came from the Beloit *Round Table* and was almost certainly written by Rollin D. Salisbury, a Beloit debater and editor of *Round Table*. The Jan. 1880 edition of the *RSM* featured a "College Societies" entry (17–19) from Colby College, unsigned but presumably from J. T. MacDonald and continued in the Feb. 1880 magazine (50–52). The article defended societies as the "intellectual gymnasium" of a school, offering extracurricular exercise for the brain and a means of encouraging a "healthy spirit of rivalry" among the participants ([Jan. 1880]: 18). Another "College Societies" article was contributed by a Wellesley College student and printed in the *RSM* (May 1880): 146–49. In May 1880 Mary Downs, 1879 valedictorian and former *RSM* editor, wrote to JA and praised her for her innovations on the magazine, especially her work with the "Clippings and Exchanges" and the introduction of the "College Societies" articles (23 May 1880, below).

4. The *Bowdoin Orient* was edited in the 1879–80 academic year by a staff of seven headed by Henry A. Wing, the managing editor, and Eliphalet Greely Spring, the business editor, both seniors. Wing (1853–1912) was born in Waterville, Maine and earned both his B.A. and M.A. degrees from Bowdoin College (1880, 1901) and became a professional journalist. Spring (1859–95) was born in Portland, Maine, and was a merchant in Boston and Portland. He earned his B.S. degree at Bowdoin in 1880, followed by a M.S. degree in 1883. The *Bowdoin Orient*, like the *RSM*, carried news of campus life and intellectual interest. Under Wing's editorship it reported on Bowdoin's literary societies, athletics (including baseball, field days, gymnastics, and boating), debating, and political clubs. It also printed poetry, news of major events such as commencement or concerts, and articles or editorials on such topics as mineralogy, physical culture, mental and moral philosophy, the marking system, and the issue of coeducation. The *Orient* was published on "every alternate Wednesday during the Collegiate Year, by the Class of '80." When Wing and Spring took over the editing of the magazine they announced that their motto would be "To censure where censure is deserving, and give praise where praise is due" (*Bowdoin Orient* [23 Apr. 1879]: 1).

5. Myra Reynolds responded on 24 Oct. 1879 that she had read JA's letter with interest and found the "plan you propose has certainly the merit of novelty." Reynolds wanted to know if Yale had "already pledged an article for the December number of your magazine, and also what other colleges have promised to join in the proposed undertaking?" She concluded that she needed the answers to those questions before she could bring the "matter before the board of editors." She signed pleasantly, wishing JA the "best of success" (SCPC, JAC; *JAPM*, 1:433–34). JA also heard from J. T. MacDonald of the Colby College *Echo*. Like Reynolds, he was intrigued but a little wary. He was interested in sending an article but wanted to be assured that, if he did so, it would be printed anonymously. He, too, wrote very cordially and with praise for the *RSM*. After the long article he submitted was published, JA and MacDonald continued to correspond. He wrote a warm letter to "My Friend Miss Addams" about their respective magazine work in early 1880 (18 Nov. 1879 and 14 Feb. 1880, SCPC, JAC; *JAPM*, 1:435, 478–81).

To Ellen Gates Starr

Rockford Sem'y [Ill.]   Nov 22" 1879

Beloved Friend

I have spent the afternoon in a long strain between the reign of Uzziah[1] and Bacon's Essays, and as we are said always to postpone our pleasures until the fag-end of the day when we will be sure to take to it sadly just as people hate dinner parties—so I settle down just about dark to write the forthcoming epistle.

I was vividly reminded of you when Uzziah was struck with the leprosy (don't be alarmed) because I at once thought how you would pour out your pity upon him—after he had done so many good things to be treated like that; and strangely enough you popped suddenly into my head when I was in the midst of Bacon's profound essay on friendship for he said something just the same thing I heard you say once (I beg you once again not to be alarmed, he said it a good deal better than you did) and so between my association of you, both with a bible-lesson and moral reflections, I conclude you must be very nearly orthodox even if you do go to hear Swing and ride <about> in street cars on Sunday, at both of which proceedings I was somewhat shocked but wished that I could do it too.

Katie Hitchcock did n't come back this year because she is n't strong enough, I miss her more than I thought I would,[2] and Miss Anderson & I for the first of the year felt quite inconsolable—it is surprising what a difference the absence of two girls like herself and Mary Downs will make. It has this advantage however that Miss Anderson and I try to make up to each other the deficency and I feel that I know her better this year than I ever did before, the more you can know of a sincere genuine character like hers the more you are led to admire and venerate; and we have had some of the best talks this year that I ever expect to have with anyone: I had never tried to talk to her before on the subject of religion— my ideas of her religion were vague but full of profound respect. One Sunday evening a little while ago, she talked for a long time and told me all about her beliefs & how she came to them: I wish you could have heard her—may be I

exaggerate but it seems to me she has kept just as true to herself and the innocence and freshness born in her as anyone could and that her reason has built
her religious principle right on from that, it seems to me it must be the source
of what we admire so much in her, it reminds <me> of that of Carlyle "every
God-created man is a hero if he only remains true to his creation."[3] Miss Anderson has done that in her religion and it has brought out all the sweetness in her;
she said "I do not think we are put into the world to be religious, we have a certain work to do, and to do that is the main thing."

I, for my part am convinced that the success of that work in a large degree
~~depends~~ depends upon our religion and that I can never go ahead and use my
best powers until I do settle it, it seems to me some-times—I suppose when I
am wrought up—could I but determine that and have it for a sure basis, that
with time and space to work in I could train my powers to anything, it would
only remain to choose what. Of course this must be a false stress <laid on reli-
gion>, but I don't fuss anymore, since I have discovered its importance, but go
ahead building up my religion where-ever I can find it, from the Bible and observation, from books and people and in no small degree from Carlyle.

Miss Potter is back and goes on with her work in the delightful way peculiar to herself, the first of the year she was all tired out and was cross that is the
only word to express it, her crossness differed from Miss Blaisdell's[4] as much as
thier characters do, but it was there just as surely, she frighten the new girls half
out of thier wits, but was a constant source of amusement and interest to me.
She did n't talk much about what she had seen and when she did mention something she had seen would flush up and grow confused, when we were all delighted because she was going to talk. One day in Eng literature she described Caxton's[5] old house (Caxton is still one of her hobbies) and <was> so embarassed
she could n't tell what century he lived in, there was something so pretty & help-
less the way she looked up at us. She is all over that now just as she is her irrat-
ability and I enjoy her as much as ever. At the last Vesperian public she gave a
little lecture, began by telling about the Italian skies & thier influence on her and
then gave her impressions in Venice—the thing I remember best is her description of a flock of doves.

I am all alone in Greek this year and am selfish enough to quite enjoy the
position,[6] I expect to begin the Iliad in a week or two and look forward to the
fact with a great deal of pleasure, there is something inspiring in the thought of
reading Homer in the same language Homer sang in, Miss Blaisdell is quite
excited over the prospect.

That reminds me I sit at Miss Blaisdells table this year (they had some new
theory about development & expansiveness and I was forcibly torn from Miss
Anderson's)[.] Corinne Williams is senior there and we have some funny sort
of times; Corinne is sort of queer this year, I think it is because she reads too much
and so omniverously it has an effect that I like to watch for there is no telling
where She is going to land, will probably turn out all right. Some of the new girls

are real nice and interesting, there is one girl who has the queerest voice I ever heard, it is all on one key and never varies one tone, although when she is excited she speaks louder, she has some good ideas on things & some original ideas but about the least expression of anyone I ever saw, I intend to gradually draw her out if I can, although her voice makes me want to fly through the key-hole.

I have not yet seen Eva although I have had one or two letters from her, have been expecting to see her almost every Friday evening but as she stated in one of her epistles she is very busy practicing & taking care of 'our boy'.[7]

Of course I was obliged to take a new room-mate unto myself (a sort of "dare-devil" spirit posessed <me>[)] and I told Miss Blaisdell that I had n't the least choice, would take the girl who happened to come next—the girl who happened to come next was Addie M. Smith[8]—do you remember her—and my fate was sealed. We get along quite swimmingly and I like the independence of it, for we go on our separate ways and tacitly compare notes.

As you told me I should not mention to Miss Blaisdell that you were using the Continental pronounciation of Latin I took particular pains to tell her and she said her interest in you was founded on something even deeper the[n] the pronounciation of Latin, that is a compliment my friend which it would be well for you to remember. I am very much obliged to you for your invitation to come to see you, I should be delighted to come if possible; Miss Anderson & I talk in a vague way, once in a while of what might happen if we could spend a Sunday in Chicago, but the vision is so far in the future that I tremble. By the way Mary Down's address is 132 Drex[el]. Boul. Chicago. I hope you will go to see her, she is one of the girls whom it pays never to lose sight of.

What made you make that curious remark concerning Mr Hazeltine? Did he say anything about me to warrent it, tell me what he said and I will report what I think of him.

Miss Anderson is going home with me for Thanksgiving, I wish you were going to be there. I did n't mean to make this letter so abomniably long, there is a second Miss Ellen Smith[9] here whom I will reserve for my next. She has one astronomy class. I am getting very much interested in astronomy and enjoy it thoroughly in spite of Miss N.[10] I am having a real nice <time> this year quiet & steady. Enjoyed your letter, would enjoy another. Yours sincerely

Jane Addams

For "recreation", I am reading Warner's "Back-log Studies",[11] nice as it can be. We have lovely times in Young's "Night Thoughts[".][12] After all my writing there were two or three things that I wanted to say & didn't, it is the effort of Bacon, he is interesting but not conducive to original thought.

ALS (SC, Starr; *JAPM*, 1:436–41).

1. Uzziah (ben Amaziah) was King of Judah in the eighth century B.C. According to II Kings 14:21 and II Chronicles 26:1, 3, Uzziah was co-regent with his father, Amaziah, from the age of sixteen to thirty-one. Under his own reign, he oversaw the reopening of the Red Sea trade

and built extensive fortifications. His reign ended ca. 750 B.C. JA was probably studying the reign of Uzziah in Greek, for she completed her course in ancient history in Feb. 1879.

2. Katie Hitchcock wrote to JA just before Christmas and expressed similar dismay over her inability to return to school: "Oh, dear Jane; I wish I could come back but I don't believe I could, or can I mean, and even if I did come I shouldn't think of graduating." Hitchcock asked especially to be remembered to Miss Blaisdell and Miss Anderson, two teachers with whom JA also had a close bond, and ended her letter by asking JA to write to her. "You have been very forbearing. Good-bye," she closed (23 Dec. 1879, SCPC, JAC; *JAPM*, 1:443–44).

3. Probably a quotation from one of Carlyle's lectures on heroism compiled in *On Heroes, Hero Worship, and the Heroic in History*. In "Lecture IV: The Hero as Priest," Carlyle observed, in the context of discussing Martin Luther's life, "If Hero mean *sincere man*, why may not every one of us be a Hero? A world all sincere, a believing world: the like has been; the like will again be. . . . Better be so reverenced as where all were True and Good!" (Carlyle, *On Great Men*, 50; see also Essay in the *RSM*, July 1879, above).

4. The phrase "taught Latin at Rockford" was inserted beside Blaisdell's name in the text of the letter. It was written by EGS to identify Sarah Blaisdell for James Weber Linn before sending it and other letters to him for use as research material as he prepared his biography of JA in 1935.

5. William Caxton (ca. 1421–91), English printer, merchant, and translator, lived in Bruges before establishing a famous press at Westminster in 1476. His house is believed to have been located on the site of the Old Almonry on Little Dean St. near Storey's Gate in London. There he printed more than a hundred books, including many of his own translations from French. Caxton was the subject of a profile written by "R." and published in the *RSM* under the title "Wm. Caxton, The First English Printer" (July 1878: 122–27).

6. In her memoirs, JA recalled feeling a sense of holiness about her private study of Greek with Blaisdell (*Twenty Years*, 51; see also introduction to part 2, above). Reading the *Iliad* was standard fare for the second-year curriculum in the Greek course at RFS.

7. References to Eva Campbell Goodrich and her young stepson, Lewis Goodrich, Jr.

8. JA included a dialogue between a "Miss Smith" and her "Room-mate" regarding how cold it was in their room in the *RSM* (Dec. 1879): 274. She also published an editorial on the proper treatment of one's roommate (*RSM* [Jan. 1881]: 282). Although JA sometimes complained about Addie M. Smith's socializing with friends in their room, she herself was quite the attraction for get-togethers. Corrine Williams, a fellow *RSM* staff member, described JA in her college years as a seemingly somber girl with "'brown hair drawn plainly back, with a decided inclination, never encouraged, to fall apart on the side,'" who quickly revealed herself to be self-possessed and have a charming personality. "'School girls are not psychologists,'" Williams continued, "'and we never speculated as to why we liked to go to her room so that it was always crowded when the sacred "engaged" sign was not hung out. We just knew there was always something "doing" where she was, and that however mopey it might be elsewhere there was intellectual ozone in her vicinity'" (recollections from 1909, quoted in Linn, *Jane Addams*, 47).

9. This Ellen Smith must have been a special student at RFS who only took the astronomy course. Her name is not listed among registered full-time students of the school in 1879–80.

10. Helen S. Norton (1839–1923) taught at RFS in the early 1870s and again in 1879–80. She was born in Dexter, Mich., and grew up on a farm. She graduated from Mt. Holyoke College and taught in Wisconsin, Michigan, and elsewhere before coming to RFS. On 29 Aug. 1879, Dr. D. Selwyn Clark wrote to fellow RFS trustee Joseph Emerson to tell him that "Miss Helen Norton of Howell, Michigan, will fill Miss Dorr's place the ensuing year" (a reference to Catherine C. Dorr, who taught mathematics at RFS in 1878–79) (BC, EB). The *RSM* announced that "Miss Helen Norton, after several years of teaching elsewhere, has again joined our corps of instructors" ([Nov. 1879]: 245). An astronomy outing received an amusing de-

scription from the journalism staff in the "Home Items" section of the same issue. Norton taught the astronomy class and was listed in the 1879–80 RFS *Catalogue* as librarian and teacher of mathematics. In the fall of 1880 she planned to become a missionary in Turkey, but because of illness she worked in Hawaii instead. She stayed for five years, becoming the principal of the Kawaiahao Seminary in Honolulu (1880–84), and then returned to the mainland, where she became a member of a board serving African American churches in the South for the Woman's Home Missionary Assn. During this period she contributed money to RFS toward the purchase of a new organ and recommended a place to find one at a discounted price. She wrote from Boston, "When I returned from my summer vacation I found a circular letter from Miss Jane Addams of the class of '81. Dear girls: how their faces rise up before me, how dear they were to me!" (Helen Norton to Sarah Anderson, 11 Oct. 1891, RC). Norton did graduate work at the Univ. of Michigan (1892–93) and the Univ. of Wisconsin, earning her M.A. at Wheaton College, Ill., in 1901. She was a professor at the Presbyterian College of Florida from 1905 to 1909. Apparently, the warmth that Norton expressed toward JA was not returned. JA implies as much here, and she wrote explicitly to her sister about her mixed feelings about Norton (see JA to SAAH, 23 [and 24] Jan. 1880, below).

11. Charles Dudley Warner (1829–1900), a Massachusetts-born attorney and writer of novels, travel accounts, biographies, and autobiographical essays, practiced law in Chicago from 1858 to 1860. He then moved to Hartford, Conn., where he edited the *Courant*. He published *Back-log Studies* in 1873 and brought out other books regularly throughout the 1870s and 1880s. His first novel, the rollicking and satirical *The Gilded Age* (1873), was written with his friend Samuel Clemens.

12. Edward Young (1683–1765), English rector, playwright, and satirist, wrote *Night Thoughts* ("The Complaint, or Night Thoughts on Life, Death, and Immortality"), an extremely long (ten thousand lines in nine books) didactic poem of blank verse between 1742 and 1745. The poem enjoyed a very warm reception.

Poem in the *Rockford Seminary Magazine*

Jane Addams and Sarah Anderson composed the following poem on the terrors of balancing the demands of seminary life for the Rockford Seminary Magazine *together, signing it with the initials of their two last names: "A.A." The piece was printed in the "School Department" section and prefaced with an explanatory editorial notation, which was bracketed and printed in small type above the title.*

[Rockford, Ill.]   NOVEMBER 1879

[Our design is to print during the year, for the benefit of our young readers, the bitter experiences and mistakes of various students. We took our idea from Sackville's "Mirror for Magistrates";[1] like that famous work, our attempt may be destined to remain unfinished, and even the fragments be more noted than read. In the following, the experience appears to be real, but we will not vouch for the rhyme.—ED.]

Sarah Anderson, a young teacher and accountant at Rockford Female Seminary, in 1879. She later served as the first official president of Rockford College from 1890 to 1896. (RC)

THE GIRL WHO HAD TOO MUCH TO DO

A Letter from father, I must read the news,
Though I ought this minute to be blacking my shoes;
"Dear daughter, no letter this week from our girl,
And mother is worried." It's a shame! what a whirl
Of confusion and hurry this whole week has been;
I ought to have written on Monday, but then
At the five o'clock hour, the time I had planned,
Mary came to my room, her Caesar in hand,
We studied till supper as hard as we could,
—It was an awful hard lesson, do what we would;
The verbs were all twisted, so we were scared
When we went to the class, and said, "not prepared.—"
After supper I practiced two hours, although
My poor head was thumping, my lesson I know
Was wretched next day—the professor said so.
I was restless all night, and dreamed of that letter;
The rising bell rang, and my head was no better.
On Tuesdays I'm busy from morning till night,
My German is extra, my essay to write
For Wednesday. It isn't because I was careless,
But what in the world could I do? I even went prayerless
To bed Thursday night, and that worried me too.
That day my room-mate was ill, and she

A breakfast must have, a dinner, her tea,
With trays to take up, and trays to bring down,
With lessons to get, and mending my gown;
No wonder to domestic work I found myself late,
And before I was through, broke a cup and a plate;
Was it strange that I broke at that very same moment
My good resolutions, and when I next went
To my room-mate so true, I scolded and fumed,
Her patience consumed, and that worried me too;
But through all of the day I thought of that letter;
In the midst of my work it came like a spectre;
In prayer-meeting that night—I do try to be good—
Every moment was thinking how ever I could
Get my history—of course I felt wicked—
How the bells rang and clashed on Friday!
At every stroke I thought of that tidy
For mother's birthday—I can't get it done—
I've no time for anything under the sun!
Do you think Friday night there's nothing on hand but glee?
Remember society calls on a faithful devotee.
You must write, you must speak, you must read;
When asked must sing, and debates must lead.
And so the week is ended, and what have I gained?
Poor lessons, no letters, and yet I have strained
Every nerve. Have I too much to do?
Can work be a failure, and hard work too?
And here I am thinking—while I ought this minute
Be studying chemistry—I see no sense in it.

A.A

PD (*RSM* [Nov. 1879]: 235–37).

1. Thomas Sackville, Lord Buckhurst, Earl of Dorset (1536–1608), poet, barrister, and member of Parliament, was also a high official at Oxford Univ. His collected poems were published in 1859. He wrote the long, medieval-style, poetical narratives "Induction" and "The Complaint of Buckingham" for *Mirror for Magistrates* (1563), a popular sixteenth-century anthology compiled by William Baldwin of Oxford, royal official George Ferrers, and others. *Mirror for Magistrates* featured tragic poems, or laments, by various authors, all organized around such themes as the downfall of famous men, the loss of prosperity, defeat and death, and the woeful impact of misfortune. *Mirror for Magistrates* went through several editions and expansions between 1559 and 1610. Sackville's work is generally seen as the most significant aspect of the collection.

From Ellen Gates Starr

Chicago, [Ill.] Dec. 25, 1879.

My dear Jane,
I cannot forbear beginning a letter to you tonight. You told me once that you thought of me when you knelt for prayer in the dining room, & it often happens that occasions of religious associations bring you into my mind—and in a decided sort of fellowship. It often seems strange to me, & perhaps a little hard, that so many strong minds, even gigantic geniuses have been troubled in the calmness of their religious faith by no disturbing doubt, at least no intellectual difficulties sufficiently formidable to form any barrier against the full & free exercise of that faith; & that it is for me to find my self so fettered. I have imagined that your experience might be something similar, I may mistake. At times I wish my reason might become passive in that one direction, or at the least not quite so suspicious, & let me enjoy my faith in peace. I attended, on Xmas eve, a midnight service at the Ascension,[1] a ritualistic Episcopal church. How beautiful it was! They have the choral service which is always pretty. That night the boys sang divinely. I put myself into harmony with the service & the occasion, & enjoyed it intensely. It was most solemn & touching & to come away thinking of the Babe of Bethlehem in any way but that way seemed sacrilege. I like the heart in the Episcopal service. I especially enjoy the communion service. Of course I cannot participate, but I like to kneel, & commune in my own way, & as best I can in my seat & I think the low, sweet music helps one to pray. I hope you do not think this foolish or restless. Generally I am not restless, but sometimes all my heart goes out toward a beautiful experience & faith, & seems to be dragged back by something, I don't quite know what. Dear Miss Holmes reminds me of Miss Blaisdell sometimes though she is very unlike her. She is very fond of me, & very solicitous for my welfare. She knelt by me in church, & she told me afterwards that she could not bear to leave me alone, when she went to the communion table. The tears came into her eyes, & it made me sort of wretched.[2]

Man can never realize his ideals. Only God has a power of performance equal to his power of conception. God realized his ideal of man in Christ.

Just as, sometimes, we are not understood until we put ourselves into some work of ours, & thus reveal ourselves, so man could never understand God until He put Himself into His Christ. In that way, I believe Christ is God.

I do not say I believe this now, I believed it when I wrote it. I know Christ is more than man. Of that I feel fully convinced. Leonardo de Vinci[3] makes us sure of that. If you have never seen a copy of the original sketch of the head of Our Lord in the Last Supper, I hope you will. The copies of the picture itself, as it has been patched up, give no idea of its divinity[.][4]

AL fragment (SCHS; *JAPM*, 1:445–49).

1. The Anglo-Catholic Church of the Ascension at LaSalle and Elm streets in Chicago was under the guidance of Rev. Arthur Ritchie, who served from 1875 until 1884, when he accepted the call of the Church of St. Ignatius in New York City.

2. Mary J. Holmes and EGS continued to travel around Chicago on Sundays to try different churches. EGS, however, remained undecided as to which seemed to best offer what she was seeking as a spiritual member. She wrote soon after Christmas 1879, "Miss Holmes & myself have been giving all our money to horse car conductors to day, as usual, instead of to the Lord. We have been to the W. side cathedral. The service is so beautiful that if we were near I should feel tempted to go all the time. I told Miss H[olmes] today that I should be obliged to invest in a prayer book if I was going to her church all the time. She said she would give me one if I would promise to go there, which of course I didn't do. The episcopal church near us I can't endure. They go through the service as if their chief aim was to get home early" (EGS to JA, 28 Dec. 1879, SCPC, JAC; *JAPM*, 1:450–51). The nearest Roman Catholic church, to which EGS possibly refers, was that of Saints Peter and Paul at Washington and Peoria streets, and the nearest Episcopal church was probably St. James at Cass and Huron streets.

3. Leonardo da Vinci (1452–1519), one of the greatest Italian painters of the High Renaissance of the sixteenth century, was also a brilliant inventor, designer, engineer, and scientist who theorized in anatomy, aeronautics, and other fields. He is best known for his drawings and sketches and for his masterpieces *The Last Supper* (painted in Milan, ca. 1497) and the *Mona Lisa* (painted in Florence, ca. 1500–1504).

4. EGS wrote perpendicular to the bottom of p. 4 of her original letter: "I am going to send this letter written Xmas ~~day~~ night. People to know each other must know each other under those phases which we generally commit to writing & throw into the fire the next morning" (*JAPM*, 1:447).

To Anna Hostetter Haldeman Addams

Rockford Sem'y [Ill.]   Jan 14" 1880

My dear Ma

I have only been here a little over a week yet some-way to look back on it the time seems endless. It will be a week always memorable to me because I begun Homer in it, I have never enjoyed the beginning and anticipation of anything as much as I have of that. Miss Hodge[1] one of the seniors had read the Iliad long ago and as she wants to review has come into the class, of course it is easy for her and I find in some respects it is more fun not to be alone. Have been unusually busy this week getting advirtisements for the magazine but of course now we are all settled for the year. Corinne Williams and I got them all as the other editors were too much afraid to start out. We were out a little while Wednesday & had eighteen; on Thursday thirteen & on Saturday six & every time make quick trips. The girls last year worried and fussed over it, but we attributed it all to our superior powers of talking busines: it was quite an experiance & I am glad I had it.

Among the new girls there is a Miss Hewett[2] from Pecatonica a friend of Eva's, and Mrs Goodrich requested me to befriend her, I haven't done so very energetically, although I did call on her, she sits at our table & is as afraid as can be of Miss Blaisdell. My room-mate[3] after all her planning has n't gone to Grin-nell, she had a telegram from her father Wednesday telling her to stay, some-thing had evidently occurred to make him change his mind, I think she is a good deal better here. On last Friday evening the girls of her set had a regular jubilee over the fact, there were eight of them and each one gave each of the others a Christmas present costing less than a quarter in addition to every thing imag-inable to eat, of course everything they had was rediculous hence our room at this minute is adorned with seven rediculous things. We had our last lesson on Milton's "Comus"[4] this morning, and we were all sorry to get through. It is supper-time & I must descend, we have had apple-sauce every single night since we came back.

With a great deal of love to Pa and yourself[.] Ever your loving daughter,

Jane Addams

ALS (JAPP, DeLoach; *JAPM*, 1:463–66).

1. A reference to Berty Hodge.

2. Carrie Hewitt (Heckman), who at various times lived in Pecatonica, Rockford, Chica-go, and Belvidere, Ill., was a first-year student at RFS in 1879–80. She taught music lessons in Pecatonica before coming to Rockford. Called home by the death of her brother in Apr. 1880, she did not return for the following school year, helping her family by teaching instead. She was back at RFS in 1882, when she participated in an oratorical contest between RFS and Beloit College and received the highest ranking from the judges (one of whom was Julia Lathrop). After graduating in 1884, Hewitt taught school for four years. She worked as a stenographer for another six years and then married Irvin J. Heckman, a physician and surgeon. She was president and founder of the Hinckley, Ill., Woman's Club and the first vice president of the RFS Alumnae Assn. in 1898–99. Eva Campbell Goodrich would inquire about her in a letter to JA written at the end of the school year (see 1 June 1880, below).

3. Addie M. Smith.

4. John Milton's (1608–74) *Comus* was a pastoral entertainment or masque presented at Ludlow Castle in 1634 upon the occasion of the Earl of Bridgewater's becoming lord presi-dent of Wales. It was published in 1637. The title character was a pagan god created by Mil-ton as son of Bacchus and Circe. He entices travelers to drink a liquid that turns their faces into those of wild animals. On JA's feelings about *Comus*, see also introduction to part 2, n. 44, above, and Draft of Essay, 28 Jan. 1880, n. 7, below. The "Literary Notes" that JA edited in the *RSM* included the following passage, printed immediately after her "The Macbeth of Shakespeare" (see Essay in the *RSM*, Jan. 1880, below). In it, JA may have been referring to herself, or to a close friend, as the "enterprising junior":

> As we study the bible by topics, [and] read many historians on one subject, why may we not be poetical by topics? An enterprising junior is trying this plan, as yet it is not man-ifest whether she will succeed or fail. The class [members] were very much interested in Milton's "Comus," especially impressed with the beautiful lady who by her very virtue was strong enough to defy all natural force. Our friend in particular was fired with am-bition to read all she could about this characteristic of womanhood, while she was "in the mood" she said. She took Milton's suggestions, and began in mythology with Diana and the stern Minerva. In history she read all she could find from that defiant Roman maiden to Joan de Arc. She also searched the sweet story of Ruth. In fiction she re-read Rebecca's career in "Ivanhoe" and Hilda in Hawthorne's "Marble Faun," she tried Des-

demona, and three or four more in Shakespeare. She expected the richest results from poetry, and at present is struggling with Chaucer having a vague remembrance of such a character in his works. We think the Junior has a good idea although her zeal bids fair to mislead her. (16–17)

To Clara B. Lutts

In this pivotal letter to an old childhood friend, Jane Addams announced the official use of the bread-giver motto for the class of 1881 and also revealed something of her own emotional nature. The idea of the bread-giver (of a life-sustaining lady who provides for others in need), which the juniors, under Jane Addams's leadership, took on as their defining identity, was a core concept in Addams's personal intellectual development toward settlement-house work.

In addition, this letter contained an unusual reference to Addams having an open disagreement with a colleague and to the discomfort she felt over the conflict. It spoke to her self-defined conservative nature and referred to an earlier exchange of letters with Vallie Beck in which she rejected the oversentimentality of schoolgirl behavior and lauded a more restrained demeanor.

Rockford Seminary [Ill.]   Jan 14" [and 17"] 1880

My Very dear Friend—[1]

Observe our class paper! the design it may be well to state is of wheat and hops, the <u>hops</u> I will admit are obscure but thier significance is deep. Our purpose is to give bread to the world in every sense we can, for it surely needs it, "bread-givers" you know is the old Saxon meaning for the word <u>lady</u>, it is a pity that it ever lost its primitive meaning, there are sixteen girls in Rockford Seminary who mean to do all they can to restore it.[2]

You don't know how glad I was to read your letter both for the letter itself (for I always enjoy yours and never say again they are not interesting) but for

The RFS class of 1881's bread-givers motif.

some-thing more than that, I think may be rememberances it suggested, for friendship depends upon something a good deal deeper and more primordial than conversation, it does n't make so much difference <u>what</u> your friend says in a letter, as the fact that she said it, that she thought of you and wanted you to know it, therefore, my dear, if you do not receive more than two letters from me during the year 1880 it will most certainly be surprising, I never save my letters but I am very sure if I could count them up <u>two</u> would be all I could find from <u>my</u> best of friends, it is most certainly shocking and should not be thus, it is just the same way that people of one family are sure of each other's love, take it for granted and never take the trouble to express it, some friends fall unconciously into the same thing and lose some of the highest joys of friendship.

I had a lovely time at home during the holidays though very short and quiet, what a lovely time <u>we</u> would have if we could both ever happen to be at Cedarville at the same time.

Jan 17"

I was writing this letter Sunday morning and thought I would have time to finish it before church, you see that I was inclined to be meditative as is becoming to Sunday, I had just finished reading a chapter in the Greek testament with Miss Blaisdell and that always makes me feel sort of solemn. Now it is Wednesday evening I feel any thing else but peaceful and contented, have been working hard all day and this afternoon went down town for advertisments with one of my sister-editors, we were very successful but on the way home had a fuss, it will not be intertaining to state particulars but I think she[3] owes me an apology & very likely she thinks the same of me, therefore it is disagrecable all around, school-life has two sides to it & I think the worst part is there is too much impetuousness among young people the conservative element is lacking. Whatever I may do I don't very often have fusses with people so it makes me feel wretched even though I think I am only maintaining self-respect. Would that you were here, I heartily endorse the idea of having you for a room-mate, I don't think I would then very often feel as I do now.

I am much obliged for the good-opinion of your ministerial friend, I am inclined to regard him with kindly feelings unless I should hear any vague rumors in regard to the his <u>friendly</u> position towards you and then I fear the youngman might find my feelings changed.

I wish I had chosen some evening to finish this letter when I was n't in such a diabolical mood, but such an offering as it is I send it. Speaking of our magazine I have been meaning all year to send you one, and will be sure to forward one of the next issue. Will mark an essay of mine not because I think it is anything wonderful but because you may like to read it more if you know who wrote it.[4] Ever your friend

Jane Addams

ALS (Private Collection, photocopy, JAPP).

1. When this letter was written, JA's old friend Clara ("Kitty") B. Lutts was living in Missouri with her family. Later in 1880, the Lutts family moved to Iowa.

2. The Feb. 1880 *RSM* reported, "The Juniors are supplied with class paper which is pronounced by the Seniors, who are supposed to be connoisseurs, as lovely" (53). The new paper featured sheaves of wheat and hops in its upper corner.

The bread-giver motif had been in the minds of the members of the RFS class of 1881 for some time before they officially chose it as their motto in their junior year. The important editorial in the July 1879 *RSM* (which has already been noted for its boldness in addressing the sequestered nature of life at the campus) had presented the motif cloaked in an argument for refinement: "Lady, in its old Saxon sense, means a giver of bread, but the bread of one who cuts her loaf in dainty, shapely slices will be more eagerly sought and relished, than that of the bread giver who distributes rough, uncut loaves" (205). The juniors carried the motif from the stationery for their class to the walls of their class parlor, which featured "sheaves of the Bread-Givers" on the wallpaper (*RSM* [Nov. 1880]: 247). They also used sheaves of wheat and poppies to adorn the stage at class presentations and used "bread-givers" in the lyrics of their class song (*RSM* [Apr. 1880]: 109–10). The motto also inspired poetry and was the theme of speeches given by class members, including JA.

JA referred to bread-giving wheat and pain-relieving poppies in her school essay "Poppy" (see Draft of Essay, [ca. 1878], above). In her memoirs she stated, "We must have found the sentiment in a book somewhere, but we used it so much that it finally seemed like an idea of our own" (*Twenty Years*, 48). The book that spawned the idea may very well have been Thomas Carlyle's *Democracy*. There, in "Past and Present," Carlyle wrote—in the context of a call for "Serene Highnesses and Majesties" to "take note" of the need among the Saxon poor for food, work, and wages—that "If no pious Lord or *Law-ward* would remember it, always some pious Lady ('*Hlaf-dig*,' Benefactress, '*Loaf-giveress*,' they say she is,—blessings on her beautiful heart!) was there, with mild mother-voice and hand, to remember it" (Abrams et al., eds., *Norton Anthology of English Literature*, 1003).

JA's identification with the bread-giver as a maternalistic ideal was also very personal and based on her own mother and on MCA, her surrogate mother, as role models. SWA, as the wife of a flour mill operator, had quite literally baked bread for neighbor women and was well known in her community, as was MCA after her, for good deeds toward others. SWA was a bread-giver in reality as well as symbolically, and her generous, other-oriented example had been held out for her daughters to emulate. The ideal of the bread-giving, uplifting, benefactress would remain with JA into her founding of Hull-House.

However lofty the sentiment behind the bread-givers motif and motto, it was fair game for satire. The Feb. 1880 *RSM* printed a comment from a "Junior Prep" to a "Sister Prep," "I don't see what makes all the classes so domestic in their mottoes. The Seniors have a *gravy bowl* and the Juniors have *bread* on their paper; when we have ours we'll have something sort of high and inspiring, won't we?" (54). The Mar. 1881 *RSM* asked, "Why will people misapply refined sentiment? The latest comes from town, where they call the Seniors the 'Servant Girls,' because of their motto—'Bread Givers'" (69).

3. The dispute was with Corrine Williams over the conduct of *RSM* business.

4. There were no signed articles by JA in the Feb. 1880 *RSM*, but she was the anonymous author of the editorial, which was on Carlyle's sense of the lost chivalry of labor, with analogy to the lack of "chivalry of study" among RFS schoolgirls (63). The manuscript version of the editorial, entitled "The Chivalry of Study (Editorial)," is extant (*JAPM*, 46:164–69).

To Sarah Alice Addams Haldeman

Rockford Sem'y [Ill.]   Jan 23" [and 24"] 1880

My dear Alice

...[1] It is Friday night and some-way I feel particularly happy and content-ed—probably it is this same blissful mood that moves me to write to you for it is a disgracefully long time since I have had an epistle from your gifted pen.

I am sitting in Miss Anderson's room and she is writing as well, my room is full of girls having a regular good time with my energetic room-mate hence I have beat a graceful retreat.

I began to read Homer as soon as I came back Christmas, and I never en-joyed any-thing more in my life, I would be willing to study Greek for ten years, even pig along in Crosby's grammar[2] all that time if I could have the fun of read-ing Homer in the end—that sounds extravagant and I wish I had n't written it, but the fact remains just the same. We have been unusually busy this month on the magazine and I don't know now when it will be out, the printers have been making mistake upon mistake and I go down to the office about every other day; Corinne Williams and myself got all the advirtisements this year, we worked for three days and I guess went into about every store in town but were very suc-cessful in the end, we are determined, if such a thing is possible, to bring the magazine to the end of next year without any debt on it—sometimes I am per-fectly sick of it and think it takes more time than it is right to give.

I have learned to stuff birds by the new method i.e. without skinning them. I have finished my lessons & glory in four birds which adorn the room, drying in all sorts of angles and positions. Miss Holmes has planned to stuff with me every Saturday morning right straight on until June.[3]

I would like to know your opinion concerning Miss Helen Norton—she is one of those people that when I think about her I like her & admire her quali-ties but when I am around her I dont like her at all. I am afraid I am degenerat-ing this epistle into gossip but what brings her into my mind so to-day in that peculiar manner is that she is trying to have me write up the "Nebular Hypoth-esis"[4] for the benefit of the astronomy class and I have had the funniest time all afternoon, divide my attention between Nebular and the study of Miss Norton, I am going to have solid-geometry with her next term.

Had a long visit with a class-mate of yours a few days since—Miss Fitch,[5] she talked & talked a long time about things as they used to be.

My room-mate & myself invested in a lounge last week, the amount of com-fort we take out of it is something surprising. I wish you could see our room, it is one of the cosiest in school.

Miss Anderson proposes chess and I am delighted. I had many more things to say into you but think I will wait until you honor me with an epistle. Miss A. sends her love. With love to Harry & yourself[.] Ever Your loving Sister

Jane Addams

P.S.

Saturday morning—[January 24]

Had a letter from Pa this morning saying he had just received one from you. I am ever so sorry Harry has been sick again, if there is anything I can get for him don't hesitate a minute to write.

Please give my love to Laura & Sadie.[6]

ALS (IU, Lilly, SAAH; *JAPM*, 1:467–72).

1. The first paragraph has been abridged. JA began her letter to her sister almost verbatim to the way she began her letter to Lutts nine days earlier (JA to Clara B. Lutts, 14 Jan. 1880, above).

2. Alpheus Crosby's (1810–74) *A Grammar of the Greek Language* (1846) went through dozens of editions and was a standard text in American schools and colleges. JA read *A Compendious Grammar of the Greek Language* (1871) as well as Crosby's two books on the *Anabasis: Greek Lessons: Selections from Xenophon's Anabasis, with Directions for the Study of Grammar, Notes . . . and Vocabulary* (1856) and *The Anabasis of Xenophon. First Four Books. . . . for the Use of Schools and Colleges* (1875). Crosby's *Lessons* and *Grammar* were required reading in the four-year Greek course at RFS (see also Katie L. Hitchcock to JA, 11 Aug. 1878, n. 5, above).

3. Here JA refers to her fascination with taxidermy, both as an art and a science. JA had been making "stuffed birds" at home in her scientifically oriented summer sojourns with stepbrother GBH (Addams, *Twenty Years*, 62), but in Mary E. Holmes she had the help of a master. Holmes had been practicing the craft for many years. Like some of JA's other passions, the taxidermy rage made its way into the pages of the *RSM*. The Feb. 1880 "Home Items" included—"Can you stuff birds?" (52)—and an announcement that "Jane Addams and May Southworth have been taking lessons of a taxidermist during the past month, and the results of their labor are most astonishing" (57). The *RSM* reported that RFS girls had been known to kill campus cats and birds in order to stuff them, and in Mar. 1880 noted, "Our amateur taxidermist"—no doubt a reference to JA—"exhibited her specimens to a small boy who inquired 'How do you kill them?' Upon her replying she had them shot he gravely remarked: 'That's very cruel, you ought to put salt on their tails, that is a great deal easier and it don't hurt them at all'" (85). JA's "Report (Account) Book" for 1879–80 included a Jan. 1880 entry for taxidermy supplies and a Mar. 1880 entry for wire, cotton, and chloroform (RC; *JAPM*, 27:327, 329).

Apparently, it was not unusual for middle-class families to preserve beloved pets through taxidermy for sentimental reasons. That this practice did not always go well is testified to by JA's friend Annie Sidwell, who wrote to JA about her pet bird's bad end: "the morning after I received your letter Claudius died and I cried all day and was in no frame of mind to write." She continued, "I took him down and had him stuffed and he looks a fright. I was disgusted beyond expression when I went to get him and the old woman told me she had put him on a long wire so that I could have him in a winter 'bokay' nice little grasses and things—very natural surrounding. . . . She made him with great big eyes and Claudy had little eyes—and he always kept them shut, too, not staring out at you like colored glass—and he always sat with his head under his wing." The results were bad enough that the dismayed Sidwell reported, "I think I will cremate him" (Sept. 1885, SCPC, JAC; *JAPM*, 2:103, 109–10).

JA became involved in taxidermy during a time of transition in the art. Holmes was schooled in the highly technical scientific methods popular in the mid-nineteenth century. That approach to zoological or naturalistic specimens emphasized the (cluttered but systematic) classification and cabinet display of objects by size and type. Leading scientists associated with major U.S. museums, both earlier and later in the century, emphasized dramatic representation over row-upon-row displays.

In addition to technique, there was the question of the gender of the practitioner. Although the leading authorities in the field were male, taxidermy was popular as an amateur decorative art and craft among middle-class women—a fact illustrated by its inclusion in M. A. Donohue's *Ladies' Manual of Art; or, Profit and Pastime: A Self Teacher in All Branches of Decorative Art, Embracing Every Variety of Painting and Drawing on China, Glass, Velvet, Canvas, Paper and Wood* (Chicago, 1890). As a woman and a scientist who practiced the craft, Mary E. Holmes crossed the boundaries between science and art. She was an excellent amateur artist as well as a scientist. Her home featured not only stuffed birds and animals—preserved for their beauty or grandeur as well as for their scientific interest—but also watercolors she had painted of natural scenes.

In the late nineteenth century, the professional practice of taxidermy (and of the diorama, or habitat panorama, with painted background behind a taxidermy display) had strong anthropocentric aspects. The animal world was interpreted in terms of human characteristics, and taxidermy displays embodied Victorian ideas about masculinity, femininity, and family. When it came to using taxidermy in zoological study, the art was no idle hobby but rather a hallmark of serious scientific inquiry, one that won some men a kind of celebrity status when their work received public display.

Despite its overtones of dry objectivity, taxidermy was a subjective process by which animals and birds were preserved in positions chosen by the scientist/artist. In the late nineteenth century, it became one of the prevailing methods by which leading male scientist-explorers and museum curators interpreted the natural world. These men, in association with the staffs of leading natural history museums, used taxidermy much as painters of the western landscape or of American natural and ornithological life used their drawings and paintings. They styled animal relations to larger mythic meanings, using science artistically to help transmit cultural values about wilderness and civilization, the family unit, gender relations (including the representation of the male as the standard of the species and the female as the deviant), and notions of dominance and submission.

While Charles Wilson Peale and his Baltimore Museum characterized the approach early in the century, by the end of the century the noted figures were men such as Carl Akeley and William Temple Hornaday, whose dramatic displays of buffalos or tigers were emblematic of the vanishing West or the exoticism and danger of the African savannah and jungle. The male answer to Donohue's *Ladies's Manual* was Hornaday's *Taxidermy and Zoological Collecting: A Complete Handbook for the Amateur Taxidermist, Collector, Osteologist, Museum-Builder, Sportsman, and Traveller* (1891).

The boom in providing public access to museums in the 1890s, with wealthy private patrons interested in using museum displays as mediums for the education of the masses, brought innovation in this type of awe-inspiring taxidermy. The field was further advanced on a private and amateur level after the turn of the century with the popular impact of the cult of masculinity fostered by Theodore Roosevelt and his network of upper-class men. As Roosevelt and his cohorts endorsed taxidermy as a trophy art—with stuffed heads displayed on the walls of studies as permanent domestic examples of the owner's masculinity and his ability to hunt, dominate, and kill large male animals in the wild—private patronage of taxidermists picked up nationwide. In Chicago, the World's Columbian Exposition of 1893 and the Field Museum of Natural History, which was incorporated the same year, were in the forefront of this cultural phenomenon. They featured well-known taxidermy displays of male animals in fierce poses that underscored the public association of maleness with untamed strength and virility.

JA's fascination with taxidermy—and her chance that came soon after this letter was written to preserve a male hawk—thus came at a time when the field was burgeoning in two directions. Mary E. Holmes, in encouraging her young student's interest in taxidermy, was in part instilling skills in what was seen as a ladylike domestic craft or hobby, to be practiced privately for the interior decoration of the home. At the same time, she helped spur JA along nontraditional paths and into the more powerful realm of public display and the scientific powers of interpretation.

JA's keenness for the practice speaks, along with her interest in medicine, to her attraction to the "masculine" characteristics associated with science and its stated objective (versus femininized and emotional) stance. There was also the decidedly unladylike aspect of the blood and gore involved, not to mention the heavy-handed use of chemicals. Holmes dealt with the latter aspects of taxidermy with some humor in an essay she wrote on cat behavior. She recalled finishing several new specimens of birds and leaving them mounted in a room to dry while she and her father went off to Sunday services. Upon their return, they found a floor strewn with feathers and one very sick cat, who in attacking the dead, preserved birds had ingested toxic doses of "arsenic, corrosive sublimate, &c., used on the skins." The cat was given an emergency purgative and was nursed successfully through a critical illness but lost all its teeth. The story leaves open questions of the possible side-effects of the chemicals used in taxidermy on the health of the human practitioners of the art ("Miss Mary Holmes and Her Cat," unidentified clipping, Sill, "Scrapbook"; see also JA to AHHA, 7 Mar. 1880, below).

4. For JA's essay on Laplace's Nebular Hypothesis, see Draft of Essay, 28 Jan. 1880, below.

5. Elizabeth Fitch was a classmate of SAA's in the RFS class of 1872. She taught at an industrial school in Charles City, Iowa, and lived for many years in Rockford. She became corresponding secretary for the RFS Alumnae Assn. in 1881.

6. References to JWA's wife Laura Shoemaker Addams and daughter Sarah ("Sadie") Weber Addams.

Draft of Essay

Jane Addams studied astronomy in her junior year at Rockford Female Seminary.[1] In this piece on Laplace's[2] Nebular Hypothesis,[3] the reigning scientific theory of her time on the origins of the solar system, Addams engaged in one of the nineteenth century's primary intellectual debates over creationism and cosmogony: Did the origins of the universe occur by divine act or by natural law? Widespread popular acceptance of Laplace's theory in the mid-nineteenth century set the stage for Darwin and biological theories of natural selection and evolution that followed. Laplace's ideas continued to be of importance to Addams. She incorporated metaphoric references to his theory into other writings, and the Nebular Hypothesis was a subject discussed in the Sunday evening science lectures offered at Hull-House.[4]

[Rockford, Ill.]   Jan 28" '80[5]

The Nebular Hypothesis.

The great Egyptian goddess[6] who was not all knowing but had a power deeper and more primordial than knowledge <&> by whose brooding power every

thing was produced, embodies man's primitive idea of the creation & beginning of the universe.

Silence & darkness with a certain life-giving power of moisture may be found
in the traditions of almost every nation, whence they thought every-thing was
evolved. This same idea has been followed up, either with a vague religious feeling or else scientific[al]ly, through century after century almost until the time
of our own era. Now we suddenly find ourselves in the midst of a revolution—
that produced by the Nebular Hypothesis. If we wished to be theoretical we
might say that in this age of intellectual force and intensive living, man spurns
the Egyptian creation of the great brooding mother to whom time & knowledge were as nothing, and claims, in his birth-right—and as the parent to whom
he can lay the most natural right—the dull heated mass extending throughout
the universe in constant & frightful motion, from which by the very persistence
of force man himself was finally evolved.[7]

Speculative philosophers such as Kant[8] <& Swendenborg>[9] were the first to
conceive the idea of a perpetual developement in the regions of space, beginning and consequently returning to—a self luminous substance of a highly attenuated nature distributed throughout the celestial realms—this in short would
lead to a Nebular Hypothesis not only in regard to our own solar system but in
regard to the processes of star formation going on in the stellar regions.

But Laplace the supporter of the "Nebular Hypothesis" in its restricted sense
is not a great philosopher simply a great mathematician; he confines his theory
to the explanation of the solar system and observes only firm facts he is sure of.

He places his observations upon the nine following coincidences—all wholly
independent of the law of gravitation—[10]

1. The sun rotates on his axsis from West to East.

2. All the planets revolve about the sun from W. to E.

3. All the planets rotate on thier axses from W. to E.

4. All the sattellites (ex[cept] those of Uranus[11] and Neptune)[12] revolve about
thier primarris[13] from W. to E.

5. All the sattellites rotate on thier axses in the same direction in which their
primarris turn on thier axses.

6. All the planets revolve about the sun nearly in the plane of the solar equator.

7. All the sattellites revol[v]e about thier primarris nearly in the planes of
the equator of thier respective planets.[14]

8. All the planets—& sattellites in like manner—have orbits of small eccentricity.[15]

9. The central mass—the sun—rotates on the his axsis in less time than any
of the planets revolve about him in their orbits, and contains a larger mass of
matter than the sum of the seperated masses—

These coincidences naturally suggest the existence of some grand comprehensive law prevading the whole solar system. A huge nebulous mass once ex-

tended throughout the space now bounded by the orbit of Neptune. This star dust or world-stuff was in a cloudy form deficient in heat or cold, consisting of discrete portions of matter of various density & bulk aggregated into special forms under the influence of mutual attraction. By the gradual condensation of these discrete particles by the effect of gravity, a central aggregation or nu-clues[16] would be formed—the germ of our sun. It is obvious that in a crowd of aggregating bodies, moved by partially-opposing impul[s]es, co<l>lision would occur, destruction of velocity & subsidence towards the centre of attraction. It is also evident that the impulse which remained would ultimately give rise to circulation or rotation of a permanent character about some axsis.

We all understand that force is correlative & indestructable, that motion is but heat transformed & to produce a certain amount of heat but a certain amount of motion is required. Thus in the process of aggregation such an amount of heat would finally be evolved that the entire mass would be can-descant—the repulsive force of heat would overcome all the inherent power of attraction, chemical affinity & cohesion. A heat so powerful would hold every atom apart & would resolve every known substance to its simplest element—airy substance—in other words, all matter is diffused in a nebulous form & when heat evolution has so far progressed that the rotating s[p]heriod[17] extend-ed far beyond the orbit of Neptune we are furnished with all the conditions assumed by Laplace.

Laplace then shows upon mechanical prinicples that as the rotating s[p]heriod] slowly contra[c]ted & condensed by the graviation of its parts to-wards the centre & the process of cooling at its surface, the rotation must nec-essarily be acclerated & the centrifugal force augmented until the centrifugal force overcome gravity. When this mechanical condition was reached a vapor-ous zone would become detached & revolve independently of the interior mass. More condensed portions of nebulous matter would be formed & thrown off until a succession of zones had become detached. Each ring would revolve around a central nucleus & would sooner or later break up into a number of globes, which by the superior attraction of the largest would ultimately coalese into one. This globe still contracting would throw off satillites & other planets all revolving in nearly the same plane & in the same direction until an entire solar system had been formed. This in brief is the theory of Laplace he alleged that all the processes were in accord with known natural & mechanical laws & could be demonstrated by mathematical caculations.

Philosophers have since gone further demonstrating it as a physical reali-ty. By the aid of Spectrum Analysis[18] nebulas masses have been discovered—relics of the original chaotic substance & worlds are formed almost under the very eye of the astronomer. In the nebulae they recognize the same elements which compose the soil we tread. Geology has proved that the earth was once a molten mass, it is not unreasonable to suppose that is may have existed pri-or to that time in a still more highly heated condition—was volatilized & diffused through space as rare & attenuated gages[19]—this is all the Nebular Hypothesis demands to establish its proof.

AMsS (UIC, JAMC, Detzer; *JAPM*, 46:155–63).

1. JA drafted "The Nebular Hypothesis" on class of 1881 bread-givers stationery. She was part of a group of girls actively interested in astronomy in her junior and senior years. The Feb. 1880 *RSM* humorously reported, "The astronomy class are writing a course of essays with such subjects as 'The Meteoric Hypothesis,' or 'Later Theories on The Tidal Actions.' Now that they are avowedly appealing to Nature for knowledge they find how hard it is to become natural in their mode of thinking. As one perplexed maiden says, 'If I didn't know anything and didn't believe anything I read in the *Popular Science Monthly* I could get along.' The words of a philosopher—'Were man but free from prejudice, having a mind delicately balanced between credulity and skepticism, he could' and so on" (50; *JAPM*, 46:179).

The *RSM* carried news in JA's junior and senior years about RFS girls studying astronomy with the help of Dr. Gearn, who lectured to them under the stars and made his powerful telescope available for their use. JA's editorial in the Feb. 1881 *RSM* gave a tongue-in-cheek account of "Girls, in their mad chase for science" being frustrated by experiments gone bad in the chemistry laboratory and then setting out for Gearn's observatory in the wee hours of the morning:

> . . . Wrestle with the heavens for a time, ease your troubled soul, become calm by the study of celestial not terrestrial bodies. You long to behold Venus in the sunlight. You wish to catch a glimpse of the subject of your next essay; the way to the observatory is long, the thermometer stands that morning at 35, but it[']s then or never. Bravely you start forth, the destination after two miles walk is reached. The observatory gentleman is not at home, but the key handed you bids you enter. There are five of you, and certainly five can arrange the massive instrument, and you will gaze to your heart's content; but the roof of the building is to be moved, and stature fails; one chair, one box, a step ladder, and five on these three do their best; 35° does not express the weather, but you labor on; the instrument is finally arranged; the finder tells you the position of your planet in view, and you gaze. One fortunately stood at the other end, and no discovery taking place, investigations are in order. A small door opens, chamois is displayed, and calmly beneath it lies the reflector. On, girls, why so stupid; look again; it must be seen; but yon heavenly body is vanishing; the instrument won't work, and clouds dim the horizon of certain heavens. Frozen and desperate you start for home, declaring eternal dissatisfaction with your wits, and assuring yourself that this episode is positively the last of the season. (54–55; see also Excerpt from Editorial in the *RSM*, Feb. 1881, below)

Apparently the "chase for science" had many manifestations. In Nov. 1879, girls coming home from observing the heavens through Gearn's telescope found "their attention was abruptly diverted from the stars by the fact that they were on the railroad bridge and the train was coming in full pursuit. The Seniors proposed competition and ran; the others laid it to the fact that they weigh 148 lbs. apiece and were afraid to be on the bridge. The Juniors cried, 'Sit down and hold fast;' but the teachers siding with the Seniors carried the day, and the railroad bridge was saved" (*RSM* [Nov. 1879]: 241).

2. Pierre-Simon Laplace (1749–1827), French mathematician, physicist, and politician, was one of the eighteenth and nineteenth centuries' pioneers in astronomy. He was among the first theorists to suggest the possibility of black holes, and he devised important theorems in mathematical physics. He is best known, however, for his concepts regarding the origins of the universe and the relations and motions of the planets. During the reign of Napoleon, Laplace served as French minister of the interior (1799) and, beginning in 1803, as chancellor

of the senate. He published his many theories regarding gravitational astronomy and celestial mechanics in the massive, five-volume *Mécanique céleste* (Celestial Mechanics, 1799, 1799, 1802, 1805, 1823–25). Laplace presented his famous cosmogony, the "Nebular Hypothesis," in which he conjectured that the solar system originated out of a great cloud of collapsing and condensing gas, in *Exposition du système du monde* (System of the World, 1796); on the hypothesis, see also n. 3.

3. True nebulae are clouds of gaseous interstellar matter opaque with cosmic dust particles. In the nineteenth century the term was often used generically to describe clusters of stars, and astronomy guides sometimes defined nebulae as "the hazy spots of light visible in the sky with a telescope" (Gore, *Astronomical Glossary*, 71). There are nebulae of several different types, characteristics, and intensities. In his hypothesis, Laplace built upon the understanding of the process of condensation in planetary nebulae developed by English astronomer William Herschel (1738–1822) from 1785 to 1790. Planetary nebulae, Herschel observed, were more or less uniform, elliptical or circular, and surrounded a central star. Through a telescope, they looked like a disk.

In the Nebular Hypothesis, sometimes referred to as the "Kant-Laplace Nebular Hypothesis" (n. 8), Laplace postulated that the creation of the sun and planets in the solar system is the result of natural laws by which vaporous nebular matter condense and flatten, forming a whirling ring around a central star—the sun. The revolving debris, by collision, gravitational attraction, and cooling processes, further condense into separate planets and their moons (or satellites). Laplace theorized that this is a natural evolutionary process in the life of a star (for further details of the hypothesis, see also nn. 14 and 15).

4. In an acceptance speech for a National Education Award on 26 Feb. 1935, JA told her audience that "a <very popular> Sunday evening course of lectures" was started at Hull-House with "'the nebular hypothesis' and went on rapidly through the sciences into human history" (SCPC, JAC; *JAPM*, 49:525). Laplace's theory dominated nineteenth-century scientific thought and debates about cosmogony. By the 1850s most educated Americans accepted it as the most plausible explanation for the formation of the solar system. The widespread acceptance of Laplace's ideas set the stage for positive popular reception of Charles Darwin's *Origins of the Species* (1859) and the concept of human evolution. Both evolutionary models were key parts of the shift in modern thought from literal to more metaphorical interpretation of the account of the Creation in Genesis and to more general beliefs about natural organic development.

In JA's time, however, creationism and science were usually not thought to be mutually exclusive. Despite the articulate opposition of fundamentalists, a majority embraced a combination of scientific evidence and theological meaning, granting the forces at work in the Nebular Hypothesis divine provenance or causation. The result of the Nebular Hypothesis was revised understanding of both the natural and supernatural.

The girls at RFS discussed and debated the relatedness of natural law to divine cause. As a poem printed in the June 1880 *RSM* put it, "'Whoever in Earth's creation / Feels music sweet possess his soul, / Has but the faint reverberation / Of that grand tune to which the planets roll'" ("The Music of the Spheres," 174). As "S.E.F" observed in the July 1878 *RSM*, "By the mysteries which the telescope has unraveled, overthrowing the speculations and theories of men, it has proven what was spoken by one of the world's greatest students: 'It is not for man to dictate, but to examine, to reason, and to confirm, if we can, what appear to be the teachings of the book of nature'" (130). In her essay "Old Dreams Realized," Helen Harrington addressed the issue of whether new scientific understanding supplanted spiritual appreciation. Idealism, she concluded, was only enhanced. "Every science in its infancy has been rocked in the cradle of superstition," she wrote. "Thus the real truth has been surrounded by fancies that it has taken the light of long years of study to dispel. . . . have we dropped from our grasp that better, more spiritual part, and lost the power to appreciate it[?] . . . It is only the image, the symbol, that is broken; the idea lives on and it is ours. To us, the stars, with their sweet influences, are burning suns in ceaseless motion, and all those old superstitions are dispelled by the grand reality" (*RSM* [May 1880]: 141–42).

Carrie Strong, in "Jupiter Is Not Now Inhabited," her Junior Exhibition speech in the spring of 1881 (which JA published as the lead article in the May 1881 *RSM*), attached a First Cause dimension when she referred to the theory "of Laplace, indorsed by the genius of the elder Herschel. We assert, then, that evidence exists that the solar system came from the hands of the Creator a fiery vapor" (130). "It has become a kind of fashion in certain quarters to denounce all scientific doctrines, to which the term development may be applied, as tending to atheism," Strong continued:

> This objection is founded on shortsightedness and in a failure to appreciate the case. The hypothesis of development simply assumes that the Creator has brought worlds into existence by the use of secondary causes, precisely as he brings a tree into existence. Does any one hesitate to admit that an oak has undergone a slow and regular development? . . . If it appears to intellects of the loftiest and broadest grasp that the Creator has evolved the solar system according to a method, and by the use of natural laws, exactly as he evolves a tree from the germ in the seed, why is atheism charged in the one case and not in the other? The only difference between the cases is that the one attributes to Deity a vaster scope of intelligence and power than the other. (131)

At RFS, astronomy and mythology were also sometimes merged, in an entertaining way, into science fiction. As Carrie Hewitt surmised in a fiery version of the chaotic origin of the solar system, printed in an essay entitled "The Man in the Moon":

> Once upon a time there was an immense ball of fire, which was in a terrible state of commotion. This ball of fire hung among the stars, and the remains of it we now call the sun. At frequent intervals this ball would get in such a fury that it would throw off pieces of itself. Numbers of these fragments set up in independent business and formed the Earth, Jupiter, Mars, and the other planets, and after a while the Moon. After many long years, this moon cooled on the outside, and became a living, inhabited place, like our own world. But after many more ages it became cooled clear through, and grew colder and colder, till all living things upon it died with the exception of a man, two dogs, and Luna, Queen of Night, who has her throne in the moon. (*RSM* [May 1880]: 143)

Laplace's theory influenced romantic and transcendentalist writers earlier in the century. Among them were Edgar Allan Poe, who in 1809 speculated about the revelations of immortality inherent in the infinity of the universe and who incorporated the Nebular Hypothesis into his *Eureka* (1848), and Ralph Waldo Emerson (1803–82), who used the theory in his ideas about nature.

5. JA signed and dated this essay "Jane Addams, Jan 28" '80" (*JAPM*, 46:163).

6. A reference to the great Egyptian mother-goddess Nut. Nut, the goddess of the sky and of moisture, was the co-originator and sustainer of an orderly, life-sustaining physical universe. According to the Egyptian creation myth, out of space and chaos Nut mated with her brother Geb, the earth god, and gave birth to other gods and goddesses. In Egyptian iconography, Nut was usually depicted in human form, arching up above the earth like a constellation. Her sexual union with Geb was symbolized by an obelisk reaching up from the earth toward her arched body in the sky. She was often drawn with a water pot, a symbol of the womb. Rain and replenishment were said to come from her, and she also was believed to supply order and containment to the earth. As one scholar has put it, "She keeps the forces of chaos from breaking through the sky and engulfing the world—her body is in fact the firmament dividing the cosmos . . . from the amorphous, primeval matter merging with which would be tantamount to non-existence" (Hart, *Dictionary of Egyptian Gods and Goddesses*, 145).

The perspective JA offers here, beginning a scientific treatise with mention of similar ideas in mythology, was reflected in an earlier essay by her friend Katie L. Hitchcock, who observed, "Before science was born Mythology reigned pre-eminent, and now that Science wields his sceptre, the history of Mythology affords us some idea of the earlier thoughts of man, scattering rays of light upon the way in which people reasoned before they had a scientific knowledge of nature" (*RSM* [Apr. 1878]: 73).

7. At the end of the school year, JA wrote a second version of this essay and entitled it "Darkness versus Nebulae" (*JAPM*, 46:207–15). Like "The Nebular Hypothesis," it was written on RFS class of 1881 bread-givers stationery. JA signed and dated it "Jane Addams June 14" '80" (*JAPM*, 46:215).

The two essays begin in almost exactly the same manner but then diverge completely in theme and substance. Instead of branching into a description of Laplace's scientific explanation of the origins of the solar system, the creation of the planets, and the relation of the planets to one another, as she did in "The Nebular Hypothesis," in "Darkness versus Nebulae" JA used the Nebular Hypothesis as a metaphor to discuss human nature and the relationship of the individual to society.

At the start of her June 1880 essay, JA copied almost verbatim the first two paragraphs of the Jan. 1880 essay as they appear above. She joined what had been the first two paragraphs in the first essay into one long one. She also spelled "scientifically" correctly in the second version instead of writing it as "scientificly," as in the Jan. 1880 essay (*JAPM*, 46:208). In addition, she made "nebular hypothesis" lowercase (46:209). Beginning with "intellectual force & knowledge," she substituted ampersands for the word *and* (46:209). After repeating the basic introduction she had used before, she departed from the previous text. This time she discussed orientations among humans instead of planets. She began with a brief look at ancient times. "We can see the belief of the ancients in a creation evolved from silence and quietude in many ways," she argued:

> In thier statues & representations of the Gods, they are in a calm invioable circle of peace as if thier divinity had never been touched by the passions & discords of human-nature. Even in thier statues of ideal women there is a coldness & quiet as if they could be alone in the world & need no other support. The ancients had nothing of that spirit which in the extremes becomes fanaticism or despondency—it is an element of later times, they did not desire death as an admission to higher thought, but lived with a feeling of completeness & security & bidding farewell to life calmly descended into the shades. They exercised thier best powers when alone & nearest their idea of creation. (46:210–11)

She then moved on to the seventeenth century. "Milton['s] lady in Comus is an embodiment of the ancient idea," she continued (referring to *Comus, a Masque, Presented at Ludlow Castle, 1634, before the Earl of Bridgewater, Lord President of Wales,* a pastoral by Milton). "[I]t was only when she was alone & unprotected that she exercised her wonderful power. Each man <in thier times> had his own religion, he worshiped with sy<m>bols but his belief itself was his own & never approached by another." She then began a new paragraph and offered a moral: "Now it [is] onnly given to the greatest to adhere strictly to thier own nature, the less gifted use the eyes of others even when they think to know themselves—" (46:211).

"It seems to be at the time of the Reformation—while Kant was suggesting the Nebular Hypothesis—" she wrote and then deleted the next lines with a series of vertical slashes down the page: "when architecture & the older arts seems powerless to speak to men & words posessed might—that the old idea of power in solitude disappeared" (46:211–12). The quality of the penmanship changed at this stage in the essay, perhaps indicating that JA stopped and commenced writing again at a later time.

Resuming, she wrote "~~Now~~ It seems <after that> as if each man's vital force was insufficient to accomplish all the work necessary to be done in the rush of events, as if the work was disproportioned to human enthusiasm & endeavor. In order to do all he must catch & echo enthusiasm from his neighbor & surroundings, &." Here she metaphorically used Laplace's idea of nebulae being compressed into planets and continued, "under this false stimulus he will for a time accomplish wonders almost worthy of the great ~~force~~ <power> & persistence of his nebular birth, for a time vital force & endeavor are common property as if in the crowded <world?> all men had fused thier hopes into one mass. But yet no one man posessed the self-reliance & self-sustaining power of the ancients & when a catastrophe occurs or some great man is removed on whom this enthusiasm depended, then the great crowd surges back again into indifference" (46:212–13). She then—harkening back to an earlier set of RFS essays on Eliot's hero—offered the strict and martyred Savonarola as an example. (On other essays regarding Savonarola, see EGS to JA, 12 [and 19] Oct. 1879, n. 13 above.)

"We can best see this spirit by illustration" she began. "[In t]he wonderful career of Savonarola in Florence such great things did he accomplish that it seemed almost possible to change the nature of men at his bidding they [burned] their vanities & reformed their government. He poured into the lives of the Florintines the fire of his own life yet at length when <u>wearied</u> he himself wished to lean upon this strength he was compelled to perceive that he solely & alone had posessed power that the enthusiasm of the people was but an echo of his own, that the same Florintines saw the savior of their liberties burned as a heritic" (46:213).

JA then leaped from fifteenth-century Florence to late-eighteenth-century revolution and ended the essay on the contemporary and perhaps somewhat autobiographical theme of college promise and the problems of living up to potential and expectation. "The terrible times of the French Revolution was an aggre[g]ate of human passion; it went beyond the bounds set to humanity, no one man felt the fury but the aggre[g]ate was that of a demon—" she wrote and then segued to the present:

> We see minor illustrations of the same thing in our own time. Brilliant & talented young men who during thier college course seem to promise such great things, so impress one with thier force & enthusiasm that thier friends think they must win high honors in the world, become great & influential. But they always dodge the a/c [accounting] become lost in the crowd or keep on promising until no one expects any thing else. The reason of this disappointment is that they show a brilliancy not thier own, mingling for 4 yrs with the best of books & cultured people they acquire an enthusiasm & force that is not thiers ~~own~~ but drawn from other sources—when these sources are removed thier spirit flags & they fail, they posess not the qualities of self-reliance & silent resources, it is here where the nebular origin is inferior to drakness [darkness]—— [ending, with a slight flourish, with the word] finis—. (46:213–14)

8. Much of the early work of Immanuel Kant (1724–1804), the great German philosopher and professor of logic and metaphysics, was dedicated to mathematical and cosmological questions. Among his first publications were *Thoughts on the True Estimation of Living Forces* (1747) and *Universal Natural History and Theory of the Heavens; or, An Essay on the Constitution and Mechanical Origin of the Entire World-Edifice Treated According to Newtonian Principles* (1755). In the latter work—which predated Laplace's Nebular Hypothesis by decades— Kant presented the theory that the orderly solar system, or cosmos, had evolved out of a crude state of chaos in which particles were initially spread throughout infinite space. Kant specifically suggested that the planets had condensed out of a cloud of primordial matter around the sun, first through a process of coherence of the particles and then by gravitational or Newtonian attraction of masses, and that their orbits and rotations around the sun were a natural corollary of this process. In his writings, Kant combined metaphysical with scientific explanations and in general sought to reconcile basic tenets of Newtonian philosophy with religious and moral life. The spiritual roots of his cosmogony were further stated in his

philosophical *The Only Possible Argument for a Demonstration of the Existence of God* (1763). Neither this nor his *Theory of the Heavens* were widely read, and Laplace was almost certainly unfamiliar with them. Kant was not credited with contributing to the Nebular Hypothesis until the popular rediscovery of his ideas in the mid-nineteenth century.

9. Emanuel Swedenborg (1688–1772), Swedish scientist, philosopher, and theologian, believed that the Bible reveals laws of continual correspondence between God and Nature, with every natural object or phenomenon being the expression of spiritual causation. Swedenborgianism, and the Church of the New Jerusalem formed by Swedenborg's followers, had a strong intellectual impact among nineteenth-century intellectuals in the United States, especially among the Transcendentalists, and was of special interest to AHHA (see also introduction to part 1, above).

10. Here JA wrote "(over)" at the bottom of the page to indicate the continuation of the essay on the other side of the paper.

11. At the time Laplace first formed the Nebular Hypothesis, Uranus was a relatively new discovery. One of the superior planets (the seventh furthest out from the sun), it was the first planet discovered by means of a telescope. English astronomers and brother and sister William and Caroline Herschel (1750–1848) identified it on 13 Mar. 1781. The Herschels also greatly extended the catalog of known nebulae—work that was continued by William's son, John Herschel (1782–1871), into JA's lifetime. In 1787 the first two satellites or moons of Uranus, Titania and Oberon, were discovered. Two more, Ariel and Umbriel, were discovered in 1851. The next, Miranda, was not identified until 1948. Uranus is now known to have at least eleven moons.

12. Throughout the last half of the nineteenth century and into the twentieth, Neptune was the outermost known planet in the solar system (Pluto was not discovered until 1930). The existence of Neptune was calculated in relation to observations of Uranus by English mathematician John Couch Adams (1819–92) and others in the 1840s, and the planet was actually identified by telescope by Johann G. Galle (1812–1910) at the Berlin Observatory on 23 Sept. 1846. At that time Neptune was known to have at least one moon or satellite, Triton, which revolved around its primary in about six days. A second moon, Nereid, was discovered in 1949. Neptune is now known to have at least eight moons.

13. Here, and in instances below, JA means "primaries," as in primary planets (the planets that revolve around the sun, i.e., Mercury, Venus, Earth, Mars, Jupiter, Saturn, Uranus, Neptune, and Pluto) as opposed to secondary planets (the satellites that revolve around the primary planets, for example, our moon is a secondary, or satellite, to the earth).

14. In forming these points, JA relied heavily on the observations made in two summary paragraphs in Laplace's *System of the World*. In first offering his hypothesis, Laplace stated:

> However arbitrary the elements of the system of the planets may be, there exists between them some very remarkable relations, which may throw light on their origin. Considering it with attention, we are astonished to see all the planets move round the Sun from west to east, and nearly in the same plane, all the satellites moving round their respective planets in the same direction, and nearly in the same plane with the planets. Lastly, the Sun, the planets, and those satellites in which a motion of rotation have been observed, turn on their own axes, in the same direction, and nearly in the same plane as their motion of projection. (2:326)

Restating these elements later in the book, he wrote, "we have the five following phenomena to assist us in investigating the cause of the primitive motions of the planetary system. The motions of the planets in the same direction, and very nearly in the same plane, the motions of the satellites in the same direction as those of the planets, the motions of rotation of these different bodies and also of the Sun, in the same direction as their motions of projection, and in planes very little inclined to each other; the small eccentricity of the orbits of the planets and satellites" (2:354).

15. Eccentricity refers to the shape of the curves of the path of an orbit, the eccentricity of an elliptical orbit being a measure of how much it deviates from being a circle. The greater the eccentricity, the greater the displacement relative to some specified center such as the sun. Kant theorized that the closer a planet is to the sun (its principal center of attraction), the less eccentric its orbit. Laplace observed in the Nebular Hypothesis that "the small eccentricity of the orbits of the planets and their satellites" is one of the remarkable phenomena of the solar system. "We are here again compelled to acknowledge the effect of a regular cause," Laplace concluded, "chance alone could not have given a form nearly circular to the orbits of all planets" ("Laplace's Nebular Hypothesis," reprinted in Numbers, *Creation by Natural Law*, appendix 2, 125).

16. JA meant to write *nucleus*.

17. Here and below JA wrote *sheriod*, meaning *spheriod*, or a solid formed by the rotation of matter in an ellipse round an axis, as in oblate (rotation around the minor axis) and prolate (rotation around the major, or longer, axis) spheroids.

18. Spectrum analysis, or the determination of the elements of a luminous body by the examination of its light passing through prisms, was used in nineteenth-century astronomical research to determine the chemical elements and motion of stars and to divide them into classes. As Carrie Strong put it in her 1881 Junior Exhibition speech, "The discovery of spectrum analysis has greatly aided the search of astronomers" (*RSM* [May 1881]: 130).

19. JA meant to write *gases*.

To Ellen Gates Starr

Rockford Sem'y [Ill.]   Jan 29" 1880

My dear friend

Occasion of religious associations—as you truly said. I only need tell you that this is "fast Day" and you will understand.

I have just come down from a prayer-meeting conducted by Miss Potter. I enjoyed it but not as much as I would have enjoyed a recitation with her, I suppose it must be—because I take less interest in the first subject than in the other; but whatever else I am I mean to be honest in the subject of religion, I have tried to-day and made a failure.[1] The services this morning in chapel were really impressive, Dr Curtis[2] lead and in addition to the usual corps of ministers there were two or three strangers, they sort of reacted on each other and so were interested.

For the first time—I am glad it happened once—I was proud of my institution, glad that I belonged to a <u>Christian school</u> and was under influence I knew were on the right side—although I must confess somewhat preverted.

Do you remember two years ago to-day, how excited we were? I see now that the idea of being injured was all in our own minds, it seems to me that I have changed since then but I do not know that I have grown very much in spiritual things—I do not mean in character but in ideals, I see more the need of knowing God but he seems further off than he did then. Have you read one of Joseph Cooke's later lectures—"The new birth a scientific necessity" if you have you will know what I mean I feel it as a <u>scientific</u> necessity but not as a <u>aesthetic</u>

necessity so to speak. I have been trying an awful experiment I did n't pray, at least formally for almost three months, and was shocked to find that I feel no worse for it, I can think about a great many other things that are noble & beautiful I feel happy and unconcerned and not in the least morbid. You see, my dear, you have progressed since two years ago for you could no more do that now than any-thing at all. I am ever so much obliged for the letter of Christmas night, and consider it a compliment because you did send it; I started a letter to you something like that a few months ago but never finished it, I wish I had now for I think I was better then, than I am to-day, "Fast Day".

You have the main idea because you long for a faith, I remember an illustration of a man who was a musician and refused to look at a fine picture because he held that the finest beauty was by the sense of hearing, the illustration is n't very good but the idea to show how absurd is the insisting upon seeing into religion by the understanding instead of by faith, which is the highest faculty given.

There is where I think we differ—you long for a beautiful faith an experiance of this kind—I only feel that I need religion in a practical sense, that if I could fix myself with my relations to God & the universe, & so be in perfect harmony with nature & deity, I could use my faculties and energy so much better & could do almost any thing. Mine is preeminantly selfish and yours is a reaching for higher things. I am so glad you have opportunity to attend the services—and any way there is some thing enlarging in a city. Sometimes when I think of being hemmed in by these four walls I grow perfectly restless, but when I think what a good quiet place it is for study I become quite contented again.

I am reading Homer and enjoy him more than I ever imagined I would, I would be willing to study Greek for ten years, even pig along in Crosby all that time if I might read Homer in the end—that sounds extravagent and I wish I had n't written it, but the fact still remains. Miss Blaisdell is quite as much interested as I am, and I shall always be thankful that I have read it with her, and inseperable in my mind will be the two names!!

Corinne Williams was in my room just before prayer-meeting and helped me with the exchanges for the next number, we have been thrown together a great deal this year on magazine work and I continually keep discovering something more about her character, although I thought I understood her a good while ago, we had a row once when we were getting advertisements which I fervently hope will never happen again.

I had just finished reading "Marble Faun"[3] a few days before your epistle arrived, a coincidence! Some of the descriptions & scence[4] will always be very vivid to me & I am glad I have them, but the effect of the entire story is most certainly peculiar; in regard to Donatello's developement I feel very much the same as the poor sculptor did—that it was sin which developed him, I think that scence by the fountain & his lost intercourse with nature is really pathetic. The way Miriam turns out is to me simply disgusting. I had one or two things in particular I wanted to write to you about Hilda but I have forgotten what they are now. Was your knowledge of modern history sufficient to solve the mystery, I must confess the personages are a deep mystery to me without the least clue.[5]

Observe, if you please, our class paper, the design it may be well to state is of wheat and hops, the hops I will admit are obscure but their significance is deep.

You don't know how sorry I am that my postal came to[o] late, it was all my carelessness for I did n't have the least idea I was a day behind time, I shall never cease to regret the same.

Your ideas on the conception of Christ I think are good but I don't believe they are exactly correct, I don't think God embodied himself in Christ to reveal himself, but that he did <n't> considering the weakness of man; that while man might occasionaly comprehend an abstract diety he couldn't live by it, it came to him only in his more exalted moments, & it was impossible for his mind to retain his own conception of God. It seems to me that a philosopher might have an abstract centre for his faith but that an ordinary man could n't. If a man can once see God through Christ then he is saved for he can never again lose him as Christ is always with him. Of course contemplating & understanding God a man must progress infinitely. This is my idea and may be it don't differ so very much from yours after all. If I could claim one promise in the Bible I would care for no other—"He restorest my soul." Carlyle says every-one must sooner or later find out it is not with work alone he must contend but with folly & sin in himself & others, I have laid too many of my plans simply for work. Am much obliged for the poem, some parts of it are lovely, some I don't like. I have had a quiet peaceful day, & that I am thankful for. Miss Anderson sends her love, ditto Miss Potter. Your friend

Jane Addams

ALS (SC, Starr; *JAPM*, 1:473–77).

1. JA recalled the discomfort she felt in regard to the regular evangelical pressure put upon her and the other "comparatively few 'unconverted' girls in the school" (Addams, *Twenty Years*, 49). Being the subject of prayer during obligatory attendance at daily chapel exercises and weekly prayer meetings and during dutiful participation in such special days of sacred observance as Fast Day was difficult to endure for those firmly rationally minded students, like JA, who did not wish to succumb to the expectations of the RFS administration. Anna P. Sill and many of the more fervent teachers hoped that during their tenure at the school all RFS girls would come to experience the joys of an emotional, unequivocal, conversion (followed, it was hoped, by dedication to work in the missionary field). Resisting general entreaties to join the ranks of the zealously converted during group exercises was one thing, being the subject of private petitions was even worse. JA "became unspeakably embarrassed when . . . [forms of emotional appeal] were presented to me at close range by a teacher during the 'silent hour'" that came at the end of each school day (49).

JA was hardly alone in these feelings. Before her younger sister, Lizzie, started school at RFS, Addie B. Smith wrote home to her about Fast Day: "It is just like Sunday and no visiting is allowed among the girls. Had services in the Chapel this forenoon to which all the Trustees, ministers and 'Friends of Education' came and strove to impress the naughty Sem. girls with the good truths. We behaved very properly & you should surely say so if you could have seen us all seated in rows across the chapel arrayed in our Sunday best. . . . Oh 'lisabeth, you wouldn't like it here. There are too many prayer meetings etc." (25 Jan. [1877], SHSW, Smith). In the next school year, Addie wrote to her mother, "Seems to me everyone is bound to convert me before they let me leave this 'institooshun' for good and they have kept at me quite beautifully." Sill had asked her to come to her room for a one-on-one talk and questioned Addie about whether her parents were churchgoers and about her own faith. She told Addie that she wished to see her "fully persuaded." Pressure to convert came not only from Sill and faculty members but also from peers. Addie commented that "the girls I go with are church members, and Mattie Thomas is a perfect little saint. Mary Blakeslee often has said she wished I would be a converted christian." Mattie Thomas was also trying to persuade Smith through the influence of a mutual friend, whom she was also trying to convert. Addie summed up her feelings in a way JA could well appreciate: "I don't desire to be good and pious like some of the girls here who pray in meeting etc. and if I can't be thought a Christian without it I don't care to be called one" (Addie B. Smith to Annie M. Jordan Smith, 8 Mar. 1878, SHSW, Smith; see also T.H. Haseltine to JA, 13 June 1880, below).

2. The Rev. Dr. William Stanton Curtis (b. 1820) was chair of the RFS Exec. Com. in JA's sophomore, junior, and senior years. He was born in Vermont and grew up in Missouri and Wisconsin. He graduated from Illinois College, Jacksonville, in 1838 and attended Yale Divinity School, New Haven, Conn. He was the pastor of the First Congregational Church of Rockford for one year (ca. 1841) before becoming pastor of the First Presbyterian Church of Ann Arbor for thirteen years. He also taught at the Univ. of Michigan. He became college pastor and professor of moral philosophy at Hamilton College, Clinton, N.Y., and then president of Knox College, Galesburg, Ill., in the 1860s. In 1869 he returned to Rockford as pastor of the Westminster Presbyterian Church. He resigned in 1875 to go abroad as a missionary and then returned to Rockford, where he worked as a visiting pastor to churches with vacant pulpits in the vicinity. He later became a director of the Theological Seminary of the Northwest in Chicago. An 1887 biographical profile of Curtis stated that as a preacher he was "metaphysical and profound, yet lucid and popular in style" (Schaff and Jackson, eds., *Encyclopedia of Living Divines*, 47).

3. Massachusetts-born Nathaniel Hawthorne's (1804–64) *The Marble Faun* (1860), which he once said he believed to be his best novel, was a tragic romance set in Italy. EGS had written to JA on 28 Dec. 1879 to say that she, too, had been reading the novel. She disapproved of Hawthorne's views on art but quoted with appreciation a passage on the nature of faith: "Christian faith is a grand cathedral with divinely pictured windows. Standing without, you see no glory, nor can possibly imagine any; standing within, every ray of light reveals a harmony of unspeakable splendors" (SCPC, JAC; *JAPM*, 1:452–53).

4. JA meant to write the word *scenes*.

5. It is possible that JA was reading *The Marble Faun* in part because of an interest in the character of Hilda. JA's essay on Macbeth was followed, in the "Literary Notes" section of the *RSM*, by an account of "an enterprising junior," perhaps JA—certainly someone reading many of the same titles to which JA refers in her letters—who was fired with interest in reading about women characters who by their "very virtue" were "strong enough to defy all natural force" after reading about the beautiful lady in Milton's *Comus* in class. She read in mythology about Diana and Minerva, and "In history she read all she could find from that defiant Roman maiden to Joan of Arc." She read the story of Ruth in the Bible, and "in fiction she re-read Rebecca's career in 'Ivanhoe' and Hilda in Hawthorne's 'Marble Faun'" as well as Desdemona and other women of Shakespeare and Chaucer ([Jan. 1880]: 16–17).

Hawthorne based his characters on elements drawn from real historical personalities. The character of Donatello shares his name with that of the fifteenth-century Florentine sculptor Donatello (1386–1466), who was considered artistically revolutionary in his time by moving toward a more natural or realistic (versus idealistic) depiction of heroic subjects. Many Victorians found his work ugly, but Hawthorne greatly admired it. The character of Miriam was based in part on the historical figure of the beautiful Beatrice Cenci, who was abused by a vicious father and willed her brother and an admirer to kill him and throw his body off a balcony to make the murder seem an accident.

Essay in the *Rockford Seminary Magazine*

This analysis of Macbeth, in which Jane Addams offered a symbolic interpretation of Shakespeare's play, was probably her favorite essay among those she wrote while a student at Rockford Female Seminary. Her approach emphasized the psychological and figurative dimensions of the play in addition to considering issues of morality and justice. Her emphasis on the symbolic aspects of the play presented something of a departure from standard nineteenth-century readings and in some ways prefigured perspectives that literary critics would more commonly use to discuss Macbeth in the twentieth century. Like Addams, Ellen Gates Starr was particularly fond of this essay. In the mid-1880s she used it as a text for her students at Miss Kirkland's School for Girls in Chicago.[1]

Rockford, Ill.   JANUARY 1880

THE MACBETH OF SHAKESPEARE

In the Eleventh Century Duncan and Macbeth were two grandsons of the reigning king of Scotland. In course of time the old king peacefully died and Duncan ascended the throne. He had but the shadow of a claim over his cousin,[2] he was not as gifted a man, he probably made no greater effort toward the crown and yet he gained it. The divine right of king was bestowed upon him while Macbeth was merely one of this subjects.[3] We should take Duncan to be one of those men who some way have the material universe on their side, a "great vague backing" in all they do and undertake, the word "luck" somewhat expresses their success, things turn out just to suit them, and honors are easily granted them. Macbeth had no doubt observed this ever since he could remember, it seemed perfectly natural for Duncan to be king and gain that which he desires. Macbeth is not envious, but he continually thinks of these things, he is a nervous man and cannot think calmly.[4]

Shakespeare leaves us to imagine all this. He does not present Macbeth until these thoughts have begun to pursue and control him; until his mind has gained that sort of exasperation which comes from using living muscle against some lifeless insurmountable resistance.

All the scenes of the play are laid at night, and we are hurried on with feverish rapidity—we do not know the Macbeth of the day time, how he appears in council or battle—we meet only the nervous high strung man at night, pursued by phantoms and ghosts, and ever poetically designing a murder.[5]

Shakespeare presents the man's thought 'ere he presents the man himself, and in the very first scene the three witches frighten us before we know what they are to represent. As Macbeth enters they hail him with the three titles his heart most desires; he starts, who wouldn't?[6] The thoughts he has been thinking and thinking, have suddenly embodied themselves, and stand before him on the bold bare heath; they have all at once grown into definite purposes, have spoken out before a third person, Banquo, and he knows that ever afterward he must acknowledge them, that they will pursue and harrass him.[7] We have all had the experience—how we prepare ourselves for sudden deeds by the intuitive choice of good and evil, or, as our thoughts go forth never to be recalled, how they increase and gain enormous proportions until we lose all control of them. But Macbeth had this experience in a way that was simply frightful; his thought grew so powerful as to assume form and shape, as to be endowed with life and a distinct physical existence to baffle and confront him. His first impulse is one of fear and terror at the metaphysical confusion in which he is entangled. He is lost in a maze of his own thoughts, he knowns not what is real and what is fantastical, he is filled with horrible imaginings and doubts; but slowly from all this confusion there arises a phantom distinctly before him, it seems afar off, he detaches it from himself, and yet he knows it is his own creation. He says:

> "Why do I yield to that suggestion,
> Whose horrid image doth unfix my hair"—[8]

That image is murder, it takes a poetical man to call it an image, but Macbeth tries to deceive himself and keep his heart of hearts pure. Here he yields to that impulse of a sort of self-preservation, that shielding of his inner character, he wishes not to harm or shock himself, he would gain a deadly end, but without the illness that should attend it; with this purpose he reorganizes the witches and phantoms, and shifts upon them the entire moral responsibility of his future actions, he follows them mechanically and saves himself—it is a phantom that murders Duncan.[9]

He discloses his purpose to Lady Macbeth, and thus gives to her the physical or material responsibility, she plans and contrives, does all cooly and calmly, for she is but murdering a man—avenging her father[10]; Macbeth meanwhile is struggling throughout with murder itself, invisible yet clinging and horrible the phantom pursues him until the last moment. Just before the final deed he soliloquizes:

> "Now o'er the one half world
> Nature seems dead, and withered murder
> Alarmed by his sentinel the wolf
> Moves like a ghost"—[11]

'Tis "withered murder" that leads him on to his destruction, and follows it as something inevitable. Macbeth has slowly prepared a splendid defense for himself, it is utterly impossible for him, murdering Duncan, to receive any conscious harm or any violent shock to his inner self, and yet he is thwarted by his own ends. He kills Duncan and comes back to his wife horror-struck and frightened, not because of the bloody deed, but because he has murdered sleep, because he has heard a voice cry "Sleep no more! Macbeth does murder sleep!"[12] No matter how often we read it, it always produces the same thrilling effect; the idea of a man murdering sleep; think of being pursued by withered murder and a sleepless sleep.

This then is the result, by getting rid of his will and following merely the poetical idea, he kills not a man, but an imaginary, an invisible horrible being; it is the only possible retribution and it is frightful.

After the death of Duncan, the rest of the play is virtually but a repetition. Macbeth is driven from murder to murder, ghosts and phantoms pursue him, he consults again the weird sisters, gains courage and is lost through his own daring[13]—a poetical man doing the worst deeds in a poetical sense—the philosophy of murder.[14]

L.J.A. '81

PD (RSM [Jan. 1880]: 13–16; JAPM, 46:137–40).[15]

1. See EGS to JA, 28 Apr. 1885, SC, Starr; JAPM, 2:50–53. Essays on Shakespeare plays appeared periodically in the RSM. An issue of the magazine in JA's first year included "A Study of Macbeth" written by Maria Nutting that focused on the qualities of character displayed by Macbeth (RSM [Oct. 1877]: 184–85). Victoria Wigren discussed the popularity of Macbeth in an essay on Julius Caesar (RSM [Jan. 1878]: 6–9).

2. Shakespeare's play was based on the lives of the real Scottish monarchs Macbeth (1005?–57) and Duncan (1001?–40). As JA points out, they were first cousins. Both were grandsons of King Malcolm II (954?–1034), who ruled the Scots from 1005 to his death, and although both had some claim by blood to the throne, Duncan had the slight preference as the son of Malcolm II's eldest daughter (Macbeth being the son of the king's second daughter), and he was chosen by Malcolm II to be his successor. Duncan, also known as Duncan I the Gracious, ruled as King of Scots from 1034 to 1040, when at the age of thirty-nine he was slain in battle by Macbeth, who succeeded him. Macbeth ruled from 1040 until he was killed on the battlefield by Duncan's eldest son, Malcolm III (Malcolm Canmore, 1031–93), who ruled Scotland from 1058 until his death.

Shakespeare based his play in part upon accounts from Raphael Holinshed's Chronicles of Scotland, the second volume of the Chronicles of England, Scotland, and Ireland (3 vols.), which was first published in 1577 and reissued in the revised edition that Shakespeare used in 1587. Shakespeare wrote the play early in the reign of King James I (1566–1625), and many have seen it as a reflection upon Elizabethan politics. James I was the son of Mary Stuart, Queen of Scots (1542–87), who had relinquished her right of inheritance to the British crown to him and was imprisoned and eventually beheaded under order of Elizabeth (1533–1603), accused as an accomplice in a 1586 plot to assassinate the English queen. Upon Elizabeth's death, James I succeeded her on the throne of England and reigned until 1625. Macbeth involved two of James I's personal interests, Scottish history and witchcraft. The play was first performed in London ca. 1606, and the first printed version appeared in folio in 1623.

3. As Macbeth characterizes his relationship to Duncan, "I am his kinsman and his subject" (act 1, sc. 7, line 13). Aside from the matter of lineage, Macbeth could have legitimately

been granted the crown instead of Duncan by virtue of election because of his superior worthiness as a thane (a Scottish feudal lord or nobleman who performed military service for the king). Macbeth was thane of Glamis before Duncan's reign, and, after battling for Duncan as his king, he was made thane of Cawdor by Duncan's decree. The assassination plot Shakespeare used in *Macbeth* was not based on the true story of the historical Macbeth and Duncan but instead adapted from an account of the heinous murder of Duff (Dubh), King of Scots from 962 to 967, by Donwald, who acted in league with his wife.

4. *Macbeth* was often read in the nineteenth century as a morality play about envy and ambition, with a focus upon the issue of character and the rise and fall of its protagonist as a tragic hero. As Macbeth puts it while contemplating the murder of Duncan, "I have no spur / To prick the sides of my intent, but only / Vaulting ambition, which o'erleaps itself / And falls on th' other" (act 1, sc. 7, lines 25–28).

5. A.C. Bradley, in his famous interpretation of the play in *Shakespearean Tragedy* (1904), similarly characterized Macbeth as a man of action who possessed the sensibility of a poet. JA, here, too, emphasizes Macbeth's poetical imagination and the ways in which his nervous thoughts become manifested in phantasmal images that are either visible or invisible to others. As she notes, *Macbeth* is permeated with eery metaphysical imagery, including dramatic meteorological phenomena; the appearance of witches, phantoms, ghostly apparitions, and portents (including a raven and an owl); the use of magical potions and incantations; and the experiences of gnawing dreams or hallucinations. The encounter with the dark side of human nature—evil, night, and the supernatural—and its contrast with everyday life was often the theme in romantic literary criticism of the play, including that written by Thomas De Quincey.

6. Act 1, sc. 1 of *Macbeth* is devoted solely to the three witches. They appear on stage accompanied by thunder and lightening and briefly plan their impending encounter with Macbeth, which occurs in act 1, sc. 3. In that scene, Macbeth makes his first entrance in the play, along with his friend and fellow thane Banquo. Macbeth is hailed by the witches in triple fashion as thane of Glamis, thane of Cawdor, and king. JA here reads the witches as projections of Macbeth's agitated mind, or as his evil thoughts or ambitions made incarnate or personified.

7. As the witches speak with Macbeth at the beginning of the play, they foretell the fate that will unfold for the drama's main characters. Their weird prophecies, given to Macbeth and Banquo in the form of riddles, both spur Macbeth on in his ambition to be king and impel him to murderousness as he attempts to circumvent the challenges to his sovereignty hinted at in the witches' predictions.

8. JA quotes here from an aside soon after Macbeth has met with the witches and received the news from a fellow nobleman that Duncan has made him thane of Cawdor. Macbeth reasons to himself: "This supernatural soliciting / Cannot be ill, cannot be good. If ill, / Why hath it given me earnest of success / Commencing in a truth? I am Thane of Cawdor. / If good, why do I yield to that suggestion / Whose horrid image doth unfix my hair / . . . Present fears / Are less than horrible imaginings" (act 1, sc. 3, lines 131–39).

9. Lady Macbeth, upon learning the news of the witches' prophesies, famously summons herself in a witchlike way to the task of murder, proclaiming: "Come, you spirits / That tend on mortal thoughts, unsex me here / And fill me from the crown to the toe top-full / Of direst cruelty! Make thick my blood; / Stop up th' access and passage to remorse, / That no compunctious visitings of nature / Shake my fell purpose, nor keep peace between / Th' effect and it! Come to my woman's breasts / And take my milk for gall, you murdering ministers, / Wherever in your sightless substances / You wait on nature's mischief! Come, thick night, / And pall thee in the dunnest smoke of Hell, / That my keen knife see not the wound it makes, / Nor heaven peep through the blanket of the dark / To cry 'Hold, hold!'" (act 1, sc. 6, lines 38–52).

10. Lady Macbeth, or Gruoch (b. 1015?), was the daughter of Boite (Bodhe or Beoedhe), the granddaughter of Kenneth III, king of Scotland from 997 to 1005, and the great-grand-daughter of Duff (Dubh). Both Macbeth and Gruoch were descendents of Malcolm I, king of Scots from 942 to 954. Gruoch's grandfather, Kenneth III, was slain in battle by Macbeth's grandfather, Malcolm II, who thereby became king, depriving Kenneth III's sons, Giric and Boite, of their possible inheritance of the throne. Sources differ on the course of Gruoch's life. She married Macbeth ca. 1032 and brought with her into the marriage a young son, Lulach (sometimes called Lulach the Fool) (b. 1030?–58), born of her first marriage to Macrory, Gillacomgan (Earl) of Moray. Lulach was briefly recognized as king of Scots in 1057, but was, like his stepfather before him, killed by Malcolm Canmore (Malcolm III). Some historians believe Gruoch, or another woman by the same name, may have married Malcolm III, and the date and circumstances of her death are unknown.

11. JA quotes here from Macbeth's soliloquy before killing Duncan, in which Macbeth ponders: "Is this a dagger which I see before me, / The handle toward my hand? Come, let me clutch thee:— / I have thee not, and yet I see thee still. / Art thou not, fatal vision, sensible / To feeling as to sight? Or art thou but / A dagger of the mind, a false creation / Proceeding from the heat-oppressed brain? / . . . It is the bloody business which informs / Thus to mine eyes.—Now o'er the one half-world / Nature seems dead, and wicked dreams abuse / The curtained sleep. Witchcraft celebrates / Pale Hecate's offerings; and withered murder, / Alarumed by his sentinel, the wolf, / Whose howl's his watch, thus with his stealthy pace, / With Tarquin's ravishing strides, towards his design / Moves like a ghost.—" (act 2, sc. 1, lines 33–39, 48–56). JA quotes parts of lines 49 and 50, followed by part of line 52, all of line 53, and the first part of line 56. "Withered murder," which she repeats, is from line 52.

12. The murder of Duncan takes place off stage, in act 2, sc. 2. When Macbeth returns from stabbing the king, he tells his wife: "Methought I heard a voice cry 'Sleep no more! / Macbeth does murder sleep!'—the innocent sleep / . . . Still it cried 'Sleep no more!' to all the house: / 'Glamis [Macbeth, Thane of Glamis] hath murdered sleep, and therefore Cawdor [Macbeth, thane of Cawdor] / Shall sleep no more, Macbeth shall sleep no more!'" (act 2, sc. 2, lines 35–36, 41–43). JA quotes here from lines 35 and 36.

The murder of Duncan is closely associated with varying levels of sleep, unconsciousness, and wakeful guilty consciences. Macbeth murders Duncan in the dead of night while the king sleeps unguarded in Macbeth's castle. Lady Macbeth drugs the king's guards into a deep drunken slumber, and Macbeth uses their own knives to kill Duncan. Macbeth then frames them for the murder by leaving their bloody daggers by their sides and smearing their sleeping bodies with blood. When the castle-dwellers awake, Macbeth murders the guards before they can speak their innocence, acting as if in a fit of rage at the discovery of their crime against the dead king. In consequence of these and subsequent acts of violence, Lady Macbeth is plagued by guilt-ridden sleepwalking nightmares and ultimately dies.

13. A chain reaction of bloodshed follows the initial murder of Duncan, finally resulting in the death of Macbeth himself. Macbeth has the suspicious Banquo assassinated, whereupon Banquo appears as a ghost to haunt Macbeth at his banquet table (act 3, sc. 3, 4). The witches reappear along with Hecate, the goddess of night and witchcraft (act 3, sc. 5; act 4, sc. 1), and Macbeth murders the family of Macduff, the thane of Fife (act 4, sc. 3), whereupon Malcolm (III) and Macduff seek their vengeance. Macduff kills and decapitates Macbeth, and the play concludes with Malcolm (III) as king (act 5, sc. 8).

14. JA's class of 1881 briefly formed a Shakespeare Club in their senior year. They met once a week in the Senior parlor and lined the bookshelves with copies of Shakespeare's plays. "'Why do they have so many Shakespeares?'" asked a preparatory student, eyeing the bookcase in the parlor. "'Don't you know,' replied a wicked Junior, 'Shakespeare was the greatest writer who ever lived, and the Seniors have mastered every body else'" (RSM [Dec. 1880]: 267). By the following spring, the RSM reported "The Shak[e]speare Club of the Senior class

is no more, but we observe books of a different character scattered in their parlor. Just now they are greatly interested in the 'Diary of a Bad Boy'" ([Apr. 1881]: 104).

15. See also the AMsS version of this essay (*JAPM*, 46:128–36).

From Ellen Gates Starr

Chicago, [Ill.]   Feb. 29, 1880.

My dear Jany;

I have just been rereading your letter, & the first thing that it occurred to me I wished to answer, was what you said in answer to me about the Incarnation. You seemed to think we differed, but what you went on to say was just about what I <u>meant</u> to say, but apparently fell a little short of. You say "I don't think God embodied himself in Christ to <u>reveal</u> himself, but that he did it considering the weakness of man." Then you go on about mankind in ordinary not being able to comprehend an "abstract Deity" which is a very bad expression, though I agree with the idea. The idea in fact is the same Macaulay has in one of his Essays I think the one on Milton.[1] Now I think, considering the weakness of man, He <u>did</u> do it to reveal Himself.

The revelation of Himself was the great object, as I see it. The reason for His chosing that way of doing it I see just as you do, "—that while man might occasionally comprehend an abstract deity he couldn't live by it; it came to him only in his more exalted moments, & it was impossible for his mind to retain his own conception of God," you say,

> "And so the Word had breath, & wrought
> With human hands the creed of creeds
> In loveliness of perfect deeds
> More strong than all poetic thought."

I do not think we are far apart. You suggested to me once that you thought I might find in the "In Memoriam" what would help me. By a coincidence, which frequently happens between us, I was at the time reading it, & found so many helpful things. The point on which I suppose I am unorthodox, is the "atonement." It seems to me God revealed Himself to us to <u>draw</u> <u>us</u> <u>away</u> from our sins, <u>to</u> <u>Him</u>. I can't understand what it is they mean by Christ <u>expiating</u> our sins, (& I don't know that I care to) or by His <u>reconciling</u> God to us.—, God <u>always</u> loved us & wanted us, to love Him.

We can imagine a parents grief for a child who has sinned, & thus <u>separated</u>, & the love reaches out across that awful gulf, that most <u>hopeless</u> gulf that can exist between two souls, that of <u>incapacity</u> on the part of one to appreciate, or meet the other. When we think of what the love was, & what the incapacity was, the inertness of not understanding, it does not seem to me to require anything more to account for the agony of the Passion. It seems a kind of sacrilege to talk of that Passion. I remember you used to feel so. I wish, my friend that you would not practice again upon yourself the kind of experiment you told me of. I can't see that any good <u>can</u> come of it, & harm <u>might</u>. If one wished, before uniting himself forever with another person, to <u>test</u> himself, he might <u>keep away</u> for a certain length of time, to try if the love would live. But when the life of the love is the life of the soul, when its existence is recognized as a necessary thing, I don't think it best to experiment. I did the same thing once, for longer than you say—very much longer. But not as an experiment. I did it because prayer, the form of prayer, was a mockery to me then, & I was too sincere to use a lifeless form. The soul has come back to it. If there is any soul in yours, don't put it away to <u>see</u> if it will live.

Miss Holmes received, a week ago today, the news of her mother's sudden death.[2] She is a person of such unquenchable cheerfullness, under ordinary circumstances, that the change is very much felt. We are alone in the house together, you know, & depend very much on each other for society. I am surprised to find how much she depends on me now, & perhaps still more surprised, certainly made very happy by finding that I can help her. I have given up all my private pursuits this week, to devote myself to her. I have been hoping all the winter that you & Miss Anderson would come to Chicago. I hardly think I shall be at commencement this year, for I think my sister will be here about that time, & as she will want me to visit her friends here with her, I shall not want to hurry away.

I often want to talk with you, about Carlyle, & about the people I hear. We attended two lectures of Dr. Gibson's, you remember him. I liked them so much, that I introduced myself, & asked him if I might go to see him sometime. He said he should be very glad to have me, & gave me his address. I went the evening he said he was generally at home, but he was out of the city. It is a long distance from here, but I shall try again sometime, I want a real good talk with him, & I know I should have it. He is such a <u>genuine</u> kind of man. I believe I told you I met Prof. Swing once. I was also invited to dinner to meet Mr. Butler, a young man that they think of calling to Mr. Collyer's church.[3] Miss Rice[4] (I give a drawing lesson once a week in her school) is a great Unitarian, & seems rather to take a fancy to me. I didn't specially admire the individual. I do wish Mr. Collyer had remained. We live too far from Dr. Gibson[5] to go there, & don't especially admire the Unity people, & the result is I go to the Ascension (ritualistic Episcopal church) as often as any where. You will perceive from the above that I am somewhat <u>liberal</u> in my views. In fact the name of the church makes very little difference to me. I have been engaged in the perusal of three old & rather standard works on all of which my early education was sadly neglected. Pilgrims Progress, Gullivers Travels,[6] & Book of Job. I presume you approve, especially of the latter. In accordance with your advice, I once began to read Froude[7] on Job, but was interrupted in the beginning, & never finished. When I finish the work itself, I shall read the article. I hope you will excuse this merciless letter, & I will promise the next time to write one totally different, I had no intention of inflicting so many of my "views" upon you, but was rather lead on. I remember you used to object to talking upon religion, & always suppressed me. If you feel so still please say so, & I will not annoy you.[8] I enjoy very much your ideas upon that subject, when you feel inclined to express them, as indeed upon all others. Believe me your appreciative friend;

Ellen Starr.

ALS (SCPC, JAC; *JAPM*, 1:484–95).

1. Thomas Macaulay (1800–1859) wrote many critical essays, many first published in the *Edinburgh Review* and collected in book form in 1843. The best known was on poet John Milton (1600–1674) and written in response to Milton's *De Doctrina Christiana*, which had been printed in 1825.

2. A reference to the death of the mother of EGS's close friend Mary J. Holmes of Chicago (not to be confused with Mary E. Holmes of RFS's mother, who died in 1890).

3. A committee of six convened from June 1879 to Nov. 1880 to consider a successor to Rev. Robert Collyer, who resigned with short notice in May 1879. They invited a series of ministers to preach at the church, and on 12 Jan. 1881 the Rev. George C. Miln of Brooklyn, N.Y., was formally installed as the new pastor. Miln tried to resign less than a year later, in Dec. 1881, but his resignation was not approved. It was later agreed, in Feb. 1882, that due to the "change in the religious opinions of Mr. Miln," he would be allowed to resign (Andreas, *History of Chicago*, 825). He was in turn replaced by the Rev. George Bachelor of Salem, Mass.

4. Rebecca S. Rice, administrator of Miss Rice's School for Young Ladies and Children at 481 N. LaSalle St. in Chicago, where EGS taught part time in 1879–80 (see EGS to JA, 27 July 1879, n. 6, above).

5. JA replied, "You spoke of Dr Gibson. I hope you saw him before he left the city. I heard him at Carrie Hood's funeral and was a little disappointed in him, although two or three things he said were very beautiful & comforting" (JA to EGS, 15 May 1880, SC, Starr; *JAPM*, 1:506). Tragedy struck the Hood family in the spring of 1880. Vocal teacher Carrie Hood, daughter of RFS music professor Daniel Hood, became very ill with consumption. Her mother, Maria Greenough Hood, took her to Florida to recover. Maria Hood contracted malaria in Florida and died on 21 Feb. 1880. Carrie Hood, who was twenty-one and engaged to be married to a young Rockford man, lingered on but died herself on 20 Mar. 1880. Her funeral was held in Rockford and reported in the Apr. 1880 edition of the *RSM*.

6. John Bunyan's (1628–88) Christian allegory *Pilgrim's Progress* (1678) and Jonathan Swift's (1667–1745) satiric *Gulliver's Travels* (1726).

7. Probably a reference to the work of Oxford scholar Richard Hurrell Froude (1803–36). Froude was a controversial figure within the Tractarian (or Oxford) movement, which helped stir popular debate over theological issues in England in the mid-1830s. Froude achieved fame and died in the midst of the controversies sparked by the movement, proponents of which attacked the prevalence of rationalist thought within the Church of England and generally supported High Church, or High Anglican, Anglo-Catholic views (views that became ever more dear to EGS as she grew older). Froude was a close friend of Oxford fellow John Henry Newman (1801–90), and he wrote with Newman, in Rome, the *Lyra Apostolica* (1836). He contributed as an author, with Newman, Edward B. Pusey, and others, three of the many-part *Tracts for the Times*, a series of writings on religious subjects published between 1833 and 1841, which were at the intellectual core of the Oxford movement. Froude's thought was capped with the publication of the *Literary Remains of Richard Hurrell Froude*, published in 1838–39, which dealt in part with issues of the Reformation. Froude's younger brother, James

Anthony Froude (1818–94), editor of *Fraser's Magazine* from 1860 to 1874, whose essays on religion, theology, travel, and English history were reprinted in *Short Studies on Great Subjects* (1867–83), was the literary executor of Thomas Carlyle's estate.

8. JA took EGS at her word and on 15 May 1880 replied:

> I believe, my friend, it would be better for us not to talk about religion any more, I enjoyed you[r] letter and am obliged to you for what you wrote, but I find it is hopeless to express myself in regard to the <u>Incarnation</u>, and in regard to the other things we wrote about my ideas are changing, I believe <u>this</u> if you will excuse a long quotation—"It is the unconscious reception of a kingly example, gentle compliance with <what> the Good and Beautiful alluringly offer & that habitual turning to the Divine as a butterfly to the sunlight which lead men mysteriously but surely on." And so I intend to yield myself to all nobility where-ever I can find it, in hopes at length I may be lead to the Perfect or Ideal man, a very simple creed and the being satisfied with it may but show how shallow my religion is. (SC, Starr; *JAPM*, 1:505–6)

From Henry W. Haldeman

The following letter is a rare example of extant correspondence between Jane Addams and her sister Alice's husband Harry Haldeman. Despite the paucity of surviving communications between Jane and the man who was both her stepbrother and her brother-in-law, Haldeman was a fairly copious letter-writer, particularly loyal in his correspondence to his mother. The body of his surviving correspondence, taken as a whole, is erratic. The handwriting is inconsistent in style, and the tone of the letters seems to shift from ebullience to despair. Harry suffered from chronic illness, some of which may have been induced by alcoholism. Anna Haldeman Addams, who referred to her son's nervousness and worried about the impact that holding a job as a country physician was having on his health, proved a mainstay through his financial and professional troubles, enabling his eventual transition from medicine to business and banking. Harry Haldeman had entered into an agreement on 23 August 1878 with Dr. A. C. Simonton of Mitchellville, Iowa, to purchase (with financial backing from his mother) from Simonton three parcels of land and Simonton's medical practice. Simonton also agreed not to practice medicine in the Mitchellville area. Apparently not all went well in carrying out the agreement. In this letter, Haldeman refers to testifying against Simonton in court and the resulting restraining order that was issued against Simonton in concurrence with the 1878 agreement between the two men.[1]

It is not surprising that Jane Addams turned to Harry Haldeman for help with her class song.[2] Music, more than medicine, was his first passion. He had studied music in Europe for two years. After his return to the United States he supported himself as a musician, music teacher, and would-be composer while preparing to be a physician.

Mitchellville Polk co [Iowa]   Mar 4th 80

Dear Jane,

Your Sisterly Epistle—came—duly forwarded by the U.S. Mail Co. I sprang at once to my Lyre. I am not lying, and just as the mus-ic—was about to enrapture me with dis-cancord & sweet sounds—a preempting call from Des Moines bode myself & wife prepare for Our Trial and an Early Appearance at Court.

In short—my Dear we have been put at Our wits Ends to get through this horrid low business—and—Congratulate us—to night—at 8<u>30</u> the following reached us: Des Moines—Mar 4th 1880. Telegram: Simonton is restrained from practicing in Mitchellville and within a radius of Six to Nine miles. Brown & Dudley. Yesterday I was on the witness stand. Alice remained at the Fort until this Evening returning at 7 oclock[.]

I at once set about composing something for your class-song being guided by what I remembered of it—while Alice set about finding the song & letter—but did not succeed—in short it is <u>lost</u>. of Course I am at a dead stop. However if it is not too late send me another copy—with instructions, vis: will the song be the opening piece on your programme? Do you want it in march time? Do you want it for <u>Solo</u> <u>and</u> Chorus—or for all the class like a common 3 or 4 part song. Will you sing at the last thing? Do you want it lively or the reverse or neither? I desire you give me an idea of what your class wishes.

When I hear from you I shall be pleased to finish at once and send by next mail. All of these points are very necessary—to be serious.

If you will send me another copy I will do my best. I cannot express my disappointment at finding the song lost. And beg a thousand pardons for not writing you sooner. However you know that nothing short of a summons from court and a bailiff could have thus prevented me from doing your biding at once.

Hoping to hear from you at once—and assuring you that the music is all but completed lacking only the finishing touches and adaptation of the <u>words</u> to make it complete. I am with many regrets & apologies Your most remiss & humblest brother

                                                    Henry Haldeman

ALS (UIC, JAMC, HJ; *JAPM*, 1:496–98).

1. The articles of agreement, drawn up in the office of A. C. Simonton, M.D., physician and surgeon, Mitchellville, Iowa, stated that Simonton agreed to sell to HWH lots 14, 15, 16 of block I at the corner of Center and 3d streets in Mitchellville, "with his Medical practice, for the sum of twenty five hundred dollars." The transaction was to take place in Sept. 1878, when Haldeman would hand over the payment in total and in return receive the deeds to the properties and "full possession of his Medical practice." Simonton also promised "<u>not</u> to <u>resettle</u> in Mitchellville as long as the said Dr. Haldeman is located there" (articles of agreement, 23 Aug. 1878, UIC, JAMC, HJ). Simonton apparently violated the last clause of the agreement, either continuing or returning to practice medicine in the Mitchellville area.

2. JA sought HWH's help with music to go with lyrics for her class song, to be used in the upcoming Junior Exhibition. The lyrics, written by Nora Frothingham and Mattie Thomas,

were printed in the *RSM* ([Apr. 1880]: 109–10; *JAPM*, 46:189–91) and in the Junior Exhibition program (*JAPM*, 27:380). The song had five stanzas, the last two of which dealt with the class motto: "Their hearts were touched with true desire / To grow in strength, and thus inspire / The world to hope and to noble deeds, / And labor to lighten its honest needs / Bread-givers of '81. O, may we all, in years to come, / Ennoble duty, but never shun / The work for us long set apart, / To give bread wrought mind and heart. / Bread-givers of '81." Possibly JA was scrambling to replace unwieldy music for the song that had been submitted along with the lyrics, for the *RSM* of Jan. 1880 stated that class songs had been handed in and the "literary editor has severely injured her vocal chords trying to hit the tune" (21). Lizzie Smith reported to her mother that class songs were all the rage at RFS. Girls sang them in their parlors and at Pierian Union meetings. The Beloit boys, when visiting the RFS campus, also serenaded girls with class songs.

To Anna Hostetter Haldeman Addams

Rockford Sem'y [Ill.]								March 7" 1880

My dear Ma—

Your letter and its astonishing contents received last evening, I was simply amazed at the silk, no other word can describe the state of my feelings. I think it is lovely of course, too nice I am afraid for just now, but if you think I need it I receive it with the utmost gratitude. I like the bunting and think that it will be very pretty made over the brown silk. I am not particular how that is made will leave it entirely to you own taste which you know is superior to mine.

I will be fitted with a lining for the silk to-morrow morning and send it instanter. I would like it buttoned behind and have the basque pretty long, if there is velvet enough. I think silk velvet-sleeves are wonderfully pretty, and I would like a square place in front of the velvet the way my blue basque something like that. I don't know whether you have planned for a velvet skirt or not but I think they are prettiest just the plain velvet and made short, of course the overskirt come down pretty far and they are a sham, and then have the overskirt slashed up in front & have the velvet show.

I don't remember ever before to have written such a long description on the subject of clothes[1] and I fear I hav n't made it very plain. Anything in my ideas that you don't like I will be perfectly contented with whatever way you may change it.

I am ever so much obliged for the silk I did n't have any idea you were going to get me any-thing so extensive.

I received an express package yesterday afternoon from some kind philanthropist—"A live hawk for Miss Addams" the expressman said at the door and I think every girl in the Seminary took up the cry and prolongly repeated it within five minutes. Down at the express office they had taken <it> out of the box because they thought it was dying and had sent it up in a basket. I wished fervently afterward that they had let it die in peace if it was so accomadating, for the killing was the very worst part of it or the best rather—for it had all the pleasure of deep excitement. After many vain endeavors I concluded to go down to Miss Holmes with him; she was very much interested considered it a treat and a privilege to work with such a noble bird, and we just did have a splendid time; we killed it with chloroform and have it all nicely cleaned and tanned ready to stuff to-morrow morning. It is one of the most beautiful things I ever saw, the feathers are beautifully shaded and the wings and tail are models of perfection; who ever sent it couldn't possibly have found any-thing to have pleased me more; I intend to put forth my best skill to-morrow morning and mount it with spread wings, they must measure three feet from tip to tip.

If Pa sent it please give him my heartfelt thanks, I am divided in my opinion between him as the donor and Web. Who ever it was I shall never cease to be eternally grateful.[2]

I don't know when I have enjoyed myself as much as I did those two hours yesterday afternoon for we discected & studied as we went along.

There is one of the alumnae visiting here with two of the sweetest little boys,[3] She knew both Martha & Alice, and was for a long time Pres of the Castalian so all things taken together we have become quite friends, she sits next me at Miss Blaisdell table.

Miss Anderson is afraid she will not be feeling well enough to go to Beloit, unless she feels better I will go with the rest of the girls by carriage, but of course will exercise jugement if the evening is unpleasant.[4] I wish you would come any-way, & know we would have a real good time. I think a plum colored silk would be the prettiest for you unless you wanted a black one be sure to get one or the other

With much love to Pa and my heartiest and deepest thanks to whom-ever sent the hawk[.] Ever Your loving daughter

Jane Addams.

ALS (private collection, photocopy, JAPP; *JAPM*, 1:499–503).

1. Conservatism and plainness in dress were encouraged by Anna P. Sill at RFS, in part to maintain a spirit of egalitarianism among the girls, who came from different walks of life. One of Sill's goals was to provide education to young women like EGS, who came from modest circumstances or from small towns and rural areas. Sill recommended that dressmaking be done at home and that parents have their daughters bring only basic and sensible clothing to Rockford. The 1877–78 RFS *Catalogue*, for example, stipulated, "No one should leave home without a supply of plain, inexpensive clothing, especially flannel; also woolen hose, and a pair of India-rubber overshoes, a water proof cloak, and an umbrella are required. Frequent shopping is not allowed. Every article of clothing or bedding should be marked with the full name. Young ladies are requested not to bring jewelry or expensive apparel. Parents or guardians are requested not to furnish their daughters or wards with unnecessary spending money." In order to try to ensure that these rules were followed, "Each pupil will be required to present a weekly account of all her expenditures" (27; *JAPM*, 27:131).

Some students had but one regular dress, which they laundered by night in their rooms. JA wrote an essay, "Dress," on 15 Mar. 1878, noting, "Although an individual may conform to the prevailing mode, yet he cannot prevent his individuality from entering his garments" (*JAPM*, 45:1729–35, quote 1733; see also *JAPM*, 45:1736–44). Despite her emphasis on relative uniformity, Sill was not immune to the idea that dress was an expression of individuality. She was known to say that "Dress is the flowering out of character," and she herself was always impeccably attired in simple but beautifully tailored clothes made from fine materials (Cedarborg, "Early History," 72). Self-expression through dress, and questions of fashion and propriety, were topics for instruction at RFS. In 1880 JA wrote, "The subject under discussion in the natural Philosophy class was Taste. The standard of taste in Dress 'dress the blossoming out of character' and so forth" ("Pocket Diary, 1875[–81]," printed date 11 Nov. 1875 [written 1880?]; *JAPM*, 28:1647).

Clearly, not all the girls subscribed to Sill's egalitarian vision of a limited and simple wardrobe. Lizzie Smith wrote frequently to her mother about ordering or having dresses made for special occasions at the school, of shopping, and of acquiring new dresses and hats for the different seasons. She carefully detailed fads and changes in fashion, from wearing caps instead of hats, to embroidering stockings, to the newest style of sleeves or fabrics. She also reported at the beginning of her senior year that her new roommate, the daughter of a shoemaker, "doesnt have but few clothes which is fortunate for me, because I can have three of the drawers and most of the closet to myself." Despite the quantity of her clothing, Lizzie disparaged other RFS girls who were too fancy in their taste—clearly implying that others dressed up even more than she. The connection between dress and self-esteem was also clear to Lizzie, who wrote of a new dress at the end of her junior year, "I looked very 'chick' for me Friday eve and had the consolation of knowing that my dress was real pretty, even if I wasn't" (Sara Elizabeth Smith to Annie M. Jordan Smith, 21 Sept. and 13 June 1880, SHSW, Smith).

A conflict between the principles attached to plainness and simplicity in dress and a desire for fancier attire existed for JA's stepmother AHHA, whose habits of dressing seem to have been curtailed by her husband JHA's spartan tastes and careful monitoring of the pocketbook. She wrote to JHA a few months after their wedding, evidently reporting in a way that was expected to please him, "I am dressed in the same waterproof dress you first met me in. . . . Yesterday I wore this same dress without the least idea or wish to change. But enjoy the liberty of wearing the gravest and most somber cloths without the slightest relief of bows or ribbons comparing well (with the miller whose wife I am proud to be) when he wears his grey coat and hat" (25 Feb. 1869, SCPC, JAC). Despite these claims and her obvious effort, at least early in her marriage, to appear in every way as a good match with her husband, AHHA loved fine clothes and the other trappings of an upper-middle-class lifestyle, and she encouraged both JA and SAAH in that regard.

JA's brown silk was likely being prepared for an upcoming special occasion—her appearance in the Junior Exhibition the next month (Introductory Speech by JA at the Junior Exhibition, 20 Apr. 1880, below). A 10 Mar. 1880 entry in JA's "Report [Account] Book" for 1879–80 indicates an expense of one dollar for a dress fitting (*JAPM*, 27:329).

2. The gift of the hawk has been attributed to JHA. The chloroform used to kill the hawk appeared as an entry in JA's Mar. 1880 list of expenses in her "Report [Account] Book" for 1879–80 (*JAPM*, 27:329). The Mar. 1880 *RSM* reported, "One day not long ago the expressman brought a queer package. A basket containing a live hawk for Miss A. The rest of the day everyone Miss A. encountered informed her that a live hawk had arrived by express for her. Those who prefer to keep a distance from live animals can now view the bird with safety at Miss A's room" (85).

3. The visitor was Ellen Shepard Dorsett, a member of the RFS class of 1868, who knew JA's sisters Martha and SAAH when they, too, were students at the school. Dorsett was a former member of the Castalian Society, and she reminisced about her experiences with the group to the current members at a reception at RFS. She "had her two little boys with her" (*RSM* [Mar. 1880]: 84–85, 91). Student Lizzie Smith wrote home to her mother Annie M. Jordan Smith

about the Castalian meeting and said that the "third hour that evening the Castalians had a reception for an old scholar, who used to be a very active Castalian and was here on a visit with her too <u>terrible</u> male <u>infants</u>" (10 Mar. 1880, SHSW, Smith). Ellen Shepard Dorsett was married to Daniel Dorsett and was a principal of a school in North Carolina.

4. Lizzie Smith also wrote about the Beloit excursion in her 10 Mar. 1880 letter to her mother:

> I wanted to go to Beloit to hear Prof. Proctor last night, only I was afraid of taking more cold if I did so staid at home. Mary [Ellwood] and Sade [Sarah Sperry], Kinke [Hattie Wells], Add [Addie M. Smith], Hattie Smith and Jane Addams are the only girls who went. A great many more were going only it snowed in the morning and they had to give up the idea of going by carriage. The girls . . . staid all night. They saw a lot of the college boys and they are coming to our Junior Exhibition and we are going to theirs which is to come off the 8th of this [next] month. (SHSW, Smith)

Introductory Speech at the Junior Exhibition

The creation of a Junior Exhibition at Rockford Female Seminary was one more step in the seminary's effort toward claiming equality with men's schools.[1] As in other landmarks in the process of the transition of the school from seminary to college, Jane Addams played a decisive leadership role.[2] As she articulated in this introductory speech at the exhibition, the issue at hand was not only woman's opportunities in education but also her greater liberty and empowerment in general. She used the bread-giver theme in her introductory statements. The stage was decorated by classmates with ferns, evergreens, and flowers, and a large banner designed by Lizzie Smith that was emblazoned with the bread-giver motif hung overhead.[3]

[Rockford, Ill.]   [20 April 1880]

FRIENDS AND CITIZENS OF ROCKFORD:—

The class of 1881 has invited you this evening to the first Junior exhibition ever given within the halls of Rockford Seminary. The fact that it is the first, seems to us a significant one, for it undoubtedly points more or less directly to a general movement which is gradually claiming the universal attention. We mean the change which has taken place during the last fifty years in the ambition and aspirations of woman. We see this change most markedly in her education, it has passed from accomplishments and the arts of pleasing, to the developement of her intellectual force, and her capabilities for direct labor. She wishes not to be a man, nor like a man, but she claims the same right to independent thought and action.[4] Whether this movement is tending toward the ballot box, or will gain simply equal intellectual advantages, no one can predict, but certain it is, that woman has received a new confidence in her possibilities and a fresher hope in her steady progress.

We, then, the class of 1881, in giving this our Junior Exhibition, are not trying to imitate our brothers in college, we are not restless and anxious for things beyond us, we simply claim the highest privileges of our time, and avail ourselves of its best opportunities.

But while on the one hand, as young women of the nineteenth century, we gladly avail ourselves of these opportunities, and proudly assert our independence, on the other hand we still retain the old ideal of womanhood—the Saxon "lady" whose mission it was to give bread unto her household. So we have planned to be "bread-givers" throughout our lives, believing that in labor alone is happiness, and that the only true and honorable life is one filled with good works and honest toil, we will strive to idealize our labor, and thus happily fulfil woman's noblest mission.

But if at any time we should falter in our trust, if under the burden of years we should for the moment doubt the high culture which comes from giving—then may be the memory of this evening, when we were young and strong, when we presented to our friends a portion of the work already accomplished, and told them of the further labor we had planned for the future, then, I say, the memory of our Junior Exhibition may come to us as an incentive to renewed effort, it may prove to us a vow by which we pledged ourselves unto our calling. And if through some turn of fortune we should be confined to the literal meaning of our words, if our destiny throughout our lives, should be but to give good, sweet, wholesome bread to our loved ones, then perchance we will do that the better, with more of conscious energy and innate power for the memory of our Junior Exhibition.

Thus, my friends, you see that this our Junior Exhibition bears to the class of 1881 a deeper significance than would at first appear, and I hope that by thus simply and openly laying our plans and purposes before you to have gained the interest and good will of the audience, secure in that, we will not apologize for the many mistakes which we may make, only expressing the further hope, that in this, our first attempt at bread-giving, our offering may not prove wholly unacceptable.[5]

PD (*RSM* [April 1880]: 110–11; *JAPM*, 46:195–97).[6]

1. Similar exhibitions were the practice at Beloit College; indeed, a history of that college went so far as to announce that the "'Junior Exhibition,' derived from Yale, was an institution of the Beloit life" (Eaton, *Historical Sketches*, 236). While women at RFS were demonstrating their ability to match the standards at the men's schools, young men at Beloit were busy showing that their small midwestern institution offered the same practices as those of the Ivy League. They were also taking advantage of the exhibitions at their respective schools as opportunities for social interaction.

Beloit College student and class of 1882 orator Roger Leavitt recalled in memoirs of his student days that RFS juniors came up to Beloit in the spring of 1881 to attend that year's Beloit Junior Exhibition. He was part of the reception committee of Beloit boys that met the girls at the train. They paired off (Leavitt with Kittie Waugh), conducted the visitors on a tour of the campus, and then escorted them to the chapel, where the exhibition took place. After the speeches, the pairs adjourned to a private supper party for juniors at a student's home. It began at about 11 P.M. and stretched into the wee hours. Apparently, the young people outdid themselves in offering witty toasts, some, Leavitt remembered, "sharp as a razor." The girls stayed at a hotel in town and were ferried back to the train station by the boys in the morning.

Later in Apr. 1881, the Beloit students went to Rockford for a return visit, and their carriage caused quite a stir. As it pulled onto the seminary grounds, Leavitt recalls looking up to see every window "filled with fairy forms looking at us." The boys were assimilated—despite many stares—into the regular dinner hour in the RFS dining room, followed by prayers and devotions. A reception was arranged for them afterward in the senior parlor while the juniors dressed for their big event. "Jane Addams was one of the Seniors we met," Leavitt recalled. "We had little thought then that she was going to become so prominent." Leavitt found the Junior Exhibition at RFS in 1881 to be impressive. After the presentations, there was a formal reception, during which the Beloit boys entertained with "college songs; then sang 'Good Night Ladies,' and departed at 11:30 P.M." Their hostesses sent them off to the train with a basket of cake. At the station, the visitors "tried to decide which of the girls was the nicest—but could not agree" (Leavitt, "Memoirs").

The Junior Exhibition—with its emphasis on oratory as a method of displaying intellectual proficiency—did not catch on easily at RFS. The class of 1882 failed to hold one, and at Beloit College the practice disappeared during the 1890s, giving way instead to an emphasis on all of the members of the graduating class speaking at commencement before receiving their degrees. Class Day exercises at both Beloit and RFS were to some extent mock versions of the Junior Exhibition, and programs were devised to poke fun at the pretensions of the more formal proceedings.

2. JA, as head of her class, gave not only the introductory speech at the first RFS Junior Exhibition but also one of the major orations. She chose as her subject Bellerophon (a Herculian hero of ancient Greek myth, whose story appears in book 6 of the *Iliad*), and she delivered the speech in Greek. Bellerophon is challenged by a series of difficult tasks, all of which are potentially lethal and include a violent battle in which he kills the Chimaera, a fire-breathing monster. Bellerophon is aided throughout his series of conquests by his winged horse, Pegasus, who helps him literally to transcend his difficulties. Once victorious, he marries the king's daughter. Bellerophon's downfall comes when, not content with earthly rewards, he attempts to ride Pegasus to heaven, and the horse throws him off, condemning him to a life of loneliness. As she recalled, "The Greek oration I gave at our Junior Exhibition was written with infinite pains and taken to the Greek professor in Beloit College [Sarah Blaisdell's brother, James J. Blaisdell] that there might be no mistakes, even after the Rockford College teacher and the most scholarly clergyman in town had both passed upon it. The oration upon Bellerophon and his successful fight with the Minotaur, contended that social evils could only be overcome by him who soared above them into idealism, as Bellerophon mounted upon the winged horse Pegasus, had slain the earthy dragon" (Addams, *Twenty Years*, 46–47). Two versions of the speech survive: see "Βελλεροφόντης" (Bellerophon), *JAPM*, 46:90–94; and "[Bellerophon]," Addams, "Pocket Diary, 1875[–81]," printed dates 3–5 and 8–14 July 1875 [written 1880?]; *JAPM*, 28:1591–92, 28:1594–97.

3. The *Rockford Register* of 21 Apr. 1880 reported that "Promptly at eight o'clock the class, numbering seventeen, ranged themselves in a semi-circle on the platform, and sang the class song which was printed on the dainty little programme, after which the class marshal, Miss Elwood [Mary Ellwood], introduced the president, Jane Addams, who delivered the following address, every word of which is pitched to the keynote of the true intellectual progress of the time." They then gave their account of the speech printed here. After detailing the rest of the events of the evening, the reporter concluded, "Rockford society cannot but be interested in these talented, self-possessed and self-respecting young women, who, in dress, carriage and deportment, speak volumes for the value of higher education." The full program for the Junior Exhibition was reprinted in the *RSM* ([Apr. 1880]: 118; see also *JAPM*, 27:378–81, 27:382).

Lizzie Smith described preparations for the "Junior X" in her letters home. "Saturday, Monday and Tuesday were spent in preparations," she wrote. The silk of the banner "was poppy red like our class colors," and "the motto Bread Givers" was done in "the same style as our class paper only of course much larger. The letters were covered with wheat and put on a background of evergreens up between the first two pillars in Chapel /drawing of sign in Chapel/ that way and an urn of ferns from the green house was by each pillar. Back against the wall was a pyramid of flowers in pots on a stand and ivies in the posts. In the evergreens over the doors in front & back & on the gas jets were little turkey red flags about four inches long with '81 stamped on them" /drawing of sample flag/. "They looked real cute if we did make them and I never saw the chapel look so pretty. Tuesday the Juniors were excused for all classes" so they could do their hair and get dressed in their special dresses (Lizzie's was light blue). "All the girls did beautifully and the first Junior X was a very great success. After it was over we had a reception in the parlors, none of the girls except the Seniors and Juniors being present. The Beloit boys about twenty five in number and a good many town boys staid. We had a splendid time. The Beloits sung us a lot of college songs and were afterward up to serenade us" (Sara Elizabeth Smith to Annie M. Jordan Smith, 22 Apr. 1880, SHSW, Smith).

4. JA had earlier used a version of this phrase in the text of one of her Pierian Union debates in which she argued the affirmative of (as she put it, with her distinctive spelling of "politics") "Resolved. That French women have had more influence through literature than polotics. Rep. women George Sand and M'de dè Staël." In one version of that debate, she stated that woman "wishes not to be a man or like a man but she claims the same right to independent thought & action. Whether this movement is tending towards the ballot box or will stop short at equal intellectual privileges, no one can predict" (JAPM, 45:1808–18).

5. Following group-singing of the class song and JA's introductory remarks, the program commenced with Mattie Thomas giving a Latin oration, "Magnus Imperator." She was followed by Emma Briggs, who gave a historical dissertation on "France and England Contrasted in the Reformation." Phila Pope gave the scientific oration, "Mountains as a Means toward Development." Alice Atkinson read a French essay on Marie Antoinette, "L'aurose de rose: et de choucs sombre." Helen Harrington gave the ethical oration, "Old Dreams Realized." Ella Browning provided German literary criticism with "Das Nibelunganlied." Annie Sidwell offered a humorous talk on junior class life, "Reminiscences of a Junior," which was followed by a solo, "Waiting Heart," sung by Kate Tanner. JA gave the Greek oration, "Bellerophon." The last oration of the evening was presented by Nora Frothingham on philosophy, "The Last Great Empire." Additional instrumental and vocal music was interspersed in the program and provided by Ella and Kate Huey, Addie M. Smith, and Martha Thomas. The closing benediction was delivered by Joseph Emerson, RFS Board of Trustees member and professor at Beloit College. For a copy of what the local newspaper had called the "dainty little program," see UIC, JAMC; JAPM, 27:378–80.

Lest all these scholarly presentations should make the evening too serious, the class of 1881 also prepared a spoof of the Junior Exhibition as a libretto. The libretto program was graced by a mock quotation from "Revised Shakespeare"—"Music hath charms to make a savage / Eat a peck of pickled cabbage"—and announced that general admission cost "nothing; reserved seats, free; reserved seats in gallery, pay as you go. PROCEEDS TO BUY NEW CLASS RIBBON." In the extant copy in the Rockford College Archives, the members of the "cast" were listed in print, with the girls' names written in by hand next to their mock title. JA headed the list as Miss Blunt, followed by Miss Black Jacket (Alice Atkinson); Miss Impenetrability (Emma Briggs); Miss Mal A. Proppe (Ella Browning); Miss Letter (Laura Ely); Miss Happy G. Lucky (Mary Ellwood); Miss Lively Small (Nora Frothingham); Miss Little Hand (Helen Harrington); Miss South Pole (Kate Huey); Miss Rattle Trap (Ella Huey); Miss Slam T. Door (Phila Pope); Miss Very Slender (Addie M. Smith); Miss Agility (Lizzie Smith); Miss Dead Silence (Annie Sidwell); Miss Friz (Katie Tanner); Miss No Bangs (Mattie Thomas); and Miss

Black (Lizzie White) (*Brief Libretto of Junior Exhibition*, 20 Apr. 1880 [printed program], *JAPM*, 27:384–87).

6. See also AMsS version, *JAPM*, 46:198–200.

Draft of Essay

This essay, perhaps prepared for a Walpurgis Night[1] program, illustrates a fantastical side to Jane Addams not hinted at in more sober and objective venues. It also reflects the Romantic fascination with Gothic subjects and Addams's interest in mythology and folklore as well as some of her struggles with Christian beliefs. Addams had often been entertained at home by Anna Haldeman Addams's gifted telling of ghost stories. Later, she would encounter some of the issues she related here in a personal way when neighbor women living near Hull-House came to believe that settlement workers were harboring a "devil baby," complete with cloven hoofs and a tail, who had been born to a neighbor girl who reportedly had been cursed by a male member of her family. Word of the devil baby's existence spread with a "contagion of emotion," and a steady stream of callers came to Hull-House to demand that the baby be put on view.[2]

[Rockford, Ill.]   [ca. 30 April 1880?]

To night is Walpurgis Night; we all realize it, the air is densly peopled with witches, goblins, spirits & demons. Impreceptibly their weird influence controls us, tonight of all nights in the year the supernatural holds supreme command. Air, earth, fire & water, the four elements, for this one night yield <to> the fifth & mightier element, the soul of the world; & this astral light within the power of the Devil, through his agents the witches exerts a fearful influence. Hence we shiver; shudder and imagine unholy sounds.

Every nation that exists or has existed, believes or has believed in the reality of fascination & all these beliefs strangely coincide or they have one common foundation. Lilith[3] was the first & lawful wife of Adam, her descendents increased & filled all the earth, but they were the race of demons. She produced the dread Titans at war with all mankind, the horrible dragons, the huge giants of superhuman strength, the monsters & goblins, griffins & pygmies.

These demons stalking ~~about~~ through<out> the earth have a mighty influence & witches are found in the tradi[ti]ons of every nation. The Persian queen who fascinated & subdued[4] all who approached, man & beast, and compelled them ~~the~~ to yield to her will, was in reality a witch. We find Wiswamitra[5] in India with remarkable deeds in scorcery & magic, Tithrambo of the Egyptians, Vivian[6] of the Anglo-Saxons, the wrinkled hags of the Norse traditions[7] & the Kratu of the Scandanavians.

The Greek Hecate[8] surroun[d]ed by her howling dogs & the Roman furries[9] with their snaky hair are types of mythological witches, but mythology threw ~~her~~ <its> poetical halo even about a witch & made her almost beautiful.

In course of time, however, these attributes instead of being regarded <as> abstract & entirely supernatural, began to be found in human beings, men & women embodied them & were possessed of demons. People discovered the strange power of calling up the dead & from them ascertaining future events,[10] this was carried to such an extent that certain women, as the witch of Endor,[11] made it a practice & it was forbidden both in the political & Mosaic law. Strange & unknown arts were tried by the wicked & wise. But modern witchcraft originated in the 10th cent, when an unknown Greek by the name of Eretychianus sold his soul to the devil & startled the world with his obscure & horrible deeds. From this time on throughout the earth we can trace the footsteps of the witches. First in the evil eye[12] which certain people posessed, fascinating & injuring all upon whom their glance fell. Then in the horrible werewolf,[13] which originated in a disease, necromachy, an abnormal craving for human flesh, men with terrible hunger haunted pest houses, & graveyards, they had a double skin & at certain times of the year became wolves in order to satisfy more easily, their insatiable appetites. From this grew the vampire,[14] bodies which were buried but still retained life, came forth from their graves at night & influenced men in their sleep. ~~Whilst these~~ The magicians during the middle centuries were an honorable class of men, they claimed Soloman[15] as the direct founder of their ~~race~~ profession & to have received from him the key explaining all mysteries. But there were two kinds of magic, the black & white, the first attained by years of study, in which the devil served the magician, the latter in which the magician sold his soul & served the devil. To the second class belonged many old women, for of course the devil would not serve a woman, hence the poor women served the devil, & with their incantations bewitched cattle, raised storms & blasted crops, in order to please their hard master.

This was the state of Europe when Christianity was introduced, its missionaries held one sole avenging God, & they condemned all other dieties; not only vampires & demons but the good as well, all the heathen gods & thier beautiful mythological characters were degraded into devils, they declared there could be no white magic but that it was all black[16] & when explosions shook the solid earth that caused the ironclad horseman to reel in his saddle, the defenceless head of woman found no protection, <they were connected with heresy & it finally rose to a [fire?],> what need to tell of the four cent. that filled Europe with bloodshed & the 9000000 of human beings who were butchered as witches.[17]

But what have these maglignant demons & horrible facts, to do with Walpurga,[18] the renow[n]ed & courageous St, who spread Christianity throughout Germany, founded a convent & protects men from ferocious beasts.

The connection is obvious. The first of May & the last night in April have ever been renow[n]ed in the annals of superstition. Among the Celts the feast to Baal, the god of fire, was held on that day, for his honor in conquering winter.[19] Ostera, the principal diety among the Saxons was celebrated on the 1st of May.[20] Great sacrifical offerings & religious processions were also held in Rome.

Christianity accepting this date, shifted the celebration of St Walpurga to agree
with the assembling of witches;[21] <to her they dedicated May day night> this
sacred night for the universal walking abroad of spirits visible & invisible. None
of us, at any minute, would be surprised to see a witch, her feet & ~~shoulders~~
<neck> anointed with the fat of unbaptized infants, her goatskin mantle thrown
over her shoulders flying through the air on a broomstick. Where she comes
from is a conjecture, whither she goes is a certainty. She flies to the summit of
the Brocken,[22] the highest point on the Hartz Mountains, to the assemblage of
evil spirits.

In the vast solitude of the Blocksberg, she meets, on this Walpurga's night,
the congregated demons & appriations of every age. The sides of the Mt are
covered with huge blocks of granite, the naked roots, white & snakelike, twine
over the slimy rocks, stagnant waters ~~flow~~ <ooze> from every crevice, between
mountain plants with thick forked leaves, salamanders gleam through the brake
with their long legs and ~~slimy~~ warty skin, the owl hoots in the distance <with
her boding scream of death>, a melancholy light of morning red glimmers
through the mountain gorges, here rises a mine damp, there float exhalations,
will o' the wisps sparkle on every side & glow worms in crowded swarms, the
storm wind sweep around the peak, you hear the mighty groaning of the trunks
& the yawning of the roots & yet an unearthly silence is over all. But now the
winds hiss & howl over the wreck covered cliffs; there are voices aloft, a raving
witch song streams along the whole Mt. The arch demon, himself, in the shape
of a <huge> goat[23] with black human countenance is seated upon the very pin-
nacle, around him on every side are the unearthly revellers, engaged in debauch-
ery & dancing, keeping time to the music of a bagpipe, made of a horse head &
a black cat's tail, they drink cold clotted blood from human skulls & gnaw the
bones of the white loathsome leper, there is whizzing, sparkling & burning. Silent corp[s]es stand in the midst <unmoved> holding lighted torches in thier
cold clammy hands. There are gibbets with their blood red axes, open coffins,
murdered infant & <~~some forms~~ blue & livid <forms>, some cadaverous &
~~others deluged in blood & impurity~~ the smell of death arises.> The dance <of
time & futurity> goes on until the first ghostly gleam of morning, then the huge
goat sets fire to his horns and slowly burns himself, the witches divide his ashes
& go forth on thier various <campaigns>.

AMs [fragment?] (UIC, JAMC, Detzer; *JAPM*, 45:1614–21).

1. Walpurgisnacht, or Walpurgis Night, is celebrated the night of 30 Apr. in tribute to the
burgeoning spring and the beginning of the summer growing season. It has its origins in
pagan tradition and in the cults surrounding St. Walburga, a healer and abbess of the double
monastery of Heidenheim, Germany (n. 18). In Bavarian, Bohemian, and Scandinavian
witch lore, the May Eve Walpurgis Night was considered the greatest of the quarterly witch's
sabbats (sabbaths), stemming from the most important pagan festival celebrating fertility. During the Middle Ages it was believed in Germany, Norway, Sweden, Finland, and other
Western Europe countries that, on Walpurgis Night, witches fly to mountaintops on their
brooms, engage in wild feasting and dancing, and, at midnight, copulate with demons

(n. 22). The festival figured in many romantic works of art. It provided the inspiration for Goethe's poetic "The First Walpurgis Night" (1799), which was, in turn, adapted for Felix Mendelssohn's (1808–47) *Die erste Walpurgisnacht*. Walpurgis Night also featured in one of the weird dreams in Thomas De Quincey's *Confessions of an Opium Eater*, read by JA and her friends at RFS (see Draft of Student Essay, [ca. 1878], above).

The origins of Walpurgis Night were discussed in the context of changing customs, holidays, and superstitions in a Jan. 1878 *RSM* article signed by "L." (possibly Laura L. Keeney) and entitled "Halloween":

> The celebration of All Saints' Day, called All Hallons by the Scotch, was formerly upon the first of May, which is also the day of the feast of Walpurgis, a German festival in memory of Walpurga, the first abbess of one of their convents. The evening before this festival, or Walpurgis' night, was supposed to be the time of the councils of the witches, when they met on the Brocken mountains for consultations, and reports of their deeds. Many traditions existed concerning this "Witches' Sabbath," as it was called, and the enchantresses were supposed on this night to have special powers and liberties. Thus the legends and traditions of these two days became so associated and interwoven that when the celebation of All Hallons was changed to the first of November, the stories and superstitions of Walpurgis' night clung to Halloween. (21)

Halloween was regularly celebrated at RFS. That girls also participated in May Day revelry is indicated by an item in the "Home Items" section of the June 1879 *RSM:* "The Junior class intended to celebrate May-day, in the true old English style. Just think of one of the Juniors being a May queen!" (161).

2. JA wrote about the devil baby story as an urban legend in "The Devil Baby of Hull-House," published in the *Atlantic Monthly* in Oct. 1916 (reprinted in *One Hundred Years at Hull-House*, ed. Bryan and Davis, 150–55; the "contagion of emotion" quotation is from 152). In the article, JA surmised that for many old women of the neighborhood who had led hard lives, the devil baby story served a subconscious purpose as

> powerful testimony that tragic experiences gradually become dressed in such trappings in order that their spent agony may prove of some use to a world which learns at the hardest; and that the strivings and sufferings of men and women long since dead, their emotions no longer connected with flesh and blood, are thus transmuted into legendary wisdom. . . . Because the Devil Baby embodied an undeserved wrong to a poor mother, whose tender child had been claimed by the forces of evil, his merely reputed presence had power to attract to Hull-House hundreds of women who had been humbled and disgraced by their children; mothers of the feebleminded, of the vicious, of the criminal, of the prostitute. In their talk it was as if their long role of maternal apology . . . had at last broken down. (153, 154)

She further noticed that the story of the devil baby had an impact on the balance of power between men and women in immigrant households and gave women an upper hand, which left men uncomfortable. Noting that a group of working men had come to Hull-House and demanded to see the baby, claiming that their womenfolk had already seen it, JA observed, "All the members in this group of hard-working men, in spite of a certain swagger toward one another and a tendency to bully the derelict showman, wore that hang-dog look betraying the sense of unfair treatment which a man is so apt to feel when his womankind makes an appeal to the supernatural . . . their talk confirmed my impression that such a story may still act as a restraining influence in that sphere of marital conduct which, next to primitive religion itself, we are told, has always afforded the most fertile field for irrational tabus and savage punishments" (154). On the Devil Baby legend, see also Addams, *Long Road*, 1–52, and Addams, *Second Twenty Years*, 49–79.

3. A Lilith figure exists by several different names in the myths and folklore of many cultures. She has been associated with the Babylonian goddess Belili and the Canaanite goddess Baalat ("mistress"), the female complement to the male god Baal (n. 19). It is from rabbinical Hebraic tradition that the Lilith legend is primarily derived. In Jewish folklore, Lilith was the first wife and sister of Adam. She was born as a siamese twin to Adam, joined with him at the back. Separated from Adam, she demanded sexual equality with him by challenging the male-superior sexual position, later championed by church authorities and more popularly called the "missionary" position. When he refused to relinquish his dominance, she left Eden in anger. She subsequently gave birth to hundreds of demon or fairy children ("djinn"). She was replaced in Eden by the more accommodating Eve, born symbolically out of Adam's rib. Lilith is considered the mother of the settled agricultural tribes, and Adam and Eve the parents of nomadic herdsmen. Lilith remains associated with fertility and female sexuality and with blood (in the form of the menstrual cycle and birth) and in the form of death and the cyclical replenishment of the earth. Hebrews described her as a Great Mother who drank the blood of Abel after he was slain by Cain.

In the Middle Ages, Lilith was seen primarily as a seductress and goddess of night. She was in part a personification of the feminine powers associated with the moon. A patron of witches, she was believed in European folk tradition to fly by night and threaten new mothers, kidnap or strangle newborns, seduce men as they slept, and rule demons and evil spirits. She was sometimes depicted as a beautiful winged vampire with clawed feet and feminine form. In Jewish and Christian tradition, it was believed that Lilith and her daughters, the *lilim* (who in Greek myth were called the "daughters of Hecate"), were gorgeous and lustful she-demons who took revenge on women in childbirth and newborn infants and induced celibate men and boys to wet dreams with their expert lovemaking. Succubi were said to gather with Lilith in nocturnal mountain fests in which she met either with her demon lover or the goat-figured satan himself. The Kabbalah warned that she was at the height of her powers when the lunar cycle was in its darkest stages. Well into the eighteenth century, new mothers and their babies were protected from Lilith by amulets and charms and by magic circles drawn around their beds.

4. Possibly a reference to the Persian queen Zemroude, who in Persian legend fascinated Fadlallah, king of Mousel. According to the Persian tales, Fadlallah learned incantations in order to be able to take on the bodies of pet animals or birds so he could be near her.

5. A reference to the Vedic priest and singer Visvamitra, who was a *purohita* (wise man or spiritual advisor), first to King Sudas and then to ten kings who opposed Sudas's rule. Visvamitra, a master of mantras and incantations, used his magical powers to protect the king from enemies and rivals. He could also cause the harmful spells of witches to revert to their creators. He was considered the earthly counterpart to Brhaspati, the lord of prayer and spells.

6. According to various Arthurian legends, Vivian (Viviane or Nimue), a Celtic water goddess, was the seducer and nemesis of the great Druidic wizard Merlin. By some accounts, she stole his magic and used the powers of enchantment to imprison him under a tree or a rock. By others, she is said to have given Merlin his magic early in his life and to have protected him with an enchanted sleep in his secret cave at the end of it. She is closely associated with Morgan Le Fay, the Fairy Queen, or the Lady of the Lake, who, it was said, raised Lancelot in France, gave Excalibur to Arthur, and was murdered by Balin because of her powers. Pagan Britons believed that Merlin slept, much like the Beltane Winter God, who spent time in the underworld (n. 19), and would return to the earth in a new age of well-being and fertility.

7. The term *hag* (holy or wise woman) may come from the Egyptian *Heq*, a matriarchal ruler with powers of incantation. In Greek myth, the hag or crone is associated with Hecate (n. 8), and in many cultures the hag is a kind of angel of death. In Jewish tradition, the daughters of Lilith were also known as "night hags." In old Norse legend, the *hagi* was a sacred grove of trees, used as a place of sacrifice, where hags were said to chop sacrificial victims into pieces for a

feast. "Hag's dish" (in Scotland, "haggis"), a reference to eating internal organs, comes from this tradition. In folklore, hags were often depicted accompanied by spinning wheels, which were considered wheels of fate. Shakespeare used the term *hagged* to mean to be bewitched.

8. The powerful Greek goddess Hecate has many characteristics in common with Lilith, including a close association with life-cycles, childbirth, sexuality, and the moon. Her name may be derived from the same Egyptian root, *heq,* as the hags of myth and legend, and she is associated with the midwife goddess Hequit (Heket or Hekat), who in Egyptian legend delivered the sun god each morning. In Greek legend, she was depicted as an intensely beautiful Fury-like queen of darkness, a creature of perverse sexuality and fertility with petrified snakes for hair and a necklace made of testicles. Alternate images gave her three heads—one of a dog, another of a snake, and the last of a horse—each facing in a different direction and associated with a unified trinity of powers. As such, she was worshiped as a goddess of crossroads. She was appeased on the last day of the month with offerings of eggs and food or, according to legend, by the blood sacrifice of newborn animals or infants. She was associated with fate, wealth, wisdom, justice, and, increasingly, with the spirit world and the dead, necromancy, and the underworld.

By the Middle Ages, Hecate was called the queen of witches and considered the patron of sorcery, black magic, and witchcraft. She was believed to posses fatal powers that she could use either to kill humans or bring them back to life. Like Lilith, her powers were considered greatest during the waning phases of the moon. She was believed to rule the night and to have authority over its spirits, including hobgoblins, poltergeists, apparitions, ghouls, demons, and evil forces. Her incantations were said to bring about nightmares and insanity. She was portrayed in just such a guise in Shakespeare's *Macbeth,* a play of special interest to JA (see Essay in the *RSM,* Jan. 1880, above). According to legend, and as JA makes reference here, Hecate was said to roam the earth at night accompanied by hounds from hell, which had glowing eyes and were visible only to dogs. When dogs howled in the night, it was a sign Hecate was near.

Hecate is sometimes described as a daughter of the Titans. By some Greek legends she is the mother of Dionysus. She was also associated with the story of Demeter and Persephone, the simultaneous rule of the sky and the underworld, and the cyclical coming of spring. She is alternately identified as the mother of Cassandra, the seer who rebuffed the advances of Apollo and was doomed to be ignored when she prophesied the fall of Troy and the death of Agamemnon. JA made Cassandra the subject of her graduating essay at the end of her senior year (see Graduation Essay, 22 June 1881, below).

9. The Furies (the Erinyes, the Eumenides), sometimes called the "holy ones" or the "kindly ones," were goddesses of vengeance in Roman and Greek myth. They were usually characterized as three cruel, avenging sisters who distributed terrifying, sadistic, but fair justice to evildoers. According to Hesiod, they were the daughters of Gaia (Earth) and Uranus (Heaven). Virgil described them as residents of the underworld who punished men for committing murder, perjury, and other crimes, especially against kindred or family members. They were usually depicted carrying torches and whips, their heads wreathed in writhing snakes.

10. Necromancy is the ancient art of conjuring the dead for the purpose of divination or foretelling future events. The dead were considered free of normal constraints and thus able to communicate supernormal information not available to them in their time on earth. Necromancers were said to be able either to raise a corpse to life or summon spirits of the dead. Closely related to Haitian vodoun, this form of magic was common in the legends of Greece, Persia, Rome, and other cultures. During the Middle Ages, necromancy was practiced by witches, magicians, and sorcerers. It was believed that necromancers, in their efforts to communicate with the dead and cross the boundaries of life and death, would eat the flesh of corpses during their rituals or wear the clothing of the deceased. Strongly condemned by the Catholic and Protestant churches, necromancy was outlawed in Elizabethan England by the Witchcraft Act of 1604.

11. The biblical story of the Witch of Endor, one of the most famous of necromancers, is related in I Samuel, 28. King Saul of Israel, in fear of impending battle, sought out the Witch of Endor, a known medium, and requested that she conjure up the dead prophet Samuel to speak to him of his fate. She then summoned Samuel's ghost, who predicted Saul's downfall and death. The next day, as feared, the Israelites were attacked by the Philistines; many died, including three of Saul's sons. Saul, in despair, fell on his own sword. David succeeded him as king of Israel.

12. The evil eye is related to the all-seeing eye of the goddess Maat of ancient Egypt, whose name meant "to see" and who was represented by a hieroglyphic of an eye. Belief in the evil eye existed in a variety of ancient Middle Eastern cultures. In Muslim and Christian tradition, the all-seeing eye was diabolized. People—especially strangers, old women, or individuals with eyes of an unusual color for the culture—were said to be able to "overlook" (or, in Ireland, to "blink") and malevolently curse animals or humans with a glance and thereby bring misfortune upon them. In some European witch trials, the association of the evil eye and witchcraft was so strong that witches were faced backward when brought before their inquisitors so as not to be able to bewitch the proceedings with their eyes. The evil eye is related, in some cultures, with taboos against women making direct eye contact with men, but its use was not believed limited to women. Pope Pius IX (1792–1878) and his successor Pope Leo XIII (1810–1903) were both popularly believed to be cursed with possession of the evil eye, or the *mal occhio*. Belief in the evil eye was particularly strong in nineteenth-century Italy and among Italian immigrants to the United States.

13. Superstitions about werewolves and lycanthropy (the assumption of the form of a wolf through magic or witchcraft) were linked to beliefs about necromancy and to accusations of cannibalism. The origins of the belief may be in various Roman wolf gods and in the wolf totems, shamans, and cults of pagan cultures. In European folk traditions, including those in Russia, Germany, Romania, the Scandinavian countries, and Slovakia, werewolves were believed to be humans who transformed or shape-shifted into a part-human, part-wolf form on moonlit nights. They would viciously attack and feast upon cattle and humans, returning to normal human form by day. During the Inquisition, individuals accused of being werewolves were sometimes forced to confess that they had devoured missing children.

14. Vampires were believed to be dead people who reanimated to life at night and perpetuated themselves by attacking and sucking the blood from the necks of the living, turning their victims into fellow vampires in the process. Vampires retreated to their graves or coffins by the light of day. Like werewolf legends, tales about vampires were closely related to ancient ideas about the power of the moon and to taboos regarding menstrual cycles, sexuality, blood, and blood sacrifice. Blood, in turn, was an essential ingredient in necromancy.

15. A reference to King Solomon of Israel (d. 932 B.C.?), son of David and Bathsheba, who reigned in the middle of the tenth century and who, according to biblical legend, God made to be a man of great wisdom: "Behold, I give you a wise and discerning mind, so that none like you has been before you and none like you shall arise after you" (I Kings 3:12). "And God gave Solomon wisdom and understanding beyond measure, and largeness of mind like the sand on the seashore, so that Solomon's wisdom surpassed the wisdom of all the people of the east, and all the wisdom of Egypt. For he was wiser than all other men. . . . And men came from all peoples to hear the wisdom of Solomon, and from all the kings of the earth, who had heard of his wisdom" (I Kings 4:29–31, 34).

Solomon also was associated with goddess worship and female influence. He was said to have "loved many foreign women. . . . He had seven hundred wives, princesses, and three hundred concubines; and his wives . . . turned away his heart after other gods" (I Kings 11:1, 3–4). According to Arab legend, Solomon held his gift of wisdom by magic and was killed by the djinni when he lost his magic powers. Solomon's legendary wisdom made him a patron of sorcerers and magicians in the Middle Ages, giving rise to such occult works as *The Key of Solomon,* a guide to the use of magic and magic signs and symbols.

16. From the eighth century on, spell-casting or sorcery was increasingly associated with harmful or "black" magic, religious heresy, and devil worship. It was condemned by the church and criminalized by law—in departure from earlier pagan views of white and black magic as morally neutral, often used for benevolent purposes, and practiced with the help of beautiful and powerful goddesses and gods. Heightened by the Inquisition, the church's campaign against religious sects and witchcraft resulted in the persecution and torture of individuals, in many cases women, who were either believed to be witches or accused of practicing witchcraft. The standard image of witches also gradually changed from one of seductive power, terror, and potent beauty associated with goddesses who meted out justice to that of a wrinkled, post-reproductive hag or crone serving the devil and bent upon doing harm. Thomas Aquinas (1225–74) helped reinforce the kinds of popular beliefs about witches that JA relates in this essay, including the ideas that witches copulated with the devil or demons, flew by night, cast spells upon others, and caused thunderstorms and other natural phenomenon. The repression of witchcraft had much to do with misogyny and fears of unbridled female power and sexuality as well as with shifts in Christian belief. Martin Luther reflected the views common in the time of the Reformation when he rather famously characterized witches as "whores of the devil."

17. The publication of the *Malleus Mallificarum* (1486) codified the prosecution and punishment of witches. Witch hunts, trials, and crazes swept various parts of the European continent, including Germany, France, the Scandinavian countries, and Switzerland, particularly from the fifteenth into the seventeenth centuries. In England and Scotland, where witchcraft was a violation of civil law, the emphasis in prosecuting witches was often upon the harm they were believed to do to others rather than on questions of religious heresy. Witch hunts peaked in Britain in the 1640s and reached into the America colonies in the same era. Modern scholars estimate that thousands of people accused as witches were tortured, imprisoned, or executed, often by being burned at the stake. Their property was frequently confiscated, and charges of witchcraft were sometimes raised in property disputes and political rivalries. Many of the accused were marginalized women, including widows or spinsters, and among them were healers, herbalists, and midwives whose power to cure, or association with various maladies or problems in childbirth, marked them for suspicion. Such women were seen as exercising free will outside strict social boundaries or possessing abilities not readily understood. Others were stigmatized as witches because of some physical mark or deformity or odd or disliked behavior. By the nineteenth century, popular conceptions of witchcraft had returned to a more or less benign fascination in folk magic, gothic tales, the supernatural, spiritualism, and sorcery, including such forms of conjuring as powwowing, popularized in the United States by German immigrants and familiar to AHHA and JA's Pennsylvania Dutch relatives.

18. St. Walburga (Walpurga, Walpurgia, Vaubourg, Falbourg) (710?–777?) was an Anglo-Saxon woman trained in medicine; she became a nun under St. Tatta at Wimbourne in Dorset, England. St. Boniface was her uncle, and her father was an under-king of the West Saxons. In 748 she followed St. Lioba to Germany at the invitation of Boniface, and there she founded, with her brother, St. Winnibald (d. 761), a double monastery (one for both men and women) at Heidenheim. Walburga was much beloved. She was believed to be able to protect crops and communicate with animals, and her powers were sought as a healer. Images sometimes present her as an earth mother with three ears of corn. When she died on 25 Feb. 777 (some sources say 778 or 779), cults quickly developed in dedication to her name, and she became one of the most popular saints in England, Germany, and France. Miracle cures were reported from ailing people who anointed themselves with a fluid known as Walburga's oil

that drained from the rock at her shrine at Eichstatt. Some scholars of the pagan tradition believe that Walburga is the original May queen of Walpurisnacht festivals, a pagan goddess of spring who was Christianized by canonical legend.

19. In Celtic and English tradition the 30 Apr. holiday lauding the beginning of summer is called "May Eve" or "Beltane" (Beltain), meaning "bright, great, or splendid fire." The Celts observed the Beltane festival by building huge bonfires and dancing around them in circles to celebrate fertility, the replenishment of the earth and the growth of crops, and the purification of cattle from disease. The fires, associated with good health, were also seen as symbols of the sun. In Britain, dance processions, ring dancing around maypoles, and ritualistic jumping over broomsticks (both the maypole and the broomstick were symbols of fertility) were related ways of celebrating the rebirth of spring and the miracle of life on May Eve and May Day. In time, the pagan celebrations of Beltane were Christianized, with churchyard ceremonies and fires lit by priests in the fields. In many Christian traditions, the blessing of a fire is part of the Easter Vigil (n. 20).

Several different gods are associated with Beltane, and the source of the name of the festival is a matter of scholarly debate. Some nineteenth-century scholars drew connections, as JA does in this essay, between the worship of the Baal of Semitic traditions and the Celtic practice of Beltane. Baal, whom the Greek historian Philo of Byblos (63?–141?) called "Zeus," was a god of the sky and of thunderstorms. His cult was widespread from Syria into Egypt. The Canaanite god of agriculture and fertility, he was said to anoint the season of rains and bring sexual and natural abundance. He was usually depicted as a bearded man wearing a horned helmet and wielding a thunderbolt or branch. The legend of Baal has much in common with the classical story of Persephone and Demeter. In Middle Eastern lore, Baal was killed and descended into the underworld, whereupon he was returned to life by the powers of his sister-lover, Anat. Baal is thus associated with the seasonal cycles and the coming of spring and crops. This was reflected in Beltane festivals, which culminated with the symbolic marriage of the Winter God and Spring Goddess (or King Winter and Queen May). Queen May, in the festivals, was a mother earth figure. The word *Baal* means lord or husband. In the mating of King Winter and Queen May, earth and sky were joined, and fertility and life were symbolically rekindled in animals, people, and nature. Baal, as a god of nature, was often condemned in Israelite literature as a rival to the supremacy of Yahweh. As one historian has put it, "Baal was a god of sexual congress whose cult sported erotic acts that offended Israelite sensitivities" (Achtemeir, ed., *Harper-Collins Bible Dictionary,* 95).

Other gods were associated with the festival and for similar reasons as Baal. One, called Cernunnos (the Horned One) by the Romans, was one of the greatest gods of Gaul. He was worshipped in Celtic tradition as a god of fertility, life, animals, wealth, and the underworld. Bearded, he had the antlers of a stag and usually carried a coin purse. He was said to be born at the winter solstice, have married the moon goddess at Beltane, and have died at summer solstice, ruling along with the goddess over cycles of day and night, death and rebirth. Another god associated with Beltane was Bel (the Druid Bile, the Gaelic Bal or Bel, or the Welsh Beli), the Celtic god of sun, fire, light, and healing, who was also the patron of cattle and sheep and associated, as was the fire festival, with the return of life and fertility to the barren, wintery world.

20. Ostera (Eostra, Eostre, Easter, Ostara) was the Anglo-Saxon goddess worshipped at Eostre, the festival of spring. The pagan holiday was adapted under the Roman calendar for the Christian observance of Easter, which commemorates the Resurrection. Many pagan aspects of the Easter celebration were maintained in the Holy Week customs of the church. The timing of the pagan festival was originally set at the first Sunday after the first full moon after the spring equinox. The Christian holiday falls on the first Sunday after the full moon that occurs on the day of the vernal equinox of 21 Mar. (between 22 Mar. and 25 Apr.). Until

the Middle Ages, the Celtic church celebrated Eostre on a different day from the Roman observance of Easter. A time of forgiving and new beginnings, Easter was observed in Rome with clemency toward those who were imprisoned. In medieval times, Easter was often greeted at the beginning of a new year, especially in France. Ostera is associated with pregnancy, and her festival involved the sharing of decorated eggs as symbols of rebirth and fertility. Painted Easter eggs are important aspects of Easter or springtime New Year festivals in several folk traditions, including in England, Germany, Persia, and Russia. Ostara ("radiant dawn") was the Germanic equivalent of the Anglo-Saxon goddess Eostra. A goddess of agriculture and healing, she was considered the personification of the rising sun and thus symbolized the beginning of the new season of spring. In traditions very similar to Beltane, she was celebrated in pagan custom with singing, rejoicing, flowers, and the lighting at dawn of fires for crop protection. The rabbit, still a symbol of Easter and of fertility, was her escort. Many Christians observe Easter with a sunrise service as an extension of this folk tradition.

21. The first of May was long the date for the fertility festival of the Druids, or Celtic priests. Although she was celebrated with feasts four times a year, the Monastic Kalendar set St. Walburga's feast day on the day of her death, 25 Feb. When the Roman office was adopted, her saint's day was moved, in the Roman martyrology, to 1 May. Some scholars of the pagan tradition claim that the dates were shifted as part of the church's effort to circumvent the power of Walpurgisnacht revels and Christianize the May Eve festival.

22. The Blocksberg(the Brocken), the highest mountaintop in the Hartz Mountains of Germany and the setting of Walpurgisnacht, was long believed to be the rendezvous point for witches and phantoms. It is strongly associated with Goethe's *Faust* and with the idea of giving one's soul over to the devil. Local Blocksbergs also existed, as nearby peaks were given the name in various locales in association with the practice of Walpurgis Night. Nordic witches' sabbats were similarly associated with Blakulla (the Blue Hill), the Scandinavian equivalent of the German Brocken.

23. The figure of a horned goat or horned god, part human and part animal, existed across time in many cultures and was known by many names, including Baphomet, Cernunnos, Mete, Pan, Robin Good-Fellow, the Black Goat, and the Judas Goat. The image of the horned god is very old, and some horned deities were considered to be more sinister than others. Man-animal figures with stag or goat horns, some presiding over dance ceremonies, were depicted in Paleolithic cave paintings and carvings and also appeared in ancient art throughout the Near and Middle East, including Egypt and India, and on into Mesopotamia, Babylon, and Assyria. In these cultures, horns on a human head were associated with divinity, royalty, sexual desire, and fertility. In Greek and Roman mythology, horned figures often represented wisdom and ecstasy, Dionysian celebration, or Bacchanalia. In the Christian era, the horned man became more narrowly identified as a devil, and the horned goat was associated with Satanism, fornication, and infidelity. The goat often appeared as the image on the devil card in Tarot decks. In ancient Egypt and in other traditions, the horned goat god was believed to have sexual relations with his women followers. That belief was paralleled in Western European ideas that the devil appeared to women as part man and part goat and that witches served the devil and fornicated with him during their sabbats. The horned god (the Black Man), who could convert himself into a goat and was believed to serve as the grand master of covens and at witches' sabbaths, figured in many depositions during witch trials. In popular observance of Beltane, follow-the-leader chain dances were often led by a black-goat figure. Ring dances were sometimes performed by female dancers who would link hands and circle a single male who wore horns and stood in the center of the circle.

From Mary B. Downs

Chicago, [Ill.]   May 23, '80

Dear Jane:—

Pardon my delay in answering your letter. I have been unusually busy during the last two weeks house cleaning etc. for you know I am a "breadgiver"— in the practical sense of the term. Your letter was a very pleasant surprise. Anniversaries, I think are pleasant—even of "awful disturbances" when they are celebrated by an assurance that some good resulted from the disturbances.[1] I am glad that you wrote to me about ours; but I hardly know how to tell you how I have thought or felt in regard to the matter.

Of course, that horrible fuss can never be a pleasant remembrance but I think, that I will never regret the stand we took, and certainly I will never think that we acted wrongly. Now without contradicting what I have said, I do not believe that I should presume to interfere in another similar case. I would or ought—it is easy enough to say so in these times of calm retrospection—to begin "at home."

Perhaps you know and perhaps you do not that I wrote to Add Merrill, last summer explaining as well, as I could, apologized for the rudeness with which I had sometimes treated her and "agreed to disagree": she answered very pleasantly and there the subject was dropped as far as the harmony of the class in concerned. I knew that I would feel better satisfied with myself—a little more "self righteous" if I wrote, whatever the result might be—and so I did. (Did feel more righteous, I mean.)

I fear that you will not have a very clear understanding of my views of this interesting subject—I can't tell them any plainer. It would be much easier and pleasanter to talk it over with Miss Anderson, Katie[2] and yourself—no offense. I am only paying due respect to the absent—. I am much obliged to Miss Anderson & Jane for their invitation and would like very much to accept, but, at present do not entertain any hopes of being able to do so. Probably the majority of our class will be there. I was surprised and much disappointed that Katie did not return this year to take charge of the Magazine—and wondered who would take her place. I soon learned that "the world could get along without us, if we would but think so." I have read the mag: with the natural interest of an ex-editor critically too, wishing that Katie and I could read them together. We would have crowed together when they were late and defended ourselves stoutly when obliged to acknowledge improvements. You are progressive, Jane—or you would not have joined the revolutionists, last year.—and your good work well merits the commendations you have received. I am not trying to flatter you. Your Exchange Department made me blush in-memoriam of mine, and the introduction of the "Society" papers is an innovation worthy of your enterprising spirit. In short, you have not disappointed my anticipations. There!

I attended a Literary of the University last week, and the president gave a summary of those papers on "Societies", in his address.[3] Did you and Miss Anderson laugh over my College Songs?[4] when I saw it in print I imagined that you would, and I longed to hear Katie's opinion concerning it.

It was gratifying to learn that the lit. editor had been moved to musical, or rather vocal, efforts and that those rediculous maidens, who wandered from Arcadia, across Achaia, crossed the Corinthian Gulf and went on the Parnassus, had at some song books. I am sorry to hear that you came out behind, thirty dollars, last year. We reckoned that there would be no arrears when the subscriptions should be payed.

You hear from Ellen Starr, I know: so do I. We carry on quite an extensive correspondence on postals all in regard to a visit which I anticipate making her: I write to assure her of my constant endeavor to see her, she writes to encourage me in "well doing" or "well trying." In the mean time we both hope on.

I have wandered from the subject of my epistle.

I have never been conscious of enduring the suffering that people seem to think I must have endured last spring. It was very exciting, very unpleasant but still I think the experience had made no very lasting effect on my disposition. Some in speaking of the matter, seem to think that I am to be pitied. I do not understand why. I wish that I could talk to you instead <of> write. I am sure that I will not make myself understood—therefore I will wait. If I am not in Rockford in June—if I am there too—I hope that you will have a pleasant reunion, that if you plan to go to Beloit you may succeed, at least, as well as Katie & I did. Do you still expect to study medicine, after a course of study at Smiths College & that "tramp" through Europe? I had almost ceased thinking of that trip to Europe when an "Itinerary" of travels through Europe, including the "Passion Play" at Ober-ammergau arrived.[5] I thought of writing to you Miss Anderson & Katie in regard to making immediate arrangements to start: fortunately I was hindered and my reason had opportunity assert its authority.

I am certainly descended from Macawber[6] and I will live in Air Castles now even if I do end my days in the wilds of Australia. Now, my friend, I don't ask you to excuse the mispelled words, for I never hope to be able to spell correctly and I can't afford to make excuses <for myself> all my life. I shall always be very glad indeed to hear from you.

Mary B. Downs

I would like very much to hear from Katie; Will you please tell her so when you write? I am uncertain about her directions.

ALS (SCPC, JAC; *JAPM*, 1:507–14).

1. It was the anniversary of Downs's graduation and of the little furor at RFS over Sill's rules about chaperoning and interaction with the Rockford community. It is not certain that that matter is the "horrible fuss" referred to here, but clearly she and JA had been in accordance on the issue in dispute at the time. It is quite likely that the end-of-the-year editorial

printed in the *RSM* ([July 1879]: 204–5), which criticized the barriers put upon social interactions at the school, was written by Mary Downs and that she was sanctioned because of it.
The issue, combined with the expulsions that happened that semester, could well have caused
factionalization and hard feelings among the students at RFS—and among the members of
editorial staff of the *RSM* over printing the editorial and winning Sill's wrath—in the spring
of 1879.

2. Sarah Anderson and Katie Hitchcock.

3. Downs probably is referring to an event at Chicago University. Often considered the first
University of Chicago, it was begun in the late 1850s and survived only until 1886. The reference is to the short series on "College Societies" that JA, as editor of the "Clippings and Exchanges" section of the *RSM*, ran in Jan.–Feb. and May 1880, using contributions from editors of student magazines at other schools (see JA to Myra Reynolds, [Oct. 1879], n. 3, above).

4. An essay on "College Songs," steeped with classical references, was printed in the *RSM*
([Jan. 1880]: 2–4). Signed simply by "'79," it was almost certainly written by Mary Downs
and is the piece to which she refers in this letter. Versions of class songs were submitted to
the *RSM* staff, and a few verses were printed in various issues of the magazine during the
spring of 1880. The class song for the class of 1881, devoted to the bread-givers theme, appeared unsigned in the Apr. issue (*RSM* [Apr. 1880]: 109–10; for a partial text see HWH to
JA, 4 Mar. 1880, n. 2, above) and in the program for the Junior Exhibition (see *JAPM*, 27:380).
"College Song No. 1 [Founded on Fact.]," also anonymous, appeared in the Mar. issue of the
RSM. It was to be sung to the tune of "Twas Off the Blue Canaries." Ghostly in theme and
set in a dormitory, its lyrics began, "Twas silent in the Seminary, / For the 'blowout' bell had
rung, / And a flood of moonlight entered / As the shutters backward swung" (*RSM* [Mar.
1880]: 78–79; *JAPM*, 46:190).

5. Every ten years, the village of Oberammergau in Upper Bavaria sponsors an elaborate
passion play as a measure of thanks for being spared by the plague during the fifteenth century. Travelers often time tours to Europe to include Oberammergau during the performance
of the play. JA visited the region around Oberammergau at the beginning of 1884 during her
first trip abroad (JA to JWA, 27 Jan. 1884, UIC, JAMC; *JAPM*, 1:1356–60).

6. A reference to the character Wilkins Micawber in Charles Dickens's *David Copperfield*.

From Eva Campbell Goodrich

Pecatonica, Ill.,   June 1, 1880.

Dearly Beloved;

Your postal was received this evening; it is post marked May 31st., so you see
I could not have seen you Saturday, not knowing that you intended going home.
I expected to visit the home friends Saturday and remain over Sunday, but the
rain prevented. I should have enjoyed a visit from the "trio",[1] but they and I seem
doomed to not meet this year. Jane, you and I must not forget that we are still
friends. You know ere this the reason that I have not visited you this spring. I
go out very little now, but I expect to go into society again after the first or middle
of July.[2] My time is fully occupied now. I do my domestic work and have sixteen music scholars. I hire my laundry work out of the house. I expect to have
a girl next week, and if she suits me I hope to keep her the coming year. If I can

carry out my plan, I expect to take lessons of Prof. Hood next year—provided he remains at the Sem.[3]

During vacation you <u>must</u> visit me.[4] If you don't come to see me I shall make you a "visitation" at your home.

Why is it that we know so little of each other this year? I have thought of you very often, and wondered if it were possible for Jane and Eva to so soon forget. You have never written me anything in regard to your school work this year, nor your intentions or rather plan for the coming year. Do you talk as strongly of going east as you did last year, or do you think to graduate at Rockford Seminary first? It was very careless in me to keep your Eng. Literature as long as I did, but I trust Carrie Hewett returned it uninjured. Can you tell me why there is nothing in Shaw's Lit.[5] about Dickens, when he was one of the greatest English novelists? Did you have any notes last year, on the "Last Days of Pompeii". If you have them please send them to me—if not too busy. I have many times wondered how Carrie Hewett is liked at the Sem. I am not intimately acquainted with her, yet I know that she is not at all popular with her classmates or lady friends here although she is quite scholarly. I like her very well, but I have not seen enough of her to know her failings. When I came to Pecatonica she had a class of nine pupils in music. I never once thought of making any effort to form a class, nor did I expect to get any scholars so long as we remained in this place. Some time in December the lady across the street called and asked me if I would give her lessons. I was very much surprised, for she and I used to be classmates in the public school here, and <u>then</u> she pretended to be quite a player, while I knew little or nothing about music. I have never made any effort to get scholars, but they have come to my home, and asked if I would give them lessons. I ask ten dollars a term while the other teachers ask but eight and nine, yet I have the largest class that any <u>one</u> teacher has ever had here, so I am told. I think Carrie Hewett has but two or three scholars now, yet I cannot feel to blame myself for their having left her. I think Carrie felt a little hard toward me at first, but after being told by a friend of hers and mine that I had done nothing toward getting her scholars, she came to see me. Jane, what I write you is for you, and <u>you</u> only. Please say nothing in regard to my class, nor that I think of taking lessons the coming year. I would like to know who are the graduates this year—and if the school is as full as it was last year. I should have been glad to have spent a few days at the Sem. about the time of your Junior Ex. but I could not. I had a little of the President's opening remarks but nothing of the Greek oration. Jane, you did nobly. "Thems my sentiments." "Where are the friends of my youth?" Where is Ada Smith? Does she still room with you?[6] Give her a little love for me. I would write a longer letter, and one more interesting, but I am almost sick.

Hoping to hear from you soon and to see you this summer, I remain, Your ever lasting friend,

Eva C.G.

P.S. Do you ever hear from Ellen Gates Starr? I have not received a line from her since last fall. Yours &c.,

Eva.

ALS (SCPC, JAC; *JAPM*, 1:524–29).

1. Who constituted the "trio" is unclear; probably it was JA, EGS, and Katie Hitchcock.

2. Eva Campbell Goodrich is speaking discretely of the advanced stage of her pregnancy. She was expecting to give birth to her first child in July.

3. Daniel Hood remained teaching at RFS after the deaths of his wife and daughter.

4. JA did go to Pecatonica, Ill., later in the summer to see the newborn.

5. Thomas B. Shaw's *English Literature*, first published in London and in its tenth edition in 1876, was a commonly assigned text in English classes at women's colleges, including RFS, during the late nineteenth century (see "Textbooks Mentioned by Women's College Catalogs since 1850," appendix 1 in Woody, *History of Women's Education*, 2:475). Shaw's (1813–62) work was published in various editions before and after his death, including *Outlines of English Literature, with a Sketch of American Literature by H. T. Tuckerman* (published in a New American edition in Philadelphia in 1853); *The Student's Manual of English Literature: A History of English Literature* (rewritten and edited with notes and illustrations by William Smith and published in London in 1864); and *A Complete Manual of English Literature*, 2d ed. (New York: Sheldon and Co., 1865). In notes jotted in her old 1875 diary while at RFS, JA wrote, "Shaw's Eng Lit P. 72 character bewailing their destiny—'The Girl who took too much'" ("Pocket Diary, 1875[–81]," printed date 26 Oct. 1875 [written 1879?]; *JAPM*, 28:1639). The comment was reminiscent of Sarah Anderson and JA's spoof on the "girl who had too much to do" (Poem in the *RSM*, Nov. 1879, above). JA's "Report [Account] Book" for 1879–80 indicates that she bought *English Literature* on 22 Sept. 1879 (*JAPM*, 27:322).

6. Addie M. Smith was JA's roommate in 1879–80.

From T. H. Haseltine

Anna Haldeman Addams's friend and Ellen Gates Starr's acquaintance, the Rev. T. H. Haseltine, functioned here as a spiritual counselor to Jane Addams.[1] Haseltine had visited the Addams family at their home in Cedarville near the start of the school year, and Jane and he no doubt had some conversations about religion at that time. Haseltine also came to Rockford in June 1880 to attend the seniors' examinations and sit in on recitations in the Latin classes.[2] In her memoirs, she referred to this period "at boarding school when under great evangelical pressure."[3] The extent of spiritual questioning and crisis in Christian faith that Addams was experiencing during her junior year was hinted at in her May 1880 response to Starr's lengthy ruminations on the divinity of Christ. Addams had asked that the two friends stop discussing religion and, in particular, the Incarnation.[4]

Warren Ill.   June. 13. 1880.

My friend Jane Addams:

The contents of your letter were not in my mind. Nor did I have time to converse of it all when I saw you. I have just reread it. Am very glad you write

so fully of yourself. I hope to be able to help you. By better personal acquaintance I could <u>talk</u> with you to better advantage. [Now?] may be do as well by
<u>writing</u>[.] 1st Don't ever let the opinions or efforts of those about you in their
treating you as <u>atheist</u> or <u>unconverted</u>. For anyone to be helped they must first
be understood. You are not understood by either of those parties.

So far as <u>thought</u> is concerned I think you <u>theist</u> & <u>christian</u>. Sometime
Christ or God are misrepresented in a persons <u>thought</u> & by the <u>rejection</u> of that
misrepresentation we do accept the real God. You say you do not pray or feel
the need of prayer. I think you misconceive <u>prayer</u> & your rejection of that
misconception is prayer. Prayer is communion of us with our Father & source
of daily soul life. The intelligent conception of that communion is not essential, but is still desirable. What you call "indifferent" is—may be—restfulness
resultant on <u>true</u> <u>faith</u>. We pass from the <u>sensible</u>, to the <u>abstract</u> then to the
<u>personal</u>, the <u>real</u>, the <u>ideal</u>, this reached we <u>rest</u> & also <u>seek</u>. This coupled with
the <u>ultimate</u> <u>aim</u>—the <u>real</u>—with <u>self</u> out of <u>sight</u>, is highest <u>life</u>. I think you are
in the right road. Wait patiently & walk on. Quietly to yourself, <u>rest</u> on & try to
<u>realise</u> the <u>real</u> God. Little by little you will succeed. In the way of this success,
cease to blame & berate yourself. God is near to and <u>wholly</u> in sympathy with
<u>all</u> <u>good</u> <u>every</u> <u>where</u>.

I am glad you appreciate Carlyle. I like him very much. Being able to appreciate him, I know you can appreciate the <u>greater</u> Christ. Dont say to yourself you are growing indifferent or hardened. I think it was in "consideration
of mans weakness" that Christ was needed to reveal God.

God, <u>personally</u> & in <u>principle</u> & in <u>sympathy</u> is <u>much</u> <u>nearer</u> you than you
think.

A dying soldier was told by his narrow chaplain to "repent & pray[.]" He said
"after a life of sin I wont be mean enough to pray just as I die because I die[.]" A
true chaplain could see <u>true</u> <u>prayer</u> & <u>true</u> faith in that soldiers reply. Dont set
bounds by <u>thoughts</u> or impressions of others related experience but remembering this nearness—not <u>local</u> nearness—let Him <u>impress</u> you. Those impressions
from the opposite source—of "indifference" &c—shut out & gradually you shall
see where you so much desire to see. Never shun thoughts or sentiments of God,
cherish them rather. After this when I see you I can talk with you.

I shall be very glad to hear from you any time that the <u>I</u> predominate as it
will. Dont study to write[.] The I will take care of itself. I have pleasant recollections of my visit at the Seminary. I would be glad often to spend an hour or
two there.

I hope you will get my meaning from my written words. Your friend

T. H. Haseltine

ALS (SCHS; *JAPM*, 1:536–38).

1. From childhood through her school years, JA also turned to her father for guidance on
religious issues. Although Haseltine here urged her to let go and make the emotional transi-

tion from the real to the ideal, from a basis in rationality to one of faith, JHA had told her (in a discussion of foreordination) to favor "mental integrity above everything else" (Addams, *Twenty Years*, 15). "I suppose I held myself aloof from all these influences," JA explained, "partly owing to the fact that my father was not a communicant of any church, and I tremendously admired his scrupulous morality and sense of honor in all matters of personal and public conduct, and also because the little group to which I have referred [those girls, like JA, who resisted conversion] was much given to a sort of rationalism, doubtless founded upon an early reading of Emerson" (50).

Significantly, Haseltine would write again upon the death of JA's father, stepping in as a paternal influence to try to comfort her, remind her of her spiritual duty in life, and advise her to try to greet the hard fact of her father's passing with faith in God's plans rather than obsession with rational explanation: "When our time arises to lay [a]side the darkly glass we shall see face to face & understand all we can only question now. This is a life of learning <u>trust</u> lessons. <u>Sight</u> lessons are in the next room. Learn these Jane as well as you may[.] The next shall reveal the how & why of these" (29 Aug. 1881, SCPC, JAC; *JAPM*, 1:751–52).

Rationalism, authenticity, and privacy remained important parts of JA's spiritual life into her adulthood. She eventually chose to become an official member of the Presbyterian church, joining the small Cedarville congregation she had attended in her youth. Once Hull-House was established, she supported quiet, internal prayer meetings and in 1891 was a charter member of the Ewing Street Church, a Congregational Church serving a culturally diverse, largely immigrant population and located in the same neighborhood as the settlement house. JA was always circumspect about her formal church involvement while devotedly applying Christian ethics in her active, lifelong dedication to social reform, social welfare, conflict resolution, and peace. Theologian Georgia Harkness has observed, "Miss Addams was a theist and a liberal Christian whose motivation came primarily from the ethical teachings of Jesus; her depths of religious insight, while not ecclesiastical or fully evangelical, were nevertheless real and powerful" ("JA in Retrospect," 39; see also Stebner, *Women of Hull House*, 76–81).

For examples of JA's writing at RFS on religious topics and prepared for her classes in "Evidences of Christianity," the Bible, or mental or moral philosophy, see "<u>Analysis of Lecture II</u> [on Christianity]," [ca. 1881]; "[Essay on the Biblical Prophets]," [ca. 1880–81]; and "<u>The Notion of Conscience</u>," [ca. 1881], all *JAPM* (46:86–89, 46:96–98, 46:99–103).

2. Haseltine's visit to Rockford at the end of the school year was reported as an item in the June 1880 *RSM*, with his name spelled "T. S. Hazeltine" (187). He conducted exercises in the RFS chapel one morning while attending a religious conference in late 1880 and also sat in on Latin classes at that time (see also EGS to JA, 12 [and 19] Oct. 1879, n. 14, above).

3. Addams, *Twenty Years*, 15.

4. JA made this request in JA to EGS (15 May 1880, SC, Starr; *JAPM*, 1:506; see also EGS to JA, 29 Feb. 1880, n. 8, above).

From Maria G. Nutting

Sem. [Rockford, Ill.]   Friday eve. [July 2, 1880(?)]

Dear Jane:

Just one week from the time I carried the matter down for our July Magazine they were deposited in the Sanctum all damp from the bindery, pretty good for Register printers isn't it. I now have them nearly ready for mailing so that my time of service is nearly over. I shall try to pack tomorrow and go home Monday. I feel like shouting glory hallelujah at the thought of seeing my dear ones so soon. Yet I have not minded staying much because I have had pleasant company, only when a letter or postal came urging me to come as soon as I could.[1]

I presume you will think the Mag. <u>looks</u> as if it were gotten up in a hurry, as I did, but the printer's rushed to make up for the holiday tomorrow, and I do not feel much like upbraiding them for its appearance as it frees me sooner. Selfish creature, am I not?

I shall try to leave the office & records in a little better order than we found them, though I confess I have nearly lost all patience in trying to arrange the utter confusion of Corinne's work.[2] She had told James[3] that she was to see about the collecting of two or three advertising bills, but no record was made, these & other things were so inexplicable that I wrote her enclosing a careful statement of the records as I found them which did not at all agree with what she left. She of course was provoked & returned my letter with an irate note, but not a sign of explanation. I then wrote again requesting her to explain to James. I am so sorry she shows such carelessness. Miss Blaisdell was quite out of patience with the way she left things and—but never mind, I mustn't fill my letter with such unpleasantness.

Probably you judged from my postal that the matter you sent was too late for publication. The first proof came up that very morning I think. I was real sorry you had not had time to prepare it before you left, as it would have quite varied the monotony of one writing so much of one Magazine. I have put the matter with other of your belongings, a letter, penknife &c, in a box in Sanctum desk. I think some of it will do for the fall numbers.

I looked up your silver as you wished and Mrs. Rogers[4] put it with what other girls had forgotten in her glass closet where I think it will stay safely till fall.

Katie Smith,[5] Mrs. Rogers, Nettie Pitman[6] & I have been alone this week until Miss Sill came back from Beloit yesterday. She was quite delighted with the exercises, with the fine orations, graceful manners, and respectful demeanor of the students. Spoke of seeing you there, wished some of our class had been there to see what Seniors <u>could</u> do. I do hope, Jane, that your class will be more of a delight to her than ours has been, will justify the high expectations she has of <u>you</u>, personally.

Last Sabbath evening I went with Miss Smith to the children's service in Westminster church. It was very pretty, though simple, on a variety of missionary topics; our little pretty girls all took part. Mr Scott[7] was to make some remarks near the close, but was suddenly called home to his wife who had an attack of rheumatism of the heart, so Mr. Wi[lliam?]s, who presided asked Mr. <u>Curtis</u>[8] if <u>he</u> had something to say. And he opened his mouth & said, & behold more wisdom came out than a lesser man could have said in twice the time. A few strong thoughts on the present hopeful outlook of Missionary work. Do you know, I had the offer Commencement day, repeated by letter yesterday, of the position of assistant lady Principal in Lenox College, Rev. Dr Hodge,[9] Pres. This offer came quite providentially while I was so despondent over the denial of the

D. school[10] Tuesday night. Write when you feel like it, or wish a word from me always remembering that I am yours in good fellowship

Maria G. Nutting.

ALS (SCPC, JAC; *JAPM*, 1:542–44).

1. *RSM* editor-in-chief Maria Nutting graduated in June 1880 and stayed in Rockford to oversee the production, printing, and distribution of the July 1880 edition of the magazine, which covered commencement activities.

2. A reference to Corrine Williams, with whom JA had experienced her own frustrations in handling the sale of advertisements.

3. A reference to James Alcock.

4. A reference to Betsy Rogers.

5. Katie Smith was a teacher in the RFS Preparatory Dept. in 1879–80 and 1880–81.

6. In Nov. 1880, the *RSM* reported that "Miss Nettie Pittman, who has been a constant indweller of the Seminary for two years past, left last week for her far-away home in Oregon. We are glad for Nettie's sake that she has gone to her friends, but her face is missed by many of us" (249).

7. The Rev. Thomas Smith Scott (1849–1912) was the new pastor of Westminster Presbyterian Church in Rockford. He and his wife Hattie were both active in providing pastoral care and attention to Presbyterian girls at RFS. Scott gave a commencement sermon for RFS in June 1880, which Nutting reprinted in the *RSM* ([July 1880]: 214–16). Thomas S. Scott was born in Enon Valley, Pa. He studied at Auburn Theological Seminary before graduating from Union Theological Seminary, in New York, in 1877. He earned a D.D. degree in 1895. He married Hattie Elizabeth Osborn of Ohio in Nov. 1877 and was pastor at the Collamer, Ohio, Presbyterian church (1877–79). He headed the Westminster Presbyterian Church of Rockford—Mary E. Holmes's church and that of many RFS students—from 1879 to 1885. He led churches in Knoxville, Tenn., and in Indiana, Illinois, and Ohio in the late 1880s and 1890s.

8. The Rev. Dr. William S. Curtis, a member of the RFS Exec. Com. and Board of Trustees, who had no regular church in Rockford at the time.

9. The Rev. Samuel Hodge, Berty Hodge's father, was from Hopkinton, Iowa, and head of the Lenox Collegiate Institute (Lenox College). Like the Scotts, Hodge was active in RFS affairs, especially while his daughter was a student there. He lectured to the RFS girls on the subject of "A Noble Career; or, A Life of Duty" in Apr. 1880.

Maria Nutting accepted Hodge's invitation to teach in Hopkinton in 1880–81. She taught mathematics at the school. Berty Hodge wrote JA from Hopkinton in Aug. to say, "Our school opens September 1st. You know Nuttie is to teach here, dont you?" (14 Aug. 1880, SCPC, JAC; *JAPM*, 1:551). Berty Hodge taught German and vocal music at the institute. News of her and Nutting's appointment in Hopkinton made the "Personals" section of the *RSM* in Nov. 1880 (249). Nutting, who remained lifelong friends with JA, wrote to her from Hopkinton. She apparently had been painfully ill during that winter of 1881 but nevertheless experienced "more deep enjoyment more satisfaction than any like period for years. More indeed than in all probability could ever have come to me but for this trial which has drawn out the kindliest side of pupils & associates & has kept me from knowledge of the rougher more disheartening moods." Nutting wrote eagerly about what she had been reading and reported that "Some time ago a Reading Club was formed of six or eight intelligent people promising to meet at my parlor as I could not go out. . . . I hope to be able to go on with my school work next term (to begin Mar. 16), expect to teach complete Algebra, Arithmetic, Geography, U.S. History & Botany, possibly Chemistry. I can not begin to tell you how deeply I enjoy my class room work" (7 Mar. 1881, SCPC, JAC; *JAPM*, 1:610, 1:612).

10. Nutting is probably referring to divinity school.

From Eva Campbell Goodrich

Pecatonica, Ill.,   Aug. 31, 1880.

Dear Jane;
Yours of the 17th was recd two weeks ago. I have twice tried to answer it, but
failed in the attempt. Fortunately we were alone most of the day that you were
here, or rather that you came the day we were alone, for we have scarcely had a
quiet day since. I had fifty-two callers and visitors the week that you were here.
Mr. Goodrich's niece came that week, but she only stayed until last Friday.

My "Beloved"[1] came last Wednesday evening. Words fail to express the joy
at meeting. He had been absent from home one month; and a long one to[o]. I
expect he will now stay at home one year. He has gone west every summer for
four years. "Herbert Bryant"[2] is improving, although he has had quite a hard
time since you were here. I cannot call it a serious time, for he grows nicely, and
sleeps well nights. For the past four days he has not had a crying spell. Jane, I
think "my baby" is "<u>awful</u>" sweet. At present he requires much attention; but
today he has asked for less than <on> any previous day. My elder son[3] is enjoying good health. His papa finds it necessary to correct him, and pretty severely
since his return. This evening he asked his papa if he could go and play with the
little Brainard girl; his papa told him <u>no</u>, and in less than five minutes we saw
the boy in Mr. Brainard's yard. Mr. Goodrich is quite lenient with his boy, but
when he comes so far short of minding, he finds it necessary to reprove him.
Mr. Goodrich was considerably disappointed in not seeing you, for he has heard
me say so much about my friend Jane. I told him that <u>we</u>—you and I,—enjoyed
our visit full as well without him or Miss Ellen Gates &c. He understood in what
way I meant it.

Please let me know what day you return to the seminary. Do you room with
Ada the coming year?[4] I expect you have seen Miss Anderson since you visited
me, for she wrote me that you told her that <u>I</u> had a son. I received the letter this
evening. I should have enjoyed the letter full as well if it had been more of pleasure and less of business; but business letters are necessary sometimes. I agree
with [you] Jane,—and did some time ago,—that Miss Anderson is "<u>perfectly
lovely</u>." Mr. Goodrich and I are now reading "The Life of James Garfield",[5] and
"Vicar of Wakefield." He brought the books on his return from Nebraska, also
two Eng. Literatures. I take a book or paper every time that I take my baby, unless
he requires my undivided attention. I have not commenced to study the history of France, for I am not real strong, and we are not fairly settled down to work
again. Our <steady> work comes when school opens. This year school does not
commence until September 20th. O Jane, we are invited to attend a wedding
tomorrow evening. I hardly see how I can go, for I have not been out of the yard
yet, and I am <u>not</u> <real> well. I believe 150 invitations are out, so <u>that</u> rather
discourages me. I like to feel well, and lively when I go into such a company. I

believe in quiet weddings. Some of the <town> people,—possibly those not invited,—call it a donation. I should not enjoy presents given in that way. You will probably not see me at the seminary until after the middle of Sept. or the first of Oct. I must not commence my music, by way of taking lessons, until I get real strong. I am feeling very much better than when you were here.

You were with me just long enough for me to begin to feel your presence. If you would have spent one week with me, I should have had a delightful time, and I trust that you would not have felt that the time was wholly wasted. Pleasure do not vanish with the day. The remembrance of these delightful hours afford much pleasure, and stimulate me to press onward and upward. When I think of your mind and its workings as compared with some others. I feel that you ought not to shut yourself up in some seminary or college unless your presence is more needed there than elsewhere. You have no idea what a stimulus your visit was. I am too tired tonight to be able to express clearly what I mean. If you cannot comprehend, wait until my head is clearer. Hoping to see you at no distant day, I remain, Your sincere friend,[6]

Eva Goodrich.

ALS (SCPC, JAC; *JAPM*, 1:554–57).

1. Eva Campbell Goodrich's husband, Lewis Goodrich.

2. Eva Campbell Goodrich's first child, Herbert Bryant Goodrich (1880–91), was born on 16 July 1880 but died while still a boy. He drowned in the Pecatonica River in 1891, just days before his parents were planning to leave town to start a new life on a farm in Fairmount, Nebr. Eva Campbell Goodrich was so distraught by her son's death that she refused to leave the place where he died, and the Goodrichs stayed on in Pecatonica for an additional year. The couple had a second child, Willard, in Pecatonica in 1882; after young Herbert's death and the move to Nebraska in 1891–92, a third son, Homer, was born. Eva Campbell Goodrich lived another twenty-four years after her husband died in Nebraska on 2 Nov. 1914.

3. Eva Campbell Goodrich's stepson, Lewis Goodrich, Jr.

4. It is not known who roomed with JA in the first part of her senior year. It is possible that Addie M. Smith, her roommate in 1879–80, also lived with her in 1880–81, but it seems that for the second half of the year JA roomed alone. Space was available, and some older girls had rooms to themselves. JA and Addie M. Smith (Strong) remained friends after graduation. They corresponded, and JA maintained Strong's address in her address book (SCPC, JAC; *JAPM*, 1:1376, 1:1393, 1:1528; 2:1033; 27:1196; see also JA to SAAH, 19 Jan. 1881, below).

5. James A. Garfield (1831–81) was nominated as the Republican candidate for the presidency of the United States in June 1880, and he won the presidential election against Democratic opponent Winfield S. Hancock and Greenback candidate James B. Weaver that fall. Several "Life of James Garfield" books were published in conjunction with the campaign (and many more a year later when Garfield died). The one to which Eva Campbell Goodrich refers may have been *The Life and Public Services of James A. Garfield* by J. M. Bundy, published by A. S. Barnes and Co. in 1880. Bundy's book was of special interest in Beloit College and RFS circles because Bundy, editor of the *New York Evening Mail*, had graduated from Beloit in the class of 1853. The book received a hearty review in the Beloit *Round Table*, and Garfield was praised in the review as inspirational in "climbing into national notice" from humble beginnings ([22 Oct. 1830]: 29).

Garfield fulfilled the popular image of a president who rose from impoverished circumstances. Born in a log cabin in a rural township near Cleveland, Ohio, he grew up in poverty and attended district schools. As a junior, he went to Williams College, Williamstown, Mass., where he had a college career that reflected interests similar to those that engaged JA at RFS. He was the school's debating champion and editor of the school magazine. He then taught classical languages and became president of the Eclectic Institute at Hiram, Ohio. He served in the Ohio state senate in 1859–61 and was a Republican U.S. representative from Ohio from 1863 to 1880. He was a colonel in the Union army during the Civil War and after the war was a strong supporter of Ulysses S. Grant. Garfield was elected president in Nov. 1880 but was assassinated in office, the victim of a shooting by Charles Julius Guiteau, a former Freeport resident and son of JHA's business associate Luther Guiteau and brother of JA's good friend Flora Guiteau (see *PJA*, 2). Garfield was popular in Winnebago Co., where he received a vote of 4,617 to Hancock's 1,511 and Weaver's 290.

6. Eva Campbell Goodrich wrote philosophically to JA about a year later. She had been unable to attend JA's graduation because of illness, and she was feeling very tangibly the different paths on which life had taken JA and herself since they were roommates together in JA's first year at RFS. While JA had gone on to excel in every way at Rockford—in academics, as a student leader, and in the wider sphere of relations with students at other colleges and universities—Goodrich reflected on the domestic focus of her own life: "Jane, my work for the past year has been the care of my home and children, music lessons, and painting" (27 June 1881, SCPC, JAC; *JAPM*, 1:663).

In the same summer of 1880 that Eva Campbell Goodrich was adjusting to motherhood with her infant son and to domestic life as the wife of a schoolteacher, JA was enjoying a lighthearted schoolgirl life and making the most of her time away from RFS. At the end of Aug. 1880, she and two young friends set off for a trip to Niagara Falls. The girls, unchaperoned, traveled from Milwaukee to Buffalo by boat. Ann Eliza Clingman noted the adventure in her diary, and Sarah Hostetter wrote about it in her memoir of JA's youth. Hostetter's charming account captures both the event and JA's personality:

> I remember distinctly a beautiful black hat trimmed with glorious dark red silk poppies (her class flower). It was most becoming and as Jane's hats were always out of the usual order this was not an exception, and something unusual almost *did* happen; it nearly fell overboard as we were dreaming in the moonlight, heads on the railing. It was rescued with a quick grab but a little book dear to Jane's heart went into Lake Michigan. A picture taken at this time (tintypes were the fashion) shows the three girls standing on a *rag rug* at the very edge of the American Falls, apparently just ready to fall over. But Jane is nearest the edge looking oh! so serious! By some unlucky fate she had lost her return ticket to Chicago, and she said the Falls said to her all day, "Lost your ticket, Lost your ticket," the cars said, "Lost your ticket, ticket"; and her worry was that her father would think her careless and carelessness he could not abide. But Jane Addams careless is an impossible idea. (Hostetter, "Home and Girlhood," 7; see also Bade and Mau, *Cedarville Clingmans*, 253)

We have been unable to locate the tintype that Hostetter describes.

Rockford Seminary Magazine.

PUBLISHED BY

THE PIERIAN UNION.

A Literary Association connected with the Rockford Seminary.

EDITORS:

JANE ADDAMS, '81,   -   -   -   -   -   -   Editor in Chief.
MARTHA THOMAS, 81, -   -   -   -   -   -   Literary.
HATTIE E. WELLS, '82,   -   -   -   Business and Exchange.
JULIA E. GARDINER, '82,   -   -   -   -   - Home Items.
ELLA L. NICHOL, '83,   -   -   -   -   -   - Personals.

The ROCKFORD SEMINARY MAGAZINE is a monthly of thirty-two pages, published during the school year.
Contributions are solicited from those who have been at any time connected with the school. Articles for publication may be addressed to Rockford Seminary. Subscriptions and all business letters may be addressed to HATTIE E. WELLS, Business Editor.

TERMS:

Single Copy, one year, in advance,   -   -   - $1 00
    "   "   "   "   after three months,   -   -   -   1 25
Single Number,   -   -   -   -   -   -   -   -   20
With ten cents added for postage.
Address   HATTIE E. WELLS, Business Editor.

The masthead for the *Rockford Seminary Magazine.*

From Mary B. Downs

Jane Addams became both class president and editor-in-chief of the Rockford Seminary Magazine *in her senior year. Here one of the former editors, Mary Downs, discussed Addams's ideas for changing the format of the magazine and also tactics for dealing with its constant financial instability. The changes Addams began to institute became visible in the December 1880 issue.[1]*

481 N. La Salle St. Chicago, [Ill.]   Nov. 14, '80.

My dear Jane:—

Your envelope appears quite business like—and speaks well for the enterprising spirit of the new editors and their chief. I stand in great admiration of the powers which have succeeded in quenching that bothersome "Alumnae Department" and given younger or more enthusiastic friends a chance to help.[2] I begin to understand why the much abused elder sisters—for some reason or other I do not yet consider myself one of them—do not respond very promptly or cheerfully to the call for "more matter." A pedagogue's life is rather prosaic to say the least and when the most romantic sphere to which a "Sem-girl" can attain, is to go to China and marry a missionary the Alumnae Department must of necessity be rather monotonous.[3] When Miss A.[,] Katie,[4] you & I (I confess that this part of my future rarely occurs to my sobered mind, and that my highest aspirations now are—not any more probable than in my younger days—only a little lower—to marry a rich man and live comfortably.)[5] Well, when we four pedestrians are making our way through the "old world" (I teach geography) we will favor the Magazine with accounts of our travels.

Does that august assembly "The <Pierian Union>"[6] conform its proceedings to parliamentary laws, now? It did not in my day, therefore you find no account of its noble deeds. However I have a distinct remembrance of that meeting two years ago. I believe that the present prudent members are in no way responsible for the rash deeds of the Union in its younger years. I cannot regret that no records are to be found. I do not see that you can do otherwise than raise the price of your labors.

Would that the wealthy spouse were at hand and I would turn benevolently to your relief. On condition that Miss S.[7] need not know, & thus be encouraged to solicit a fund for the "Art Hall" which she took occasion to mention in our last class letter. So much for what might be, now for what is.

Victoria Wigren is teaching in Dayton, Iowa. Mary Earle, I hear, is teaching in some public school not far from me. I wish that I knew her address—I know nothing more worth mentioning—I am sorry that there will be <u>no</u> reunion for I hoped that I might have the oportunity to see you and Miss Anderson & Miss Blaisdell or Miss Potter. However, chance may bring you here before the close of the year and if so don't fail to come to see me. I am not quite sure that I would enjoy a visit to the Seminary. Each year makes so much change there; still I may visit Rockford before the year closes. If the spirit moves, I will do myself the pleasure of contributing to the new department before very long. I shall look for Katie's signature to some very profound article before long. I am so glad that the way is open to her. I am very comfortably situated and but for my own perverse spirit which is as unmanageable as ever & persists in making me not quite satisfied, I would be quite happy. I live in a very pleasant family & have for a chum an Oberlin girl who is very pleasant in spirit and quite Amazonian in body. The other members of the family are firstly, Fraulein, our chief, an American but educated in Germany & very German in manner; we salute her with a kiss at morning & even: secondly, Madame, the French teacher; & thirdly, a musician, a kindergarten teacher, & your humble servant, who all speak English with a smattering of French & Dutch.[8]

I answer your letter soon because ~~your~~ I am staying home from church and feel in the spirit. I hope that an unanswered letter does not "weigh on your mind" for though I should be glad to hear from you often, I have not so far forgotten the duties of one in your position, as to expect much attention. I think that you will understand my meaning, although not very clearly <u>put</u>. I wish that I could help you in some way but my powers are limited. Be sure of my sympathy. Is the Seminary as conservative as ever?[9] How much better it would be if the town people could be interested in the school. Your Magazine work would be so much easier and much better appreciated if you knew some thing about each other. If you could rely a little more upon some one else than the poor Alumnae, you might feel a little safer in raising the subscription fee, if it would be necessary. However, I don't see what else you can do. It is so easy to see & say things. How glad I am that I need not <u>do</u>! I am glad that I am where I can't be bothered; for your letter has awakened a little troublesome enthusiasm & scheming in regard to ways & means. I did not mean to write so much. Give my love to Miss Blaisdell and Miss Anderson. Yours truly

Mary B. Downs.

ALS (SCPC, JAC; *JAPM*, 1:558–63).

1. One of the innovations JA made in the Dec. 1880 issue was to print a masthead for the *RSM* that listed the editorial staff. In past years staff members had worked more or less anonymously, sometimes making an appearance in items signed with initials or, occasionally, with full names. The new masthead was printed just above the editorial for the magazine. It proclaimed the periodical as the "Rockford Seminary Magazine, Published by the Pierian Union, a Literary Association connected with the Rockford Seminary." JA was listed as editor-in-chief, Martha Thomas as literary editor, Hattie E. Wells as business and exchange editor, Julia E. Gardiner as editor of the "Home Items" section, and Ella L. Nichol as editor of the "Personals" section. The magazine was further described as "a monthly of thirty-two pages, published during the school year." Contributions were solicited from "those who have been at any time connected with the school." In her first editorial that appeared with the new masthead JA announced:

> We have planned various changes in the magazine for next year, and in this number as nearly as possible are represented the proposed changes. The first is in the order and size of the various departments. We think the new one will prove both convenient and satisfactory. It is also more in accordance with the usual college publication, without giving up our magazine form. . . . As last year, we will publish nine numbers, publishing every month excepting August, September and October; *our year beginning in January, and all debts to be paid within the first six months.* Hoping these changes will meet with the approval of our patrons, we solicit their renewed subscriptions. (*RSM* [Dec. 1880]: 280, 282; *JAPM*, 46:264, 46:266)

2. The rather stodgy "Alumnae Dept.," which featured essays, articles, and poems from graduates, had long run on the front page of the magazine. The section appeared in its accustomed spot in the first issue of the 1880–81 school year (Nov. 1880), but in Dec. 1880 the "Literary Dept." was given the front-page position and "Alumnae Dept." was nowhere to be seen. "Alumnae department has been abolished, and in its stead we plan a Contributors' department," JA told readers, "to be sustained by the Alumnae as well as all those who are in any way interested in the institution. We have reason to believe that by thus broadening the interest it will receive a more hearty support. For the coming year we have planned a series of articles by the Alumnae on practical subjects, thus hoping to make the department an incentive, as well as a source of literary benefit" (*RSM* [Dec. 1880]: 282; *JAPM*, 46:266, see also 46:263–66). The first Contributors' Dept. immediately followed JA's editorial and featured EGS's essay, "Soul Culture" (284–86; see also JA to EGS, 11 Aug. 1879, n. 12, above).

3. This is just what Sarah B. Clapp did—go to China and marry a missionary—and those facts were well documented in the "Alumnae Dept." news of the 1879–80 *RSM*. The Nov. 1880 issue featured Clapp's "A Short Trip into Mongolia" and an announcement of her marriage to the Rev. Chauncey Goodrich (229–34; see also Eva Campbell to JA, 18 June 1879, n. 6, above).

4. References to Sarah Anderson and Katie Hitchcock.

5. Mary Downs did not marry. She taught in the Chicago area for many years and lived with various family members in that vicinity and in Elgin, Ill. She kept in touch with JA's activities. Her sister, Jessie Downs (d. 1940), taught at the Elgin Academy before marrying William H. Goodrow (d. 1930) and moving to Chicago in the mid-1890s. On 27 Jan. 1896, Mary Downs told Sarah Anderson that she was living with her sister in Chicago, not far from Hull-House (first on Dearborn St. and then on Walnut St.). "Jane is fulfilling the promises of youth, isn't she. Her work and her influence have accomplished wonders," Downs observed (SCPC, JAC; *JAPM*, 3:31). Downs had been an outstanding scholar at RFS, and JA admired her intellect. Because of her high merit and family's modest circumstances, Downs had been admitted to RFS with a special financial aid arrangement. She was still paying installments to Sarah Anderson on the costs of her education in the 1890s. She moved to Oak Park, Ill., with the Goodrows in 1910, where she lived until her death in 1940 (see also n. 8).

6. Nov. and Dec. 1880 were active times for JA in regard to Pierian Union affairs. When Lizzie Smith wrote to her mother to complain about her course work, she reported, "To top all I have had to write a debate for this evenings society. Jane Addams and I had the affirmative, and Helen Harrington and Alice Atkinson the negative. Our subject was Resolved: That the British form of government tends to produce better statesmen then the form of government of the U.S. Our side came out ahead" (Sara Elizabeth Smith to Annie M. Jordan Smith, Nov. 1880, SHSW, Smith; see also JA, "Resolved: 'That the British form of government tends to develope better statesmen than the American form.' Aff.," 19 Nov. 1880, *JAPM*, 46:253–62).

JA organized a Pierian Union fair and sociable for Christmas in order to raise money for the magazine and for literary society programs. In the spirit of encouraging alumnae of some means to contribute more to the literary aspects of RFS life, she wrote to SAAH on 9 Dec. 1880, urging that she come to see former classmates and friends (SCPC, JAC; *JAPM*, 1:564–65). Lizzie Smith described the preparations for the fair to her mother: "We are to have a fair here before Christmas to raise money for the magazine. I'm on the senior class committee so will ask you, if you wouldn't consider it a pleasure to knit a pair of mittens. . . . We are going to do the work in classes and of course the Senior Class would like to have the nicest booth. We are thinking of sending invitations to the Beloit boys as several of them have expressed a wish to come" (Sara Elizabeth Smith to Annie M. Jordan Smith, 28 Nov. 1880, SHSW, Smith).

The fair was held in the RFS chapel on Monday evening, 20 Dec. 1880, just before the winter holiday, which extended from 24 Dec. to 2 Jan. 1881. JA's seniors combined with the junior class to make a gypsy tent with a fortune teller. Visitors paid ten cents admission and sampled wares from candy and food stands, as well as arts and crafts. JA apparently set up shop amid all the merriment. Somewhere between the art gallery on the stage and the oyster stand, "In the most appropriate, viz: the most conspicuous place, stood the sanctum, fully furnished, scrap basket, desk, placard, ink, hard-working editor and all." The social helped put the magazine's operations back on solid financial footing, and JA pronounced it "a decided success" (*RSM* [Jan. 1881]: 16). In the Mar. 1881 issue, she announced as part of her editorial that "we have money in the bank, and draw interest," and the "fair given by the Pierian Union counted generous returns, more than enough to pay the debt, and so why not become a capitalist?" (86; *JAPM*, 46:307; for the entire editorial, see *JAPM*, 46:305–8; for the last portion, see Excerpt from Editorial in the *RSM*, Mar. 1881, below). In her May 1881 editorial, JA used the Pierian Union Fair and Sociable as an example of how everything at RFS had to be done by appealing to class loyalty or else nothing would be accomplished (*JAPM*, 46:349–54).

7. A reference to Anna P. Sill.

8. The Nov. 1880 *RSM* reported, "Mary Downs, of '79, is teaching in a private school in Chicago" (249). Downs had joined the staff of Miss Rice's School at 481 N. LaSalle St., entering the same world of private school teaching that EGS had joined the year before. While EGS had taught drawing at the school in 1879–80, Downs became a geography instructor in 1880.

Rebecca S. Rice's school was thriving and in its fifth year of operation in 1880–81. By 1884 it would outgrow its quarters and move to larger facilities. Downs joined a faculty of seven or eight teachers. No catalogs for the school are apparently extant from the 1881–87 period, and it is not known who taught French at Miss Rice's School in 1880–81. It is also not known where Downs roomed and whether her housemates were employed at the school or elsewhere in Chicago.

Miss Rice's School did offer all the specialities that Downs mentions in connection with the unnamed individuals. The school emphasized teaching modern languages (in addition to Latin) to children at a young age and offered instruction, for an extra fee, in French, German, and Italian. It had a music department "supplied from the ablest instructors in the city," and a kindergarten class for which tuition was fifty dollars an academic year ("Young Ladies' School," 2). Alice A. Farrar was the kindergarten teacher in 1879–80. Downs's friend from Oberlin has not been identified. School principal Rebecca S. Rice had studied at Heidelberg in 1870–71 and taught daily oral lessons in German at the school to all levels of students, including the kindergarten, in 1879–80. By 1888 Frl. Anna Wullweber had taken over the duties of teaching German at the Girls' Higher School, Mlle. Helene Belle taught French, and Miss Lilian Greenleaf and Miss Agnes Ingersoll headed the kindergarten and music departments (see also EGS to JA, 27 July 1879, n. 6, above).

9. JA made this issue of the conservatism of RFS the subject of her editorial for the Jan. 1881 edition of the *RSM* (see Excerpt from Editorial in the *RSM*, Jan. 1881, below).

From Rollin D. Salisbury

Beloit Wis.   Jan 15 '81

Miss Adams:

Prof. E. S. Morse,[1] whom you doubtless know as one of the leading Scientists of the Evolution School is to lecture in Beloit next Thursday Evening. Thinking possibly that some of the students of the Seminary might like to hear him, as Proctor[2] last season, I write you this note. If you desire it, I will reserve seats as early as possible, though by course of mail I presume it will be as late as Wednesday before an answer can reach Beloit.[3] I will enclose a brief press notice. Yours respectfully,

R. D. Salisbury.[4] Chm Com.

[Enclosure][5]

ALS (SCHS; *JAPM*, 1:573–75).

1. Scientist Edward Sylvester ("E.S.") Morse (1838–1925), a prominent and versatile zoologist, was born in Maine and studied with Louis Agassiz at Harvard. He earned his doctorate at Yale and was a professor of comparative anatomy and zoology at Bowdoin College in 1871–74. He taught at the Imperial Univ. in Tokyo, Japan, from 1877 to 1880, establishing a museum and zoological station there. In 1880 he returned to the United States and became director of the Peabody Museum in Salem, Mass. He was an authority on Japanese ceramics. In addition to his research and writing in zoology, he was an expert on the topic of astronomy and a popular lecturer on many other scientific subjects. He paid for his scientific research and inventions partly through lecturing. He was "a representative American evolutionist, who facilitated the acceptance by his countrymen of the Darwinian theory, both by his able ad-

vocacy and by the collection of a large body of confirmatory facts" (*NCAB*, 24:407). As an ethnologist, he served on the juries for Expositions in Chicago (1893), Buffalo (1901), and St. Louis (1904), all of which promoted a social-Darwinist vision of civilizations.

As editor of the school magazine, Rollin D. Salisbury gave Morse's lecture good advance publicity in the pages of the Beloit *Round Table*. It was reported in the 8 Oct. 1880 edition that "Prof. Morse will lecture in Beloit in behalf of the High School and the Archaean Union some time in December" (20). By the 17 Dec. 1880 edition, it was announced that Morse's lecture had been rescheduled for 17 Jan. 1881, and a clipping Salisbury enclosed with his letter to JA indicates that it may have been rescheduled yet again, to 20 Jan. (n. 5). Morse, whom Salisbury praised as an eminent scientist who could make science interesting to a popular audience, was to lecture on "Wonders of Growth in Animals." Because Morse was an avowed evolutionist, his appearance in evangelical Beloit was a landmark. His presentation was part of a series of lectures on evolution given on campus in connection with the Scientific Course in the spring of 1881. Salisbury encouraged the readers of the 18 Mar. 1881 *Round Table* to consider that the creationism of the Bible and evolutionary theory need not be seen as antagonistic ways of understanding life's origins.

2. JA had traveled up to Beloit to hear a lecture during the previous school year (JA to AHHA, 7 Mar. 1880, n. 4, above).

3. JA replied to Salisbury on 18 Jan. 1881, "The Powers that Be have quietly decided the question for us." Despite the prospect of "good sleighing & fine lecture" that had made them initially decide "in favor of science (a la Morse)," the juniors and seniors at RFS had to "respectfully plead 'pressure of school duties'" (SCHS; *JAPM*, 1:576). In the Mar. 1881 *RSM* it was noted, "Though invitations were sent us from Beloit to attend the lectures on 'The Wonder of Growth of Animals,' given by Prof. Morse, the weather was so unfavorable that the expedition was abandoned" (71). The 21 Jan. 1881 *Round Table* reported that the audience for the lecture was "composed chiefly of students and H.S. girls, with an occasional gray head visible among the 'youth and beauty,' assembled at the Opera House . . . the speaker's manner on the stage was easy and pleasant, and his style unique and spicy" (81).

4. There is no doubt that JA was well acquainted with Rollin D. Salisbury by her senior year, when they both were editors of their respective college magazines. Salisbury (1858–1922), who attended Beloit College with Addams's stepbrother GBH but was not a special friend of his, has been rumored to have proposed marriage to JA, probably in their senior year. This lore originates with James Weber Linn's authorized biography of his aunt. Linn claimed that Salisbury proposed but that JA refused him, and, he implied, Salisbury remained unmarried for the rest of his life because of her refusal (*Jane Addams*, 50).

It is true that, like JA, Salisbury never married. For both, success as leaders in college was an indication of greater successes to come. Both rose to positions of public stature in their respective fields. Both lived most of their adult lives in Chicago, some six miles apart from one another. Although Linn says that they had no contact and that Salisbury "never entered" the door of Hull-House, Salisbury did in fact visit the settlement and lectured there in its early days. The *Hull-House Bulletin* records that on 10 Mar. 1896 he presented a stereopticon lecture on "Arctic Exploration." He lectured again, on Greenland, at Hull-House on 2 Feb. 1897. Even though they lived and worked in close proximity, no particular friendship seems to have been maintained between Salisbury and JA, and when he died she was not among those listed as having sent flowers or a note of condolence to his family. There is no evidence to support Linn's claim regarding the romantic link between them. Salisbury's niece felt Linn's claim had been fabricated and knew of no evidence to support it in her family history. JA never expressed interest in Salisbury in any extant letters to family or friends, nor did Salisbury express interest in her in his extant personal correspondence. His 1880–92 correspondence to close friends who were students with him at Beloit indicates that he was interested in a series of young women during his years at the college. Salisbury wrote particularly freely and frankly to Horace Spencer Fiske about his affections and the status of his relationships with particular women, and there is no reason to believe that he would not have shared similar news of his interest in JA had such an attraction existed.

While teaching at Beloit, Salisbury became engaged to Annie Laura Chapin (1867–1903), the daughter of Beloit College president and RFS trustee Aaron Lucius Chapin and his wife, Fanny L. Coit (b. ca. 1840). The Chapins had married in their home state of Connecticut on 26 Aug. 1861. Annie, the third of the couple's five children, was born in Beloit on 9 Jan. 1867. She was a brilliant student, an accomplished scientific illustrator, and valedictorian of the class of 1885 at Beloit High School. She has been remembered as "the whole world wiser than any man" (notes on Annie L. Chapin by Helen D. Richardson, n.d., BC). Although considered "delightfully all right" by Theodore Lyman Wright, one of Salisbury's close friends, Chapin broke the engagement; her mother apparently disapproved of the match. Chapin later married Barney C. Batchellor in 1900. She died in childbirth in 1903. Rumors of Salisbury becoming engaged to other women continued to circulate. In 1892 his friend Edward C. Ritscher, a Chicago lawyer, wrote of a visit to Beloit and commented on the Chapin family: "Miss Mary Porter spoke of your engagement to a Chicago lady in as matter of fact a manner as she did of the engagement of [James] Simmons some weeks before." Salisbury's fame, Porter had observed, did not shield him from being the object of gossip. Porter had gotten the news from the "Chapin girls." Ritscher had discretely replied that he had heard that Salisbury had an "engagement to Chicago University" (referring to Salisbury's new job), and "I was abusing no confidence in saying it was a fact" (Ritsher to Salisbury, 29 Aug. 1892, BC).

Salisbury became a distinguished professor of the sciences. In many ways during his student years at Beloit he was the male counterpart to JA at RFS. While she began college in 1877–78, he entered Beloit College in 1878; both were seniors and graduates in 1881. While she edited the RSM in her senior year, he edited the Beloit college newspaper, Round Table, from Sept. 1880 through Jan. 1881. Like JA, Salisbury was the top scholar of his class, becoming, like her, class valedictorian in 1881. His valedictory oration, "Conflict the Law of Progress," praised as "strong in matter, vigorous in style . . . manly in tone," was reprinted in part in the Round Table (1 July 1881, 179). He and JA also held many interests in common. Like her, he was active in a campus literary society (he was president of the Alethean Society in 1880); a good debater (he represented Wisconsin at the Interstate Oratorical Contest at Jacksonville, Ill., in May 1881, a contest that JA attended as a spectator); and very interested in the sciences. Both thought during their senior years that they were headed for careers in science, he in geology, she in medicine.

Their similarities went beyond academic and extracurricular interests. Both experienced profound religious doubts at their respective Christian schools. Salisbury was one of the "unconverted" at Beloit until, unlike JA, he succumbed (apparently temporarily because later he was described as an agnostic) to the evangelical pressure so prevalent at both Beloit College and RFS. He was, he declared, saved.

Salisbury was born in Spring Prairie, Wis., on 17 Aug. 1858, the son of farmers Daniel and Lucinda Salisbury. His father, a former teacher, instilled good study habits in his young son. Salisbury was educated in a country school and at Whitewater Normal School before he became a rural school master in Port Washington, Wis. He taught for a year in the Port Washington village school before entering Beloit College at the age of twenty. He did some teaching at the college during his senior year, and after graduation he became a professor of geology, zoology, and botany at his alma mater, succeeding his teacher and mentor Thomas C. Chamberlin on the faculty in 1883. One student described Salisbury as "tall, dark-eyed, the picture of life and energy." He was a favorite because of the dynamic energy he brought to the classroom and his mastery of the "art of expression" (Patterson, "Rollin Salisbury," 5).

Pedagogy remained one of Salisbury's primary concerns throughout his career. He did graduate work in Germany in 1887 and became a full professor of geology at Beloit in 1889.

His work on the glacial history of Wisconsin led to appointment as an assistant geologist at the U.S. Geological Survey in 1889, where he served as a member of its Glacial Division until 1891. He taught at the Univ. of Wisconsin in 1890–91, and in 1892 he joined Chamberlin as a member of the founding faculty at the Univ. of Chicago.

Salisbury enjoyed a long career at the university, serving as chair of the geology dept. and dean of the Ogden School of Science. He trained many of the nation's top graduate students in the field of geology. He specialized in promoting what was called higher geography as an interdisciplinary approach that incorporated methods and research questions from the fields of geology, biology, political economy, and history. In addition, he was an organizer and the first president of the Geographic Society of Chicago (1898–99). Chamberlin and Salisbury's textbook series *Geology* (3 vols., 1904, 1906) was considered canonical in its time.

Like JA, Salisbury served on the board of his undergraduate alma mater. He was a charter member of the Assn. of American Geographers (1904) and became vice president of the organization in 1908 and president in 1912. He was a managing editor of the *Journal of Geology*, specializing in landform research and related topics, from its first issue in 1892 until his death. In 1907 he published *Physiography*, a textbook containing his university lectures on the same topic. The book was produced for high school use in 1908 and 1910.

Salisbury suffered a coronary thrombosis near the end of the 1921–22 academic year. He died in Chicago on 15 Aug. 1922, leaving copious publications based on his fieldwork and other research as well as textbooks and laboratory guides. His personal papers are stored in Special Collections at the Joseph Regenstein Library at the Univ. of Chicago.

5. Salisbury enclosed a clipping from a Beloit newspaper—a notice entitled "Scientific Lecture" that announced the impending 20 Jan. 1881 talk by E. S. Morse. Morse was to repeat his lecture on "The Wonder of Growth in Animals," which had gone well in Philadelphia. The announcement quoted at length from the *Philadelphia Evening Bulletin's* description of the event. Morse was praised for his skill in translating scientific data into "familiar discourse" and for the "singular beauty" of his illustrations, which he drew to portray the growth process of the organisms he described. "From the first to the last the delighted audience passed from surprise to surprise at the wonders of created life," the enthusiastic reviewer concluded. The Beloit lecture was to begin at eight in the evening, with general admission going for fifty cents a ticket, twenty-five cents for school children. The occasion was, as Salisbury had reported, a benefit to raise funds for the Archaean Union and Beloit High School.

To Sarah Alice Addams Haldeman

Rockford Sem'y [Ill.]　　　　　　　　　　　　　　　Jan 19" 1881

My Beloved Sister—

Your happy letter deserved a quick and appreciative reply, but as usual the things you want to do most are left until the things you are tired of doing are done. Thus it has been. I am glad Harry enjoyed the medical works for Ma took a great deal of pains selecting them, and I think feels hurt that she has not had a special reply of thanks, I wish you, my dear, would write her a real nice letter even if it did take an effort—that is the only way to gain a growing insight and sympathy. I know that you could do nothing to please Pa more, generousness and faithfulness touch every-one even if they cause self renouncing motives. Excuse this little "preach" I did n't mean it to sound so but "the responsibility of tolerance lies with those of the deepest insight" and it would only be a proof of your wider culture if you could advance the tolerance.

It has always been a pet idea of mine to have you here when I graduate & I find myself planning what we will do just as soon as you come, although I was wonderfully disappointed about Christmas still I believe we will enjoy June more.

Our class just now are revolving great plans, among them the abolishment of Commencement exercises as such, it remains to be seen how we will succeed, but our ideas for Class-day are already extended and striking.[1]

I have just finished Geo Eliot's "Mill on the Floss"[2] was disappointed in the characters but not their ideas; I was in the midst of "Theophrastus Such" when Geo Eliot died[3] and some way or other the news seemed particularly striking so that I suppose just now I am over sensitive in reading her. Miss Hill,[4] our German teacher is giving us a review of German literature so exceedly rapid and withal so deep that it is quite confusing as it were. She has a perfect passion for having us learn poems and review whole plays in one lesson. It seems to me that I have gained more from her in this short time than <I> did in all the years from Fraulein Emerson.[5] I wish that you could come in time next June to meet the new teachers and get to know them, they would be worth the effort, while it would be a great source of pride & pleasure to me to present you. My little room-mate did not come back after the holidays. I miss her more than I thought I would and hardly know how to study when I don't hear her talking continually.

I have been having a good deal of trouble with my eyes lately. Dr Clark[6] said that there was nothing organic but that they were strained from over use and being a little run down[.] I felt it there first. I at once dropped by[7] Greek and began to take iron so that by this time I am feeling quite refreshed.

I think you will enjoy Bryant's Homer,[8] I would sooner part with any thing else I have gained in school than the Homer I have read.

I wish I could get a view of the office with the coal-stove and the new table, I was so sleepy and tired when we were there in the summer that it is hard for me to form definite conception of <the> place[.] Miss Sill inquires about you often, she comes to my room a good deal this year—the magazine is the pride of her heart. Miss Anderson sends her love. With love to Harry & Yourself. Your devoted Sister

Jane Addams.

P.S. I do wish you might see our youngest niece,[9] she is without exception the very sweetest baby I have ever seen, I am so afraid she will lose some of it by summer.

ALS (UIC, JAMC; *JAPM*, 1:577–82).

1. Rebellion seemed to be the rule of the day under JA's leadership of her class. The seniors did indeed want to abolish commencement day as it had usually been conducted. Their desire sent Anna P. Sill to the RFS Board of Trustees. "One thing More," she wrote to Joseph Emerson the same day JA wrote this letter to SAAH. "The Class 1881 are very anxious to abolish

commencement day as far as they are concerned and substitute an address by some one distinguished and simply receive their diplomas on that day. They will prepare essays on themes given them to read before a Committee or the Faculty and will have Class Day as usual. Should not a change of this kind be decided by the Board of Trustees? and, if made, be a permanent one and the successive classes follow it? Please give us your opinion at an early day and oblige" (19 Jan. 1881, BC, EB). Apparently, the push for innovation was not successful. The 1881 commencement seems to have gone off more or less as usual, with members of the class each presenting an oral essay on graduation day as part of the commencement exercises.

2. George Eliot's tragedy *The Mill on the Floss* (1860) is the story of a conflict of personality between brother and sister Tom and Maggie Tulliver and presents the theme of the redeeming quality of woman's selflessness.

3. *The Impressions of Theophrastus Such* (1879), a satire, was one of Eliot's last works. She died in Dec. 1880, less than a year after marrying John Walter Cross. JA noted in the Mar. 1881 edition of the *RSM* (misspelling both "Eliot" and "Shakespeare") that *"The Kansas Review* contains an excellent tribute to the memory of George Elliot. The author rightfully calls her the 'flower of this age, the Shakspeare of her century'" (84).

4. Ella M. Hill was a new German and French teacher at RFS in 1880–81. From Ann Arbor, she was hired for the Dept. of Modern Languages at RFS. She married in the summer of 1881 and was "Mrs. Kingsley" by the beginning of Oct. and had left her post at RFS. Ella Hill was immediately popular with the less conservative girls at RFS, both because of her challenging professionalism in the classroom and her congeniality outside it. Lizzie Smith wrote home to her sister Addie, "we have a new teacher, Miss Hill, whom I think we will like. She seems very thorough and just the one we need." The next month, Lizzie told her mother that despite Anna P. Sill's strict injunctions against dancing, Miss Kendall, a teacher of Latin and gymnastics as well as music, "is a treasure, she lets us dance whenever we want to and even dances herself. One evening not long ago we had her and Miss Hill both dancing. Deda [Deda Mealey, a first-year student from Monticello, Minn.] took Miss Hill and I Miss K and we learned them to dance the 'Racket.' I don't believe Miss Sill knew what she was doing when she got such teachers." During the next semester, Lizzie and friends danced for and then serenaded Miss Hill and Miss Williams on combs (Sara Elizabeth Smith to Addie B. Smith, 21 Sept. 1880; and Sara Elizabeth Smith to Annie M. Jordan Smith, 20 Nov. 1880 and 6 Feb. 1881, all SHSW, Smith). Ella C. Williams, a mathematics teacher and recent graduate of the Univ. of Michigan, and a Miss Kendall, a graduate of Oberlin in the class of 1880, joined Ella M. Hill as the new young members of the RFS teaching staff in Jan. 1881 (on Williams, see JA to JHA, 6 Mar. 1881, n. 8, below).

5. Charlotte Emerson, JA's German teacher at RFS in 1879–80, retired from teaching in June 1880. She married the Rev. William Bryant Brown in Rockford on 20 July 1880 (introduction to part 2, n. 40, above).

6. D. Selwyn Clark was personal physician to Anna P. Sill.

7. JA evidently meant to write "my" instead of "by."

8. William Cullen Bryant (1794–1878), Massachusetts poet, prepared translations of both Homer's *Iliad* (1870) and the *Odyssey* (1871–72). The translations were praised for their simplicity and dignity of tone.

9. A reference to Esther Margaret Linn, the new daughter of JA's sister MCAL, born 7 Aug. 1880.

Excerpt from Editorial in the
Rockford Seminary Magazine

Continuing on the note of innovation Jane Addams introduced in December 1880, this declaration of independence from Rockford Female Seminary norms was written in the spirit of a delayed reply to the controversy that had enveloped former editor Mary Downs in the spring of 1879.[1]

[Rockford, Ill.]

JANUARY 1881

. . . It was high advice which an old sage once gave to his young disciple: "Always do what you are afraid to do." Unfortunately we are not at all sage like, neither are our readers inclined to be admiring disciples, still we are emboldened to repeat the ancient advice, in hopes that the somewhat dangerous motto may work a reformation which is sadly needed among us.

The conservative element seems to predominate, and thus there is growing a tameness and monotony in our opinions and ideas which has a decidedly depressing influence. We are like those children who "shut the door after, and always do as they're bid."

Far be it from us to stir up an insurrection in the keeping of the rules, or to inspire any one with that most detestable of all motives—a trying to be odd and unlike other people; but we do wish that a spirit of individuality might be increased, and the tendency to act in masses checked.

The teacher at table makes some general remark or advances an idea, a bland smile of approval beams on every face, and each one agrees exactly with that idea; the teacher meanwhile gasps for a breath of fresh air.

A remark is made, or a question is asked, on a subject of which the class are totally ignorant. Nobody says, "I don't know;" but every one looks wise, and mods their heads at the right place. A girl brings a book back to the library, and announces that it is "perfectly splendid;" immediately six other girls rush up to the librarian to take it for the next week.

It is certainly unnatural for one hundred girls from different homes, and different parts of the country, to agree so beautifully in their literary tastes and general opinions. Just because we eat breakfast by the hundred and go to bed by the hundred, probably there is an unconscious feeling that it is dangerous to attempt anything alone.

Some one says or does something a little unusual, and is surprised by the attention it attracts, and the stir it makes: she thus begins to look at the effect of an act instead of the act itself, and at the next opportunity for action she grows conservative. The *Magazine,* just now, feels very like adopting the former motto of the *Globe* newspaper—"The world is governed too much."

PD (*RSM* [Jan. 1881]: 25–26; *JAPM,* 46:282–83).

1. See Mary B. Downs to JA, 14 Nov. 1880, above.

Announcement in the
Rockford Seminary Magazine

As president of the senior class, Jane Addams, along with Mary Ellwood and Mattie Thomas, organized a surprise Friday afternoon fete in honor of American educator Mark Hopkins's eightieth birthday.[1] The event, which added some spark to dragging students at examination time, was also a celebration of the seniors' successful completion of study of Hopkins's Lectures on the Evidences of Christianity *(1846), a text for their "Evidences of Christianity" class directed by Anna P. Sill. Seniors were invited to their parlor, not expecting much, and were greeted by an elaborate feast.[2]*

[Rockford, Ill.]　　　　　　　　　　　　　　　　　　　　[4 Feb. 1881]

The "Evidences" are conclusive that the Seniors have enjoyed the most elegant affair of the season. The officers of the class fully understood "the thing to be done," and in extending invitations to the members of [the] class to a "Birthday Fete in Honor of Mark Hopkins," they provided "a perfect standard" for the guidance of all following. In response to the dainty invitations,[3] the Seniors appeared in full dinner toilet, and the honored gentleman himself extended, by letter, his appreciation of the honor and regrets for his non-attendance.[4] A most delightful repast, together with numerous toasts, occupied the attention of the guests from 4:30 to 7 P.M. *Hoch, uebermal hoch*[5] resounded through the halls in response to "Our President, Jane Addams," and to "Mark Hopkins and his mighty work 'Evidences of Christianity.'" The following was the *menu:*

SOUP.—	Lobster. Chowder.
FISH.—	Oysters (Raw and Fried.)
POULTRY.—	Turkey.
VEGETABLES.—	Potatoes (a la Saratoga.) Celery.
RELISHES.—	Chow Chow and Jelly
BREAD.—	Rolls [(]Hot and Cold.)
DESSERT.—	Ice Cream and Cake.
FRUITS.—	Oranges and Figs.
Nuts. Coffee.	

PD (*RSM* [Mar. 1881]: 77).

1. Mark Hopkins (1802–87), physician, educator, religious philosopher, and Congregationalist minister, was born on 4 Feb. 1802 in Stockbridge, Mass. He was the president of Williams College, Williamstown, Mass., from 1836 to 1872 and a professor of philosophy at Williams for fifty-seven years. He graduated from Williams in 1824 and from Pittsfield Medical College, Mass., in 1829 and joined the Williams faculty in 1830. In addition to his best-known *Evidences of Christianity,* he wrote *The Law of Love and Love as a Law* (1869) and *Teachings and Counsels* (1884). Anna P. Sill knew him as an educator and through his capacity as the president of the American Board of Commissioners for Foreign Missions from 1857 to 1887.

2. "We did not expect anything very extra, but were disappointed" senior Lizzie Smith wrote with enthusiasm to her mother about the birthday fete. "They had a long table set with china and loaded down with good things. At each plate was a Chinese paper napkin and on it the printed bill of fare, the headings of which were Soup, Fish, Poultry, Vegetables, Relishes, Bread, Dessert & Fruits." Lizzie went on to describe the delicious lobster chowder, fried oysters, turkey, Saratoga potatoes, and other specialties served up to the girls. The party ended with the singing of class songs. In this case at least, the "sober" JA had successfully defied her classmates' expectations (Sara Elizabeth Smith to Annie M. Jordan Smith, 6 Feb. 1881, SHSW, Smith).

3. *Birthday Fete In Honor of Mark Hopkins, L.L.D., Feb. 4, 1802–Feb. 4, 1881. Compliments of Class Officers to Class 1881. Senior Parlors. . . . DINNER HOUR, 4.30 P.M.* Printed invitation on class of 1881 bread-givers stationery and listing the same bill of fare as given above (*JAPM*, 27:414–15).

4. The Mar. 1881 *RSM* printed a transcription of a 10 Feb. 1881 letter written by Hopkins "to the Senior Class in Rockford Seminary." In it, he expressed gratification "on hearing, as I have just done, through the kindness of Miss Sill, of the honor you have done me by celebrating my birthday." It "gives me the opportunity now in my eightieth year of testifying to you," he continued, "not only my increasing sense of the truth of the religion, but of is unutterable value to each one who receives it. With the wish and prayer that each one of you may receive it fully, and be the means of spreading it, I am Sincerely yours, Mark Hopkins" (74). In contacting Hopkins, Anna P. Sill did her best to make sure that a moral lesson regarding Christian conversion was conveyed along with the evening's food and fun.

5. A German expression of cheer or well-wishing, meaning "cheers."

To Ellen Gates Starr

Rockford Sem'y [Ill.]   Feb 13 1881

My dear Girl

Your espistle quite delighted me, I fancy your progress must be rapid if you can spend a couple of hours each week in wonder & admiration, after all it is the only thing that gives energy to culture; above all things deliver me from a "nil admirair",[1] they most certainly will never produce a thing and never have a chance to transcend their own natures[.] You see that I highly approve your admiration of the drama, if we can't find character, we can <at least> bring ourselves in contact with genius in any form it may present itself and get as much as it can give us. But don't flatter yourself that I agree with you in your latent vein of hero-worship, I don't, I would rather get my inspiration from a dodecahedral crystal than even a genius because it would take a stronger mind to see a principle embodied by cohesion than <embodied> by vital personal force, but as I am destitute of either & you have splendidly found the one, I congratulate you my dear, on what I regard as unmistakable signs of advancement.

Carlyle is dead and if I don't get to Mass[.] before Emerson dies,[2] and don't have the opportunity of seeing him, I shall have to give up the one experiment I would like to try above all others alas! "time is fleeting, experiment slipping judgement difficult" and art continually appears longer and longer.[3]

We have had a "revival season" here,[4] of course I felt the influence more or less for no matter if I agree with people or not, we are hunting after the same thing and have cause for a mutual distrust, I shall always look back with peculiar sensations on the month of Jan 1881.

I have been <reading> John Stuart Blackie[5] ~~some~~, my former vague dream to study medicine[6] for a year in Edinburgh is growing into a settled passion, I have an idea that to live in Edinburgh with all the splendid men that are there now, would be next thing to old Athens itself. Germany is very fine but still it is mostly learning.

I suppose the limit of sentimentality is Mathew Arnold[7] but I am there now, tell me if this don't exactly express the ideal you have had of a self poised, mighty life

Unaffrighted by the silence round them
Undistra[c]ted by the sights they see
These demand not that the things without them
Yield them love, anusement sympathy.[8]

I am much obliged for your kind invitation to come to see you Easter week, but it cannnot be. I am afraid, this year is a solid dig to make up all the odds & ends for Smiths,[9] such little things a spherical trigenometry & the Memorabilia, my comfort is leisure next year & Boston to spend it in.

Miss Anderson is a source of unfailing delight to me, I wish you could come & see <u>us</u> before the big hub bub in June. Yours &c

Jane Addams.

ALS (SC, Starr; *JAPM*, 1:584–88).

1. JA means *nil admirari*, Latin for "to be astonished (or to wonder) at nothing."

2. Thomas Carlyle died on 4 Feb. 1881, the week before this letter was written. Ralph Waldo Emerson, the Transcendentalist philosopher and New England poet, died in Concord, Mass., on 27 Apr. 1882.

3. A reference to Henry Wadsworth Longfellow's "A Psalm of Life," published in *Voices of the Night* (1839). Stanza 4, line 1, reads, "Art is long, and Time is fleeting." Longfellow's didactic poem urged the young to realize that "Life is real! Life is earnest!" and make the most of it with lives of action and "be up and doing, / With a heart for any fate; / Still achieving, still pursuing, / Learn to labor and to wait." The poem was a popular one among JA's schoolmates, who, like JA, were busy sorting out their destinies. JA also liked to allude to it (see also Katie Hitchcock to JA, 11 Aug. 1878, n. 11, above, and Excerpt from Editorial in the *RSM*, Feb. 1881, below). Indeed, JA liked to quote stanzas of poetry on a regular basis to her friends and was known, in response to a quotation game they enjoyed playing, to have one handy in response to any given letter of the alphabet. Over time, friends grew familiar with her favorites. Sarah Hostetter reported, "If Jane got the letter *P* we expected to hear: 'Pleasures are like poppies spread,/ You seize the flower, its bloom is shed; / Or like the snowfall on the river, / A moment seen then lost forever; / Or like the Borealis face, / Evanishing, ere you can point their place.' Or if an *A* turned up: 'All the world's a stage,' etc. No matter what the letter, I am sure even *X* and *Z* had quotations" ("Home and Girlhood," 7).

4. Feb. 1881 was set aside as a month of prayer at RFS, and the situation turned into a revival. Anna P. Sill must have been pleased. She had noted in a letter to Joseph Emerson that

27 Jan. 1881 was the "Day of Prayer for Higher Institutions," and she had written to a former RFS student (who had become a missionary in Persia) during the previous school year that she wished some religious enthusiasm would manifest itself at RFS. "We have daily prayer meetings," she wrote, "but no marked religious interest. Pray for us constantly, daily, that the fountain may be kept pure and the streams make glad the city of our God" (Anna P. Sill to Loretta E. Van Hook, 18 Mar. 1880, RC, Anna P. Sill Papers).

5. John Stuart Blackie (1809–95) was a specialist in Greek and English literature and a proponent of the philosophy of self-culture, especially for students. His works included *Four Phases of Morals: Socrates, Aristotle, Christianity, Utilitarianism* (1871); *On Self-Culture, Intellectual, Physical, and Moral* (1874); and *Language and Literature of the Scottish Highlands* (1876). He later wrote a life of Robert Burns (1888) and a study of Scottish song (1889).

6. JA had repeatedly told friends and peers that she hoped to study medicine. She recalled, "towards the end of our four years' course we debated much as to what we were to be, and long before the end of my school days it was quite in my mind that I should study medicine and 'live with the poor'" (*Twenty Years*, 60–61).

7. English poet, essayist, cultural critic, and educational reformer Matthew Arnold (1822–88) was a professor of poetry at Oxford College from 1857 to 1867. He published several volumes of poems and books of literary and cultural criticism including *Culture and Anarchy* (1869) as well as lectures on Greek and Celtic literature and reports on school systems in Europe. On Arnold's influence regarding nineteenth-century concepts of culture, see the introduction to part 2, above.

8. JA alludes to the last line of the seventh stanza ("These attain the mighty life you see") and quotes (or slightly misquotes) the fifth stanza or Matthew Arnold's "Self-Dependence," first published in *Empedocles on Etna, and Other Poems* (1852). She loved the passage and made it the focus of one of her last editorials as editor-in-chief of the *RSM*. In May 1881 she reminded readers:

> . . . We must confess that the latter heroism has its magnificent inspiring side, but that the danger of young people is to lose altogether the ancient self-centered enthusiasm, and to depend largely upon the excitement of external circumstances. If we gain this habit while at school it will take a desperate effort to exert ourselves when external excitements are taken away. Mat[t]hew Arnold realizes that startling defect when he is standing at the prow of a ship, and looking at the stars, as it so exactly expresses the ideal to be attained, we will commit the uneditorial act of quoting:

> > "Unaffrighted by the silence around them,
> > Unaffected by the sights they see,
> > These demand not, that the things without them,
> > Yield them love, amusement, sympathy." (154–55)

Little did JA know when she wrote this letter to EGS or her editorial in the school magazine that Arnold's themes would so closely match the emotional challenges that would face her throughout the decade following graduation. In addition to losing the community of women she had so enjoyed at school, she would deal with family death, illness, and depression as well as her stepmother's expectations before finally charting a course of self-determination (see *PJA*, 2).

9. JA's plan in her senior year was to finish school at RFS and then go on to Smith College in Northampton, Mass., for a year before proceeding to medical school. Fate and ill-health intervened, however, and the plan went through several permutations. She never attended Smith (see *PJA*, 2).

Excerpt from Editorial in the
Rockford Seminary Magazine

[Rockford, Ill.]   FEBRUARY 1881

... We are often forcibly reminded in our school work of our first attempt at sewing. How often the stitches had to be taken out and the work that cost us a long hour of sitting quietly indoors, had to be done all over again, if we had been in a hurry and had not come up to the requirements of the patient mother. Over-particular, doubtless, it then seemed to us. And again we find ourselves obliged to repeat much of our work. What we think we have stowed away carefully in our memory will not always come forth from its hiding-place when bidden, and thus we find that if we would master the subject we must study it in all its bearings, and by repeatedly turning our attention to it make it our own. But we cannot, with study as with our sewing, undo it all and begin over again, if at any time we become dissatisfied with our progress. It must remain with all its errors, as a continual reminder to us of the imperfectness of even our best endeavors. So with life, in all its various phases; the days come and go, bearing with them an evil or good report, we cannot live them over even though we think we could better them, but, profiting by our failures, must toil on, striving so to "act that each to-morrow finds us farther than to-day."[1]

PD (*RSM* [Feb. 1881]: 55; *JAPM*, 46:292).

1. Here JA quotes, again, from Henry Wadsworth Longfellow's "A Psalm of Life," originally published in *Voices of the Night* (1839). Stanza 3 reads: "Not enjoyment, and not sorrow, / Is our destined end or way; / But to act, that each to-morrow / Find us farther than to-day." Longfellow urged, "In the world's broad field of battle, / In the bivouac of Life, / Be not like dumb, driven cattle! / Be a hero in the strife!" (stanza 5). For another essay by JA regarding study and effort, see "[The Chivalry of Study]," *RSM* version (*JAPM*, 46:170–72; AMs, *JAPM*, 46:164–69).

To John Huy Addams

Rockford Sem'y [Ill.]   March 6 1881

My dear Pa—

We are snowed in so comfortably and are so self-centred naturally that the only way we really feel the storm is by the dreadful delay of letters & hence the array of home sick girls who imagine all sorts of things are happening to the home-folks. I must confess that I feel most nervous when I think of the melting time and imagine the water sprite of Cedar Creek exulting in a demolished dam.

I went to Mary's[1] last Saturday afternoon and so had my share of adventure, I meant to come back Saturday night but it was too stormy to think of that, on Monday morning the train was stuck in a drift about a mile and a half beyond

Winnebago—20 rods long. By dint of two snow-plows and about one hundred men shoveling the came[2] through by half past one and we were the first train to pass triumphantly over the road. Dr Curtis[3] was with me and I felt a firm confidence in his powers, though I fail to see what good learning could have done in case of accident & as for <u>action</u> he is certainly the slowest of men. Of course I got here too late for lessons, but Miss Sill was away the rest were very lenient and so I am none the worse for it in any sense.

Last Friday evening we went to hear Signor Gavazzi[4] an Italian who has been quite prominent in the late revolutions and is now fighting against the power of the Roman Catholic Church in Italy. It was simply a missionary address with the usual statements and statistics but I could fancy a hero after all, for his manner was peculiar and impressive; the church was very full and the crowd enthusiastic.

We have begun swimmingly under Miss Holmes, object & argue in the finest manner possible and she dare not oppose too actively, for as she always says "well! I hav'n't looked the matter up"![5]

Last Friday was Nora Frothingham's birthday, she was twenty one and that it should occur on Garfield inauguration we thought should not be without a celebration.[6] Mattie[,] Helen[7] & myself gave a brunc[h] in her honor and to give tone to the affair invited the too new teachers Miss Williams & Miss Hill,[8] it was evidently a new experiance to them & they enjoyed it immensely. Mary had supplied me with a piece of dri[e]d beef, Mattie had a can of pears, Helen brought rolls and oranges & with popcorn & cho[c]alate we had a gay time, good & select company—certainly in all my experiance in this seat of learning there has never been such a need of impromptu feasts, for the table has been growing steadily worse since Christmas,[9] Mr Dickerman[10] has an economical humor I believe, but it is reported that Mrs Rogers has been making it so uncomfortable that he meditates a speedy reform.[11] The check was duly received, I am very much obliged & will inclose a receipt for the Sem'y fund. Of my semi-annual report, I wish you would please write me what my too marks were, they have been very silent this year about them and I naturally feel a curiosity on the subject.[12]

With much love to Ma & Yourself & with a hope that you are not hopelessly snowed in. Ever Your loving Daughter

Jane

ALS (JAPP, DeLoach; *JAPM*, 1:590–95).

1. A reference to MCAL in Winnebago.
2. JA evidently meant to write "By dint of two snow-plows, and about one hundred men shoveling the rails, we came through by half past one."
3. Probably the Rev. Dr. William Curtis, vice president of the RFS Board of Trustees in 1880–81 and chair of the RFS Exec. Com.
4. Alessandro Gavazzi (1809–99), Italian political and church reformer during the Risorgimento, was a former monk and professor of rhetoric who fell out of favor with the Catholic

hierarchy because of his liberal views. He became an international lecturer in the 1850s. He spoke out against the priesthood in his periodical the *Gavazzi Free Word* and in his lectures, which in more than one Catholic stronghold provoked what became known as the Gavazzi Riots. Gavazzi gradually converted to Evangelicalism and became the organizer of the Italian Protestants in England before returning to Italy in 1860. He became head of the Free Church of Italy in 1870 and in 1875 founded the Free Church Theological College in Rome. His main message was one of doctrinal simplicity and the importance of attention to social problems.

5. A reference to practicing debating under the supervision of Mary E. Holmes.

6. Nora Frothingham and Mattie Thomas were very close friends. Helen Harrington and Mary Ellwood also came to the celebration, which took place on 4 Mar. 1881, the day James A. Garfield was inaugurated as president. Frothingham's was one of a series of Mar. birthdays among the RFS girls in the dormitories. Lizzie Smith wrote to her mother, Annie M. Jordan Smith, on 12 Mar. 1881, "Nora Frothingham had a box sent her for her birthday that did not arrive till a week after. That reminds me that I am almost twenty years old, and soon will have left my 'teens' behind me. I don't like the idea but must make the best of it. Mary Ellwood's birthday is only a few days from mine so 'the girls' said that if we would furnish them something to eat Friday night they would give us presents. We are afraid that the presents won't be worth as much as the necessary eatables would come to" (SHSW, Smith).

7. Helen Harrington (Alderson) (1860–1943) graduated in the class of 1881. Born on a farm in Wisconsin, she was a classmate of JA's at RFS in their junior and senior years, and the two remained lifelong friends. Harrington's family lived in Cedar Fall, Wis., and Caldwell, Kans. She came to RFS knowing no one, and on her first lonely Sunday at the school JA approached her and invited her to walk beside her to church—an honor and also a ritual in a school where students went to church in lines of two, older girls matched with first-year students and sophomores. Harrington was lauded at RFS for her "poetic genius" (*RSM* [July 1881]: 198). Indeed, she was the author of the class poem "Our Lady," a tribute to the theme of the breadgiver (reprinted *RSM* [July 1881]: 201–2). Harrington was one of the first RFS students to earn a B.A. degree at the school. She taught briefly at RFS after graduation and then for several years in a rural Wisconsin district school. She went to Europe at the same time that JA made her second trip there in 1887–88, visiting France, Spain, Italy, and England, including Toynbee Hall. JA asked her to be among the "original group at Hull House," and, Harrington recalled, "I was very much gratified to be invited . . . and would have done so at the time had there not seemed to be insurmountable objections in my way. In the first place, I had no independent fortune, and felt I must earn my living for the present" (Alderson, "Memoirs," 48–49). She was also falling in love. On 20 Apr. 1890 she married William M. Alderson (d. 1920). A son of English immigrants, he mined and farmed in the area of Wisconsin where she grew up. They lived on the Oklahoma frontier for three years, then farmed and ranched in Nebraska and later in the Colorado mountains. The Aldersons had a son and a daughter.

8. Teachers Ella Hill and Ella Williams also joined the party in Frothingham's honor. Ella Cornelia Williams (1854–1935) was born in Watkins, N.Y. She entered the Univ. of Michigan in 1877 and earned her master's degree in the School of Literature, Science and the Arts in June 1880. She was hired in the Dept. of Mathematics at RFS in the fall of 1880 and also served as school librarian. She was called from her teaching duties for a time in Dec. 1880 because of the death of her father. Helen Harrington later informed JA that Williams was the first woman to earn a master's degree at the Univ. of Michigan. Harrington thought that what was often seen as conceit on the part of Williams was actually "self-sufficient pride," which, Harrington believed, the university had fostered (Helen Harrington to JA, 9 Mar. 1882, SCPC; *JAPM*, 1:888–91). Williams, who remained single all her life, went on to teach mathematics at the New Hampshire State Normal School in Plymouth and at a school in Arlington, Mass., before taking a post at Miss Spence's School in New York, N.Y. She worked with the U.S. Draft

Board in the summer of 1918 and with the Red Cross throughout World War I. She was a member of the Episcopal church.

9. The concern with food and eating seems to have been universal among RFS students. JA, like her sisters before her, anticipated boxes of food from home with great pleasure, and she sometimes charged apples as a dietary supplement to her monthly account. A strict regimen was observed in the dining hall, with assigned seating mixing teachers and students and food carefully apportioned. Addie B. Smith wrote:

> Dinner is over now and we had fish, mashed potatoes & rice pudding. Every thing is dished out in nice even little rations to each one and there is just enough to go 'round once. Of course we never take twice of anything because it is not polite here to eat all we want. So Aggie [possibly Agnes Mary Baker of Harvard, Ill.] and I come up to our room after meals & eat apples and I guess we are not the only ones that do. Some of the girls eat something in their rooms and then go down to meals and pretend they are not very well and can't eat much. I think that is a very nice way to make believe you are dainty. (Addie B. Smith to Annie M. Jordan Smith, 28 Sept. [1876?], SHSW, Smith)

In the next academic year, she begged her mother to send her and her sister Lizzie some food, disguising it if she had to in a box of clothes: "I wish we could just have a little something good to eat because I'm getting so tired of this plain Sem. fare and I think Lizzie is too. . . . [everything is] alike everyday. Everything is so strictly healthful. . . ." (Addie B. Smith to Annie M. Jordan Smith, 3 Mar. 1878, SHSW, Smith). Three years later, Lizzie Smith was writing home with the same complaint, dreaming of boxes of food being sent and reporting, "Last Wednesday one of the girls in our class went down to the basement about five o'clock and stole a loaf of brown bread right out of the oven and brought it up to the Senior parlor. Another girl got some butter and we all pitched into that bread as though our lives depended on our devouring it in a certain number of minutes" (Sara Elizabeth Smith to Annie M. Jordan Smith, 6 Feb. 1881, SHSW, Smith).

The issue of the food at RFS seems to have been more than schoolgirl complaints. Rockford College historian Hazel Cedarborg has observed that "food was very poor and poorly cooked" and also spare in portions ("Early History," 118; see also Vallie E. Beck to JA, 2 [and 4] May 1878, n. 1, above). Partying in separate dormitory rooms often involved food, including fudge- and taffy-making. In Jan. 1880, a spoof about illicit candy-making was published in the RSM, written in homage to Poe's "The Raven" (on JA's familiarity with Poe's poem, see also JA to Vallie E. Beck, 3 Aug. 1878, n. 2, above). In the schoolgirl version, instead of the raven it is a suspicious teacher who comes to tap at the door: "'O, girls! it sticks,' the Junior said, / When suddenly there came a tapping, / As of some one gently rapping, / Rapping at their chamber door. / CHORUS: O, candy rich! O, candy rare! / We're caught, we're caught, I do declare, / For study hours we did not care. / Run, girls, run." The guilty girls quickly crowd into the closet with the candy, while the resident of the room innocently presents herself alone at her door: "Inquiring, there a teacher stood, / 'Seems to me I heard a rumbling, / As if some one gently tumbling / Here within the chamber door.' / 'Surely not! only me and nothing more.' / CHORUS: O, candy rich! O, candy rare! / In spite of all we'll have our tear / For study hours we do not care / Eat, girls, eat" (22).

10. Worcester ("W.A.") Dickerman (b. 1820) was a general insurance agent, merchant, and banker in Rockford and the general agent of the RFS Board of Trustees in 1880–81. He was born in Lexington, N.Y., and came to Rockford in 1844 and opened a mercantile business with G. A. Sanford. He was in the banking business for several years and in 1877 was a director of the Second National Bank in Rockford. He married Caroline M. Thomas of Rockford in 1847, and they had two children. He served as county superintendent of schools for two years, and the couple was active in the Second Congregational Church of Rockford. It is not known exactly how involved Dickerman was in the question of RFS food and finances (or Domes-

tic Dept. personnel), but he certainly had a hand in managing RFS money. JA later told GBH that she and other senior class members had been invited to dinner at the Dickermans' and that the trustees had been invited too.

11. Betsy Rogers, superintendent of the Domestic Dept. and RFS cook, left her position within the month (JA to JHA, 20 Mar. 1881, below).

12. Grade reports were sent straight home to parents rather than given directly to students on campus. JA earned the following marks in what was called the "First Series," or first semester, of 1880–81: "Mental Philosophy," 9.8; "Evidences of Christianity," 9.7; German, 10.0; chemistry, 9.9; and Bible, 9.8. In the "Second Series," her final semester at RFS, she would be graded as follows: geology-mineralogy, 10.0; German, 10.0; spherical trigonometry, 9.9; "Crit. Rdg. Anc't. Lit. Comp." [Critical Reading in Ancient Literature, and Composition], 9.5; Latin (Tacitus), 9.9; "Moral Philosophy," 9.9; and Bible, 9.9.

To John Huy Addams

Rockford Sem'y [Ill.]   Mar 20" 1881

My dear Pa

In addition to the storm this week we have had excitement of another character viz—the prospect of starvation[.] Miss Rogers has left[1] and the new cook shows that she share[s] the usual failure of 19" cent women viz—blissful ignorance of the culinary branch of science. Mrs Rogers had recov[er]ed from her sick attack but her son came for her & insisted upon her leaving, I was very sorry to see her go for she has always been a stanch friend of mine and occasionaly in a substantial manner. I received Ma's graphic account of the fete to the orchestra, you must have had a splendid time, music! toasts! and refreshments! what more can there be at court of a King. I wish I had been there, I should have made my best bow to the toast-master & heartily applauded the brilliant and polished response.

Our life has been extremely uneventful, I am engaged just now in antiquarian efforts to dig up from by brain a deep & mature(?) graduating essay,[2] the result has not been extremely flattering but as there is no haste I calmly wait for an inspiration.

Had a letter from Cousin Joe Weber[3] the other day, containing a picture of his graceful countenance, as he very urgently requested a reply I shall make the effort as soon as possible trusting that it will equal his.

The family compact between Miss De Pue[4] and myself seems to prosper, she is exceedingly diligent and as I am naturally very perverse I find myself inclined to be quite the opposite when ever I see her too deeply engaged. We are trying to dress alike Commencement day or rather trying to decide how we shall dress, as there are such marked difference in the finances of the members it seems positively necessary to have our gowns alike, I never realized before how paramount a girl[']s interest in dress is to all others & never in my class-Presidency have I made such mighty efforts to keep some kind of order and peace.[5] We have

finally worked it down to this, that they shall be white and that the entire out-
fit—gloves shoes fans &c shall come within twenty five dollars. One always finds
a great deal in books about the hopes & fears of the "last half" or last term of
your school life, I think I am beginning to realize it.

I hope that this last storm will not [be] severe enough to affect at last the
telephone.

With love to Ma & Yourself[.] Ever Your loving daughter

Jane Addams.

ALS (JAPP, DeLoach; *JAPM*, 1:613–16).

1. "Mrs. Rogers, who has been quite ill for the past two weeks, is slowly improving, we are
glad to say," reported the *RSM* in Mar. 1881 (78). Despite the improvement, Rogers was encouraged by her family to leave her position at RFS. As the official announcement explained
the departure:

> We are sorry to announce that Mrs. Betsy Rogers, who has been matron in the Semi-
> nary for the past seven years, left for her home in Carthage, Mo., a few weeks since. Mrs.
> Rogers suffered from an attack of pneumonia in the winter, and although recovered,
> thought it prudent to leave her work here, and rest for a year or two. Many of the Rock-
> ford students [and] alumnae will deeply regret this vacancy; those who remember her
> kindness and generosity in times past, and those of us who will now miss her motherly
> attention. The work Mrs. Rogers has done in the Seminary will be long remembered.
> (*RSM* [May 1881]: 146)

2. JA's graduating essay was on "Cassandra" and "her tragic fate 'always to be in the right,
and always to be disbelieved and rejected'" (Addams, *Twenty Years*, 61). For the text, see Graduation Essay, 22 June 1881, below.

3. Joseph Weber (b. 1855?) was the son of SWA's brother the Rev. George Weber, Jr., and
Maria Hoffeditz Weber of Vinton, Iowa. The U.S. census of 1880 indicated that he lived at
home and worked on a farm. He probably helped support the Weber family and care for his
paralyzed mother. He eventually lived in Fairsberg, Nebr.

4. Possibly a reference to an informal family arrangement with Lucy Depue, a RFS graduate (class of 1857), who was living in Rockford when JA was a student there. Lucy Depue
married a physician, J. Baldwin Lyman, and moved to Salem, Mass. She lived in Rockford
and Elgin, Ill., before the move to Salem.

5. Lizzie Smith wrote to her mother, Annie M. Jordan Smith, on 7 Apr. 1881 about discussions of how the senior class should dress at commencement:

> I have never told you the idea of our class with regard to graduating dresses because I
> had no faith in its being carried out. . . . a few of the girls set their hearts upon <us>
> having <nice> graduating dresses alike and <u>we</u> decided, that is a majority, decided to have
> them so then we afterward reconsidered the question & decided as long as the dressing
> alike served mostly to be for the sake of lessening the expense some of us suggested that
> calico would be cheaper & the seventeenth girl to read would not look so badly if it was
> the 17th calico dress as if the 17th nice <plain> white dress, so we decided to have calico
> dresses. Miss Sill does not like the idea of our graduating in calico, so we will probably
> end by giving up the idea of dressing alike & dress like sensible mortals, in which case I
> don't know what to get and would be glad to have suggestions. (SHSW, Smith)

JA ended up with a dress of blue silk draped with crepe (see JA to AHHA, 2 June 1881, below).

Excerpt from Editorial in the
Rockford Seminary Magazine

Rockford, Ill. MARCH 1881

...All the world just now thinks of Carlyle with peculiar reverence, and even his most extravagant sayings sound pathetic. He once wrote a sentence to this effect, that the main good many young men gain from a university career is the opportunity to have a fire of their own, and time to think quietly for themselves.[1] Certainly, this is not the least of the benefits which we obtain here, but of late we have had a suspicion that this privilege is being abused, and our leisure time filled up in a peculiar manner. We have noticed a passion for reading the stories in bound magazines, such as the *Eclectic, Home and Fireside,* or even *Harper's* and *Scribner's*.[2] These stories are entertaining and life-like, and in many cases keen and instructive, but, after all, in the long run they will hardly count in our intellectual make-up.[3] We have noticed in various rooms, books poorly bound and printed, in bluish or pinkish paper—in short, we have seen a good deal of trash. We do not mean that many of those books handed so eagerly from girl to girl are absolutely vicious and degrading—such an existent evil would call for a remedy and lecture far beyond our powers—but that these books are enervating and foolish.[4] A hero and heroine are madly in love—it is not very clear to the reader why they are, for both are destitute of qualities eminently lovable—they have a misunderstanding, in which a dark rival figures, suffer untold trials, and are united with a dash of marriage-bells. This story is repeated, with endless variations, and is hardly an ennobling theme to spend one's leisure hours over. While we have a fire to ourselves and time to think, we had better be diligent to gain a clue to an intellectual life, which we can hold fast to when we no longer have a fire to ourselves and time to think, when it may require all our tact and principle to hold fast to our reserved store of beautiful ideas, and will not care a cent whether Imogene married Victor or Clarence. We most heartily endorse the old advice given for a course of reading, viz: "Here are books, fall to!" But, after all, a vitiated taste once formed will be a disgrace and a hinderance to us throughout our lives. "Fall to" with a will, but avoid trash as you would be strong.

PD (*RSM* [Mar. 1881]: 88–89; *JAPM,* 46:308).

1. JA drafted this editorial in 1881, writing on the back pages of her old 1875 diary ("Pocket Diary, 1875[–81]," printed dates 28, 29, and 30 Nov. 1875 [written Mar. 1881?]; *JAPM,* 28:1656–57). She was responding in part to the views of Thomas Carlyle on books. He wrote in "Hero as Man of Letters" and other publications of those things "called 'bits of paper with traces of black ink'" as, ideally, the *"purest* embodiment a Thought of man can have." He also stressed the awesome responsibility of the "Priesthood of the Writers of Books" ("Hero as Man of Letters," 142, 144). In his famous summation of the impact of printing on the democratization of knowledge in the nineteenth century, Carlyle observed that the "true Uni-

versity of these days is a Collection of Books. . . . Once invent Printing, you metamorphosed all Universities, or superseded them! The teacher needed not now to gather men personally round him, that he might *speak* to them what he knew: print it in a Book, and all learners far and wide, for a trifle, had it each at his own fireside, much more effectually to learn it!" ("Hero as Man of Letters," 140, 139).

2. *Eclectic, Our Home and Fireside, Scribner's,* and *Harper's Monthly* were all popular nineteenth-century literary magazines. Specializing in family reading, *Our Home and Fireside* was published in the 1880s by H. Hallett and Co. out of Portland, Me. The *Eclectic* was a monthly digest of foreign literature, science, and art and carried reprints of writing by primarily British authors. Published from the East Coast under various names from 1819 to 1844 and under the *Eclectic* title from 1844 to 1907, it was for many years edited and published by Eliakim Littell (1797–1870). At the end of 1898, the New York–based magazine was sold to one of its rivals, the Boston-based weekly *Living Age.* It was published with dwindling success out of Boston until 1905, ending the last two years of its life back in New York. *Scribner's Monthly* was a literary journal founded by New York publisher Charles Scribner (1821–71) and edited by J. G. Holland (1819–81). It was published from 1870 to 1881. *Scribner's Magazine,* however, begun by the elder Scribner's son (also named Charles) (1854–1930) in 1887 and published until 1939, was geared specifically to a highly educated, intellectual, and professional audience.

Like *Scribner's,* the Harper's periodicals were produced as part of a New York publishing conglomerate and geared toward various audiences. Harper's periodicals in 1881 included *Harper's Monthly* magazine, *Harper's Weekly, Harper's Bazaar,* and *Harper's Young People.* Although it focused on current events and sharp-witted political commentary, *Harper's Weekly* also carried serialized fiction, often as a promotion of Harper and Brothers book publications. The Mar. 1881 issues of the weekly featured illustrations and coverage of James Garfield's presidential inauguration and his cabinet selections (see, e.g., *Harper's Weekly* 25 [19 Mar. 1881]: 181, 184–85; and 25 [26 Mar. 1881]: 204–5) as well as news of such events as the assassination of Czar Alexander II (1818–81) of Russia in St. Petersburg at the beginning of the month ([26 Mar. 1881]: 197). The featured serialized works of fiction in Mar. 1881 were chapters from *Christowell: A Dartmoor Tale* by R. D. (Richard Doddridge) Blackmore (1825–1900), author of *Mary Anerley* (New York: Harper, 1880) and *Lorna Doone* (New York: Harper and Bros., 1874); portions of *Asphodel* (New York: G. Munro, 1881) by "Miss M. E. Braddon" (Mrs. Mary Elizabeth Braddon Maxwell) (b. 1837); and *Into the Shade* (New York: Harper and Bros, 1881) by Mary Cecil Hay (1840?-86). In the latter, a schoolgirl roommate of the protagonist exclaims, "You have left your studies at last, Eve; I'm so glad!" and the girls share their dreams in their bedroom before leaving school (*Harper's Weekly* 25 [19 Mar. 1881]: 186). The 19 Mar. 1881 issue of the weekly listed new books from Harper and Brothers, including a study of Mme. de Staël, and the 26 Mar. 1881 issue advertised their publication of the works of Thomas Carlyle, including the American release of *Reminiscences* (194, 207).

Vols. 61 and 62 of *Harper's Monthly,* published during JA's senior year at RFS, included issues produced from June to Nov. 1880 and from Dec. 1880 to May 1881. Featured fiction writers and poets included Sarah Orne Jewett, Henry Wadsworth Longfellow, Rose Terry Cooke, Robert Burns, Rebecca Harding Davis, Elizabeth Stuart Phelps, Alfred, Lord Tennyson, James Russell Lowell, and Walt Whitman. Essays by such intellectuals as Charles Francis Adams and Moncure D. Conway offered opinions on American education (including the expansion of women's education and scientific education) or profiles of figures who loomed in JA's own education and private reading, including John James Audubon, Thomas Carlyle, and George Eliot. JA could also find good sources of reference for future trips in articles on the English Lake District and information about its writers (including Thomas De Quincey). In addition, there were descriptions of master works of Christian Italian art and places of historical significance in the life of Martin Luther as well as profiles of the belles of Baltimore.

Special departments were echoed in smaller, more parochial scale in JA's own "Home Items" or other departments featured under her editorship of the *RSM*. The Editor's Literary Record included a review (in Oct. 1880) of Joseph Cook's new collection of Monday lectures and announcement in the Editor's Historical Record (in Mar. 1881) of the 22 Dec. 1880 death of George Eliot, at age sixty, in London.

Art history and urban history both had a place in the era's feature writing. Articles appeared on the Dutch masters; "ladies'" arts (porcelain painting, lace making); major cities, including Chicago and Washington, D.C.; and on urban living and labor conditions. The latter foreshadowed issues that would be the focus of JA's life at Hull-House, including reports on Italian street life, immigrant squatter life in New York, and working women's labor. William H. Rideing's "Working-Women in New York" in June 1880 was a discussion of sweatshops and factory work, artificial flower making, book binding, millinery, cigar making, and working as a seamstress or shop girl.

3. It is likely that JA grew up familiar with the offerings of *Harper's Monthly*. A run of the magazine, beginning with the first volume in 1850, was among the titles in SAAH's library upon her death. We suppose that this periodical was originally the property of the Addams family in Cedarville. *Harper's Monthly* published short stories and serialized novels that appealed on different levels, varying from what would become recognized as canonical literature to popular romantic fiction, regionalism, and dialect stories. Serialized novels that appeared in the magazine during JA's senior year included Henry James's *Washington Square* and Thomas Hardy's *A Laodicean*. In a more popular vein were the installments of William Black's *White Wings: A Yachting Romance*, R. D. Blackmore's *Mary Amerley* (chap. 48 was entitled "Short Sighs, and Long Ones"), and Constance Fenimore Woolson's *Anne* (with an illustration captioned "Dear me! what can be done with such a young Savage?").

Such stories were wickedly lampooned in William H. Baker's "A Helpmeet for Him," printed in the Mar. 1881 issue of *Harper's Monthly* (596–603). It featured a romance-writing heroine, Matilda, who, "If her intellect was narrow and not too vigorous, at least she had not burdened it with learning too heavy" (601). Matilda's character exemplifies the principle JA propounded in her Mar. 1881 *RSM* editorial. Matilda's intellect is "A frail spark at best," but "she had heaped upon it the chaff of the lightest of literature, there had been so very much of such fuel also, that the flame, if she was not to suffocate, must find outlet." She does so by writing an impassioned "story in which the hero was to do deeds more daring than man ever conceived of before. As he was to be the handsomest of men, the heroine was to surpass all women in loveliness, devotion, [and] desperate daring" (602). When Matilda has "got hero and heroine through whirlwinds of tribulation, and married them at last, enormously rich, universally beloved by their happy peasantry, with strong likelihood of their ascending the throne of their own land, the gifted writer was all of a tremble." She must lie down to rest for the remainder of the afternoon (602).

Undone by her flimsy literary efforts, Matilda is even worse off in her marriage. When she who "had always been the frailest of vines" and has no strength of her own confronts the death of he who "had been the sturdiest of oaks," she dies—a dire warning for girls not to follow in a similar, mindless path (603). Aside from satirizing sentimental female roles and the standard paradigms of romance fiction, the story also illustrates popular prejudices about women writers and ideas about women's ill-health and frailty. Mental activity, for example, was thought to wear away at the weak female brain and nervous system. It would take quite some time before Virginia Woolf's woman writer with a room of her own would take her place beside Thomas Carlyle's male student and enjoy the intellectual quiet of his fireside.

4. The widespread reading of popular fiction was a not-very-well-kept secret among RFS schoolgirls. JA jotted down a scene drawn from campus life: "The sophmores in class were discussing that scene in 'Guy Mannering' when Bertram <1st> lands on the estate of his forefathers, one student expressed it as her opinion that ~~it~~ <~~the [scene?]~~> was overdrawn 'My,'

she says, 'it is just like ~~dozens~~ those affected ~~of such~~ scenes that I've read ~~in~~ <dozens of> in cheap novels' & a warning pinch stop[ped] her[.] 'Dont confess it,' whisper her neighbors ~~modestly wishing~~ to conceal her knowlege & the class generally look scared" ("Pocket Diary, 1875[–81]," printed date 15 Sept. 1875 [written 1879?]; *JAPM*, 28:1619).

To John Huy Addams

Shortly before she wrote the letter to her father printed below, Jane Addams had been to see her family in Cedarville for a brief spring-break visit. On May 8, she wrote to tell her father about her experiences traveling to the Interstate Oratorical Association contest at Jacksonville, Illinois.[1] The regional contest was sponsored that year by Illinois College,[2] with related events held at the cluster of other schools in the small city. Quite a bit was at stake in the trip, for Addams went to Jacksonville not only to cover the interstate contest for her magazine but also to politick among the powers-that-be within the leadership of the state and regional oratorical associations in order to help win approval for Rockford to enter their ranks.

In Addams's senior year, Anna P. Sill was anxious for Rockford Female Seminary to be accepted as an official member of the (Illinois) Intercollegiate Oratorical Association. Beginning in the 1870s, the organization encouraged debating contests between participating Illinois colleges. It organized an annual contest between orators from member colleges within the state, the winner of which went on to represent Illinois in an annual regional competition sponsored by the Interstate Oratorical Association.[3] In 1881–82, Rockford vied to become the only all-female school among the colleges involved in the organization. All the other affiliated institutions were coeducational[4] with the exception of Jacksonville's own Illinois College—a men's college and a debating powerhouse.

Mastery of the persuasive techniques of oratory and debate was considered an important benchmark of a good late-nineteenth-century education. As George Bowman Haldeman well knew, social life in the societies at the all-male Beloit College centered on lively weekly debates. At Rockford Female Seminary, a professional elocution teacher came in to drill girls in preparation for their public addresses, including their Junior Exhibition speeches and the oratory of commencement week. Debates and oratorical essays were regular features of Vesperian and Castalian Society programs, and debating arguments were drafted in classes, where girls were assigned to argue positions pro or con on a given issue. Memorization— of poetry or meaningful quotations from major thinkers—was part of being prepared for public speaking. The emphasis on reasoning on one's feet extended into the oral examinations that Rockford students had to pass before their committee of examiners at the end of each school term. Beyond that, what the Beloit Round Table called "the culture and discipline of the debate" set intellectual standards and helped prepare participants—especially males—for influential roles in public or civic life, whether as ministers, attorneys, missionaries, teachers, or local politicians.[5]

Anna P. Sill's desire to earn an equal voice for the Rockford girls in oratory contests was but one part of her larger campaign to bring education at Rockford Female Seminary completely up to the standards of men's schools. It was also one more mark on the measuring stick of the rivalry that existed between the women students at Rockford and the male students at Beloit College and a chance for seminary students to demonstrate that they could stand against orators of either sex from other Illinois institutions, including the larger state schools.

Cultural attitudes about intellectual excellence, aptitude, and gender lay behind the push to gain the opportunity to compete in oratorical association meetings. Sill and students like Jane Addams recognized that oratorical contests were a chance for young women to exhibit their powers of logic and persuasion and argue positions and ideas in open forums. Integrating college women and men in major speaking competitions in the 1870s and 1880s was no small endeavor. Earlier in the century, women were effectively barred from public speaking, and traditionalists still frowned upon those who addressed audiences from stages, podiums, and pulpits during Jane Addams's time at Rockford Female Seminary. The Rockford girls' efforts to gain admission to the association thus meant struggling against established popular opinion. It also meant countermanding the prejudice of some young male oratorical association officers who opposed the inclusion of women in what was often a boys' club or fraternitylike atmosphere. As the Round Table *explained, "The social benefits of such societies are perhaps as great as their literary value."[6] For many leaders in the oratorical organizations, male camaraderie was part of the point. From their viewpoint, the presence of women compromised the competitive enterprise and changed and crimped fraternal style.[7] There was also the matter of circumventing the doubts of conservative members of Rockford Female Seminary's all-male Board of Trustees, including Beloit College president Aaron Lucius Chapin, about expanding the role of women at the school and elevating the status of the institution in comparison to men's colleges.*

Jane Addams succinctly summed up the process in her memoirs: "In line with this policy of placing a woman's college on an equality with the other colleges of the state, we applied for an opportunity to compete in the intercollegiate oratorical contest of Illinois, and we succeeded in having Rockford admitted as the first woman's college."[8] The change came in 1882 after Addams had graduated from the seminary, but the admission of women was set in motion partly by her persistence as a representative of Rockford in her senior year.[9]

The details of Addams's exact role as an orator in the intercollegiate context are contradictory and open to some conjecture. Although no extant documentation definitively reveals her as a contestant in competitions between colleges, in Twenty Years *she wrote—decades after the actual events—about representing Rockford Female Seminary in intercollegiate competition. The details of that account imply that the contest was in Jacksonville.[10] She recalled her self-consciousness at the time. She was speaking not just as an individual or as a pathbreaking delegate of a women's college but as a representative of "women in general" who was in the service of the "progress of Woman's Cause."[11]*

Addams used a self-deprecating tone of amusement in her rich recollection of her performance as an orator carrying the standard for women in competition with men. She reported being told ahead of time that she "had an intolerable habit of dropping [her] . . . voice at the end of a sentence in the most feminine, apologetic and even deprecatory manner which would probably lose Woman the first place." When the judges' votes were in at the end of the particular contest, she recalled, she found herself ranked "fifth, exactly in the dreary middle."[12] While she busied herself with other appointments after the contest, garlands her friends had prepared for the victory celebration wilted along with their high hopes. Addams observed wryly that she felt her median ranking was quite appropriate and that failing to come out at the top in the contest was not entirely due to her not-yet perfected speaking mannerisms. She pointed out that one of the competitors who placed above her was none other than William Jennings Bryan,[13] who later became recognized as the greatest orator of his generation. Although male competitors worried about the emotional edge female orators might gain over the judges, just the opposite happened in the competition in question. According to Addams, Bryan upstaged her when he "thrilled" his auditors "with a moral earnestness which we had mistakenly assumed would be the unique possession of the feminine orator."[14]

In recounting her efforts to represent her sex against the best that male oratory students had to offer, Addams may have conflated more than one situation in her memory. Her appearance in the same contest with Bryan must have been an intercollegiate meeting between Illinois contestants and not an Interstate Oratorical Association meeting such as that which pitted representatives from different states at Jacksonville in May 1881. Neither she nor Bryan competed in the interstate meet, which she attended as an auditor and in her capacity as editor of the Rockford Seminary Magazine *and not as a speaker. Her memories were possibly of an earlier (Illinois) Intercollegiate Oratorical Association event such as the one held at Knox College in Galesburg in the autumn of her senior year.[15] Nevertheless, Addams made the most of her May 1881 trip to Jacksonville. The contacts she formed there helped lead to the official inclusion of Rockford Female Seminary in intercollegiate competitions during the following academic year.*

Rockford Semy [Ill.]   May 8" 1881

My dear Pa—

Your kind letter came yesterday, I am glad Ma had a longer visit at Carroll and I hope that Mary came home Saturday. I have been on a journey since my last letter and have a long story to tell; I have some times doubted the wisdom of it and I hope it won't seem to you sudden and erratic.[16]

The editors of the Magazine received an invitation to the Inter State Oratorical Contest held at Jacksonville last Wednesday evening[17] and at the same time there was to be held a Conclave of the College Editors from the same six states viz. Wis. Iowa. Ill. Minn. Ind and Ohio. Miss Sill has been anxious for some time to have Rockford Sem'y enter the State Contest, <so> she was very desirous to have two of the Editors go to open negotiations, and like wise to bring forward the institution ~~to~~ <by> bringing forward the magazine. The Pierian Union raised $20 & delegated Hattie Wells[18] and myself to go and we forth with started on Wednesday morning on the C. & Q. road,[19] we expected to change at Aurora for Peoria to Galesburg, but found after we started that we could not make connections at Galesburg and so went on to Chicago & took the Chicago & Alton, this brought us into Jacksonville in the evening and so we missed half of the contest but were in time to hear the successful orator from Indiana,[20] he took the first prize a gold medal $75., and to share all the excitement in the decision of the judges, I never realized before what a bond of sympathy college & state ties represent. The second prize was taken by Minn,[21] the Iowa orator was a lady[22] <who stood 3d> her subject was Hypatia & the criticism offered was that she was over oratorical almost theatrical. Much to our disappointment Ill stood last,[23] The <Ill orator> was very kind to us indeed gave us all necessary directions in our arrangements for next year, he was very cool over his defeat but seemed to feel very much disgraced. Of course after Ill we were interested in Beloit College and that orator stood next to the last to our disgust. He was Mr Salisbury[.][24] You have probably heard George speak of him as he boards at Mr Greenleaf's,[25] I never saw anyone more dispondent than he was after the contest, & all the time he was talking about it we could hear the Indiana men out-side singing college songs of triumph. The Committee of Entertainment had us in charge and showed us every possible attention and politeness, the next day we met the officials, most of the orators & a great many of the editors and accomplished our business satisfactorily, received more compliments on the magazine than we had ever dreamed of & only hope they were all sincere. Visited the Deaf & Dumb Asylum & two of the college[26] & Thursday evening attended a contest between the two societies of Knox & Ill College[27] escorted thither by two editors of the "College Rambler,"[28] the committee of intertainment provided entertainment for all the editors—that is paid our hotel bills, & we could not possibly have been better provided for. It was <an> experiance entertaining and decidedly different from any thing I ever had before, we got more into the spirit of College life than I had ever dreamed of. We wanted to stop at Springfield but thought we ought to get back on Friday, the Chicago train Friday morning was three hours late but even then we would have made connections with the north-western if the Wells St bridge had n't been turned & we missed it.[29]

Hattie Wells' home is in Geneva and as we were tired she insisted on our going out there all night—about an hours ride—& taking the train next morning. Her father & mother are very pleasant indeed, we rested splendidly & came on Saturday as fresh as could be. Miss Sill & the Pierian Union seem perfectly satisfied with our report,[30] & we certainly had a good time, Jacksonville seems to me one of the prittiest towns I ever was in. Of course I would have felt much

better satisfied & comfortable if there had been time to write home & see what
you & Ma thought of such an undertaking—but unfortunately there wasn't
time. I know a great deal more about the colleges in the six states & the internal
workings of the oratorical ass. than I ever did before, and I hope the added experiance & information will make up for the lost time here.[31] We think the[32] fully
sustained our dignity & after our negotiations it ought to be very easy for the
school to enter the State contest next year at [Bloomington, Ill.?], after this long
a/c[33] I won't expatiate any more until I see you. Give my love to Mary, kisses to
Web & Esther.[34] With much love to Ma & Yourself[.] Ever Your loving daughter

Jane Addams.

P.S. Our class appointments have been decided, the 2n Honor or Salutatorian is Nora Frothingham,[35] the Valedictorian is your most humble servant &
most loving daughter.[36] Do not think I am puffed up, I too will realize how little it is worth or signifies, the only gorund[37] of satisfaction is—that I hope the
home folks will be pleased. Mrs Forbes[38] gives the Alumnae Essay, it is somewhat of a coincidence, is n't it?

Please tell Ma I am having my gingham dress fixed & so won't need a new
calico. Inclosed please find my bill for the full school year.[39] Miss Anderson forgot to put in my drawing which I added.

ALS (UIC, JAMC; *JAPM*, 1:621–28).

1. The Jacksonville contest had been anticipated at RFS for a year. The "Clippings and
Exchanges" section of the June 1880 *RSM* provided a brief synopsis of the results of the May
1880 Interstate Oratorical Assn. meeting at Oberlin, Ohio. Five states were represented, Illinois, Indiana, Iowa, Ohio, and Wisconsin (Missouri did not send a representative). The top
two prizes went to male speakers. L. C. Harris of Grinnell College, representing Iowa, placed
first with an oration on Poe. Second prize went to Richard Yates of Illinois College, who spoke
on "The Evolution of Government." The *RSM* announced that the next annual meeting
would be held in 1881 in Jacksonville (191).

2. Illinois College, located on West College Ave. in Jacksonville, was founded in 1829 by a
group of seven Yale Univ. graduates who were interested in offering Christian education in
the state and wanted to establish an institution for men on the Yale model. Edward Beecher
(1803–95), the brother of Henry Ward Beecher, Catherine Beecher, and Harriet Beecher Stowe,
was the first president of the college. Illinois College was among the first colleges in the state
to graduate a class of scholars. It went coeducational in 1903 when it merged with the Jacksonville Female Academy, founded 1835.

3. The formation of state- and regional-level collegiate oratorical associations was an outgrowth of the emphasis on public speaking in campus-based literary and debating societies
(like RFS's Castalian and Vesperian societies or Pierian Union). The (Illinois) Intercollegiate
Oratorical Assn., founded in 1873, fostered intercollegiate contests between teams of orators
from various member colleges within the state of Illinois. Each fall it sponsored an annual
contest at a different location within Illinois, wherein the best orators from the member
schools competed against one another and crowned a first-place winner or state champion.
The Interstate Oratorical Assn., organized in 1874 and involving six states in 1880–81, provided opportunities for those orators who reached the top echelons in statewide intercollegiate competitions to represent their respective states in an annual regional contest, which
was held in a different state each spring.

4. Although most of the (Illinois) Intercollegiate Oratorical Assn. member colleges were coeducational, the majority of active orators were young men, and men dominated the leadership of the oratorical associations. Rivalry was keen. When the association became solidly established during the mid-1870s, eight schools participated: (what was then called) Chicago Univ. (later the Univ. of Chicago); Illinois College; Illinois Wesleyan; Industrial Univ. (later the Univ. of Illinois); Knox College; Monmouth College; Northwestern Univ.; and Shurtleff College. The number and exact nature of participating colleges fluctuated somewhat over the years because some less prestigious schools had difficulty maintaining approval for their admission.

5. "College Societies," reprinted in "Clippings and Exchanges" (*RSM*, Dec. 1879): 270–72, quotation on 272. The article dealt with the relative merits of extracurricular oratory in Beloit education. Beloit had two debating societies—the Alethean and the Delian—which each Wednesday held debates and united under Archaean Union auspices for inter-society debates three times a year, much as the Vesperians and Castalians debated each other in Pierian Union programs at RFS. The author of the "College Societies" article described the weekly gatherings "at which a question is discussed by four men previously chosen, and then by any members of the society voluntarily, after which the president gives his decision." He then explored a question: "what are the beneficial and what the injurious influences of the debate[?]" On the down side, he observed, learning information through debate tended to make "research one-sided, a study after arguments to support a given side, instead of a search after truth. Such study overlooks some truths and perverts others, and is wholly unscholarly. . . . 'Read not to contradict and confute . . . but to weigh and consider.' Bacon's wise, oft-quoted words apply as well to hearing as to reading." On the positive side, however, he concluded, that the "practice of extemporaneous debate cultivates a readiness of speech and a quickness of thought which are always valuable. It sharpens the wit and the tongue. . . . It moreover clears one's ideas of vagueness. It brings what one only thinks he knows to the keen test of expression; a man knows only what he can tell" (270–71).

6. "College Societies," 272.

7. Sexism in the oratorical associations took many forms. As at RFS, there was a close association between the personnel of college debating societies and college magazines. Thus leaders of oratorical associations often were the same young men—or close friends with them—who held the power to report on oratorical contests. Some male editors of college journals maintained a covert political silence about female oration and refrained from mentioning women's participation in events. Other opposition was more overt, such as the unsuccessful movement within the business wing of the Intercollegiate Oratorical Assn. in 1880 to officially bar females from participation. Young men who opposed the participation of women claimed inherent superiority over their female counterparts as a reason for excluding them. Women's participation, they charged, lowered the quality of competition. They simultaneously cried foul, however, when women did participate. It was widely believed that when women won or were ranked high in contests it was not because they were deserving but because judges unfairly favored them out of chivalry—or because they made manipulative, "womanish" use of sentiment and emotion. At issue, in part, was the subjective evaluation of male and female styles and the ways that individual judges reacted to various choices of theme and uses of emotion on the part of men and women speakers.

8. Addams, *Twenty Years*, 53. RFS may have been the first all-women's college to become an institutional member in the intercollegiate association, but individual women's abilities to succeed in the contests had already been proved. The first woman orator (a student from coeducational Monmouth College) participated in an Intercollegiate Oratorical Assn. contest in 1876, and a woman won the state contest in 1878.

9. RFS prepared to compete in the fall 1881 intercollegiate contest but due to a technicality did not participate until the following academic year (n. 31).

10. JA recalled that after the contest she went to visit the "state institutions, one for the Blind and one for the Deaf and Dumb," which she did in conjunction with covering the oratorical contests in Jacksonville in May 1881 (*Twenty Years*, 54; see also n. 26). She told her father in this 8 May 1881 letter that she had "Visited the Deaf & Dumb Asylum & two of the college[s]" in Jacksonville.

11. Addams, *Twenty Years*, 53.

12. Addams, *Twenty Years*, 53. JA implied here that there were either nine or ten participants in the contest, a detail of significance in identifying the specific contest in which she appeared with William Jennings Bryan.

13. William Jennings Bryan (1860–1925), a student at Illinois College in Jacksonville and a member of the class of 1881, was a superb college orator. He was vice president of the (Illinois) Intercollegiate Oratorical Assn. and influential in its internal politicking. He and JA would both go on to become famous public speakers. They had a good deal in common. They were born in the same year, and both were raised in small Illinois towns (Bryan was from Salem, Ill.). Both of their fathers were civic leaders and state senators, and each died when Bryan and JA were in their twenties. Bryan and JA both became outstanding orators at their respective colleges and graduated in the same year as valedictorians of their classes. While JA went to medical school in Philadelphia after finishing at RFS, Bryan attended the Union College of Law in Chicago and graduated in 1883. He went on to become a member of Congress from Nebraska, serving two terms, from 1891 to 1895; a popular Democratic party presidential candidate in 1896, 1900, and 1908; a leading Populist intellectual; and, like JA, a major spokesperson for peace and nonviolence. Bryan never achieved his goal of the presidency, but he served as secretary of state in the Wilson administration from 1913 to 1915. He was world-renowned for powerful political oratory and earned a fervent political following. His "Cross of Gold" speech, advocating a silver standard (to which JA alludes in *Twenty Years*, 53), which he delivered at the Chicago Democratic National Convention in 1896, is one of the most famous addresses in American history. Bryan is also remembered for his highly publicized legal defense of the principle of religious fundamentalism in the Scopes trial of 1925. In that trial, which occurred at the end of his life, Bryan represented the state's position in the successful prosecution of John T. Scopes, a Tennessee public school teacher being tried for teaching Darwinian theory in a biology classroom. Scopes's defense team included Chicago-based attorney Clarence Darrow (1857–1938). Although Bryan won the case and Scopes was convicted, the conviction was overturned on a technicality, and the publicity of the case influenced statutes on religious freedom across the nation. Bryan died in Dayton, Tenn., on 26 July 1925, five days after the conclusion of the trial.

14. Addams, *Twenty Years*, 53.

15. It is possible that JA may have represented RFS—and competed against Bryan—in the annual Intercollegiate Oratorical Assn. meeting sponsored by Knox College and held in Galesburg, Ill., on 13 Oct. 1880. Documentation for this period of JA's life and of the fall contest is scanty. Although school newspaper accounts do not mention JA, Bryan was definitely a participant. He placed second, much to the surprise of his Illinois College classmates, who felt his was the most moving address of the day. The Jan. 1881 *RSM* carried the following notice in the "Clippings and Exchanges" section: "The *Rambler* devotes a good deal of space to an interesting account of the oratorical contest held at Galesburg, Wed., Oct. 13. The first prize was awarded to Erskine, of Monmouth; the second to Bryan, of Illinois College" (20).

Part of the confusion over the course of these events is that there is no known extant JA correspondence from the autumn 1880 period and thus no letter from her describing her experiences in that time frame, which might have made mention of Galesburg. Nor is there any Knox College archival record of her presence at Galesburg in Oct. The Galesburg contest is not mentioned in either the Nov. or Dec. 1880 issues of the *RSM*, which JA was editing. Some biographers have attributed the version of the contest with Bryan that JA gave in

Twenty Years to faulty memory blurred by hindsight and the passage of decades between the writing of the memoirs and the actual events. Others accept circumstantial evidence that supports her participation at the Galesburg intercollegiate event.

The conflated version of events that JA presented in *Twenty Years* in 1910 was further impressed into the public mind when Bryan's biographers reprinted, during the 1920s, a photograph of him from his college oratory days. Pictured with him are seven young men and one young woman, the latter identified as JA. As M. R. Werner captioned the photograph in an article on Bryan printed in *Liberty* (12 Jan. 1929), "Bryan as an Illinois College student, representing his alma mater on a debating team. He is standing, fourth from the left. The girl is Jane Addams, later of Hull House" (9). A copy of the same photograph had earlier been reprinted in Bryan's *Memoirs* (1925). Probably captioned by his widow, Mary Baird Bryan, who prepared the memoirs for publication after her husband's death, the photograph was identified as "Intercollegiate debating team, representing six middle-western colleges. The lady is Miss Jane Addams; the tallest figure standing is that of Mr. Bryan" (84f).

Winifred Wise further advanced the photograph as evidence of a JA-Bryan oratorical encounter when she described it in detail (in a synopsis of JA's account of the oratorical experience from *Twenty Years*) in Wise's authorized biography, *Jane Addams of Hull-House*, which was finished before JA's death in 1935 (83–84). In *Jane Addams*, Linn, who did not use the photograph, describes JA in the Interstate Oratorical Contest with both Rollin D. Salisbury and William Jennings Bryan and dates the event in June 1881 (53). Wise placed the contest in Galesburg.

Doubts persist about the provenance of the photograph. It is not certain that the young woman depicted is JA or that all those pictured were orators rather than the attendees at an oratorical event. The caption in Bryan's *Memoirs* implies that only six of the nine people in the picture were speakers. Although the woman shown is certainly slight and dark-haired, like JA—and it could perhaps be she—her identity has not been definitively established. The Interstate Oratorical Assn. contest that JA witnessed at Jacksonville in May 1881 included six contestants, only one of whom, Minnie Bronson of Iowa, was a woman.

Another first-person account of the contest supports both JA's memories of her big moment onstage as well as the photograph's caption. In 1917, after recently re-reading *Twenty Years*, one of the other individuals pictured wrote a letter of appreciation to JA. Writing on 9 Apr. 1917 from Willows, Calif., Henry W. Read placed the event that JA described in her memoirs in Galesburg. He had been, he told JA, "on the reception committee at Knox College, at the time of [the] contest you speak of." Read remembered "quite distinctly how you looked on the platform that night; also the tall, <u>slim</u> lad with the scholarly face, who represented Ill. College" (the "tall, slim lad" was Bryan). "I remember, too," he went on, "how scared we boys were for fear the judges would award you the prize 'just because you were a girl.'" Read graduated from Knox College (the "Athens of the West") the following year and joined its faculty as a Greek instructor. As a faculty member, he helped sponsor oratorical events. The controversy about whether to include girls in oratorical competitions continued, he confessed, to be a source of conflict. Contrary to not being good enough, girls were often too good. Boys ascribed girls' success not to merit but to favoritism. "[W]e of the Knox faculty were early beset by the question," Read reported, of "what to do about the girls in declamation contests. They were taking all the prizes & the boys were calling loudly 'unfair!'. Hence separate contests for girls were established" (SCPC, JAC; *JAPM*, 10:1055–56).

16. This introductory passage of JA's letter seems to indicate that she was unsure how her father would react to news of her activities. It is also clear that she received no specific parental consent before traveling to Jacksonville.

17. The contest in Jacksonville was held on 4 May 1881.

18. Former Vesperian Society president Hattie Wells of the RFS class of 1882 was the "Business and Exchange" editor of the *RSM*. She promoted the seminary magazine and managed

the "Clippings and Exchanges" section, which featured exchanges of news from the magazines produced by other colleges. The contacts she had through her role on the magazine staff made her an obvious choice to help negotiate for RFS in Jacksonville. Wells, also an excellent debater, gave "The Power to Perceive Beauty" at the Junior Exhibition of 1881. Anna P. Sill preserved a copy of Wells's graduation speech, "The Great Man Theory," in her scrapbook.

19. The Chicago, Burlington, & Quincy Railroad.

20. It is often incorrectly said that the successful orator from Indiana was William Jennings Bryan. It was not. The first-place orator was Charles F. Coffin of Asbury Univ. (now DePauw Univ.) in Greencastle, Ind., who represented Indiana. Bryan was from Illinois. Coffin spoke on "The Philosophy of S[k]epticism." JA described his delivery as "individual and forcible" (RSM [June 1881]: 174) and reprinted his winning entry in full (taken from Illinois College's College Rambler) in the same issue (184–90; see also JAPM, 46:362). Bryan was present at the proceedings in Jacksonville in 1881, but as a consequence of his second-place ranking in the intercollegiate contest in Galesburg in Oct. he was not one of the speakers. JA may have heard him debate at a separate intercollegiate contest held between Illinois College and Knox College at the Illinois State School for the Deaf on the day after the interstate competition concluded.

21. The representative from Minnesota was the second orator of the evening, Owen Morris, of Carleton College, St. Olaf, Minn. Morris spoke on "Progress, Its Sources and Laws."

22. Minnie Bronson, the orator from Iowa, was the lone woman in the contest. She spoke on "'Hypatia,' drawing around her the momentous forces of the fifth century. The only criticism offered on this oration, was that the delivery was too dramatic" (RSM [June 1881]: 173; JAPM, 46:361).

23. The Illinois representative was J. S. E. Erskine, who spoke on "'The People in History.' The oration was pre-eminently thoughtful and logical, but the delivery attempted too much of the Websterian, and largely detracted from the impressions of the oration" (RSM [June 1881]: 173–74; JAPM, 46:361–62).

24. Rollin D. Salisbury, editor of the Beloit Round Table, with whom JA was already well acquainted. Salisbury had previously won the Wisconsin state oratorical contest in 1880. At the Jacksonville contest he "delivered the third oration of the evening, his subject 'Two Englishmen,—a Scotchman and a Jew.' His delivery was pronounced and impressive. Gladstone and Disraeli were closely compared and contrasted" (RSM [June 1881]: 173; JAPM, 46:361). The entry was reprinted in the Round Table ([6 May 1881]: 134–37; see also Collie and Densmore, Chamberlin and Salisbury, 73–74). One observer gave a frank evaluation that on the evening of the contest Salisbury was "too matter of fact in delivery to stand high as an orator." He further observed that dramatic style was not a key indicator of good intellect, as Salisbury's subsequent career as a public intellectual proved (Collie and Densmore, Chamberlin and Salisbury, 72). The pressure to succeed at the contest must have been great for Salisbury.

The fact that Beloit College would be representing the state of Wisconsin at the interstate contest was front-page news in the 18 Mar. 1881 issue of the Round Table, and Beloit friends Roger Leavitt and Harry Williams accompanied Salisbury to Jacksonville for the contest under the Archaean Union's sponsorship. The trip turned out to be a fortunate one for Leavitt. He met William Jennings Bryan on the train on his way to the event. Bryan subsequently backed Leavitt's successful candidacy as president of the Interstate Oratorical Assn. for 1882. Leavitt was elected at the business meeting that took place the day after the contest. Happy for himself, he was only "sorry that Rollin did not win the prize!" (Leavitt, "Memoirs," 44).

The final orator, whom JA does not mention, was R. S. Lindsay of Oberlin College, the representative of Ohio. He spoke on "Byron."

25. Salisbury boarded at the home of the L. L. Greenleaf family in Beloit, along with GBH.

He had taken his meals at the Greenleafs since he began school at Beloit College in Sept. 1878. Roger Leavitt also lived at the Greenleafs for part of his time at Beloit (from 1878 to 1881). He remembered that his northeast "room at Mrs. Greenleaf's . . . was cozy and comfortable. The pipe from the coal-stove below ran through my room and helped warm it. I had a little cast-iron box stove which easily warmed the room. The room was so small that my wood-box stood in the hall. We boys all sawed our own wood." Later the Greenleafs moved from that house "just north of Prof. Porter's" to one "just east of the city park, formerly occupied by the Plants" (Leavitt, "Memoirs," 18, 28). There, Leavitt had the "front parlor on the first floor facing the west," a larger room than that he had occupied in the other residence.

The Greenleaf home was the site of some heavy-handed attempts to bring Salisbury—who, like JA at RFS, was "unconverted"—into the evangelical fold. Leavitt recalled to a Salisbury biographer (and former classmate) that he saw Salisbury at the Greenleafs every day and took the opportunity to go to his room frequently and, "Again and again we discussed what it meant to be a Christian, but he could not see it as I did. . . . He said he was an infidel, did not believe the Bible. I made poor work explaining its statements." While JA retained her position of passive resistance against constant evangelical pressure from faculty and peers, Salisbury "fought the battle in his room" and eventually stood up at a meeting and made a public proclamation of his acceptance of "Jesus Christ as his Saviour" (quoted in Collie and Densmore, *Chamberlin and Salisbury*, 67).

The humble life that Luther ("L.L.") Greenleaf (1821?–84) and his wife Elizabeth M. Greenleaf (b. 1819?) led in Beloit hinted little at their former social stature. Both were born in Vermont. When he was young, L.L. Greenleaf worked in the Boston house of Fairbanks & Co. before he came west in 1868 to establish the mercantile firm of Fairbanks, Greenleaf, & Co. of Chicago. He took up residence in Evanston, Ill., where he engaged extensively in real estate business and became a major benefactor to philanthropic causes and to Northwestern University. Prominent in university development, his gifts to the school included the twenty-thousand-volume Greenleaf library of classical literature, art, philosophy, and religion. His business fortunes as well as his emotional and physical health were destroyed by the effects of the Great Chicago Fire of 1871 and the financial panic of 1872. His wife Elizabeth, a strong supporter of female education in Evanston, managed what was left of Greenleaf's business affairs, and in the mid-1870s the family retired to Beloit, where they lived quite simply in protection of L.L. Greenleaf's health. The Greenleafs took in students as boarders, enjoying their company and supporting student endeavors on campus, and Greenleaf cared for Prof. Joseph Emerson's horse.

The Greenleafs had been longtime temperance advocates and Temperance Alliance volunteers. They were early influences upon WCTU president and Evanston resident Frances Willard, whose brother, Oliver, attended Beloit College and who was a guest in the Greenleafs' Beloit home in 1878. Willard, in her history of Evanston, remembered the Greenleaf of old as a "man of senatorial face, figure and bearing; one to be noted anywhere, even as was Saul among the prophets; a model of ethical exactitude, warm with brotherly kindness and open-handed in deeds of charity—such was L. L. Greenleaf, long the leader among 'men of means' in Evanston. . . . He was foremost in all our enterprises, looked with manly zeal and pride upon the growth of Evanston, and was, no doubt, our favorite citizen" (*Classic Town*, 224, see also 225).

The Greenleafs had a direct impact on Willard's WCTU activism as well as a hand in her career as an educator, for Willard read Temperance Alliance literature as a young teacher and attended an Alliance social at which she took her first temperance pledge. She later taught both Greenleaf daughters, Mary and Helen, at Northwestern Female College, where Elizabeth Greenleaf was a member of the board of trustees. The Greenleafs also had a son, who died during their years in Evanston. Helen Greenleaf, an artist, married James Simmons, a friend of Rollin D. Salisbury's and a Beloit graduate in 1883. Simmons became a professor of psychology at Grinnell College, Grinnell, Iowa, in 1889. Mary Greenleaf, a favorite of both Salisbury and GBH and a visitor to the Addams family in Cedarville, was an 1875 graduate of the RFS Conservatory of Music. She taught school before she married businessman James C. Plant in Sept. 1882. Her husband had attended Beloit College in the class of 1874 but did not graduate. He was working in Minneapolis when he courted Mary Greenleaf. The Plants' wedding ceremony was performed by the Rev. James J. Blaisdell, Sarah Blaisdell's brother.

L. L. Greenleaf died and was buried in Beloit. He was lauded as a "highly cultured, benevolent, enterprising gentleman" who was "very highly regarded by his business associates and by society" in the obituary run by the *Evanston Index* on 29 Nov. 1884, which gave "nervous prostration" after a decade of failing health as the cause of his death.

Elizabeth M. Greenleaf, a favorite among Beloit students, was a reliable patron of the college's debating societies. In 1881 she gave the juniors an engraving, the "Signing of the Emancipation Proclamation," for the Delian Society room at the school, and she and her husband regularly sponsored parties for the boys, including a grand one given for the junior class in Feb. 1881. It featured sleigh rides around the city before a sit-down dinner, with music and orations in the parlor after the meal. The party was considered the "Juniors' debut into society as a class" (*Round Table* [4 Feb. 1881]: 91). After her husband's death, Elizabeth Greenleaf remained living at 204 Church St. in Beloit. Both she and her daughter Helen were listed as at that address in the 1891 Beloit city directory (86).

26. References to the Illinois State School for the Deaf, probably the Illinois Female College (now MacMurray College), and the Illinois State School for the Blind, all located in Jacksonville. The Illinois State School for the Deaf opened in 1843 with a small student body and grew over the years into one of the largest schools for the deaf in the country, with a large campus on the west end of College Ave. The Illinois State School for the Blind, founded in 1847, was well known for its excellent music school and opera performances. The Illinois Female College (originally the Illinois Conf. Female Academy) was established on State St. in 1846. The Methodist Episcopal school for women was renamed MacMurray College in 1930 after a senator who contributed generously to the institution. In 1881, Illinois College boys came over to campus to help the girls at Illinois Female College decorate the grounds with Chinese paper lanterns on the occasion of a reception for delegates of the Interstate Oratorical Assn. contest. The *Jacksonville Journal* proclaimed the evening one of great beauty and brilliance.

27. The Illinois State School for the Deaf was host to a contest between the literary societies of Illinois College and Knox College. The Phi Alpha Society of Illinois won the debate, but Knox's Adelphi Society won the essay, declamation, and oratory contests, emerging as the champion.

28. JA was squired about in part by A. W. Small, an Illinois College student active in oratorical association politics and part of the group of Intercollegiate Oratorical Assn. members in charge of a reception at the Jacksonville contest. Among the other events there was a sit-down banquet and a huge dance. Small, like JA, was editor of his college newspaper, *College Rambler*. The *Rambler* was regularly featured in the "Clippings and Exchanges" section of the *RSM*. The *Rambler* staff produced a special interstate edition of their magazine in honor of the oratorical contest, and the *Round Table* referred readers to it: "[The] Jacksonville *Rambler*, containing a full account of the Inter-State contest and giving the first three orations in full, is on the exchange table in the reading room" ([20 May 1881]: 151).

JA formed a good working relationship with Small at the Jacksonville event. He promised to keep her posted with inside information about who delegates would be to future contests. He wrote to her after she had returned to Rockford to tell her of his personal support for RFS's efforts to enter the Intercollegiate Oratorical Assn., although, he cautioned, his position was unofficial: "As for myself I do not see why Rockford should be refused admittance: but others may differ." Small included a copy of his special *Rambler* edition on the interstate contest and closed with "Hoping that you enjoyed your trip and regretting that you labored under so many disadvantages" (11 May 1881, SCPC, JAC; *JAPM,* 1:638). When the time was right, Small kept his word and did his part to help the RFS women's cause. He wrote an editorial endorsing the RFS request for admission into the oratorical association and published it in the *College Rambler* on 1 Oct. 1881 (79).

29. JA and Hattie Wells were changing railroad lines in Chicago, and therefore train stations. They had apparently arrived at a station located south of the Chicago River. The Chicago and North Western Railroad lines left from a station north of the river. The Wells St. bridge over the Chicago River was a center-pier swing bridge. It was evidently turned so that tall-masted vessels could move freely on the river on their way to and from Lake Michigan.

30. The June 1881 *RSM* carried a full synopsis of the interstate oratorical contest (173–74).

31. RFS did indeed leap into action. As the June 1881 *RSM* reported:

> [The] result of the trip by the representatives to the Inter-State Contest at Jacksonville, was itself the cause of numerous mass meetings of the school. Arrangements were discussed for the honor contest, with a view to being admitted into the State Assn. in the fall. Many of Rockford's loyal students are very anxious for this, their alma mater, to be identified with this association. We can but trust that by the friendly aid of our brothers, we may stand hand in hand with them in their many struggles and victories. Our home contest will probably take place June 10th, when music will be interspersed between orations, and all we hope will "go merry as a marriage bell." (169–70)

The practice oratorical contest took place on 14 June 1881 and included only girls who would be students at RFS the following year. Appointments were made in May, and those chosen to partipate were juniors Kittie Waugh, Minnie Marks, and Julia Gardiner; sophomores Mary Waddell and May Brown; and freshman Hattie Fay. The contestants appeared on the platform along with the four class presidents, including JA. Waugh spoke on "The Decline of Absolutism," Gardiner on "Heroism in the 19th C.," Waddell on "The Influence of Great Minds," and Marks on "Difference of Opinion." The judges chose Kittie Waugh as the orator to represent RFS in the intercollegiate contest in 1881–82; Minnie Marks was selected as the alternate. "That Rockford may obtain a right to compete in the State and Inter-State contests," the *RSM* staff editorialized, "and that her representatives may do her as much honor abroad as at home, must, we are sure, be the desire of every one who heard the orations on Tuesday evening" ([July 1881]: 206–7).

The *Rockford Register* greeted the event, "the first oratorical contest ever held in the institution," along with Class Day and Junior Exhibition events that had been newly added to the annual tradition at RFS, as one more sign of the raised standards of the seminary and proof that the "vigorous young womanhood represented there is certainly proving itself worthy of the highest opportunities which can be offered it. . . . Next fall, in the city of Bloomington, will be held a State Collegiate oratorical contest, to which six colleges of Illinois are allowed to send contestants. Among these six, it is not unlikely that Rockford Seminary, the first female college ever admitted, will be permitted to appear. The colleges which win appointments in the State contest are allowed to enter the lists in the Inter-State contest which occurs every spring. Tuesday evening's orations, then, were delivered for the purpose of electing an orator to the State contest at Bloomington, which is itself a preliminary to the inter-State contest of next year." The newspaper then described the content of each young woman's oration and explained that the presentations were judged on the basis of "thought, composition, and oratory" ("Collegiate Contest," undated newspaper clipping, ca. 15 June 1881, Sill, "Scrapbook").

RFS was admitted into the Intercollegiate Oratorical Assn. at the association business meeting held in conjunction with the annual contest at Bloomington, Ill., in Oct. 1881, but the admittance came too late for a RFS delegate to compete in that contest. RFS participated in the next state competition, held in Oct. 1882. That contest was historic in that four of the eight colleges participating—Illinois Wesleyan, Illinois Industrial Univ. (now the Univ. of Illinois), and Chicago Univ. joined RFS in sending female orators. Moreover, the winner was a woman: Myra Pollard of Chicago Univ. (Monmouth College *Collegian* [14 Oct. 1882]: 7–11).

The large showing and success of women provoked a backlash. Pollard's win was contested as a scoring error on the part of the judges and, in an association ruling, overthrown. She was thus replaced by a male contestant as the Illinois representative in the spring interstate oratorical contest. In 1883 the association business meeting again considered a motion to ban women officially from participation in intercollegiate association contests. Although the motion did not pass, its spirit was still effective. At the end of the decade all orators in the state competition were male.

32. JA meant to write "we think we fully sustained."

33. Abbreviation for the word *account.*

34. MCAL, with two of her children, son James Weber and baby daughter Esther Margaret, was visiting in Cedarville.

35. Nora Frothingham gave the salutatory to open the commencement exercises "in flowing Latin clearly enunciated" (clipping, June 1881, Sill "Scrapbook"). She also spoke on the subject of "Monopolies."

36. JA closed the commencement program with her valedictory and her address on Cassandra (see 22 June 1881 documents, below).

37. JA probably meant to write the word *ground.*

38. The Addams family's friend, Laura Jane ("Jennie") Gorham Forbes, for whom JA was probably named, was an 1858 graduate of RFS. She gave the alumnae speech at the 1881 commencement. Entitled "After the Snow Banks," it was delivered at the end of the program, just before JA's valedictory comments and oration.

39. The enclosure is not extant.

To George Bowman Haldeman

"Puffed up" or not, Jane Addams was justly proud of being named valedictorian of her class. Although she imparted the information to her father in a carefully low-key manner through the artful use of a postscript, she communicated the deep pleasure of her success to her stepbrother George more directly, and he did not follow her instructions to burn the letter. This letter contains Jane's first hint that Anna P. Sill favored her receiving a collegiate degree—a process that would not reach fruition until the end of the next academic year.

Rockford Semy [Ill.]   May 8" 1881

Dear George

You have probably heard from the Beloit delegation of my journey southward and my condition of mind therein. Suffice it to say that we had all possible attentions and politeness shown to us, at the same time accomplishing the object for which we were sent and which Miss Sill so earnestly desires. I enjoyed the trip and felt all the excitement of a college contest, sometimes doubt the wisdom of the undertaking & it seems a little bit erratic, but as I had a very pleasant experience and since my return feel vivified and strengthened I do not regret the time lost; I will enlarge on the subject when I see you at present more important matter[s] claim my attentions[.] The appointments are for Salutatorian Nora Frothingham, & your most humble servant gives the Vale Dictum, I do not feel puffed up, in short it appears of less consequence to me now than it ever did, & it was never a passionate ambition, please say nothing at home for I am going home in a few weeks & will then disclose,—Now comes my important object of writing, on this you will please swear eternal secrecy & likewise give to me your most mature and deliberate opinion for I need it, and although you may not know it, I have great confidence in your judgement on these kinds of questions.

The Trustees & Faculty will add this year a post-graduate course of one year, and whoever takes this course is entitled to the degree of B.A. in other words is a college graduate. Now I have had a little more than a <full> years extra work & thereupon Miss Sill has offered to me this degree if I want to take it next Commencement,[1] of course it has not yet been offered by the Trustees & Miss Sill may be immature in her offer, I simply want to made up my mind what to do if it comes regularly endorsed by the officers.[2] I know better than any one else how little my scholarship is worth, & I do hate a spread especially if I have the first class honor & too if I ever take a degree at Smiths it will be perfectly absurd to have had this one first. On the other hand I think it would rather please Pa, & the class would of course be anxious to have me do it, for there are two girls in the next class who will run something of a chance for it, & it is natural to want to be the first class. Miss Sill puts stress on it as being important to have a girl do it at once, bring forward the rank of the institution & incite other girls to try for it; she thinks now I have refused but will undoubtedly renew the subject. This is as I stand, remember you are the first to be taken into the confidence of the subject & I would like your honest ideas.

This epistle is mostly about myself, not from egotism, but because from necessity just now my thoughts are largely subjective. Your loving Sister

Jane Addams

I think this epistle had better be consigned to the flames.

ALS (JAPP, DeLoach; *JAPM*, 1:629–32).

1. Although JA ended up being at the center of the issue of RFS degrees, the hoped-for transition of RFS from girls' seminary to a degree-granting college had begun well before she entered the school and did not find full fruition until the 1890s. Many students, including JA, felt that the school's curriculum and research facilities were not being modernized and improved fast enough. Anna P. Sill worked continually behind the scenes to strengthen the collegiate aspects of RFS education. She lengthened coursework to four years to match that of nearby men's colleges and the women's colleges of the East. She also did what she could to raise faculty salaries in order to attract the most highly qualified teachers available, in each case attempting to match the offerings and quality of instruction of Beloit College.

On 30 June 1877, during the summer before JA began school at RFS, Sill wrote to RFS trustee Joseph Emerson that she could "see no remedy now but that the Seminary takes a college rank in form as soon as practicable and give degrees as such, asserting full college powers. I care nothing for the name <u>college</u> or <u>seminary</u>. I only want the fact" (BC, EB). As it happened, the granting of degrees preceded the official changes in name of the insitution. JA's class of 1881 was the "first class which takes the standard of the advanced course." In 1882, JA was among the first few RFS graduates granted a collegiate degree (Anna P. Sill to Loretta C. Van Hook, 18 Mar. 1880, RC).

2. The RFS Board of Trustees authorized the granting of individual bachelor's and master's degrees effective the 1881–82 academic year. JA returned to RFS and received her A.B. at the June 1882 commencement exercises. For more on the decisions and actions of the RFS Board of Trustees and the first degree-granting commencement at RFS, see RFS Board of Trustees, "Minutes of the Annual Meeting," 1882; *RSM* (July 1882): 230, 233–37; and *Rockford Register,* 21 June 1882 (see also *PJA,* 2).

To George Bowman Haldeman

Rockford Sem'y [Ill.]   May 29" 1881

My dear George

I plead guilty to a long pause in our correspondence, but I wish you could be induced to write as usual, for I feel the need of cheering influences now if ever before—for I am tired and rather worn out, though in much better trim than I was last year.

Had a lovely visit home last Sunday with three of the girls, I intend to do all I can and go every-where I can from now until Commencement, and see if I can mantain respectable health and spirits.

We will have our Senior examinations a week from next Wednesday,[1] and from that time on will be mainly engaged with elocution and class-day work, there is a certain charm in the prospect and our last few weeks promise to be happy ones for the girls are unusualy gentle and obedient to their unworthy Pres in particular & to everyone in general.

My essay is ready for the finishing touches, I am disappointed in it because I have had to cut it down over & over again, until it seems to me crude and a little obscure—which I hate above all things—but there is a certain satisfaction in knowing on that day that you are not saying nearly all you want to say on your subject. I wish you would write me a little dissertation on your idea of the Scientific method of education, on the results and habits of mind gained from the study of natural science.[2] I think it would help me just where I am obscure. Don't think I mean to plagiarize.

The Senior Class & teachers were invited out the other evening at Mr Dickerman's,[3] met the trustees & others having a delightful time where we had rather anticipated a bore.

I am reading Kingsley's <u>Hypatia</u>,[4] of course find it exciting but hardly as powerful as I had anticipated. Excuse this short letter. Your loving Sister

Jane Addams

ALS (UIC, JAMC; *JAPM,* 1:642–43).

1. Lizzie Smith informed her mother, Annie M. Jordan Smith, on 5 June 1881, that "Tuesday afternoon and Wednesday morning [7 and 8 June 1881] we have our final examinations, after that no more studies for us" (SHSW, Smith). The members of the RFS Board of Examiners for 1881, all from Illinois, were: the Rev. Edward Eaton of Oak Park, the Rev. Charles Caverno of Lombard, the Rev. Henry M. Curtis of Belvidere, the Rev. C. R. Lathrop of Rockford, Prof. C. S. Richards of Washington, the Rev. H. J. Ferris of Stillman Valley, and the Rev. M. F. Sargent of Winnebago. The time between examinations and commencement on 22 June was taken up with Class Day festivities and the 14 June 1881 RFS oratorical contest.

2. GBH was able to lend his stepsister some expertise not only in methodology and science, his field of specialty, but also in approaches to public speaking. In the 1880–81 academic year, he was active in Beloit College's Alethean Society and participated in debates sponsored by the Archaean Union (Beloit College's counterpart to the Pierian Union at RFS). GBH was featured in a Archaean debate in Nov. 1880, and in Feb. 1881 he had become vice president of the Alethean Society. If he replied in writing to this letter from JA, the reply is not extant.

3. RFS General Agent Worcester ("W.A.") Dickerman.

4. Charles Kingsley (1819–75), an English curate and novelist, was a vicar in Hampshire and professor of modern history at Cambridge (1860–69). His *Hypatia; or, New Foes with an Old Face*, published in *Fraser's Magazine* in 1851 and in book form in 1853, is set in fifth-century A.D. Alexandria and centers on the character of the beautiful Hypatia, daughter of the mathematician Theon. Hypatia was a teacher of Neoplatonic Greek philosophy. As a result of her outspoken intellectualism, she was killed by a mob of enraged Christians. Minnie Bronson, the lone female contender, had made Hypatia the subject of her oration in the Interstate Oratorical Contest in May. Perhaps JA's interest in Hypatia arose from that encounter.

Announcement in the
Rockford Seminary Magazine

Under Jane Addams's editorial direction, the "Home Items" section of the seminary magazine included the following notice about the appearance of the Transcendentalist thinker and innovative educator Bronson Alcott,[1] who was appearing in Rockford as part of a lecture tour. His visit caused quite a stir among RFS students who, like Addams, had read Little Women *and other favorites by Louisa May Alcott during their childhoods.*

[Rockford, Ill.]   MAY 1881

A. Bronson Alcott, a famous philosopher of the Concord school, was in Rockford almost a week, quickening the intellectual pulse of the entire community. Many of the students heard him Sunday evening, April 12th, on the immortality of the soul, its descent from God, passage through the earth and return thither. The hero worship, and enthusiasm there created, steadily increased until Tuesday evening. The lecturer's subject was "Methods of Study," but there was a constant expectation and hope among the younger members that he would "tell us of his daughter Louise and the rest of the little women," and they were not disappointed. We will not try to reproduce the lecture. Mr. Alcott first pre-

sented the threefold aspect of the human mind, and the development and culture necessary to each, the great quickening and vivifying power for women is
through the affections, intuition is to be guarded as one of her highest endow-
ments. He then illustrated, by the education of his own four daughters, they
began to keep journals as soon as they could write, and above all things their
individuality was fostered. He closed with incidents, and the manifold experiences of Louise Alcott. We feel confident that the effects of this one lecture will
be long felt in Rockford Seminary.

PD (*RSM* [May 1881]: 139).

1. Amos Bronson Alcott (1799–1888), the neighbor of Ralph Waldo Emerson and father of
Louisa May Alcott (called "Louise" in the *RSM* account of his visit), was founder of the Temple
School in Boston (1834–39), a superintendent of schools in Concord, Mass. (beginning in
1859), and the operator of the experimental Concord School of Philosophy (1879–88). Alcott
developed systems of education that stressed aesthetic appreciation and the beauty of the
environment, the use of imagination and play, and the development of conversational skills
and self-expression. Many of his ideas were considered too radical by parents, but they were
admired by his friends Emerson and Thoreau and by many educators who followed him. The
chosen topic of his lecture in Rockford (on the nature of the mind) involved one of his favorite philosophical subjects. Alcott's utopian dedication to alternative philosophies and
approaches was not a lucrative way of life, and his family was largely supported by the writings of his daughter Louisa, whose first novels about family life in New England, including
Little Women, were published when JA was a child in Cedarville (see also introduction to part
1, n. 167, and JA to Vallie E. Beck, 30 Mar. [and 2 Apr.] 1876, nn. 2 and 3, above). Louisa May
Alcott supported her elderly father throughout the 1880s and continued to publish until her
death. Her last novels, *Jo's Boys* and *Garland for Girls,* appeared in 1886 and 1888.

Announcement in the
Rockford Seminary Magazine

[Rockford, Ill.]   MAY 1881

The subject for the last public society given by the Castalians was "Lectures."
Six were given during the evening—brief but explicit. The first on the program
was a lecture on Temperance[1]—illustrated by diminutive sketches of underground caverns; the catacombs of the metropolis, beer, wine and ale; inscriptions on the various casks.—Lizzie Smith. The second—The Sunday School
Man,—in which was portrayed the average man of the times, with his usual
sayings—Alice Atkinson.[2] Following this was a stump speech; sticks or wood;
high boxes being prepared for the orator; said orator an advocate, *pro tem,* of
the Democratic ticket.—Julia Gardiner.[3] The fourth was a Phrenological lecture;
the secretary of the society was the victim for the evening, whose several bumps
were sadly deficient in places where wise men protrude; a skull present declared
the degeneracy of mankind.—Jane Addams.[4] Fifth, the beneficial results of
elocutionary drill were ably shown by the recitation of Old Mother Hubbard;

"Tears were seen trickling down every nose," and the audience was swayed by every utterance.—Miss Anderson.[5] The sixth and last for the evening was a lecture on Morals; the flirt and model girl were shown as living illustrations of the lecturer's sound words. The speaker announced before closing that if any questions were to be propounded, the audience might remain, but no autographs would be given.—Edith Evans.[6] Music by Lola Manatte[7]—strictly literary—closed the *resumi* thus briefly given of the lecture course this winter.

PD (*RSM* [May 1881]: 136).

1. The temperance movement was strong in Rockford and among Missionary Society activists on the RFS campus. It built momentum in the town with the Women's Crusade of 1874, a prayer and saloon-intervention movement facilitated by women through the churches and spurred in part by the general evangelical revival that swept Illinois in the mid-1870s, bringing with it a new spirit of social consciousness that had a significant impact on educational and religious practice. The movement received support from faculty at RFS and, in Wisconsin, at Beloit College, where professors like the Blaisdells came from families that had a long tradition of temperance reform. Like the Addams family, most educators and students at RFS supported the Republican party, one wing of which had formally endorsed temperance as part of its political platform.

In the city of Rockford, meanwhile, the temperance movement received particular support from the Swedish immigrant community. By the 1890s the majority of backers of "dry" businesses were residents of Rockford's Swedish wards. A special referendum in 1881 allowed local women to voice their opinions against the licensing of dram shops. Men were more ambivalent, however. JA, in the May 1881 *RSM*, offered the following editorial opinion on the referendum:

> The ladies of Rockford, at the late city election, obtained a shadow of their "rights" long clamored for. They were allowed the privilege of putting in their votes, but the votes could not count. There must have been some satisfaction in going to the polls, for there certainly was none in thinking their votes helped along the good cause. We suppose, however, this is step toward eventual suffrage, and as such ought to be applauded, but at present it seems but a mockery. The license party triumphed. We suppose each one is at liberty to draw his own conclusions, and put his own construction to the matter. (155; *JAPM*, 46:354)

The success of a later anti-drinking referendum in 1914 made Rockford officially a temperance town and established an "anti-saloon" section of the city where liquor was banned. Frances Willard, the driving force behind the WCTU, was a presence in Illinois temperance policy in the mid-1870s, when she headed the Chicago WCTU and was president of the Illinois Union before becoming national president of the WCTU in 1879. In Oct. 1881 the WCTU formally linked the causes of temperance and woman suffrage during their Washington, D.C., convention.

2. Alice Atkinson (Sprague), class of 1881, was described as "a blonde, with a gentle, calm expression shining from that placid countenance" (*RSM* [July 1881]: 194). She specialized in art, music, and French studies; at the Junior Exhibition of 1880 she read a paper on Marie Antoinette and sang a song in French. She was from West Salem, Wis. After graduation she taught at RFS, and during the 1880s she taught art and painting in La Crosse, Wis., and Astoria, Oreg. She married Clark W. Sprague, a sea captain and shiploader, in Seattle, Wash., in 1891, and made her home in that city. She died in Tacoma, Wash., in 1952.

3. Julia Evangeline Gardiner (1860–83) was one of the outstanding members of the class

of 1882. She had attended Wellesley College, Mass., in 1877–78 before coming to Rockford. She was an editor of the "Home Items" section of the *RSM* under JA's direction in 1880–81. Like Alice Atkinson, she was interested in French studies and gave the French oration at the Junior Exhibition in 1881 and wrote on topics of French history for the *RSM*. She was vice president of the Presbyterian Society at RFS in 1880–81 and one of the school's leading debaters. Gardiner was the youngest daughter of the Rev. A. S. and Caroline Gardiner of Lena, Ill. She was ill at the time of her graduation, when she earned her B.A. She moved east with her family to New Hampshire, where her father took up a new post as a pastor immediately after her graduation. She died in Nashua of consumption on 26 Aug. 1883. In 1886 her father published the lecture that he gave at RFS for her senior class on 22 Feb. 1882, dedicating it lovingly in her honor. Anna P. Sill was "deeply attached to the industrious, painstaking, and accomplished graduate" (clipping, Sill, "Scrapbook").

4. JA at this point in her life was apparently able to poke fun at the neo-science of phrenology, which had fascinated her stepmother (if not herself when a teenager). She was able to speak with some authority, having had a phrenological reading of her head done five years before (see Phrenological Reading, 28 Jan. 1876, above). Phrenology, like temperance, the water cure movement or hydropathy, the anti-tobacco movement, dress reform, vegetarianism, and other theories about health and social ills, was linked to a reform mentality and political progressivism. In terms of aesthetics, it also appealed to avant-garde intellectuals and literary elites, such as Poe or De Quincey, who were interested in psychology, magnetism, mesmerism, the occult, and altered states. In its belief in physical, inherited causes for emotional and psychological behavior it was also connected to emerging evolutionary theories in ethnography, biology, and anthropology that prescribed notions of superiority and inferiority to perceived stages of "civilization" and cultures—the categorization not of the head's bumps and crannies but of "Races, Tribes, and Families of men" (quoted in Stern, *Heads and Headlines*, 213).

5. Sarah Anderson.

6. Edith Hood Evans of Buda, Ill., was a special student at RFS in 1879–80. She studied in the Dept. of Drawing and Painting in 1879–80 and 1880–81 and was a sophomore in the Collegiate Dept. and also a member of the graduating class of the RFS Conservatory of Music in 1880–81.

7. Lola A. Manatt (sometimes spelled "Manatte" or "Monatt") of Brooklyn, Iowa, was a RFS Preparatory Dept. and Conservatory of Music student in 1879–80. She returned to Rockford after her studies to teach and accompany, including events at RFS. The Jan. 1881 *RSM* reported, "Miss Lola Monatt, one of our last year's students, is again in the city, and pays her attention to music exclusively" (44).

To Anna Hostetter Haldeman Addams

Rockford Semy [Ill.]   June 2 1881.

My dear Ma

We can't come, one thing is adding up on another until it is impossible to do anything outside, I never realized before just exactly what the last of the Senior year meant. Had a letter from Miss Greenleaf[1] saying she had laid her plans to come, but has since receivid word of cousins who were coming to spend next Sunday & so she gave up the idea of course. In order to keep up the see-saw of invitations she invited me to spend the Beloit Commencement week with her, making it very kind & urgent, of course I refused but it amused me. The Rockford people are coming out splendidly to our class, as they have never done before—much to Miss Sill's delight. We are invited to Mr Talcotts[2] next Friday evening & on Tuesday evening to Mrs Gregory's[3] on Tuesday evening to meet the Beloit Seniors[4] & the first of the week we have our examinations. My essay is <u>completed</u>! to my relief, I wanted to read it to you and Pa when I came home this time & now that is impossible. I send you a sample of my dress & hope you will like it, the entire thing is to made of blue silk & draped with the crape, it will [be] a great deal more becoming I suppose than the dead white although not as elegant. I found that the best white silk (the kind if wanted) was $4. < 4.20 a yard bringing the goods up to about $76.00 which was absurd, the goods <u>proper</u> now have cost $32.00 and the whole thing complete will be under $50.00, my first experiance in buying a dress has been rather a nove[5] one but I have not been worried or restless about it.

Last Friday evening we were invited to Mr Dickerman's[6] with quite a large company, had one of the nicest times I ever had out in Rockford.

I send you one of my proof to give you a faint idea of the struggles I am having for a picture, I did n't take that one rather objecting to mouth & Miss Blaisdell assertion that I looked 14.[7]

Hope that you have not made plans for us & will not be disappointed. With love to Pa & Yourself

Jane

ALS (SCPC, JAC; *JAPM*, 1:650–53).

1. Mary Greenleaf was the daughter of L. L. and Elizabeth M. Greenleaf, with whom GBH boarded in Beloit (not to be confused with Mary Irvine Hostetter Greenleaf, JA's step-cousin). She taught in Beloit and had been invited to Cedarville for a visit. There was some discussion with GBH about the invitation, which Greenleaf accepted in July. She wrote to JA about her trip to Chicago and sent her a copy of Rollin D. Salisbury's valedictory address (JA to GBH, 31 May 1881, UIC, JAMC; *JAPM*, 1:644; Mary Greenleaf to JA, 21 July 1881, SCPC, JAC; *JAPM*, 1:676–79). GBH and Mary Greenleaf remained friends, and he mentioned her in letters to his mother, AHHA, later in 1881 and in early 1882.

2. Talcott was a significant family name in Rockford and RFS history and remained so for generations. The family of William Talcott (whose sons were Thomas, Wait, Sylvester, and Henry Talcott) was among the first white settlers of the Rock River region in the 1830s. They came from Rome, N.Y., in 1835 and in 1837 took up residence at Rockton, Ill. The Talcott saw and grist mills, which opened in Rockton in 1839, were the first to be operated on the power of the Rock River. Wait Talcott (1807–90), one of William's sons, was a strong proponent in the 1830s and 1840s of the establishment of Beloit College and a Rockford-area female seminary and served as a state senator from 1854 to 1858. He was one of the incorporators of RFS in Feb. 1847 and involved in hiring Anna P. Sill. Talcott married Elizabeth Anna Norton. In 1858 their daughter, Adaline Elizabeth Talcott, married Ralph Emerson (b. 1831), a lawyer and wealthy businessman who invested widely in Rockford manufacturing, textiles, and lumber industries as well as insurance companies, banks, and electric power companies. He was a longtime member of the RFS Board of Trustees.

William ("W.A.") Talcott (d. 1900) was a prominent Rockford businessman; his wife, Fanny

Jones Talcott (d. 1925), was a RFS graduate. The couple were key supporters of RFS. W.A. Talcott was an owner of Emerson, Talcott & Co., a manufacturing company started by Wait and Sylvester Talcott, along with Ralph Emerson and others, in 1854. The company, which produced reapers, was a leader in the burgeoning Rockford farm implement industry. W.A. Talcott also owned the property on which the Rockford Country Club was founded in 1900. The Talcotts were members of the Rockford social elite, philanthropists, and strong supporters of education. They were frequent hosts of social events related to RFS and Beloit College.

The Talcotts moved in similar social circles with other RFS board members, and their home at 436 North Main St. was a center of hospitality for RFS students, faculty, administrators, and benefactors and for the social events related to RFS and Beloit College. Among other influential individuals involved in the seminary and college faculties and administrations, the Talcotts were close to the Emerson families of Rockford and Beloit; the Lathrops; the Perrys; and Beloit College president (and RFS Board of Trustees member and original incorporator) Aaron Lucius Chapin (1817–92).

Both of the Talcotts were important fund-raisers for RFS, active in the RFS Endowment Com. and themselves generous donors to the school. W.A. Talcott was a member of the RFS Board of Trustees from 1883 to 1900. He became a member of the RFS Exec. Com. in 1888 and served as president of the board from 1894 until his death shortly before Christmas in 1900. He and Ralph Emerson donated the money to build the Emerson Music House building on the RFS campus in 1892. Throughout the 1880s and 1890s, Talcott worked hard to build the school's endowment and encouraged—often in jovial fashion—wealthy friends to contribute as well, usually in the form of monetary gifts targeted for specific purposes, whether books for RFS classes or a new organ for the Conservatory of Music.

Fanny Jones Talcott joined Anna P. Sill in donating reference books and a art-photograph filing system for the RFS art dept. She was active in the RFS Alumnae Assn. in Rockford and often hosted meetings and parties. At the 22 June 1881 RFS Alumnae Assn. meeting she presented a resolution "That the Alumnae appreciate the benefit that would accrue to this institution by the erection of a hall for scientific purposes, pledge their co-operation with the trustees in raising the necessary funds." The resolution was adopted, and Fanny Talcott was appointed to the committee of three "to carry into effect the above resolution" ("Alumnae Meeting" clipping, June 1881, Sill, "Scrapbook").

The desire to improve scientific education at RFS was not the only cause that Talcott championed that also concerned JA. As she was preparing to graduate, Talcott was firmly lobbying for another cause dear to her heart—the inclusion of women on the RFS Board of Trustees. That issue would be won, with both JA's and Talcott's participation, in the following year (see RFS Board of Trustees, "Minutes, 10 May 1883"; see also PJA, 2).

Fanny Jones Talcott was the recipient of an honorary degree from RFS in June 1882. In 1885 she became the first president of a newly formed organization, the Student's Aid Society, an outgrowth of the older Rockford Education Society. The group, whose slate of officers included Anna P. Sill and Sarah Anderson, raised money for scholarships, scholastic prizes, and financial aid to needy students.

The Talcotts were devoted friends of Sarah Anderson, and they actively and kindly supported her administration when she became principal of the school in the 1890s. Fanny Jones Talcott (called "Mrs. W. A. Talcott" or "Madame Talcott" in Rockford circles) supported the school into the administration of William Arthur Maddox (1883–1933), who became president of the college in 1919 and was a close friend. She was lauded for the "intellectual, spiritual, and financial impetus which she has given to the institution during the three-score years as alumna and a score of years of service as member of the board" upon the occasion of the sixtieth anniversary of her graduation in 1920 (Rockford Star, 15 June 1920, quoted in Rockford College, ed. Nelson, 110). She was memorialized for her "spirit of exaltation" and her perpetually charming, youthful, and vivacious manner by Maddox, who eulogized her "as one of the rare women of her time" at a special campus memorial service upon her death in 1925 (Maddox, "Eulogy").

The Talcotts maintained a high profile on campus. The first floor of Chapel Hall, an assembly hall originally built in 1866 and one of RFS's main buildings (used for assemblies as well as for chapel and such public events as commencements), was renovated with Talcott funds and renamed the William A. Talcott Memorial Chapel after he died in 1901. The Talcotts had six children, only one of whom, Wait (1866–1942), lived past 1904.

Fanny Jones Talcott made her home with her son in Rockford after the death of her husband. Her granddaughter, Elizabeth Talcott McMenemy (1894–1981), daughter of Wait and Grace Forbes Talcott and herself a Rockford graduate in the class of 1909, succeeded her grandmother on the Rockford College Board of Trustees and served from 1926 to 1955. A cameo of W.A. Talcott was hung in the Talcott Memorial Chapel in 1901, and a portrait of Fanny Jones Talcott was placed in Middle Hall in 1926. The Talcott Cross Alumnae Award, given for meritorious service to Rockford College over a span of years, was established in 1948.

3. Lucy E. Spafford (d. 1888), daughter of Daniel and Julia Spafford, who had settled in Rockford in 1844, married the Rev. Lewis B. Gregory (b. 1820). He was the son of the Rev. Harry Gregory, a Methodist minister, and the nephew of Eliphalet and Samuel and had come to Rockford in 1843 from New York and begun a school. He soon became involved in water-powered industry along the Rock River. The couple had six children, one of whom died in infancy. The others settled in Rockford, Beloit, and Chicago. The Gregory family—including brothers Eliphalet (1804–76) and Samuel (d. 1886)—were, like the Talcotts, among the original pioneer settlers of Rockford in the mid-1830s and became influential in the town's churches, educational institutions, and businesses.

4. JA's last issue as editor of the *RSM* reported, "Seniors were overwhelmed before leaving the Forest City, by delightful invitations, to tea, from Mrs. [Caroline M. Thomas] Dickerman, Mrs. [Fanny Jones] Talcott, Mrs. [Adaline Elizabeth Talcott] Emerson and Mrs. [Lucy Spafford] Gregory, in turn extending their kindness. One after another came their invitations to an evening party, and the Seniors gladly and gracefully accepted" (*RSM* [July 1881]: 203). Lizzie Smith wrote about the parties to her mother, Annie M. Jordan Smith, on 5 June 1881: "I have not yet written you of Friday evening which we seniors spent at Mrs. Talcotts. Everything is very refined looking about the house and quite elegant. She has lovely, delicate china. . . . Most of the people there were quite old, but her Sunday school class, boys, were there and were the greenest specimens I ever saw. The other Mr. Talcott took us out rowing a little while. Altogether we spent a very pleasant evening. Tuesday evening we are invited to Mrs. Gregory to meet the Beloit Seniors. I expect we will have a very jolly time with them" (SHSW, Smith).

5. JA probably meant to write *novel*.

6. Worcester ("W.A.") Dickerman.

7. All of JA's classmates had their photographs taken in preparation for graduation. The photograph collection associated with SCPC, JAC, contains her set of these portraits. Her own picture was taken by G. W. Barnes of Rockford.

To George Bowman Haldeman

Rockford Sem'y [Ill.]   June 11 1881

My dear George

I don't apologize any longer for not answering letters, but I don't believe you will enjoy Commencement day very much if you don't get here before 10 A.M., the exercises open at nine & the chapel is always <u>crowded</u>, I think you would enjoy it more if you could make an effort to come very early,—say by eight or half past & so have a chance to collect yourself & get a good post of observation, of course you would be in plenty of time to hear me but I want you to enjoy the day & the class.[1] I expect Alice next Saturday in time for the class-day exercises in the evening. I wish that you could come down then, but of course if you can only be here once save it for June 22. We have been the gayest of the gay lately, ~~have been~~ <were> invited to Miss Emerson's last Thursday to a young people's party, yesterday a reception here, & it promises to go on thusly until the finis.[2]

I will not have time to write again until I see you, unless you need any further information. Excuse brevity. Your loving Sister

                                                                        Jane Addams.

ALS (UIC, JAMC; *JAPM*, 1:656–57).

1. AHHA wrote to GBH on 14 June 1881, "[W]e will not go to Beloit until commencement if at all. But we will see you at Rockford when Jane graduates <u>without fail</u>. How glad we will be to see you all home again" (UIC, JAMC, HJ). She cautioned her son to dress nicely for the Rockford occasion. Class Day exercises took place on Saturday, 18 June 1881, followed by the baccalaureate sermon on Sunday morning (given by the Rev. F. P. Woodbury of Rockford) and the Missionary Society address that evening (given by the Rev. Charles Caverno of Lombard on the topic of the religion of the future). A concert of conservatory music directed by Prof. Daniel Hood took place Monday night, and the anniversary address before the literary societies was scheduled for Tuesday (given by the Rev. Simeon Gilbert of Chicago on "World Sociability, and how the fact of it conditions the true education of the women of our time") (E.D.E., "Commencement at Rockford Seminary," undated newsclipping, ca. June 1881, Sill, "Scrapbook"). Commencement took place on Wednesday morning, 22 June 1881, followed by an alumnae banquet on Wednesday evening (UIC, JAMC; *JAPM*, 27:418, 27:419, 27:420–21). The "Personals" section of the July 1881 RSM reported, "Mr. and Mrs. Addams" and "Mrs. Dr. Halderman [Haldeman], '72" were in attendence at commencement (213, 212).

2. Charlotte Emerson made it a point to invite RFS students to parties and programs at her house in order to allow them to mix with young people in the town. "Tuesday evening we spent with the Beloit Seniors as I think I mentioned in my last letter," Lizzie Smith wrote. "Thursday eve our class spent at Mrs. Emerson's where we met all the nicest young men in town and several town young ladies. We had a very nice supper and dancing singing and promenading on the lawn afterward. I enjoyed it more than any evening I have spent out in Rockford" (Sara Elizabeth Smith to Annie M. Jordan Smith, 12 June 1881, SHSW, Smith).

From Rollin D. Salisbury

Beloit. [Wis.]   June. 11, 1881.

Miss Addams:

Some of our class are very anxious to get an elocutionist for a few days just before Commencement, and if we conclude to do so, we would like to know something of the gentleman who is at the Seminary.[1] Probably he is the most available man we could find and you have probably had opportunity to judge of his efficiency. If you will be kind enough to let us know something of his work we shall be very much obliged.

Pardon me if I speak also of another matter. Several of us were very much mortified the other evening at Rockford, by one or two of the songs sung—not by the class,—but by individual members, under the leadership of one member. To my knowledge, several of the class did not know that there were such songs in the book, and we have, never as a class, practiced them at any time. I hope this breach of courtesy and respect may not be looked upon as a class action,—although I donot know that you had reason to look upon it otherwise,—for I assure you that a large majority of the class were and are still indignant over the affair, and we have not been sparing of rebuke.[2]

Perhaps it is unbecoming in me to speak thus of my own classmates, but it seems to me the occasion warrants it. You know there is little class feeling among us,—perhaps you see a reason,—one reason—now. Yours very respectfully,

Rollin D. Salisbury.

P.S. Mr. Fiske[3] (Junior) has just come in, and wants to know who the victorious contestant of last night is.[4]

R.D.S.

ALS (SCPC, JAC; JAPM, 1:659–61).

1. A reference to elocution teacher Prof. J. R. J. Anthony from Princeton, Ill., who helped RFS students train to give their orations for commencement. JA had taken lessons from him the previous spring, and the lessons were noted in an Apr. 1880 entry in her "Report [Account] Book" for 1879–80 (JAPM, 27:300). She also made an entry in the pages of her old diary: "Prof Anthony, of Princeton—drill—'Young man boat ahoy'" ("Pocket Diary, 1875[–81]," printed date 12 Oct. 1875 [written 1880?]; JAPM, 28.1632).

2. Beloit boys and RFS girls, as was typical, had been sparring in a friendly fashion all semester. A notice in the "Clippings and Exchanges" section of the Mar. 1881 RSM noted: "We are sorry The Round Table is not able to say positively that our 'new and gay dress' is pretty. The Exchange department is evidently presided over by a more amiably disposed individual, or a more polished one, than it has been for some time past. We hope that in the future we will act more like cousins than we have in the past, for we have always agreed with that distinguished individual Tradition in his theory that sisters fights like cats and dogs" (81). News of happy encounters had appeared in the 22 Apr. 1881 issue of the Round Table, when Beloit students enjoyed "wit and sense in the parlors" at RFS while attending the Junior Exhibition on 19 Apr. 1881. In the "Local" column the Round Table's editors went so far as to announce, "Rockford Sem. and Beloit College have———kissed each—other?" ([22 Apr. 1881]: 130). In the same column it was noted that the fact a "Rockford Sem. girl was in the city Friday night" was enough to adjourn the meeting of the Delian Society so members could concentrate their energies elsewhere.

Earlier, during the winter, the "Local" column had given news that the RSM had recommended holding up one foot as a cure for drowsiness. "Thanks, we knew there was some cause for the Sems' vivacity" was the Beloit response. The column also featured news of a sleigh ride to Rockford and printed the following missive: "A Rockford Junior accidentally disclosed the following laconic but significant telegram: 'Thursday instead of Tuesday. Maggie.' No elucidation needed" ([18 Feb. 1881]: 100).

In the 20 May 1881 issue, the *RSM* responded to the *Round Table*'s request for news: "Although we would never have dared contribute to the columns of the *Round Table* unasked, in fact would never have thought of doing so, yet when the request to furnish something for that far-famed periodical met our ears, we immediately recognized the propriety and 'rush to print.'" There followed three-quarters of a page of banter signed "Alienum Elementum" (147–48). On 4 June 1881, Anna P. Sill had forbidden the first-year RFS students (class of 1884) to go to Beloit for a visit, making her ruling in order to break a tie vote among the faculty on the issue. The class sent a letter of regret to Beloit to explain the situation and the "decision of our 'Mother Superior'" (Olive Chick, secretary, class of 1884, to Beloit College Class of 1884, 4 June 1881, TMs, BC).

Both Beloit College and RFS had songbooks, and GBH had served on a Beloit committee that collected various school songs and published them for use by Beloit boys. Serenading, often in a sardonic or mocking fashion, part flirtation, part competition, was an element of the social interaction between Beloit and RFS students. Whether Salisbury's stated indignation over the songbook affair was real or feigned in a humorous fashion is not known. The *Round Table* did publish an acerbic statement in the "Editor's Table" column in its next issue (17 June 1881): "As for the *Rockford Sem. Mag.*, we are disappointed at its uncongenial attitude. We had been so rash as to hope that the sensitively fastidious creature would some time condescend, at least for one number, to play the part of a gentle sister, with friendly works; but under its present exchange writer the *Mag.* has exhibited nothing toward Beloit except persistent antipathy and lofty austerity" (170).

The brother-sister language used in the editorial statement was typical of the way RFS and Beloit students addressed each other; indeed, administrators often stressed the sibling relationship of the two schools. Sill argued for raised standards at RFS so the curriculums there and at Beloit would be on a par; she also urged continuance of the separate school status. In a pivotal letter to Joseph Emerson on 3 July 1879, she ironically appealed to chivalry in order to win Beloit support for RFS's continued autonomy: "Let Beloit College steadily pursue its course—it is the Yale of the West. Can it not afford to be the gallant brother to defend and aid the younger sister?" (BC, EB).

3. Horace Spencer Fiske (1859–1940) was a close friend and confidant of Rollin D. Salisbury at Beloit. He followed in his friend's footsteps in his senior year, appearing as the representative of Wisconsin in the 1882 Interstate Oratorical Contest and speaking as valedictorian of his class when he graduated, a year after Salisbury, in 1882. He went on to teach and write. Fiske earned a M.A. in English from the Univ. of Michigan in 1885. Like Salisbury, he taught for a time in Beloit before eventually moving on to establish a career in Chicago. After graduation, he worked as an instructor in Greek, political economy, and civics at Beloit Academy before teaching at Wisconsin State Normal School from 1887 to 1893. He married Ida Peck Nettleton of Lancaster, N.C., on 22 June 1889. After a fellowship at the Univ. of Wisconsin in 1892, he was a student at Oxford Univ. in the 1893–94 academic year. Returning from the year abroad, Fiske became a lecturer in English literature in the extension division of the Univ. of Chicago. He served as literary editor of the *World Review* in Chicago in 1901–2 and became the editor of the *University Record* in 1903. He was the author of a series of books of poetry and literary criticism, including *Provincial Types in American Fiction* (1903), *Chicago in Picture and Poetry* (1903), and *Poems on Athletics* (1905). He was described in a history of Beloit College as a "depicter in poetry of the higher aspects of the life of Chicago" (Eaton, *Historical Sketches*, 265).

4. Fiske was probably interested in the outcome of the oratory contest that was held to choose a representative to compete at the state collegiate contest in Bloomington, Ill., in the fall of 1881. The contest to choose a delegate, in which Kittie Waugh was the victor, was originally planned for 10 June 1881 but took place on 14 June 1881. Waugh graduated in the RFS class of 1882. Like JA and Salisbury, she had a professional life in Chicago (see also *PJA*, 2).

Excerpt from Article in the
Rockford Seminary Magazine

The graduation issue of the Rockford Seminary Magazine *began with a transcription of* Sage and Sibyl, *the comic spoof done during Class Day exercises about the foreseen future of each member of the Rockford Female Seminary class of 1881. The light-hearted Class Day program took place on the Saturday evening before commencement.[1] In the dialogue, "Sage" related an amusing short history of each girl, which was followed by "Sibyl's" psychic predictions about the "destiny of these maidens."[2] The spoof was preceded in the program by class president Jane Addams and vice-president Mary Ellwood doing "an interesting oracular duet in which the former told what the class '81 did and the latter what they didn't do."[3] The following excerpt is what Sage and Sibyl had to say about Jane Addams.*

[Rockford, Ill.]   [18 June] 1881

SAGE— . . . I will inquire as to the fate of Jane Addams, the president of this class of '81. As her brain is larger than her body, I will give the history of her brain. At three she read with fluency, and before she was six had read the thousand and one Arabian nights. At ten she plunged into fiction, and at the age of twelve had devoured it all from the works of Mrs. Holmes to Jean Paul Friederich Richter. Her mind was almost swamped in this case, but rebounded at the age of fifteen into Emerson's essays; here she delved and lingered long, and after passing through a scientific infection came to Byron, DeQuincey and Carlyle. From the time of her entering R.F.S., four years ago, to the present time, she has been wearied and troubled about many matters. Weary with class business, she re sorts, for recreation, to writing editorials for the magazine, or to the laboratory, there to analyze some poisonous compound. Tell 'me, O Sibyl, what will be the fate of this prodigious intellect.

Sibyl—What would we expect of our honored president, our valedictorian, with all her grand ideas and vast conceptions—her life-work is so *broad,* the star of her destiny I see now here, now there, brightening, glimmering, but never disappearing. All her thoughts and energies have finally centered on this grand undertaking, this great benefit to mankind. She will make glass eyes for dolls, bushels and bushels of the most perfect blue eyes for dolls. . . .[4]

PD (*RSM* [July 1881]: 193–94).

1. Class Day, with its "farci[c]al revelations" was held on Saturday evening, 18 June 1881, and reported in the July 1881 *RSM* (207–10, quote 207) and the *Rockford Register.* The local newspaper described it as a "sparkling prelude to Commencement week" wherein "History and prophecy joined mirthful partnership" (clipping, "Commencement at Rockford Seminary," June 1881, Sill, "Scrapbook"). The speeches were humorous, and the music featured selections of *The Pirates of Penzance.* Nora Frothingham's talk illustrates the silliness and satire of the proceedings. She demonstrated "by inductive and deductive methods, internal and external evidence that Chaucer was certainly a woman, ending with the profound syllogism

Jane Addams with some of her friends from the class of 1881 of Rockford Female
Seminary. Left to right, back row (standing): Nora Frothingham, Laura Ely, Kate
Tanner, and Jane Addams (holding parasol); middle row (seated): Phila Pope, Ella
Browning, and Mattie Thomas; bottom row (seated): Helen Harrington and Annie
Sidwell. Addams remained lifelong friends with many classmates. (RC)

that he either was a woman or he was not a woman he was not a woman therefore he was a
woman" (*RSM* [July 1881]: 208). During the presentation of comic degrees, JA was awarded
"a gilt pony upon which to gallop better over the Roman and Grecian fields" (209). For a
copy of the invitation to Class Day, which also listed the other events of the week of commencement, see UIC, JAMC, Detzer; *JAPM*, 27:418.

    2. *RSM* (July 1881): 193.

    3. *RSM* (July 1881): 209. Whatever JA said, Ellwood contradicted: "The president referred
to their ambition and intelligence, the vice-president called into notice their conceit and
ugliness. The one referred touchingly to the institution of the Senior parlors; the other said
they fought over curtains, and only put in three chairs and two foot-stools. . . . Numerous
other undertakings during the class' course were brought to light by the president only to be
thrown from its high pedestal by the caustic illusions of the second officer" (209).

    4. The Class Day Sibyl and Sage chose a frivolous future for JA, but the fate they allotted
to Mattie Thomas and Addie M. Smith (a destiny of urban social work and joint institution-
founding) turned out to be a more accurate prediction of the actual future awaiting JA and
EGS. "Behold in the conjugation of planets," Sibyl predicted, Thomas and Smith were "destined to shine in the annals of philanthropy; thousands of little street arabs shall rise up and

call them blessed. Together they will found an asylum, a broad and beneficent one" (*RSM* [July 1881]: 199).

Of the sixteen members of the 1881 RFS graduating class besides JA, Alice Atkinson married a businessman and moved to the Northwest; Emma Briggs went to medical school in Philadelphia; Ella Browning became a teacher before marrying a storekeeper and lived in Iowa and Illinois; Annie Ellers did postgraduate work in nursing in Boston, studied medicine, and became a medical missionary in Korea; Mary Ellwood traveled in Europe with JA, married a banker, and became a leader in the women's club and missionary movements in De Kalb; Laura Ely married a professor and was active in the work of the Congregational church; Nora Frothingham married a minister and became a missionary educator in Japan; Helen Harrington taught school before marrying a farmer and farming in Oklahoma, Nebraska, and Colorado; sisters Kate Huey and Mary Ella Huey both married merchants; Phila D. Pope was a teacher at RFS until her marriage to a grain and coal merchant in 1890; Anna W. Sidwell made a career in teaching in Illinois, Iowa, and Nebraska; Addie M. Smith married a Chicago stockbroker and became, like JA, a trustee of RFS; Lizzie Smith became a librarian; Kate Tanner, the class beauty from Rockford, married a Chicago high school principal and became an acclaimed concert soloist; and Mattie Thomas married a physician and lived in Dubuque, Iowa, and Urbana, Ill. Emma Briggs, Mary Ellwood, Kate and Mary Huey, Phila Pope, Addie M. Smith, and Kate Tanner all were first-year students at RFS in 1878 when JA was in her second year. JA remained in touch with many of these women, and in 1931 she joined eleven of them in celebrating the fiftieth anniversary of their graduation.

Graduation Essay

Jane Addams's essay on Cassandra,[1] delivered as part of the 1881 Rockford Female Seminary commencement exercises in Chapel Hall on Wednesday, 22 June 1881, dealt boldly with the status of opportunities for women in the nineteenth century. In choosing this theme, she addressed the major issue underlying institutional politics at Rockford Female Seminary during her years there. Strengthening the school's curriculum, applying for admission to intercollegiate and interstate oratorical associations, inaugurating a Junior Exhibition, and lobbying for bachelor's degrees were all steps toward greater opportunity for women through education.

Addams was directly involved in all these efforts. Her graduation essay—which proclaimed, through both content and example, the talents of women and their ability to speak with authority in public—was, like these previous measures, a demonstration of women's abilities. In it as well were the roots of Addams's later dedication to social science and to social-scientific ways of understanding. As the local newspaper put it, her essay was "excellent," as were the presentations by the other young women. The commencement performances provided one more piece of public evidence that Rockford Female Seminary was ready to be granted collegiate status. "In clearness and shrewdness of thought, aptness of illustration, dignity and grace of bearing," the newspaper report concluded, "it would not be altogether easy to match these speakers upon a college platform."[2]

[Rockford, Ill.]

CASSANDRA

Upon the broad Trojan plain for ten years the mighty warriors of Greece and Troy fought hand to hand for honor and justice. Safe within the city walls the stately Trojan dames ever wove with golden threads the history of the conflict. To one of these beautiful women, to Cassandra, daughter of Priam, suddenly came the power of prophecy. Cassandra fearlessly received the power, with clear judgment and unerring instinct she predicted the victory of the Greeks and the destruction of her father's city. But the brave warriors laughed to scorn the beautiful prophetess and called her mad. The frail girl stood conscious of Truth but she had no logic to convince the impatient defeated warriors, and no facts to gain their confidence, she could only assert and proclaim until at last in sooth she becomes mad.

This was the tragic fate of Cassandra—always to be in the right, and always to be disbelieved and rejected. Three thousand years ago this Trojan woman represented pure intuition, powerful and God-given in itself but failing to accomplish. She, who might have changed the entire destiny of the ancient world, becomes only a curse and a thorn to her brethren. I would call this a feminine trait of mind—an accurate perception of Truth and Justice which rests contented in itself, and will make no effort to confirm itself, or to organize through existing knowledge. Permit me to repeat my subject; a mighty intuitive perception of Truth which yet counts nothing in the force of the world.

The nineteenth century is distinguished by the sudden acquisition of much physical knowledge. The nineteenth century has proclaimed the duty of labor and the bond of brotherhood. These acquisitions and high thoughts of the century have increased each man's responsibility, but as yet have added nothing to the vitality and spontaneous motives of mankind. With increasing demands the force of society tends to be mechanical and conscious, rather than vital. In other words, while men with hard research into science, with sturdy and unremitting toil, have shown the power and magnificence of knowledge, somewhere, some one has shirked to perform for intuition the same hard labor.

Knowledge is reverenced, and the old beautiful force which Plato taught is treated with contempt. Intuition is not telling on the world. Occasionally a weak woman, striving to use her high gift, will verge out into spiritualism and clairvoyance, others will become sentimentalists or those women who bear through life a high discontent, because of their very keen-sightedness, yet have not power to help those around them. The world looks upon such women with mingled pity and contempt; they continually reinact the fate of the fearless, unfortunate Cassandra, because they failed to make themselves intelligible; they have not gained what the ancients called *auethoritas,* right of speaker to make themselves heard, and prove to the world that an intuition is a force in the universe, and a part of nature; that an intuitive perception committed to a woman's charge is not a prejudice or a fancy, but one of the holy means given to mankind in their search for truth.

I will make one exception—there is one means which has hitherto saved this force from complete loss and contempt. The divine force of love which ever exalts talent and cultivates woman's insight. A loving woman believes in ministering spirits; the belief comes to her that her child's every footstep is tenderly protected by a guardian angel. Let her not sit and dreamily watch her child; let her work her way to a sentient idea that shall sway and ennoble those around her. All that subtile force among women which is now dreaming fancy, might be changed into creative genius.

There is a way opened, women of the nineteenth century, to convert this wasted force to the highest use, and under the feminine mind, firm and joyous in its intuitions; a way opened by the scientific ideal of culture; only by the accurate study of at least one branch of physical science can the intuitive mind gain that life which the strong passion of science and study, feeds and forms, more self-dependent that love, confident in errorless purpose. With eyes accustomed to the search for Truth, she will readily detect all self-deceit and fancy in herself; she will test whether her intuition is genuine and a part of nature, or merely a belief of her own. She will learn silence and self-denial, to express herself not by dogmatism, but by quiet, progressive development. And besides this training, there is certainly a place in science reserved for this stamp of mind; there are discoveries to be made which cannot come by induction, only through perception, such as the mental laws which govern suggestion, or the place that rhythm holds in nature's movements. These laws have remained undiscovered for lack of the needed intuitive minds. Could an intuitive mind gain this scholarly training, or discover one of these laws, then she would attain her *aucthor itas*. Men would see that while the searching for Truth, the patient adding one to one is the highest and noblest employment of the human faculties. Higher and nobler than even this, and infinitely more difficult, is the intuitive seeing of Truth, the quick recognition of the true and genuine wherever it appears.

Having gained accuracy, would woman bring this force to bear throughout morals and justice, then she must take the active, busy world as a test for the genuineness of her intuition. In active labor she will be ready to accept the promptings that come from growing insight, and when her sympathies are so enlarged that she can weep as easily, over a famine in India as a pale child at her door, then she can face social ills and social problems as tenderly and as intuitively as she can now care for and understand a crippled factory child.

The actual Justice must be established in the world by trained intelligence; by broadened sympathies toward the individual man and woman who crosses one path, only an intuitive mind has a grasp comprehensive enough to embrace the opposing facts and forces.

The opening of the ages has long been waiting for this type of womanhood. The Egyptians called her Neith; the Hebrews, Sophis, or Wisdom; the Greeks,

Athene; the Romans, Justicia, holding in her hands the scale pans of the world; the Germans called her the Wise-woman, who was not all knowing, but had a power deeper and more primordial than knowledge. Now is the time for a faint realization of this type, with her faculties clear and acute, from the study of science, and with her hand upon the magnetic chain of humanity. Then the story of Cassandra will be forgotten, which now constantly meets and stirs us with its proud pathos.

JANE ADDAMS.

PD (*Rockford Seminary: Thirtieth Commencement, Essays of Graduating Class*, 36–39, UIC, JAMC; *JAPM*, 46:267–71).[3]

1. Cassandra, tragic heroine of Greek myth, was the daughter of Hecuba and Priam, king of Troy. She received the gift of prophecy, but when she slighted Apollo he ensured that her predictions would not be given credence. She predicted the fall of Troy, was captured in the Temple of Athena during the conquest, and raped. She was taken as a captive to Greece to serve as a concubine to Agamemnon, leader of the Greek forces in the Trojan War. She foretold his murder by his wife, Clytemnestra, at whose hands she also died.

2. Clipping, "Commencement at Rockford Seminary," June 1881, Sill, "Scrapbook."

3. For AMs fragments of this essay, see UIC, JAMC, Detzer; *JAPM*, 46:317–18, 46:319–33, 46:334–36, 46:337–48. The graduation essays of the seventeen graduating members of the class of 1881 were printed in booklet form by the News Stream Press in De Kalb, Ill., (1881), compliments of class member Mary Ellwood, who sent copies to each classmate by the fall of 1881. JA's essay on "Cassandra" was included but not her valedictory address, neither were Nora Frothingham's salutatory and Jennie L. Forbes's alumnae essay. Kate Tanner's copy of the booklet later became part of the Hull-House Association library in Chicago and is the version used here (*JAPM*, 27:424–61). In late summer 1881 Ellwood wrote to JA, "I have given the essays to the Printer but have not seen even the proof yet—I am afraid they will not be done before I go [away to school at Smith College]—I would not undertake the job again for half a dozen classes of '81" (28 Aug. 1881, SCPC, JAC; *JAPM*, 1:748). Four autograph manuscript, or fragmentary, versions of JA's talk on "Cassandra" also are extant (UIC, JAMC, Detzer; *JAPM*, 46:317–48). The program for RFS's thirtieth commencement in 1881 was reprinted in *RSM* ([July 1881]: 211–12; see also *JAPM*, 27:420–21).

The topics JA's classmates chose for their commencement presentations reveal the perspectives they held after four years of schooling and shed light on themes JA chose for her own composition. The commencement program began with a chant and prayer, followed by the Latin salutatory address by Nora Frothingham. Senior presentations were interspersed with musical selections. The talks began with Phila Pope on "For Value Received I Promise to Pay" (*Rockford Seminary: Thirtieth Commencement Essays*, 5–7), an essay on progress and contributions to society ("Each individual has his own duty to perform, every age has its own debt to pay" [5]). Kate Huey spoke in "Ambition Leads Men to Work" (7–8) on the urge toward self-improvement ("Every man has a vague belief in a destiny. . . . A noble man compares and estimates himself by an ideal which is higher than himself" [7]). "There's Magic in It," (8–10), presented by Annie Sidwell, dealt with the nature of appearances and how bitterness or idealism shape perceptions of society in different ways ("and though such has been the motive power of much that is bright and beautiful in the thoughts and deeds of men, so revenge paints with fearful truthfulness the dark creations of a mind embittered by disappointed ambition or misplaced affection" [10]). Lizzie Smith spoke on "The Slavery of To-Day" (11–12), which despite its title and Smith's interests in missionary outreach to African Americans, did not deal with racial rights issues or post-Emancipation politics but with applying the principle of moderation to even the exercise of virtues ("The slavery of to-day lies in excess; our freedom in following the old Greek motto which says: 'Do nothing too much'" [12]). Annie Ellers's talk was "Man, Know Thyself," (12–14), on the duty of individuals to make the most of themselves with the talents they have been given ("Every one by his peculiar mental faculties and special gifts is adapted to some kind of work, and whenever that kind of work is found, we shall have that which will give us the best development" [14]). Ella Huey chose as her topic "Under the Snow Lie the Daisies," which was on the grandeur of Egyptian civilization and the arrogance of believing in a steady march of progress to the present ("Now while winter reigns supreme over the far distant Egypt, while the mantle of snow has shrouded that land nearly from our view, shall we turn aside, and give the entire praise of our present attainments to some more modern nation?" [15]). Laura Ely presented an essay on the topic of free trade, "Dependence and Independence" (16–18), in which she argued against protectionism ("True independence consists in being able to throw our land open to foreign influence and foreign commerce; to command the products of every land because we can supply their wants in return" [17]).

Kate Tanner's essay "Too Many Gates to Swing On" (19–20) stands out in that Tanner chose to comment on very immediate issues of women's proper roles in Victorian society and her interpretation of the meaning of the class of 1881's bread-giver theme. Her talk centered on the impropriety of women desiring a place in the public realm ("women who protest against womanhood and wildly strain to throw off their most lovable characteristics. They want power, political power, and yet the world is entirely what their home influence has made it. . . . At home is where woman's influence is needed, and not in the public assemblies" [19, 20]). She praised the high and sacred calling of being "a true woman, one highly educated and fitted" to raise good citizens ("Where is due the greater honor, to the man who has attained the summit of public station and power, or with the mother whose care and labor through years of self denial struggled to educate the man for this position in life?" [20]), and she used the bread-giver motto to support her position. She concluded by describing the womanly norms and values that JA's mother SWA had so well embodied—norms and values that JA would ultimately radically revise for herself in dedication to social reform and public action:

Thus it appears that woman has already all she can successfully accomplish at home, in the social and literary circles without constantly striving for more avenues to power, more opportunities for employment and more gates to swing out upon into the political world. If at home she fills the mission of the Saxon lady who was a "Bread Giver" and feeder of the poor, she has fullfilled woman's noblest work on earth and rightly claims the name of lady, not merely title alone but the grand office and duty signified by it.

But when she neglects her own best interests at home in order to reform the world and when political ambition leads her into worldly strife, she then is no more a lady and "Bread Giver" but like many another restless element in human society she is found, as the small boy, upon too many open gates swinging to and fro upon the turbulent highways. (20)

The program continued upon the theme of women's nature and proper roles with Ella Browning's "The Two Georges" (20–23), a talk contrasting George Sand and George Eliot. Browning praised Eliot's ability to depict the "true nature of woman," especially in her creation of the self-sacrificing, stoic Romola, a "model of filial devotedness" and "purity of character" [21]). The topic of literature having been introduced, Mary Ellwood followed Browning with a talk about "The Novel" (22–25) and the importance of literature as the expression of a national culture ("We study a nation through its literature" [24]) and of the emerging recognition of American writers in this respect. She lauded Nathaniel Hawthorne and Harriet Beecher Stowe as among America's greatest novelists. Helen Harrington chose a philosophical subject in "No Metamorphoses Can Hide a God from a God" (25–27), feeling and appreciating the gifts of the world around one and aspiring toward greater uplift ("happiness is the highest good—that happiness which comes from the most perfect development of man's God-given nature—from broad benevolence and helpfulness and charity— from the constant exercise of those higher faculties of mind and heart which mark the divinity of man" [26–27]). Next, speaking on a more practical plane, came Nora Frothingham on "Monopolies" (26–30), a critique of the influence powerful corporations wielded upon legislatures and the courts and their role in eroding the significance of the workingman and the "great middle class" as voices in the government of the nation ("One of the greatest dangers to be feared as coming through these monopolists is the extremes of wealth caused by the accumulation of money in the hands of the few" [28–29]). Mattie Thomas took things back into the clouds with her "Essential Truth Always Known" (31–32), which, like Ella Huey's earlier talk about Egypt, questioned the idea that "We have been taught from childhood to believe that this is the most enlightened era, and we the most civilized people the world has ever seen" (30). Thomas concentrated on examples from Greek, Egyptian, and Chinese history to demonstrate "the spirit of progress even among the ancients" (32). Addie M. Smith followed with similar themes in "The Titans Overcome by the Gods" (32–34), which considered the great civilizations of the past and their achievements and discoveries. Alice Atkinson asked in "Who Is Oedipus?" (34–36) what spurs humankind toward achievement and adventure ("More of the highest life is suppressed in every one of us than ever is revealed, and it is these inward suppressions which constitute the chief tragedy of history" [35]).

Atkinson set the stage for JA's essay on "Cassandra" (37–39), in which JA synthesized many of the evening's major themes, including the debates over women's proper nature, the example of ancient civilizations and the question of advancement in the present time, and the means of striving toward higher ideals. She gave a female face to heroism and called for a new standard of womanhood, far separated from Kate Tanner's woman improperly swinging on a gate. JA's valedictory address (Valedictory, 22 June 1881, below) immediately followed her speech on Cassandra. The diplomas were presented to the class of 1881 after JA's address, and the program closed with a benediction.

Valedictory

As class valedictorian, Jane Addams capped the pre-diploma portion of the commencement program with her speech on Cassandra, followed by the valedictory to Rockford residents and Rockford Female Seminary students and faculty. She reprinted the full text of the valedictory as part of her last editorial as editor-in-chief of the Rockford Seminary Magazine. *It appeared in the July 1881 issue, which focused on accounts of graduation events. Addams touched on several important themes. She spoke in a discreet way of the administration's policies of carefully chaperoning and restricting the seminary girls' participation in the life of the town. Then she stepped directly into the hotbed of internal board politics concerning upgrading the collegiate status of the seminary, granting degrees to graduates, and admitting women to the Board of Trustees.[1] She paid respectful tribute to Anna P. Sill and said farewell to one of her favorite teachers, Sarah Blaisdell, whom she had admired as a child and who would in the years ahead remain her friend. She closed the chapter of her student life at Rockford Female Seminary, fittingly, with the words "Good-bye."*

[Rockford, Ill.]   [22] June 1881

To the Citizens of Rockford:

In a quiet part of your busy city for four years a class of girls have lived, studied some, planned and dreamed much more, and to all appearances have added nothing to the society or working force of your citizens. A student's life is necessarily an isolated one; they have had but little contact with you, and your direct influence on them has been small. Yet they hold to Rockford the peculiar affection felt only by a student to his college town, where he loves the very streets and trees which have witnessed his highest dreams and his young ambitions. They have felt for four years the helpful influence of your cultured citizens, they have been sheltered by your churches, they have been stirred by the hum of your manufactories, they have been excited over your city elections—until in future years and in other regions, never can they hear the name of dear old Rockford, without a responsive thrill owning their relationship to the forest city and its kindly inhabitants who once adopted them.

To the Gentlemen of the Board of Trustees:

The class of '81 receives from you to-day testimonials of a completed course of study; as this is but the last one of the many high benefits we have received from your hands, it is fitting that we publicly express to you our gratitude and appreciation, you to whom we are indebted for the basis and authority of our education. We know the past history of the institution—the struggles to maintain its footing and the hard labor which every dollar of its property represents. During the last year we have read for ourselves the economy and wise management exercised by the board and the self-sacrifice of its patrons and friends. But we have also felt increasing demands, there has been, as it were, in the very air an awaking of college spirit, seen in the higher standards of admission and scholarships, in the enlarged course of study and in the ambitions of the students. Rockford Seminary from its organization has possessed a legal college charter, but has never yet been distinctly recognized as a college, nor its alumnae received as college graduates.[2] Do not now, we beg of you, stint this newly awakened college life through want of encouragement or funds. We have admired and respected your past works only from a distance, but to-day we approach you in some sense as co-operators, henceforth having in common the same cause, so with our gratitude for what we have received, to you we feel rather like extending a greeting than a farewell. And in your future appeals to your alumnae for assistance and support, may you never find the class of '81 disloyal to their Alma Mater.[3]

Miss Sill, our honored principal: Your life has been one of constant endeavor and wise planning for others. By the mysterious law of the culture which comes from giving each year, you have had more to give, a richer blessing to bestow. Hence we your latest class have received from your hands, not only the training and teaching which was our individual need, but we have come into the fullness of your life. When we see how much and how freely you have given us and remember that we are but one class out of the thirty classes you have sent forth, then we gain a faint conception of the magnitude and worthiness of your life-work. Bearing with them this rich legacy, the daily remembrances of a life of noble purpose steadily fulfilled, the class of '81, the youngest of your many daughters, go forth, perchance to pay back again to the world the much good they have received from you.[4]

Miss Blaisdell: You are about to sever your connection with Rockford Seminary and crowned with your seventeen years of work, to go forth with our class. To you is due the highest meed of our praise. For if in future years any of us stand firm where it would be easier to fall, if we are moved by principle while those around us are swayed by impulse, in short if we are in any degree true to your teachings and at length attain the character you have so carefully trained us in and so constantly shown us—to you will redound the glory of that character. With the hard lessons in Latin and Greek, you have taught us the harder lessons of thoroughness and uprightness.[5]

To the Teachers of Rockford Seminary:

Next to the deep, everlasting force of kinship moving through society, the purest and strongest relation the world acknowledges is that between earnest teachers and their pupils—a bond wrought by the exchange of high thought and the molding of life convictions. We recognize the strength of sympathy of this world-acknowledged bond between you and us. Added to this are domestic ties. We have lived under one roof, and in one family, until to the debt of guidance and help in many cases we add the holier one of friendship. Thanking you for what we have received, and humbly acknowledging how far short we have come from your endeavor, the class of '81 says, Farewell.

To the Undergraduates of Rockford Seminary.

If our course as a class has ever seemed to you rather on the material, selfish side; if we have appeared more anxious to do striking things than to be scholarly and steadfast, then we beg of you to-day to forget that side of our character, and to think of us only as the students we aimed to be. And in the college life we all enjoy, and the opening achievements we are all so proud of, do not you repeat our mistake, do not you forget that it is alone the deep regions of meditation whence proceeds power. We wish you all the highest success possible—permanent scholarship in your studies, and happiness in your class relations. So the class of '81 goes forth from among you, with sorrow, truly, but with no foreboding of evil, when they commit to your hands their share of the character and reputation of Rockford Seminary.

And now to you, my classmates, the glorious Seventeen, with whom I have worked and planned and studied for four years—the happiest years of our lives, they say—knowledge labored for together has bred between us sympathy and helpful friendship. On different days when we have been touched and stirred, we have expressed to each other higher and nobler things than we have probably ever said to any one else, and these years of our young lives being past, better than we will say again. So that we stand to-day in possession of each other's best impulses and highest hopes of what each can attain. Henceforth, let the remembrance of those days become to you a help and inspiration. If you are tempted to flag and grow weary of "bread-giving," remember the sixteen girls of '81 who believe and expect higher things of you. We stand united to-day in a belief in beauty, genius and courage, and that these can transform the world. If you each are true to these beliefs, and never lose confidence in your possibilities there, the class of '81 will be undivided throughout their entire lives. Then the old class loyalty and helpful friendship will never be withdrawn. So to you, my friends, I will only say, "God be with us," which is the older and better form of "Good-bye."

PD (*RSM* [July 1881]: 219–22; *JAPM*, 46:383–86).[6]

1. These debates were happening at a fast and furious pace during commencement week 1881. The last issue of the *RSM* that JA prepared as editor (July 1881) ended with a full transcript of her valedictory speech, which was directly followed in the last three pages of the issue by a report of the RFS Alumnae Assn. meeting of 22 June 1881 on the effort to win representation for women on the RFS Board of Trustees. It was, in effect, JA's last word as editor and the beginning of her active stance as an alumna.

The RFS activists had support from many in the Rockford community. Among the pragmatic arguments that entered public discussion in favor of allowing women's membership on the board was the fact that women were important donors to the school's fund-raising drives. Proponents also noted the irony of preparing girls for lives of usefulness and then curbing their usefulness in regard to the very school that had educated them—not to mention the contradictions involved in having a school full of women regulated by a governing body of men. The local newspaper linked the issue of women board members directly to that of the collegiate status of the school. After lauding improvements in the curriculum and noting the continued need for better library and scientific tools, the reporter who covered the 1881 commencement asked, "Why should our Western girls, capable and eager as they are, be handicapped in the race? And why should not wide-awake women, like the Alumnae Master of this year [Laura Jane ("Jennie") Forbes], be added to the Trustees? All our colleges are now calling Alumni to their Boards of Trust; why should a college whose regular Faculty and students are wholly ladies, be regulated wholly by men?" (clipping, "Commencement at Rockford Seminary," June 1881, Sill, "Scrapbook").

The women of the RFS Alumnae Assn., led by Julia Clark, Eva Townsend Clark, Adeline Potter Lathrop, Marie Thompson Perry, Fanny Jones Talcott and others (some of whom had husbands who were long-term members of the RFS Board of Trustees or who had served on the RFS Visiting Com., which reviewed how policies were working on campus) were dedicated to changing the sex-restricted nature of the RFS governing board. They wanted reform, but they wanted it to occur in a way that would build consensus. Before the events of commencement week, Clark, Lathrop, and Mrs. G. A. Sanford, acting as representatives of the RFS Alumnae Assn., petitioned the RFS Board of Trustees, "proposing and advising the election of women to the membership of the Board." A subcommittee was appointed by the trustees to consider the women's request. These two men—Lathrop's husband William, who was a prominent lawyer in Rockford, and Hiram Foote, a local minister—weighed in on the side of the women. They reported to the board at the annual meeting on 21 June 1881 in favor of the proposal, stating that "there is no legal obstacle to women's occupying the position of trustees" and "insomuch as the institution is solely for the education of women, your committee thinks that there is an eminent propriety in giving women such representation, and would recommend that three discreet and competent women be elected to fill existing vacancies upon the Board" (*RSM* [July 1881]: 223; see also "Alumnae Meeting," clipping, ca. 22 June 1881, Sill, "Scrapbook").

The subcommittee report caused something of a furor among board members. Some ardently supported the change, whereas others—led by Aaron Lucius Chapin of Beloit College, who was long a champion of male administration of the female school—just as strongly objected to it. After heated discussion, the subcommittee's recommendation was overruled by the board at large. The trustees then prepared a substitute resolution, upholding the traditional gendered division of labor in the operation of the school and ignoring in the process the existing involvement of women as fund-raisers, donors, and alumnae volunteers in the development and financial aspects of the school's operation. They stated that it was the "settled policy" of the school to leave "educational work, the training and discipline of its pupils, and its internal administration and government to the faculty of teachers, constituted of women, and to leave its business arrangements, its property trusts, and general exterior management to a board of trustees consisting of men." Therefore, the board "did not deem it expedient to change the constitution of the Board of Trust, as it has existed for the past thirty years." It was resolved that the matter be "laid over for further consideration until the next annual meeting of the board" in June 1882 (*RSM* [July 1881]: 223; see also "Alumnae Meeting," clipping, ca. 22 June 1881, Sill, "Scrapbook").

The RFS Alumnae Assn. meeting duly gathered for its own annual business meeting on the evening of commencement day. Among the items on the agenda was the reading of the resolutions presented by the Board of Trustees and the drafting of a response. Fanny Jones Talcott presented a resolution that the group at large adopted:

> *Resolved*, That the Alumnae acknowledge the receipt of the communication from the board of trustees relative to the election of women as members of that body, and disdain any desire for a change in the membership of that board as shall in any degree impair the harmonious and efficient action of all the members of that board of trust, and of the patrons of the institution, in carrying on the work as successfully in the future as in the past, and therefore we do not desire to make any change in said membership unless there can be perfect unanimity among the board itself. (*RSM* [July 1881]: 224; see also "Alumnae Meeting," clipping, ca. 22 June 1881, Sill, "Scrapbook")

Women were not admitted to the RFS Board of Trustees until 1883, and at first only on a provisional, honorary basis. Full membership was won only gradually. JA, Fanny Jones Talcott, and Marie Thompson Perry were among the first female trustees, beginning in May 1883 (see RFS Board of Trustees, "Minutes of Special Meeting, 10 May 1883," *JAPM*, 1A:150–51; see also *PJA*, 2).

2. The granting of bachelor's degrees at RFS, like the representation of women on the Board of Trustees, was a spearhead issue for those favoring college status. JA was directly involved in both these endeavors. As a Board of Trustees member, she was present through some of the negotiations about changing the formal designation of the school from seminary to college. The name was changed from RFS to Rockford Seminary in June 1887 (see RFS Board of Trustees, "Minutes of the Annual Meetings," 21 June 1887, *JAPM*, 1A:153). Anna P. Sill, who saw the resolution as a half-way action that fell short of recognizing the collegiate quality of Rockford, was among the three board members who voted in opposition to the measure. At the same 1887 meeting, the board set standards for the granting of a M.A. degree. The transition to collegiate status was finally given official sanction when the name of the institution was changed to Rockford College in 1892 (see RFS Board of Trustees, "Minutes of the Annual Meetings," 21 June 1887 and 12 June 1894, *JAPM*, 1A:152, 1A:184–88).

3. As an alumna, JA remained a stalwart supporter of RFS. In addition to serving as a member of the Board of Trustees, she promoted the school in the Rockford community and

Chicago and made gifts to the school, including "a draft for one thousand dollars payable to your treasurer on his order" to be "expended upon the library and a preference given to scientific works" granted to the trustees with a note from JA on 20 June 1887 (see RFS Board of Trustees, "Minutes of the Annual Meetings," 21 June 1887; see also *RSM* [May 1887]: 194). She was an active member of the RFS Reunion Assn. and led her class in soliciting contributions to the college from former classmates (see *JAPM*, 27:412). Voted a full trustee in 1887, she used the college's buildings for the Hull-House Summer School in the 1890s. JA was among those who reorganized and modernized the board in 1901 by leading the move to limit trustees' terms to three years (see *JAPM*, 1A:153; RFS Board of Trustees, "Minutes of the Annual Meetings," 1882–1901, *JAPM*, 1A:149–50, 1A:151, 1A:153, 1A:155, 1A:169–70, 1A:186, 1A:197–98, 1A:205–8, 1A:217–21).

4. Anna P. Sill was nearing the end of her life and career. She had suffered frequent bouts of ill-health since the early 1870s, and in Aug. 1879 D. Selwyn Clark urged her to resign as principal of the school. Sill took a leave of absence in 1883 and announced her resignation in Jan. 1884. From Europe on 22 June 1884 JA told SAAH that she was thinking about the events that were going on that week at the seminary and looked "for a long account of the Rockford Commencement, and poor Miss Sill[']s last day on the rostrum" (UIC, JAMC; *JAPM*, 1:1539). Sill died in her rooms at Linden Hall on 22 June 1889.

5. Sarah Blaisdell retired because of ill-health. It was apt that JA should say the formal goodbyes to her from the student body. Although many RFS girls feared Blaisdell, she and JA had worked closely together and JA had been one of her best students. JA appreciated the mentorship Blaisdell had provided and continued a warm correspondence with her former teacher, whom she also visited. Blaisdell moved to Beloit to be near her brother James and his family. She built her own home there and lived in Beloit until her death.

6. See also *JAPM*, 46:363–80 for the AMs and an AMs fragment of JA's Valedictory.

BIOGRAPHICAL PROFILES

Parents, Step-Parent, Siblings, and

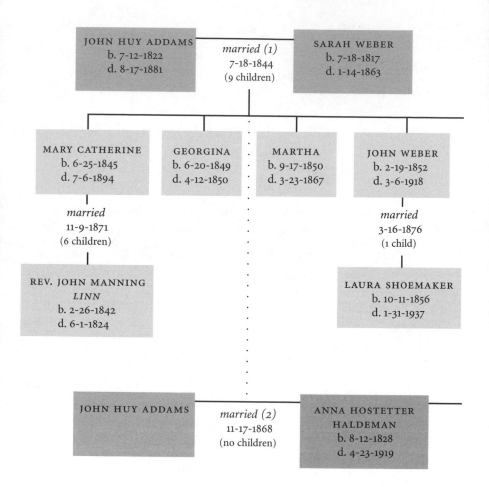

JOHN HUY ADDAMS
b. 7-12-1822
d. 8-17-1881

married (1)
7-18-1844
(9 children)

SARAH WEBER
b. 7-18-1817
d. 1-14-1863

MARY CATHERINE
b. 6-25-1845
d. 7-6-1894

GEORGINA
b. 6-20-1849
d. 4-12-1850

MARTHA
b. 9-17-1850
d. 3-23-1867

JOHN WEBER
b. 2-19-1852
d. 3-6-1918

married
11-9-1871
(6 children)

married
3-16-1876
(1 child)

REV. JOHN MANNING
LINN
b. 2-26-1842
d. 6-1-1824

LAURA SHOEMAKER
b. 10-11-1856
d. 1-31-1937

JOHN HUY ADDAMS

married (2)
11-17-1868
(no children)

ANNA HOSTETTER
HALDEMAN
b. 8-12-1828
d. 4-23-1919

Step-Siblings of Jane Addams

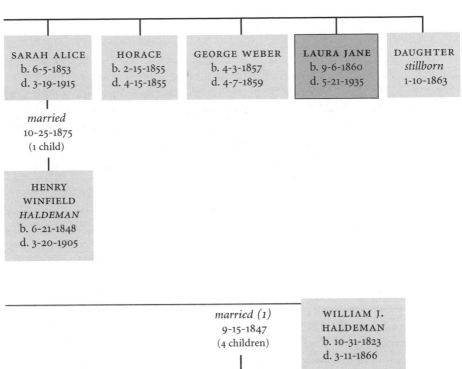

SARAH ALICE	HORACE	GEORGE WEBER	LAURA JANE	DAUGHTER
b. 6-5-1853	b. 2-15-1855	b. 4-3-1857	b. 9-6-1860	*stillborn*
d. 3-19-1915	d. 4-15-1855	d. 4-7-1859	d. 5-21-1935	1-10-1863

married
10-25-1875
(1 child)

**HENRY
WINFIELD
*HALDEMAN***
b. 6-21-1848
d. 3-20-1905

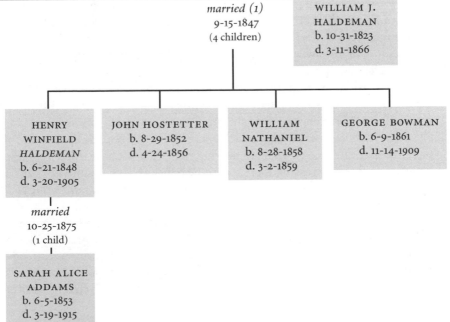

married (1)
9-15-1847
(4 children)

WILLIAM J.
HALDEMAN
b. 10-31-1823
d. 3-11-1866

HENRY WINFIELD *HALDEMAN*	JOHN HOSTETTER	WILLIAM NATHANIEL	GEORGE BOWMAN
b. 6-21-1848	b. 8-29-1852	b. 8-28-1858	b. 6-9-1861
d. 3-20-1905	d. 4-24-1856	d. 3-2-1859	d. 11-14-1909

married
10-25-1875
(1 child)

SARAH ALICE
ADDAMS
b. 6-5-1853
d. 3-19-1915

Addams, Anna Hostetter Haldeman (1828–1919)

Anna Hostetter was born on 12 August 1828 in Lancaster County, Pennsylvania. Ann or Annie, as she was called by family and close friends, was the daughter of Magdalena B. Lichty Hostetter (1793–1835) and Abraham (or Abram) Hostetter (1777–1843), both of German ancestry, who wed on 4 June 1811. At least six other children were born to the couple. The eldest was Susanna ("Susan") (1812–83), who was followed by Jacob (b. 1812), Abraham (1818–73), John Lichty (1821–77), and Noah (1824–1901). The youngest was Barbara (1832?–35), who died from "brain fever" on the same day and a few hours before her mother. In later years Anna Hostetter recalled that she had loved her little sister dearly. After she had been in her dying mother's room where Barbara shared her mother's bed, Anna "would come from the room and go sit alone and ponder over the great wrong that was done" to her. "I thought, am I not, a poor little girl too that will have no mother—and my little sister—the light of my life— to die, too. Oh! These were sadest of, all sad days, that, could come in a childs life" (AHHA to HWH, 25 May 1884, UIC, JAMC, HJ). Toward the end of her life, as she was recounting stories of her youth to a nephew, Anna admitted that on that particular occasion the housekeeper (perhaps the same Irish woman who taught her Irish ballads and stories) had chided her for pouting. She responded, "I am not always pouting when I cry" ([C. L. Hostetter], "[Notes from a conversation with AHHA]").

We know little about the early life of Anna Hostetter, because the record that survives for those years is so slight. After her mother's death, Anna, a precocious child who could read by the time she was five, was raised by her siblings. Mary Fry, who became Anna Hostetter Haldeman Addams's housekeeper and companion beginning in 1890, recalled hearing "her tell how she learned to manipulate her peers by playing on their sympathy to get what she wanted. 'That's all right,' she'd say, 'They buried my mother and left room for my father, but that's all right, you just go ahead and swing'" (Fry, Generous Spirit, 35).

Some time after her sister Susan wed George Bowman in 1836, Anna went to live with them. There, on a farm across the Susquehanna River from Harrisburg in Cumberland County, Pennsylvania, Anna grew to maturity and attended school. The parallels between her early life and that of Jane Addams are striking. Not only did Anna lose the special guidance and attention that her mother might have given, but she also, like Jane, found herself in the care of an elder sister who acted as surrogate mother. In 1847, as Anna was contemplating her marriage to William J. Haldeman and anticipating leaving her sister's home permanently, she wrote, "A feeling of sadness steals o'er—[me?] when I think of leaving my Mother—my sister. She indeed has ever manifested a motherly affection for me, and seems deeply interested in my welfare" ("Diary, 1846[–62]," 1 Feb. 1847).

When Anna Hostetter was fourteen she left school to become her sister's helper, taking on household chores and caring for the Bowman's children. Indeed, she seems to have spent time as a helper in the homes of each of her married siblings while she was being educated in female household responsibilities. It is uncertain who determined that it was time for her formal education to come to an end, but perhaps it was the Bowmans. Later in life she would recall with great sadness and some resentment the fact that she was unable to continue attending school. "I ought to have a repreive, from all kitchen, and cooking work for I begun—at fourteen, to do—all, manner of house work—the age when most girls of any—standing—are going to school. no matter, my—deploma is awaiting me—and, will read, 'Well done good and, faithful servant, enter into the joys of thy rest[']" (AHHA to HWH, 8 Feb. 1894, UIC, JAMC, HJ). Yet her education was far from over. For the remainder of her life she continued to educate herself by reading books and periodicals; attending lectures, plays, and musical events; and traveling.

Like her brothers Abraham and John L. Hostetter, Anna was raised on the religious doctrines and teachings of the New Jerusalem Church. Both brothers were dedicated New Church advocates, and mentions of New Church philosophy and activities permeate their correspondence. Between 1843 and 1847 John sent Anna a series of letters about what he called the "science of life." Two of his special letters to her survive. These reflect not only New Church teachings but also the hopes and expectations of their father, who before his death had presented Anna with a document of instruction about the responsibilities of being an adult female (see Abrm Hostetter, "A father's advice to his daughter").

The philosophy of her brother and father echos and re-echos throughout her diary and in her letters to friends, children, and stepchildren during the remainder of her life. John L. Hostetter stated his basic message in his initial letter: "The great business of life is to do all the good we can, without any reference to external circumstances. The benefits we dispense to those around us whether by our kindnes[s] or good actions, will return to [us] multiplied, in the approval of our understandings. If this be true, then it follows that we can only be happy in proportion as we render others. And reasoning by analogy, we infer that the greatest misery which human beings may endure arises from a conciousness that we have m[ade] others miserable." He also suggested that she avoid vanity and know that there is value in "s[oun]d sense, amiability of temper, cheerfulness without nonsen[se,] grace without affectation, intelligence free from pedant[ry,] and modesty free from blundering bashfulness" (Nov. 1843, JAPP, AHHA).

A year later, he continued his instruction, apparently reiterating portions of advice that he thought particularly pertinent for his sister:

> One of the most attractive qualities of the human mind is amiability of disposition. If it were for no other purpose than to secure the esteem of our fellow beings, a good temper would be well worthy of acquisition; for nothing draws us so irresistibly towards a person as this attribute of goodness and nothing is so repulsive as a boisterous, spleenic, overbearing disposition. Believe me that all over the world goodness of heart is preferable to brilliancy of mind; or, in other words, moral worth is every where more valued, than flashing Wit—but thrice fortunate is that person in whom both are combined. . . . The will is indeed a powerful regulator of actions—and if not restrained by the understanding, it obeys the impulse of feeling and feeling alone is a feeble criterion to judge of the correctness of the motive. (24 June 1844, JAPP, AHHA)

Other members of the Hostetter family might have applauded that advice. Among family materials, there is a description of the prominent personality traits that the Hostetter family associated with Anna: "high temp[ered], dictatorial, Fascinating" and with a "fine mem[ory], literary & poetical" ([Family Genealogical Chart], JAPP, Hostetter Genealogy File).

Anna and John L. Hostetter remained close as brother and sister all their lives. Their relationship seems to have been special. They shared a love of music, literature, good conversation, and friends. It was to John that Anna turned for advice—much as one might a father—in times of stress and momentous decision. She sought his views about both of her marriages, for example, and consulted him about her son Harry Haldeman's marriage to Sarah Alice Addams. His advice—that which has survived in correspondence—was direct and accompanied by the rationale for his suggestions. Although she might not always act on his recommendations, she continued to seek his counsel, indicating that she valued his perspective.

When Abraham and John L. Hostetter determined to emigrate west from their Pennsylvania homes, they convinced a reluctant Susan Bowman to let Anna Hostetter go with them. The travelers, including their friend Alexander Officer and Abraham Hostetter's family, arrived in Mount Carroll, Illinois, on 15 April 1845. They came from Pennsylvania by way of canal up the Susquehanna Valley and over the mountains by inclined plane (via the Portage Railroad line operated by the state of Pennsylvania). In Pittsburgh, they experienced the great fire of 1845 and almost lost their lives as the fire raced to consume the wooden bridge on which they crossed the river to escape the burning city. Steamboats brought them down the Ohio and, after a brief stop in St. Louis, up the Mississippi River to Savanna, Illinois. Then it was only a few miles overland to Mount Carroll.

"Here there are cottages dotted along on the slooping side of this beautiful

Prarie," wrote Anna of Mount Carroll soon after she arrived, "and a stream winding close by, with a waterfall, which, with its murmurmering, at evening hours, lulls all things into silence and repose, except the old Mill which occasionally chimes in, to make some variations, in the almost melancholy music, of the old Mill stream," ("Diary, 1846[–62]," 5 Mar. [1846]). She and John settled into a cottage in the village, where he continued to offer Anna lessons in the "science of life." While John and his brother Abraham began their medical practice, Anna took up housekeeping. She was seventeen.

On 1 January 1846 she began to keep a diary. It reveals that her days were filled with household chores and with visits to friends. On Sundays, she usually attended a church service. Anna may have taught Sunday School for a brief time after she came to Mount Carroll. She spent her evenings around the fireside with conversation, games (among them blind-man's bluff, cards, and chess), reading aloud, and musicales as entertainments. Anna and her brother received callers, who were often her suitors, at their cottage, or they went out into the village visiting friends. Sometimes they attended lectures and readings associated with temperance meetings or the local lyceum organization. Anna described one pleasant evening when her brother John played the clarinet to Alexander Officer's flute while she sang in what she described wittily and perhaps proudly as a "melodious voice" ("Diary, 1846[–62]," 11 Mar. [1846]).

When the Hostetter party came up the Mississippi River on the *Sara Ann* to Illinois for the first time, a concert violinist was on board. When he heard Anna sing he commented to her brother, "if I had a sister who could sing like that I would take her on the first boat to Europe" ([C. L. Hostetter], "Aunt Ann's Discription of Pittsburg Fire" 6 Nov. 1909). Music became one of Anna Hostetter's life-long passions. It was in January 1862 that she received a guitar as a belated Christmas gift. She learned to play it and used it for the remainder of her life when she sang and played for friends and children.

Anna was a popular young woman. She was tall and slender with long, "burnished chestnut" hair and "often restless" hazel eyes (M. Haldeman-Julius, "Two Mothers," 12). According to Marcet Haldeman-Julius, who, by her own admission worshiped her grandmother, "Her hands were arrestingly beautiful. . . . I never saw her do anything more useful with her hands than adjust objects in a room, care for her flowers and strum a guitar when she sang the ballads of Moore and Burns" (12).

Anna saw herself as "a social being" and stated that she would "try to cultivate social feelings, toward those, among whom my lot is cast" ("Diary, 1846[–62]," 12 Feb. [1846]). "I do certainly enjoy the spice of life, if it exists in variety," she confided to her diary on 28 February 1846 ("Diary, 1846[–62]"). She loved the attention of others and found conversation in which she could participate most entertaining. In an entry for 29 January 1846, she wrote, "when we are all seated around our cottage fire side conversing upon subjects that elevate the mind and purify the affections, I forget my distant home [in Pennsylvania], in the enjoyment of one that is equally pleasant" ("Diary, 1846[–62]"). On another, less satisfying occasion when her brother Abraham came to call, she recorded that she was pleased to see him "although his society added but little to my enjoyment, for he and John were speaking of things, that did not interest <u>me</u>" ("Diary, 1846[–62]," 4 Mar. [1846]).

During the first five months of 1846 Anna received at least three proposals of marriage, two of which she rejected. The third was tendered by William J. Haldeman, whom she may have met shortly after she arrived in Mount Carroll. He was an attentive suitor, coming to visit or to take her to meetings or to visit friends three or four times each week. Their attraction for one another must have been mutual. He made his intentions known on 22 February 1846, for she recorded in her diary on that date: "This evening Mr. Halderman [Haldeman] spent here, and to me there were some unexpected revelations made, which will not easily be erased from, my mind. I do not know but, <that> I should have doubted, the authenticity of those revalations; Had not the true saying of the wise Solomon come into my mind, 'from the fullness of the heart the mouth speaketh'" ("Diary, 1846[–62]").

Even before he revealed his feelings she seems to have been partial to William Haldeman. On 18 January 1846 she wrote, "the world has given the latter one to me as an intended husband and no doubt will take him away from me again. I would rather see time prove such matters than to here tell of them—for I am inclined to think such reports are always fullfilled in contrary manner" ("Diary, 1846[–62]"). Haldeman was certainly on her mind, for a day later, on 19 January, Anna noted, "I have a particular regard for him, on account of the many good qualities, he posesses. This is not love I am speaking of for that operates (if I understand the definition of it) differently" ("Diary, 1846[–62]"). Two weeks later, on 3 February, after being at her brother Abraham's home where Haldeman was also in attendance, she recorded, "He and I being there together has caused them to think, that some relationship is going to take place between us, but to me it is all imaginery" ("Diary, 1846[–62]"). By 10 March 1846 Anna may have indicated her true feelings for him as well. On that day she had received an unwanted call from a Mr. Robinson, who pronounced his intention to court her with the idea of marriage. She reported that she felt enormous relief when her brother John came in and interrupted the presentation. That night her diary received the following: "The evening Mr. Halderman [Haldeman] called in and no one was so glad to see him as I. An open confession is good for the soul—" ("Diary, 1846[–62]").

From the time that Anna arrived in Mount Carroll, she seems to have been homesick for her friends and family in Pennsylvania. On 12 February 1846 she wrote, "How happy I will <be> if once more, landed safely on the shore of my native land. Once more to be surrounded with friends, who so dearly loved me in bygone days, and shall I see them all or are they gone? some perhaps to distant countries, or to the <u>Land</u> of <u>love</u>, and if even so; their bonds of love, with me, are still not broken[.] Nor shall those friendships, ever: by me, be forgotten" ("Diary, 1846[–62]"). Even with her growing interest in William Haldeman, she wrote on 5 March 1846, "Oh how I long to leave Mount Carroll, with all its pleasures and endearments, to dwell again in my own native clime" ("Diary, 1846[–62]").

Anna apparently experienced numerous mood swings and admonished herself frequently to be more even-tempered. On 20 January 1846 her reaction to gloomy weather caused her to "indulge in melancholy thoughts," and she made a new resolution: "I will hereafter (as far as I can overcome human nature) enjoy the present, let come what may, and will have it as a motto imprinted on my mind, so that, if the most adverse circumstances should frown upon me, I shall even then enjoy peace and tranquility" ("Diary, 1846[–62]"). Her private writings are peppered with reminders to respond to life situations, whatever they were, in a positive way. On 7 February 1846 she recorded, "[T]his day has been a stereotyped addition of monotony and sameness. The only way I could calm my troubled spirit, Was to put in practice my resolution, and by so doing I became perfectly reconciled to my lot" ("Diary, 1846[–62]"). She was often in search of "peace and tranquility" as she described it for the remainder of her life.

From time to time, Anna reminded herself how much she enjoyed being alone. "I enjoy myself very well (when I have interesting books to read,) quite alone" ("Diary, 1846[–62]," 9 Feb. [1846]). Apparently, she was trying to put into practice lessons she had learned from her brother's "science of life" curriculum. "I this day have again realized the fact," she wrote on 22 January 1846, "[t]hat true happiness alone can flow, from <doing> kind and benevolent acts to others—" ("Diary, 1846[–62]"). "I shall endevor to have sun shine and smiles to accompany me through life, for sorrow and sighing, come without calling," she recorded three days later ("Diary, 1846[–62]," 25 Jan. [1846]). Although on 6 February 1846 she indicated that she particularly liked domestic chores because they kept her busy and made it easier to deal with homesickness, by 25 March 1846 she was reporting that washday work "corresponded with the weather, for both were disagreeable" ("Diary, 1846[–62]"). One of the reasons she may have looked forward to going home, as she put it, was that she would "have a long rest from all such labours [as laundry]" ("Diary, 1846[–62]," 4 May [1846]).

When she carried out her planned return to her sister's home in Pennsylvania in May 1846 she worried about leaving her intended behind. Her brother John counseled that all would be well. Although the couple expected to wed in the next spring, their plans were altered. Susan Bowman was uncertain that William J. Haldeman was an appropriate or potentially successful enough provider for her sister. She apparently hoped that Anna would find a mate in Pennsylvania. It is likely that the Bowmans even presented a potential candidate in a relative named John D. Bowman. Haldeman wrote to Anna that he could not "blame your sister for her opposition for it is but the natural outpouring of an affectionate heart" (24 Jan. 1847, UIC, JAMC, HJ).

The two lovers carried out an extensive correspondence, sharing their hopes and feelings. "True happiness you are well aware," wrote Anna on Valentine's Day in 1847, "cannot flow from the love of self—neither can any one enjoy perfect peace of mind without paying a strict regard to truth. . . . It is my desire and aim, to live a useful life—and as you possess a still more generous nature than mine—I trust, with our combined efforts we may, while passing through—life, do something for the amelioration—of the cause of human suffering, among those among whom our lot is cast. I have not found love to be a raging passion as some devine it, but <it> seems like a gentle stream, flowing in upon my mind which waves on with the fleeting years getting deeper and deeper the nearer it approaches the goal" (JAPP, AHHA). "Would that I could lay this pen aside and clasp you to my heart," William wrote on 14 December 1846, "words would not be needed then to tell how much my life, my being is wraped up in yours—how much my happiness, my all depends on you. . . . You know that my whole heart is yours, that I regard you indeed as a part of my better being. If so, our mutual confidence will never be shaken, for I know I feel, that in your very heart you love me, and that nothing but a few unmeasured leagues prevent us from being one in evry sence" (UIC, JAMC, HJ). "[I]f the hope of seeing you, and if being yours—were cut off, then, I fear, I should become weary—of living, and earth with all its beauties, could not fill the aching void within my breast," Anna wrote in the spring of 1847 (9 Apr. 1847, JAPP, AHHA). Romance and William J. Haldeman, "with the gentle heart of a poet," finally won Anna's hand in marriage (M. Haldeman-Julius, "Two Mothers," 10). William made the journey to Cumberland County, Pennsylvania, to wed Anna on 15 September 1847, and the young couple returned to make their home among relatives in Mount Carroll.

Although the Haldemans found their livelihood in Mount Carroll, both referred to the community as "dull." They probably began keeping house in a little cottage near the one in which Anna had lived with John L. Hostetter. The social affairs, educational opportunities, friendships, and general life of the community had changed little since she had left in 1846. Quickly pregnant, she was caught up in household chores, which were still not among her favorite activities. When at home with her sister in Pennsylvania, she reported on 8 March 1847 that the hired girl left and that she had to take her place. Entries in her diary from 9 through 17 March 1847, when the entries cease, indicate an increasingly unhappy Anna. She was "very tired of" her "occupation" ("Diary, 1846[–62]," 16 Mar. [1847]) and weary and lonesome, for she "had to work hard" ("Diary, 1846[–62]," 17 Mar. [1847]).

The newlyweds received and made calls. They still spent evenings around the hearth, reading, discussing what they read, and gossiping. They had parties and musicales. There were also trips to Chicago to visit their friend Alexander Officer, his wife, and his sister and to attend New Jerusalem Church functions and entertainments. Yet Anna Haldeman never quite relinquished her attachment to Pennsylvania relatives and friends. For several years, especially while a relatively new bride, she went to stay with relatives in Pennsylvania (including Haldeman kin) from late fall until spring while husband William remained in Mount Carroll managing his mercantile business. Her first long trip east seems to have taken place beginning in 1849, when she was accompanied by her six-month-old son, Henry Winfield Haldeman, born on 21 June 1848 in Mount Carroll. Until the George Bowman family moved to the Mount Carroll area in the late 1850s Anna Haldeman went east for large segments of time almost every year that she was not expecting a child.

The Haldemans had three other children. John Hostetter Haldeman, born in Mount Carroll on 29 August 1852, was almost four when he died from scarlet fever on 24 April 1856 in Mount Carroll. William Nathaniel Haldeman was born on 28 August 1858 after the couple had settled in Freeport and died on 22 March 1859. Initially, both children were buried in Mount Carroll, but in 1919 their remains were moved to the Cedarville Cemetery. In memory of her two middle sons, Anna recorded in a 2 January 1862 diary entry, "This day has been anything but a happy one. Memory buisy with the past has brought up my dear little boys to my mental view and, then did I fall into a reverie about those little icy forms laid away into the 'silent land' where, one has slept under the white chrisp winter snow almost three winters, the older one almost twice as long, but, their bright spirits are oh so happy, in the—Kingdom of Heaven, be calm my Mothers heart" ("Diary, 1846[–62]"). The Haldemans' last child, George Bowman Haldeman, was born near Mount Carroll on 9 June 1861.

In 1857 William J. Haldeman, who knew as early as 1856 that he had "lung disease," sold his Mount Carroll store, which had long been associated with the Haldeman mill in the same town. He moved his family to Freeport, where he owned and operated the new Stone Steam Flour Mill. It is difficult to know what precipitated this move. It may have been a simple matter of a better business opportunity or wishing to be more separate from the Haldeman and Hostetter families. Or it may have been an attempt to put the sadness of the death of their second child behind them. The Haldemans settled in a house in the Second Ward of Freeport with one servant and began to make friends in their new community.

By 1861 Anna was pregnant again and fearful that the child she carried might die. She was convinced that her baby would have a better chance of survival if, both before and after the child was born, she was near what she considered competent medical help. And so she left Freeport, her husband, and his new business to be near her physician brothers in Mount Carroll. There she settled with her sister-mother Susan Bowman and her family at their home, Oakland, to await the birth of her last child. Initially, her son Harry, about thirteen and attending school in Mount Carroll, was with her at the Bowmans. He apparently became so unmanageable when her new son was born, however, that she sent Harry to be with his father in Freeport.

After George Bowman Haldeman was born, Anna remained at the Bowmans' home for almost a year despite frequent pleas from William to return to

Freeport. In December 1861 he told her that he was "tired of Bachelor—or rather widdower life—and am looking round in hopes of finding some kind of a bird cage to gather you all in" (William J. Haldeman to AHHA, 15 Dec. 1861, UIC, JAMC, HJ). His letters in early 1862 reveal that he was offering her an assortment of dwellings and hoping that one would entice her to leave Mount Carroll for Freeport. She assured him of her love and devotion and recorded in her diary that she hoped "every wife might have so kind a husband—without a vice to taint him—all nobleness of soul all real worth" ("Diary, 1846[–62]," 12 Jan. 1862). "[M]y friend of friends," she wrote. "I love to write his name in full and, I am the happier and better woman for being loved by him" ("Diary, 1846[–62]," 28 Feb. 1862).

An unpleasant confrontation between Anna and her sister Susan eventually precipitated Anna's return to Freeport. Anna's diary entry for 5 March 1862, the day of the clash, reads in part:

> You have been an unhappy day "brought forth fruit—meat for repentance," and I trust that few may be the hurricanes of indignation that shall sweep across my soul, such as I contended with this evening—and, the desolation—of affection and of love—that, will follow, for,—"who can minister to a mind—diseased, pluck from the heart a rooted sorrow" but trust on brave heart all will be well some day, and bright will be your day star when it downs. "Life is short and, time is fleeting and the grave is not its goal" so if we do not get our due amount of happiness here I trust to—be happy in eternity if God will pardon my sins—and make me fitt to enter in at the strait gait—"for strait is the gait and narrow is the way and few their be who find it." ("Diary, 1846[–62]")

Susan's daughter Anna Martha, who might be expected to take her mother's part, reported in her diary on the same day that "Aunt Ann has been talking so ugly to Mother and it makes me feel bad. She has been here at our house a year. And I think Mother has taken her share of ugly talk from Aunt Ann. I can take my share of it but it is strength from above and not mine through which I hear it. I hope I may ever be able to conquer ugly feelings which rise in me" (Bowman, "Diary, 1862[–83]"). Hiding little of her pleasure in her Aunt Anna's discomfort, three days later Anna Martha Bowman reported that her Uncle William and Cousin Harry came unexpectedly on Sunday, March 8, and "Aunt Ann did not have her room cleaned and she was not dressed in her best. People will sometimes be taken unawares as it happened Sunday," and on 12 April 1862 she recorded that "Uncle William wrote to Mother that he and Aunt Ann are comfortably situated in their new house with a good hyred girl. I am glad they have. May joy go with them" (Bowman, "Diary, 1862[–83]").

During the next few years, the Haldemans seemed to have settled more comfortably in Freeport. The cloud on the horizon was William Haldeman's health. By the fall of 1865 he was back in Mount Carroll, being cared for by one of his Haldeman relatives and struggling with the end stage of tuberculosis. From the late fall of 1865 through his death from the disease on 6 March 1866, Anna and her two sons lodged in Mount Carroll with William's brother Nathaniel. Distraught and disconsolate at the loss of her husband, she shared her anguish with brother John, who advised, "[T]he world is cold—and rough, we cannot help. . . . It is only by sometimes forgetting our own wants and troubles, and intently searc[h]ing to benefit the neighbor that we are enabled to see how much need they have as well as we for kindness, forbearance and instruction" (26 May 1866, IU, Lilly, SAAH).

Anna Haldeman found herself a thirty-eight-year-old widow with two sons to raise. Harry, who had been a student at Mount Carroll Seminary, was eighteen, and George, barely five, was almost ready for school. In his will, William J. Haldeman had made Anna and Nathaniel co-executors of his estate. In addition, Anna was to be the legal guardian of their children unless she remarried. In that case, Nathaniel would become the sole executor of the estate and the guardian of the children until each reached majority.

The estate was composed of the real property on which the Stone Steam Flour Mill was built, one additional lot in Freeport (on which one hundred of the three-hundred-dollar purchase price was still owed), the milling operation itself with its assets and receivables, and U.S. bonds. The estate's estimated value on 20 March 1866 was $24,760.60. By August, Nathaniel Haldeman had requested that the court of Stephenson County discharge him from his responsibility as co-executor, leaving Anna as the sole executor of her husband's estate.

A little more than two years later, on 18 November 1868, when Anna relinquished her position as executor as a result of her marriage to John Huy Addams, the condition of the estate she passed into the hands of the reinstated executor Nathaniel Haldeman had been altered considerably. The mill, which burned about six months after William's death, was still being carried on the estate books as having the same value, fifteen thousand dollars, that it did when it was fully operational. For the two years that she had charge of the estate Anna had tried, unsuccessfully, to sell the property. She also submitted a list of articles that she declared had been stolen from the mill and produced a list of William Haldeman's accounts receivable that she had been unable to collect. In addition, uncollected receivables had accrued, and she also gave an accounting of "Other Monies Paid" out. These amounted to a total of $6,249.38 and included more than $2,000 to support Harry, who was studying music and medicine in Europe; approximately $1,800 in expenses associated with protecting and operating the mill; approximately $500 to support George; taxes of more than $500; a payment of $500 to Nathaniel for his services; and the purchase of a cemetery plot for $345. When Nathaniel received the estate, there was little in liquid assets available from which he could pay taxes or maintain the insurance on the mill property. There was no accounting of the funds Anna Haldeman had expended to support herself during her tenure as executor.

During the two years after William J. Haldeman's death, Anna continued to live in Freeport. There, she tried to secure millers to operate the Stone Steam Flour Mill; looked after her son George; and, according to Jane Addams's biographer James Weber Linn, gave music lessons to Freeport children. There, too, a new suitor came into her life. Addams family lore contends that on the very day that William J. Haldeman lay dying an acquaintance of both men stopped John Huy Addams to tell him that news. Suddenly and apparently with some chagrin—at least in retrospect—John Addams had the idea that Anna Hostetter Haldeman would be an appropriate wife for him and mother for his children. It seems that his daughter Martha, who had been taking piano lessons, had been practicing in the Haldeman home (the Addamses having no piano at the time). Anna had won Martha's admiration with her quick wit, sparkling eyes, and love of music, and Martha would come home to regale her father and siblings with flattering stories of Mrs. Haldeman.

Although Addams may have had his eye on Anna as soon as she was widowed, he apparently waited an appropriate length of time for mourning before he began to present himself as a potential suitor. It seems likely that to begin with she rejected him. "Permit me to frankly say that I sincerely regret that your sympathies do not accord with my own," he wrote to "Mrs. Halderman [.] Dear Madam" on 30 June 1868. "I cannot but admire the frankness and generous kindness with which you decline the sentiment for which I had hoped might be favorably considered," he continued. "In requesting an interview (perhaps persistently) had contemplated what would naturally occur to you, both of us having families, but cherished the idea that proper explanations could be made" (SCPC, JAC).

By the end of the summer, however, Anna had changed her mind. Vicenta Fensely wrote to her that she was certain Anna "enjoyed the company of" her "warmhearted friend very much" (26 July 1868, UIC, JAMC, HJ Supp.). Indeed, Anna Haldeman was looking at John Addams with a great deal more interest. He was established, he was powerful, and he was wealthy. She and her children would be secure. In addition, she could relinquish the burdensome responsibility of the estate of her first husband. John Hostetter thought that the marriage made sense and that, if she would, she could make John Addams happy and herself as well. With little romance in the relationship—at least on her part—the couple were wed on 17 November 1868, and Anna and her sons moved to Cedarville.

The next thirteen years of her life, the years of her marriage to John Huy Addams, may not have been very happy ones. In an 1871 letter to her stepdaughter Alice she confided some of her disappointments and at the same time chided Alice for continuing to focus on clothes and food:

I many—many—times—mentally leave Cedarville—and travel into the past—there to revel in the rich store house, that, Memory ever contains for me: And on wings of hope, fly down the future believing—it too hold many a happy day in store.

The present has so many somber realities—to contend with—I sometimes wonder—what all the—daily routine means—when so much goes (for—the attain-
ment of) <u>something</u> to <u>eat</u> and to <u>wear</u>—. The imortal part, the higher spiritual,
faculties, all—dragged—down, to meet the exegencies of the case. And thus un-
less we constantly watch we become of the <u>earth</u>—<u>more</u> <u>earthy</u> every day. (12 Sept.
1871, UIC, JAMC, HJ Supp.)

As a new bride, Anna Addams began to establish herself in her new household and community. She called on Cedarville neighbors and set about becoming John Huy Addams's wife. Initially, she went with her new husband to Springfield for sessions of the Illinois General Assembly, but that social outlet was soon
closed to her. To her dismay, her husband decided not to seek reelection to the
Illinois senate. James Weber Linn indicates, in text that Jane Addams read and
approved, that Senator Addams did not go back to the General Assembly because "there had been social wars and rumors of wars" associated with his new
wife "disturbing to the Senator's mind" (*Jane Addams*, 30). Linn was of the
opinion that Anna Addams nagged her husband to take further political office
but that he declined. Marcet Haldeman-Julius believed that the women of
Springfield were jealous of the beauty and wit of the new Mrs. Addams.

Anna Addams apparently never achieved the level of intellectual intimacy
and friendship with John Huy Addams that she had with William J. Haldeman.
The few surviving letters between them indicate that Anna's letters to John at
the beginning of their marriage were warm and affectionate, but no extant later ones or diary entries reveal the progression of her feelings. John addressed
letters to "My dear Wife" and signed them "Affectionately" during his last term
in the General Assembly. Pleasant and respectful, they are not full of the open
ardor that she seems to have achieved with William or expected from John.

John and Anna Addams were a union of opposites in personality and interests. She was emotional, given to outbursts of feeling, lively, fun-loving, outgoing, self-centered, full of imagination, and willing to investigate new ideas;
he was calm, conservative, even, pragmatic, logical, determined, concerned for
others, and smart but not intellectual. He was dedicated to public service; she
was not. She was apparently not a woman who joined or participated in clubs
or women's groups for her own benefit or that of her community. Although he
did read at least one novel that Anna recommended during their first year of
marriage, he preferred to read history, biography, philosophy, and practical how-
to books, whereas she loved literature and poetry. They did not share the same
commitment to traditional religious practice or the same pleasure in the theater or music. Anna Addams ran John Addams's household, and he provided
the financial means by which she did it. He participated in her family's special
occasions and she in his. They vacationed together and held social events for
friends and family. They attended their children's exhibitions and graduation
ceremonies—especially those of George and Jane. In 1881, after the death of

George Haldeman's legal guardian Nathaniel Haldeman, John Addams made plans to assume that guardianship until George reached maturity. The couple's concern for the welfare of their children was likely the major element of bonding in their life together, and because of the difficulties they experienced with their blended family they had to work at that part of their relationship, too.

When Anna Addams was denied the social life she craved in Springfield, she pursued one at home, where she entertained members of her own family—some from the East but most from Mount Carroll. Among her favorite nieces and nephews were Charles Linnaeus Hostetter and Mamie Hostetter Greenleaf. Both followed intellectual interests that mirrored her own, the former in history and literature and the latter in music. Although Marcet Haldeman-Julius asserted that Anna was "frankly, a man's woman" ("Two Mothers," 15) and adored men—which she did—she also had close female friends. Among them were Laura Malburn of Freeport; Vicenta Fensley, who lived in various places in Illinois until she moved from Illinois to the West Coast; Sarah Officer, sister of Alexander Officer, who settled in Chicago; and an assortment of women she met during her travels. Almost all of the women with whom she maintained a friendship were, like Anna, cultured and interested in arts and literature.

She was never able to establish many close friendships with neighbors in Cedarville, however. Marcet Haldeman-Julius believed that "[i]n the village of Cedarville her fondness for the arts, her easy familiarity with books and classical music, gave rise to the suspicion that she was (though the term was not then invented) 'highbrow.'" Moreover, "Her poise and manner were regarded, by those who did not like her, as 'putting on airs.' Her interest in social life, which arose entirely from her pleasure in mentally stimulating companionship, was distorted into the vulgar interpretation of 'climbing'" ("Two Mothers," 14–15). And she was so very different from the first Mrs. Addams. Mary Fry, who became her devoted companion and housekeeper, recalled being frightened when, as a young girl of twelve, she presented herself to Anna Addams for the first time. "Mary . . . knew Mrs. Addams by reputation," Paul Fry remembered in his biography of his special aunt. He added that Anna Addams's "haughtiness was a topic of conversation in the village, as was her quick temper" (*Generous Spirit*, 34). The village also knew Anna to be a difficult employer who had trouble keeping help. Jane Addams herself seems to have admonished James Weber Linn for "being too hard on her stepmother" in his initial treatment of her. "Mrs. Addams," Jane said, "was just in the wrong place to be appreciated." She also apparently "realized that people in the village [of Cedarville] were still talking about her stepmother, fifteen years after her death" (Fry, *Generous Spirit*, 9).

Anna Addams began to solidify her position as a stepmother as soon as she returned from her honeymoon trip to the East. She launched efforts to influence the intellectual, social, and cultural development of the Addams children and to inform and improve their manners, as she did those of her own sons. John Weber Addams, responding to one of her corrections, wrote, "I am very much obliged to you for your kind <u>hint</u> in respect to <the> use of my fork and I will strive to improve by it" (JWA to AHHA, 21 Feb. 1869, UIC, JAMC, HJ). While Alice Addams was visiting relatives in Pennsylvania during the summer of 1871, Anna wrote a series of letters to her. Those that survive are full of advice. "Study '<u>men</u>, and, <u>things</u>,' (as well—as women, and particularly, the young <u>girl</u> of the <u>period</u>). Making a <u>long period</u>—in favor of, the one with <u>good</u> <u>com-</u> <u>mon</u> **sense**. The latter type, I hope my Alice can be classed in—," stepmother Anna suggested (6 July 1871, IU, Lilly, SAAH). In the next month she offered Alice more counsel, particularly on the matter of selfishness. The goal, she told Alice, was to

> develope <u>our</u> Allie into a <u>nobler</u> <u>wiser</u>, and <u>better</u> <u>woman</u>, for, we are constantly progressing—or retrograding. . . . Development, development, is the soul's demand. The <u>highest</u> <u>development</u>—is to see and know the Lord in all His works.
>
> To love Him above all things—and fellow beings as our selves. For this high end we must lose sight of our selfishness, by trying to make others—as happy as we would wish to be; (that is to do all in our power, to make others so).
>
> Not wishing to moralize I could not help saying what—I have, because I see so many <u>heartless</u> young people growing up selfish and, <u>perfectly</u> <u>regardless</u> of any one; But <u>themselves</u> and their own enjoyment. (19 Aug. 1871, UIC, JAMC, HJ Supp.)

Sons George and Harry were also treated to their share of her direction.

One by one, all of the children whom John Huy Addams initially placed in Anna's care left home to begin independent lives—all, that is, save Jane Addams and her own George Haldeman. Mary Catherine Addams wed John Manning Linn in the fall of 1871 and left the Addams home. Although she returned to Cedarville for visits while her father was living, she seems not to have visited the widow Addams after his death. Nor were her children, with the possible exception of Esther Margaret Linn, who spent time in the John Weber Linn household in Cedarville, close to their step-grandmother Addams. By 1869 John Weber Addams had also left the Addams home. The precipitating occasion was a major disagreement with his stepmother, probably exacerbated by his developing mental illness. For the remainder of his life, when not resident in a mental institution he lived in the Cedarville area. Although the home he built for his family was just across Cedar Creek from the Addams home and the road between them short and direct, the John Weber Addams family and Anna Addams were apparently not especially close or supportive family or neighbors. Anna evidently saw Laura and Sarah Addams from time to time but with no regularity. In 1894 she complained to son Harry that Laura and her brother Will Shoemaker "drove by yesterday he (Shoemaker) returned without his sister in the evening, and today I was told she is gone for a visit—Maybe to Hull House. I never know only what others tell me. I have not been on the Hill since the funeral [of Mary Catherine Addams Linn]" (AHHA to HWH, 7 Oct. 1894, UIC, JAMC, HJ Supp.).

Initially, the relationship between Alice Addams and her stepmother seems to have been affectionate; it cooled considerably, however, when Harry Haldeman determined to wed Alice. This Miss Addams was apparently not the choice of a wife that Anna would have made for her elder son. When the couple produced Anna's only grandchild, Anna Marcet Haldeman, her relationship with Alice improved. Alice brought Marcet to visit her grandmother and uncle George Haldeman in Cedarville almost yearly. In addition, Anna Addams must have been grateful for Alice's help in caring for George Haldeman, who was in Girard, Kansas, for long periods of time while Harry tried to cure him of depression. Anna castigated Alice, however, for what she believed to be unwifely treatment of Harry as the couple aged in their marriage and Alice became more independent. She also faulted Alice's attachment to her sister Jane, for her commitment to social work in Girard, and for managing her own financial affairs without permitting Harry access to her funds. After Harry died in 1905, however, the aging Anna Addams reconciled with Alice, and the two became close again. Alice served as Anna's trusted financial advisor and helped oversee the management of the Addams home.

By early 1870, Harry, his mother's favorite and eldest, was also gone from the Addams home. John Huy Addams apparently believed that it was time for Harry to be gainfully employed. Harry, however, wanted to complete his education and become a physician like his Hostetter uncles. He set out on his own to achieve that dream. Anna Addams mourned his loss and kept up with his progress as a musician and physician for the remainder of his life through correspondence and periodic visits. "I get homesick to see him it will soon be a year since he went away, and, as, he is not so far away [in Mendota, Illinois] it seems harder not to have him come. But 'all is well, that, ends well[.]' And as he is doing, well, in his profession—and has been so successful in making so many warm friends among strangers, I will try and be content," she wrote to Alice (19 Aug. 1871, UIC, JAMC, HJ Supp.). Mother and son had similar personalities and shared many interests. Before he became a practicing physician, Anna tried to help him publish his poetry and music. After the death of her brother John L. Hostetter in 1873, Harry became a special confidante and advisor. Although she did not like his alcoholism and counseled him frequently about drinking, the two found little else to disagree about. Perhaps their most significant difference of opinion came over his choice of Alice Addams as a wife.

Throughout her life, Anna Addams continued to help her eldest son. In 1878 she, perhaps with John Huy Addams's blessing, bought Harry a medical practice in Mitchellville, Iowa. After Addams died in 1881 she may also have helped Harry purchase farm property in Iowa. When the Haldeman couple left the life of a country physician behind in Mitchellville in 1884 for banking in Girard, Kansas, Anna was so relieved that she helped them buy the Bank of Girard in 1886. As she had in Iowa, she permitted her son to invest her widow's inheritance in notes primarily secured by land in the Girard area.

As mother and son aged, their relationship became stronger and emotionally more intimate. She consulted Harry constantly about George's condition and progress. They also conferred about financial and real estate matters, about Marcet, about Harry's own physical and emotional health, and about Haldeman and Hostetter family matters. Anna became the sounding board for Harry's marital problems, and she, better than almost anyone else, understood his love of music and literature. In the summer of 1894 she wrote to him, "life would seem too dismal for me to live on in without you my dear dear son. You have been my comforter always—and what would George do—we two—would be so bereft—that nothing would lend happiness to life" (UIC, JAMC, HJ). Three years later, Anna had drawn even closer to Harry:

> I begin too feel so forcibly the help and need of your presence and—effeciency—that, my soul cries out—to you in ways, that, you must feel it. Oh! Harry! Harry! why—must we—be so sepperated? And life so short and fleeting—atleast—at my age? The thirteen years we were boon-companions before George came as a factor in our family life, gave you the presidence as my advisor and counselor—and knitted our love—and interests—with "Hooks of steel" (which only death can break)[.] Am just as true and devoted a Mother to George, but never dared lean upon him—in emergencys as I have done with you. The shadings are so delicate, that make <up> the difference—betwen you—that you will understand, while I can not express all I feel. (7 May 1897, JAPP, DeLoach)

By 1871, with the three oldest Addams children and her own Harry away from the Addams home, Anna had time to direct her considerable energies, hopes, ambitions, and knowledge into the two youngest children in her care, Jane Addams and George Haldeman. She taught them manners and appropriate dress and personal hygiene and encouraged their social friendships. She saw that they had household responsibilities and began to learn the male and female culture of the day. She also entertained them with stories, songs, and games. A child who grew up visiting Anna Addams recalled that to be read to by her "was such a special treat . . . because . . . [Anna Addams] read every story with such drama that it was like a trip to the theater" (Fry, *Generous Spirit*, 110). Jane Addams herself wrote of an evening in 1875: "It is pretty cold and looks as if it was going to storm, this evening we were all sitting in the room in dark or rather moonlight, and talked and Ma told us stories and so on until I went to see what time it was and lo and behold it was twenty minutes to nine when it did not seem more than seven" ("Pocket Diary, 1875[–81]," 15 Mar. 1875; *JAPM*, 28:1536). In the winter, Anna led her charges in mind-building games played around the fire or the dining table. In the summer, she encouraged outdoor play. "Kate Miller . . . and the children are out playing croquet," she reported. "Kate and Jennie against George with two balls. Last evening George and I beat Kate and Jennie[.] I do not know how the game will end this morning, or who will win" (AHHA to SAA, 19 Aug. 1871, UIC, JAMC, HJ Supp.). Anna fostered the physical well-being of the children through play. An expert horsewoman herself, she required her stepdaughter to take up the practice of riding.

Until Jane Addams went away to Rockford Female Seminary, she was almost constantly under the guidance and watchful eye of her stepmother. For the whole of each of their lives, however, only three letters from Anna to Jane seem to be extant. The earliest was written by Anna at the end of the 1878 school year, when Jane anticipated returning home from her first year at the seminary. In addition to directions about packing her bedding and other furnishings from her room for storage over the summer, Anna offered gossip about former teachers and neighbors and advice:

> Am glad my child is so cheerful,—and feels happy, in making a retrospect of the past—that, her school work has been well-done,—and gives her content—so far as she has gone; But alas! we can but push open a crevic, (thro' the great barrier of ignorance)—by patient labor and, steady endevor—and find the great labyrinths of knowledge, winding in devious ways, far beyond our mortal ken. . . . Do without fail get your bedding—and, other things, you do not use in, a shape to pack carefully before the last—week (or days). . . . but see to it yourself or it may get lost. (AHHA to JA, 11 June [1878], IU, Lilly, SAAH; *JAPM*, 1:301)

After Jane graduated from Rockford Female Seminary, she remained under her stepmother's roof as daughter and companion, although she began spending more and more time away from Cedarville with her siblings, with Addams and Weber relatives, and with friends she had made in seminary.

Anna Addams understood that George required special support and encouragement. He and Jane had grown up together and were treated to similar teachings and influences. They seem to have become ready playmates and sibling-like friends. Anna believed her son to be extraordinarily intelligent yet not physically robust. She was proud of his scholastic achievements but fussed constantly about the state of his health, even as she encouraged him to pursue a career in science. She also worried about his emotional stability and prodded him, unsuccessfully it seems, to become more outgoing and social. Although she may have tried, Anna also failed at instilling a sense of independence in George. Ultimately, he seemed to find security only within a circle of the immediate and familiar Addams/Haldeman family that included his mother and Jane. As he became more and more reclusive, George would remain especially tied to his mother for the remainder of his life.

With John Huy Addams's unexpected death in August 1881, Anna inherited one-third of his estate and retained possession of the Addams homestead. Although she had hoped to replace her husband as a director of the Second National Bank that he had founded in Freeport, she was thwarted in that goal when, much to her dismay, John Weber Addams was appointed instead. She did, however, have control of considerable assets and set out to have the entertaining cultural and social life she so craved.

After spending the fall and winter of 1881–82 in Philadelphia, accompanying Jane Addams and Sarah Alice and Harry Haldeman, all of whom were in medical school, she returned to Cedarville to continue recuperating from surgery she had undergone in Philadelphia. By the next winter she and George vacationed in Florida while Jane recovered from back surgery performed by Harry Haldeman in Iowa. It was the first of what would be several more visits that Anna would make to Green Cove Springs and its surrounding area in Florida. Again back in Cedarville, she gathered the rest of the immediate family, and they went to Beloit, Wisconsin, where they had the pleasure of seeing George graduate from Beloit College.

Because George anticipated going to graduate school at Johns Hopkins University in Baltimore, Anna and Jane, still recovering from back surgery, planned their first European trip. After Anna spent the summer with George in Annisquam, Massachusetts, the two women left for Europe in the fall of 1883, accompanied by Anna's niece Sarah Hostetter and in a party with three other women. During two years in Europe, Anna was often ill, suffered at least one serious fall, enjoyed and taught Jane to appreciate opera and classical music, and had the pleasure of sharing travel experiences with George, who joined them in the summer of 1884. For the winters of 1885 and 1886, she and Jane, whom Anna had begun to visualize as her companion, lived in Baltimore, forming the familiar family unit in support of George.

It must have delighted Anna to have her youngest children together and with her. While George was in school, she and Jane experienced a very active social life. They were called upon by an assortment of intelligent and educated women, and they entertained and were entertained by them. They had card parties and teas, went to musicales and plays, and attended lectures. They also had the social and intellectual company of George's professors and their wives and George's bright young classmates. Except for worry about her son's health, Anna Addams seemed to enjoy this period of her life immensely.

After George left Johns Hopkins University in the early winter of 1887 without graduating, he and Anna went once more to Florida so that he could rest. His hopes of going immediately to study in Leipzig, Germany, were placed on hold. Harry and Alice were expecting their first—and as it turned out their only—child. Anna Addams wanted her family in place and with no distractions for this special event. George Haldeman reported to Harry on the birth of Anna Marcet Haldeman that "Mother seems wrapt in a quiet joy which she is careful not to betray but which only shows the more how deeply she is affected—by the auspicious occasion. . . . Mother says she is opposed to Anna but no doubt she would be pleased to have it named so" (23 June 1887, UIC, JAMC, HJ). In celebration, Anna copied a poem and sent it to her granddaughter. It was, she said, "one of the sweetest things ever written for a baby—in the English language" ("To Baby by George Macdonald," copied by AHHA, [June 1887], JAPP, DeLoach). For the remainder of her life, Anna Addams doted on her granddaughter, whom she addressed in correspondence as "My precious pearl of great price." She looked forward to Anna Marcet's visits and anxiously awaited all information about her development and activities.

After the baby's arrival in the summer of 1887, George was on his way to Germany but stayed only a few weeks before returning home ill. "George come back to us four weeks ago," his mother reported, "and I am so happy—he is looking quite well now, but—he made me very anxious about his health when he first arrived home—the climate of Germany was too damp and it chilled him constantly—no fires and damp linnen sheets were a source of continual colds at last a cough set in, and tis only in the last ten days that he is free from hacking" (AHHA to Laura Malburn, 8 Nov. 1887, UIC, JAMC, HJ Supp.). Little did she know that George, for the rest of his life, would live in Cedarville and that, for the most part, she would be responsible for his care.

Anna and her youngest son settled down in Cedarville together, and Jane Addams left for her second tour of Europe in December 1887. Much to Anna's dismay, George seemed unable to decide on a choice of career. During this period of uncertainty he may have been looking for ways to declare independence from his mother. In June 1888, after they had disagreed, George simply walked away from home without telling Anna where he was going. A distraught Anna telegraphed Harry for help, who, in turn, joined the Stephenson County sheriff in the search for George. They finally located him in Iowa and brought him home to a relieved and thankful mother. Mother and son settled down in the Addams home in Cedarville to await the return of Jane.

By July 1888 Jane Addams was on her way home from Europe. Anna's friend Mrs. A. M. Rowell was probably correct when she wrote to Anna from Ripon, England, "How you must long for Jane, and how glad you will be to welcome her home. I can truly say from the depthes of my heart I think her the most unselfish loveliest character I ever knew" (17 July 1888, IU, Lilly, SAAH). Another friend who had visited her in Cedarville commented on Anna's good fortune in having Jane at home: "I am glad to learn that your dear daughter Jane—is with you—and please give her my love. I certainly do like and admire her very much. A lovely character I think" (Julia Tompkins to AHHA, 18 Nov. [1888], IU, Lilly, SAAH).

Jane did not remain long, however. By the first of 1889 she and Ellen Gates Starr had moved to Chicago to begin their settlement project, and Anna and George were reduced to housekeeping together. By late spring, George was attempting once again to find his way toward a life's work. He left for Colorado to explore the countryside and opportunities for employment and advancement there. This time he let Anna know where he was. Although she left him alone in the West, she did send him money on which to live. He was uncertain about what to do and unable or unwilling to find permanent employment there. After a short time on his own, George begged his mother to join him in Colorado. She declined, and he decided to return to Cedarville.

From 1889 until she died in 1919, Anna Addams spent most of her life in the Addams home in Cedarville. Her last years were increasingly full of worry, loneliness, boredom, and poor health. Initially, her primary concern was the care of George, who lived with her and was becoming more and more troubled and reclusive, until his death in 1909. On his return home from his sojourn in Colorado in 1889, Anna had a brick cottage built to the south of the Addams home, supposing that her son might like a separate living space and that he might use it as a place to continue his studies. He never lived or studied there, however. Instead, mother and son continued to share the Addams home and kept one another company by reading aloud and playing cards and chess. They traveled to Florida together once more in the winter of 1890 and infrequently attended village functions.

By the early 1890s it had become clear that George Haldeman was unwell. Anna turned to Harry to effect a cure and devoted all of her energy to George's welfare. "The last three years my whole soul has been concentrated on his recovery—and, the promise has been—that—'George will get well.' 'Hope deferred' sometimes makes my heart faint, and sick," pronounced Anna (AHHA to IIWH, 8 Feb. 1894, UIC, JAMC, HJ). As time went on and George became more depressed and reclusive, Anna's hope that he could be made well dwindled and she became more disheartened. Loneliness weighed on her. Despite the fact that, according to the local newspaper of 9 January 1895, there were 240 visitors at the Addams home during 1894, Anna wrote to Harry, perhaps in the hope that he would visit, "Alas! no one ever comes—no one cares. . . . We are very lonely to be sure but, useless in repining" (7 Oct. 1894, UIC, JAMC, HJ Supp.). Two weeks later, she confided that "sometimes I nearly go wild[.] I can not eat or sleep my power to resi[s]t depressing emotions is growing daily less—and the need for more endurance, and strength greater. I have not one person who can give me any comfort or solace. No real sympathetic friend as I used to have in Mrs. [Laura] Malburn" (25 Oct. 1894, UIC, JAMC, HJ).

Three years later, Anna was still overwhelmed by "a constant vigilance—and anxiety" that "hung over" her because of George and because of "the care of the place—the house in all its details (as its keeper) and, seldom seeing any one" (AHHA to HWH, 7 May 1897, JAPP, DeLoach). Early in 1898 she related that she had not been out of the house for six weeks and looked for three more months of "dreary days" during the Illinois winter (AHHA to HWH, 28 Jan. 1898, UIC, JAMC, HJ). "I read myself hoarse and—blind nearly—for it is more to George than food," she reported in March. "Wonder if I shall always read to others instead of being read to (as I sometimes think I should be) in my old age" (AHHA to HWH, 11 Mar. 1898, UIC, JAMC, HJ Supp.). Later in the same year, ill with vertigo, she protested, "I have too much to do, and if I could rest more, think that my strength—would improve: quite too old—to have care of a house" (AHHA to HWH, 26 May 1898, UIC, JAMC, HJ). "That he [George] almost tires of me having me constantly by him for—nearly eleven years—is not strange:

nor a case to be questioned. The multitude come, and pass by—but we go on—without change; wish he and I could go————'up in a baloon boys' or have a chariot and many horses to drag us out of the 'sloug of despond'" she wrote to Harry of her long travail ([ca. Feb. 1902], UIC, JAMC, HJ).

Anna Addams had long envisioned having an appropriate female companion to help run the house and keep her company during the remainder of her life. Of the girl who finally became her companion she wrote, "She should be my personal attendant—and then have a good housekeeper beside—but alas!" (AHHA to HWH, 7 Oct. 1894, UIC, JAMC, HJ Supp.). Anna had planned on grooming one of the Addams sisters for that role. Not quite two years into her marriage to John Huy Addams, she wrote to her stepdaughter Alice, "I long for you my dear Allie. I need heartfelt companionship in one daughter at least—and Mary will never be more, lost, to me when married and gone" (27 Aug. 1871, UIC, JAMC, HJ Supp.). Yet she may have determined that Alice would not be suited as her companion, even before her son Harry and Alice determined to wed. With Jane the one female Addams child left, it is likely that Anna poured all of her hopes for an appropriate companion into her. A hint of that comes through when she informed Jane that she might accompany John Huy Addams's sister, Jane Addams Mull, to Kansas to visit the recently married Mull son and his new wife "If I were well—and my little housekeeper at home would like to go with her[.] All prospects—turn a dark side—for me—and if they have a silver linning for some one else all the better for some body" (11 June [1878], IU, Lilly, SAAH; *JAPM*, 1:302).

In 1890 Anna Addams finally secured the female companion she craved. Twelve-year-old Mary Fry, whose mother had recently died, was sent by her father to help. She stayed with Anna Addams and George Haldeman, becoming a near family member, until Anna died in 1919. For her part, Anna Addams was exceedingly good to the child, who grew into an intelligent, competent, loyal, caregiver. Much as she had with her own and the Addams children, Anna Addams taught Mary household skills and manners, cared for her when she was ill, and educated her. She encouraged Mary's interest in music and literature and sent her to local school, then to Shimer College in Mount Carroll, and finally to the University of Chicago. In short, Anna treated her almost like a daughter, and George found her soothing and acceptable. When she was away at school in Mount Carroll, Anna missed her as helper and companion. Anna often complained about how difficult it was to get good household help. When Mary returned, Anna was very relieved to turn over the running of the Addams home to her. She saw Mary as her comfort, her "prop and standby . . . (tender and true)" (AHHA to HWH, 29 Dec. 1899, UIC, JAMC, HJ). Mary's nephew Paul Fry reported that "Mary, too, was tied to Mrs. Addams by bonds of duty and affection" (*Generous Spirit,* 68). Perhaps it was primarily through Mary Fry that the lives of several of her Fry siblings became interwoven with the Addams family. When Anna Addams agreed to educate Mary's brother John as a physician, Mary promised never to leave Anna, and she did not.

Anna Addams was exceedingly displeased when Jane left Cedarville permanently for Chicago. "When Jane declined George's proposal [of marriage] and he reacted so strongly [his emotional distress and Colorado venture], his mother was terribly disturbed," reported Paul Fry as family lore gleaned from his Aunt Mary. "Although she may not have blamed Jane for his emotional collapse, she was unhappy when—at the same time—Jane made plans that took her away from the family. . . . In addition," Fry continued, "she did not understand so she could not support—Jane's idealistic plan for the Settlement in a Chicago slum" (*Generous Spirit*, 33). Harry agreed wholeheartedly with his mother and believed that Jane had abandoned George and her. "Mary, early on, heard her [Anna's] expressions of bitterness; she also heard George sadly begging his mother to drop the matter. . . . In time, Mrs. Addams grew to understand, and to be proud of Jane's accomplishments," reported Paul Fry (34). In 1912 Anna revealed to Marcet Haldeman something of her feelings toward the end of her life for her youngest stepdaughter: "Jane, dear old Aunt Jane. My heart grows young again, when I hear of her <u>dear</u> <u>soul</u> being still incased in the same body I embrased and kissed and so dearly loved; and still love. Providence so rules our destinies there can be no mistake—and all things work together for good" (3 Apr. 1912, UIC, JAMC, HJ).

Jane Addams continued to visit Cedarville throughout the 1890s; when she did, however, she lodged with her brother John Weber Addams's family at their home, Cedar Cliff. "It was during this period that Miss Addams'[s] relationship with her stepmother was strained," wrote Paul Fry (*Generous Spirit*, 60). In the beginning, both Jane Addams and Ellen Gates Starr invited Anna to visit their new enterprise, and it seems likely that she did visit the settlement at least once before Christmas 1891. In her letter of thanks for the "very pretty little platter" that Anna had sent to her as a Christmas present in 1891, Jane wrote encouragingly, "I wish very much that when Sarah [Hostetter] comes to Cedarville this winter, that you could come in and make another visit longer than your first one" (JA to AHHA, 28 Dec. 1891, JAPP, DeLoach; *JAPM*, 2:1293). During the summer of 1893, Anna Addams and Mary Fry attended the World's Columbian Exposition, and "For many years they went in regularly to the opera [in Chicago], and stayed at the Sherman House" (Fry, *Generous Spirit*, 62). There is no evidence that they ever visited Hull-House or saw Jane on any of those occasions. Anna was aware that other members of the family were gathering for Christmas at Hull-House in 1893 but reported to Harry that she did not care that she had not been invited, too.

In 1895, when Anna was shown the letter that Ellen Gates Starr wrote to John Weber Addams's family about the appendectomy that Jane underwent, she copied it verbatim to send to Harry Haldeman. She added her own opinion for his benefit:

Tis only the beginning of the end that, you have long prophicied every—selfish end, no matter how it takes the form of an "angle of light" meets its downfall— surely it is no fault of ours if they sow the wind and reap the whirl wind. I am so broken in health and spirits all for want of a little help that was my due—for the help and care I gave when they were young—and I could extend my powers and, put my whole mind into their interests—all to be spurned—and neglected in old age. If only you and George—can bury me quietly—and no hypocritical hands laid upon me, I will feel that all is well. (13 Sept. 1895, IU, Lilly, SAAH)

A reconciliation of sorts between Jane Addams and Alice Haldeman on the one hand and Anna Addams on the other seems to have taken place when all three were gathered in Cedarville for Harry Haldeman's funeral in March 1905. Anna was devastated by Harry's unexpected death and the loss of her son and best friend. Mary Fry "had a special role in comforting Mrs. Addams. . . . She also helped Jane Addams and S. Alice Haldeman to heal old wounds from past disagreements and make a complete reconciliation with their stepmother. Marcet gave Mary special credit for her involvement in this process" (Fry, *Generous Spirit*, 71).

A second blow came with the death of George Haldeman in November 1909 from a stroke. Once again, the family gathered in the Addams home for the funeral followed by burial in the Cedarville Cemetery. Now, only Anna Addams and Mary Fry remained in the Addams home. Over the winter of 1911–12, Anna, accompanied by Mary Fry and her brother John Fry, who had graduated from Northwestern University Medical School in June 1911, went to stay in Florida. Anna had not vacationed there since the early 1900s. Although they spent time in St. Augustine, Fort Lauderdale, and other south Florida venues, the trio finally settled back in Green Cove Springs at the Qui-Si-Sana Spa and Hotel.

It would be Anna's final visit to Florida. On her return to Illinois in April 1912 she stopped in Terre Haute, Indiana, as she usually did on her journey back from Florida, to visit Noah Hostetter's children. She then continued on to Cedarville and an extensively remodeled Addams home that included new plumbing and hardwood floors. Silas B. McManus, a journalist and former Indiana state legislator, came upon Anna Addams during this period of her life while he was seeking the birthplace of Jane Addams. He recorded his reaction to Anna in the Addams home. "Here she sits at her book-piled table, a splendid and beautiful presence, a large, white-haired dignified woman whose years one forgets in the resplendence of the youth of her mind. In her white dress with no stint of clingy lace, one fancies they are looking upon a portrait rather than upon a living and loving reality" (quoted in Gustason, "Looking Back," 21 June 1997).

Throughout the years Anna's health had worsened. Her letters indicate that as a young woman she was frequently unwell. She was bothered by outbreaks of erysipelas, especially during her marriage to John Huy Addams. As a widow, she continued to experience health-related problems. She submitted to unspecified but probably gynecological or intestinal surgery in Philadelphia early in 1882, and her bouts with erysipelas continued. "My nose has been sore for a week and have daily fears it may spread over my face. I dread Erysipeles more than death. I have suffered so intens[e]ley," she wrote to Alice Haldeman on 30 October 1882 (IU, Lilly, SAAH). By the late 1890s she had trouble controlling her writing hand. She informed Harry Haldeman that she was "nervous in the extreme," and "the muscles of my hand and arm often fly about involentarily—then I can not write—have no appetite—and—do not feel—n[o]urished" (7 May 1897, UIC, JAMC, HJ). "If my hand would only be steady and not whirl about like a reed broken by the wind," she complained to Harry (28 Jan. 1898, UIC, JAMC, HJ). By the early 1900s the apparent weakness in her writing hand made her letters difficult to read. She had suffered from intestinal and bowel trouble for a great part of her adult life. Sometime after 1900 she indicated that it was difficult for her to walk because she endured a prolapsed rectum complicated by hemorrhoids. As she aged, she gained more weight and began to spend more and more time chair-bound.

After Harry Haldeman died, Anna Addams had to rely on other physicians for medical advice. In 1905 she agreed to send John Fry to medical school. He completed high school in 1906, took the required science courses from Bradley Polytechnic Institute in Bloomington, Illinois, and entered medical school at Northwestern University in Evanston, Illinois, in the fall of 1906. From his graduation until her death in 1919, John Fry saw to Anna's health care, even after he married and opened his own medical practice first in Chicago and later in Iowa.

In the early part of 1914 John Fry and his fiancée, Genevieve Buck, planned to take Anna to Chicago for a visit and to see Marcet Haldeman, who had become a professional actress, in a stage play. In early April 1914, Anna and Mary Fry journeyed to Chicago, where they planned to stay for a week, lodging at the familiar Sherman House. Anna was entertained by Jane Addams's close friends Mary Rozet Smith and Louise de Koven Bowen and at Hull-House. Jane Addams visited her stepmother almost daily.

The day Anna returned to Cedarville, she suffered a stroke, and her mental and physical condition deteriorated over the next five years. "In the spring of 1917 Mary [Fry] wrote to Marcet that her grandmother seemed physically quite well, but apathetic mentally. Then, at times, she rallied and was quite alert" (Fry, *Generous Spirit*, 105). Mary Fry, ably assisted by Cedarville resident Bird Rutter, remained her faithful nurse and companion. Sometimes Mary slept on the foot of Anna's bed to be near in case Anna needed her quickly. After Alice Haldeman's death in March 1915, Marcet Haldeman gave up her acting career and took her mother's place managing the assets she had inherited and those of her grandmother as well. Jane Addams visited Anna Addams in Cedarville as frequently as possible and made special attempts to attend Anna's birthdays and holiday occasions. The last time the women saw each other was early in April 1919, when Jane visited Cedarville just before preparing to leave for Europe. It is doubtful that Anna knew that her youngest stepdaughter was at her bedside. Anna Addams, ninety-one, died on 23 April 1919.

The funeral was conducted in Cedarville from the living room of the Addams family home. Anna was clothed in a silver-grey dress and lay in a grey casket. Around her shoulders was a soft lace shawl that Jane had given her in 1917; Jane's last present for her, a small pillow, was under her head. The service included an address by a local minister, a song rendered by long-time Addams family friend Flora Guiteau, and the recitation of the favorite Haldeman family chapter from the Bible, Ephesians 4. Jane Addams was out of the country, but she was represented by Mary Rozet Smith. The small gathering included Mary Fry, Marcet Haldeman-Julius and her husband Emanuel, and Laura Addams with her daughter Sarah and niece Esther Margaret Linn, Anna's step-grandchild. James Weber Linn, who recalled that Anna "was still handsome, in a terrifying sort of way, when she died," was not there (*Jane Addams*, 29). The only Hostetter in attendance was Anna's niece, Susan Hostetter McKay. Anna Addams was buried in the Cedarville Cemetery in the Addams plot among the family she loved best, husband William J. Haldeman and their children.

The net value of Anna Addams's estate on 22 September 1921 was $58,410.81. She had executed her last will on 18 June 1912, the birthday of her only and beloved granddaughter Marcet Haldeman, her sole heir. Mary Fry, faithful to Anna even after her death, was to serve as administrator with the assistance of attorney Robert A. Hunter. The estate was composed of real property, notes payable in the amount of more than forty-four thousand dollars and a small bank account. Before her death, Anna Addams had planned to give Mary Fry twenty-five thousand dollars in recognition for her lifetime of service. In addition, through an understanding with Marcet Haldeman, Mary was to consider the Addams home as hers for as long as she wished.

Addams, John Huy (1822–81)

John Huy Addams was born on 12 July 1822 at Sinking Spring in Berks County, Pennyslvania. He was the seventh child and third son of Catherine Huy Addams (1787–1866) and Samuel Addams (1782–1854). His ancestors had come from England and Germany. Several served in the colonial forces during the American Revolution, and through the years several others were elected to public office.

It is likely that Robert Adams of Ledwell, Oxfordshire, England, who acquired five hundred acres of land from William Penn in 1681, was John Huy Addams's first American male ancestor. By the 1730s, William Adams (1703 or 1705–73), a descendant of Robert Adams, had married Anne Lane (or Lare) of Philadelphia and moved to Cocalico Township, Lancaster County, Pennyslvania, where he owned and operated a mill, laid out Adamsburry (later to be named Adamstown), and built a three-story stone homestead that by the twentieth century had become an inn.

One of their sons, Isaac Addams (1747–1809), who, according to family lore, was the first of the family to add a second *d* to the Adams name, making it Addams, married Barbara Ruth Addams (1744–1832), widow of his brother, William, who died in 1774. She was of German ancestry. They established a farm at the eastern end of Sinking Spring in Lancaster County near what was to become the inn at Sinking Spring. Eventually the couple moved to Reading, Pennyslvania, where he became a successful merchant. One of their sons, Samuel, wed Catherine Huy, who was likely descended from German immigrants. She was the first-born daughter of Margaret Gernant (1765–1843) and John Huy, who were married in 1786 and operated the inn at Sinking Spring. Samuel and Catherine Addams had ten children and made their home in Sinking Spring, where Samuel was a miller, farmer, merchant, and innkeeper.

John Huy Addams grew up in a large family in the small village of Sinking Spring, which also was home to an assortment of his aunts and uncles, great aunts and great uncles, cousins, and second cousins. He attended Sinking Spring schools and received advanced training during 1838 and 1839 at the Washington Hall Collegiate Institute, a boarding academy located in Trappe, Montgomery County, Pennsylvania. Among the subjects he studied were surveying and higher mathematics. Although his teachers encouraged him to become a teacher, about 1840 he apprenticed himself to Enos L. Reiff, a Quaker miller in Ambler, Upper Dublin, Montgomery County, Pennslvania, to learn the mill trade. While he was there and during his shift in the mill, which began at 3 A.M., he continued his education by reading through a library in the village.

While visiting Ambler in 1886, Jane Addams reported that she "had a splendid ride over the turnpike, past the little public library Pa read through, and Saunders Square where he bought wheat" (JA to SAAH, 31 Mar. 1886, UIC, JAMC). After he completed his apprenticeship, he returned to the Sinking Spring area to assist his father and to teach. In 1843 he had forty-nine students. Yet John Huy Addams seemed to long for the opportunities he thought available through milling and farming in the newly formed states west of the Allegheny Mountains near the Mississippi River. He hoped to visit the West during the summer of 1843, although there is no evidence that he did.

Instead, he seems to have spent that time in pursuit of a life-long companion. His efforts resulted in success, and on 18 July 1844 John Huy Addams wed Sarah Weber at her home in Kreidersville, Pennsylvania. His bride was five years his senior and the sister of Enos L. Reiff's wife Elizabeth. He and Sarah had become acquainted during her visits to the Reiff home while he was learning to be a miller. The couple left the new Mrs. Addams's family home on 29 July for a new life in Illinois. John Huy Addams's father-in-law, Col. George Weber, a farmer and miller who was also excited by business prospects in the West, accompanied the newlyweds on their honeymoon trek to Illinois. Weber hoped to establish milling interests there and to move other members of his family from Pennsylvania to Illinois.

The trio set off by horse-drawn conveyance to a rail line in New Jersey that carried them by train into New York City. A journey by steamboat up the Hudson River to Albany and on to Buffalo, New York, where they visited Niagara Falls, was followed by another steamer ride through the Great Lakes to Chicago and thence overland by horse-drawn buggy to Freeport, Illinois. Distant cousins, members of the Reitzell and Miller families, whom John Huy Addams had known in Sinking Spring, had established themselves as farmers and millers in Stephenson County, Illinois, during 1839 and 1840. Philip and Mary Ruth Reitzell, with whom the Addams couple initially lodged, had purchased the Whitehall Mills on Richland Creek in what would become Buena Vista in Stephenson County, several miles to the northwest of Freeport.

The day after the travelers arrived, John Huy Addams and Colonel Weber began to investigate mill sites and operating mills that were for sale in the area around Freeport. Although John Huy Addams was partial to the Cedar Creek Mills operation about six miles north of Freeport and a few miles southeast of Whitehall Mills, Weber preferred a site at what would become Como, Illinois, some sixty miles south of Freeport on the Rock River, where he would eventually purchase milling property with a store.

Addams required the assistance of his father in order to purchase the mill site he favored. "Told Father [by means of a letter] I liked the property but could not see it Through Save he would say that he would go my halves—and so left it," he recorded in "Journal, 1844" on 12 July [Aug.]. He had considered several other less expensive and less appealing mill sites, initially because the owners of the Cedar Creek Mills property did not wish to sell and because he feared that his father had abandoned his commitment to help. That fear, exacerbated by the difficulties in communication because of the unreliable and slow postal service between Freeport and Sinking Spring, proved unfounded.

During what must have seemed to them an interminable wait for word from Sinking Spring, the newlyweds, their first child on the way, experienced grave anxiety concerning their future. Entries in the diary that John Huy Addams kept during this period reflect hope, dismay, and depression and indicate that he admonished himself frequently to put his faith in God. On 10 September 1844 he wrote, "Prospects this evening look very dark[.]" He continued, "my mind is moody—owing probably in part of not having a letter [from his father]" ("Journal, 1844"). On 1 October 1844, after seeing Sinking Spring friends who had visited the Addams couple in Stephenson County, onto the steamer in Savanna, Illinois, for their return home via the Mississippi and Ohio rivers, Addams recorded: "I returned to the inn rather with a heavy heart went to my bedroom and there lifted up my soul to 'God' until my eyes were filled with tears with the firm resolution that all would be right" ("Journal, 1844").

On 12 October 1844, after the longed-for supportive letter from his father arrived, he thanked God. Then, on 18 October, he wrote that he trusted "in God that my mind may be directed aright[.] My spirits are very much depressed and want much comfort but safely trust in our devine benefactor, the Giver of all Good and the Presence of all that my purchase may yet end for the better—May

God help us, keep us through this life and preserve us from all Evil and in death accept of us through Christ our dear Redeemer, Amen" ("Journal, 1844"). His solace during this period of uncertainty, in addition to faith, came from the support of family and friends in Stephenson County; helping his cousins with their farms and milling operation; and a growing friendship with the first Presbyterian minister in Freeport, the Rev. Calvin Waterbury, who advised Addams to settle among the Pennsylvania German population of the Stephenson County area.

The Cedar Creek Mills consisted of a sawmill and a gristmill. As Addams described his acquisition, "The property I purchased contains 675 acres with three mill seats . . . [.] I am satisfied [that it is] one of the best water powers in this Northern part of Ill—The improvements are 3 Small houses and a Frame Mill with 2 run of stones which we are now runing Day & night—doing altogether custom work and which I shall for the present continue on—. . . I pay the man about $4600 for this property—and as far as I have come am highly pleased with it" (JHA to Elizabeth Weber and Enos L. Reiff, 12 Jan. 1845, IU, Lilly, SAAH).

The mills had been constructed on the south bank of Cedar Creek by Dr. Thomas Van Valzah from Lewistown, Pennsylvania, in 1837 on a claim initiated by the first settler in the area, John Goddard. David Neidigh had begun purchasing the milling operation and property from Van Valzah in 1842, and he, in turn, was selling it to Conrad Epley and John W. Shuey, who were working and purchasing the mill property when John Addams bought it from them on 18 December 1844. Addams took immediate possession of the property and began to work the mills. It is likely that one of the three structures on the property was a cabin, originally constructed by John Goddard and used by Van Valzah, that became the first home Sarah and John Addams owned.

By May 1845, shortly after the couple moved into a new log cabin that would be their home for the next nine years, John Huy Addams began to purchase farmland in the surrounding area, a practice he continued for the remainder of his life. He secured his first additional eighty-acre tract at a federal sale for $1.25 an acre. The land was located a few miles east of his mill site. Succeeding purchases came through federal land sales as well as through purchases from private owners. Eventually, some of his farms would be operated by his son and by tenant farmers. At his death, he owned more than 2,600 acres of farmland in Canada, Iowa, and Illinois, almost 1,800 acres of it in Stephenson County.

At the same time, Addams began to plan for additions and improvements to his milling operation. Securing his means of livelihood was paramount for the young Mr. Addams. By 1846, as he farmed and continued to buy more land, he was able to rebuild the gristmill, adding at least one run of stone and other improvements costing approximately four thousand dollars. He constructed a large barn in 1848 (which was still standing on its original foundations in 1997). It was not until 1854 that the family moved from their cabin with two rooms, a sleeping loft, and a lean-to kitchen to a commodious two-story brick home of at least eight rooms (which was still in its original location and being used as a home in 1997). The new house was anchored solidly on the hillside on the east side of the road to Red Oak and surveyed the mill site to the west below. Having seen to the comfort of his family, John Huy Addams turned once again to business development.

In the early 1850s he and two partners constructed a flaxseed oil mill on his property about two miles east and upstream on Cedar Creek from his home and millpond. The partners operated this mill until 1859, when they converted the three-story frame building measuring 35 by 40 feet into a woolen mill. Woolen fabric was in especially great demand during the Civil War, and their efforts were apparently both patriotic and profitable. The mill was operated by Joseph F. Jackson, one of the partners, until the 1880s. Then, in 1858, John Huy Addams turned once again to his own milling operation. He replaced the improved Van Valzah mill with a large, three-and-one-half-story frame gristmill that had three run of stone, grain storage, and a flour bolter. It all cost ten thousand dollars. This was the mill he continued to operate for the remainder of his life, sometimes through millers who leased the facility.

As a farmer and miller, Addams realized soon after he settled in Stephenson County the importance of getting crops and products from the area to larger markets quickly and cost-effectively. Accordingly, he led the effort begun in 1847 to bring the Galena and Chicago Union Railroad through Stephenson County. It would be the first rail line to cross that portion of northern Illinois. The successful effort was accomplished by subscription among settlers throughout the region. John Huy Addams canvassed the countryside, selling twenty thousand dollars worth of stock to bring the railroad to Freeport. After a struggle with the builders to keep the road from bypassing Stephenson County altogether and heading to Savanna on the Mississippi River by another route, its tracks reached Freeport from Rockford in 1853. The line eventually became part of the Chicago and Northwestern Railroad system. Regular service began on 31 August 1853. Initially, travel to Chicago—a journey that had taken John Huy Addams and his bride approximately three days—took only six hours. For years the road made handsome profits for investors. As a result of his success at spearheading the railroad company venture, Addams was chosen as a director of the Savanna Branch Rail Road Company in January 1853. His leadership in these railroad efforts, in addition to his growing stature as a businessman and community leader in northern Illinois, made his election to the senate of the Illinois General Assembly as a Whig in 1854 almost a certainty.

John Huy Addams had long been intrigued with politics. In addition to comments about land, farming, and milling, his early letters contain observations on politics in Pennsylvania, Illinois, and in the rest of the country. It is hardly surprising that the man who decried the Democrats as locofocos to his brother-in-law Enos L. Reiff in Pennsylvania would enter politics as a Whig and then move to the Republican Party. In fact, he was one of the founders of the Republican Party. He was present at Rockford on 30 August 1854 when citizens from the northern tier of Illinois counties gathered to explore ways to prevent the further extension of slavery and protect the interests of free labor. He also attended numerous other gatherings, some as a delegate, that led to the formation of the Republican Party. Addams was a fiscal conservative, an advocate for high tariffs, and a supporter of temperance. He favored expanded legal rights, but not suffrage, for women and was dedicated to abolition.

He served for sixteen years in the senate of the Illinois General Assembly, representing his and nearby counties and assuming an increasing leadership role there until his retirement in 1870. Among the committees on which he served were Education, Public Roads, Township Organization and Counties, Saline and Swamplands, Geology, Agriculture, Internal Navigation, Finance, Banks and Corporations, State Institutions, Printing, and Penitentiary. He also shepherded local bills through the legislature, including those that created local public improvements and those that incorporated local businesses. In addition, he visited educational, penal, and mental institutions and was on the legislative committee that established the University of Illinois and mandated improved conditions at the state penitentiary at Joliet following a public scandal. Moreover, he was instrumental in helping pass legislation protecting the property rights of women.

John Huy Addams, an ardent supporter of Abraham Lincoln, worked for him during Lincoln's 1858 effort to secure election to the U.S. Senate from Illinois. He was also a leader in organizing Lincoln's debate with rival Stephen A. Douglas in Freeport. Addams and Lincoln maintained a correspondence, although none of it is apparently extant, and pictures of Lincoln adorned the walls of the Addams home. When Lincoln died, Addams openly mourned for his loss. His admiration for Lincoln and for his memory was so great that Jane Addams echoed it for the rest of her life, reverently holding the Great Emancipator and his dedication to humanity as a role model.

Addams often spoke at Republican conventions, mass meetings, and rallies, especially in his northern Illinois district. His repertoire ran from the history of the Republican Party to repeal of the Illinois Black Laws. In the fall of 1872 he defended President U. S. Grant and his administration. Grant, Addams argued, was in favor of true civil service reform; he answered charges of corruption in the Grant administration by stating that taxes were being reduced while public debt was being paid off. He did admit, however, that internal revenue and tariff laws needed to be tightened and money not squandered after it was collected. "His speech," reported the *Freeport Journal* on 25 September 1872, "was earnest and eloquent, and full of that kind of logic which plain and sensible men could understand and appreciate."

As early as 1854, journalists began to recognize the leadership qualities of John Huy Addams, calling him a man "of fine ability and unquestionable integrity" (*Freeport Journal*, 7 Sept. 1854). After more than twelve years in the state legislature, he was termed an "honorable, high-minded, and conscientious gentleman" by another journalist, even though the writer disagreed with Addams's stand against canal legislation proposed in 1867 (*Freeport Journal,* 13 Mar. 1867). In 1869, just as he was about to retire from active political life, he was described as one "whose public record is as pure as crystal, who has not an enemy in the country" (*Freeport Journal,* 24 Mar. 1869). At the end of his life, "Honest John Addams," as he was apparently often labelled, was known as experienced and able in his understanding and use of the political system but not as a politician. At Addams's death, Andrew Shuman, editor of the *Chicago Evening Journal,* described him as "not a man of great education nor of pretention to superior wisdom, but 'a plain, blunt man,' whose honesty of purpose was above suspicion, whose integrity was proverbial, and whose soundness of judgment was recognized in the halls of legislation, in the counsels of politics and in business circles. He was a modest man—a quiet, conscientious and dignified gentleman, who shrunk from publicity, and yet, as a matter of duty, was never slow to 'act well his part' in connection with public affairs as a citizen" (quoted in *Freeport Budget,* 27 Aug. 1881).

John Huy Addams staunchly and patriotically embraced the Union cause, although he did not serve in the military because mill products were considered so valuable to the cause that the lives of millers were not to be risked in battle. Yet he participated in the war effort by actively recruiting troops, by raising and equipping a company of infantry called the "Addams Guards," by continuing to serve in the state legislature, and by leading the effort after the war to erect a monument honoring those from Stephenson County who gave their lives in the struggle.

Before Addams achieved public acclaim as a state senator—some said to such a degree that he was sought after as a congressional or gubernatorial candidate—he was active in the development of Cedarville and its immediate surrounding area. He was instrumental in the opening and the construction of the community's first school through subscription in 1846. In the late 1850s he was the main force behind the creation of the Cedarville select school. A high school for village children, it existed into the 1860s when schools in the area became public. Then, Addams served as one of the three directors of School District No. 5. He and two friends also organized the Cedar Creek Union Library Company during the same year that the first school was organized. The library was lodged in his home, and Addams served as treasurer and librarian.

Addams's interest in education continued throughout his life. From 1875 through 1877 he served as a trustee for the Rockford Female Seminary, where four of his daughters were students. He was also one of the organizers and officers of the Old Settlers' Association in Stephenson County, a group that met annually for a time in a grove on his property. In addition, he helped establish the village cemetery and in 1855 provided the land on which it is located.

A vital element in the life of John Huy Addams was his relationship with God. Although he termed himself a Hicksite Quaker, he supported all organized religious efforts in the small community. He helped secure funds for at least two church structures, the Methodist Church and the Presbyterian parsonage, and attended all four Cedarville churches—Methodist, Presbyterian, Lutheran, and German Reform. He seemed particularly partial to the Presbyterian denomination, and in 1846 became one of a small committee that led an attempt to organize the German Presbyterian Society of Richland to serve the north central part of Stephenson County. Later, in the late 1860s and in 1870, he served as a trustee in the successful effort to create the Presbyterian Church in Cedarville. He took the lead in establishing the Union Sunday School in the village and became one of its teachers. He often hosted Sunday School teacher meetings during the week and on weekends spent a great deal of time in meetings associated with religion. He attended Saturday evening community sings in the Methodist Church and services and Sunday School on Sunday, often hosted a minister for Sunday dinner, and sometimes returned for other church-related activities during the evening. He also attended revivals and was an ardent supporter of temperance. A thirty-year member of the Cedar Creek Bible Society and the Stephenson County Bible Society, he was an officer in each.

John Huy Addams helped create the Stephenson County Agricultural Society, which initiated the local agricultural fair and provided an organization where farmers could share new techniques and marketing data. Farm loss from fire was an issue of importance. Early in 1867 Addams sponsored legislation that passed the Illinois General Assembly and enabled the creation of rural mutual assessment insurance companies. Almost immediately, he became the temporary president of the Buckeye Mutual Fire Insurance Company, which began operations on 24 May 1867. His brother James Huy Addams became one of its board of governors and the first agent for the enterprise. In 1870 the Buckeye Mutual Fire Insurance Company, still in existence, reported more than twenty million dollars' worth of property insured.

Addams was also instrumental in helping create a second insurance firm, the Protection Life Insurance Company, which was incorporated by act of the Illinois General Assembly on 7 March 1867 to operate in Freeport. It seems likely that in April 1867 he was selected as president and John R. Lemon was chosen secretary. The venture into the insurance business was definitely not a successful one for Addams. After two years, effective 8 March 1869, the home office and leadership of the company were moved to Chicago by legislative act. It was probably at this time that John Huy Addams relinquished the presidency of the company. The Western Historical Company's *History of Stephenson County, Illinois* conspicuously identified no individuals associated with the firm when it reported,

The Protection Life operated in Freeport until March 7, 1867 [8 March 1869], when its base of supplies and distribution was removed to Chicago. After two years of apparently fruitful labors, the Protection Life, as will be remembered by most every resident of Stephenson County, was described as hanging upon the verge of ruin. This cheerful picture was at first disputed by friends of the corporation, but claimants insisted such was the case, and clamorously demanded an investigation. These demands were finally ordered, and the examination made resulted in the discovery of facts which were not thought to have existed before. The institution was reported as not only on the verge of ruin, but so hopelessly in that condition as that its recovery was a question of chance rather than possibility. The law was appealed to to unravel the skein of circumstances, and ascertain what had become of the premiums presumably to the credit of the assured, but thus far without results. A Receiver was appointed, and other things done that seemed proper and right, but thus far nothing has been born of the proceedings but trials, troubles and vexations of spirit. (429–30)

The Protection Life Insurance Company was licensed by the state of Illinois on 15 December 1870 to operate in Chicago, beginning in January 1871. At the time, it was one of eight life insurance companies created under Illinois law and licensed to operate in that state. Its president was S. Edwin Skinner. Its license to conduct business in Illinois was canceled on 6 August 1877 after an investigation by the state of Illinois indicated massive insurance fraud and bankruptcy.

In May 1864 John Huy Addams, in concert with a group of Freeport businessmen, formed the Second National Bank of Freeport with an initial capital of fifty thousand dollars, which was increased to one hundred thousand by 1866. Until the end of his life he served as a director and president of that institution. Although his office for his milling and farming businesses were in his home, Addams maintained an office at the bank building in Freeport and conducted business there at least two days a week. At his death, he owned 310 shares of its stock, which were valued at one hundred dollars each.

Addams was a slender man of more than medium height but appeared taller because of the shiny black top hat he often wore in public beginning in the 1860s. He had a shock of dark-brown hair above grey eyes, even features, and a cleft chin over a neck beard. Jane Addams recalled that her "father . . . was a most imposing figure in his Sunday frock coat, his fine head rising high above all the others" (*Twenty Years*, 6–7). Her own grey eyes and cleft chin resembled her father's. John Huy Addams's hands bore the marks of a miller: a thumb flattened from testing grain and milled produce and faint red and purple flecks, the result of stone fragments spit from dressing millstones. His step-niece Sarah Hostetter recalled him as a "fine, stately gentleman, wearing high silk hat and black stock. . . . Everybody knew Mr. Addams, and the ring of good cheer and cordiality in his greeting was a treat to hear. It was all so exact, so orderly and correct, as were all his business and social methods" (*Home and Girlhood*, 4). A serious, logical man, he approached life with determination, persistence, honesty, and faith in God's will. He was noted for his forthright and upright dealings with others, for his sense of justice, for his moral nature, and his personal commitment to do what was right. He was earnest in his wish to help others and known for his inability to do "anything mean and unworthy" (Isaac Carey to JA, 21 Aug. 1881, SCPC, JAC; *JAPM*, 1:713). He was firm but not stern in his interactions with family, friends, and business associates. Kind to others, John Huy Addams was a gentle man with an enormous will to succeed. He usually kept personal feelings in check in a public setting and led family and friends by example. At the time of his death, a friend recalled, "Oftentimes human language was not adequate to express the feelings of his heart. A member of the Bible class which he . . . taught continuously for 25 years in the Sunday School, told me a few weeks since that on a certain day when he was recounting the sufferings and trials of our Savior, and contrasting them with the ingratitude of the human heart, that the tears rolled down his cheeks. He said, 'the affection of that heart manifested in those tears were more of an incentive and inspiration to me than anything that has ever been brought to bear upon me'" (*Freeport Budget*, 27 Aug. 1881). John Huy Addams valued "mental integrity above everything else" (Addams, *Twenty Years*, 15), and he taught his children to be honest with themselves as well as with other people.

If Addams knew success in business and politics, he also knew sadness in his personal life. Of the nine children he and Sarah had, only five outlived their mother, who died shortly after the stillbirth of their ninth child in January 1863. The few letters between the couple that survive indicate that their marriage was comfortable and loving, a true partnership in which the couple worked and grew together. Addams remained a widower for nearly five years, and during that time another one of his children died.

Then, on 17 November 1868, John Huy Addams remarried. His choice was Anna Hostetter Haldeman, the widow of William Haldeman, who had been a competitor as the operator of the Freeport Stone Steam Flour Mill. Senator Addams began to court the initially reluctant Mrs. Haldeman in the spring of 1868, and their surviving correspondence indicates that he had won her to the idea of marriage by the early fall. The new Mrs. Addams brought with her into the Addams home two sons by her first husband: Henry "Harry" Winfield Haldeman and George Bowman Haldeman.

For Addams, the marriage was apparently not as loving, comfortable, agreeable, or as placid as his first. He and his new bride were temperamental opposites and worked to develop their relationship. Both had entered the marriage for good reason—he, to secure a mother for his children, especially the three younger ones, Weber, Alice, and Jane, and perhaps a charming, entertaining wife for himself; she, to gain a father and breadwinner for her family. Anna Addams was very different in personality and in social and intellectual interests from her predecessor.

After the first few months of the new arrangement, relationships among the members of the two blended families became troublesome. John Huy Addams and Harry Haldeman were soon at odds. Addams did not like Harry's use of alcohol nor what he probably saw as Harry's unacceptable bohemian lifestyle. For his part, Harry saw his mother's new and wealthy husband as unjust in his unwillingness to support his effort to continue his education and become a physician. Addams's relationship with George, the younger Haldeman son, however, seems to have been very fatherlike. As soon as George Haldeman's legal guardian, his uncle Nathaniel Haldeman, died in 1880, Addams began proceedings to take his place.

John Huy Addams's relationship with his own children seems to have been supportive and loving. He kept in touch through letters and, after they left home as adults, through frequent visits. He provided a secure environment for them, was supportive of their educational and community activities, and provided ample opportunity for them to socialize with and entertain friends at home. Their letters to him are affectionate and indicate an easy, respectful relationship between child and parent. They shared information about their daily lives and the details of their friendships. They were also comfortable with asking for money or other necessary things from home while they were students at seminary and college. The few letters that survive from John Huy Addams to his children are rather stiff, direct, almost businesslike, and brief yet kind and affectionate.

He was concerned for the welfare of all of his children, especially for that of his only surviving son. By 1869 John Weber Addams began to experience the paranoid schizophrenia that would plague him for the remainder of his life. The symptoms were evident for several years before his father was finally forced to commit him to a state mental institution for the first time in 1872. The public process, carried out under the guidance of a judge in Freeport, must have been heartbreaking for the whole family. John Huy Addams seems to have been an especially sensitive, supportive, and hopeful parent with regard to his son's illness. Always expecting that he would improve and be able to achieve a satisfactory life, John Addams assisted him in learning the mill trade and in becoming a livestock farmer.

Addams also seems to have been concerned that his daughters secure successful marriages. When Sarah Alice Addams determined to wed her stepbrother Harry Haldeman, her father was disappointed and so troubled that for a time his attendance at the wedding was apparently in doubt. Although he did not like the pairing, he did not abandon his daughter. He kept in touch with the young couple and visited them in their home in Iowa. Perhaps he was pleased with daughter Mary Catherine Addams's choice for a husband, Presbyterian minister John Manning Linn. Yet he must have been worried at her husband's meager earnings and the simple, spartan surroundings in which she lived as the couple moved to his various postings throughout northern Illinois. That Jane Addams doted on her father and considered him a role model is certain. Her treatment of him and his influence on her childhood in the first volume of her autobiography *Twenty Years at Hull-House* leaves little doubt. From the surviving correspondence, it is also clear that he loved and supported her as she grew to maturity. As his youngest child, she probably did have a special place in his heart.

After his marriage to Anna Haldeman, Addams continued to develop various business ventures, including farming, milling, insurance, and banking. He retired from the General Assembly but continued to be involved in state and local politics. During the 1870s, three of his children married. In 1871, Mary Catherine Addams wed John Manning Linn; in 1876, John Weber Addams married Laura Shoemaker and Sarah Alice Addams became the wife of Harry Haldeman. He became a grandfather when the Linns had children in 1872, 1876, and 1880 and the young Addams couple had their only child in 1877.

Most summers, John Huy Addams and his family vacationed in the states north of Illinois, where he sought business opportunities. During the summer of 1881 he had taken Anna, Jane, and George with him on a journey to the Lake Superior area to investigate mining and real estate in northern Michigan and Wisconsin. The group left Cedarville on 4 August 1881 and by 11 August was in Marquette, Michigan, where Addams was investigating copper mines. George, who returned to Cedarville on Saturday, 13 August, reported that on Thursday, 11 August, Addams suffered a sudden "bilious attack, which was not thought to be serious at the time" (*Freeport Daily Bulletin*, 18 Aug. 1881). Apparently John Huy Addams thought it would pass, and the travelers moved on to Green Bay, Wisconsin. There he became very ill and despite the attendance of a physician died on 17 August, apparently of a ruptured appendix. His body, accompanied by his widow and daughter Jane, was returned to Cedarville by train on 18 August.

The funeral took place on Saturday, 20 August 1881 in a yard of the Addams home. A huge crowd from throughout Illinois heard the Rev. John C. Irvine, pastor of the Cedarville Presbyterian Church for some three years, and the Rev. Lewis H. Mitchell of Portage, Wisconsin, the church's former pastor, deliver eulogies. After that, people passed into the Addams home to view John Huy Addams's remains. A procession was formed, and pallbearers carried him to the family burial plot, where he was laid to rest.

Because John Huy Addams died intestate his estate was managed and apportioned according to the inheritance law that he had helped pass while he was in the Illinois General Assembly. By a document signed and lodged with the court in Stephenson County on 23 August 1881, Anna Haldeman Addams relinquished her right to administer the estate in favor of Edward P. Barton, the family's attorney. At the time the estate was appraised, she and family members living with her were allotted personal goods, including family pictures, wearing apparel and jewelry, books, one sewing machine, beds and bedding, stoves and cooking utensils, and household and kitchen furniture as well as two milk cows and calves, ten sheep, one horse, a saddle and bridle, provisions for one year for the family, food for the stock for six months, and fuel for three months—all in the amount of $2,309. The remainder of the estate consisted of real estate, assets from the various businesses, promissory notes, stocks, bonds, and life insurance. For appraisal purposes, the real estate, consisting of property held in Illinois ($96,394 worth in Stephenson County), Iowa, and Canada was valued at $193,709.41. The remainder had a value of approximately $193,869.

When the estate was finally closed on 16 June 1886, Anna Addams had received a one-third share less expenses; the four living Addams children had equally divided two-thirds of the estate less expenses. During the time the estate was kept open, the executor tried to collect promissory notes, some of which he was forced to identify as bad debt, and he had his fees and expenses as well as those associated with settling the estate. It is difficult to determine exactly how much everyone received. If the total estate was valued at approximately $400,000, then Anna Addams would have received $133,333 and the four Addams children would have divided $266,666, less expenses. That would have meant that each Addams child would have received approximately $66,666, less expenses. According to an accounting kept by Sarah Alice Addams Haldeman, Jane received real estate valued at $22,860. She would also have received other assets valued at approximately $44,000, less executor's expenses.

The fact that John Huy Addams was the primary family anchor for the young Jane Addams and that he held an august place in her life and heart made his unexpected death especially difficult for her. It came at a time when she had just graduated from Rockford Female Seminary and was considering what her next step in the world might be. It is unclear just exactly what her father had thought it should be, but he may have known and approved of her plan to attend medical school in the fall of 1881. Shortly after his funeral, Jane's brother-in-law John Manning Linn indicated that he hoped she would continue with her plans despite her father's death. The fact that approximately one month later she was on her way to medical school in Philadelphia could indicate that she had planned all along, with her father's agreement, to undertake the study of medicine.

The accolades offered by friends and the press must have been of some comfort to the Addams family, especially to his youngest, most vulnerable child. There were personal letters of condolence and lengthy obituaries in the area newspapers. Colleagues from competitor banks, the directors of his bank, and members of both bible societies offered resolutions of condolence. Although few who issued public statements saw Addams as a formally educated leader of great intellectual acumen, all identified his honesty, integrity, and innate goodness. In retrospect, one of the most historically provocative summations of his strengths and influence was offered by John Irvine at his funeral and appeared in the *Freeport Budget* on 27 August 1881. Although he had not known John Huy Addams long, Irvine recalled, he had loved him for

the combination of the noble elements of character which he possessed, and the degree to which he perfected them. The foundation of all these elements was thoughtfulness, that righteous thoughtfulness which is so admirable in society, such a mighty factor in stimulating truth, in accomplishing good, in acquiring a competence. We remember Mr. Addams to-day, not so much because of his intellectual ability, not so much because of his successful financial career, but because of his thoughtfulness; his thoughtfulness for the State; his thoughtfulness for the country—he was identified with all the best interests of the State and community. His thoughtfulness for the poor, his heart was always full of love and sympathy for the poor. His thoughtfulness for the young, his visits to the school room were weekly, his interest in the young of the community constant. His thoughtfulness for the church, his support was liberal, and his seat never empty. . . . His thoughtfulness for the Sunday School in which he had labored so long and earnestly. His thoughtfulness for himself and family. In truth his thoughtfulness for humanity. The world was his field; of humanity he thought; for humanity he acted. . . . "Thou has loved righteousness and hated iniquity." This was the guiding principle of his life—the love of right and the hatred of evil.

This particular memory of her father may have been a powerful incentive for the young and impressionable Jane Addams as she set forth to structure her life and find a place in the world.

Addams, John Weber (1852–1918)

John Weber Addams, born on 19 February 1852 in Cedarville, Illinois, was called Web or Weber, which was pronounced "Weeb" or "Weeber." He was the fourth child and only living son of Sarah Weber Addams and John Huy Addams. Weber attended the public and select schools in Cedarville and Freeport, Illinois, between 1857 and 1867. He went to Beloit Academy in Beloit, Wisconsin, between 1867 and 1869 for a preparatory course of study for college. Due to illness, he returned home in the spring of 1869 before he completed the school year. He did not graduate from Beloit Academy. Family letters during 1869 and the early 1870s mention digestive problems, high fever, and boils, which he treated with shoe wax. It is likely that this episode of illness followed by another in the fall, with their attendant physical problems, was also the first significant evidence of the mental illness that was to plague Weber in increasingly severe episodes for the remainder of his life.

It is difficult to know just when the disorder first appeared. By the description of his niece Marcet Haldeman-Julius, Weber was an obstreperous child. He was apparently adventuresome, inquisitive, and headstrong. On many occasions he tried the patience of his mother, Sarah, enough to require discipline. He recalled detention in the dark closet under the stairs to the second floor of the Addams home as punishment. He also seemed to have learning problems. In at least one letter from Beloit Academy to his father in January 1869 he carefully explained a routine he had established so he could focus on his studies. In the fall of 1869 he decided to go directly to the University of Michigan at Ann Arbor as a college student in the Latin Scientific course. He hoped to be well enough to stand the stress of competition and meet academic standards. He was not.

He returned, ill once again, to Cedarville in October. His home within the confines of the blended Addams-Haldeman family, however, proved no safe haven. He and his stepmother Anna Haldeman Addams apparently had an explosive falling out that involved her children and her relatives, one of whom,

Mary Peart, was visiting in the Addams home. Harry Haldeman, Anna's son who left the Addams home for good at this time, wrote to his mother from his new home in Mendota, Illinois, on 18 January 1870, advising her not to be concerned about her relationship with Weber. "Be happy, don't try to be miserable—you have everything necessary to make you So. Mr A I am sure loves you—and as for Mary—I think She does Allice and Jennie I am sure do—Weber is an ass—and you cant expect anything of him" (IU, Lilly, SAAH).

John Huy Addams sent Weber, accompanied by his older sister Mary Catherine, to stay with the Col. Henry C. Forbes family near Cobden in Union County, Illinois, where they remained for most of December. The Forbeses, who had taught in Cedarville between 1859 and 1866, seemed familiar with Weber's problems. According to a Cobden druggist, Weber took a medication "intended to steady the nerves." He got plenty of outdoor exercise, chopping wood and walking and riding long distances. He explored the mills in the area, and he and his sister took a riverboat trip on the Mississippi from Cairo, Illinois, into Kentucky. On returning from the excursion, Mary Addams wrote to her father that she was still concerned about Weber's stability, although he was improving. "Sometimes he worries me a little," she reported. "I told you in my letter on Monday about his writing so steadily in his Memorandum; Yesterday morning at Cairo he did not seem very well, . . . after dinner, some time after he had taken his medicine, he wanted to take a nother dose, as he said the druggist at Cobden had said it was a very good medicine, . . . but I told him not to take more, then he laughed and gave it to me to put in the satchel: I think he did it more in sport than anything else however." Colonel Forbes cautioned that Weber should not go home until he was well "if home matters was what troubled Weber" (Friday evening [10 Dec. 1869], JAPP, Hulbert).

In the evenings, Weber read and wrote letters and shared family time with the Forbes family. All watched carefully for his improvement. On 15 December 1869, Mary discussed the future with Weber and reported to her father the next day that he would like to learn the mill trade. John Huy Addams brought his son home to live on a farm north and east of the Addams home and, giving up the idea of a formal education, to learn to be a miller and stock farmer.

Weber's health may have improved temporarily, although by the summer of 1872 his mental condition had deteriorated once again. This time it was to such a degree that his father was forced to commit him for treatment in the Illinois State Hospital for the Insane in Elgin. This began a series of commitments, in some instances by his sisters Jane and Alice. According to data provided at the time of the last commitment of Weber Addams, dated 6 October 1906, all records of his previous commitments had been lost. Interviewed in December 1909, he recalled that his first commitment was at the Illinois Hospital for the Insane in Elgin and had lasted from 26 May to 11 November 1872. In 1883 he was sent to a private hospital operated by Dr. George McFarland and his son in Jacksonville, Illinois, and when they could not help he was once again returned to

Elgin. He remained there, he recalled, from 16 April to 2 July 1883. He also reported being committed to the Elgin State Hospital between 16 August and 2 December 1885, from 16 November 1892 for 156 days, from 16 July to 16 December 1896, and from April 1900 to 14 March 1902. In March 1902 he was transferred to the Illinois State Hospital for the Insane in Kankakee, where he remained until 22 October 1906 before being sent to the Illinois Hospital for the Insane at Watertown, where he died.

The events that eventually resulted in his commitment usually consisted of periods of high excitability sometimes characterized by exaltation and complete lack of personal control. He sometimes heard voices and often felt threatened. He was classified by the Watertown Hospital as having "dementia praecox (paranoid type)." His record indicates that he was "periodically disturbed; at such times becoming quite obscene, profane in his language, noisy, and suffering intensely from hallucinations, more especially those of hearing" ("Statistical Data: John Weber Addams" and "Summary: John Weber Addams").

Between episodes of mental illness, Weber attempted to live a normal life. In the spring of 1870 he wrote an argument entitled "Res. That Women should be allowed the right of suffrage. Negative" for presentation in the Cedarville debating society. The young men and women of the village formally organized on 13 December 1870 as the Nestor Debating Club. Their announcement in the *Freeport Journal* on 11 January 1871 reported that the question of "Woman Suffrage" had been decided in favor of women. None of the debaters was identified by name.

Weber learned the mill trade in his father's mills. In addition, he and his father entered a stock-raising partnership. One of his responsibilities as a boy had been rounding up cattle from the fields in the evening and seeing that they were sheltered for the night. As he grew older, his experience and knowledge of livestock increased. By the late 1870s, J. Weber Addams and Company was offering yearlings for sale and providing pasturage for one hundred head of cattle on Addams's ground that surrounded the woolen mill operated by Joseph Jackson two miles east of Addams's mill on Cedar Creek.

On 16 March 1876 John Weber Addams married Laura Shoemaker from Lena, Illinois. We know nothing about their courtship or their personal feelings for each other. No personal diaries or correspondence between them are extant. Their only child, Sarah Weber Addams, was born on 26 February 1877. In 1881, with the death of his father, Weber Addams's plans to resettle his family in the West were dashed. He purchased the Cedarville mill from his father's estate and continued its operation as Addams' Roller Mills. He also continued to raise thoroughbred cattle on Cedar Creek Farm. In 1882 he moved his family into Cedar Cliff, a large frame home built for them on the north side of Cedar Creek.

After the house was completed, Addams began a series of improvements to the mill in 1883, upgrading the machinery to remain as competitive as possible in a milling business climate that was changing rapidly. Processing tasks that had always been done by local mills were being mechanized and refined in larger mills in centrally located, urban settings where good rail transport was available. The improvements were costly, and the process of reconstruction highly stressful. Weber endured another severe attack of mental illness, the first that Laura had experienced. When he was committed as a patient in Elgin in 1883, she and his sister Jane assumed responsibility for overseeing the completion of the mill renovation then underway. It continued to operate until 1905, finally being reduced to handling only grinding for stock feed.

Weber was active in his community. He served as a representative of Buckeye Township on the Stephenson County Board of Supervisors. After his father's death, he was selected, much to Anna Haldeman Addams's dismay (she had hoped to be chosen to replace her husband), as a director of the Second National Bank of Freeport. With his wife and child, he was a member of the Presbyterian Church. Between 1866 and 1872 he was a member of the temperance organization, Independent Order of Good Templars, Constance Lodge, and he became a member of Evergreen Lodge No. 170, A.F. & A.M., Freeport Chapter No. 23, R.A.M., and Freeport Consistory.

As Weber's health deteriorated, Laura began to take more responsibility for maintaining the household, educating their daughter, and managing the farms and business. Little by little, the family's holdings were sold to support the family and Weber in the mental hospital. When possible, other family members purchased his property. In November 1888, Jane Addams bought some of Weber's farmland for $6,800, and by 1913 she owned at least 230 acres in sections 31, 32, and 33 to the north and east of Cedarville. In 1915 Laura, Weber's conservator, sold their last piece of property other than their home to Anna Haldeman Addams for three thousand dollars.

As a child, Jane Addams's relationship with her brother was marked by the concern of a much older brother for the welfare of his youngest sister. They corresponded from the time that Weber was away at Beloit and throughout his life when he was at Cedarville. By the time Jane left for her first European trip in 1883, she had become his wife's helpmate in the struggle to keep her family together and their business solvent and cope with his increasing bouts with mental illness. She understood that her brother was fundamentally afflicted. Throughout his life, however, she remained concerned for his welfare and sympathetic to his infirmities. She visited him when he came home to Cedar Cliff and was emotionally and financially supportive of his wife and child. She also made interest-free loans to Weber, ten thousand dollars in 1899 and three thousand dollars in 1900. In addition, she purchased real estate that the Weber Addams family was forced to sell. After Jane Addams left Cedarville permanently in 1889, it was to Cedar Cliff and her brother's family that she returned when she visited.

According to his death certificate, John Weber Addams died of dementia praecox with chronic nephritis in the Illinois Hospital for the Insane at Watertown on 6 March 1918. An infected elbow, the result of an accidental fall, is listed as a contributing factor. Jane recalled that he had always hoped to die at home. After a funeral conducted in his home in Cedarville, he was buried in the Addams family plot in the Cedarville Cemetery. Mary Fry, the housekeeper and companion of Anna Addams, provided an account of the occasion for Marcet Haldeman-Julius:

> I looked at Aunt Jane standing by the open grave [and] I realized how she must feel to be the last member of her family. It must be a relief to her and Aunt Laura to know that suffering is ended but it will be agony for some time to come to think of Mr. Addams dying there alone. He was sick almost a week and they didn't know it. The letter written to Aunt Laura didn't reach her until after his death. He was conscious at the end and might have longed to see his family. . . . O it is sad and no one will ever be able to comfort Aunt Laura on that. She feels very bitter toward the Authorities for not wiring her of his condition. He had a septic poisoning terminating in a fatal dysentary. (quoted in Fry, *Generous Spirit,* 108–9)

Addams, Laura Shoemaker (1856–1937)

Laura Shoemaker Addams was born in Mifflin County, Pennsylvania, on 11 October 1856. She was the eldest of six children of Henrietta Bupp Shoemaker (1839–81), also born in Mifflin County, Pennsylvania, and John L. Shoemaker (1831–69), born in Lancaster County, Pennsylvania, who were wed on 27 December 1855. Her father was a part-time blacksmith and a farmer. The Shoemakers had come to Illinois in 1857 and settled near Lena in Stephenson County, where Laura and her siblings grew up and attended school. After her father's death, she helped her mother raise her brothers: Charles (b. 1858?), Frank (b. 1861?), Edward (1863–1941), and William (b. 1865?). The youngest child, a girl named Sarah, had died as an infant before 1870.

Laura Shoemaker and John Weber Addams were married in Lena at the Shoemaker home on 16 March 1876. Their only child, Sarah Weber Addams (1877–1937), was born on 26 February 1877. By 1882 the family had moved into a large, rambling, frame home they built and named Cedar Cliff. It was located on a bluff on the north side of Cedar Creek, above the Addamses' millpond. Laura Addams assumed the usual assortment of tasks associated with maintaining a home and with motherhood, but she soon had additional responsibility thrust upon her.

In 1883 Laura experienced the first of her husband's several hospitalizations for paranoid schizophrenia. Devastated by this turn of events, she also legally became his conservator. With the help of her sister-in-law Jane, she began to assume control of the family's farming and milling interests. Each time Weber Addams was institutionalized as a private patient, even though he was treated in state mental hospitals, he and his family were responsible for paying for his room, board, clothing, and amenities. Eventually, Laura and her husband sold most of their assets except their home to pay for his care, provide a family livelihood, and maintain the home.

Very few letters or documents created by Laura Shoemaker Addams are extant, but she is mentioned in the letters of other Addams family members. It is likely that a mutual concern for Weber Addams brought Jane and Laura close as friends. In the beginning, the two women shared the burden of managing his business and financial concerns. It was in letters to Laura during two winters in Baltimore and a trip to Europe that Jane revealed her growing interest in social welfare. It was also during this time that Laura became a member and treasurer of the Women's Home Missionary Society organized in the Cedarville Presbyterian Church on 3 August 1886. The two women also had a mutual interest in self-education. Between 1885 and 1886, while Jane was studying German in Baltimore, Laura undertook the study of German with a small group of women in the Cedarville area (many with German roots in the recent past). She reported on her progress to Jane and sought her advice about texts.

When Jane visited in Cedarville after she founded Hull-House, it was with Laura, Weber, and their daughter that she lodged. As the years went by, Laura gradually became involved in activities at Hull-House and spent portions of several years in work at the settlement. In March 1900, after Laura had returned to Cedar Cliff from a winter at Hull-House, Jane wrote to her sister Alice Haldeman, "I miss her very much and am sorry to have the visit come to a close" (IU, Lilly, SAAH; *JAPM*, 3:1516).

After the death of her sister-in-law Mary Catharine Addams Linn in July 1894, Laura Addams became a surrogate mother to Mary's daughter. Esther Margaret Linn began attending Rockford Female Seminary, where Sarah Weber Addams was also a student. The two cousins became friends, and Esther, who seems to have been difficult for Jane Addams to manage, grew close to Laura. When Esther left the University of Chicago to marry and begin her family in 1901, her wedding took place at Cedar Cliff, and Laura went to be with her in St. Louis for the birth of her first two children. For the remainder of her life Laura maintained a close relationship with Esther and her family. For long periods they apparently corresponded weekly, although only a letter or two of that exchange are extant.

With her daughter at the University of Chicago beginning in 1896 and with her husband often hospitalized, Laura Addams was persuaded by Jane Addams to spend increasing amounts of time at Hull-House. A kind, thoughtful, but shy person, Laura led what Jane considered to be a lonely life. She seems to have had little to do with Alice and Harry Haldeman or with Anna Haldeman Addams who lived in Cedarville just across Cedar Creek from her. Anna Addams complained to her son Harry that she sometimes saw Laura pass by on her way home but seldom had visits from anyone at Cedar Cliff and knew nothing about the family's doings. Alice Addams apparently worried about Laura, too. She wrote to Jane that she did not want Laura to stay at Cedar Cliff alone. She suggested that Jane arrange for Laura to visit in Girard, Kansas, indicating she would pay her railroad fare. She also admitted that she knew Jane would have difficulty making the arrangements because Laura and Weber seemed not to let anyone help them except Jane.

In January 1902, when daughter Sarah left home for a teaching position at the woman's college in Oxford, Ohio, Laura Addams settled at Hull-House more permanently. From 1902 until at least 1913 she was listed as a Hull-House resident. For the next twelve years the settlement was her winter home, and Cedar Cliff remained her summer location. She began a three-month course in domestic science training at the Lewis Institute in Chicago in January 1902, and although she felt great sadness at her husband's worsening condition she kept busy at the settlement. In May 1902 she began to teach a series of separate cooking classes for adults and children, a project she continued through at least 1907. Jane Addams reported to Alice on 19 May 1902 that Laura, a reluctant teacher, "begins today with some fear and trembling" (IU, Lilly, SAAH; *JAPM*, 4:381). She must have been a success, for children's classes, initially given in the kitchen only on Wednesday at 4 P.M., by 1906 were being held Monday through Thursday at 4. Classes for adults were also a hit. By 1906 three adult class offerings had been increased to daily classes in the kitchen at 7:30 P.M.

At the start of her Hull-House residency, Laura Addams was the director of the Garfield Club, a social group of approximately twenty teenagers. In addition, she taught sewing first once a week in the kitchen during the evening and then later in the textile room of the Hull-House shops. In the summer of 1902, when her daughter joined her as a settlement resident, Laura served as director of the Coffee House. By 1903 she had given up the sewing class for her expanding cooking classes and to learn more about textiles. In a 26 January 1903 letter to Alice Haldeman, Jane Addams remarked on Laura's growing skill as a dyer. Shortly after that, Laura was identified as the settlement resident responsible for the Labor Museum, a position she held for several years. From 1905 until sometime between 1913 and 1916, she was in charge of the textile room of the Hull-House shops. There, under her leadership four women made blankets, drapery fabric, patterned towels, and rugs for sale out of flax and wool that they produced by spinning and weaving.

When Laura Addams returned to Cedarville during summers, she worked hard to maintain her household. Writing to Marcet Haldeman in the late spring of 1908, she remarked, "I have been so busy and so tired when evening came that I hadn't one single idea in my head but just how tired I felt." She was, she continued, becoming an "'expert'" farmer. Among her accomplishments were planting "corn, cowpeas, sugar beets potatoes &c&c" and raising sheep, pigs, and chickens. "When you get back [from Europe] I will be a typical farmer with only one single idea the price of corn, pigs &c" ([28 May 1908?], JAPP, DeLoach).

Although Jane Addams purchased the Weber Addams's 240-acre farm to help keep his family solvent, she and Laura seemed to have a special business arrangement by which Laura had use of a portion of land as a stock farm. In her will, Jane left the farm to Laura for her use during her life, with the proviso that after Laura's death it was to be divided in four equal shares among the living children of John Manning and Mary Catherine Addams Linn (Weber, Esther, and Stanley) and Weber and Laura's daughter, Sarah. The only year she had this benefit, Laura split net profits of two thousand dollars from the farm with her tenant farmer.

After the death of her husband in 1918, Laura Addams was more free to travel and visit friends. For most of the last years of her life she lived with her daughter and son-in-law Ernest Adams Young (1876–1938) in San Antonio, Texas, and visited Cedarville usually only briefly during the summers. She died from pneumonia in Chicago on 31 January 1937. She was cremated, and after a brief service in Cedarville at the home of friends she was buried on 3 February 1937 beside her husband in the Cedarville Cemetery.

Her daughter, Sarah Weber Addams Young, who had no children, lived in San Antonio until her death on 19 December 1951. She, too, was cremated, and on 10 May 1952 her ashes were buried next to those of her husband, whose remains had been placed in the Cedarville Cemetery near other members of the Addams family on 16 May 1939, several months after he died suddenly in San Antonio on 6 December 1938.

Addams, Martha (1850–67)

Martha Addams, born 17 September 1850, was the third child of John Huy and Sarah Weber Addams. Until she was four years old, she knew the Addamses' two-room log cabin as home and shared its sleeping loft with her sister, Mary Catherine, and her brother, John Weber. Hearsay identifies her as the family beauty. She seems to have been intelligent, kind-hearted, and responsible. When she was fourteen, her older sister Mary, accompanied by younger sister Sarah Alice, visited relatives in Pennsylvania, leaving Martha in charge of Weber, then thirteen, and Jane, only four.

Like the other Addams children, Martha attended school in Cedarville, and, like her older sister Mary, she was a student of Laura Jane Gorham Forbes at her select school. By 1866 she had become a student in the Collegiate Department and in the Conservatory of Music at Rockford Female Seminary. She was a senior in 1867 at the time of her death at Rockford from typhoid fever on 23 March.

Among the scant records of her life are a few essays she wrote as a student in Cedarville, as well as a letter or two that reached her from childhood playmates and select-school classmates who came from such communities at Mount Morris, Shelbyville, and Warren, Illinois, and Cadiz, Wisconsin. In an 1860 essay, she identified the importance of reading. She prepared an essay entitled "Search After Happiness" for oral presentation in her select-school public examinations on 6 April 1864. In it, she revealed her perspective on the importance of patience, mercy, and Christian teachings weighted against wealth, pleasure, and fame.

By the fall of 1864, she was taking music, piano, and voice lessons from Sophia F. B. Hill. One family story insists that Martha Addams practiced her piano lessons in Freeport on the instrument owned by the Haldeman family. She was so entranced by the elegant, musically literate Anna Hostetter Haldeman that she sang her praises to John Addams and encouraged his attention toward Anna Haldeman after Anna's husband, William, died in 1866.

Addams, Sarah Weber (1817–63)

Sarah Weber Addams, the mother of Jane Addams, was born on 18 July 1817, the fourth child of Sarah Beaver Weber (1786–1846) and Col. George Weber (1790–1851). The Beaver and Weber families had arrived in Pennsylvania from Europe during the early eighteenth century. George Weber's great-grandfather was Christian Weber (1695–1778), who came in 1727 from his birthplace in Amsterdam, Holland, with his wife Apolonia, aboard the ship *Good Will* to settle in Worcester, Pennsylvania. Sarah Beaver was the great-granddaughter of George Bieber (1698–1775) and his wife Margaret. They came in 1744 on the *Friendship* from Rotterdam, Holland, and settled in Tredyffrin Township in Chester County, Pennsylvania.

Compared to information left by her husband John Huy Addams and by her children, the written record from which to construct a biography of Sarah Weber Addams is slight. When this biographical note was written, fewer than ten documents composed largely of parts of letters written by or about some aspect of her life were available from public sources. Snippets from her husband's 1844 diary and from a series of seventeen letters John Huy Addams wrote to her in 1857 while she was expecting their sixth child and he was representing his district in the senate of the Illinois General Assembly in Springfield provide a small window on their relationship. Marcet Haldeman-Julius, a granddaughter born nearly twenty-five years after Sarah Weber Addams died, became curious about her. After conducting an informal oral history about 1910 among the few and aged friends and family members still living who remembered Sarah Weber Addams, she wrote her description of Grandmother Sarah in a manuscript entitled "The Two Mothers of Jane Addams."

The most complete record of events in Sarah Weber Addams's life are in her husband's diary for the first six months of their married life and in documents relating to her death, which in retrospect became one of the defining moments in the life of her youngest child, Jane. A stark picture of that particular event emerges from the letter that Sarah's brother George Weber, Jr., wrote to their siblings in Pennsylvania describing it. A brief, one-paragraph obituary also appeared in the 21 January 1863 *Freeport Journal* and an even briefer obituary in the German-language newspaper *Deutscher Anzeiger,* also of Freeport, for the same date.

In all of the prose Jane Addams devoted to her childhood, there is almost no mention of her mother, stepmother, or siblings, whereas stories about her father abound. In *Twenty Years at Hull-House,* the first volume of her autobiography, she mentions her mother and stepmother only once: "My mother had died when I was a baby and my father's second marriage did not occur until my eighth year" (11). There are two chapters of reminiscences about her father.

That her mother's death was mysterious and traumatic for twenty-eight-month-old Jane there can be no doubt. Later in life she recalled horrible nightmares centered on the theme of abandonment. She also believed that she recalled the specific occasion of the death itself. The family must have remembered and exchanged stories about Sarah. In addition, her older children, husband, and Polly Beer, the family's helper who had been nurse to the child Sarah Weber, must have shared with Jane Addams tidbits of Sarah's wit and the character-building rules by which she ran her home and raised her children.

Although it is likely that Sarah remained an influence in the Addams home and in the development of her children even after her death, there is unfortunately no evidence of that in the written record handed down in family correspondence or in Jane Addams's public writing or extant personal records. Perhaps the memories of her mother were too distant, too blurred, and too much hearsay by the time she could write about her. Sarah Weber Addams's position as primary caregiver was of necessity superseded by others who became more immediate and lasting mother-figures to Jane, for example, her oldest sister Mary Catherine and Polly Beer. Perhaps Jane's store of sibling- or parent-generated memories was too personal, delicate, and revealing to share in her public prose.

Sarah Weber Addams grew to maturity in the eastern Pennsylvania village of Kreidersville in Allen Township, Northampton County, where the Webers were millers and merchants. After she attended local school, Colonel Weber sent his daughter to a boarding school to complete her education. (Although one source indicates it was located in Philadelphia, it could have been the Female Seminary founded in 1841 in Easton, Pennsylvania, where her father was a trustee of Lafayette College.) She was twenty-two when she joined the Reformed Church on 7 November 1839. By the standards of her day, Sarah was old when, on her twenty-seventh birthday in 1844, she was married by Jacob Christian Becker of the Reformed Church in Kreidersville to the twenty-two-year-old John Huy Addams of Sinking Spring, Pennsylvania.

They had met through her sister, Elizabeth Weber Reiff, and Elizabeth's miller husband Enos. Sarah often visited the Reiffs, where John Huy Addams was apprenticed to learn the mill trade. Much later, Addams's sister Susan Jane Addams Mull recalled that Sarah had already suffered "a disappointment" in love when she encountered John. Family lore indicates that her father judged her first serious suitor as unacceptable and that she made up her own mind about John. According to Elizabeth Weber Reiff, both families wondered at the pairing. The Webers were certain she could have done better by choosing an older, better-established partner. Jane Addams Mull hinted that the Addams family believed she had "ensnared him."

In Sarah Weber, Addams had found a true helpmate, one who complimented his personality, his high moral standards, his personal commitment to God, his will to succeed, and his dedication to family and community. "The understanding between them seems to have been without cloud or rift," pronounced Marcet Haldeman-Julius. It is likely that John was struck by Sarah's maturity and intellect as well as by her family connections and looks. According to Haldeman-Julius, Sarah was "good-looking. She was tall, with smooth, light brown hair which, parted in the middle and combed down softly over her ears, she gathered into a loose knot. Her forehead was noble, her nose straight; her kindly eyes were set in triangular sockets. Her height made her seem more slender than she was. A very old lady, who knew her well, said. . . . 'You wouldn't call her spare. She was well-fleshed, though she was never heavy.'" Jane Addams Mull recalled years later that "there was often a shine of merriment in [the] quiet depths" of Sarah's eyes. Her voice, she added, "had a winning overtone of warmth and cordiality," and when she heard either Jane or Alice Addams speak she could "'almost believe I hear Sarah talking'" ("Two Mothers," 2, 7).

Until 1854, when Sarah and John Huy Addams moved into a large two-story brick home built for them, Sarah kept house, gave birth to at least five children, and raised them in a log home with two rooms, a lean-to kitchen, and a sleeping loft. She created and maintained a garden each year, and after the orchard had matured she preserved a large amount of her family's food from those two sources. Like many frontier women, she sewed, cleaned, cooked, cared for the sick, and saw to the education and responsible upbringing of the eight Addams children who lived some portion of a year or more. It is likely that Sarah Addams had several miscarriages and physical illness as well. She also experienced the death from illness of three of her children. She was active in the community, in the development of religion in Cedarville, and a leader among the women of the village.

The comforting security of the well-ordered Addams home was dealt a major blow when Sarah died after giving premature birth. Her brother George Weber, Jr., described the details in a letter dated 17 January 1863, the day she was buried at 11 A.M. in the Cedarville Cemetery:

> Their Millers Wife was about being confined Sarah was called upon being in the family way herself having yet two months time for her confinement in her over exertion she was taken sick the Physician in attendance was obliged to lead her home this hapend a week ago to <yester>day on Friday afternoon She was taken very ill & her eye sight faild her she said to her daughter Mary that it was growing so dark & took her by the hand & said dear Mary is this the last time that I ever shall see you again she soon had convulsions a Messenger came for me I got to her bed side about Midnight oh it was very hard to see her have the convulsions her features had entirely changed she had ten or a Dozen attacks towards morning the Doctors removed the child a daughter well formed the convulsions ceased she lay

unconcious untill Sunday about 11 oClock the first we noticed of any conciousness was the little daughter Jenny cried with a loud shriek Sarah raised up in bed
but oh the wild look she had she soon sank back again I called her by name she
opened her eyes I gave her something to drink she recd it. John had arved in the
Morning (Sunday) from Springfield towards evening she Knew us both we all
thought she might possibly get well again I returned home in the night our daughter Mary being very sick of Typhoid fever. on Monday afternoon I again went to
see Sarah and found the change still for the better as we supposed she named me . . .
at night I returned home again & as Mary was growing worse I did not get to see
Sarah on Tuesday. On Wednesday morning James Addams bro to John drove up
to my door have a long stick in the Buggy I well knew what it meant but could
hardly think it possible that the Measure was for a Coffin for our Sister John wished
me to come along with his brother to see him he takes it severely to heart & is much
perplexed what to do in regard of his dear family being obliged to return to Springfield to fill his Seat in the Senate Polly Beer will stay with the Children & Mrs Forbs
a school teacher who formerly boarded there. Sarahs Corpse looked very life like
her featurs had fully returned again. (George Weber, Jr. to Brothers and Sister
[Devault Weber, John Harrison Weber, and Elizabeth Weber Reiff], SCPC, JAC)

The *Freeport Journal* and brother George agreed in their account of the funeral that it was unusually large and well attended. In part, that may have been
a result of the prominence of the Addams family and the prestige of John Huy
Addams. It was also no doubt due to the reputation for kindness and helpfulness that Sarah had engendered by her work in the community. As the *Freeport
Journal* reported on 21 January 1863, "Mrs. Addams was a woman who will be
missed everywhere—at home, in society, in the church, in all places where good
was to be done, and suffering to be relieved. Possessed of means, and with a heart
ever alive to the wants of the poor, she was always present when sympathy was
needed or aid required."

Through Sarah Weber Addams's portion of the estate of her father, Col.
George Weber, the Addams children each received $32.70 when the estate was
settled in 1867. John Huy Addams served as guardian for the minor Addams
children and managed the portion for each, giving it to them at majority. In 1874
John Weber Addams received $56.20, in 1877 Sarah Alice Addams Haldeman
received $66.85, and in 1878 Jane Addams was given $70.68.

Ainsworth, Sarah Anderson (1849–1932)

Sarah Anderson (Ainsworth) was a teacher and administrator at Rockford Female Seminary when Jane Addams was a student at the seminary, and the two
became confidantes and close friends. Of Scots-Irish descent, Anderson was
born in Bucyrus, Ohio. Lauded by Rockford schoolgirls for her amiable demean-
or and striking looks, she had dark auburn hair and a fair complexion. She was
the daughter of John Anderson and his second wife, Mary Andrews Anderson,

who was from Ashland, Ohio. The couple were married in 1845 and had five children. Her father's first wife, Sarah Redburn Anderson, had died in 1844, leaving two children. Sarah grew up in Geneseo, Illinois, where her father was a prominent businessman, real estate developer, and farmer. She was raised within an environment of activism and reform; family members were abolitionist Republicans, Congregationalists, and supporters of the temperance cause.

Sarah Anderson was educated at Rockford Female Seminary and graduated in 1869. When she first began teaching at Rockford, she specialized in physical education and calisthenics. She also taught English and the history of art and was for many years the financial secretary of the seminary. Each student had the experience of paying tuition and settling her monthly budget with Miss Anderson. Student Addie B. Smith wrote to her father in 1877 that Miss Anderson "is a real little business woman and as pleasant as can be and ever since that first day when we were arranging about the bill down there in the office I have grown to like her more and more" (Addie B. Smith to Papa [Benjamin Smith], 18 June [1877], SHSW, Smith). Former student Emma Goodale (Garvin) remembered that she "liked Miss Anderson very much—I think she did not teach but was in the office. She had such pretty hair and would laugh and talk with the girls" (Emma Goodale Garvin to Hazel Cedarborg, 22 Mar. 1925, RC).

Anderson continued teaching calisthenics in the late 1870s. She was appointed secretary and treasurer of the Society of Mission Inquiry in December 1878 and remained active as an officer in the group, including stints as recording secretary of the Congregational Board of Ladies of the Society of Mission Inquiry and as president of the Society of Mission Inquiry's Home Missions Society auxiliary. In Addams's junior year, the 1879–80 Rockford Female Seminary *Catalogue* listed her as "Sarah F. Anderson, Accountant and English Language, Preparatory Dep't." She and Jane became very close, especially in Jane's senior year. They traveled together during the summer when Addams was a student, and they remained good friends and correspondents after she left Rockford. A colleague in the Rockford Female Seminary administration remembered that Anderson "had so much to do in helping Jane Addams get her ideas into shape," a fact that Addams confirmed in her own correspondence to Ellen Gates Starr (Martha Hillard [MacLeish] to Karl Bickel [Anderson's nephew and the president of the United Press], 18 Mar. 1935, RC).

Anderson and Addams were both active in the Chicago Rockford Female Seminary Reunion Association, and they traveled together with Ellen Gates Starr in Europe in 1887–88. Art prints collected during that trip later graced the walls of both the seminary and Hull-House. This aspect of her contribution to the school was highlighted in the Rockford College profile of Anderson's term as principal, in which it was noted that "she had been commissioned to buy photographs of paintings and sculpture for the Seminary and had accompanied Jane Addams to Europe in 1888, returning with an impressive collection" (*Profiles of the Principals of Rockford Seminary*, 13).

Like Addams, Anderson had ambitions for postgraduate study in medicine in 1881–82. She confided in Addams regarding the dilemmas she faced in deciding whether to leave Rockford Female Seminary to pursue graduate studies or to remain and try to convince Anna P. Sill that she should be allowed release time from her seminary duties in order to take coursework in Chicago. She decided to stay at Rockford and served as secretary for the seminary's Executive Committee and financial secretary for the school's Board of Trustees. A decade after Addams's graduation, Anderson headed the school.

Anderson became temporary principal of Rockford Female Seminary in June 1890, when Anna Bordwell Gelston left that position. She was appointed "Upon motion of Miss Jane Addams seconded by Mr. T. D. Robertson" by act of the Rockford Female Seminary Executive Committee and Board of Trustees (William A. Talcott to Sarah Anderson, 24 June 1890, RC). A formal printed announcement signed by William A. Talcott on 1 August 1890 proclaimed that Anderson was the "first graduate of the Seminary to act as its Principal" (RC). The job was made permanent in 1891, when the Board of Trustees approved the following motion: "Resolved: We commend the administration of Sarah F. Anderson as acting principal during the past year, and deeming such action for the best interest of the school we hereby appoint and confirm her Principal" (RFS Board of Trustees, "Minutes of the Annual Meetings," 25 June 1891; *JAPM*, 1A:175). At the time of her appointment, Anderson had been with the school for twenty-one years.

It was under Anderson's presidency that the name of Rockford Seminary was changed to Rockford College in 1892. She also oversaw the building of Adams Hall and major improvements to the college's laboratories and studios. Fellow administrator Martha Hillard MacLeish (who succeeded Anna P. Sill as the seminary's principal) acknowledged Anderson for putting the school on a sound financial basis, much to the benefit of the administrations that followed her. Anderson was also credited with increasing faculty salaries and updating library holdings. She remained principal of Rockford College until 1896. When she resigned at the end of the 1895–96 academic year, the Board of Trustees paid tribute to "a mind well trained, a character exalted, and a manner sympathetic and unselfish" (quoted in *Profiles of the Principals of Rockford Seminary,* 13).

Anderson was given an honorary master's degree by Beloit College in the midst of her tenure as Rockford College principal in 1894. She resigned on 14 April 1896 in order to marry a widower, Henry A. ("Harry") Ainsworth (1833–1914). She and Ainsworth had been friends for many years—indeed, they had been family. Ainsworth's first wife, Sarah Andrews Ainsworth, was Anderson's aunt (her mother's sister). Sarah Andrews had married Ainsworth in Ashland, Ohio, in 1858, and she died in Chicago in 1891. The couple had a daughter and a son, both of whom were educated at Oberlin College, Oberlin, Ohio. Henry A. Ainsworth was a former New Englander who was president of the Moline Trust and Savings Bank and the Williams and White Company (a steam hammer and tool manufacturing business) in Moline, Illinois. He had been a general merchandise, hardware, and agricultural implement dealer in Geneseo, Illinois, from 1853 to 1870, when he moved to Moline. In addition, he was very active in Republican Party politics. He served as a delegate to party conventions and was appointed or elected to various state and local political positions. He was an Ohio state senator from 1882 to 1886.

After her marriage to Henry A. Ainsworth on 30 June 1896, Sarah Anderson Ainsworth became a member, with Jane Addams, of the Rockford College Board of Trustees. She was also active in the kindergarten movement. She helped begin the first kindergarten in Moline, raising money for the school with a local women's club. She was a frequent visitor to Hull-House and contributed funds to Addams to help Hull-House weather the economic depression of 1894. The Ainsworths were also active members of the First Congregational Church of Moline.

The Ainsworths had a second home in Daytona Beach, Florida, where Sarah lived after her husband's death. She wrote a book about Florida birds before dying at the age of eighty-two, nearly twenty years after he did. She was buried in Geneseo.

Beer, Mary ("Polly") (1802–77)

Mary ("Polly") Beer (the spelling used on her grave marker) Bier or Behr was an important figure in the Addams home. She was a major link between Jane and the other Addams children and their mother Sarah Weber Addams and their Weber kin.

It is likely that Polly Beer, born in Pennsylvania, became a fixture in the home of George and Sarah Beaver Weber in Kreidersville, Pennsylvania, at a young age. All of Sarah Weber Addams's siblings remembered Polly fondly as their childhood nurse. While the Weber children grew up and began to marry and move away, Polly Beer remained in the Weber home with Sarah Beaver Weber. After her sudden death in July 1846, Polly lodged for a time with one of her former charges, Margaret Weber.

In 1848 the thirty-eight-year-old Polly and a fourteen-year-old servant, Louise ("Lucy") Hensy, accompanied another Weber child, John Harrison ("Harry") and his wife, the former Caroline Catherine Houck, to join Col. George Weber, Harry's father, in the milling business he had purchased in Como, a small village centered around the mill on the Rock River in Whiteside County in northwestern Illinois. Polly, Lucy, and the Webers lived in a two-story frame house constructed for them near the mill site. Soon, Polly was once again a family nurse. The Harry Webers had their first child, George A. Weber, in 1848, shortly after their arrival at Como. Another of Colonel Weber's sons, George Weber, Jr., and his wife Maria (or Mariah) W. Hoffeditz, married in November 1848, joined the Como enterprise in 1849. Their firstborn, John T. Weber, died in June 1850, a few months after his birth.

Polly and the Webers stayed in Como until Colonel Weber's death on 21 June 1851. During the next few years the family dispersed. Harry Weber and his family moved to Chicago, where he became a merchant. George Weber, Jr., became a missionary minister for the Reformed Church and traveled the Midwest. In all probability, Polly lived partially with his family during the 1850s, helping Maria Weber cope with her brood of children, which eventually reached ten, only five of whom lived to maturity. It is likely that Polly spent increasing periods in the Addams household, for during the 1850s the George Weber, Jr., family lived in Orangeville and Freeport, both just a few miles from Cedarville in northern Illinois. She is listed with the John H. Humphrey family in the U.S. census of 1860. Cousins of Beer, the family members were John H., a farmer, age fifty-six; his wife Frances, age fifty; a son, John H., twenty-four; and a daughter, Mary J., nineteen. All were born in Pennsylvania; a son, Milton, seven, was born in Illinois.

Polly probably came to live permanently in the Addams home about the time of Sarah Weber Addams's death in 1863. She is listed with the Addams family in the Illinois census of 1865. By that time it had become clear that the George Weber, Jr., family could not afford to feed and house a servant. The Addams family could and also had great need. John Huy Addams was often away from home as a businessman and state legislator, and the Addams children, except for Mary Catherine, were relatively young. They needed someone who knew all of the household chores that had to be completed and could both undertake them and instruct others in carrying them out. Polly helped sew, knit mittens and caps, and cook and preserve food. She kept the house in order and served as a nurse and caretaker for the children. Jane Addams described her as "the face familiar from my earliest childhood and associated with homely household cares" (*Twenty Years*, 19). Her near-family position and significance to young Jane is also reflected in part by Jane's inclusion of Polly's name in her childhood letters to other family members (*JAPM*, 1:115, 1:123, 1:128, 1:133, 1:138, 1:146).

On 7 January 1877, while was visiting the John H. Humphrey family who lived on a farm four miles north of Cedarville, Polly became ill. Sixteen-year-old Jane went to her and was her only attendant when she died. It was an unforgettable experience for Jane, and she wrote to at least two of her mother's siblings to report the death of their former nurse. Responses from uncles Harry Weber on 24 January 1877 (SCHS; *JAPM*, 1:203–9) and Devault Weber (Devault Weber to JA, 3 Sept. 1877, above) are extant, although the letters Jane wrote are not. Her description of her experience at Polly's death appears in her memoirs (*Twenty Years*, 19–20). Polly Beer was buried in the Addams family plot in the Cedarville Cemetery.

Haldeman, George Bowman (1861–1909)

George Bowman Haldeman, youngest son of Anna Hostetter Haldeman and William J. Haldeman, was born on 9 June 1861 at Oakland, the home of Anna's sister and brother-in-law, Susanna ("Susan") Hostetter Bowman and George Bowman, near Mount Carroll in Carroll County, Illinois. He spent the first year of his life there with his mother, aunt, and the uncle for whom he was named. While her husband and her eldest child, Henry ("Harry") Winfield Haldeman, remained in Freeport, Illinois, where William J. Haldeman ran the steam flour mill and Harry went to school and took music lessons, Anna Haldeman lived with the infant George at the home of the sister who had raised and mothered her after their own mother had died. Two children born to the Haldemans after Harry's birth had died, and Anna was fearful about this fourth child. She insisted that she would feel more secure near her siblings, two of whom were physicians in Mount Carroll.

By the time George was a year old, his father had persuaded Anna to join him in Freeport. There they made their home, George growing up under the watchful eye of his parents and brother thirteen years his senior. In 1866, when George was only five, his father died of tuberculosis. Several months later, his brother Harry, who was eighteen and in school at Mount Carroll Academy, left the United States for two years of musical and scientific study in Leipzig, Germany. The new widow Haldeman and young George remained in Freeport, where George began to attend the local public school.

George Haldeman was a slight, sandy-haired youth who challenged himself mentally and physically. He was often unwell, experiencing fevers and frequent nosebleeds. After Anna Haldeman married John Huy Addams in November 1868, George went with his mother to live in the Addams's Cedarville home. He seems to have integrated himself into the blended family with more ease than she did. Although he became acquainted with other Cedarville youths and joined them in play in the schoolyard and in the barns and fields around the community, his primary playmate was Jane. She was only slightly older than he, and he became her constant companion and intellectual peer. The two wrote letters at the same time, played cards and board games together (including chess, which the Haldeman family introduced to the Addams family), studied the same subjects in school, created make-believe games and secret organizations that had special alphabets and symbols only they knew, and romped and played in the Cedarville countryside in all seasons. While he was a graduate student at Johns Hopkins University in Baltimore, George Haldeman watched neighborhood boys sledding and nostalgically recalled a happier time: "I enjoy watching the boys coasting it recalls pleasant memories of when Mamie Gardiner used to help Jane and me in that pastime" (GBH to AHHA, 30 Dec. 1883, JAPP, DeLoach).

Like Jane, George Haldeman attended Sunday School and church in Cedarville with the Addams family. He also seems to have received a generous dose of New Jerusalem Church doctrine from his mother and her siblings. Eventually, he began to read a Greek Bible and frequently read the New Testament, exclaiming later in life on the power and mystery of the Book of Revelation. By 1889 he reflected that "all Knowledge and science confirmed Christianity" and indicated that he hoped he would honor God with his life (GBH to AHHA, 7 May 1889, UIC, JAMC, HJ).

Along with Jane, George studied natural history, Latin, mathematics, spelling, history, and English in the Cedarville school and participated in public examinations and presentations. The step-siblings made similar grades, although George was a much better speller than Jane. During the spring of 1875, and perhaps until he graduated in 1877, he also served as school janitor, sweeping the schoolrooms and bringing in fuel for the stove, for which he received ten cents a day.

Anna Haldeman Addams encouraged her son to develop the artistic elements of his personality. All his life he wrote poetry; his earliest extant work was penned in 1870 when he was nine. He and Jane both took piano and singing lessons. "He was not an accomplished pianist as his brother was, but he was proficient enough to have memorized all the Mozart piano sonatas" (Fry, *Generous Spirit*, 38). In addition, and perhaps more important, he achieved an appreciation for music that gave him much pleasure. Later in life he exclaimed to his mother, "I love music so much. . . . There seems to be a mysterious connection between music and thought" (10 Feb. 1884, JAPP, DeLoach). He also began to hone his drawing skills, making sketches of Cedarville sites and the places he visited or lived. His drawing ability was especially useful during graduate studies in biology at Johns Hopkins University. Some of his drawings appeared in *Report on the Stomatopoda . . .* (1886), which was written by his primary professor, William Keith Brooks (1848–1908), a zoologist.

Harry Haldeman was a particularly important influence on George and Jane's educations. He encouraged both children to study science, languages, and mathematics. Excellence in those subjects was associated with a high and rigorous intellect and with the ability to achieve success in a university curriculum. When George visited his brother each summer while Harry was studying to be a physician—and after he had established himself as one—Harry encouraged him in scientific study, helping him learn about chemistry, pharmaceuticals, and the human body.

By 1877 George Haldeman and Jane Addams had exhausted all the educational opportunities in Cedarville. When Jane went to Rockford Female Seminary to continue her education, George matriculated at Beloit Academy and College. He did not attend Mount Carroll Academy as Harry had done, because by 1877 the school was no longer accepting male students.

George Haldeman arrived in Beloit, Wisconsin, in September 1877 to attend the Academy or Preparatory School of Beloit College, from which he graduated in 1879. Making sufficiently high grades, he was admitted to Beloit College in the fall of 1879. He specialized in the study of science and languages, and when he graduated in June 1883 he presented the salutatory address in Latin for his graduating class of four. It was during his seven years in Beloit that George firmly established his dedication to the study of foreign languages. Although he read

Latin and German, he was proudest of his ability to read Greek, an achievement he practiced for the remainder of his life.

While at Beloit, George Haldeman lived in a rented room and ate his meals in a boardinghouse. He led an intellectually active life, writing articles for the college magazine, the *Round Table*, and participating in debates. Among the topics for which he prepared arguments were the affirmative position for "Resolved, that the higher branches (the languages & higher mathematics) should not be taught in our High School" and the negative position for "Resolved, that the U.S. is governed by the general law of the decay of nations." "Resolved, that the Tribal Relations of our Indians should be Abolished" was the subject of a debate held on 19 November 1880 at a public meeting of the Archaean Union of scholarly societies. Haldeman, known as "Dens," represented the Alethean Society in arguing the negative position. His mother and stepfather were in the audience of the Opera House in Beloit to hear the debate and to see H. M. Herrick and George declared victorious.

The Alethean Society was one of two literary and debating organizations that composed the Archaean Union (the Delian Society was the other). George served as treasurer of the Archaean Union in 1879. He became vice president of the Alethean Society in 1881 and president for the 1882–83 academic year. In the spring of 1882 he was a member of the Committee of College Songs, which selected and published songs written about Beloit College by former students as well as songs from other colleges. Haldeman also wrote and presented a number of orations. At the Junior Exhibition of his class, held on 20 December 1881, he offered an oration in Greek: "To Nomimon Dikaion Einai." He was keeping up with Jane, who had presented her Junior Exhibition oration in Greek just the year before.

George Haldeman submitted one of his most prophetic orations on 7 May for presentation on 21 May 1881. He entitled it "The College Hermit." As if describing a personal dilemma with which he already grappled, one that would consume his adult life, George suggested:

> There are traits manifesting themselves now and then which point too plainly towards the hermit. Where social relations stand merely upon policy and convenience, not upon community and oneness of interests; there will be seen the individual seeking for his own aggrandizement, contracting within the narrow shell of his own existence; senseless and callous to external relations. . . . Many an unfortunate has been driven to despair by the sad revelation of himself, in vain endeavoring to escape his own <dreaded> existence. In the hermit of old there was much of virtue. . . . So his modern representative is not devoid of excellence but cherishes a purpose far above many ignoble aims and though he may not hold the sympathy of mankind let him still be regarded as one that "loved not wisely but too well." (JAPP, DeLoach)

In the fall of 1881 Jane Addams, Harry Haldeman, and Alice Addams Haldeman went to Philadelphia, where they enrolled in medical schools. Anna

Haldeman Addams accompanied them. For the first time in his life George was completely alone, depending on his own reserves and abilities for health and emotional stability. By early 1882, about the time that Anna underwent surgery and Jane was exploring S. Weir Mitchell's cure for nervous prostration, George indicated to his brother that he was tiring of Beloit and would be content there only one more year. He wished to go to Cedarville to be with his mother and stepsister when they returned home at the end of March. Instead, he remained in school and spent the summer of 1882 in Cedarville and visiting Alice and Harry Haldeman in Mitchellville, Iowa.

At the end of the first term in his final year at Beloit he accompanied his mother on a trip to Florida while his brother and Alice operated on Jane Addams's spinal curvature and saw to her recuperation. During December 1882 and into the spring of 1883, mother and son went to Green Cove Springs, Florida, and visited St. Augustine and Palatka. George then returned to complete his final term at Beloit. His senior essay "The Augur," which he presented at his graduation exercise in June 1883, foretold his lifelong interest in the classical world of Greece and Rome as well as his curiosity about religion. His family, including his mother, brother Harry, brother-in-law John M. Linn, and stepsister Jane, attended the occasion.

Young George Haldeman was faced with the decision of what he should do next. Although few letters for this period are extant, it seems certain that he and Harry had been considering his future—especially where and with whom he would live. Showing concern for their mother and indicating a family role for his brother, Harry wrote: "[F]rom now On You and Ma will be together. It is My De[a]r Boy best. It is fitting that You and She Should make a home for Each other and I hope Nothing Will occurr to Separate you. Jane has Mary's and Webers and our Home to go to and Mother has no place Except her own Home which I hope She Will always keep, but Keep alone. We Will put our heads together and See about that in the Spring" ([Dec. 1883], UIC, JAMC, HJ).

George and Anna summered at Annisquam, Massachusetts, on Cape Ann in 1883. He enrolled in the Annisquam Laboratory summer session organized by Massachusetts Institute of Technology professor Alpheus Hyatt (1838–1902) and conducted research in marine biology. By early October 1883, however, George was in Baltimore, enrolled in the recently organized Johns Hopkins University and working toward a Ph.D. He chose to specialize in marine biology. He secured a room with Cornelia Mayer, widow of Brantz Mayer (1809–79), a historian and founder of the Maryland Historical Society, and her family; ate his meals in a boardinghouse; and became Brooks's student, focusing on the morphology of marine animals.

During the first two of George Haldeman's Johns Hopkins years, his mother and stepsister traveled and lived in Europe. He buried himself in study and laboratory work, taking in musical entertainment and plays from time to time but leading an increasingly isolated and solitary life. Instead of going to the home of his step-aunt and step-uncle Young and their family in Philadelphia for Christmas, he stayed in Baltimore with the Mayers. "I lead a quiet life as usual," he reported to his mother, "and spend many idle moments musing by the fire-side, and will confess have some pleasant melancholy in longing and gazing at those two dear faces which seemed never sweeter to me than they do now" (30 Dec. 1883, JAPP, DeLoach). Evidently, Anna replied and chided him for being unsocial, because late in January 1884 he responded: "The motive and inducement and I may say the return for moving in 'Society' is small, very small," he told his mother. "It is a waste I fear, an extravagance which I can't afford. It is a difficult thing to be sociable. The honest friendly social man is a good type. I will try to imitate it" (28 Jan. 1884, JAPP, DeLoach). He was not, however, successful.

During the summer of 1884 George Haldeman joined the Addams party in Europe. They meandered through France and Switzerland before he returned for another year of study at Johns Hopkins that seems to have passed much like the 1883–84 academic year. In the late summer of 1885, under Brooks's leadership, Haldeman went to the Chesapeake Zoology Laboratory in Beaufort, North Carolina, where he investigated and gathered marine life specimens for study during the 1885–86 academic year. By the time his mother arrived in Baltimore in mid-November 1885 to take up residence for the winter and spring, he was once again focused on study.

Her presence—and, by Christmas, Jane's—provided George once again with a social environment with which he was both familiar and comfortable. So far as his mother was concerned, his health continued to be a problem. (His letters to his mother while she was in Europe are full of assurances that he was healthy and feeling well. Hers to him indicate constant concern for his strength and well-being, both physical and mental.) Shortly after her arrival in Baltimore, Anna Haldeman Addams determined, "Tis good for George I came—and, he needs recreation; he looked pale—and, had constant attacks of nose bleedings used to come on very suddenly, even when sitting quietly; A long siege of nearly nine years of hard study, I find is, breaking him down and, my coming—was a merciful Providence because—he had no social life—no friend to break in upon his studious habit" (AHHA to SAAH, 16 Dec. 1885, IU, Lilly, SAAH).

George realized that he was different from other students. He knew he created no friendships and believed that he was incapable of doing so. Anna seemed to agree and, looking on the positive side, thought the fact that he was so alone might be a "safe guard to his talent, and genius, that otherwise would be frittered away on society and its trivialities that now go in to social work" (AHHA to HWH, 2 Apr. 1886, UIC, JAMC, HJ).

George Haldeman did seem to impress older women. When she discovered that he would no longer be rooming at her home, Cornelia Mayer wrote to his mother. "He was the most gentle—respectful and considerate person I ever knew," she said. "So you cannot wonder at my partiality for one—who has been ever my true and steadfast friend—as well—as my highly esteemed boarder"

(17 June 1886, UIC, JAMC, HJ Supp.). As Anna, ever proud and protective of her son, exclaimed to her daughter-in-law Alice, "George does all for me, in his power, as a lady in the house said the other day—'Why seldom a daughter is so devoted to a Mother, as your son is to you'" (16 Dec. 1885, IU, Lilly, SAAH).

The spring and summer of 1886 saw George back in Beaufort to gather more biological material. "My constitution is improving here. I am more robust," he assured his mother shortly after he arrived there in mid-April (26 Apr. 1886, UIC, JAMC, HJ). Although George had planned to go with Professor Brooks's expedition to Nassau, he finally decided not to interrupt his Beaufort investigations. Instead, he and Edmund B. Wilson (1856–1939), who would become a distinguished zoologist but at the time was a young scholar teaching at Bryn Mawr College, rented a laboratory building for ten dollars per month and settled in. Although Anna probably thought the social interaction with other scientists as well as a definite change of venue might help her son's mental health, she was unable to change his mind about going to the West Indies.

Toward the end of August, George left the "Marine Laboratory" in Beaufort to meet his mother in Maryland, where they vacationed together. Afterward, they met Jane at Harpers Ferry, West Virginia, and returned to Baltimore. Jane and her stepmother rented a three-room flat in a house where George had a room, and the family settled down for what would become George Haldeman's last semester at Johns Hopkins. When Anna indicated to him that Mrs. Brooks thought he would graduate in 1887, George hastened to inform his mother that she was

much mistaken, . . . no doubt she is not well acquainted with the requirements. I had not anticipated taking my degree before 1888 as I think I told you last winter, that will make a stay of five years at the university. The degree is not the main thing by any means, and the time is so much more profitable to me when I go a little slower and really fix some of the overwhelming mass of facts. My studying capacity is of a certain amount but I either overexert or else do not know as much by trying to shorten my course of study by several years. It is certainly a great danger to young men to seek positions and titles prematurely giving better opportunity to display their asinine qualities. (26 June 1886, UIC, JAMC, HJ)

George Haldeman was comfortable as a student and unwilling to be hurried.

With his mother's financial support, George had planned to study in Europe beginning in the spring of 1887. When Anna Addams discovered, however, that Harry and Alice Haldeman were expecting a child in June 1887 she decided that neither she nor George would go to Europe but remain in the United States to await the birth of her first grandchild. Jane Addams commented on the effect this decision had on George. "I think it was natural in Harry to tell Ma and I have no doubt it seriously influenced her plans," she wrote to Alice. "George will probably build up in Florida and be all the more ready for his European plans. I am more sorry for him than I can express, he gets so utterly discouraged" (9 Feb. 1887, IU, Lilly, SAAH; JAPM, 2:438–39).

George joined his mother to spend the spring in Melrose, Florida. By early June, both were back in Cedarville, and once again George was recovering from poor health. Cornelia Mayer, who corresponded with Anna Haldeman Addams early in June, wondered if his illness was caused by malaria and indicated how sorry she was that he could not return to Johns Hopkins.

On 23 June 1887 George wrote to his brother and indicated he would not return to the university. "I hope to get some where in quiet, so that I can study and collect my thoughts. I hardly know what to think of the various phases that events have taken. Suggestions are usually plentiful except when requested then there is no response" (UIC, JAMC, HJ). It is not clear just what George meant by "various phases that events have taken." In addition to illness and his mother's about-face on his trip to Europe, perhaps he was discouraged from further study by his primary professor. Before the beginning of the next academic year the focus of his intellectual interest had altered in a significant way, and he had given up the study of marine biology.

After spending the summer in Cedarville with his mother, in September 1887 George set out without her to study in Leipzig. His decision may have been taken because brother Harry had studied there, as had some of his professors and fellow students at Johns Hopkins. Perhaps he saw Leipzig as an academic step up from Hopkins and wanted an opportunity to experience, and hopefully excel at, a highly respected German institution.

His goal was to study with Wilhelm Max Wundt (1832–1922), the German physiologist and psychologist who founded the first laboratory for experimental psychology and taught at Leipzig from 1875. Wundt had applied scientific methods within psychology, particularly the use of introspection. George, who planned to attend five lecture series, prepared by reading the texts before the lectures began. Living in Leipzig, he was immediately confronted by a language barrier. Reading German was one thing but speaking and understanding it were other matters. He was probably one of the few Americans attending the university. During the previous year there had been only thirty-seven students from the United States among the 3,054 enrolled in the university at Leipzig. He was not impressed with Leipzig, with the German people, or with their customs. Apparently, he felt more isolated than ever, and by November he had returned to Cedarville.

According to his mother, George became too ill to function as a student and thus returned home. Harry's response to the return was that George might prove helpful to Anna. George's reply indicates his sense of failure:

It is pleasant to know that my return meets with your approval, I hope that it may prove advantageous to mother. I did not realize how deeply she seemed to feel my absence nor how inadequate your sympathy was to alleviate the situation. Of course I will stay with her as long as she says or as long as it does not conflict with the family harmony.

At any time I am willing to earn a humble living for myself. I doubt if you appreciate mother's intense admiration and devotion to you which should be a source of your keenest pleasure. It is but natural that my failure should recall the trying circumstances and the successful outcome of your student days in Leipzig. (12 Nov. 1887, UIC, JAMC, HJ)

His comment about "family harmony" may well have indicated a major change in the previously familiar and supportive relationships that Anna, George, and Jane had shared during the first year they spent together in Baltimore. Now, loving mentions of stepsister Jane Addams were missing from his letters to their shared kin.

As Jane Addams left for her second European adventure in December 1887, George was still searching ineffectually for a livelihood and a purpose. He rejected Harry's suggestion that he might join him at the Girard bank or that he might help manage their mother's assets. He hoped to find something to do that would permit him to use his training but told Harry that for the time being he would stay with their mother. "She seems to have use for me here as a companion and consequently I have no present intention of seeking employment," he wrote. He determined to bend himself to study "not . . . to astonish the world but to keep myself in a state of continual awe before the silent and incontrovertible testimony of fact." He expected to share his intellectual investigations with Harry because of their similar experiences and their "brotherly love" and because their "kinship" permitted them "to investigate psychology more closely than <on> any other of the human species" (2 Dec. 1887, UIC, JAMC, HJ).

While Anna attempted to become a companion to her son (George told Harry that he and his mother were reading the *Odyssey* and that she thought she would like to learn Greek), it was with Harry and no one else that George maintained an intellectual relationship. Through their correspondence they played chess, posed and solved geometrical theorems, and discussed religion, philosophy, and science. George also began to investigate the leaders, writers, events, and conditions of Greek and Roman history, with which he would remain intrigued for the remainder of his life.

On 8 June 1888, when he might have been receiving his Ph.D. from Johns Hopkins University, without telling his mother or anyone else George abruptly disappeared from the Addamses' Cedarville home. Harry and Stephenson County Sheriff Benjamin F. Timms, who went in search of him, discovered that George had set off walking west and reached Dubuque, Iowa, where he disappeared. Sarah Hostetter went to stay with Anna during the crisis, and Alice wrote frequent letters of support and consolation. In her letter of 25 June 1888, Alice told Anna that she "did so dreadfully fear a morbid condition," and her fears were based on George's "morbid condition of mind" (IU, Lilly, SAAH). "Dear George," Alice lamented in a letter to her husband, "we have all been so complacently proud of his achievements—and here he has thought we did not care"

(22 June 1888, IU, Lilly, SAAH). Jane, writing from Europe, believed that George would not intentionally hurt himself but that he might forget to eat. She was distressed for Anna Haldeman Addams but certain that George would reappear in due course—as he did. Harry and Sheriff Timms found him "'two miles east of Waterloo, Iowa. His clothes were ragged and dirty'" (Fry, *Generous Spirit*, 37).

The *Freeport Weekly Democrat* carried several articles about his disappearance. According to the first article on 22 June 1888, George's reason for leaving was "his being morbidly sensitive in regard to the matter of dependence." A final article on 6 July revealed that he had worked for a week on a farm in Iowa and that a "tiff" with his mother was the event that precipitated his leaving (Fry, *Generous Spirit*, 36–37).

By 6 July 1888 George had returned to Cedarville and had begun trying to interact normally with other town residents and family, attending local social functions and family gatherings. In August he and his mother visited Harry and Alice in Girard, Kansas, and they returned to Cedarville to meet Jane when she came back from her European trip in July. He was also once again reading the classics and holding intellectual discussions on philosophy and psychology with Harry.

In April 1889, as Jane Addams was making a firm commitment to carry out her plans to develop Hull-House, George set off to the West once again. Perhaps he was jolted into the journey not only by guilt at having no means of livelihood and by the actions of Jane, who was creating one for herself, but also by conversations they may have had. "Let Jane not think that I took her 'wish' as a <u>challenge</u> should I go on to the very Pacific Coast" he informed his mother from Colorado (14 May 1889, UIC, JAMC, HJ). "It seemed to me too easy a life, and too ideal to stay there with you and study, and something seemed to forbid it," he wrote to Anna on 17 May (UIC, JAMC, HJ).

This time he combined walking with rail travel. Arriving in Denver on 2 May, he secured inexpensive lodging. "I am a little uncertain what to do next. I would like employment because I abhor the idleness, and yet I am almost indifferent about an occupation, could I only have time to think." He knew he owed his mother an explanation for his behavior and vowed that he would write about the "theory" of what he was doing, especially since she had listened to "his long discourse last winter" (GBH to AHHA, 4 May 1889, UIC, JAMC, HJ).

George, broad-shouldered, six feet tall, and approaching thirty, trudged among the towns at the base of Pikes Peak—Colorado Springs, Manitou, and Pueblo—sometimes walking forty miles a day. "When I am among the rocks, I feel <u>a</u> new vigor breathed into me, there is so much of the wild free life in it; and yet after all, I am sedentary, if I had my way would stay in my room and study and never take more than a stroll. But nature seems to drive me to what I would avoid" (GBH to AHHA, 7 May 1889, UIC, JAMC, HJ). He struggled with what to do as he rambled daily, holding conversations with himself, sometimes singing to the ravines and rivers and mountains and always reading from the pocket testament he carried with him. He continued "perfectly at sea as regards an occupation" (GBH to AHHA, 12 May 1889, UIC, JAMC, HJ). He was not ready to publish, wondered if farming would be better than teaching, and indicated that he could not stand the idea of applying to educational bureaus. Recognizing his inability to grasp a goal or present a direction that others could understand, on 13 May he wrote to his mother, "I may write pages and yet not tell you what I would because I do not know what I would tell you; and yet I would know if you had been told the unknown bit of information that I would impart to you" (UIC, JAMC, HJ).

While he continued to beg Anna to join him in the West, telling her that her letters made him almost regret that he had gone away, he also began, rather plaintively, to request that she tell him what to do, that if she needed or wanted him at home he would come. She must have encouraged him to explore opportunities in Colorado, and to make his life more secure she began sending him money. Only three weeks into his adventure he wrote to her, "I think you are still trying to kill me in a mild way with such kindness. I would not need any more money for perhaps several months: and think that it is a great deal if I even have the interest on the shares of Bank Stock that you gave me" (6 May 1889, UIC, JAMC, HJ). He reminded her that her support could steal from him the "poetry and romance; which thrives on scantiness, and compensates for it by enriching everything by touches of fancy" (10 May 1889, UIC, JAMC, HJ).

By the end of May, George Haldeman had totally given up the idea of finding work west of the Mississippi River. He realized that neither his mother nor Jane was coming to rescue him, and after a sixty-mile trek by foot to Marshall's Pass and Parlin, Colorado, he felt "no inducement to go further," for he did not want to cause Anna "unnecessary apprehension" (GBH to AHHA, 26 May 1889, UIC, JAMC, HJ Supp.). "As long as we undergo the disagreeable voluntarily, all the bitterness is gone" (GBH to AHHA, 12 May 1889, UIC, JAMC, HJ). "I would stay with you as long as you would have me," he promised Anna. Perhaps referring to his lack of success at wooing Jane as well as his inability to achieve a life independent of his mother, he continued, "I think that I must feel much as you do; and gladly deny myself the pleasure that natural prompting makes easiest and seemingly best: but I suppose there is some law that regulates it for the best" (26 May 1889, UIC, JAMC, HJ Supp.).

On his way east, he stopped in Girard, Kansas, and he and Harry returned to Pikes Peak to climb it together. By now, the Haldeman and Addams families acknowledged that George was not well. He remained with Alice and Harry in Girard, and Harry attempted to improve his spirits and health. "Do try the Electricity; and let him use the best olive oil. John [Weber] Addams is getting well on oil, has used about 14 bottles," Anna urged (Oct. 1889, IU, Lilly, SAAH). Alice Addams Haldeman brought her daughter Marcet to visit Anna in Cedarville for Christmas in 1889 while Harry and George remained in Girard. Jane stayed in Chicago at her newly established social settlement, Hull-House.

In 1890 George Haldeman returned once more to his mother, Cedarville, and study. He became more reclusive and unresponsive to any social contact, including Anna's. Physical illness and mental instability continued to plague him, and in the spring of 1891 he returned to Girard and spent a year with Harry, Alice, and Marcet. Harry Haldeman was determined to cure his brother. He reported to his mother in April that although George did not speak he was eating three meals a day, with medicine at mid-day and a brandy toddy at breakfast. Alice described George's condition for Anna:

> George seems very much better. Harry left off the opium yesterday all day—When he first came out of the opium he looked better than I have seen him since he came. He seemed quite responsive, except he did not talk, but he smiled & seemed his old self.
>
> This morning when I first went into the room, he looked up pleasantly, but when I offered to read to him he screwed up his forehead and rolled up his eyes & kept his eyes rolled up & fixed while I straightened the room & arranged the fire & other bedroom. (4 Apr. 1891, JAPP, DeLoach)

A year later, Harry admonished Anna that "all unnecessary attention drives him out of his skin . . . I have found out the real Disease—but not the Cause of it and it will be a long pull of patient Care before he recovers" (19 Apr. 1892, IU, Lilly, SAAH). Unfortunately, Harry never specifically identified George's malady, yet he explained that his opium treatment did not work and that George was on belladonna treatment. He informed Anna that he would not know for six months or more if the belladonna had worked because George would not talk or respond. She must "Simply Consider his fate Sealed forever. . . . He looks better Every Way—Since We left You a year ago—and his Mind is better a great deal better and We are gaining Slowly all the time but it can not be Magnatized— nor wash'd or ridden into him—Patience a long wait and cheerfullness are the Main remedies and all the rest he wants" (19 Apr. 1892, IU, Lilly, SAAH).

In mid-1893 George returned to Cedarville, where he lived for the remainder of his life. He seemed, Anna told Harry, to be improving and was more like he used to be years earlier, but on very stormy days he seemed to withdraw into himself. He became comfortable with Mary Fry, who was Anna Haldeman Addams's companion, housekeeper, and nurse. He particularly liked his niece Marcet and would often attempt to be present for a time during her visits. He also seemed to present himself for Sarah Hostetter, whose singing he seemed to enjoy. But for most visitors—and, according to Anna, as the years went by there were few except for family—George kept to his room. Sometimes he refused to bathe and later to shave, growing a lengthy, fuzzy, unkempt beard. When Jane in the summer of 1895 paid one of her infrequent visits to her former Cedarville home, Anna wrote to Harry that George refused her entrance to his room, although "she would 'rush in where angles [angels] fear to tread' if she dare" (15 July 1895, UIC, JAMC, HJ Supp.). Toward the end of 1895, Anna reported to Harry that "George was down to dinner he looked at all the gifts—but after dinner he returned to bed, he does that almost every day, some days he does not come down at all" (24 Dec. 1895, UIC, JAMC, HJ).

George Haldeman, his mother, and Mary Fry settled into a quiet and routine life centered on the Addamses' Cedarville home. By 1900 Anna Addams had a cottage built on the lot south of the home, hoping that George might use it as a study. He did not. By the early 1900s his life had become quite simple. In good weather he walked some, Anna read to him, and they played chess and card games. Sometimes family came to call. George spent large amounts of time closeted in his room, silent or in bed. When Harry died in 1905, his closest intellectual friend disappeared.

There is no doubt that George Haldeman grew to maturity comfortable with and close to only a few people, and all of them were part of the Addams-Haldeman families. With the exception of his mother and brother, the person to whom he was closest during his childhood, teenage, and college years was Jane Addams. It is not surprising that he hoped to secure permanently what had become a vital and stabilizing relationship for him. Apparently his brother and mother expected that outcome, too. Marriage to Jane would satisfy George's emotional dependency, provide a home for the remaining unmarried Addams daughter, secure an acceptable lifetime companion for Anna Haldeman Addams, and keep the money Jane Addams had inherited from her father within the confines of the family structure. Jane admitted that George and the family expected that they would marry, but she rejected the idea.

Although there is no definite evidence for when a confrontation—if there ever was just one confrontation—over the future of their relationship took place, it was likely that Jane Addams knew by the time George Haldeman graduated from Beloit that she would not marry him. It was probably her time in Europe with Anna and George and the two years spent supporting George emotionally in Baltimore that validated her decision. Hints appear here and there in the correspondence between them. Alice must have asked Jane in the fall of 1885, when Anna left for Baltimore and Jane stayed behind to help Laura Shoemaker Addams and Mary Addams Linn, if her actions signaled a break with Anna and George. That was not the case, Jane reassured her. That Alice was even thinking that a break could occur indicated Jane's growing independence and her rejection of a traditional role as a wife and companion. George's emotional instability when he was away from his mother and Jane was equally unappealing. In extant letters Jane Addams mentions his nervousness and suspicion of others as weaknesses and flaws. By the time George blundered toward an attempt at independence on his two unannounced solo trips west, Jane was weary of his antics and saddened by them. She felt pity but little sense of responsibility. Initially, George's attachment to her continued even after she rejected him. He was curious about her progress at Hull-House and the purpose she was finding in life, even as he walked the countryside of Colorado searching for a rationale to his. According to Marcet Haldeman-Julius, George always defended Jane within the family circle despite the fact that his brother and mother were cool toward her. When Anna would speak "harshly of" Jane, "he would say 'Now, now,' in a tone of gentle pacification" (*Jane Addams as I Knew Her*, 6).

George Bowman Haldeman never recovered from his failures, whether at Johns Hopkins, in Leipzig, in securing independence from his mother, or in making Jane Addams his life's partner. He died of a stroke on 14 November 1909. Mary Fry, companion to Anna Haldeman Addams, recalled that when Jane arrived at the homestead for his funeral on 17 November she asked her to accompany her to George's bedroom, where he was laid out for burial. Jane "pulled up a chair by the bed and sat for a long time. She finally put her hand on his and simply said, 'We did have good times, old boy, didn't we[?]'" (Fry, *Generous Spirit*, 73). George Haldeman was buried in the Cedarville Cemetery. His executor was Alice Addams Haldeman, followed by Mary Fry. Marcet Haldeman inherited the only asset in his estate, an undivided one-half interest in five lots in Freeport that he had obtained through his father's estate.

Haldeman, Henry Winfield (1848–1905)

Henry Winfield Haldeman, born on 21 June 1848 in Mount Carroll, Illinois, was the first child of Anna Hostetter Haldeman and her first husband, merchant and miller, William J. Haldeman. He spent his childhood in Mount Carroll and Freeport, Illinois, but received the majority of his primary and secondary education in Mount Carroll schools. "Harry," as he was known, seems to have been a creative and precocious but willful, somewhat unruly, and demanding child. He must have been difficult for both parents to manage. While Anna Haldeman was pregnant with her last child, George Bowman, and for a year after his birth, she lived with her sister and brother-in-law, Susanna ("Susan") Hostetter Bowman and George Bowman, near Mount Carroll. During that time, William Haldeman stayed in Freeport, where he owned and operated a steam flour mill, visiting her as his business permitted.

At the start of this arrangement Harry lived with his mother, but the difficult thirteen-year-old was soon placed in the care of his father. After receiving a letter from Anna complaining about Harry's behavior, William replied:

> If he does not conduct himself as he should and try to do what is right he will have to come home where I can see to him my self. . . . In the mean time remember that self will is constitutional with him—having inherited no small share from both parents—and therefore make no more commands than are really necessary—and these as little given in public as possible. With a nature like Harries—a kind request is much more likely to be complied with than a positive command. . . . A strong will is rather an inconvenient thing in a child—yet without it—a man is

nothing. Harries vulnerable point is his—sympathies. . . . but he is one of those strange natures—who would rather labour to conseal a feeling—than to show it by demonstrations ~~such~~ as most people do. (11 May 1861, UIC, JAMC, HJ)

William added that he had seen Harry "assume the dignity, judgment, and thoughtfullness of a person of mature years" when he was ill and Harry was attempting to minister to him. "What ever there is about Harry which may seem wrong, is all on the out side and he will—and allways has—recd more blame than many worse children. But we should judge him correctly if the world does not, and be thankful that he has a large warm and affectionate heart . . . rather than a smooth and pliable exterior with a narrow—deseitful [deceitful] and selfish heart."

During the last half of 1861 and 1862 Harry Haldeman remained with his father in Freeport. The duo lodged for a time in the Brewster House Hotel and finally moved to a boardinghouse. Harry was frequently with his father at the mill. Harry had "converted the Book Case into a Billiard table," reported William, "where he is enjoying a game of Billiards all by him self—indeed he never plays with boys any more but amuses himself when not at school in various ways" (William J. Haldeman to AHH, 30 Oct. 1861, UIC, JAMC, HJ). Harry also continued with the piano lessons he had begun taking sometime earlier.

Nearly eighteen years old when his father died in 1866, Harry Haldeman persuaded his mother to let him go to Germany to study at the Leipzig Conservatory of Music, where, according to one Hostetter relative, "the best talents are." (A. H. Lichty to AHH, 14 May 1866, UIC, JAMC, HJ Supp.). Harry had an aptitude for music. As he grew older he added violin lessons to his piano study and continued to receive instruction in both instruments while he was a student at the Mount Carroll Seminary in 1865 and 1866. In the fall of 1866 he left for Germany in the company of two seminary teachers who saw him settled in Leipzig. He lived on funds his mother sent him.

In Leipzig between the fall of 1866 and 1868 Harry not only studied music but also began a science curriculum in preparation for becoming a physician. The fact that his favorite uncle, John L. Hostetter, was a doctor may have influenced him. As he began his second year in Leipzig he reminded his mother, "[Y]ou say it Has cost 1,300 Hundred dollars—this year . . . I am sor[r]y it costs so much—but I must have—something in my branes or—I never would amount to any thing[.] I hope in two years more—to be able to do something; in fact I am sure by that time I can suport the family but we must have pateance" (HWH to AHH and GBH, 16 Aug. 1867, JAPP, DeLoach).

Many of Harry Haldeman's surviving letters from Europe reveal that he frequently requested money from his mother. He often apologized for having to ask her to pay the postage on letters requesting her support. He seems to have enjoyed himself, however, while he was a student; his letters are full of descriptions of his accommodations, sightseeing trips, and friends. In 1867 he suggested that his mother sell the Freeport mill, bring brother George, and join him in Europe. She did not. Harry was unable to stay a final year in Leipzig, perhaps because Anna could no longer support him there. She had growing financial worries because of a mill she could neither run nor sell.

Harry returned home in 1868 before his mother wed John Huy Addams and associated himself with Dr. Levi A. Mease in Freeport in an effort to continue his medical education. It was also during this period that he may have taught music briefly in Bloomington, Illinois. For the next year, he remained in the Freeport and Cedarville area, working with Levi Mease.

Although the U.S. census for 1870 indicates that Harry Haldeman resided with the Addams family in Cedarville and was employed as an agent for the Metalic Roofing Company, extant correspondence shows that he was living in Mendota, Illinois. There he continued his study of medicine with the Drs. Edgar P. and Charles E. Cook. To support himself he gave music lessons and concerts and tuned pianos. He began to write poetry and music that he and his mother attempted, unsuccessfully, to have published in New York City, Boston, and Chicago. By October 1871 he had completed a play, a group of sonnets, a 260-line poem, and a short lyric play. "Pirosa a Poem," written in January 1872, a few additional poems, and a number of sonnets, also in manuscript form, are extant. "The only reason for wishing to make money by my writings," he reminded his mother, "is that I may have Sufficient means when the time comes, to Send Brother off—to College and give him—those advantages so necessry to insure—Success at this age of the world. . . . When I look back—Mother, it makes me Shiver—you little know what I have gone through—in the last two years, My future now looks comparatively bright—though no So promising— as it might be" (8 Oct. 1871, IU, Lilly, SAAH).

The early 1870s were a difficult time for Harry. He refused to visit in Cedarville, where he no longer felt welcome, apparently because of a major disagreement with the Addams men. It seems likely that John Huy Addams wanted him to give up the idea of becoming a musician or a doctor and may have refused to support Harry in further medical education. Harry Haldeman was determined to be successful on his own terms and to make his living by doing what he wanted. Separated from his mother and brother and struggling to live independently, he was often disappointed, depressed, or unwell. "I am perfectly discontended," he confided to Anna, "every thing looks—as it has for the last four or five years—ladened—with—all sorts of disagreeabilaties" (10 May 1873, IU, Lilly, SAAH). On 28 June 1874 he reported, "I am not feeling at all well, but suppose its—depression of spirits more than anything" (IU, Lilly, SAAH). He wrote often of his "case of the blues" or "low spirits." By 1875 he was dismayed about his lack of success as a musician and wrote to his mother, "Music, it is worthless like a bad investment, and spoils one for active pursuits, I wish I had never struck a note" (14 Feb. 1875, IU, Lilly, SAAH).

After almost four years of apprenticeship with the doctors in Mendota, and after attending the University of Michigan medical school for a semester in 1873 on money that he had saved working in Mendota, Harry settled in Fontanelle, Iowa, where he established himself as a practicing physician. "My life has been made up of disappointment, at least—not much that was encourrageing," he informed his mother. "I Set out to be a Doctor—but fate seemed against me, however I guess I'll be one—after all. . . . I shall never rest—untill I get a degree! which—I mean to have—in a year or so" (3 Jan. 1875, UIC, JAMC, HJ Supp.). By January 1875 he had earned $180.50, and had more than $500 in savings. Much to the Addamses' dismay, on 25 October 1875 he married his stepsister Sarah Alice Addams in the family home in Cedarville. The couple went to live in Fontanelle. After two years Harry entered the Medical School of Northwestern University, from which he graduated in the spring of 1878 with an M.D. At long last Harry Haldeman had achieved his goal.

To start him off properly in his chosen career, his mother helped him purchase the medical practice and real property of Dr. A. C. Simonton in Mitchellville, Iowa, for twenty-five hundred dollars. The Haldemans moved to Mitchellville, also the home of Harry's cousin Virginia Hostetter Reichard and her husband D. Harvey Reichard, and began to practice medicine. Simonton signed a no-compete agreement, which by 1880 Harry was obliged to enforce by suing. He returned once again to music. In 1880 Jane Addams asked him to compose the music for her Rockford Female Seminary graduating class song and sent him the words. If he composed the music, however, it is no longer extant.

In the fall of 1881 the Haldemans accompanied recently widowed Anna Haldeman Addams and Jane Addams to Philadelphia. There Harry entered the University of Pennsylvania Medical School as a third-year student and graduated with his second M.D. on 15 March 1882. He was able to enter as a senior because he already had an M.D. from Northwestern University. The third-year curriculum at the University of Pennsylvania Medical School, with its emphasis on obstetrics, gynecology, surgery, and diseases of women and children, meshed nicely with Harry Haldeman's interest in medical problems concerning women. His senior essay was entitled "Evacuation of Exposed Ovarian Cysts."

The Haldemans returned to practice medicine in Mitchellville, Alice as her husband's nurse-helper. In the fall of 1882 Harry operated on Jane Addams's spinal curvature to correct it. According to Alice, it was not the first such surgery he had undertaken. His previous experience treating a malformed spine for a former soldier was judged as successful. While Jane was in residence and recovering from the procedure, the Haldemans were also hosts to Mary Peart, Anna Addams's distant cousin who would marry one of Harry's Hostetter uncles, and to James Weber Linn, one of Mary Addams Linn's children, who was being monitored for a childhood problem. In addition, Harry continued to treat his regular patients.

By the summer of 1884, Harry Haldeman was worn out and ready to quit his medical practice in Mitchellville. The life of a country physician was tiring.

It called for long hours and difficult travel by horse or horse and buggy over a sometimes roadless terrain in miserable weather at all hours of the day or night. Anna Addams was concerned that Harry was overburdened and wrote to Alice that she wanted her son "to stop night riding" (30 Oct. 1882, IU, Lilly, SAAH). She offered him a two-year, interest-free loan to use in reestablishing himself in a Des Moines practice.

His poor health and inability to continue a strenuous work pace were in all likelihood exacerbated by alcoholism. Various Addams and Hostetter family members recognized Harry's problem, as did Mary Fry, companion to Anna Addams from 1890 until the end of her life. His drinking problem was likely one of the reasons that John Huy Addams did not favor him as a son-in-law. To his mother, his physical condition, in part from drink, was a lifelong worry. As early as his student days in Leipzig she had begun to counsel control of, if not abstinence from, liquor. He had been in Leipzig only four months when he reassured her that he had "stoped drinking Beer since the could wether set in." He continued, "I do not drink any Kind of—liquor—now" (HWH to AHHA and GBH, 3 Dec. 1866, JAPP, DeLoach). As Anna Addams set out for Europe with Jane Addams and Sarah Hostetter, she admonished her Harry, "When I return . . . meet me a . . . sober man and die so" (11 Aug. 1883, UIC, JAMC, HJ). Anna also wrote to him from Europe between 1883 and 1885 to encourage him to stop drinking.

Although Harry must have tried to control his use of alcohol and perhaps other readily available habit-forming drugs such as opium, he was unsuccessful. Several incoherent, rambling letters written in varying handwriting styles may provide a hint of his addiction. By 1894 his mother admonished his apparently unsympathetic wife, "Dear Alice the book I sent for your birth day gift <Inebrity a disease>—has much wisdom contained in it—and if read without prejudice— you will find it will lead your mind to deal charitably with what is a direful disease (Physically) and mentally. 'All is well that ends well and constant kindness is the only remedy'" (AHHA to SAAH, 18 Oct. 1894, UIC, JAMC, HJ Supp.).

After a visit to the hills of Virginia during the summer of 1884, perhaps in an attempt to extricate himself from his addictions, Harry, accompanied by his wife, settled in Girard, Kansas. They identified 12 September 1884 as the day they arrived in their new community. It is difficult to know why they chose Girard. A Mr. A. Smith, a banker and businessman whom Harry joined as a banking partner in the private Bank of Girard, may have encouraged the move. The 1885 census for Girard, which is in Crawford County, identifies Harry as a farmer. The Haldemans had farmland in Iowa and may have purchased some in Kansas. Yet that same census shows them as living next to A. Smith, Mrs. Carrie Smith, and Kitty Baldwin, all of the same household, and having come to Kansas from Iowa. A. Smith and Kitty Baldwin are identified as a bankers.

In 1886 the Haldemans purchased Smith's share of the Bank of Girard, and Harry became its sole proprietor. As a banker, he settled into the civic life of Girard. He joined the Masonic and Odd Fellows organizations and became active in politics. Between April 1895 and April 1899, Harry Haldeman served two terms as mayor of Girard. On achieving his first victory, one of his former mentors, Dr. Edgar P. Cook, wrote, "Congratulations. We rejoice with you in your victory over the hosts of misrule—boodleism &c. In your tryumph in the interests of Municipal reform &c. . . . Later we will be prepared to hear that Kansas needs you in the Gubernatorial Chair or has wisely selected you to represent her interests in the United States Senate" (14 Apr. 1895, UIC, JAMC, HJ). Neither the governorship nor a Senate seat ever materialized for Harry Haldeman.

Ironically, among the battles that Mayor Harry Haldeman and his city treasurer Oscar Schaeffer (also the cashier of his bank) fought was to control the public liquor interests in Girard. Shortly after winning his first election, Harry wrote to his mother of his plans. "When I . . . proclaim against Liquor and its Sale—Which I shall do—Blessed by Jupeter—if I live so long—then indeed the mighty—We—the Mob—Will howl and Many will assist them the perodoxical idea exists that Saloons Make a town rich—that Drunkenness and Dirt are conducive to happiness and prosperity I regard as the Cause I am about to take as Dangerous[.] I have already received letters of Warning and threats of my life if I prosecute the Whiskey Element but by the Mother of Jesus—I shall do it all the Same—!!" (22 Apr. 1895, IU, Lilly, SAAH). A year later he was still at work on battling the liquor interests: "There is nothing new here nothing but the Whiskey ring to fight—So far I have held my own and altho twelve Saloons are in full blast at Pittsburg—Our Neighbor city and the cry here is for Saloons—I have remained firm—and unbendable" (HWH to AHHA, 25 Feb. 1896, IU, Lilly, SAAH).

During his twenty years in Girard, Harry Haldeman continued to practice medicine occasionally. He had a penchant for special or unique cases and for assisting those in need. A disaster in the 1890s at a coal mine near Girard brought him out to help. In 1893 he reported on a potential patient: "I have just finished the arduous task of listening to a tale of Woe—Miss D—a lover a clover field—Dusk—and—the rest—Miss D—is not in any immediate danger of being a fond Mother—altho insisting to the contrary—Sic. . . . Life in the Wild and Wully West—has now and then its diversions" (HWH to AHHA, 26 Oct. 1893, IU, Lilly, SAAH).

Harry paid particular and detailed attention to the mental and physical disabilities suffered by his brother George, who spent parts of three years with the Haldemans in Girard while Harry tried unsuccessfully to cure him:

> No one could be more anxious than I am—Was and always have been to get him up and Well—but he So Conducted himself that it was absolutely impossible to arrive at a definite Diagnosis. . . . If George will State his case—or reply—to questions put him regarding his Condition—he can be cured[.] But he seems to be opposed to getting well—Except in his own way. . . . [I]f he hates himself let him reconstruct his pychic being and after such a fashon that he will become his own lover—Bless the Boy I will do anything for him and if We cant Work out his Case it is no fault of mine. (HWH to AHHA, 26 Dec. 1893, IU, Lilly, SAAH)

The brothers had always been close. As a child and young man George had visited Harry over his school vacations, and Harry had encouraged his brother in the study of science and languages and in his graduate education. The two shared intellectual interests and during their adult years served as each other's peer group.

Harry and his mother were soul mates and had an almost romantic attachment for one another. "I miss you very much the older I get—and hate every day that chains me away from you," he wrote (9 Nov. 1894, IU, Lilly, SAAH). They shared a love of music, poetry, literature, and games along with a concern for George; they also formed a Haldeman-Hostetter family sphere within the larger Addams family group. They enjoyed the companionship of the same members of the Hostetter family and shared an interest in genealogy. Harry often thought of himself as Anna's child or young man rather than as an independent adult. "I was my dear Mother most agreeably surprised by a letter from you day before yesterday," he wrote. "So great was my delight—that—like a good overgrown—or underchild boy that I am, I put off answering it—'till today" (18[21] Sept. 1873, IU, Lilly, SAAH). Many of his letters to his mother are peppered with similar images and language. Before he wed Alice Addams, his mother was almost his sole emotional support as he struggled to achieve independence as either a physician or musician. "[W]e have not—So many years to be to gether—whats twenty or more—years—and they pass Swift enough—. oh—that we could be allowed my dear Mother to pass the remainder of our lives—near each other—read together and enjoy those things—which pertain to our higher being in—discourse," he wrote in 1873 (10 Aug. 1873, UIC, JAMC, HJ Supp.). Their bond experienced an emotional dip when he chose Alice Addams as his wife, but as the marriage became more troubled he turned once again with more frequency to confide in and seek the approval of his mother. That was especially true after the birth of Alice and Harry's only child, Anna Marcet, in June 1886. Anna Addams gave him the emotional, and to some degree financial, support he needed, for she invested her money through the Bank of Girard. Harry visited her and George in Cedarville at least once a year—usually without Alice and Marcet.

His relationship with Alice, begun with devotion and with respect, over time turned to resentment and sarcastic displeasure, in part the result of unmet needs and expectations. After the birth of Anna Marcet, the couple's relationship spiraled into ever-increasing unpleasantness. Harry apparently resented Alice's public life, full of civic and social activities and resulting in time away from their home and from child and family responsibility. He may also have disliked the fact that she was wealthier than he and that she used the money she had inherited from John Huy Addams for her own purposes although she expected him to support their household. Then there was the issue of her sister Jane.

Harry grew to disapprove of Jane Addams, her activities, and her fame, and he did not hesitate to make it known. "There is nothing new to Say about the folks [Alice and Marcet Haldeman]," he informed his mother and George, add-

ing in a meanly witty manner, "[T]hey are going to the Chataqua Assembly to
hear Miss Jane Addams deliver an address—on god knows what—I don't[.] I
have Seen intimations that She has a <u>book</u> <u>out</u>—gave one to Alice for her birthday present—don't know the Subject but judge from reports of her condition
physically that it is on <u>Osteology</u>—but can't Say" (26 June 1893, IU, Lilly, SAAH).
When the portrait of Jane that Alice Kellogg Tyler (1866–1900) painted for Alice arrived at their Girard house, Harry was overwhelmed. With what his mother
might have called "a vein of satire" (AHHA to HWH, 7 Oct. 1894, UIC, JAMC,
HJ Supp.), he gave it a scathing review:

> The next picture is on the plan—<u>gigantique</u>—and—is a fine—very fine full Sized
> oil—life size—clothes and all—of Miss Laura Jenny Addams—Now called Jane—
> Side face—With best eye—towards the observer—Hands—clasped—over the as—
> coccyx—or in that neighborhood—Head—Slightly—Elevated—a la—Pointer—
> on the Scent—or on the as sent—I Cant really Say Which—General tone of features
> gentle—Alive or old gold—joundice—tinge with Sweat glands—clased—Mag-
> nificet fore-head—With large and fully developed frontal—or <u>Snot-pouches</u>—
> gently—sloping—backward toward the pharynx—or receptaculure Snotdi. There
> is no abdominal enlargement—but—Old Virginey Never—tire—up and Down—
> preSentation—Breast's flat—and throat clasped—by Globulous Tosteincus—pro-
> tuberance—Chin Well-Stuck forward—gladly Angulor—agressive—and a little to
> much on the Jaw to perfectly Satisfactory in Short the whole is good and an excel-
> lent picture of Miss Addams—the Frame is what it Should be Heavy—beamy—
> obtrusive—With good Plank—backing—the Whole weighing probably 3 or 4
> times as much as the Original—and requiring the Woole family—and a few neigh-
> bors—to manage the Whole Art Product.
>   This is now a prominent Household Shrine—all the family meet at its feet in
> the Morning and part at its feet at night[.] With Mr Linn—John Addams Linn, I
> beg your pardon—always with me and this Alive—Jaundiced Specter I feel as tho'
> I Was in very fairy land—or Close to its Borders—God bless Our home. (20 May
> 1894, UIC, JAMC, HJ)

Years later Marcet Haldeman reported that her father and aunt simply saw
the world in very different terms. She described her father as a cynic who had
little reverence for anything. She recalled his quick temper, that he was "silent
on social questions," and that he was "radical and picturesque in his unconventional expression of opinion." He "regarded [Jane Addams's] work as sentimental and futile" and was "unsympathetic with the fundamental optimism of [Jane
Addams's] character and viewpoint." Harry was concerned that Jane had abandoned his brother and mother when she should have accepted her family responsibility and stayed in Cedarville with them. Marcet reported that he was
angered because Jane and Alice failed to "realize the turmoil and heartbreak of
grandmother's [Anna Addams] unusual situation" with regard to George and
to act in a "more understanding and forgiving" manner (*Jane Addams as I Knew
Her*, 6). He may also have been jealous that Jane Addams had achieved a fame

that eluded him. Moreover, he no doubt sensed Jane's probable displeasure at his drinking and at the life he evolved separately from that of his wife. He would have understood that Jane would take Alice's point of view in disagreements between himself and Alice.

No matter what his relationship with his wife and Jane Addams, he was devoted to Marcet and to her welfare. He recorded her growth and antics for his mother and seemed an attentive father, proud of her development. He had chosen her name, providing Anna Addams with a namesake and paying special homage to one of his distant Haldeman relatives, the writer Jane Haldimand Marcet (1769–1858), known as "Mrs. Marcet."

Among his hobbies and interests were philosophy, paleontology, chess, reading and collecting books, especially those by Mrs. Mareet, and Haldeman family genealogy. Yet music remained a primary interest in Harry's adult life. Although he apparently never published any music, he continued to compose. An assortment of works are mentioned in his correspondence, but none seem to be extant. He continued to teach both violin and piano in the Girard area and to keep up with former musician friends. From time to time, former students or fellow musicians would come to Girard for lengthy stays to practice and learn from Harry. He sometimes gave concerts with them, not only in Girard but also in the surrounding area. His mother wrote to him that she wished he would stop touring because it was dangerous. Perhaps it was.

During the mid-1890s Harry fell in love with one musical partner. Her name was Luella Totten, and their relationship may have lasted until his death. When not in personal contact they communicated through letters. By 1898 she had received more than five hundred letters from Harry. Hers to him—supportive, passionate love letters revealing their shared interest in music—arrived in lock box 81 at the Bank of Girard. During the fall of 1898 her letters were written from Pittsburg, Kansas, but apparently the couple sometimes trysted in St. Louis. A hint that Alice Haldeman knew of their meetings appeared in a letter Jane Addams wrote to her sister: "Harry's mother said that he had gone to St Louis on business and I could not tell what she knew of his whereabouts. I am so sorry that you have had this worry again" (JA to SAAH, 31 Dec. 1898, IU, Lilly, SAAH; JAPM, 3:1259–60).

Between December 1897 and October 1898 Harry Haldeman wrote a series of love poems to Luella. She copied fifty-five of them and had them bound into a book entitled *Poems by Henry Winfield Haldeman*. The title page reads, "Poems—An Luella von Heinrich-1898," and an inscription signed "Luella" reads, "My thanks to Heinrich. If lovely thoughts are blossoms of the Soul— / Dear Heinrich—then a garden I possess— / Through which I wander—breathing in Desire, / And fragrant Joy's bewildering lovliness." It is likely that Harry shared some information about his relationship with Totten with his mother in 1896. "My trouble is not business," he wrote, "it is Some thing Different and yet Money is not all together out of the question[.] I Want to See you—I am Hungury to see you—I dream of you and think of you Constantly—I must See you" (21 July 1896, IU, Lilly, SAAH). Anna Addams wrote to Luella Totten after Harry's death and received a reply from Baltimore, thanking her. "O—I can never tell you how glorious it is," Luella wrote. "[Y]our blessed son was perfect—and as we wished it—so our conquest of Self was, through God" (27 Oct. 1905, UIC, JAMC, HJ Supp.).

During the last years of his life Harry Haldeman's health was even more precarious. He experienced pleurisy, insomnia, and at one point he warned his mother that he might die from kidney failure. In 1902, after receiving a letter from Alice telling her that Harry was ill, she wrote to him that the letter was "so full of subterfuge" that she was uncertain what Alice had actually meant. "Why don't you come home," she continued, "it is due to us—and to yourself for you need a rest and change! Alice . . . thinks the house ought to be closed while she and Marcet are away—surely, you would then have no abiding place—no meals[,] no comforts—now come home" (9 July 1902, UIC, JAMC, HJ Supp.). Harry evidently agreed, for he went to Cedarville and stayed for almost two months—recuperating.

Harry Winfield Haldeman's death on 20 March 1905 was apparently the result of a massive heart attack that took place in his bedroom at home in Girard. According to one newspaper account, he had been experiencing heart disease for some time. His funeral was held on 21 March 1905 in his home, and his remains were taken by train to Cedarville for burial in the Cedarville Cemetery. He left an estate valued at twenty-four thousand dollars, with Alice Haldeman serving as executor.

An obituary that appeared in the *Girard News* on the day of his death described him as "eccentric to an unusual degree but possessed many excellent qualities and was given to kindly deeds of which few people knew." Another obituary that appeared the day after his burial in Cedarville called him "a man of varied gifts":

> Recognized as a physician of undoubted skill and judgment, his counsel was often sought by the prof[e]ssion, and ungrudgingly given. Many in this community remember with gratitude the aid rendered their loved ones when life hung in the balance. As a business man he was sagacious and thorough. Himself a musician of great ability, he encouraged, aided in all ways, and personally instructed many struggling aspirants. A linguist and a lover of science, philosophy and belles lettres, he surrounded himself with books dealing with his favorite problems, and possessed himself of their contents. In regarding such a mind and such attainments, we may naturally ask, "Can mind ever die?" ("[Haldeman, Henry Winfield], Obituary," unidentified publication)

Haldeman, Sarah Alice Addams (1853–1915)

Sarah Alice Addams (Haldeman) was born on 5 June 1853 to Sarah Weber Addams and John Huy Addams in their two-room log cabin in Cedarville, Illinois.

She joined two older sisters, Mary Catherine and Martha, and a brother, John Weber, when the family moved into its two-story brick home in 1854. Alice, or "Allie" as she was often called, attended local schools in Cedarville, including Laura Jane Gorham Forbes's select school. She was an active and sturdy little girl with direct, grey-blue eyes and long, light-brown hair. Alice and her frequent playmate Weber roamed the precincts of the Addams mill and farm in search of adventure and excitement. Evidently, the two often found what they were seeking. Family lore recalls them often being the focus of disciplinary action by their mother. Later in life Alice would also remember playing childhood games with her younger sister Jane in their father's mill.

Alice was nine when her mother died. It is difficult to know her reaction to that event, for she left no extant childhood letters or diaries. She came under the kind yet firm ministrations of her sister Mary, who assumed the role of surrogate mother. After the summer of 1866, when she and Mary went to visit Addams and Weber relatives in Pennsylvania, Alice, along with their older sister Martha, enrolled at Rockford Female Seminary. Although few of her letters from this period have survived, a number that Mary Addams wrote to her at school are extant. They indicate that Alice was a self-absorbed young woman who knew her own mind and was determined to have what she wanted when she wanted it. She was bright, creative, assertive, and charming but apparently more difficult to manage than the ladylike, more mature Martha. Alice seems to have required considerable coaching, because Mary was often advising, encouraging, or admonishing her.

Shortly after Alice returned to Rockford Female Seminary after her Christmas holiday in 1869, Mary reminded her, "I think that to a very great extent we can make ourselves either happy or unhappy just as we will: I think we are very apt to forget that we have many, very many blessings that are denied to others; who are just as good as we are" (25 Jan. 1869, UIC, JAMC, HJ). Alice received more than one prompt in this vein. After she had returned to Rockford Female Seminary for another year and discovered a roommate not quite to her liking, her sister advised, "I think if you try to do your part towards making it pleasant, you & Miss [Emma] Faris will get along very well: We should always try to remember that we have our happiness very much in our own hands" (30 Sept. 1869, UIC, JAMC, HJ). "Am glad that you receive so many letters," wrote Mary, "but I think you allow yourself to think to[o] much about them and thus attract your attention from your studies; it is all right and proper to be glad to receive letters and appreciate our friends kindness, but we should never allow these to distract our thoughts from our present duties" (25 Jan. 1869, UIC, JAMC, HJ). Mary often reminded her charge to live each day as it came. Writing about a proposed visit from two of Alice's Freeport friends, she suggested, "hope you did not feel too much disappointed if they did not come: as we must all learn sooner or later, to bear disappointments; and I think that by bearing these little daily annoyance[s] with a proper spirit we strengthen our Christian character:

and I do not that[think] that there is any thing that we have to bear or do, so small that we may not ask and receive the blessing or help of our heavenly Father" (1 Feb. 1869, UIC, JAMC, HJ).

Even as a school girl, Alice had a tendency to be "fleshy." She often asked for special foods from home and was apparently displeased if they were not sent. Mary admonished from Cedarville: "Sent you some lemons and sugar, do not make your self sick drinking too much lemonade" (8 Feb. 1869, UIC, JAMC, HJ). The following month, Mary wrote, "Without meaning to offend you at all, I do think that you allow your thoughts to run too much on something to eat, and if you are not careful it will grow on you, and finally make you appear very disagreeably in the eyes of those around you" (15 Mar. 1869, UIC, JAMC, HJ).

Throughout her life, Alice seemed to have had difficulty heeding her sister's advice about food, and she became a very large woman with a thick body and broad face, topped by long hair drawn back in a bun. In group photographs later in life she nearly always sought to hide her bulk behind others. As they grew older, Jane and she developed similar body shapes and also evidently had similar voices. A Girard, Kansas, resident who heard Jane Addams speak and knew Alice Haldeman "said that if you closed your eyes you would think it was Mrs. Haldeman talking, their voices were so much alike" (Cuthbertson, *Genesis of Girard*, 115). According to her Aunt Mary Addams Van Reed, Alice's facial features strongly resembled those of her father. On seeing Alice, she exclaimed "'oh my, there is John!!'" That pleased Alice, who wrote to her father proudly that "every one tells me I look like you more and more every day" (3 Oct. 1875, SCPC, JAC).

Alice's relationship with Anna Haldeman Addams, her stepmother, was initially warm and loving. Anna joined Mary Addams in providing instruction and advice, although she discovered that she could not easily bend Alice to her wishes. One wonders if the clash of wills was not part of the reason that Alice returned to Rockford Female Seminary after she graduated in 1872, serving as a resident graduate and tutor and continuing to study art during 1874 and 1875.

After she graduated from Rockford Female Seminary, Alice and her stepbrother Harry Haldeman began a serious romantic relationship. By 1875 they had decided to wed despite the fact that both parents were against the union. Surviving correspondence indicates that Anna Addams tried to dissuade her son from his choice. Although there is no extant correspondence between Alice and her father or siblings on this subject, one might suppose that they, too, tried to talk her out of the relationship. In part to put more time and space between the pair, Anna and John Huy Addams permitted Alice to go with a group of Rockford Female Seminary students and teachers on a tour of Europe. From May until October 1875 she had a jolly, exciting time taking art lessons in Berlin and jaunting through Germany, Switzerland, Italy, France, Belgium, and Great Britain. The extant letters describing her trip are addressed only to her father.

Sarah Alice Addams and Harry Winfield Haldeman were married at the Addams home in Cedarville on 25 October 1875. "Mary [Fry, Anna's housekeeper

and companion for many years] remembered Mrs. Addams telling of the day
the young couple drove away after their wedding. As she and Mr. Addams stood
on the front porch waving to them, tears were running down Mr. Addams' face.
She coolly said, 'I don't feel a bit more sorry for your Allie than I do for my
Harry.' Apparently no one in the family felt it was a marriage made in heaven"
(Fry, *Generous Spirit*, 38). The couple established themselves in Fontanelle, a
village in southwestern Iowa, where Harry had been practicing medicine. On
17 November 1875, Alice wrote to Harry's cousin Virginia and her druggist husband, D. Harvey Reichard, whom the newlyweds had visited in Mitchellville,
Iowa, a small town west of Des Moines:

> When we reached Stewart found all the horses in the place were sick with the
> Epogotic and consequently stage not running. So we took noon train to Casey
> where after dinner we were enabled to find an open spring wagon drawn by two
> poor lean horses to take us twenty miles over the cold bleak prairies and dreadful
> roads after the severe snow storm. Still we had a good time. Once our driver was
> thrown out of the wagon and when within five miles of Fontanelle, we broke down.
> Fortunately near a farm house, so we procured a heavy lumber wagon and reached
> our new home about half past eight in the evening.
> Our goods did not reach here until the following Friday night. So Saturday we put
> down our carpets and settled in our new home. Our wood did not come until the
> following Wednesday so we lived at Home and took meals at the Hotel until Wednes-
> day. Since then we have enjoyed our home most thoroughly. (JAPP, DeLoach)

In Fontanelle, Alice became Harry's nurse-helper and took an active role in
the social life of their community. Shortly after the newlyweds arrived, Alice
reported:

> I enjoy housekeeping so much and "Doctor is the happiest & proudest man of the
> town . . ." the people say. Harry claims all my time. We have taken up Latin and
> German studies together and are reading Bulwers "Strange Story." The society here
> is very pleasant. The ladies have been very kind & prompt to call. We have been out
> to dinner & invited to tea serveal times. Last evening took tea & spent the evening
> with the Lawyer & his wife Mr and Mrs James Gow. . . . [W]e think we have a gem
> of a <u>home</u>, and wish our friends could but see how nicely we are situated. Harry's
> practice is good and increasing. We [are] happy and contented. Have identified our-
> selves with the people. Last Saturday evening some of our German friends took tea
> with us and in the evening we made six gallons of Sour Krout. (SAAH to Virginia
> Hostetter and D. Harvey Reichard, 17 Nov. 1875, JAPP, DeLoach)

Prophetically, Alice had written to her father from Europe that "Great cities are no delight to[o] me to many heart aches anxieties interests at stake, too
much rushing pushing and jarring. The country is my home be it the broad
expansive wide prairie or the quiet hillsides by brooks, streams rivers or quiet
lakes, or in the Grand sublime mountain districts, I could not live long in a city.

It makes me feel cramped & narrow, But under the broad heavens midst nature would I make my home" ([July–Aug. 1875], SCPC, JAC). For the remainder of her life Alice Addams Haldeman found her home primarily on the midwestern prairies and in the small towns that developed on them.

As pleasant as their situation might have been in Fontanelle, by 1878 the Haldemans had moved to Mitchellville, where the Reichards had established themselves in the early 1870s. "I may say without any attempt at boasting and without taking a long breath," Harry announced to his mother, "that Alice— has more friends—than any other person in the country and is by far the most popular woman—within miles—if she hasn't a natural gift for manipulating people no one has—the more of them the better." He continued, discussing Alice's role in their medical practice, "Alice does Considerable practicing and the people have <u>boundless</u> confidence in Her—judgement and with good Reason." According to Harry, one of their patients refused to go to the drugstore because he thought the druggist (probably D. Harvey Reichard) careless in preparing prescriptions "and <u>insisted</u> on Alice filling it here for him . . . this is only one of many incidents—I could relate—showing in what esteem she is held" (8 Jan. 1880, IU, Lilly, SAAH). Anna Addams's physician brother John L. Hostetter had understood before their marriage that Alice wanted to become a "<u>true helpmate</u> to Harry" (John L. Hostetter to AHHA, 22 Jan. 1875, JAPP, DeLoach).

When their father died in August 1881, Alice and her siblings divided his estate, each receiving assets valued at approximately sixty-six thousand dollars composed of a farm and timberland and sharing in the proceeds from stocks, bonds, and notes as well as in jointly owned real estate. Through Alice's inheritance, the Haldemans had become relatively well-to-do. They could afford to leave their practice in Mitchellville for a time so both could secure more medical training. Accordingly, they went with Jane and Anna Addams to Philadelphia in the fall of 1881. There, Jane and Alice entered the Woman's Medical College of Pennsylvania and Harry became a student at the medical school of the University of Pennsylvania. According to Rachel L. Bodley, dean of the Woman's Medical College of Pennsylvania, from 17 October 1881 until 1 March 1882 Alice Haldeman "performed one dissection upon the cadaver and attended the Quiz Classes in Physiology and Chemistry" (Rachel L. Bodley to To Whom It May Concern, 20 Mar. 1882, IU, Lilly, SAAH).

The Haldemans returned to Mitchellville and resumed their medical practice. In addition to serving as her husband's nurse, Alice also became his anesthetist. In the fall of 1882, at Alice's urging, Jane Addams went to Mitchellville so Harry could surgically correct her spinal curvature. For nearly six months Alice nursed her bedridden sister. Joined by Mary Peart, a distant cousin of Anna Addams and soon to be the wife of Harry's cousin, Charles Linneaus Hostetter, the women chatted, read, and watched the antics of James Weber Linn, one of sister Mary Addams Linn's children, who was also staying with the Haldemans during Mary's pregnancy with Stanley Ross Linn.

By 1883 Harry Haldeman's health, which had been deteriorating for some time, began to affect his ability to practice medicine. He was tiring of his strenuous schedule as a country physician. In 1884 the couple left Iowa for Girard, Kansas, where they settled permanently. Located on the rolling prairie of southeastern Kansas in Crawford County and near the Missouri border, Girard was started in 1868 and incorporated in 1869. It developed around a town square that had the usual complement of scales, general stores, banks, hotels, hardware, blacksmith, and bakery shops, and churches, as well as a dairy, a water company, and a school. At first the terminus of the Missouri River, Fort Scott, and Gulf Railroad, Girard became one of the stops on that line and a shipping center for agricultural products and manufactured goods from the surrounding area. Farms on the periphery of the community and throughout the county produced grain and cattle. Among the manufacturing efforts established in the new community by the early 1880s were a foundry, new brush factory, and the Girard Albumen Works.

By 1886 Alice and Harry Haldeman had purchased a private bank in Girard, and Harry was its proprietor. Banking was part of their heritage. John Huy Addams had started a bank in Freeport, Illinois, and Hostetters and Haldemans were associated with banking in Mount Carroll, Illinois. As Alice wrote to Anna Addams, "It was hard deciding but we feel confident it will prove wisely" (12 Aug. 1886, IU, Lilly, SAAH). When Harry was away from Girard, Alice oversaw the banking operation.

In the spring of 1886 the Haldemans bought a pleasant two-story frame home on the corner of St. John and Cherokee streets, and they began housekeeping there; Jane and Anna visited during that summer. At the end of the visit, Alice and Jane toured the Denver and Pikes Peak area of Colorado, viewing the natural wonders of the West that so fascinated American tourists, and visited friends and acquaintances in the area. The sisters returned to Girard through Kansas City, Missouri, where they saw their cousin Charles Young and his family.

Although she had not planned to, Jane returned to Girard and the Haldeman household for a large part of the next summer. The occasion was special. Alice and Harry Haldeman were expecting their first and only child. Alice, thrilled to be pregnant, told Jane the news before the third month of pregnancy but swore her to secrecy. She apparently had anticipated previous pregnancies that had not materialized, or perhaps she had experienced miscarriages and may have wanted to avoid the public and family commiseration that another loss would cause. After several months, when she was certain that she would likely carry the baby to term, she relented and told her sister Mary Linn. Alice Haldeman's girth, which had grown throughout her years of marriage, hid her pregnancy. Shortly after Jane arrived in Girard at the end of May, she reported that Alice's "figure is so unchanged that I do not wonder the Girard people are blinded" (JA to Laura Shoemaker Addams, 8 June 1887, SCPC; JAPM, 2:497–504). The Haldemans' new baby was apparently a surprise to some Girard residents.

Anna Marcet Haldeman, called Marcet, was born on 18 June 1887 after a lengthy labor that Harry described in some detail to his mother in a letter of 19 June 1887 (IU, Lilly, SAAH). According to Alice Haldeman's granddaughter Alice DeLoach, who was told the story by her mother, Anna Marcet Haldeman-Julius (and also according to Mary Fry), Marcet was the product of artificial insemination. Techniques for artificial insemination were known to doctors of the 1880s in America and Europe. American gynecologist J. Marion Sims, who practiced in New York and became the first president of the American Medical Association, had reported extensive experience with techniques by 1886. Another report indicated that Dr. William Pancoast of Philadelphia recorded the first use of donor sperm in 1884. Given his recent attendance at the University of Pennsylvania Medical College, where he specialized in the study of gynecology, it is entirely possible that Harry Haldeman was aware of appropriate procedures to achieve successful human artificial insemination.

Marcet immediately became the focus of attention and affection for a small family circle that included her Uncle George Haldeman, Grandmother Anna Addams, and parents. Jane Addams was also a doting aunt. In the first of two baby books Jane gave to Alice to record Marcet's progress, Alice wrote, "Aunt Jennie Addams was here from June 5th until baby was 6 weeks old. Such a happiness to all to have her!" (Bray, *The Baby's Journal,* filled out by SAAH for Anna Marcet Haldeman and listed as no. 642 in the catalog of the library of SAAH). For the remainder of Jane Addams's life and as Marcet grew to maturity, the Haldemans made sure that their daughter and her close Illinois relatives saw each other regularly. Alice Haldeman took her to visit family in Illinois at least once each year, usually during the summer. They customarily stayed for a time with Jane Addams at Hull-House and also stopped in Cedarville with Weber and Laura Shoemaker Addams so Marcet could visit her grandmother Anna Addams and Uncle George Haldeman.

As Marcet grew, her parents kept Jane and Anna Addams and George Haldeman apprised of her progress through frequent letters describing her precocious achievements. During the first two years of Marcet's life, Alice recorded her daughter's development in a diary. The proud parents sent photographs of Marcet at three weeks, five months, ten months, one year, and fifteen months to an assortment of close family and friends that included Aunt Jane. Both Haldemans doted on their daughter and gave her every educational and social advantage and nurtured her sense of independence.

Alice Haldeman hoped that Marcet and Jane would have a strong, lifelong bond. Probably much to the dismay of her husband and his mother, in 1890 she wrote and signed a statement indicating that in the event of her death it was her "most earnest sincere desire and often expressed wish that she [Marcet] shall be given into the entire care of my sister Jane Addams" (5 June 1890, JAPP; *JAPM,* 27:719). It was apparently not until after Alice's death in 1915, however, that Marcet and Jane developed a close relationship. Then, Marcet made Jane her confidante regarding financial and marital problems. Before that time, among the factors influencing Marcet's feelings about her famous Aunt Jane may have been the fact that Marcet adored her father and her grandmother Addams, both of whom were critical of Jane and may have made their views known to Marcet. In addition, Marcet had apparently felt herself in a frequent emotional struggle with Alice, perhaps exacerbated by her father's critical perspective of her mother. "Marcet harbored a lot of unresolved feelings about S. Alice," Mary Fry's nephew Paul Fry wrote. "Twenty[-]four years after her mother's death she would still write about her feelings of guilt and inadequacy, about never having been able to please her mother" (*Generous Spirit*, 90). A rebellious Marcet might well have had difficulty taking her mother's view of Jane.

Alice Haldeman ran her household with at least one full-time helper, sometimes augmented by a cook. She oversaw the expansion of her home to include additional rooms after her daughter was born and lovingly attended to its decoration. With her fine artist's eye, she arranged and rearranged furniture, books, paintings, sculpture, and decorative fabrics according to the style of her day to create a warm, hospitable atmosphere. She continued to carry out special nursing duties when necessary, especially for family members. In addition to Jane Addams, Alice nursed George Haldeman for at least two lengthy periods during the late 1880s and the early 1890s. In 1894 her nephew John Addams Linn received her care. She also looked after her personal business, which included managing the farm she had inherited from her father as well as other real estate she acquired primarily from siblings and their children.

Sometimes, although infrequently, Jane Addams succeeded in getting Alice to join her in travel. In 1894 she accompanied Jane to California on a series of public appearances. She also went with her sister on shorter trips in the Chicago area when she was visiting her there. In 1897 Alice asked Harry if she and Marcet could have the money to go with Jane to Toronto, Canada, visiting Niagara Falls along the way. He agreed, and mother and daughter also saw Montreal before returning to Girard.

"[Alice] was not only personally loyal at all times to Aunt Jane, but she shared her ideals, approved of her methods and was proud of her achievements" wrote Marcet in 1936 (*Jane Addams as I Knew Her*, 6). The two sisters maintained a close and generally supportive relationship. They shared similar interests in family, early friends, educational experiences, and adult vocations. Both sought and achieved a public life in civic responsibility and social welfare. They turned to one another with regard to health issues and consulted about financial matters and investments.

Alice recorded Jane's first two European trips, copying her circular travel letters in journals for her. For a time, she amassed and maintained a large file about Jane's public work and writing from periodical clipping agencies. (These clippings compose the core of the Jane Addams Clippings File, SCPC, JAC; JAPM, reels 55–71.) The correspondence of the two sisters was certainly regular and voluminous. Worried that she had not heard from Alice in three weeks, Jane begged, "Why don't you drop me a letter or a postal card, I have n't heard for a very long time" (18 May 1897, IU, Lilly, SAAH; *JAPM*, 3:610). Unfortunately, a great deal of their correspondence has been lost. No more than ten of Alice Haldeman's letters to Jane Addams appear to have survived, although more than four hundred letters written by Jane to Alice are extant. In several cases the letters offer tantalizing hints about personal situations that Alice apparently discussed in detail during visits with, or in letters to, Jane. The sisters spent time together each year and certainly conferred with one another about family matters. Most often Alice visited Jane in Chicago; if Jane was going west, however, she sometimes saw Alice in Kansas.

Although Alice was supportive and proud of her famous sister, their relationship had its ups and downs. Alice could be demanding and opinionated and especially assertive if family transactions involved money. When Jane purchased items for Alice during her early travels in Europe, she seemed concerned that what she had selected might not be acceptable to her sister. Her constant worry about how Alice would receive her choices and their cost, as well as Alice's reaction to her gifts for others, may indicate that Alice had firm opinions about what was suitable and acceptable, that she wanted good value for her money, and that she wanted to receive as many quality items as other family members did. Jane had a difficult time getting Alice to pay a medical bill (something Alice had apparently agreed to do) for their brother John Weber Addams after he was a patient in a private mental hospital in Jacksonville, Illinois, in 1883.

The sisters also disagreed over Jane's handling of Mary Addams Linn's estate. "What is in your mind and why are your letters so reproachful?" the dismayed Jane wrote to her sister on 16 February 1896. "I cannot imagine why you would say 'that I fear that the children and finances are cutting you off from your natural sister.' Why do you feel cut off? It seems to me that I deserve an explanation." Alice must also have complained about the Linn children, who were not fond of her, for Jane continued, "I am sorry that the children show this lack of tenderness, no one could have been more shocked by the manifestation of it on both sides than I was last summer, and no one could deplore it more. . . . Of course I am fearfully worried but it seems to me a little ungenerous to reproach me with my 'guardian' duties when I most need your counsel and sisterly help" (IU, Lilly, SAAH; *JAPM*, 3:54–59). In the same letter, Jane suggested that the two meet to work out their misunderstanding, and Alice apparently traveled to Chicago in March for that purpose. Weber Addams reported to Jane that Esther "would die before she would go and live with her Aunt Alice" (28 Feb. 1896, SCPC, JAC; *JAPM*, 3:68–70).

Jane Addams's friends at Hull-House must have seen the difficulties and differences between the two. Among settlement house residents, opinion on Alice varied. Mary Keyser, who had been a nurse in Mary Addams Linn's home when the Linns lived in Geneseo, Illinois, and who had come to the settlement as one of its first three residents to oversee household chores for Jane Addams and Ellen Gates Starr, wrote lovingly to Alice, for whom she seemed to have genuine affection. "The house [Hull-House] seems very lonely without you and Marcet. You were lovely to me and I miss you very much. [James] Weber [Linn] and John [Addams Linn] were here to-day and seemed very nice. I think your visit has been a wonderful help to us all" ([13 Oct. 1895], IU, Lilly, SAAH). Settlement resident Gertrude Barnum, writing to Mary Rozet Smith in 1899 about another of Alice's visits, pronounced that she did not "think Mrs. Haldeman has been altogether easy—too more different individuals will hardly be found than she & her sister—I wish she felt called to assume some of the Linns—I believe she is to do some little thing for Esther this year" (16 Aug. 1899, SCPC, JAC; *JAPM*, 3:1410–18). "I have many faults but I am sure I am not snobbish and so it [is] always hard for me to comprehend why you imagine me sensitive about my relatives," Jane wrote to Alice after a misunderstanding in the fall of 1900. "I was really a little hurt by your first letter when you said you took pains not to say [publicly] you were my sister. . . . We will simply have to go on, dear, understanding each other as best we can with a little blindness apparently on both sides" (23 Sept. 1900, UIC, JAMC; *JAPM*, 3:1658–60).

The seeds for their differences had been sown in childhood, for it is likely that Alice Haldeman perceived Jane to be the sister who was coddled and always had her own way. Marcet certainly assumed that was so. She described Jane Addams as "a delicate, rather spoiled but very lovable child" and her mother as "an irrepressible hoydenish girl" and indicated that "individual members" of the family "were forceful and ambitious, had strong characters and were highly temperamental" (*Jane Addams as I Knew Her*, 4).

Marcet's descriptions came not only from her experience within the family but also from comments made by her parents and her grandmother. Although her mother supported Jane, her father and grandmother criticized her. That difference in perspective must have been terribly difficult for Alice, who for a time may have been torn between loyalty to her husband or to her sister. In addition, while Jane Addams's fame grew, the fact that Alice remained locked in relative obscurity in a difficult marriage in Girard, Kansas, may not have been easy for her to accept. Moreover, friction between the two strong sisters may have been generated by Jane's close relationship with the Linn children. Alice seems to have felt that she and Marcet competed with them for Jane's limited time and attention.

Alice and Harry Haldeman began their married life with great affection and love for one another. Knowing his mother's concerns about his wife, Harry continually encouraged Anna Addams to give Alice a chance. Early in 1875 he announced, "I love Alice Sincerely—She is a true woman, and I hope you will appreciate her—and be—kind to her" (3 Jan. 1875, UIC, JAMC, HJ Supp.). Five months later, shortly after Alice had left for Europe, Harry continued, "To besure Alice loves me did n't you know that before? But—I think more of her than she does of me, and allways expect to" (8 May 1875, IU, Lilly, SAAH). "I would not do, nor be guilty of a mean action on her account for the world," he assured Anna (3 Jan. 1875, UIC, JAMC, HJ Supp.).

By the 1890s, however, the couple's relationship had changed drastically. In 1892, when Marcet seemed quite ill and her parents were not certain she would live, Harry wrote to his mother, "Alice has her religion and I my Philosophy— and no doubt we will each seek our sources of comfort if the case is one of extremis" (29 Feb. 1892, IU, Lilly, SAAH). On 23 April 1892 he responded to an accusing letter from Anna, no longer extant, that may have referred to complaints Alice had made about him:

> We are having a nice run of business and are popular in every way—You see I still feel sore over the beastly unkind letter you wrote me. It seems pretty rough when one is doing their very best to make others happy and comfortable to have such horrible accusations made on foundations unstable and rotten when closely examined[.] I have never set up for a Saint and never expect to—but I do live an Honest upright life—in Every way and have no apologies to make to any one on earth. I suppose I have some rights and some liberties—these I shall allow no one to trespass on. (IU, Lilly, SAAH)

Some surviving letters may indicate a troubled marriage. Although none of the very few extant letters written by Alice Haldeman during this period reports problems from her perspective, a few from Jane to Alice suggest the detailed accounts, no longer extant, of marital problems that Alice may have described to her sister. In November 1896 Jane wrote that her heart ached for Alice, "I simply can't write a reply to your letter, there is so much that I want to say but it must be said and not written" (15 Nov. 1896, IU, Lilly, SAAH; *JAPM*, 3:499–500). The next month she advised, "Geo. Eliot says that we have to take pains with our affections and friendships as we do with our other treasures" (4 Dec. 1896, IU, Lilly, SAAH; *JAPM*, 3:518–19). It seems likely that these veiled references concerned Harry's affair with musician Luella Totten, a relationship that began in the mid-1890s and continued for the remainder of his life (see also Biographical Profiles: Haldeman, Henry Winfield).

Anna Haldeman Addams, an early and willing critic of Alice Addams Haldeman, had become her son's confidante. A few extant letters between them indicate his unhappiness with his mate. Most of his complaints centered on his perceptions that Alice was ignoring her responsibilities as a wife for more public pursuits and that she gave little thought to his wants or needs. During the late summer of 1893, as he struggled to get his bank through the business depression of that period, he wrote to his mother about his financial problems and indicated that Alice and Marcet were visiting the Linn family in Storm Lake, Iowa. "They Expect to be 'Home!' by the 29# perhaps Earlier—they are Well— I know very little about the occourences of their trip—'they have met very agreeable people—during the Summer &c &c' I have nothing to say!" (15 Aug. 1893, IU, Lilly, SAAH).

He complained of Alice's daily schedule in Girard, which he believed gave little consideration to him and Marcet:

The House has been over run for the last week with Sufferage Women—big time parades—Bands—Bugles and Wind. . . . We run an Hotel—or have been doing so—and I confess I am—tired. Yesterday Alice—Started out in the morning to a Committee Meeting Dined in the country—Spent the evening at a reception— and Sat on the School Board until Eleven at night—Baby and I read "Under the Lilacs["] and had a good time—Ben—Bob—and Betty and Mrs Morris—and the Dog Sancho. Amusing us greatly—Sic!! God bless Our Home! Loyalty is the virtue that is wanting—but let it want. (9 Nov. 1894, IU, Lilly, SAAH)

In the same letter Harry continued, "The Chicago crowd—give me endless trouble if it was not for Baby I Would soon Wind things up and quit but—go— &twist." His frequent refrain "God bless Our Home!" often appeared in correspondence at the end of some protest about Alice, so that it became a code for his cynical view of their relationship.

A year later, in 1895, after Marcet had again experienced a severe childhood illness, Harry wrote to Anna that "Her appetite is good & her digestion excellent—I think her Sickness has been a good thing for her taking it all arround— Her Mother is More careful and attentive than before—not more attentive probably but more thoughtful—Being Strong and robust herself she forgets Sometimes how frail the rest of us are—I am a walking skeleton myself and So troubled With insomnia I cant at least don't pick up" (7 June 1895, IU, Lilly, SAAH). In a witty yet biting fashion he ranted about the birthday gift Alice and Marcet sent him from Chicago in June 1893. "I also receved a Book from Marcet and Alice, Darwin's Autobiography & letters what you and George read while here—I also have a copy of it at the House—I can now read it again right and left handed—and not go ploding through the Same book—twice—which will be a great convenience and saving of eye sight—as well as resting the arms. I know very little of what is going on at Chicago—or any where else—Every body seems to be doing as they please—the main end of life" (21 June 1893, IU, Lilly, SAAH).

It is also likely that Harry resented the fact, as did Anna, that Alice would not give him access to her inherited wealth to use as he saw fit in managing the bank. Instead, she used her funds to develop additional assets for herself and help the Addamses. At the same time, she relied on her husband to support Marcet and her. Anna opined:

I gave Mr [Reuben B.] Siegfried a check for 40 dollars to be paid to Alice for wood I bought—of her, and, with the other proceeds of the large farm—it will make up a goodly sum to help Hull House, and the L[inn] family. A wrong is a wrong and a right—is a right,—eternally! You ought soon to quit; and, take life easy and, restful, we know how to live within our means—and why not close up—and stop working (and, <u>sowing</u> for others to <u>reap</u>, and <u>waste</u>.) And take some of the fruits of your labor—and enjoy it, by coming home—and, resting and lending good cheer to us—who are so isolated, and, comfortless,—so far as others think of us. (7 Oct. 1894, UIC, JAMC, HJ Supp.)

Several notes indicate that Alice did lend money to the bank.

Anna Addams and Alice Haldeman maintained a distant and apparently warily cordial relationship, but Harry Haldeman was the focal point of disagreement and disappointment between the two until after his death. As he became his mother's best friend and she his, Anna never hesitated to scold Alice for her shortcomings as a wife and daughter-in-law. She appears to have taken Harry's view of the couple's problems and criticized Alice in letters to both Harry and Alice. In 1894 she complained to Harry, "Alas! no one ever comes—no one cares[.] Alice has not written us the first line—since she was home with Marcet, if she does not care for us tis more honest—not, to pretend, and, so we are not deceived. We are very lonely to besur[e] but, useless is repining" (7 Oct. 1894, UIC, JAMC, HJ Supp.). A week later she directed her angry remarks to Alice:

> The "Magic wand—that—would have <u>consoled</u> him" and given comfort for every suffering was broken—<u>no unity</u> in the home—meals eaten in bitterness so that the very bread of life, turned to stone from indigestion, rushing out into to the cold unsympathizing world with <u>no heart</u>—to do any thing, but <u>wrong</u> because the <u>highest</u> incentive, was dead—<u>love</u>, that "day star from Heaven which lights the darkest night." Oliver Wendell Holmes—just dead says "No home can be Christian that does not practice the courtesies and amenities in its domestic round[.] 'Tis shocking sin to have progress before discord enough to make angles[angels] weep, and devils laugh, to see how Christianity is practiced after leaving the church portals" simply make the few quotations—to let us "see ourselves as others see us" for if we were not sometimes shown up in the critic's mirror, we would never— see our <u>own discrepencies</u>—but, only have a keen sense of the wrongs that others do. The greatest touch stone of goodness is to "forgive <and do <u>good</u>—> to those who dispitefully use you, and persecute you." (18 Oct. 1894, UIC, JAMC, HJ Supp.).

In another letter five months later she complained to Alice, "[N]o doubt you find your time—taken up in ways you enjoy more than <in> writing to—<u>two—lonely</u> people—an old—Woman—and <an> <u>afflicted man</u>, (whose patience—and endurance,—is Saint like, and rises to the sublime)" and signed herself "Affectionately MA" (21 Mar. 1895, IU, Lilly, SAAH).

In Girard, Alice Haldeman was becoming a civic leader. Upon her arrival, she identified herself with the Presbyterian Church. She served on its board of trustees until her death and as its treasurer for twenty-eight years, supported its foreign mission efforts, and taught in and served as superintendent of its Sunday School for many years. Alice organized her own large collection of books and periodicals as a lending library for the town. In the back of a notebook in which she recorded notes on the books she had studied is a list of those she lent during 1885. Once again Alice began to paint and draw, and by 1886 she had gathered a small group of women who met together weekly to study the history of art. Soon she was asked by Anna M. Leonard, founder of Girard's oldest women's group, the Ladies Reading Club, organized in April 1883, to join, a membership she held until her death. Anna Leonard, wife of merchant and banker Joseph T. Leonard, became one of Alice's close Girard friends.

Alice Haldeman served two terms, from 1888 until 1898, as president of the Girard board of education. In 1899 she initiated an effort that resulted in the creation of a Carnegie public library for the town. She began the process with the Ladies Reading Club. When she realized that it alone was not strong enough to lead the fight for a public library, however, she enlisted the support of the three other literary organizations in the community. At her home on 21 January 1899 representatives of these organizations formed a Girard City Federation of Women's Study Clubs with Alice as president. A week later the organization created a library association, and again Alice Haldeman was chosen as president. With the support of many civic-minded leaders, she convinced the Girard city council to place the matter of a tax levy for the maintenance of a public library before the citizens of Girard. The proposition passed, and a new library building was dedicated in 1901. During the ten years that Alice Haldeman was president of the Girard Library Association she also helped establish the Kansas Traveling Library Commission, on which she served for a time.

Alice Haldeman was a dedicated club woman. She believed "in club life" as "an avenue of constant usefulness, both for enthusiastic study and loyal friendships" ([Addams and M. Haldeman], "[Haldeman, (Mrs.) Sarah Alice (Addams)]," 3). "Although a very busy woman, Friday afternoons were devoted to club [Ladies Reading Club]. She treated all of the members with sweet courtesy. It was hers to do and say the kindest thing in the kindest way," wrote a member of the Ladies Reading Club ([Memorial to S. Alice Haldeman by a member], [Mar. 1915], UIC, JAMC, HJ). In addition to the Girard City Federation of Women's Study Clubs, Alice was a member of the State Federation of Women's Clubs. She served as president of the third district of the Kansas Federation of Women's Clubs (1900–1901) and as a member of the civic committee of the General Federation of Women's Clubs (1904–6), although poor health apparently kept her from accepting the nomination as president of the Kansas Federation. Wishing to develop more club opportunities for the women of her area, she organized the Twentieth Century clubs of Girard and Walnut, Kansas, in 1901 and continued to attend their meetings until health prevented her from doing so. She became a member of the National Society of the Daughters of the American Revolution (DAR) in May 1902 and was associated with the Topeka Chapter. It was through Alice, who submitted her candidacy, that Jane Addams received membership in the DAR, also in the Topeka Chapter, in August 1902. Alice was selected by the National Child Labor Committee as a member of the Kansas Committee in 1908.

The welfare of children was high on Alice's list of community priorities. Her

concerns were reflected by a boys' club and by creating summer camping opportunities for youths, two projects she organized shortly after she arrived in Girard
and continued throughout her life; her dedication to quality education for the
young people of Girard; and her commitment to a public library. Seattle attorney L. Frank Brown, one of the children she charmed and influenced, wrote,
"Your life is so beautifully woven into the Brown family's larger vision of life that
any sorrow that enters your life, reacts upon us all. You can never realize how in
the formative periods of all our lives, you gave that touch of culture and experience that has left an impress on all our lives, and while time and distance have
seperated me from you, my love and remembrance are just as keen as when a
youngster you brightened my narrow Girard vision" ([1915?], UIC, JAMC, HJ).

Speaking at a memorial service for Alice Haldeman, Mrs. F. A. Gerken of the
Girard City Federation of Women's Study Clubs recalled, "'If I were an artist I
would paint for you a portly dignified woman with smiling face driving a black
horse to a one seated fringe top phaeton. I say one seat but she had a seat up
against the dash board for children and for some of the younger club members
who could double up their legs'" ("Observations," *Girard Press*, 4 Oct. 1962).
At her memorial service in Girard shortly after her death, her minister spoke
of her conveyance, which he said was often in the service of those in need as "'the
chariot of the Lord'" ([Addams and M. Haldeman], "[Haldeman, (Mrs.) Sarah Alice (Addams)]," 4).

Among Alice's hobbies were painting and drawing, photography, collecting intricate and unusual lace and basketry, maintaining her library, and reading. A few of her paintings survive in private hands, as do some of her early
photographs. During the 1890s she photographed rooms and activities of Hull-
House, and some of her work was used in early settlement publications.

After the death of her husband in 1905, Alice Haldeman reorganized the
Haldemans' private bank into the State Bank of Girard. She took her husband's
place as president, with her mother-in-law as vice president, and served as head
of the bank until her death. Although the couple had purchased it from Mr. A.
Smith piecemeal, Alice promoted the idea that her husband had created the
bank. "'My husband became interested in the banking business shortly after we
came here and he founded a bank of his own. We are the oldest bank in the
county and have weathered three panics,'" she proudly told a reporter for the
Kansas City (Mo.) *Star* on 8 October 1911.

Alice Haldeman was recognized as the first woman bank president in Kansas and honored by the Kansas State Bankers Association in 1914 by being selected as vice president of that organization. After almost two years as a banker,
she told a reporter for the *Chicago Evening Journal*, "'I do not see why banking
should not be a business suitable for women who must engage in business of
some kind'" (4 Jan. 1907, clipping, IU, Lilly, SAAH). *American Banker* published
a summary of the entire interview on 10 January 1907.

Ever more frequently after 1905, Alice Haldeman shuttled back and forth between Kansas and Illinois, not only to oversee the management of her large stock farm near Cedarville but also to tend to the financial affairs of her mother-in-law, who was growing older and more feeble, and of her stepbrother, the reclusive George Haldeman. When George died in 1909 she served as his executor. During the last ten years of her life, Alice Haldeman and Anna Addams grew to respect one another. It was almost as if, without Harry to fight over, the two women, both with strong personalities and quick minds, could achieve peaceful accommodation. Alice helped Anna's companion Mary Fry renovate and redecorate the Addams home.

By 1910 Alice Haldeman's health had begun to fail noticeably. Obese during most of her adult life, she had also suffered from rheumatism. She underwent her first cancer surgery in 1910 at Augustana Hospital in Chicago attended by Dr. Ludwig Hektoen and Dr. Edward H. Ochsner and then returned to Girard. Initially she grew better but was again treated for cancer in 1913. By the end of 1914 she was desperately ill from the spread of the disease. "I am sorry to say I have not been having a bed of ease—Every other night a[I] grow nearly wild with the burning 'Aftermath of Radium' they call it, but the cure is worse than the desease," she wrote to her daughter. "Miss [Elvira] Hartvigh is constant and faithful and I don't know what I would do without her—and the paliative douches" (21 Jan. 1915, UIC, JAMC, HJ). After the removal of another tumor, she slipped into a coma and died on 19 March 1915 in Augustana Hospital, her daughter Marcet and sister Jane at her side. Her body was taken to Cedarville, and after a brief service in the Addams home she was buried near her husband in the Cedarville Cemetery. Marcet was the heir of her estate.

Jane Addams and Marcet Haldeman recalled that "her blue grey eyes were ever alight with jolity and sympathy and her laugh was as infectous as irresistable—the entire personality <was that> of a big, joyous soul." They remarked on her ability to draw friends to her and hold them. "The trouble[d], the vexed, the worried, the afflicted came to her, and, aided by a rare judgment, she gave freely of kindness, of sympathy and of advice, and, when needed, of financial assistance, possessing such an unusual ability to enter sympathetically into the experiences of others and to give of her own strong, serene spirit that the recipient experienced an up-lift that might be likened to a new birth." They also pointed out "her great charity of judgment towards others, even in situations where bitterness and personal resentment on her part would have been natural and readily excused" ("[Haldeman, (Mrs.) Sarah Alice (Addams)]," 4–5). In addition, they lauded her calmness, poise, and self-control and identified her inner strength and ability to organize and direct others.

Hostetter, Sarah (1856–1938)

Sarah Hostetter was the daughter of Catherine Bowman Hostetter and Dr. Abraham Hostetter and the niece of Anna Hostetter Haldeman Addams. She was born on 17 January 1856 in Mount Carroll, Illinois, where she grew up and attended school. She went to Cedarville often to visit the Addams family. With her sister, Susan Mattie Hostetter, she had been a student at the Swedenborgen school, Waltham New-Church School, Massachusetts, for two years. She graduated from Mount Carroll Seminary in 1878, having studied advanced voice, piano and harmony, and literature. A talented musician, she played both piano and organ. She traveled in Europe with Jane Addams and Anna Haldeman Addams in 1883–84. Between 1884 and 1886 she taught music at the newly established Groton Collegiate Institute in North Dakota, where Mary Addams Linn's husband, John Manning Linn, was president. Later (1896–98) she taught music, including voice, organ, piano, and harmony at the Breck School, which the Episcopal Church had opened in Wilder, Minnesota, in 1889. She undertook a study of domestic science at the Lewis Institute in Chicago and in 1899–1900 at Bradley Polytechnic Institute in Bloomington, Illinois. After serving as principal of the Domestic Science Department of the high school in Janesville, Wisconsin, she founded the Domestic Science Department at Shimer College, the former Mount Carroll Seminary, between 1902 and 1904 and became a teacher there.

Sarah Hostetter never married, but after the death of Linneaus Hostetter's wife Mary Peart Hostetter in 1902 she returned to her brother's home, Wilderberg, to serve as his hostess. Among her family she was noted for thoughtfulness and "unusual generosity . . . generous with money when needed, but generous also in giving of . . . [herself]. Sarah did for all members of the family, big and little, old and young" ([C. L. Hostetter and R. Hostetter], "Sarah," in ["Hostetter Family"]). During World War I she headed the Red Cross effort in Mount Carroll and was active in the local woman's club. She was a member of the New Jerusalem Church. Although she visited at Hull-House and was interested in Jane Addams's social experiment, she remained in Mount Carroll, where she died on 15 March 1938. She is buried among her family in Oak Hill Cemetery in Mount Carroll.

Three of the reminiscences of family events and relationships that Sarah wrote are extant. One records descriptions of her aunts, uncles, and cousins, their homes, and special family occasions. The other two concern Jane Addams. One is a reminiscence of the Addams family and Jane as a teenager, and the other is a partial account of Hostetter's European tour with Jane and Anna.

Linn, John Manning (1842–1924)

John Manning Linn was born in Ickesburg, Perry County, Pennsylvania on 26 February 1842. His parents were John Ross Linn (1817[18?]–92) and Margaret Isabel McKee (1809–74[76?]), both native Pennsylvanians of Scottish ancestry. The Linns emigrated to Byron Township, Ogle County, Illinois, in 1867, where they bought and worked a farm. Before that, John Ross Linn had been a salesman in Perryville, Pennsylvania, and then during the Civil War was the steward and overseer of the four-hundred-acre farm associated with the Pennsylvania Agricultural College (which became Pennsylvania State College in 1874) in Centre County. He was a Republican and a Presbyterian. In addition to their eldest, John Manning, the Linns had two other children. Mary Elizabeth (1845–1903) became the wife of Matthew P. Bull, a farmer in Byron Township, Ogle County; James Clopper (b. 1847?) married Anna Jones of Ogle County and purchased his father's farm but lived in Chicago, where he worked as a salesman at the Chicago Fireplace Company and later at the Central West Advertising Bureau. After the death of his children's mother, John Ross Linn wed twice more, first to Ann L. McClure (d. 1879?) of Perry County, Pennsylvania, and then to Mary E. Wilson, who had been a teacher and missionary among Native Americans on the frontier. He and Mary lived in Rockford, Illinois.

John Manning Linn joined the Presbyterian Church when he was fourteen and attended the Tuscarora Academy and the Airy View Academy in Port Royal, Pennsylvania, in preparation for studies at Jefferson College in Cannonsburg, Pennsylvania, from which he graduated in 1863. After serving eight months in the 21st Pennsylvania Cavalry of the Union army during the Civil War, Linn briefly became a teacher at Pennsylvania Agricultural College. He entered the Princeton Theological Seminary in New Jersey in 1864, graduating three years later; he remained there as a graduate student and taught Hebrew until the summer of 1868.

John Manning Linn's career as a minister in the Presbyterian Church began in June 1866 when he was licensed to preach by the Presbytery of Huntingdon. He was ordained in September 1868 by the Presbytery of Rock River after returning to his parents' home in Illinois. Thereafter he served in a multitude of churches, many with small congregations just getting started. He moved frequently throughout the Midwest as both a called and supply pastor. He served in Cedarville and Dakota, Illinois (as supply) in 1868–71; Durand and Shannon, Illinois (as supply) in 1871–72; Lena, Illinois (as supply) in 1872–75; Winnebago, Illinois (his first pastorate) in 1875–81; Harvard, Illinois (as supply) in 1881–84; Ellendale, Dakota Territory (as supply) in 1884–85; Geneseo, Illinois (as pastor) in 1886–91; Storm Lake, Iowa (as pastor) in 1892–94; at the Chicago Lawn Church (as pastor) in 1894–95; at the First Church of Quincy, Illinois (as pastor) in 1895–96; in Inwood, Iowa (as supply) in 1896–1900; Charter Oak, Iowa (as pastor) in 1900–1902; Colfax, Iowa (as pastor) in 1902–3; Panora, Iowa (as supply) in 1903–4; Casey, Iowa (as pastor) in 1905–7; at the First Church of Houghton, Michigan (as supply) in 1907–10; and in Florence, Wisconsin (as pastor) in 1910–12.

Linn became involved with three colleges during his career. While he was serving in Ellendale, Dakota Territory, the Presbytery of Aberdeen, meeting at Ellendale, determined to create a college. The site chosen was Groton, and Linn was selected to establish the Groton Collegiate Institute. Its first classes met in the fall of 1885. The first year there were eighty students, and the curriculum included classical, scientific, normal, commercial, and musical studies. The music teacher was Jane Addams's step-cousin Sarah Hostetter, who braved cold winters, uncertain travel, and spartan living conditions to assist in this mission-like attempt to bring higher education to the frontier. By the end of 1885 Linn had so displeased the trustees that he was forced to resign, even though the student body, with whom he was a favorite, petitioned the board to reconsider. The financial burden of maintaining the school proved too much for Presbyterian churches of the immediate area, and shortly after it graduated its first class of two in June 1887 the Groton Collegiate Institute closed.

Linn went from his Groton experience to become fiscal agent for Lake Forest College during the next two years. His daughter Esther Margaret Linn Hulbert later identified him as an "advertising officer" for the school. As she observed, "he wasn't too successful either in raising money or students and went back to preaching" (E. M. L. Hulbert, "Autobiography of an Unknown"). Linn was not again involved with an institution of higher education until he accepted an offer from Buena Vista College in Storm Lake, Iowa, to become its second president. The college had been operating at Storm Lake since the fall of 1891 under the guidance of its first president, Loyal Y. Hays, who died in the spring of 1892.

Linn, characterized as an "aggressive man with a 'bristling red moustache, short stout figure and Irish features'" (Cumberland, *History of Buena Vista College*, 41), came to his new duties with much hope. Soon, however, he was overwhelmed by the school's financial problems, which were exacerbated by the economic recession of 1893. By mid-1893 he was spending all but the first two weeks of each term away from Buena Vista in an attempt to raise the money required to keep the school afloat and faculty salaries, including his own of $1,250, paid. He was also away from his family, who had moved to Storm Lake with him and bought property there. With funds provided by his wife, they constructed their own home, which became known as the "President's House." The Presbyterian organizations that supported the institution demanded that the school limit itself to academy status, undertake only the first two years of college, work toward developing an endowment, and raise sufficient funds so indebtedness would not be increased by current expenses. Linn resigned in June 1894. His wife was desperately ill, his salary was unguaranteed, and he had no prospect of being able to succeed immediately in the task of carrying Buena Vista College forward.

John Manning Linn met his first wife—Jane Addams's eldest sister Mary Catherine—at his first assignment for the Presbyterian Church in Cedarville, Illinois. They were wed on 9 November 1871. When the Linns established themselves in their first home in Durand, John admitted to his new sister-in-law Alice Addams just how much he did not know about husbandly responsibilities:

> We are fixed very well and the house is running regularly. . . . All our things came safely and although every [thing] is not yet quite in its place, we know where everything is. The change to housekeeping independently of every other consideration is in itself a pleasant change to me. I make fires, fetch water, attend a horse,

carry wood, & go to market. I was not ever brought up to these things with any regularity at home and school days ought to have not only obliterated all ideas of how to do it . . . but created a feeling against it. But as I was brought up to business, it is just as natural for me to do the little things required as it is for the good "Land Lord" "to keep a hotel." (28 Nov. 1871, UIC, JAMC, HJ)

The Linns had at least six children, four of whom lived to maturity (see Biographical Profiles: Linn, Mary Catherine Addams). The family moved frequently to meet Linn's job requirements, but he was not noted in the Addams family as a good provider. Mary's inheritance from her father supplemented his often-meager earnings. The money made it possible for the family to secure more appropriate lodging than might ordinarily have been available to a small-town minister. Linn was often away from his family, especially when he served more than one community at a time, when he was attending conventions or meetings, or when his job took him to the frontier or on fund-raising expeditions.

The Addams siblings and their spouses understood, however, that Mary was committed to her children and her marriage, and they continued to be supportive of those commitments even as her health deteriorated. The family must have questioned Linn's judgment on many occasions, as he himself evidently did in 1920 when he recalled his decision to take the presidency of Buena Vista College. "'It was a big, difficult place to fill,'" he observed in hindsight. "'I had a much easier place offered me at the same time in Ann Arbor, Michigan, with a ten thousand dollar house to move my family into. What blunders we make! I accepted a pastorate and presidency without realizing the tremendous tasks before me'" (JML to Elizabeth Ensign, *Tack*, 14 Dec. 1920, quoted in Cumberland, *History of Buena Vista College*, 41). Jane Addams had recommended her brother-in-law for the position he refused at Tappen Hall in Ann Arbor. She described Linn as having "a fondness for young people" and being "rather happy in his relations with them" (JA to Anna B. Gelston, 29 Aug. 1891, UM, BHL; *JAPM*, 2:1264–66).

When Mary died in 1894, Jane became the executor of her estate as well as guardian of the minor Linn children. The eldest, John Addams Linn, had already reached legal majority and would soon enter Western Theological Seminary to become an Episcopal priest. Jane found it impossible to let the youngest children remain with their father, especially after she discovered the rude dwelling he planned for them while he served as pastor of the Chicago Lawn Church. James Weber Linn was a student at the University of Chicago, Esther Margaret went to Cedarville to stay with Laura Shoemaker Addams and her daughter Sarah, and Stanley Linn settled with his Aunt Jane at Hull-House. The Linn children saw their father by visiting him periodically and by joining him during his visits to Hull-House, usually at a holiday such as Thanksgiving or Christmas. They apparently saw little of him after he was remarried on 9 July 1896 in Chicago to Mary L. Hochschild, with whom he had two daughters. From the time of his second marriage until he retired, most of Linn's pastoral assignments were in Iowa, Michigan, or Wisconsin. He lived in the Chicago area from his retirement in 1913 until 1923 and in Arlington, California, until his death at eighty-three. He was buried in Memorial Cemetery in Evanston, Illinois.

From the few John Manning Linn letters or writings available, it seems likely that he may have been more interested in practical Christian service than in the ritual or the philosophical issues associated with religion. At the death of John Huy Addams, he offered very practical and supportive advice to Jane. He reminded her that her father had been proud of her achievements and supportive of her goals and that she should carry on as he would have wished.

The death of his daughter Mary Addams Linn in 1888 from whooping cough seems to have been an extraordinary trial for Linn, perhaps even a test of his faith. Although his wife saw "Little Mary" as "safe and happy" in heaven, he grieved that "[Jesus] took her until she vanished and sad, sad our sorrow she went out into what seems to us a cold Eternity. Surley Jesus has a warm bosom somewhere for her little tired head to rest upon" (JML and MCAL to JA, 31 Jan. 1888, SCPC, JAC; *JAPM*, 2:705).

When Linn preached his final sermon on Sunday, 31 May 1891, before leaving for Storm Lake, Iowa, it was reported in local Geneseo, Illinois, newspapers that his church was filled not only with its own members but also with many from other community churches. One local paper reported that the sermon was "full of thought and impressive. It was attentively and devoutly listened to" (*Geneseo Republic*, 5 June 1891, IU, Lilly, SAAH). Another indicated that it "was an able exposition of the loving side of the gospel message" ([*Henry County News?*], 5 June 1891, IU, Lilly, SAAH). Both publications commented more fully on the Linns' dedication to charity. The *Geneseo Republic* intoned that Linn's "usefulness has not been confined to the church, but has been felt in secular and benificent ways." Including particularly Mary Addams Linn in its praise, it continued, "Many bowed in want and sorrow, many sick and weary, will miss the unexpected call, the kindly words and material aid bestowed by these workers of silent and unselfish charity" (5 June 1891, IU, Lilly, SAAH).

Linn, observed the *Geneseo Republic,* was "one of those persons rarely met with who combines in himself much learning and ardent love of study with the sensible, practical and useful affairs of life" (5 June 1891, IU, Lilly, SAAH). The county's other newspaper agreed. "His ministry here has been marked by exact scholarship, a devotion to the great truths of scripture, a broad and Catholic spirit, and a bold and fearless stand against all unrighteousness" ([*Henry County News?*], 5 June 1891, IU, Lilly, SAAH). It is not surprising that on her return from Europe in 1888 Jane Addams would have discussed her plans for what was to become Hull-House with Mary and John Manning Linn. She must have believed that in them she would find practical yet sympathetic listeners for her plan.

Linn, Mary Catherine Addams (1845–1894)

Mary Catherine Addams (Linn), the first child of John Huy Addams and Sarah Weber Addams, was born on 25 June 1845 in Stephenson County, Illinois, in the community that would become Cedarville. She spent the first nine years of her life with her parents and siblings in a two-room log cabin with a lean-to kitchen and a sleeping loft and in 1854 moved with them to the grand two-story brick home that would be her home until she was twenty-six.

She grew to maturity under the watchful eye of her mother, Sarah Weber Addams, who taught her such skills as sewing, cooking, gardening, maintaining a home, caring for children, tending the sick, and participating in community organizations and activities. Mary Addams attended the local school that her father had helped create for the area in 1846, and in 1859 she began attending the select school that he also helped found in that year. Laura Jane Gorham, the select school's teacher, lived with the Addams family during the 1860s, and she and Mary became good friends.

Mary's hope of going on with her education was thwarted by the unexpected death of her mother in childbirth in January 1863. Her thirst for education continued, however. She wrote to her sister Alice at Rockford Female Seminary, "Hope you will keep well and contented & appreciate the opportunity of going to school, for I assure you it is a great privilege, and one for which you should be thankful: I would be very glad if I could have gone a year or two more, . . . but I suppose it was all for the best or it would not have been so" (19 Nov. 1869, UIC, JAMC, HJ). A few years later, she wrote again to Alice, encouraging her to take advantage of the education she was getting in Rockford: "I feel painfully at times what I have lost in the way of school-days: hope I do not complain as I want to make the most of what advantages that I have, and I have & have had much to be thankful for; but I cannot help feeling like urging every girl that <u>can</u> go to school to make the most of her time: for things that we treasure in our minds cannot be taken from us; and it is not so much, what we <u>have</u> as what we <u>are</u> <that> will make us happy and useful" (29 Feb. 1872, UIC, JAMC, HJ).

With the help of Sarah Weber Addams's childhood nurse Mary ("Polly") Beer, Mary took her mother's place as the female head of the household. She managed the Addams home, keeping it clean and in good order; saw that the gardens were planted, tended, and harvested; that the clothes were washed, mended, and sewn; and that food was cooked and preserved. She also kept her father informed about family and community happenings. In addition, she took her mother's place in the community, providing help to the ill and infirm and solace to families who experienced death and helping friends prepare for weddings and other happy social events. All the younger Addams children—Martha, Weber, Alice, and Jane—were initially under Mary's care. All except Jane attended school either in Cedarville or in Freeport, Illinois, until 1866, when

Martha and Alice went off to boarding school at Rockford Female Seminary, and Weber left for Beloit Academy in Wisconsin.

Jane Addams remained at home in the loving care of Polly Beer and Mary Addams, who treated her indulgently according to family lore. She came to see her oldest sister as a mother figure. Years later a distant relative would recall, "I remember how much more acceptable to you [Jane] was the service of love from your eldest sister, than the word of authority from your step-mother. You doubtless in time, became more attached to the latter, but I am sure your love for your sister never grew less. For one could not know her and not love her" (Sarah C. T. Uhl to JA, 16 Nov. 1896, SCPC, JAC; *JAPM*, 3:501–02).

Like her mother before her, Mary Addams became very involved with religious activities in Cedarville. She participated in social events organized by women to support the Union Sunday School in which she taught and attended social functions to support the fundraising efforts of other religious organizations. She regularly participated in religious services no matter what the denomination, although her preference was for the Presbyterian Church. She attended Sunday School conventions in Bloomington in 1869 and Chicago in 1871 and was active in Sunday School teachers' meetings held in Cedarville and the surrounding area. A member of the Good Templars temperance organization, she encouraged the participation and membership of her siblings and their friends until the organization failed in Cedarville in 1872. Her commitment to temperance, like that of her father and mother, never wavered. She had joined the Presbyterian Church in 1867 and counseled her brother and sisters to do likewise, praising them when they did.

Motherlike, Mary Addams kept in touch with her siblings while they were away at school, writing each more than weekly and on a prearranged schedule. Although she was responsible for keeping up with Weber, it was with her sisters Martha and Alice that she seems to have had the most interaction by correspondence. Her letters were full of motherly advice. Martha apparently required little guidance, for she seems to have been a model sister and young woman. Alice, however, was different. It was to Alice that Mary Addams poured out motherwit, likely gleaned from their own mother, in almost every letter. Constant themes concerned reminding Alice not to see herself as better than others, to manage even small disappointments as if they were nothing, and to remember that she, Alice, was responsible for her own happiness. Mary believed that Alice was always looking "outside" herself for happiness rather than "inside" and that she was always looking ahead rather than finding joy in the moment. The result was that Alice was unhappy, lonely, and always disappointed. "You must learn to be contented without always looking forward to something ahead in the future," Mary counseled (15 Mar. 1869, IU, Lilly, SAAH). "I do not want you to think I am trying to lecture you," she advised. "I have always found that when I was lonely or rather discouraged, to think that I had only <u>one</u> day to live at a time & only one <u>minute</u> of that at one time, and if I tried to get all the enjoyment & good of that I could, I could not help but be happy all the time; but just as soon as we allow our thoughts to run on and wonder how we will do this and that time, so soon are we apt to become discouraged" (25 Jan. 1869, UIC, JAMC, HJ). (For more advice from Mary Addams to Alice, see Biographical Profiles: Haldeman, Sarah Alice Addams.) Mary sometimes visited her sisters at Rockford Female Seminary and took young Jane with her. She sewed clothing for them and cooked, packed, and sent boxes of food to her siblings at both schools.

Mary must have given Jane the same kind of advice and attention that she showered on the other Addams children, yet it must have been more carefully and lovingly administered, for Mary would always be mindful that the young Jane had barely known their mother. She wanted to make up for that loss. No doubt Mary, bolstered by the ever-vigilant Polly Beer, imbued Jane with standards of behavior, cleanliness, manners, and politeness along with the moral values that Sarah Weber Addams had shared with her. She also instructed her young charge in simple household skills, taught her to sew, helped with her homework from school, tended her when she was ill, and guided her early friendships. A special loving relationship developed between the two that neither time nor distance could diminish. Later, as she was about to marry and move permanently away from the Addamses' Cedarville home, Mary wrote to Alice of the strong feelings that her imposed "motherhood" position had engendered. "What an intense earnest longing I have had for you all, all these years God only knows: When I have erred, (which I know has been very often) it has been an error of the head and not of the heart: My interest in you all I often think must be more that of a Mother than a sister: at any rate it seems to me I could not endure to have it much more keen" (21 Aug. 1871, UIC, JAMC, HJ).

When John Huy Addams wed Anna Hostetter Haldeman in November 1868, Mary's life altered dramatically. She was no longer the female head of the family, no longer the decision-maker in the woman's realm of children and home. Anna Addams immediately inserted herself into that role, and Mary tried her best to help her new stepmother and her brothers and sisters make the transition a smooth one. She continued to write regularly and offer sisterly as well as motherly advice to siblings away at school. In the beginning, Anna spent some time in Springfield with John as he represented his district in the Illinois senate, and Mary and Polly became caregivers to the youngest of the new Mrs. Addams's children. George Haldeman, about a year younger than Jane, had come into the Addams household with his mother. Mary Addams also continued to undertake those household chores that Anna found disagreeable, especially sewing, cooking, and cleaning. But as Anna Addams spent more and more time in Cedarville or nearby Mount Carroll Mary became less responsible for family matters and was more able to lead her own life.

Just past mid-year 1869, Mary Addams went east on an extended visit to Weber and Addams relatives in Pennsylvania. When her brother Weber became ill in Cedarville, however, she was called home in November to accompany him to southern Illinois, where everyone hoped he would recover in the care of Henry C. and Laura Jane Gorham Forbes who lived in Union County near Cobden. She and the Forbeses watched Weber carefully and kept John Huy Addams informed of his progress. Home once again by Christmas, Mary spent 1870 and 1871 attending Rockford Female Seminary for one semester, visiting friends and family, continuing to attend to religious activities, and being courted by John Manning Linn. Linn had come to Cedarville in 1869, just ordained by the Rock River Presbytery, to organize a Presbyterian Church and serve the community of Dakota, Illinois.

Before Linn left for his new post, supply minister to Durand and Shannon, Illinois, in September 1871, he and Mary became engaged. They wed in Cedarville on 9 November 1871. After a wedding trip to southern Illinois, where they stayed with the Forbes family (one of whose children, "Little Mary," was probably named for Mary Addams Linn), they settled in a small home in Durand, Illinois. Mary was twenty-six and her husband was twenty-nine. Within a month, she began to write about Linn's absences due to his ministerial duties, something that would be a constant refrain in her letters for the remainder of her life. "I shall be very glad if he once gets where he can be home every Sunday, but I presume I ought not complain, for things might be much more unpleasant than they are: there is nothing really unpleasant about it, only I would like him home all the time" (MCAL to SAA, 20 Mar. 1872, UIC, JAMC, HJ). Little did Mary know how much more difficult her life would become and that Linn would seldom be home more than he was during his first posting.

Before the couple left Durand for their next home in Lena, Illinois, they were visited by both sets of parents and by siblings, including Jane Addams, and Mary Linn was pregnant with their first child. The move to Lena, where Linn served as supply minister until 1875, took place during the summer of 1872, and the couple's first child, John Addams Linn, was born on 9 September. At least one miscarriage followed. Even as a child Mary Addams Linn had not been robust; her son James Weber Linn indicated that she had weighed only forty-nine pounds when she was nine. Early in her married life she began to experience what would become increasingly poor health.

By 1875 John Linn had secured his first pastorate. It was in Winnebago, Illinois, where the couple lived until 1881. During that time Mary Linn gave birth to two more children: James Weber was born on 11 May 1876 and Esther Margaret on 7 August 1880. Because the Linns lived within a day's easy travel of Cedarville, they had frequent visits from Addams relatives and Mary Linn and her children could easily visit the Addams home.

With the unexpected death of her father in August 1881, Mary Linn inherited real and personal property from his estate valued at approximately sixty-six thousand dollars. It came to her as a 240-acre farm in Lancaster Township; fifty-three acres of timber in Harlem Township and five acres in Freeport, all in Stephenson County, Illinois; and financial instruments and cash. For the remainder of her life she used the inheritance to enhance her growing family's quality of life, primarily by purchasing larger and better dwellings in each of the communities in which the Linns lived. She purchased her first home in Harvard, Illinois, where John Linn settled between 1881 and 1884 as a supply minister.

Despite her increasingly poor health, probably due at least in part to her frequent pregnancies, Mary Linn remained active as a minister's wife. Her certainty of God's love mingled with almost empathetic concern for those less fortunate than she. She had often admonished her siblings—and one imagines her friends as well—to be grateful to God for his blessings. To sister Alice Addams she wrote, "we are never near as thankful as we ought to be; coming on the [train] cars from Bloomington I saw a little blind girl just from Jacksonville; she was quite talkative and very intelligent and interesting looking; and seemed perfectly happy; I then thought what a blessing sight is to us and yet we rarely, if ever think of thanking our heavenly Father for it" (14 June 1869, IU, Lilly, SAAH. The Illinois School for the Blind was located in Jacksonville, Illinois). A year later she shared other heartfelt concerns with Alice: "It is very cold indeed this evening . . . : I cannot help thinking of the many thousands of homeless and freezing people this evening: How thankful we should be for all our Heavenly Fathers kindness to us; and how willing we should be to work for him, and consecrate ourselves to His service, for it is a very small return for His kindness to us" (17 Jan. 1870, IU, Lilly, SAAH).

It is likely that she saw her marriage to John Manning Linn as something of a mission partnership. He reported to Alice that Mary, after their first Sunday service together in Durand, had remarked, "'This makes me feel like going to work'" (28 Nov. 1871, UIC, JAMC, HJ). In addition to keeping house and tending her children, she led church women in various social and educational activities and always attended services. In Harvard, she became a member of the Woman's Christian Temperance Union when it was formed in 1883 and initiated a "Woman's Lecture Course" that survived for twelve years after her departure from the town.

After the birth of Stanley Ross Linn on 21 May 1883, the Addams siblings seemed particularly concerned about Mary Linn's health. Anticipating that birth, Jane Addams had planned to bring John Addams Linn and James Weber Linn to stay with her in Cedarville. By the time she could have retrieved the children, however, Stanley Ross had been born. When she visited her sister she found Mary "looking very well indeed, brighter more hopeful than I have seen her for a long long time" (JA to SAAH, 5 June 1883, UIC, JAMC, HJ; *JAPM*, 1:1099–1100). By early July, however, it seemed that she had taken a turn for the worse, and Jane planned to go to her, for Mary herself seemed "to feel as if she needed some one" (JA to SAAH, 2 July 1883, UIC, JAMC, HJ; *JAPM*, 1:1111). When she arrived, she found Mary better again. "She does n't cough one fourth as much as she did last summer but the dropsical tendency is quite pronounced," she wrote to Alice. "Nothing will induce her to wean the baby before fall. . . . I will do all I can for Mary while I am here & will try to provide for help for her the coming winter—she ought to have some one to take complete charge of the baby as soon as he is weaned" (18 July 1883, UIC, JAMC, HJ; *JAPM*, 1:1124).

By December 1883 Jane Addams, away in Europe, knew from Mary Linn's letters that her sister was "all broken down . . . feeling much worse than usual" (JA to SAAH, 17 Jan. [1884], UIC, JAMC, HJ; *JAPM*, 1:1339). Mary's sisters felt that her husband was not taking proper care of her and his family. In all likelihood he was in the process of negotiating what he thought might be a better position for all of them in the Dakota Territory. Alice Addams Haldeman must have written to Jane and complained, for Jane urged caution and support for the Linn family: "I am sorry that you [are] disappointed in Mr Linn . . . but Mary is so devoted to him that her sole happiness is knowing and feeling that he is happy and contented. So I know that you wont let her feel however indirectly, that he is not doing for her or others what you expect, for it only grieves her and can do him no possible good now" (17 Jan. [1884], UIC, JAMC, HJ; *JAPM*, 1:1340).

By May, physicians caring for Mary Linn were convinced that her problem could be solved by surgery. Jane, still traveling in Europe, wrote to Alice: "It is just three weeks to day since Mary's operation, and the most danger, must be over. It hardly seems as if Mary was strong enough to stand so severe an operation. She wrote in her last letter, that the feeling of exhaustion sometimes amounted to positive suffering" ([10] June 1884, UIC, JAMC, HJ; *JAPM*, 1:1531).

Exhausted or not, when her husband and eldest son set off for the Dakota Territory in September 1885, where John Linn was the supply minister for Ellendale and where he became the short-term first president of Groton Collegiate Institute in Groton, Mary remained behind in Harvard with the Linns' three other children. Once again she was pregnant. On 28 May 1885 Mary Addams ("Little Mary") Linn was born. Mary Linn sold the family's Harvard home in February 1886, for she anticipated joining John and their son in the Dakota Territory. Instead, they returned to Illinois, and, when John Linn secured a position as fiscal agent for Lake Forest College, the family moved to Lake Forest. Mary bought another home for the family there. She remained in Lake Forest until the birth of her last child, Charles Hodge Linn, on 18 February 1887 during her eighth month of pregnancy. Shortly afterward, and with Jane to help her, she moved her family into a house she purchased for twenty-five hundred dollars in Geneseo, Illinois.

The Linn family remained in Geneseo until 1892, when they followed John Linn to a position in Storm Lake, Iowa. It was in Geneseo that their two youngest children died. Charles Hodge died in May 1887. He had difficulty from birth with breathing and was almost continuously ill after the family moved to Geneseo. Little Mary died of complications from whooping cough in January 1888 while Jane was away in Europe. A stoic Mary Linn accepted both deaths as God's will, told herself that the children were safely in heaven, and struggled on with her life. Despite increasingly poor health, she was as active as possible in community and church affairs in her new community. She was also apparently much loved, especially by the women of Geneseo.

During Mary's confinements and bouts of particularly poor health the Linns sent their children to stay with siblings or friends. Most of these arrangements were made by Mary Linn. Sometimes Esther Margaret visited Laura Shoemaker Addams and her daughter Sarah in Cedarville. On at least one occasion, the Linn boys were placed in the care of Alice and Harry Haldeman; they also stayed with the James Goddard family in Harvard when Mary Linn had surgery. When she could, Jane Addams took them to Cedarville or came to stay with Mary, especially when John was away, and helped care for them. Mary Linn also tried to keep a nurse and maid/cook to manage the children and the house. More than once Jane helped search for appropriate employees.

Between 1892 and 1894 the Linn family lived in Storm Lake, where John Linn served as the second president of Buena Vista College. With funds provided by his wife, he built a home there that would become known in the community as the "President's House." Mary Linn's health continued its downward slide, and doctors convinced John that she needed complete bed rest. With guidance from Jane Addams, whose good friend and mentor Sarah Anderson had retreated there for rest and recuperation, he decided that Mary Linn should seek treatment and rest at the Pennoyer Sanitarium in Kenosha, Wisconsin. Jane made the arrangements in March 1894. Mary Keyser, who had become attached to the Linn family in Geneseo, went to Storm Lake to become their housekeeper, and by 8 April Mary was in the sanitarium. According to Jane, who went to her immediately after her husband took her to Kenosha, she was in need of constant care because of her helplessness. She was also incredibly homesick for her children. Jane wrote to Alice frequently about Mary's condition. In almost every letter she requested her sister's help with the financial burden of keeping Mary at Pennoyer. "Mary must have absolutely no worry about the bills and poor Mr Linn has been able to collect no money at all," Jane wrote, although to no avail (16 Apr. 1894, UIC, JAMC, HJ; *JAPM*, 2:1526). She borrowed money to pay Mary's Pennoyer bills, but there is no evidence that Alice Addams Haldeman ever assisted or reimbursed her.

At first Mary Linn seemed to improve. Jane visited her as frequently as possible despite the Pullman Car Company strike that tied up rail lines (during which Jane served as a member of the arbitration committee). Late in June, however, she was told that Mary had developed "heart weakness" (JA to MRS, 29 June 1894, SCPC, JAC; *JAPM*, 2:1550). Mary died intestate on 6 July 1894 of a cerebral hemorrhage and was buried two days later in the Cedarville Cemetery near her parents and the two Linn children who had died. The Rev. Lewis H. Mitchell from South Chicago, who had been a young minister in Cedarville between 1874 and 1878, conducted her service.

Mary Linn left assets valued at $33,600 and easily identifiable liabilities of $8,060. There were also assorted expenses associated with her last illness and death, as well as taxes to pay on the real estate that made up the bulk of her estate. Jane was named executor of the estate, which was kept open until 1898. She also became the guardian of the Linns' minor children: James Weber, Esther Margaret, and Stanley Ross.

Memorial services were held for Mary Addams Linn by the congregations she and her husband had served in Harvard, Geneseo, and Winnebago, Illinois. "She passed thro[u]gh so much suffering," Cousin Miranda Addams recalled, "and with it all, so uncomplaining. . . . [H]er crown was ready for her—it was well earned, her life was a fitting example for all who were privileged to know her" (Miranda E. Addams to SAAH, 8 July 1895, UI, Lilly, SAAH).

Starr, Ellen Gates (1859–1940)

Schoolmate and lifelong friend of Jane Addams, Ellen Gates Starr was the cofounder with Addams of Hull-House. During her long association with Addams in Chicago, Starr was also a labor activist, teacher, master craftsman in book arts, promoter of public art and art education, Christian Socialist, and fervent Roman Catholic convert. She was born on 19 March 1859 at Spring Park, her family's farm near Laona, Illinois.

Starr came from a New England farming family. Her parents were Unitarians, and religion was an important part of Starr's life from her early years. Her ancestors had arrived in America from England in the 1600s, and the family lived in New England for many generations. Starr's parents, Susan Gates Childs Starr (1821–1900) and Caleb Allen Starr (1822–1915), grew up in rural Deerfield, Massachusetts, where they married and began their own family. They migrated along with other Starr family members to Illinois four years before Ellen was born. Their third child and second daughter, she grew up on the farm where she was born and attended a nearby one-room school. Although family funds were tight, there was an emphasis upon good education. For one academic year beginning in September 1877, Starr attended Rockford Female Seminary in Rockford, Illinois, where she became close friends with Jane Addams. She left Rockford because of economic pressures, and in 1878 began making an independent living as a teacher. In that same year, when Ellen was eighteen, her parents moved into the town of Durand, Illinois, where her father went into business as a druggist (for more details on the lives of Starr's family members, see EGS to JA, 11 Aug. 1878, nn. 5, 7, 8, and 9 above).

Like Jane Addams, Ellen Gates Starr was profoundly influenced by her childhood relationship with her father. The reformist vigor, socialist principles, and belief in opportunities for women that would become cornerstones of Starr's later life were all values and behaviors she had seen modeled by her Republican parents, particularly by her activist father, who supported abolition, women's rights, and suffrage. A local leader in the grange movement, Caleb Starr was also an advocate of collective farming and marketing among low-income owners of small farms and farm laborers and a proponent of other forms of mutual economic aid among farm families. As an adult, Starr memorialized her father as "consistently democratic and opposed to privilege" (quoted in Carrell, "Reflections in a Mirror," 41). He was also progressive in his stance toward opportunities for women. When Starr was a child, her father took her to a meeting of local farmers, where he introduced Elizabeth Cady Stanton and Susan B. Anthony as speakers. Unlike John Huy Addams, who was privately contemptuous of female women's rights advocates, Caleb Starr admired women activists who spoke out and encouraged his daughter to respect them as positive role models.

Starr and Addams were also alike in having thoroughly domestic mothers. Despite the affirmative view of women in public political roles held within the Starr family, Ellen's mother led a very private life as a farm wife and later as a resident of the town of Durand. Highly artistic in nature, her skills were channeled into practical and domestic arts, including sewing, tailoring, and elaborate embroidery. She imparted to all of her children a lasting love of beauty and a sensitivity to aesthetics. The three eldest Starr children spent their lifetimes involved in the arts. Mary Houghton Starr Blaisdell (1849–1934) studied painting in Cambridge, Massachusetts, and Paris before marrying and working as a portrait painter in Chicopee, Massachusetts. William Wesley Starr (1851–1913) studied drawing and painting in Chicago, Boston, and Rome and at the Lowell Institute of Art, Boston, Massachusetts. He became a professional artist and sought-after sculptor for public arts projects in the Chicago area. Ellen's younger brother, Albert Childs Starr (1861–1935), was attracted to the sciences and business rather than to the arts. He studied pharmacy and then became a cotton broker with his sister Mary's husband Charles Blaisdell in Massachusetts. His daughter, Josephine Starr (1894–1991), would in adulthood become close to her aunt Ellen, if not entirely understanding of her politics.

The strongest inspiration for the development of artistic skills and sensibilities among the Starr children came from their paternal aunt, Eliza Allen Starr (1824–1921), who was particularly close to Ellen and William (on the biography of Eliza Allen Starr, see EGS to JA, 11 Aug. 1878, n. 9). Ellen Gates Starr proved to be much more like her aunt than like her mother. She shared her aunt's enthusiasms, particularly her devotion to art and religion.

The fervency of Eliza Allen Starr's belief and her primary focus on Christian symbolism and the aesthetics of religious iconography in her evaluation of artistic excellence had a strong impact upon her niece. As a frequent visitor and sometime resident of her aunt's home in Chicago, young Ellen was exposed firsthand to the combination of her aunt's urban, artistic lifestyle and conservative religious viewpoints. Eliza Allen Starr's professional, independent, unmarried life among networks of women was quite a contrast to Ellen's mother's more insular, rural, and marriage-and-family-centered choices.

There was much about her aunt's simultaneously more cosmopolitan and more ideological and spiritual example that Ellen Gates Starr seized upon with enthusiasm. Much of her own life at Hull-House as a teacher and promoter of the arts, living in a communal setting and working closely on projects with Chicago women in a position to provide financial support, was congruent with the kind of life her aunt had led in the generation preceding. Like her aunt, Ellen Gates Starr never married. Her views regarding worthwhile interpretation of art—disdaining modern art in favor of medieval and Renaissance works—and her somewhat tortured course of spiritual seeking that led to a zealous conversion from the Protestant to Roman Catholic faith, and to lay membership in a religious order, almost eerily matched Eliza Allen Starr's earlier path. Both women channeled their literary skill into writing for religious publications and lectured to increase public awareness of the significance of religious art. In these ways as well as in others, Ellen Gates Starr carried her aunt's mantle into the world.

Although her father and aunt were important early mentors and she developed many close friendships later in life, the most formative relationship in Ellen Gates Starr's life was her friendship with Jane Addams. After the two discovered one another at Rockford Female Seminary in 1877–78 they carried on an intimate association that would prove pivotal for both women throughout the rest of their lives. Each discovered in the other a kind of soulmate and a source of lasting affection and motivation to high ideals. They shared opinions and quests for meaning in classical and romantic literature, sorted through questions about social reform and women's proper roles in society, and confided their inner emotions and thoughts to one another.

However they shored one another up as mutual confidantes, Starr and Addams's experiences and perspectives were always somewhat at odds. The contrasts evident in their youthful correspondence grew as they continued their relationship into middle age. In their early twenties, Starr had less opportunity for education and travel than Addams but lived a more independent, profession-directed life. Family economic differences that cut short Starr's seminary education and perpetuated Addams's continued to play a somewhat complicated role in their separate life experiences. While Addams was supported as a student by her family, and at the death of her father came into an early inheritance, Starr made her own way in the world as a teacher and tutor, craftswoman, and well-known lecturer on the arts. None of these were lucrative fields, and she became increasingly dependent in adulthood on patronage from wealthier friends, including Addams.

The livelihood issue was not the only dividing line that shaped the nearly life-long relationship between the two close friends. Although not as evident when they were girls at Rockford together, they differed quite markedly in personality and physique. Starr was direct and energetic, zealous and passionate in her politics, and a strong believer in candid, articulate confrontation and direct protest actions. Weighing less than one hundred pounds, she was elegant, charming, and grammatically precise. When she was thirty she was described in a *Woman's Journal* article of 5 May 1889, a few months before the founding of Hull-House, as "full of vivacity, a rare conversationalist, and one who never loses sight of the humorous side of things. . . . Petite, graceful, brilliant, even to sparkling," she was "a great favorite in society, with young and old, men and women" (clipping, Hull-House Scrapbook, vol. 1, 1889–94; *JAPM,* Addendum 10).

Years later, when Starr was in her sixties and her involvement in Hull-House had waned, she was honored for her dynamic presence and effectiveness. "I remember most of all" recalled an observer, her "fresh laughter, her passage with head thrown a little back, and a touch of whiteness at throat and wrists." She was "one whose fearlessness, whose ardor for beauty, stirred many a young person to a new zeal" (Hackett, "Hull-House," 70). Despite such testimonials, Starr easily intimidated people with her forthrightness and was, especially late in life, frequently accused of being haughty or demanding. As one who knew her well put it after Starr's death, Ellen could be something of a martinet.

Starr's and Addams's paths diverged for a decade between their time together at Rockford and the founding of Hull-House. While Addams continued as a student at the seminary, Starr embarked on a teaching career. After leaving Rockford in June 1878, she taught Latin and French classes for an academic year at Mount Morris Seminary in Mount Morris, Illinois. During the summer of 1879 she tutored children in Harlem, Illinois, a small town near Rockford. Both positions made possible short visits into Rockford to see friends, including Jane Addams, who were still enrolled at the seminary. In September 1879 Starr began teaching in Chicago. She worked with educators Mary J. Holmes and Rebecca Rice. After some part-time instructing, she settled into a regular position at the prestigious Miss Kirkland's School for Girls, which was founded by Elizabeth Stansbury Kirkland (1828–96) and her sister Cordelia Kirkland (b. 1835) and located on Huron Street near Ellen's Aunt Eliza's home and studio (see *PJA,* 2). Starr taught several subjects, including Latin, literature, and geography, but she specialized in drawing, art history, and art appreciation classes. In the process of teaching at Miss Kirkland's, she formed close friendships with other teachers and became acquainted with the wealthy parents of many of her students. Those contacts later became important in the promotion and realization of plans to establish Hull-House.

Both Addams and Starr maintained hopes of furthering their postseminary education in the East. While Addams set her sights on Smith College and briefly attended the Woman's Medical College of Pennsylvania (1881–82), Starr made a try at Harvard University. She studied privately with a tutor in Chicago to prepare (probably Greek and Hebrew scholar Dr. Edward Cushing Mitchell [1829–1900], see *PJA,* 2), and she attempted to take regional entrance examinations for Harvard in the summer of 1883. She was rebuffed, however, because she was a woman (see *PJA,* 2; see also *JAPM,* 1:900, 1:945, 1:1112). She planned to try again the following summer but apparently did not do so, remaining at work among a close circle of culturally sophisticated friends in Chicago.

One of the earliest friendships Starr developed through those circles was with

Mary J. Holmes. Holmes—and later another teacher, the young Mary Runyan—in some ways in the late 1870s and early 1880s supplanted Addams in Starr's affections. Starr and Holmes were involved in reading groups together, and Starr became close to Holmes's mother, living for a time in the Holmes home. Holmes was a southern-bred Episcopalian, and unlike Addams she shared Starr's keen interest in church. She joined Starr during the 1879–80 period in exploring various churches and parishes throughout the Chicago area, searching for a church home that Starr felt could meet her needs. They attended Robert Collyer's Church of the Unity and heard the controversial David Swing preach at Chicago's Central Music Hall; they also visited Congregational and Anglican services.

Starr eventually chose to join the Episcopal Church. She was officially baptized and confirmed as an Episcopalian in 1884, all the while "protesting actively" on certain questions of dogma (E. Starr, "Bypath into the Great Roadway," 5). She grew close to Mary Runyan in 1882 and was devastated when Runyan moved away from Chicago to teach kindergarten in St. Louis. The two women continued to visit, however, and saw each other in the summer of 1883. Starr confided to Jane Addams that she was heartsick with the pain of losing Runyan and that people around her did not understand the intensity of her loss in the same way they would had Runyan been a man (see also PJA, 2). Like Addams, Starr also kept in touch with seminary friends, especially Sarah Anderson, corresponding with her and visiting frequently in Rockford and Chicago.

Religion was one of the lifelong points of friendly contention between Starr and Addams. Starr's questing about institutional religion, and the private pressure she began to put upon Addams to experience the joys and rewards she had found in Christ-centered conversion and devotions, caused a degree of emotional difficulty between the friends as they corresponded between Rockford and Starr's various teaching posts. Yet both thought that human beings, women included, had a moral responsibility to seek fulfillment by finding and doing work in the world.

The decade of the 1880s, between Starr's year at Rockford and the founding of Hull-House, was a very difficult one for Addams, and she repeatedly turned to Starr for inspiration and encouragement. Starr helped her to recover from bouts of depression and was privy more than anyone else (except, perhaps, Sarah Anderson and possibly Flora Guiteau) to Addams's inner recesses, private struggles, and musings. She gave Addams confidence and provided a sounding board for many ideas, observations, and resolves that Addams apparently did not readily share with family members or other friends. Addams could turn to Starr for safe expression of self, and in doing so she was able to maintain an intellectual and emotional identity independent and separate from the burdens and expectations that the circumstances of Addams family life placed upon her, which became more and more complicated and demanding after her graduation and return to Cedarville in 1881.

A turning point came in 1887–88, when the two friends joined Sarah Anderson in a tour of Europe. Addams helped fund Starr's way. It was the first of eight or nine trips to Europe that Starr made during her lifetime. As she visited cathedrals, monasteries, and catacombs and the group wandered separately or together through Italy, Spain, northern France, and England, Addams moved more solidly toward a conviction that she must act on the social values to which she was dedicated intellectually. Sharing Ruskin's *Unto This Last* (a collection of essays on social ethics and political reform) and discussing Tolstoy, Starr and Addams became ever more convinced of the efficacy of Christian Socialism.

The trip turned out to be a crossroads for both of them. When they returned to the United States, it was with a plan of life in mind. In January 1889 they moved together into a rooming house in Chicago. They then set out to do the promotional groundwork that would make possible the beginning of their grand experiment as it had been conceived by Addams and shared with her traveling companions during the trip. That experiment was to be a settlement house where college-trained women and men could use their educations for the good of others and, in the process, bring to full realization their own talents and abilities. The experiment officially began on 18 September 1889 with the opening of Hull-House on South Halsted Street.

Starr and Addams took up residence at Hull-House, along with former Linn family housekeeper Mary Keyser. At first they shared the first floor with a manufacturing firm and had the use of the entire second floor. They had new windows put in, mended and finished the wooden floors, laid oriental rugs, and varnished and rehung the doors. In pursuit of creating a calm and inspiring oasis of beauty and taste amid surrounding urban working-class squalor, the Hull-House hallways were repainted in various delicate terra-cotta tints and the rooms in ivory and gold. Starr painted her own two-room living space blue and added William Morris wallpaper. She hung prints of Italian and Flemish pictures on the walls. A copy of Botticelli's *Primavera*—the feminist and spiritual aspects of which Starr much admired and later wrote about—was featured in a prominent spot over her bookcases.

One of Starr's first activities as a Hull-House resident was a throwback to Rockford seminary days. She began a reading group for young women based on an old Rockford favorite: George Eliot's *Romola*. She also offered courses to neighborhood immigrant working women on Dante and Browning. Soon other residents led Shakespeare and Plato clubs. The Working People's Social Science Club provided a forum for workers to come, hear, and debate information presented by a series of speakers, including Starr's aunt Eliza Allen Starr, John Dewey, Susan B. Anthony, and others. Former students of Starr's from Miss Kirkland's School came to Hull-House and volunteered to teach classes and help with various clubs. Starr made a collection of framed photographs of master paintings available on loan to neighborhood women and began what became a very popular series of art appreciation courses for working women and men. Prints of Botticellis, Fra Angelicos, and others were delivered to tenement households to comfort mourning family members when deaths had taken place, and immigrant women were encouraged to tack up reproductions of master paintings on their walls for inspiration as they worked at home. The books and reproductions of fifteenth-century Florentine art that Starr loaned to the neighborhood were meant to be means by which exhausted factory girls could transcend their condition, at least in imagination (Addams, "Art-Work," 40).

As the settlement house became more established, art outreach was continually expanded. The first additional building erected as part of the settlement was an art gallery (Butler Gallery, constructed in 1891). Starr was instrumental in attracting the philanthropic funding for the building from a leading Chicago patron of the arts, and she helped supervise its design. Chicago matrons were encouraged to loan artwork from their private collections, and Starr mounted the first of several biannual Hull-House exhibits in June 1891. Gothic, Pre-Raphaelite, Greek Revival, Romanesque, and sacred art was emphasized in the exhibitions, because these works met Starr's standards of artistic excellence and ideals regarding artistic production. They also were chosen in order to make a more direct connection to the Greek, Russian, and Italian residents of the Halsted neighborhood, who could appreciate and admire them as part of their personal cultural heritage.

By 1893 art studios were established at Hull-House, with studio lessons taught by resident artists. Addams credited Starr with being the central "vital influence" in the "many-sided experiment" of arts at Hull-House, explaining to Forum readers in 1895 that Starr "not only feeds her own mind and finds her highest enjoyment in Art, but . . . believes that every soul has a right to be thus fed and solaced." Addams also spoke of Starr's influence as a dynamic and popular teacher. "There is abundant testimony," she concluded in describing the students who had attended Starr's art history courses for the past four years, "that the lectures and pictures have quite changed the tone of their minds" ("Art-Work," 40).

In providing the instigation behind the development of Hull-House arts programs, Starr endeavored to carry out principles already well defined in the writings and lectures of William Morris (1834–96) and John Ruskin (1819–1900), for whom art was indivisible from social ethics. As Starr explained in her talks and essays, aesthetics shaped character and beauty reinforced morality, but the key factors were the ways in which aesthetics intersected with social reform. At issue in particular was the nature of work and the control and shape of the processes of production and consumption.

In planning the settlement house's art programs, Starr hoped that far more than her students' minds would be reshaped or uplifted through viewing the grace and beauty of masterpieces and gaining knowledge of the historical traditions that had produced them—or even that they, like she, would come to feel that "all great art is praise," evidence of the connection between the human and the divine (E. G. Starr, "Art and Labor," 167). She hoped that the apprenticeshiplike opportunities offered in Hull-House studios could free some workers from industrial jobs, helping to replace assembly-line work with skilled, self-directed labor. She also hoped to see the replacement of cheaply manufactured, machine-made consumer goods with handmade objects of beauty and worth.

Starr's idealistic goals for transforming the urban-industrial economy by reforming the nature of work soon ran up against the limitations of reality. Art could neither feed nor clothe families. For most impoverished workers involved in artistic efforts at Hull-House studios, learning new skills came on top of working twelve-hour days. As Addams put it in *Twenty Years*, "the Settlement soon discovers how difficult it is to put a fringe of art on the end of a day spent in a factory" (375). Short of winning broad-reaching economic changes, Hull-House art classes and programs provided immigrants with chances to experience "restorative power" through the "exercise of a genuine craft" (376). Painting, drawing, silversmithing, sculpting, and throwing pottery offered creative outlets and provided windows of liberation from the enforced drudgery of jobs and the uglier, dingier sides of tenement living. Starr believed the opportunity to develop artistic talents counteracted the deadening psychic costs of working in monotonous manufacturing jobs that afforded little chance for self-expression or, as she put it, "wasting human life in the making of valueless things" (E. G. Starr, "Art and Labor," 178).

The arts emphasis at Hull-House was continually evolving. While Starr used reproductions to teach European art history courses to adults in the evenings and students drew from casts in Hull-House studios, children were taken on daytime excursions to see a variety of work in museums or participated in outdoor classes, sketching from nature at lake-front property on Lake Michigan. The new appreciation of primitive and folk arts that swept fashionable circles as a consequence of the American arts and crafts movement (at its heyday from the founding of Hull-House through the 1920s) also led Hull-House to shift away from its initial emphasis on European arts and recognize the artistic contributions of Native America and Mexico. Emphasis on mounting and viewing exhibitions also shifted to the active demonstration of arts and to the blurring lines between art and craft.

Starr's campaign to use Hull-House programs to bring art to the masses (and the masses to art), changing society in the process, was expanded in several ways beyond the settlement house into the Chicago community at large. The public relations involved in contacting and organizing artists and collectors to loan paintings to Hull-House's 1897 Easter Art Exhibit and in attracting artists-in-residence for studio work at the settlement led to the creation of the Chicago Arts and Crafts Society. Starr turned expressly to women's clubs to see that the methods being carried out in Hull-House exhibits and arts education programs were extended to public schools. She spearheaded the formation of the Chicago Public School Art Society (CPSAS) in 1893 and became its first president, serving from 1894 to 1897. The CPSAS existed well into the late twentieth century and worked to place art on the walls of public school classrooms in the Hull-House area. It eventually expanded within the city of Chicago by sending art history teachers into public school classes and promoting field trips to the Art Institute of Chicago, bringing children face to face with original paintings, sculpture, textiles, furniture, and Asian art.

Starr's concerns for promoting public art were closely linked to those for promoting public health. As the CPSAS worked to bring beauty in the abstract to urban school children Starr and Addams lobbied for public parks, open spaces, safe and clean public transit, street cleaning, and garbage removal—all ways to change the dirty, crowded conditions and dilapidation that dominated children's experience of the city environment. Starr promoted these ideas in lectures. She became well known in the 1890s as a speaker at chautauquas, women's clubs, church groups, and schools. Her subjects ranged from the settlement house movement to the arts, labor rights, or the relationship between the arts and democracy. She varied her emphasis on the arts, religion, labor, or social justice issues, depending on her audience. A typed draft of one talk on art and democracy is hand-labeled "For a socialist audience." She spoke to teachers and art critics in New York on the work of the CPSAS in January 1897 before arriving in Detroit in early February. In Detroit she spoke on settlement houses to a Baptist Church group by day and, with stereopticon illustrations, on "The Artist's Part in the Social New Birth" and "The Relation of Art to Life" at a Detroit Museum of Art lecture series in the evenings. Her trip had been sponsored by the Young Woman's Home of Detroit, and her talks were free. She was touted in Detroit as "one of the most talented lady lecturers in the land" and advised that "as the gifted lady is a staunch friend of organized labor, workingmen should turn out in large numbers to hear her" ("Intellectual Treat").

Even the most prosaic of Starr's opinions could become a cause of controversy. When she spoke on schools and the arts in New York during the 1897 tour, a vigorous debate ensued. "The wave of interest in art that there is in the principal American cities just now was illustrated by the vehement way in which Miss Starr's ideas on schoolroom decoration were attacked and defended at the Public Education Association yesterday afternoon" reported the New York Evening Post on 16 January. Conservatives in the audience were vocal in their opposition to the idea of introducing reproductions into schools because they thought that doing so would dull the senses of those traveling to Europe to see the originals. One female debate participant reminded naysayers that "our public schools could not be treated from the point of view of those children who make trips to Europe" and, furthermore, it was her experience that even those Americans who did have a chance for European travel were more apt to be "interested in the originals and most aware of the difference between them and copies" if they had prior exposure to reproductions. Starr told one of her favorite anecdotes at the occasion, the story of the "little Chicago girl who crossed the river with a companion, and said 'My, I hate rivers,' and the other answered, 'Yes, so do I;

they smell so,'" illustrating that children grasp "meaning only as far as they had experienced" and that to impart an enlarged knowledge of nature and the world through exposure to pastoral landscape paintings is but one of the "reasons for giving city children some insight into the beautiful." Starr was virtually citing the motto of her arts work as well as her social philosophy when she assured listeners that what she sought was "the Best for Everybody."

Not long after returning from the 1897 lecture tour, Starr determined to carry some of her principles about art and labor into practice. As she explained in an 1890 Hull-House pamphlet, "I began to feel that instead of talking, it would be a great deal better to make something myself, ever so little, thoroughly well, and beautiful of its kind" (Starr, "A Note of Explanation," 2; see also E. G. Starr, "Hull-House Bookbindery"). What she decided to make combined her love of literature and ideas with her love of art and craft. Ellen Gates Starr became a master binder of books. In 1897 she secured a rare apprenticeship with T. J. Cobden-Sanderson (1840–1922) at the Doves Bindery in Hammersmith, London, which he had established in a small house opposite William Morris's Kelmscott Press in March 1893. She was the first woman to do so (she had been preceded by Douglas Cockerell, who left in 1897, and the sewing and headbanding at the bindery was done for many years by Bessie Hooley). Cobden-Sanderson was renowned as one of the greatest bookbinders of his era. A philosopher and former lawyer, he was a friend of Morris and an important figure in the British arts and crafts movement. Backed by money from a close friend and patron, the Chicago socialite and activist Mary Wilmarth, Starr moved to England. She trained at Cobden-Sanderson's workshop in the house called The Nook at 15 Upper Mall on the Thames. She worked there seven days a week for fifteen months (ca. 1897–98) until Cobden-Sanderson deemed her workmanship at master quality. Her goal was not merely to learn the trade well enough to teach it to others but to achieve excellence in her product. As she humbly put it, she wanted "to produce something of a kind worth making" (E. G. Starr, "A Note of Explanation," 5).

Starr's intention was to return to Hull-House and offer extension courses there in bookbinding. During 1898 she returned to Chicago, set up a bindery workshop by combining her two bedrooms on the second floor of Hull-House, and immediately began to see that she had not thoroughly thought through all the practical and political implications of her plan. The manual training extension classes she envisioned proved impossible. The tools and materials needed for binding books were very expensive. Binding was also extremely time-intensive, involving so many hours per task that the process was "too long for those who only give an evening or two or three evenings a week" on top of their wage-work jobs (E. G. Starr, "A Note of Explanation," 6). She also found that teaching the process involved so much detailed and personal attention that it was impossible to take more than a few students at once. The result was that she operated her workshop, taking contracts for bindings from a wealthy clientele, and took on a select group of apprentices whom she trained to help her. "I earn my living," she reported in 1900, "not by talking about other people's work—that I still do for pleasure—but by binding and ornamenting a few books as well as I can do it, and by teaching three private pupils as well as I can teach them" ("A Note of Explanation," 6). Her apprentices, committed to work intensively with her for at least a year at a time, were taught, as Starr's niece put it, "with meticulous precision to the accompaniment of almost continuous laughter" (J. Starr, "Notes," 5). Key among them was Mary Kelly, a working-class neighborhood girl who began with Starr in 1902. Peter Verburg, Jr., himself a noted designer, joined Starr as an associate. Starr and Verburg also taught summer workshops at a working bindery on Verburg's father's farm in Troy, New Hampshire, near Mount Monadnock and the Green Mountains.

Starr was particular about what books she worked on. Among those she bound for patrons in Detroit, Cleveland, New York, Chicago, and elsewhere between 1898 and 1904 were Shakespeare's sonnets, books on Sappho and about Charles and Mary Lamb, *In Memoriam, Democracy and Social Ethics, The Art of William Morris, The Song of Hiawatha, Daphnis and Chloe,* and *Everyman.* She also did collections of poetry, songs, drawings, woodcuts, children's books, and books on gothic architecture. Many of the titles were produced, ready for leather rebinding, by Morris's Kelmscott Press. Loving in particular English romantic texts, Starr proclaimed, "Naturally, I only bind books which seem to me worthy to last" ("A Note of Explanation," 7).

The museum-quality bindings soon received critical acclaim. Exhibited in Chicago, they received favorable notice in such publications as *Brush and Pencil* and *House Beautiful.* Newspapers ran stories about her workshop. Orders came in for books from Addams's companions and Hull-House supporters Mary Rozet Smith and Mary Wilmarth and from members of Chicago society, such as Nettie Fowler (Mrs. Cyrus) McCormick and Charles Scribner. Starr did an edition of *Lost Letters from Lesbos* for the Chicago women's Fortnightly Club (1904). Her bindings may be identified by her initials with the date stamped on the inside back cover. She often submitted work for exhibit and judging and had several bindings in the third public exhibition of the Society of Arts and Crafts in January 1903 in Minneapolis. *Seven Poems* and *Two Translations by Alfred Lord Tennyson,* bound by Starr in 1923, won first prize at the exhibition of fine bindings at the Art Institute of Chicago in 1924. She became a member of the prestigious Guild of Book Workers during the 1930s, when many of her best bindings were being conserved in storage for her through private arrangement at the City Museum of New York.

Starr ultimately became discouraged with the book arts, precisely because the economics of the situation meant that she could produce beautiful work for only the private collections of the rich. The elitism of the practice itself also caused her dismay. "The gravest practical difficulty for the painstaking handicraftsman and minor artist, as indeed for the artist major as well," she explained in "Bookbinding as an Art, and as a Commercial Industry," "is that of connecting his work at all closely with the life of the day. Our art has long ceased to be in any sense democratic. Artists as a class (they should not be a class)—live a life apart, more or less posed and sophisticated. They minister not to the community at large as a normal art should do, but to exclusive circles of the rich and 'cultivated.' Only by such are their ministrations sought to an appreciable extent, only by such is it made possible for them to continue doing their work" (7–8). After the turn of the century, Starr supplemented her interests in the transformative powers of art by becoming increasingly involved in supporting the labor movement.

Starr befriended one of the first working-class residents of Hull-House, Mary Kenney, who was an organizer for the Women's Book Binders Union and held regular meetings for trade unions at Hull-House. She also worked with Florence Kelley in campaigning for legislation to abolish sweatshops, end child labor, and promote an eight-hour day for women workers. Starr and Kelley did not always see eye-to-eye, however, on the proper extent of hands-on involvement of Hull-House workers in their neighbors' lives. While Starr and Addams were having some difficulty sorting out what the Hull-House role would be in providing health care and other personal services to neighborhood women, Kelley out-voiced the vocal Starr on whether emphasis should be given to ameliorating individual need or working for broad-based social change. On one occasion, when Starr was leaving Hull-House to wash and dress the body of a neighborhood child who had recently died, Kelley reprimanded, "Sister Starr, if we [want to] bring about a change in this country peaceably, we've got to hustle. I believe it's a solemn duty to wash the dead, but it's mighty incidental!" (EGS to Mary Blaisdell, 25 July 1892, SC, Starr; also quoted in Sklar, *Florence Kelley*, 195; see also Starr's comments on "personal ministration to the sick and needy," child care, and education versus working for larger structural changes and political reform such as changes in laws regulating factories ["College Settlement Work," 2]).

Starr did not give up personal ministrations, however. Over the decades numerous neighborhood women in times of need—whether pregnant, mentally ill, or suffering from disfiguring illness—were housed temporarily on cots in her private quarters. Instead of concentrating on the reform aspects of legislation and regulation, she became directly engaged in union work, especially in organizing strike support. She was a charter member of the Illinois branch of the National Women's Trade Union League (WTUL) formed at Hull-House in 1903, and she was deeply involved in a series of textile worker strikes in 1896, 1910, and 1915 in Chicago. During the strikes she was a whirlwind of activity, "organizing mass meetings, collecting money, delivering flaming speeches, protesting to the mayor and to the newspapers, bringing clothing and food to the needy, and marching in the picket lines" (Davis, "Ellen Gates Starr," 353). Starr used invitations to lecture as chances to advocate trade unionism, telling audiences, "We must join hands with those in the labor movement—imperfect as it is—if we would accomplish social regeneration of the masses. There is need of the fostering of mutuality of interest in social organizations. Trades unionism to-day furnishes the best illustration of this feature of the work of ameliorating the condition not only of the wage-earners, but of those who are out of employment" (quoted in "Social Settlements: Miss Starr Says Join in the Labor Movement").

In writing of Starr's "aspirational, shining" demeanor, Addams's nephew and Hull-House resident James Weber Linn observed that she grew more and more ardent and vivid as she grew older: "Her interest in the unionization of women became intense. She concerned herself directly with strikes and women-strikers. She picketed. She harangued" (*Jane Addams*, 131). She also won added publicity for labor rights by having herself arrested. She was arrested in con-junction with the 1914 Henrici Restaurant strike, and, when defended by her friend Mary Wilmarth's son-in-law Harold Ickes, legal counsel for the WTUL, she turned the trial into a forum on the rights of women workers in the food industry. Ickes (1874–1952) was the second husband of Anna Wilmarth Thomp-son Ickes (1873–1935), a leader, along with Starr and Addams, in Chicago suf-frage, urban reform, and labor rights circles. She had often picketed beside Starr on WTUL picket lines and regularly posted bail for arrested demonstrators. Both Anna and Harold Ickes were involved with Addams in the formation of the Progressive Party. Anna became a Republican Illinois state legislator and advo-cate for Native American rights, and Harold became secretary of the interior in the Democratic Franklin D. Roosevelt administration.

When the Amalgamated Clothing Workers of America (ACWA) instigated a long strike in 1915, Starr, experienced and ready, was put in charge of picket lines. The strike, which began at the end of September 1915, included a conglom-eration of workers of several ethnicities employed at dozens of factories, cloth-ing stores, and tailor shops. Starr employed the tactic she had used on a very small scale in the Henrici strike and recruited many professional friends to walk the lines at the various locations. "[D]octors, lawyers, clergymen and profes-sors, as well as other social workers and residents at Hull House" came out and took stints marching with the strikers, attracting media attention in the process, and providing strikers with some measure of protection from violent interfer-ence from city police or private security hired by the manufacturers to break the strike" (Clark, "Ellen Gates Starr, O.S.B." 447). On October 12 the pickets were supported by a mass demonstration in which a "one-mile long parade, the majority women, marching four abreast, stretched along Chicago's streets" (Ahlbach, "To Be Catholic and Radical," 47).

More than eight thousand arrests were reportedly made during the course of the strike. Starr made frequent speeches decrying police brutality in the ar-rests and was herself arrested repeatedly. She befriended and worked closely during the strike with ACWA leaders Sidney Hillman (1887–1946) and Jacob Potofsky (1894–1979). At strike's end, Potofsky praised her energy in soliciting funds, arranging for relief and shelter for striking families, speaking at meetings and rallies, and stirring positive press coverage for the strikers in addition to organizing picket lines. As a tribute after the strike was over, the ACWA declared Starr an honorary life member.

It was during this time of intensive labor activism that Starr joined the Socialist Party and in 1916 ran for alderman of Chicago's Nineteenth Ward on the Socialist Party ticket. The 10 February 1940 *Chicago Daily News* reported that she "declared openly that she did not particularly want the job, explaining her candidacy on the grounds that 'there was no other Socialist in the ward to go on the ticket, and so I couldn't reasonably decline.'" During the campaign, in which she was defeated, she "declared that neither a woman nor a Socialist could be elected, explaining that she had become a candidate solely for 'educational' purposes" (*New York Times*, 10 Feb. 1940). A leaflet she produced for distribution during the campaign read "Vote for Ellen Gates Starr—April 4, 1916—and you will elect an alderman that will represent YOU and not private and public utility corporations" (J. Starr, "Notes," 9).

Starr wrote a personal campaign statement entitled "Why I Am a Socialist" for the "Daily Campaign Edition" of a local newspaper. In it, she referred to the influence of William Morris, who, she explained, had come to socialism through art but then departed from these roots in explaining her own allegiance to the Socialist Party. "I became a Socialist because I was a Christian," she explained succinctly. "The Christian religion," she went on to say, "teaches that all men are to be regarded as brothers, that no one should wish to profit by the loss or disadvantage of others; as all winners must do under a competitive system; that 'none should enjoy "two coats" while others are coatless[']; that, in effect, 'none should have cake till all have bread.'" What possibilities existed, Starr asked, "to abolish privilege, to stem the tide of concentrating wealth and power, steadily increasing and intensifying in the hands of a smaller and more terribly oppressive minority, while the majority increased in ratio and suffering[?]" The answer, for her, was support for the Socialist Party platform. "The Socialist Party proposed, without violence, quite lawfully, by the ballot, to tax away these preposterous aggregations of money and power," she wrote:

> It proposed that all necessary things should be made for the use of all, not for concentrating power over their fellow men in the hands of those few who control manufacture and distribution. It proposed to allow all who were able the opportunity to do these things for themselves. And those who were unable, through youth or age or feebleness, it proposed to care for in comfort and with respect. The methods were modern, practical, scientific, and peaceable. The object was such a society as Christian precept could be practiced in; even Christians admit that it is impossible under present conditions to carry out the teachings of Christ. (clipping, SC, Starr)

Starr's leftist allegiances and militant tactics, and her insistence on the importance of direct action and social activism, posed an increasing problem for

Jane Addams. Not only did these approaches not fit well with Addams's personality but they also contrasted with her carefully developed strategies. Addams's penchant for pragmatism, and for recognizing and working within gray areas, often by quietly power-brokering behind the scenes, was a source of irritation to Ellen Gates Starr, who saw the world as much more black and white. As Linn explained, "there arose a militancy in her that found tolerance difficult, and welcome to certain ideas almost distasteful" (*Jane Addams*, 132). To Starr, Addams's perspective was filled with compromise. "Jane if the devil himself came riding down Halsted Street with his tail waving out behind him," she once exclaimed in exasperation, "you'd say 'what a beautiful curve he has in his tail'" (quoted in Davis, *American Heroine*, 115).

During the World War I era Starr became increasingly detached from Hull-House matters, and somewhere between 1918 and 1920 (ironically, at the height of Addams's international organizing for peace, when public outcry about her radicalism was at its highest) she ended her long connection as a resident. She and Addams were still cordial, however, and she continued to visit Hull-House periodically until late 1929. After that, when Starr had become chronically ill and was no longer able to travel, Addams visited her several times a year. Starr continued, during these visits, to serve as a personal consultant as Addams mulled over Hull-House affairs.

Although the women remained dear to one another, the close partnership they had enjoyed in the founding of Hull-House was diluted over time by their friendships with others, especially by the arrival of Mary Rozet Smith into Jane Addams's life. Starr, on her part, counted among her many friends and political/spiritual soulmates Mary Wilmarth, Vida Scudder, and Frances Crane Lillie.

Mary Hawes Wilmarth (1837–1919) was one of the original trustees of Hull-House, a supporter of suffrage, president of the Fortnightly Club and of the Illinois branch of the Consumers' League, and delegate, along with Jane Addams, to the Progressive National Convention in 1912. She had wanted to come to Hull-House as a resident but was prevented from doing so by her wealthy family's disapproval. Instead, she became a volunteer teacher and an important patron of the settlement—and of Starr in particular. She worked out an arrangement by which Starr lived in the Hull-House duplex apartment Wilmarth had planned and furnished for herself. Starr also received a small stipend that Wilmarth supplied to support Starr's political activities. In addition to funding Starr's training as a bookbinder and her 1916 campaign for alderman, Wilmarth also was on call for such incidents as Starr's arrest during labor strikes, whether to post bail or secure a lawyer.

In many ways Vida Scudder and Starr led parallel lives. Scudder (1861–1954) was a professor of English at Wellesley College and a founder of the College Settlements Association in the Boston area. She was, like Starr, active in a lay order of the Episcopalian church and the Socialist Party, an activist with the WTUL, and a leader in promoting feminist and Christian Socialist thought. Charles

H. A. Wager (1869–1939), a professor of English at Oberlin College, and Elizabethean scholar Eleanor Grace Clark (b. 1895), who earned her Ph.D. from Bryn Mawr in 1928, were two more of Starr's friends who shared a love of poetry and literature with her as well as interests in labor and religion. Frances Crane Lillie (1869–1958) was Starr's best friend between 1906 and 1940 and shared her spiritual and political convictions. She was married to Frank Rattray Lillie (1870–1947), a biologist on the faculty at the University of Chicago and a chief researcher at the Marine Biological Laboratory at Wood's Hole, Massachusetts. Starr was a frequent guest in the Lillies' home in Chicago and during the summers at Cape Cod and became godmother to one of their daughters. Lillie joined Starr in shifting her religious affiliation from the Anglican to the Roman Catholic Church, and the Lillies did much to help support Starr financially as she grew older.

In the process of moving from the Anglican to the Roman Catholic Church, Starr had several close spiritual guides and friends, among them was the Rev. James O. S. Huntington (1854–1935), founder of the Order of the Holy Cross, who was very interested in the idea of reviving "monasticism as a means of achieving social reform" (Chrisman, "To Bind Together," 8). Huntington, a leader in the Anglican Catholic branch of the Episcopal Church, led Starr in 1894 to membership in the Society of the Companions of the Holy Cross (SCHC). Founded in Boston in 1884 by friends Emily M. Morgan and Adelyn Howard, the SCHC was an Anglican lay order that focused on intercessory prayer, the building of spiritual community among women, social justice, and simple, communal forms of living. Admirers of the teachings of St. Francis, members of the order encouraged simplicity in material things and the development of "religious discipline as a way of life" (8). The lay order was closely allied in its membership with supporters of the settlement-house movement. Several members were residents or volunteers at settlements, and, like many settlement-house workers, a good proportion of the Companions were unmarried, college-educated, women. The lay order supported women in the workforce and the professions as well as the cause of labor generally. In policy statements issued over the years, Companions voiced support for strikes and boycotts, guilds, and trade unions. Membership grew internationally, and several Companions were involved abroad in helping run medical missions and schools. The order attracted as members teachers, nurses, physicians, social workers, and women in the arts and law. Starr helped found the Chicago–Midwest Chapter of the Companions in 1901, and in the early 1900s she often attended retreats at the Companions' communal residence, Adelynrood, in South Byfield, Massachusetts.

Starr had become increasingly disenchanted with the official policies of the Episcopal Church, the minority status of Anglican Catholics within the church, and the lack of commitment of the church to social justice issues. In 1919 she began an active quest for spiritual guidance from a series of Roman Catholic advisors, and in the spring of 1920 she officially converted to Catholicism. She was baptized into the church on 2 March 1920 at the Benedictine Abbey in St.

Benedict, Louisiana, and took her first Holy Communion as a Catholic the next day. She was later confirmed in the church on May 23 in the Holy Name Cathedral in Chicago.

The beginning of Starr's official life as a Catholic was also the end of her long affiliation as a resident of Hull-House. Her militancy on both things political and things religious had increasingly alienated her from other residents, many of whom were liberal Protestants who neither embraced direct individual political action nor were particularly open to spiritual practices outside a middle-class Protestant tradition. There were also deeper, spiritual, personal reasons. Starr wanted to focus on a directed devotional life. As she confided to Charles Wager early in 1920, she feared "Inertia," the "Tendency to remain where one is," that "Disturbing sense of stability," and, she added jokingly, "(The sense of stability at this writing is profoundly disturbed)!" The bottom line, she confessed, was "a longing for peace for the last [years] of life; to cease pulling against the stream and to go with one's impulse and inclination" (4 Jan. 1920, SC, Starr; also quoted in Alhbach, "To Be Catholic and Radical," 57).

Like her aunt before her, Starr began writing for Catholic publications. She focused during the 1920s on topics in sacred art, shrines, cathedrals, and devotional literature. She also continued to travel and visit scores of friends—including those at Hull-House—when she was able, but she was increasingly hampered by physical disability. She was in and out of hospitals in New York and Chicago, although she conducted herself with her former vigor between hospitalizations. "In later years," Josephine Starr remembered, "she dressed entirely in purples and lavenders all of which blended delightfully into one another" and wore a hat made of a brim "with a purple veil which streamed out behind with her rapid advance. One of the last times I saw her active (within a month she was paralyzed from the waist down) [ca. December 1929] was when meeting a family in sorrow from a death, she all but flew down the La Salle Street station platform, the purple wings behind her, her little feet skimming the ground" (J. Starr, "Notes," 6).

Although Starr was plagued by declining health during the last decade of her life, it was also a period often characterized by serenity. In 1929 she was struck by partial paralysis while on a visit to Hull-House. Taken to Billings Hospital, she underwent an operation for a tubercular abscess on her spine. The surgery did not go well. Parts of two vertebrae were removed in the process of excising the tumor, and, although her physicians expected her to regain the ability to walk, there was permanent damage. In extreme pain, Starr spent months recovering, first at a Maryknoll convent, then at an orthopedic hospital in New York, and finally for a few weeks at Eleanor Grace Clark's New York apartment. It was Clark who suggested that she move to the Convent of the Holy Child, a Benedictine school and convent in Suffern, New York. Starr took up residence there in 1930 and lived at the convent for the rest of her life. She was supported by a small pension from Hull-House arranged by Jane Addams and supplemented by monthly allotments from two private sources, one of which was the Lillie family.

Wheelchair-bound and wearing a steel and leather brace designed for her by her doctors, she enjoyed the yard at the convent, drew, and taught painting and pastels to the sisters. She lived in a small room wallpapered in orchid, her Aunt Eliza's crucifix on the wall. She attended mass and greeted a steady stream of visitors, including Addams, Frances Crane Lillie, and churchmen from the House of Blessed Sacrament Fathers down the road.

News of Addams's death from cancer in May 1935 devastated Starr. She spent the day alone in anguished seclusion in the convent chapel and emerged to plan a requiem mass in her lifelong friend's memory. When asked to write a statement to be read at the 2 June 1935 tribute to Addams sponsored by the National Federation of Settlements, she focused on the contribution Addams had made in "her work for peace, in war time," the bravery that doing so had entailed, and the "friends swept away" and estranged without Addams knowing that in time some would return and that her public reputation would have a renaissance. Starr was glad that her dear friend had withdrawn from the scene of life "in a blaze of glory amidst the plaudits of the world, on the occasion of the anniversary of her founding an international peace society." This "dramatic justice" was "not too much," Starr observed. "She has earned it" ("Memorial statement"). Starr herself was feted much more quietly four years later on the occasion of her eightieth birthday. Greeted at the convent by friends old and new, she received many letters from "Hull House neighbors who remembered and told what she had been to them" (J. Starr, "Notes," 11).

Ellen Gates Starr died on the tenth day of February 1940 at the Convent of the Holy Child. She was eighty-one. A requiem mass was held for her at the convent chapel, and she was buried in the convent cemetery. Back home in Chicago, a memorial for Starr was held on Wednesday afternoon, 8 May 1940, at the Hull-House Theatre.

Bibliography

This bibliography is divided into eight categories: "Unpublished Documents, Clippings, and Individual Manuscripts"; "Printed and Manuscript Sources of Genealogy and Vital Statistics, and Government Records, Reports, and Returns"; "Artifact and Rare Books Collections"; "Photograph Collections"; "Directories, Published Minutes, and Annual Catalogs"; "Newspapers and Magazines"; "Journal and Magazine Articles and Chapters from Books"; and "Books." For a bibliography of the writings and speeches of Jane Addams, consult Mary Lynn McCree Bryan, Nancy Slote, and Maree De Angury, *The Jane Addams Papers: A Comprehensive Guide* (1996). For a full list of symbols for manuscript collections and repositories, see pages xlix–lii of this volume.

1. Unpublished Documents, Clippings, and Individual Manuscripts

[Addams], Anna Hostetter. "Memories. Diary Book beginning on January 1st A.D. 1846 by Ann Hostetter in the 17teenth year of her age, Mount Carroll, Carroll County, Illinois." 1846[–62]. AMsS, 180 pp., JAPP, DeLoach.

Addams, Jane. "[Account Book for Estate of Mary Catherine Addams Linn]." 1894–97. AD, 242 pp., UIC, JAMC; *JAPM*, 27:883–944.

———. "[Address Book, 1883–98]." H and ADS, 122 pp., SCPC, JAC; *JAPM*, 27:1150–1209.

———. "[Address on Illinois Geography]." 26 May [1878]. AMsS, 8 pp., UIC, JAMC, Detzer; *JAPM*, 45:1779–87.

———. "Affirmative. Resolved; that the French women have had more influence through literature than polotics. Rep. women. George Sand and Mdé Dé Staël." [ca. 13 Nov. 1878.] AMsS, 16 pp., UIC, JAMC, Detzer; *JAPM*, 45:1795–1807.

———. "An Allogory." n.d. [ca. 1877–81.] AMsS, 7 pp., UIC, JAMC, Detzer; *JAPM*, 45:1603–8.

———. "Analysis of Lecture II [on Christianity]." [ca. 1881.] AMsS, 4 pp., UIC, JAMC, Detzer; *JAPM*, 46:86–89.

———. "Βελλεροφόντης" (Bellerophon). [Spring 1880.] AMsS, 6 pp., UIC, JAMC, Detzer; *JAPM*, 46:90–94; another AMs version in Addams, "Pocket Diary, 1875[–81]," printed dates 3–5 and 8–14 July 1875 [written 1880?], CAHS; *JAPM*, 28:1591–92, 28:1594–97.

———. "Blindness is preferable to deafness." 5 Jan. 1878. AMsS, 8 pp., UIC, JAMC, Detzer, *JAPM*, 45:1708–14.

———. "Caesar's Commentaries on the Gallic War. As translated by Jane Addams. Book I from Chapter I to XLV." Cedarville, Ill., Oct. 1876. AMsS, 84 pp., RC; *JAPM*, 27:20–65.

———. "Caesar's Commentaries on the Gallic War. As translated by Jane Addams. From Bk. I Chap. XLV to Bk[.] III, Chap. VIII." Cedarville, Ill., May 1877. AMsS, 78 pp., RC; *JAPM*, 27:66–106.

———. "Caesar's Commentaries on the Gallic War. As translated by Jane Addams. From Bk[.] IV Chap. XXVII to [Chap. XXXVI]." [Cedarville, Ill., 1877.] AMsS, 12 pp., RC; *JAPM*, 27:107–13.

———. "Cassandra." [ca. May-June 1881.] AMs, 11 pp., and AMs fragments, 1 p., 14 pp., 2 pp., UIC, JAMC, Detzer; *JAPM*, 46:317–48.

———. "The Chivalry of Study" (editorial). [ca. Feb. 1880.] AMs, 6 pp., UIC, JAMC, Detzer; *JAPM*, 46:164–69.

———. "Cicero and Caesar." 10 Nov. 1879. AMsS, 13 pp., UIC, JAMC, Detzer; *JAPM*, 46:62–75.

———. "Compilers." 1881. AMsS, 9 pp., UIC, JAMC, Detzer; *JAPM*, 46:272–79.

———. "Conservatism of the Japanese." 12 Jan. 1880. AMsS, 5 pp., UIC, JAMC, Detzer; *JAPM*, 46:149–54.

———. "[Copybook, 1878–May 1879]." AMs, SCPC; *JAPM*, 27:147–71.

———. [Correspondents, 1877.] AMs, 1 p., CAHS; *JAPM*, 27:139.

———. "Darkness versus Nebulae." 14 June 1880. AMsS, 8 pp., UIC, JAMC, Detzer; *JAPM*, 46:207–15.

———. "Dress." 15 Mar. 1878. AMsS, 8 pp., UIC, JAMC, Detzer; *JAPM*, 45:1729–35, and 2d version, 45:1736–44.

———. "[1880 Notebook]." 1880[–82]. AMs, 41 pp., SCPC; *JAPM*, 27:352–77.

———. "[Essay on the Biblical Prophets]." [ca. 1880–81.] AMsS, fragment, 4 pp., UIC, JAMC, Detzer; *JAPM*, 46:96–98.

———. "[Essay on Johann Wolfgang von Göethe]." [ca. 1879?] AMs, 4 pp., UIC, JAMC, Detzer; *JAPM*, 45:1610–13.

———. "[Essay on Walpurgis Night]." [ca. 1 May 1880?] AMs, fragment, 10 pp., UIC, JAMC, Detzer; *JAPM*, 45:1614–21.

———. "[Fable]." [1877–78?] AMs, 2 pp., UIC, JAMC, Detzer; *JAPM*, 45:1578–80.

———. "Fear—as a conservative Element." 22 Nov. 1879. AMsS, 7 pp., UIC, JAMC, Detzer; *JAPM*, 46:76–82, and 2d version, 7 Jan. 1880, AMs, 7 pp.; *JAPM*, 46:141–48.

———. "'Follow thou thy Star.'" 26 Feb. 1879. AMsS, 7 pp., UIC, JAMC, Detzer; *JAPM*, 45:1831–37.

———. "George Eliot's view of Savonarola." n.d. [ca. 1877–81.] AMs, 1 p., UIC, JAMC, Detzer; *JAPM*, 45:1622–23.

———. "The Gipsies of Romance. Meg Merrilies thier queen." ca. 15 Oct. 1879. AMsS, 8 pp., UIC, JAMC, Detzer; *JAPM*, 46:40–48, and 2d version, 9 pp., *JAPM*, 46:49–56.

———. "Guy Mannering." [ca. 15 Oct. 1879.] AMs, 2 pp., UIC, JAMC, Detzer; *JAPM*, 27:339–40.

———. "Hannibal." [ca. 1877–81.] AMsS, 8 pp., UIC, JAMC, Detzer; *JAPM*, 45:1624–30.

———. "'High trees take the wind.'" [ca. 1877–81.] AMsS, 5 pp., UIC, JAMC, Detzer; *JAPM*, 45:1631–35.

———. *The Jane Addams Papers* edited by Mary Lynn McCree Bryan et al. Ann Arbor: University Microfilms International, 1985–86. Microfilm, 82 reels, with published guide.

———. "The McBeth of Shakespeare." [ca. Jan. 1880.] AMsS, 10 pp., UIC, JAMC, Detzer; *JAPM*, 46:128–36.

———. "The Magnificence of Character." 5 Oct. 1880. AMsS, 8 pp., UIC, JAMC, Detzer; *JAPM*, 46:219–25.

———. "The Nebular Hypothesis." 28 Jan. 1880. AMsS, 10 pp., UIC, JAMC, Detzer; *JAPM*, 46:155–63.

———. "The night hath Stars (To develope the imagination)." 20 Feb. 1878. AMsS, 7 pp., UIC, JAMC, Detzer; *JAPM*, 45:1722–28.

———. "The Notion of Conscience." [ca. 1881.] AMsS, 4 pp., UIC, JAMC, Detzer; *JAPM*, 46:99–103.

———. "The Office of Rivers." 24 Nov. 1877. AMsS, 7 pp., UIC, JAMC, Detzer; *JAPM*, 45:1677–83.

———. "[Opening Address at the Junior Exhibition, RFS]." [ca. Mar. 1880.] AMs, 2 pp., UIC, JAMC, Detzer; *JAPM*, 46:198 200.

———. "Our debts; and how shall we pay them." [ca. 1880.] AMs (fragment?), 9 pp., UIC, JAMC, Detzer; *JAPM*, 46:104–12.

———. "Paris—The Perfect Gentleman (The law of beauty opposed to force)." 4 Feb. 1881. AMsS, 12 pp., UIC, JAMC, Detzer; *JAPM*, 46:295–304.

———. "The Passion of revenge and mercy as a producing element in Literature." [1880–81?] AMsS, 7 pp., UIC, JAMC, Detzer; *JAPM*, 46:113–19.

———. "Plated Ware." Jan. 1878. AMsS, 8 pp., and fragment, AMsS, 2 pp., UIC, JAMC, Detzer: *JAPM*, 45:1697–1707.

———. "Pocket Diary, 1875[–81]; Published for the Trade." [ca. 1875–81.] AMs, PD. [Blank book pages printed with 1875 dates; A entries written ca. 1875–81.] 371 pp., CAHS; *JAPM*, 28:1483–1671.

———. "Poppy." [1878.] AMsS, 6 pp., UIC, JAMC, Detzer; *JAPM*, 45:1691–96.

———. "The Present Policy of Congress." 5 Dec. 1877. AMsS, 7 pp., UIC, JAMC, Detzer; *JAPM*, 45:1684–90.

———. "Proverbs." 28 May 1878. AMsS, 6 pp., UIC, JAMC, Detzer; *JAPM*, 45:1788–94.

———. "'Quid sum quia cogito' (What I think, that I am)." [ca. 1877–81.] AMsS, 9 pp., UIC, JAMC, Detzer; *JAPM*, 45:1636–43.

———. "Report [Account] Book, [1879–80]." AMs, PD [Blank book by H. H. Waldo, Co., Rockford, Ill; with A entries.] RC; *JAPM*, 27:320–32.

———. "Resolved. The Civilization of the 19" cent. tends to fetter intellectual life and Expression. Aff." 18 Feb. 1880. AMsS, 6 pp., UIC, JAMC, Detzer; *JAPM*, 46:180–85.

———. "Resolved. That French women have had more influence through literature than polotics. Rep. women. George Sand and M'de dè Staël." [13 Apr. 1880?] AMs, 10 pp., UIC, JAMC, Detzer; *JAPM*, 45:1808–18.

———. "Resolved. That French women have had a wider influence through literature than polotics. Representative Women. George Sand and M'de De Staël." n.d. AMs, fragment, 4 pp., UIC, JAMC, Detzer; *JAPM*, 45:1819–23.

————. "Resolved: 'That the British form of government tends to develope better statesmen than the American form.' Aff." 19 Nov. 1880. AMs, 12 pp., UIC, JAMC, Detzer; *JAPM*, 46:253–62.

————. "Resolved; that the invention & use of machinery is a hinderance to the increase of wealth in a country." [ca. Apr. 1879?] AMsS, 10 pp., UIC, JAMC, Detzer; *JAPM*, 45:1644–52.

————. "Resolved[:] that the Ornamental branches are necessary to a Complete Education. negative." Feb. 1878. AMsS, 8 pp., UIC, JAMC, Detzer; *JAPM*, 45:1715–21.

————. "Savonarola." n.d. [ca. 1877–81.] AMs, 8 pp., UIC, JAMC, Detzer; *JAPM*, 45:1653–61.

————. "Self Tradition." 2 Nov. 1880. AMsS, 12 pp., and [ca. 2 Nov. 1880], AMs fragments, 2 pp., 2 pp., 5 pp., 2 pp., UIC, JAMC, Detzer; *JAPM*, 46:229–52.

————. "Slavery—an Allogory." 24 Mar. [1879?] AMsS, 8 pp., UIC, JAMC, Detzer; *JAPM*, 46:1–7.

————. "[Statement on John H. Addams]." n.d. AMs, 1 p., UIC, JAMC, Detzer.

————. "The study of Nature." [June 1879.] AMsS, 5 pp., UIC, JAMC, Detzer; *JAPM*, 46:24–29.

————. "Teeth." [ca. 1877–81.] AMsS, 9 pp., UIC, JAMC, Detzer; *JAPM*, 45:1662–69.

————. "Tramps." 10 Apr. 1878. AMsS, 6 pp., UIC, JAMC, Detzer; *JAPM*, 45:1757–62.

————. "Unknown Quantities." 15 May 1878. AMsS, 7 pp., SCPC; *JAPM*, 45:1772–78.

————. "[Valedictory.]" At Rockford Female Seminary. [ca. 22 June 1881.] AMs, 14 pp. and AMs fragment, 2 pp., UIC, JAMC, Detzer; *JAPM*, 46:366–80, 363–65.

————. "The Village Schoolmaster." 1 Nov. 1877. AMsS, 7 pp., UIC, JAMC, Detzer; *JAPM*, 45:1670–75.

————. "'We miss the abstract when we comprehend.'" 6 Jan. 1879. AMsS, 7 pp., UIC, JAMC, Detzer; *JAPM*, 45:1824–30.

————, and others. "The Origin of Chess." [Apr. 1878.] AMs, 4 pp., UIC, JAMC, Detzer; *JAPM*, 45:1745–49.

[Addams, Jane, and Marcet Haldeman]. "[Haldeman, (Mrs.) Sarah Alice (Addams)]," [ca. Mar. 1915?]. (Likely prepared for *Cyclopedia of American Biography* 8 [1918], pp. 279–81.) TMs with A annotations, 5 pp., JAPP, DeLoach.

Addams, John Huy. "Journal of John H. Addams." Vol. 1, 28 June–Sept. 7, 1844, ADS, 123 pp.; vol 2., 8 Sept.–19 Dec., 1844, ADS, 118 pp., SCPC, JAC.

Addams, John Weber. "Fetching the Cows." n.d. AMsS, 2 pp., JAPP, Hulbert.

————. "Res. That Woman should be allowed the right of suffrage. Negative." 21 May 1870. AMsS, 10 pp., JAPP, Hulbert.

————. [Promissory notes to Jane Addams.] 5 May 1899 and 12 Sept. 1900. ADS, 2 pp., UIC, JAMC; *JAPM*, 27:1144–5.

[Addams, Sarah Weber, obituary.] *Deutscher Anzeiger* (Freeport, Ill.), 21 Jan. 1863. PD, clipping, photocopy, JAPP.

Ahlbach, Mary F. "To Be Catholic and Radical: A Study of Three Catholic Laywomen: Ellen Gates Starr, Margaret Foley, and Dorothy Day." M.A. Thesis, Graduate Theological Union and Franciscan School of Theology, Berkeley, Calif., 1987.

Alderson, Helen Harrington. "The Memoirs of Helen Harrington Alderson." n.d. TMs, RC.

"Annie Ellers Bunker, '81, Dies Last Fall in Korea." *Rockford College Alumna* 15, no. 2 (Mar. 1939): 24. PD, clipping, RC.

"Art for the School Children: Public Education Association Learns What Has Been Accomplished in Chicago." Unidentified newspaper, ca. Jan. 1897. PD, clipping, SC, Starr.

[Articles of Agreement between Dr. Simonton and Dr. Haldeman.] 23 Aug. 1878. HD in hand of S. Alice Haldeman, 4 pp., UIC, JAMC, HJ.

Birthday Fete in Honor of Mark Hopkins, L.L.D., Feb. 4, 1802.–Feb. 4, 1881, Compliments of Class Officers to Class 1881. Senior Parlors. 4 Feb. 1881. PD [printed invitation and Bill of Fare], 4 pp., UIC, JAMC; *JAPM,* 27:414–15.

"Books in Addams Home Were Part of Pioneer Community Library." *Freeport* (Ill.) *Journal-Standard.* n.d. PD, clipping, JAPP.

Bosch, Jennifer Lynne. "The Life of Ellen Gates Starr, 1859–1940." Ph.D. diss., Miami University, Coral Gables, Fla., 1990.

Bowman, Anna Martha. "The Diary of Anna Martha Bowman, Mount Carroll Seminary, Room No. 27." 1862–[83]. TMs, 26 pp., UIC, JAMC, HJ.

Brace, Julia Eastman. "Sidelights on Life of Jane Addams as Related by Her First Teacher." *Freeport* (Ill.) *Journal-Standard,* 13 Jan. 1932. PD, clipping, photocopy, JAPP.

Brauer, Gerald J. "A Manual for Guides at the Ellwood House: The Mansion Tour." 1998. TMS, 22 pp., Ellwood House Museum, De Kalb, Ill.

Brief Libretto of Junior Exhibition [Rockford Female Seminary], 20 Apr. 1880. PD [printed program], 8 pp., RC; *JAPM,* 27:384–87.

Brush, Mary Isabel. "John W. Gates Tells How Col. El[l]wood and His Wife Made World's First Barbed Wire with a Coffee Mill." *Chicago Tribune,* 18 Sept. 1910. PD, clipping, Ellwood House Museum, De Kalb, Ill.

Carrell, Elizabeth Hutcheson. "Reflections in a Mirror: The Progressive Woman and the Settlement Experience." 2 vols. Ph. D. diss., University of Texas at Austin, 1981.

Castalian Society Programme, Chapel, October 10, 1879. PD [printed program], 1 p., UIC, JAMC; *JAPM,* 27:336.

"Catherine Waugh McCulloch" [obituary] Unidentified newspaper, ca. 20 Apr. 1945. PD, clipping, RC, McCulloch Vertical File.

Cedarborg, Hazel Paris. "The Early History of Rockford College." M.A. thesis, Wellesley College, Mass., 1926.

Cedar Creek Bible Society. "[Resolution on death of John H. Addams]." 30 July 1882. HDS, 2 pp., SCPC, JAC.

Cedarville, Ill., Public School. "Report for the Month Ending June 9, 1875." PD, 1 p., UIC, JAMC, Smith; *JAPM,* 27:19.

"Cedarville 'A Day in the Village.'" Walking tour booklet. [Cedarville, Ill.?]: N.p, 1 Oct. 1977. Mimeograph, JAPP.

"Chocolate Creams." n.d. HD, 1 p. and cover. *JAPM,* 27:145–46.

Chrisman, Miriam U. "To Bind Together: A Brief History of the Society of the Companions of the Holy Cross." n.d., n.p. TMs, 92 pp., photocopy, JAPP.

"City Loses a Leader." *Freeport* (Ill.) *Weekly Bulletin,* 21 June 1901. PD, clipping, photocopy, JAPP.

Class Song [Rockford Female Seminary Class of '81], Apr. 1880. PD [printed program], UIC, JAMC; *JAPM,* 27:380.

"Collegiate Contest: Miss Kittie Waugh the Successful Contestant in the Oratorical Exercises at the Seminary." Unidentified Rockford newspaper, ca. June 1881. PD, clipping, Anna P. Sill, "Scrapbook," RC.

"The Correspondence of Rollin D. Salisbury with Horace Spencer Fiske, Beloit College, 1882." 1880–1892. TMs, ca. 168 pp. [AMsS correspondence transcribed by Helen Louisa (Drew) Richardson, 1940], BC.

"C. R. Mower Dies at Home Early Today." *Rockford* (Ill.) *Gazette*, 19 Oct. 1927. PD, clipping, photocopy, JAPP.

Dean, Erma Mae Sawtell. "The First Hundred Years Are the Hardest: The History of the Chicago-Midwest Chapter of the Society of the Companions of the Holy Cross." July 1983. TMs, gift of Beverly Scott to the Archives of the Diocese of Chicago; photocopy, JAPP.

"Death Calls Mary E. Holmes." Unidentified Rockford newspaper, ca. 13 Feb. 1906. PD, clipping, Presbyterian Church (U.S.A.), Department of History, Philadelphia, Pa.

"Death of Col. H. C. Forbes." *Tri-County Press* (Polo, Ill.), 15 Jan. 1908. PD, clipping, photocopy, JAPP.

"Death of John H. Addams." *Lena* (Ill.) *Star*, 19 Aug. 1881. PD, clipping, photocopy, JAPP.

"Death of Miss Rebecca Rice." *Yellow Springs* (Ohio) *News*, 5 May 1911. PD, clipping, photocopy, JAPP.

"Death Was Sudden" [J. Brown Taylor obituary]. *Freeport* (Ill.) *Daily Democrat*, 24 Feb. 1897. PD, clipping, photocopy, JAPP.

"Degree Conferred on Mrs. Douglas [Corrine Williams Douglas] by Illinois School." *Atlanta Journal*, [ca. 14 June 1930]. PD, clipping, RC, Williams Vertical File.

"A Discussion about Art: Stories to Illustrate the Need of It in City Schools." *Evening Post* (New York), 16 Jan. 1897. PD, clipping, SC, Starr.

[Downs, Mary B., obituary.] *Oak Leaves* (Oak Park, Ill.), 9 May 1940. PD, clipping, JAPP.

[Downs, Mary B., obituary.] *Rockford* [College] *Alumna*, 17 (Nov. 1940). PD, clipping, RC.

"Dr. W. H. Haldeman Dead." Unidentified newspaper, 20 Mar. 1905. PD, clipping, IU, Lilly, SAAH.

"Ellen G. Starr, Cofounder of Hull House, Dies." *Chicago Daily News*, 10 Feb. 1940. PD, clipping, SC, Starr.

"Ellen Starr, Co-founder of Hull House, Dies." *Chicago Times*, 11 Feb. 1940. PD, clipping, SC, Starr.

"Ellen Starr, Co-founder of Hull House, Dies." *New York Times*, [ca. 10 Feb. 1940]. PD, clipping, SC, Starr.

"Elizabeth S. Kirkland, 1828–96." n.d. TMs, 3 pp., JAPP.

Farrell, James T. "James Weber Linn—a Memoir." *Chicago*, Oct. 1955, PD 2pp., JAPP.

"The Final Farewell" [Carrie Hood obituary]. Unidentified Rockford newspaper, 28 Mar. 1883. PD, clipping, Anna P. Sill, "Scrapbook," RC.

"Four Generations of the Ellwood Family." *A Walk through Ellwood House*. [ca. 1964?], 4. PD [pamphlet guide], Ellwood House Museum, De Kalb, Ill.

Freeport, Ill., Bankers. "[Resolution on Death of John H. Addams]." 19 Aug. 1881. HDS, 3 pp., SCPC, JAC.

Giovangelo, Florence. "Miss Starr, Godly Light in the Dark Lives of the Poor." SC, Starr.

Grade cards [for Jane Addams], Cedarville, Ill., Public School, 1870–75. HD, 6 cards. CAHS; *JAPM*, 27:13–18.

Grade cards [for Jane Addams], Rockford Female Seminary, 1878–81. HD, 58 cards. SCHS.

Haldeman, George Bowman. "Account Book, 1875–76." A and HD, 26 pp., IU, Lilly, SAAH.

———. Beloit College Essays and Orations, 1878–82. JAPP, DeLoach.

———. "The College Hermit." 5 May 1881 for 21 May 1881 oration. AMsS, 8 pp., JAPP, DeLoach.

———. "G.B.H. Things of Interest in Madison Wis." Drawings, [summer? 1873]. ADS, CAHS; *JAPM*, 27: 5–6.

———. "The Science of Almanacs Association." 27 Dec. 1873. AMsS, 1 p., CAHS; *JAPM*, 27:7.

Haldeman, Henry Winfield. "Poems an Luella von Heinrich—1898 (Poems to Luella from Henry)." Written by Henry Winfield Haldeman between Dec. 1897 and Sept. 1898 and copied in the hand of Luella Totten. HMs bound in leather, photocopy, 58 pp., JAPP, DeLoach.

[Haldeman, Henry Winfield, obituary.] *Girard* (Kans.) *News,* 20 Mar. 1905. PD, clipping, JAPP, DeLoach.

[Haldeman, Henry Winfield], "Obituary." Unidentified publication, ca. Mar. 1905. PD, clipping, 1 p., JAPP, DeLoach.

Haldeman, Marcet. [Correspondence and writings from the copy books of Sarah Alice Addams Haldeman, her mother], 26 vols. (1904–13). HMs, UIC, JAMC, HJ.

Haldeman, Sarah Alice. "[Account Book, 1881]." AMs, UIC, JAMC; *JAPM*, 27:687–707.

———. "[Address Book]." [ca. 1910–15.] AD, 118 pp., UIC, JAMC, HJ.

———. Birthdays of family and friends entered by date. [ca. 1890–1915.] In *The Whittier Birthday-Book.* Arranged by Elizabeth S. Owen. Boston: Houghton, Mifflin and Co., [1881]. HD, photocopy, 402 pp., JAPP.

———. "[Catalog of the Library of Sarah Alice Addams Haldeman] Note Book No. 64." n.d. AMsS, 72 pp., JAPP, DeLoach.

———. [Note Book, Addresses and Gift Lists], [ca. 1904–11]. AD, 55 pp., UIC, JAMC, HJ.

Haldeman-Julius, Marcet. "Two Mothers of Jane Addams." n.d. TMs, 18 pp., SCPC, JAC.

Hostetter, Abrm. "A father's advice to his daughter." n.d. HMsS, 3 pp., JAPP, AHHA.

[Hostetter, Charles Linneaus.] "Aunt Ann's Discription of Pittsburg Fire." 6 Nov. 1909. TMs, 2 pp., JAPP, DeLoach.

———. [Notes from a conversation with Anna Hostetter Haldeman Addams.] 15 Nov. 1914. TMs, 1 p., JAPP, Hostetter Family Genealogy File.

[Hostetter, Charles Linneaus, and Ross Hostetter.] "[Hostetter Family]." n.d. TMs, photocopy, 42 pp., JAPP, Hostetter Genealogy File.

Hostetter, Sarah. "Few Reminiscences of Jane Addams Home and Girlhood." [1916?] AMsI, 16 pp., JAPP, Schneider.

———. "[Reminiscences]." [ca. 1920.] TMs, transcript, produced by David Alexander Sandberg from manuscript written by his mother, Harriet Hostetter Burquist Sandberg, and dictated by Sarah Hostetter. Feb. 1969. Photocopy, 12 pp., JAPP, Hostetter Family Genealogy File.

Hulbert, Esther Margaret Linn. "Autobiography of an Unknown." Notes. n.d. AMs, 16 pp., JAPP, Hulbert.

Hull-House Association. Hull-House Scrapbook. 3 vols., 1889–97. PD [scrapbook of clippings and documents]. UIC, JAMC, HH Assn.; *JAPM*, Addendum 10.

"In Memoriam. Elizabeth Stansbury Kirkland, Died July 30, 1896." Chicago, Ill. Read before a special meeting of the Kirkland Association, 3 Dec. 1896. [Chicago, 1896.] PD, CHS.

"In Memoriam: Mary Ellwood Lewis." [De Kalb, Ill.?]: First Congregational Church, De Kalb, Ill., 1904. PD, Ellwood House Museum, De Kalb, Ill.

"Intellectual Treat: Miss Ellen G. Starr Will Lecture Here Next Week." Unidentified Detroit newspaper, n.p., n.d. PD, clipping, SC, Starr.

"In the Tomb" [Joseph Marcus Beck obituary]. *Fort Madison* (Iowa) *Evening Democrat*, 6 June 1893. PD, clipping, photocopy, JAPP.

"Isaac Leonard Ellwood . . . Death Last Evening." *De Kalb* (Ill.) *Chronicle*, 12 Sept. 1910, PD, clipping, Ellwood House Museum, De Kalb, Ill.

"James Alcott" [obituary]. *Rockford* (Ill.) *Register*, June 1883. PD, clipping, Anna P. Sill, "Scrapbook," RC.

"James Griswold Merrill: Pastor-Friend." n.d. TMs, Merrill Papers, Special Collections, Fisk University, Nashville, Tenn.

"James W. Linn Will Be Buried at Cedarville." *Freeport* (Ill.) *Journal-Standard*, [ca. 17 July 1939]. PD, clipping, JAPP.

"James Weber Linn." Editorial. *Freeport* (Ill.) *Journal-Standard*, [ca. July 1939]. PD, clipping, JAPP.

Jewett, Milo P. "Origin of Vassar College." Mar. 1879. TMs, Vassar College Archive, Poughkeepsie, N.Y.

"John L. Capen, M.D., Phrenologist." Broadside. Philadelphia: [John L. Capen], n.d., 1 p., College of Physicians of Philadelphia, Pa.

"[John Manning Linn Preaches Last Sermon in Geneseo, Illinois]." *Geneseo* (Ill.) *Republic*, 5 June 1891. PD, clipping, IU, Lilly, SAAH.

"John W. Henney, Manufacturer, Dies Suddenly." *Freeport* (Ill.) *Journal-Standard*, 17 May 1926. PD, clipping, photocopy, JAPP.

"Josiah O. Stearns, Long Prominent in Business Enterprises, Dies Here." *Grays Harbor Washingtonian* (Hoquiam, Wash.), 24 Apr. 1936. PD, clipping, photocopy, JAPP.

"Judge Barton Is Dead." *Freeport* (Ill.) *Daily Journal*, 28 Dec. 1893. PD, clipping, photocopy, JAPP.

"Julia Gardiner" [obituary]. *Rockford* (Ill.) *Register*, 31 Aug. 1881. PD, clipping, Anna P. Sill, "Scrapbook," RC.

Junior Exhibition, Rockford Seminary, Rockford, Ills., Seminary Chapel, Tuesday Evening, April 20, 1880. PD [printed program], 4 pp., UIC, JAMC; *JAPM*, 27:379–80.

K., M. [Kelly, Mary]. "Notes on Bookbinding, with Examples by Ellen G. Starr." *Brush and Pencil* (n.d.): 178–82. PD, clipping, SC, Starr.

Kahler, Bruce R. "Art and Life: The Arts and Crafts Movement in Chicago, 1897–1910." Ph.D. diss, Purdue University, Lafayette, Ind., 1986.

Kansas State College Library. "The Library of E. Haldeman-Julius." Pittsburgh, Kans.: Kansas State College Library, [ca. 1971]. Mimeograph, 178 pp., PSU, EHJ.

"Kirkland School." *Chicago Tribune*, 6 July 1902. PD, clipping, CHS.

Ladies Reading Club of Girard, Kansas. [Memorial to S. Alice Haldeman by a member.] [Mar. 1915.] HD, 6 pp., UIC, JAMC, HJ.

"The Last Call. Hon. John H. Addams of Cedarville Died at Green Bay, Wis., after a Brief Illness." *Freeport* (Ill.) *Daily Bulletin*, 18 Aug. 1881. PD, clipping, JAPP.

"The Late John A. Wright." *Freeport* (Ill.) *Daily Democrat*, 10 Oct. 1889. PD, clipping, photocopy, JAPP.

Leavitt, Roger. "Memoirs of Roger Leavitt." n.d. TMs, BC.

———. [Scrapbook of Roger Leavitt.] [ca. 1923?] PD, clippings scrapbook, BC.

"Life's Work Well Done" [Linn, Mary Catherine Addams obituary]. *Winnebago* (Ill.) *Reflector*, 20 July 1894. PD, clipping, IU, Lilly, SAAH.

McDonald, George. "'To Baby' by George McDonald." HMs copied in the hand of Anna Hostetter Haldeman Addams, [June 1887], 2 pp., JAPP, DeLoach.

McIlhaney, Asa K. "Historical Notes from the Writings of Asa K. McIlhaney." n.d. TMs, pp. 1–3, 65–67, Easton Area Public Library and District Center, Easton, Pa.

Maddox, William Arthur. "Eulogy of Mrs. W. A. Talcott." 1925. TMs, RC.

"Memorial Rites Tomorrow for Ellen G. Starr." *Chicago Daily News*, 7 May 1940. PD, clipping, SC, Starr.

"Milestones" [death notice of Ellen Gates Starr]. *Time*, 19 Feb. 1940, 42. PD, clipping, SC, Starr.

"Miss Beck Is Taken by Death." *Fort Madison* (Iowa) *Evening Democrat*, 9 Nov. 1933. PD, clipping, photocopy, JAPP.

"Miss Blaisdell Passes Away." *Beloit* (Wis.) *Daily News*, 12 Oct. 1906. PD, clipping, Peter T. Maiken Private Collection, Beloit, Wis.; photocopy, JAPP.

"Miss Blaisdell Passes Away Today." *Beloit* (Wis.) *Daily Free Press*, 12 Oct. 1906. PD, clipping, Peter T. Maiken Private Collection, Beloit, Wis.; photocopy, JAPP.

"Miss Downs Dies Four Months after Her Sister" [Mary B. Downs obituary]. *Oak Leaves* (Oak Park, Ill.), 25 Jan. 1940. PD, clipping, photocopy, JAPP.

"Miss Sarah Smith . . . Outstanding in Community Life." Unidentified De Pere, Wis., newspaper, Aug. 1939. PD, clipping, De Pere Historical Society/White Pillars Museum, De Pere, Wis.

"Miss Starr's Lectures." Unidentified Detroit newspaper, n.p., n.d. PD, clipping, SC, Starr.

"Mrs. Mary Rinehart." *Fort Madison* (Iowa) *Weekly Plain Dealer*, 9 Nov. 1871. PD, clipping, photocopy, JAPP.

"Mrs. Mower, Eighty-three, Dies Suddenly at Chautauqua." *Rockford* (Ill.) *Register-Republic*, 20 Aug. 1936. PD, clipping, photocopy, JAPP.

"Mrs. Penfield Dies in East." *Rockford* (Ill.) *Daily Register Gazette*, 30 Oct. 1908. PD, clipping, photocopy, JAPP.

"Narrative of Administration: James Griswold Merrill." n.d. TMs, Merrill Papers, Special Collections, Fisk University.

Oglio, Donna Marianne. "The American Reformer: Psychological and Sociological Origins: A Comparative Study of Jane Addams, Louis Brandeis, and William Jennings Bryan." Ph.D. diss., City University of New York, 1979.

Parr, Samuel Wilson. "Graduate's Record, University of Illinois." June 1905. ADS, 3 pp., UIUC.

Patterson, William D. "Rollin D. Salisbury, 1858–1922." 1981. TMs, 33 pp., BC and University of Chicago, Special Collections.

"Phrenological Office and Bookstore." Broadside. Philadelphia: [John L. Capen], [1876?] PD, photocopy, 1 p., JAPP, DeLoach; *JAPM*, 28:729.

"President Sarah Anderson." n.d. TMs, 11 pp., RC, Anderson Vertical File.

"Prof. Blaisdell's Aunt Dies" [Sarah E. Blaisdell obituary]. *Round Table*, 17 Oct. 1906, 33. PD, clipping, BC.

"Prof. J. W. Linn, Educator and Legislator, Dies." *Chicago Tribune*, 17 July 1939. PD, clipping, JAPP.

"Professor S. W. Parr, '84, Dies at His Home in Urbana." Unidentified newspaper, June 1931. PD, clipping, UIUC.

"Public School Association: Miss Starr, of Chicago, Lectures on the Public School Art Society." *New York Daily Tribune*, 16 Jan. 1897. PD, clipping, SC, Starr.

Purdy, James. "The Linns." n.d. TMs, 8 pp., JAPP, Hulbert.

"Report of the Examining Committee." Unidentified Rockford newspaper, ca. June 1881. PD, clipping, Anna P. Sill, "Scrapbook," RC.

"Rev. Theodore Ludwig Hoffeditz, D.D., 1783–1858." *Fathers of the Reformed Church*. N.p., n.d. PD, clipping, photocopy, JAPP.

Rockford College Board of Trustees. "Minutes of the Annual Meeting of the Rockford College Board of Trustees." 1915. AMs, RC.

"Rockford College Gives Degree to Atlanta Woman. Mrs. Hamilton Douglas, Sr. [Corrine Douglas Williams] Honored for Educational Work." *Chicago Evening Post*, 15 June 1927. PD, clipping, RC, Williams Vertical File.

Rockford Female Seminary Board of Trustees. "Minutes of the Annual Meetings of the Rockford Female Seminary[/Rockford College] Board of Trustees." 1882–1908. AMs, RC; *JAPM*, 1A:148–86.

———. "Minutes of Special Meeting of the Rockford Female Seminary Board of Trustees, 10 May 1883." AMs, RC; *JAPM*, 1A:150.

Rockford Female Seminary Executive Committee. "Minutes of the Executive Committee Meetings of the Rockford Female Seminary Board of Trustees." 1864–82. AMs, RC.

Rockford Seminary, Thirtieth Commencement at the Chapel Hall, Wednesday, June 22, 1881. PD [printed program], 4 pp., UIC, JAMC; *JAPM*, 27:420–21.

"Series of Lectures." Given by Ellen Gates Starr. Unidentified Detroit newspaper, n.p., n.d. PD, clipping, SC, Starr.

[Sidwell, Annie W., obituaries.] *Lincoln* (Nebr.) *Daily Star*, 13 Feb. 1907; *Nebraska State Journal*, 14 Feb. 1907. PD, clippings, Nebraska Historical Society, Lincoln, Nebr.

Sill, Anna P. "Scrapbook of Miss Anna P. Sill." PD [scrapbook of newspaper clippings and miscellany], RC.

Simons, Kenneth L. "Vignette of a Long-Time Book Man." Unidentified Pittsburg, Kans. newspaper, 15 Jan. 1969. PD, clipping, JAPP, DeLoach.

"A Sketch of the Life and Ministerial Labors of the Rev. Theodore Ludwig Hoffeditz, D.D." Pts. 1–3. *German Reform Messenger* [Lancaster, Pa.], 8, 15, and 28 Sept. 1858. PD, clipping, photocopy, JAPP.

[Smith, Lathrop E., obituary.] *Beloit* (Wis.) *Alumnus* 22, no. 4 (Jan. 1921). PD, photocopy, JAPP.

[Smith, Lucy M., obituary.] *Beloit* (Wis.) *Daily News*, 1 Feb. 1909. PD, clipping, photocopy, JAPP.

———. *Wisconsin State Journal* (Madison), 1 Feb. 1909. PD, clipping, photocopy, JAPP.

"Social Settlements: Miss Starr Says Join in the Labor Movement." Unidentified Detroit newspaper, , n.p., n.d. PD, clipping, SC, Starr.

"Society of Mission Inquiry, Rockford Female Seminary, Minutes." 1871–82. HMsS [entries signed by various secretaries], RC.

Song Recital by Katherine Tanner Fisk, Rockford College Chapel, Thursday Evening, September 22, 1910. PD [printed program], RC.

"Sorry to See Him [Rev. John Manning Linn] Go." [Henry County (Ill.) News?], 5 June 1891. PD, clipping, IU, Lilly, SAAH.

[Soule, Thomas T., obituary.] Washington Historian 2 (Oct. 1900): 52, photocopy, JAPP.

"Speech of Hon. John H. Addams." Freeport (Ill.) Journal, 23 Oct. 1872. PD, clipping, photocopy, JAPP.

Starr, Ellen Gates. "Art and Democracy." n.d. TMs, 8 pp., SC, Starr.

———. "Bookbinding as an Art, and as a Commercial Industry." n.d. TMs, 8 pp., SC, Starr.

———. "A Bypath into the Great Roadway." Catholic World (May 1924): 177–86, and (June 1924). PD, clipping, 44 pp., SC, Starr.

———. "Cheap Clothes and Nasty." Ms written for the New Republic. Unpublished, n.d. SC, Starr.

———. "College Settlement Work: Hull House." Society of the Companions of the Holy Cross, Fourth Paper. 1895. PD [leaflet], 3 pp., SC, Starr.

———. "Efforts to Standardize Chicago Restaurants—The Henrici Strike." Survey, 23 May 1914. PD, clipping, SC, Starr.

———. "Handicraft Bookbinding and a Possible Modification." The Sketch Book (n.d.): 311–16. PD, clipping, SC, Starr.

———. "Memorial statement on the death of Jane Addams." [ca. 2 June 1935.] AD, SC, Starr.

———. "A Note of Explanation [on Bookbinding]." n.d. PD, [Hull-House booklet], SC, Starr.

———. "The 'Primavera' of Botticelli." Chicago, Hull-House, Easter, 1906. PD, SC, Starr.

———. "Settlements and the Church's Duty." Publications of the Church Social Union. 15 Aug. 1896. PD, clipping, SC, Starr.

———. "The Teachings of Christ on Industrial Orders, Work, Wages, Hours, and the Common Welfare." Address to the Bible Study Dept. of the Hinsdale Women's Club, n.p, n.d. TD, 14 pp., SC, Starr.

———. "This 'Stupendous Lapse from Civilization.'" Unidentified Chicago newspaper, letter to the editor, 27 Dec. n.y. PD, clipping, SC, Starr.

———. "Why I Am a Socialist." Unidentified Chicago newspaper, daily campaign edition, n.p., n.d. [ca. 1916?]. PD, clipping, SC, Starr.

———. Will and testament. 17 Feb. 1925. TMsS, with A emendations, SC, Starr.

———. Will and testament. n.d. TMsS, with Emendations [on Hull-House letterhead, Chicago], SC, Starr.

———. Will and testament. May 1937. AD [on Holy Child Convent letterhead, Suffern, N.Y.]. SC, Starr.

Starr, Josephine. "Notes on Ellen Gates Starr." Apr. 1960. TMs, SC, Starr.

Stephenson County Bible Society. [Resolution on Death of John H. Addams.] 11 Sept. 1881. HDS by C. Rich Bickenbach, 2 pp., SCPC, JAC.

"A Sudden Summons" [John A. Wright obituary]. *Lena* (Ill.) *Star*, 11 Oct. 1889. PD, clipping, photocopy, JAPP.

"Summer School at Rockford Seminary, Rockford, Ill., in Connection with the College Extension Classes of Hull-House, June 23d to July 23d, 1892." PD [pamphlet], RC.

Thompson, Barney. "Column Left: Roots in Long Past [Calvin R. Mower]." Unidentified Rockford newspaper, 17 Oct. 1927. PD, clipping, Rockford Public Library, Rockford, Ill.

Union Library Company of Cedar Creek Mills. *Rules and By-Laws of the Cedar Creek Union Library Company; Passed March 7, 1846.* Freeport: S. D. Carpenter, Printer, 1847. PD, photocopy, 8 pp., JAPP, DeLoach; *JAPM*, 28:852–56.

"'Unity's' Tribute to Miss Rebecca Rice." [*Unity?*], 23 June 1911. PD, clipping, CHS.

University School for Girls, Chicago, Ill. [Announcement.] 1897–98. PD, CHS.

Van Reed, J. "1776 Centennial Book 1876 of Reminiscences, Traditions, Recollections, Habits, Manners, and Customs, and of What I Know of the Olden Times, Written Expressly for the Van Reed Family." 1876. AMs, Historical Society of Berks Co., Reading, Pa.

Vestal, Pearl Gordon. "Wildcat Springs at Hamilton [Illinois] Owned by Browns for Century." Unidentified newspaper, 15 Dec. 1954. PD, clipping, Keokuk Public Library, Iowa.

Walshe, Frances. "Chicago Public School Art Society." 26 Apr. 1940. TD, SC, Starr.

"W. A. Talcott Memorial." ca. 26 Jan. 1901. PD [printed for Rockford College, Rockford, Ill.], RC.

[Weber, George, Jr., obituary.] *Reformed Church Messenger*, 28 Nov. 1888. PD, clipping, photocopy, JAPP.

"William Beck Dies Monday." *Fort Madison* (Iowa) *Democrat*, 18 May 1936. PD, clipping, photocopy, JAPP.

Williams, Corrine. "Debate—Resolved: That French women have exerted a greater influence through Literature than Politics. Representative Women—George Sand and Madame de Stael . . . Negative." 13 Nov. 1878. AMsS, fragment, 16 pp. UIC, JAMC, Detzer; *JAPM*, 27:197–212.

2. *Printed and Manuscript Sources of Genealogy and Vital Statistics, and Government Records, Reports, and Returns*

Addams Family Genealogy Files. JAPP.

Anderson, Marian, comp. *De Kalb County, Illinois, Index to Death Register 1: January 1878–June 1903.* Sycamore, Ill.: Genealogical Society of De Kalb County, Ill., 1982.

Barber, Edwin Atlee. *Genealogy of the Barber Family, the Descendants of Robert Barber of Lancaster County, Pennsylvania.* Philadelphia: Privately printed, 1890.

Beaver, I. M. *History and Genealogy of the Bieber, Beaver, Biever, Beeber Family.* Reading, Pa.: I. M. Beaver, 1939.

"Blaisdell Genealogy." Oct. 1968. Prepared by Allen C. Blaisdell and Phyllis Butler for the Blaisdell Association. TD, Peter T. Maiken Private Collection, Beloit, Wis.; photocopy, JAPP.

Carroll County, Ill., Clerk of the Circuit Court, Mt. Carroll, Ill. Estate records for Haldeman and Hostetter families.

Carroll County Genealogical Society. "Carroll County Cemetery Inscriptions, Oak Hill Cemetery." Mt. Carroll, Ill.: Carroll Co. Genealogical Society, n.d. Mimeograph, Carroll County Genealogical Society.

Cedarville, Ill., Cemetery. Burial Records, 1850–1994. n.d. HMs, photocopy, 64 pp. and index, JAPP.

Cook County, Ill., Clerk of the Circuit Court, Probate Division. [Estate records of Mary Catherine Addams Linn, 1894–97.] *JAPM,* 27:734–882.

De Garmo, Lois, Eleanor Holland, Eliza Kammer, and Martin Voss, comps. "Lena Burial Park." [Lena, Ill.]: 1983. Mimeograph, Freeport Public Library, Freeport, Ill.

"Edwards Family Genealogy." n.d. TMs, ISU, Edwards Papers.

"Elmwood Cemetery, Section 32, City of Sycamore, Township of Sycamore, County of De Kalb, State of Illinois." Information taken from cemetery tombstones and other cemetery records. Sycamore, Ill.: Genealogical Society of De Kalb County, Ill., 1982.

Ft. Madison, Iowa, Census returns, 1856. Mimeograph, Old Fort Genealogical Society, Inc., Ft. Madison, Iowa.

Ft. Madison, Iowa, City Cemetery Inscriptions. n.d. HMs, Old Fort Genealogical Society, Inc., Ft. Madison, Iowa.

Haldeman Family Genealogy File. JAPP.

Hostetter Family Genealogy File. JAPP.

Illinois, State of. Department of Public Health, Death Certificates. ISA, RS 205.14.

———. General Assembly Records. *Journal of the Senate.* 19th–26th General Assemblies, 1855–70, 8 vols. ISA, RG 600.101.

———. *Reports Made to the General Assembly of Illinois at Its Thirtieth Regular Session.* Vol. 1, pt. 2. Springfield: D. W. Lusk, 1877. "Ninth Annual Insurance Report of the Auditor of Public Accounts of the State of Illinois. Part 2: Life and Accident Insurance, 1877" and "Protection Life Insurance Company: Year Ending December 31, 1876." PD, 36–37. ISA.

———. *Reports to the General Assembly of Illinois, 1877.* Vol. 1. Springfield: D. W. Lusk, 1878. "Tenth Annual Insurance Report of the Auditor of Public Accounts of the State of Illinois. Part 2: Life and Accident Insurance, [1878]." PD, 5–11. ISA.

———. *Reports to the General Assembly of Illinois, at Its Twenty-seventh Session, Convened January 4, 1871.* Vol. 4. Springfield: Illinois Journal Printing Office, 1872. "Part 2: Life Insurance Companies. Insurance Report, Part 2: Life and Accident Insurance." PD, 221–305. ISA.

———. "An Act in Relation to the Rights of Married Women in Certain Cases." Approved 14 Feb. 1857. HD, 2 pp., Illinois. General Assembly. Enrolled Acts. ISA, RS 103.032.

———. "An Act to Amend an Act Entitled an Act to Incorporate the Protection Life Insurance Company, Approved March 7, 1867." Approved 8 Mar. 1869. HD, 5 pp., Illinois. General Assembly. Enrolled Acts. ISA, RS 103.032.

———. "An Act to Incorporate the Protection life Insurance Company." Approved 7 Mar. 1867. HD, 11 pp., Illinois. General Assembly. Enrolled Acts. ISA, RS 103.032.

———. Census returns, De Kalb County, 1865. Microfilm.

———. Census returns, Stephenson County, 1865. Microfilm.

———. East Moline State Hospital (Watertown State Hospital), Case File. John Weber Addams. n.d. HD, 4 pp. ISA, RS 262.3.

———. Land Records. "Illinois Public Domain Land Sales from the First Half of the Nineteenth Century." ISA, Database.

Laurel Hill Cemetery, Philadelphia, Pa. Lot Records, Internments, ca. 1836–1982. Microfilm.

"Master Index, Carroll County [Ill.] Cemeteries." Carroll County Genealogy Society, n.d. Mimeograph, Carroll County Genealogy Society.

Pierce, Frederick Clifton. Forbes and Forbush Genealogy. Chicago: Published for the author, 1892.

Philadelphia, Pa., City of. Registration of Deaths, 1890. Microfilm reel 25, file 2, vol. A, 1890, Department of Records, City of Philadelphia.

Stephenson County, Ill., Clerk of Circuit Court, Freeport. Records including probate and insanity hearings relating to Addams, Haldeman, and Weber families.

Stephenson County, Ill., County Clerk, Freeport. Death, birth, marriage records for various Cedarville and Freeport families, including those of Addams and Haldeman.

Stephenson County Genealogical Society. Cemetery Inscriptions Stephenson County, Illinois, vol. 5: Freeport City Cemetery, Freeport, Ill. Freeport: Stephenson County Genealogical Society, [1992?].

Stephenson County, Ill., Recorder, Freeport. Records relating to land bought or sold by Addams, Haldeman, and Weber families.

United States of America. Census returns, Beloit, Wis., 1850. Microfilm.

———. Census returns, Carroll County, Ill., 1850, 1860, 1870, 1880, 1900. Microfilm and mimeograph.

———. Census returns, Cook County, Ill., 1860, 1870, 1880, 1900. Microfilm.

———. Census returns, Crawford County, Kans., 1870, 1880. Microfilm.

———. Census returns, De Kalb County, Ill., 1860, 1870, 1880. Microfilm.

———. Census returns, Lee County, Iowa, 1860, 1870. Microfilm.

———. Census returns, McLean County, Ill., 1850, 1860, 1870, 1880. Microfilm.

———. Census returns, Madison, Wis., 1900. Microfilm.

———. Census returns, Ogle County, Ill., 1850, 1860, 1870, 1880. Microfilm.

———. Census returns, Philadelphia, Pa., 1850, 1860, 1900, 1910. Microfilm.

———. Census returns, Stephenson County, Ill., 1850, 1860, 1870, 1880, 1900, 1910. Microfilm and mimeograph.

———. Census returns, Whiteside County, Ill., 1850. Microfilm.

Washington State, Board of Health, Bureau of Vital Statistics. Forbes, Laura Jane. [Death certificate.] 1 Dec. 1914. D, photocopy, JAPP.

Weber family genealogy files. JAPP.

Whiteside County Genealogists. Cemetery Records of the Eastern Half of Whiteside Co., Illinois. n.p.: Whiteside County Genealogists, n.d. Mimeograph.

3. Artifact and Rare Books Collections

Addams family library. Rare Book Room, Coleman Library, Rockford College, Rockford, Ill.

Collected books from the library of Jane Addams. CAHS; Rare Book Room, Coleman Library, Rockford College, Rockford, Ill.; SCPC; UIC, JAMC.

Collected books of George Bowman Haldeman. UIC, JAMC.
Collected books from the Union Library Company of Cedar Creek Mills. CAHS; Rare Book Room, Coleman Library, Rockford College, Rockford, Ill.; UIC, JAMC.
Library of Emanuel Haldeman-Julius. EHJ, PSU.
Needlecraft by, and other artifacts of, Jane Addams. CAHS; UIC, JAMC; UIC, Hull-House.

4. Photograph Collections

CAHS; Ellwood House Museum, De Kalb, Ill.; JAMC, UIC; JAPP; RC; SC, Starr; SCHS; SCPC; De Pere Historical Society/White Pillars Museum, De Pere, Wis.

5. Directories, Published Minutes, and Annual Catalogs

Allen's Beloit City Directory for 1872–73. Beloit, Wis., 1872.
"Alumni Register, Illinois State Normal University, 1860–1927." *Normal School Quarterly* ser. 26, no. 104 (July 1927).
Beloit College and Academy. *Catalog of Beloit College; Its Officers, Students and Alumni.* Beloit, Wis.: Beloit College, 1884–85, 1885–86.
Beloit, Wis., city directories, 1890–95.
Board of Missions for Freedmen. *Annual Report.* n.p., 1891.
Brown, W. Norman, comp. *The Johns Hopkins Half-Century Directory.* Baltimore: Johns Hopkins University Press, 1926.
Catalogue of the Trustees, Officers, and Students of the University of Pennsylvania, 1881–2. Philadelphia: Press of Edward Stern and Co., 1882.
Catalogue of the Trustees, Officers, and Students of the University of Pennsylvania, 1882–3. Philadelphia: Collins, Printer, 1883.
Chicago, Ill., *City Directories.* Chicago, 1856–70.
Costa, Isaac, comp. *Gopsill's Philadelphia City Directory for 1877.* Philadelphia: James Gopsill, 1877.
Elgin, Ill. *City Directories.* Elgin, Ill., 1881–95.
Girls' Higher School [catalog], 1888–89. Chicago: Miss Rice's School for Young Ladies and Children, [1888].
Glendale Female College. *Catalogue, 1896–97.* Cincinnati, Ohio: Elm Street Printing Co., [1896].
Gould's McLean County Directory for 1875–76. Bloomington, Ill.: David B. Gould, [1875?].
Hostetter's Illustrated United States Almanac. Pittsburgh: Hostetter Co., 1861–1909.
Illinois Blue Book. 1913–94. Springfield: Illinois Secretary of State, 1913–94.
Illinois State Normal University. *Catalogue, 1869–70.* Normal, Ill.: Illinois State Normal University, [1869].
Kane County Business Directory, 1887–88. [Chicago?], [1887].
Kane County Gazetteer and Directory for 1889–90. Chicago, [1889].
Kirkland Association. *Annual Reports.* 1st-3d. Chicago, 1891–94.
Lake Forest College. *Lake Forest College Bulletin Alumni Directory.* Lake Forest, Ill.: Lake Forest College, 1931.
———. *Lake Forest College Roll of Graduates and Students.* Lake Forest, Ill.: Lake Forest College, 1914.

Lake Forest University. *Annual Registers*. Lake Forest, Ill.: Lake Forest University, 1884–98.

———. *Catalogue*, 1896–97.

Lakeside Annual Directory of the City of Chicago. Chicago, 1874–1914.

Methodist Episcopal Church, Rock River Annual Conference. *Minutes of the Fifty-Sixth Session of the Rock River Annual Conference of the Methodist Episcopal Church Held in First Church, Elgin, Illinois, Sept. 25–Oct. 1, 1895*. Rockford, Ill.: Monitor Publishing Co., 1895.

Miss Rice's School for Young Ladies and Children. *Catalogue, 1879–80*. Chicago: Miss Rice's School, [1879].

Mt. Morris (Ill.) Seminary. *Catalogues*. Various years. Manchester College, North Manchester, Ind.

National Council of the Congregational Churches of the United States. *Congregational Year-Book*. Boston: Congregational Publishing Society, 1879–1903, 1906–11, 1915.

Oak Park, Ill., city directories, 1910–30.

Prairie Farmer's Reliable Directory of Farmers and Breeders, Stephenson County. Chicago: Prairie Farmer, [1917].

Presbyterian Church, U.S.A. *Minutes of the General Assembly of the Presbyterian Church in the United States*. Philadelphia: Presbyterian Church [U.S.A.], 1842–74.

Presbyterian Theological Seminary, Chicago. *Annual Register of Officers and Students, the McCormick Theological Seminary of the Presbyterian Church in the U.S.A*. Chicago: Presbyterian Theological Seminary, 1928.

Rockford Female Seminary. *Catalogues of the Officers and Students of Rockford Seminary, Rockford, Ill*. Rockford, Ill.: Rockford Female Seminary, 1863–84.

Rockford and Winnebago County Directory. [Rockford?], Ill., 1903–4, 1911, 1915, 1918–21.

Rock River Seminary. *Catalogue*. Mt. Morris, Ill.: Rock River Seminary, 1874–77. Manchester College, North Manchester, Ind.

Social Welfare History Group. *Annual Bibliography of Scholarship in Social Welfare History*. 1980–97.

Stoneipher, John F. *Biographical Catalogue of Lafayette College, 1832–1912*. Easton, Pa.: Chemical Publishing Co., 1913.

Stowe's Clerical Directory of the American Church 1917. Minneapolis: Andrew David Stowe, [1917].

Straker, Robert. *Directory of Antioch College, 1850–1934*. [Yellow Springs, Ohio, 1934].

United States Military Academy, West Point, New York. *Sixty-fifth Annual Report of the Association of Graduates at the United States Military Academy at West Point, New York, June 11, 1934*. Newburgh, N.Y.: Moore Printing Co., [1934].

———. *Seventieth Annual Report of the Association of Graduates of the United States Military Academy at West Point, New York, June 10, 1939*. Newburgh, N.Y.: Moore Printing Co., Inc., [1939].

———. *Forty-first Annual Reunion of the Association Graduates of the United States Military Academy, at West Point, New York. June 14, 1910*. Saginaw, Mich.: Seemann and Peters, Printers and Binders, 1910.

University of Pennsylvania. *Catalogue of the Trustees, Officers, and Students of the University of Pennsylvania, 1881–83*.

University School for Girls. *Catalogues*. Chicago, 1899–1904.

Young Ladies' School [catalog]. Chicago: Miss Kirkland's School for Girls, [1879?].

6. Newspapers and Magazines

Atlanta (Ga.) *Constitution*
Aurora (Ill.) *Beacon*
Beloit (Wis.) *Daily Free Press*
Beloit (Wis.) *Daily News*
Beloit Magazine
Boston Journal
Bowdoin Orient (Bowdoin College, Bowdoin, Maine)
Carroll County (Ill.) *Mirror* (Mt. Carroll)
Catholic World
Champaign (Ill.) *News-Gazette*
Chicago Daily News
Chicago Evening Journal
Chicago Evening Post
Chicago Times
Chicago Tribune
Colby Echo (Colby College, Waterville, Maine)
College Rambler (Illinois College, Jacksonville)
Collegian (Monmouth College, Monmouth, Ill.)
Congregational Quarterly n.s., 6–10 (1874–78)
De Kalb (Ill.) *Chronicle*
Deutscher Anzeiger (Freeport, Ill.)
Dunn Co. (Wis.) *News*
Eclectic Magazine
Evanston (Ill.) *Index*
Evening Post (New York)
German Reformed Messenger (Lancaster, Pa.)
Freeport (Ill.) *Budget*
Freeport (Ill.) *Bulletin*
Freeport (Ill.) *Daily Bulletin*
Freeport (Ill.) *Daily Democrat*
Freeport (Ill.) *Daily Journal & Republican*
Freeport (Ill.) *Journal*
Freeport (Ill.) *Journal-Standard*
Freeport (Ill.) *Republican*
Freeport (Ill.) *Weekly Bulletin*
Freeport (Ill.) *Weekly Democrat*
Freeport (Ill.) *Weekly Journal*
Fort Madison (Iowa) *Daily Democrat*
Fort Madison (Iowa) *Democrat*
Fort Madison (Iowa) *Evening Democrat*
Fort Madison (Iowa) *Weekly Democrat*
Fort Madison (Iowa) *Weekly Plain Dealer*
Geneseo (Ill.) *Republic*
Girard (Kans.) *News*
Harper's Monthly Magazine

Harper's Weekly Magazine
Henry County (Ill.) *News* (Geneseo)
Hull-House Bulletin (Chicago, Ill.)
Illinois Monitor (Freeport, Ill.)
Jacksonville (Ill.) *Journal*
Kansas City (Mo.) *Star*
Lena (Ill.) *Star*
Leslie's Illustrated Magazine
The Liberator
Lincoln (Nebr.) *Daily Star*
Menomonie (Wis.) *Times*
National Republican (Washington, D.C.)
New York Daily Tribune
New York Evening Post
New York Herald
New York Times
Oak Leaves (Oak Park, Ill.)
Peru (Ill.) *Republican*
Philadelphia (Pa.) *Public Ledger*
Purple Parrot (Rockford College, Rockford, Ill.)
Rockford Alumna (Rockford College, Rockford, Ill.)
Rockford Collegian (Rockford College, Rockford, Ill.)
Rockford (Ill.) *Daily Register Gazette*
Rockford (Ill.) *Gazette*
Rockford (Ill.) *Morning Star*
Rockford (Ill.) *Register*
Rockford (Ill.) *Register-Republican*
Rockford Seminary Magazine (Rockford Female Seminary, Rockford, Ill.) (*RSM*)
Round Table (Beloit College, Beloit, Wis.)
Savannah (Ga.) *Morning News*
Scribner's Magazine
Scribner's Monthly
Tri-County Press (Polo, Ill.)
Vassar Miscellany (Vassar College, Poughkeepsie, N.Y.)
Volante (University of Chicago)
Wisconsin State Journal (Madison)
Yellow Springs (Ohio) *News*

7. *Journal and Magazine Articles and Chapters from Books*

Adams, James N., comp. "List of Illinois Place Names." *Illinois Libraries* 50 (Apr.–June 1968): iii–vi, 275–596.

Addams, Jane. "The Art-Work Done by Hull-House, Chicago." *Forum* 19 (July 1895): 614–17. Reprinted in *One Hundred Years at Hull-House,* edited by Mary Lynn McCree Bryan and Allan F. Davis, 40–42. Bloomington: Indiana University Press, 1990.

———. "Cassandra." In *Rockford Seminary, Thirtieth Commencement, Essays of Graduating Class, Wednesday, June 22, 1881*, 36–39. De Kalb, Ill.: "News" Steam Press, 1881.

———. "[The Chivalry of Study]." *Rockford Seminary Magazine* 8 (Feb. 1880): 63–64.

———. "The Devil Baby at Hull-House." *Atlantic Monthly* (Oct. 1916): 441–48, 451. Reprinted in *One Hundred Years at Hull-House*, edited by Mary Lynn McCree Bryan and Allan F. Davis, 150–55. Bloomington: Indiana University Press, 1990.

———. "Editorial." *Rockford Seminary Magazine* 8 (Nov. 1880): 254–56.

———. "Editorial." *Rockford Seminary Magazine* 8 (Dec. 1880): 280–82.

———. "Editorial." *Rockford Seminary Magazine* 9 (Jan. 1881): 23–26.

———. "Editorial." *Rockford Seminary Magazine* 9 (Feb. 1881): 52–57.

———. "Editorial." *Rockford Seminary Magazine* 9 (Mar. 1881): 85–89.

———. "Editorial." *Rockford Seminary Magazine* 9 (Apr. 1881): 113–16.

———. "Editorial." *Rockford Seminary Magazine* 9 (May 1881): 151–55.

———. "Editorial." *Rockford Seminary Magazine* 9 (June 1881): 179–83.

———. "Editorial." *Rockford Seminary Magazine* 9 (July 1881): 217–18.

———. "The Element of Hopefulness in Human Nature." *Rockford Seminary Magazine* 7 (May 1879): 120–22.

———. "Follow Thou Thy Star." *Rockford Seminary Magazine* 7 (July 1879): 183–85.

———. "[Homage to the Vesperian Society from the President of the Castalian Society]." *Rockford Seminary Magazine* 7 (Nov. 1879): 242.

———. "The Macbeth of Shakespeare." *Rockford Seminary Magazine* 8 (Jan. 1880): 13–16.

———. "Marks." *Rockford Seminary Magazine* 7 (May 1879): 130.

———. "One Office of Nature." *Rockford Seminary Magazine* 7 (June 1879): 154–56.

———. "[Opening Address at the Junior Exhibition, Rockford Female Seminary]." *Rockford Seminary Magazine* 8 (Apr. 1880): 110–11.

———. "Plated Ware." *Rockford Seminary Magazine* 6 (Apr. 1878): 60–62.

———. "The Play Instinct and the Arts." In *The Second Twenty Years at Hull-House*, 343–79. New York: Macmillan, 1930.

———. "Self Tradition." *Rockford Seminary Magazine* 9 (Apr. 1881): 97–100.

———. "Valedictory." *Rockford Seminary Magazine* 9 (July 1881): 219–22.

———, ed. "Clippings and Exchanges." *Rockford Seminary Magazine* 7 (Nov. 1879): 246–48.

———, ed. "Clippings and Exchanges." *Rockford Seminary Magazine* 7 (Dec. 1879): 282–84.

———, ed. "Clippings and Exchanges." *Rockford Seminary Magazine* 8 (Jan. 1880): 25–29.

———, ed. "Clippings and Exchanges." *Rockford Seminary Magazine* 8 (Feb. 1880): 58–62.

———, ed. "Clippings and Exchanges." *Rockford Seminary Magazine* 8 (Mar. 1880): 92–94.

———, ed. "Clippings and Exchanges." *Rockford Seminary Magazine* 8 (Apr. 1880): 121–23.

———, ed. "Clippings and Exchanges." *Rockford Seminary Magazine* 8 (May 1880): 155–57.

————, ed. "Clippings and Exchanges." *Rockford Seminary Magazine* 8 (June 1880): 188–91.

————, ed. "Clippings and Exchanges." *Rockford Seminary Magazine* 8 (July 1880): 211–13.

————, ed. "Home Items." *Rockford Seminary Magazine* 7 (June 1879): 158–63.

————, ed. "Home Items." *Rockford Seminary Magazine* 7 (July 1879): 199–202.

————, ed. "Literary Notes." *Rockford Seminary Magazine* 8 (Jan. 1880): 16–17.

————, ed. "Literary Notes." *Rockford Seminary Magazine* 8 (Feb. 1880): 49–50.

————, Eleanor Frothingham, and Martha Thomas. "Class Song." *Rockford Seminary Magazine* 8 (Apr. 1880): 109–10.

————, Ellen Gates Starr, and Florence Kelley. "Hull-House: A Social Settlement." In *Hull-House Maps and Papers,* by Jane Addams et al., 207–30. New York: Crowell, 1895.

————, et al. "The Origin of Chess." *Rockford Seminary Magazine* 6 (Apr. 1878): 69–71.

Angle, Paul M. "Hardy Pioneer: How He Lived in the Early Middle West." In *History of Medical Practice in Illinois,* vol. 2: *1850–1900,* edited by David J. Davis, 26–35. Chicago: Illinois State Medical Society, 1955.

Arnold, Lois Barber. "American Women in Geology." *Geology* 5 (Aug. 1970): 493–94.

Baym, Nina. "Creating a National Literature." In *Making America: The Society and Culture of the United States,* edited by Luther S. Luedtke, 219–35. Chapel Hill: University of North Carolina Press, 1992.

————. "Women and the Republic: Emma Willard's Rhetoric of History." *American Quarterly* 43 (Mar. 1991): 1–23.

Bowen, A. L. "The World Is Better That This Woman Lives." *New Age Illustrated* 11 (Nov. 1927): 27.

Breckinridge, Frank P. "James Weber Linn: An Appreciation by an 'Old Grad.'" *University of Chicago Magazine* 32 (Oct. 1939): 8–9.

Byrne, Archibald J. "Eliza Allen Starr." In *Notable American Women, 1607–1950,* edited by Edward T. James, Janet Wilson James, and Paul S. Boyer, 3:350–51. Cambridge: Harvard University Press, 1971.

Capen, Charles L. "A Sketch of the Illinois Normal University; from the Quarter-Centennial Celebration, Aug. 24, 1882." In *Transactions of the McLean [County, Illinois] Historical Society,* 2:176–86. Bloomington, Ill.: McLean Historical Society by Pantagraph Printing and Stationery Co., 1903.

Carlyle, Thomas. "The Hero as Man of Letters." Lecture 5 [19 May 1840] in *On Heroes, Hero-Worship, and the Heroic in History,* edited by Murray Baumgarten et al., 133–67. Berkeley: University of California Press, 1993.

Cavallo, Dominick. "Sexual Politics and Social Reform: Jane Addams from Childhood to Hull-House." In *New Directions in Psychohistory: The Adelphi Papers in Honor of Erik H. Erikson,* edited by Mel Albin. Lexington, Mass.: D. C. Heath and Co., 1980.

Clark, Eleanor Grace. "Ellen Gates Starr, O[rder]. [of] S[t.] B[enedict]. (1859–1940): An Account of the Life of the Co-Foundress of Hull House." *Commonweal,* 15 Mar. 1940, 444–47.

Clark, Virginia. "Rockford Chosen as Seminary Site." In *Rockford College: A Retrospective Look,* edited by C. Hal Nelson, Joan Surrey, Isy Nelson, Leona Carlson, and Betty Asprooth, 31–34. Rockford, Ill.: C. Hjalmar Nelson and Rockford College, 1980.

Clarke, W. S. "Eliza Allen Starr: Poet, Artist, and Teacher of Christian Art." *Catholic World* 66 (Nov. 1897): 254–60.

Conway, Jill K. "Perspectives on the History of Women's Education in the United States." *History of Education Quarterly* 14 (Spring 1974): 1–12.

Cook, Blanche Wiesen. "Female Support Networks and Political Activism: Lillian Wald, Crystal Eastman, Emma Goldman." *Chrysalis* 3 (1977): 43–61.

Davis, Allen F. "Ellen Gates Starr." In *Notable American Women, 1607–1950*, edited by Edward T. James, Janet Wilson James, and Paul S. Boyer, 3:351–53. Cambridge: Harvard University Press, 1971.

"Eliza Allen Starr." In *The National Cyclopaedia of American Biography*, 13:564. New York: James T. White and Co., ca. 1897–1906.

Fee, Elizabeth. "Nineteenth-Century Craniology: The Study of the Female Skull." *Bulletin of the History of Medicine* 53 (1979): 415–33.

"Focus on Alums: Doris J. Malkmus, '76." *Shimer College Symposium* (Fall 1997): 10–11.

Fraser, Stephen. "Amalgamated Clothing Workers of America." In *Encyclopedia of the American Left*, edited by Mari Jo Buhle, Paul Buhle, and Dan Georgakas, 16–18. New York: Garland, 1990.

Gordon, Lynn D. "From Seminary to University: An Overview of Women's Higher Education, 1870–1920." In *Gender and Higher Education in the Progressive Era*, chap. 1, 13–51. New Haven: Yale University Press, 1990.

Gustason, Harriett. "Looking Back: Damsel's Decision Affects Freeport's Future." *Freeport* (Ill.) *Journal-Standard*, 11–12 Feb. 1989.

———. "Looking Back: Visitor Was Not Impressed with Freeport." *Freeport* (Ill.) *Journal-Standard*, 21 June 1997.

Hackett, Francis. "Hull-House: A Souvenir." *Survey*, 1 June 1925, 275–79. Reprinted in *One Hundred Years at Hull-House*, edited by Mary Lynn McCree Bryan and Allan F. Davis, 67–73. Bloomington: Indiana University Press, 1990.

Hamilton, Alice. "Hull-House Within and Without." In *Exploring the Dangerous Trades*, Boston: 1943, 68–87. Reprinted in *One Hundred Years at Hull-House*, edited by Mary Lynn McCree Bryan and Allan F. Davis, 108–16. Bloomington: Indiana University Press, 1990.

Harkness, Georgia. "Jane Addams in Retrospect." *Christian Century*, 13 Jan. 1960, 39–41.

Henderson, Harold. "Big Ideas [Shimer College]." Reprinted from the *Chicago Reader* by Shimer College, 17 June 1988 and updated Feb. 1997.

Henderson, Mary C. "Against Broadway: The Rise of the Art Theatre in America (1900–1920)." In *1915, the Cultural Moment: The New Politics, the New Woman, the New Psychology, the New Art, and the New Theatre in America*, edited by Adele Heller and Lois Rudnick, 233–49. New Brunswick: Rutgers University Press, 1991.

High, Edwin Van Reed. "Van Reed Family, and the Van Reed Paper Mills." *Historical Review of Berks County* 7 (Jan. 1942): 49–51.

"History of School Libraries." *Illinois Libraries* 50 (Nov. 1968): 853–972.

"History of the Seminary." In *Catalogue of Rock River Seminary, Mount Morris, Illinois*. Freeport, Ill., 1874.

Holmes, Mary Emilie. "Methods of Presenting Geology in Our Schools and Colleges." *Science*, 19 Sept. 1893, 175–79.

[Horrocks, Thomas A.] "'Know Thyself': A Phrenological Character Reading." *Fugitive Leaves from the Historical Collections, Library of the College of Physicians of Philadelphia.* 3d ser., 2 (Fall 1987): 1–5.

Hostetter, Sara[h]. "Home and Girlhood of Jane Addams." *Frances Shimer Record* 7 (Feb. 1916): 3–8.

Hunt, James B. "Jane Addams: The Presbyterian Connection." *American Presbyterian* 68 (Winter 1990): 231–44.

"James Griswold Merrill." *Princeton Theological Seminary Bulletin* 15 (Aug. 1921): 89–90.

"John Manning Linn." In "Necrological Report to the Alumni Association of the Princeton Theological Seminary at Its Annual Meeting May 12, 1925." *Princeton Theological Seminary Bulletin* 19, no. 2 (1925): 249–50.

Kahler, Bruce K. "Ellen Gates Starr." In *Handbook of American Women's History,* edited by Angela Howard Zophy and Frances M. Kavenik, 573–74. New York: Garland, 1990.

Kelley, Mary. "Reading Women/Women Reading: The Making of Learned Women in Antebellum America." *Journal of American History* 83 (Sept. 1996): 401–24.

Kenney, Mary. "Mary Kenney Is Invited In" [memoirs of Mary Kenney]. Excerpt from unpublished autobiographical ms. at the Schlesinger Library, Radcliffe College, Cambridge, Mass. Reprinted in *One Hundred Years at Hull-House,* edited by Mary Lynn McCree Bryan and Allan F. Davis, 21–23. Bloomington: Indiana University Press, 1990.

Kerber, Linda. "Separate Spheres, Female Worlds, Women's Place: The Rhetoric of Women's History." *Journal of American History* 75 (June 1988): 9–39.

Knight, Louise W. "An Authoritative Voice: Jane Addams and the Oratorical Tradition." *Gender and History* 10 (Aug. 1998): 217–51.

———. "Jane Addams and the Settlement House Movement." In *Against the Tide: Women Reformers in American Society,* edited by Paul A. Cimbala and Randall M. Miller. Westport, Conn.: Greenwood Press, 1997.

Knowlton, D. A. (Mrs.). "Presbyterianism in Stephenson County, Illinois." *Journal of the Illinois State Historical Society* 11 (Apr. 1918): 193–209.

Kohlstedt, Sally Gregory. "Curiosities and Cabinets: Natural History Museums and Education on the Antebellum Campus." *Isis* 79 (Sept. 1988): 410–20.

———. "In from the Periphery: American Women in Science, 1830–80." *Signs* 4 (1978): 81–96.

Ladenson, Alex. "Bringing Books to People in Illinois." *Histories of Public Libraries: Illinois Libraries* 50 (Sept. 1968): 597–604.

"Laplace's Nebular Hypothesis." Appendix 2 in Ronald Numbers, *Creation by Natural Law,* 124–32. Seattle: University of Washington Press, 1977. An excerpt from Pierre Simon Laplace, *The System of the World,* translated by Henry H. Harte, 2:316–29, 2:331–33, 2:336–37, 2:354–62. 1796. Reprint. Dublin: University Press, 1830.

Lasser, Carol. "Let Us Be Sisters Forever: The Sororal Model of Nineteenth-Century Female Friendship." *Signs* 14 (Autumn 1988): 158–81.

Marks, Nora. "Two Women's Work." *Chicago Tribune,* 19 May 1890. Reprinted in *One Hundred Years at Hull-House,* edited by Mary Lynn McCree Bryan and Allan F. Davis, 16–19. Bloomington: Indiana University Press, 1990.

Meyer, Ernest. "The Art Industries of America, [Part] 6: The Binding of Books." *Brush and Pencil* 16 (Aug. 1905): 35–45.

Miller, Paul L. "Visit to the Sinking Spring." *Historical Review of Berks County* 54 (Spring 1989): 77–79, 94–96.

"Miss Lucy M. Smith." In *The Forester*, 2:138–39. [Lake Forest, Ill.]: Class of 1895 of Lake Forest College, [1895?].

Morgenstern, George. "Mr. Linn and Mr. Aldis' Shirt." *University of Chicago Magazine* 32 (Oct. 1939): 10–11, 26.

Murdoch, William. "Frederic Francois Chopin." In *The International Cyclopedia of Music and Musicians*, edited by Oscar Thompson et al. 11th ed., 407–11. New York: Dodd, Mead and Co., 1985.

"Nelson A. Pennoyer, M.D." In Francis H. Lyman, *The City of Kenosha and Kenosha County, Wisconsin*. . . . Vol. 2. Chicago: S. J. Clarke Publishing Co., 1916.

Rea, Annabeel M. "George Sand (1804–1876)." In *French Women Writers*, edited by Eva Martin Sartori and Dorothy Wynne Zimmerman, 399–411. Westport, Conn.: Greenwood Press, 1991.

Rice, Wallace. "Miss Starr's Bookbinding." *House Beautiful* 12 (June 1902): 12–14.

Riegel, Robert E. "Introduction of Phrenology to the United States." *Journal of American History* 39 (1933–34): 73–78.

Rudnick, Lois. "A Feminist American Success Myth: Jane Addams' Twenty Years at Hull House." In *Tradition and the Talents of Women*, edited by Florence Howe, 145–67. Urbana: University of Illinois Press, 1991.

Rupp, Leila J. "'Imagine My Surprise': Women's Relationships in Historical Perspective." *Frontiers* 5 (1980): 61–70.

Ryan, Mary P. "The Power of Women's Networks: A Case Study of Female Moral Reform in Antebellum America." *Feminist Studies* 5 (Spring 1979): 66–85.

Sahli, Nancy. "Smashing: Women's Relationships before the Fall." *Chrysalis* 17 (Summer 1979): 17–27.

"Sarah Anderson, 1890–1896." In *Profiles of the Principals of Rockford Seminary and Presidents of Rockford College, 1847–1947*, 13. Rockford, Ill.: Rockford College, 1947.

Schor, Naomi. "Idealism in the Novel: Recanonizing Sand." *Yale French Studies* 75 (1988): 56–73.

Schwager, Sally. "Educating Women in America." *Signs* 12 (Winter 1987): 333–72.

Scott, Anne Firor. "The Ever-Widening Circle: The Diffusion of Feminist Values from the Troy Female Seminary, 1822–72." *History of Education Quarterly* 19 (Spring 1979): 3–25.

Sedeen, Maggie. "Anna Peck Sill Founds Seminary." In *Rockford College: A Retrospective Look*, edited by C. Hal Nelson, Joan Surrey, Isy Nelson, Leona Carlson, and Betty Asprooth, chap. 2, 35–52. Rockford, Ill.: C. Hjalmar Nelson and Rockford College, 1980.

Simmons, Christina. "Companionate Marriage and the Lesbian Threat." *Frontiers* 4 (1979): 54–59.

Sitwell, Sacheverell. "Franz Liszt." In *The International Cyclopedia of Music and Musicians*, edited by Oscar Thompson et al. 11th ed., 1262–67. New York: Dodd, Mead and Co., 1985.

Smith-Rosenberg, Carroll. "The Female World of Love and Ritual: Relations between Women in Nineteenth-Century America." *Signs* 1 (Autumn 1975): 1–14.

Spiegel, Allan D. "Role of Gender, Phrenology, Discrimination and Nervous Prostration in Clara Barton's Career." *Journal of Community Health* 20 (Dec. 1995): 501–27.

Starr, Eliza Allen. "Scourging and the Crowning with Thorns in Art." *Catholic World* 66 (Mar. 1898): 95–107.

Starr, Ellen Gates. "Art and Labor." In *Hull-House Maps and Papers,* by Jane Addams et al., 165–79. New York: Crowell, 1895.

———. "The Chicago Clothing Strike." *New Review* (Mar. 1916): 62–64.

———. "Hull-House Bookbindery." *Hull-House Bulletin* (May 1890). Reprinted in *Commons* (June 1900): 5–6, and in *One Hundred Years at Hull-House,* edited by Mary Lynn McCree Bryan and Allan F. Davis, 84–86. Bloomington: Indiana University Press, 1990.

———. "The Renaissance of Handicraft." *International Socialist Review* 2 (Feb. 1902): 570–74.

———. "Shrines Old and New." *Abbey Chronicle* 8 (Aug. 1929): 113–14.

———. "Soul Culture." *Rockford Seminary Magazine* (Dec. 1880): 284–86.

———. "Two Pilgrim Experiences." *Catholic World* (Sept. 1930): 680–84.

Surrey, Joan, Ted Babcox, and Nancy Babcox. "Jane Addams." In *Rockford College: A Retrospective Look,* edited by C. Hal Nelson, Joan Surrey, Isy Nelson, Leona Carlson, and Betty Asprooth, chap. 3, 53–64. Rockford, Ill.: C. Hjalmar Nelson and Rockford College, 1980.

Szmurlo, Karyna. "Germaine Necker, Baronne De Staël (1766–1817)." In *French Women Writers,* edited by Eva Martin Sartori and Dorothy Wynne Zimmerman, 463–72. Westport, Conn.: Greenwood Press, 1991.

———. "Le jeu et le discours féminines: la danse de l'héroïne staëlienne." *Nineteenth-Century French Studies* 15 (Fall–Winter 1986–87): 1–13.

Thwing, Charles F. "Recent Movements in Woman's Education." *Harper's Monthly* 62 (Dec. 1880): 101–7.

Townsend, Lucy F. "The Education of Jane Addams: Myth and Reality." *Vitae Scholastica: The Bulletin of Educational Biography* 5 (1986): 225–46.

———. "The Gender Effect: The Early Curricula of Beloit College and Rockford Female Seminary." *History of Higher Education Annual* 10 (1990): 69–90.

Townsend, Lucy F., and Linda O'Neil. "Things beyond Us: A Freirian Analysis of Jane Addams's Seminary Experience." *Journal of the Midwest History of Education Society* 21 (1994): 13–26.

Vaile, Adeline. "Appreciation of the Late Rollin D. Salisbury." *University of Chicago Magazine* 17, no. 9 (1922): 356–57.

Van Valen, Nelson. "Friend of the Earth . . . Prof. James J. Blaisdell. . . ." *Beloit Magazine* (Sept. 1991): 11.

Vicinus, Martha. "Distance and Desire: English Boarding School Friendships." *Signs* 3 (Summer 1978): 856–69.

Visher, Stephen S. "Rollin D. Salisbury and Geography." *Annals of the Association of American Geographers* 43 (Mar. 1953): 4–11.

Washburne, Marion Foster. "A Labor Museum." *Craftsman* (Sept. 1904): 570–79. Reprinted in *One Hundred Years at Hull-House,* edited by Mary Lynn McCree Bryan and Allan F. Davis, 74–84. Bloomington: Indiana University Press, 1990.

Willard, Frances E., and Mary A. Livermore. "Eliza Allen Starr." In *A Woman of the Century,* 679. Chicago: Charles Wells Moulton, 1893.

Wood, Ann Douglas. "The Fashionable Diseases: Women's Complaints and Their Treatment in Nineteenth-Century America." *Journal of Interdisciplinary History* 4 (Summer 1973): 25–52.

Wright, Mary Page. "Woman's Life in Asiatic Turkey." In *The Congress of Women Held in the Woman's Building World's Columbian Exposition, Chicago, USA, 1893*, edited by Mary Kavanaugh Oldham Eagle, 305. Philadelphia: International Publishing Co./W. W. Houston and Co. and Mammoth Publishing Co., 1895.

Yeich, Edwin. "Jane Addams." *Historical Review of Berks County* 27 (Oct. 1951): 10–13.

8. Books

Abir-Am, Pnina, and Dorinda Outram, eds. *Uneasy Careers and Intimate Lives: Women in Science, 1789–1979*. New Brunswick: Rutgers University Press, 1987.

Abrams, M. H. et al., eds. *The Norton Anthology of English Literature*. 5th ed. New York: Norton, 1986.

Addams, Jane. *Democracy and Social Ethics*. 1902. Reprint. Urbana: University of Illinois Press, 2002.

———. *Long Road of Woman's Memory*. 1916. Reprint. Urbana: University of Illinois Press, 2002.

———. *My Friend Julia Lathrop*. New York: Macmillan, 1935.

———. *The Second Twenty Years at Hull-House*. New York: Macmillan, 1930.

———. *Twenty Years at Hull-House, with Autobiographical Notes*. New York: Macmillan, 1910.

Adamstown, Pa. *Two-Hundredth Anniversary, 1761–1961; Historical Book*. Adamstown, Pa.: Adamstown Bicentennial Com., [1961].

Ahlstrom, Sydney E. *Religious History of the American People*. New Haven: Yale University Press, 1972.

Ainsworth, Dorothy S. *The History of Physical Education in Colleges for Women*. New York: A. S. Barnes and Co., 1930.

Akeley, Carl. *Taxidermy and Sculpture: The Work of Carl E. Akeley in the Field Museum of Natural History*. Chicago: Field Museum of Natural History, 1927.

Alger, William Rounseville. *The Friendships of Women*. Boston: Roberts Brothers, 1868.

Allison, Alexander et al., eds. *The Norton Anthology of Poetry*. 1st ed. New York: Norton, 1970.

Andreas, A. T. *History of Chicago from the Earliest Period to the Present Time in Three Volumes*. Chicago: A. T. Andreas Co., 1884–86.

Ankarloo, Bengt, and Gustav Henningsen, eds. *Early Modern European Witchcraft*. New York: Oxford University Press, 1990.

Ashmead, Henry Graham. *History of Delaware County, Pennsylvania*. Philadelphia: L. H. Everts and Co., 1884.

Atlas of Lee County, Iowa. [Harlan, Iowa: R. C. Booth Enterprises?], 1914.

Auerbach, Nina. *Communities of Women: An Idea in Fiction*. Cambridge: Harvard University Press, 1978.

Bade, Jim, and Mary Ellen Mau, eds. *The Cedarville Clingmans*. [San Benito, Tex.]: Privately printed, 1997.

Bade, Jim, Mary Ellyn Mau, and Vera Robinson, eds. *Cedarville Clingmans: Diaries and Letters of a Nineteenth-Century Midwest Rural Family.* [San Benito, Tex.]: Privately printed, 1999.

Bailey, Robert E., and Elaine Shemoney Evans. *Descriptive Inventory of the Archives of the State of Illinois.* 2d ed. Springfield: Illinois State Archives, Office of the Secretary of State, 1997.

Bailey, Robert E., Elaine Shemoney Evans, Barbara Heflin, and Karl R. Moore. *Summary Guide to Local Governmental Records in the Illinois Regional Archives.* Springfield: Office of the Secretary of State, 1992.

Bailey, William F., ed. *History of Eau Claire County, Wisconsin.* Chicago: C. F. Cooper and Co., 1914.

Barker-Benfield, G. J. *The Horrors of the Half-Known Life: Male Attitudes toward Women and Sexuality in Nineteenth-Century America.* New York: Harper and Row, 1976.

Barnes, Robert. *Medical and Surgical Diseases of Women.* Philadelphia: H. C. Lea, 1874.

Barrère, Albert, and Charles G. Leland. *Dictionary of Slang, Jargon and Cant.* London: George Beel and Son, 1897.

Barrett, Mrs. John W. (Mary X.), and Philip L. Keister, eds. *History of Stephenson County, 1970.* Freeport, Ill.: County of Stephenson, 1972.

Barstow, Anne Llewellyn. *Witchcraze: A New History of the European Witch Hunts.* New York: Pandora Press/Harper-Collins, 1994.

Bastian, Wayne. *Whiteside County.* Illinois sesquicentennial edition. Morrison, Ill.: Whiteside County Board of Supervisors, 1968.

Batty, Joseph H. *Practical Taxidermy and Home Decoration; Together with General Information for Sportsmen.* New York: Orange Judd and Co., 1879.

Baym, Nina. *Novels, Readers and Reviewers: Responses to Fiction in Antebellum America.* Ithaca: Cornell University Press, 1984.

Beam, Ronald. *Cedarville's Jane Addams . . . Her Early Influences.* Freeport, Ill.: Wagner Printing Co., [1966].

Bean, Theodore W., ed. *History of Montgomery County, Pennsylvania.* Philadelphia: Everts and Peck, 1884.

Beauman, Katherine Bentley. *Women and the Settlement Movement.* New York: St. Martin's Press, 1996.

Beecher, Catharine. *Educational Reminiscences and Suggestions.* New York: J. B. Ford and Co., 1874.

———. *Physiology and Calisthenics.* New York: Harper and Brothers, 1856.

The Bench and Bar of Chicago: Biographical Sketches. [Chicago: American Biographical Co., 1883?].

Bent, Charles, ed. *History of Whiteside County, Illinois.* 1877. Reprint. Dixon, Ill.: The Print Shop and the Sterling–Rock Falls Historical Society, n.d.

Biographical Encyclopedia of Illinois of the Nineteenth Century. Philadelphia: Galaxy Publishing Co., 1875.

Biographical and Historical Memoirs of Story County Iowa. Chicago: Goodspeed Publishing Co., 1890.

Biographical Record of McLean County, Illinois. Chicago: S. J. Clarke Publishing Co., 1899.

Blackwell, Elizabeth. *The Laws of Life with Special Reference to the Physical Education of Girls.* New York: G. P. Putnam, 1852.

Blain, Virginia, Patricia Clements, and Isobel Grundy, eds. *The Feminist Companion to Literature in English*. London: B. T. Batsford, 1990.

Blaisdell, James Arnold. *The Story of a Life: A Biography*. Claremont, Calif.: Claremont University Center, 1984.

Blaisdell, James Joshua. *Brief Essays from the Writings and Public Address of Professor J. J. Blaisdell*. Boston: Congregational Sunday-School and Publishing Society, [1897].

———. *Lectures in Ethics*. Beloit, Wis.: Beloit College, 1894.

Block, Marguerite Beck. *The New Church in the New World: A Study of Swedenborgianism in America*. New York: Octagon, 1968.

Boardman, John et al., eds. *The Cambridge Ancient History*. 8 vols. New York: Cambridge University Press, 1988–94.

Boas, Louise Schutz. *Woman's Education Begins: The Rise of the Women's Colleges*. 1935. Reprint. New York: Arno Press, 1971.

Boatner, Mark Mayo. *Civil War Dictionary*. New York: David McKay Co., 1962.

Bogart, Ernest Ludlow, and Charles Manfred Thompson. *Industrial State 1870–1893*. Vol. 4 of *Centennial History of Illinois*. Edited by Clarence Walworth Alvord. Springfield: Illinois Centennial Comm., 1920.

Boies, Henry L. *History of De Kalb County, Illinois*. Chicago: O. P. Bassett, Printers, 1868.

Boone, Richard G. *Education in the United States*. New York: D. Appleton and Co., 1894.

Borghese, Susanna, Caroline F. Schimmel, and Mary C. Schlosser. *The Guild of Book Workers: Seventy-fifth Anniversary Exhibition*. New York: Guild of Book Workers, 1981.

Boris, Eileen. *Art and Labor: Ruskin, Morris, and the Craftsman Ideal in America*. Philadelphia: Temple University Press, 1986.

Bowden, Henry Warner. *Dictionary of American Religious Biography*. Westport, Conn.: Greenwood Press, 1977.

Brooks, William Keith. "Report on the Stomatopoda Collected by H.M.S. *Challenger* during the Years 1873–76." In Johns Hopkins University, *Memoirs from the Biological Laboratory*, vol. 1. Baltimore: Johns Hopkins University, 1887.

Bross, William. *History of Chicago*. Chicago: Jansen, McClurg and Co., 1876.

Brown, Thomas. *The Taxidermist's Manual; or, The Art of Collecting, Preparing, and Preserving Objects of Natural History: Designed for the Use of Travellers, Conservators of Museums, and Private Collectors*. 26th ed. London: A. Fullarton and Co., 1875.

Browne, Walter, ed. *Who's Who on the Stage: The Dramatic Reference Book and Biographical Dictionary of the Theatre*. New York: Dodge, 1908.

Bryan, Mary Lynn McCree, and Allen F. Davis. *One Hundred Years at Hull-House*. Bloomington: Indiana University Press, 1990.

Bryan, Mary Lynn McCree, Nancy Slote, and Maree de Angury. *The Jane Addams Papers: A Comprehensive Guide*. Bloomington: Indiana University Press, 1996.

Bryan, William Jennings, and Mary Baird Bryan. *The Memoirs of William Jennings Bryan*. Chicago: Winston, 1925.

Bryant, Margaret E. *The Unexpected Revolution: A Study in the History of Education of Women and Girls in the Nineteenth Century*. London: University of London, 1979.

Burstyn, Joan N. *Victorian Education and the Ideal of Womanhood*. Totowa, N.J.: Barnes and Noble Books, 1980.

Calasibetta, Charlotte Mankey. *Fairchild's Dictionary of Fashion*, 2d ed. New York: Fairchild Pub., 1988.

Callen, Anthea. *Women Artists of the Arts and Crafts Movement, 1870–1914*. New York: Pantheon, 1979.

Capen, John L. *New Illustrated Self-Instructor and Physiology; with Over One Hundred Engravings; Together with the Chart and Character of Miss Jane Addams, Mr. George B. Haldeman as Marked by John L. Capen July 31, 1876*. New York: S. R. Wells and Co., 1876.

Carlyle, Thomas. *On Great Men*. New York: Penguin, 1995.

———. *Heroes and Hero Worship*. Chicago: W. B. Conkey and Co., 1900.

———. *Past and Present, Chartism, and Sartor Resartus, Complete in One Volume*. New York: Harper, 1877.

Cedarville's Heritage. [Freeport, Ill.?]: Cedarville Bi-Centennial Comm., [1976].

Chamberlin, Rollin T. *Memorial of Rollin D. Salisbury*. New York: Geological Society of America, 1931.

Church, Charles A. *History of Rockford and Winnebago County, Illinois*. Rockford, Ill.: New England Society of Rockford, W. P. Lamb, Printer, 1900.

———. *History of the Republican Party in Illinois, 1854–1912 with a Review of the Aggressions of the Slave-Power*. Rockford, Ill.: Wilson Brothers Co., [1912].

Cimbala, Paul A., and Randall M. Miller. *Against the Tide: Women Reformers in American Society*. New York: Praeger, 1997.

Clancy, Herbert J. *The Presidential Election of 1880*. Chicago: Loyola University Press, 1958.

Clark, Robert Judson, ed. *The Arts and Crafts Movement in America: 1876–1916*. Princeton: Princeton University Press, 1972.

Clayton, John. *Illinois Fact Book and Historical Almanac, 1673–1968*. Carbondale: Southern Illinois University Press, 1970.

Cobden-Sanderson, T. J. *The Closing of the Doves Press*. Prepared in conjunction with the "Exhibition of Cobden-Sanderson Bindings, Books from Doves Press and Doves Bindery," Stanford University, Apr. 1969. San Francisco: Grabhorn-Hoyem, 1969.

———. *Four Lectures by T. J. Cobden-Sanderson*. Edited and with an introductory essay by John Dreyfus. San Francisco: Book Club of California, 1974.

———. *The Journals of Thomas James Cobden-Sanderson, 1879–1922*. New York: B. Franklin Press, 1969.

Coffin, Seldon J. *Men of Lafayette, 1826–1898*. Easton, Pa.: George W. West, 1891.

Cole, Arthur C. *A Hundred Years of Mount Holyoke College: The Evolution of an Educational Ideal*. New Haven: Yale University Press, 1940.

Collie, George L., and Hiram D. Densmore. *Thomas C. Chamberlin and Rollin D. Salisbury: A Beloit College Partnership* [also published as *Chamberlin and Salisbury: Life Partners in Science Work*]. Madison: State Historical Society of Wisconsin, 1932.

Combination Atlas Map of Stephenson County Illinois, Compiled, Drawn, and Published from Personal Examinations and Surveys. Geneva, Ill.: Thompson and Everts, 1871.

Combined 1871 Combination Atlas Map of Stephenson County, Illinois, 1913 Standard Atlas and 1894 Plat Book. 1913. Reprint. Evansville, Ind.: Whipporwill Publications for the Stephenson Co. Genealogical Society, 1986.

Complete Guide to the Centennial Exposition Fairmont Park and the City of Phildel-phia. Philadelphia: Wm. Butt and Co., 1876.

Conway, Jill K. *The First Generation of American Women Graduates.* New York: Garland Publishing, Inc., 1987.

Cook, E. T., and Alexander Wedderburn, eds. *The Works of John Ruskin.* London: George Allen, 1904.

Cotkin, George. *Reluctant Modernism: American Thought and Culture, 1880–1900.* New York: Twayne Publishers, 1992.

Courtwright, David T. *Dark Paradise: Opiate Addiction in America before 1940.* Cambridge: Harvard University Press, 1982.

Cumberland, William H. *History of Buena Vista College.* 2d ed. Ames: Iowa State University Press, 1991.

Cuthbertson, William C. *The Genesis of Girard [Kansas].* Fort Scott, Kans.: Sekan Publications Co., [1993].

Davidson, Alexander, and Bernard Stuvé. *A Complete History of Illinois from 1673 to 1884.* . . . Springfield: H. W. Rokker, 1884.

Davies, Emily. *Thoughts on Some Questions Relating to Women, 1860–1908.* 1910. Reprint. New York: Kraus, 1971.

Davies, John Dunn. *Phrenology, Fad and Science: A Nineteenth-Century American Crusade.* New Haven: Yale University Press, 1955.

Davis, Allen F. *American Heroine: The Life and Legend of Jane Addams.* New York: Oxford University Press, 1973.

Davis, David J., ed. *History of Medical Practice in Illinois,* vol. 2: *1850–1900.* Chicago: Illinois State Medical Society, 1955.

Davis, William W. *History of Whiteside Country, Illinois.* Chicago: Pioneer Publishing Co., 1908.

De Gregorio, William A. *The Complete Book of U.S. Presidents.* New York: Dembner Books, 1984.

De Quincey, Thomas. *Confessions of an English Opium Eater.* London: Taylor and Hessey, 1822.

Dick, Charles, and James E. Homans, eds. *The Cyclopaedia of American Biography.* Revised and enlarged edition of *Appleton's Cyclopaedia of American Biography,* originally edited by James Grant Wilson and John Fiske, 6 vols. 1886. Reprint. New York: Press Association Compilers, Inc., 1915.

Dolbow, Sandra W. *Dictionary of Modern French Literature.* New York: Greenwood, 1986.

Donald, David Herbert. *Lincoln.* New York: Simon and Schuster, [1995].

Donohue, M. A. et al. *Ladies' Manual of Art; or, Profit and Pastime: A Self Teacher in All Branches of Decorative Art, Embracing Every Variety of Painting and Drawing on China, Glass, Velvet, Canvas, Paper and Wood.* Chicago: Donohue, Henneberry and Co., 1890.

Donovan, Mary Sudman. *A Different Call: Women's Ministries in the Episcopal Church.* Philadelphia: Morehouse, 1986.

Douglass, Frederick. *The Frederick Douglass Papers,* series 1, Speeches, Debates, and Interviews. Vol. 2: *1847–54,* edited by John W. Blassingame, Richard Carlson, Clarence L. Mohr, Julie S. Jones, John R. McKivigan, David Roediger, and Jason H. Silverman. New Haven: Yale University Press, 1982.

————. *The Frederick Douglass Papers,* series 1, Speeches, Debates, and Interviews. Vol. 4: *1864–80,* edited by John W. Blassingame, John R. McKivigan, Richard G. Carlson, Suzanne Selinger, and Gerald W. Fulkerson. New Haven: Yale University Press, 1991.

Drachman, Virginia G. *Women Lawyers and the Origins of Professional Identity in America: The Letters of the Equity Club, 1887 to 1890.* Ann Arbor: University of Michigan, 1993.

Dudden, Faye E. *Women in the American Theatre: Actresses and Audiences, 1790–1870.* New Haven: Yale University Press, 1994.

Duis, E. *The Good Old Times in McLean County, Illinois.* Bloomington: Leader Publishing and Printing Co., 1874.

Eagle, Mary Kavanaugh Oldman, ed. *The Congress of Women Held in the Women's Building, World's Columbian Exposition, Chicago, 1893.* Official Edition. Philadelphia: International Publishing Co., 1895.

Eaton, Edward Dwight. *Historical Sketches of Beloit College, with Chapters by Members of the Faculty.* New York: A. S. Barnes, 1928.

Edelman, Hope. *Motherless Daughters: The Legacy of Loss.* New York: Dell Publishing, 1994.

Eden, John. *The Mount Holyoke Hand-book and Tourist's Guide: For Northampton and Its Vicinity.* Northampton, Mass.: Bridgman and Co., 1851.

Ehrenreich, Barbara, and Deirdre English. *Complaints and Disorders: The Sexual Politics of Sickness.* Old Westbury, N.Y.: Feminist Press, 1973.

————. *For Her Own Good: 150 Years of Experts' Advice to Women.* Garden City, N.Y.: Anchor Press, 1978.

Ellis, Franklin, and Samuel Evans. *History of Lancaster County, Pennsylvania. . . .* Philadelphia: Everts and Peck, 1883.

Ellsworth, Spencer. *Records of the Olden Time; or, Fifty Years on the Prairies . . . [of Marshall and Putnam Counties].* Lacon, Ill.: Home Journal Steam Printing Establishment, 1880.

Emerson, Benjamin Kendall. *The Ipswich Emersons, A.D. 1636–1900.* Boston: David Clapp and Son, 1900.

Emerson, Joseph. *Female Education: A Discourse Delivered at the Dedication of the Seminary Hall in Saugus, January 15, 1822.* Boston, n.p., 1823.

Epstein, Barbara Leslie. *The Politics of Domesticity: Women, Evangelism, and Temperance in Nineteenth-Century America.* Middletown, Conn.: Wesleyan University Press, 1981.

Eschbach, Elizabeth Seymour. *The Higher Education of Women in England and America, 1865–1920.* New York: Garland, 1993.

Exhibition of a Collection of Bookbindings by Ellen Gates Starr . . . Hull-House Bindery, March 18th to March 25th. Chicago: Hollister Brothers, 19[06?].

Faderman, Lillian. *Surpassing the Love of Men: Romantic Friendship and Love between Women from the Renaissance to the Present.* New York: William Morrow, 1981.

Faran, Angeline Loveland, ed. *Glendale, Ohio: 1855–1955.* Cincinnati, Ohio: McDonald Printing Co., n.d.

Farnham, Christie Anne. *The Education of the Southern Belle: Higher Education and Student Socialization in the Antebellum South.* New York: New York University Press, 1994.

Farrell, John C. *Beloved Lady: A History of Jane Addams' Ideas on Reform and Peace.* Baltimore: Johns Hopkins University Press, 1967.

Federal Writers' Project, Illinois. *Illinois: A Descriptive and Historical Guide.* Compiled and written by the Federal Writers' Project of the Work Projects Administration for the State of Illinois. Sponsored by Henry Horner, governor. Chicago: A. C. McClurg and Co., 1939.

Ffrench, Florence. *Music and Musicians in Chicago.* 1899. Reprint. New York: DaCapo Press, 1979.

Finegold, Wilfred J. *Artificial Insemination.* Springfield: Charles C. Thomas Publisher, [1964?].

First Presbyterian Church (Freeport, Ill.). *Centennial Celebration, Nov. 8–15, 1942.* [Freeport, Ill.: First Presbyterian Church, 1942].

Fish, Daniel W. *Robinson's Progressive Practical Arithmetic.* Chicago: Ivison, Blakeman, Taylor and Co., 1872.

Fisher, D. Jerome. *The Seventy Years of the Department of Geology, University of Chicago, 1892–1961.* Chicago: University of Chicago Press, 1963.

Fisher, Lois H. *A Literary Gazetteer of England.* New York: McGraw-Hill, 1980.

Fiske, Fidelia. *Recollections of Mary Lyon, with Selections from Her Instructions to the Pupils in Mt. Holyoke Female Seminary.* Boston: American Tract Society, 1866.

Foght, Harold W. *American Rural School.* New York: Macmillan Co., 1918.

Foner, Philip S. *The Life and Writings of Frederick Douglass,* vol. 4: *Reconstruction and After.* New York: International Publishers, 1955.

Forbes, John Ripley. *In the Steps of the Great American Zoologist: William Temple Hornaday.* New York: M. Evans and Philadelphia: Lippincott, [1966].

Ford, Henry. *History of Putnam and Marshall Counties. . . .* Lacon, Ill.: Ford, 1860.

Forrester, George, ed. *Historical and Bibliographical Album of the Chippewa Valley, Wisconsin.* Chicago: A. Warner Pub., 1891–92.

Foster, Frank. *Ferns to Know and Grow.* New York: Hawthorn Books, 1971.

France, Peter, ed. *The New Oxford Companion to Literature in French.* New York: Oxford University Press, 1995.

Frank, Charles. *Pioneer's Progress: Illinois College, 1829–1979.* Carbondale: Southern Illinois University Press, 1979.

Frankfort, Roberta. *Collegiate Women: Domesticity and Career in Turn-of-the-Century America.* New York: New York University Press, 1977.

Frederick, Peter J. *Knights of the Golden Rule: The Intellectual as Christian Reformer in the 1890s.* Lexington: University Press of Kentucky, 1976.

Fry, Paul E. *Generous Spirit: The Life of Mary Fry.* [Washington, D.C.]: Paul E. Fry, [1991].

Fulwider, Addison L. *History of Stephenson County, Illinois.* Chicago: S. J. Clarke Publishing Co., 1910.

Gardner, E. A. *History of Ford County, Illinois, from Its Earliest Settlement to 1903.* Chicago: S. J. Clarke Publishing Co., 1908.

General Biographical Catalogue of Auburn Theological Seminary 1818–1918. Auburn, N.Y.: Auburn Seminary Press, 1918.

General Catalogue of Bowdoin College and the Medical School of Maine: A Biographical Record of Alumni and Officers, 1794–1950. Brunswick, Maine.: Bowdoin College, 1950.

Gillett, Charles Ripley, comp. *Alumni Catalogue of the Union Theological Seminary in the City of New York, 1836–1926.* New York: Association of the Alumni, 1926.

Ginzberg, Lori D. *Women and the Work of Benevolence: Morality, Politics, and Class in the Nineteenth-Century United States.* New Haven: Yale University Press, 1990.

Godwin, William. *Lives of the Necromancers.* London: Frederick Mason, 1834.

Goodsell, Willystine, ed. *Pioneers of Women's Education in the United States.* New York: McGraw-Hill, 1931.

Goodspeed, Thomas Wakefield. *The Story of the University of Chicago, 1890–1925.* Chicago: University of Chicago Press, 1925.

Gordon, Lynn D. *Gender and Higher Education in the Progressive Era.* New Haven: Yale University Press, 1990.

Gore, J. E. *An Astronomical Glossary; or, Dictionary of Terms Used in Astronomy.* London: Crosby, Lockwood, and Son, 1893.

Green, Elizabeth Alden. *Mary Lyon and Mount Holyoke: Opening the Gates.* Hanover, N.H.: University Press of New England, 1979.

Gregory, James M. *Frederick Douglass, the Orator.* Springfield, Mass.: Willey and Co., 1893.

Gross, Lewis M. *Past and Present of De Kalb County, Illinois.* 2 vols. Chicago: Pioneer Publishing Co., 1907.

Gross, Margaret Geissman. *Dancing on the Table: A History of Lake Erie College.* Burnsville, N.C.: Celo Valley Books, 1993.

Gue, Benjamin F. *History of Iowa.* Vol. 4, *Iowa Biography.* New York: Century History Co., [1903].

Guiley, Rosemary Ellen. *The Encyclopedia of Witches and Witchcraft.* New York: Facts on File, 1999.

Gustason, Harriett. *Looking Back: From the Pages of the Journal-Standard,* vol. 1: *1982–1985.* Freeport, Ill.: Stephenson Co. Historical Society, 1994.

Gutwirth, Madelyn. *Madame de Staël: The Emergence of the Artist as Woman.* Urbana: University of Illinois Press, 1978.

Haldeman-Julius, Marcet. *Jane Addams as I Knew Her.* Reviewer's Library no. 7. Girard, Kans.: Haldeman-Julius Co., [1936].

Halttunen, Karen. *Confidence Men and Painted Women: A Study of Middle-Class Culture in America, 1830–70.* New Haven: Yale University Press, 1983.

Hanscom, Elizabeth Deering, and Helen French Greene. *Sophia Smith and the Beginnings of Smith College.* Northampton, Mass.: Smith College, 1925.

Hamilton, Gail [Mary Abigail Dodge]. *Twelve Miles from a Lemon.* New York: Harper and Brothers, 1874.

Harlan, Edgar Rubey. *Narrative History of the People of Iowa, . . .* Vol. 5. Chicago: American Historical Society, 1931.

Hart, George. *A Dictionary of Egyptian Gods and Goddesses.* London: Routledge and Kegan Paul, 1986.

Hart, James D., ed. *The Oxford Companion to American Literature.* 4th ed. New York: Oxford University Press, 1965.

Hartt, Frederick. *Art: A History of Painting, Sculpture, Architecture.* 3d ed. New York: Harry N. Abrams, 1989.

Harvey, Paul, and Dorothy Eagle, eds. *The Oxford Companion to English Literature.* 4th ed. New York: Oxford University Press, 1967.

Hastie, W. *Kant's Cosmogony; as in His Essay on the Retardation of the Rotation of the Earth and His Natural History and Theory of the Heavens.* Glasgow: James Maclehose and Sons, 1900.

Henson, Clyde E. *Joseph Kirkland.* New Haven: College and University Press, 1962.

Hetherington, Norriss S., ed. *Encyclopedia of Cosmology: Historical, Philosophical, and Scientific Foundations of Modern Cosmology.* New York: Garland, 1993.

Historic Manual of the Presbyterian Churches of Cedarville and Dakota, Illinois, 1906. Freeport, Ill.: Journal Printing Co., 1906.

Historic Rock Island County. Rock Island, Ill.: Kramer and Co., 1908.

History Committee of Brown County, S.D., Museum and Historical Society. *Brown County, South Dakota, History, 1980.* Aberdeen, S.D.: The Society, 1980.

History of Carroll County Illinois. . . . Chicago: H. F. Kett and Co., 1878.

The History of Cincinnati and Hamilton County, Ohio: Their Past and Present. Cincinnati: S. B. Nelson and Co., 1894.

History of Dunn County, Wisconsin. Compiled by F. Curtiss-Wedge. Minneapolis–Winona, Minn.: H. C. Cooper, Jr. and Co., 1925.

History of Lee County, Iowa. Chicago: Western Historical Co., 1879.

History of McHenry County, Illinois. Chicago: Inter-State Publishing Co., 1885.

History of Medicine of Polk County, Iowa. [Des Moines]: Council of the Des Moines Academy of Medicine and Polk Co. Medical Society, 1951.

History of Ogle County, Illinois, Containing a History of the County—Its Cities, Towns, etc. . . . Portraits of Early Settlers and Prominent Men. Chicago: H. F. Kett and Co., 1878.

History of Polk County, Iowa. . . . Des Moines, Iowa: Union Historical Co., 1880.

History of Stephenson County, Illinois. Chicago: Western Historical Co., 1880.

History of Winnebago Country, Illinois, Its Past and Present. Chicago: H. F. Kett and Co., 1877.

Holber, Harriet Wells, Carolina A. Potter Brazee, Nellie Rose Caswell, Catharine Waugh McCullough, and Mabel Walker Herrick, comps. and eds. *Jubilee Book: Commemorating the Fiftieth Anniversary of the Graduation of the First Class, 1854–1904.* Rockford, Ill.: Alumnae Assn. of Rockford College, 1904.

[Holmes, Mary E.] *Aida Rocksbege and the White Stone: Today's Problem, a Presbyterial Romance.* Rockford, Ill.: Calvert Brothers, 1897.

[Holmes, Mary E. et al.]. *His Father's Mantle, by the Ten.* Rockford, Ill.: Empire Book Co., 1895.

Holmes, Oliver Wendell, Sr. *Pages from an Old Volume of Life: A Collection of Essays, 1857–81.* Boston: Houghton, Mifflin and Co., 1883.

Holt, Glen E., and Dominic A. Pacyga. *Chicago, a Historical Guide to the Neighborhoods: The Loop and South Side.* Chicago: Chicago Historical Society, 1979.

Hornaday, William Temple. *Taxidermy and Zoological Collecting: A Complete Handbook for the Amateur Taxidermist, Collector, Osteologist, Museum-builder, Sportsman, and Traveller.* New York: Charles Scribner's Sons, 1891.

Horowitz, Helen Lefkowitz. *Alma Mater: Design and Experience in the Women's College from their Nineteenth-Century Beginnings to the 1930s.* 1985. Reprint. Amherst: University of Massachusetts Press, 1993.

———. *Culture and the City: Cultural Philanthropy in Chicago from the 1880s to 1917.* 2d ed. Chicago: University of Chicago Press, 1989.

Houghton, Walter E. *The Victorian Frame of Mind, 1830–1870.* New Haven: Yale University Press, 1985.

Howe, Daniel Walker. *Making the American Self: Jonathan Edwards to Abraham Lincoln.* Cambridge: Harvard University Press, 1997.

Howe, Florence, ed. *Tradition and the Talents of Women.* Urbana: University of Illinois Press, 1991.

Hunter, Robert, and Charles Morris, eds. *Universal Dictionary of the English Language.* New York: P. F. Collier and Son, 1903.

Illinois Sesquicentennial Commission. *Illinois Guide and Gazetteer.* Chicago: Rand, McNally and Co., 1969.

Illustrated Freeport. Freeport, Ill.: Freeport Journal, 1896.

In the Foot-Prints of the Pioneers of Stephenson County, Ill.: A Genealogical Record. Freeport, Ill.: Pioneer Publishing Co., 1900.

Industrial Chicago, vol 6: *Bench and Bar.* Chicago: Goodspeed Publishing Co., 1896.

Ingram, J. S. *The Centennial Exposition Described and Illustrated.* Philadelphia: Hubbard Bros., 1876.

Inness, Sherrie A. *Intimate Communities: Representation and Social Transformation in Women's College Fiction, 1895–1910.* Bowling Green, Ohio: Bowling Green State University Popular Press, 1995.

Iowa Historical Dept. *Annals of Iowa.* Vol. 1, 3d ser. Des Moines: Historical Dept. of Iowa, 1903.

James, Edward T., Janet Wilson James, and Paul S. Boyer, eds. *Notable American Women, 1607–1950.* 3 vols. Cambridge: Harvard University Press, 1971.

Janson, H. W. *History of Art.* 3d ed. Rev. and expanded by Anthony F. Janson. New York: Harry N. Abrams/Englewood Cliffs, N.J.: Prentice-Hall, 1986.

Jay, Charles D. *Sesquicentennial One Hundred and Fifty Years of Illinois Education.* Springfield: Office of the Superintendent of Public Instruction, [1968].

Jobes, Gertrude. *Dictionary of Mythology Folklore and Symbols.* New York: Scarecrow Press, 1961.

Johnson, Allen, and Dumas Malone, eds. *Dictionary of American Biography.* 1929. Reprint. New York: Charles Scribner's Sons, 1937.

Johnson, Edgar. *Charles Dickens: His Tragedy and Triumph.* 2 vols. New York: Simon and Schuster, 1952.

Johnson, Nan. *Nineteenth-Century Rhetoric in North America.* Carbondale: Southern Illinois University Press, 1991.

Johnston, William J. *Sketches of the History of Stephenson County, Ill. and Incidents Connected with the Early Settlement of the North-West.* Freeport, Ill.: J.O.P. Burnside, 1854.

Karénine, Wladimir. *George Sand, sa vie et ses oeuvres.* 4 vols. Paris: Ollendorff and Plon-Nouritt, 1899–1912.

Kauffman, Horace G., and Rebecca H. Kauffman, eds. *Historical Encyclopedia of Illinois.* 2 vols. Chicago: Munsell Publishing Co., 1909.

Kaufman, Martin, Stuart Galishoff, and Todd L. Savitt, eds. *Dictionary of American Medical Biography.* 2 vols. Westport, Conn.: Greenwood Press, 1984.

Keister, Philip L. *Stephenson County Roads.* Freeport, Ill.: Stephenson Co. Historical Society, [1955?].

Kett, Joseph F. *The Pursuit of Knowledge under Difficulties: From Self-Improvement to Adult Education in America, 1750–1990.* Stanford, Calif.: Stanford University Press, 1994.

Kilburn, Lucian M., ed. *Iowa and Its People.* 2 vols. Chicago: Pioneer Publishing Co., 1915.

Kilner, Colleen Brown. *Joseph Sears and His Kenilworth.* Kenilworth, Ill.: Kenilworth Historical Society, 1969.

Laplace, Pierre Simon. *The System of the World.* Trans. Henry H. Harte. Dublin: University Press, 1830.

Lasch, Christopher. *New Radicalism in America [1889–1963]: The Intellectual as a Social Type.* New York: Alfred A. Knopf, 1965.

Lee, R., Mrs. *Taxidermy; or, The Art of Collecting, Preparing, and Mounting Objects of Natural History. For the Use of Museums and Travellers.* London: Longman, Hurst, Rees, Orme, and Brown, 1820.

Leibowitz, Herbert. *Fabricating Lives: Explorations in American Autobiography.* New York: Alfred A. Knopf, 1989.

Levine, Daniel. *Jane Addams and the Liberal Tradition.* Madison: State Historical Society of Wisconsin., 1971.

Linn, James Weber. *Jane Addams: A Biography.* New York: D. Appleton-Century Co., Inc., 1935.

Longfellow, Henry Wadsworth. *Poems.* Philadelphia: Carey and Hart, 1845.

Lundin, Jon W. *Rockford: An Illustrated History.* Chatsworth, Calif.: Windsor Publications, Inc., 1989.

Lyman, Francis H. *The City of Kenosha and Kenosha County, Wisconsin. . . .* 2 vols. Chicago: S. J. Clarke Publishing Co., 1916.

MacCulloch, J. A. *The Celtic and Scandinavian Religions.* London: Hutchinson's University Library, [1948].

Macleod, Diane. *Art and the Victorian Middle Class.* New York: Cambridge University Press, 1996.

McCarthy, Kathleen. *Noblesse Oblige: Charity and Cultural Philanthropy in Chicago, 1849–1929.* Chicago: University of Chicago Press, 1982.

———. *Women's Culture: American Philanthropy and Art, 1830–1930.* Chicago: University of Chicago Press, 1991.

McDonald, Lucile Saunders. *Where the Washingtonians Lived.* Seattle: Superior Publishing Co., 1969.

McGovern, James J., ed. *Life and Letters of Eliza Allen Starr.* Chicago: Lakeside Press, 1905.

Manton, Walter Porter. *Taxidermy without a Teacher, Comprising a Complete Manual of Instruction for Preparing and Preserving Birds, Animals and Fishes.* 2d rev. ed. Boston: Lee and Shepard, New York: C. T. Dillingham, 1882.

Marchalonis, Shirley. *College Girls: A Century in Fiction.* New Brunswick: Rutgers University Press, 1995.

Marrs, Edwin, Jr., ed. *Letters of Thomas Carlyle to His Brother Alexander.* Cambridge: Harvard University Press, 1968.

Martin, Wendy. *The American Sisterhood: Writings of the Feminist Movement from Colonial Times to the Present.* New York: Harper and Row, 1972.

Mayer, Harold M., and Richard C. Wade. *Chicago: Growth of a Metropolis.* Chicago: University of Chicago Press, 1969.

Memorials of Anna P. Sill, First Principal of Rockford Female Seminary, 1849–1889. Rockford, Ill.: Daily Register Electric Print Co., 1889.

Mickel, John. *Home Gardeners' Book of Ferns.* New York: Rinehart and Winston, 1979.

Mihesuah, Devon A. *Cultivating the Rosebuds: The Education of Women at the Cherokee Female Seminary, 1851–1909.* Urbana: University of Illinois Press, 1993.

Miller, Paul L. *Seventy-fifth [Anniversary] Borough of Sinking Spring 1913–1988.* [Sinking Spring, Pa.]: [Sinking Spring Area Historical Society], [1989].

Miller, Wallace J. *South-western Washington; Its Topography, Climate, Resources, Productions, Manufacturing . . . with Illustrated Reviews of the Principal Cities and Towns, and Pen Sketches of Their Representative Business Men. Also, Biographical Sketches of Prominent State, County, and Municipal Officials. . . .* Olympia, Wash.: Pacific Publishing Co., 1890.

Minnich, Elizabeth, Jean O'Barr, and Rachel Rosenfeld, eds. *Reconstructing the Academy: Women's Education and Women's Studies.* Chicago: University of Chicago Press, 1988.

Moses, John. *Illinois, Historical and Statistical. . . .* 2 vols. Chicago: Fergus Printing Co., 1889.

Mount Morris: Past and Present, an Illustrated History of the Village of Mount Morris, Ogle County, Illinois. 2d ed. Mt. Morris: Kable Brothers Co., 1938.

Mullin, Donald, comp. and ed. *Victorian Actors and Actresses in Review . . . 1837–1901.* Westport, Conn.: Greenwood Press, 1983.

Murray, Margaret Alice. *The God of the Witches.* London: Sampson Low, Marston amd Company, 1933.

Murray, Peter, and Linda Murray. *The Penguin Dictionary of Art and Artists.* Rev. ed. New York: Penguin Books, 1989.

The National Cyclopeadia of American Biography: Being the History of the United States as Illustrated in the Lives of the Founders, Builders, and Defenders of the Republic, and of the Men and Women Who Are Doing the Work and Moulding the Thought of the Present Time. New York: James T. White and Co., 1897.

Nelson, C. Hal, Joan Surrey, Isy Nelson, Leona Carlson, and Betty Asprooth, eds. *Rockford College: A Retrospective Look.* Rockford, Ill.: C. Hjalmar Nelson and Rockford College, 1980.

Nelson, C. Hal, comp. and ed. *Sinnissippi Saga: A History of Rockford and Winnebago County, Illinois.* Rockford: Winnebago County Illinois Sesquicentennial Committee, 1968.

Nevin, Alfred. *Encyclopedia of the Presbyterian Church in the United States of America.* Philadelphia: Presbyterian Encyclopedia Publishing Co., 1884.

Newcomer, Mabel. *A Century of Higher Education for Women.* New York: Harper, 1959.

Newspapers in the [Illinois State] Historical Library. Springfield: Illinois State Library, Office of the Secretary of State, 1994.

Norton, Charles Eliot, ed. *Early Letters of Thomas Carlyle.* 2 vols. New York: Macmillan and Co., 1886.

Numbers, Ronald. *Creation by Natural Law: Laplace's Nebular Hypothesis in American Thought.* Seattle: University of Washington Press, 1977.

One Hundred and Fifty Years of Presbyterianism in the Ohio Valley, 1890–1940. Cincinnati: n.p., 1941.

Orton, James, ed. *The Liberal Education of Women.* New York: Barnes, 1873.

Osborne, Georgia L. *Brief Biographies of the Figurines on Display in the Illinois State Historical Library.* Springfield: State of Illinois, 1932.

Osborne, William S. *Caroline M. Kirkland.* New York: Twayne, 1972.

Palmer, John M., ed. *The Bench and the Bar of Illinois: Historical and Reminiscent.* 2 vols. Chicago: Lewis Publishing, 1899.

Palmieri, Patricia Ann. *In Adamless Eden: The Community of Women Faculty at Wellesley.* New Haven: Yale University Press, 1995.

Palmieri, Robert, and Margaret W. Palmieri, eds. *Encyclopedia of Keyboard Instruments,* vol. 1: *The Piano.* New York: Garland, 1994.

Parker, Inez Moore. *The Rise and Decline of the Program of Education for Black Presbyterians of the United Presbyterian Church, USA, 1865–1970.* San Antonio: Trinity University Press, 1977.

Perrin, William Henry, ed. *History of Alexander, Union and Pulaski Counties, Illinois.* Chicago: O. L. Baskin and Co., 1883.

Pfeffer, Naomi. *The Stork and the Syringe: A Political History of Reproductive Medicine.* N.p.: Polity Press, Blackwell Publishers, 1993.

Pfeifer, Helen E. *Something of a Faith: A Brief History of Mary Holmes College.* West Point, Miss.: Mary Holmes College, 1982.

Pickard, Madge E., and R. Carlyle Buley. *Midwest Pioneer: His Ills, Cures, and Doctors.* New York: Henry Schuman, 1946.

Picken, Mary Brooks. *The Fashion Dictionary.* New York: Funk and Wagnalls, 1957.

Pierce, Bessie Louise. *A History of Chicago.* 3 vols. New York: Alfred A. Knopf, 1937, 1940, 1957.

Plummer, Mark A. *Lincoln's Rail-Splitter: Governor Richard J. Oglesby.* Urbana: University of Illinois Press, 2001.

Pollard, Lancaster. *History of the State of Washington.* Vol. 3. Lloyd Spencer, editor-in-chief. New York: American Historical Society, 1937.

Porter, Will. *Annals of Polk County, Iowa and City of Des Moines.* Des Moines: Geo. A. Miller Printing Co., 1898.

Porterfield, Amanda. *Mary Lyon and the Mount Holyoke Missionaries.* New York: Oxford University Press, 1997.

Portrait and Biographical Album of De Kalb County, Illinois. . . . Chicago: Chapman Brothers, 1885.

Portrait and Biographical Album of Henry County, Illinois. Chicago: Biographical Publishing Co., 1885.

Portrait and Biographical Album of Lee County, Iowa. . . . Chicago: Chapman Brothers, 1887.

Portrait and Biographical Album of Ogle County, Illinois. . . . Chicago: Chapman Brothers, 1886.

Portrait and Biographical Album of Stephenson County, Ill. 1888. Reprint. Mt. Vernon, Ind.: Windmill Publications, Inc., 1990.

Portrait and Biographical Album of Whiteside Co., Illinois. . . . Chicago: Chapman Brothers, 1883.

Portrait and Biographical Record of Winnebago and Boone Counties, Illinois. . . . Chicago: Biographical Publishing Co., 1892.

Post, Robert C., ed. *Treatise upon Selected Aspects of the Great International Exhibition Held in Philadelphia on the Occasion of Our Nation's One-Hundredth Birthday, with Some Reference to Another Exhibition Held in Washington Commemorating That Epic Event, and Called 1876 a Centennial Exhibition.* Washington: National Museum of History and Technology, Smithsonian Institution, 1976.

Power, John Carroll, and Mrs. S. A. Power. *History of the Early Settlers of Sangamon County, Illinois.* Springfield: Edwin A. Wilson and Co., 1876.

Pratt, Anne. *Flowers and Their Associations.* London: C. Knight, 1840.

Pratt, Anne, and Thomas Miller. *Language of Flowers; Popular Tales of Flowers.* London: Simpkin, Marshall, Hamilton, Kent and Co., [18?]

Profiles of the Principals of Rockford Seminary and Presidents of Rockford College, 1847–1947. Rockford, Ill.: Rockford College, 1947.

Prosser, William Farrand. *A History of the Puget Sound County [Washington].* Vol. 1. New York: Lewis Publishing Co., 1903.

Rammelkamp, Charles Henry. *Illinois College: A Centennial History, 1829–1929.* New Haven: Published for Illinois College by Yale University Press, 1928.

Reid, Joyce M. H., ed. *The Concise Oxford Dictionary of French Literature.* New York: Oxford University Press, 1976.

Rockford Seminary, Thirtieth Commencement, Essays of Graduating Class, Wednesday, June 22, 1881. De Kalb, Ill.: News Steam Press, 1881.

Rockford Today: Historical, Descriptive, Biographical, Illustrated. Rockford, Ill.: Clark Company Press for the Rockford Morning Star, Co., 1903.

Rogal, Samuel J. *The Educational and Evangelical Missions of Mary Emilie Holmes (1850–1906): "Not to Seem, but to Be."* Lewiston, Maine: E. Mellen, 1994.

Rosenberg, Charles E. *Trial of The Assassin Guiteau.* Chicago: University of Chicago Press, 1968.

Rothman, David J., and Sheila M. Rothman. *The Dangers of Education: Sexism and the Origins of Women's Colleges.* New York: Garland, 1987.

Ryals, Clyde de L., Kenneth J. Fielding, Ian Campbell, Aileen Christianson, and Hilary J. Smith, eds. *The Collected Letters of Thomas and Jane Welsh Carlyle,* vol. 16: *January–July 1843.* Durham: Duke University Press, 1990.

Sargent, Dudley Allen. *Health, Strength, and Power.* New York: H. M. Caldwell, 1904.
———. *Physical Education.* Boston: Ginn and Co., 1906.

Sartori, Eva Martin, and Dorothy Wynne Zimmerman, eds. *French Women Writers: A Bio-Bibliographical Source Book.* Westport, Conn.: Greenwood Press, 1991.

Schaff, Philip, and Samuel M. Jackson, eds. *Encyclopedia of Living Divines and Christian Workers of All Denominations in Europe and America.* New York: Funk and Wagnalls, 1887.

Schellen, A. M. C. M. *Artificial Insemination in the Human.* Amsterdam: Elsevier Publishing Co., 1957.

Schmidt-Kunsemuller, Friedrich Adolf. *T. J. Cobden-Sanderson as Bookbinder.* Pamphlet trans. from German by I. Grafe. Esher, Germany: Tabard Press, 1966.

Seaton, Beverly. *Language of Flowers: A History.* Charlottesville: University Press of Virginia, 1995.

Seidenhelm, Harriet Joy. *Brief History of the First Congregational Church of Wilmette, Illinois, Prepared for the Fiftieth Anniversary.* [Wilmette]: [First Congregational Church], 1925.

Selby, Paul, and Newton Bateman, eds. *Historical Encyclopedia of Illinois and History of Carroll County.* Chicago: Munsell Publishing Co., 1913.

Semi-Centennial History of the Illinois State Normal University, 1857–1907. Normal: Illinois State Normal University, 1907.

Shattock, Joanne. *The Oxford Guide to British Women Writers.* New York: Oxford University Press, 1993.

Showalter, Elaine. *Sister's Choice: Tradition and Change in American Women's Writing.* New York: Oxford University Press, 1991.

Sklar, Kathryn Kish. *Florence Kelley and the Nation's Work: The Rise of Women's Political Culture, 1830–1900.* New Haven: Yale University Press, 1995.

Sloat, Jerry. *Lee County Iowa: A Pictorial History.* Virginia Beach, Va.: Donning Co., 1993.

Smith, Eva Munson. *Woman in Sacred Song: A Library of Hymns, Religious Poems and Sacred Music by Woman.* Boston: D. Lothrop, 1885.

Smith-Rosenberg, Carroll. *Disorderly Conduct: Visions of Gender in Victorian America.* New York: Oxford University Press, 1985.

Solomon, Barbara Miller. *In the Company of Educated Women: A History of Women and Higher Education in America.* New Haven: Yale University Press, 1985.

Somerville, Mrs. [Mary]. *Mechanism of the Heavens.* London: John Murray, 1831.

Southwestern Washington. [Seattle?]: Pacific Publishing Co., 1890.

Sparling, Henry Halliday. *The Kelmscott Press and William Morris, Master-Craftsman.* New York: Macmillan and Co., 1924.

Spender, Dale, ed. *The Education Papers: Women's Quest for Equality in Britain, 1850– 1912.* New York: Routledge and Kegan Paul, 1987.

Springen, Donald K. *William Jennings Bryan: Orator of Small-town America.* Westport, Conn.: Greenwood Press, 1991.

Stacey, Robert, ed. *The Earthly Paradise: Arts and Crafts by William Morris and His Circle.* Toronto: Key Porter Books, 1993.

Stebner, Eleanor J. *The Women of Hull House: A Study in Spirituality, Vocation, and Friendship.* Albany: State University of New York Press, 1997.

Stern, Madeleine. *Heads and Headlines: The Phrenological Fowlers.* Norman: University of Oklahoma Press, 1971.

———, comp. *Phrenological Dictionary of Nineteenth-Century Americans.* Westport, Conn.: Greenwood Press, 1982.

Stevenson, Burton Egbert, ed. *Home Book of Verse: American and English.* 7th ed. New York: Henry Holt and Co., 1940.

Stow, Sarah D. Locke. *History of Mount Holyoke Seminary, South Hadley, Mass., during its First Half Century, 1837–1887.* Springfield, Mass.: Springfield Printing Co., 1887.

Stutley, Margaret. *Ancient Indian Magic and Folklore.* Boulder: Great Eastern, 1980.

Sullivan, Jack, ed. *The Penguin Encyclopedia of Horror and the Supernatural.* New York: Viking, 1986.

Swedenborg, Emanuel. *The Earths in Our Solar System, which are Called Planets and the Earths in the Starry Heavens Their Inhabitants and Spirits and Angels Thence.*

English trans. by Garrett P. Serviss. 1758 (in Latin). Reprint. Boston: B. A. Whittemore, 1928.

Sylvester, S. H. *The Taxidermists' Manual, Giving Full Instructions in Mounting and Preserving Birds, Mammals, Insects, Fishes, Reptiles, Skeletons, Eggs, &c.* 3d ed. Middleboro, Mass.: Sylvester, 1865.

Taber's Cyclopedia Medical Dictionary. 15th ed. Philadelphia: F. A. Davis Co., 1981.

Taylor, James Monroe. *Before Vassar Opened.* Boston: Houghton Mifflin Co., 1914.

Thiem, E. George, ed. *Carroll County—A Goodly Heritage.* Mt. Morris, Ill.: Kable Printing Co., 1968.

Thompson, Susan Otis. *American Book Design and William Morris.* 2d ed. London: Oak Knoll Press, 1997.

Tidcombe, Marianne. *The Bookbindings of T. J. Cobden-Sanderson.* London: British Library, 1984.

———. *The Doves Bindery.* London: British Library, New Castle, Del.: Oak Knoll Books, 1991.

Todd, Janet, ed. *British Women Writers.* New York: Frederick University, 1989.

Townsend, Lucy Forsyth. *The Best Helpers of One Another: Anna Peck Sill and the Struggle for Women's Education.* Chicago: Educational Studies Press, 1988.

Tracks of Time; Mendota, Illinois, 1853–1978. Mendota: Mendota Area Chamber of Commerce, 1978.

A Twentieth-Century History and Biographical Record of Crawford County, Kansas. Chicago: Lewis Publishing Co., 1905.

Turnbull, David. *Phrenology, the First Science of Man.* Geelong, Vict., Australia: Deakin University Press, 1982.

Twain, Mark. *Innocents Abroad.* Hartford, Conn.: American Publishing Co., 1869.

Valparaiso University, 1859–1984: One Hundred Twenty-five Years. [Valparaiso, Ind.?]: [Valparaiso University?], [ca. 1984?].

Van Kleeck, Mary. *Women in the Bookbinding Trade.* New York: Russell Sage Foundation, 1913.

Vassar Miscellany Monthly. *A Book of Vassar Verse: Reprints from the Vassar Miscellany Monthly, 1894–1916.* Poughkeepsie, N.Y.: Vassar Miscellany Monthly, 1916.

Verbugge, Martha H. *Able-Bodied Womanhood: Personal Health and Social Change in Nineteenth-Century Boston.* New York: Oxford University Press, 1988.

Vicinus, Martha. *A Widening Sphere: Changing Roles of Victorian Women.* Bloomington: Indiana University Press, 1972.

Vogel, Virgil J. *Indian Place Names in Illinois.* Springfield: Illinois State Historical Society, 1963.

Voters and Tax-Payers of De Kalb County, Illinois. Chicago: H. F. Kett and Co., 1876.

Waite, Joslyn R. *History of Kane County.* Chicago: Pioneer Publishing Co., 1908.

Walker, Barbara G. *The Woman's Encyclopedia of Myths and Secrets.* New York: Harper and Row, 1983.

Walser, G. H. *Boquet.* Lincoln, Nebr.: G. H. Walser, 1897.

[Ward], Elizabeth Stuart Phelps. *Doctor Zay.* 1882. Reprint with afterword by Michael Sartisky. New York: Feminist Press at the City University of New York, 1987.

———. *Gates Ajar.* 1868. Reprint edited by Helen S. Smith. Cambridge: Harvard University Press, 1964.

Warren, Joyce, ed. *The (Other) American Traditions: Nineteenth-Century Women Writers*. New Brunswick: Rutgers University Press, 1993.

Watters, Mary. *The First Hundred Years of MacMurray College*. Springfield, Ill.: MacMurray College for Women and Williamson Printing Co., 1947.

Webster's New Geographical Dictionary. Springfield, Mass.: Merriam-Webster, Inc., 1988.

Welter, Barbara. *Dimity Convictions: The American Woman in the Nineteenth Century*. Athens: Ohio University Press, 1976.

Whitney, William Dwight, ed. *Century Dictionary and Cyclopedia*. 10 vols. New York: Century Co., 1897.

Who Was Who in America. 7 vols. Chicago: Marquis-Who's Who, Inc., 1981.

Who Was Who in America, 1607–1896: A Companion Volume of Who Was Who in American History. Chicago: Marquis, 1963.

Willard, Frances E. *A Classic Town: The Story of Evanston*. Chicago: Woman's Temperance Publishing Association, 1891.

———. *Glimpses of Fifty Years: The Autobiography of an American Woman*. Chicago: Woman's Temperance Publication Assn. and H. J. Smith and Co., 1889.

Willard, Frances E., and Mary A. Livermore, eds. *A Woman of the Century . . . Sketches of Leading American Women in All Walks of Life*. Buffalo: Charles Wells Moulton, 1893.

Willard, George O. *History of the Providence Stage, 1762–1891*. Providence, R.I.: n.p., 1891.

Williams, E. Melvin. *Lancaster County Pennsylvania: A History*. Vol. 2. Edited by H. M. J. Klein. New York: Lewis Historical Publishing Co., 1924.

Williams, Randolph. *The New Church and Chicago: A History*. Chicago: W. B. Conkey, 1906.

Wise, Winifred E. *Jane Addams of Hull-House*. New York: Harcourt, Brace and Co., 1935.

Woody, Thomas. *A History of Women's Education in the United States*. 2 vols. 1929. Reprint. New York: Octagon Books, 1966.

Writers' Program, Pennsylvania. *Pennsylvania: A Guide to the Keystone State*. Compiled by workers of the Writers' Program of the Work Projects Administration in the State of Wisconsin. New York: Oxford University Press, 1940.

Writers' Program, Wisconsin. *Wisconsin: A Guide to the Badger State*. 2d ed. Compiled by workers of the Writers' Program of the Work Projects Administration in the State of Wisconsin. Sponsored by the Wisconsin Library Assn. New York: Duell, Sloan and Pearce, 1941.

Zophy, Angela Howard, and Frances M. Kavenik, eds. *Handbook of American Women's History*. New York: Garland, 1990.

Index

MARY LYNN MCCREE BRYAN led the team of editors who produced the microfilm edition of *The Jane Addams Papers* and *The Jane Addams Papers: A Comprehensive Guide.* Coeditor with Allen F. Davis of *One Hundred Years at Hull-House,* she was curator of the Jane Addams Hull-House at the University of Illinois at Chicago until 1983, when the Jane Addams Papers Project became associated with the history department of Duke University. A lecturer on documentary editing and Jane Addams and her era, she has been active in the development of the Cumberland Community Foundation in Fayetteville, N.C., and in other community organizations and projects.

BARBARA BAIR is a historian at the Library of Congress and a longtime documentary editor. She is the author of *Though Justice Sleeps: African Americans, 1880–1900* and of the introduction to the University of Illinois Press edition of *Hull-House Maps and Papers,* as well as a contributor to several collections of essays on women in social movements and social reform. She has also been active in community organizing and social services in Santa Cruz, California, and with the Women's International League for Peace and Freedom.

MAREE DE ANGURY was a member of the group of editors who produced *The Jane Addams Papers: A Comprehensive Guide.* She has been associated with the Jane Addams Papers Project for more than a decade and helped prepare them for publication. She is also involved with the Girl Scouts of America as a camp ranger and leader.

The University of Illinois Press
is a founding member of the
Association of American University Presses.

Composed in 10.5/12.5 Minion
with Burlington display
by Jim Proefrock
at the University of Illinois Press
Designed by Copenhaver Cumpston
Manufactured by Thomson-Shore, Inc.

University of Illinois Press
1325 South Oak Street
Champaign, IL 61820-6903
www.press.uillinois.edu